**elf-Study:**

**Scalable Cisco Internetworks (BSCI)**

**Edition**

Paquet

re

t © 2004 Cisco Systems, Inc.

ed by:

Press

East 96th Street

anapolis, IN 46240 USA

Printed in the United States of America 6 7 8 9 0

Sixth Printing  June 2006

Library of Congress Cataloging-in-Publication Number: 2003105057

ISBN: 1-58705-146-x

## Warning and Disclaimer

This book is designed to provide information about building scalable Cisco internetworks. Every effort has been
made to make this book as complete and accurate as possible, but no warranty or fitness is implied.

The information is provided on an "as is" basis. The authors, Cisco Press, and Cisco Systems, Inc. shall have neither
liability nor responsibility to any person or entity with respect to any loss or damages arising from the information
contained in this book or from the use of the discs or programs that may accompany it.

The opinions expressed in this book belong to the authors and are not necessarily those of Cisco Systems, Inc.

| | |
|---|---|
| The Cisco Press self-study book series is as described, intended for self-study. It has not been designed for use in a classroom environment. Only Cisco Learning Partners displaying the following logos are authorized providers of Cisco curriculum. If you are using this book within the classroom of a training company that does not carry one of these logos, then you are not preparing with a Cisco trained and authorized provider. For information on Cisco Learning Partners please visit:www.cisco.com/go/authorizedtraining. To provide Cisco with any information about what you may believe is unauthorized use of Cisco trademarks or copyrighted training material, please visit: http://www.cisco.com/logo/infringement.html. |  CISCO SYSTEMS ‖‖‖‖‖‖‖® &#124; Learning Solutions Partner<br><br>CISCO SYSTEMS ‖‖‖‖‖‖‖® &#124; Learning Partner |

## Trademark Acknowledgments

All terms mentioned in this book that are known to be trademarks or service marks have been appropriately
capitalized. Cisco Press or Cisco Systems, Inc. cannot attest to the accuracy of this information. Use of a term in
this book should not be regarded as affecting the validity of any trademark or service mark.

## Corporate and Government Sales

Cisco Press offers excellent discounts on this book when ordered in quantity for bulk purchases or special sales. For
more information, please contact:

**U.S. Corporate and Government Sales** 1-800-382-3419 corpsales@pearsontechgroup.com

For sales outside of the U.S., please contact:
**International Sales** international@pearsontechgroup.com

# CCNP Self-Study:

## Building Scalable Cisco Internetworks (

Second Edition

**Catherine Paquet**
**Diane Teare**

**Cisco Press**

Cisco Press
800 East 96th Street
Indianapolis, Indiana 46240 USA

# Feedback Information

At Cisco Press, our goal is to create in-depth technical books of the highest quality and value. Each book is crafted with care and precision, undergoing rigorous development that involves the unique expertise of members of the professional technical community.

Reader feedback is a natural continuation of this process. If you have any comments about how we could improve the quality of this book, or otherwise alter it to better suit your needs, you can contact us through e-mail at feedback@ciscopress.com. Please be sure to include the book title and ISBN in your message.

We greatly appreciate your assistance.

| | |
|---|---|
| Publisher | John Wait |
| Editor-in-Chief | John Kane |
| Executive Editor | Brett Bartow |
| Cisco Representative | Anthony Wolfenden |
| Cisco Press Program Manager | Nannette M. Noble |
| Production Manager | Patrick Kanouse |
| Development Editor | Andrew Cupp |
| Project Editor | Marc Fowler |
| Copy Editor | Gayle Johnson |
| Technical Editors | Elan Beer, Patrick Lao, Joseph Triolo |
| Team Coordinator | Tammi Barnett |
| Cover Designer | Louisa Adair |
| Composition | Interactive Composition Corporation |
| Indexer | Larry Sweazy |

**CISCO SYSTEMS**

**Corporate Headquarters**
Cisco Systems, Inc.
170 West Tasman Drive
San Jose, CA 95134-1706
USA
www.cisco.com
Tel: 408 526-4000
    800 553-NETS (6387)
Fax: 408 526-4100

**European Headquarters**
Cisco Systems International BV
Haarlerbergpark
Haarlerbergweg 13-19
1101 CH Amsterdam
The Netherlands
www-europe.cisco.com
Tel: 31 0 20 357 1000
Fax: 31 0 20 357 1100

**Americas Headquarters**
Cisco Systems, Inc.
170 West Tasman Drive
San Jose, CA 95134-1706
USA
www.cisco.com
Tel: 408 526-7660
Fax: 408 527-0883

**Asia Pacific Headquarters**
Cisco Systems, Inc.
Capital Tower
168 Robinson Road
#22-01 to #29-01
Singapore 068912
www.cisco.com
Tel: +65 6317 7777
Fax: +65 6317 7799

Cisco Systems has more than 200 offices in the following countries and regions. Addresses, phone numbers, and fax numbers are listed on the **Cisco.com Web site at www.cisco.com/go/offices.**

Argentina • Australia • Austria • Belgium • Brazil • Bulgaria • Canada • Chile • China PRC • Colombia • Costa Rica • Croatia • Czech Republic Denmark • Dubai, UAE • Finland • France • Germany • Greece • Hong Kong SAR • Hungary • India • Indonesia • Ireland • Israel • Italy Japan • Korea • Luxembourg • Malaysia • Mexico • The Netherlands • New Zealand • Norway • Peru • Philippines • Poland • Portugal Puerto Rico • Romania • Russia • Saudi Arabia • Scotland • Singapore • Slovakia • Slovenia • South Africa • Spain • Sweden Switzerland • Taiwan • Thailand • Turkey • Ukraine • United Kingdom • United States • Venezuela • Vietnam • Zimbabwe

# About the Authors

**Catherine Paquet** is a freelancer in the field of internetworking and security. She has in-depth knowledge of security systems, remote access, and routing technology. She is a Cisco Certified Security Professional (CCSP), a Cisco Certified Network Professional (CCNP), and a Cisco Certified Systems Instructor (CCSI) with one of Cisco's largest learning partners. She started her internetworking career as a LAN manager, moved to MAN manager, and eventually became the nationwide WAN manager. She was the course director/master instructor for the Building Cisco Remote Access Networks (BCRAN) and Managing Cisco Network Security (MCNS) courses at one of Cisco's largest learning partners. She was recently the Director of Technical Resources for the same company, where she was responsible for the instructor corps and the equipment offerings in Canada, including Cisco courses. She also teaches Cisco Secure PIX Firewall Advanced (CSPFA). In 2002 and 2003, she volunteered with the UN mission in Kabul, Afghanistan to train Afghan public servants in the area of networking. Paquet has a master's degree in business administration with a major in management information systems (MBA [MIS]). She coauthored Cisco Press's *Building Scalable Cisco Networks* and *CCNP Self-Study: Building Scalable Cisco Internetworks (BCSI)* and edited *Building Cisco Remote-Access Networks*.

**Diane Teare** is a consultant in the networking, training, and e-learning fields. She has more than 20 years of experience in designing, implementing, and troubleshooting network hardware and software and has also been involved in teaching, course design, and project management. She was the course director/master instructor for the Designing Cisco Networks (DCN) and Building Scalable Cisco Networks (BSCN) courses at one of the largest authorized Cisco learning partners. She was recently the Director of e-Learning for the same company, where she was responsible for planning and supporting all the company's e-learning offerings in Canada, including Cisco courses. Teare has a bachelor's degree in applied science in electrical engineering (BASc) and a master's degree in applied science in management science (MASc). She was a CCSI and currently holds her CCNP and Cisco Certified Design Professional (CCDP) certifications. She edited *Designing Cisco Networks*, authored *CCDA Self-Study: Designing for Cisco Internetwork Solutions (DESGN)*, and coauthored *Building Scalable Cisco Networks* and *CCNP Self-Study: Building Scalable Cisco Internetworks (BSCI)*, all from Cisco Press.

## About the Technical Reviewers

**Elan Beer,** CCIE No. 1837, is president and founder of Synaptic Solutions, Inc. For the past 15 years, he has held several key positions within the telecommunications industry, including senior telecommunications consultant, project manager, and telecommunications instructor, as well as Canadian training manager with Global Knowledge. Through his global consulting and training engagements, he is recognized internationally as a telecommunications industry expert. His strong technical skills have enabled him to attain several top-level industry certifications, including Cisco Certified Internetwork Expert. As one of the first product-based public Cisco instructors in the world, Beer has used his expertise in multiprotocol internetworking; LAN, WAN, and MAN technology; network management; and software engineering to provide training and consulting services to many of Canada's top companies. As a senior trainer and course developer, he has designed and presented intensive public and implementation-specific technical courses for clients in North America, Europe, Australia, Asia, and Scandinavia.

**Patrick Lao** has been a Cisco Systems education specialist since 1998. He has Cisco Certified Internetwork Expert (CCIE No. 4952), CCSI, CCNP, and CCNA certifications. As part of the BSCN and BSCI development teams, he developed all the labs for the BSCN and BSCI instructor-led courses. He has a bachelor of science degree in electrical engineering technology from Cal Poly Pomona and a master of science degree in telecommunications management from Golden Gate University.

**Joseph Triolo** has been focused on the internetworking and telecommunications field since 1987. He holds CCNP and CCSI certifications. He is currently employed at Global Knowledge Network Canada as a senior network architect and technical instructor, where he is the BSCI course director and teaches BSCI regularly. He also instructs other courses throughout North America, including CIT, BCMSN, OSPF, BGP, and multicast. He has specialized in Cisco training since 1999, after spending two years as a 3Com Certified Technical Trainer and more than 11 years in the telecommunications industry. There he held several positions, including telecommunications manager and network designer. An experienced professional, he today works with his consulting clients and in training services.

# Dedications

If a man empties his purse into his head, no man can take it away from him. An investment in knowledge always pays the best interest.

—Benjamin Franklin

From Diane:

This book is dedicated to my loving husband, Allan Mertin, who has given me remarkable encouragement and support; to our enchanting son, Nicholas, who never ceases to amaze us; and to my parents, Syd and Beryl, for their continuous warm thoughts and support.

From Catherine:

To my parents and sister, Maurice, Florence, and Hélène Paquet, for your continuous support: Thank you. To my children, Laurence and Simon: "Develop a passion for learning. If you do, you will never cease to grow."—Anthony J. D'Angelor. And, finally, to Pierre Rivard, my soul mate, husband, and an eternal learner: Your enthusiasm is contagious. Thanks for sharing it with us.

# Acknowledgments

We would like to thank many people for helping us put this book together:

**The Cisco Press team:** Brett Bartow, the executive editor, was the catalyst for this project, coordinating the team and ensuring that sufficient resources were available for the completion of the book. Drew Cupp, the development editor, has been invaluable in producing a high-quality manuscript. His great suggestions and keen eye caught some technical errors and really improved the presentation of the book. We would also like to thank Marc Fowler, the project editor, and Gayle Johnson, the copy editor, for their excellent work in shepherding this book through the editorial process.

**The Cisco Systems team:** Many thanks to the other members of the development team of the original BSCN and BSCI courses, including Patrick Lao, Kip Peterson, Keith Serrao, Kevin Calkins, Won Lee, and Imran Quershi.

**The technical reviewers:** We would like to thank the technical reviewers of this book—Elan Beer, Patrick Lao, and Joseph Triolo—for their thorough, detailed review and very valuable input.

**Global Knowledge Network (Canada):** Thanks to Eric Dragowski and Mark Martinovic for providing us with equipment and support when we needed to run some tests.

**Our families:** Of course, this book would not have been possible without the constant understanding and patience of our families. They have always been there to motivate and inspire us. We thank you all.

**Each other:** Last, but not least, this book is a product of work by two friends, which made it even more of a pleasure to complete.

# Contents at a Glance

# Table of Contents

# Foreword

*CCNP Self-Study: Building Scalable Cisco Internetworks (BSCI)*, Second Edition, is a Cisco-authorized, self-paced learning tool that helps you understand foundation concepts covered on the CCNP BSCI exam. This book was developed in cooperation with the Cisco Internet Learning Solutions group, the team within Cisco responsible for the development of the CCNP exams. As an early-stage exam preparation product, this book presents a detailed and comprehensive introduction to the use of advanced IP addressing and routing in implementing scalability for Cisco routers connected to LANs and WANs. Whether you are studying to become CCNP certified, or you are simply seeking to gain a better understanding of advanced routing protocol concepts, configuration, and management, you will benefit from the information presented in this book.

Cisco Systems and Cisco Press present this material in text-based format to provide another learning vehicle for our customers and the broader user community in general. Although a publication does not duplicate the instructor-led or e-learning environment, we acknowledge that not everyone responds in the same way to the same delivery mechanism. It is our intent that presenting this material via a Cisco Press publication will enhance the transfer of knowledge to a broad audience of networking professionals.

Cisco Press will present other books in the Certification Self-Study series on existing and future exams to help achieve the Cisco Internet Learning Solutions Group's principal objectives: to educate the Cisco community of networking professionals and to enable that community to build and maintain reliable, scalable networks. The Cisco Career Certifications and classes that support these certifications are directed at meeting these objectives through a disciplined approach to progressive learning.

To succeed with Cisco Career Certifications and in your daily job as a Cisco-certified professional, we recommend a blended learning solution that combines instructor-led training with hands-on experience, e-learning, and self-study training. Cisco Systems has authorized Cisco Learning Partners worldwide that can provide you with the most highly qualified instruction and invaluable hands-on experience in lab and simulation environments. To learn more about Cisco Learning Partner programs available in your area, go to www.cisco.com/go/authorizedtraining.

The books Cisco Press creates in partnership with Cisco Systems meet the same standards for content quality demanded of our courses and certifications. It is our intent that you will find this and subsequent Cisco Press certification self-study publications of value as you build your networking knowledge base.

Thomas M. Kelly
Vice President, Internet Learning Solutions Group
Cisco Systems, Inc.
March 2004

# Introduction

Internetworks are growing at a fast pace to support more protocols and users and are becoming more complex. As the premier designer and provider of internetworking devices, Cisco Systems is committed to supporting these growing networks.

This book teaches you how to design, configure, maintain, and scale a routed network. It focuses on using Cisco routers connected in LANs and WANs typically found at medium-to-large network sites. After completing this book, you will be able to select and implement the appropriate Cisco IOS services required to build a scalable, routed network.

In this book, you will study a broad range of technical details on topics related to routing, including advanced IP addressing issues such as variable-length subnet masks (VLSMs), route summarization, network address translation (NAT), and IP version 6 (IPv6). You will also examine principles of routing protocols before studying in detail the following routing protocols: Enhanced Interior Gateway Routing Protocol (EIGRP), Open Shortest Path First (OSPF), Intermediate System-to-Intermediate System (IS-IS), and Border Gateway Protocol (BGP). Running multiple routing protocols and controlling the information passed between them are also examined. Configuration examples and sample verification outputs demonstrate troubleshooting techniques and illustrate critical issues surrounding network operation. Chapter-ending Configuration Exercises and Review Questions illustrate and help solidify the concepts presented in this book.

This book starts you down the path toward attaining your Cisco Certified Network Professional (CCNP), Cisco Certified Internetwork Professional (CCIP), or Cisco Certified Design Professional (CCDP) certification, because it provides in-depth information to help you prepare for the BSCI exam.

The commands and configuration examples presented in this book are based on Cisco IOS Releases 12.0 and 12.1.

## Who Should Read This Book

This book is intended for network architects, network designers, systems engineers, network managers, and network administrators who are responsible for implementing and troubleshooting growing routed networks.

If you are planning to take the BSCI exam toward your CCNP, CCIP, or CCDP certification, this book provides you with in-depth study material.

To fully benefit from this book, you should be CCNA certified or should possess the following knowledge:

- A working knowledge of the OSI reference model.

- An understanding of internetworking fundamentals, including commonly used networking terms, numbering schemes, topologies, distance vector routing protocol operation, and when to use static and default routes.

- The ability to operate and configure a Cisco router, including displaying and interpreting a router's routing table, configuring static and default routes, enabling a WAN serial connection using High-Level Data Link Control (HDLC) or PPP, configuring Frame Relay permanent virtual circuits (PVCs) on interfaces and subinterfaces, configuring IP standard and extended access lists, and verifying router configurations with available tools, such as **show** and **debug** commands.

- Working knowledge of the TCP/IP stack, configuring IP addresses, and configuring Routing Information Protocol (RIP) and Interior Gateway Routing Protocol (IGRP).

If you lack this knowledge and these skills, you can gain them by completing Cisco's Introduction to Cisco Networking Technologies (INTRO) and Interconnecting Cisco Network Devices (ICND) courses or by reading the related Cisco Press books. See Appendix C for a listing of some of the Cisco router and switch IOS commands you might find in ICND, organized in various categories.

## What's New in This Edition

This book is an update to *CCNP Self-Study: Building Scalable Cisco Internetworks (BSCI)* (ISBN 1-58705-084-6). This second edition addresses changes to the BSCI course. The following are the major changes between books:

- Each topic has been rewritten. Any items that were removed from the main portion of the previous edition because of course changes have been put in an appendix or sidebar, as appropriate.
- New topics include IPv6 and NAT.
- Configuration Exercises now use four routers per pod (previously there were three routers per pod). All configuration exercises have changed and have been redone on this new configuration.
- The order in which the routing protocols are presented has changed. The previous order was OSPF, IS-IS, EIGRP, BGP, optimizing routing updates. The order in this book is EIGRP, OSPF, IS-IS, manipulating routing updates, BGP.
- The JKL case study was deleted.
- A supplement was added to Appendix A to offer extra IS-IS information.

## Objectives of This Book

When you complete the readings and exercises in this book, you will be able to describe advanced IP addressing issues, including VLSMs, route summarization, classless interdomain routing (CIDR), basic IPv6 concepts, route maps, and NAT. You will also be able to describe advanced IP routing principles, including static and dynamic routing characteristics and the concepts of classful and classless routing and address summarization. You will be able to configure EIGRP for a scalable network, OSPF and IS-IS for scalable multiarea networks, and basic BGP for internal and external connections. You will also be able to manipulate routing updates and packet flow using redistribution, distribution lists, administrative distance, route maps, and policy-based routing.

## Summary of Contents

The chapters and appendixes in this book are as follows:

Chapter 1, "Advanced IP Addressing," discusses various aspects of IP addressing, including VLSMs, route summarization, CIDR, NAT, and IPv6.

Chapter 2, "Routing Principles," covers the principles of routing, including classful and classless routing, and the differences between distance vector and link-state routing protocol behavior.

Chapter 3, "Configuring Enhanced Interior Gateway Routing Protocol," introduces EIGRP. Topics include EIGRP features, modes of operations, and configuring and verifying EIGRP.

Chapter 4, "Configuring the Open Shortest Path First Protocol in a Single Area," introduces the OSPF routing protocol. Topics include OSPF terminology and operation in a broadcast multiaccess topology, a point-to-point topology, and an NBMA topology.

Chapter 5, "Interconnecting Multiple Open Shortest Path First Areas," covers the use, operation, configuration, and verification of OSPF in multiple areas.

Chapter 6, "Configuring the Intermediate System-to-Intermediate System Protocol," provides an overview of IS-IS technology and its structures and protocols, as well as basic configuration examples.

Chapter 7, "Manipulating Routing Updates," discusses different ways to control routing update information. Route redistribution to interconnect networks that use multiple routing protocols is explained. You can control information between the protocols by using distribute lists and route maps and by changing the administrative distance. Policy-based routing using route maps is also explained. The configuration of each of these techniques is discussed in this chapter.

Chapter 8, "Configuring Basic Border Gateway Protocol," introduces BGP, including BGP terminology and the fundamentals of BGP operation.

Chapter 9, "Advanced Border Gateway Protocol Configuration," starts with a discussion of BGP route summarization, followed by a study of BGP path manipulation using route maps. Connecting an autonomous system (AS) with more than one BGP connection is called multihoming, and different ways to accomplish this are explored.

Appendix A, "Job Aids and Supplements," contains job aids and supplements for the following topics: IPv4 addressing, EIGRP, OSPF, IS-IS, BGP, and route optimization.

Appendix B, "Router Password Recovery Procedure," contains the procedure for password recovery on Cisco routers.

Appendix C, "Summary of ICND Router and Switch Commands," lists some of the Cisco router and switch IOS commands covered in the ICND course, organized in various categories.

Appendix D, "Summary of BSCI Router Commands," lists some of the Cisco router IOS commands you might find in this book, organized in various categories.

Appendix E, "OSI Reference Model," is a brief overview of the Open System Interconnection (OSI) seven-layer model.

Appendix F, "Common Requests for Comments," lists some common RFCs.

Appendix G, "Answers to Review Questions," contains the answers to the review questions that appear at the end of each chapter.

Appendix H, "Configuration Exercise Equipment Requirements and Initial Configurations," contains information on the equipment requirements for the Configuration Exercises, along with the initial configuration commands for the routers.

The glossary defines networking terms and acronyms used throughout this book.

## Configuration Exercises and Review Questions

Configuration exercises at the end of the chapters let you practice configuring routers with the commands presented. If you have access to real hardware, you can try these exercises on your routers; refer to Appendix H for a list of recommended equipment and initial configuration commands for the routers. However, even if you don't have access to any routers, you can go through the exercises and keep a log of your own running configurations on separate sheets of paper. Commands used and solutions to the Configuration Exercises are provided after the exercise sections.

At the end of each chapter, you can test your knowledge by answering review questions on the subjects covered in that chapter. You can compare your answers to the answers provided in Appendix G to find out how you did and what material you might need to study further.

# Icons Used in This Book

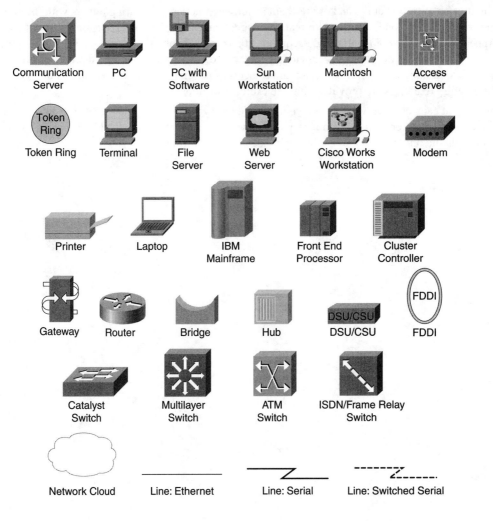

# Command Syntax Conventions

The conventions used to present command syntax in this book are the same conventions used in the IOS Command Reference. The Command Reference describes these conventions as follows:

- **Bold** indicates commands and keywords that are entered literally as shown. In actual configuration examples and output (not general command syntax), bold indicates commands that are manually input by the user (such as a **show** command).
- *Italic* indicates arguments for which you supply actual values.
- Vertical bars (|) separate alternative, mutually exclusive elements.
- Square brackets ([ ]) indicate an optional element.
- Braces ({ }) indicate a required choice.
- Braces within brackets ([{ }]) indicate a required choice within an optional element.

# Author's Notes, Key Points, Sidebars, and Cautions

The notes, sidebars, and cautions found in this book provide extra information on a subject. The key points highlight specific points of interest.

This chapter discusses the following advanced IP addressing topics:

- IP Address Planning
- Hierarchical Addressing Using Variable-Length Subnet Masks
- Route Summarization
- Classless Interdomain Routing
- Network Address Translation
- Understanding IP Version 6

# Advanced IP Addressing

Scalable, well-behaved networks are not accidental; they are the result of good network design and effective implementation planning. A key element for effective scalable network implementation is a well-conceived and scalable IP addressing plan. The purpose of a scalable IP addressing plan is to maximize the amount of IP address space available in deployed networks (this address space is shrinking) and to minimize the size of routing tables.

As a network grows, the number of subnets and the volume of network addresses required increase proportionally. Without advanced IP addressing techniques such as summarization and classless interdomain routing (CIDR), the size of the routing tables increases, which causes a variety of problems. For example, networks require more CPU resources to respond to each topology change in the larger routing tables. In addition, larger routing tables can cause delays while the CPU sorts and searches for a match to a destination address. Both of these problems are solved by summarization and CIDR.

To effectively use summarization and CIDR to control the size of routing tables, network administrators employ other advanced IP addressing techniques such as Network Address Translation (NAT) and variable-length subnet masking (VLSM).

NAT allows the use of a private addressing space within an organization while using globally unique addresses for routing across the Internet and between independent divisions of the organization. Different address pools may be used to track groups of users, which makes it easier to manage interconnectivity.

VLSM allows the network administrator to subnet a previously subnetted address to make the best use of the available address space.

Another long-standing problem that network administrators must overcome is the exhaustion of available IP addresses caused by the increase in Internet use. Although the current solution is to use NAT, the long-term solution is to migrate from the IP version 4 (IPv4) 32-bit address space to the IP version 6 (IPv6) 128-bit address space. Gaining insight into IPv6 functionality and deployment will prove valuable for network administrators in the not-too-distant future.

After completing this chapter, you will be able to describe the concepts of network design and explain the benefits and characteristics of an effective scalable IP addressing plan. You will also be able to describe the role of VLSM addressing in a scalable network and calculate VLSM addresses for a network. You will be able to demonstrate the principles of route summarization and CIDR by summarizing a given range of network addresses into larger IP address blocks. You will also be able to configure NAT for multiple address pools using access lists and route maps. Finally, you will be able to describe the features and benefits of using IPv6.

# IP Address Planning

A well-designed large-scale internetwork with an effective IP addressing plan has many benefits. It is scalable, flexible, predictable, and can reduce the routing table size through summarization.

## Scalable Network Design

An understanding of scalable network design concepts is imperative for understanding proper IP address planning.

Corporate organizational structure should affect network design. The structure of a scalable network design reflects a corporation's information flow and is called a *hierarchical network design*.

There are two types of hierarchical network design: functional and geographic.

---

**NOTE**   The design concepts discussed in this section are only a very small part of good network design from the perspective of the IP addressing plan. For a full discussion of internetwork design, refer to *CCDA Self-Study: Designing for Cisco Internetwork Solutions (DESGN)* (Cisco Press, 2003).

---

### Functional Structured Design

Some corporations have independent divisions that are responsible for their own operations, including networking. These divisions interact with one another and share resources; however, each division has an independent chain of command.

This type of corporate structure is reflected in a functional network design, as illustrated in Figure 1-1. In this example, the different divisions of the corporation have their own networks and are connected according to their functional purpose within the corporate structure. The network architecture can follow the corporate organizational chart.

**Figure 1-1**    *In a Functional Design, Networks Are Connected According to Their Functional Purpose*

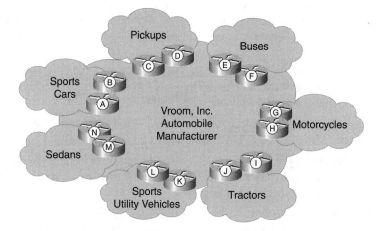

## Geographic Structured Design

Many retail corporations are organized by the geographic location of their stores. Within the corporate structure, each local retail store reports to a district consolidation point. These district consolidation points report to regional consolidation points; the regional consolidation points then report to corporate headquarters. Networks are organized along geographic boundaries, such as countries, states, or provinces.

This type of corporate structure is reflected in a geographic network design, as illustrated in Figure 1-2. In this example, the divisions of the corporation have their own networks and are connected according to their location.

**Figure 1-2**    *In a Geographic Design, Networks Are Connected According to Their Location*

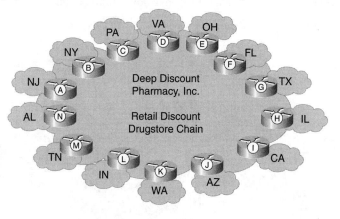

**NOTE**    From a networking point of view, a geographic network structure is cost-effective because fewer network links require long-haul carriers, often a considerable added expense.

## Hierarchical Layers

Within the functional or geographic networks, the following three primary layer elements are involved in a hierarchical scalable network design:

- **Access layer**—Provides local and remote workgroup, end-user, and customer access to the network. Virtual LANs (VLANs), firewalls, and access lists maintain security for this layer.

- **Distribution layer**—Provides policy-based connectivity and is the consolidation point for access layer devices and corporate services. Host services required by multiple access layer devices are assigned to this layer.

- **Core (or backbone) layer**—Provides high-speed transport to satisfy the connectivity and transport needs of the distribution layer devices. The circuits with the fastest bandwidth are in the core layer of the network. Redundancy occurs more frequently at this layer than at the other layers.

There are many different ways of designing these hierarchical layers. Some of the considerations are identified in this section.

## Fully Meshed Core Layer

The core layer is designed to provide quick and efficient access to headquarters and other divisions within a company. Because the core is usually critical to the network, redundancy is often found in this layer. In a fully meshed core layer design, shown in Figure 1-3, each division has redundant routers at the core layer. The core sites are fully meshed, meaning that all routers have direct connections to all other routers. This connectivity allows the network to react quickly when it must route data flow from a downed link to another path.

**Figure 1-3**    *In a Fully Meshed Core, All Routers Are Connected to All Other Routers*

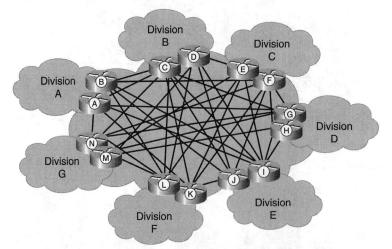

For a small core with a limited number of divisions, this core layer design provides robust connectivity. However, a fully meshed core layer design is very expensive for a corporation with many divisions.

**NOTE**    The number of links in a full mesh is $n(n-1)/2$, where $n$ is the number of routers. As the number of routers increases, the cost of full-mesh connectivity might become prohibitive.

### Hub-and-Spoke Core Layer

As a network grows, fully meshing all the core routers can become difficult. At that point, consolidation into geographically separate data centers might be appropriate. For example, in many companies, data travels to a centralized headquarters where the corporate databases and network services reside. To reflect this corporate centralization, the core layer hub-and-spoke configuration establishes a focal point for the data flow at a key site. The hub-and-spoke design, illustrated in Figure 1-4, supports the traffic flow through the corporation.

**Figure 1-4**    *In a Hub-and-Spoke Core, Each Division Is Connected Only to the Headquarters*

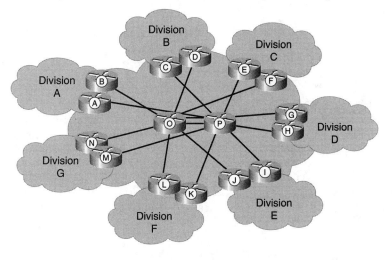

**NOTE**    A partial-mesh design is also possible, including some nodes connected in a full mesh and some connected in hub-and-spoke fashion.

### Access and Distribution Layers

Remote sites are points of entry to the network for end users and customers. Within the network, remote sites gain access to network services through the access layer. The distribution layer consolidates the services and devices that the access layer needs to process the activity that is generated by the remote sites. Figure 1-5 illustrates this process.

**Figure 1-5**   *The Distribution Layer Consolidates Access Layer Connectivity*

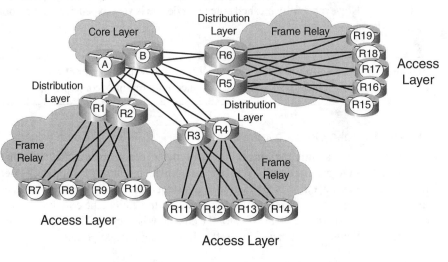

Frame Relay, shown in Figure 1-5, is a WAN access protocol commonly used to interconnect geographically dispersed sites.

Services should be placed in the distribution layer when there is no benefit to having duplicated services at the remote sites. These services may include Dynamic Host Configuration Protocol (DHCP), Domain Name System (DNS), human resources, and accounting servers. One or more distribution layers can connect to each entry point at the core layer.

You can fully mesh connectivity between remote sites at the access layer. However, using a hub-and-spoke configuration by connecting remote sites to at least two distribution layer devices provides redundancy and is relatively easy to administer.

# Benefits of a Good Network Design

An effective network design accommodates unexpected growth and quick changes in the corporate environment. The network design can be adapted to accommodate mergers with other companies, corporate restructuring, and downsizing with minimal impact on the portions of the network that do not change.

The following are characteristics of a good IP addressing plan implemented in a well-designed network:

- **Scalability**—A well-designed network allows for significant increases in the number of supported sites.

- **Predictability**—A well-designed network exhibits predictable behavior and performance.
- **Flexibility**—A well-designed network minimizes the impact of additions, changes, or removals within the network.

These characteristics are described further in the following sections.

## Scalability of a Good Network Design

Private addresses are reserved IPv4 addresses to be used only internally within a company's network. These private addresses are not to be used on the Internet, so they must be mapped to a company's external registered address when you send anything to a recipient on the Internet.

---

### Key Point: IPv4 Private Addresses

RFC 1918, *Address Allocation for Private Internets* (available at www.cis.ohio-state.edu /cgi-bin/rfc/rfc1918.html), has set aside the following IPv4 address space for private use:

- **Class A network**—10.0.0.0 to 10.255.255.255
- **Class B network**—172.16.0.0 to 172.31.255.255
- **Class C network**—192.168.0.0 to 192.168.255.255

---

**NOTE**    The examples in this book use only private addressing.

---

The current proliferation of corporate mergers emphasizes the design issues inherent in private IPv4 addressing. For example, if two companies merge, and both use network 10.0.0.0 addresses, there will likely be some overlapping addressing space.

A scalable network that integrates private addressing with a good IP addressing plan minimizes the impact of additions or reorganizations of divisions to a network. A scalable network allows companies that merge to connect at the core layer. Implementing NAT on routers allows the network administrator to translate overlapping network numbers to an unused address space as a temporary solution. Then, the overlapping network numbers can be changed on the devices and/or on the DHCP server in the network.

Good network design also facilitates the process of adding routers to an existing network. For example, in Figure 1-6, two companies have merged. Both companies were using network 10.0.0.0 for addressing. One correct way to merge the two networks would be as follows:

- Attach routers P and Q in the new domain to the other routers in the core layer of the network (routers A, D, J, K, X, and Y).

- Configure NAT on routers P and Q to change the IP address space of the new company from network 10.0.0.0 to network 172.16.0.0.

- Change the DHCP servers to reflect the newly assigned address space in the new network.

- Remove NAT from routers P and Q.

**Figure 1-6**   *A Good IP Addressing Design Minimizes the Impact of Merging Networks*

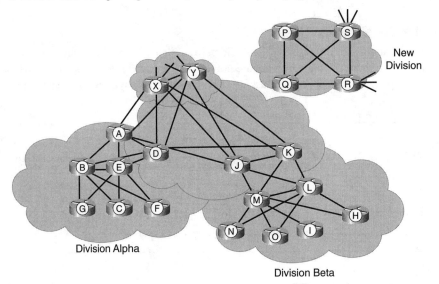

## Predictability of a Good Network Design

The behavior of a scalable network is predictable.

Packets load-balance across the internetwork if equal-cost paths exist between any two routers in the internetwork. When a circuit or router fails, an alternative equal-cost path to the destination that exists in every routing table can be used, without any recalculation. This alternative path reduces convergence times and route recalculation to typically less than 1 second after the failed circuit or router is discovered.

Depending on the routing protocol used, the equal cost is determined based on hop count and/ or bandwidth. For example, if the Routing Information Protocol (RIP) is used in the network shown in Figure 1-6, the routing table for router C will have two best paths to X: three hops through B and three hops through E. Routers B and E each have two best paths to the networks behind router X: Both have two hops through either routers A or D. If router D fails, routers B and E do not need to discover alternative routes because the preferred route exists in the routing table. Thus, if router D fails, the routes to X in router C's routing table do not change.

If a routing protocol that uses bandwidth in its calculation is used (for example, Interior Gateway Routing Protocol [IGRP]), the bandwidth should be configured equally on all interfaces within a layer at each site. For example, in Figure 1-6, routers B and E are consolidation points for the access layer routers (G, C, and F in the example). Routers C, B, and E all have the same bandwidth configured on the links that connect them so that load balancing can be used.

The paths between routers B and E and routers A and D need larger-bandwidth pipes to consolidate the traffic between corporate divisions. Because routers A and D consolidate multiple distribution points for a division, the connections for these routers to other divisions in the company need the largest bandwidth.

The result is a predictable traffic pattern. This level of network behavior predictability is a direct benefit of a scalable network design.

### Flexibility of a Good Network Design

A scalable network also needs to be flexible. For example, corporate reorganizations can have minimal impact on the rest of the network when implemented in a scalable network. In the sample network shown in Figure 1-6, assume that Frame Relay is used at the remote sites and that Division Beta is sold and merged with another company, except for remote site H, which becomes part of Division Alpha.

The network administrator in this sample network could accommodate the corporate reorganization with the following process:

- Install two additional virtual circuits from router H to routers B and E.
- Following a successful installation, remove the virtual circuits to routers M and L.
- Perform NAT on the router H interfaces to routers B and E to use the address space of Division Alpha.
- Remove the circuits from routers J and K to the other core routers A, D, X, and Y (and P and Q if they are connected).
- Change the user addresses for router H to the Division Alpha block of addresses.

## Benefits of an Optimized IP Addressing Plan

An optimized IP addressing plan uses hierarchical addressing.

Perhaps the best-known addressing hierarchy is the telephone network. The telephone network uses a hierarchical numbering scheme that includes country codes, area codes, and local exchange numbers. For example, if you are in San Jose, California, and you call someone else in San Jose, you dial the San Jose local exchange number, 528, and the person's four digit number. Upon seeing the number 528, the central office recognizes that the destination telephone is within its area, so it looks up the four digit number and transfers the call.

**NOTE** In many places in North America now, the area code must also be dialed for local calls. This is because of changes in the use of specific digits for area codes and local exchange numbers. The telephone network is suffering from *address exhaustion*, just like the IP network. Changes in how telephone numbers are used is one solution being implemented to solve this problem.

In another example (see Figure 1-7), to call Aunt Judy in Alexandria, Virginia, from San Jose, you dial 1, and then the area code 703, and then the Alexandria prefix 555, and then Aunt Judy's local number, 1212. The central office first sees the number 1, indicating a remote call, and then looks up the number 703. The central office immediately routes the call to a central office in Alexandria. The San Jose central office does not know exactly where 555-1212 is in Alexandria, nor does it have to. It needs to know only the area codes, which summarize the local telephone numbers within an area.

**Figure 1-7**  *The Telephone Network Uses an Addressing Hierarchy*

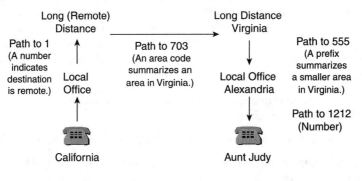

**NOTE** As you might have noticed, the telephone number used in this example is the number for international directory assistance; it is used for illustration purposes to ensure that Aunt Judy's personal number is not published.

If there were no hierarchical structure, every central office would need to have every telephone number worldwide in its locator table. Instead, the central offices have summary numbers, such as area codes and country codes. A summary number (address) represents a group of numbers. For example, an area code such as 408 is a summary number for the San Jose area. In other words, if you dial 1-408 from anywhere in the U.S. or Canada, followed by a seven-digit telephone number, the central office routes the call to a San Jose central office. Similarly, a routed network can employ a hierarchical addressing scheme to take advantage of those same benefits.

Here are some of the benefits of hierarchical addressing:

- **Reduced number of routing table entries**—Whether it is with your Internet routers or your internal routers, you should try to keep your routing tables as small as possible by using route summarization. Route summarization is a way of having a single IP address represent a collection of IP addresses; this is most easily accomplished when you employ a hierarchical addressing plan. By summarizing routes, you can keep your routing table entries (on the routers that receive the summarized routes) manageable, which offers the following benefits:

  - More efficient routing
  - A reduced number of CPU cycles when recalculating a routing table or sorting through the routing table entries to find a match
  - Reduced router memory requirements
  - Reduced bandwidth required to send the fewer, smaller routing updates
  - Faster convergence after a change in the network
  - Easier troubleshooting
  - Increased network stability

- **Efficient allocation of addresses**—Hierarchical addressing lets you take advantage of all possible addresses because you group them contiguously. With random address assignment, you might end up wasting groups of addresses because of addressing conflicts. For example, classful routing protocols (discussed in the later section "Implementing VLSM in a Scalable Network") automatically create summary routes at a network boundary. Therefore, these protocols do not support discontiguous addressing (as you will see in Chapter 2, "Routing Principles"), so some addresses would be unusable if not assigned contiguously.

Within the context of hierarchical addressing, the IP addressing plan must include provisions for summarization at key points. Summarization (also called aggregation or information hiding) is not a new concept. When a router announces a route to a given network, the route is a summarization of the addresses in the routing table for all the host devices and individual addresses that reside on that network.

Summarization helps reduce routing-table size and helps localize topology changes. This promotes network stability because a reduced routing-table size means that less bandwidth, memory, and CPU cycles are required to calculate the best path selection. Because summarization limits the propagation of detailed routes, it also reduces the impact to the network when these detailed routes fail.

## Scalable Network Addressing Example

The network illustrated in Figure 1-8 shows an example of scalable addressing. In this example, a U.S. national drugstore chain plans to have a retail outlet in every city in the country with a population greater than 10,000. Each of the 50 states has up to 100 stores, with two Ethernet LANs in each store:

- One LAN is used to track customer prescriptions and pharmacy inventory and reorder stock.

- The second LAN is used to stock the rest of the store and connect the cash registers to a corporate-wide, instantaneous point-of-sale evaluation tool.

**Figure 1-8**  *Scalable Addressing Allows Summarization*

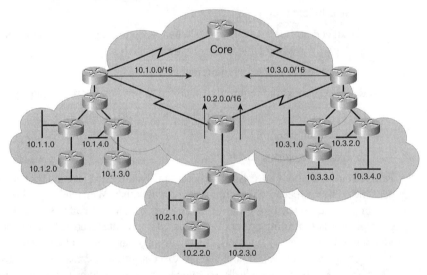

The total number of Ethernet LAN networks is 50 states * 100 stores per state * 2 LANs per store = 10,000. (An equal number of serial links interconnect these stores.)

Using a scalable design and creating 51 divisions (one for each state and one for the backbone interconnecting the divisions), the corporation can assign each division a block of IP addresses 10.x.0.0 /16. Each LAN is assigned a /24 subnet of network 10.0.0.0, and each division has 200 such subnets (two for each of the 100 stores). The network will have 10,000 subnets; without summarization, each of the 5000 routers will have all these networks in their routing tables.

If each division router summarizes its block of networks 10.x.0.0 /16 at the entry point to the core network, any router in a division has only the 200 /24 subnets within that division, plus the 49 10.x.0.0 /16 summarizations that represent the other divisions, in its routing table. This results in a total of 249 networks in each IP routing table.

## Nonscalable Network Addressing

In contrast to the previous example, if a hierarchical addressing plan is not used, summarization is not possible, as is the case in Figure 1-9. Problems can occur in this network related to the frequency and size of routing table updates and how topology changes are processed in summarized and unsummarized networks. These problems are described next.

**Figure 1-9**  *Nonscalable Addressing Results in Large Routing Tables*

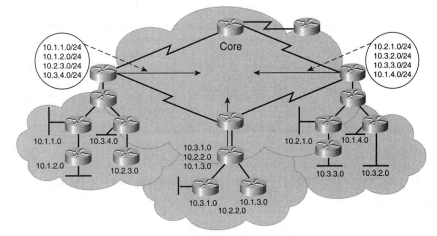

## Update Size

Routing protocols such as RIP and IGRP, which send a periodic update every 30 and 90 seconds, respectively, use valuable bandwidth to maintain a table without summarization. A single RIP update packet is limited to carrying 25 routes; therefore, 10,000 routes means that RIP on every router must create and send 400 packets every 30 seconds. With summarized routes, the 249 routes means that only 10 packets need to be sent every 30 seconds.

## Unsummarized Internetwork Topology Changes

A routing table with 10,000 entries constantly changes. To illustrate this constant change, consider the sample network with a router at each of 5000 different sites. A power outage occurs at site A, a backhoe digs a trench at site B, a newly-hired system administrator begins work at site C, a Cisco IOS software upgrade is in progress at site D, and a newly-added router is being installed at site E.

Every time a route changes, all the routing tables must be updated. For example, when using a routing protocol such as Open Shortest Path First (OSPF), an upgrade or topology change on the internetwork causes a shortest path first (SPF) calculation. The SPF calculations are large because each router needs to calculate all known pathways to each of the 10,000 networks. Each change a router receives requires time and CPU resources to process.

## Summarized Network Topology Changes

In contrast to an unsummarized network, a summarized network responds efficiently to network changes. For example, in the sample drugstore network with 200 routes for each division, the routers within the division see all the subnets for that division. When a change occurs on one of the 200 routes in the division, all other routers in the division recalculate to reflect the topology change of those affected networks. However, the core router of that division passes a summarized /16 route and suppresses the /24 networks from advertisement to the core routers of other divisions. The summarized route is announced as long as any portion of the summarized block can be reached from that core router. The more-specific routes are suppressed so that changes from this division are not propagated to other divisions.

In this scenario, each router has only 200 /24 networks, compared to the 10,000 /24 networks in an unsummarized environment. Obviously, the amount of CPU resources, memory, and bandwidth required for the 200 networks is less than the 10,000 networks. With summarization, each division hides more-specific information from the other divisions and passes only the summarized route that represents that overall division.

# Hierarchical Addressing Using Variable-Length Subnet Masks

VLSM is a crucial component of an effective IP addressing plan for a scalable network. This section introduces VLSM, provides examples, and discusses methods of determining the best subnet mask for a given address requirement.

## Network Mask and Prefix Length

The concept and definition of a network mask and the prefix length field relate to hierarchically addressed network implementation. This section discusses the purpose of the network mask and the prefix length and describes their use within a network.

### IP Addressing and Subnetting

---

**NOTE**      This section is an overview of IP addressing and subnetting. Appendix A, "Job Aids and Supplements," includes a more detailed review of these topics.

---

A subnet mask is a 32-bit value that identifies which bits in an address represent network bits and which represent host bits. To create a subnet mask for an address, use a 1 for each bit of the address that you want to represent the network or subnet portion of the address, and use a 0 for each bit of the address that you want to represent the node portion of the address. Note that the 1s in the mask are contiguous. The default subnet masks for Classes A, B, and C addresses are as shown in Table 1-1.

**Table 1-1**    *IP Address Default Subnet Masks*

| Class | Default Mask in Binary | Default Mask in Decimal |
|-------|------------------------|-------------------------|
| A | 11111111.00000000.00000000.00000000 | 255.0.0.0 |
| B | 11111111.11111111.00000000.00000000 | 255.255.0.0 |
| C | 11111111.11111111.11111111.00000000 | 255.255.255.0 |

When contiguous 1s are added to the default mask, making the all-1s field in the mask longer, the definition of the network part of an IP address is extended to include subnets. Adding bits to the network part of an address decreases the number of bits in the host part. Thus, creating additional networks (subnets) is done at the expense of the number of host devices that can occupy each network segment.

The number of bits added to a default routing mask creates a counting range for counting subnets. Each subnet is a unique binary pattern.

The number of subnetworks created is calculated by the formula $2^n$, where $n$ is the number of bits by which the default mask was extended. Subnet 0 (where all the subnet bits are 0) must be explicitly allowed using the **ip subnet-zero** global configuration command in Cisco IOS releases before 12.0. In Cisco IOS Release 12.0 and later, subnet 0 is enabled by default.

---

**NOTE**    This book describes the formula for obtaining the number of subnets differently than some previous Cisco courses and books. Previously, the same formula that was used to count hosts, $2^n - 2$, was used to count subnets. Now $2^n$ subnets and $2^n - 2$ hosts are available. The $2^n$ rule for subnets has been adopted because the all-1s subnet has always been a legal subnet according to the RFC, and subnet 0 can be enabled by a configuration command on Cisco routers (and, in fact, it's on by default in Cisco IOS Release 12.0 and later). Note, however, that not all vendor equipment supports the use of subnet 0.

---

The remaining bits in the routing mask form a counting range for hosts. Host addresses are selected from these remaining bits and must be numerically unique from all other hosts on the subnetwork.

The number of hosts available is calculated by the formula $2^n - 2$, where $n$ is the number of bits in the host portion. In the host counting range, the all-0s bit pattern is reserved as the subnet identifier (sometimes called *the wire*), and the all-1s bit pattern is reserved as a broadcast address, to reach all hosts on that subnet.

Both the IP address and the associated mask contain 32 bits. Routers are similar to computers in that both use the binary numbering scheme to represent addresses. Network administrators, however, typically do not use binary numbers on a daily basis and therefore have adopted other formats to represent 32-bit IP addresses. Some common formats include decimal (base 10) and hexadecimal (base 16) notations.

The generally accepted method of representing IP addresses and masks is to break the 32-bit field into four groups of 8 bits (octets) and to represent those 8-bit fields in a decimal format, separated by decimal points. This is known as 32-bit *dotted-decimal notation*.

---

**NOTE**    Although dotted-decimal notation is commonly accepted, this notation means nothing to routing or computing devices, because devices internally use the 32-bit binary string. All routing decisions are based on the 32-bit binary string.

---

Subnet masks are used to identify the number of bits in an address that represent the network, subnet, and host portions of the address. Another way of indicating this information is to use a *prefix*. A prefix is a slash (/) followed by a numeric value that is the number of bits in the network and subnet portions of the address—in other words, the number of contiguous 1s that are in the subnet mask. For example, assume you are using a subnet mask of 255.255.255.0. The binary representation of this mask is 11111111.11111111.11111111.00000000, which is 24 1s followed by eight 0s. Thus, the prefix would be /24, for the 24 bits of network and subnet information, the number of 1s in the mask.

## Use of the Network Mask

If a PC has an IP address of 192.168.1.67 with a mask of 255.255.255.240 (or a prefix length of /28), it uses this mask to determine the valid host addresses for devices on its local connection. These devices have the first 28 bits in their IP address in common (the range of these local devices is 192.168.1.65 through 192.168.1.78). If communication with any of these devices is necessary, the PC uses Address Resolution Protocol (ARP) to find the device's corresponding media access control (MAC) address (assuming that it does not already have a destination MAC address for the IP address in its MAC table). If a PC needs to send information to an IP device that is not in the local range, the PC instead forwards the information to its default gateway. (The PC also uses ARP to discover the MAC address of the default gateway.)

A router behaves in a similar manner when it makes a routing decision. A packet arrives on the router and is passed to the routing table. The router compares the packet's destination IP address to the entries in the routing table. These entries have a prefix length associated with them. The router uses the prefix length as the minimum number of destination address bits that must match to use the corresponding outbound interface that is associated with a network entry in the routing table.

## Network Mask Example

Consider a scenario in which an IP packet with a destination address of 192.168.1.67 is sent to a router. The router's IP routing table is shown in Example 1-1.

**Example 1-1**  *IP Routing Table for Network Mask Example*

```
192.168.1.0 is subnetted, 4 subnets
O 192.168.1.16/28 [110/1800] via 172.16.1.1, 00:05:17, Serial 0
C 192.168.1.32/28 is directly connected, Ethernet 0
O 192.168.1.64/28 [110/10] via 192.168.1.33, 00:05:17, Ethernet 0
O 192.168.1.80/28 [110/1800] via 172.16.2.1, 00:05:17, Serial 1
```

In this scenario, the router determines where to send a packet that is destined for 192.168.1.67 by looking at the routing table. The routing table has four entries for network 192.168.1.0. The router compares the destination address to each of the four entries for this network.

The destination address of 192.168.1.67 has the first three octets in common with all four entries in the routing table, but it is not clear by looking at the decimal representation which of those entries is the best match to route this packet. A router handles all packets in binary, not dotted-decimal, notation.

Following is the binary representation of the last octet for destination address 192.168.1.67 and the binary representation of the last octet for the four entries in the IP routing table. Because the prefix length is 28 and all four entries match at least the first 24 bits of 192.168.1, the router must find the routing table entry that matches the first 4 bits (bits 25 to 28) of the number 67. It is not important if the last 4 bits match, so the target is 0100*xxxx*. The routing entry 64, which has a value of 0100 in the first 4 bits, is the only one that matches the requirement:

- 67—**0100**0011
- 16—**0001**0000
- 32—**0010**0000
- 64—**0100**0000
- 80—**0101**0000

The router therefore uses the 192.168.1.64 entry in the routing table and forwards this packet to the next router (192.168.1.33) on the Ethernet 0 interface.

# Implementing VLSM in a Scalable Network

---

### Key Point: Classful Versus Classless Routing

A major network (also known as a classful network) is a Class A, B, or C network.

With classful routing, routing updates do not carry the subnet mask. Therefore, only one subnet mask must be in use within a major network. This is known as Fixed-Length Subnet Masking (FLSM). Examples of classful routing protocols are RIP version 1 (RIPv1) and IGRP.

With classless routing, routing updates do carry the subnet mask. Therefore, different masks may be used for different subnets within a major network. This is known as VLSM. Examples of classless routing protocols are RIP version 2 (RIPv2), OSPF, Intermediate System-to-Intermediate System (IS-IS), and Enhanced Interior Gateway Routing Protocol (EIGRP).

---

| NOTE | Classful and classless routing protocols are discussed further in Chapter 2. |
|---|---|

VLSM allows more than one subnet mask within a major network and enables the subnetting of a previously subnetted network address.

The network shown in Figure 1-10 is used to illustrate how VLSM works.

**Figure 1-10** *Network for the VLSM Example*

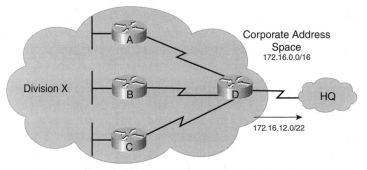

172.16.12.0/22 has been assigned to Division X.
Range of Addresses: 172.16.12.0 to 171.16.15.255

The following are some characteristics that permit VLSMs to conserve IP addresses:

- **Efficient use of IP addresses**—Without the use of VLSMs, companies are locked into implementing a single subnet mask within an entire Class A, B, or C network number.

  For example, suppose a network architect decides to use the 172.16.0.0/16 address space to design a corporate network. The architect determines that 64 blocks of addresses with up to 1022 hosts in each are required. Therefore, 10 host bits ($2^{10} - 2 = 1022$) and 6 subnet bits ($2^6 = 64$) are required for each block. The mask is therefore 255.255.252.0; the prefix is /22.

  The network architect assigns address block 172.16.12.0/22 to Division X, as shown in Figure 1-10. The prefix mask of /22 indicates that all addresses within that range have the first 22 bits in common (when reading from left to right). The prefix mask provides Division X with a range of addresses from 172.16.12.0 through 172.16.15.255. The details of the range of addresses available to Division X are shown in the center block of Figure 1-11. Within Division X, the networks are assigned addresses in this range, with varying subnet masks. Details of these address assignments are provided in the next section.

- **Greater capability to use route summarization**—VLSMs allow for more hierarchical levels within an addressing plan and thus allow better route summarization within routing tables. For example, in Figure 1-10, address 172.16.12.0/22 summarizes all the subnets that are further subnets of 172.16.12.0/22.

**Figure 1-11**  *Range of Addresses for VLSM for Division X in Figure 1-10*

| Dotted Decimal Notation | Binary Notation |
|---|---|
| 172.16.11.0 | 10101100. 00010000.0000101 1.00000000 |

(Text Omitted for Continuation of Bit/Number Pattern)

| | |
|---|---|
| 172.16.12.0 | 10101100. 00010000.000011 00.00000000 |
| 172.16.12.1 | 10101100. 00010000.000011 00.00000001 |
| 172.16.12.255 | 10101100. 00010000.000011 00.11111111 |
| 172.16.13.0 | 10101100. 00010000.000011 01.00000000 |
| 172.16.13.1 | 10101100. 00010000.000011 01.00000001 |
| 172.16.13.255 | 10101100. 00010000.000011 01.11111111 |
| 172.16.14.0 | 10101100. 00010000.000011 10.00000000 |
| 172.16.14.1 | 10101100. 00010000.000011 10.00000001 |
| 172.16.14.255 | 10101100. 00010000.000011 10.11111111 |
| 172.16.15.0 | 10101100. 00010000.000011 11.00000000 |
| 172.16.15.1 | 10101100. 00010000.000011 11.00000001 |
| 172.16.15.255 | 10101100. 00010000.000011 11.11111111 |

(Text Omitted for Continuation of Bit/Number Pattern)

| | |
|---|---|
| 172.16.16.0 | 10101100. 00010000.000100 00.00000000 |

- **Reduced number of routing table entries**—In a hierarchical addressing plan, route summarization allows a single IP address to represent a collection of IP addresses. When VLSM is used in a hierarchical network, it allows summarized routes, which keeps routing table entries (on the routers that receive the summarized routes) manageable and provides the following benefits:
  - More-efficient routing
  - Reduction in the number of CPU cycles to sort through the routing table entries to find a match and for routing table recalculation
  - Reduction in router memory requirements
  - Reduced bandwidth required to send the fewer, smaller routing updates
  - Faster convergence after a change in the network
  - Easier troubleshooting
  - Increased network stability

Because of the reduced router requirements, it also might be possible to use some less-powerful (and therefore less-expensive) routers in the network.

The address 172.16.12.0/22 represents all the addresses that have the same first 22 bits as 172.16.12.0. Figure 1-11 displays the binary representation of networks 172.16.11.0 through 172.16.16.0. Notice that 172.16.12.0 through 172.12.15.255 all have the first 22 bits in common, whereas 172.16.11.0 and 172.16.16.0 do not have the same first 22 bits. Therefore, the address 172.16.12.0/22 represents the range of addresses 172.16.12.0 through 172.16.15.255.

## VLSM Calculation Example

You can best understand the design and implementation of a scalable IP address plan if you study a detailed example of how a VLSM network is laid out.

Figure 1-12 shows a detailed view of the same Division X shown in Figure 1-10.

**Figure 1-12** *Detailed IP Addressing of Division X in Figure 1-10*

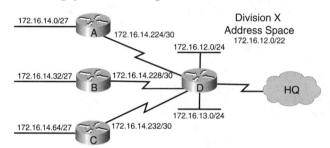

In Division X, the following exist:

- One VLAN on each of the two Ethernet ports of Router D, each with 200 users.

- Three remote sites, at Routers A, B, and C, each with a 24-port Cisco 2924 10/100 switch. Corporate management guarantees that the number of users at each remote site does not exceed 20.

- Three serial links to the remote sites. The serial links are point-to-point Frame Relay and require an address on each side.

VLSM allows you to further subnet the 172.16.12.0/22 address space, using variable masks, to accommodate the network requirements. For example, because point-to-point serial lines require only two host addresses, you can use a subnetted address that has only two host addresses and therefore does not waste scarce subnet numbers.

To start the VLSM process, determine the number of subnets necessary for the networks to which you need to assign IP addresses, and determine the number of hosts necessary per subnetwork. You can determine the number of hosts by checking corporate policy to see if a limit is set per segment or VLAN, checking the physical number of ports on a switch, and checking the current size of the network or networks at other sites that fulfill the same role.

---

**NOTE**     The decimal-to-binary conversion chart in Appendix A might be helpful when you are calculating VLSMs.

---

## LAN Addresses

Because IP addresses are binary, they are used in blocks of powers of 2. A block of addresses contains 2, 4, 8, 16, 32, 64, 128, 256, 512, 1024, 2048, and so on addresses. Two addresses are lost each time you create a subnet: one for the network (wire) address and the other for the broadcast address.

The lowest address of the range, where the host bits are all 0s, is known as the network number or the wire address. The top of the address range, where the host bits are all 1s, is the broadcast address. The number of addresses in a block that can be assigned to devices is $2^n - 2$, where $n$ is the number of host bits. For example, with 3 host bits, $2^3 - 2 = 8 - 2 = 6$ addresses can be assigned.

To determine the size of the block of addresses needed for a subnet, follow these steps:

**Step 1**    Calculate the maximum number of hosts on that subnet.

**Step 2**    Add 2 to that number for the broadcast and subnet numbers.

**Step 3**    Round up to the next higher power of 2.

In this example, the VLANs each have 200 users; therefore, the number of addresses required is $200 + 2 = 202$. Rounding up to the next power of 2 gives you 256. Thus, 8 ($2^8 = 256$) host bits are required for the VLANs; therefore, the prefix is /24 (32 bits – 8 bits for the host = 24 bits). The network administrator subnets the 172.16.12.0/22 into four /24 subnets on router D. 172.16.12.0/24 is assigned to VLAN 1, and 172.16.13.0/24 is assigned to VLAN 2. This leaves two /24 subnets, 172.16.14.0/24 and 172.16.15.0/24, to use for the switches at the three remote sites and the three serial point-to-point links.

The number of addresses required for the LANs at each remote site is $20 + 2 = 22$. Rounding this up to the next power of 2 gives you 32. Thus, 5 host bits ($2^5 = 32$) are required to address the remote users at each site. Therefore, the prefix to use is /27 (32 bits – 5 bits for the host = 27).

You cannot use the 172.16.12.0/24 or 172.16.13.0/24 networks, because they are assigned to VLANs 1 and 2 on router D. The process to further subnet 172.16.14.0/24 into /27 subnets is shown in Figure 1-13. The first three subnets calculated in Figure 1-13 are used on the LANs in Figure 1-12.

**Figure 1-13**    *Calculating Subnet Addresses for the LANs in Figure 1-12*

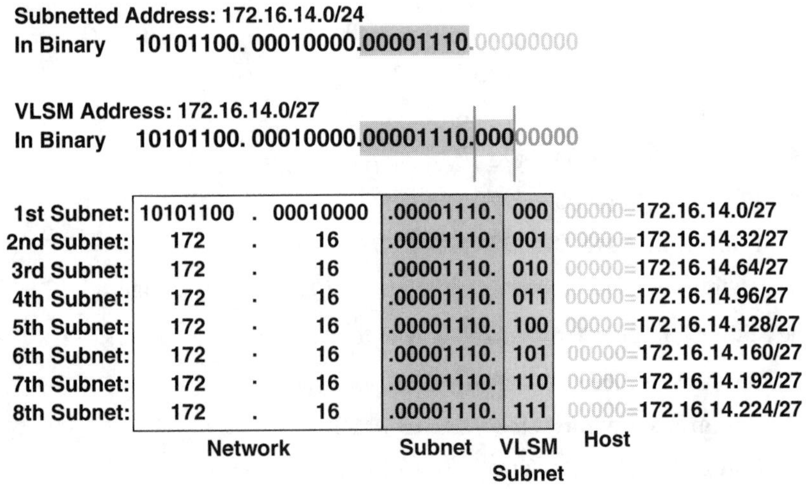

**Subnetted Address: 172.16.14.0/24**
**In Binary    10101100. 00010000.00001110**.00000000

**VLSM Address: 172.16.14.0/27**
**In Binary    10101100. 00010000.00001110.000**00000

| | | | | | |
|---|---|---|---|---|---|
| **1st Subnet:** | 10101100 . | 00010000 | .00001110. | 000 | 00000=172.16.14.0/27 |
| **2nd Subnet:** | 172 . | 16 | .00001110. | 001 | 00000=172.16.14.32/27 |
| **3rd Subnet:** | 172 . | 16 | .00001110. | 010 | 00000=172.16.14.64/27 |
| **4th Subnet:** | 172 . | 16 | .00001110. | 011 | 00000=172.16.14.96/27 |
| **5th Subnet:** | 172 . | 16 | .00001110. | 100 | 00000=172.16.14.128/27 |
| **6th Subnet:** | 172 . | 16 | .00001110. | 101 | 00000=172.16.14.160/27 |
| **7th Subnet:** | 172 . | 16 | .00001110. | 110 | 00000=172.16.14.192/27 |
| **8th Subnet:** | 172 . | 16 | .00001110. | 111 | 00000=172.16.14.224/27 |
| | **Network** | | **Subnet** | **VLSM** **Subnet** | **Host** |

## Serial Line Addresses

After you establish the addresses for the LANs at the remote sites, you must address the serial links between the remote sites and router D. Because the serial links require two addresses, the number of addresses required is 2 + 2 = 4 (the two additional addresses are for the network number and the broadcast address).

In this case, there is no need to round up, because 4 is a power of 2. Therefore, 2 host bits will allow for two hosts per subnet. A network mask of /30 (32 bits – 2 host bits = 30 bits) is used. This prefix allows for only two hosts—just enough hosts for a point-to-point connection between a pair of routers.

To calculate the subnet addresses for the WAN links, further subnet one of the unused /27 subnets. In this example, 172.16.14.224/27 is further subnetted with a prefix of /30. The three additional subnet bits result in $2^3$ = 8 subnets for the WAN links.

---

### Key Point: Further Subnet Only Unused Subnets

It is important to remember that only *unused* subnets should be further subnetted. In other words, if you use any addresses from a subnet, that subnet should not be further subnetted. In Figure 1-12, three subnet numbers are used on the LANs. Another, as-yet unused subnet, 172.16.14.224/27, is further subnetted for use on the WANs.

---

The WAN addresses derived from 172.16.14.224/27 are as follows. The shaded bits are the 3 additional subnet bits:

- 172.16.14.11100000 = 172.16.14.224/30
- 172.16.14.11100100 = 172.16.14.228/30
- 172.16.14.11101000 = 172.16.14.232/30
- 172.16.14.11101100 = 172.16.14.236/30
- 172.16.14.11110000 = 172.16.14.240/30
- 172.16.14.11110100 = 172.16.14.244/30
- 172.16.14.11111000 = 172.16.14.248/30
- 172.16.14.11111100 = 172.16.14.252/30

The first three of these subnets are used on the WANs shown in Figure 1-12.

The address information for the router A to router D link is as follows:

- **Network number**—172.16.14.224
- **Router A serial interface**—172.16.14.225
- **Router D serial interface**—172.16.14.226
- **Broadcast address**—172.16.14.227

The address information for the router B to router D link is as follows:

- **Network number**—172.16.14.228
- **Router B serial interface**—172.16.14.229
- **Router D serial interface**—172.16.14.230
- **Broadcast address**—172.16.14.231

The address information for the router C to router D link is as follows:

- **Network number**—172.16.14.232
- **Router C serial interface**—172.16.14.233
- **Router D serial interface**—172.16.14.234
- **Broadcast address**—172.16.14.235

Note that to provide the most flexibility for future growth, the 172.16.14.224/27 subnet was selected for the WANs instead of using the next available subnet, 172.16.14.96/27. For example, if the company purchases more switches, the next IP segment could be assigned the 172.16.14.96/27 subnet, and the new remote site would be connected to router D with the 172.16.14.236/30 serial subnet.

The 172.16.15.0/24 block could have been used for these /30 subnets, but only three subnets are currently needed, so a lot of the address space would be unused. The 172.16.15.0/24 block is now available to use on another LAN in the future.

## Summary of Addresses Used in the VLSM Example

Figure 1-14 summarizes the addresses, in binary, used in this example.

**Figure 1-14**  *Binary Representation of the Addresses Used in Figure 1-12*

| VLSM Addresses for /24 for 172.16.12.0–172.16.15.255: | | | |
|---|---|---|---|
| 172.16.12.0 | 10101100. 00010000.000011 | 00 .00000000 | VLAN 1 |
| 172.16.13.0 | 10101100. 00010000.000011 | 01 .00000000 | VLAN 2 |
| 172.16.14.0 | 10101100. 00010000.000011 | 10 .00000000 | Nodes |
| 172.16.15.0 | 10101100. 00010000.000011 | 11 .00000000 | Not Used |
| VLSM Addresses for /27 for 172.16.14.0–172.16.14.255: | | | |
| 172.16.14.0 | 10101100. 00010000.000011 | 10 .000 00000 | Nodes Site A |
| 172.16.14.32 | 10101100. 00010000.000011 | 10 .001 00000 | Nodes Site B |
| 172.16.14.64 | 10101100. 00010000.000011 | 10 .010 00000 | Nodes Site C |
| VLSM Addresses for /30 for 172.16.14.224–172.16.14.255: | | | |
| 172.16.14.224 | 10101100. 00010000.000011 | 10 .111 000 00 | A-D Serial |
| 172.16.14.228 | 10101100. 00010000.000011 | 10 .111 001 00 | B-D Serial |
| 172.16.14.232 | 10101100. 00010000.000011 | 10 .111 010 00 | C-D Serial |
| 172.16.14.236 | 10101100. 00010000.000011 | 10 .111 011 00 | Not Used |
| 172.16.14.240 | 10101100. 00010000.000011 | 10 .111 100 00 | Not Used |
| 172.16.14.244 | 10101100. 00010000.000011 | 10 .111 101 00 | Not Used |
| 172.16.14.248 | 10101100. 00010000.000011 | 10 .111 110 00 | Not Used |
| 172.16.14.252 | 10101100. 00010000.000011 | 10 .111 111 00 | Not Used |

Original Prefix

Mask      Mask 2      Mask 3
(VLAN)   (Nodes)   (Serial Links)

## Another VLSM Example

This section illustrates another example of calculating VLSM addresses. In this example, you have a subnet address 172.16.32.0/20, and you need to assign addresses to a network that has ten hosts. With this subnet address, however, you have $2^{12} - 2 = 4094$ host addresses, so you would be wasting more than 4000 IP addresses. With VLSM, you can further subnet the address 172.16.32.0/20 to give you more subnetwork addresses and fewer hosts per network, which would work better in this network topology. For example, if you subnet 172.16.32.0/20 to 172.16.32.0/26, you gain 64 ($2^6$) subnets, each of which can support 62 ($2^6 - 2$) hosts.

To further subnet 172.16.32.0/20 to 172.16.32.0/26, do the following, as illustrated in Figure 1-15:

**Step 1**  Write 172.16.32.0 in binary.

**Step 2**  Draw a vertical line between the 20th and 21st bits, as shown in Figure 1-15.

**Step 3**  Draw a vertical line between the 26th and 27th bits, as shown in Figure 1-15.

**Step 4**  Calculate the 64 subnet addresses using the bits between the two vertical lines, from lowest to highest. Figure 1-15 shows the first five subnets available.

**Figure 1-15**  *Further Subnetting a Subnetted Address*

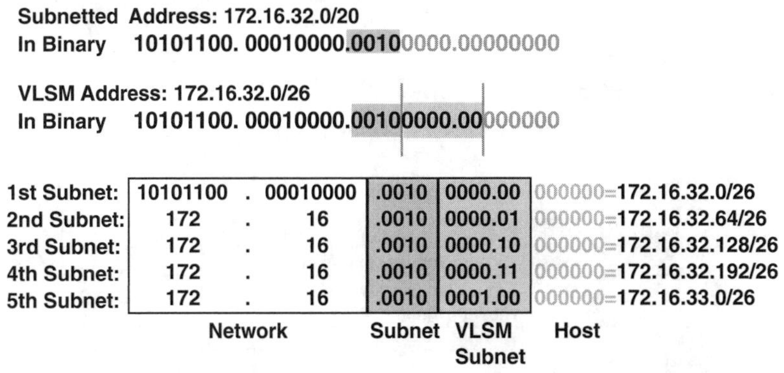

```
Subnetted Address: 172.16.32.0/20
In Binary    10101100. 00010000.0010 0000.00000000

VLSM Address: 172.16.32.0/26
In Binary    10101100. 00010000.0010 0000.00 000000
```

| | Network | | Subnet | VLSM Subnet | Host | |
|---|---|---|---|---|---|---|
| 1st Subnet: | 10101100 . | 00010000 | .0010 | 0000.00 | 000000 | =172.16.32.0/26 |
| 2nd Subnet: | 172 . | 16 | .0010 | 0000.01 | 000000 | =172.16.32.64/26 |
| 3rd Subnet: | 172 . | 16 | .0010 | 0000.10 | 000000 | =172.16.32.128/26 |
| 4th Subnet: | 172 . | 16 | .0010 | 0000.11 | 000000 | =172.16.32.192/26 |
| 5th Subnet: | 172 . | 16 | .0010 | 0001.00 | 000000 | =172.16.33.0/26 |

**NOTE**  VLSM calculators are available on the web. The following URL contains the one offered by Cisco: www.cisco.com/cgi-bin/Support/IpSubnet/home.pl. (Note that you need to have an account on Cisco's website to use this calculator.)

# Route Summarization

As the result of corporate expansion and mergers, the number of subnets and network addresses in routing tables is increasing rapidly. This growth taxes CPU resources, memory, and bandwidth used to maintain the routing table. Route summarization and CIDR techniques can manage this corporate growth much like Internet growth has been managed. With a thorough understanding of route summarization and CIDR, you can implement a scalable network. This section describes summarization; CIDR is covered in the later section "Classless Interdomain Routing." The relationship between summarization and VLSM is also examined. With VLSM, you break a block of addresses into smaller subnets; in route summarization, a group of subnets is rolled up into a summarized routing table entry.

## Route Summarization Overview

In large internetworks, hundreds, or even thousands, of network addresses can exist. It is often problematic for routers to maintain this volume of routes in their routing tables. Route summarization (also called *route aggregation* or *supernetting*) can reduce the number of routes that a router must maintain, because it is a method of representing a series of network numbers in a single summary address.

For example, in Figure 1-16, router D can either send four routing update entries or summarize the four addresses into a single network number. If router D summarizes the information into a single network number entry, the following things happen:

- Bandwidth is saved on the link between routers D and E.
- Router E needs to maintain only one route and therefore saves memory.
- Router E also saves CPU resources, because it evaluates packets against fewer entries in its routing table.

**Figure 1-16**   *Routers Can Summarize to Reduce the Number of Routes*

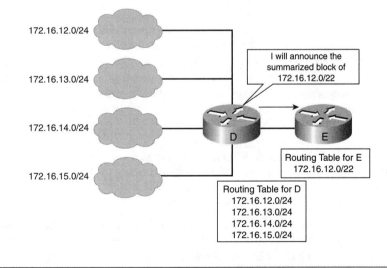

**Key Point: Summary Routes**

A summary route is announced by the summarizing router as long as at least one specific route in its routing table matches the summary route.

NOTE   Router D in Figure 1-16 is advertising that it can route to network 172.16.12.0/22, including all subnets of that network. However, if there were other subnets of 172.16.12.0/22 elsewhere in the network (for example, if 172.16.12.0 were discontiguous), summarizing in this way might not be valid.

Another advantage of using route summarization in a large, complex network is that it can isolate topology changes from other routers. For example, in Figure 1-16, if a specific link (such as 172.16.13.0/24) is *flapping* (going up and down rapidly), the summary route (172.16.12.0/22) does not change. Therefore, router E does not need to continually modify its routing table as a result of this flapping activity.

NOTE   Flapping is a common term used to describe intermittent interface or link failures.

Route summarization is possible only when a proper addressing plan is in place. Route summarization is most effective within a subnetted environment when the network addresses are in contiguous blocks in powers of 2. For example, 4, 16, or 512 addresses can be represented by a single routing entry because summary masks are binary masks—just like subnet masks—so summarization must take place on binary boundaries (powers of 2). If the number of network addresses is not contiguous or not a power of 2, you can divide the addresses into groups and try to summarize the groups separately.

Routing protocols summarize or aggregate routes based on shared network numbers within the network. Classless routing protocols (such as RIPv2, OSPF, IS-IS, and EIGRP) support route summarization based on subnet addresses, including VLSM addressing. Classful routing protocols (RIPv1 and IGRP) automatically summarize routes on the classful network boundary and do not support summarization on any other bit boundaries. Classless routing protocols support summarization on any bit boundary.

NOTE   Summarization is described in RFC 1518, *An Architecture for IP Address Allocation with CIDR*, available at www.cis.ohio-state.edu/cgi-bin/rfc/rfc1518.html.

As an example of the power of summarization, imagine a company that operates a series of pizza shops, with 200 stores in each of the 50 states in the U.S. Each store has a router with an Ethernet and a Frame Relay link connected to headquarters. Without route summarization, the routing table on any of those routers would have 200 * 50 = 10,000 networks.

Instead, if each state has a central site to connect it with all the other states, and each of these routes is summarized before being announced to other states, every router sees its 200 state subnets and 49 summarized entries representing the other states. This results in less CPU, memory, and bandwidth usage.

## Route Summarization Calculation Example

Router D in Figure 1-16 has the following networks in its routing table:

- 172.16.12.0/24
- 172.16.13.0/24
- 172.16.14.0/24
- 172.16.15.0/24

To determine the summary route on router D, determine the number of highest-order (leftmost) bits that match in all the addresses. To calculate the summary route, follow these steps:

**Step 1**   Convert the addresses to binary format and align them in a list.

**Step 2**   Locate the bit where the common pattern of digits ends. (It might be helpful to draw a vertical line marking the last matching bit in the common pattern.)

**Step 3**   Count the number of common bits. The summary route number is represented by the first IP address in the block, followed by a slash, followed by the number of common bits. As Figure 1-17 illustrates, the first 22 bits of the IP addresses from 172.16.12.0 through 172.16.15.255 are the same. Therefore, the best summary route is 172.16.12.0/22.

**Figure 1-17**   *Summarizing Within an Octet, for Router D in Figure 1-16*

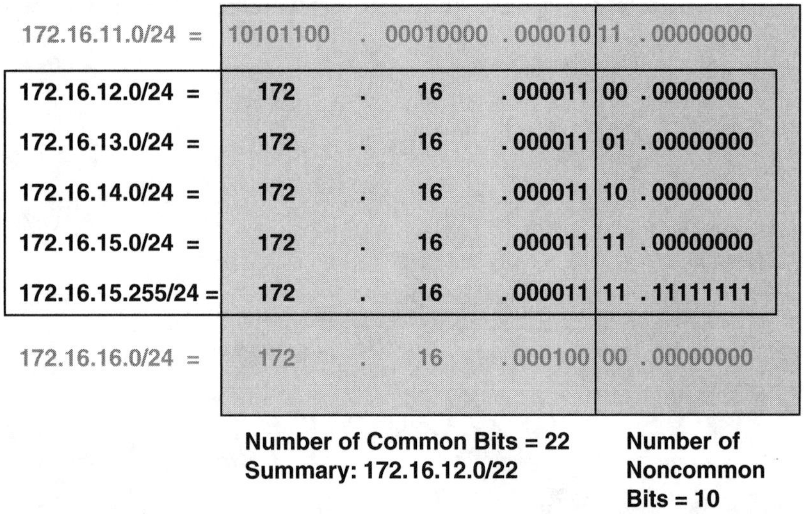

| | | | | |
|---|---|---|---|---|
| 172.16.11.0/24 = | 10101100 | . 00010000 | . 000010 | 11 . 00000000 |
| 172.16.12.0/24 = | 172 | . 16 | . 000011 | 00 . 00000000 |
| 172.16.13.0/24 = | 172 | . 16 | . 000011 | 01 . 00000000 |
| 172.16.14.0/24 = | 172 | . 16 | . 000011 | 10 . 00000000 |
| 172.16.15.0/24 = | 172 | . 16 | . 000011 | 11 . 00000000 |
| 172.16.15.255/24 = | 172 | . 16 | . 000011 | 11 . 11111111 |
| 172.16.16.0/24 = | 172 | . 16 | . 000100 | 00 . 00000000 |

Number of Common Bits = 22
Summary: 172.16.12.0/22

Number of
Noncommon
Bits = 10

| | |
|---|---|
| **NOTE** | In this network, the four subnets are contiguous, and the summary route covers all the addresses in the four subnets and only those addresses. Consider, for example, what would happen if 172.16.13.0/24 were not behind router D, but instead were used elsewhere in the network, and only the other three subnets were behind router D. The summary route 172.16.12.0/22 should no longer be used on router D, because it includes 172.16.13.0/24 and might result in confusing routing tables. (However, this depends on how other routers in the network summarize. If the 172.16.13.0/24 route is propagated to all routers, they choose the route with the most bits that match the destination address and should route properly. This is further described in the section "Route Summarization Operation in Cisco Routers.") |

| | |
|---|---|
| **NOTE** | In Figure 1-17, the subnets before and after the subnets to be summarized are also shown. Observe that they do not have the same first 22 bits in common and therefore are not covered by the 172.16.12.0/22 summary route. |

## Summarizing Addresses in a VLSM-Designed Network

A VLSM design allows for maximum use of IP addresses as well as more-efficient routing update communication when using hierarchical IP addressing. In Figure 1-18, route summarization occurs at the following two levels:

- Router C summarizes two routing updates from networks 10.1.32.64/26 and 10.1.32.128/26 into a single update: 10.1.32.0/24.

- Router A receives three different routing updates. However, router A summarizes them into a single routing update, 10.1.0.0/16, before propagating it to the corporate network.

**Figure 1-18**  *VLSM Addresses Can Be Summarized*

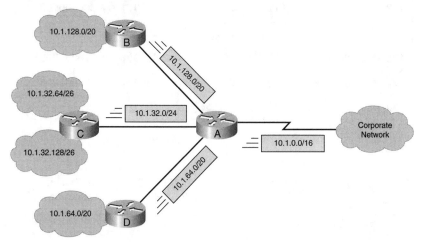

# Route Summarization Implementation

Route summarization reduces memory use on routers and routing protocol network traffic, because it results in fewer entries in the routing table (on the routers that receive the summarized routes). For summarization to work correctly, the following requirements must be met:

- Multiple IP addresses must share the same highest-order bits.

- Routing protocols must base their routing decisions on a 32-bit IP address and a prefix length that can be up to 32 bits.

- Routing updates must carry the prefix length (the subnet mask) along with the 32-bit IP address.

# Route Summarization Operation in Cisco Routers

This section discusses generalities of how Cisco routers handle route summarization. Details about how route summarization operates with a specific protocol are discussed in the corresponding protocol chapter of this book.

Cisco routers manage route summarization in two ways:

- **Sending route summaries**—Routing information advertised out an interface is automatically summarized at major (classful) network address boundaries by RIP, IGRP, and EIGRP. Specifically, this automatic summarization occurs for routes whose classful network addresses differs from the major network address of the interface to which the advertisement is being sent. For OSPF and IS-IS, you must configure summarization.

  Route summarization is not always a solution. You would not want to use route summarization if you needed to advertise all networks across a boundary, such as when you have discontiguous networks. When using EIGRP and RIPv2, you can disable this automatic summarization.

- **Selecting routes from route summaries**—If more than one entry in the routing table matches a particular destination, the longest prefix match in the routing table is used. Several routes might match one destination, but the longest matching prefix is used.

  For example, if a routing table has the paths shown in Figure 1-19, packets addressed to destination 172.16.5.99 are routed through the 172.16.5.0/24 path, because that address has the longest match with the destination address.

**Figure 1-19**  *Routers Use the Longest Match When Selecting a Route*

| | | |
|---|---|---|
| 172.16.5.33 | /32 | host |
| 172.16.5.32 | /27 | subnet |
| 172.16.5.0 | /24 | network |
| 172.16.0.0 | /16 | block of networks |
| 0.0.0.0 | /0 | default |

When running classful protocols (RIPv1 and IGRP), you must enable **ip classless** if you want the router to select a default route when it must route to an unknown subnet of a network for which it knows some subnets. Refer to the section "The **ip classless** Command" in Chapter 2 for more details.

Note that by default (and for historical reasons) the routing table on Cisco routers acts in a classful manner, as described in the sidebar "The Routing Table Acts Classfully" in Chapter 2.

## Route Summarization in IP Routing Protocols

Table 1-2 summarizes the route summarization support available in the various IP routing protocols.

**Table 1-2**   *Routing Protocol Route Summarization Support*

| Protocol | Automatic Summarization at Classful Network Boundary? | Capability to Turn Off Automatic Summarization? | Capability to Summarize at Other Than a Classful Network Boundary? |
|---|---|---|---|
| RIPv1 | Yes | No | No |
| RIPv2 | Yes | Yes | No |
| IGRP | Yes | No | No |
| EIGRP | Yes | Yes | Yes |
| OSPF | No | — | Yes |
| IS-IS | No | — | Yes |

NOTE    Cisco IOS 12.0 introduced RIPv2's manual summarization feature with the **ip summary-address rip** command. This command provides limited summarization support; RIPv2 advertises a summarized local IP address pool on the specified interface to dialup clients.

More information on this feature is available in *IP Summary Address for RIPv2* at www.cisco.com /en/US/products/sw/iosswrel/ps1830/products_feature_guide09186a0080087ad1.html.

# Classless Interdomain Routing

CIDR is a mechanism developed to help alleviate the problem of exhaustion of IP addresses and growth of routing tables. The idea behind CIDR is that blocks of multiple addresses (for example, blocks of Class C address) can be combined, or aggregated, to create a larger classless set of IP addresses, with more hosts allowed. Blocks of Class C network numbers are allocated to each network service provider; organizations using the network service provider for Internet connectivity are allocated subsets of the service provider's address space as required. These multiple Class C addresses can then be summarized in routing tables, resulting in fewer route advertisements. (Note that the CIDR mechanism can be applied to blocks of Class A, B, and C addresses; it is not restricted to Class C.)

CIDR is described further in RFC 1518, *An Architecture for IP Address Allocation with CIDR,* and RFC 1519, *Classless Inter-Domain Routing (CIDR): An Address Assignment and Aggregation Strategy*, available at www.cis.ohio-state.edu/cgi-bin/rfc/rfc1519.html. RFC 2050, *Internet Registry IP Allocation Guidelines*, specifies guidelines for the allocation of IP addresses. It is available at www.cis.ohio-state.edu/cgi-bin/rfc/rfc2050.html.

Most CIDR debates revolve around summarizing blocks of Class C networks into large blocks of addresses. As a general rule, Internet service providers (ISPs) implement a minimum route advertisement standard of /19 address blocks. A /19 address block equals a block of 32 Class C networks. (In some cases, smaller blocks might be advertised, such as with a /21 mask [eight Class C networks].) Addressing is now so limited that networks such as 12.0.0.0/8 are being divided into blocks of /19 that are assigned to major ISPs, which allows further allocation to customers. CIDR combines blocks of addresses regardless of whether they fall within a single classful boundary or encompass many classful boundaries.

## CIDR Example

Figure 1-20 shows an example of CIDR and route summarization. The Class C network addresses 192.168.8.0/24 through 192.168.15.0/24 are being used and are being advertised to the ISP router. When the ISP router advertises the available networks, it can summarize these into one route instead of separately advertising the eight Class C networks. By advertising 192.168.8.0/21, the ISP router indicates that it can get to all destination addresses whose first 21 bits are the same as the first 21 bits of the address 192.168.8.0.

**Figure 1-20**  *CIDR Allows a Router to Summarize Multiple Class C Addresses*

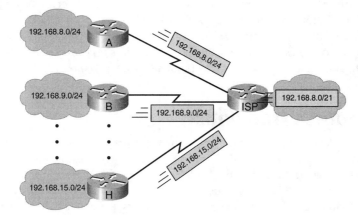

The mechanism used to calculate the summary route to advertise is the same as shown in the "Route Summarization" section. The Class C network addresses 192.168.8.0/24 through 192.168.15.0/24 are being used and are being advertised to the ISP router. To summarize these addresses, find the common bits, as shown here (in bold):

| | |
|---|---|
| 192.168.8.0 | 192.168.**00001**000.00000000 |
| 192.168.9.0 | 192.168.**00001**001.00000000 |
| 192.168.10.0 | 192.168.**00001**010.00000000 |
| . . . | |
| 192.168.14.0 | 192.168.**00001**110.00000000 |
| 192.168.15.0 | 192.168.**00001**111.00000000 |

The route 192.168.00001*xxx.xxxxxxxx* or 192.168.8.0/21 (also written as 192.168.8.0 255.255.248.0) summarizes these eight routes.

In this example, the first octet is 192, which identifies the networks as Class C networks. Combining these Class C networks into a block of addresses with a mask of less than /24 (the default Class C network mask) indicates that CIDR, not route summarization, is being performed.

---

**Key Point: CIDR Versus Route Summarization**

The difference between CIDR and route summarization is that route summarization is generally done within, or up to, a classful boundary, whereas CIDR combines several classful networks.

---

In this example, the eight separate 192.168.*x*.0 Class C networks that have the prefix /24 are combined into a single summarized block of 192.168.8.0/21. (At some other point in the network, this summarized block may be further combined into 192.168.0.0/16, and so on.)

Consider another example. A company that uses four Class B networks has the IP addresses 172.16.0.0/16 for Division A, 172.17.0.0/16 for Division B, 172.18.0.0/16 for Division C, and 172.19.0.0/16 for Division D. They can all be summarized as a single block: 172.16.0.0/14. This one entry represents the whole block of four Class B networks. This process is CIDR; the summarization goes beyond the Class B boundaries.

# Network Address Translation

IP address depletion is a key problem facing the Internet. To assist in maximizing the use of registered IP addresses, Cisco IOS Release 11.2 and later implement NAT. This feature, which is Cisco's implementation of RFC 1631, *The IP Network Address Translator* (available at www.cis.ohio-state.edu/cgi-bin/rfc/rfc1631.html), is a solution that provides a way to use the same IP addresses in multiple internal stub networks, thereby reducing the need for registered IP addresses.

NAT is an important function in most scalable networks and is mandatory for the majority of companies that have Internet connections. ISPs have hundreds of users accessing the Internet, yet commonly are assigned only 8 or 16 individual addresses. The ISPs use NAT to map the hundreds of inside addresses to the few globally unique addresses assigned to that company. After introducing NAT terminology and features, this section demonstrates the following:

- How to use basic NAT and a standard access list to assign separate address space to different users.

- How to use an extended access list to check a packet's destination address and assign different source addresses based on it.

- How to use a Cisco IOS software tool called a route map to create a fully extended address translation in an IP NAT table. The IP NAT table tracks the original address and its translation as well as the destination address and the Transmission Control Protocol (TCP) and User Datagram Protocol (UDP) ports for each.

## NAT Terminology and Features

This section first introduces the terminology that is necessary to understand NAT and then explains NAT's various features.

### NAT Terminology

The terms *inside network* and *outside network* are used with NAT, as shown in Figure 1-21. NAT terminology, as used in Figure 1-21, is defined in Table 1-3.

**Figure 1-21** *Network Address Translation Is Used to Translate Addresses Between the Inside and Outside Networks*

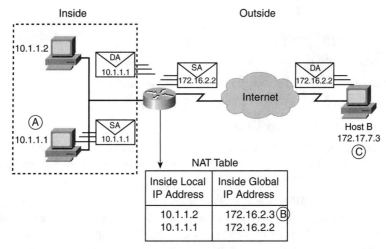

**Table 1-3**    *NAT Terminology*

| Term | Definition |
| --- | --- |
| Inside local IP address (A) | The IP address assigned to a host on the inside network. (The address was either globally unique but obsolete, allocated from RFC 1918, or randomly picked.) |
| Inside global IP address (B) | A legitimate IP address (typically assigned by a service provider) that represents one or more inside local IP addresses to the outside world. (The address was allocated from a globally unique address space, typically provided by the ISP.) |
| Outside global IP address (C) | The IP address that was assigned to a host on the outside network by its owner. (The address was allocated from a globally routable address space.) |
| Outside local IP address (not shown) | The IP address of an outside host as it appears to the inside network. (The address was allocated from address space routable on the inside or possibly was allocated from RFC 1918, for example.) An example of when an outside local IP address is required is given in the "Handling Overlapping Networks" sidebar later in this section. |
| Simple translation entry | A translation entry that maps one IP address to another. This is the type of entry shown in the NAT table in Figure 1-21. |
| Extended translation entry (not shown) | A translation entry that maps one IP address and port pair to another. |

A NAT entry is built in the IP NAT table as the packet goes from an IP NAT inside interface. A NAT entry usually changes the source IP address in the packet from an inside address to an outside address. When a device on the outside responds to the packet, the destination IP address of the returning packet is compared to the entries in the IP NAT table. If a match is found, the destination IP address is translated to the correct inside address and is sent to the routing table to be routed to the correct IP NAT inside interface. If no match is found, the packet is discarded.

NAT is performed when a packet is routed between the following interfaces:

- IP NAT inside interface to an IP NAT outside interface
- IP NAT outside interface to an IP NAT inside interface

A NAT table may contain the following information:

- **Protocol**—IP, TCP, or UDP.
- **Inside local IP address:port**—The IP address and port number used by the inside host before any translations. The inside local IP address is usually the private addressing defined in RFC 1918.
- **Inside global IP address:port**—The IP address and port number used by the inside host as it appears to the outside network; this is the translated IP address and port. Addresses are allocated from a globally unique address space, typically provided by the ISP if the enterprise connects to the global Internet.

- **Outside global IP address:port**—The configured globally unique IP address assigned to a host in the outside network, and the port number used.

- **Outside local IP address:port**—The IP address and port number of an outside host as it appears to the inside network.

**NOTE**    Simple NAT entries consist of only the inside local IP address and the inside global IP address.

## Features Supported by NAT

Supported NAT features include the following:

- **Static address translation**—Establishes a one-to-one mapping between inside local and global addresses.

- **Dynamic source address translation**—Establishes a dynamic mapping between the inside local and global addresses. This is accomplished by describing the local addresses to be translated, the pool of addresses from which to allocate global addresses, and associating the two. The router creates translations as needed.

- **Address overloading**—Can conserve addresses in the inside global address pool by allowing source ports in TCP connections or UDP conversations to be translated. When different inside local addresses map to the same inside global address, each inside host's TCP or UDP port numbers are used to distinguish between them.

**NOTE**    When the router determines that a packet's path is from an IP NAT inside interface to an IP NAT outside interface, an entry is built to include both the original source IP address and the original TCP for UDP port number. Each of these entries is assigned a unique TCP/UDP source port number to distinguish it from the others. When a packet returns to the IP NAT outside interface, it is compared to the IP NAT table. Although the packet destination address could match thousands of entries, NAT checks the destination TCP/UDP port for the correct entry for the returning packet. After the correct entry is found, the current destination address and port number change to the appropriate IP NAT inside destination address and port number.

- **TCP load distribution**—A dynamic form of destination translation that can be configured for some outside-to-inside traffic. After a mapping is defined, destination addresses matching an access list are replaced with an address from a rotary pool. Allocation is done on a round-robin basis, and only when a new connection is opened from the outside to the inside. All non-TCP traffic is passed untranslated (unless other translations are in effect).

---

### Handling Overlapping Networks

Figure 1-22 illustrates NAT operation when addresses in the inside network overlap with addresses that are in the outside network; in this case, outside local IP addresses are used.

**Figure 1-22** *Handling Overlapping Networks*

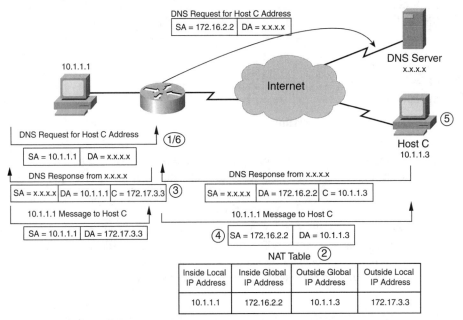

The following describes this process of handling overlapping addresses:

**Step 1**  The user at 10.1.1.1 opens a connection to Host C (10.1.1.3), causing 10.1.1.1 to perform a name-to-address lookup to a DNS server.

**Step 2**  If there is an overlap, the router intercepts the DNS reply and translates the returned address. In this case, 10.1.1.3 overlaps with an inside address. To translate the return address of Host C, the router creates a simple translation entry that maps the overlapping address 10.1.1.3 to an address from a separately configured outside local address pool. In this example, the address is 172.17.3.3.

**Step 3**  The router forwards the DNS reply to Host 10.1.1.1. The reply has Host C's address as 172.17.3.3. At this point, 10.1.1.1 opens a connection to 172.17.3.3.

**Step 4**  When the router receives the packet for Host C (172.17.3.3), it sets up a translation that maps the inside local and global addresses and the outside global and local addresses by replacing the source address of 10.1.1.1 with the inside global address 172.16.2.2 and replacing the destination address of 172.17.3.3 with Host C's outside global address, 10.1.1.3.

**Step 5**   Host C receives a packet and continues the conversation.

**Step 6**   For each packet sent between Host 10.1.1.1 and Host C, the router performs
a lookup, replaces the destination address with the inside local address, and
replaces the source address with the outside local address.

# Configuring NAT with Access Lists

This section explains the IP NAT commands to configure IP NAT with access lists. It provides
a sample IP NAT configuration and two specific examples of configuring IP NAT with access
lists. The first example demonstrates how to use access lists to determine whether an IP address
needs translation based on the original source address. The second example demonstrates how
to use an access list to assign a NAT source IP address based on the source and destination
addresses of the original packet.

The following commands are used to configure IP NAT with access lists:

- **ip nat {inside | outside}**—This interface configuration command marks the IP networks
  attached to that interface as either internal or external to the controlled network. Only packets
  arriving on an interface marked as IP NAT inside or outside are subject to translation.

- **ip nat inside source list** {*access-list-number* | *access-list-name*} **pool** *pool-name*—When
  a packet comes in on an interface marked as IP NAT inside, this global configuration
  command causes the router to compare the source IP address in the packet to the access list
  referenced in the command. The access list indicates whether the router should translate that
  source IP address to the next available address in the *pool-name* listed. NAT translates an
  address that is permitted in the access list. Addresses that are not permitted by the access
  list are not translated, and the packet is routed normally.

- **ip nat pool** *pool-name starting-ip-address ending-ip-address* {**prefix-length** *prefix-length* |
  **netmask** *netmask*}—This global configuration command creates the translation pool
  referenced by the previous command. This command includes the starting and ending
  addresses for translation and either the prefix length or network mask associated with this
  range of addresses.

## Standard Access List Translation Example

In Figure 1-23, when an IP packet comes in on Ethernet 0 of Router A with a source address of
10.1.2.*x*, the router translates it from the NAT pool of addresses defined by the name **sale_pool**.
If the packet has a source address of 10.1.3.*x*, the router translates it from the NAT pool of
addresses defined by the name **acct_pool**.

In this example, the Information Services (IS) department maps different groups of users
to different blocks of NAT addresses. The IS department determines the percentage of
users per department who can use the NAT interface and assigns an appropriate number
of addresses. The percentage of users can typically be determined using accounting or
security software.

**Figure 1-23** *Translating with Standard Access Lists*

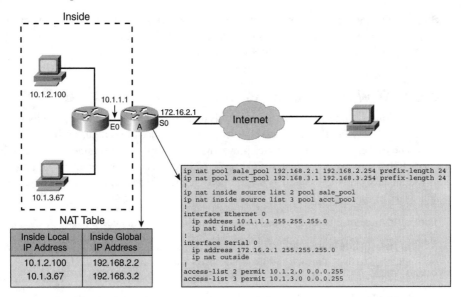

## Extended Access List Translation Example

The network used in this example is the same as that shown in Figure 1-23. However, in this configuration example, the extended access lists 102 and 103 are used to control NAT decisions. Instead of making the decision based only on the source address, an extended access list makes the decision based on the source and destination addresses of all packets coming in on interface Ethernet 0.

The configuration used on Router A is shown in Example 1-2.

**Example 1-2** *NAT Example Using Extended Access Lists on Router A in Figure 1-23*

```
ip nat pool trusted_pool 192.168.2.1  192.168.2.254 prefix-length 24
ip nat pool untrusted_pool 192.168.3.1 192.168.3.254 prefix-length 24
!
ip nat inside source list 102 pool trusted_pool
ip nat inside source list 103 pool untrusted_pool
!
interface ethernet 0
 ip address 10.1.1.1 255.255.0.0
 ip nat inside
!
interface serial 0
 ip address 172.16.2.1 255.255.255.0
 ip nat outside
!
access-list 102 permit ip  10.1.1.0 0.0.0.255  172.16.1.0 0.0.0.255
access-list 102 permit ip  10.1.1.0 0.0.0.255  192.168.200.0 0.0.0.255
access-list 103 permit ip  10.1.1.0 0.0.0.255  any
```

In this example, if the packet is not from the 10.1.1.0/24 subnet, the packet's source IP address is not translated. If the packet is from the 10.1.1.0/24 subnet and the destination address matches either 172.16.1.0/24 or 192.168.200.0/24, the source IP address is translated to the next available address in the trusted_pool, which is the 192.168.2.0/24 network.

If the packet is from the 10.1.1.0/24 subnet and the destination address does not match either 172.16.1.0/24 or 192.168.200.0/24, the source IP address is translated to the next available address in the untrusted_pool, which is the 192.168.3.0/24 network.

In this example, the outside NAT environment has both trusted and untrustworthy sites. For example, the company might be attached to an industry internetwork where it exchanges information with corporate partners and competitors. 172.16.1.0/24 and 192.168.200.0/24 are addresses of trusted networks on the industry internetwork, but all other destination addresses are considered untrustworthy. (A firewall system may also be added to allow greater control over the trusted sites.)

## Configuring NAT with Route Maps

A route map is a Cisco IOS software function that serves a variety of purposes. This section explains route maps and compares the results of using NAT with a route map to the results of using NAT with only an access list.

---

**NOTE**    Route maps are discussed in more detail in Chapter 7, "Manipulating Routing Updates."

---

When you use only access lists for NAT, as described in the previous section, the resulting NAT table has only simple translation entries, identifying only which inside local address is being translated to which inside global address. Example 1-3 shows simple translation entries using the **show ip nat translations** command. The simple translation entry contains only local and global IP address entries. It does not include any TCP or UDP port information or the packet's destination address.

**Example 1-3**  *Simple IP Address Translation Entries*

```
Router#show ip nat translations
Pro Inside global      Inside local      Outside local      Outside global
--- 192.168.2.1        10.1.2.100        ---                ---
--- 192.168.3.1        10.1.3.67         ---                ---
```

The entries in this IP NAT translation table are called simple entries because they track only the original source address (the inside local address) and the address to which it is translated (the inside global address). The other fields in the table are left blank. It is difficult to troubleshoot connectivity using simple address entries, because you do not see the destination address or the application (port) associated with each NAT translation. This might also prevent proper translation among multiple address pools. The first address pool matched creates a simple NAT entry; a second session initiated by the same source to a different host already matches the simple entry, thereby preventing proper translation to the second address pool. (Configuration Exercise 1-2, at the end of this chapter, includes an example of this translation problem.)

To get an extended translation entry in the NAT table, you must either configure NAT for overloading (using the **overload** keyword on the **ip inside source** command) or use a Cisco IOS software tool called a route map. Example 1-4 shows an example of an extended translation entry. The extended translation entry identifies the source and destination addresses with their appropriate translations, the transport layer protocol used, and the port (or application) used for the session.

**Example 1-4** *IP Address Translation with Route Maps*

```
Router#show ip nat translations
Pro Inside global      Inside local      Outside local     Outside global
udp 192.168.2.1:1024   10.1.2.100:1024   172.16.1.20:69    172.16.1.20:69
tcp 192.168.2.1:4097   10.1.2.100:4097   172.16.1.20:21    172.16.1.20:21
tcp 192.168.2.1:1084   10.1.2.100:1084   172.16.1.20:20    172.16.1.20:20
tcp 192.168.3.1:1024   10.1.3.67:1024    172.16.1.20:23    172.16.1.20:23
tcp 192.168.3.1:5553   10.1.3.67:5553    172.16.1.20:80    172.16.1.20:80
```

## Understanding Route Maps

Route maps are complex access lists that allow some conditions to be tested against the packet or route in question using **match** commands. If the conditions match, some actions can be taken to modify attributes of the packet or route. These actions are specified by **set** commands.

A collection of route map statements that have the same route map name are considered one route map. Within a route map, each route map statement is numbered and therefore can be edited individually.

The statements in a route map correspond to the lines of an access list. Specifying the match conditions in a route map is similar to specifying the source and destination addresses and masks in an access list.

---

### Key Point: Route Maps Versus Access Lists

One big difference between route maps and access lists is that route maps can modify the route by using **set** commands.

---

The **route-map** *map-tag* [**permit** | **deny**] [*sequence-number*] global configuration command can be used to define the conditions for NAT. This command is explained in detail in Table 1-4.

**Table 1-4**    **route-map** *Command*

| Command | Description |
|---|---|
| *map-tag* | Name of the route map |
| **permit** \| **deny** | Optional parameter that specifies the action to be taken if the route map match conditions are met |
| *sequence-number* | Optional sequence number that indicates the position that a new route map statement will have in the list of route map statements already configured with the same name |

The default for the **route-map** command is **permit**, with a *sequence-number* of 10.

---

### Route Map Sequence Numbering

If you leave out the sequence number when configuring all statements for the same route map name, the router will assume that you are editing and adding to the first statement, sequence number 10. Route map sequence numbers do not automatically increment!

---

A route map may be made up of multiple route map statements. The statements are processed top-down, similar to an access list. The first match found for a route is applied. The sequence number is used for inserting or deleting specific route map statements in a specific place in the route map.

The **match** *condition* route map configuration commands are used to define the conditions to be checked. The **set** *condition* route map configuration commands are used to define the actions to be followed if there is a match and the action to be taken is permit. (The consequences of a deny action depend on how the route map is being used.)

A single match statement may contain multiple conditions. At least one condition in the match statement must be true for that match statement to be considered a match. A route map statement may contain multiple match statements. All match statements in the route map statement must be considered true for the route map statement to be considered matched.

---

### Key Point: Route Map Match Conditions

Only one match condition listed on the same line must match for the entire line to be considered a match.

---

For example, IP standard or extended access lists can be used to establish match criteria using the **match ip address** {*access-list-number* \| *name*} [...*access-list-number* \| *name*] route map configuration command. (If multiple access lists are specified, matching any one results in a match.) A standard IP access list can be used to specify match criteria for a packet's source address; extended access lists can be used to specify match criteria based on source and destination addresses, application, protocol type, type of service (ToS), and precedence.

The sequence number specifies the order in which conditions are checked. For example, if two statements in a route map are named MYMAP, one with sequence 10 and the other with sequence 20, sequence 10 is checked first. If the match conditions in sequence 10 are not met, sequence 20 is checked.

Like an access list, an implicit deny any appears at the end of a route map. The consequences of this deny depend on how the route map is being used.

Another way to explain how a route map works is to use a simple example and see how a router would interpret it. Example 1-5 shows a sample route map configuration. (Note that on a router, all the conditions and actions shown would be replaced with specific conditions and actions, depending on the exact **match** and **set** commands used.)

**Example 1-5** **route-map** *Command*

```
route-map demo permit 10
  match x y z
  match a
  set b
  set c
route-map demo permit 20
  match q
  set r
route-map demo permit 30
```

The route map named **demo** in Example 1-5 is interpreted as follows:

> If {(x or y or z) and (a) match} then {set b and c}
> Else
> > If q matches then set r
> > Else
> > > Set nothing

## NAT with Route Maps Example

The **ip nat inside source route-map** *route-map-name* **pool** *pool-name* global configuration command causes the router to compare the source IP address in the packet to the route map referenced in the command. The route map indicates whether the router should translate that source IP address to the next available address in the *pool-name* listed. NAT translates an address that is matched in the route map.

Example 1-6 provides an alternative configuration for Router A in Figure 1-23. Two route maps have been added to the configuration shown in Figure 1-23. In this example, the what_is_sales_doing route map is linked to the sales_pool using the **ip nat inside source route-map what_is_sales_doing pool sales_pool** command.

**Example 1-6**  *Alternative Configuration for Router A in Figure 1-23*

```
ip nat pool sales_pool 192.168.2.1 192.168.2.254 prefix-length 24
ip nat pool acct_pool 192.168.3.1 192.168.3.254 prefix-length 24
!
ip nat inside source route-map what_is_sales_doing pool sales_pool
ip nat inside source route-map what_is_acct_doing pool acct_pool
!
interface ethernet 0
  ip address 10.1.1.1 255.255.0.0
  ip nat inside
!
interface serial 0
  ip address 172.16.2.1 255.255.255.0
  ip nat outside
!
route-map what_is_sales_doing permit 10
  match ip address 2
!
route-map what_is_acct_doing permit 10
  match ip address 3
access-list 2 permit 10.1.2.0 0.0.0.255
access-list 3 permit 10.1.3.0 0.0.0.255
```

Following the path of a packet through this configuration is the best way to understand it. An IP packet with a source address of 10.1.2.100 arrives on interface Ethernet 0, which is an IP NAT inside interface. The **ip nat inside source route-map what_is_sales_doing pool sales_pool** command causes the router to send the packet to the what_is_sales_doing route map. Sequence 10 of this route map matches the packet's source IP address, 10.1.2.100, against access list 2, which permits the packet and therefore matches the route map. The router then queries the NAT pool sales_pool and obtains the next address to which to translate the 10.1.2.100 packet.

The what_is_acct_doing route map together with the **ip nat inside source route-map what_is_acct_doing pool acct_pool** command causes the router to look for source IP addresses in the 10.1.3.0/24 range and change them to source IP addresses in the 192.168.3.0/24 range.

As discussed, to examine the IP NAT translation table, use the **show ip nat translations** command. When using just an access list (as in the configuration shown in Figure 1-23), the router creates only a simple translation entry, one entry per application, without the TCP and UDP ports; Example 1-3 shows a simple translation entry. However, when using a route map, the router creates a fully extended translation entry in the IP NAT translation table, which includes the source and destination TCP or UDP port numbers. The extended translation entry shown in Example 1-4 results from the configuration in Example 1-6.

Notice in Example 1-4 that each session has individual entries; the IP address of each user and the applications in use can be determined from these entries. The local device with IP address 10.1.2.100 has three sessions with an outside device that has IP address 172.16.1.20. Example 1-4 shows that 10.1.2.100 has a TFTP session (UDP port 69) and an FTP session (TCP ports 20 and 21) with 172.16.1.20. Local device 10.1.3.67 has two sessions with the same remote device (172.16.1.20). Its two sessions are Telnet (TCP port 23) and HTTP (TCP port 80).

# Understanding IP Version 6

The ability to scale networks for future demands requires a new generation of IP addresses. IPv6 combines expanded addressing with a more efficient and feature-rich header to meet the demands for scalable networks in the future. This section describes the functionality and benefits of IPv6.

## Benefits of IPv6

IPv6 is a powerful enhancement to IPv4. Its primary features are as follows:

- The larger address space provides new global reachability, flexibility, aggregation, multihoming, autoconfiguration, plug and play, and renumbering. IPv6 increases the IP address size from 32 bits to 128 bits, allowing more support for addressing hierarchical levels, a much greater number of addressable nodes, and simpler autoconfiguration of addresses.

- The simpler, fixed-size header enables better routing efficiency, performance, and forwarding rate scalability.

- The numerous possibilities to transition from IPv4 to IPv6 allow existing IPv4 capabilities to exist with the added features of IPv6. Various mechanisms are defined for transitioning to IPv6, including dual stack, tunneling, and translation.

- Mobility and security ensures compliance with Mobile IP and IP Security (IPSec) standards.

Mobility is an important feature in networks. Mobile IP is an Internet Engineering Task Force (IETF) standard available for both IPv4 and IPv6. This standard lets mobile devices move without breaks in current connections. In IPv6, mobility is built in, which means that any IPv6 node can use it when necessary. However, mobility is not provided in IPv4; you must add it. IPv6's routing headers make mobile IPv6 much more efficient for end nodes than mobile IPv4.

IPSec is the IETF standard for IP network security. It enables integrity, authentication, and confidentiality. IPSec is available for both IPv4 and IPv6. Although the functionality is essentially identical in both environments, IPSec is mandatory in IPv6.

IPSec is enabled on every IPv6 node and is available for use, resulting in the IPv6 Internet being more secure. IPSec also requires keys for each party, which implies global key deployment and distribution.

**NOTE**    RFC 2460, *Internet Protocol, Version 6 (IPv6) Specification* (available at www.cis.ohio-state.edu /cgi-bin/rfc/rfc2460.html), defines the IPv6 standard.

You can find information on IPv6 features supported in specific Cisco IOS releases by following the links on the *Cisco IOS IPv6* page, at www.cisco.com/warp/public/732/Tech/ipv6/.

# IPv6 Addressing

IPv6 increases the number of address bits by a factor of 4, from 32 to 128. During the IPv6 design specification, factoring to 64, 128, and 160 bits was considered. Ultimately, the design team selected 128 bits as the most appropriate factoring choice, resulting in a very large number of addressable nodes. (However, as in any addressing scheme, not all the addresses are used.)

---

### Key Point: IPv6 Addresses Are 128 Bits

The 128 bits of an IPv6 address provide a much larger address space than IPv4.

---

IPv6 can provide approximately $3.4 * 10^{38}$ addresses (340,282,366,920,938,463,374,607,432,768,211,456), or approximately $5 * 10^{28}$ addresses for every person on the planet!

Increasing the number of bits for the address also increases the header size. Because each IP header contains a source and a destination address, the sizes of the header fields that contain the addresses are 64 bits for IPv4 and 256 bits for IPv6.

IPv6 allows hosts to have multiple IPv6 addresses and networks to have multiple IPv6 prefixes, thereby facilitating connection to multiple ISPs, for example.

## IPv6 Address Format

IPv6 addresses are represented as a series of 16-bit hexadecimal fields separated by colons (:), in the format *x:x:x:x:x:x:x:x*. Techniques are available to shorten written IPv6 addresses:

- The leading 0s within a field are optional.

- IPv6 addresses often contain successive hexadecimal fields of 0s. To shorten IPv6 addresses, two colons (::) may be used to compress and represent successive hexadecimal fields of 0s. This can be done at the beginning, middle, or end of an IPv6 address, but it is allowed only once in an address. To determine the number of missing 0s in an IPv6 address, write the two parts of the address separately, and fill in between with 0s until you have 128 bits.

**NOTE**   An address parser identifies the number of missing 0s by separating the two parts and entering 0 until the 128 bits are complete. If two :: notations are placed in the address, there is no way to identify the size of each block of 0s.

For example, the IPv6 address 2031:**0000**:130F:**0000:0000:0**9C0:876A:130B can be written as 2031:**0**:130F**::**9C0:876A:130B. An *incorrect* way to write this address is 2031::130F::9C0:876A:130B; two colons are allowed only once in an address.

The address 0:0:0:0:0:0:0:0 can be written as :: because it contains all 0s.

**NOTE**   The IPv6 addressing architecture is described in RFC 2373, *IP Version 6 Addressing Architecture,* available at www.cis.ohio-state.edu/cgi-bin/rfc/rfc2373.html.

Like the IPv4 prefix, the IPv6 prefix represents the *network* part of the address. The IPv6 prefix is written in *prefix/prefix-length* format; the *prefix-length* is a decimal value indicating the number of higher-order bits in the address that are included in the prefix. For example, 1080:5E40::/32 indicates that the higher-order 32 bits represent the network part of the address.

## IPv6 Address Types

**Key Point: IPv6 Address Types**

IPv6 addresses can be *unicast* (one-to-one), *anycast* (one-to-nearest), or *multicast* (one-to-many); IPv6 has no concept of a broadcast address.

**NOTE**   Broadcasting in IPv4 results in a number of problems, including interrupting every computer on the network and, in some cases, completely hanging up an entire network (this is called a *broadcast storm*).

IPv6 *unicast* addresses are the same as IPv4 unicast: A single source sends data to a single destination. A packet sent to a unicast IPv6 address is delivered to the interface identified by that address.

An IPv6 *multicast* address is the same as in IPv4 multicast: an address for a set of interfaces (in a given scope) that typically belong to different nodes. A packet sent to a multicast address is delivered to all the interfaces identified by the multicast address (in a given scope). (IPv6 uses a 4-bit scope ID to specify address ranges reserved for multicast addresses for each scope.) Multicast addresses enable efficient network operation by using a number of functionally specific multicast groups to send requests to a limited number of computers on the network. The multicast groups prevent the majority of problems related to broadcast storms in IPv4. The range of multicast addresses in IPv6 is larger than in IPv4. For the foreseeable future, allocation of multicast groups is not being limited.

IPv6 defines a new type of address called an *anycast* address. It identifies a list of interfaces that typically belong to different nodes. A packet sent to an anycast address is delivered to the *closest* interface, as defined by the routing protocols in use, identified by the anycast address. In other words, devices that share the same characteristics are assigned the same anycast address. A sender interested in contacting a device (a receiver) with those characteristics sends a packet to the anycast address, and the routers deliver the packet to the receiver nearest to the sender. Anycast can be used for service location. For example, an anycast address could be assigned to a set of replicated FTP servers. A user in China who wants to retrieve a file would be directed to the Chinese server, and a user in Europe would be directed to the European server.

Anycast addresses are allocated from the unicast address space and must not be used as the source address of an IPv6 packet. To devices that are not configured for anycast, these addresses appear as unicast addresses. When a unicast address is assigned to more than one interface, thus turning it into an anycast address, the nodes to which the anycast address is assigned must be explicitly configured to know that it is an anycast address.

An example of anycast use in a Border Gateway Protocol (BGP) multihomed network is when a customer has multiple connections to multiple ISPs. The customer uses a different anycast address for each ISP; each router for that ISP has the same configured anycast address. The source device can choose which ISP to send the packet to. However, the routers along the path determine the closest router to reach that ISP using the anycast address.

Another use for an anycast address is when a LAN is attached to multiple routers, and the routers are all configured with the same anycast address. Distant devices need to specify only the anycast address, and then intermediate devices can choose the best path to reach the closest entry point to that LAN.

## IPv6 Address Aggregation

A larger address space means that larger address allocations can be made to ISPs and organizations. As for IPv4, IPv6 summarization (or aggregation) reduces the routing table size and results in an efficient and scalable routing table. Scalable routing is necessary to connect to various devices and networks on the Internet in the future.

An ISP aggregates all its customers' prefixes into a single prefix and announces that single prefix to the IPv6 Internet, as shown in Figure 1-24.

**Figure 1-24** *IPv6 Address Summarization*

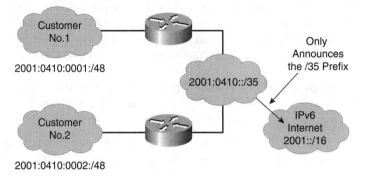

## IPv6 Autoconfiguration

A much larger address space allows IPv6 engineers to design a better way to enable autoconfiguration of the addresses and maintain their global uniqueness. The *stateless autoconfiguration* method is one way to do this. With stateless autoconfiguration, a router on the local link sends network-type information, such as the prefix of the local link and the default route, to all its nodes. An IPv6-enabled host uses the prefix advertised by the router as the top 64 bits of the address; the remaining 64 bits contain the 48-bit MAC address in an extended universal identifier 64-bit (EUI-64) format. This autoconfiguration produces a full 128-bit address that can be used on the local link and that guarantees global uniqueness.

**NOTE**    IPv6 detects duplicate addresses in special circumstances to avoid address collision.

---

**The EUI-64 Format**

The EUI-64 format interface ID is derived from the 48-bit link-layer MAC address by inserting the hex number FFFE between the upper 3 bytes (the Organizational Unique Identifier [OUI] field) and the lower 3 bytes (the serial number) of the link-layer address. To make sure that the chosen address is from a unique MAC address, the seventh bit in the high-order byte is set to 1 (equivalent to the IEEE G/L bit) to indicate the uniqueness of the 48-bit address.

The information in this sidebar is derived from Cisco's "The ABCs of IP Version 6," available at www.cisco.com/warp/public/732/abc/docs/abcipv6.pdf.

---

Autoconfiguration enables a plug-and-play feature, which connects devices (such as DHCP servers) to the network without configuration. Plug and play is a key feature to deploy new devices on the Internet, including cell phones, wireless devices, home appliances, and networks.

Stateless autoconfiguration is accomplished via a handshake between the host and the router. As illustrated in Figure 1-25, the host sends a router solicitation (RS) at boot time to ask the router to send an immediate router advertisement (RA) on the local link. The router sends an RA immediately after the host sends an RS. The host therefore receives the autoconfiguration information without waiting for the next scheduled RA.

**Figure 1-25**  *Stateless Autoconfiguration Means That IPv6 Can Be Plug and Play*

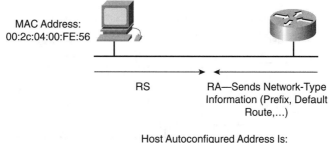

MAC Address:
00:2c:04:00:FE:56

RS        RA—Sends Network-Type
Information (Prefix, Default
Route,...)

Host Autoconfigured Address Is:
Prefix Received + Link-Layer Address

Routers also send RAs periodically, upon request, on all their configured interfaces. The router sends an RA to the *all-nodes* multicast address. Information contained in the RA message includes the following:

- One or more prefixes to use on the link
- A prefix's lifetime
- Flags that indicate the kind of autoconfiguration that hosts perform
- Default router information, including existence and lifetime
- Other types of host information

RA timing and other parameters can be configured on the routers.

## IPv6 Renumbering

RAs may announce the pending retirement of an old node prefix with a short lifetime and the use of a new node prefix. Decreasing the lifetime of the old prefix tells the nodes to begin using the new prefix and, at the same time, to continue maintaining connections opened with the old prefix for a period. During that period, nodes have two unicast addresses that they can use. When the old node prefix is retired (its lifetime decreases to 0), the RA announces only the new node prefix.

If you are renumbering an entire site, you must also renumber the routers. A router renumbering protocol is currently under review by the IETF. Renumbering an entire site also requires changes to the DNS entries; the introduction of new DNS records for IPv6 facilitates this process.

# IPv6 Packet Format

As illustrated in Figure 1-26, the new IPv6 header is less complicated than the IPv4 header in the following ways:

- It contains half of the previous IPv4 header fields. Fewer fields means easier packet processing, enhanced performance, and routing efficiency.

- It enables direct routing data storage and faster routing data retrieval with 64-bit aligned fields.

**Figure 1-26** *The IPv6 Header Is Simpler and More Efficient Than the IPv4 Header*

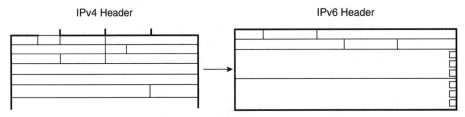

IPv6 header enhancements enable hardware-based processing that provides forwarding rate scalability for the next generation of high-speed lines. In the long term, it is clear that IPv6 improves routing efficiency. In the short term, however, the impact of the larger, 128-bit addressing remains unclear.

## IPv4 Header Format

As illustrated in Figure 1-27, the IPv4 header contains 12 basic header fields, followed by an Options field and a data portion (usually the transport layer segment). The basic IPv4 header has a fixed size of 20 octets. The variable-length Options field increases the size of the total IP header.

**Figure 1-27** *IPv4 Header Format*

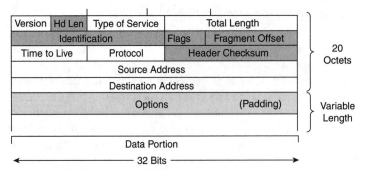

IPv6 contains fields similar to seven of the 12 IPv4 basic header fields. The IPv6 header does not require the other fields for the following reasons:

- Routers handle fragmentation in IPv4, which causes a variety of processing issues. IPv6 routers no longer perform fragmentation. Instead, a discovery process is used to determine the most optimum maximum transmission unit (MTU) to use during a given session, as follows:

— In the discovery process, the source IPv6 device attempts to send a packet at the size specified by the upper IP layers—for example, the transport and application layers. If the device receives an "ICMP packet too big" message, it tells the upper layer to discard the packet and to use the new MTU. The "ICMP packet too big" message contains the proper MTU size for the pathway. Each source device needs to track the MTU size for each session. Generally, the tracking is done by creating a cache based on the destination address; however, it also can be built using the flow label. If source-based routing is performed, the tracking of the MTU size can be built using the source address.

— The discovery process is beneficial because as routing paths change, a new MTU can be more appropriate. When a device receives an "ICMP packet too big" message, it decreases its MTU size if the ICMP message contains a recommended MTU less than the device's current MTU. A device can perform MTU discovery every 5 minutes to see if the MTU has increased along the path.

— Applications and transport layers for IPv6 accept MTU reduction notifications from the IPv6 layer. If they do not, IPv6 has a mechanism to fragment packets that are too large. However, upper layers are encouraged to avoid sending messages that require fragmentation.

• Most currently implemented link-layer technologies already do checksum and error control. Because link-layer technologies are relatively reliable, an IP header checksum is considered redundant. Without the IP header checksum, the upper-layer optional checksums, such as UDP, are now mandatory.

## IPv6 Header Format

The IPv6 header is illustrated in Figure 1-28.

**Figure 1-28** *IPv6 Header Format*

---

**Key Point: IPv6 Header**

The IPv6 header has 40 octets in contrast to the 20 octets in IPv4. IPv6 has a smaller number of fields, and the header is 64-bit aligned to enable fast processing by current processors. The IPv6 address fields are four times larger than in IPv4.

---

The IPv6 header contains these fields:

- **Version**—A 4-bit field, the same as in IPv4, that indicates the IP version. It contains the number 6 for IPv6 instead of the number 4 for IPv4.

- **Traffic Class**—An 8-bit field similar to the ToS field in IPv4. It tags the packet with a traffic class that it uses in differentiated services. These functions are the same for IPv6 and IPv4.

- **Flow Label**—A new 20-bit field. It tags a flow for IP packets. It can be used for multilayer switching techniques and faster packet-switching performance.

- **Payload Length**—A 16-bit field similar to the Total Length field in IPv4. This field indicates the total length of the packet's data portion.

- **Next Header**—An 8-bit field similar to the Protocol field in IPv4. The value of this field determines the type of information following the basic IPv6 header. It can be a transport layer segment, such as TCP or UDP, or it can be an extension header.

- **Hop Limit**—This 8-bit field specifies the maximum number of hops that the IP packet can traverse. It is similar to the Time To Live (TTL) field in IPv4. Each hop or router decreases this field by 1. Because the IPv6 header has no checksum, the router can decrease the field without recomputing the checksum. (On IPv4 routers, the recomputation costs processing time.)

- **Source Address**—This field has 16 octets or 128 bits and contains the packet's source address.

- **Destination Address**—This field has 16 octets or 128 bits and contains the packet's destination address.

The extension headers, if any, and the packet's data portion follow the eight fields. The number of extension headers is not fixed, so the total length of the extension header chain is variable.

## Stream Control Transmission Protocol

IPv6 also uses Stream Control Transmission Protocol (SCTP) at the transport layer. SCTP is a reliable transport service like TCP and supports sequence and acknowledgment functions. SCTP was built to overcome TCP's limitations—for example, the TCP requirement for a strict order of transmission that can cause head-of-line blocking.

The main difference between the two protocols lies in SCTP's purpose. SCTP is used for multihomed nodes and to combine several streams within a single data connection. TCP sends a stream of bytes, and SCTP sends a stream of messages. In TCP, the application has to know how to divide the stream of bytes into usable segments. SCTP is designed to provide a general-purpose transport protocol for message-oriented applications, such as signaling used in the public telephone network. If multiple streams are integrated into one connection and one of these streams has reliability problems, all the streams in TCP have difficulty. SCTP is aware of the messages in the connection, and functionality is provided with SCTP to selectively acknowledge SCTP packets.

In multihoming, clients and servers can have multiple network interface cards (NICs), and each can be reached through a variety of physical pathways. During SCTP setup, the client informs the server of all its IP addresses. The client needs to know only a single address for the server, because when the server responds to the client, it has in its acknowledgment a list of addresses to use to reach it. SCTP monitors all paths between the devices with a heartbeat function and identifies one path as the primary. Secondary paths can be used for retransmissions or in case the primary path fails.

SCTP has greater security than TCP, because SCTP uses a cookie function for each session and is immune to a TCP SYN attack. For example, if Device A wants to set up an SCTP session with Device B, the following steps occur:

- Device A creates an initialization request and sends it to Device B. Device A then waits for a message from Device B.

- Device B receives the request, generates an encrypted key and a message authentication code (indicating who created the message), and puts these into a cookie message. It sends the cookie to Device A.

- Device A receives the cookie and sends it back to Device B in a cookie echo message. Device A again waits for a message from Device B.

- Device B receives the cookie echo message and examines it to ensure that the message authentication code indicates that it was indeed Device B that created the cookie. It sends a cookie acknowledgment to Device A. Only then does Device B initiate the SCTP session; it is now in a state in which it can accept and send data.

- Device A receives the cookie acknowledgment and enters a state in which it can accept and send data.

---

**NOTE**     RFC 2960, *Stream Control Transmission Protocol*, available at www.cis.ohio-state.edu/cgi-bin /rfc/rfc2960.html, further describes SCTP.

---

## IPv6 Extension Headers

There are many types of extension headers. Each extension header is 64-bit aligned. The extension headers form a chained list of headers; the Next Header field of the previous header identifies each header, as shown in Figure 1-29.

**Figure 1-29** *IPv6 Extension Headers Form a Chained List of Headers*

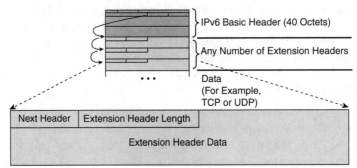

When multiple extension headers are used in the same packet, their order is as follows:

1 IPv6 header

2 Hop-by-Hop Options header

3 Destination Options header (when using the Routing header)

4 Routing header

5 Fragment header

6 Authentication header

7 Encapsulating Security Payload header

8 Destination Options header

9 Upper-layer header

# IPv6 to IPv4 Interoperability

The transition from IPv4 to IPv6 will be a slow process, but fortunately it does not require upgrades on all nodes at the same time. Meanwhile, IPv4 and IPv6 must coexist.

Many transition mechanisms enable smooth integration of IPv4 and IPv6. Other mechanisms that allow IPv4 nodes to communicate with IPv6 nodes are available.

---

**Key Point: IPv6 Transition Techniques**

The two most common techniques to transition from IPv4 to IPv6 are as follows:

— **Dual stack**—IPv4 and IPv6 stacks run on a system. The system can communicate with both IPv4 and IPv6 devices.

— **Tunneling**—The most common type of tunneling used is IPv6 to IPv4 (6to4) tunneling to encapsulate IPv6 packets in IPv4 packets.

---

A third method uses an extension of IP NAT to translate an IPv4 address to an IPv6 address and an IPv6 address to an IPv4 address.

## Dual-Stack Transition

A dual stack enables both the IPv4 and IPv6 protocols. Cisco IOS software is IPv6-ready. As soon as IPv4 and IPv6 basic configurations are complete on an interface, the interface is dual stacked, and it forwards IPv4 and IPv6 traffic.

As shown in Figure 1-30, using IPv6 on a Cisco IOS software router requires the global configuration command **ipv6 unicast-routing**. This command enables the forwarding of IPv6 datagrams. All interfaces that forward IPv6 traffic must have an IPv6 address, assigned with the interface configuration command **ipv6 address** *IPv6-address* [*/prefix length*]. This command specifies the IPv6 address to be assigned to the interface and enables IPv6 processing on the interface.

**Figure 1-30**  *Assigning IPv4 and IPv6 Addresses Creates a Dual-Stack Interface*

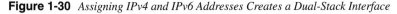

## Overlay Tunnels

Tunnels are often used to overlay an incompatible protocol on an existing network. Tunneling IPv6 traffic over an IPv4 network requires one edge router to encapsulate the IPv6 packet inside an IPv4 packet and another router to decapsulate the packet. This process lets you interconnect IPv6 islands without converting the entire network to IPv6, as illustrated in Figure 1-31.

**Figure 1-31**  *Tunneling Encapsulates an IPv6 Packet in an IPv4 Packet*

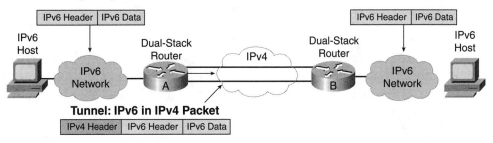

When you tunnel, remember the following:

- If the IPv4 header does not contain an optional field, the MTU effectively decreases by 20 octets.

- A tunneled network is often difficult to troubleshoot. Tunneling is a *transition* technique that should be used only where it is appropriate; do not consider it a final architecture. Using native IPv6 throughout the network is still the final goal.

Tunnels can be either manually or automatically configured.

## Manually Configured Tunnel

In a manually configured tunnel, you configure both the IPv4 and IPv6 addresses statically on the routers at each end of the tunnel, as illustrated in Figure 1-32. These end routers must be dual-stacked, and the configuration does not change dynamically as network and routing needs change. Routing must be set up properly to forward a packet between the two IPv6 networks.

**Figure 1-32** *A Manually Configured Tunnel Has Static Addresses*

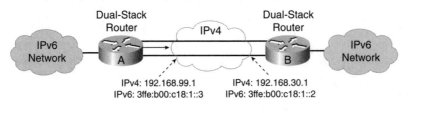

**NOTE**      Tunnel endpoints can be unnumbered, but unnumbered endpoints make troubleshooting difficult. The IPv4 practice of saving addresses by using unnumbered tunnel endpoints is no longer an issue.

## 6to4 Tunneling

The 6to4 tunneling method automatically establishes and enables the connection of IPv6 islands through an IPv4 network, as illustrated in Figure 1-33. The 6to4 tunneling method assigns a valid IPv6 prefix to each IPv6 island, which enables the fast deployment of IPv6 in a corporate network without obtaining addresses from the ISPs or registries.

**Figure 1-33** *6to4 Tunneling Automatically Establishes Connections*

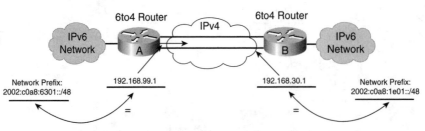

The 6to4 tunneling method requires configuration of the edge routers, but the IPv6 hosts and routers inside the 6to4 site do not require new features to support 6to4.

---

**Key Point: 6to4 Tunnel Addresses**

The 6to4 tunnel treats the IPv4 network as a virtual link. Each 6to4 edge router has an IPv6 address with a /48 prefix, which is the concatenation of 2002::/16 and the edge router's IPv4 address (in hexadecimal); 2002::/16 is a specially assigned address range for the purpose of 6to4. The edge routers automatically build the tunnel using the IPv4 addresses imbedded in the IPv6 addresses.

---

For example, if the edge router's IPv4 address is 192.168.99.1, the prefix of its IPv6 network is 2002:c0a8:6301::/48, because c0a86301 is the hexadecimal representation of 192.168.99.1.

When the edge router receives an IPv6 packet with a destination address in the range of 2002::/16, it determines from its routing table that the packet must go through the tunnel. The router extracts the IPv4 address embedded as the third to sixth octets inclusive in the IPv6 next-hop address; this is the IPv4 address of the 6to4 router at the other end of the tunnel. The router encapsulates the IPv6 packet in an IPv4 packet with the extracted IPv4 address of the destination edge router. The packet then goes through the IPv4 network. The destination edge router decapsulates the IPv6 packet from the received IPv4 packet and forwards the IPv6 packet to its final destination. (To be able to reach a native IPv6 Internet, a 6to4 relay router, which offers traffic forwarding to the IPv6 Internet, is needed.)

# IPv6 Routing Protocols

This section introduces IPv6 routing protocols and compares them to their IPv4 counterparts.

The routing protocols available in IPv6 include interior gateway protocols (IGPs), for within an autonomous system, and exterior gateway protocols (EGPs), for between autonomous systems. The following routing protocols or draft proposals are available:

- IGPs:
  - RIP new generation (RIPng)
  - OSPF version 3 (OSPFv3)
  - Integrated IS-IS version 6 (IS-ISv6)
- EGP—BGP4+

---

**NOTE**    Routing protocols for IPv4 are discussed in detail in other chapters.

---

## RIPng

RIPng is a distance-vector protocol with a limit of 15 hops that uses split horizon and poison reverse to prevent routing loops. IPv6 features include the following:

- RIPng is based on the IPv4 RIPv2 and is similar to RIPv2.
- RIPng uses an IPv6 prefix and next-hop IPv6 address.
- A multicast group, FF02::9, is the all-RIP-routers multicast group and is used as the destination address for RIP updates.
- RIPng uses IPv6 for transport.

| | |
|---|---|
| **NOTE** | RIPng is defined in RFC 2080, *RIPng for IPv6*, available at www.cis.ohio-state.edu/cgi-bin/rfc /rfc2080.html. |

## OSPFv3

OSPFv3 is a new protocol implementation for IPv6. It has the following features:

- OSPFv3 is similar to the IPv4 version of OSPF.
- OSPFv3 carries IPv6 addresses.
- OSPFv3 uses IPv6 link-local unicast addresses as source addresses. (A link-local unicast address can serve as a method of connecting devices on the same local network without the need for either site-local or globally unique addresses.)
- OSPFv3 uses IPv6 for transport.

| | |
|---|---|
| **NOTE** | OSPFv3 is defined in RFC 2740, *OSPF for IPv6*, available at www.cis.ohio-state.edu/cgi-bin /rfc/rfc2740.html. |

## Integrated IS-ISv6

The large address support in Integrated IS-ISv6 facilitates the IPv6 address family. IS-ISv6 is the same as IS-IS for IPv4, with the following extensions added for IPv6:

- Two new types, lengths, values (TLVs):
  - IPv6 reachability
  - IPv6 interface address
- A new protocol identifier

## BGP4+

Multiprotocol extensions for BGP4 let other protocols besides IPv4 be routed, including IPv6. Other IPv6-specific extensions also are included in BGP4+, including the definition of a new identifier for the IPv6 address family.

---

**NOTE**    Multiprotocol extensions to BGP are defined in RFC 2858, *Multiprotocol Extensions for BGP-4*, available at www.cis.ohio-state.edu/cgi-bin/rfc/rfc2858.html. BGP4+ for IPv6 is defined in RFC 2545, *Use of BGP-4 Multiprotocol Extensions for IPv6 Inter-Domain Routing*, available at www.cis.ohio-state.edu/cgi-bin/rfc/rfc2545.html.

---

---

**NOTE**    Cisco routers support the RIPng, IS-ISv6, and BGP4+ routing protocols. OSPFv3 is also supported on some platforms. You can find information on IPv6 features supported in specific Cisco IOS releases and platforms by following the links on the *Cisco IOS IPv6* page, at www.cisco.com/warp/public/732/Tech/ipv6/.

---

In the Cisco 12000 Internet Router Series, IPv6 routing is supported in the Cisco IOS 12.0(22)S configuration and later. In all other platforms, the IPv6 routing protocols are supported in IOS 12.2(2)T and later. Redistribution is not supported between IPv4 routing protocols and IPv6 routing protocols.

The largest use of IPv6 is across the Internet using BGP extensions for IPv6.

# Summary

In this chapter, you learned that networks must be designed to support the benefits of advanced IP routing protocols. Well-designed networks allow corporations to react quickly to changes in their networking requirements, including mergers, reorganizations, and downsizing.

There are two types of hierarchical network design: functional and geographic. In a functional network design, the different divisions of a corporation have their own networks and are connected according to their functional purpose within the corporate structure. In a geographic network design, the divisions of a corporation have their own networks and are connected according to their location.

The access, distribution, and core layers comprise a hierarchical scalable network design.

In a fully meshed core layer design, all routers in the core have direct connections to all other routers in the core. A core layer hub-and-spoke configuration establishes a focal point for the data flow at a key site.

A good IP addressing plan implemented in a well-designed network provides scalability, predictability, and flexibility.

RFC 1918 has set aside the following IPv4 address space for private use:

- **Class A network**—10.0.0.0 to 10.255.255.255
- **Class B network**—172.16.0.0 to 172.31.255.255
- **Class C network**—192.168.0.0 to 192.168.255.255

The benefits of hierarchical addressing include a reduced number of routing table entries and efficient allocation of addresses.

A subnet mask is a 32-bit value that identifies which bits in an address represent network bits and which represent host bits. To create a subnet mask for an address, use a 1 for each bit of the address that you want to represent the network or subnet portion of the address, and use a 0 for each bit of the address that you want to represent the node portion of the address. The number of subnetworks created by adding $n$ bits to the default mask is calculated by the formula $2^n$. The number of hosts available is calculated by the formula $2^n - 2$, where $n$ is the number of bits in the host portion.

A prefix is a slash (/) followed by a numeric value that is the number of bits in the network and subnet portions of the address—in other words, the number of contiguous 1s that would be in the subnet mask.

A major network is a Class A, B, or C network. With classful routing, routing updates do not carry the subnet mask. Therefore, only one subnet mask must be in use within a major network; this is known as FLSM. With classless routing, routing updates do carry the subnet mask. Therefore, different masks may be used for different subnets within a major network; this is known as VLSM.

With VLSM, it is important to remember that only *unused* subnets should be further subnetted. In other words, if you use any addresses from a subnet, that subnet should not be further subnetted.

Route summarization (also called *route aggregation* or *supernetting*) can reduce the number of routes that a router must maintain, because it is a method of representing a series of network numbers in a single summary address. Route summarization is most effective within a subnetted environment when the network addresses are in contiguous blocks in powers of 2.

Routing information advertised out an interface is automatically summarized at major (classful) network address boundaries by RIP, IGRP, and EIGRP. When using EIGRP and RIPv2, you can disable this automatic summarization. For OSPF and IS-IS, you must configure summarization.

CIDR is a mechanism developed to help alleviate the problem of exhaustion of IP addresses and growth of routing tables. The idea behind CIDR is that blocks of multiple addresses (for example, blocks of Class C address) can be combined, or aggregated, to create a larger classless set of IP addresses, with more hosts allowed.

The difference between CIDR and route summarization is that route summarization is generally done within, or up to, a classful boundary, whereas CIDR combines several classful networks.

NAT terminology includes the following:

- **Inside local IP address**—The IP address used by the inside host before any translations.
- **Inside global IP address**—The IP address used by the inside host as it appears to the outside network; this is the translated IP address.
- **Outside global IP address**—The configured globally unique IP address assigned to a host in the outside network.
- **Outside local IP address**—The IP address of an outside host as it appears to the inside network.

When you use only access lists for NAT, the resulting NAT table has only simple translation entries, identifying only which inside local address is being translated to which inside global address. To get an extended translation entry in the NAT table, you must either configure NAT for overloading or use route maps.

Route maps are complex access lists that allow some conditions to be tested against a packet or route in question using **match** commands. If the conditions match, some actions can be taken to modify attributes of the packet or route. These actions are specified by **set** commands.

IPv6 addresses have 128 bits. The IPv6 header has 40 octets in contrast to the 20 octets in IPv4. IPv6 has a smaller number of fields, and the header is 64-bit aligned to enable fast processing by current processors. The IPv6 address fields are four times larger than in IPv4.

IPv6 addresses are represented as a series of 16-bit hexadecimal fields separated by colons (:), in the format $x:x:x:x:x:x:x:x$. The leading 0s within a field are optional. Two colons (::) may be used to compress successive hexadecimal fields of 0s. This can be done at the beginning, middle, or end of an IPv6 address, but it is allowed only once in an address.

IPv6 addresses can be *unicast* (one-to-one), *anycast* (one-to-nearest), or *multicast* (one-to-many); IPv6 has no concept of a broadcast address.

With IPv6 *stateless autoconfiguration,* a router on the local link sends network-type information to all its nodes. An IPv6-enabled host uses the prefix advertised by the router as the top 64 bits of the address; the remaining 64 bits contain the 48-bit MAC address in an extended universal identifier 64-bit (EUI-64) format. This autoconfiguration produces a full 128-bit address that can be used on the local link and that guarantees global uniqueness.

The two most common techniques to transition from IPv4 to IPv6 are as follows:

- **Dual stack**—IPv4 and IPv6 stacks run on a system. The system can communicate with both IPv4 devices and IPv6 devices.
- **Tunneling**—The most common type of tunneling used is IPv6 to IPv4 (6to4) tunneling, to encapsulate IPv6 packets in IPv4 packets. Each 6to4 edge router has an IPv6 address with a /48 prefix, which is the concatenation of 2002::/16 and the edge router's IPv4 address (in hexadecimal). The edge routers automatically build the tunnel using the IPv4 addresses imbedded in the IPv6 addresses.

The following routing protocols or draft proposals are available for IPv6: RIPng, OSPFv3, IS-ISv6, and BGP4+.

# References

For additional information, refer to these resources:

* Cisco IP Version 6 Solutions, www.cisco.com/univercd/cc/td/doc/cisintwk/intsolns/ipv6_sol/index.htm.

* Cisco IOS IPv6, www.cisco.com/warp/public/732/Tech/ipv6.

* "The ABCs of IP Version 6," www.cisco.com/warp/public/732/abc/docs/abcipv6.pdf.

# Configuration Exercise 1-1: Basic Connectivity

In this exercise, you give the routers in your pod a basic configuration.

---

### Introduction to the Configuration Exercises

This book uses Configuration Exercises to help you practice configuring routers with the commands and topics presented. If you have access to real hardware, you can try these exercises on your routers. See Appendix H, "Configuration Exercise Equipment Requirements and Initial Configurations," for a list of recommended equipment and initial configuration commands for the routers. However, even if you don't have access to any routers, you can go through the exercises and keep a log of your own running configurations or just read through the solution. Commands used and solutions to the Configuration Exercises are provided after the exercises.

In the Configuration Exercises, the network is assumed to consist of two pods, each with four routers. The pods are interconnected to a backbone. You configure pod 1. No interaction between the two pods is required, but you might see some routes from the other pod in your routing tables in some exercises if you have it configured (the Configuration Exercise answers show the routes from the other pod). In most of the exercises, the backbone has only one router; in some cases, another router is added to the backbone. Each Configuration Exercise assumes that you have completed the previous chapters' Configuration Exercises on your pod.

---

**NOTE**    Throughout this exercise, the pod number is referred to as $x$, and the router number is referred to as $y$. Substitute the appropriate numbers as needed.

---

## Objectives

Given that the routers in your pod are properly cabled, your task is to do the following:

* Provide an initial configuration on your edge routers, P$x$R1 and P$x$R2, so that you can connect to the TFTP server in the core.

- Connect to the TFTP server in the core from the P*x*R1 and P*x*R2 routers.
- Download a configuration file and complete the setup of your edge routers.

## Visual Objective

Figure 1-34 illustrates the topology used in this exercise. You will configure only the P*x*R1 and P*x*R2 routers in this exercise.

**Figure 1-34**  *Basic Configuration Exercise Topology*

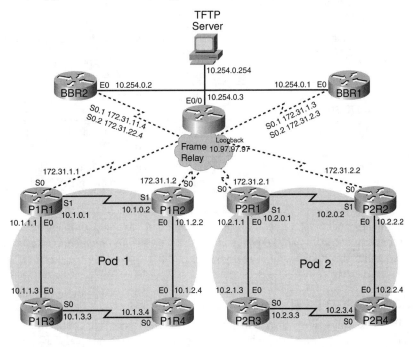

---

**NOTE**   Backbone Router 2 (BBR2), shown in Figure 1-34, is not used until a later Configuration Exercise.

---

## Command List

In this exercise, you use the commands in Table 1-5, listed in logical order. Refer to this list if you need configuration command assistance during the exercise.

**CAUTION** Although the command syntax is shown in this table, the addresses shown are typically for the P*x*R1 and P*x*R3 routers. Be careful when addressing your routers! Refer to the exercise instructions and the appropriate visual objective diagram for addressing details.

**Table 1-5** *Basic Configuration Exercise Commands*

| Command | Description |
|---------|-------------|
| (config-if)#**encapsulation frame-relay** | Enables Frame Relay encapsulation. |
| (config-if)#**ip address 172.31.**x.y **255.255.255.0** | Assigns an IP address. |
| (config-if)#**frame-relay map ip 172.31.**x.**3 1**xy **broadcast** | Maps a next-hop IP address to a permanent virtual circuit (PVC). |
| (config-if)#**no shutdown** | Brings up an interface. |
| (config)#**ip route 10.0.0.0 255.0.0.0 172.31.**x.**3** | Creates a static route. |
| #**copy tftp run** | Copies the configuration file into the running configuration from a TFTP server. |
| #**copy run start** | Copies the running configuration file (in RAM) into the startup configuration file (in NVRAM). |

**NOTE** Refer to Appendix C, "Summary of ICND Router and Switch Commands," for a listing of the Cisco IOS router commands covered in the Cisco Press *Interconnecting Cisco Network Devices* book, which this book assumes that you are familiar with.

## Task: Setting Up the Edge Routers

In this task, you will use a terminal utility to establish a console connection to the equipment. You will establish connectivity between the edge routers in your pod (P*x*R1 and P*x*R2) and the BBR1 router. Then you will download configurations to these routers from the TFTP server in the core. Complete the following steps:

**Step 1** Connect to each of your pod routers; they should not have configurations on them. If a router does have a configuration, delete the configuration using the **erase start** command, and then use the **reload** command to reboot.

> **NOTE** In this exercise, you will apply some minimal addressing and routing information so that your routers can reach the TFTP server.

**Step 2** Connect to each of your pod edge routers (P*x*R1 and P*x*R2). Configure the serial s0 interface of these routers for Frame Relay by turning on Frame Relay encapsulation.

**Step 3**   Assign an IP address to your serial 0 interface. Your IP address is 172.31.*x*.*y*/24 (where *x* is your pod number and *y* is your router number).

**Step 4**   Inverse ARP has been turned off in the core Frame Relay network. Manually map a data-link connection identifier (DLCI) to BBR1 (172.31.*x*.3). The DLCI number will be in the form 1*xy*, where *x* is your pod number and *y* is your router number. For instance, P2R1 will use DLCI 121.

| NOTE | Remember to specify the **broadcast** keyword so that the Frame Relay mapping supports broadcasts and multicasts, such as routing protocol traffic. |
|------|------|

**Step 5**   Use the **no shutdown** command on the interface, and exit configuration mode.

**Step 6**   Verify successful connectivity from your P*x*R1 and P*x*R2 router to the core BBR1 router (172.31.*x*.3) using the **ping** command.

**Step 7**   The goal of this exercise is to download a file from the TFTP server (at 10.254.0.254), which is connected to BBR1. Look at your P*x*R1 and P*x*R2 routing tables. Is there a route to the network that the TFTP server is located on? Why not?

**Step 8**   Add a static route to 10.0.0.0/8 on your edge routers, through BBR1 (172.31.*x*.3), to provide a path to the TFTP server. Verify that the edge routers can see this route.

**Step 9**   Verify successful connectivity to the TFTP server (10.254.0.254) from your P*x*R1 and P*x*R2 router using the **ping** command.

**Step 10**  Retrieve the configuration file for your router from the TFTP server. The file should be named P*x*R*y*.txt. (For example, Pod 1 Router 2 will download P1R2.txt.)

| NOTE | Filenames are not case-sensitive. |
|------|------|

| NOTE | The configuration files include the **no ip classless** command to force your router to behave classfully (although this command is on by default in IOS 12.0 and later). These files also include all required IP addresses and enable all required interfaces. Remember that files copied to running-config are merged, so this configuration complements what is already in your running-config. |
|------|------|

| NOTE | The initial configuration files for the routers are provided in Appendix H. |
|------|------|

**Step 11**  Save your configuration before proceeding.

## Exercise Verification

You have successfully completed this exercise if you can ping the core BBR1 router and the TFTP server from your edge routers (P*x*R1 and P*x*R2) and if you have downloaded the configuration files for your edge routers from the TFTP server.

# Configuration Exercise 1-2: NAT Using Access Lists and Route Maps

In this exercise, you will use NAT to allow your internal routers (P*x*R3 and P*x*R4) to download a configuration file from the TFTP server.

---

**NOTE**    Throughout this exercise, the pod number is referred to as *x*, and the router number is referred to as *y*. Substitute the appropriate numbers as needed.

---

## Objectives

After completing this exercise, you will be able to

- Demonstrate the uses and limits of access control list (ACL)-based NAT
- Demonstrate the usefulness of NAT with route maps by implementing separate concurrent translations
- Connect the internal router to the TFTP server or the opposite edge router using appropriate translation
- Download a configuration file for the internal routers

## Visual Objective

Figure 1-35 illustrates the topology used in this exercise.

---

**NOTE**    Backbone Router 2 (BBR2), shown in Figure 1-35, is not used until a later Configuration Exercise.

---

## Command List

In this exercise, you will use the commands in Table 1-6, listed in logical order. Refer to this list if you need configuration command assistance during the exercise.

**Figure 1-35** *NAT Configuration Exercise Topology*

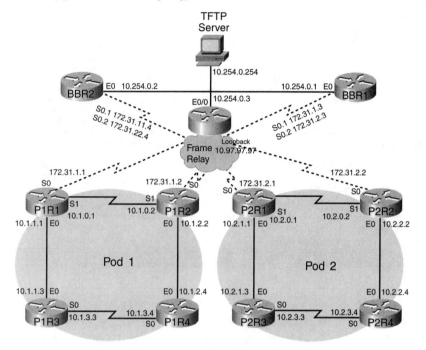

CAUTION    Although the command syntax is shown in this table, the addresses shown are typically for the P*x*R1 and P*x*R3 routers. Be careful when addressing your routers! Refer to the exercise instructions and the appropriate visual objective diagram for addressing details.

**Table 1-6**    *NAT Configuration Exercise Commands*

| Command | Description |
|---|---|
| (config)#**access-list 100 permit ip 10.1.*x*.0 0.0.0.255 10.254.0.0 0.0.0.255** | Creates an access list that specifies the traffic that should be translated. |
| (config)#**ip nat pool BBR 192.168.*x*.1 192.168.*x*.254 netmask 255.255.255.0**<br>or<br>(config)#**ip nat pool BBR 192.168.*x*.1 192.168.*x*.254 prefix-length 24** | Creates a named pool of addresses for use by NAT. |
| (config)#**ip nat inside source list 100 pool BBR** | Translates inside addresses that match the access list into this pool. |

*continues*

**Table 1-6**    *NAT Configuration Exercise Commands (Continued)*

| Command | Description |
|---|---|
| (config-if)#**ip nat inside** | Identifies an inside NAT address. |
| (config-if)#**ip nat outside** | Identifies an external NAT address. |
| (config)#**ip route 0.0.0.0 0.0.0.0 e0** | Creates a default route pointing out interface E0. |
| #**show ip nat translations** | Views the translation table. |
| #**debug ip icmp** | Starts the console display of ICMP events. |
| #**debug ip packet** | Starts the console display of IP packet events. |
| (config)#**route-map TO_BBR permit 10**<br>(config-route-map)#**match ip address 100** | Creates a route map to match the source address with addresses permitted by the access list. |
| #**clear ip nat translation *** | Removes all address translations from the NAT table. |
| (config)#**ip nat inside source route-map TO_POD pool POD** | Specifies a route map to be used for NAT. |
| #**debug ip nat detailed** | Starts the console display of translation entries being created. |

# Task 1: Connecting the Internal Router to the Edge Router

In this task, you will connect the internal routers in your pod, P*x*R3 and P*x*R4, to the edge routers, P*x*R1 and P*x*R2. Complete the following steps:

**Step 1**    The internal routers (P*x*R3 and P*x*R4) should not have a configuration. If a configuration is present, use the **erase start** and **reload** commands to clear the configuration and reload the router.

**Step 2**    Connect to your internal routers. Supply an IP address to the Ethernet interface, and enable the interface. The Ethernet address of P*x*R3 should be 10.*x*.1.3/24, and the Ethernet address of P*x*R4 should be 10.*x*.2.4/24.

**Step 3**    P*x*R1 has an Ethernet address of 10.*x*.1.1, and P*x*R2 has an Ethernet address of 10.*x*.2.2. Verify connectivity to the Ethernet-attached edge router from each internal router.

# Task 2: Setting Up ACL-Based NAT

In this task, you will configure one-to-one NAT using an access list on the edge routers (P*x*R1 or P*x*R2). The access list translates the internal router Ethernet address using either 192.168.*x*.0/24 or 192.168.*xx*.0/24.

---

**NOTE**    BBR1 has static routes for 192.168.*x*.0/24 and 192.168.*xx*.0/24. It does not have any remote routes for the pod 10.*x*.0.0 addresses, only its local TFTP server network 10.254.0.0.

---

Complete the following steps:

**Step 1** On the P*x*R1 and P*x*R2 routers, configure the sources to be translated using extended access list 100. Access list 100 should match traffic sourced from the network on your edge router's Ethernet interface, destined for the network that the TFTP server is located on. For example, P*x*R1 should match traffic sourced from 10.*x*.1.0/24, and P*x*R2 should match traffic sourced from 10.*x*.2.0/24. The access list must match only packets with a destination of 10.254.0.0/24.

**Step 2** On the P*x*R1 and P*x*R2 routers, create a pool of addresses called **BBR** for use by NAT, using the **ip nat pool** command. P*x*R1 should use the address range of 192.168.*x*.0/24, and P*x*R2 should use 192.168.*xx*.0/24. For example, P2R1 would use 192.168.2.1 through 192.168.2.254, and P2R2 would use 192.168.22.1 through 192.168.22.254.

**Step 3** On the P*x*R1 and P*x*R2 routers, use the **ip nat inside source list** command to specify that packets that match access list 100 should have their source addresses translated into the BBR pool.

**Step 4** On the P*x*R1 and P*x*R2 routers, define which interfaces are inside or outside for NAT translation purposes.

**Step 5** On the P*x*R3 and P*x*R4 routers, configure a default route pointing to the attached edge router e0 interface. This configuration allows the internal router to reach the core network.

**Step 6** From the P*x*R3 and P*x*R4 routers, verify connectivity to the TFTP server (10.254.0.254) using the **ping** command.

---

**CAUTION**    You will not be able to reach the TFTP server if the NAT translation is not done correctly.

---

**Step 7** View the NAT translation table on the edge router (P*x*R1 and P*x*R2).

## Task 3: Translating to the Other Edge Router

In this task, you will translate traffic from the odd half of the pod (P*x*R1 and P*x*R3) to the even half of the pod (P*x*R2 and P*x*R4) and vice versa. Because you are not running a routing protocol, you will translate the internal addresses to addresses that would be appropriate on the serial link between P*x*R1 and P*x*R2. Complete the following steps:

**Step 1** On the P*x*R1 and P*x*R2 routers, configure the source addresses to be translated using extended access list 101. Access list 101 should match traffic sourced from the network on your edge router's Ethernet interface, bound for any destination. For instance, P*x*R1 should match traffic from 10.*x*.1.0/24, and P*x*R2 should match traffic from 10.*x*.2.0/24. The access list must match packets with a destination to any network.

**Step 2**  On the P*x*R1 and P*x*R2 routers, create a pool of addresses named **POD** for use by NAT. P*x*R1 should use the address range 10.*x*.0.64 to 10.*x*.0.95, and P*x*R2 should use the address range 10.*x*.0.96 to 10.*x*.0.127.

**Step 3**  On the P*x*R1 and P*x*R2 routers, specify that packets that match access list 101 should have their source addresses translated into the POD pool.

**Step 4**  At the P*x*R1 and P*x*R2 routers, define the S1 interface of each router as the NAT outside interface by using the **ip nat outside** command so that traffic from the respective internal routers is translated.

**Step 5**  From one internal router, ping the Serial 1 interface of the nonconnected edge router. (For example, from P*x*R3, ping the Serial 1 address of P*x*R2.) Is the ping successful?

**Step 6**  Look at the IP translation table on the edge routers to help explain the result of the previous ping.

**Step 7**  From the nonconnected edge router, use the **debug ip icmp** and **debug ip packet** commands while the pings are still active. Observe the output to help explain the results of the previous ping. Turn off all debugging when you are finished.

**Step 8**  Look at the routing table on the nonconnected edge router. Is there a route back to the destination address of the ping echo reply message?

**Step 9**  What does a router do when it does not find an appropriate address?

## Task 4: Using a Route Map with NAT to Translate Internal Addresses

In this task, you will configure NAT using a route map to match traffic. You saw in Task 3 that when NAT uses an access list without overloading addresses, the translation entry contains only local and global inside IP addresses. When a route map is used with NAT, the translation entry contains both the inside and outside (local and global) address entries and any TCP or UDP port information. This translation entry lets the router recognize different conversations.

In this exercise, traffic needs to be translated based on destination. Traffic to the TFTP server and the core should still be translated to 192.168.*x*.0/24 or 192.168.*xx*.0/24, but traffic to the other edge router should be translated to an IP address in the 10.*x*.0.0 subnet. This address will appear to be local to the serial 1 interface of the other edge and will have a path entered in the routing table (connected routes are automatically in the routing table). To prevent confusion, P*x*R1 uses the address range of 10.*x*.0.64/24 through 10.*x*.0.95/24, and P*x*R2 uses the address range of 10.*x*.0.96/24 through 10.*x*.0.127/24.

Complete the following steps:

**Step 1**  Create a route map that will be used to conditionally translate traffic based on the packet's destination.

**Step 2**  Replace the translation commands from Task 3 with route map-based commands to perform the required translation.

---

**NOTE**   If the router reports "%Dynamic mapping in use, cannot remove," simply go to privileged mode and enter the **clear ip nat translation \*** command to remove all mappings. You then can configure the router.

---

**Step 3**  Ping from one internal router to the opposite edge router and to the TFTP server to verify that the previous step was successful. Turn on **debug ip nat detailed** debugging on the edge routers to see the translation.

**Step 4**  Use the **show ip nat translations** command on each edge router to see the resulting NAT translation table.

## Task 5: Downloading a Configuration File

Now that NAT is properly configured and working, you will download a configuration for the internal routers (P*x*R3 and P*x*R4).

On the internal routers, use TFTP to download the configuration file called P*x*R*y*.txt from the TFTP server to the running-config.

---

**NOTE**   The configurations for P*x*R3 and P*x*R4 include the command **no ip classless** in preparation for the next Configuration Exercise at the end of the next chapter. If you try to communicate with the TFTP server now, it will not work. The reasoning behind this behavior is examined in the next Configuration Exercise.

---

## Exercise Verification

You have successfully completed this exercise when you achieve the following results:

- Your internal router can ping the TFTP server using a translation to 192.168.*x*.0/24.
- Your internal router can ping the opposite edge router using a translation to 10.*x*.0.0/24.
- You have demonstrated the limitations of access list-based NAT and have overcome those limitations by configuring NAT using a route map.
- You have connected to the TFTP server through NAT and have downloaded a configuration file for your internal routers.

# Solution to Configuration Exercise 1-1: Basic Connectivity

This section provides the answers to the questions in the Configuration Exercise.

---

**NOTE**    Some answers provided cover multiple steps; the answers are given after the last step for which that answer applies.

---

## Solution to Task: Setting Up the Edge Routers

**Step 1**    Connect to each of your pod routers; they should not have configurations on them. If a router does have a configuration, delete the configuration using the **erase start** command, and then use the **reload** command to reboot.

---

**NOTE**    In this exercise, you will apply some minimal addressing and routing information so that your routers can reach the TFTP server.

---

**Step 2**    Connect to each of your pod edge routers (P*x*R1 and P*x*R2). Configure the serial s0 interface of these routers for Frame Relay by turning on Frame Relay encapsulation.

**Step 3**    Assign an IP address to your serial 0 interface. Your IP address is 172.31.*x.y*/24, where *x* is your pod number and *y* is your router number.

**Step 4**    Inverse ARP has been turned off in the core Frame Relay network. Manually map a DLCI to BBR1 (172.31.*x*.3). The DLCI number will be in the form 1*xy*, where *x* is your pod number and *y* is your router number. For instance, P2R1 will use DLCI 121.

---

**NOTE**    Remember to specify the **broadcast** keyword so that the Frame Relay mapping supports broadcasts and multicasts, such as routing protocol traffic.

---

**Step 5**    Use the **no shutdown** command on the interface and exit configuration mode.

**Solution:**

The following shows how to perform the required steps on the P1R1 router:

```
Router>en
Router#conf t
Enter configuration commands, one per line.  End with CNTL/Z.
Router(config)#int s0
Router(config-if)#encapsulation frame-relay
Router(config-if)#ip address 172.31.1.1 255.255.255.0
Router(config-if)#frame-relay map ip 172.31.1.3 111 broadcast
Router(config-if)#no shutdown
```

**Step 6**    Verify successful connectivity from your P*x*R1 and P*x*R2 router to the core
BBR1 router (172.31.*x*.3) using the **ping** command.

**Solution:**

The following shows the ping from the P1R1 router:

```
Router#ping 172.31.1.3
Type escape sequence to abort.
Sending 5, 100-byte ICMP Echos to 172.31.1.3, timeout is 2 seconds:
!!!!!
Success rate is 100 percent (5/5), round-trip min/avg/max = 36/36/36 ms
Router#
```

**Step 7**    The goal of this exercise is to download a file from the TFTP server (at
10.254.0.254), which is connected to BBR1. Look at your P*x*R1 and P*x*R2
routing tables. Is there a route to the network that the TFTP server is located
on? Why not?

**Solution:**

The following shows the routing table on P1R1. There is no route to the 10.254.0.0 network.
P1R1 only has a route to its connected S0 interface; it does not have any other interfaces
configured, and it has not learned any other routes from other routers.

```
Router#show ip route
<output omitted>
     172.31.0.0/24 is subnetted, 1 subnets
C       172.31.1.0 is directly connected, Serial0
Router#
```

**Step 8**    Add a static route to 10.0.0.0/8 on your edge routers, through BBR1 (172.31.*x*.3),
to provide a path to the TFTP server. Verify that the edge routers can see
this route.

**Solution:**

The following configuration and output are on the P1R1 router. P1R1 now has a route to the
10.0.0.0 network.

```
Router#conf t
Enter configuration commands, one per line.  End with CNTL/Z.
Router(config)#ip route 10.0.0.0 255.0.0.0 172.31.1.3
Router(config)#exit

Router#show ip route
<output omitted>
     172.31.0.0/24 is subnetted, 1 subnets
C       172.31.1.0 is directly connected, Serial0
S    10.0.0.0/8 [1/0] via 172.31.1.3
Router#
```

**Step 9**    Verify successful connectivity to the TFTP server (10.254.0.254) from your
PxR1 and PxR2 router using the **ping** command.

**Solution:**

The following ping is from the P1R1 router; the ping is successful:

```
Router#ping 10.254.0.254
Type escape sequence to abort.
Sending 5, 100-byte ICMP Echos to 10.254.0.254, timeout is 2 seconds:
.!!!!
Success rate is 80 percent (4/5), round-trip min/avg/max = 32/35/40 ms
Router#
```

The following ping is from the P1R2 router; the ping is successful:

```
Router#ping 10.254.0.254
Type escape sequence to abort.
Sending 5, 100-byte ICMP Echos to 10.254.0.254, timeout is 2 seconds:
!!!!!
Success rate is 100 percent (5/5), round-trip min/avg/max = 32/44/96 ms
Router
```

**Step 10**   Retrieve the configuration file for your router from the TFTP server. The file should
be named PxRy.txt. (For example, Pod 1 Router 2 will download P1R2.txt.)

| NOTE | Filenames are not case-sensitive. |
|------|-----------------------------------|

| NOTE | The configuration files include the **no ip classless** command to force your router to behave classfully (although this command is on by default in IOS 12.0 and later). These files also include all required IP addresses and enable all required interfaces. Remember that files copied to running-config are merged, so this configuration complements what is already in your running-config. |
|------|------|

**Solution:**

The following output is from the P1R1 router. The download was successful.

```
Router#copy tftp run
Address or name of remote host []? 10.254.0.254
Source filename []? P1R1.txt
Destination filename [running-config]?
Accessing tftp://10.254.0.254/P1R1.txt...
Loading P1R1.txt from 10.254.0.254 (via Serial0): !
[OK - 1334/2048 bytes]
1334 bytes copied in 25.184 secs (53 bytes/sec)
P1R1#
```

| NOTE | The initial configuration files for the routers are provided in Appendix H. |
|------|------|

**Step 11** Save your configuration before proceeding.

**Solution:**

The following output is from the P1R1 router. The configuration was saved successfully.

```
P1R1#copy run start
Destination filename [startup-config]?
Building configuration...
[OK]
P1R1#
```

## Exercise Verification

You have successfully completed this exercise if you can ping the core BBR1 router and the TFTP server from your edge routers (PxR1 and PxR2) and you have downloaded the configuration files for your edge routers from the TFTP server.

# Solution to Configuration Exercise 1-2: NAT Using Access Lists and Route Maps

This section provides the answers to the questions in the Configuration Exercise.

---

**NOTE**    Some answers provided cover multiple steps; the answers are given after the last step for which that answer applies.

---

## Solution to Task 1: Connecting the Internal Router to the Edge Router

**Step 1** The internal routers (PxR3 and PxR4) should not have a configuration. If a configuration is present, use the **erase start** and **reload** commands to clear the configuration and reload the router.

**Step 2** Connect to your internal routers. Supply an IP address to the Ethernet interface, and enable the interface. The Ethernet address of PxR3 should be 10.x.1.3/24, and the Ethernet address of PxR4 should be 10.x.2.4/24.

**Solution:**

The following example shows the configuration of P1R3:

```
Router(config)#int e0
Router(config-if)#no shutdown
Router(config-if)#ip address 10.1.1.3 255.255.255.0
```

The following example shows the configuration of P1R4:

```
Router(config)#int e0
Router(config-if)#no shutdown
Router(config-if)#ip address 10.1.2.4 255.255.255.0
```

**Step 3** P*x*R1 has an Ethernet address of 10.*x*.1.1, and P*x*R2 has an Ethernet address of 10.*x*.2.2. Verify connectivity to the Ethernet-attached edge router from each internal router.

**Solution:**

To verify connectivity, the edge routers are pinged from the appropriate internal router.

The following output is from the P1R3 router. The ping was successful.

```
Router#ping 10.1.1.1
Type escape sequence to abort.
Sending 5, 100-byte ICMP Echos to 10.1.1.1, timeout is 2 seconds:
.!!!!
Success rate is 80 percent (4/5), round-trip min/avg/max = 4/4/4 ms
Router#
```

The following output is from the P1R4 router. The ping was successful.

```
Router#ping 10.1.2.2
Type escape sequence to abort.
Sending 5, 100-byte ICMP Echos to 10.1.2.2, timeout is 2 seconds:
.!!!!
Success rate is 80 percent (4/5), round-trip min/avg/max = 4/5/8 ms
Router#
```

# Solution to Task 2: Setting Up ACL-Based NAT

**NOTE**   BBR1 has static routes for 192.168.*x*.0/24 and 192.168.*xx*.0/24. It does not have any remote routes for the pod 10.*x*.0.0 addresses, only its local TFTP server network 10.254.0.0.

**Step 1** On the P*x*R1 and P*x*R2 routers, configure the sources to be translated using extended access list 100. Access list 100 should match traffic sourced from the network on your edge router's Ethernet interface, destined for the network that the TFTP server is located on. For example, P*x*R1 should match traffic sourced from 10.*x*.1.0/24, and P*x*R2 should match traffic sourced from 10.*x*.2.0/24. The access list must match only packets with a destination of 10.254.0.0/24.

**Step 2** On the P*x*R1 and P*x*R2 routers, create a pool of addresses called **BBR** for use by NAT, using the **ip nat pool** command. P*x*R1 should use the address range of 192.168.*x*.0/24, and P*x*R2 should use 192.168.*xx*.0/24. For example, P2R1 would use 192.168.2.1 through 192.168.2.254, and P2R2 would use 192.168.22.1 through 192.168.22.254.

**Step 3**  On the P*x*R1 and P*x*R2 routers, use the **ip nat inside source list** command
to specify that packets that match access list 100 should have their source
addresses translated into the BBR pool.

**Step 4**  On the P*x*R1 and P*x*R2 routers, define which interfaces are inside or outside
for NAT translation purposes.

**Solution:**

Because the traffic to be translated will come from the Ethernet interface, that will be the
inside NAT interface. Translated traffic will leave via the Serial0 interface, so S0 will be
the outside interface for NAT purposes. The following example shows the configuration on the
P1R1 router:

```
P1R1(config)#access-list 100 permit ip 10.1.1.0 0.0.0.255 10.254.0.0 0.0.0.255
P1R1(config)#ip nat pool BBR 192.168.1.1 192.168.1.254 netmask 255.255.255.0
P1R1(config)#ip nat inside source list 100 pool BBR
P1R1(config)#int e0
P1R1(config-if)#ip nat inside
P1R1(config-if)#exit
P1R1(config)#int s0
P1R1(config-if)#ip nat outside
```

**Step 5**  On the P*x*R3 and P*x*R4 routers, configure a default route pointing to the
attached edge router e0 interface. This configuration allows the internal
router to reach the core network.

**Solution:**

The following example shows the configuration on the P1R3 router:

```
Router(config)#ip route 0.0.0.0 0.0.0.0 e0
```

**Step 6**  From the P*x*R3 and P*x*R4 routers, verify connectivity to the TFTP server
(10.254.0.254) using the **ping** command.

**Solution:**

The following output shows the result of the **ping** command on the P1R3 router; the ping is
successful.

```
Router#ping 10.254.0.254
Type escape sequence to abort.
Sending 5, 100-byte ICMP Echos to 10.254.0.254, timeout is 2 seconds:
!!!!!
Success rate is 100 percent (5/5), round-trip min/avg/max = 36/36/36 ms
Router#
```

---

**CAUTION**    You will not be able to reach the TFTP server if the NAT translation
is not done correctly.

---

**Step 7** View the NAT translation table on the edge router (P*x*R1 and P*x*R2).

**Solution:**

The following output shows the NAT translation table on the P1R1 router. From this output, you can see that one address has been translated.

```
P1R1>show ip nat translations
Pro Inside global     Inside local      Outside local      Outside global
--- 192.168.1.1       10.1.1.3          - - -              - - -
P1R1>
```

# Solution to Task 3: Translating to the Other Edge Router

**Step 1** On the P*x*R1 and P*x*R2 routers, configure the source addresses to be translated using extended access list 101. Access list 101 should match traffic sourced from the network on your edge router's Ethernet interface, bound for any destination. For instance, P*x*R1 should match traffic from 10.*x*.1.0/24, and P*x*R2 should match traffic from 10.*x*.2.0/24. The access list must match packets with a destination to any network.

**Step 2** On the P*x*R1 and P*x*R2 routers, create a pool of addresses named **POD** for use by NAT. P*x*R1 should use the address range 10.*x*.0.64 to 10.*x*.0.95, and P*x*R2 should use the address range 10.*x*.0.96 to 10.*x*.0.127.

**Step 3** On the P*x*R1 and P*x*R2 routers, specify that packets that match access list 101 should have their source addresses translated into the POD pool.

**Step 4** At the P*x*R1 and P*x*R2 routers, define the S1 interface of each router as the NAT outside interface by using the **ip nat outside** command so that traffic from the respective internal routers is translated.

**Solution:**

The following example shows the configuration of the P1R1 and P1R2 routers:

```
P1R1(config)#access-list 101 permit ip 10.1.1.0 0.0.0.255 any
P1R1(config)#ip nat pool POD 10.1.0.64 10.1.0.95 netmask 255.255.255.0
P1R1(config)#ip nat inside source list 101 pool POD
P1R1(config)#int s1
P1R1(config-if)#ip nat outside

P1R2(config)#access-list 101 permit ip 10.1.2.0 0.0.0.255 any
P1R2(config)#ip nat pool POD 10.1.0.96 10.1.0.127 netmask 255.255.255.0
P1R2(config)#ip nat inside source list 101 pool POD
P1R2(config)#int s1
P1R2(config-if)#ip nat outside
```

**Step 5** From one internal router, ping the Serial 1 interface of the nonconnected edge router. (For example, from P*x*R3, ping the Serial 1 address of P*x*R2.) Is the ping successful?

**Solution:**

The following example is a ping from the P1R3 router to the P1R2 router's Serial 1 address:

```
Router>ping 10.1.0.2
Type escape sequence to abort.
Sending 5, 100-byte ICMP Echos to 10.1.0.2, timeout is 2 seconds:
.....
Success rate is 0 percent (0/5)
```

The ping is unsuccessful.

**Step 6**   Look at the IP translation table on the edge routers to help explain the result of the previous ping.

**Solution:**

The following output is from the P1R1 router:

```
P1R1#show ip nat translations
Pro Inside global      Inside local      Outside local      Outside global
--- 192.168.1.1        10.1.1.3          ---                ---
P1R1#
```

As you can see in the translation table, the P1R1 router has already translated the 10.1.1.3 source address, in Task 2, to 192.168.1.1. The router doesn't recognize that ping is a separate conversation, to a different destination, so it doesn't translate the traffic again for the new destination. You need a way to distinguish between different conversations.

**Step 7**   From the nonconnected edge router, use the **debug ip icmp** and **debug ip packet** commands while the pings are still active. Observe the output to help explain the results of the previous ping. Turn off all debugging when you are finished.

**Solution:**

The following output is from the P1R2 router while the pings from P1R3 to the P1R2 Serial 1 address are ongoing:

```
P1R2#debug ip icmp
ICMP packet debugging is on
P1R2#debug ip packet
IP packet debugging is on
P1R2#
Feb 28 21:44:55 EST: IP: s=192.168.1.1 (Serial1), d=10.1.0.2 (Serial1),
    len 100, rcvd 3
Feb 28 21:44:55 EST: ICMP: echo reply sent, src 10.1.0.2, dst 192.168.1.1
Feb 28 21:44:55 EST: IP: s=10.1.0.2 (local), d=192.168.1.1, len 100, unroutable
```

P1R2 receives a packet with source address 192.168.1.1 and tries to reply to this packet. However, P1R2 reports that 192.168.1.1 is unroutable.

**Step 8** Look at the routing table on the nonconnected edge router. Is there a route back to the destination address of the ping echo reply message?

**Solution:**

The following output is from the P1R2 router:

```
P1R2#sh ip route
<output omitted>
     172.31.0.0/24 is subnetted, 1 subnets
C       172.31.1.0 is directly connected, Serial0
     10.0.0.0/8 is variably subnetted, 3 subnets, 2 masks
C       10.1.0.0/24 is directly connected, Serial1
C       10.1.2.0/24 is directly connected, Ethernet0
S       10.0.0.0/8 [1/0] via 172.31.1.3
```

There is no route in P1R2's routing table to 192.168.1.1; this is why P1R2 cannot reply to the ping.

**Step 9** What does a router do when it does not find an appropriate address?

**Solution:**

The router drops the packet.

# Solution to Task 4: Using a Route Map with NAT to Translate Internal Addresses

**Step 1** Create a route map that will be used to conditionally translate traffic based on the packet's destination.

**Solution:**

The following example shows the configuration on P1R1:

```
P1R1(config)#route-map TO_BBR permit 10
P1R1(config-route-map)#match ip address 100
P1R1(config-route-map)#exit
P1R1(config)#route-map TO_POD permit 10
P1R1(config-route-map)#match ip address 101
```

**Step 2** Replace the translation commands from Task 3 with route map-based commands to perform the required translation.

---

**NOTE** If the router reports "%Dynamic mapping in use, cannot remove," simply go to privileged mode and enter the **clear ip nat translation \*** command to remove all mappings. You then can configure the router.

---

**Solution:**

The following configuration is from the P1R1 router:

```
P1R1#clear ip nat translation *
P1R1#conf t
Enter configuration commands, one per line.  End with CNTL/Z.
P1R1(config)#no ip nat inside source list 100 pool BBR
P1R1(config)#no ip nat inside source list 101 pool POD
P1R1(config)#ip nat inside source route-map TO_BBR pool BBR
P1R1(config)#ip nat inside source route-map TO_POD pool POD
```

**Step 3**   Ping from one internal router to the opposite edge router and to the TFTP
server to verify that the previous step was successful. Turn on **debug ip nat
detailed** debugging on the edge routers to see the translation.

**Solution:**

The following ping output is from the P1R3 internal router to the TFTP server. (The P1R4
internal router produced the same result.)

```
Router#ping 10.254.0.254
Type escape sequence to abort.
Sending 5, 100-byte ICMP Echos to 10.254.0.254, timeout is 2 seconds:
!!!!!
Success rate is 100 percent (5/5), round-trip min/avg/max = 36/38/48 ms
```

The following debug output is from the P1R1 router while the preceding ping from P1R3 to the
TFTP server was ongoing. This output shows the translation using the BBR pool:

```
P1R1#debug ip nat detailed
IP NAT detailed debugging is on
P1R1#
Feb 28 21:59:37 EST: NAT: map match TO_BBR
Feb 28 21:59:37 EST: NAT: map match TO_BBR
Feb 28 21:59:37 EST: NAT: i: icmp (10.1.1.3, 2567) -> (10.254.0.254, 2567) [65]
Feb 28 21:59:37 EST: NAT: s=10.1.1.3->192.168.1.1, d=10.254.0.254 [65]
Feb 28 21:59:37 EST: NAT*: o: icmp (10.254.0.254, 2567) -> (192.168.1.1, 2567) [189]
Feb 28 21:59:37 EST: NAT*: s=10.254.0.254, d=192.168.1.1->10.1.1.3 [189]
```

The following ping output is from the P1R3 internal router to the P1R2 router's Serial 1
interface. (The same results were obtained when P1R4 pinged the P1R1 router
Serial 1 interface.)

```
Router#ping 10.1.0.2
Type escape sequence to abort.
Sending 5, 100-byte ICMP Echos to 10.1.0.2, timeout is 2 seconds:
!!!!!
Success rate is 100 percent (5/5), round-trip min/avg/max = 52/54/60 ms
```

The following debug output is from the P1R1 router while the preceding ping from P1R3 to P1R2 was ongoing. This output shows the translation using the POD pool:

```
P1R1#debug ip nat detailed
IP NAT detailed debugging is on
P1R1#
Feb 28 22:03:45 EST: NAT: map match TO_POD
Feb 28 22:03:45 EST: NAT: map match TO_POD
Feb 28 22:03:45 EST: NAT: i: icmp (10.1.1.3, 330) -> (10.1.0.2, 330) [85]
Feb 28 22:03:45 EST: NAT: s=10.1.1.3->10.1.0.64, d=10.1.0.2 [85]
Feb 28 22:03:45 EST: NAT*: o: icmp (10.1.0.2, 330) -> (10.1.0.64, 330) [85]
Feb 28 22:03:45 EST: NAT*: s=10.1.0.2, d=10.1.0.64->10.1.1.3 [85]
```

**Step 4**    Use the **show ip nat translations** command on each edge router to see the resulting NAT translation table.

**Solution:**

The following output is from the P1R1 and P1R2 routers:

```
P1R1#show ip nat translations
Pro Inside global       Inside local      Outside local       Outside global
icmp 10.1.0.64:1652     10.1.1.3:1652     10.1.2.2:1652       10.1.2.2:1652
icmp 10.1.0.64:1653     10.1.1.3:1653     10.1.2.2:1653       10.1.2.2:1653
icmp 10.1.0.64:1654     10.1.1.3:1654     10.1.2.2:1654       10.1.2.2:1654
icmp 10.1.0.64:1655     10.1.1.3:1655     10.1.2.2:1655       10.1.2.2:1655
icmp 10.1.0.64:9208     10.1.1.3:9208     10.1.0.2:9208       10.1.0.2:9208
icmp 10.1.0.64:9209     10.1.1.3:9209     10.1.0.2:9209       10.1.0.2:9209
icmp 10.1.0.64:9210     10.1.1.3:9210     10.1.0.2:9210       10.1.0.2:9210
icmp 10.1.0.64:9211     10.1.1.3:9211     10.1.0.2:9211       10.1.0.2:9211
icmp 10.1.0.64:9212     10.1.1.3:9212     10.1.0.2:9212       10.1.0.2:9212
icmp 192.168.1.1:133    10.1.1.3:133      10.254.0.254:133    10.254.0.254:133
icmp 192.168.1.1:134    10.1.1.3:134      10.254.0.254:134    10.254.0.254:134
icmp 192.168.1.1:135    10.1.1.3:135      10.254.0.254:135    10.254.0.254:135
icmp 192.168.1.1:136    10.1.1.3:136      10.254.0.254:136    10.254.0.254:136
icmp 192.168.1.1:137    10.1.1.3:137      10.254.0.254:137    10.254.0.254:137
P1R2#show ip nat translations
Pro Inside global       Inside local      Outside local       Outside global
icmp 192.168.11.1:5005  10.1.2.4:5005     10.254.0.254:5005   10.254.0.254:5005
icmp 192.168.11.1:5006  10.1.2.4:5006     10.254.0.254:5006   10.254.0.254:5006
icmp 192.168.11.1:5007  10.1.2.4:5007     10.254.0.254:5007   10.254.0.254:5007
icmp 192.168.11.1:5008  10.1.2.4:5008     10.254.0.254:5008   10.254.0.254:5008
icmp 192.168.11.1:5009  10.1.2.4:5009     10.254.0.254:5009   10.254.0.254:5009
icmp 10.1.0.96:1481     10.1.2.4:1481     10.1.0.1:1481       10.1.0.1:1481
icmp 10.1.0.96:1482     10.1.2.4:1482     10.1.0.1:1482       10.1.0.1:1482
icmp 10.1.0.96:1483     10.1.2.4:1483     10.1.0.1:1483       10.1.0.1:1483
icmp 10.1.0.96:1484     10.1.2.4:1484     10.1.0.1:1484       10.1.0.1:1484
icmp 10.1.0.96:1485     10.1.2.4:1485     10.1.0.1:1485       10.1.0.1:1485
```

Notice that the NAT translation table is completely developed. The inside and outside local and global addresses are included in the table, along with the TCP and UDP port numbers. Much more troubleshooting information is available within this table than with the table shown in Task 3.

## Solution to Task 5: Downloading a Configuration File

On the internal routers, use TFTP to download the configuration file called P*x*R*y*.txt from the TFTP server to the running-config.

**Solution:**

The following configuration and output are from the P1R3 router. Notice that the router's name, P1R3, is configured after the configuration is downloaded:

```
Router#copy tftp run
Address or name of remote host []? 10.254.0.254
Source filename []? p1r3.txt
Destination filename [running-config]?
Accessing tftp://10.254.0.254/p1r3.txt...
Loading p1r3.txt .from 10.254.0.254 (via Ethernet0): !
[OK - 1085/2048 bytes]
1085 bytes copied in 31.956 secs (35 bytes/sec)
P1R3#
```

The following configuration and output are from the P1R4 router. Again, notice that the router's name changes after the configuration is loaded:

```
Router#copy tftp run
Address or name of remote host []? 10.254.0.254
Source filename []? p1r4.txt
Destination filename [running-config]?
Accessing tftp://10.254.0.254/p1r4.txt...
Loading p1r4.txt .from 10.254.0.254 (via Ethernet0): !
[OK - 1085/2048 bytes]
1085 bytes copied in 31.992 secs (35 bytes/sec)
P1R4#
```

**NOTE**    The configurations for P*x*R3 and P*x*R4 include the command **no ip classless** in preparation for the Configuration Exercise in the next chapter. If you try to communicate with the TFTP server now, it will not work. The reasoning behind this behavior is examined in the next Configuration Exercise.

## Exercise Verification

You have successfully completed this exercise when you achieve the following results:

- Your internal router can ping the TFTP server using a translation to 192.168.*x*.0/24.

- Your internal router can ping the opposite edge router using a translation to 10.*x*.0.0/24.

- You have demonstrated the limitations of access list-based NAT and have overcome those limitations by configuring NAT using a route map.

- You have connected to the TFTP server through NAT and have downloaded a configuration file for your internal routers.

# Review Questions

Answer the following questions, and then refer to Appendix G, "Answers to Review Questions," for the answers.

1   When networks are connected based on their location, is this a functional or geographic network design?

2   Describe the role of each layer in the hierarchical network model.

3   Name an advantage and a disadvantage of a fully meshed core layer.

4   At what layer are DHCP and DNS servers typically found?

5   What are three benefits of a good IP address design?

6   What are private IP addresses, and what are they used for?

7   How does route summarization benefit a network?

8   Given a host address 10.1.17.61/28, what is the range of addresses on the subnet that this host is on?

9   How does VLSM allow a more efficient use of IP addresses?

10   What range of addresses is represented by the summary route 172.16.16.0/21?

11   You are in charge of the network shown in Figure 1-36. It consists of five LANs with 25 users on each LAN and five serial links. You have been assigned the IP address 192.168.49.0/24 to allocate addressing for all links.

**Figure 1-36**   *Network for Address Assignment*

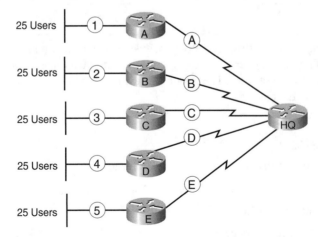

Write down the addresses you would assign to each of the LANs and serial links

| LAN 1 | |
|---|---|
| LAN 2 | |
| LAN 3 | |
| LAN 4 | |
| LAN 5 | |
| WAN A | |
| WAN B | |
| WAN C | |
| WAN D | |
| WAN E | |

**12**  Figure 1-37 shows a network with subnets of the 172.16.0.0 network configured. Indicate in the following table where route summarization can occur in this network and what the summarized addresses would be.

**Figure 1-37**  *Network for Route Summarization*

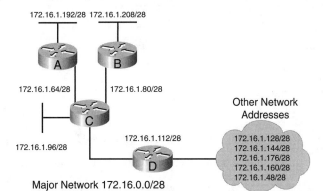

| Router C Routing Table Entries | Summarized Routes That Can Be Advertised to Router D from Router C |
|---|---|
| | |
| | |
| | |
| | |
| | |
| | |

**13**   Figure 1-38 shows a network with subnets of the 172.16.0.0 network configured. Indicate in the following table where route summarization can occur in this network and what the summarized address would be.

**Figure 1-38**   *Network for Route Summarization*

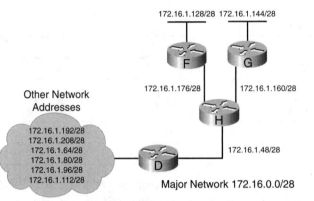

| Router H Routing Table Entries | Summarized Routes That Can Be Advertised to Router D from Router H |
|---|---|
|  |  |
|  |  |
|  |  |
|  |  |
|  |  |

**14**   When selecting a route, which prefix match is used?

**15**   What is the difference between route summarization and CIDR?

**16**   The following networks are in Router A's routing table:

192.168.12.0/24

192.168.13.0/24

192.168.14.0/24

192.168.15.0/24

Using CIDR, what route could Router A advertise to its neighbor?

**17**   What is the difference between a NAT inside local IP address and an inside global IP address?

**18**   Which command indicates that NAT translation is to be done for packets arriving on an interface?

**19**  In the following configuration example, what does the first line do? What does the fourth line do?

```
ip nat pool our_pool 192.168.4.1  192.168.4.254 prefix-length 24
ip nat pool their_pool 192.168.5.1 192.168.5.254 prefix-length 24
!
ip nat inside source list 104 pool our_pool
ip nat inside source list 105 pool their_pool
!
interface ethernet 0
 ip address 10.1.1.1 255.255.0.0
 ip nat inside
!
interface serial 0
 ip address 172.16.2.1 255.255.255.0
 ip nat outside
!
access-list 104 permit ip  10.1.1.0 0.0.0.255  172.16.1.0 0.0.0.255
access-list 104 permit ip  10.1.1.0 0.0.0.255  192.168.200.0 0.0.0.255
access-list 105 permit ip  10.1.1.0 0.0.0.255  any
```

**20**  Describe how a route map works.

**21**  What are some differences between IPv4 and IPv6?

**22**  What is the difference between the IPv4 header and the IPv6 header?

**23**  What features does the larger address space of IPv6 provide?

**24**  Write the shortest legal format for the following IPv6 address:

2210:0000:0011:ABCD:0000:0000:0000:0101

**25**  Write out the following IPv6 address completely:

2214::15:ABCD

**26**  Describe how IPv6 stateless autoconfiguration works.

**27**  Name two IPv4 packet header fields that are no longer defined in the IPv6 packet header.

**28**  Describe how 6to4 transition works.

**29**  What does dual stack mean?

**30**  What is the difference between an IPv6 anycast address and an IPv6 multicast address?

**31**  What is the IPv6 broadcast address?

**32**  What does the 2001::/16 summary route mean?

**33**  The IPv6 header is aligned on what bit boundary?

This chapter discusses advanced IP routing principles. It covers the following topics:

- IP Routing Overview
- Characteristics of Routing Protocols
- IP Routing Protocol Comparisons

# CHAPTER 2

# Routing Principles

This chapter covers advanced IP routing principles, including static and dynamic routing characteristics, classful and classless routing, and manual and automatic route summarization across network boundaries. It explains the difference between distance-vector, link-state, and hybrid routing protocols. Also included is a comparison of IP routing protocols.

## IP Routing Overview

Routers forward packets toward destination networks. To forward the packets, routers must understand these remote networks and determine the best way to reach them. This section addresses the ways in which routers learn about networks and how routers can also incorporate static and dynamic routes.

## Principles of Static Routing

This section explains the situations in which static routes are the most appropriate to use.

Routers must be aware of destination networks to be able to forward packets to them. A router knows about the networks directly attached to its interfaces; it looks at the network address configured on its interface and deduces the network number for that link. But for networks not directly connected to one of its interfaces, the router must rely on outside information. There are two ways a router can be made aware of remote networks: an administrator can manually configure the information (static routing), or a router can learn from other routers (dynamic routing). A routing table can contain both static and dynamically recognized routes.

Network administrators can use static routing, dynamic routing, or a combination of both. A static route can be used in the following circumstances:

- When it is undesirable to have dynamic routing updates forwarded across slow-bandwidth links, such as a dialup link.
- When the administrator needs total control over the routes used by the router.
- When a backup to a dynamically recognized route is necessary.

- When it is necessary to reach a network accessible by only one path (a stub network). For example, in Figure 2-1, there is only one way for router A to reach the 10.2.0.0/16 network on router B. You can configure a static route on router A to reach the 10.2.0.0/16 network via 10.1.1.1.

**Figure 2-1** *Configuring Static Routing*

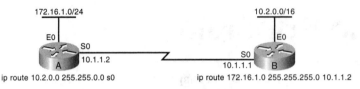

- When a router is underpowered and does not have the CPU or memory resources necessary to handle a dynamic routing protocol.

- When a route should appear to the router as a directly connected network.

A perfect match for static routing is a hub-and-spoke design, with all remote sites defaulting back to the central site and the one or two routers at the central site having a static route for all subnets at each remote site. However, without proper design, as the network grows into hundreds of routers, with each router having numerous subnets, the number of static routes on each router also increases. Each time a new subnet or router is added, an administrator must add a static route to the new networks on a number of routers. The administrative burden to maintain this network can become excessive, making dynamic routing a better choice.

---

**NOTE**

Later in this chapter, we will also discuss the use of default routes to alleviate the configuration required by the administrator and to simplify routing tables on some perimeter and internal routers.

---

Another drawback of static routing is that when a topology change occurs on the internetwork, an administrator might have to reroute traffic by configuring new static routes around the problem area. With dynamic routing, the routing process automatically discovers whether any alternative routes exist and reroutes without administrator intervention, thereby providing speedier convergence.

---

### Key Point: Convergence

Convergence represents the speed and ability of a group of internetworking devices running a specific routing protocol to agree on the topology of an internetwork after a change in that topology. (Source: www.cisco.com/univercd/cc/td/doc/cisintwk/ita/c12.htm)

---

The **ip route** command creates a static route. The **show ip route** command verifies the resulting static entry in the IP routing table. If no dynamic routing protocol is used on a link connecting two routers, such as in Figure 2-1, a static route must be configured on the routers on both sides of the link. Otherwise, the remote router will not know how to return the packet to its originator located on the other network. There will be only one-way communication.

While configuring a static route, either a next-hop IP address or an exit interface needs be specified to notify the router which direction to send traffic. Both configuration scenarios are shown in Figure 2-1. If the next-hop IP address is used, it should be the IP address of the interface of the router on the other end of the link. If the exit interface is used, the local router sends data to the router on the other end of its attached link. When an exit interface is specified, the router considers this a directly-connected route.

The following command, explained in Table 2-1, is used to create static routes:

```
RouterA(config)#ip route prefix mask {address | interface} [distance]
    [permanent] [tag tag]
```

**Table 2-1**    **ip route** *Command*

| ip route Command | Description |
|---|---|
| *prefix mask* | The IP network and subnet mask for the remote network to be entered into the IP routing table. |
| *address* | The IP address of the next hop that can be used to reach the destination network. |
| *interface* | The local router outbound interface to be used to reach the destination network. |
| *distance* | (Optional) The administrative distance to be assigned to this route. |
| **permanent** | (Optional) Specifies that the route will not be removed from the routing table, even if the interface associated with the route goes down. |
| **tag** *tag* | (Optional) A value that can be used as a match value in route maps. |

**NOTE**    Use static routes pointing to an interface on point-to-point interfaces only, because on multiaccess interfaces the router will not know the specific address to which to send the information. On point-to-point interfaces, the information is sent to the only other device on the network.

In Figure 2-1, router A is a stub router: it has no other routers beyond it. If router B sends data to any device in the 172.16.1.0/24 network, it must be sent through router A. Similarly, if router A needs to send data to any device in the 10.2.0.0/16 network, it must go through router B. Figure 2-1 shows the static routes created on both router A and router B to accomplish this connection.

Router A recognizes the directly connected networks 172.16.1.0 and 10.1.1.0. It needs a route to the remote network 10.2.0.0. Router B knows about the directly connected networks 10.2.0.0 and 10.1.1.0; it needs a route to the remote network 172.16.1.0. Notice that on router B, the next-hop IP address of the router A serial interface has been used. On router A, however, the **ip route** command specifies its own Serial 0 interface as the exit interface.

## Configuring a Static Default Route

In some circumstances, a router does not need to recognize the details of remote networks. The router is configured to send all traffic, or all traffic for which there is no entry in the routing table, in a particular direction. That particular direction is called a default route. Default routes are either dynamically advertised using routing protocols or statically configured.

To create a static default, use the normal **ip route** command. However, the destination network (the *prefix* in the command syntax) and its subnet mask (the *mask* in the command syntax) are both 0.0.0.0. This address is a type of wildcard designation; any destination network will match. Because the router tries to match the longest common bit pattern, a network listed in the routing table is used before the default route. If the destination network is not listed in the routing table, the default route is used.

In Figure 2-2, on router A, the static route to the 10.2.0.0 network has been replaced with a static default route pointing to router B. On router B, a static default route has been added, pointing to its Internet service provider (ISP). Traffic from a device on the router A 172.16.1.0 network bound for a network on the Internet is sent to router B. Router B recognizes that the destination network does not match any specific entries in its routing table and sends that traffic to the ISP. It is then the ISP's responsibility to route that traffic to its destination.

**Figure 2-2** *Configuring the Static Default Route*

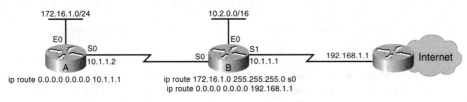

In Figure 2-2, to reach the 172.16.1.0/24 network, router B still needs a static route pointing out its S0 interface.

Entering the **show ip route** command on router A in Figure 2-2 returns the information shown in Example 2-1.

**Example 2-1**  **show ip route** *Command*

```
RouterA#show ip route
(text omitted)
Gateway of last resort is not set
C    172.16.1.0 is directly connected, Ethernet 0
C    10.1.1.0 is directly connected, Serial 0
S*   0.0.0.0/0 [1/0] via 10.1.1.1
```

# Principles of Dynamic Routing

Dynamic routing allows the network to adjust to changes in the topology automatically, without administrator involvement. This section describes standard dynamic routing principles. The **network** statement is a necessary part of configuring most IP routing protocols, but its function is often misunderstood.

A static route cannot respond dynamically to changes in the network. If a link fails, the static route is no longer valid if it is configured to use that failed link. A new static route must be configured. If a new router or new link is added, that information must also be configured on every router in the network. In a very large or unstable network, these changes can lead to considerable work for network administrators. It can also take a long time for every router in the network to receive the correct information. In situations like these, it might be better to have the routers receive information about networks and links from each other using a dynamic routing protocol.

When using a dynamic routing protocol, the administrator configures the routing protocol on each router, as shown in Figure 2-3. The routers then exchange information about the reachable networks and the state of each network. Routers exchange information only with other routers running the same routing protocol. When the network topology changes, the new information is dynamically propagated throughout the network, and each router updates its routing table to reflect the changes. Here are some examples of dynamic routing protocols:

- Routing Information Protocol (RIP)
- Enhanced Interior Gateway Routing Protocol (EIGRP)

**Figure 2-3**  *Principles of Dynamic Routing*

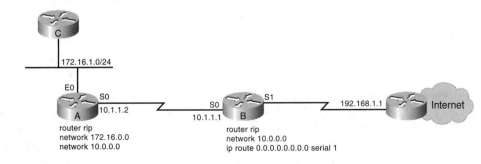

- Intermediate System-to-Intermediate System (IS-IS)
- Open Shortest Path First (OSPF)
- Border Gateway Protocol (BGP)

The distance to the network, which is called the metric or cost, is included in the information exchanged by routers. Different routing protocols base their metric on different measurements: hop count, interface speed, or more-complex metrics. Most routing protocols maintain databases containing all the networks that each routing protocol recognizes and all the paths to each network. If a router recognizes more than one way to reach a network, it compares the metric for each different path and chooses the path with the lowest metric. If multiple paths have the same metric, a maximum of six can be installed in the routing table, and the router can perform load balancing between them. Interior Gateway Routing Protocol (IGRP) and EIGRP can also perform load balancing between unequal-cost paths.

---

**Key Point: Definition of Metric**

A *metric* is a standard of measurement (such as path length) that routing algorithms use to determine the optimal path to a destination. (Source: "Internetwork Technology Overview," Cisco Systems document, October 1994, page 2-1)

---

To configure an IP dynamic routing protocol, use the **router** protocol command. Protocols other than RIP also require specification of either an autonomous system or a process number. You also need the **network** command under the router configuration mode of all routing protocols except IS-IS and BGP, which use the **network** command in a different context.

For RIP, IGRP, EIGRP, and OSPF, the **network** command tells the router which interfaces are participating in that routing protocol. Any interface that has an IP address that falls within the range specified in the **network** statement is considered active for that protocol. In other words, the router sends updates from the specified interfaces and expects to receive updates from the same interfaces. Some protocols look for neighbors by sending hello packets out those interfaces. Thus, because a **network** statement identifies interfaces on the local router, it is configured only for directly connected networks. A router also originates advertisements for the networks connected to the specified interfaces.

RIP and IGRP use only major classful networks to determine which interfaces are participating in the protocol. EIGRP and OSPF permit exact specification of interfaces with a combination of a subnet or interface address and a wildcard mask.

The network statement functions differently in BGP. The following will be explained in detail in Chapter 8, "Configuring Basic Border Gateway Protocol." BGP requires its neighbors to be statically configured. The **network** statement in BGP tells the router to originate an advertisement for that network. Without a **network** statement, BGP passes along advertisements it receives from other routers, but it does not originate any network advertisements itself. In BGP, the network listed in the **network** statement does not have to be directly connected, because it does not identify interfaces on the router, as it does in other protocols.

Integrated IS-IS does not use the **network** statement. Instead, interfaces participating in the IS-IS routing process are identified under interface configuration mode.

Figure 2-3 shows the topology used in Example 2-2. Both routers A and B are configured with RIP. Router A has two directly attached networks and needs RIP to search for neighbors on both of those interfaces. Therefore, **network** statements are configured for both the 172.16.1.0 network and the 10.1.1.0 network. Because RIP is a classful routing protocol, only the major network numbers of these two networks are configured as part of the **network** command, as shown in Example 2-2. Router A sends RIP packets out interfaces E0 and S0. The neighbors also receive an advertisement for the networks that are attached to those interfaces.

**Example 2-2**  *Configuring RIP*

```
routerA(config)#router rip
routerA(config-router)#network 172.16.0.0
routerA(config-router)#network 10.0.0.0

routerB(config)#ip route 0.0.0.0 0.0.0.0 serial 1
routerB(config)#router rip
routerB(config-router)#network 10.0.0.0
```

Router B also has two directly attached networks. However, router B wants only the network it shares with router A to participate in RIP. Therefore, a **network** statement is configured only for the 10.1.1.0 network. As explained earlier, with RIP, only the major network number is actually used in the **network** command. Router B has a static default route pointing toward its ISP to reach other networks. Router B sends RIP packets out its interface S0, but not out interface S1. It does not advertise the 192.168.1.0 network attached to S1 or the static default route unless specifically configured to do so.

# Principles of On-Demand Routing

A drawback of static routes is that they must be manually configured and updated when the network topology changes. A drawback of dynamic routing protocols is that they use network bandwidth and router resources. In a hub-and-spoke network with hundreds of spokes, both the configuration needed for static routes and the resource usage of dynamic routing can be considerable.

There is a third option—On-Demand Routing (ODR). ODR uses the Cisco Discovery Protocol (CDP) to carry network information between spoke (stub) routers and the hub. ODR provides IP routing information with minimal overhead compared to a dynamic routing protocol. ODR requires less manual configuration than static routes.

ODR is applicable in a hub-and-spoke topology only. In this type of topology, each spoke router is adjacent only to the hub. Another term for this is stub router. The stub router may have some

LAN networks connected to it and typically has a WAN connection to the hub router. The hub router needs to recognize the networks connected to each spoke, but the spokes need only a default route pointing to the hub.

When ODR is configured, the stub routers use CDP to send IP prefix information to the hub router. Stub routers send prefix information for all their directly connected networks. ODR reports the subnet mask, so it supports variable-length subnet masking (VLSM).

The hub router, in turn, sends a default route to the spokes that points back to itself. It installs the stub networks reported by ODR in its routing table, and the hub router can be configured to redistribute them into a dynamic routing protocol. For a next-hop address, the hub router uses the IP address of the spoke routers as reported to it by CDP.

ODR is not a true routing protocol because the information exchanged is limited to IP prefixes and a default route. ODR reports no metric information; the hub router uses a hop count of 1 as the metric for all routes reported via ODR. However, by using ODR, routing information for stub networks can be obtained dynamically without the overhead of a dynamic routing protocol, and default routes can be provided to the stub routers without manual configuration.

## Configuring ODR

ODR is configured on the hub router using the global **router odr** command.

On the stub router, no IP routing protocol must be configured. In fact, from the standpoint of ODR, a router is automatically considered a stub when no IP routing protocols have been configured. Figure 2-4 shows a hub-and-spoke topology.

**Figure 2-4**    *Hub-and-Spoke Topology: Configuring ODR*

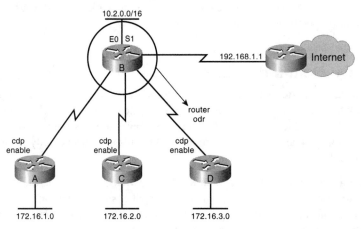

You might want to tune ODR with some of the optional commands. You can place a distribute list in router configuration mode to control the network information that is recognized through ODR. You can adjust the ODR timers with the **timers basic** command in router configuration mode.

Because the spoke routers receive only a default route from the hub router, all network information beyond their own stub networks is hidden from them. If information about the stub networks needs to be propagated to other parts of the enterprise, the hub router can redistribute it into dynamic routing protocols with an appropriate metric.

ODR relies on the CDP to carry the information between the hub router and the spoke routers. Therefore, CDP must be enabled on the links between the hub router and spokes. Cisco routers by default have CDP enabled both globally and per interface. However, on some WAN links, such as ATM, CDP must be explicitly enabled.

The CDP updates are sent as multicasts. On WAN links that require mappings, such as dialer links and Frame Relay, it is important to use the **broadcast** keyword in the mapping statements. Allowing broadcasts also allows multicasts across the link. CDP uses Subnetwork Access Protocol (SNAP) frames, so it runs on all media that support SNAP.

CDP updates are sent every 60 seconds by default. This setting might be too infrequent in rapidly changing networks or too often in stable ones. The timers can be adjusted by the **cdp timer global** command.

CDP settings can be verified by using the **show cdp interface** command.

As soon as ODR is configured and running, routes from the stub routers are identified in the routing table, shown in Example 2-3 at the hub router with an o character. Notice in the example that the metric is 1, and the administrative distance for ODR is 160. Also, do not confuse the o character of ODR routes with the O character of OSPF routes.

**Example 2-3**   *Routing Table with ODR Routes*

```
Router B#show ip route
<output omitted>
172.16.0.0/16 is subnetted, 4 subnets
o    172.16.1.0/24 [160/1] via 10.1.1.2, 00:00:23, Serial0
o    172.16.2.0/24 [160/1] via 10.2.2.2, 00:00:03, Serial1
o    172.16.3.0/24 [160/1] via 10.3.3.2, 00:00:16, Serial2
o    172.16.4.0/24 [160/1] via 10.4.4.2, 00:00:45, Serial3
```

The routing table for each spoke router contains only its connected networks and a static default route injected by ODR from the hub router.

# Characteristics of Routing Protocols

Routing protocols share many features with each other, but they can be classified into different categories such as link state, distance vector, or a hybrid of these two. IP routing protocols can also be classified as either classful or classless.

# Classful Routing Protocol Concepts

When classful protocols were originally developed, networks were very different from those used now. The best modem speed was 300 bps, the largest WAN line was 56 kbps, router memory was less than 640 KB, and processors were running in the kHz range. Routing updates had to be small enough not to monopolize the WAN link bandwidth. In addition, routers did not have the resources to maintain up-to-date information about every subnet.

A classful routing protocol does not include subnet mask information in its routing updates. Because no subnet mask information is known, when a classful router sends or receives routing updates, the router makes assumptions about the subnet mask being used by the networks listed in the update. These assumptions are based on IP address class. Upon receiving a routing update packet, a router running a classful routing protocol determines the network portion of the route by applying the following rules:

- If the routing update information contains the same major network number that is configured on the receiving interface, the router applies the subnet mask that is configured on the receiving interface.

- If the routing update information contains a different major network than the one configured on the receiving interface, the router applies the default classful mask by IP address class. The IP address classes and their default classful masks are as follows:

  — For Class A addresses, the default classful mask is 255.0.0.0.

  — For Class B addresses, the default classful mask is 255.255.0.0.

  — For Class C addresses, the default classful mask is 255.255.255.0.

All subnets of the same major network—Classes A, B, and C—must use the same subnet mask when using a classful routing protocol. Otherwise, routers might assume incorrect subnet information. Routers running a classful routing protocol perform automatic route summarization across network boundaries.

## Automatic Network-Boundary Summarization in a Classful Routing Protocol

Classful routing protocols make assumptions about networks based on their IP address class. These assumptions lead to automatic summarization of routes when routers send updates across major classful network boundaries.

Routers send update packets from their interfaces to other connected routers. The router sends the entire subnet address when an update packet involves a subnet of the same classful network as the IP address of the transmitting interface. The router assumes that the network and the interface use the same subnet mask.

The router that receives the update also makes the same assumption. If that route is using a different subnet mask, the router will have incorrect information in its routing table. Thus, when using a classful routing protocol, it is important to use the same subnet mask on all interfaces belonging to the same classful network.

When a router using a classful routing protocol sends an update about a subnet of a classful network across an interface belonging to a different classful network, the router assumes that the remote router will use the default subnet mask for that class of IP address. Therefore, when the router sends the update, it does not include the subnet information. The update packet contains only the classful network information. This process is autosummarization across the network boundary. The router sends a summary of all the subnets in that network by sending only the major network information. Classful routing protocols automatically create a classful summary route at major network boundaries. Classful routing protocols do not allow summarization at other points within the major network address space.

The router that receives the update behaves in a similar fashion. When an update contains information about a different classful network than the one in use on its interface, the router applies the default classful mask to that update. The router must determine the correct subnet mask to apply, because the update does not contain subnet mask information.

In Figure 2-5, router A advertises the 10.1.0.0 subnet to router B because the interface connecting them belongs to the same major classful 10.0.0.0 network. Router B uses a 16-bit subnet mask on the interface between itself and router A. When router B receives the update packet, it assumes that the 10.1.0.0 subnet uses the same 16-bit mask as the one used on its 10.2.0.0 subnet.

**Figure 2-5**    *Network Summarization in Classful Routing*

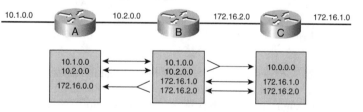

Routers B and C include the subnet information when they exchange information about the 172.16.0.0 network, because the interface connecting them belongs to the same major classful 172.16.0.0 network. Therefore, router B's routing table has information about all the subnets that are in use in the network.

However, router B summarizes 10.1.0.0 and 10.2.0.0 subnets to 10.0.0.0 before sending the routing information to router C. This summarization occurs because the update crosses a major network boundary. The update goes from a subnet of network 10.0.0.0, subnet 10.2.0.0, to a subnet of another major network, network 172.16.0.0.

Router B summarizes the 172.16.1.0 and 172.16.2.0 subnets to 172.16.0.0 before sending them to router A. Therefore, router A's routing table contains summary information about only the 172.16.0.0 network. Router C's routing table contains summary information about only the 10.0.0.0 network.

## Summarizing Routes in a Discontiguous Network

Discontiguous subnets are subnets of the same major network that are separated by a different major network.

Recall that RIP, IGRP, and EIGRP summarize automatically at network boundaries. This behavior, which cannot be changed with Routing Information Protocol version 1 (RIPv1) and IGRP, has important results:

- Subnets are not advertised to a different major network.

- Discontiguous subnets are not visible to each other.

In the example shown in Figure 2-6, routers A and B do not advertise the 172.16.5.0 255.255.255.0 and 172.16.6.0 255.255.255.0 subnets, because RIPv1 cannot advertise subnets across a different major network; both router A and router B advertise 172.16.0.0. This leads to confusion when you route across network 192.168.14.16/28. Router C, for example, receives routes about 172.16.0.0 from two different directions; it therefore might make an incorrect routing decision.

**Figure 2-6**    *Classful Routing Protocols Do Not Support Discontiguous Subnets*

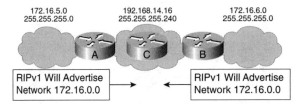

This situation can be resolved by using Routing Information Protocol version 2 (RIPv2), OSPF, IS-IS, or EIGRP and not using summarization, because the subnet routes will be advertised with their actual subnet masks. Advertisements can be configured when using OSPF and EIGRP, but not RIPv2.

The Cisco IOS software also provides an IP unnumbered feature that permits noncontiguous subnets to be separated by an unnumbered link; this feature is discussed in Supplement 1 of Appendix A, "Job Aids and Supplements."

## Route Summarization Cautions in Discontiguous Networks

Be careful when using route summarization in a network that has discontiguous subnets, or if not all the summarized subnets can be reached via the advertising router. If a summarized route indicates that certain subnets can be reached via a router, when in fact those subnets are discontiguous or cannot be reached via that router, the network might have problems similar to those shown in Figure 2-6 for a RIPv1 network. For example, in Figure 2-7, EIGRP is being used, and both router A and router B are advertising a summarized route to 172.16.0.0/16. Router C therefore receives two routes to 172.16.0.0/16 and does not know which subnets are attached to which router.

**Figure 2-7**    *Care Is Also Needed When Summarizing with Classless Routing Protocols*

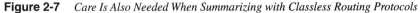

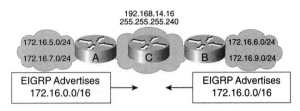

This problem can be resolved if you are using a classless routing protocol, because automatic summarization can be turned off (if it is on by default). Because routers running classless routing protocols use the longest prefix match when selecting a route from the routing table, if one of the routers advertises without summarizing, other routers will see subnet routes as well as the summary route. The other routers can then select the longest prefix match and follow the correct path. For example, in Figure 2-7, if router A continues to summarize to 172.16.0.0/16, and router B is configured not to summarize, router C will receive explicit routes for 172.16.6.0/24 and 172.16.9.0/24, along with the summarized route to 172.16.0.0/16. All traffic for router B's subnets will then be sent to router B, and all other traffic for the 172.16.0.0 network will be sent to router A. This will be true for any other classless protocol.

## Route Summarization Summary

Table 2-2 summarizes the route summarization support available in the various IP routing protocols discussed.

**Table 2-2**    *Routing Protocol Route Summarization Support*

| Protocol | Automatic Summarization at Classful Network Boundary? | Ability to Turn Off Automatic Summarization? | Ability to Summarize at Other Than Classful Network Boundary? |
|---|---|---|---|
| RIPv1 | Yes | No | No |
| RIPv2 | Yes | Yes | No |
| IGRP | Yes | No | No |
| EIGRP | Yes | Yes | Yes |
| OSPF | No | — | Yes |
| IS-IS | No | — | Yes |

### Examining a Classful Routing Table

Example 2-4 shows an example of the output from the **show ip route** command executed on a router running RIP.

**Example 2-4** *Interpreting the IP Routing Table with a Classful Protocol*

```
p1r3#show ip route
<output omitted>
Gateway of last resort is 0.0.0.0 to network 0.0.0.0
     10.0.0.0/24 is subnetted, 3 subnets,
R       10.1.1.0/24 [120/1] via 10.1.2.2, 00:00:05, Ethernet0
C       10.1.2.0/24 is directly connected, Ethernet0
R       10.1.3.0/24 [120/2] via 10.1.2.2, 00:00:05, Ethernet0
R     192.168.24.0/24 [120/2] via 10.1.2.2, 00:00:16, Ethernet0
R     172.16.0.0/16 [120/3] via 10.1.2.2, 00:00:16, Ethernet0
R*    0.0.0.0/0 [120/3] via 10.1.2.2, 00:00:05, Ethernet0
```

What would the router do with traffic that is bound for various destinations? Here are some examples of traffic destinations:

- 192.168.24.3
- 172.16.5.1
- 10.1.2.7
- 200.100.50.0
- 10.2.2.2

The routing table contains routes to the first three of these destination networks. There is no route to the fourth destination, 200.100.50.0, but there is a default route. The router uses the default route for the fourth destination.

The fifth destination, 10.2.2.2, is bound for an unknown subnet of a major network that is in the routing table. By default, a classful routing protocol assumes that it knows about all subnets of a network in its routing table. It discards traffic routed to any unknown subnets, so the packet to 10.2.2.2 is discarded by default.

The behavior of the classful routing protocol changes when you use the **ip classless** command.

---

### The Routing Table Acts Classfully

The routing table itself acts classfully and therefore does not forward a packet unless all subnets are known. For example, assuming that you have no routing protocols, only static routes, you still would not be able to reach a subnet of a known major network using a default route unless you entered the **ip classless** command. So this is not a function of a classful routing protocol, but rather a function of the routing table, which by default (and for historical reasons) acts in a classful nature.

A CCIE technical reviewer of this book performed the following test using two Cisco 2520 routers running Cisco IOS c2500-i-l.122-8.T5.bin. The two routers, R1 and R2, were connected via interface E0, and no routing protocols were enabled on either router.

**Router 1 configuration:**

```
!
int lo 0
ip address 10.1.0.1 255.255.0.0
int lo 1
ip address 10.2.0.1 255.255.0.0
int e 0
ip address 10.3.0.1 255.255.0.0
!
ip route 0.0.0.0 0.0.0.0 10.3.0.2
!
no ip classless
```

**Router 2 configuration:**

```
!
int lo 0
ip address 10.4.0.1 255.255.0.0
int e 0
ip address 10.3.0.2 255.255.0.0
!
```

**Test 1:**

As you can see, R1 has a default route pointing to R2 and has the **no ip classless** command. The test is to ping from R1 to R2-L0, which fails. When the **ip classless** command is entered on R1, the ping from R1 to R2-L0, via the default route, succeeds. This test proves that even though no routing protocols are used, the table acts classfully.

**Test 2:**

The second step is to test the classful nature of the routing table using a classless routing protocol. OSPF, a classless routing protocol, is used for the following test. OSPF is turned on for all interfaces on R1 but is activated only on R2's Ethernet link.

R2's OSPF then injects a default route into R1 using the **default-information originate always** command (which is covered in detail in Chapter 5, "Interconnecting Multiple OSPF Areas"). R1 therefore has a default route pointing to R2 that is introduced via OSPF. The pings from R1 to R2-L0 succeed regardless of the **ip classless** command. Therefore, turning on OSPF, a classless protocol, acts to override the router's classful nature.

## The **ip classless** Command

When running classful protocols (RIPv1 and IGRP), you must enable **ip classless** if you want the router to select a default route when it must route to an unknown subnet of a network for which it knows some subnets. For example, consider a router's routing table that has entries for subnets 10.5.0.0/16 and 10.6.0.0/16 and a default route of 0.0.0.0. If a packet arrives for a destination on the 10.7.0.0/16 subnet and **ip classless** is not enabled, the packet is dropped. Classful protocols assume that if they know some of the subnets of network 10.0.0.0, they must know all that network's existing subnets. Enabling **ip classless** tells the router that it should follow the best supernet route or the default route for unknown subnets of known networks, as well as for unknown networks.

The following command is used to activate the classless IP behavior:

```
RouterA(config)#ip classless
```

Note that classless IP is enabled by default in Release 12.0 of the Cisco IOS software; in previous releases it is disabled by default.

# Classless Routing Protocol Concepts

Classless routing protocols can be considered second-generation protocols because they are designed to address some of the limitations of the earlier classful routing protocols. One of the most serious limitations in a classful network environment is that the subnet mask is not exchanged during the routing update process. Therefore, the same subnet mask must be used on all subnetworks within the same major network. Here are some examples of classless routing protocols:

- Routing Information Protocol version 2 (RIPv2)
- EIGRP
- OSPF
- IS-IS
- Border Gateway Protocol version 4 (BGPv4)

With classless routing protocols, different subnets within the same major network can have different subnet masks. The use of different subnet masks within the same major network is called variable-length subnet masking (VLSM). If more than one entry in the routing table matches a particular destination, the longest prefix match in the routing table is used. For example, if a routing table has different paths to 172.16.0.0/16 and to 172.16.5.0/24, packets addressed to 172.16.5.99 are routed through the 172.16.5.0/24 path, because that address has the longest match with the destination network.

Another limitation of the classful approach is the need to automatically summarize to the classful network boundary at major network boundaries. In the classless environment, the route summarization process can be controlled manually and can usually be invoked at any bit position within the address. Because subnet routes are propagated throughout the routing domain, manual route summarization might be required to keep the size of the routing tables manageable.

## Classless Subnetting Requirements

With classful routing protocols, a consistent subnet mask must be applied to all router interfaces within the same major network, resulting in inefficient use of host addresses. Classless routing protocols allow VLSM, which enables a more appropriate allocation of address space. The subnet mask can be customized to allow the appropriate number of hosts in a network.

In Figure 2-8, the serial link is configured with a subnet mask of /30, which properly supports the point-to-point serial link requirement for only two host addresses. Meanwhile, the Ethernet links are configured with a subnet mask of /27, which supports up to 30 host addresses each.

**Figure 2-8**    *Classless Subnetting Requirements*

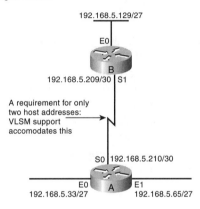

## Automatic Network-Boundary Summarization Using RIPv2 and EIGRP

Some classless routing protocols do not automatically advertise every subnet. But by default, classless routing protocols, such as RIPv2 and EIGRP, perform automatic network summarization at classful boundaries, just like a classful protocol does. Automatic summarization lets RIPv2 and EIGRP be backward-compatible with their predecessors, RIPv1 and IGRP.

The difference between these protocols and their predecessors is that you can manually turn off automatic summarization. To turn off automatic summarization, use the **no auto-summary** command under the routing process. You don't need this command when you are using OSPF or IS-IS, because neither protocol performs automatic network summarization by default. As a matter of fact, automatic summarization cannot be configured on OSPF and IS-IS even if you want to.

The automatic summarization behavior can cause problems in a network that has discontiguous subnets or if some of the summarized subnets cannot be reached via the advertising router. If a summarized route indicates that certain subnets can be reached via a router, when in fact those subnets are discontiguous or unreachable via that router, the network might have problems similar to those caused by a classful protocol. For example, in Figure 2-9, both router A and router B are advertising a summarized route to 172.16.0.0/16. Router C therefore receives two routes to 172.16.0.0/16 and cannot identify which subnets are attached to which router.

**Figure 2-9** *Automatic Network-Boundary Summarization*

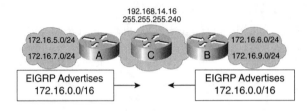

You can resolve this problem by disabling automatic summarization when running RIPv2 or EIGRP. Classless routers use the longest prefix match when selecting a route from the routing table; therefore, if one of the routers advertises without summarizing, the other routers see subnet routes as well as the summary route. The other routers can then select the longest prefix match and follow the correct path. For example, in Figure 2-9, if router A continues to summarize to 172.16.0.0/16 and router B is configured not to summarize, router C receives explicit routes for 172.16.6.0/24 and 172.16.9.0/24, along with the summarized route to 172.16.0.0/16. All traffic for router B subnets is sent to router B, and all other traffic for the 172.16.0.0 network is sent to router A. This treatment of traffic applies for any other classless protocol.

## The **auto-summary** Command for RIPv2 and EIGRP

The default behavior for RIPv2 and EIGRP is to summarize networks at major classful boundaries, even though the subnet mask information is contained in routing updates.

In the RIPv2 network illustrated in Figure 2-10, router B is attached to subnet 172.16.1.0/24. Therefore, if router B recognizes any network on this interface that is also a subnet of the 172.16.0.0 network, it correctly applies the subnet mask of 255.255.255.0 to that recognized network.

However, notice how router C, which is attached to router B via the 192.168.5.0/24 network, handles routing information about network 172.16.0.0. Router B automatically summarizes the 172.16.1.0/24 and 172.16.2.0/24 subnets to 172.16.0.0 before sending the route to router C, because it is sent over an interface in a different network. Rather than using the subnet mask known to router B (/24), router C applies the default classful mask for a Class B address (/16) when it receives information about 172.16.0.0.

In the OSPF network shown in Figure 2-11, router B passes the subnet and subnet mask information to router C, and router C puts the subnet details in its routing table. Router C does not need to use default classful masks for the received routing information because the subnet mask is included in the routing update, and OSPF does not automatically summarize networks.

**Figure 2-10**  *Effect of the* **auto-summary** *Command*

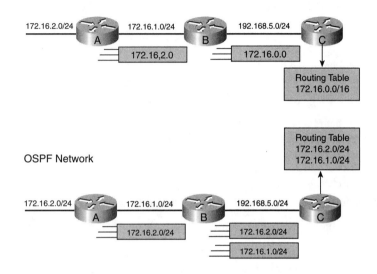

RIPv2 Network with Default Behavior

OSPF Network

**Figure 2-11**  *Effect of the* **no auto-summary** *Command*

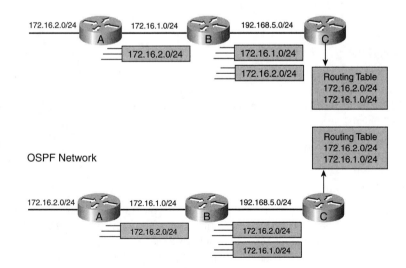

RIPv2 Network with "no auto-summary"

OSPF Network

When automatic summarization is disabled, RIPv2 and EIGRP forward subnet information, even over interfaces belonging to different major networks. In Figure 2-11, automatic summarization has been disabled. Notice that now the routing table is the same for both the RIPv2 and the OSPF routers.

To disable automatic summarization in RIPv2, use the following commands:

```
router(config)#router rip
router(config-router)#version 2
router(config-router)#no auto-summary
```

Use the following commands to disable automatic summarization in EIGRP:

```
router(config)#router eigrp 100
router(config-router)#no auto-summary
```

## Characteristics of RIPv1

RIPv1 is described in RFC 1058. Its key characteristics include the following:

- Hop count is used as the metric for path selection.

- The maximum allowable hop count is 15.

- Routing updates are broadcast every 30 seconds by default.

- RIP can load-balance over as many as six equal-cost paths—four paths by default.

- It has no authentication support.

RIPv1 is a classful routing protocol that does not send the subnet mask in its updates. Therefore, RIPv1 does not support VLSM.

## Characteristics of RIPv2

RIPv2 is a classless distance-vector protocol defined in RFCs 1721, 1722, and 2453. The purpose of RIPv2 is to update and enhance the RIPv1 protocol. The most significant addition to RIPv2 is the inclusion of the mask in the RIPv2 routing update packet. By sending the mask, RIPv2 has the following capabilities:

- Classless routing

- VLSM

- Manual route summarization

Additionally, RIPv2 uses multicast addressing for more efficient periodic updating on each interface. RIPv2 uses the 224.0.0.9 multicast address to advertise to other RIPv2 routers. This approach is more efficient, because when RIPv1 uses a 255.255.255.255 broadcast address, all devices, including PCs and servers, process this packet. They perform the checksum on the Layer 2 packet and pass it up their IP stack. IP sends the packet to the User Datagram Protocol (UDP) process, and UDP checks to see if RIP port 520 is available. Most PCs and servers do not have any process running on this port and discard the packet. RIP can fit up to 25 networks and subnets in each update, and updates are dispatched every 30 seconds. For example, if the routing table has 1000 subnets, 40 packets are dispatched every 30 seconds (80 packets a minute). With each packet being a broadcast, all devices must look at it; most of the devices discard the packet.

The IP multicast address for RIPv2 has its own multicast MAC address. Devices that can distinguish between a multicast and a broadcast at the MAC layer read the start of the Layer 2 frame and determine that the destination MAC address is not for them. They can then discard all these packets at the interface level and not use CPU resources or buffer memory for these unwanted packets. Even on devices that cannot distinguish between broadcast and multicast at Layer 2, the worst that will happen is that the RIP updates will be discarded at the IP layer instead of being passed to UDP, because those devices are not using the 224.0.0.9 address.

Security was added between RIP routers using message-digest or clear-text authentication. It is implemented in interface configuration mode. Security features are not covered in this book.

---

**NOTE**  RIP is sometimes used as a gateway discovery technique in TCP/IP services, such as UNIX and Windows.

---

## RIPv2 Configuration Commands

To activate the RIP process (version 1 by default), use the following command:

```
Router(config)#router rip
```

By default, the Cisco IOS software receives both RIPv1 and RIPv2 packets; however, it sends only version 1 packets. To configure the software to send and receive packets from only one version, use the **version {1 | 2}** command.

To select participating attached networks, use the following command, where you will enter the major classful network number:

```
Router(config-router)#network network-number
```

Regardless of the version, a **network** command is required under the RIP routing process using the classful network number.

Although the RIP **version** command controls RIP's overall default behavior, you might need to control the version of RIP on a per-interface basis. To control the version of RIP on each interface, use the **ip rip send version** and **ip rip receive version** interface commands. Version control per interface might be required when you are connecting legacy RIP networks to newer networks.

```
Router(config-if)#ip rip {send | receive} version {1 | 2 | 1 2}
```

By default, automatic summarization across network boundaries is activated for all networks in both versions of RIP. Manually summarizing routes in RIPv2 improves scalability and efficiency in large networks. The more-specific routes are not advertised, only the summary routes, thus reducing the size of the IP routing table and allowing the router to handle more routes.

Networks are automatically summarized at their classful boundaries. Manual summarization is done at the interface. One limitation of RIPv2 is that routes can be summarized only up to the classful network boundary. RIPv2 does not support CIDR-type summarization to the left of the classful boundary. To summarize RIP routes on nonclassful boundaries, do the following:

- Turn off autosummarization using the **no auto-summary** command under the RIP process.

- Use the **ip summary-address rip** interface command, and define a network number and mask that meet the particular requirement.

Figure 2-12 illustrates how RIPv1 and RIPv2 coexist in the same network. Router A is running RIPv2, and router C is running RIPv1. Router B runs both versions of RIP to bring the two versions together. Notice that the **ip rip send version 1** and **ip rip receive version 1** commands are required only on interface serial 3 of router B, because RIPv2 is configured as the primary version for all interfaces. The serial 3 interface has to be manually configured to support RIPv1 so that it can connect correctly with router C.

**Figure 2-12** *RIPv2 Configuration Example*

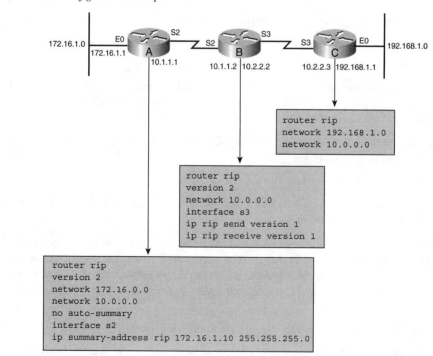

An **ip summary-address rip** command is configured on router A with the **no auto-summary** option. The combination of these two commands allows router A to send the 172.16.1.0 subnet detail to router B. Because router B is in a different network (10.0.0.0), the default behavior for router A is to send only the classful summarization (172.16.0.0) to router B.

---

NOTE    In Figure 2-12, the **ip summary-address rip 172.16.1.0 255.255.255.0** command is unnecessary because the **no auto-summary** command is also applied. The moment that the **no auto-summary** command is used, the subnet 172.16.1.0 is advertised as such because it uses a 24-bit mask.

---

# IP Routing Protocol Comparisons

Each IP routing protocol has its own unique characteristics. These protocols also share characteristics with other protocols. This section compares and contrasts the various IP routing protocols. It also illustrates the qualities of IP routing protocols, such as administrative distance and floating static routes.

## Administrative Distance

Most routing protocols have metric structures and algorithms that are incompatible with other protocols. It is critical that a network using multiple routing protocols be able to seamlessly exchange route information and be able to select the best path across multiple protocols. Cisco routers use a value called administrative distance to select the best path when they learn of two or more routes to the same destination from different routing protocols.

Administrative distance rates a routing protocol's believability. Cisco has assigned a default administrative distance value to each routing protocol supported on its routers. Each routing protocol is prioritized in the order of most-to-least-believable. Here are some examples of prioritization:

- Prefer manually configured routes (static routes) to dynamically learned routes
- Prefer protocols with sophisticated metrics to protocols with more-deterministic metrics
- Prefer External Border Gateway Protocol (EBGP) over most other dynamic protocols

Table 2-3 lists the default administrative distance of the protocols supported by Cisco routers. It is a value between 0 and 255. The lower the administrative distance value, the higher the protocol's reliability.

**Table 2-3**    *Administrative Distance of Routing Protocols*

| Route Source | Default Distance |
|---|---|
| Connected interface | 0 |
| Static route out an interface | 0 |
| Static route to a next-hop address | 1 |
| EIGRP summary route | 5 |
| External BGP | 20 |
| Internal EIGRP | 90 |
| IGRP | 100 |
| OSPF | 110 |
| IS-IS | 115 |
| RIPv1, RIPv2 | 120 |
| Exterior Gateway Protocol (EGP) | 140 |
| ODR | 160 |
| External EIGRP | 170 |
| Internal BGP | 200 |
| Unknown | 255 |

**NOTE**    Static routes are configured with the **ip route** *prefix mask {address | interface} [distance]* [**permanent**] [**tag** *tag*] global configuration command, described in the "Principles of Static Routing" section earlier in this chapter. If the *address* parameter is used in this command, it specifies the address of the next-hop router to use to reach the destination network, and the default administrative distance is 1. If the *interface* parameter is used instead, specifying the local router outbound interface to use to reach the destination network, the router considers this a directly-connected route, and the default administrative distance is 0.

**NOTE**    Administrative distance is an 8-bit variable—thus, the decimal values ranging from 0 to 255.

For example, in Figure 2-13, if router A receives a route to network 10.0.0.0 from RIP and also receives a route to the same network from OSPF, the router compares RIP's administrative distance, 120, with OSPF's administrative distance, 110. The router uses the administrative distance value to determine that OSPF is more reliable and adds the OSPF version of the route to the routing table.

**Figure 2-13** *Route Selection and Administrative Distance*

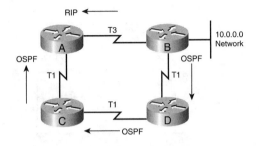

## Floating Static Routes

Based on administrative distance, routers believe static routes over any dynamically learned route. A directly connected interface is the only default administrative distance lower than that of a static route. There might be times when default behavior is not the desired behavior.

When you configure a static route as a backup to a dynamically learned route, the static route should not be used as long as the dynamic route is available. First, consider that the syntax for configuring a static route is as follows:

```
ip route prefix mask {address | interface} [distance]
```

The optional administrative distance value in this command can be manipulated to make the static route appear less desirable. Administrative distance can also be manipulated to make one static route appear less desirable than another static route. A static route that appears in the routing table only when the primary route goes away is called a floating static route.

---

**NOTE**     It is important to remember that the lower the administrative distance, the more reliable the protocol is assumed to be.

---

In Figure 2-14, routers A and B have two connections—a point-to-point serial connection that is the primary link, and an ISDN link to be used if the other line goes down. Both routers use EIGRP but do not route the ISDN 172.16.1.0 network link.

A static route has been created on each router that points to the ISDN interface of the other router. Because EIGRP has an administrative distance of 90, the static route has been given an administrative distance of 100. As long as router A has an EIGRP route to the 10.0.0.0 network, it appears more believable than the static route, and the EIGRP route is used. If the serial link goes down and disables the EIGRP route, router A inserts the static route into the routing table. A similar process happens on router B with its route to the 172.17.0.0 network.

**Figure 2-14** *Floating Static Routes*

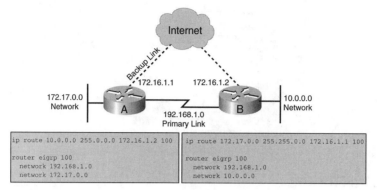

## Criteria for Inserting Routes in the IP Routing Table

One intriguing aspect of Cisco routers is how the router chooses the best route among those presented by routing protocols, manual configuration, and various other means. Although route selection is not difficult, understanding it completely requires some knowledge of how Cisco routers work. The router must consider the following four criteria:

- **Valid next-hop IP address**—As each routing process receives updates and other information, the router first verifies that the route has a valid next-hop IP address.

- **Metric**—If the next hop is valid, the routing protocol chooses the best path to any given destination based on the lowest metric. The routing protocol attempts to install this path into the routing table. For example, if EIGRP learns of a path to 10.1.1.0/24 and decides that this particular path is the best EIGRP path to this destination, the routing protocol tries to install the learned path into the routing table.

- **Administrative distance**—The next consideration is administrative distance. If more than one route exists for the same network, the router decides which route to install based on the administrative distance of the route's source. If the routing protocol that is presenting the path to a particular destination has the lowest administrative distance compared to the other ways the router has learned about this network, the router installs the route in the routing table. If that route does not have the best administrative distance, it is rejected.

- **Prefix**—The router looks at the prefix being advertised. If there is no exact match to that prefix in the routing table, the route is installed. For example, suppose the router has three routing processes running on it, and each process has received the following routes:

    — EIGRP (internal)—192.168.32.0/26

    — RIP—192.168.32.0/24

    — OSPF—192.168.32.0/19

Because each route has a different prefix length, also known as the subnet mask, the routes are considered different destinations and are installed in the routing table.

## Comparing Routing Protocol Charts

IGRP, EIGRP, and OSPF are transport-layer protocols that run directly over IP. IGRP uses connectionless delivery for its routing updates. Routers receiving IGRP updates do not need to acknowledge the receipt of these updates. EIGRP and OSPF have more reliability built into their update processes. They both require the acknowledgment of one update before they send another. Thus, they have a 1-to-1 window—one update and one acknowledgment. This section provides comparative summaries of routing protocols. Table 2-4 lists protocol numbers, port numbers, and reliability of routing protocols.

**Table 2-4**    *Protocols, Ports, and Reliability of Routing Protocols*

| Routing Protocol | Protocol Number | Port Number | Update Reliability |
|---|---|---|---|
| IGRP | 9 | — | Best-effort delivery |
| EIGRP | 88 | — | 1-to-1 window |
| OSPF | 89 | — | 1-to-1 window |
| RIP | — | UDP 520 | Best-effort delivery |
| BGP | — | TCP 179 | Uses TCP windowing |

RIP and BGP both reside at the application layer. RIP uses UDP as its transport protocol; its updates are sent unreliably with best-effort delivery.

BGP uses TCP as its transport protocol. It takes advantage of TCP's reliability mechanisms and windowing, which is important when you consider the number of routes a BGP router sends in its updates. BGP routers often carry more than 100,000 routes in their routing tables. If OSPF or EIGRP has to send updates for 100,000 routes with their 1-to-1 window, it will take a long time. Even if information for 100 routes can fit in one update, it will still take 1000 updates to send the entire table. Each update will have to be acknowledged before another is sent. On the other hand, BGP routers using TCP have a 65,536-byte window limit for their updates. The routers can send information with many more routes in each update than either OSPF or EIGRP.

**NOTE**    IS-IS is a network-layer protocol and does not use the services of IP to carry its routing information. IS-IS packets are encapsulated directly into a data-link layer frame.

RIPv2 is a distance-vector protocol, but it is classless and supports VLSM. RIPv2 automatically summarizes routes at major classful network boundaries; however, summarization can be disabled, and some manual summarization is possible. RIPv2 uses hop count, the number of routers between the router and the destination network, as its metric. The maximum allowable hop count is 15. RIP uses timers to prevent loops, but these also slow down network convergence.

EIGRP is an advanced distance-vector routing protocol; however, it demonstrates some of the same characteristics as link-state protocols, such as maintaining a topological table and neighbor relationships. EIGRP automatic route summarization is enabled by default, but you can disable it and configure manual route summarization. EIGRP uses a composite metric: bandwidth and delay by default. Although hop count is not part of the composite metric, EIGRP has a maximum hop count of 255 (the default is 100). EIGRP generally has the fastest convergence time, because it maintains a feasible successor (a backup route) in its topology table. If the best path fails, EIGRP immediately switches to the feasible successor without performing additional best-path calculations.

Table 2-5 compares the characteristics of the different routing protocols.

**Table 2-5**    *Routing Protocol Comparison*

| Characteristic | RIPv2 | EIGRP[*] | IS-IS | OSPF | BGP[**] |
|---|---|---|---|---|---|
| Distance-vector | ✓ | ✓ | | | ✓ |
| Link-state | | | ✓ | ✓ | |
| Hierarchical topology required | | | ✓ | ✓ | |
| Automatic route summarization | ✓ | ✓ | | | ✓ |
| Manual route summarization | ✓ | ✓ | ✓ | ✓ | ✓ |
| VLSM support | ✓ | ✓ | ✓ | ✓ | ✓ |
| Classless | ✓ | ✓ | ✓ | ✓ | ✓ |
| Metric | Hops | Composite metric | Cost | Cost | Path attributes |
| Convergence time | Slow | Very fast | Fast | Fast | Slow |

[*]EIGRP is an advanced distance-vector protocol with some characteristics also found in link-state protocols.

[**]BGP is a path-vector protocol.

OSPF and IS-IS are both classless link-state protocols that support VLSM. They require a hierarchical topology with a backbone that carries interarea traffic. OSPF and IS-IS use the Dijkstra shortest path first (SPF) algorithm to calculate the best paths through the network. They use cost as their metric. The cost of OSPF is based on bandwidth in Cisco routers. The IS-IS cost metric has a maximum value of 1023, and Cisco uses a default value of 10 for all types of WAN and LAN links. With OSPF and IS-IS, route summarization must be manually configured. Network convergence after a topology change is fairly fast, because routers already recognize all the links in their area.

BGP is a classless routing protocol that keeps track of paths to autonomous systems. BGP has a highly complicated metric based on a prioritized evaluation of the attributes of each path. With BGP, the prime consideration is reliability; convergence time is not as imperative.

Some documentation states that BGP automatically summarizes routes at major classful network boundaries and that you can disable this automatic summarization. However, this does not tell the whole story, as BGP works differently than the other protocols. The **network** command for BGP permits BGP to advertise a network if it is present in the IP routing table. This command allows classless prefixes; the router can advertise individual subnets, networks, or supernets. The default mask is the classful mask and results in only the classful network number being announced; note that at least one subnet of the specified major network must be present in the IP routing table in order for BGP to start announcing the classful network. However, if you specify the network-mask, an exact match to the network (both address and mask) must exist in the routing table in order for the network to be advertised. The BGP **auto-summary** command determines how redistributed routes are handled by BGP; the **no auto-summary** router configuration command turns off BGP autosummarization. When enabled (with **auto-summary**), all redistributed subnets will be summarized to their classful boundaries in the BGP table. When disabled (with **no auto-summary**), all redistributed subnets will be present in their original form in the BGP table. BGP route summarization is discussed further in Chapter 9, "Advanced Border Gateway Protocol Configuration."

All routing protocols use timers, which have default values. Table 2-6 summarizes default timer values. Distance-vector protocols send their routing updates on a regular basis. Distance-vector protocols use routing updates to maintain neighbor relationships. Routing protocols are responsible for advertising routes learned by the routing process, subject to the rules of split horizon. RIP sends updates every 30 seconds; IGRP sends updates every 90 seconds. The update interval affects the holddown for these protocols. Holddown, invalid, and flush times are as follows:

- **Holddown**—An interval, in seconds, during which routing information about a worse or equivalent metric path is suppressed. It should be at least 3 times the value of the update argument. A route enters a holddown (possibly down) state when it receives an update packet that indicates an unreachable route. The route is marked inaccessible and is advertised as unreachable. However, the route is still used to forward packets. When holddown expires, routes advertised by other sources with a worse or equivalent metric are accepted, and the route is no longer inaccessible. In RIP, the default is 180 seconds.

- **Invalid**—An interval, in seconds, after which a route is declared invalid; it should be at least 3 times the value of the update argument. A route becomes invalid when there is an absence of updates that refresh the route. The route then enters a holddown state. The route is marked inaccessible and is advertised as unreachable. However, the route still forwards packets. In RIP, the default is 180 seconds.

- **Flush**—An amount of time, in seconds, that must pass before the route is removed from the routing table; the interval that is specified should be greater than the value of the invalid argument. If it is less than the value of the invalid argument, the proper holddown interval cannot elapse, which results in the acceptance of a new route before the holddown interval expires. In RIP, the default is 240 seconds.

**Table 2-6**    *Comparison of Default Timers*

| Routing Protocol | Update Frequency | Hello Frequency | Other Timers |
|---|---|---|---|
| RIP | 30 sec plus triggered | — | Hold and invalid timers—180 sec<br>Flush—240 sec |
| IGRP | 90 sec plus triggered | — | Hold timers—280 sec<br>Invalid timers—270 sec<br>Flush timers—630 sec |
| EIGRP | Triggered | 60 sec for multipoint T1 or less<br>5 sec for others | Hold timers—180 sec for multipoint T1 or less<br>15 sec for others<br>(3 × hello interval) |
| IS-IS | Triggered<br>Also, link-state database synchronizing on the LAN every 10 sec and at startup on point-to-point | 10 sec | Hold timers—30 sec |
| OSPF | Triggered<br>Also link-state advertisements (LSAs) flooded every 30 min | 30 sec— nonbroadcast multiaccess (NBMA)<br>10 sec—others | Dead—120 sec NBMA, 40 sec others (4 × hello interval) |
| BGP | Triggered | 60 sec | Hold—180 sec |

Protocols that do not regularly advertise their routing tables—EIGRP, IS-IS, OSPF, and BGP— must have some way of establishing and maintaining neighbor relationships. EIGRP, IS-IS, OSPF, and BGP establish and maintain neighbor relationships by exchanging hello packets on a regular basis (BGP calls these keepalive messages). For EIGRP and OSPF, the hello interval varies according to the type of link between the two neighboring routers. Faster links receive more-frequent hellos.

Link-state protocols refresh the link-state database at intervals, even if there have been no link-state changes, to ensure that the information has not become corrupted while in a database. With OSPF, when an LSA is 30 minutes old, the router originating the LSA refloods the information. With IS-IS, the link-state database on a LAN link is synchronized every 10 seconds with a multicast complete sequence number PDU (CSNP). On point-to-point links, this synchronization is done at startup.

Hold time has a different meaning for these protocols compared to holddown for distance-vector protocols. If a router does not receive a hello packet from a neighbor within the specified hold time, that neighbor is down, and routes through that neighbor are unavailable. For OSPF, the equivalent term is dead interval.

All these timers can be configured, or you can use the defaults. For example, the default values for the hold time and dead interval time depend on the frequency of hellos, but they are generally 3 to 4 times the hello value. For some applications, 3 to 4 times the hello value might be an inappropriate value.

A network administrator should consider several issues before changing the default timers. Hold timers must not be set so low that neighbor relationships are torn down unnecessarily. On the other hand, longer hold times might delay network convergence. This delay is because of the long down time for a router before the neighbor's hold timer expires and it notices the topology change. Similarly, the smaller the hello interval, the faster the topological changes are detected, although more routing protocol traffic ensues.

# Summary

In this chapter, you learned how to select and implement the most effective method of IP routing for your network topology and its requirements. You also learned how to compare and contrast the concepts, characteristics, and operation of classful and classless IP routing protocols and how to determine the appropriate IP routing protocol for your network.

# References

For additional information, refer to this resource:

*Dictionary of Internetworking Terms and Acronyms*, Cisco Press, ISBN: 1587200457

# Configuration Exercise: Migrating to a Classless Routing Protocol

In this exercise, you set up RIPv2.

**Introduction to the Configuration Exercises**

This book uses Configuration Exercises to help you practice configuring routers with the commands and topics presented. If you have access to real hardware, you can try these exercises on your routers. See Appendix H, "Configuration Exercise Equipment Requirements and Initial Configurations," for a list of recommended equipment and initial configuration commands for the routers. However, even if you don't have access to any routers, you can go through the exercises and keep a log of your own running configurations or just read through the solution. Commands used and solutions to the Configuration Exercises are provided after the exercises.

In the Configuration Exercises, the network is assumed to consist of two pods, each with four routers. The pods are interconnected to a backbone. You configure one of the pods, pod 1. No interaction between the two pods is required, but you might see some routes from the other pod in your routing tables in some exercises if you have it configured (the Configuration Exercise answers show the routes from the other pod). In most of the exercises, the backbone has only one router; in some cases, another router is added to the backbone. Each Configuration Exercise assumes that you have completed the previous chapters' Configuration Exercises on your pod.

---

**NOTE**    Throughout the exercise, the pod number is referred to as *x*, and the router number is referred to as *y*. Substitute the appropriate numbers as needed.

---

# Objectives

After completing this exercise, you will be able to

- Connect to other devices in the network and have full network visibility using RIPv2 as a routing protocol

- Recognize RIPv2 support for default routes, VLSM, and route summarization

- Determine how VLSM contributes to network efficiency

# Visual Objective

Figure 2-15 illustrates the topology used in this exercise.

---

**NOTE**    Backbone router 2 (BBR2), shown in Figure 2-15, is not used until a later Configuration Exercise.

---

**Figure 2-15**  *Configuration Exercise Topology*

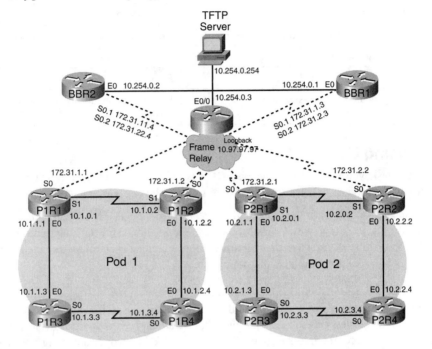

## Command List

In this exercise, you use the commands in Table 2-7, listed in logical order. Refer to this list if you need configuration command assistance during the exercise.

---

**CAUTION**   Although the command syntax is shown in this table, the addresses shown are typically for the P*x*R1 and P*x*R3 routers. Be careful when addressing your routers! Refer to the exercise instructions and the appropriate visual objective diagram for addressing details.

---

**Table 2-7**   *Configuration Exercise Command List*

| Command | Description |
| --- | --- |
| (config)#**router rip** | Turns on RIP. |
| (config-router)#**version 1** | Runs RIPv1. |
| (config-router)#**network 172.31.0.0** | Specifies a classful network that RIP should run within. |
| (config-router)#**network 10.0.0.0** | Specifies a classful network that RIP should run within. |

*continues*

**Table 2-7** *Configuration Exercise Command List (Continued)*

| Command | Description |
|---|---|
| (config-router)#**default-information originate** | Advertises the default route through RIP. |
| (config)#**ip classless** | Instructs the router to behave classlessly. |
| (config-router)#**version 2** | Runs RIPv2. |
| (config-router)#**no auto-summary** | Does not automatically summarize routes at classful boundaries. |

# Task 1: Cleaning Up

In this task, you establish a connection to the exercise equipment and clean up the configuration from the exercises in Chapter 1 to prepare for this exercise. Complete the following steps:

Manually remove from the routers all access lists, route maps, NAT statements, and static routes. The easiest way to do this for the edge routers is to copy the configuration file from the TFTP server (P*x*R*y*.txt) into the **startup-config** and reload each router. For the internal routers, it is only necessary to remove the static routes.

NOTE    Important: If you chose to download the configuration files to the internal routers, you must enable **ip classless** on the internal routers before attempting to do the download. Copy the configuration for the internal routers before you reload the edge routers, or you won't be able to connect to the TFTP server from the internal routers.

CAUTION    When you are reloading a router, if you see the following message:

```
System configuration has been modified. Save? [yes/no]
```

enter **no**, or your configuration will be resaved.

# Task 2: Exploring Classful Routing

In this task, you explore classful routing. Follow these steps:

Step 1    On all the routers within your assigned pod, configure RIPv1 for the classful pod network (10.0.0.0) and the Class B 172.31.0.0 Frame Relay network.

Step 2    Explicitly specify RIPv1 using the **version 1** command. The default sends version 1 advertisements and receives versions 1 and 2. Setting the router to version 1 prevents confusion—the backbone router runs both versions.

Step 3    Verify that your routers accept only version 1 advertisements using the **show ip protocols** command.

Step 4    Test connectivity to the TFTP server (10.254.0.254 /24) from the internal router using the **ping** command. Does the ping work?

**Step 5**    To investigate the results of the previous step, use the **debug ip rip** and **show ip route** commands to examine the routers' behavior.

Can your internal router reach the core router? Why or why not?

**Step 6**    One thing you might try to allow the internal routers to reach the core is to advertise a default route from the edge router through RIP using the **default-information originate** command (under the router RIP configuration).

**Step 7**    Look at the routing table on the internal router. Is there a path now? Remember that RIP is slow to converge. You might need to wait up to a minute, even in this small network, before the default route appears on the internal router. To force convergence, you can issue the **clear ip route \*** command.

**Step 8**    Again, test connectivity from the internal router to the TFTP server using **ping**. Does the ping work now?

## Task 3: Exploring Classless Forwarding

The ping to the TFTP server in the last task did not work because the behavior of classful routing is to look for known routes within the connected classful network (10.0.0.0 in this case) and to not consider less-specific routes, such as a default route. Given that classful behavior is the cause of the problem, this task explores classless behavior. Follow these steps:

**Step 1**    The TFTP server cannot be reached because the router has been instructed to route classfully with the command **no ip classless**. Enable classless IP on each router to explore classless behavior.

**Step 2**    Test connectivity from the internal router to the TFTP server. Does the ping work now?

**Step 3**    To fix the connectivity problem, change to the classless version of RIP, RIPv2, and turn off RIP automatic route summarization at the edge routers.

**Step 4**    One more time, test connectivity from the internal router to the TFTP server. Does the ping work now?

## Task 4: Optimizing Classless Routes for Scalability

As the network grows, large routing tables are inefficient because of the memory required to store them. Any routing event (such as a flapping line) must be propagated throughout the network for each route in the routing table. Summarization limits the update traffic and minimizes the size of the routing tables of all routers. In this task you configure summarization on your edge routers. Follow these steps:

**Step 1**    From the internal router, use Telnet to connect to BBR1 (172.31.x.0); the password is cisco. Notice that all your pod's networks are listed in BBR1's routing table.

**Step 2**    Configure the edge routers to announce a summary route of 10.x.0.0 255.255.0.0 to BBR1. Where should you place the appropriate command?

**Step 3**    Review the routing table on BBR1 again. What is the difference now? Remember that RIP is slow to converge, so you might need to wait up to a minute, even in this small network, before the summaries appear on BBR1.

**Step 4**    Examine the output from **show ip protocols** for details about the operation of RIP.

## Exercise Verification

You have completed this exercise when you achieve the following results:

- You can set up RIPv2, and you have full network visibility using RIPv2 as a routing protocol.

- You understand RIPv2 support for default routes, VLSM, and route summarization.

- You understand how VLSM contributes to network efficiency.

# Solution to Configuration Exercise: Migrating to a Classless Routing Protocol

This section provides the answers to the questions in the Configuration Exercise.

---

**NOTE**    Some answers cover multiple steps; the answers are given after the last step to which that answer applies.

---

## Solution to Task 1: Cleaning Up

In this task, you establish a connection to the exercise equipment and clean up the configuration from the exercises in Chapter 1 to prepare for this exercise. Complete the following steps:

Manually remove from the router all access lists, route maps, Network Address Translation (NAT) statements, and static routes. The easiest way to do this for the edge routers is to copy the configuration file from the TFTP server (P*x*R*y*.txt) into the **startup-config** and reload each router. For the internal routers, it is only necessary to remove the static routes.

---

**NOTE**    Important: If you chose to download the configuration files to the internal routers, you must enable **ip classless** on the internal routers before attempting to do the download. Copy the configuration for the internal routers before you reload the edge routers, or you won't be able to connect to the TFTP server from the internal routers.

---

**CAUTION**    When you are reloading a router, if you see the following message:

```
System configuration has been modified. Save? [yes/no]
```

enter **no**, or your configuration will be resaved.

**Solution:**

The following shows how to download the configuration and reload the P1R1 and P1R2 routers:

```
P1R1#copy tftp start
Address or name of remote host []? 10.254.0.254
Source filename []? p1r1.txt
Destination filename [startup-config]?
Accessing tftp://10.254.0.254/p1r1.txt...
Loading p1r1.txt from 10.254.0.254 (via Serial0): !
[OK - 1334/2048 bytes]
[OK]
1334 bytes copied in 11.404 secs (121 bytes/sec)
P1R1#
Feb 28 22:48:17 EST: %SYS-5-CONFIG_NV_I: Nonvolatile storage configured from
  tftp://tftp/p1r1.txt by console
P1R1#reload
Proceed with reload? [confirm]

P1R2#copy tftp start
Address or name of remote host []? 10.254.0.254
Source filename []? p1r2.txt
Destination filename [startup-config]?
Accessing tftp://10.254.0.254/p1r2.txt...
Loading p1r2.txt from 10.254.0.254 (via Serial0): !
[OK - 1313/2048 bytes]
[OK]
1313 bytes copied in 11.428 secs (119 bytes/sec)
P1R2#
Feb 28 22:49:41 EST: %SYS-5-CONFIG_NV_I: Nonvolatile storage configured from
  tftp://tftp/p1r2.txt by console
P1R2#
P1R2#reload
Proceed with reload? [confirm]
```

For the internal routers, it is only necessary to remove the static routes. Here are the configuration steps for the P1R3 and P1R4 routers:

```
P1R3#conf t
Enter configuration commands, one per line.   End with CNTL/Z.
P1R3(config)#no ip route 0.0.0.0 0.0.0.0 e0
P1R3(config)#^Z
*Feb 28 22:51:17 EST: %SYS-5-CONFIG_I: Configured from console by console
P1R3#copy run start
Destination filename [startup-config]?
Building configuration...
[OK]
```

*continues*

```
P1R4#conf t
Enter configuration commands, one per line.  End with CNTL/Z.
P1R4(config)#no ip route 0.0.0.0 0.0.0.0 e0
P1R4(config)#^Z
P1R4#
*Feb 28 22:52:25 EST: %SYS-5-CONFIG_I: Configured from console by console
P1R4#copy run start
Destination filename [startup-config]?
Building configuration...
[OK]
P1R4#
```

# Solution to Task 2: Exploring Classful Routing

In this task, you explore classful routing. Complete the following steps:

**Step 1**    On all the routers within your assigned pod, configure RIPv1 for the classful
pod network (10.0.0.0) and the Class B 172.31.0.0 Frame Relay network.

**Solution:**

The following configuration is for the pod 1 routers:

```
P1R1(config)#router rip
P1R1(config-router)#version 1
P1R1(config-router)#network 10.0.0.0
P1R1(config-router)#network 172.31.0.0

P1R2(config)#router rip
P1R2(config-router)#version 1
P1R2(config-router)#network 10.0.0.0
P1R2(config-router)#network 172.31.0.0

P1R3(config)#router rip
P1R3(config-router)#version 1
P1R3(config-router)#network 10.0.0.0

P1R4(config)#router rip
P1R4(config-router)#version 1
P1R4(config-router)#network 10.0.0.0
```

**Step 2**    Explicitly specify RIPv1 using the **version 1** command. The default sends
version 1 advertisements and receives versions 1 and 2. Setting the router
to version 1 prevents confusion—the backbone router runs both versions.
You entered this command in Step 1.

**Step 3**    Verify that your routers accept only version 1 advertisements using the **show
ip protocols** command.

**Solution:**

The following sample output is from the P1R1 router. Note that under the Recv column, only version 1 is displayed.

```
P1R1#show ip protocol
Routing Protocol is "rip"
  Sending updates every 30 seconds, next due in 14 seconds
  Invalid after 180 seconds, hold down 180, flushed after 240
  Outgoing update filter list for all interfaces is not set
  Incoming update filter list for all interfaces is not set
  Redistributing: rip
  Default version control: send version 1, receive version 1
    Interface           Send  Recv  Triggered RIP  Key-chain
    Ethernet0           1     1
    Serial0             1     1
    Serial1             1     1
  Automatic network summarization is in effect
  Maximum path: 4
  Routing for Networks:
    10.0.0.0
    172.31.0.0
  Routing Information Sources:
    Gateway         Distance      Last Update
    10.1.1.3             120      00:00:18
    10.1.0.2             120      00:00:15
    172.31.1.3           120      00:00:07
  Distance: (default is 120)
```

**Step 4**    Test connectivity to the TFTP server (10.254.0.254 /24) from the internal router using the **ping** command. Does the ping work?

**Solution:**

The following sample output is from the P1R3 router. The ping did not work.

```
P1R3#ping 10.254.0.254
Type escape sequence to abort.
Sending 5, 100-byte ICMP Echos to 10.254.0.254, timeout is 2 seconds:
.....
Success rate is 0 percent (0/5)
P1R3#
```

**Step 5**    To investigate the results of the previous step, use the **debug ip rip** and **show ip route** commands to examine the routers' behavior.

Can your internal router reach the core router? Why or why not?

**Solution:**

The internal router cannot reach the core because it does not have a route for the 10.254.0.0 subnet in its routing table. Classful routing protocols such as RIPv1 do not exchange subnet mask information and either assume a constant mask throughout the classful network or advertise the entire classful network. Advertisements between the pod edge routers and BBR1 go across the 172.31.0.0 network. Therefore, all three routers summarize the subnets of network 10.0.0.0 and advertise network 10.0.0.0 to each other. Each router ignores this advertisement, because it already has a route to the 10.0.0.0 network. Classful routing behavior is to look for known routes within the connected classful network (10.0.0.0 in this case) and to not consider less-specific routes. (You can verify this behavior with the **debug ip rip** command.) Verify this by displaying the routing table on the internal router. Look for a route to the 10.254.0.0 network:

```
P1R1#debug ip rip
RIP protocol debugging is on
P1R1#
*Feb 28 19:19:07 EST: RIP: received v1 update from 10.1.0.2 on Serial1
*Feb 28 19:19:07 EST:     10.1.2.0 in 1 hops
*Feb 28 19:19:07 EST:     10.1.3.0 in 2 hops
*Feb 28 19:19:07 EST:     172.31.0.0 in 1 hops
P1R1#
*Feb 28 19:19:15 EST: RIP: sending v1 update to 255.255.255.255 via Ethernet0
  (10.1.1.1)
*Feb 28 19:19:15 EST: RIP: build update entries
*Feb 28 19:19:15 EST:     subnet 10.1.0.0 metric 1
*Feb 28 19:19:15 EST:     subnet 10.1.2.0 metric 2
*Feb 28 19:19:15 EST:     network 172.31.0.0 metric 1
*Feb 28 19:19:15 EST: RIP: sending v1 update to 255.255.255.255 via Serial0
  (172.31.1.1)
*Feb 28 19:19:15 EST: RIP: build update entries
*Feb 28 19:19:15 EST:     network 10.0.0.0 metric 1
*Feb 28 19:19:15 EST:     subnet 172.31.1.0 metric 1
*Feb 28 19:19:15 EST:     subnet 172.31.2.0 metric 2
*Feb 28 19:19:15 EST: RIP: sending v1 update to 255.255.255.255 via Serial1
  (10.1.0.1)
P1R1#
*Feb 28 19:19:15 EST: RIP: build update entries
*Feb 28 19:19:15 EST:     subnet 10.1.1.0 metric 1
*Feb 28 19:19:15 EST:     subnet 10.1.3.0 metric 2
*Feb 28 19:19:15 EST:     network 172.31.0.0 metric 1
P1R1#
*Feb 28 19:19:19 EST: RIP: received v1 update from 172.31.1.3 on Serial0
*Feb 28 19:19:19 EST:     10.0.0.0 in 1 hops
*Feb 28 19:19:19 EST:     172.31.2.0 in 1 hops
*Feb 28 19:19:19 EST: RIP: ignored v2 packet from 172.31.1.3 (illegal version)
P1R1#

P1R1#show ip route
<output omitted>
     172.31.0.0/24 is subnetted, 2 subnets
R       172.31.2.0 [120/1] via 172.31.1.3, 00:00:26, Serial0
C       172.31.1.0 is directly connected, Serial0
     10.0.0.0/24 is subnetted, 4 subnets
R       10.1.3.0 [120/1] via 10.1.1.3, 00:00:14, Ethernet0
R       10.1.2.0 [120/1] via 10.1.0.2, 00:00:11, Serial1
```

```
C       10.1.1.0 is directly connected, Ethernet0
C       10.1.0.0 is directly connected, Serial1
P1R1#

P1R3#
P1R3#show ip route
<output omitted>
R    172.31.0.0/16 [120/1] via 10.1.1.1, 00:00:16, Ethernet0
     10.0.0.0/24 is subnetted, 4 subnets
C       10.1.3.0 is directly connected, Serial0
R       10.1.2.0 [120/1] via 10.1.3.4, 00:00:04, Serial0
C       10.1.1.0 is directly connected, Ethernet0
R       10.1.0.0 [120/1] via 10.1.1.1, 00:00:16, Ethernet0
P1R3#
```

**Step 6**   One thing you might try to allow the internal routers to reach the core is to advertise a default route from the edge router through RIP using the **default-information originate** command (under the router RIP configuration).

**Solution:**

```
P1R1(config)#router rip
P1R1(config-router)#default-information originate
P1R2(config)#router rip
P1R2(config-router)#default-information originate
```

**Step 7**   Look at the routing table on the internal router. Is there a path now? Remember that RIP is slow to converge. You might need to wait up to a minute, even in this small network, before the default route appears on the internal router. To force convergence, you can issue the **clear ip route \*** command.

**Solution:**

Your display should resemble the following for P1R3:

```
P1R3#show ip route
<output omitted>
Gateway of last resort is 10.1.1.1 to network 0.0.0.0

R    172.31.0.0/16 [120/1] via 10.1.1.1, 00:00:26, Ethernet0
     10.0.0.0/24 is subnetted, 4 subnets
C       10.1.3.0 is directly connected, Serial0
R       10.1.2.0 [120/1] via 10.1.3.4, 00:00:14, Serial0
C       10.1.1.0 is directly connected, Ethernet0
R       10.1.0.0 [120/1] via 10.1.1.1, 00:00:26, Ethernet0
R*   0.0.0.0/0 [120/1] via 10.1.1.1, 00:00:26, Ethernet0
```

**NOTE**   You will notice a default route in the routing table of P*x*R3 and P*x*R4. This default route is the result of the pod's edge routers, P*x*R1 and P*x*R2, advertising themselves as default with the **default-information originate** command.

Your display should resemble the following for P1R4:

```
P1R4#show ip route
<output omitted>
Gateway of last resort is 10.1.3.3 to network 0.0.0.0

R    172.31.0.0/16 [120/1] via 10.1.2.2, 00:00:17, Ethernet0
     10.0.0.0/24 is subnetted, 4 subnets
C       10.1.3.0 is directly connected, Serial0
C       10.1.2.0 is directly connected, Ethernet0
R       10.1.1.0 [120/1] via 10.1.3.3, 00:00:14, Serial0
R       10.1.0.0 [120/1] via 10.1.2.2, 00:00:17, Ethernet0
R*    0.0.0.0/0 [120/2] via 10.1.3.3, 00:00:14, Serial0
                 [120/2] via 10.1.2.2, 00:00:17, Ethernet0
```

Notice that only one route to the 0.0.0.0 default route appears in the routing table for P1R3, whereas P1R4 has two equal-cost routes to 0.0.0.0. This is because P1R3 advertises its default route to P1R4 first (because P1R1 is the first to be configured); because of split horizon, P1R4 does not advertise the default route back to P1R3. The routing table for P1R2 also has the default route, learned from P1R1; P1R1 does not have the default route from P1R2, again due to split horizon.

**Step 8**  Again, test connectivity from the internal router to the TFTP server using **ping**. Does the ping work now?

**Solution:**

The following sample output is from the P1R3 and P1R4 routers. The pings still do not work. The reasoning behind this is examined in the next task.

```
P1R3#ping 10.254.0.254
Type escape sequence to abort.
Sending 5, 100-byte ICMP Echos to 10.254.0.254, timeout is 2 seconds:
.....
Success rate is 0 percent (0/5)

P1R3#
P1R4#ping 10.254.0.254
Type escape sequence to abort.
Sending 5, 100-byte ICMP Echos to 10.254.0.254, timeout is 2 seconds:
.....
Success rate is 0 percent (0/5)
P1R4#
```

# Solution to Task 3: Exploring Classless Forwarding

The ping to the TFTP server in the last task did not work because the behavior of classful routing is to look for known routes within the connected classful network (10.0.0.0 in this case) and to not consider less-specific routes, such as a default route. Given that classful behavior is the cause of the problem, this task explores classless behavior. Follow these steps:

**Step 1**   The TFTP server cannot be reached because the router has been instructed to route classfully with the command **no ip classless**. Enable classless IP on each router to explore classless behavior.

**Solution:**

The following sample configuration is on the pod 1 routers:

```
P1R1#conf t
Enter configuration commands, one per line.  End with CNTL/Z.
P1R1(config)#ip classless

P1R2#conf t
Enter configuration commands, one per line.  End with CNTL/Z.
P1R2(config)#ip classless

P1R3#conf t
Enter configuration commands, one per line.  End with CNTL/Z.
P1R3(config)#ip classless

P1R4#conf t
Enter configuration commands, one per line.  End with CNTL/Z.
P1R4(config)#ip classless
```

**Step 2**   Test connectivity from the internal router to the TFTP server. Does the ping work now?

**Solution:**

The following outputs are from the P1R3 and P1R4 routers. The pings do not work.

```
P1R3#ping 10.254.0.254
Type escape sequence to abort.
Sending 5, 100-byte ICMP Echos to 10.254.0.254, timeout is 2 seconds:
U.U.U
Success rate is 0 percent (0/5)

P1R4#ping 10.254.0.254
Type escape sequence to abort.
Sending 5, 100-byte ICMP Echos to 10.254.0.254, timeout is 2 seconds:
UU.UU
Success rate is 0 percent (0/5)
```

The "U" result for the pings indicates that this router has a valid route in its routing table (the default route), but the echo reply still was not received. Although you changed the router behavior, RIPv1 still is a classful routing protocol and still is autosummarizing across the Frame Relay link. The BBR1 router does not have a route back to the 10.x.1.0/24 or 10.x.2.0/24 subnets, so the ping does not work.

**Step 3** To fix the connectivity problem, change to the classless version of RIP, RIPv2, and turn off RIP automatic route summarization at the edge routers.

**Solution:**

The following sample configuration is on the pod 1 routers:

```
P1R1(config)#router rip
P1R1(config-router)#version 2
P1R1(config-router)#no auto-summary

P1R2(config)#router rip
P1R2(config-router)#version 2
P1R2(config-router)#no auto-summary

P1R3(config)#router rip
P1R3(config-router)#version 2
P1R3(config-router)#no auto-summary

P1R4(config)#router rip
P1R4(config-router)#version 2
P1R4(config-router)#no auto-summary
```

**Step 4** One more time, test connectivity from the internal router to the TFTP server. Does the ping work now?

**Solution:**

The following sample output is from the P1R3 and P1R4 routers. The pings now work.

```
P1R3#ping 10.254.0.254
Type escape sequence to abort.
Sending 5, 100-byte ICMP Echos to 10.254.0.254, timeout is 2 seconds:
!!!!!
Success rate is 100 percent (5/5), round-trip min/avg/max = 32/33/36 ms
P1R3#

P1R4#ping 10.254.0.254
Type escape sequence to abort.
Sending 5, 100-byte ICMP Echos to 10.254.0.254, timeout is 2 seconds:
!!!!!
Success rate is 100 percent (5/5), round-trip min/avg/max = 36/36/40 ms
P1R4#
```

# Solution to Task 4: Optimizing Classless Routes for Scalability

As the network grows, large routing tables are inefficient because of the memory required to store them. Any routing event (such as a flapping line) must be propagated throughout the network for each route in the routing table. Summarization limits the update traffic and minimizes the size of the routing tables of all routers. In this task you configure summarization on your edge routers. Follow these steps:

**Step 1**   From the internal router, use Telnet to connect to BBR1 (172.31.x.0); the password is cisco. Notice that all your pod's networks are listed in BBR1's routing table.

**Solution:**

The following sample output is from the BBR1 router:

```
BBR1>show ip route
<output omitted>
Gateway of last resort is not set

     172.31.0.0/24 is subnetted, 4 subnets
B        172.31.22.0 [20/0] via 10.254.0.2, 00:00:13
C        172.31.2.0 is directly connected, Serial0.2
C        172.31.1.0 is directly connected, Serial0.1
B        172.31.11.0 [20/0] via 10.254.0.2, 00:00:13
S     192.168.11.0/24 [1/0] via 172.31.1.2
     10.0.0.0/24 is subnetted, 6 subnets
R        10.1.3.0 [120/2] via 172.31.1.2, 00:00:09, Serial0.1
                  [120/2] via 172.31.1.1, 00:00:13, Serial0.1
R        10.1.2.0 [120/1] via 172.31.1.2, 00:00:09, Serial0.1
R        10.1.1.0 [120/1] via 172.31.1.1, 00:00:13, Serial0.1
B        10.97.97.0 [20/0] via 10.254.0.3, 00:00:13
R        10.1.0.0 [120/1] via 172.31.1.2, 00:00:09, Serial0.1
                  [120/1] via 172.31.1.1, 00:00:13, Serial0.1
C        10.254.0.0 is directly connected, Ethernet0
S     192.168.22.0/24 [1/0] via 172.31.2.2
S     192.168.1.0/24 [1/0] via 172.31.1.1
S     192.168.2.0/24 [1/0] via 172.31.2.1
BBR1>
```

**NOTE**   The 10.97.97.0 subnet is a loopback address, configured on the Frame Relay switch router, for use in a later lab.

**Step 2**   Configure the edge routers to announce a summary route of 10.x.0.0 255.255.0.0 to BBR1. Where should you place the appropriate command?

**Solution:**

The following sample configuration is on the P1R1 and P1R2 routers. The summarization commands are placed on the S0 links, the interfaces that connect to the BBR1 router.

```
P1R1(config)#int s0
P1R1(config-if)#ip summary-address rip 10.1.0.0 255.255.0.0

P1R2(config)#int s0
P1R2(config-if)#ip summary-address rip 10.1.0.0 255.255.0.0
```

**Step 3**   Review the routing table on BBR1 again. What is the difference now? Remember that RIP is slow to converge, so you might need to wait up to a minute, even in this small network, before the summaries appear on BBR1.

**Solution:**

The following sample output is from the BBR1 router:

```
BBR1>show ip route
<output omitted>
Gateway of last resort is not set

     172.31.0.0/24 is subnetted, 4 subnets
B       172.31.22.0 [20/0] via 10.254.0.2, 00:00:08
C       172.31.2.0 is directly connected, Serial0.2
C       172.31.1.0 is directly connected, Serial0.1
B       172.31.11.0 [20/0] via 10.254.0.2, 00:00:08
S    192.168.11.0/24 [1/0] via 172.31.1.2
     10.0.0.0/8 is variably subnetted, 3 subnets, 2 masks
B       10.97.97.0/24 [20/0] via 10.254.0.3, 00:00:08
R       10.1.0.0/16 [120/1] via 172.31.1.2, 00:00:08, Serial0.1
                    [120/1] via 172.31.1.1, 00:00:00, Serial0.1
C       10.254.0.0/24 is directly connected, Ethernet0
S    192.168.22.0/24 [1/0] via 172.31.2.2
S    192.168.1.0/24 [1/0] via 172.31.1.1
S    192.168.2.0/24 [1/0] via 172.31.2.1
```

**Step 4**   Examine the output from **show ip protocols** for details about the operation of RIP.

**Solution:**

The following sample output is from the P1R2 router. It shows that RIP version 2 is running for network 10.0.0.0, and autosummarization is off:

```
P1R2#show ip protocols
Routing Protocol is "rip"
  Sending updates every 30 seconds, next due in 16 seconds
  Invalid after 180 seconds, hold down 180, flushed after 240
  Outgoing update filter list for all interfaces is not set
  Incoming update filter list for all interfaces is not set
  Redistributing: rip
  Default version control: send version 2, receive version 2
    Interface          Send  Recv  Triggered RIP  Key-chain
    Ethernet0          2     2
```
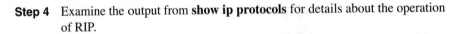

```
    Serial0                   2    2
    Serial1                   2    2
Automatic network summarization is not in effect
Address Summarization:
  10.1.0.0/16 for Serial0
Maximum path: 4
Routing for Networks:
  10.0.0.0
  172.31.0.0
Routing Information Sources:
  Gateway          Distance       Last Update
  10.1.0.1              120       00:00:22
  10.1.2.4              120       00:00:06
  172.31.1.3           120       00:00:08
Distance: (default is 120)
P1R2#
```

## Exercise Verification

You have completed this exercise when you achieve the following results:

- You can set up RIPv2, and you have full network visibility using RIPv2 as a routing protocol.

- You understand RIPv2 support for default routes, VLSM, and route summarization.

- You understand how VLSM contributes to network efficiency.

# Review Questions

Answer the following questions, and then refer to Appendix G, "Answers to Review Questions," for the answers.

**1** Which of the following is not a scenario in which static routes would be used?

  a. When the administrator needs total control over the routes used by the router

  b. When a backup to a dynamically recognized route is necessary

  c. When rapid convergence is needed

  d. When a route should appear to the router as a directly connected network

**2** What are two drawbacks of static routes?

  a. Reconfiguring to reflect topology changes

  b. Complex metrics

  c. Involved convergence

  d. Absence of dynamic route discovery

**3** What is used by traffic for which the destination network is not specifically listed in the routing table?

    a. Dynamic area

    b. Default route

    c. Border getaway

    d. Black hole

**4** The **show ip route** command usually provides information on which of the following two items?

    a. Next hop

    b. Metric

    c. CDP

    d. Host name

**5** When using dynamic routing protocols, what does the administrator configure the routing protocol on?

    a. Each area

    b. Each intermediate system

    c. Each router

    d. Each gateway of last resort

**6** Which of the following is not a dynamic routing protocol?

    a. IS-IS

    b. CDP

    c. EIGRP

    d. BGP

    e. RIPv2

**7** What is a metric?

    a. A standard of measurement used by routing algorithms

    b. The set of techniques used to manage network resources

    c. Interdomain routing in TCP/IP networks

    d. Services limit the input or output transmission rate

**8** Which two routing protocols use only major classful networks to determine the interfaces participating in the protocol?

    a. RIPv2

    b. EIGRP

    c. RIPv1

    d. IS-IS

    e. BGP

    f. OSPF

    g. IGRP

**9** ODR uses what to carry network information between spoke (stub) routers and the hub?

    a. Metric

    b. BGP

    c. Convergence

    d. CDP

**10** Which of the following is not a classification of routing protocols?

    a. Link-state

    b. Default

    c. Hybrid

    d. Distance-vector

**11** What is the default subnet mask of a Class B address?

    a. 255.255.255.255

    b. 255.255.255.0

    c. 255.255.0.0

    d. 255.0.0.0

**12** What do you call the process when the router, using a classful routing protocol, sends an update about a subnet of a classful network across an interface belonging to a different classful network and assumes that the remote router will use the default subnet mask for that class of IP address?

    a. Autosummarization

    b. Default routing

    c. Classful switching

    d. Tunneling

**13** True or false: Discontiguous subnets are subnets of the same major network that are separated by a different major network.

**14** Classless routing protocols allow _____.

    a. QoS

    b. VLSM

    c. VPN

    d. RIP

**15** What is the command to turn off autosummarization?

    a. **no auto-summarization**

    b. **enable classless**

    c. **ip route**

    d. **no auto-summary**

**16** What is the OSPF default administrative distance value?

    a. 90

    b. 100

    c. 110

    d. 120

**17** When a static route's administrative distance is manually configured to be higher than the default administrative distance of dynamic routing protocols, that static route is called what?

    a. Semistatic route

    b. Floating static route

    c. Semidynamic route

    d. Manual route

**18** Which protocols are considered "best-effort"?

    a. RIPv1

    b. QoS

    c. IS-IS

    d. IGRP

    e. EIGRP

**19**  Which variables can be used to calculate metrics?

   a.  Hops

   b.  Convergence time

   c.  Administrative distance

   d.  Path attributes

   e.  Cost

**20**  What is an interval, in seconds, during which routing information about a worse or equivalent metric path is suppressed?

   a.  Invalid timer

   b.  Holddown timer

   c.  Flush timer

   d.  Dead-detection timer

This chapter introduces you to Enhanced Interior Gateway Routing Protocol (EIGRP). This chapter covers the following topics:

- EIGRP Overview
- EIGRP Operation
- Configuring and Verifying EIGRP

# CHAPTER 3

# Configuring Enhanced Interior Gateway Routing Protocol

In present-day and future routing environments, Enhanced Interior Gateway Routing Protocol (EIGRP) offers benefits and features over historic distance vector routing protocols, such as Routing Information Protocol version 1 (RIPv1) and Interior Gateway Routing Protocol (IGRP). These benefits include rapid convergence, lower bandwidth utilization, and multiple-routed protocol support.

This chapter introduces EIGRP terminology and concepts, as well as basic EIGRP configuration and troubleshooting.

After completing this chapter, you will be able to describe EIGRP features, benefits, metric calculation and operation and how EIGRP selects a successor and a feasible successor. You will also be able to configure basic EIGRP and advanced options and verify EIGRP connectivity and operation. You will also be able to implement an effective scalable network with EIGRP.

## EIGRP Overview

EIGRP is a Cisco-proprietary protocol that combines the advantages of link-state and distance vector routing protocols. Features of this hybrid protocol include the following:

- **Rapid convergence**—EIGRP uses the Diffusing Update Algorithm (DUAL) to achieve rapid convergence. A router running EIGRP stores all available backup routes so that it can quickly adapt to changes in the network. If no appropriate route or backup route exists in the local routing table, EIGRP queries its neighbors to discover an alternative route. These queries are propagated until an alternative route is found, or it is determined that no alternative route exists.

- **Reduced bandwidth usage**—EIGRP does not send periodic updates. Instead, it uses partial updates when the path or the metric to a destination changes. When the route information changes, DUAL sends an update about only that link rather than the entire routing table. In addition, the information is passed only to routers that require it, in contrast to link-state protocol operation, which sends a change update to all routers within an area.

- **Multiple network layer support**—EIGRP supports IP, AppleTalk, and Novell NetWare Internetwork Packet Exchange (IPX) using protocol-dependent modules (PDMs) that are responsible for protocol requirements specific to the network layer. EIGRP's rapid convergence and sophisticated metric offer superior performance and stability when implemented in IPX and AppleTalk networks.

- **Seamless connectivity across all data link layer protocols and topologies**—EIGRP does not require special configuration to work across any Layer 2 protocols. Other routing protocols, such as Open Shortest Path First (OSPF), require different configurations for different Layer 2 protocols, such as Ethernet and Frame Relay. EIGRP was designed to operate effectively in both local-area network (LAN) and wide-area network (WAN) environments. In multiaccess topologies, such as Ethernet and Token Ring, neighbor relationships are formed and maintained using reliable multicasting. EIGRP supports all WAN topologies: dedicated links, point-to-point links, and nonbroadcast multiaccess (NBMA) topologies. EIGRP accommodates differences in media types and speeds when neighbor adjacencies form across WAN links and can limit the amount of bandwidth that EIGRP uses on WAN links.

---

**NOTE**    Only the IP implementation of EIGRP is thoroughly covered in this chapter. EIGRP for AppleTalk and IPX is covered in Appendix A, "Job Aids and Supplements."

---

EIGRP has its roots as a distance vector routing protocol. Like its predecessor, IGRP, EIGRP is easy to configure and is adaptable to a wide variety of network topologies. What makes EIGRP an advanced distance vector protocol is its addition of several link-state features, such as dynamic neighbor discovery.

EIGRP is an *enhanced* IGRP because of its rapid convergence and the guarantee of a loop-free topology at all times. IGRP performs periodic updates, which might consume bandwidth unnecessarily. IGRP also performs triggered updates in case of a change in network topology. EIGRP generates only partial routing updates and only upon topology changes. Distribution of these EIGRP partial updates is bounded so that only routers that need the information are updated.

As a classless routing protocol, EIGRP advertises a routing mask for each destination network, enabling support of discontiguous subnetworks and variable-length subnet masking (VLSM), thus promoting efficient allocation of IP addresses. EIGRP supports both hierarchical and nonhierarchical IP addressing. Secondary addresses can be applied to interfaces to solve particular addressing issues, although all routing overhead traffic is generated through the primary interface address.

Like most IP routing protocols, EIGRP relies on IP packets to deliver routing information. (Integrated Intermediate System-to-Intermediate System [IS-IS] is the exception, as you will see in Chapter 6, "Configuring the Intermediate System-to-Intermediate System Protocol.") The EIGRP routing process is a transport layer function of the Open System Interconnection (OSI) reference model. IP packets carrying EIGRP information use protocol number 88 in their IP header, as illustrated in Figure 3-1.

**Figure 3-1**    *EIGRP Is a Transport Layer Function*

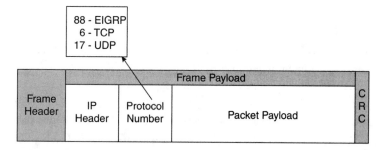

By default, EIGRP performs route summarization at major network boundaries, as shown in Figure 3-2. Administrators can also configure manual summarization on arbitrary bit boundaries (as long as a more-specific route exists in the routing table) to shrink the size of the routing table. EIGRP supports the creation of supernets or aggregated blocks of addresses (networks).

**Figure 3-2**    *EIGRP Performs Route Summarization by Default*

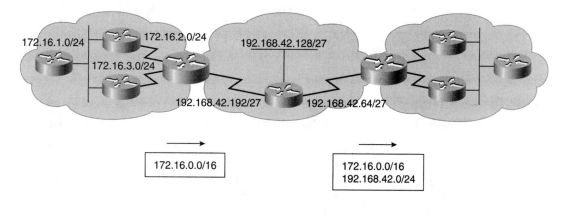

---

**Key Point: EIGRP Features**

In summary, the following are the key features of EIGRP:

- Rapid convergence
- Reduced bandwidth usage
- Support for multiple network-layer protocols
- Support for LANs and WANs
- Advanced distance vector capabilities

- 100 percent loop-free
- Easy configuration
- Incremental updates
- Support for VLSM, discontiguous networks, and classless routing
- Compatibility with IGRP

EIGRP offers many advantages over traditional distance vector routing protocols; one of the most significant is in the area of bandwidth utilization. With EIGRP, operational traffic is multicast and unicast, rather than broadcast. As a result, end stations are unaffected by routing updates or queries.

EIGRP uses the IGRP algorithm for metric calculation, although the value is represented in 32-bit format, providing additional granularity for route selection. The EIGRP metric is the IGRP metric multiplied by 256. A significant advantage of EIGRP (and IGRP) over other protocols is its support for unequal metric load balancing that allows administrators to better distribute traffic flow in their networks.

Some of the EIGRP operational characteristics are borrowed from link-state protocols. For example, EIGRP allows administrators to create summary routes at any bit position within the network (as long as a more-specific route exists in the routing table), rather than allowing only the traditional distance vector approach of performing classful summarization at major network number boundaries. EIGRP also supports route redistribution from other routing protocols.

# EIGRP Terminology

The following terms are related to EIGRP and are used throughout the rest of this chapter:

- **Neighbor table**—Each EIGRP router maintains a neighbor table that lists adjacent routers. This table is comparable to the neighborship (adjacency) database used by link-state routing protocols. It serves the same purpose—ensuring bidirectional communication between each of the directly connected neighbors. EIGRP keeps a neighbor table for each network protocol supported, such as an IP neighbor table, an IPX neighbor table, and an AppleTalk neighbor table.

- **Topology table**—An EIGRP router maintains a topology table for each network protocol configured: IP, IPX, and AppleTalk. All learned routes to a destination are maintained in the topology table.

- **Routing table**—EIGRP chooses the best routes to a destination from the topology table and places these routes in the routing table. The router maintains one routing table for each network protocol configured.

- **Successor**—This is the neighbor that provides the primary route used to reach a destination. Successor routes are kept in the routing table.

- **Feasible successor (FS)**—This is a neighbor that is downstream from the destination, but it is not the least-cost path and, thus, is not used to forward data. In other words, this is the neighbor that provides a backup route to the destination. These feasible successor routes are selected at the same time as successors but are kept in the topology table. The topology table can maintain multiple feasible successors for a destination.

EIGRP routers use the following procedure to populate their IP topology and routing tables, as shown in Figure 3-3:

**Step 1**    Each router forwards a copy of its IP routing table to all its adjacent EIGRP neighbors, as specified in its EIGRP neighbor table.

**Step 2**    Each router stores the routing tables of the adjacent neighbors in its EIGRP topology table (database).

**Step 3**    Each router examines its EIGRP topology database and determines the best route and other feasible routes to every destination network.

**Step 4**    The best route (the successor route) to each destination is selected from the topology table and is put into the routing table.

**Figure 3-3**    *EIGRP Maintains a Neighbor Table, a Topology Table, and a Routing Table*

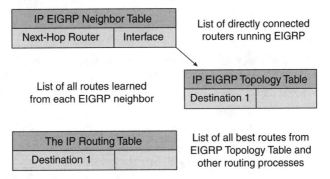

## EIGRP Operation

EIGRP sends out five different types of packets. They are used to establish the initial adjacency between neighbors and to keep the topology and routing tables up-to-date. When troubleshooting an EIGRP network it is important for network administrators to understand what EIGRP packets are used for and how they are exchanged. For example, if routers running EIGRP do not form neighbor relationships, those routers do not exchange EIGRP updates with each other. Without EIGRP routing updates, users cannot connect to services across the internetwork.

EIGRP packets and mechanisms are explained in this section, along with initial route discovery, route selection, and how the DUAL algorithm functions.

# EIGRP Packets

EIGRP uses the following five types of packets:

- **Hello**—Hello packets are used for neighbor discovery. They are sent as multicasts and carry an acknowledgment number of 0.

- **Update**—An update is sent to communicate the routes that a particular router has used to converge; an update is sent only to affected routers. These updates are sent as multicasts when a new route is discovered and when convergence is completed (when the route becomes passive). To synchronize topology tables, updates are sent as unicasts to neighbors during their EIGRP startup sequence. Updates are sent reliably.

- **Query**—When a router is performing route computation and does not find a feasible successor, it sends a query packet to its neighbors, asking if they have a feasible successor to the destination. Queries are always multicast and are sent reliably.

- **Reply**—A reply packet is sent in response to a query packet. Replies are unicast to the originator of the query and are sent reliably.

- **Acknowledge (ACK)**—The ACK is used to acknowledge updates, queries, and replies. ACKs are hello packets sent as unicasts. They contain a nonzero acknowledgment number. (Note that hello and ACK packets do not require acknowledgment.)

## EIGRP Hello Packets

The router sends hello packets out of interfaces configured for EIGRP. The EIGRP multicast address used is 224.0.0.10. When an EIGRP router receives a hello packet from a router belonging to the same autonomous system (AS), it establishes a neighbor relationship (adjacency).

---

**Key Point: Hello Packets**

By default, hello packets are sent every 60 seconds on T1 or slower multipoint interfaces and every 5 seconds on LANs and other serial interfaces.

---

The time interval of hello packets varies depending on the medium. Hello packets are released every 5 seconds on a LAN link such as Ethernet, Token Ring, and FDDI. The default interval is also set to 5 seconds for point-to-point links such as PPP, High-Level Data Link Control (HDLC), point-to-point Frame Relay, and ATM subinterfaces, and for multipoint circuits with bandwidth greater than T1, including ISDN PRI, Switched Multimegabit Data Service (SMDS), ATM, and Frame Relay. Hello packets are sent out less frequently on lower-speed links, such as multipoint circuits with a bandwidth less than or equal to T1, including ISDN BRI, Frame Relay, SMDS, ATM, and X.25. Hellos are generated at 60-second intervals on these types of interfaces.

Through the hello protocol, an EIGRP router dynamically discovers other EIGRP routers directly connected to it. Information learned about neighbors, such as the address and interface they use, is maintained in the neighbor table. The rate at which hello packets are sent, called the hello interval, can be adjusted per interface with the **ip eigrp hello-interval** *as-number seconds* interface configuration command.

The neighbor table also maintains the hold time.

---

### Key Point: Hold Time

The hold time is the amount of time a router considers a neighbor up without receiving a hello or some other EIGRP packet from that neighbor. Hello packets report the hold-time value.

---

The hold-time interval is set by default to 3 times the hello interval. Therefore, the default hold-time value is 15 seconds on LAN and fast WAN interfaces and 180 seconds on slower WAN interfaces. The hold time can also be adjusted with the **ip eigrp hold-time** *as-number seconds* interface configuration command.

**NOTE**    The hold time is not automatically adjusted after a hello interval change. If you change the hello interval, you must manually adjust the hold time to reflect the configured hello interval.

---

If a packet is not received before the expiration of the hold time, the neighbor adjacency is deleted, and all topology table entries learned from that neighbor are removed, as if the neighbor had sent an update stating that all the routes are unreachable. If the neighbor is a successor for any destination networks, those networks are removed from the routing table, and alternative paths, if available, are computed. This lets the routes quickly reconverge if an alternative feasible route is available.

---

### Key Point: Passive Versus Active Routes

A route is considered *passive* when the router is not performing recomputation on that route. A route is *active* when it is undergoing recomputation (in other words, when it is looking for a new successor).

Note that *passive* is the operational state.

---

## EIGRP Neighbors

It is possible for two routers to become EIGRP neighbors even though the hello and hold time values do not match; this means that the hello interval and hold-time values can be set independently on different routers.

EIGRP will not build peer relationships over secondary addresses, because all EIGRP traffic uses the interface's primary address. To form an EIGRP adjacency, all neighbors use their primary address as the source IP address of their EIGRP packets. Adjacency between EIGRP routers takes place if the primary address of each neighbor is part of the same IP subnet. In addition, peer relationships are not formed if the neighbor resides in a different autonomous system or if the metric-calculation mechanism constants (the K values) are misaligned on that link. (K values are discussed in the "EIGRP Metric Calculation" section.)

## Neighbor Table

EIGRP (like OSPF) routers multicast hello packets to discover neighbors and exchange route updates. Only adjacent routers exchange routing information. Each router builds a neighbor table from hello packets it receives from adjacent EIGRP routers running the same network layer protocol. The IP neighbor table can be displayed with the **show ip eigrp neighbors** command, as shown in Example 3-1.

**Example 3-1** *Sample Output for the* **show ip eigrp neighbors** *Command*

```
p2r2#show ip eigrp neighbors
IP-EIGRP neighbors for process 400
H Address         Interface  Hold Uptime   SRTT  RTO Q  Seq
                             (sec)         (ms)      Cnt Num
1 172.68.2.2      To0        13 02:15:30    8    200 0  9
0 172.68.16.2     Se1        10 02:38:29   29    200 0  6
```

EIGRP maintains a neighbor table for each configured network-layer protocol. This table includes the following key elements:

- **H (handle)**—A number used internally by the Cisco IOS to track a neighbor.
- **Neighbor address**—The neighbor's network-layer address.
- **Interface**—The interface on this router through which the neighbor can be reached.
- **Hold Time**—The maximum time, in seconds, that the router waits to hear from the neighbor without receiving anything from a neighbor before considering the link unavailable. Originally, the expected packet was a hello packet, but in current Cisco IOS software releases, any EIGRP packets received after the first hello from that neighbor resets the timer.
- **Uptime**—The elapsed time, in hours, minutes, and seconds since the local router first heard from this neighbor.
- **Smooth Round Trip Timer (SRTT)**—The average number of milliseconds it takes for an EIGRP packet to be sent to this neighbor and for the local router to receive an acknowledgment of that packet. This timer is used to determine the retransmit interval, also known as the retransmit timeout (RTO).
- **RTO**—The amount of time, in milliseconds, that the router waits for an acknowledgment before retransmitting a reliable packet from the retransmission queue to a neighbor.

- **Queue count**—The number of packets waiting in the queue to be sent out. If this value is constantly higher than 0, a congestion problem might exist. A 0 indicates that no EIGRP packets are in the queue.

- **Seq Num**—The sequence number of the last update, query, or reply packet that was received from this neighbor.

## EIGRP Reliability

EIGRP's reliability mechanism ensures delivery of critical route information to neighboring routers. This information is required to allow EIGRP to maintain a loop-free topology. For efficiency, only certain EIGRP packets are transmitted reliably.

---

### Key Point: Reliable Packets

All packets carrying routing information (update, query, and reply) are sent reliably, which means that a sequence number is assigned to each reliable packet and an explicit acknowledgment is required for that sequence number.

---

Reliable Transport Protocol (RTP) is responsible for guaranteed, ordered delivery of EIGRP packets to all neighbors. It supports intermixed transmission of multicast and unicast packets. For example, on a multiaccess network that has multicast capabilities, such as Ethernet, it is not necessary to send hello packets to all neighbors individually, so EIGRP sends a single multicast hello packet containing an indicator that informs the receivers that the packet need not be acknowledged. Other types of packets, such as updates, indicate in the packet that acknowledgment is required. All packets that carry routing information (update, query, and reply) are sent reliably, because they are not sent periodically. Each packet that is sent reliably has an assigned sequence number and requires an explicit acknowledgment.

RTP ensures that ongoing communication is maintained between neighboring routers. As such, a retransmission list is maintained for each neighbor. This list indicates packets not yet acknowledged by a neighbor within the RTO. It is used to track all the reliable packets that were sent but not acknowledged.

---

### Key Point: RTO Timer

If the RTO expires before an ACK packet is received, the EIGRP process transmits another copy of the reliable packet, up to a maximum of 16 times or until the hold time expires.

---

The use of reliable multicast packets is efficient. However, a potential delay exists on multiaccess media where multiple neighbors reside. The next reliable multicast packet cannot be transmitted until all peers have acknowledged the previous multicast. If one or more peers are slow to respond, this adversely affects all peers by delaying the next transmission. RTP is designed to handle such exceptions: Neighbors that are slow to respond to multicasts have the unacknowledged multicast packets retransmitted as unicasts. This allows the reliable multicast operation to proceed without delaying communication with other peers, helping to ensure that convergence time remains low in the presence of variable-speed links.

The multicast flow timer determines how long to wait for an ACK packet before switching from multicast to unicast. The RTO determines how long to wait between the subsequent unicasts. The EIGRP process for each neighbor calculates both the multicast flow timer and RTO, based on the SRTT. The formulas for the SRTT, RTO, and multicast flow timer are Cisco-proprietary.

In a steady-state network where no routes are flapping, EIGRP waits the specified hold-time interval before it determines that an EIGRP neighbor adjacency is down. By default, EIGRP waits up to 15 seconds on high-speed links and up to 180 seconds on low-speed, multipoint links. When EIGRP determines that a neighbor is down and the router cannot reestablish the adjacency, the routing table removes all networks that could be reached through that neighbor. The router attempts to find alternative routes to those networks so that convergence can occur.

The 180-second hold timer on low-speed links can seem excessive, but it accommodates the slowest-speed multipoint links, which are generally connected to less-critical remote sites. In some networks with mission-critical, time-sensitive applications, even on high-speed links, 15 seconds is too long. The point to remember is that other conditions can override the hold timer and allow the network to converge quickly.

For example, if the network is unstable and routes are flapping elsewhere because a remote site is timing out on its adjacency, EIGRP hold timers begin counting down from 180 seconds. When the upstream site sends the remote site an update, and the remote site does not acknowledge the update, the upstream site attempts 16 times to retransmit the update. The retransmission occurs each time the RTO expires. After 16 retries, the router resets the neighbor relationship. This causes the network to converge faster than waiting for the hold time to expire.

RTO is a dynamic timer that adjusts over time. It is based on the SRTT, which specifies how many milliseconds it takes a neighbor to respond to an EIGRP acknowledgment. As more unacknowledged updates are sent, the SRTT gets higher and higher, which causes the RTO to increase exponentially.

## Topology Table

When the router dynamically discovers a new neighbor, it sends an update about the routes it knows to its new neighbor and receives the same from the new neighbor. These updates populate the topology table. The topology table contains all destinations advertised by neighboring routers. The **show ip eigrp topology all-links** command displays all the IP entries in the topology table. The **show ip eigrp topology** command displays only the successor(s) and feasible successor(s) for IP routes. It is important to note that if a neighbor is advertising a destination, it must be using that route to forward packets. This rule must be strictly followed by all distance vector protocols.

The topology table also maintains the metric that the neighbors advertise for each destination and the metric that this router uses to reach the destination. The metric used by this router is the cost of this router to reach the best neighbor for this destination, plus the best neighbor's metric to reach the destination.

The topology table is updated when a directly connected route or interface changes, or when a neighboring router reports a change to a route.

## Initial Route Discovery

EIGRP combines the process of discovering neighbors and learning routes. Figure 3-4 illustrates the initial route discovery process.

**Figure 3-4**  *Initial Route Discovery*

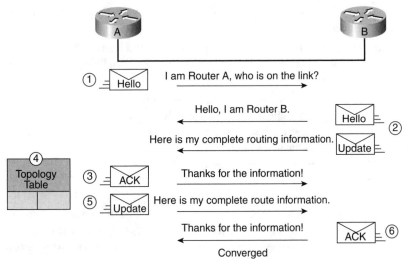

The following describes the initial route discovery process:

1.  A new router (Router A) comes up on the link and sends out a hello packet through all of its interfaces.

2.  Routers receiving the hello packet on one interface (Router B in Figure 3-4) reply with update packets that contain all the routes they have in their routing table, except those learned through that interface (split horizon). Router B sends an update packet to Router A, but a neighbor relationship is not established until Router B sends a hello packet to Router A. The update packet from Router B has the initial bit set, indicating that this is the initialization process. The update packet contains information about the routes that a neighbor is aware of, including the metric that the neighbor is advertising for each destination.

3.  After both routers have exchanged hellos, and the neighbor adjacency is established, Router A replies to each neighbor with an ACK packet, indicating that it received the update information.

4   Router A inserts update packet information in its topology table. The topology table includes all destinations advertised by neighboring (adjacent) routers. It is organized so that each destination is listed, along with all the neighbors that can get to the destination and their associated metrics.

5   Router A exchanges update packets with each of its neighbors.

6   Upon receiving the update packets, each router sends an ACK packet to Router A. When all updates are received, the router is ready to choose the primary and backup routes to keep in the topology table.

---

### Split Horizon

Split horizon controls the sending of IP EIGRP update and query packets. When split horizon is enabled on an interface, these packets are not sent for destinations for which this interface is the next hop. This reduces the possibility of routing loops. By default, split horizon is enabled on all interfaces.

Split horizon blocks information about routes from being advertised by a router out of any interface from which that information originated. This behavior usually optimizes communications among multiple routers, particularly when links are broken.

When a router changes its topology table in such a way that the interface through which the router reaches a network changes, it turns off split horizon and poison reverses the old route out of all interfaces (indicating that the route is unreachable). This ensures that other routers will not try to use the now invalid route.

---

## Route Selection

The EIGRP route selection process is perhaps what most distinguishes it from other routing protocols. EIGRP selects primary (successor) and backup (feasible successor) routes and injects those into the topology table (up to six per destination). The primary (successor) routes are then moved to the routing table.

EIGRP supports several types of routes: internal, external, and summary. Internal routes originate within the EIGRP AS. External routes are learned from another routing protocol or another EIGRP AS. Summary routes are routes encompassing multiple subnets.

EIGRP uses DUAL to calculate the best route to a destination. DUAL selects routes based on the composite metric and ensures that the selected routes are loop-free. DUAL also calculates backup routes (feasible successor routes) to a destination that are loop-free. If the best route fails, EIGRP immediately uses a backup route without any need for holddown, because the backup route is loop-free; this results in fast convergence.

### EIGRP Metric Calculation

The EIGRP metric calculation can use five variables, but EIGRP uses only two by default:

*   **Bandwidth**—Smallest bandwidth between the source and destination.

*   **Delay**—Cumulative interface delay along the path.

The following criteria, although available, are not commonly used, because they typically result in frequent recalculation of the topology table:

- **Reliability**—Worst reliability between the source and destination based on keepalives.

- **Loading**—Worst load on a link between the source and destination based on the packet rate and the interface's configured bandwidth.

- **Maximum transmission unit (MTU)**—Smallest MTU in the path. (MTU is included in the EIGRP update but is not used in the metric calculation.)

EIGRP calculates the metric by adding together weighted values of different variables of the link to the network in question. The default constant weight values are K1 = K3 = 1, and K2 = K4 = K5 = 0, where weights are attributed to the variables as follows: K1 = bandwidth, K2 = load, K3 = delay, K4 = reliability, and K5 = MTU.

In EIGRP metric calculations, when K5 is 0 (the default), variables (bandwidth, bandwidth divided by load, and delay) are weighted with the constants K1, K2, and K3. The following is the formula used:

metric = (K1 * bandwidth) + [(K2 * bandwidth) / (256 − load)] + (K3 * delay)

If these K values are equal to their defaults, the formula becomes

metric = (1 * bandwidth) + [(0 * bandwidth) / (256 − load)] + (1 * delay)
metric = bandwidth + [0] + delay
metric = bandwidth + delay

If K5 is not equal to 0, the following additional operation is performed:

metric = metric * [K5 / (reliability + K4)]

K values are carried in EIGRP hello packets. Mismatched K values can cause a neighbor to be reset. (Only K1 and K3 are used, by default, in metric compilation.) These K values should be modified only after careful planning; changing these values can prevent your network from converging and is generally not recommended.

---

**Key Point: Delay and Bandwidth Values**

The format of the delay and bandwidth values is different from those displayed by the **show interfaces** command. The EIGRP delay value is the sum of the delays in the path, in tens of microseconds, multiplied by 256. The **show interfaces** command displays delay in microseconds.

The bandwidth is calculated using the minimum bandwidth link along the path, represented in kilobits per second (kbps). Divide $10^7$ by this value, and then multiply the result by 256.

---

EIGRP represents its metrics in a 32-bit format instead of the 24-bit representation used by IGRP. This representation allows a more granular decision to be made when determining the successor and feasible successor. Present-day bandwidth ranges from 9600 to 9,984,000,000 bits per second (almost 10 gigabits [Gb]); the EIGRP 32-bit metric accommodates this range better than the IGRP 24-bit number.

The EIGRP metric value ranges from 1 to 4,294,967,296. The IGRP metric value ranges from 1 to 16,777,216. When integrating IGRP routes into an EIGRP domain using redistribution, the router multiplies the IGRP metric by 256 to compute the EIGRP-equivalent metric. When sending EIGRP routes to an IGRP routing domain, the router divides each EIGRP metric by 256 to achieve the proper 24-bit metric.

## EIGRP Metric Calculation Example

In Figure 3-5, Router A has two paths to reach the networks behind Router D. The bandwidths (in kbps) and the delays (in tens of microseconds) of the various links are also shown.

**Figure 3-5**    *EIGRP Metric Calculation Example*

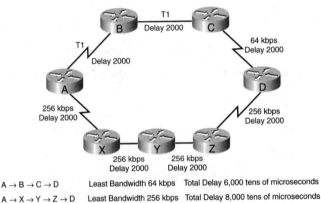

A → B → C → D       Least Bandwidth 64 kbps    Total Delay 6,000 tens of microseconds
A → X → Y → Z → D   Least Bandwidth 256 kbps   Total Delay 8,000 tens of microseconds

The least bandwidth along the top path (A → B → C → D) is 64 kbps. The EIGRP bandwidth calculation for this path is as follows:

bandwidth = $(10^7$ / least bandwidth in kbps) * 256
bandwidth = (10,000,000 / 64) * 256 = 156,250 * 256 = 40,000,000

The delay through the top path is as follows:

delay = [(delay A → B) + (delay B → C) + (delay C → D)] * 256
delay = [2000 + 2000 + 2000] * 256
delay = 1,536,000

Therefore, the EIGRP metric calculation for the top path is as follows:

metric = bandwidth + delay
metric = 40,000,000 + 1,536,000
metric = 41,536,000

The least bandwidth along the lower path (A → X → Y → Z → D) is 256 kbps. The EIGRP bandwidth calculation for this path is as follows:

bandwidth = $(10^7$ / least bandwidth in kbps) * 256
bandwidth = (10,000,000 / 256) * 256 = 10,000,000

The delay through the lower path is as follows:

delay = [(delay A → X) + (delay X → Y) + (delay Y → Z) + (delay Z → D)] * 256
delay = [2000 + 2000 + 2000 + 2000] * 256
delay = 2,048,000

Therefore, the EIGRP metric calculation for the lower path is as follows:

metric = bandwidth + delay
metric = 10,000,000 + 2,048,000
metric = 12,048,000

Router A therefore chooses the lower path, with a metric of 12,048,000, over the top path, with a metric of 41,536,000. Router A installs the lower path with a next-hop router of X and a metric of 12,048,000 in the IP routing table.

The bottleneck along the top path, the 64-kbps link, can explain why the router takes the lower path. This slow link means that the rate of transfer to Router D would be at a maximum of 64 kbps. Along the lower path, the lowest speed is 256 kbps, making the throughput rate up to that speed. Therefore, the lower path represents a better choice, such as to move large files quickly.

# Routing Table and EIGRP DUAL

DUAL is the finite-state machine that selects which information is stored in the topology and routing tables. As such, DUAL embodies the decision process for all EIGRP route computations. It tracks all routes advertised by all neighbors; uses the metric to select an efficient, loop-free path to each destination; and inserts that choice in the routing table.

## Advertised Distance and Feasible Distance

To determine the successor (the best route) and the feasible successor (the backup route) to a destination, EIGRP uses the advertised distance (AD) and the feasible distance (FD).

---

**Key Point: Advertised Distance Versus Feasible Distance**

The AD is the EIGRP metric for an EIGRP *neighbor router* to reach a particular network. This is the metric between the next-hop neighbor router and the destination network.

The FD is the EIGRP metric for *this router* to reach a particular network. This is the sum of the AD for the particular network learned from an EIGRP neighbor, plus the EIGRP metric to reach that neighbor.

---

A router compares all FDs to reach a specific network in its topology table. The route with the lowest FD is placed in its IP routing table; this is the successor route. The FD for the chosen route becomes the EIGRP routing metric to reach that network in the routing table.

For example, in Figure 3-6, Routers A and B send their routing tables to Router C, whose tables are shown in the figure. Both Routers A and B have paths to network 10.1.1.0/24 (among many others that are not shown).

**Figure 3-6**    *EIGRP Chooses the Route with the Lowest Feasible Distance*

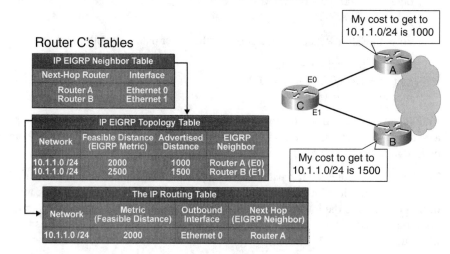

The routing table on Router A has an EIGRP metric of 1000 for 10.1.1.0/24. Router A advertises 10.1.1.0/24 to Router C with a metric of 1000. Router C installs 10.1.1.0/24 from Router A in its EIGRP topology table with an AD of 1000. Router B has network 10.1.1.0/24 with a metric of 1500 in its IP routing table. Router B advertises 10.1.1.0/24 to Router C with an AD of 1500. Router C places the 10.1.1.0/24 network from Router B in the EIGRP topology table with an AD of 1500.

Router C in Figure 3-6 has two entries to reach 10.1.1.0/24 in its topology table. The EIGRP metric for Router C to reach either Router A or B is 1000. This cost (1000) is added to the respective AD from each router, and the results represent the FDs that Router C must travel to reach network 10.1.1.0/24. Router C chooses the least-cost FD (2000) and installs it in its IP routing table as the best route to reach 10.1.1.0/24. The EIGRP metric in the routing table is the best FD from the EIGRP topology table.

## Successor and Feasible Successor

**Key Point: Successor**

A successor is a neighboring router used for packet forwarding that has a least-cost path to a destination that is guaranteed not to be part of a routing loop.

A router is chosen as a successor because it has the lowest FD of all possible paths to that destination network. The successor is the next router in line to reach that destination. In other words, it is the router with the best path to reach that destination network.

An EIGRP router selects the best path to reach a given network and then installs the destination network, the metric to reach that network, the outbound interface to reach the next-hop router, and the IP address of the next-hop router into the IP routing table. If the EIGRP topology table has many entries that have an equal-cost FD to a given destination network, all successors (up to four by default) for that destination network are installed in the routing table. Note that it is the FD, not the AD, that affects the selection of the best routes for incorporation in the routing table; the AD is used only to calculate the FD.

All routing protocols can install only the next-hop router information in the routing table; information about the subsequent routers in the path is not put in the routing table. Each router counts on the next-hop router to make a reliable decision to reach a specific destination network. The hop-by-hop path through a network goes from one router to the next. Each router makes a path selection to reach a given network and installs the best next-hop address along the path to reach that destination network. A router trusts a route's successor (the best next-hop router) to send traffic toward that destination address.

The routing table is essentially a subset of the topology table; the topology table contains more detailed information about each route, backup routes, and information used exclusively by DUAL.

---

### Key Point: Feasible Successor

A feasible successor (FS) is a router providing a backup route. The route through the feasible successor must be loop-free; in other words, it must not loop back to the current successor.

---

FSs are selected at the same time the successors are identified. These FS routes are kept in the topology table; the topology table can retain multiple FS routes for a destination.

---

### Key Point: Feasible Successor Requirements

An FS must be mathematically proven. To qualify as an FS, a next-hop router must have an AD less than the FD of the current successor route for the particular network.

---

This requirement ensures that the FS cannot use a route through the local router (which would be a routing loop), because the AD through the FS is less than the best route through the local router. More than one feasible successor can be kept at a time in the EIGRP topology table. For example, in Figure 3-7, Router B is an FS, because the AD through Router B (1500) is less than the FD of the current successor, Router A (2000).

**Figure 3-7**    *Feasible Successor's AD Must Be Less Than the Successor's FD*

| EIGRP Topology Table | | | |
|---|---|---|---|
| Network | FD (EIGRP Metric) | AD | EIGRP Neighbor |
| 10.1.1.0/24 | 2000-Successor | 1000 | Router A (E0) |
| 10.1.1.0/24 | 2500 | 1500 | Router B (E1) |
|  |  | Feasible Successor |  |

When a router loses a route, it looks at the topology table for an FS. If one is available, the route does not go into an active state; rather, the best FS is promoted as the successor and is installed in the routing table. The FS can be used immediately, without any recalculation. If there are no FSs, a route goes into active state, and route computation occurs. Through this process, a new successor is determined. The amount of time it takes to recalculate the route affects the convergence time.

Figure 3-8 illustrates another example. Router C's initial topology table is shown at the top of the figure. Router B is the successor for network 10.1.1.0/24, and Router D is the FS.

**Figure 3-8**    *With a Feasible Successor, EIGRP Can Recover Immediately from Network Failures*

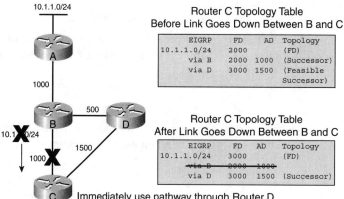

In Figure 3-8, the link between Router B and Router C fails. Router C removes the route 10.1.1.0/24 through Router B from its routing table and searches the EIGRP topology table for an FS; Router D is an FS. Because Router D can still reach the network and does not send an update or query packet to inform Router C of the lost route, Router C immediately uses the path through Router D. Router C chooses this path because the AD through router D (1500) is less than the FD of the best route, through Router B (2000); this path is guaranteed to be loop-free.

## DUAL Example

The mathematical formula to ensure that the FS is loop-free requires that the AD of the backup route be *less than* the FD of the successor. When the AD of the second-best route is greater than or equal to the FD of the successor, an FS cannot be chosen. In this case, a discovery process that uses EIGRP queries and replies must be used to find any alternative paths to the lost networks.

The following example examines partial entries for network 10.1.1.0/24 of the topology tables for Routers C, D, and E in Figure 3-9 to give you a better understanding of EIGRP behavior. The partial topology tables shown in Figure 3-9 indicate the following:

- **FD**—The feasible distance is equal to the sum of the costs of the links to reach network 10.1.1.0/24.

- **AD**—The advertised distance is equal to the link cost of the path to network 10.1.1.0/24 as advertised by neighboring routers.

- **Successor**—The forwarding path used to reach network 10.1.1.0/24. The cost of this path is equal to the FD.

- **FS**—The feasible successor is an alternative loop-free path to reach network 10.1.1.0/24.

**Figure 3-9**  *DUAL Example, Step 1*

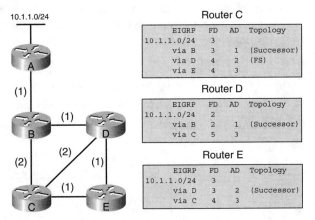

The network shown in Figure 3-9 is stable and converged.

---

**NOTE**  As mentioned earlier, EIGRP implements split horizon. For example, Router E does not pass its route for network 10.1.1.0/24 to Router D, because Router E uses Router D as its next hop to network 10.1.1.0/24.

---

In Figure 3-10, Routers B and D detect a link failure. After being notified of the link failure, DUAL does the following, as shown in Figure 3-10:

- At Router D, it marks the path to network 10.1.1.0/24 through Router B as unusable.

**Figure 3-10** *DUAL Example, Step 2*

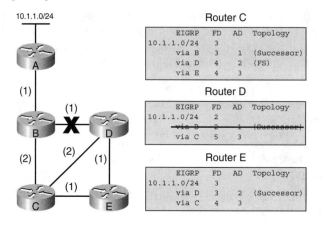

The following steps then occur, as shown in Figure 3-11:

- At Router D, there is no FS to network 10.1.1.0/24, because the AD via Router C (3) is greater than the FD via Router B (2). Therefore, DUAL does the following:
  - Sets the metric to network 10.1.1.0/24 as unreachable (–1 is unreachable).
  - Because an FS cannot be found in the topology table, the route changes from the passive state to the active state. In the active state, the router sends out queries to neighboring routers looking for a new successor.
  - Sends a query to Routers C and E for an alternative path to network 10.1.1.0/24.
  - Marks Routers C and E as having a query pending (q).
- At Router E, DUAL marks the path to network 10.1.1.0/24 through Router D as unusable.
- At Router C, DUAL marks the path to network 10.1.1.0/24 through Router D as unusable.

**Figure 3-11** *DUAL Example, Step 3*

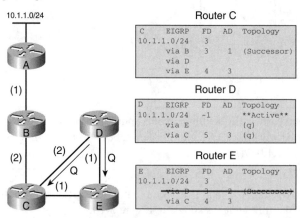

The following steps then occur, as shown in Figure 3-12:

- At Router D:

    — DUAL receives a reply from Router C that indicates no change to the path to network 10.1.1.0/24.

    — DUAL removes the query flag from Router C.

    — DUAL stays active on network 10.1.1.0/24, awaiting a reply from Router E to its query (q).

- At Router E, there is no FS to network 10.1.1.0/24, because the AD from Router C (3) is not less than the original FD (also 3).

    — DUAL generates a query (q) to Router C.

    — DUAL marks Router C as query pending (q).

- At Router C, DUAL marks the path to network 10.1.1.0/24 through Router E as unusable.

**Figure 3-12**  *DUAL Example, Step 4*

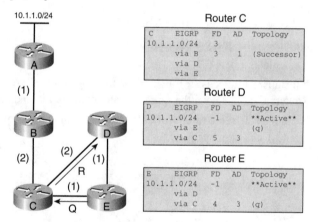

The following steps then occur, as shown in Figure 3-13:

- At Router D, DUAL stays active on network 10.1.1.0/24, awaiting a reply from Router E (q).

- At Router E:

    — DUAL receives a reply from Router C indicating no change.

    — It removes the query flag from Router C.

    — It calculates a new FD and installs a new successor route in the topology table.

    — It changes the route to network 10.1.1.0/24 from active to passive (converged).

**Figure 3-13** *DUAL Example, Step 5*

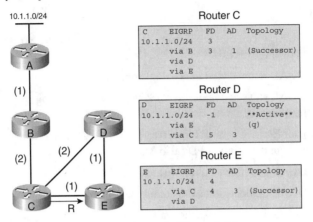

The following steps then occur, as shown in Figure 3-14:

- At Router D:
  - DUAL receives a reply from Router E.
  - It removes the query flag from Router E.
  - It calculates a new FD.
  - It installs new successor routes in the topology table. Two routes (through Routers C and E) have the same FD, and both are marked as successors.
  - It changes the route to network 10.1.1.0/24 from active to passive (converged).

**Figure 3-14** *DUAL Example, Step 6*

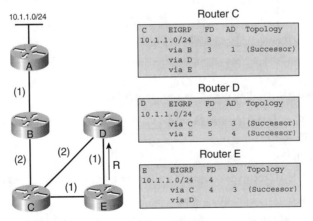

The following steps then occur, as shown in Figure 3-15:

- At Router D, two successor routes are in the topology table for network 10.1.1.0/24. Both successor routes are listed in the routing table, and equal-cost load balancing should be in effect.
- The network is stable and converged.

**Figure 3-15**  *DUAL Example, Step 7*

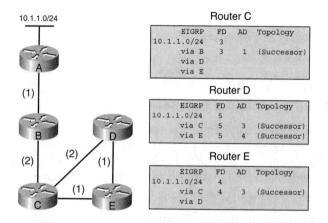

Figure 3-9, the original topology before the link failure, shows traffic from Router E passing through Routers D and B. In Figure 3-15, the new topology shows traffic from Routers D and E going through Routers C and B. Notice that throughout the entire convergence process, routes to network 10.1.1.0/24 become active only on Routers D and E. The route to network 10.1.1.0/24 on Router C remains passive because the link failure between Routers B and D does not affect the successor route from Router C to network 10.1.1.0/24.

**NOTE**    When DUAL decides that a packet needs to be transmitted to a neighbor, the packets are not actually generated until the moment of transmission. Instead, the transmit queues contain small, fixed-size structures that indicate which parts of the topology table to include in the packet when it is finally transmitted. This means that the queues do not consume large amounts of memory. It also means that only the latest information is transmitted in each packet. If a route changes state several times, only the last state is transmitted in the packet, thus reducing link utilization.

# Configuring and Verifying EIGRP

This section covers the commands used to configure EIGRP features. The following topics are discussed:

- Basic EIGRP configuration
- Configuring EIGRP default routes
- Route summarization
- EIGRP load balancing

- EIGRP and WAN links
- Using EIGRP in a scalable internetwork
- Verifying EIGRP operation

# Basic EIGRP Configuration

Follow these steps to configure basic EIGRP for IP:

**Step 1**    Enable EIGRP, and define the autonomous system using the **router eigrp**
*autonomous-system-number* global configuration command. In this command,
the *autonomous-system-number* identifies the autonomous system and is
used to indicate all routers that belong within the internetwork. This value
must match on all routers within the internetwork.

**Step 2**    Indicate which networks are part of the EIGRP autonomous system using the
**network** *network-number* [*wildcard-mask*] router configuration command.
Table 3-1 summarizes this command.

**Table 3-1**    **network** *Command*

| network Command | Description |
| --- | --- |
| *network-number* | This parameter can be the network address, the subnet, or the address of an interface. It determines which links on the router to advertise to, which links to listen to advertisements on, and which networks are advertised. |
| *wildcard-mask* | (Optional) An inverse mask used to determine how to interpret the network number. The mask has wildcard bits, where 0 is a match and 1 is don't care. For example, 0.0.255.255 indicates a match in the first 2 bytes. |

If you do not use the optional wildcard mask, the EIGRP process assumes
that all directly connected networks that are part of the major network will
participate in the EIGRP routing process, and EIGRP will attempt to establish
EIGRP neighbor relationships from each interface that is part of the overall
Class A, B, or C network.

Use the optional wildcard mask to identify a specific IP address, subnet, or
network. The router interprets the network number using the wildcard mask
to determine which connected networks will participate in the EIGRP routing
process. If you're specifying the interface address, use the mask 0.0.0.0 to
match all 4 bytes of the address. An address and wildcard mask combination
of 0.0.0.0 255.255.255.255 matches all interfaces on the router.

**Step 3**   If you're using serial links, especially for Frame Relay or SMDS, define the link's bandwidth for the purposes of sending routing update traffic on the link. If you do not change the bandwidth value for these interfaces, EIGRP assumes that the bandwidth on the link is of T1 speed. If the link is slower, the router might not be able to converge, or routing updates might become lost. (The later section "EIGRP and WAN Links" provides more details on why this is so.) To define the bandwidth, use the **bandwidth** *kilobits* interface configuration command. In this command, *kilobits* indicates the intended bandwidth in kbps.

For serial interfaces such as PPP and HDLC, set the bandwidth to match the line speed. For Frame Relay point-to-point interfaces, set the bandwidth to the committed information rate (CIR). For Frame Relay multipoint connections, set the bandwidth to the sum of all CIRs. If the permanent virtual circuits (PVCs) have different CIRs, set the bandwidth to the lowest CIR multiplied by the number of PVCs for the multipoint connection.

## Basic EIGRP Configuration Example

Figure 3-16 shows a sample network, including the configuration of Router A for EIGRP. All routers in the figure are part of AS 109. (For EIGRP to establish a neighbor relationship, all neighbors must be in the same autonomous system.)

**Figure 3-16**   *Basic EIGRP Configuration Sample Network*

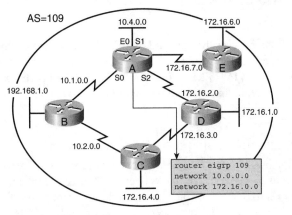

Because the wildcard mask is not used in Router A's configuration, all interfaces on Router A that are part of network 10.0.0.0/8 and network 172.16.0.0/16 participate in the EIGRP routing process. In this case, this includes all four interfaces. Note that network 192.168.1.0 is not configured in the EIGRP configuration on Router A, because Router A does not have any interfaces in that network.

Instead, suppose that the configuration in Example 3-2 were entered onto Router A.

**Example 3-2** *Alternative Configuration of Router A in Figure 3-16*

```
routerA(config)#router eigrp 109
routerA(config-router)#network 10.1.0.0
routerA(config-router)#network 10.4.0.0
routerA(config-router)#network 172.16.7.0
routerA(config-router)#network 172.16.2.0
```

Router A would automatically summarize the network commands to classful networks, and the resulting configuration would be as shown in Example 3-3.

**Example 3-3** *Router A's Interpretation of the Configuration in Example 3-2*

```
router eigrp 109
 network 10.0.0.0
 network 172.16.0.0
```

Instead, consider if the configuration shown in Example 3-4 was entered onto Router A.

**Example 3-4** *Another Alternative Configuration of Router A in Figure 3-16*

```
routerA(config)#router eigrp 109
routerA(config-router)#network 10.1.0.0 0.0.255.255
routerA(config-router)#network 10.4.0.0 0.0.255.255
routerA(config-router)#network 172.16.2.0 0.0.0.255
routerA(config-router)#network 172.16.7.0 0.0.0.255
```

In this case, Router A uses the wildcard mask to determine which directly connected interfaces participate in the EIGRP routing process for AS 109. All interfaces that are part of networks 10.1.0.0/16, 10.4.0.0/16, 172.16.2.0/24, and 172.16.7.0/24 participate in the EIGRP routing process for AS 109; in this case, all four interfaces participate.

## EIGRP Configuration Example Using the Wildcard Mask

Figure 3-17 shows another sample network that runs EIGRP in AS 100. The configuration for Router C uses the wildcard mask, because Router C connects to a router external to this network on its serial interface, and you do not want to run EIGRP with the same autonomous system number there. Router C has subnets of Class B network 172.16.0.0 on all interfaces. Without using the wildcard mask, Router C would send EIGRP packets to the external network. This would waste bandwidth and CPU cycles and would provide unnecessary information to the external network. The wildcard mask tells EIGRP to establish a relationship with EIGRP routers from interfaces that are part of network 172.16.3.0/24 or 172.16.4.0/24, not 172.16.5.0/24.

**Figure 3-17**  *EIGRP Configuration with Wildcard Mask Example*

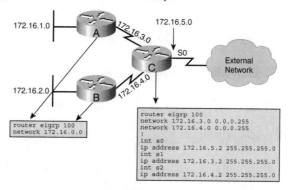

## Configuring EIGRP Default Routes

The EIGRP default route can be created with the **ip default-network** *network-number* command. A router configured with this command considers the *network-number* the last-resort gateway that it will announce to other routers. The network must be reachable by the router that uses this command before it announces it as a candidate default route to other EIGRP routers. The network number in this command must also be passed to other EIGRP routers so that those routers can use this network as their default network and set their gateway of last resort to this network. This means that the network must either be an EIGRP-derived network in the routing table or be generated with a static route and redistributed into EIGRP.

Multiple default networks can be configured; downstream routers then use the EIGRP metric to determine the best default route.

For example, in Figure 3-18, Router A is directly attached to external network 172.31.0.0/16. Router A is configured with the 172.31.0.0 network as a candidate default network using the **ip default-network 172.31.0.0** command. Router A also has that network listed in a **network** command under the EIGRP process and, therefore, passes it to Router B. Notice that the routing table for Router A does not set the gateway of last resort; the **ip default-network** command does not benefit Router A directly. On Router B, the EIGRP-learned 172.31.0.0 network is flagged as a candidate default network (indicated by the * in the routing table). Router B also sets the gateway of last resort as 10.64.0.2 (Router A) to reach the default network of 172.31.0.0.

| NOTE | When you configure the **ip default-network** command, a static route (the **ip route** command) is generated in the router's configuration; however, the IOS doesn't display a message to indicate that this has been done. The entry appears as a static route in the routing table of the router where the command is configured (Router A in the example). This can be confusing when you want to remove the default network; the configuration must be removed with the **no ip route** command. |
| --- | --- |

**Figure 3-18** *EIGRP* **ip default-network** *Sample Network*

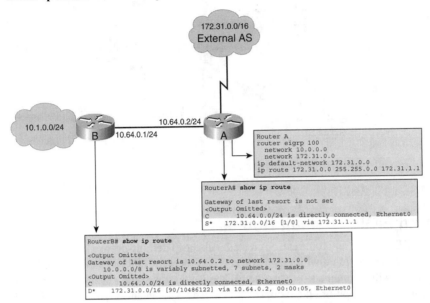

**NOTE**    EIGRP and IGRP behave differently than RIP when using the **ip route 0.0.0.0 0.0.0.0**
command. For example, EIGRP does not redistribute the 0.0.0.0 0.0.0.0 default route by
default. However, if the **network 0.0.0.0** command is added to the EIGRP configuration, it
redistributes a default route as a result of the **ip route 0.0.0.0 0.0.0.0** *interface* command
(but not as a result of the **ip route 0.0.0.0 0.0.0.0** *address* or **ip default-network** command).
For example, the configuration shown in Example 3-5 illustrates a router with the 0.0.0.0 route
passed to EIGRP neighbors.

**Example 3-5**    *EIGRP Passes a Default Route Only If It Is Configured to Do So*

```
interface loopback 0
 ip address 192.168.2.1 255.255.255.0
ip route 0.0.0.0 0.0.0.0 loopback 0
!
router eigrp 100
 network 0.0.0.0
```

# Route Summarization

Some EIGRP features, such as automatically summarizing routes at a major network
boundary, have distance vector characteristics. Traditional distance vector protocols, which

are classful routing protocols, must summarize at network boundaries. They cannot presume the mask for networks that are not directly connected, because masks are not exchanged in the routing updates.

---

### Key Point: EIGRP Summarization

EIGRP automatically summarizes on the major network boundary by default; this feature can be turned off. In addition, EIGRP summary routes can be configured on any bit boundary within the network as long as a more-specific route exists in the routing table.

---

Summarizing routes at major boundaries (classful) creates smaller routing tables. Smaller routing tables, in turn, make the routing update process less bandwidth-intensive. Cisco distance vector routing protocols have autosummarization enabled by default. As mentioned earlier, EIGRP has its roots in IGRP and, therefore, summarizes at the network boundary by default. For EIGRP, this feature can be turned off.

The inability to create summary routes at arbitrary boundaries with a major network has been a drawback of distance vector protocols since their inception. EIGRP has added functionality to allow administrators to create one or more summary routes within a network on any bit boundary (as long as a more specific route exists in the routing table).

When summarization is configured on a router's interface, a summary route is added to that router's routing table, with the route's next-hop interface set to null0—a directly connected, software-only interface. The use of the null0 interface prevents the router from trying to forward traffic to other routers in search of a more precise, longer match, thus preventing traffic from looping within the network. For example, if the summarizing router receives a packet to an unknown subnet that is part of the summarized range, the packet matches the summary route based on the longest match. The packet is forwarded to the null0 interface (in other words, it is dropped or sent to the *bit bucket*). This prevents the router from forwarding the packet to a default route and possibly creating a loop.

For effective summarization, blocks of contiguous addresses (subnets) should funnel back to a common router so that a single summary route can be created and then advertised. The number of subnets that can be represented by a summary route is directly related to the number of bits by which the subnet mask has been pulled back toward the major network mask. The formula $2^n$, where $n$ equals the number of bits by which the subnet mask has been reduced, indicates how many subnets can be represented by a single summary route. For example, if the summary mask contains 3 fewer bits than the subnet mask, eight ($2^3 = 8$) subnets can be aggregated into one advertisement.

When creating summary routes, the administrator needs to specify the IP address of the summary route and the summary mask. The Cisco IOS handles the details of proper implementation, such as metrics, loop prevention, and removal of the summary route from the routing table if none of the more specific routes are valid.

## Configuring Summarization

EIGRP automatically summarizes routes at the classful boundary, but, as discussed, in some cases you might want to turn off this feature. For example, if you have discontiguous subnets, you need to disable autosummarization. Note that an EIGRP router does not perform automatic summarization of networks in which it does not participate.

To turn off automatic summarization, use the **no auto-summary** router configuration command.

Use the **ip summary-address eigrp** *as-number address mask* interface configuration command to manually create a summary route at an arbitrary bit boundary, as long as a more specific route exists in the routing table (or for networks in which your router does not participate). Table 3-2 summarizes this command.

**Table 3-2** **ip summary-address eigrp** *Command*

| ip summary-address eigrp Command | Description |
|---|---|
| *as-number* | EIGRP autonomous system number. |
| *address* | The IP address being advertised as the summary address. This address does not need to be aligned on Class A, B, or C boundaries. |
| *mask* | The IP mask being used to create the summary address. |

For example, Figure 3-19 shows a discontiguous network 172.16.0.0. Because by default both Routers A and B summarize routes at the classful boundary, Router C has two equally good routes to network 172.16.0.0 and performs load balancing between Router A and Router B.

**Figure 3-19** *Summarizing EIGRP Routes*

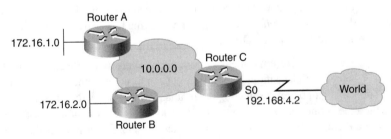

As shown in Example 3-6, you can disable the automatic route summarization feature so that Router C knows precisely that 172.16.1.0 is reached via Router A and that 172.16.2.0 is reached only via Router B.

**Example 3-6** *Turning Off EIGRP Autosummarization on Routers A and B in Figure 3-19*

```
router eigrp 1
  network 10.0.0.0
  network 172.16.0.0
  no auto-summary
```

An EIGRP router autosummarizes routes for only networks to which it is attached. If a network was not autosummarized at the major network boundary, as is the case in this example on Routers A and B because autosummarization is turned off, all the subnet routes are carried into Router C's routing table. In turn, Router C sends routing information about the 172.16.1.0 subnet and the 172.16.2.0 subnet to the WAN.

Forcing a summary route out Router C's interface s0, as shown in Example 3-7, helps reduce route advertisements about network 172.16.0.0 to the world.

**Example 3-7**  *Forcing Summarization on Router C in Figure 3-19*

```
router eigrp 1
  network 10.0.0.0
  network 192.168.4.0
!
int s0
  ip address 192.168.4.2 255.255.255.0
  ip summary-address eigrp 1 172.16.0.0 255.255.0.0
```

**NOTE**  For manual summarization, the summary is advertised only if a component (a more specific entry that is represented in the summary) of the summary route is present in the routing table.

**NOTE**  IP EIGRP summary routes are given an administrative distance value of 5. Standard EIGRP routes receive an administrative distance of 90, and external EIGRP routes receive an administrative distance of 170.

You will notice the EIGRP summary route with an administrative distance of 5 only on the local router performing the summarization with the **ip summary-address eigrp** command. You can see this administrative distance on the router doing the summarization using the **show ip route** *network* command, where *network* is the specified summarized route.

# EIGRP Load Balancing

### Key Point: Load Balancing

Load balancing is a router's capability to distribute traffic over all of its network ports that are the same distance from the destination address.

Good load balancing algorithms use both line-speed and reliability information. Load balancing increases the utilization of network segments, thus increasing effective network bandwidth.

By default, the Cisco IOS balances between a maximum of four equal-cost paths for IP. Using the **maximum-paths** *maximum-path* router configuration command, you can request that up to six equally good routes be kept in the routing table. (Set *maximum-path* to 1 to disable load balancing.) When a packet is process-switched, load balancing over equal-cost paths occurs on a per-packet basis. When packets are fast-switched, load balancing over equal-cost paths is on a per-destination basis.

**NOTE**   Load balancing is performed only on traffic that passes *through* the router, not traffic generated by the router.

**NOTE**   If you are testing load balancing, do not ping to or from the routers with the fast-switching interfaces, because these locally router-generated packets are process-switched rather than fast-switched and might produce confusing results.

EIGRP can also balance traffic across multiple routes that have different metrics; this is called unequal-cost load balancing. The amount of load balancing that is performed can be controlled by the **variance** *multiplier* router configuration command. The multiplier is a variance value, between 1 and 128, used for load balancing. The default is 1, which means equal-cost load balancing. The multiplier defines the range of metric values that are accepted for load balancing. For example, in Figure 3-20, a variance of 2 is configured, and the range of the metric values (the FDs) for Router E to get to Network Z is 20 to 45. This range of values is used in the procedure to determine the feasibility of a potential route.

---

**Key Point: Feasible Route with Variance**

A route is feasible if the next router in the path is closer to the destination than the current router and if the metric for the entire path is within the variance.

---

**Figure 3-20**  *EIGRP Load Balancing with a Variance of 2*

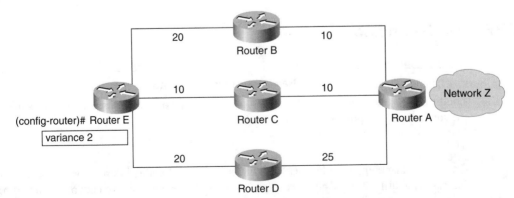

Only paths that are feasible can be used for load balancing (the routing table indicates only feasible paths). The two feasibility conditions are as follows:

- The local best metric (the current FD) must be greater than the best metric (the AD) learned from the next router. In other words, the next router in the path must be closer to the destination than the current router; this prevents routing loops.

- The variance multiplied by the local best metric (the current FD) must be greater than the metric through the next router (the alternative FD).

If both these conditions are met, the route is called feasible and can be added to the routing table.

---

### Traffic Sharing

To control how traffic is distributed among routes when multiple routes exist for the same destination network and they have different costs, use the **traffic-share** router configuration command. With the keyword **balanced**, the router distributes traffic proportionately to the ratios of the metrics associated with the different routes. With the keyword **min**, the router uses only routes that have minimum costs. (In other words, all routes that are feasible and within the variance are kept in the routing table, but only those with the minimum cost are used.)

---

In Figure 3-20, Router E uses Router C as the successor because its FD is lowest (20). With the **variance 2** command applied to Router E, the path through Router B meets the criteria for load balancing. In this case, the FD through Router B is less than twice the FD for the successor (Router C). Router D is not considered for load balancing because the FD through Router D is greater than twice the FD for the successor (Router C). Also, because Router D's AD of 25 is greater than Router E's FD of 20, Router D is not considered closer to the destination than Router E.

In another example of unequal load balancing, four paths to a destination have the following different metrics:

- Path 1: 1100
- Path 2: 1100
- Path 3: 2000
- Path 4: 4000

By default, the router routes to the destination using both Paths 1 and 2. To load-balance over Paths 1, 2, and 3, you would use the **variance 2** command, because 1100 * 2 = 2200, which is greater than the metric through Path 3. Similarly, to also include Path 4, you would issue the **variance 4** command.

# EIGRP and WAN Links

EIGRP operates efficiently in WAN environments. EIGRP is scalable on both point-to-point links and NBMA multipoint and point-to-point links. Because of the inherent differences in links' operational characteristics, default configuration of WAN connections might not be optimal. A solid understanding of EIGRP operation coupled with knowledge of link speeds can yield an efficient, reliable, scalable router configuration.

## EIGRP Link Utilization

---

### Key Point: EIGRP Bandwidth on an Interface

By default, EIGRP uses up to 50 percent of the bandwidth declared on an interface or subinterface. EIGRP uses the bandwidth of the link set by the **bandwidth** command, or the link's default bandwidth if none is configured, when calculating how much bandwidth to use.

---

You can adjust this percentage on an interface or subinterface with the **ip bandwidth-percent eigrp** *as-number percent* interface configuration command. The *percent* parameter is the percentage of the configured bandwidth that EIGRP can use. You can set it to a value greater than 100. This is useful if the bandwidth is configured artificially low for routing policy reasons. Example 3-8 shows a configuration that allows EIGRP to use 40 kbps (200 percent of the configured bandwidth) on the interface. It is essential to make sure that the line is provisioned to handle the configured capacity. (The section "Examples of EIGRP on WANs" provides more examples of when this command is useful.)

**Example 3-8**  *Adjusting the EIGRP Link Utilization*

```
interface serial0
 bandwidth 20
 ip bandwidth-percent eigrp 1 200
```

The Cisco IOS treats point-to-point Frame Relay subinterfaces in the same manner as any serial interface when it comes to bandwidth. The IOS assumes that those serial interfaces and subinterfaces are operating at full T1 link speed. In many implementations, however, only fractional T1 speeds are available. Therefore, when configuring these subinterfaces, set the bandwidth to match the contracted CIR.

When configuring multipoint interfaces (especially for Frame Relay), remember that the bandwidth is shared equally by all neighbors. That is, EIGRP uses the **bandwidth** command on the physical interface divided by the number of Frame Relay neighbors connected on that physical interface to get the bandwidth attributed to each neighbor. EIGRP configuration should reflect the correct percentage of the actual available bandwidth on the line.

Each installation has a unique topology, and with that comes unique configurations. Differing CIR values often require a hybrid configuration that blends the characteristics of point-to-point circuits with multipoint circuits. When configuring multipoint interfaces, configure the bandwidth to represent the minimum CIR times the number of circuits. This approach might not fully use the higher-speed circuits, but it ensures that the circuits with the lowest CIR will not be overdriven. If the topology has a small number of very low-speed circuits, these interfaces should be defined as point-to-point so that their bandwidth can be set to match the provisioned CIR.

## Examples of EIGRP on WANs

In Figure 3-21, the interface has been configured for a bandwidth of 224 kbps. In a pure multipoint topology, each circuit is allocated one-quarter of the configured bandwidth on the interface, and this 56-kbps allocation matches the provisioned CIR of each circuit.

**Figure 3-21**  *Frame Relay Multipoint in Which All VCs Share the Bandwidth Evenly*

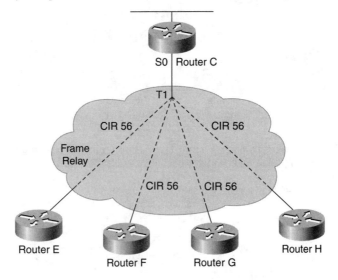

• All VCs share bandwidth evenly: 4 x 56 = 224

Example 3-9 shows the configuration for Router C's Serial 0 interface.

**Example 3-9**  *Adjusting the **bandwidth** Command on an Interface on Router C in Figure 3-21*

```
interface serial 0
encapsulation frame-relay
  bandwidth 224
```

In Figure 3-22, one of the circuits has been provisioned for a 56-kbps CIR, and the other circuits have a higher CIR. This interface has been configured for a bandwidth that represents the lowest CIR multiplied by the number of circuits being supported (56 * 4 = 224). This configuration protects against overwhelming the slowest-speed circuit in the topology.

**Figure 3-22** *Frame Relay Multipoint in Which VCs Have Different CIRs*

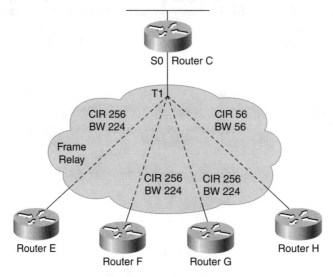

- Lowest CIR x # of VC: 56 x 4 = 224

Figure 3-23 presents a hybrid solution. There is only one low-speed circuit, and other VCs are provisioned for a higher CIR.

**Figure 3-23** *Frame Relay Multipoint and Point-to-Point*

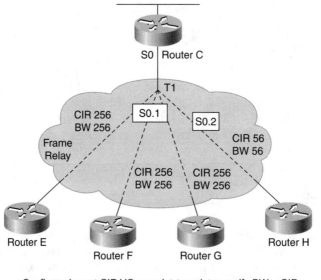

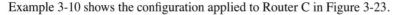

- Configure lowest CIR VC as point-to-point, specify BW = CIR
- Configure higher CIR VCs as multipoint, combine CIRs

Example 3-10 shows the configuration applied to Router C in Figure 3-23.

**Example 3-10** *Adjusting the Bandwidth for a Frame Relay Subinterface on Router C in Figure 3-23*

```
interface serial 0.1 multipoint
  bandwidth 768

interface serial 0.2 point-to-point
  bandwidth 56
```

Example 3-10 shows the low-speed circuit configured as point-to-point. The remaining circuits are designated as multipoint, and their respective CIRs are added up to set the interface's bandwidth.

Figure 3-24 illustrates a common hub-and-spoke oversubscribed topology with ten VCs to the remote sites. (Only four of the ten remote sites are shown in the figure.)

**Figure 3-24**  *Frame Relay Hub-and-Spoke Topology*

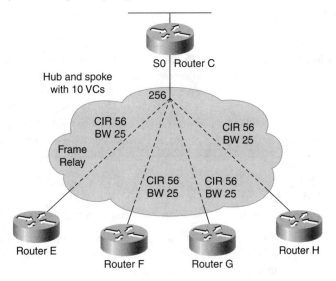

- Configure each VC as point-to-point, specify BW = 1/10 of link capacity
- Increase EIGRP utilization to 50% of actual VC capacity

The circuits are provisioned as 56-kbps links, but there is insufficient bandwidth at the interface to support the allocation. In a point-to-point topology, all VCs are treated equally and are configured for exactly one-tenth (25 kbps) of the available link speed.

Example 3-11 shows the configuration used on Routers C and G of Figure 3-24.

**Example 3-11** *EIGRP WAN Configuration: Point-to-Point Links on Routers C and G in Figure 3-24*

```
RouterC(config)#interface serial 0.1 point-to-point
RouterC(config-subif)#bandwidth 25
RouterC(config-subif)#ip bandwidth-percent eigrp 63 110
<output omitted>
RouterC(config)#interface serial 0.10 point-to-point
RouterC(config-subif)#bandwidth 25
RouterC(config-subif)#ip bandwidth-percent eigrp 63 110
```

*continues*

**Example 3-11** *EIGRP WAN Configuration: Point-to-Point Links on Routers C and G in Figure 3-24 (Continued)*

```
RouterG(config)#interface serial 0
RouterG(config-if)#bandwidth 25
RouterG(config-if)#ip bandwidth-percent eigrp 63 110
```

By default, EIGRP uses 50 percent of a circuit's configured bandwidth. As mentioned, EIGRP configuration should reflect the correct percentage of the actual available bandwidth on the line. Therefore, in an attempt to ensure that EIGRP packets are delivered through the Frame Relay network in Figure 3-24, each subinterface has the EIGRP allocation percentage raised to 110 percent of the specified bandwidth. This adjustment causes EIGRP packets to receive approximately 28 kbps of the provisioned 56 kbps on each circuit. This extra configuration restores the 50-50 ratio that was tampered with when the bandwidth was set to an artificially low value.

---

NOTE    Suppressing ACKs also saves bandwidth. An ACK is not sent if a unicast data packet is ready for transmission. The ACK field in any reliable unicast packet (RTP packet) is sufficient to acknowledge the neighbor's packet, so the ACK packet is suppressed to save bandwidth. This is a significant feature for point-to-point links and NBMA networks, because on those media, all data packets are sent as unicasts and, thus, can carry an acknowledgment themselves (this is also known as a piggyback ACK). In that instance, there is no need for an ACK packet.

---

## Using EIGRP in a Scalable Internetwork

The following are some of the many variables that affect network scalability:

- **The amount of information exchanged between neighbors**—If more information than necessary is exchanged between EIGRP neighbors, unnecessary compilation work during routing startup and topology changes results.

- **Number of routers**—When a topology change occurs, the quantity of resources consumed by EIGRP is directly related to the number of routers that must be involved in the change.

- **The topology's depth**—The topology's depth can affect the convergence time. Depth refers to the number of hops that information must travel to reach all routers. For example, a multinational network without route summarization has a large depth and increased convergence time.

  A three-tiered network design is highly recommended for all IP routing environments. There should never be more than seven hops between any two routing devices on an internetwork. The propagation delay across multiple hops and the query process when changes occur can slow down the convergence of the network when routes are lost.

- **The number of alternative paths through the network**—A network should provide alternative paths to avoid single points of failure. However, too many alternative paths can create problems with EIGRP convergence, because the EIGRP routing process, using queries, needs to explore all possible paths for lost routes. This complexity creates an ideal condition for a router to become stuck in active (described in the section after the next one) as it awaits a response to queries that are being propagated through these many alternative paths.

As an advanced distance vector routing protocol, EIGRP relies on its neighbors to provide routing information. If a route is lost and no FS is available, EIGRP queries its neighbors about the lost route.

## Tiered Network Design

Summarization in the three tiers of the hierarchical network model can provide the following benefits:

- **At the core**—Summarized routes reduce the size of the routing table held by core routers. These smaller tables make for efficient lookups, thus helping provide a fast-switching core.

- **At the regional head offices**—Summarized routes at the regional head office help in the selection of the most efficient path by reducing the number of entries to be checked.

- **At the remote offices**—Proper allocation of blocks of addresses to remote offices lets local traffic remain local and not unnecessarily burden other portions of the network.

## Active and Stuck in Active

Recall that when a router loses a route and does not have an FS in its topology table, it looks for an alternative path to the destination. This is known as *going active* on a route. (A route is considered passive when a router is not performing recompilation on that route.) Recompiling a route involves sending query packets to all neighbors on interfaces other than the one used to reach the previous successor (split horizon), inquiring whether they have a route to the given destination. If a router has an alternative route, it answers the query with the path in a reply packet and does not propagate it further. If a neighbor does not have an alternative route, it queries each of its own neighbors for an alternative path. The queries then propagate through the network, thus creating an expanding tree of queries. When a router answers a query, it stops the spread of the query through that branch of the network; however, the query can still spread through other portions of the network as other routers attempt to find alternative paths, which might not exist.

Because of the reliable multicast approach used by EIGRP when searching for an alternative to a lost route, it is imperative that a reply be received for each query generated in the network. In other words, when a route goes active and queries are initiated, the only way this route can come out of the active state is by receiving a reply for every generated query. Therefore, a route transitions from active to passive state when the router receives a reply for every generated query.

---

### Key Point: Stuck in Active

If the router does not receive a reply to all the outstanding queries within 3 minutes (the default time), the route goes to the stuck-in-active (SIA) state.

---

When the route goes to SIA state, the router then resets the neighbor relationships for the neighbors that failed to reply. This causes the router to go active on all routes known through that neighbor and to readvertise all the routes it knows about to that neighbor. Limiting the scope of query propagation through the network (the query range), also known as query scoping, helps reduce incidences of SIA. Keeping the query packets close to the source reduces the chance that an isolated failure in another part of the network will restrict the convergence (query/reply) process.

**NOTE**    You can change the active-state time limit from its default of 3 minutes using the **timers active-time** [*time-limit* | **disabled**] router configuration command. The *time-limit* is in minutes.

**NOTE**    Use the **eigrp log-neighbor-changes** command to enable the logging of neighbor adjacency changes to monitor the routing system's stability and to help detect problems related to SIA.

One erroneous approach for decreasing the chances of a stuck-in-active route is to use multiple EIGRP autonomous systems to bound the query range. Many networks have been implemented using multiple EIGRP autonomous systems (to somewhat simulate OSPF areas), with mutual redistribution between the different autonomous systems. Although this approach changes how the network behaves, it does not always achieve the results intended. If a query reaches the edge of the AS (where routes are redistributed into another AS), the original query is answered. However, then the edge router initiates a new query in the other AS. Therefore, the query process has not been stopped; the querying continues in the other AS, where the route can potentially go in SIA.

**NOTE**    Another misconception about autonomous system boundaries is that implementing multiple autonomous systems protects one autonomous system from route flaps in another autonomous system. If routes are redistributed between autonomous systems, route transitions from one autonomous system are detected in the other autonomous systems.

## Update and Query Example

Remote routers rarely need to know all the routes advertised in an entire network. Therefore, it is the network manager's responsibility to look at what information is necessary to properly route user traffic and to consider the use of a default route.

Examples of mechanisms used to limit what information is provided to other routers include filters on routing updates and the **ip summary-address eigrp** command on the router's outbound interfaces.

For example, in Figure 3-25, Router B notices the loss of network 10.1.8.0 and sends a query to Routers A, C, D, and E. In turn, these routers send queries to their neighbors, requesting an FS for

10.1.8.0. When the query process starts, each path receives duplicate queries because of the redundant topology. Therefore, not only are the remote routers required to respond to queries from the head office, but they also continue the search by reflecting the queries back toward the head office's other router. This significantly complicates the convergence process on the network.

**Figure 3-25**  *Effect of the EIGRP Update and Query Process*

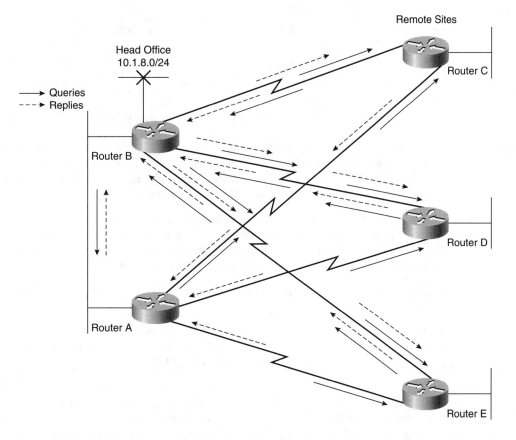

In this sample network with only two regional and three remote routers, the problem might not be very significant. In a network with hundreds of remote offices, the problem can be severe.

Examine the query process for the 10.1.8.0/24 subnet. Router B advertises 10.1.8.0/24 to all other routers. The best path for Router A to reach 10.1.8.0/24 is over the Ethernet link to Router B. The remote routers (C, D, and E) use the serial link to B as their preferred path to reach 10.1.8.0/24 but still learn about an alternative path through Router A. For this example, assume that the EIGRP metric for Ethernet is 1000 and the metric for a serial link is 100,000.

Table 3-3 shows the content of the IP EIGRP topology table for Routers C, D, and E for network 10.1.8.0/24. Table 3-4 shows the content of the IP EIGRP topology table for Router A for network 10.1.8.0/24.

**Table 3-3**   *IP EIGRP Topology Table for Routers C, D, and E in Figure 3-25*

| Neighbor | FD | AD |
|----------|----|----|
| Router A | 102,000 | 2000 |
| Router B | 101,000 | 1000 |

**Table 3-4**   *IP EIGRP Topology Table for Router A in Figure 3-25*

| Neighbor | FD | AD |
|----------|----|----|
| Router B | 2000 | 1000 |
| Router C | 201,000 | 101,000 |
| Router D | 201,000 | 101,000 |
| Router E | 201,000 | 101,000 |

Note that Routers C, D, and E determine that for network 10.1.8.0/24, Router B is the successor and Router A is an FS (because the AD is 2000 through Router A, which is less than the FD through Router B). Also, note that Router A does not have an FS, because all paths through the remote routers have an AD larger than the FD through Router B.

When Router B loses the path to network 10.1.8.0/24, it queries all four of its neighbors. When the remote sites receive this query, they automatically install the path through Router A in their routing tables and respond to Router B with their supposedly good path through Router A. They also remove the bad path through Router B from their topology tables.

Router B now has responses to three of its four queries, but it must wait until Router A responds as well.

When Router A receives the query from Router B for network 10.1.8.0/24, Router A creates a query and sends it to routers C, D, and E, because Router A does not have an FS but knows that a path exists through each remote site to reach 10.1.8.0/24.

Routers C, D, and E receive the query from Router A and check their topology tables for alternative paths. However, none of these routers currently has another path, because Router B has just informed them that it does not have a path to this network. Because the remote routers do not have an answer to the query from Router A, routers C, D, and E create a query and send it to all neighbors except the neighbor (interface) that these routers received the original query from. In this case, the remote routers send the query only to Router B.

Router B learns from these queries that none of the remote routers has a path to network 10.1.8.0/24, but it cannot respond that it does not know of a path, because Router B is waiting for Router A to reply to a query. Router A is waiting for either Router C, D, or E to reply to its query, and these remote sites are waiting for Router B to reply to their queries. Because Router B sent out the first query, its SIA timer expires first, and Router B reaches the SIA state for network 10.1.8.0/24 first (in 3 minutes by default). Router B resets its neighbor relationship with Router A. As soon as the neighbor relationship goes down, Router B can respond to Routers C, D, and E immediately, saying that Router B does not have a path to 10.1.8.0/24. Routers C, D, and E can then respond to Router A that they do not have a path.

After the EIGRP neighbor relationship between Routers A and B is reestablished (just after the adjacency is reset), Router B, which no longer has a path to 10.1.8.0/24, does not pass the 10.1.8.0/24 network to Router A. Router A learns that the remote sites do not have a path to 10.1.8.0/24, and the new relationship with Router B does not include a path to 10.1.8.0/24, so Router A removes the 10.1.8.0 network from its IP EIGRP topology table.

In Figure 3-25, the network architect provides redundancy with dual links from the head office to remote sites. The architect does not intend for the traffic to go from the head office to the remote office and back to the head office, but unfortunately this is the situation. The design of the network shown in Figure 3-25 is sound, but because of EIGRP behavior, remote routers are involved in the convergence process.

If the remote sites are not acting as transit sites between the regional sites, the regional routers can be configured to announce only a default route to the remote routers. The remote routers can be configured to announce only their directly connected stub network to the regional routers to reduce the complexity and the EIGRP topology table and routing table size.

The following section describes other solutions for limiting the EIGRP query range.

## Limiting the EIGRP Query Range

The network manager determines the necessary information to properly route user traffic to the appropriate destination. The amount of information needed by the remote routers to achieve the desired level of path selection must be balanced against the bandwidth used to propagate this information. When you achieve maximum stability and scalability, the remote routers can use a default route to reach the core. If some specific networks need knowledge of more routes to ensure optimum path selection, a business decision is necessary to determine whether the benefits of propagating the additional routing information outweigh the additional bandwidth required to achieve this goal.

In a properly designed network, each remote site has redundant WAN links to separate distribution sites. If both distribution sites pass a default route to the remote site, the remote site load balances to all networks behind the distribution sites. This maximizes bandwidth utilization and allows the remote router to use less CPU and memory, which means that a smaller and less expensive remote router can be used at that site.

If the remote site can see all routes, the router can select a path that is best to reach a given network. However, depending on the number of routes in the internetwork and the amount of bandwidth connecting the remote site to the distribution sites, this approach can mean that higher-bandwidth links or large routers are needed to handle the additional overhead.

After you determine the minimum routing requirements, you can make EIGRP more scalable. Two of the best options are the following:

* Configure route summarization using the **ip summary-address eigrp** command on the outbound interfaces of the appropriate routers.
* Configure the remote routers as stub EIGRP routers.

Summarizing routes limits the queries' scope by limiting a router's knowledge of a network's subnets. If a subnet goes down, queries go only as far as the routers that had knowledge of the subnet.

A remote router configured as an EIGRP stub tells upstream distribution routers not to pass queries to this EIGRP stub router, because it has no downstream EIGRP neighbors and, thus, does not have alternative paths for lost routes. Therefore, upstream routers do not query EIGRP stub routers for lost routes.

Other methods to limit query range include route filtering and interface packet filtering. For example, if specific EIGRP routing updates are filtered to a router and that router receives a query about those filtered (blocked) networks, the router indicates that the network is unreachable and does not extend the query any further.

### Limiting Query Range with Summarization

One of the best solutions to limit the EIGRP query range is to use route summarization.

For example, in Figure 3-26, Router B sends a summary route of 172.30.0.0/16 to Router A. When network 172.30.1.0/24 goes down, Router A receives a query from Router B about that network. Because Router A has received only a summary route, that specific network is not in the routing table. Router A replies to the query with a "network 172.30.1.0/24 unreachable" message and does not extend the query any further.

**Figure 3-26** *EIGRP Summarization Can Limit Query Range*

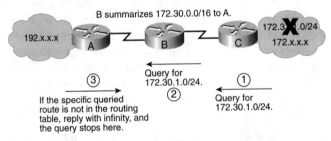

The query range is not a common reason for SIA routes. The most common reasons are as follows:

- The router is too busy to answer the query, generally as a result of high CPU usage. Or the router has memory problems and cannot allocate the memory to process the query or build the reply packet.

- The link between the two routers is not good, so some packets are lost between the routers. The router receives an adequate number of packets to maintain the neighbor relationship, but the router does not receive all queries or replies.

- A failure causes traffic on a link to flow in only one direction. This is called a unidirectional link.

These problems can be beyond the network administrator's control. However, by performing summarization, you can minimize the size of the routing table, which means less CPU usage to manage it and less bandwidth to transmit the information. Summarization reduces the chance of networks becoming SIA. By limiting the query range with summarization, you reduce the number of routers that see each query, so the chance of a query encountering one of these issues is also reduced.

**Key Point: Query Range**

A remote router extends the query about a network only if it has an exact match in the routing table.

Figure 3-27 illustrates how route summarization can affect the network shown in Figure 3-25. The **ip summary-address eigrp** command is configured on the outbound interfaces of Routers A and B so that Routers A and B advertise the 10.0.0.0/8 summary route to the remote Routers C, D, and E.

**Figure 3-27** *Limiting Updates and Queries Using Summarization*

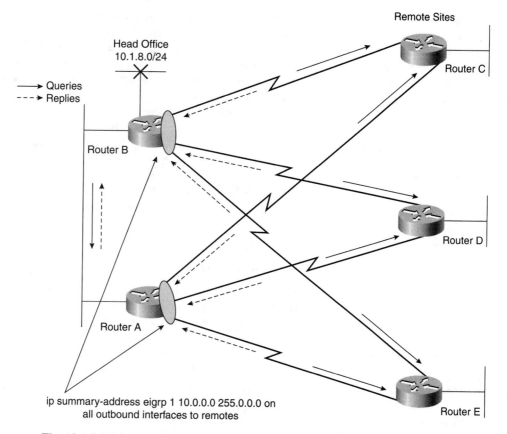

ip summary-address eigrp 1 10.0.0.0 255.0.0.0 on
all outbound interfaces to remotes

The 10.1.8.0/24 network is not advertised to the remote routers. Therefore, the remote routers (C, D, and E) do not extend the queries about the 10.1.8.0/24 network back to the regional routers (A and B), reducing the convergence traffic (queries and replies) caused by the redundant topology. When Routers A and B send the query for 10.1.8.0/24 to Routers C, D, and E, these routers immediately reply to Routers A and B that the destination is unreachable. Queries for the lost 10.1.8.0/24 networks are not propagated beyond the remote sites, preventing Routers A and B from becoming SIA waiting for the query process to receive all the replies.

## Limiting Query Range Using a Stub

Hub-and-spoke network topologies commonly use stub routing. In this topology, the remote router forwards all traffic that is not local to a hub router; the remote router does not need to retain a complete routing table. Generally, the hub router needs to send only a default route to the remote routers.

In a hub-and-spoke topology, having a full routing table on the remote routers serves no functional purpose, because the path to the corporate network and the Internet is always through the hub router. Additionally, having a full routing table at the spoke routers increases the amount of memory required. Route summarization and route filtering can also be used to conserve bandwidth and memory requirements on the spoke routers.

Traffic from a hub router should not use a remote router as a transit path. A typical connection from a hub router to a remote router has significantly less bandwidth than a connection at the network core; attempting to use the connection to a remote router as a transit path typically results in excessive congestion. The EIGRP stub routing feature can prevent this problem by restricting the remote router from advertising the hub router's routes back to other hub routers. For example, routes recognized by the remote router from hub Router A are not advertised to hub Router B. Because the remote router does not advertise the hub routes back to the hub routers, the hub routers do not use the remote routers as a transit path. Using the EIGRP stub routing feature improves network stability, reduces resource utilization, and simplifies stub router configuration.

---

**Key Point: EIGRP Stub**

Only the remote routers are configured as stubs. The stub feature does not prevent routes from being advertised to the remote router.

---

The EIGRP stub feature was first introduced in IOS Release 12.0(7)T.

A stub router sends a special peer information packet to all neighboring routers to report its status as a stub router. Any neighbor that receives a packet informing it of the stub status does not query the stub router for any routes. Therefore, a router that has a stub peer does not query that peer.

---

**Key Point: EIGRP Stub Routers Are Not Queried**

Stub routers are not queried. Instead, hub routers connected to the stub router answer the query on behalf of the stub router.

---

The EIGRP stub routing feature can help provide significant network stability. In the event of network instability, this feature prevents EIGRP queries from being sent over limited-bandwidth links to nontransit routers, thus reducing the chance of further network instability because of congested or problematic WAN links.

The EIGRP stub routing feature also simplifies the configuration and maintenance of hub-and-spoke networks. When stub routing is enabled in dual-homed remote configurations, you do not have to configure filtering on remote routers to prevent them from appearing as transit paths to the hub routers.

---

**CAUTION**   EIGRP stub routing should be used on stub routers only. A stub router is defined as a router connected to the network core or hub layer through which core transit traffic should not flow. A stub router should have hub routers only for EIGRP neighbors. Ignoring this restriction causes undesirable behavior.

---

To configure a router as an EIGRP stub, use the **eigrp stub [receive-only | connected | static | summary]** router configuration command. A router configured as a stub with this command shares information about connected and summary routes with all neighbor routers by default. Table 3-5 describes the four optional keywords that can be used with the **eigrp stub** command to modify this behavior.

**Table 3-5**    **eigrp stub** *Command*

| eigrp stub Command | Description |
|---|---|
| **receive-only** | The **receive-only** keyword restricts the router from sharing any of its routes with any other router within an EIGRP autonomous system. This keyword does not permit any other keyword to be specified, because it prevents any type of route from being sent. |
| **connected** | The **connected** keyword permits the EIGRP stub routing feature to send connected routes. If a **network** command does not include connected routes, it might be necessary to redistribute connected routes with the **redistribute connected** command under the EIGRP process. This option is enabled by default. |
| **static** | The **static** keyword permits the EIGRP stub routing feature to send static routes. Redistributing static routes with the **redistribute static** command is still necessary. |
| **summary** | The **summary** keyword permits the EIGRP stub routing feature to send summary routes. You can create summary routes manually with the **ip summary-address eigrp** command or automatically at a major network border router with the **auto-summary** command enabled. This option is enabled by default. |

The optional parameters in this command can be used in any combination, with the exception of the **receive-only** keyword. If any of the keywords (except **receive-only**) is used individually, the connected and summary routes are not sent automatically.

In Example 3-12, the **eigrp stub** command is used to configure the router as a stub that advertises connected and summary routes.

**Example 3-12** **eigrp stub** *Command to Advertise Connected and Summary Routes*

```
router eigrp 1
 network 10.0.0.0
 eigrp stub
```

In Example 3-13, the **eigrp stub receive-only** command is used to configure the router as a stub. Connected, summary, or static routes are not sent.

**Example 3-13** *eigrp stub Command to Receive Only Routes*

```
router eigrp 1
 network 10.0.0.0 eigrp
 eigrp stub receive-only
```

The EIGRP stub feature does not automatically enable route summarization on the hub router. The network administrator should configure route summarization on the hub routers if desired.

If a true stub network is required, the hub router can be configured to send a default route to the spoke routers. This approach is the most simple and conserves the most bandwidth and memory on the spoke routers.

---

**NOTE**   When you configure the hub router to send a default route to the remote router, use the **ip classless** command on the remote router. By default, the **ip classless** command is enabled in all Cisco IOS images that support the EIGRP stub routing feature.

---

Without the stub feature, EIGRP sends a query to the spoke routers if a route is lost somewhere in the network. If there is a communication problem over a WAN link between the hub router and a spoke router, an EIGRP SIA condition can occur and cause instability elsewhere in the network. The EIGRP stub routing feature allows a network administrator to prevent sending queries to the spoke router under any condition. Cisco highly recommends using both EIGRP route summarization and EIGRP stub features to provide the best scalability.

Figure 3-28 illustrates how using the EIGRP stub feature affects the network shown in Figure 3-25. Each of the remote routers is configured as a stub. Queries for network 10.1.8.0/24 are not sent to Routers C, D, or E, thus reducing the bandwidth used and the chance of the routes being stuck in active.

**Figure 3-28** *Limiting Updates and Queries Using the EIGRP Stub Feature*

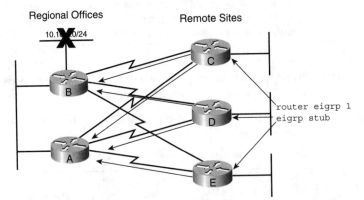

Using the EIGRP stub feature at the remote sites allows the hub (regional) sites to immediately answer queries without propagating the queries to the remote sites, saving CPU cycles and bandwidth, and lessening convergence time even when the remote sites are dual-homed to two or more hub sites.

## EIGRP Scalability Rules

EIGRP has many features that allow for the creation of very large internetworks. Solid design principles are the foundation on which the network infrastructure rests.

Route summarization is most effective with a sound address allocation. Having a two- or three-layer hierarchical network design, with routers positioned by function rather than by geography, greatly assists traffic flow and route distribution.

**NOTE**    For a full discussion of internetwork design, refer to *Designing for Cisco Internetwork Solutions (DESGN)* (Cisco Press, 2003).

Figure 3-29 shows the topology of a nonscalable internetwork in which addresses (subnets) are either randomly assigned or assigned by historical requirements. In this example, multiple subnets from different major networks are located in each cloud, requiring many subnet routes to be injected into the core. In addition, because of the random assignment of addresses, query traffic cannot be localized to any portion of the network, thus increasing convergence time. Administration and troubleshooting are also more complex in this scenario.

**Figure 3-29**  *Nonscalable Internetwork*

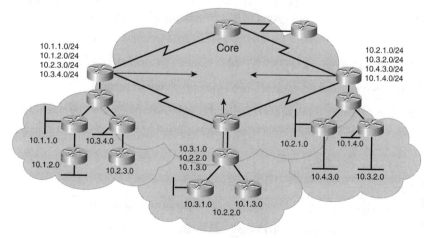

Figure 3-30 illustrates a better-designed network. Subnet addresses from individual major networks are localized within each cloud. This allows summary routes to be injected into the core. As an added benefit, the summary routes act as a boundary for the queries generated by a topology change.

**Figure 3-30** *Scalable Internetwork*

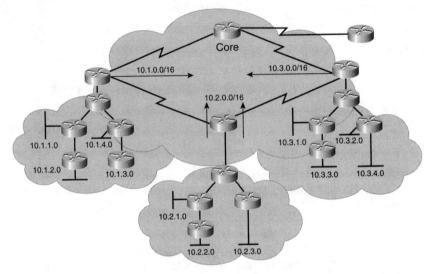

Some common design principles should be followed for proper EIGRP operation. Routers located at convergence points within the network need sufficient memory to buffer a large number of packets and to support numerous processes related to routing large volumes of traffic.

On WAN links, and especially with the hub-and-spoke topology, enough bandwidth should be provided to prevent router overhead traffic from interfering with normal user-generated traffic. In this respect, the impact of EIGRP packets being lost because of contention for bandwidth might be greater than application delays experienced by some users.

## Verifying EIGRP Operation

This section discusses commands used to verify EIGRP operation.

Table 3-6 describes some **show** commands used to verify EIGRP operation. Other options might be available with these commands. Use the Cisco IOS's integrated help feature to see the full-command syntax.

**Table 3-6** *EIGRP **show** Commands*

| Command | Description |
|---|---|
| **show ip eigrp neighbors** | Displays neighbors discovered by EIGRP. |
| **show ip eigrp topology** | Displays the EIGRP topology table. This command shows the topology table, the active or passive state of routes, the number of successors, and the FD to the destination. |
| **show ip route** | Displays the current entries in the IP routing table for all configured routing protocols. |

**Table 3-6**    *EIGRP* **show** *Commands (Continued)*

| Command | Description |
|---------|-------------|
| **show ip route eigrp** | Displays the current EIGRP entries in the IP routing table. |
| **show ip protocols** | Displays the parameters and current state of the active routing protocol processes. For EIGRP, this command shows the EIGRP autonomous system number, filtering and redistribution numbers, and neighbors and distance information. |
| **show ip eigrp traffic** | Displays the number of EIGRP packets sent and received. This command displays statistics on hello packets, updates, queries, replies, and acknowledgments. |

Table 3-7 describes **debug** commands used to verify EIGRP operation. Other options might be available with these commands. Use the Cisco IOS's integrated help feature to see the full command syntax.

**Table 3-7**    *EIGRP* **debug** *Commands*

| Command | Description |
|---------|-------------|
| **debug eigrp packets** | Displays the types of EIGRP packets sent and received. A maximum of 11 packet types can be selected for individual or group display. |
| **debug eigrp neighbors** | Displays neighbors discovered by EIGRP and the contents of the hello packets. |
| **debug ip eigrp** | Displays packets that are sent and received on an interface. Because this command generates large amounts of output, use it only when traffic on the network is light. |
| **debug ip eigrp summary** | Displays a summarized version of EIGRP activity. It also displays filtering and redistribution numbers and neighbors and distance information. |

The following sections provide sample output from some of these commands.

## show ip route for EIGRP Example

You can use the **show ip route** command to verify whether the router recognizes EIGRP routes for any neighbors, as shown in Example 3-14.

**Example 3-14** **show ip route** *Command Output for EIGRP Routes*

```
RouterA#show ip route
 Codes: C - connected, S - static, I - IGRP, R - RIP,
    D - EIGRP, EX - EIGRP external, O - OSPF,
    (text omitted)
    * - candidate default,
Gateway of last resort is not set
```

*continues*

**Example 3-14** show ip route *Command Output for EIGRP Routes (Continued)*

```
      172.16.0.0/24 is subnetted, 1 subnets
D        172.16.1.0 [90/10639872] via 10.1.2.2, 06:04:01, Serial0/0
      10.0.0.0/24 is subnetted, 4 subnets
D        10.1.3.0 [90/10514432] via 10.1.2.2, 05:54:47, Serial0/0
D        10.3.1.0 [90/10639872] via 10.1.2.2, 06:19:41, Serial0/0
C        10.1.2.0 is directly connected, Serial0/0
C        10.1.1.0 is directly connected, Ethernet0/0
```

The **show ip route** command displays all the routes in the IP routing table. Using the highlighted line in Example 3-14 as an example, the fields in the routing table are interpreted as follows:

- Internal EIGRP routes are identified with a D in the leftmost column. (External EIGRP routes, not shown in this example, are identified with a D EX in the leftmost column.)

- The next column is the network number (10.1.3.0 in this example).

- After each network number is a field in brackets (90/10514432 in this example).

  The first number, 90 in this case, is the administrative distance. Recall from Chapter 2, "Routing Principles," that administrative distance is used to select the best path when a router learns two or more routes to the same destination from different routing protocols. For example, assume that this router uses RIP as well as EIGRP. If RIP has a route to network 10.1.3.0 that is three hops away, the router, without the administrative distance, cannot compare three hops to an EIGRP metric of 10,514,432. The router does not know the bandwidth associated with hops, and EIGRP does not use hop count as a metric. To correct this problem, Cisco established an administrative distance for each routing protocol: the lower the value, the more preferred the route is. By default, EIGRP internal routes have an administrative distance of 90, and RIP has an administrative distance of 120. Because EIGRP has a metric based on bandwidth and delays, it is preferred over RIP's hop count metric. As a result, in this example, the EIGRP route would be installed in the routing table.

  The second number in brackets is the EIGRP metric. As discussed in the "EIGRP Metric Calculation" section earlier in this chapter, the default EIGRP metric is the least-cost bandwidth plus the delay. The EIGRP metric for this network is the same as its FD in the EIGRP topology table.

- The 10.1.2.2 address is the next-hop router to which this router passes packets destined for 10.1.3.0; 10.1.3.0 is a network behind that next-hop router. The next-hop address in the routing table is the same as the successor in the EIGRP topology table.

- The route also has a time associated with it; this is the length of time since EIGRP last advertised this network to this router. EIGRP does not refresh routes periodically; it resends the routing table only when neighbor adjacencies change.

- The interface, serial 0/0 in this case, indicates the interface out which packets for 10.1.3.0 are sent.

## show ip protocols Example

Use the **show ip protocols** command to examine EIGRP settings. As shown in Example 3-15, the command output displays any route filtering occurring on EIGRP outbound or inbound updates. It also identifies whether EIGRP is generating a default network or receiving a default network in EIGRP updates and provides information about additional settings for EIGRP, such as default K values, hop count, and variance.

**Example 3-15** show ip protocols *Command Output*

```
RouterA#show ip protocols
Routing Protocol is "eigrp 100"
  Outgoing update filter list for all interfaces is not set
  Incoming update filter list for all interfaces is not set
  Default networks flagged in outgoing updates
  Default networks accepted from incoming updates
  EIGRP metric weight K1=1, K2=0, K3=1, K4=0, K5=0
  EIGRP maximum hopcount 100
  EIGRP maximum metric variance 1
  Redistributing: eigrp 100
  Automatic network summarization is not in effect
  Maximum path: 4
  Routing for Networks:
    10.1.0.0/16
    10.0.0.0
  Routing Information Sources:
    Gateway         Distance      Last Update
    10.1.2.2             90       05:50:13
  Distance: internal 90 external 170
```

**NOTE**    Because the routers must have identical K values for EIGRP to establish an adjacency, the **show ip protocols** command helps determine the current K-value setting before an adjacency is attempted.

The output in Example 3-15 also indicates that automatic summarization is disabled and that the router is allowed to load-balance over a maximum of four paths.

The router in this example routes for networks 10.1.0.0/16 and 10.0.0.0. Therefore, the following commands are configured on this router:

```
router eigrp 100
  network 10.1.0.0 0.0.255.255
  network 10.0.0.0
```

The routing information source portion of this command output identifies all other routers that have an EIGRP neighbor relationship with this router. The **show ip eigrp neighbors** command provides a detailed display of EIGRP neighbors.

The **show ip protocols** command output also provides the two administrative distances for EIGRP. An administrative distance of 90 applies to networks from other routers inside the same autonomous system number; these are considered internal networks. An administrative distance of 170 applies to networks introduced to EIGRP for this autonomous system through redistribution; these are external networks.

## show ip eigrp topology Example

Example 3-16 is an example of **show ip eigrp topology** command output.

**Example 3-16** show ip eigrp topology *Command Output*

```
RouterA#show ip eigrp topology
 IP-EIGRP Topology Table for AS(100)/ID(10.1.2.1)
Codes: P - Passive, A - Active, U - Update, Q - Query, R - Reply,
        r - reply Status, s - sia Status
P 10.1.3.0/24, 1 successors, FD is 10514432
         via 10.1.2.2 (10514432/28160), Serial0/0
P 10.3.1.0/24, 1 successors, FD is 10639872
         via 10.1.2.2 (10639872/384000), Serial0/0
P 10.1.2.0/24, 1 successors, FD is 10511872
         via Connected, Serial0/0
P 10.1.1.0/24, 1 successors, FD is 2190
         via Connected, Ethernet0/0
P 172.16.1.0/24, 1 successors, FD is 10639872
         via 10.1.2.2 (10639872/384000), Serial0/0
```

The command output lists the networks known by this router through the EIGRP routing process. Example 3-16 is from a router (10.1.2.1) in autonomous system 100. (The EIGRP ID is the highest IP address on an active interface for this router.) The codes used in the first column of this output are as follows:

- **Passive (P)**—This network is available, and installation can occur in the routing table. Passive is the state for a stable network.

- **Active (A)**—This network is currently unavailable, and installation cannot occur in the routing table. Being active means that this network has outstanding queries.

- **Update (U)**—This code applies if a network is being updated (placed in an update packet). This code also applies if the router is waiting for an acknowledgment for this update packet.

- **Query (Q)**—This code applies if this network has an outstanding query packet. This code also applies if the router is waiting for an acknowledgment for a query packet.

- **Reply (R)**—This code applies if the router is generating a reply for this network or is waiting for an acknowledgment for the reply packet.

- **Stuck in active (S)**—This code signifies an EIGRP convergence problem for the network with which it is associated.

The number of successors available for a route is indicated in the command output. All networks in Example 3-16 have one successor; if there were equal-cost paths to the same network, a maximum number of six paths would be allowed. The number of successors corresponds to the number of best routes with equal cost. The routing table contains all the equal-cost best routes (up to six for the same network). For each network, the FD is listed next, followed by the next-hop address.

After the next-hop address is a field in brackets. The first number is the FD for that network, and the second number is the AD from the next-hop router.

## debug eigrp packets Examples

You can use the **debug eigrp packets** command to verify EIGRP connectivity. This command displays the types of EIGRP packets sent and received by the router that this command is executed on. A maximum of 11 packet types can be selected for individual or group display. Example 3-17 shows some output from this command.

**Example 3-17** **debug eigrp packets** *Command Output for Normal EIGRP Processing*

```
RouterA#debug eigrp packets
01:38:29: EIGRP: Sending HELLO on Serial0/0
01:38:29: AS 100, Flags 0x0, Seq 0/0 idbQ 0/0 iidbQ un/rely 0/0
01:38:31: EIGRP: Received HELLO on Serial0/0 nbr 10.1.2.2
01:38:31: AS 100, Flags 0x0, Seq 0/0 idbQ 0/0 iidbQ un/rely 0/0
    peerQ un/rely 0/0
01:38:33: EIGRP: Received UPDATE on Serial0/0 nbr 10.1.2.2
01:38:33: AS 100, Flags 0x0, Seq 23/37 idbQ 0/0 iidbQ un/rely 0/0 peerQ
    un/rely 0/0
01:38:33: EIGRP: Enqueueing ACK on Serial0/0 nbr 10.1.2.2
01:38:33: Ack seq 23 iidbQ un/rely 0/0 peerQ un/rely 1/0
01:38:33: EIGRP: Sending ACK on Serial0/0 nbr 10.1.2.2
01:38:33: AS 100, Flags 0x0, Seq 0/23 idbQ 0/0 iidbQ un/rely 0/0 peerQ
    un/rely 1/0
01:38:33: EIGRP: Enqueueing UPDATE on Serial0/0 iidbQ un/rely 0/1 serno 75-75
01:38:33: EIGRP: Sending UPDATE on Serial0/0 nbr 10.1.2.2
01:38:33: AS 100, Flags 0x0, Seq 38/23 idbQ 0/0 iidbQ un/rely 0/0 peerQ un/rely
    0/1 serno 75-75
01:38:33: EIGRP: Received ACK on Serial0/0 nbr 10.1.2.2
01:38:33: AS 100, Flags 0x0, Seq 0/38 idbQ 0/0 iidbQ un/rely 0/0 peerQ
    un/rely 0/1
```

The **debug eigrp packets** command traces transmission and receipt of EIGRP packets. The output in Example 3-17 shows normal transmission and receipt of EIGRP packets. The serial link is an HDLC point-to-point link; therefore, the default hello time interval is 5 seconds. Hello packets are sent unreliably, so the sequence number (Seq) does not increment.

When Router A in this sample output receives an update from the 10.1.2.2 neighbor, values appear in the sequence number field. Seq 23/37 indicates that 10.1.2.2 is sending this packet as sequence number 23 to Router A and that sequence number 37 has been received from Router A by neighbor 10.1.2.2. 10.1.2.2 is expecting to receive sequence number 38 in the next reliable packet from Router A.

Router A returns an ACK packet with Seq 0/23. The acknowledgment is sent as an unreliable packet, but the neighbor unreliable/reliable flag (un/rel 1/0) is set. This means that the acknowledgment was sent in response to a reliable packet.

The serial number (serno 75-75) reflects the number of changes that the two neighbors register in their EIGRP topology tables. A single update can contain more than 100 networks that all produce an update, because all are now unavailable.

---

**Key Point: Sequence Number Versus Serial Number**

The sequence number increments each time a query, update, or reply packet is sent, whereas the serial number increments each time the topology table changes. Therefore, when the topology table has more than 100 changes, the serial number increases substantially, but the sequence number increases by only 1.

---

In Example 3-18, an interface on Router B (EIGRP neighbor 10.1.2.2) is shut down. Router B then sends a query packet to Router A to determine if Router A knows a path to the lost network. Router A responds with an ACK packet to acknowledge the query packet. A reliable packet must be explicitly acknowledged with an ACK packet. Router A also responds to the query with a reply packet. The serial number reference (74) represents the number of changes to the routing table since the start of the neighbor relationship between these two EIGRP neighbors.

**Example 3-18** **debug eigrp packets** *Command Output When the Neighbor Interface Is Shut Down*

```
RouterA#debug eigrp packets
01:38:11: EIGRP: Received QUERY on Serial0/0 nbr 10.1.2.2
01:38:11: AS 100, Flags 0x0, Seq 22/36 idbQ 0/0 iidbQ un/rely 0/0 peerQ
    un/rely 0/0
01:38:11: EIGRP: Enqueueing ACK on Serial0/0 nbr 10.1.2.2
01:38:11: Ack seq 22 iidbQ un/rely 0/0 peerQ un/rely 1/0
01:38:11: EIGRP: Sending ACK on Serial0/0 nbr 10.1.2.2
01:38:11: AS 100, Flags 0x0, Seq 0/22 idbQ 0/0 iidbQ un/rely 0/0 peerQ
    un/rely 1/0
01:38:11: EIGRP: Sending REPLY on Serial0/0 nbr 10.1.2.2
01:38:11: AS 100, Flags 0x0, Seq 37/22 idbQ 0/0 iidbQ un/rely 0/0 peerQ
    un/rely 0/1 serno 74-74
01:38:11: EIGRP: Received ACK on Serial0/0 nbr 10.1.2.2
01:38:11: AS 100, Flags 0x0, Seq 0/37 idbQ 0/0 iidbQ un/rely 0/0 peerQ
    un/rely 0/1
```

Example 3-19 is another example using the **debug eigrp packets** command. This output indicates that the router received a hello packet from neighbor 10.1.2.2 with mismatched K values. In this case, the neighbor configuration is K1 = 1, K2 = 1, K3 = 1, K4 = 1, and K5 = 1. Router A's configuration is the default K values. An adjacency between these two neighbors is not formed until the K values are equal.

**Example 3-19** debug eigrp packets *Command Output with Mismatched K Values*

```
RouterA#debug eigrp packets
01:39:13: EIGRP: Received HELLO on Serial0/0 nbr 10.1.2.2
01:39:13: AS 100, Flags 0x0, Seq 0/0 idbQ 0/0 iidbQ un/rely 0/0 peerQ
   un/rely 0/0
01:39:13:        K-value mismatch
```

## debug ip eigrp Examples

You can use the **debug ip eigrp** command to verify EIGRP operation. This command displays EIGRP packets that this router sends and receives.

Example 3-20 shows the contents of the updates that are reported when you use the **debug ip eigrp** command to monitor a stable network.

**Example 3-20** debug ip eigrp *Command Output*

```
RouterA#debug ip eigrp
IP-EIGRP Route Events debugging is on

01:57:23: IP-EIGRP: Processing incoming UPDATE packet
01:57:23: IP-EIGRP: Int 172.16.1.0/24 M 10639872 - 9999872 640000
         SM 384000 - 256000 128000
```

In this example, an internal route (indicated by "Int") for 172.16.1.0/24 is advertised to Router A. Recall that by default the EIGRP metric is equal to the bandwidth plus the delay.

The EIGRP process uses the source metric (SM) information in the update to calculate the AD and place it in the EIGRP topology table. In this example, the SM information is SM 384,000 - 256,000 128,000, which means the source metric (the AD) = 384,000 = 256,000 (the bandwidth) + 128,000 (the delay).

The EIGRP metric calculation for the total delay uses the metric (M) information in the update. In this example, the M information is M 10,639,872 - 9,999,872 640,000, which means the metric (the FD) = 10,639,872 = 9,999,872 (the bandwidth) + 640,000 (the delay).

The EIGRP metric for this route is equal to the FD and, therefore, is 10,639,872.

Example 3-21 illustrates what occurs when a router processes an incoming query packet for network 172.16.1.0/24 when the interface on the neighboring router that leads to that network is shut down. (Note that comments have been added to this output for easier understanding; they are indicated with an exclamation point.) The neighbor previously advertised 172.16.1.0/24 to this router. The query performs the following two functions:

- Router A discovers that its neighbor no longer knows how to get to network 172.16.1.0/24. The metric value (4,294,967,295) is the highest possible value. It indicates that the route is unreachable. Router A removes this entry from the EIGRP topology table and looks for alternative EIGRP routes.

- The debug output indicates that the routing table is not updated; this means that EIGRP did not find an alternative route to the network. The next statement verifies that the EIGRP process has removed the old route and that the route is not in the IP routing table. Router A then informs the neighbor that it does not have a path to this network either.

**Example 3-21**  debug ip eigrp *Command Output*

```
RouterA#debug ip eigrp
 IP-EIGRP Route Events debugging is on
!Shut down an EIGRP neighbor interface for network 172.16.1.0/24
!Router A receives a query looking for a lost path from Router B
01:56:57: IP-EIGRP: Processing incoming QUERY packet
01:56:57: IP-EIGRP: Int 172.16.1.0/24 M 4294967295 - 0 4294967295
     SM 4294967295 - 0 4294967295
!Router A realizes that if it cannot use B for 172.16.1.0/24,
! it does not have an entry in the routing table to get to that network
01:56:57: IP-EIGRP: 172.16.1.0/24 routing table not updated
01:56:57: IP-EIGRP: 172.16.1.0/24 - not in IP routing table
!Router A sends an update to Router B saying it does not know how to reach that
! network either
01:56:57: IP-EIGRP: Int 172.16.1.0/24 metric 4294967295 - 9999872 4294967295
```

# Summary

In this chapter, you learned about Cisco's own EIGRP, an advanced distance vector routing protocol that is easy to configure. It has many advanced features, including rapid convergence, reduced bandwidth usage, multiple network layer support, and support for all data link layer protocols and topologies. EIGRP is a classless routing protocol that guarantees a loop-free topology and that supports VLSM and incremental bounded updates.

EIGRP uses three tables in the path-selection process: the EIGRP neighbor table, the EIGRP topology table, and the IP routing table. The neighbor table contains a list of directly connected EIGRP routers that have established an adjacency with a given router. The topology table includes route entries for all destinations the router has learned. The EIGRP DUAL finite state machine embodies the decision process for all route computations. DUAL tracks all routes advertised by all EIGRP neighbors, chooses the best routes to a destination from the topology table, and places these routes in the routing table. The neighbor that provides the best route is called the successor. A neighbor that provides backup routes is called a feasible successor.

EIGRP supports five packet types: hello, update, query, reply, and acknowledgment. Update, query, and reply packets are sent reliably and require acknowledgment. Hello and acknowledgment packets are sent unreliably and do not require acknowledgment. Fields in the hello packet build adjacencies between EIGRP neighbors. By default, hello packets are sent every 60 seconds on T1 or slower multipoint interfaces and every 5 seconds on LANs and other serial interfaces.

The hold time is the amount of time a router considers a neighbor up without receiving a hello or some other EIGRP packet from that neighbor. Hello packets report the hold-time value. The hold-time interval is set by default to 3 times the hello interval.

A route is considered passive when the router is not performing recomputation on that route; the route is active when it is undergoing recomputation.

If the RTO expires before an ACK packet is received, the EIGRP process retransmits another copy of the reliable packet, up to a maximum of 16 times or until the hold time expires.

EIGRP uses DUAL to calculate the best route to a destination. DUAL selects routes based on the composite metric and ensures that the selected routes are loop-free. EIGRP uses the same basic algorithm for metric calculation as IGRP, which allows EIGRP to be backward-compatible with IGRP. For both protocols, the default calculation relies on bandwidth and delay. EIGRP represents its metrics in a 32-bit format instead of the 24-bit representation used by IGRP.

The AD is the EIGRP metric for an EIGRP neighbor router to reach a particular network. This is the metric between the next-hop neighbor router and the destination network. The FD is the EIGRP metric for this router to reach a particular network. This is the sum of the AD for the particular network learned from an EIGRP neighbor plus the EIGRP metric to reach that neighbor.

The route with the lowest FD is placed in the IP routing table; this is the successor route. If a route's AD is less than the FD of the current successor route, that route is an FS and can be used immediately if the path through the successor for a network becomes unavailable. If there is no FS for a given network and the path through the successor becomes unavailable, a query/reply process is automatically executed to find a loop-free path to the lost network.

When configuring EIGRP, if you do not use the optional wildcard mask in the **network** command, the EIGRP process assumes that all directly connected networks that are part of the major network will participate in the EIGRP routing process. EIGRP attempts to establish EIGRP neighbor relationships from each interface that is part of the overall Class A, B, or C network.

A router configured with the **ip default-network** command for EIGRP does not set the gateway of last resort; this command affects routers that receive EIGRP updates from this router.

Advanced configuration options for EIGRP include manual route summarization, unequal path-cost load balancing, and limiting EIGRP bandwidth utilization on WAN links.

EIGRP performs automatic network-boundary summarization, but this can be disabled, and manual route summarization can be configured on any bit boundary (as long as a more-specific route exists in the routing table).

By default, EIGRP uses up to 50 percent of the bandwidth declared on an interface or subinterface.

If the router does not receive a reply to all of the outstanding queries within 3 minutes (the default time), the route goes to the stuck-in-active (SIA) state.

EIGRP is not plug-and-play for large networks. Like other major routing protocols, it must be designed and configured properly. EIGRP can be scaled in large and growing internetworks by limiting the range of EIGRP queries using route summarization and the EIGRP stub feature.

For scaling EIGRP, the proper resources such as bandwidth, CPU cycles, and memory also have to be available. The network should have good IP address allocation for summarization and a hierarchical design.

# Reference

For additional information, refer to this resource:

- EIGRP protocol home page,
  *www.cisco.com/en/US/customer/tech/tk365/tk207*
  */tech_protocol_family_home.html*

---

**NOTE**   You must be a registered user to access this document.

---

# Configuration Exercise: Configuring and Tuning EIGRP

In this exercise, you configure EIGRP and investigate its default behavior. You then configure summarization, a stub, and a default route.

---

### Introduction to the Configuration Exercises

This book uses Configuration Exercises to help you practice configuring routers with the commands and topics presented. If you have access to real hardware, you can try these exercises on your routers. See Appendix H, "Configuration Exercise Equipment Requirements and Initial Configurations," for a list of recommended equipment and initial configuration commands for the routers. However, even if you don't have access to any routers, you can go through the exercises, and keep a log of your own running configurations, or just read through the solution. Commands used and solutions to the Configuration Exercises are provided after the exercises.

In the Configuration Exercises, the network is assumed to consist of two pods, each with four routers. The pods are interconnected to a backbone. You configure pod 1. No interaction between the two pods is required, but you might see some routes from the other pod in your routing tables in some exercises if you have it configured (the Configuration Exercise answers show the routes from the other pod). In most of the exercises, the backbone has only one router; in some cases, another router is added to the backbone. Each Configuration Exercise assumes that you have completed the previous chapters' Configuration Exercises on your pod.

---

---

**NOTE**   Throughout this exercise, the pod number is referred to as *x*, and the router number is referred to as *y*. Substitute the appropriate numbers as needed.

---

## Objectives

Your task in this Configuration Exercise is to set up EIGRP and investigate its default behavior. You will then optimize the EIGRP configuration.

## Visual Objective

Figure 3-31 illustrates the topology used in this exercise.

**Figure 3-31**  *EIGRP Configuration Exercise Topology*

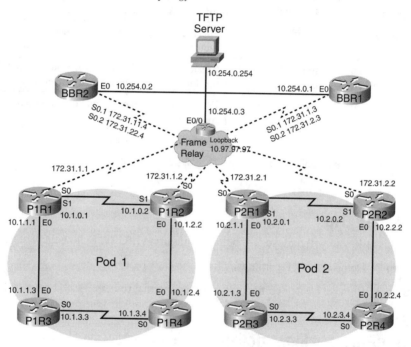

## Command List

In this exercise, you use the commands in Table 3-8, listed in logical order. Refer to this list if you need configuration command assistance during the exercise.

---

**CAUTION**    Although the command syntax is shown in this table, the addresses shown are typically for the P*x*R1 and P*x*R3 routers. Be careful when addressing your routers! Refer to the exercise instructions and the appropriate visual objective diagram for addressing details.

---

**Table 3-8**   *EIGRP Configuration Exercise Commands*

| Command | Description |
|---|---|
| (config)#**router eigrp 1** | Enters configuration mode for EIGRP in AS 1. |
| (config-router)#**network 10.x.0.0 0.0.255.255** | Specifies that EIGRP should run within network 10.x.0.0/16. |
| (config-router)#**no auto-summary** | Turns off automatic summarization at classful network boundaries. |
| (config-if)#**ip summary-address eigrp 1 10.x.0.0 255.255.0.0** | Creates and advertises a summary route 10.x.0.0/16 for EIGRP AS 1 out of this interface. |
| (config-router)#**eigrp stub** | Specifies that this router should behave as an EIGRP stub router. |
| (config-if)#**ip summary-address eigrp 1 0.0.0.0 0.0.0.0** | Creates and advertises a default route for EIGRP AS 1 out of this interface and suppresses all other specific routes. |
| #**show ip protocols** | Displays the parameters and current state of the active routing protocol process. |
| #**debug ip eigrp** | Displays EIGRP updates. |
| #**show ip eigrp neighbors detail** | Displays detailed EIGRP neighbor information. |

# Task 1: Cleaning Up

In this task, you will remove RIP before configuring EIGRP. Follow these steps:

**Step 1**   Remove all RIP commands from the edge routers.

**Step 2**   Remove all RIP commands from the internal routers.

# Task 2: Configuring Basic EIGRP

In this task, you will set up and investigate the operation of EIGRP. Follow these steps:

**Step 1**   Configure EIGRP on each router in your pod using AS 1, using the appropriate network and wildcard values to include all interfaces in the EIGRP routing process. Disable autosummarization on the edge routers.

**Step 2**   Verify that the routers are set up correctly using the **show ip protocols** command. Make sure that the AS number is correct and that all neighbors are exchanging routes.

**Step 3**   Verify that the routes from other routers in your pod are being recognized via EIGRP on each router.

**Step 4**   Use **debug ip eigrp** on the internal routers in your pod to monitor the EIGRP queries.

**Step 5**   Shut down the serial interface between the edge routers (the S1 interface on P*x*R1 and P*x*R2).

**Step 6**   View the EIGRP queries sent to internal routers.

**Step 7**   Turn off all debugging.

**Step 8**   Reenable the serial interface between the edge routers (the S1 interface on P*x*R1 and P*x*R2).

## Task 3: Configuring EIGRP Summarization

In this task, you will configure EIGRP route summarization. This will add stability and speed convergence to the network by controlling the scope of queries, minimizing update traffic, and routing table size. Follow these steps:

**Step 1**   Manually configure the edge routers (P*x*R1 and P*x*R2) to summarize the pod EIGRP routes to BBR1 into a single 10.*x*.0.0/16 advertisement (where *x* is your pod number).

**Step 2**   Telnet to BBR1 (172.31.*x*.3) (the password is **cisco**) and verify that you see only the summary route and not the more specific routes from your pod. If both edge routers are configured correctly, you should see two equal-cost paths available to BBR1.

## Task 4: Configuring the EIGRP Stub

Having optimized the routing table in the core BBR1 router by summarizing the routes from the pod's edge routers to the core BBR1 router, you will now limit the query traffic from the pod's edge routers to its internal routers. Follow these steps:

**Step 1**   Configure the internal routers (P*x*R3 and P*x*R4) as EIGRP stubs. Remember that this binds queries but does not affect the routing table.

**Step 2**   Verify that the edge router recognizes its internal EIGRP neighbor as a stub.

**Step 3**   The stub designation binds query traffic and helps the router avoid getting stuck in active, where EIGRP is unable to resolve routes for long periods. To demonstrate this, use the **debug ip eigrp** command on the internal router.

**Step 4**   Shut down the serial interface between the edge routers (the S1 interface between P*x*R1 and P*x*R2).

**Step 5**   Compared to the time before the internal routers were configured as stubs, notice that no queries are now being sent to the internal router. You should *not* see the "processing incoming QUERY" debug message on the internal routers, because they are configured as stub routers.

**Step 6** Reenable the serial interface between the edge routers (the S1 interface between PxR1 and PxR2).

**Step 7** Turn off debugging on the internal routers (PxR3 and PxR4).

## Task 5: Configuring the EIGRP Default Route

In this task, you will advertise a default route from the edge router to the internal router via EIGRP. This change will add stability and speed convergence to the network by minimizing update traffic and routing table size. Follow these steps:

**Step 1** Send a default route from the edge router to the internal router, and filter all specific routes. You can do this by configuring a summary route of 0.0.0.0 0.0.0.0 from the edge router to the internal router.

**Step 2** Examine the routing table on the internal routers. You should see the default route, the connected routes, and the EIGRP route learned from the other internal router. Other routes received from the edge router should have been filtered.

## Exercise Verification

You have successfully completed this exercise when you achieve the following results:

- You have successfully implemented EIGRP and have seen EIGRP query traffic.
- You have summarized your pod addresses to the core.
- You have optimized performance on the internal routers.

# Solutions to the Configuration Exercise: Configuring and Tuning EIGRP

This section provides the answers to the questions in the Configuration Exercise.

---

**NOTE**     Some answers provided cover multiple steps; the answers are given after the last step to which that answer applies.

---

## Solution to Task 1: Cleaning Up

**Step 1** Remove all RIP commands from the edge routers.

**Solution:**

The following shows the required configuration commands on the P1R1 and P1R2 routers:

```
P1R1(config)#no router rip
P1R1(config)#int s0
P1R1(config-if)#no ip summary-address rip 10.1.0.0 255.255.0.0

P1R2(config)#no router rip
P1R2(config)#int s0
P1R2(config-if)#no ip summary-address rip 10.1.0.0 255.255.0.0
```

**Step 2**   Remove all RIP commands from the internal routers.

**Solution:**

The following shows the required configuration commands on the P1R3 and P1R4 routers:

```
P1R3(config)#no router rip
P1R4(config)#no router rip
```

# Solution to Task 2: Configuring Basic EIGRP

**Step 1**   Configure EIGRP on each router in your pod using AS 1, using the
appropriate network and wildcard values to include all interfaces in the
EIGRP routing process. Disable autosummarization on the edge routers.

**Solution:**

The following shows the required configuration commands on the pod 1 routers:

```
P1R1(config)#router eigrp 1
P1R1(config-router)#network 10.1.0.0 0.0.255.255
P1R1(config-router)#network 172.31.1.0 0.0.0.255
P1R1(config-router)#no auto-summary

P1R2(config)#router eigrp 1
P1R2(config-router)#network 10.1.0.0 0.0.255.255
P1R2(config-router)#network 172.31.1.0 0.0.0.255
P1R2(config-router)#no auto-summary

P1R3(config)#router eigrp 1
P1R3(config-router)#network 10.1.0.0 0.0.255.255
P1R3(config-router)#no auto-summary

P1R4(config)#router eigrp 1
P1R4(config-router)#network 10.1.0.0 0.0.255.255
P1R4(config-router)#no auto-summary
```

**Step 2**   Verify that the routers are set up correctly using the **show ip protocols**
command. Make sure that the AS number is correct and that all neighbors are
exchanging routes.

**Solution:**

The following is the output from the P1R1 router, showing that the entire configuration is correct:

```
P1R1#show ip protocols
Routing Protocol is "eigrp 1"
  Outgoing update filter list for all interfaces is not set
  Incoming update filter list for all interfaces is not set
  Default networks flagged in outgoing updates
  Default networks accepted from incoming updates
  EIGRP metric weight K1=1, K2=0, K3=1, K4=0, K5=0
  EIGRP maximum hopcount 100
  EIGRP maximum metric variance 1
  Redistributing: eigrp 1
  Automatic network summarization is not in effect
  Maximum path: 4
  Routing for Networks:
    10.1.0.0/16
    172.31.1.0/24
  Routing Information Sources:
    Gateway         Distance      Last Update
    (this router)         90      00:02:41
    10.1.1.3              90      00:00:51
    10.1.0.2              90      00:00:51
    172.31.1.3           90      00:00:51
  Distance: internal 90 external 170
```

**Step 3** Verify that the routes from other routers in your pod are being recognized via EIGRP on each router.

**Solution:**

The following sample output is from the P1R1 router. The highlighted EIGRP routes are from other routers in the pod.

```
P1R1#show ip route
<output omitted>
Gateway of last resort is not set

     172.31.0.0/24 is subnetted, 2 subnets
D       172.31.2.0 [90/41024000] via 172.31.1.3, 00:02:02, Serial0
C       172.31.1.0 is directly connected, Serial0
     10.0.0.0/24 is subnetted, 9 subnets
D       10.1.3.0 [90/40537600] via 10.1.1.3, 00:02:01, Ethernet0
D       10.2.0.0 [90/41536000] via 172.31.1.3, 00:02:02, Serial0
D       10.1.2.0 [90/40537600] via 10.1.0.2, 00:02:02, Serial1
D       10.2.1.0 [90/41049600] via 172.31.1.3, 00:02:02, Serial0
D       10.2.2.0 [90/41049600] via 172.31.1.3, 00:01:48, Serial0
C       10.1.1.0 is directly connected, Ethernet0
D       10.2.3.0 [90/41561600] via 172.31.1.3, 00:01:57, Serial0
C       10.1.0.0 is directly connected, Serial1
D       10.254.0.0 [90/40537600] via 172.31.1.3, 00:02:03, Serial0
P1R1#
```

---

**NOTE**    In this output, pod 1 and 2 routers are configured for EIGRP.

Don't be confused by this routing table! Subnets 10.1.0.0 and
10.2.0.0 are not summary routes; they are the subnets on the serial
interfaces between P*x*R1 and P*x*R2 in pods 1 and 2.

---

**Step 4**    Use **debug ip eigrp** on the internal routers in your pod to monitor the EIGRP
queries.

**Solution:**

The following example is from the P1R3 router:

```
P1R3#debug ip eigrp
IP-EIGRP Route Events debugging is on
P1R3#
```

**Step 5**    Shut down the serial interface between the edge routers (the S1 interface on
P*x*R1 and P*x*R2).

**Solution:**

The following sample configuration is from the P1R1 router:

```
P1R1(config)#int s1
P1R1(config-if)#shutdown
```

**Step 6**    View the EIGRP queries sent to internal routers.

**Solution:**

The following sample output is from the P1R3 router. P1R3 receives a query for network
10.1.0.0/24 from P1R1. 10.1.0.0/24 is unreachable, as indicated by the infinite metric,
4294967295. P1R3 replies to the query with 10.1.0.0/24 as unreachable.

```
Mar  1 13:57:05 EST: IP-EIGRP: Processing incoming QUERY packet
Mar  1 13:57:05 EST: IP-EIGRP: Int 10.1.0.0/24 M 4294967295 - 0 4294967295
   SM 4294967295 - 0 4294967295
Mar  1 13:57:05 EST: IP-EIGRP: Int 10.1.2.0/24 M 4294967295 - 40000000
   4294967295 SM 4294967295 - 40000000 4294967295
Mar  1 13:57:05 EST: IP-EIGRP: Int 10.1.0.0/24 metric 4294967295 - 0 4294967295
Mar  1 13:57:05 EST: IP-EIGRP: 10.1.0.0/24 - do advertise out Serial0
Mar  1 13:57:05 EST: IP-EIGRP: Int 10.1.0.0/24 metric 4294967295 - 0 4294967295
Mar  1 13:57:05 EST: IP-EIGRP: 10.1.2.0/24 - do advertise out Ethernet0
Mar  1 13:57:05 EST: IP-EIGRP: Int 10.1.2.0/24 metric 40537600 - 40000000 537600
Mar  1 13:57:05 EST: IP-EIGRP: Processing incoming REPLY packet
Mar  1 13:57:05 EST: IP-EIGRP: Int 10.1.0.0/24 M 4294967295 - 0 4294967295 SM
   4294967295 - 0 4294967295
Mar  1 13:57:05 EST: IP-EIGRP: Processing incoming REPLY packet
Mar  1 13:57:05 EST: IP-EIGRP: Int 10.1.0.0/24 M 41049600 - 40000000 1049600
   SM40537P1600 - 40000000 537600
```

*continues*

```
Mar  1 13:57:05 EST: IP-EIGRP: 10.1.0.0/24 routing table not updated
Mar  1 13:57:05 EST: IP-EIGRP: 10.1.0.0/24 - do advertise out Ethernet0
Mar  1 13:57:05 EST: IP-EIGRP: Int 10.1.0.0/24 metric 41049600 - 40000000 1049600
Mar  1 13:57:05 EST: IP-EIGRP: Int 10.1.0.0/24 metric 41049600 - 40000000 1049600
Mar  1 13:57:05 EST: IP-EIGRP: Processing incoming UPDATE packet
Mar  1 13:57:05 EST: IP-EIGRP: Int 10.1.2.0/24 M 4294967295 - 40000000 4294967295
    SM 4294967295 - 40000000 4294967295
Mar  1 13:57:05 EST: IP-EIGRP: 10.1.0.0/24 - do advertise out Ethernet0
Mar  1 13:57:05 EST: IP-EIGRP: Int 10.1.0.0/24 metric 41049600 - 40000000 1049600
Mar  1 13:57:05 EST: IP-EIGRP: Processing incoming UPDATE packet
Mar  1 13:57:05 EST: IP-EIGRP: Int 10.1.0.0/24 M 4294967295 - 40000000 4294967295
    SM 4294967295 - 40000000 4294967295R3
Mar  1 13:57:07 EST: IP-EIGRP: Processing incoming QUERY packet
Mar  1 13:57:07 EST: IP-EIGRP: Int 10.1.0.0/24 M 4294967295 - 0 4294967295
    SM 4294967295 - 0 4294967295
Mar  1 13:57:07 EST: IP-EIGRP: 10.1.0.0/24 - do advertise out Ethernet0
Mar  1 13:57:07 EST: IP-EIGRP: Int 10.1.0.0/24 metric 4294967295 - 0 4294967295
Mar  1 13:57:07 EST: IP-EIGRP: Processing incoming REPLY packet
Mar  1 13:57:07 EST: IP-EIGRP: Int 10.1.0.0/24 M 4294967295 - 0 4294967295
    SM 4294967295 - 0 4294967295
Mar  1 13:57:07 EST: IP-EIGRP: 10.1.0.0/24 routing table not updated
Mar  1 13:57:07 EST: IP-EIGRP: 10.1.0.0/24 - do advertise out Serial0
Mar  1 13:57:07 EST: IP-EIGRP: Int 10.1.0.0/24 metric 4294967295 - 0 4294967295
```

**Step 7**   Turn off all debugging.

**Solution:**

The following example shows how to turn off debugging on the P1R3 router:

```
P1R3#no debug all
All possible debugging has been turned off
P1R3#
```

**Step 8**   Reenable the serial interface between the edge routers (the S1 interface on PxR1 and PxR2).

**Solution:**

The following example shows how to reenable the S1 interface on the P1R1 router:

```
P1R1(config)#int s1
P1R1(config-if)#no shutdown
```

# Solution to Task 3: Configuring EIGRP Summarization

**Step 1**   Manually configure the edge routers (PxR1 and PxR2) to summarize the pod EIGRP routes to BBR1 into a single 10.x.0.0/16 advertisement (where x is your pod number).

**Solution:**

The following example shows the required configuration on the P1R1 and P1R2 routers:

```
P1R1(config)#int s0
P1R1(config-if)#ip summary-address eigrp 1 10.1.0.0 255.255.0.0

P1R2(config)#int s0
P1R2(config-if)#ip summary-address eigrp 1 10.1.0.0 255.255.0.0
```

**Step 2**    Telnet to BBR1 (172.31.x.3) (the password is **cisco**) and verify that you see only the
summary route and not the more specific routes from your pod. If both edge routers
are configured correctly, you should see two equal-cost paths available to BBR1.

**Solution:**

The following sample output is from the BBR1 router. The highlighted routes are two equal-
cost routes for the pod 1 network.

```
BBR1>show ip route
<output omitted>
Gateway of last resort is not set

     172.31.0.0/24 is subnetted, 4 subnets
B       172.31.22.0 [20/0] via 10.254.0.2, 00:00:18
C       172.31.2.0 is directly connected, Serial0.2
C       172.31.1.0 is directly connected, Serial0.1
B       172.31.11.0 [20/0] via 10.254.0.2, 00:00:18
S    192.168.11.0/24 [1/0] via 172.31.1.2
     10.0.0.0/8 is variably subnetted, 4 subnets, 2 masks
D       10.2.0.0/16 [90/40537600] via 172.31.2.1, 00:00:18, Serial0.2
                    [90/40537600] via 172.31.2.2, 00:00:18, Serial0.2
B       10.97.97.0/24 [20/0] via 10.254.0.3, 00:00:18
D       10.1.0.0/16 [90/40537600] via 172.31.1.2, 00:00:18, Serial0.1
                    [90/40537600] via 172.31.1.1, 00:00:18, Serial0.1
C       10.254.0.0/24 is directly connected, Ethernet0
S    192.168.22.0/24 [1/0] via 172.31.2.2
S    192.168.1.0/24 [1/0] via 172.31.1.1
S    192.168.2.0/24 [1/0] via 172.31.2.1
BBR1>
```

# Solution to Task 4: Configuring the EIGRP Stub

**Step 1**    Configure the internal routers (P*x*R3 and P*x*R4) as EIGRP stubs. Remember
that this bounds queries but does not affect the routing table.

**Solution:**

The following example shows the required configuration on the P1R3 and P1R4 routers:

```
P1R3(config)#router eigrp 1
P1R3(config-router)#eigrp stub

P1R4(config)#router eigrp 1
P1R4(config-router)#eigrp stub
```

**Step 2** Verify that the edge router recognizes its internal EIGRP neighbor as a stub.

**Solution:**

The following sample output is from the P1R1 router. The highlighted line indicates that this router sees P1R3 (10.1.1.3) as a stub.

```
P1R1#show ip eigrp neighbor detail
IP-EIGRP neighbors for process 1
H   Address               Interface    Hold Uptime    SRTT   RTO  Q  Seq Type
                                       (sec)          (ms)        Cnt Num
1   10.1.1.3              Et0             13 00:00:24  690   4140  0  86
    Version 12.1/1.2, Retrans: 0, Retries: 0
    Stub Peer Advertising ( CONNECTED SUMMARY ) Routes
2   10.1.0.2              Se1             10 00:04:39   30   2280  0  114
    Version 12.1/1.2, Retrans: 2, Retries: 0
0   172.31.1.3           Se0            154 00:24:35   42   2280  0  121
    Version 12.1/1.2, Retrans: 10, Retries: 0
P1R1#
```

**Step 3** The stub designation binds query traffic and helps the router avoid getting stuck in active, where EIGRP is unable to resolve routes for long periods. To demonstrate this, use the **debug ip eigrp** command on the internal router.

**Solution:**

The following shows the **debug** command on the P1R3 router:

```
P1R3#debug ip eigrp
IP-EIGRP Route Events debugging is on
P1R3#
```

**Step 4** Shut down the serial interface between the edge routers (the S1 interface between PxR1 and PxR2).

**Solution:**

The following shows the required configuration on the P1R1 router:

```
P1R1(config)#int s1
P1R1(config-if)#shutdown
```

**Step 5** Compared to the time before the internal routers were configured as stubs, notice that no queries are now being sent to the internal router. You should *not* see the "processing incoming QUERY" debug message on the internal routers, because they are configured as stub routers.

**Solution:**

The following sample output is from the P1R3 router. Queries are no longer being sent to the internal routers. P1R1 only sends the Update packet to P1R3, and P1R3 responds with the Reply packet.

```
P1R3#
Mar  1 14:35:09 EST: IP-EIGRP: Processing incoming UPDATE packet
Mar  1 14:35:09 EST: IP-EIGRP: Int 10.1.0.0/24 M 4294967295 - 0 4294967295
    SM 4294967295 - 0 4294967295
Mar  1 14:35:09 EST: IP-EIGRP: Int 10.1.2.0/24 M 4294967295 - 40000000
    4294967295 SM 4294967295 - 40000000 4294967295
Mar  1 14:35:09 EST: IP-EIGRP: Int 10.1.0.0/24 metric 4294967295 - 0 4294967295
Mar  1 14:35:09 EST: IP-EIGRP: 10.1.0.0/24 - denied by stub
Mar  1 14:35:09 EST: IP-EIGRP: Processing incoming REPLY packet
Mar  1 14:35:09 EST: IP-EIGRP: Int 10.1.0.0/24 M 4294967295 - 0 4294967295
    SM 4294967295 - 0 4294967295
Mar  1 14:35:09 EST: IP-EIGRP: 10.1.0.0/24 - denied by stub
Mar  1 14:35:09 EST: IP-EIGRP: 10.1.0.0/24 - denied by stub
```

**Step 6**    Reenable the serial interface between the edge routers (the S1 interface between P*x*R1 and P*x*R2).

**Solution:**

The following example shows the reenabling of the P1R1 S1 interface and the debug output from the P1R3 router. Queries are not being sent to the internal routers.

```
P1R1(config)#int s1
P1R1(config-if)#no shutdown

P1R3#
Mar  1 14:36:13 EST: IP-EIGRP: Processing incoming UPDATE packet
Mar  1 14:36:13 EST: IP-EIGRP: Int 10.1.0.0/24 M 40537600 - 40000000 537600
    SM 40512000 - 40000000 512000
Mar  1 14:36:13 EST: IP-EIGRP: Int 10.1.0.0/24 metric 40537600 - 40000000 537600
Mar  1 14:36:13 EST: IP-EIGRP: 10.1.0.0/24 - denied by stub
Mar  1 14:36:19 EST: IP-EIGRP: Processing incoming UPDATE packet
Mar  1 14:36:19 EST: IP-EIGRP: Int 10.1.2.0/24 M 40563200 - 40000000 563200
    SM 40537600 - 40000000 537600
Mar  1 14:36:19 EST: IP-EIGRP: 10.1.2.0/24 routing table not updated
```

**Step 7**    Turn off debugging on the internal routers (P*x*R3 and P*x*R4).

**Solution:**

The following example shows how to turn off debugging on the P1R3 router:

```
P1R3#no debug all
All possible debugging has been turned off
```

# Solution to Task 5: Configuring the EIGRP Default Route

**Step 1**  Send a default route from the edge router to the internal router, and filter all specific routes. You can do this by configuring a summary route of 0.0.0.0 0.0.0.0 from the edge router to the internal router.

**Solution:**

The following example shows the required configuration on the P1R1 and P1R2 routers:

```
P1R1(config)#int e0
P1R1(config-if)#ip summary eigrp 1 0.0.0.0 0.0.0.0

P1R2(config-if)#int e0
P1R2(config-if)#ip summary eigrp 1 0.0.0.0 0.0.0.0
```

**Step 2**  Examine the routing table on the internal routers. You should see the default route, the connected routes, and the EIGRP route learned from the other internal router. Other routes received from the edge router should have been filtered.

**Solution:**

The following output is from the P1R3 and P1R4 routers; the highlighted lines indicate the default route from the edge routers. Note that the gateway of last resort is also now set on the P1R3 and P1R4 routers.

```
P1R3#show ip route
<output omitted>
Gateway of last resort is 10.1.1.1 to network 0.0.0.0

     10.0.0.0/24 is subnetted, 3 subnets
C       10.1.3.0 is directly connected, Serial0
D       10.1.2.0 [90/40537600] via 10.1.3.4, 00:08:20, Serial0
C       10.1.1.0 is directly connected, Ethernet0
D*   0.0.0.0/0 [90/307200] via 10.1.1.1, 00:02:17, Ethernet0
P1R3#

P1R4#show ip route
<output omitted>
Gateway of last resort is 10.1.2.2 to network 0.0.0.0

     10.0.0.0/24 is subnetted, 3 subnets
C       10.1.3.0 is directly connected, Serial0
C       10.1.2.0 is directly connected, Ethernet0
D       10.1.1.0 [90/40537600] via 10.1.3.3, 00:09:00, Serial0
D*   0.0.0.0/0 [90/307200] via 10.1.2.2, 00:03:27, Ethernet0
P1R4#
```

## Exercise Verification

You have successfully completed this exercise when you achieve the following results:

- You have successfully implemented EIGRP and have seen EIGRP query traffic.
- You have summarized your pod addresses to the core.
- You have optimized performance on the internal routers.

# Review Questions

Answer the following questions, and then refer to Appendix G, "Answers to Review Questions," for the answers.

1   What are some features of EIGRP?

2   Is EIGRP operational traffic multicast or broadcast?

3   How do IGRP and EIGRP differ in their metric calculation?

4   What is in the EIGRP topology table?

5   Describe the five types of EIGRP packets.

6   How often are EIGRP hello packets sent?

7   What is the difference between the hold time and the hello-time interval?

8   What is the difference between a passive route and an active route? Which is the desired type of route in a stable network?

9   Which command is used to see the RTO and hold timers?

10  Why are EIGRP routing updates described as reliable?

11  What units are the bandwidth and delay parameters in the EIGRP metric calculation?

12  What is the difference between an AD and an FD?

13  What does it mean when a route is marked as an FS?

14  In the following table, place the letter of the description next to the term the description describes. The descriptions may be used more than once.

Descriptions:

a.  A network protocol that EIGRP supports.

b.  A table that contains FS information.

c.  The administrative distance determines routing information that is included in this table.

d.  A neighbor router that has the best path to a destination.

    e.  A neighbor router that has the best alternative path to a destination.

    f.  An algorithm used by EIGRP that ensures fast convergence.

    g.  A multicast packet used to discover neighbors.

    h.  A packet sent by EIGRP routers when a new neighbor is discovered and when a change occurs.

| Term | Description Letter |
|------|--------------------|
| Successor | |
| Feasible successor | |
| Hello | |
| Topology table | |
| IP | |
| Update | |
| AppleTalk | |
| Routing table | |
| DUAL | |
| IPX | |

**15**  Answer true or false to the following statements:

    — EIGRP performs autosummarization.

    — EIGRP autosummarization cannot be turned off.

    — EIGRP supports VLSM.

    — EIGRP can maintain three independent routing tables.

    — The EIGRP hello interval is an unchangeable fixed value.

**16**  What is the recommended practice for configuring bandwidth on a Frame Relay point-to-point subinterface?

**17**  Router A has three interfaces with IP addresses 172.16.1.1/24, 172.16.2.3/24, and 172.16.5.1/24. What commands would be used to configure EIGRP to run in AS 100 on only the interfaces with addresses 172.16.2.3/24 and 172.16.5.1/24?

**18**  Router A, connected to Router B, is configured with the **ip default-network 172.17.0.0** command for EIGRP. What does this command do on Router A?

**19**  Routers A and B are connected and are running EIGRP on all their interfaces. Router A has four interfaces, with IP addresses 172.16.1.1/24, 172.16.2.3/24, 172.16.5.1/24, and 10.1.1.1/24. Router B has two interfaces, with IP addresses 172.16.1.2/24 and 192.168.1.1/24. (Other routers in the network are running EIGRP on each of the interfaces on these two routers.) Which summary routes does Router A generate automatically?

**20**   Router A has four EIGRP paths to a destination with the following EIGRP metrics:

       — Path 1: 1100

       — Path 2: 1200

       — Path 3: 2000

       — Path 4: 4000

If the command **variance 3** is configured on Router A, which paths are included for load balancing?

**21**   Router A has the following configuration:

```
interface s0
  ip bandwidth-percent eigrp 100 40
  bandwidth 256
router eigrp 100
  network 10.0.0.0
```

What is the maximum bandwidth that EIGRP uses on the S0 interface?

**22**   What is the default stuck-in-active timer?

**23**   How can EIGRP queries be limited?

**24**   Why does summarization limit the query range?

**25**   How does the stub feature limit the query range?

**26**   What does the **eigrp stub receive-only** command do?

**27**   What command displays EIGRP-learned IP routes?

**28**   The following is part of the output of the **show ip eigrp topology** command:

```
P 10.1.3.0/24, 1 successors, FD is 10514432
        via 10.1.2.2 (10514432/28160), Serial0/0
```

What are the two numbers in parentheses?

**29**   What command displays the types of EIGRP packets as they are received from EIGRP neighbors?

**30**   What command displays EIGRP packets as they are sent and received?

This chapter discusses Open Shortest Path First (OSPF) in a single area. It covers the following topics:

- OSPF Protocol Overview
- OSPF Packet Types
- Configuring Basic OSPF for a Single Area
- OSPF Network Types

# CHAPTER 4

# Configuring the Open Shortest Path First Protocol in a Single Area

This chapter examines the Open Shortest Path First (OSPF) routing protocol, which is one of the most commonly used interior gateway protocols in IP networking. OSPF is an open-standard protocol based primarily on RFC 2328. OSPF is a fairly complex protocol made up of several protocol handshakes, database advertisements, and packet types.

## OSPF Protocol Overview

This section introduces each of the major components that makes up OSPF. It defines the major characteristics of the OSPF routing protocol and provides a brief definition of link-state routing protocols, link-state adjacencies, and shortest path first (SPF) calculations.

## Link-State Routing Protocols

The need to overcome the limitations of distance-vector routing protocols led to the development of link-state routing protocols. Link-state routing protocols have the following characteristics:

- They respond quickly to network changes.

- They send triggered updates when a network change occurs.

- They send periodic updates, known as link-state refresh, at long time intervals, such as every 30 minutes.

Link-state routing protocols generate routing updates only when a change occurs in the network topology. When a link changes state, the device that detected the change creates a link-state advertisement (LSA) concerning that link, as shown in Figure 4-1. The LSA propagates to all neighboring devices using a special multicast address. Each routing device takes a copy of the LSA, updates its link-state database (LSDB), and forwards the LSA to neighboring devices. This flooding of the LSA ensures that all routing devices update their databases before updating routing tables to reflect the new topology.

As shown in Figure 4-1, the LSDB is used to calculate the best paths through the network. Link-state routers find the best paths to a destination by applying Dijkstra's algorithm, also known as SPF, against the LSDB to build the SPF tree. The best paths are then selected from the SPF tree and are placed in the routing table.

**Figure 4-1** *Components of Link-State Protocols*

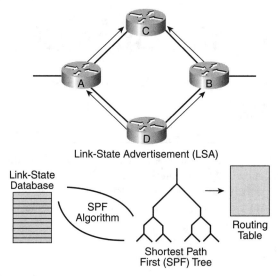

OSPF and Integrated Intermediate System-to-Intermediate System (IS-IS) are classified as link-state routing protocols because of the manner in which they distribute routing information and calculate routes.

Link-state routing protocols collect routing information from all other routers in the network or from within a defined area of the network. After link-state routing protocols have collected this information from all routers, each router independently calculates its best paths to all destinations in the network using Dijkstra's (SPF) algorithm. Incorrect information from any particular router is less likely to cause confusion, because each router maintains its own view of the network.

For all the routers in the network to make consistent routing decisions, each router must keep a record of the following information:

- **Its immediate neighbor routers**—If the router loses contact with a neighbor router, within a few seconds it invalidates all paths through that router and recalculates its paths through the network. Adjacency information about neighbors is stored in the neighbor table, also known as an adjacency database, in OSPF.

- **All the other routers in the network, or in its area of the network, and their attached networks**—The router recognizes other routers and networks through LSAs, which are flooded through the network. LSAs are stored in a topology table (an LSDB).

- **The best paths to each destination**—Each router independently calculates the best paths to each destination in the network using Dijkstra's (SPF) algorithm. All paths are kept in the LSDB. The best paths are then offered to the routing table or forwarding database. Packets arriving at the router are forwarded based on the information held in the routing table.

The memory resources needed to maintain these tables is one drawback to link-state protocols. However, because the topology table is identical for all OSPF routers in an area and contains full information about all the routers and links in an area, each router can independently select a loop-free and efficient pathway, based on cost, to reach every network in the area. This benefit overcomes the "routing by rumor" limitations of distance-vector routing.

| | |
|---|---|
| **NOTE** | With distance-vector routing protocols, the routers rely on routing decisions from the neighbors. Routers do not have the full picture of the network topology. |
| | With link-state routing protocols, each router has the full picture of the network topology, and it can independently make a decision based on an accurate picture of the network topology. |

# Defining an OSPF Area

In small networks, the web of router links is not complex, and paths to individual destinations are easily deduced. However, in large networks, the resulting web is highly complex, and the number of potential paths to each destination is large. Therefore, the Dijkstra (SPF) calculations comparing all of these possible routes can be very complex and can take significant time.

Link-state routing protocols usually reduce the size of the Dijkstra calculations by partitioning the network into areas. The number of routers in an area and the number of LSAs that flood only within the area are small, which means that the link-state or topology database for an area is small. Consequently, the Dijkstra calculation is easier and takes less time.

Link-state routing protocols use a two-layer area hierarchy:

- **Transit area**—An OSPF area whose primary function is the fast and efficient movement of IP packets. Transit areas interconnect with other OSPF area types. Generally, end users are not found within a transit area. OSPF area 0, also known as the backbone area, is by definition a transit area.

- **Regular area**—An OSPF area whose primary function is to connect users and resources. Regular areas are usually set up along functional or geographic groupings. By default, a regular area does not allow traffic from another area to use its links to reach other areas. All traffic from other areas must cross a transit area such as area 0. An area that does not allow traffic to pass through it is known as a regular area, or nonbackbone area. It can have a number of subtypes, including a stub area, a totally stubby area, and a not-so-stubby area.

OSPF forces a rigid two-layer area hierarchy. The network's underlying physical connectivity must map to the two-layer area structure, with all nonbackbone areas attaching directly to area 0.

## OSPF Areas

In link-state routing protocols, all routers must keep a copy of the LSDB. The more OSPF routers that exist, the larger the LSDB. It can be advantageous to have all information in all routers, but this approach does not scale to large network sizes. The area concept is a compromise. Routers inside an area maintain detailed information about the links and routers located within that area and only general or summary information about routers and links in other areas.

When a router or link fails, that information is flooded along adjacencies to only routers in the local area. Routers outside the area do not receive this information. By maintaining a hierarchical structure and limiting the number of routers in an area, an OSPF autonomous system (AS) can scale to very large sizes.

OSPF areas require a hierarchical structure, meaning that all areas must connect directly to area 0. In Figure 4-2, notice that links between area 1 routers and area 2 or 3 routers are not allowed. All interarea traffic must pass through the backbone area—area 0. The optimal number of routers per area varies based on factors such as network stability, but Cisco recommends no more than 50 to 100 routers per area.

**Figure 4-2**  *OSPF Areas*

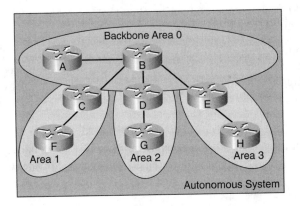

### OSPF Area Characteristics

The OSPF area characteristics are as follows:

- It minimizes routing table entries.
- It localizes the impact of a topology change within an area.
- Detailed LSA flooding stops at the area boundary.
- It requires a hierarchical network design.

Routers that make up area 0 are known as backbone routers. Hierarchical networking defines area 0 as the core. All other areas connect directly to backbone area 0.

An area border router (ABR) connects area 0 to the nonbackbone areas. An OSPF ABR plays a very important role in network design. An ABR has the following characteristics:

- It separates LSA flooding zones.
- It becomes the primary point for area address summarization.
- It functions regularly as the source of default routes.
- It maintains the LSDB for each area with which it is involved.

The ideal design is to have each ABR connected to two areas only—the backbone and another area. Three areas are the recommended upper limit.

## Defining OSPF Adjacencies

A router running a link-state routing protocol must first establish neighbor adjacencies with selected neighbor routers. A router achieves this neighbor adjacency by exchanging hello packets with the neighbor routers, as shown in Figure 4-3. In general, routers establish adjacencies as follows:

- The router sends and receives hello packets to and from its neighbor routers. The format of the destination address is typically multicast.

- The routers exchange hello packets subject to protocol-specific parameters, such as checking whether the neighbor is in the same area, using the same hello interval, and so on. Routers declare the neighbor up when the exchange is complete.

- After two routers establish neighbor adjacency using the hello packets, they synchronize their LSDB by exchanging LSAs, and confirm the receipt of LSAs from the adjacent router. The two neighbor routers now recognize that they have synchronized their LSDBs with each other. For OSPF, this means that the routers are now in full-adjacency state with each other.

- If necessary, the routers forward any new LSAs to other neighbor routers, ensuring complete synchronization of link-state information inside the area.

**Figure 4-3**    *Hello Exchange on the Broadcast Network*

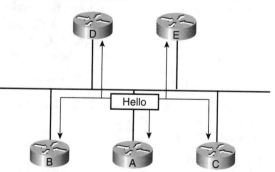

The two OSPF routers on a point-to-point serial link, usually encapsulated in High-Level Data Link Control (HDLC) or Point-to-Point Protocol (PPP), form a full adjacency with each other.

LAN links elect one router as the designated router (DR) and another as the backup designated router (BDR). All other routers on the LAN form full adjacencies with these two routers and pass LSAs only to them. The DR forwards updates received from one neighbor on the LAN to all other neighbors on that same LAN. One of the main functions of a DR is to ensure that all the routers on the same LAN have an identical database.

The DR passes its database to any new routers that join that link. It is inefficient to have all the routers on that LAN pass the same information to the new router, so one router represents the other routers to a new router on the LAN or to other routers in the area. The DR and BDR routers also maintain a partial-neighbor relationship, a two-way adjacency state, with the other non-DR and non-BDR routers (DROTHERs) on the LAN.

The exchange of link-state information occurs through LSAs, which are also called link-state protocol data units (PDUs). LSAs report the state of routers and the links between routers—hence the term link state. Link-state information must be synchronized between routers, which means the following:

- LSAs are reliable; there is a method for acknowledging their delivery.

- LSAs are flooded throughout the area.

- LSAs have a sequence number and a set lifetime, so each router recognizes that it has the most up-to-date version of the LSA.

- LSAs are periodically refreshed to confirm topology information before they age out of the LSDB.

Only by reliably flooding link-state information can every router in the area or domain ensure that it has the latest, most accurate view of the network. Only then can the router make reliable routing decisions that are consistent with the decisions of other routers in the network.

## OSPF Calculation

Edsger Dijkstra designed a mathematical algorithm for calculating the best paths through complex networks. Link-state routing protocols use Dijkstra's algorithm to calculate the best paths through a network. By assigning a cost to each link in the network, and by placing the specific node at the root of a tree and summing the costs toward each given destination, the branches of the tree can be calculated. For OSPF, the default behavior is that the interface cost is calculated based on its configured bandwidth. An OSPF cost can also be manually defined for each interface, which overrides the default cost value calculated based on the configured bandwidth.

Figure 4-4 is an example of a Dijkstra calculation. The following steps occur:

- Router H advertises its presence to Router E. Router E passes Router H's and its own advertisements to its neighbors (Routers C and G). Router G passes these and its own advertisements to D, and so on.

- Router E does not advertise Router H's LSAs back to Router H.

- Router x has four neighbor routers: A, B, C, and D. From these routers, it receives the LSAs for all other routers in the network. From these LSAs, it can also deduce the links between all routers and draw the web of routers shown in Figure 4-4.

- Each Ethernet link in Figure 4-4 is assigned an OSPF cost of 10. By summing the costs to each destination, the router can deduce the best path to each destination.

- The right side of Figure 4-4 shows the resulting best paths (SPF tree). From these best paths, shown with solid lines, routes to destination networks attached to each router are offered to the routing table; for each route, the next-hop address is the appropriate neighbor router (A, B, C, or D).

**Figure 4-4**    *SPF Calculations*

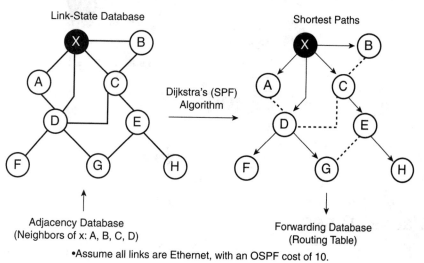

Link-State Database

Shortest Paths

Dijkstra's (SPF) Algorithm

Adjacency Database
(Neighbors of x: A, B, C, D)

Forwarding Database
(Routing Table)

•Assume all links are Ethernet, with an OSPF cost of 10.

Each LSA entry has its own aging timer, which the link-state age field carries. The default timer value for OSPF is 30 minutes (expressed in seconds in the link-state age field). After an LSA entry ages, the router that originated the entry sends a link-state update (LSU) about the network to verify that the link is still active, as shown in Figure 4-5. The LSU can contain one or more LSAs. The LSA validation method saves on bandwidth compared to distance-vector routers, which send their entire routing table at short, periodic intervals.

When each router receives the LSU, it does the following:

- If the entry does not already exist, the router adds the entry to its LSDB, sends back a link-state acknowledgment (LSAck), floods the information to other routers, runs SPF, and updates its routing table.

- If the entry already exists and the received LSU has the same information, the router ignores the LSA entry.

- If the entry already exists but the LSU includes newer information, the router adds the entry to its LSDB, sends back an LSAck, floods the information to other routers, runs SPF, and updates its routing table.

- If the entry already exists but the LSU includes older information, it sends an LSU to the sender with its newer information.

**Figure 4-5** *LSA Operations*

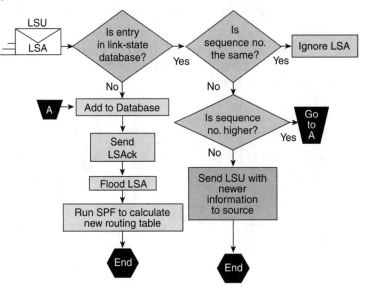

# OSPF Packet Types

Table 4-1 describes the five types of OSPF packets.

**Table 4-1** *OSPF Packets*

| Type | Packet Name | Description |
|------|-------------|-------------|
| 1 | Hello | Discovers neighbors and builds adjacencies between them. |
| 2 | Database description (DBD) | Checks for database synchronization between routers. |
| 3 | Link-state request (LSR) | Requests specific link-state records from another router. |
| 4 | Link-state update (LSU) | Sends specifically requested link-state records. |
| 5 | Link-state acknowledgment (LSAck) | Acknowledges the other packet types. |

All five OSPF packets are encapsulated directly into an IP payload, as shown in Figure 4-6. The OSPF packet does not use Transmission Control Protocol (TCP) or User Datagram Protocol (UDP). OSPF requires a reliable packet transport scheme. Because TCP is not used, it defines its own acknowledgment routine using an acknowledgment packet (OSPF packet type 5).

**Figure 4-6**    *OSPF Packet Header Format*

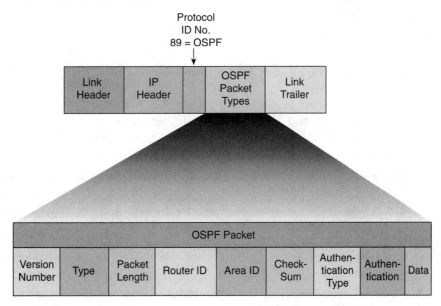

In the IP header, a protocol identifier of 89 defines all OSPF packets. Each OSPF packet begins with the same header format. This header has the following fields:

- **Version Number**—For OSPF version 2.
- **Packet Type**—Differentiates the five OSPF packet types.
- **Packet Length**—The length of the OSPF packet in bytes.
- **Router ID**—Defines which router is the packet's source.
- **Area ID**—Defines the area where the packet originated.
- **Checksum**—Used for packet header error detection to ensure that the OSPF packet was not corrupted during transmission.
- **Authentication Type**—An option in OSPF that describes either no authentication, cleartext passwords, or encrypted Message Digest 5 (MD5) formats for router authentication.
- **Data (for the hello packet)**—Contains a list of known neighbors.
- **Data (for the DBD packet)**—Contains a summary of the LSDB, which includes all known router IDs and their last sequence number among a number of other fields.
- **Data (for the LSR packet)**—Contains the type of LSU needed and the router ID of the needed LSU.
- **Data (for the LSU packet)**—Contains the full LSA entry. Multiple LSA entries can fit in one OSPF update packet.
- **Data (for the LSAck packet)**—This is empty.

## OSPF Neighbor Adjacency Establishment: Hello

Neighbor OSPF routers must recognize each other on the network before they can share information, because OSPF routing depends on the status of a link between two routers. This process is done using the Hello protocol. The Hello protocol establishes and maintains neighbor relationships by ensuring bidirectional communication between neighbors. Bidirectional communication occurs when a router sees itself listed in the hello packet received from a neighbor.

Each interface participating in OSPF uses the IP multicast address 224.0.0.5 to send hello packets periodically, as shown in Figure 4-7. A hello packet contains the following information:

- **Router ID**—A 32-bit number that uniquely identifies the router, selected at the start of the OSPF process. The highest IP address on an active interface is chosen by default unless a loopback interface or the router ID is manually configured. For example, IP address 172.16.12.1 would be chosen over 172.16.1.1. This router identification is important in establishing neighbor relationships and coordinating LSU exchanges. Also, the router ID breaks ties during the DR and BDR selection processes if the OSPF priority values are equal.

- **Hello and dead intervals**—The hello interval specifies how often in seconds a router sends hello packets (10 seconds is the default on multiaccess networks). The dead interval is the amount of time in seconds that a router waits to hear from a neighbor before declaring the neighbor router out of service (four times the hello interval by default). These timers must be the same on neighboring routers.

- **Neighbors**—The Neighbors field lists the adjacent routers with established bidirectional communication. This bidirectional communication is indicated when the router sees itself listed in the Neighbors field of the hello packet from the neighbor.

- **Area ID**—To communicate, two routers must share a common segment, and their interfaces must belong to the same OSPF area on that segment (they must also share the same subnet and mask). These routers all have the same link-state information.

- **Router priority**—An 8-bit number that indicates a router's priority. Priority is used when selecting a DR and BDR.

- **DR and BDR IP addresses**—If known, the IP addresses of the DR and BDR for the specific multiaccess network.

- **Authentication password**—If router authentication is enabled, two routers must exchange the same password. Authentication is not required, but if it is enabled, all peer routers must have the same password.

- **Stub area flag**—A stub area is a special area. Two routers must agree on the stub area flag in the hello packets. A stub area is a technique that reduces routing updates by replacing them with a default route.

**Figure 4-7**  *Establishing Neighborship*

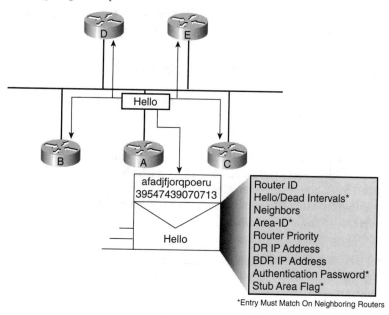

*Entry Must Match On Neighboring Routers

**NOTE**    After a DR and BDR are selected, any router added to the network establishes adjacencies with the DR and BDR only.

## Exchange Process and OSPF Neighbor Adjacency States

When routers running OSPF initialize, an exchange process using the Hello protocol is the first step, as shown in Figure 4-8. The exchange process that happens when routers come up on the network is as follows:

1  Router A is enabled on the LAN and is in a down state because it has not exchanged information with any other router. It begins by sending a hello packet through each of its interfaces participating in OSPF, even though it does not know the identity of the DR or of any other routers. The hello packet is sent out using the multicast address 224.0.0.5.

2  All directly connected routers running OSPF receive the hello packet from Router A and add Router A to their list of neighbors. This state is the init state.

3  All routers that received the hello packet send a unicast reply packet to Router A with their corresponding information. The Neighbor field in the hello packet includes all other neighboring routers, including Router A.

**4**  When Router A receives these hello packets, it adds all the routers that had its router ID in their hello packets to its own neighborship database. This is called the two-way state. At this point, all routers that have each other in their lists of neighbors have established bidirectional communication.

**5**  If the link type is a broadcast network, generally a LAN link such as Ethernet, next you must select a DR and BDR. The DR forms the bidirectional adjacencies between all other routers on the LAN link. This process must occur before the routers can begin exchanging link-state information.

**6**  Periodically (every 10 seconds by default on broadcast networks) the routers in a network exchange hello packets to ensure that communication is still working. The hello packets include the DR, the BDR, and the list of routers whose hello packets have been received by the router. Remember that "received" means that the receiving router recognizes itself as one of the neighbor list entries in the received hello packet.

**Figure 4-8**   *Establishing Bidirectional Communication*

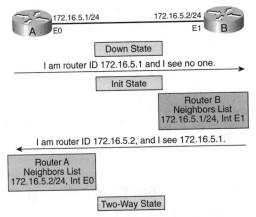

After the DR and BDR have been selected, the routers are considered to be in the exstart state. They are ready to discover the link-state information about the internetwork and create their LSDBs. The process used to discover the network routes is the exchange protocol, and it gets the routers to a full state of communication. The first step in this process is for the DR and BDR to establish adjacencies with each of the other routers. As soon as adjacent routers are in a full state, they do not repeat the exchange protocol unless the full state changes.

The exchange protocol, shown in Figure 4-9, operates as follows:

**1**  In the exstart state, a master and slave relationship is created between each router and its adjacent DR and BDR. The router with the higher router ID acts as the master during the exchange process.

---

**NOTE**    Only the DR exchanges and synchronizes link-state information with the
routers to which it has established adjacencies. Having the DR represent the
network in this capacity reduces the amount of routing update traffic.

---

**2**  The master and slave routers exchange one or more DBD packets (also called DDPs). The
routers are in the exchange state.

A DBD includes information about the LSA entry header that appears in the router's
LSDB. The entries can be about a link or about a network. Each LSA entry header
includes information about the link-state type, the address of the advertising router, the
link's cost, and the sequence number. The router uses the sequence number to determine
the "newness" of the received link-state information.

**3**  When the router receives the DBD, it performs the following actions, as shown in
Figure 4-10:

- It acknowledges the receipt of the DBD using the LSAck packet.

- It compares the information it received with the information it has in its
  own LSDB. If the DBD has a more up-to-date link-state entry, the router
  sends an LSR to the other router. The process of sending LSRs is called the
  loading state.

- The other router responds with the complete information about the requested
  entry in an LSU packet. Again, when the router receives an LSU, it sends an
  LSAck.

**4**  The router adds the new link-state entries into its LSDB.

**Figure 4-9**    *Discovering the Network Routes*

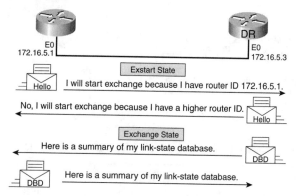

**Figure 4-10** *Adding Link-State Entries*

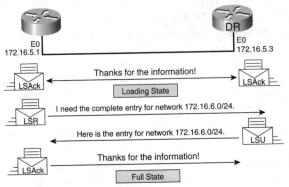

As soon as all LSRs have been satisfied for a given router, the adjacent routers are considered synchronized and in a full state. The routers must be in a full state before they can route traffic. At this point, all the routers in the area should have identical LSDBs.

## Maintaining Routing Information

In a link-state routing environment, it is very important for the link-state topological databases of all routers to stay synchronized. When there is a change in a link state, as shown in Figure 4-11, the routers use a flooding process to notify the other routers in the network of the change. LSUs provide the mechanism for flooding LSAs.

**Figure 4-11** *Maintaining Routing Information*

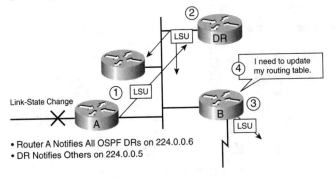

• Router A Notifies All OSPF DRs on 224.0.0.6
• DR Notifies Others on 224.0.0.5

---

**NOTE**    Although it isn't shown in Figure 4-11, all LSUs are acknowledged.

---

In general, the following are the flooding process steps in a multiaccess network:

   1  A router notices a change in a link state and multicasts an LSU packet that includes the updated LSA entry to 224.0.0.6 to all OSPF DRs and BDRs. An LSU packet might contain several distinct LSAs.

**2** The DR acknowledges the receipt of the change and floods the LSU to others on the network using the OSPF multicast address 224.0.0.5. After receiving the LSU, each router responds to the DR with an LSAck. To make the flooding procedure reliable, each LSA must be acknowledged separately.

**3** If a router is connected to another network, it floods the LSU to other networks by forwarding the LSU to the DR of the multiaccess network or to the adjacent router if in a point-to-point network. The DR, in turn, multicasts the LSU to the other routers in the network.

**4** The router updates its LSDB using the LSU that includes the changed LSA. It then recomputes the SPF algorithm against the updated database after a short delay (SPF delay) and updates the routing table as necessary.

OSPF simplifies the synchronization issue by requiring only adjacent routers to remain synchronized.

Summaries of individual link-state entries, not the complete link-state entries, are sent every 30 minutes to ensure LSDB synchronization. Each link-state entry has a timer to determine when the LSA refresh update must be sent.

Each link-state entry also has a maximum age of 60 minutes. If a link-state entry is not refreshed within 60 minutes, it is removed from the LSDB.

---

**NOTE**    In a Cisco router, if a route already exists, the routing table is used at the same time the SPF algorithm is calculating. However, if the SPF is calculating a new route, the use of the new route occurs after the SPF calculation is complete.

---

## OSPF Link-State Sequence Numbers

The Sequence Number field in a link-state record is 32 bits long. Beginning with the leftmost bit set, the first legal sequence number is 0x80000001. It is used to detect old or redundant LSA records. The larger the number, the more recent the LSA.

To ensure an accurate database, OSPF periodically floods (refreshes) each LSA record every 30 minutes, an interval called the LSRefreshTime. Each time a record is flooded, the sequence number is incremented by 1. An LSA record resets its maximum age when it receives a new LSA update. An LSA never remains in the database longer than the maximum age of 1 hour without a refresh.

It is possible for an LSA to exist in the database for long periods of time, being refreshed every 30 minutes. At some point the sequence number needs to wrap back to the starting sequence number. When this process occurs, the existing LSA is prematurely aged out (the maxage timer is immediately set to 1 hour) and flushed. The LSA then restarts its sequencing at 0x80000001.

The **show ip ospf database** output in Example 4-1 is an example of how the LS age and LS sequence numbers are kept in the database. The first router LSA entry in the OSPF database suggests that the router LSA with link ID 203.250.15.67 has been updated eight times (because the sequence number is 0x80000008) and that the last update occurred 48 seconds ago.

**Example 4-1**   *LSA Database Sequence Numbers and Maxage*

```
RTC#show ip ospf database
OSPF Router with ID (203.250.15.67) (Process ID 10)
        Router Link States (Area 1)
Link ID            ADV Router        Age  Seq#          Checksum  Link count
203.250.15.67      203.250.15.67     48   0x80000008    0xB112    2
203.250.16.130     203.250.16.130    212  0x80000006    0x3F44    2
```

The **debug ip ospf packet** command is used to troubleshoot and verify that OSPF packets are flowing properly between two routers. The output of this **debug** command is shown in Example 4-2. Notice that the fields in the OSPF header are not described in any detail. Table 4-2 describes each field of an OSPF packet header.

**Example 4-2**   *Debug of a Single Packet*

```
Router#debug ip ospf packet
 OSPF: rcv. v:2 t:1 l:48 rid:200.0.0.117
     aid:0.0.0.0 chk:6AB2 aut:0 auk:
```

**Table 4-2**   **debug ip ospf packet** *Command*

| Field | Description |
|-------|-------------|
| v: | Provides the version of OSPF. |
| t: | Specifies the OSPF packet type: <br> 1—Hello <br> 2—DBD <br> 3—LSR <br> 4—LSU <br> 5—LSAck |
| l: | Specifies the OSPF packet length in bytes. |
| rid: | Provides the OSPF router ID. |
| aid: | Shows the OSPF area ID. |
| chk: | Displays the OSPF checksum. |
| aut: | Provides the OSPF authentication type: <br> 0—No authentication <br> 1—Simple password <br> 2—MD5 |
| auk: | Specifies the OSPF authentication key. |
| keyid: | Displays the MD5 key ID. |
| seq: | Provides the sequence number. |

# Configuring Basic OSPF for a Single Area

To configure the OSPF process, do the following:

**Step 1**    Enable the OSPF process on the router using the **router ospf** command as follows:

```
router(config)#router ospf process-id
```

Table 4-3 describes the *process-id* parameter of the **router ospf** command.

**Table 4-3**    **router ospf** *Command*

| Parameter | Description |
|---|---|
| *process-id* | An internally used number that identifies the OSPF routing process. The *process-id* does not need to match process IDs on other routers. Running multiple OSPF processes on the same router is not recommended, because it creates multiple database instances that add extra overhead. |

**Step 2**    Identify which interfaces on the router are part of the OSPF process using the **network** command. For each network, identify the OSPF area to which the network belongs. The network value is either the network address supported by the router or the specific interface addresses that are configured. The router interprets the address by comparing the address to the wildcard mask. The command is

```
router(config-router)#network address wildcard-mask area area-id
```

Table 4-4 describes the parameters of the **network** command in the context of OSPF.

**Table 4-4**    *Parameters for the* **network** *Command with OSPF*

| Parameter | Description |
|---|---|
| *address* | Either the network address, subnet, or the interface's address. This address instructs the router to recognize which links to advertise to, which links to check for advertisements, and what networks to advertise. |
| *wildcard-mask* | Determines how to read the address. The mask has wildcard bits, in which 0 is a match and 1 is "don't care." For example, 0.0.255.255 indicates a match in the first 2 bytes. |
| | If you're specifying the interface address, use the mask 0.0.0.0 to match all 4 bytes of the address. |
| | An address and wildcard mask combination of 0.0.0.0 255.255.255.255 matches all interfaces on the router. |
| *area-id* | Specifies the OSPF area to be associated with the address. This command can be a decimal number or can be in dotted-decimal notation similar to an IP address A.B.C.D. |

Figure 4-12 describes OSPF configuration for Ethernet broadcast networks and serial point-to-point links. All three routers in Figure 4-12 are assigned to area 0 and are configured for network 10.0.0.0.

**Figure 4-12** *Configuring OSPF on Internal Routers of a Single Area*

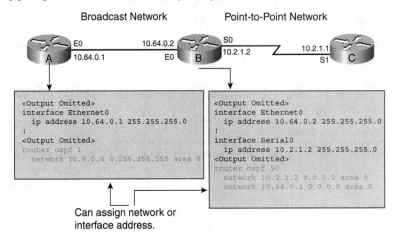

Router A uses a general **network 10.0.0.0 0.255.255.255** statement. This technique assigns all interfaces defined in the 10.0.0.0 network to OSPF process 1.

Router B uses a specific host address technique. The wildcard mask of 0.0.0.0 requires a match on all 4 bytes of the address. This technique allows the operator to define which specific interfaces will run OSPF.

Although the two examples shown in Figure 4-12 are a commonly used combination of a **network** statement and a wildcard mask, others could also work. For instance, a range of subnets could be specified. The **network** statement and wildcard mask are not used for route summarization purposes. The **network** statement is used strictly to turn on OSPF for an interface or multiple interfaces.

# Verifying OSPF Operations

To verify that OSPF has been properly configured, use the following **show** commands:

- The **show ip protocols** command displays IP routing protocol parameters about timers, filters, metrics, networks, and other information for the entire router.

- The **show ip route ospf** command displays the OSPF routes known to the router. This command is one of the best ways to determine connectivity between the local router and the rest of the internetwork.

- The **show ip ospf interface** command verifies that interfaces are configured in the intended areas. In addition, this command displays the timer intervals (including the hello interval), OSPF cost, and neighbor adjacencies.

- The **show ip ospf** command displays the OSPF router ID (RID), OSPF timers, the number of times the SPF algorithm has been executed, and LSA information.

- The **show ip ospf neighbor detail** command displays a detailed list of neighbors, including their RID, their OSPF priorities, their neighbor adjacency state (such as init, exstart, or full), and the dead timer.

Use the **show ip route ospf** command to verify the OSPF routes in the IP routing table. The O code represents OSPF routes. In Example 4-3, the 10.2.1.0 subnet is recognized on Ethernet 0 via neighbor 10.64.0.2.

The [110/10] in the routing table represents the administrative distance assigned to OSPF (110) and the total cost of the route to subnet 10.2.1.0 (cost of 10).

**Example 4-3**  show ip route ospf *Command*

```
RouterA#show ip route ospf

Codes:   C - connected, S - static, I - IGRP, R - RIP, M - mobile,
   B - BGP, D - EIGRP, EX - EIGRP external, O - OSPF,
   IA - OSPF inter area, E1 - OSPF external type 1,
   E2 - OSPF external type 2, E - EGP, i - IS-IS, L1 - IS-IS
   level-1, L2 - IS-IS level-2, * - candidate default

Gateway of last resort is not set
     10.0.0.0 255.255.255.0 is subnetted, 2 subnets
O      10.2.1.0 [110/10] via 10.64.0.2, 00:00:50, Ethernet0
```

The **show ip ospf interface** command, shown in Example 4-4, displays OSPF-related interface information:

```
RouterA#show ip ospf interface [type number]
```

**Example 4-4**  show ip ospf interface *Command*

```
RouterA#show ip ospf interface e0

Ethernet0 is up, line protocol is up
  Internet Address 10.64.0.1/24, Area 0
  Process ID 1, Router ID 10.64.0.1, Network Type BROADCAST, Cost: 10
  Transmit Delay is 1 sec, State BDR, Priority 1
  Designated Router (ID) 10.64.0.2, Interface address 10.64.0.2
  Backup Designated router (ID) 10.64.0.1, Interface address 10.64.0.1
  Timer intervals configured, Hello 10, Dead 40, Wait 40, Retransmit 5
    Hello due in 00:00:04
  Neighbor Count is 1, Adjacent neighbor count is 1
    Adjacent with neighbor 10.64.0.2  (Designated Router)
  Suppress hello for 0 neighbor(s)
```

Table 4-5 contains information about the parameters of this command.

**Table 4-5**     show ip ospf interface *Command*

| Parameter | Description |
|-----------|-------------|
| *type* | (Optional) Interface type |
| *number* | (Optional) Interface number |

This **show ip ospf** interface command describes Router A from the configuration shown in Example 4-4. The OSPF details of Ethernet interface 0 are shown in Example 4-4. This command verifies that OSPF is running on a particular interface and shows the OSPF area it is in. It also displays other information, such as the OSPF process ID, the RID, the OSPF network type, DR and BDR, timers, and neighbor adjacency information.

The **show ip ospf neighbor** command displays OSPF neighbor information for each interface:

```
RouterB#show ip ospf neighbor [type number] [neighbor-id] [detail]
```

Table 4-6 contains information about the parameters of this command.

**Table 4-6**   show ip ospf neighbor *Command*

| Parameter | Description |
|---|---|
| *type* | (Optional) Interface type |
| *number* | (Optional) Interface number |
| *neighbor-id* | (Optional) Neighbor ID |
| **detail** | (Optional) Displays a detailed list of all neighbors |

One of the most important OSPF troubleshooting commands is **show ip ospf neighbor**. OSPF does not send or receive updates without having full adjacencies between neighbors.

In Example 4-5, Router B has two neighbors. The first entry in the table represents the adjacency formed on the Ethernet interface. A full status means that the LSDB has been exchanged successfully. Broadcast networks select a DR and a BDR to facilitate the exchange of LSAs.

**Example 4-5**   show ip ospf neighbor *Command*

```
RouterB#show ip ospf neighbor

Neighbor ID   Pri   State      Dead Time   Address      Interface
10.64.0.1     1     FULL/BDR   00:00:31    10.64.0.1    Ethernet0
10.2.1.1      1     FULL/-     00:00:38    10.2.1.1     Serial0
```

In Example 4-5, Router B is the DR on the Ethernet with only one neighbor, which is the BDR. If there are other neighbors on the Ethernet, Router B has a two-way/DROTHER adjacency with the other neighbors. DROTHER signifies a router that is not a DR or BDR.

The second line of output in Example 4-5 represents the neighbor of Router B on the serial interface. DR and BDR are not used on point-to-point interfaces (indicated by -).

# Manipulating OSPF Router ID

The OSPF routing process chooses a router ID for itself when it starts up. The router ID is a unique IP address that can be assigned in the following ways:

- The highest IP address of any physical interface is chosen as the router ID. The interface does not have to be part of the OSPF process, but it has to be up. There must be at least one "up" IP interface on the router for OSPF to use as the router ID. If no up interface with an IP address is available when the OSPF process starts, the following error message occurs:

```
p5r2(config)#router ospf 1
2w1d: %OSPF-4-NORTRID: OSPF process 1 cannot start.
```

- A loopback address is always preferred over an interface address, because a loopback address never goes down. If there is more than one loopback address, the highest loopback address becomes the router ID.

- A **router-id** command is the preferred procedure to manually set the router ID and is always used over the other two procedures.

---

**NOTE**    The OSPF database uses the RID to uniquely describe each router in the network. Remember that every router keeps a complete topology database of all routers and links in an area and network. The router ID should not be duplicated.

---

As soon as the RID is set, it does not change, even if the interface that it is using for the router ID goes down. The RID changes only if the router reloads or if the OSPF routing process restarts.

## Loopback Interfaces

To modify the RID to a loopback address, first define a loopback interface as follows:

```
Router(config)#interface loopback number
```

Configuring an IP address on a loopback interface overrides the highest IP address used as the router ID. OSPF is more stable if a loopback interface is configured, because the interface is always active and cannot fail, as opposed to a real interface. For this reason, you should use the loopback address on all key routers. If the loopback address is published with the **network** command, the other routers can ping this address for testing purposes, and a private IP address can be used to save registered public IP addresses.

---

### OSPF Router ID Stability

As mentioned earlier, if a physical interface fails, the router ID does not change. But if the physical interface fails and the router (or OSPF process) is restarted, the router ID changes. This change in router ID makes it more difficult for network administrators to troubleshoot and manage. The stability provided by using a loopback interface for the router ID comes from the router ID's staying the same regardless of the state of the physical interfaces.

---

| | |
|---|---|
| **NOTE** | A loopback address requires a different subnet for each router, unless the host address itself is advertised. By default, OSPF advertises loopbacks as /32 host routes. |

To determine a router's router ID, enter the **show ip ospf** command.

The **router-id** OSPF subordinate command ensures that OSPF selects a planned router ID.

Use the following commands to ensure that OSPF selects a preconfigured router ID:

```
Router(config)#router ospf process-id
Router(config-router)#router-id ip-address
```

After the **router-id** command is configured, use the **clear ip ospf process** command. This command restarts the OSPF routing process, so it reselects the new IP address as its router ID.

| | |
|---|---|
| **CAUTION** | Remember that the **clear ip ospf process** command temporarily disrupts an operational network. |

### Key Point: Loopback Interface as Router ID

OSPF is more stable if a loopback interface is configured, because the interface is always active and cannot fail, as opposed to a real interface.

Use the **show ip ospf** command, shown in Example 4-6, to verify the RID. You can also use this command to check OSPF timer settings and other statistics.

**Example 4-6   show ip ospf** *Command*

```
RouterW#show ip ospf
Routing Process "ospf 1" with ID 1.1.3.1
 Supports only single TOS(TOS0) routes
 SPF schedule delay 5 secs, Hold time between two SPFs 10 secs
 Number of DCbitless external LSA 0
 Number of DoNotAge external LSA 0
 Number of areas in this router is 1. 1 normal 0 stub 0 nssa
    Area BACKBONE(0) (Active)
        Number of interfaces in this area is 2
        Area has no authentication
        SPF algorithm executed 10 times
        Area ranges are
        Link State Update Interval is 00:30:00 and due in 0:07:16
        Link State Age Interval is 00:20:00 and due in 00:07:15
        Number of DCbitless LSA 0
        Number of indication LSA 0
        Number of DoNotAge LSA 0
```

# OSPF Network Types

Understanding that an OSPF area is made up of different types of network links is important. The adjacency behavior is different for each network type, and OSPF must be properly configured to function correctly over certain network types.

## Adjacency Behavior for a Point-to-Point Link

A point-to-point network joins a single pair of routers. A T1 serial line configured with a link-layer protocol such as PPP or HDLC is an example of a point-to-point network.

On point-to-point networks, the router dynamically detects its neighboring routers by multicasting its hello packets to all SPF routers using the address 224.0.0.5. On point-to-point networks, neighboring routers become adjacent whenever they can communicate directly. No DR or BDR election is performed, because a point-to-point link can have only two routers, so there is no need for a DR or BDR.

Usually, the IP source address of an OSPF packet is set to the address of the outgoing interface on the router. It is possible to use IP unnumbered interfaces with OSPF. On unnumbered interfaces, the IP source address is set to the IP address of another interface on the router. The concept of IP unnumbered is covered in detail in Appendix A, "Job Aids and Supplements."

The default OSPF hello and dead intervals on point-to-point links are 10 seconds and 40 seconds, respectively.

## Adjacency Behavior for a Broadcast Network

An adjacency is the relationship that exists between a router and its DR and BDR on a multiaccess broadcast network such as Ethernet. Adjacent routers have synchronized LSDBs. A common media segment is the basis for adjacency, such as two routers connected on the same Ethernet segment. When routers first come up on the Ethernet, they perform the hello process and then elect the DR and BDR. The routers then attempt to form adjacencies with the DR and BDR.

The routers on a segment must elect a DR and BDR to represent the multiaccess broadcast network. The BDR does not perform any DR functions when the DR is operating. Instead, the BDR receives all the information, but the DR performs the LSA forwarding and LSDB synchronization tasks. The BDR performs the DR tasks only if the DR fails. If the DR fails, the BDR automatically becomes the DR, and a new BDR election occurs.

The DR and BDR add value to the network in the following ways:

- **Reducing routing update traffic**—The DR and BDR act as a central point of contact for link-state information exchange on a given multiaccess broadcast network; therefore, each router must establish a full adjacency with the DR and the BDR only. Instead of each router exchanging link-state information with every other router on the segment, each router sends the link-state information to the DR and BDR only. The DR represents the multiaccess broadcast network in the sense that it sends link-state information from each router to all other routers in the network. This flooding process significantly reduces the router-related traffic on a segment.

- **Managing link-state synchronization**—The DR and BDR ensure that the other routers on the network have the same link-state information about the internetwork. In this way, the DR and BDR reduce the number of routing errors.

---

### Benefits of Having a DR

What is the real benefit of having a DR to reduce update traffic? As an example, if a new router uses the multiaccess address 224.0.0.6 to reach the DR, all routers on that segment hear that packet because it's a shared segment, even if they don't process that frame. The DR then accepts the packet and retransmits the information to 224.0.0.5, and again all routers on that segment hear that frame, and accept it. It seems from this behavior that it would be easier for the new router to simply advertise its new routes to 224.0.0.5 itself, thereby reducing the number of frames on the shared segment. In this case, it almost seems that having a DR is a disadvantage, not an advantage. The benefit of having a DR to reduce update traffic comes from the *n squared* aspect of neighbor relationships.

---

## Electing a DR

To elect a DR and BDR, the routers view the OSPF priority value of the other routers during the hello packet exchange process and then use the following conditions to determine which router to select:

- The router with the highest priority value is the DR, as shown in Figure 4-13.

**Figure 4-13** *Electing the DR and BDR*

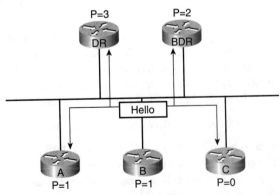

- The router with the second-highest priority value is the BDR.
- The default for the interface OSPF priority is 1. In case of a tie, the router ID is used. The router with the highest router ID becomes the DR. The router with the second-highest router ID becomes the BDR.
- A router with a priority of 0 cannot become the DR or BDR. A router that is not the DR or BDR is a DROTHER.
- If a router with a higher priority value gets added to the network, it does not preempt the DR and BDR. The only time a DR or BDR changes is if one of them is out of service. If the DR is out of service, the BDR becomes the DR, and a new BDR is selected. If the BDR is out of service, a new BDR is elected.

To determine if the DR is out of service, the BDR uses the wait timer. This timer is a reliability feature. If the BDR does not confirm that the DR is forwarding LSAs before the wait timer expires, the BDR assumes that the DR is out of service.

**NOTE**    The highest IP address on an active interface is normally used as the router ID; however, as mentioned earlier, you can override this selection by configuring an IP address on a loopback interface or by using the **router-id** command.

In a multiaccess broadcast environment, each network segment has its own DR and BDR. A router connected to multiple multiaccess broadcast networks can be a DR on one segment and a regular (DROTHER) router on another segment.

**NOTE**    Remember, the DR concept is at the link level; a DR is selected for every multiaccess broadcast link in the OSPF network.

## Setting Priorities for the DR

Use the **ip ospf priority** command to designate which router interfaces on a multiaccess link are the DR and the BDR. The highest priority interface becomes the DR, and the second-highest priority interface becomes the BDR. Any interfaces set to 0 priority cannot be involved in the DR or BDR election process.

The commands are as follows:

```
Router(config)#interface Ethernet 0
Router(config-if)#ip ospf priority 10
```

**NOTE**    An interface's priority takes effect only when the existing DR goes down. A DR does not relinquish its status just because a new interface reports a higher priority in its hello packet.

## Adjacency Behavior for a Nonbroadcast Multiaccess Network

When a single interface interconnects multiple sites over a nonbroadcast multiaccess (NBMA) network, the network's nonbroadcast nature can create reachability issues. NBMA networks can support more than two routers, but they have no broadcast capability. For example, if the NBMA topology is not fully meshed, a broadcast or multicast sent by one router does not reach all the other routers. Frame Relay, ATM, and X.25 are examples of NBMA networks.

To implement broadcasting or multicasting, the router replicates the packets to be broadcast or multicast and sends them individually on each permanent virtual circuit (PVC) to all destinations. This process is CPU- and bandwidth-intensive.

OSPF considers the NBMA environment to function similarly to other broadcast media such as Ethernet. However, NBMA clouds are usually built-in hub-and-spoke topologies using PVCs or switched virtual circuits (SVCs). A hub-and-spoke topology means that the NBMA network is only a partial mesh. In these cases, the physical topology does not provide the multiaccess capability like Ethernet, on which OSPF relies.

The election of the DR becomes an issue in NBMA topologies because the DR and BDR need to have full physical connectivity with all routers in the NBMA network. The DR and BDR also need to have a list of all the other routers so that they can establish adjacencies.

---

**Key Point: NBMA Adjacencies**

OSPF cannot automatically build adjacencies with neighbor routers over NBMA interfaces.

---

## Frame Relay Topologies

With Frame Relay, remote sites interconnect in a variety of ways, as shown in Figure 4-14. By default, interfaces that support Frame Relay are multipoint connection types. The following examples are types of Frame Relay topologies:

- **Star topology**—A star topology, also known as a hub-and-spoke configuration, is the most common Frame Relay network topology. In this topology, remote sites connect to a central site that generally provides a service or application. The star topology is the least-expensive topology because it requires the fewest PVCs. The central router provides a multipoint connection because it typically uses a single interface to interconnect multiple PVCs.

- **Full-mesh topology**—In a full-mesh topology, all routers have virtual circuits (VCs) to all other destinations. This method, although costly, provides direct connections from each site to all other sites and allows for redundancy. As the number of nodes in the full-mesh topology increases, the topology becomes increasingly expensive. To figure out how many VCs are needed to implement a full-mesh topology, use the formula $n(n - 1)/2$, where $n$ is the number of nodes in the network.

- **Partial-mesh topology**—In a partial-mesh topology, not all sites have direct access to a central site. This method reduces the cost of implementing a full-mesh topology.

**Figure 4-14**  *Frame Relay Topologies*

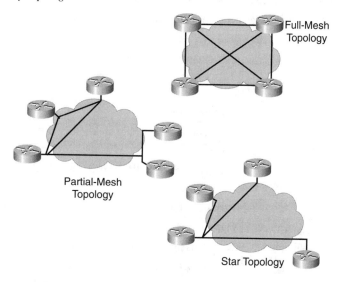

## OSPF Over NBMA Topology Modes of Operation

As described in RFC 2328, OSPF runs in one of the following two official modes in NBMA topologies:

- **NBMA**—NBMA (nonbroadcast) mode simulates the operation of OSPF in broadcast networks. Neighbors must be configured manually, and DR and BDR election is required. This configuration is used with full-mesh or partial-mesh networks.

- **Point-to-multipoint**—Point-to-multipoint mode treats the nonbroadcast network as a collection of point-to-point links. In this environment, the routers automatically identify their neighboring routers but do not elect a DR and BDR. This configuration is typically used with partial-mesh networks.

The choice between NBMA and point-to-multipoint modes determines how the Hello protocol and flooding work over the nonbroadcast network.

The main advantage of point-to-multipoint mode is that it requires less manual configuration. The main advantage of NBMA mode is that there is less overhead traffic compared to point-to-multipoint mode.

Additionally, Cisco offers the following modes:

- Point-to-multipoint nonbroadcast
- Broadcast
- Point-to-point

# OSPF Commands for NBMA Frame Relay

The **ip ospf network** interface command has four main options for NBMA, as described in Table 4-7.

```
Router(config-if)#ip ospf network {broadcast | non-broadcast | point-to-point |
    point-to-multipoint [non-broadcast]}
```

**Table 4-7**    **ip ospf network** *Command Options for NBMA*

| Command Options | Description |
|---|---|
| **broadcast** (Cisco mode) | Makes the WAN interface appear to be a LAN. One IP subnet. Uses a multicast OSPF hello packet to automatically discover the neighbors. DR and BDR are elected. Requires a full-mesh topology. |
| **non-broadcast** (NBMA) (RFC-compliant) | One IP subnet. Neighbors must be manually configured. DR and BDR are elected. DR and BDR need to have full connectivity with all other routers. Typically used in a partial-mesh topology. |
| **point-to-point** (Cisco) | One IP subnet. No DR or BDR election. Used when only two routers need to form an adjacency on a pair of interfaces. Interfaces can be either LAN or WAN. |
| **point-to-multipoint** (RFC-compliant) | One IP subnet. Uses a multicast OSPF hello packet to automatically discover the neighbors. DR and BDR are not required. The router sends additional LSAs with more information about neighboring routers. Typically used in a partial-mesh topology. |
| **point-to-multipoint non-broadcast** (a subset of **point-to-multipoint**) (Cisco) | If multicast and broadcast are not enabled on the VCs, the RFC-compliant point-to-multipoint mode cannot be used, because the router cannot dynamically discover its neighboring routers using the hello multicast packets. Neighbors must be manually configured in this case. DR and BDR election is not required. |

## ip ospf network point-to-point Configuration with NBMA

This configuration can be used in the case of a single PVC on a serial interface where point-to-point behavior is desired. For example, this could be used to track PVC when Hot Standby Router Protocol (HSRP) is used.

Example 4-7 shows a sample configuration of a Frame Relay router in a full-mesh topology, with the broadcast mode of operation defined.

**Example 4-7**    *Frame Relay Router in OSPF Broadcast Mode with Full-Mesh Topology*

```
Interface serial 0
encapsulation frame-relay
ip ospf network broadcast
```

## Configuration in Nonbroadcast Mode

In NBMA (nonbroadcast) mode, OSPF emulates operation over a broadcast network. A DR and BDR are elected for the NBMA network, and the DR originates an LSA for the network. In this environment, the routers are usually fully meshed to facilitate the establishment of adjacencies among them. If the routers are not fully meshed, the DR and BDR should be selected manually to ensure that the selected DR and BDR have full connectivity to all other neighbor routers. Neighboring routers are statically defined to start the DR/BDR election process. When using NBMA mode, all routers are on one IP subnet.

When flooding out over a nonbroadcast interface, the LSU packet must be replicated for each PVC. As defined in the neighborship table, the updates are sent to each of the neighboring routers on the interface.

When there are few neighbors in the network, NBMA mode is the most efficient way to run OSPF over NBMA networks, because it has less overhead than point-to-multipoint mode.

The **neighbor** command is used to statically define adjacent relationships in NBMA networks using nonbroadcast mode:

```
Router(config-router)#neighbor247 ip-address [priority number] [poll-interval
sec]
  [cost number] database-filter all
```

The **neighbor** command options are shown in Table 4-8.

**Table 4-8**    **neighbor** *Command*

| Parameter | Description |
|---|---|
| *ip-address* | The IP address of the neighboring router. |
| **priority** *number* | A priority command with a priority number. 0 means that the neighboring router does not become the DR. |
| **poll-interval** *sec* | How long an NBMA interface waits before sending hellos to the neighbors even if the neighbor is inactive. The poll interval is defined in seconds. |
| **cost** *number* | (Optional) Assigns a cost to the neighbor in the form of an integer from 1 to 65535. Neighbors with no specific cost configured assume the cost of the interface based on the **ip ospf cost** command. For point-to-multipoint interfaces, the **cost** keyword and the *number* argument are the only options that are applicable. This keyword does not apply to NBMA networks. |

Figure 4-15 shows how to statically define adjacencies. All three routers are using nonbroadcast mode on their Frame Relay interfaces; therefore, each must manually configure its neighboring routers. The **priority** command should be set to 0 for the two rightmost routers, because a full-mesh topology does not exist. This configuration ensures that Router A becomes the DR, because only Router A has full connectivity to the other two routers. No BDR is elected in this case.

**Figure 4-15** neighbor *Command*

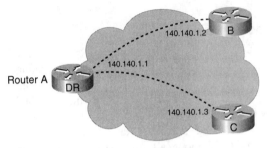

```
RouterA(config)# router ospf 100
RouterA(config-router)# network 140.140.0.0 0.0.255.255 area 0
RouterA(config-router)# neighbor 140.140.1.2 priority 0
RouterA(config-router)# neighbor 140.140.1.3 priority 0
```

In an NBMA network, **neighbor** statements are required only on the DR and BDR. In a hub-and-spoke topology, **neighbor** statements must be placed on the hub, which must additionally be configured to become the DR by being assigned a higher priority. **neighbor** statements are not mandatory on the spoke routers, because neighbors are discovered dynamically. In a full-mesh NBMA topology, you might need **neighbor** statements on all routers unless the DR and BDR are statically configured using the **priority** command.

**NOTE**

The **neighbor** command became somewhat obsolete with the introduction of the capability to configure other network modes for the interface, regardless of the underlying physical topology.

Source: *CCNP Self-Study: Building Scalable Cisco Internetworks (BSCI)* (Cisco Press, 2003)

The following command displays OSPF neighbor information on a per-interface basis:

```
RouterA#show ip ospf neighbor [type number] [neighbor-id] [detail]
```

Table 4-9 describes the parameters of the **show ip ospf neighbor** command.

**Table 4-9** show ip ospf neighbor *Command*

| Parameter | Description |
|---|---|
| *type* | (Optional) Interface type. |
| *number* | (Optional) Interface number. |
| *neighbor-id* | (Optional) ID of the neighboring router. |
| **detail** | (Optional) Displays a detailed list of all neighboring routers. |

In Figure 4-16, a router has two serial interfaces: Serial 0 is a point-to-point interface, and serial 1 is a Frame Relay NBMA interface. The neighbor learned for serial 0 has a status of FULL/-, which means that it has successfully exchanged LSDB information with the router using the **show ip ospf neighbor** command and that no DR or BDR is required on a point-to-point network type.

**Figure 4-16**  **show ip ospf neighbor** *Command*

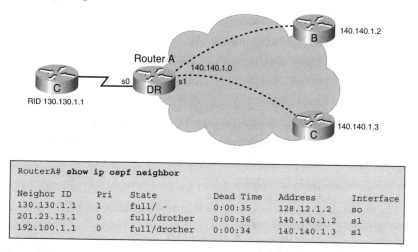

```
RouterA# show ip ospf neighbor

Neighor ID     Pri   State         Dead Time   Address       Interface
130.130.1.1    1     full/ -       0:00:35     128.12.1.2    so
201.23.13.1    0     full/drother  0:00:36     140.140.1.2   s1
192.100.1.1    0     full/drother  0:00:34     140.140.1.3   s1
```

The serial 1 interface on Router A in Figure 4-16 shows two neighbors. Both have a status of FULL/DROTHER. DROTHER means that the neighboring router is not a DR or BDR.

## Point-to-Multipoint Mode

Networks in point-to-multipoint mode are designed to work with partial-mesh or star topologies. In point-to-multipoint mode, OSPF treats all router-to-router connections over the nonbroadcast network as if they are point-to-point links. In point-to-multipoint mode, DRs are not used, and a type 2 network LSA is not flooded to adjacent routers.

Instead, OSPF point-to-multipoint works by exchanging additional LSUs that are designed to automatically discover neighboring routers, and add them to the neighbor table.

In large networks, using point-to-multipoint mode reduces the number of PVCs required for complete connectivity, because you are not required to have a full-mesh topology. In addition, not having a full-mesh topology also reduces the number of neighbor entries in your neighborship table.

Point-to-multipoint mode has the following properties:

- **Does not require a full-mesh network**—This environment allows routing to occur between two routers that are not directly connected but that are connected through a router that has VCs to each of the two routers. All three routers in Figure 4-15 could be configured for point-to-multipoint. Point-to-multipoint and nonbroadcast modes use a 30-second hello timer, and point-to-point mode uses a 10-second hello timer. The hello and dead timers on the neighboring interfaces must match for the neighbors to form successful adjacencies.

- **Does not require a static neighbor configuration**—In NBMA mode, neighboring routers are statically defined to start the DR election process, and allow the exchange of routing updates. However, because point-to-multipoint mode treats the network as a collection of point-to-point links, multicast hello packets discover neighboring routers dynamically. Statically configuring neighboring routers is not necessary.

- **Uses one IP subnet**—As in NBMA mode, when using point-to-multipoint mode, all routers are on one IP subnet.

- **Duplicates LSA packets**—Also as in NBMA mode, when flooding out a nonbroadcast interface in point-to-multipoint mode, the router must replicate the LSU. As defined in the neighborship table, the LSU packet is sent to each of the interface's neighboring routers.

Example 4-8 shows partial configurations from the point-to-multipoint example of Routers A and B. Frame-Relay Inverse ARP is enabled by default. This configuration does not require subinterfaces and uses only a single subnet. In point-to-multipoint mode, a DR or BDR is not required; therefore, DR and BDR election and priorities are not a concern.

**Example 4-8**  *Point-to-Multipoint Configuration of Routers A and B*

```
RouterA(config)#interface serial 0
RouterA(config-if)#encapsulation hdlc
RouterA(config-if)#ip address 120.120.1.1 255.255.255.0
RouterA(config)#interface serial 1
RouterA(config-if)#encapsulation frame-relay
RouterA(config-if)#ip address 140.140.1.1 255.255.255.0
RouterA(config-if)#ip ospf network point-to-multipoint

RouterB(config)#interface serial 0
RouterB(config-if)#ip address 140.140.1.2 255.255.255.0
RouterB(config-if)#encapsulation frame-relay
RouterB(config-if)#ip ospf network point-to-multipoint
```

The **show ip ospf interface** command, shown in Example 4-9, displays key OSPF details for the point-to-multipoint interface S1.

**Example 4-9**  **show ip ospf interface** *Command*

```
RouterA#show ip ospf interface s1
Serial1 is up, line protocol is up
  Internet Address 140.140.1.1/24, Area 1
  Process ID 100, Router ID 120.120.1.1, Network Type Point-To-Multipoint,
Cost: 64
  Transmit Delay is 1 sec, State: Point_To_Multipoint
  Timer intervals configured,Hello 30, Dead 120, Wait 120, Retransmit 5
  Hello due in 00:00:11
  Neighbor count is 2, Adjacent neighbor count is 2
  Adjacent with neighbor 140.140.1.2
  Adjacent with neighbor 140.140.1.3
```

The OSPF network type, area number, cost, and state of the interface are all displayed. The hello interval for a point-to-multipoint interface is 30 seconds with a dead interval of 120 seconds. The listed adjacent neighboring routers are all dynamically learned. The manual configuration of neighboring routers does not necessarily use point-to-multipoint mode.

## Cisco-Specific Modes for OSPF Neighborship

Cisco defines additional modes for OSPF neighborship:

- **Point-to-multipoint nonbroadcast**—This mode is a Cisco extension of the RFC-compliant point-to-multipoint mode. You must statically define neighbors, and you can modify the cost of the link to the neighboring router to reflect the different bandwidths of each link. RFC point-to-multipoint mode was developed to support underlying point-to-multipoint VCs that support multicast and broadcast; therefore, this mode allows dynamic neighboring router discovery. If multicast and broadcast are not enabled on the VC, RFC-compliant point-to-multipoint mode cannot be used, because the router cannot dynamically discover its neighboring routers using the hello multicast packets.

- **Broadcast**—This mode is a workaround for statically listing all existing neighboring routers. The interface is set to broadcast and behaves as if the router connects to a LAN. DR and BDR election is still performed; therefore, take special care to ensure either a full-mesh topology or a static election of the DR based on the interface priority.

- **Point-to-point**—This mode is used when only two nodes exist on the NBMA network. Point-to-point mode is typically used only with point-to-point subinterfaces. Each point-to-point connection is one IP subnet. An adjacency forms over the point-to-point network with no DR or BDR election.

## Using Subinterfaces

A physical interface can be split into multiple logical interfaces called subinterfaces. Each subinterface is defined as a point-to-point or point-to-multipoint interface. Subinterfaces were originally created to better handle issues caused by split horizon over NBMA for distance vector-based routing protocols. A point-to-point subinterface has the properties of any physical point-to-point interface.

Define subinterfaces using the following command:

```
Router(config)#interface serial number.subinterface-number
    {multipoint | point-to-point}
```

Table 4-10 lists the parameters of the **interface serial** command.

**Table 4-10**    interface serial *Command*

| Parameter | Description |
| --- | --- |
| *number.subinterface-number* | The interface number and subinterface number. The subinterface number is in the range of 1 to 4294967293.<br><br>The interface number that precedes the period (.) must match the interface number to which this subinterface belongs. |
| **multipoint** | On multipoint subinterfaces routing IP, all routers are in the same subnet. |
| **point-to-point** | On point-to-point subinterfaces routing IP, each pair of point-to-point routers is in its own subnet. |

The default OSPF mode on a point-to-point Frame Relay subinterface is a point-to-point mode; the default OSPF mode on a Frame Relay point-to-multipoint subinterface is a nonbroadcast mode. The default OSPF mode on a main Frame Relay interface is also a nonbroadcast mode.

In Figure 4-17, although all three routers have only one physical serial port, Router A appears to have two logical ports. Each logical port (subinterface) has its own IP address and operates as a point-to-point OSPF network type. Each subinterface is on its own IP subnet. This type of configuration avoids the need for a DR or BDR and removes the requirement to statically define the neighbors.

**Figure 4-17** *OSPF Subinterface Example*

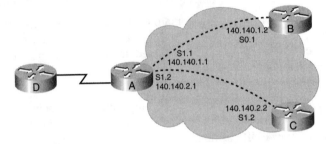

## Multipoint Subinterface

Multipoint Frame Relay subinterfaces default to the nonbroadcast OSPF network type. The nonbroadcast OSPF network type requires neighbors to be statically configured, and DR and BDR election is required.

During the configuration of subinterfaces, you must choose the point-to-point or multipoint keywords. The choice of modes affects the operation of OSPF.

Define multipoint subinterfaces using the following command:

```
Router(config)#interface serial 0.x multipoint
```

In Figure 4-18, Router A has one subinterface using point-to-point mode and a second subinterface using multipoint. The multipoint subinterface supports two other routers in a single subnet. OSPF treats the multipoint interface as NBMA by default.

**Figure 4-18** *Multipoint Subinterface Example*

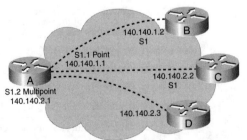

OSPF treats the point-to-point subinterface as the point-to-point OSPF network type by default. OSPF treats the multipoint interface as the nonbroadcast OSPF network type by default.

## The debug ip ospf adj Command

Use the **debug ip ospf adj** command to track OSPF adjacencies as they come up or go down. Debugging allows you to see exactly what OSPF packets are being sent between routers. The ability to see packets as they are sent over a link is an invaluable tool to the troubleshooter.

**NOTE**     The last parameter in this command is **adj**, not **adjacency**.

In Example 4-10, the partial debug output describes a serial interface in point-to-point mode. No DR/BDR election occurs; however, the adjacency forms, allowing DBD packets to be sent during the exchange process. Notice that the neighbor relationship passes through the two-way phase and into the exchange phase. After database description packets are sent between routers, the neighbors move into the final state: full adjacency.

**Example 4-10** debug ip ospf adj *Command Output for a Serial Link*

```
RouterA#debug ip ospf adj
Point-to-point interfaces coming up: No election
%LINK-3-UPDOWN: Interface Serial1, changed state to up
OSPF: Interface Serial1 going Up
OSPF: Rcv hello from 192.168.0.11 area 0 from Serial1 10.1.1.2
OSPF: End of hello processing
OSPF: Build router LSA for area 0, router ID 192.168.0.10
OSPF: Rcv DBD from 192.168.0.11 on Serial1 seq 0x20C4 opt 0x2 flag 0x7 len 32
  state INIT
OSPF: 2 Way Communication to 192.168.0.11 on Serial1, state 2WAY
OSPF: Send DBD to 192.168.0.11 on Serial1 seq 0x167F opt 0x2 flag 0x7 len 32
OSPF: NBR Negotiation Done. We are the SLAVE
OSPF: Send DBD to 192.168.0.11 on Serial1 seq 0x20C4 opt 0x2 flag 0x2 len 72
```

Example 4-11 is a partial **debug ip ospf adj** output illustrating the DR/BDR election process on an Ethernet interface. The OSPF default behavior on an Ethernet link is broadcast mode. First, the DR and BDR are selected, and then the exchange process occurs.

**Example 4-11** debug ip ospf adj *Command Output for an Ethernet Link*

```
RouterA#debug ip ospf adj
Ethernet interface coming up: Election
OSPF: 2 Way Communication to 192.168.0.10 on Ethernet0, state 2WAY
OSPF: end of Wait on interface Ethernet0
OSPF: DR/BDR election on Ethernet0
OSPF: Elect BDR 192.168.0.12
OSPF: Elect DR 192.168.0.12
     DR: 192.168.0.12 (Id)   BDR: 192.168.0.12 (Id)
OSPF: Send DBD to 192.168.0.12 on Ethernet0 seq 0x546 opt 0x2 flag 0x7 len 32
<...>
```

*continues*

**Example 4-11** **debug ip ospf adj** *Command Output for an Ethernet Link (Continued)*

```
OSPF: DR/BDR election on Ethernet0
OSPF: Elect BDR 192.168.0.11
OSPF: Elect DR 192.168.0.12
        DR: 192.168.0.12 (Id)    BDR: 192.168.0.11 (Id)
```

## OSPF Over NBMA Topology Summary

Table 4-11 briefly compares the different modes of operation for OSPF over NBMA topologies.

**Table 4-11**     *OSPF Over NBMA Topology Summary*

| OSPF Mode | NBMA Preferred Topology | Subnet Address | Hello Timer | Adjacency | RFC or Cisco | Example |
|---|---|---|---|---|---|---|
| NBMA | Fully meshed | Same | 30 sec | Manual configuration DR/BDR elected | RFC | Frame Relay configured on a serial interface |
| Broadcast | Fully meshed | Same | 10 sec | Automatic DR/BDR elected | Cisco | LAN interface such as Ethernet |
| Point-to-multipoint | Partial mesh or star | Same | 30 sec | Automatic No DR/BDR | RFC | OSPF over Frame Relay mode that eliminates the need for a DR |
| Point-to-multipoint nonbroadcast | Partial mesh or star | Same | 30 sec | Manual configuration No DR/BDR | Cisco | OSPF over Frame Relay mode that eliminates the need for a DR |
| Point-to-point | Partial mesh or star using a subinterface | Different for each subinterface | 10 sec | Automatic No DR/BDR | Cisco | T1 serial interface |

# Summary

In this chapter you learned the following:

- OSPF is a link-state routing protocol that builds three tables: a neighbor table, an LSA topology database, and a routing table or forwarding database.

- OSPF uses a two-tier hierarchical network structure in which the network is divided into areas. This area structure separates the LSDB into more manageable sizes.

- OSPF routers build adjacencies using the Hello protocol. Over these logical adjacencies, LSUs are sent to exchange database information between adjacent OSPF routers. SPF is run against the LSDB, and the outcome is a table of best paths known as the routing table. Link-state records are advertised on change but also are sent periodically.

- OSPF defines a variety of network types: point-to-point, broadcast, nonbroadcast multiaccess, point-to-multipoint, and point-to-multipoint nonbroadcast.

# References

For additional information, refer to these resources:

- OSPF design guide:

  www.cisco.com/en/US/partner/tech/tk365/tk480
  /technologies_design_guide09186a0080094e9e.shtml

- OSPF white papers:

  www.cisco.com/en/US/partner/tech/tk365/tk480/tech_white_papers_list.html

- OSPF configuration examples:

  www.cisco.com/en/US/partner/tech/tk365/tk480/tech_configuration_examples_list.html

# Configuration Exercise: Configuring and Examining OSPF in a Single Area

In this exercise, you will configure your pod as an OSPF single area.

---

### Introduction to the Configuration Exercises

This book uses Configuration Exercises to help you practice configuring routers with the commands and topics presented. If you have access to real hardware, you can try these exercises on your routers. See Appendix H, "Configuration Exercise Equipment Requirements and Initial Configurations," for a list of recommended equipment and initial configuration commands for the routers. However, even if you don't have access to any routers, you can go through the exercises and keep a log of your own running configurations or just read through the solution. Commands used and solutions to the Configuration Exercises are provided after the exercises.

In the Configuration Exercises, the network is assumed to consist of two pods, each with four routers. The pods are interconnected to a backbone. You configure pod 1. No interaction between the two pods is required, but you might see some routes from the other pod in your routing tables in some exercises if you have it configured (the Configuration Exercise answers show the routes from the other pod). In most of the exercises, the backbone has only one router; in some cases, another router is added to the backbone. Each Configuration Exercise assumes that you have completed the previous chapters' Configuration Exercises on your pod.

---

| | |
|---|---|
| **NOTE** | Throughout this exercise, the pod number is referred to as *x*, and the router number is referred to as *y*. Substitute the appropriate numbers as needed. |

## Exercise Objective

After completing this exercise, you will be able to

- Configure OSPF for a single area
- Configure a stable RID

## Visual Objective

Figure 4-19 illustrates what you will accomplish in this exercise.

**Figure 4-19** *Configuring and Examining OSPF in a Single Area*

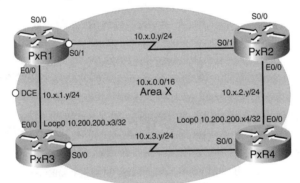

## Command List

In this exercise, you use the commands in Table 4-12, listed in logical order. Refer to this list if you need configuration command assistance during the exercise.

**Table 4-12** *Routing Protocol Route Summarization Support*

| Command | Description |
|---|---|
| (config)#**router ospf 1** | Turns on OSPF. The process number is not communicated to other routers. |
| (config-router)#**network 10.*x*.0.0 0.0.255.255 area 1** | Specifies the interfaces on which OSPF will run. |
| #**show ip ospf** | Shows OSPF process parameters. |
| (config-router)#**router-id 10.0.0.*xy* | Configures the OSPF RID. |
| #**clear ip ospf process** | Resets the OSPF process. |

**Table 4-12**    *Routing Protocol Route Summarization Support (Continued)*

| Command | Description |
|---|---|
| #**show ip ospf neighbor** | Shows all OSPF neighbors. |
| #**debug ip ospf events** | Shows OSPF process evolution. |
| (config-if)#**ip ospf priority 0** | Removes a router from contention as the DR or BDR. |

**CAUTION**    Although the command syntax is shown in Table 4-12, the addresses shown are typically for the P*x*R1 and P*x*R3 routers. Be careful when addressing your routers! Refer to the exercise instructions and the appropriate visual objective diagram for addressing details.

## Task 1: Cleaning Up

Before starting to investigate OSPF, you need to remove Enhanced Interior Gateway Routing Protocol (EIGRP).

Disable EIGRP on all the routers in your pod. Ensure that the **ip classless** command is on each router. (Alternatively, you might instead copy the router setup file [P*x*R*y*.txt] to **startup-config** and then **reload** the router. After the router restarts, add the command **ip classless**.)

## Task 2: Configuring Single-Area OSPF Within Your Pod

Follow these steps:

**Step 1**    Shut down the Frame Relay connection (serial 0 on edge routers P*x*R1 and P*x*R2).

**Step 2**    Configure OSPF on all your pod routers as Area *x*, where *x* is your pod number. To avoid problems in a later exercise, use the **network** command for your pod network 10.*x*.0.0 rather than the entire 10.0.0.0 network.

**Step 3**    Use the proper **show** command to verify the OSPF RID on the pod routers. The RID is the highest active IP address on the router. Notice that P*x*R1 and P*x*R2 have not chosen their Frame Relay IP addresses, because those interfaces are not active.

What is the OSPF RID of your pod routers? Is it what you expected it to be?

**Step 4**    Configure a loopback 0 interface on P*x*R3 and P*x*R4 with the IP address 10.200.200.*xy* /32, where *x* is the pod number and *y* is the router number.

**Step 5**    Use the proper **show** command to verify the OSPF RID on the internal router. The RID is supposed to be the highest loopback address or, if there is no loopback address, the highest active address. What is the OSPF RID of your pod's internal routers now? Is it what you expected it to be?

**Step 6**   Notice that in the previous step the RID did not change; this is a stability feature of Cisco IOS. If the RID changed, the LSAs would be invalid, and the router would have to reconverge. Save your configuration, and reload the internal routers to get the RID to change, because the loopback interface was configured after the OSPF process was configured.

**Step 7**   Use the proper **show** command to verify that the RID changed to the loopback 0 interface after the internal routers reloaded.

**Step 8**   On the P*x*R1 and P*x*R2 routers, set the OSPF RID to 10.0.0.*xy*, where *x* is the pod number and *y* is the router number, using the **router-id** command in the OSPF router configuration mode. Reset the OSPF process with the privileged mode command **clear ip ospf process** to make the **router-id** command take effect. The **router-id** command is another way to set the OSPF RID. This command was introduced in Cisco IOS Release 12.0(1)T.

> **NOTE**   Changing a RID by configuring a loopback interface requires either rebooting the router or disabling and then enabling OSPF. Changing a RID by configuring the RID under the OSPF process requires only that the OSPF process be cleared, a much less drastic move.

**Step 9**   Use the proper **show** command to verify that the RID of the edge router changed to 10.0.0.*xy* after the OSPF process was reset.

**Step 10**  Before finishing, make sure that all neighbors are in communication (in the FULL state) on all your pod routers. This will help you avoid problems in future exercises.

**Step 11**  Display the IP routing table to be sure that you are getting OSPF routes.

## Task 3: Understanding the OSPF Process

Follow these steps:

**Step 1**   Examine the OSPF process with the **debug ip ospf events** command.

**Step 2**   Reset the OSPF process with the **clear ip ospf process** command, and examine the OSPF adjacency building and the election of a DR and BDR.

## Task 4: Understanding OSPF DR and BDR Election

Follow these steps:

**Step 1**   Determine the default OSPF priority and which router is the DR on the Ethernet segment using the **show ip ospf neighbor** command.

**Step 2**    Change the DR by adjusting the OSPF priority to 0 for the appropriate router's Ethernet interface. Doing so removes this router from the election process. Observe the results when the edge router is elected as the DR (**debug ip ospf events** is still running).

**Step 3**    After you have seen the DR and BDR election, turn off the debug.

**Step 4**    Verify the results of the election by displaying the neighbor database.

## Exercise Verification

You have completed this exercise when you achieve the following results:

- EIGRP is removed from the routers.
- OSPF is running, and all pod routes are being passed.
- You understand how to control RID.
- You can witness OSPF neighborship formation.
- You can administratively determine the DR and BDR.

# Solution to Configuration Exercise: Configuring and Examining OSPF in a Single Area

This section provides the answers to the questions in the Configuration Exercise.

---

**NOTE**    Some answers provided cover multiple steps; the answers are given after the last step to which that answer applies.

---

## Solution to Task 1: Cleaning Up

Before starting to investigate OSPF, you need to remove EIGRP.

Disable EIGRP on all the routers in your pod. Ensure that the **ip classless** command is on each router. (Alternatively, you might instead copy the router setup file [P*x*R*y*.txt] to **startup-config**, and then **reload** the router. After the router restarts, add the command **ip classless**.)

**Solution:**

```
P1R4(config)#no router eigrp 1
P1R3(config)#no router eigrp 1
P1R2(config)#no router eigrp 1
P1R1(config)#no router eigrp 1
```

# Solution to Task 2: Configuring Single-Area OSPF Within Your Pod

**Step 1** Shut down the Frame Relay connection (serial 0 on edge routers P*x*R1 and P*x*R2).

**Solution:**

```
P1R1(config)#int s0
P1R1(config-if)#shutdown

P1R2(config)#int s0
P1R2(config-if)#shutdown
```

**Step 2** Configure OSPF on all your pod routers as Area *x*, where *x* is your pod number. To avoid problems in a later exercise, use the **network** command for your pod network 10.*x*.0.0 rather than the entire 10.0.0.0 network.

**Solution:**

```
P1R1(config)#router ospf 1
P1R1(config-router)#network 10.1.0.0 0.0.255.255 area 1

P1R2(config)#router ospf 1
P1R2(config-router)#network 10.1.0.0 0.0.255.255 area 1

P1R3(config)#router ospf 1
P1R3(config-router)#network 10.1.0.0 0.0.255.255 area 1

P1R4(config)#router ospf 1
P1R4(config-router)#network 10.1.0.0 0.0.255.255 area 1

P1R1#sh ip route
<output omitted>
Gateway of last resort is not set

     10.0.0.0/24 is subnetted, 4 subnets
O       10.1.3.0 [110/1572] via 10.1.1.3, 00:00:35, Ethernet0
O       10.1.2.0 [110/1572] via 10.1.0.2, 00:00:35, Serial1
C       10.1.1.0 is directly connected, Ethernet0
C       10.1.0.0 is directly connected, Serial1
P1R1#
```

**Step 3** Use the proper **show** command to verify the OSPF RID on the pod routers. The RID is the highest active IP address on the router. Notice that P*x*R1 and P*x*R2 have not chosen their Frame Relay IP addresses, because those interfaces are not active.

What is the OSPF RID of your pod routers? Is it what you expected it to be?

**Solution:**

```
P1R1#show ip ospf
 Routing Process "ospf 1" with ID 10.1.1.1 and Domain ID 0.0.0.1
 Supports only single TOS(TOS0) routes
 Supports opaque LSA
```

```
SPF schedule delay 5 secs, Hold time between two SPFs 10 secs
Minimum LSA interval 5 secs. Minimum LSA arrival 1 secs
Number of external LSA 0. Checksum Sum 0x0
Number of opaque AS LSA 0. Checksum Sum 0x0
Number of DCbitless external and opaque AS LSA 0
Number of DoNotAge external and opaque AS LSA 0
Number of areas in this router is 1. 1 normal 0 stub 0 nssa
External flood list length 0
    Area 1
        Number of interfaces in this area is 2
        Area has no authentication
        SPF algorithm executed 1 times
        Area ranges are
        Number of LSA 9. Checksum Sum 0x51F17
        Number of opaque link LSA 0. Checksum Sum 0x0
        Number of DCbitless LSA 0
        Number of indication LSA 0
        Number of DoNotAge LSA 0
        Flood list length 0

P1R1#
```

The RIDs of the pod 1 routers are as follows:

- **RID of P*x*R1** — 10.1.1.1

- **RID of P*x*R2** — 10.1.2.2

- **RID of P*x*R3** — 10.1.3.3

- **RID of P*x*R4** — 10.1.3.4

**Step 4**    Configure a loopback 0 interface on P*x*R3 and P*x*R4 with the IP address
10.200.200.*xy* /32, where *x* is the pod number and *y* is the router number.

**Solution:**

```
P1R3(config)#int loopback 0
P1R3(config-if)#ip address 10.200.200.13 255.255.255.255

P1R4(config)#int loopback 0
P1R4(config-if)#ip address 10.200.200.14 255.255.255.255
```

**NOTE**    A mask of /32 is used so that the two loopback addresses do not appear to be on the same subnet.

**Step 5**    Use the proper **show** command to verify the OSPF RID on the internal router.
The RID is supposed to be the highest loopback address or, if there is no
loopback address, the highest active address. What is the OSPF RID of your
pod's internal routers now? Is it what you expected it to be?

**Solution:**

```
P1R3#show ip ospf
 Routing Process "ospf 1" with ID 10.1.3.3 and Domain ID 0.0.0.1
 Supports only single TOS(TOS0) routes
 Supports opaque LSA
 SPF schedule delay 5 secs, Hold time between two SPFs 10 secs
 Minimum LSA interval 5 secs. Minimum LSA arrival 1 secs
 Number of external LSA 0. Checksum Sum 0x0
 Number of opaque AS LSA 0. Checksum Sum 0x0
 Number of DCbitless external and opaque AS LSA 0
 Number of DoNotAge external and opaque AS LSA 0
 Number of areas in this router is 1. 1 normal 0 stub 0 nssa
 External flood list length 0
    Area 1
        Number of interfaces in this area is 2
        Area has no authentication
        SPF algorithm executed 6 times
        Area ranges are
        Number of LSA 10. Checksum Sum 0x5308D
        Number of opaque link LSA 0. Checksum Sum 0x0
        Number of DCbitless LSA 0
        Number of indication LSA 0
        Number of DoNotAge LSA 0
        Flood list length 0
```

The RID of P*x*R3 is 10.1.3.3 (you might have expected it to be 10.200.200.13).
The RID of P*x*R4 is 10.1.3.4 (you might have expected it to be 10.200.200.14).

**Step 6**   Notice that in the previous step the RID did not change; this is a stability
feature of Cisco IOS. If the RID changed, the LSAs would be invalid, and the
router would have to reconverge. Save your configuration, and reload the
internal routers to get the RID to change, because the loopback interface was
configured after the OSPF process was configured.

**Solution:**

```
P1R4#copy run start
Destination filename [startup-config]?
Building configuration...
[OK]
P1R4#reload
Proceed with reload? [confirm]
```

**Step 7**   Use the proper **show** command to verify that the RID changed to the
loopback 0 interface after the internal routers reloaded.

**Solution:**

```
P1R3#show ip ospf
 Routing Process "ospf 1" with ID 10.200.200.13 and Domain ID 0.0.0.1
 Supports only single TOS(TOS0) routes
 Supports opaque LSA
 SPF schedule delay 5 secs, Hold time between two SPFs 10 secs
```

```
Minimum LSA interval 5 secs. Minimum LSA arrival 1 secs
Number of external LSA 0. Checksum Sum 0x0
Number of opaque AS LSA 0. Checksum Sum 0x0
Number of DCbitless external and opaque AS LSA 0
Number of DoNotAge external and opaque AS LSA 0
Number of areas in this router is 1. 1 normal 0 stub 0 nssa
External flood list length 0
   Area 1
       Number of interfaces in this area is 2
       Area has no authentication
       SPF algorithm executed 2 times
       Area ranges are
       Number of LSA 8. Checksum Sum 0x474A1
       Number of opaque link LSA 0. Checksum Sum 0x0
       Number of DCbitless LSA 0
       Number of indication LSA 0
       Number of DoNotAge LSA 0
       Flood list length 0

P1R3#
P1R4#show ip ospf
 Routing Process "ospf 1" with ID 10.200.200.14 and Domain ID 0.0.0.1
 Supports only single TOS(TOS0) routes
 Supports opaque LSA
 SPF schedule delay 5 secs, Hold time between two SPFs 10 secs
 Minimum LSA interval 5 secs. Minimum LSA arrival 1 secs
 Number of external LSA 0. Checksum Sum 0x0
 Number of opaque AS LSA 0. Checksum Sum 0x0
 Number of DCbitless external and opaque AS LSA 0
 Number of DoNotAge external and opaque AS LSA 0
 Number of areas in this router is 1. 1 normal 0 stub 0 nssa
 External flood list length 0
    Area 1
        Number of interfaces in this area is 2
        Area has no authentication
        SPF algorithm executed 5 times
        Area ranges are
        Number of LSA 8. Checksum Sum 0x474A1
        Number of opaque link LSA 0. Checksum Sum 0x0
        Number of DCbitless LSA 0
        Number of indication LSA 0
        Number of DoNotAge LSA 0
        Flood list length 0

P1R4#
```

**Step 8**   On the P*x*R1 and P*x*R2 routers, set the OSPF RID to 10.0.0.*xy*, where *x* is the pod number and *y* is the router number, using the **router-id** command in OSPF router configuration mode. Reset the OSPF process with the privileged mode command **clear ip ospf process** to make the **router-id** command take effect. The **router-id** command is another way to set the OSPF RID. This command was introduced in Cisco IOS Release 12.0(1)T.

| NOTE | Changing a RID by configuring a loopback interface requires either rebooting the router or disabling and then enabling OSPF. Changing a RID by configuring the RID under the OSPF process requires only that the OSPF process be cleared, a much less drastic move. |
|------|---|

**Solution:**

```
P1R1(config)#router ospf 1
P1R1(config-router)#router-id 10.0.0.11
Reload or use "clear ip ospf process" command, for this to take effect
P1R1(config-router)#^Z
P1R1#
Mar  1 15:16:06 EST: %SYS-5-CONFIG_I: Configured from console by console
P1R1#clear ip ospf process
Reset ALL OSPF processes? [no]: y
P1R1#
Mar  1 15:16:19 EST: %OSPF-5-ADJCHG: Process 1, Nbr 10.1.2.2 on Serial1 from
    FULL to DOWN, Neighbor Down: Interface down or detached
Mar  1 15:16:19 EST: %OSPF-5-ADJCHG: Process 1, Nbr 10.200.200.13 on Ethernet0
    from FULL to DOWN, Neighbor Down: Interface down or detached

P1R2(config)#router ospf 1
Mar  1 15:16:31 EST: %OSPF-5-ADJCHG: Process 1, Nbr 10.0.0.11 on Serial1 from
    LOADING to FULL, Loading Done
P1R2(config-router)#router-id 10.0.0.12
Reload or use "clear ip ospf process" command, for this to take effect
P1R2(config-router)#^Z
P1R2#
Mar  1 15:16:54 EST: %SYS-5-CONFIG_I: Configured from console by console
Mar  1 15:16:59 EST: %OSPF-5-ADJCHG: Process 1, Nbr 10.1.1.1 on Serial1 from
    FULL to DOWN, Neighbor Down: Dead timer expired
P1R2#clear ip ospf process
Reset ALL OSPF processes? [no]: y
P1R2#
Mar  1 15:17:10 EST: %OSPF-5-ADJCHG: Process 1, Nbr 10.0.0.11 on Serial1 from
    FULL to DOWN, Neighbor Down: Interface down or detached
Mar  1 15:17:10 EST: %OSPF-5-ADJCHG: Process 1, Nbr 10.200.200.14 on Ethernet0
    from FULL to DOWN, Neighbor Down: Interface down or detached
P1R2#
Mar  1 15:17:13 EST: %OSPF-5-ADJCHG: Process 1, Nbr 10.200.200.14 on Ethernet0
    from LOADING to FULL, Loading Done
P1R2#
Mar  1 15:17:19 EST: %OSPF-5-ADJCHG: Process 1, Nbr 10.0.0.11 on Serial1 from
    LOADING to FULL, Loading Done
P1R2#
```

**Step 9**  Use the proper **show** command to verify that the RID of the edge router changed to 10.0.0.*xy* after the OSPF process was reset.

**Solution:**

```
P1R1#show ip ospf
 Routing Process "ospf 1" with ID 10.0.0.11 and Domain ID 0.0.0.1
 Supports only single TOS(TOS0) routes
 Supports opaque LSA
 SPF schedule delay 5 secs, Hold time between two SPFs 10 secs
 Minimum LSA interval 5 secs. Minimum LSA arrival 1 secs
 Number of external LSA 0. Checksum Sum 0x0
 Number of opaque AS LSA 0. Checksum Sum 0x0
 Number of DCbitless external and opaque AS LSA 0
 Number of DoNotAge external and opaque AS LSA 0
 Number of areas in this router is 1. 1 normal 0 stub 0 nssa
 External flood list length 0
    Area 1
        Number of interfaces in this area is 2
        Area has no authentication
        SPF algorithm executed 20 times
        Area ranges are
        Number of LSA 14. Checksum Sum 0x8874E
        Number of opaque link LSA 0. Checksum Sum 0x0
        Number of DCbitless LSA 0
        Number of indication LSA 0
        Number of DoNotAge LSA 0
        Flood list length 0

 P1R1#
```

**Step 10** Before finishing, make sure that all neighbors are in communication (in the FULL state) on all of your pod routers. This will help you avoid problems in future exercises.

**Solution:**

```
P1R1#show ip ospf neighbor
Neighbor ID     Pri   State       Dead Time   Address     Interface
10.200.200.13    1    FULL/DR     00:00:31    10.1.1.3    Ethernet0
10.0.0.12        1    FULL/  -    00:00:36    10.1.0.2    Serial1
P1R1#
P1R2#show ip ospf neig

Neighbor ID     Pri   State       Dead Time   Address     Interface
10.200.200.14    1    FULL/DR     00:00:34    10.1.2.4    Ethernet0
10.0.0.11        1    FULL/  -    00:00:30    10.1.0.1    Serial1
P1R2#
P1R3#show ip ospf neig
Neighbor ID     Pri   State       Dead Time   Address     Interface
10.0.0.11        1    FULL/BDR    00:00:33    10.1.1.1    Ethernet0
10.200.200.14    1    FULL/  -    00:00:39    10.1.3.4    Serial0
P1R3#
P1R4#show ip ospf neig
Neighbor ID     Pri   State       Dead Time   Address     Interface
10.0.0.12        1    FULL/BDR    00:00:38    10.1.2.2    Ethernet0
10.200.200.13    1    FULL/  -    00:00:34    10.1.3.3    Serial0
P1R4#
```

**Step 11** Display the IP routing table to be sure that you are getting OSPF routes.

**Solution:**

```
P1R1#show ip route
<output omitted>
Gateway of last resort is not set

     10.0.0.0/24 is subnetted, 4 subnets
O       10.1.3.0 [110/1572] via 10.1.1.3, 00:03:37, Ethernet0
O       10.1.2.0 [110/1572] via 10.1.0.2, 00:03:37, Serial1
C       10.1.1.0 is directly connected, Ethernet0
C       10.1.0.0 is directly connected, Serial1
P1R1#
```

# Solution to Task 3: Understanding the OSPF Process

**Step 1** Examine the OSPF process with the **debug ip ospf events** command.

**Solution:**

```
P1R1#debug ip ospf events
OSPF events debugging is on
```

**Step 2** Reset the OSPF process with the **clear ip ospf process** command, and examine OSPF adjacency building and the election of a DR and BDR.

**Solution:**

```
P1R1#
Mar  1 15:22:46 EST: OSPF:  from 10.200.200.13 area 1 from Ethernet0 10.1.1.3
Mar  1 15:22:46 EST: OSPF: End of hello processing
Mar  1 15:22:50 EST: OSPF: Rcv hello from 10.0.0.12 area 1 from Serial1 10.1.0.2
Mar  1 15:22:50 EST: OSPF: End of hello processing
P1R1#clear ip ospf process
Reset ALL OSPF processes? [no]: y
P1R1#
Mar  1 15:22:55 EST: OSPF: Flushing External Links
Mar  1 15:22:55 EST: OSPF: Flushing Opaque AS Links
Mar  1 15:22:55 EST: OSPF: Flushing Link states in area 1
Mar  1 15:22:55 EST: OSPF: Interface Serial1 going Down
Mar  1 15:22:55 EST: %OSPF-5-ADJCHG: Process 1, Nbr 10.0.0.12 on Serial1
     from FULL to DOWN, Neighbor Down: Interface down or detached
Mar  1 15:22:55 EST: OSPF: Interface Ethernet0 going Down
Mar  1 15:22:55 EST: OSPF: Neighbor change Event on interface Ethernet0
Mar  1 15:22:55 EST: OSPF: DR/BDR election on Ethernet0
Mar  1 15:22:55 EST: OSPF: Elect BDR 0.0.0.0
Mar  1 15:22:55 EST: OSPF: Elect DR 10.200.200.13
Mar  1 15:22:55 EST: OSPF: Elect BDR 0.0.0.0
Mar  1 15:22:55 EST: OSPF: Elect DR 10.200.200.13
Mar  1 15:22:55 EST:         DR: 10.200.200.13 (Id)    BDR: none
Mar  1 15:22:55 EST: %OSPF-5-ADJCHG: Process 1, Nbr 10.200.200.13 on Ethernet0
     from FULL to DOWN, Neighbor Down: Interface down or detached
Mar  1 15:22:55 EST: OSPF: Neighbor change Event on P1R interface Ethernet0
Mar  1 15:22:55 EST: OSPF: DR/BDR election on Ethernet0
Mar  1 15:22:55 EST: OSPF: Elect BDR 0.0.0.0
Mar  1 15:22:55 EST: OSPF: Elect DR 0.0.0.0
```

```
Mar  1 15:22:55 EST:        DR: none    BDR: none
Mar  1 15:22:55 EST: OSPF: Remember old DR 10.200.200.13 (id)
Mar  1 15:22:55 EST: OSPF: Interface Serial1 going Up
Mar  1 15:22:55 EST: OSPF: Interface Ethernet0 going Up
Mar  1 15:22:56 EST: OSPF: Rcv hello from 10.200.200.13 area 1 from
    Ethernet0 10.1.1.3
Mar  1 15:22:56 EST: OSPF: 2 Way Communication to 10.200.200.13 on
    Ethernet0, state 2WAY
Mar  1 15:22:56 EST: OSPF: Backup seen Event before WAIT timer on Ethernet0
Mar  1 15:22:56 EST: OSPF: DR/BDR election on Ethernet0
Mar  1 15:22:56 EST: OSPF: Elect BDR 10.0.0.11
Mar  1 15:22:56 EST: OSPF: Elect DR 10.200.200.13
Mar  1 15:22:56 EST: OSPF: Elect BDR 10.0.0.11
Mar  1 15:22:56 EST: OSPF: Elect DR 10.200.200.13
Mar  1 15:22:56 EST:        DR: 10.200.200.13 (Id)   BDR: 10.0.0.11 (Id)
Mar  1 15:22:56 EST: OSPF: Send DBD to 10.200.200.13 on Ethernet0 seq 0x26B8 opt
    0x42 flag 0x7 len 32
Mar  1 15:22:56 EST: OSPF: End of hello processing
Mar  1 15:22:56 EST: OSPF: Rcv DBD from 10.200.200.13 on Ethernet0 seq 0x22E8
    opt 0x42 flag 0x7 len 32  mtu 1500 state EXSTART
Mar  1 15:22:56 EST: OSPF: NBR Negotiation Done. We are the SLAVE
Mar  1 15:22:56 EST: OSPF: Send DBD to 10.200.200.13 on Ethernet0 seq 0x22E8 opt
    0x42 flag 0x2 len 52
Mar  1 15:22:56 EST: OSPF: Rcv DBD from 10.200.200.13 on Ethernet0 seq 0x22E9
    opt 0x42 flag 0x3 len 172  mtu 1500 state EXCHANGE
Mar  1 15:22:56 EST: OSPF: Send DBD to 10.200.200.13 on Ethernet0 seq 0x22E9 opt
    0x42 flag 0x0 len 32
Mar  1 15:22:56 EST: OSPF: Database request to 10.200.200.13
Mar  1 15:22:56 EST: OSPF: sent LS REQ packet to 10.1.1.3, length 84
Mar  1 15:22:56 EST: OSPF: Rcv DBD from 10.200.200.13 on Ethernet0 seq 0x22EA
    opt 0x42 flag 0x1 len 32  mtu 1500 state EXCHANGE
Mar  1 15:22:56 EST: OSPF: Exchange Done with 10.200.200.13 on Ethernet0
Mar  1 15:22:56 EST: OSPF: Send DBD to 10.200.200.13 on Ethernet0 seq 0x22EA opt
    0x42 flag 0x0 len 32
Mar  1 15:22:56 EST: OSPF: Synchronized with 10.200.200.13 on Ethernet0,
    state FULL
Mar  1 15:22:56 EST: %OSPF-5-ADJCHG: Process 1, Nbr 10.200.200.13 on Ethernet0
    from LOADING to FULL, Loading Done1#
P1R1#
Mar  1 15:23:00 EST: OSPF: Rcv hello from 10.0.0.12 area 1 from Serial1 10.1.0.2
Mar  1 15:23:00 EST: OSPF: 2 Way Communication to 10.0.0.12 on Serial1,
    state 2WAY
Mar  1 15:23:00 EST: OSPF: Send DBD to 10.0.0.12 on Serial1 seq 0x14D5 opt
    0x42flag 0x7 len 32
Mar  1 15:23:00 EST: OSPF: End of hello processing
Mar  1 15:23:00 EST: OSPF: Rcv DBD from 10.0.0.12 on Serial1 seq 0x738 opt
    0x42flag 0x7 len 32  mtu 1500 state EXSTART
Mar  1 15:23:00 EST: OSPF: NBR Negotiation Done. We are the SLAVE
Mar  1 15:23:00 EST: OSPF: Send DBD to 10.0.0.12 on Serial1 seq 0x738 opt
    0x42 flag 0x2 len 172
Mar  1 15:23:00 EST: OSPF: Rcv DBD from 10.0.0.12 on Serial1 seq 0x739 opt
    0x42flag 0x3 len 152  mtu 1500 state EXCHANGE
Mar  1 15:23:00 EST: OSPF: Send DBD to 10.0.0.12 on Serial1 seq 0x739 opt
    0x42 flag 0x0 len 32
Mar  1 15:23:00 EST: OSPF: Database request to 10.0.0.12
```

*continues*

```
Mar  1 15:23:00 EST: OSPF: sent LS REQ packet to 10.1.0.2, length 12
Mar  1 15:23:00 EST: OSPF: Rcv DBD from 10.0.0.12 on Serial1 seq 0x73A opt
    0x42 flag 0x1 len 32  mtu 1500 state EXCHANGE
Mar  1 15:23:00 EST: OSPF: Exchange Done with 10.0.0.12 on Serial1
Mar  1 15:23:00 EST: OSPF: Send DBD to 10.0.0.12 on Serial1 seq 0x73A opt
    0x42 flag 0x0 len 32
Mar  1 15:23:00 EST: OSPF: Synchronized with 10.0.0.12 on Serial1,
    state FULL
Mar  1 15:23:00 EST: %OSPF-5-ADJCHG: Process 1, Nbr 10.0.0.12 on Serial1
    from LOADING to FULL, Loading Done
P1R1#
Mar  1 15:23:06 EST: OSPF: Rcv hello from 10.200.200.13 area 1 from
    Ethernet0 10.1.1.3
Mar  1 15:23:06 EST: OSPF: Neighbor change Event on interface Ethernet0
Mar  1 15:23:06 EST: OSPF: DR/BDR election on Ethernet0
Mar  1 15:23:06 EST: OSPF: Elect BDR 10.0.0.11
Mar  1 15:23:06 EST: OSPF: Elect DR 10.200.200.13
Mar  1 15:23:06 EST:         DR: 10.200.200.13 (Id)    BDR: 10.0.0.11 (Id)
Mar  1 15:23:06 EST: OSPF: End of hello processing
P1R1#
Mar  1 15:23:10 EST: OSPF: Rcv hello from 10.0.0.12 area 1 from Serial1 10.1.0.2
Mar  1 15:23:10 EST: OSPF: End of hello processing
P1R1#
Mar  1 15:23:16 EST: OSPF: Rcv hello from 10.200.200.13 area 1 from
    Ethernet0 10.1.1.3
Mar  1 15:23:16 EST: OSPF: End of hello processing
P1R1#
Mar  1 15:23:20 EST: OSPF: Rcv hello from 10.0.0.12 area 1 from Serial1 10.1.0.2
Mar  1 15:23:20 EST: OSPF: End of hello processing
P1R1#
Mar  1 15:23:26 EST: OSPF: Rcv hello from 10.200.200.13 area 1 from
    Ethernet0 10.1.1.3
Mar  1 15:23:26 EST: OSPF: End of hello processing
P1R1#
Mar  1 15:23:30 EST: OSPF: Rcv hello from 10.0.0.12 area 1 from Serial1 10.1.0.2
Mar  1 15:23:30 EST: OSPF: End of hello processing
P1R1#
Mar  1 15:23:36 EST: OSPF: Rcv hello from 10.200.200.13 area 1 from
    Ethernet0 10.1.1.3
Mar  1 15:23:36 EST: OSPF: End of hello processing
P1R1#
Mar  1 15:23:40 EST: OSPF: Rcv hello from 10.0.0.12 area 1 from Serial1 10.1.0.2
Mar  1 15:23:40 EST: OSPF: End of hello processing
P1R1#
Mar  1 15:23:46 EST: OSPF: Rcv hello from 10.200.200.13 area 1 from
    Ethernet0 10.1.1.3
Mar  1 15:23:46 EST: OSPF: End of hello processing
P1R1#
Mar  1 15:23:50 EST: OSPF: Rcv hello from 10.0.0.12 area 1 from Serial1 10.1.0.2
Mar  1 15:23:50 EST: OSPF: End of hello processing
P1R1#
Mar  1 15:23:56 EST: OSPF: Rcv hello from 10.200.200.13 area 1 from
    Ethernet0 10.1.1.3
Mar  1 15:23:56 EST: OSPF: End of hello processing
P1R1#
```

# Solution to Task 4: Understanding OSPF DR and BDR Election

**Step 1**    Determine the default OSPF priority and which router is the DR on the Ethernet segment using the **show ip ospf neighbor** command.

**Solution:**

```
P1R1#show ip ospf neighbor
Neighbor ID       Pri   State         Dead Time   Address     Interface
10.200.200.13      1    FULL/DR       00:00:31    10.1.1.3    Ethernet0
10.0.0.12          1    FULL/   -     00:00:36    10.1.0.2    Serial1
P1R1#
```

P1R3 is the DR on the Ethernet segment, because it has the highest OSPF RID.

**Step 2**    Change the DR by adjusting the OSPF priority to 0 for the appropriate router's Ethernet interface. Doing so removes this router from the election process. Observe the results when the edge router is elected as the DR (**debug ip ospf events** is still running).

**Solution:**

```
P1R3(config)#int e0
P1R3(config-if)#ip ospf priority 0

P1R1#
Mar  1 15:39:16 EST: OSPF: Rcv hello from 10.200.200.13 area 1 from
    Ethernet0 10.1.1.3
Mar  1 15:39:16 EST: OSPF: Neighbor change Event on interface Ethernet0
Mar  1 15:39:16 EST: OSPF: DR/BDR election on Ethernet0
Mar  1 15:39:16 EST: OSPF: Elect BDR 10.0.0.11
Mar  1 15:39:16 EST: OSPF: Elect DR 10.0.0.11
Mar  1 15:39:16 EST: OSPF: Elect BDR 0.0.0.0
Mar  1 15:39:16 EST: OSPF: Elect DR 10.0.0.11
Mar  1 15:39:16 EST:         DR: 10.0.0.11 (Id)    BDR: none
Mar  1 15:39:16 EST: OSPF: Remember old DR 10.200.200.13 (id)
Mar  1 15:39:16 EST: OSPF: End of hello processing
P1R1#
Mar  1 15:39:20 EST: OSPF: Rcv hello from 10.0.0.12 area 1 from Serial1 10.1.0.2
Mar  1 15:39:20 EST: OSPF: End of hello processing
P1R1#
Mar  1 15:39:26 EST: OSPF: Rcv hello from 10.200.200.13 area 1 from
    Ethernet0 10.1.1.3
Mar  1 15:39:26 EST: OSPF: Neighbor change Event on interface Ethernet0
Mar  1 15:39:26 EST: OSPF: DR/BDR election on Ethernet0
Mar  1 15:39:26 EST: OSPF: Elect BDR 0.0.0.0
Mar  1 15:39:26 EST: OSPF: Elect DR 10.0.0.11
Mar  1 15:39:26 EST:         DR: 10.0.0.11 (Id)    BDR: none
Mar  1 15:39:26 EST: OSPF: End of hello processing
P1R1#
Mar  1 15:39:30 EST: OSPF: Rcv hello from 10.0.0.12 area 1 from Serial1 10.1.0.2
Mar  1 15:39:30 EST: OSPF: End of hello processing
P1R1#
P1R1#
Mar  1 15:39:36 EST: OSPF: Rcv hello from 10.200.200.13 area 1 from
    Ethernet0 10.1.1.3
Mar  1 15:39:36 EST: OSPF: End of hello processing
```

**Step 3**   After you have seen the DR and BDR election, turn off the debug.

**Solution:**

```
P1R1#no debug all
All possible debugging has been turned off
P1R1#
```

**Step 4**   Verify the results of the election by displaying the neighbor database.

**Solution:**

```
P1R1#sho ip ospf neighbor

Neighbor ID    Pri   State          Dead Time   Address      Interface
10.200.200.13   0    FULL/DROTHER   00:00:35    10.1.1.3     Ethernet0
10.0.0.12       1    FULL/   -      00:00:39    10.1.0.2     Serial1
P1R1#
Mar  1 15:39:40 EST: OSPF: Rcv hello from 10.0.0.12 area 1 from Serial1 10.1.0.2
Mar  1 15:39:40 EST: OSPF: End of hello processing
```

## Exercise Verification

You have completed this exercise when you achieve the following results:

- EIGRP is removed from the routers.

- OSPF is running, and all pod routes are being passed.

- You understand how to control RID.

- You can witness OSPF neighborship formation.

- You can administratively determine the DR and BDR.

# Review Questions

Answer the following questions, and then refer to Appendix G, "Answers to Review Questions," for the answers.

   1  Which of the following is not a characteristic of link-state routing protocols?

      a.  They respond quickly to network changes.

      b.  They broadcast every 30 minutes.

      c.  They send triggered updates when a network change occurs.

      d.  They send periodic updates, known as link-state refresh, at long time intervals, such as every 30 minutes.

   2  For all the routers in the network to make consistent routing decisions, each router must keep a record of all of the following items except which one?

      a.  Its immediate neighbor routers

      b.  All of the other routers in the network, or in its area of the network, and their attached networks

   c.  The best paths to each destination

   d.  The version of the routing protocol used

**3**  Link-state routing protocols use a two-layer area hierarchy composed of which two areas?

   a.  Transit area

   b.  Transmit area

   c.  Regular area

   d.  Linking area

**4**  Which of the following is not a characteristic of an OSPF area?

   a.  It minimizes routing table entries.

   b.  It requires a flat network design.

   c.  It localizes the impact of a topology change within an area.

   d.  Detailed LSA flooding stops at the area boundary.

**5**  True or false: An ABR connects area 0 to the nonbackbone areas.

**6**  When each router receives the LSU, it does not do which of the following?

   a.  If the entry does not already exist, the router adds the entry to its LSDB, sends back an LSAck, floods the information to other routers, runs SPF, and updates its routing table.

   b.  If the entry already exists and the received LSU has the same information, the router overwrites the information in the LSDB with the new LSA entry.

   c.  If the entry already exists but the LSU includes newer information, the router adds the entry to its LSDB, sends back an LSAck, floods the information to other routers, runs SPF, and updates its routing table.

   d.  If the entry already exists but the LSU includes older information, it sends an LSU to the sender with its newer information.

**7**  What is an OSPF Type 2 packet?

   a.  Database Description (DBD), which checks for database synchronization between routers

   b.  Link-State Request (LSR), which requests specific link-state records from router to router

   c.  Link-State Update (LSU), which sends specifically requested link-state records

   d.  Link-State Acknowledgment (LSAck), which acknowledges the other packet types

**8**  Which of the following is true of hellos and dead intervals?

   a.  They don't need to be the same on neighboring routers, because the lowest common denominator is adopted

   b.  They don't need to be the same on neighboring routers, because the highest common denominator is adopted

    c. They don't need to be the same, because it is a negotiated interval between neighboring routers

    d. They need to be the same

**9** In which state do the DR and BDR establish adjacencies with each router in the network?

    a. Init state

    b. Exstart state

    c. Exchange state

    d. Loading state

    e. Full state

**10** Which IP address is used to send an updated LSA entry to OSPF DRs and BDRs?

    a. **unicast 224.0.0.5**

    b. **unicast 224.0.0.6**

    c. **multicast 224.0.0.5**

    d. **multicast 224.0.0.6**

**11** To ensure an accurate database, how often does OSPF flood (refresh) each LSA record?

    a. Every 60 minutes

    b. Every 30 minutes

    c. Every 60 seconds

    d. Every 30 seconds

    e. Flooding each LSA record would defeat the purpose of a link-state routing protocol, which strives to reduce the amount of routing traffic it generates.

**12** What command is used to display router ID, timers, and statistics?

    a. **show ip ospf**

    b. **show ip ospf neighbors**

    c. **show ip ospf stats**

    d. **show ip ospf neighborship**

**13** Which of the following is not a way in which the router ID (a unique IP address) can be assigned?

    a. The highest IP address of any physical interface

    b. The lowest IP address of any physical interface

    c. A loopback address is always preferred over an interface address, because a loopback address never goes down.

    d. A **router-id** command is the preferred procedure to set the router ID and is always used over the other two procedures.

**14** True or false: On point-to-point networks, the router dynamically detects its neighboring routers by multicasting its hello packets to all SPF routers using the address 224.0.0.6.

**15** An adjacency is the relationship that exists where?

    a. Between routers located on the same physical network

    b. Between routers in different OSPF areas

    c. Between a router and its DR and BDR on different networks

    d. Between a backbone DR and a transit BDR

**16** To elect a DR and BDR, a router does not use which of the following conditions to determine which router to select?

    a. The router with the highest priority value is the DR.

    b. The router with the second-highest priority value is the BDR.

    c. If all routers have the default priority, the router with the lowest router ID becomes the DR.

    d. The router with a priority set to 0 cannot become the DR or BDR.

**17** Which of the following is not true of point-to-multipoint mode?

    a. It does not require a full-mesh network.

    b. It does not require a static neighbor configuration.

    c. It uses multiple IP subnets.

    d. It duplicates LSA packets.

**18** What is the default OSPF mode on a point-to-point Frame Relay subinterface?

    a. Point-to-point mode

    b. Multipoint mode

    c. Nonbroadcast mode

    d. Broadcast mode

**19** What is the default OSPF mode on a Frame Relay point-to-multipoint subinterface?

    a. Point-to-point mode

    b. Multipoint mode

    c. Nonbroadcast mode

    d. Broadcast mode

**20** What is the default OSPF mode on a main Frame Relay interface?

    a. Point-to-point mode

    b. Multipoint mode

    c. Nonbroadcast mode

    d. Broadcast mode

This chapter discusses how to interconnect multiple OSPF areas. It covers the following topics:

- Types of OSPF Routers and LSAs
- Interpreting the OSPF LSDB and Routing Table
- OSPF Route Summarization Techniques
- OSPF Virtual Links

# CHAPTER 5

# Interconnecting Multiple Open Shortest Path First Areas

This chapter introduces the use, operation, configuration, and verification of Open Shortest Path First (OSPF) in multiple areas. After completing this chapter, you will be able to describe issues related to interconnecting multiple areas. You will see the differences among the possible types of areas and how OSPF supports the use of variable-length subnet masking (VLSM). By the end of this chapter, you should be able to explain how OSPF supports the use of route summarization in multiple areas.

## Types of OSPF Routers and LSAs

The two core concepts of OSPF are the link-state database (LSDB) and link-state advertisements (LSAs). You will learn common LSA types and how they form the layout of the OSPF LSDB. You will also learn about OSPF router types, backbone routers, area border routers (ABRs), autonomous system boundary routers (ASBRs), and internal routers.

## Types of OSPF Routers

Issues arise if an OSPF single area expands into hundreds of networks, as shown in Figure 5-1.

**Figure 5-1** *Issues with Maintaining a Large OSPF Network*

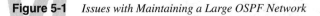

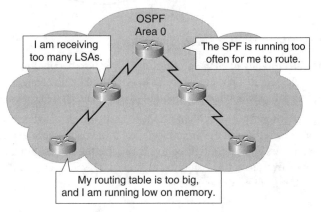

If an expansion occurs, the following issues need to be addressed:

- **Frequent shortest path first (SPF) algorithm calculations**—In a large network, changes are inevitable; therefore, the routers spend many CPU cycles recalculating the SPF algorithm and updating the routing table.

- **Large routing table**—OSPF does not perform route summarization by default. If the routes are not summarized, the routing table can become very large, depending on the size of the network.

- **Large link-state database (LSDB)**—Because the LSDB covers the topology of the entire network, each router must maintain an entry for every network in the area, even if not every route is selected for the routing table.

A solution to these issues is to divide the network into multiple OSPF areas. OSPF allows the separation of a large area into smaller, more manageable areas that still can exchange routing information.

Hierarchical area routing, shown in Figure 5-2, is OSPF's ability to separate a large internetwork into multiple areas. Using this technique, interarea routing still occurs, but many of the internal routing operations, such as SPF calculations, remain within individual areas. For example, if area 1 is having problems with a link going up and down, routers in other areas do not need to continually run their SPF calculation, because they are isolated from the problem in area 1.

**Figure 5-2**  *The Solution: OSPF Hierarchical Routing*

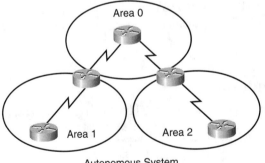

Using multiple OSPF areas has several important advantages:

- **Reduced frequency of SPF calculations**—Because detailed route information exists within each area, it is not necessary to flood all link-state changes to all other areas. Therefore, only routers that are affected by the change need to recalculate SPF.

- **Smaller routing tables**—With multiple areas, detailed route entries for specific networks within an area remain in the area. Instead of advertising these explicit routes outside the area, routers can be configured to summarize the routes into one or more summary addresses. Advertising these summaries reduces the number of LSAs propagated between areas but keeps all networks reachable.

- **Reduced link-state update (LSU) overhead**—LSUs contain a variety of LSA types, including link-state and summary information. Rather than send an LSU about each network within an area, a router can advertise a single summarized route or a small number of routes between areas, thereby reducing the overhead associated with LSUs when they cross areas.

Certain types of OSPF routers control the traffic types that go in and out of various areas. The following are the four router types, as shown in Figure 5-3:

- **Internal router**—Routers that have all of their interfaces in the same area have identical LSDBs.

- **Backbone router**—Routers that sit in the perimeter of the backbone area and that have at least one interface connected to area 0. Backbone routers maintain OSPF routing information using the same procedures and algorithms as internal routers.

- **ABR**—Routers that have interfaces attached to multiple areas maintain separate LSDBs for each area to which they connect and route traffic destined for or arriving from other areas. ABRs are exit points for the area, which means that routing information destined for another area can get there only via the ABR of the local area. ABRs can be configured to summarize the routing information from the LSDBs of their attached areas. ABRs distribute the routing information into the backbone. The backbone routers then forward the information to the other ABRs. An area can have one or more ABRs.

- **ASBR**—Routers that have at least one interface attached to an external internetwork (another autonomous system [AS]), such as a non-OSPF network. ASBRs can import non-OSPF network information to the OSPF network and vice versa; this process is called route redistribution.

**Figure 5-3** *Types of OSPF Routers*

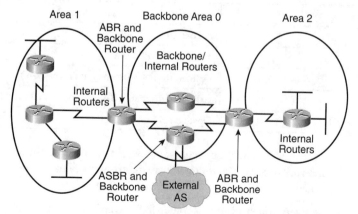

A router can exist as more than one router type. For example, if a router interconnects to area 0 and area 1, as well as to a non-OSPF network, it is both an ABR and an ASBR.

A router has a separate LSDB for each area to which it connects. Therefore, an ABR will have one LSDB for area 0 and another LSDB for the other area in which it participates. Two routers belonging to the same area maintain identical LSDBs for that area.

An LSDB is synchronized between pairs of adjacent routers. On broadcast networks such as Ethernet, an LSDB is synchronized between the DROTHER (a router that is not a designated router [DR] or a backup designated router [BDR]) and its DR and BDR.

---

### OSPF Design Guidelines

Studies and real-world implementations have led to the following OSPF design guidelines, as documented in the Cisco Press book *OSPF Network Design Solutions:*

| | | | |
|---|---|---|---|
| **Routers in a domain** | Minimum 20 | Mean 510 | Maximum 1000 |
| **Routers per single area** | Minimum 20 | Mean 160 | Maximum 350 |
| **Areas per domain** | Minimum 1 | Mean 23 | Maximum 60 |

---

# OSPF LSA Types

LSAs are the building blocks of the OSPF LSDB. Table 5-1 summarizes types of LSAs.

**Table 5-1**    *Summary of OSPF LSA Types*

| Link State Types | Descriptions |
|---|---|
| 1 | Router link advertisement |
| 2 | Network link advertisement |
| 3 or 4 | Summary link advertisement |
| 5 | AS external link advertisements |
| 6 | Multicast OSPF LSA |
| 7 | Defined for not-so-stubby areas (NSSAs) |
| 8 | External attributes LSA for Border Gateway Protocol (BGP) |
| 9, 10, or 11 | Opaque LSAs |

Individually, LSAs act as database records; in combination, they describe the entire topology of an OSPF network or area. The following are descriptions of each type of LSA. LSA types 1 to 5 are explained in more detail in the following sections.

- **Type 1**—Every router generates router-link advertisements for each area to which it belongs. Router-link advertisements describe the states of the router's links to the area and are flooded only within a particular area. All types of LSAs have 20-byte LSA headers. One of the fields of the LSA header is the link-state ID. The link-state ID of the type 1 LSA is the router's originating ID.

- **Type 2**—DRs generate network link advertisements for multiaccess networks, which describe the set of routers attached to a particular multiaccess network. Network link advertisements are flooded in the area that contains the network. The link-state ID of the type 2 LSA is the DR's IP interface address.

- **Types 3 and 4**—ABRs generate summary link advertisements. Summary link advertisements describe the following interarea routes:

  - Type 3 describes routes to networks and aggregates routes.

  - Type 4 describes routes to ASBRs.

  The link-state ID is the destination network number for type 3 LSAs and the router ID of the described ASBR for type 4 LSAs.

  These LSAs are flooded throughout the backbone area to the other ABRs. Type 3 and type 4 link entries are not flooded into totally stubby areas or NSSAs. Stub areas and NSSAs are discussed later in this chapter.

- **Type 5**—ASBRs generate AS external link advertisements. External link advertisements describe routes to destinations external to the AS and are flooded everywhere except to stub areas and NSSAs. The link-state ID of the type 5 LSA is the external network number.

- **Type 6**—These LSAs are used in multicast OSPF applications.

- **Type 7**—These LSAs are used in an NSSA.

- **Type 8**—These LSAs are used to internetwork OSPF and BGP.

- **Types 9, 10, and 11**—These LSA types are designated for future upgrades to OSPF. The opaque LSAs are types 9, 10, and 11, which are used for application-specific purposes. For example, Cisco uses opaque LSAs for Multiprotocol Label Switching (MPLS) with OSPF. Standard LSDB flooding mechanisms are used to distribute opaque LSAs. Each of the three types has a different flooding scope.

## LSA Type 1: Router LSA

A router advertises a type 1 LSA that floods to all other routers in the area where it originated, as shown in Figure 5-4. A type 1 LSA describes the collective states of the router's directly connected links (interfaces).

**Figure 5-4**   *LSA Type 1: Router LSA*

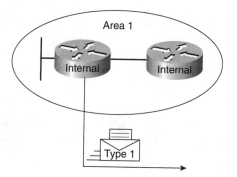

The router ID identifies each type 1 LSA. The LSA describes each link by its network number and mask, known as the link ID.

Type 1 LSA links are described in Table 5-2.

**Table 5-2**    *LSA Type 1 Links*

| Link Type | Description | Link ID |
|-----------|-------------|---------|
| 1 | Point-to-point | Neighbor router ID |
| 2 | Transit network | DR's interface address |
| 3 | Stub network | IP network number |
| 4 | Virtual link | Neighbor router ID |

A stub network is a dead-end link that has only one router attached. A virtual link is a special case in OSPF.

## LSA Type 2: Network LSA

A type 2 LSA is generated for every transit network within an area. A transit network has at least two directly attached OSPF routers, as shown in Figure 5-5. A multiaccess network such as Ethernet is an example of a transit network. A type 2 network LSA lists each of the attached routers that make up the transit network.

**Figure 5-5**    *LSA Type 2: Network LSA*

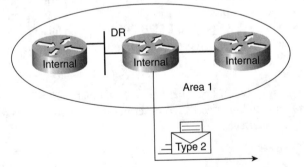

The transit link's DR is responsible for advertising the network LSA. The type 2 LSA then floods to all routers within the transit network area. Type 2 LSAs never cross an area boundary. The LSA ID for a network LSA is the IP interface address of the DR that advertises it.

## LSA Type 3: Summary LSA

The ABR sends type 3 summary LSAs. A type 3 LSA advertises any networks owned by an area to the rest of the areas in the OSPF AS, as shown in Figure 5-6.

**Figure 5-6** *LSA Type 3: Summary LSA*

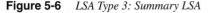
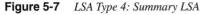

By default, OSPF does not automatically summarize groups of contiguous subnets, or even summarize a network to its classful boundary. The network operator, through configuration commands, must specify how the summarization will occur. Therefore, by default, a type 3 LSA is advertised into the backbone area for every subnet defined in the originating area, which can cause significant flooding problems. Consequently, manual route summarization at the ABR should always be considered. ABRs flood summary LSAs regardless of whether the routes listed in the LSAs are summarized.

## LSA Type 4: Summary LSA

A type 4 summary LSA is used only when an ASBR exists within an area. A type 4 LSA identifies any ASBR and provides a route to it. All traffic destined for an external AS requires routing table knowledge of the ASBR that originated the external routes.

In Figure 5-7, the ASBR sends a type 1 router LSA with a bit (known as the E bit) that is set to identify itself as an ASBR. When the ABR (identified with the B bit in the router LSA) receives this type 1 LSA, it builds a type 4 LSA and floods it to the backbone, area 0.

**Figure 5-7** *LSA Type 4: Summary LSA*

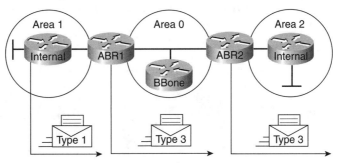
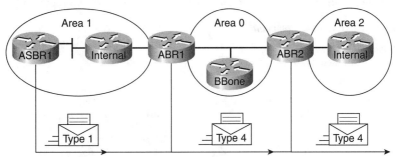

## LSA Type 5: External LSA

Type 5 external LSAs describe routes to networks outside the OSPF AS. Type 5 LSAs are originated by the ASBR and are flooded to the entire AS, as shown in Figure 5-8. Because of the flooding scope and depending on the number of external networks, lack of route summarization can also be a major issue with external LSAs. The network operator should always attempt to summarize blocks of external network numbers at the ASBR to reduce flooding problems.

**Figure 5-8** *LSA Type 5: External LSA*

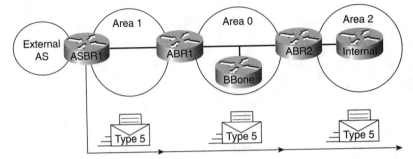

# Interpreting the OSPF LSDB and Routing Table

This section explains the relationship between the LSDB and generating entries for the routing table.

## OSPF LSDB

Example 5-1 and Figure 5-9 show an example of an OSPF LSDB. The router link states are type 1 LSAs, the net link states are type 2 LSAs, and the summary net link states are type 3 LSAs.

Example 5-1 shows the OSPF database for the topology shown in Figure 5-9.

**Example 5-1** **show ip ospf database** *Command*

```
P1R3#show ip ospf database
       OSPF Router with ID (10.64.0.1) (Process ID 1)

               Router Link States (Area 1)
    Link ID         ADV Router      Age        Seq#        Checksum Link count
    10.1.2.1        10.1.2.1        651        0x80000005 0xD482    4

               Net Link States (Area 1)
    Link ID         ADV Router      Age        Seq#        Checksum
    10.64.0.1       10.64.0.1       538        0x80000002 0xAD9A

               Summary Net Link States (Area 1)
    Link ID         ADV Router      Age        Seq#        Checksum
    10.2.1.0        10.2.1.2        439        0x80000002 0xE6F8
```

**Figure 5-9**    *Interpreting the OSPF Database*

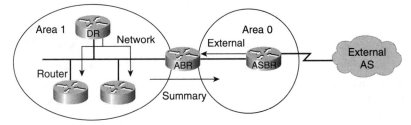

The database columns from Example 5-1 are as follows:

- **Link ID**—Identifies each LSA.
- **ADV Router**—Advertising router—the LSA's source router.
- **Age**—The maximum age counter in seconds. The maximum age is 1 hour, or 3600 seconds.
- **Seq#**—The LSA's sequence number. It begins at 0x80000001 and increases with each update of the LSA.
- **Checksum**—Checksum of the individual LSA to ensure reliable receipt of that LSA.
- **Link count**—The total number of directly attached links used only on router LSAs. The link count includes all point-to-point, transit, and stubby links. Except for point-to-point serial links, which count as two, all other serial link counts as one, and each Ethernet link also counts as one.

## OSPF Routing Table and Types of Routes

Table 5-3 defines each of the OSPF routing designators. Router and network LSAs describe the details within an area. The routing table reflects this link-state information with a designation of O, meaning that the route is an intra-area.

**Table 5-3**    *Types of OSPF Routes*

| Route Designator | | Description |
|---|---|---|
| O | OSPF intra-area (router LSA) | Networks from within the router's area. Advertised by way of router LSAs. |
| O IA | OSPF interarea (summary LSA) | Networks from outside the router's area but within the OSPF autonomous system. Advertised by way of summary LSAs. |
| O E1 | Type 1 external routes | Networks outside the router's autonomous system. |
| O E2 | Type 2 external routes | Advertised by way of external LSAs. |

When an ABR or ASBR receives summary or external LSAs, it adds them to its LSDB and floods them to their local area. The internal routers then assimilate the information into their databases. Summary LSAs appear in the routing table as I/A (interarea) routes. External LSAs appear in the routing table marked as external type 1 (E1) or external type 2 (E2) routes.

The SPF algorithm is then run against the LSDB to build the SPF tree, which is used to determine the best paths. Here is the order in which the best paths are calculated:

1 All routers calculate the best paths to destinations within their area (intra-area) and add these entries to the routing table. These are the type 1 and type 2 LSAs, which are noted in the routing table with a routing designator of O (OSPF).

2 All routers calculate the best paths to the other areas in the internetwork. These best paths are the interarea route entries, or type 3 and type 4 LSAs. They are noted with a routing designator of O IA (interarea).

3 All routers except those that are in the form of a stub area calculate the best paths to the external AS (type 5) destinations. They are noted with either an O E1 or O E2 route designator, depending on the configuration.

At this point, a router can communicate with any network within or outside the OSPF AS.

## Calculating the Costs of E1 and E2 Routes

The cost of an external route varies, depending on the external type configured on the ASBR, as shown in Figure 5-10.

**Figure 5-10** *Calculating the Costs of E1 and E2 Routes*

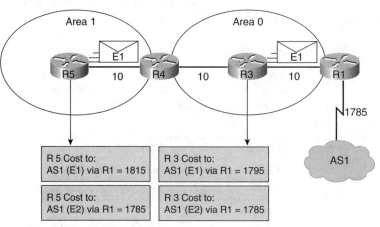

The following external packet types can be configured:

- **E1**—Type O E1 external routes calculate the cost by adding the external cost to the internal cost of each link the packet crosses. Use this type when multiple ASBRs are advertising an external route to the same AS to avoid suboptimal routing.

- **E2 (default)**—The external cost of O E2 packet routes is always the external cost only. Use this type if only one ASBR is advertising an external route to the AS.

The **show ip route** command shown in Example 5-2 depicts both external type routes (O E2) and interarea (O IA) routes. The last entry (O*E2) is a default route from the ABR.

**Example 5-2**  **show ip route** *Command with External OSPF Routes*

```
RTA#show ip route
Codes:   C - connected, S - static, I - IGRP, R - RIP, M - mobile,
    B - BGP, D - EIGRP, EX - EIGRP external, O - OSPF,
    IA - OSPF inter area, E1 - OSPF external type 1,
    E2 - OSPF external type 2, E - EGP, i - IS-IS, L1 - IS-IS
    level-1, L2 - IS-IS level-2, * - candidate default

Gateway of last resort is 203.250.15.67 to network 0.0.0.0
     203.250.16.0 255.255.255.192 is subnetted, 1 subnets
O E2    203.250.16.128 [110/10] via 203.250.15.67, 00:00:50, Ethernet0
     203.250.13.0 255.255.255.255 is subnetted, 1 subnets
C    203.250.13.41 is directly connected, Loopback0
     203.250.15.0 255.255.255.192 is subnetted, 3 subnets
O IA    203.250.15.0 [110/74] via 203.250.15.67, 00:00:50, Ethernet0
C    203.250.15.64 is directly connected, Ethernet0
C    203.250.15.192 is directly connected, Ethernet1
O*E2    0.0.0.0 0.0.0.0 [110/10] via 203.250.15.67, 00:00:50, Ethernet0
```

The two numbers in brackets [110/10] are the administrative distance and the total cost of the route to a specific destination network. In this case, the administrative distance is set to a default of 110 for all OSPF routes, and the total cost of the route has been calculated as 10.

# Changing the Cost Metric

By default, OSPF calculates the OSPF metric for an interface according to the interface's inverse bandwidth. In general, the cost in Cisco routers is calculated using the formula 100 Mbps/bandwidth. For example, a 64-kbps link gets a metric of 1562, and a T1 link gets a metric of 64. However, the cost is calculated based on a maximum bandwidth of 100 Mbps, which is a cost of 1. If you have faster interfaces, you might want to recalibrate the cost of 1 to a higher bandwidth.

When you are using the interface's bandwidth to determine OSPF cost, always remember to use the **bandwidth** interface command to accurately define the bandwidth per interface:

```
RouterA(config-if)#bandwidth value
```

If interfaces that are faster than 100 Mbps are being used, you should consider the **auto-cost reference-bandwidth** command under the OSPF process. Use this command on all routers in the network to ensure accurate route calculations.

```
RouterA(config-router)#auto-cost reference-bandwidth ref-bw
```

The parameter for **auto-cost reference-bandwidth** is described in Table 5-4.

**Table 5-4**     **auto-cost reference-bandwidth** *Command Parameter*

| Parameter | Description |
|---|---|
| *ref-bw* | The rate in Mbps (bandwidth). The range is from 1 to 4,294,967; the default is 100. |

To override the default cost, manually define the cost using the **ip ospf cost** command on a per-interface basis:

```
RouterA(config-if)#ip ospf cost value
```

*value* is an integer from 1 to 65,535. The lower the number, the better (and more preferred) the link.

---

**Key Point: Manipulating the OSPF Metric**

The cost metric default is the inverse of the bandwidth defined on an interface. The **ospf cost**, **bandwidth**, and **auto-cost reference-bandwidth** commands can manipulate the cost metric.

---

# OSPF Route Summarization Techniques

Route summarization involves consolidating multiple routes into a single advertisement.

By this point, however, a network operator should realize the importance of proper route summarization in a network. Route summarization directly affects the amount of bandwidth, CPU, and memory resources consumed by the OSPF routing process.

Without route summarization, every specific-link LSA is propagated into the OSPF backbone and beyond, causing unnecessary network traffic and router overhead. Whenever an LSA is sent, all affected OSPF routers have to recompute their LSDB and the SPF tree using the SPF algorithm.

With route summarization, only summarized routes propagate into the backbone (area 0), as shown in Figure 5-11. This summarization is important because it prevents every router from having to rerun the SPF algorithm, increases the network's stability, and reduces unnecessary LSA flooding. Also, if a network link fails, the topology change is not propagated into the backbone (and other areas by way of the backbone). LSA flooding outside the area does not occur.

**Figure 5-11** *Benefits of Route Summarization*

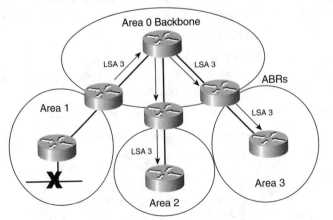

| NOTE | Summary LSAs (type 3 LSAs) do not always contain summarized routes. By default, summary LSAs are not summarized. |
|---|---|

The two types of summarization are as follows:

- **Interarea route summarization**—Interarea route summarization occurs on ABRs and applies to routes from within each area. It does not apply to external routes injected into OSPF via redistribution. To perform effective interarea route summarization, network numbers within areas should be assigned contiguously so that these addresses can be summarized into a minimal number of summary addresses. Figure 5-11 illustrates interarea summarization at the ABR.

- **External route summarization**—External route summarization is specific to external routes that are injected into OSPF via route redistribution. Again, it is important to ensure the contiguity of the external address ranges that are being summarized. Summarizing overlapping ranges from two different routers can cause packets to be sent to the wrong destination. Only ASBRs generally summarize external routes.

OSPF carries subnet mask information and, therefore, supports multiple subnet masks for the same major network. OSPF also supports discontiguous subnets, a classless routing protocol that as such gives subnet masks part of the LSDB. However, other protocols, such as Routing Information Protocol version 1 (RIPv1) and Interior Gateway Routing Protocol (IGRP), do not support VLSMs or discontiguous subnets. If the same major network crosses the boundaries of an OSPF and RIPv1 or IGRP domain, VLSM information redistributed into RIPv1 or IGRP is lost, and static routes have to be configured in the RIPv1 or IGRP domains.

### Contiguous Address Assignment

Network numbers in areas should be assigned contiguously to ensure that these addresses can be summarized into a minimal number of summary addresses.

For example, in Figure 5-12, the list of 12 networks in Router B's routing table can be summarized into two summary address advertisements. The block of addresses from 172.16.8.0 to 172.16.15.0/24 can be summarized using 172.16.8.0/21, and the block from 172.16.16.0 to 172.16.19.0/24 can be summarized using 172.16.16.0/22.

**Figure 5-12**  *Using Route Summarization*

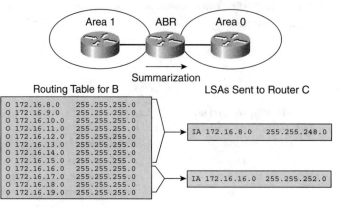

## OSPF Route Summarization Commands

OSPF is a classless routing protocol; therefore, it does not perform autosummarization. Manual summarization for OSPF is off by default. To manually configure IA route summarization on the ABR, use the following procedure:

**Step 1**   Configure OSPF.

**Step 2**   Use the **area range** command, described in Table 5-5, to instruct the ABR to summarize routes for a specific area before injecting them into a different area via the backbone as type 3 summary LSAs.

```
Router(config-router)#area area-id range address mask
```

**Table 5-5**      **area range** *Command Parameters*

| Parameter | Description |
|-----------|-------------|
| *area-id* | Identifies the area subject to route summarization. |
| *address* | The summary address designated for a range of addresses. |
| *mask* | The IP subnet mask used for the summary route. |

To configure manual route summarization on an ASBR to summarize external routes, use the following procedure:

**Step 1**   Configure OSPF.

**Step 2**   Use the **summary-address** command, described in Table 5-6, to instruct the ASBR or the ABR to summarize external routes before injecting them into the OSPF domain as type 5 external LSA.

```
Router(config-router)#summary-address {{address mask} | {prefix mask}}
   [not-advertise] [tag tag]
```

**Table 5-6**    **summary-address** *Command Parameters*

| Parameter | Description |
|---|---|
| *address* | The summary address designated for a range of addresses. |
| *mask* | The IP subnet mask used for the summary route. |
| *prefix* | The IP route prefix for the destination. |
| *mask* | The IP subnet mask used for the summary route. |
| **not-advertise** | (Optional) Used to suppress routes that match the prefix/mask pair. |
| **tag** *tag* | (Optional) A tag value that can be used as a "match" value to control redistribution via route maps. |

## Route Summarization Configuration Example at the ABR

Figure 5-13 shows that route summarization can occur in both directions—from a nonbackbone area to area 0 and from area 0 to a nonbackbone area. In Example 5-3, the R1 configuration specifies the following summarization:

- **Area 0 range 172.16.96.0 255.255.224.0**—Identifies area 0 as the area containing the range of networks to be summarized into area 1. ABR R1 summarizes the range of subnets from 172.16.96.0 to 172.16.127.0 into one range: 172.16.96.0 255.255.224.0.

- **Area 1 range 172.16.32.0 255.255.224.0**—Identifies area 1 as the area containing the range of networks to be summarized into area 0. ABR R1 summarizes the range of subnets from 172.16.32.0 to 172.16.63.0 into one range: 172.16.32.0 255.255.224.0.

**Figure 5-13** *Route Summarization Example at the ABR*

**Example 5-3**  *Enabling OSPF Routing*

```
Router1(config)#router ospf 100
Router1(config-router)#network 172.16.32.1 0.0.0.0 area 1
Router1(config-router)#network 172.16.96.1 0.0.0.0 area 0
Router1(config-router)#area 0 range 172.16.96.0 255.255.224.0
Router1(config-router)#area 1 range 172.16.32.0 255.255.224.0

Router2(config)#router ospf 100
Router2(config-router)#network 172.16.64.1 0.0.0.0 area 2
Router2(config-router)#network 172.16.127.1 0.0.0.0 area 0
Router2(config-router)#area 0 range 172.16.96.0 255.255.224.0
Router2(config-router)#area 1 range 172.16.64.0 255.255.224.0
```

The configuration for R2 works similarly.

## Route Summarization Configuration Example at the ASBR

Figure 5-14 depicts route summarization at the ASBR. On the left, an external AS running RIPv2 has its routes redistributed into OSPF. Because of the contiguous subnet block in the external RIP network, it is possible to summarize the 32 different subnets into one summarized route.

**Figure 5-14**  *Route Summarization Example at the ASBR*

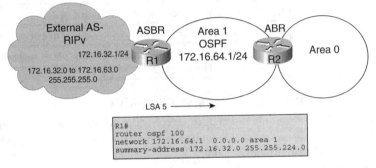

```
R1#
router ospf 100
network 172.16.64.1  0.0.0.0 area 1
summary-address 172.16.32.0 255.255.224.0
```

Instead of 32 external type 5 LSAs flooding into the OSPF network, there is only one.

## Creating a Default Route in OSPF

Figure 5-15 shows how OSPF injects a default route into a normal area. Any OSPF router can originate default routes injected into a normal area. The OSPF router does not, by default, generate a default route into the OSPF domain. For OSPF to generate a default route, you must use the **default-information originate** command.

**Figure 5-15**  *Default Routes in OSPF*

There are two ways to advertise a default route into a normal area. The first is to advertise 0.0.0.0 into the OSPF domain, provided that the advertising router already has a default route. The second is to advertise 0.0.0.0 regardless of whether the advertising router already has a default route. The second method can be accomplished by adding the keyword **always** to the **default-information originate** command.

A default route shows up in the OSPF database as an external LSA type 5, as shown in Example 5-4.

**Example 5-4**  *Default Route in the OSPF Database*

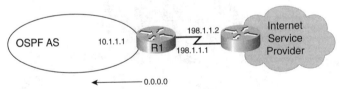

| Type-5 AS External Link States | | | | | |
|---|---|---|---|---|---|
| Link ID | ADV Router | Age | Seq# | Checksum | Tag |
| 0.0.0.0 | 198.1.1.1 | 601 | 0x80000001 | 0xD0D8 | 0 |

---

### How Does OSPF Generate Default Routes?

How OSPF generates default routes (0.0.0.0) varies depending on the type of area the default route is being injected into—a normal area, stub area, totally stubby area, or NSSA.

By default, in normal areas, routers don't generate default routes. To have an OSPF router generate a default route, use the **default-information originate** [**always**] [**metric** *metric-value*] [**metric-type** *type-value*] [**route-map** *map-name*] command. This generates an E2 link with link-state ID 0.0.0.0 and network mask 0.0.0.0, which makes the router an ASBR.

There are two ways to inject a default route into a normal area. If the ASBR already has the default route, you can advertise 0.0.0.0 into the area. If the ASBR doesn't have the route, you can add the keyword **always** to the **default-information originate** command, which then advertises 0.0.0.0.

For stub and totally stubby areas, the ABR to the stub area generates a summary LSA with the link-state ID 0.0.0.0. This is true even if the ABR doesn't have a default route. In this scenario, you don't need to use the **default-information originate** command.

The ABR for the NSSA generates the default route, but not by default. To force the ABR to generate the default route, use the **area** *area-id* **nssa default-information-originate** command. The ABR generates a type 7 LSA with the link-state ID 0.0.0.0. If you want to import routes only into the normal areas, not into the NSSA area, you can use the **no-redistribution** option on the NSSA ABR.

---

## The **default-information originate** Command

To generate a default external route into an OSPF routing domain, use the **default-information originate** router configuration command:

```
Router(config-router)#[no] default-information originate [always]
    [metric metric-value] [metric-type type-value] [route-map map-name]
```

To disable this feature, use the **no** form of the command. Table 5-7 explains the options of the **default-information originate** command.

**Table 5-7**    **default-information originate** *Command Parameters*

| Parameter | Description |
|---|---|
| **always** | (Optional) Always advertises the default route regardless of whether the router has a default route in the routing table. |
| **metric** *metric-value* | (Optional) A metric used for generating the default route. If you omit a value and do not specify a value using the **default-metric** router configuration command, the default metric value is 10. |
| **metric-type** *type-value* | (Optional) An external link type associated with the default route advertised into the OSPF routing domain. It can be one of the following values:<br><br>**1**—Type 1 external route<br><br>**2**—Type 2 external route<br><br>The default is type 2 external route (O*E2). |
| **route-map** *map-name* | (Optional) The routing process generates the default route if the route map is satisfied. |

---

### default-information originate Command Actual Behavior

The Cisco.com documentation for the **default-information originate** command mentions that if you omit a value for the *metric* variable and do not specify a value using the **default-metric** router configuration command, the default metric value for the **default-information originate** command is 10.

The following tests to verify the default value of *metric* when using **default-information originate** were performed again on Ethernet, serial high-level data link control (HDLC), and serial Frame Relay links. In all cases, the metric was 1, although Cisco's documentation indicates that it should be 10.

The following is one of the tests:

```
Router 1
interface Serial1
 no ip address
 encapsulation frame-relay
 !
interface Serial1.1 multipoint
 ip address 1.0.0.1 255.0.0.0
 ip ospf network broadcast
 frame-relay interface-dlci 120
!
router ospf 10
 log-adjacency-changes
 network 1.0.0.0 0.0.0.255 area 0
 default-information originate always

Router 2
interface Serial0
 ip address 1.0.0.2 255.0.0.0
 encapsulation frame-relay
 ip ospf network broadcast
 no fair-queue
 clockrate 2000000
 frame-relay interface-dlci 120
 frame-relay intf-type dce
 !
router ospf 10
network 1.0.0.0 0.0.0.255 area 0
```

The following is the routing table on Router 2, where the command **default-information originate** was issued without specifying a value for the *metric* variable. The metric appearing in the routing table for the default route is 1, not 10 as mentioned in the documentation.

```
P5R2>sh ip route
Codes: C - connected, S - static, I - IGRP, R - RIP, M - mobile, B - BGP
       D - EIGRP, EX - EIGRP external, O - OSPF, IA - OSPF inter area
       N1 - OSPF NSSA external type 1, N2 - OSPF NSSA external type 2
       E1 - OSPF external type 1, E2 - OSPF external type 2, E - EGP
       i - IS-IS, L1 - IS-IS level-1, L2 - IS-IS level-2, ia - IS-IS
    inter area
       * - candidate default, U - per-user static route, o - ODR
       P - periodic downloaded static route
```

```
Gateway of last resort is 1.0.0.1 to network 0.0.0.0

C    1.0.0.0/8 is directly connected, Serial0
O*E2 0.0.0.0/0 [110/1] via 1.0.0.1, 00:18:49, Serial0
```

Figure 5-16 shows an OSPF network multihomed to dual Internet service providers (ISPs). The optional **metric** command has been used to prefer the default route to ISP A. The default route being generated has a *metric-type* of E2 by default, so the metric does not increase as it goes through the area. As a result, all routers, regardless of their proximity to the border router, prefer ISP A over ISP B.

**Figure 5-16**  *Default Route Example*

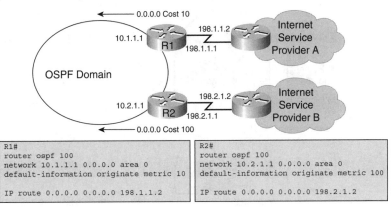

# OSPF Special Area Types

The characteristics assigned to an area control the type of route information it receives. The possible area types, shown in Figure 5-17, are as follows:

- **Standard area**—This default area accepts link updates, route summaries, and external routes.

- **Backbone area (transit area)**—The backbone area is the central entity to which all other areas connect. The backbone area is labeled area 0. All other areas connect to this area to exchange and route information. The OSPF backbone has all the properties of a standard OSPF area.

- **Stub area**—This area does not accept information about routes external to the AS, such as routes from non-OSPF sources. If routers need to route to networks outside the AS, they use a default route, noted as 0.0.0.0. Stub areas cannot contain ASBRs.

- **Totally stubby area**—This area does not accept external AS routes or summary routes from other areas internal to the AS. If the router needs to send a packet to a network external to the area, it sends the packet using a default route. Totally stubby areas cannot contain ASBRs.

- **NSSA**—NSSA is an addendum to the OSPF RFC. This area defines a special LSA type 7. NSSA offers benefits that are similar to those of a stub or totally stubby area. However, NSSAs allow ASBRs, which is against the rules in a stub area.

**Figure 5-17**  *Types of Areas*

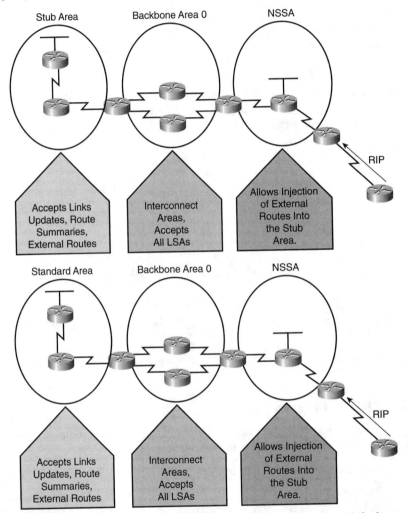

The general purpose behind all three types of stub areas is to inject default routes into an area so that external or summary LSAs are not flooded in. Stub and totally stubby areas do not carry any external routes, known as type 5 LSAs. An area qualifies as stub or totally stubby if it has the following characteristics:

- It has either a single exit point from that area or multiple exits, such as ABRs routing to the outside of the area that do not have to take an optimal path. If the area has multiple exits, one or more ABRs inject a default into the stub area. In this situation, routing to other areas or autonomous systems can take a suboptimal path to reach the destination by exiting the area via a point that is farther from the destination than other exit points.

- All OSPF routers inside the stub area, including ABRs and internal routers, must be configured as stub routers before they can become neighbors and exchange routing information.

- The area is not needed as a transit area for virtual links.
- No ASBR is inside the stub area.
- The area is not the backbone area (area 0).

## Stub Areas

Configuring a stub area reduces the size of the LSDB inside an area, resulting in reduced memory requirements for routers in that area. External network LSAs (type 5), such as those redistributed from other routing protocols into OSPF, are not permitted to flood into a stub area, as shown in Figure 5-18. Routing from these areas to a route external to the OSPF AS is based on a default route (0.0.0.0). In the case of a default route, if a packet is addressed to a network that is not in the route table of an internal router, the router automatically forwards the packet to the ABR that originates a 0.0.0.0 LSA. Forwarding the packet to the ABR allows routers within the stub area to reduce the size of their routing tables, because a single default route replaces many external routes.

**Figure 5-18**  *Using Stub Areas*

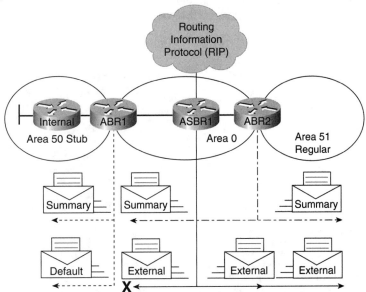

A stub area is typically created using a hub-and-spoke topology, with the spoke being the stub area, such as a branch office. In this case, the branch office does not need to know about every network at the headquarters site, because it can use a default route to reach the networks.

```
RouterA(config-router)#area area-id stub
```

To configure an area as stub, use the following procedure:

**Step 1**   Configure OSPF.

**Step 2**   Define an area as stub or totally stubby by adding the **area** *area-id* **stub** command to all routers within the area.

Example 5-5 shows a stub area configuration example.

**Example 5-5**    *Stub Area Configuration Example*

```
router ospf 10
    network 130.130.32.0 0.0.31.255 area 1
    network 130.130.0.0 0.0.31.255 area 0
    area 1 stub
```

Table 5-8 describes the parameter of the **area stub** command.

**Table 5-8**    **area stub** *Command Parameter*

| Parameter | Description |
|---|---|
| *area-id* | The identifier for the stub or totally stubby area. The identifier can be either a decimal value or in dotted-decimal format, like an IP address. |

Area 2 in Figure 5-19 is defined as the stub area. No routes from the external AS are forwarded into the stub area.

**Figure 5-19**    *OSPF Stub Area*

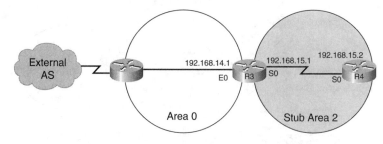

Example 5-6 shows the configuration commands to enable an OSPF stub area.

**Example 5-6**    *OSPF Stub Area Configuration*

```
R3(config)#interface Ethernet 0
R3(config-if)#ip address 192.168.14.1 255.255.255.0
R3(config)#interface Serial 0
R3(config-if)#ip address 192.168.15.1 255.255.255.252

R3(config)#router ospf 100
R3(config-router)#network 192.168.14.0.0 0.0.0.255 area 0
R3(config-router)#network 192.168.15.0.0 0.0.0.255 area 2
R3(config-router)#area 2 stub

R4(config)#interface Serial 0
R4(config-if)#ip address 192.168.15.2 255.255.255.252

R4(config)#router ospf 100
R4(config-router)#network 192.168.15.0.0 0.0.0.255 area 2
R4(config-router)#area 2 stub
```

The last line in each configuration (**area 2 stub**) defines the stub area. The R3 router (ABR) automatically advertises 0.0.0.0 (the default route) with a default cost metric of 1 into the stub area.

Each router in the stub area must be configured with the **area stub** command.

The routes that appear in the routing table of R4 are as follows:

- Intra-area routes, which are designated with an O in the routing table
- The default route and interarea routes, which are both designated with an IA in the routing table
- The default route, which is also denoted with an asterisk (O*IA)

**NOTE**    The **area** *area-id* **stub** command determines whether the routers in the stub become neighbors. This command is enabled on all routers in the stub to permit the exchange of routing information. The hello packet contains a stub area flag that must match on neighboring routers.

## Totally Stubby Areas

A totally stubby area is a Cisco-specific feature that further reduces the number of routes in the routing table. A totally stubby area blocks external type 5 LSAs and summary type 3 and type 4 LSAs (interarea routes) from entering the area, as shown in Figure 5-20. By blocking these routes, the totally stubby area recognizes only intra-area routes and the default route of 0.0.0.0. ABRs inject the default summary link 0.0.0.0 into the totally stubby area. Each router picks the closest ABR as a gateway to everything outside the area.

**Figure 5-20**  *Using Totally Stubby Areas*

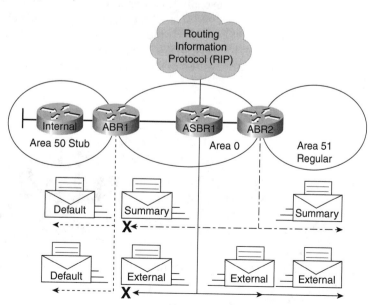

Totally stubby areas minimize routing information further than stub areas and increase stability and scalability of OSPF internetworks. Using totally stubby areas is typically a better solution than using stub areas as long as the ABR is a Cisco router.

To configure an area as totally stubby, do the following:

**Step 1**   Configure OSPF.

**Step 2**   Define an area as stub or totally stubby by adding the **area** *area-id* **stub** command to all routers in the area.

**Step 3**   At the ABR only, add **no-summary** to the **area** *area-id* **stub** command:

```
RouterA(config-router)#area area-id stub no-summary
```

Table 5-9 explains the **area** *area-id* **stub** command.

**Table 5-9**   **area** *area-id* **stub** *Command Parameters*

| Parameter | Description |
|-----------|-------------|
| *area-id* | The identifier for the stub or totally stubby area. It can be either a decimal value or in dotted-decimal format like an IP address. |
| **no-summary** | In addition to stopping external LSA flooding, the **no-summary** command keeps summary LSAs from flooding into the totally stubby area. |

The ABR advertises a default route with a cost of 1. An option is to change the cost of the default route by using the **area** *area-id* **default-cost** command:

```
RouterA(config-router)#area area-id default-cost cost
```

Figure 5-21 shows a topology for a totally stubby area. The configuration is shown in Example 5-7. All routes advertised into area 1 (from area 0 and the external AS) default to 0.0.0.0. The default route cost is set to 5 on router 2 and to 10 on router 4. Both default routes are advertised into area 1. However, the default route from router 2 is advertised with a lower cost to make it more preferable if the internal cost from R3 to R4 and R2 is the same.

**Figure 5-21**   *Totally Stubby Example*

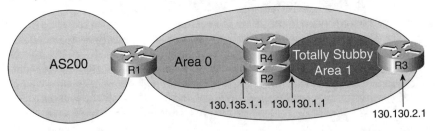

Example 5-7 shows a totally stubby configuration.

**Example 5-7**   *Totally Stubby Configuration*

```
Router2(config)#router ospf 10
Router2(config-router)#network 130.135.0.0 0.0.255.255 area 0
Router2(config-router)#network 130.130.0.0 0.0.255.255 area 1
Router2(config-router)#area 1 stub no-summary
Router2(config-router)#area 1 default-cost 5
Router2(config-router)# ! Router2 is the preferred ABR

Router3(config)#router ospf 10
Router3(config-router)#network 130.130.0.0 0.0.255.255 area 1
Router3(config-router)#area 1 stub

Router4(config)#router ospf 10
Router4(config-router)#network 130.135.0.0 0.0.255.255 area 0
Router4(config-router)#network 130.130.0.0 0.0.255.255 area 1
Router4(config-router)#area 1 stub no-summary
Router4(config-router)#area 1 default-cost 5
```

Notice that router 3 requires the **area 1 stub** command, yet the **no-summary** extension is not required. Only ABRs use **no-summary** to keep summary LSAs from being propagated into another area.

---

**CAUTION**      Remember that all routers in a stub or totally stubby area must be configured as stubs. An OSPF adjacency does not form between stub and nonstub routers.

---

Example 5-8 shows how the routing table of an OSPF router without stub or totally stubby configuration might look. Intra-area, interarea, and external routes are all maintained in a normal area without stub configuration.

**Example 5-8**   *Routing Tables with Different Areas*

```
p1r3#show ip route
<output omitted>
Gateway of last resort is not set

      10.0.0.0/8 is subnetted, 15 subnets
O IA    10.3.1.0 [110/148] via 10.64.0.2, 00:03:12, Ethernet0
C       10.1.3.0 is directly connected, Serial0
O IA    10.2.1.0 [110/74] via 10.64.0.2, 00:31:46, Ethernet0
C       10.1.2.0 is directly connected, Serial1
O IA    10.3.3.0 [110/148] via 10.64.0.2, 00:03:12, Ethernet0
O IA    10.2.2.0 [110/138] via 10.64.1.2, 00:31:46, Ethernet0
O       10.1.1.0 [110/128] via 10.1.3.1, 00:31:46, Serial0
                 [110/128] via 10.1.2.1, 00:31:46, Serial1
O IA    10.3.2.0 [110/212] via 10.64.0.2, 00:03:12, Ethernet0
O IA    10.2.3.0 [110/74] via 10.64.0.2, 00:31:46, Ethernet0
O IA    10.4.2.0 [110/286] via 10.64.0.2, 00:02:50, Ethernet0
```

*continues*

**Example 5-8** *Routing Tables with Different Areas (Continued)*

```
O IA    10.4.3.0 [110/222] via 10.64.0.2, 00:02:50, Ethernet0
O IA    10.4.1.0 [110/222] via 10.64.0.2, 00:02:50, Ethernet0
O E2    10.66.0.0 [110/60] via 10.64.0.2, 00:02:51, Ethernet0
C       10.64.0.0 is directly connected, Ethernet0
O E2    10.65.0.0 [110/60] via 10.64.0.2, 00:03:19, Ethernet0
p1r3#
```

Examples 5-9 and 5-10 compare routing tables that result from the use of route summarization, stub areas, and totally stubby areas. Note the interarea 0.0.0.0 default routes that appear in the stub and totally stubby area routers. Also, notice that the totally stubby routers have the smallest routing table. All interarea summary routes, as well as all external routes, have been removed.

**Example 5-9** *Routing Tables for Stub Areas*

```
p1r3#show ip route
<output omitted>
Gateway of last resort is 10.64.0.2 to network 0.0.0.0

     10.0.0.0/8 is variably subnetted, 9 subnets, 2 masks
O IA    10.2.0.0/16 [110/74] via 10.64.0.2, 00:11:11, Ethernet0
C       10.1.3.0/13 is directly connected, Serial0
O IA    10.3.0.0/16 [110/148] via 10.64.0.2, 00:07:59, Ethernet0
C       10.1.2.0/24 is directly connected, Serial1
O       10.1.1.0/24 [110/128] via 10.1.3.1, 00:16:51, Serial0
                    [110/128] via 10.1.2.1, 00:16:51, Serial1
O IA    10.4.0.0/16 [110/2222] via 10.64.0.2, 00:09:13, Ethernet0
C       10.64.0.0/24 is directly connected, Ethernet0
O*IA 0.0.0.0/0 [110/11] via 10.64.0.2, 00:16:51, Ethernet0
```

**Example 5-10** *Routing Tables for a Totally Stubby Area*

```
p1r3#show ip route
<output omitted>
Gateway of last resort is 10.64.0.2 to network 0.0.0.0

     10.0.0.0/8 is variably subnetted, 9 subnets, 2 masks
C       10.1.3.0 is directly connected, Serial0
C       10.1.2.0 is directly connected, Serial1
O       10.1.1.0/24 [110/128] via 10.1.3.1, 00:16:51, Serial0
                    [110/128] via 10.1.2.1, 00:16:51, Serial1
C       10.64.0.0/24 is directly connected, Ethernet0
O*IA 0.0.0.0/0 [110/11] via 10.64.0.2, 00:16:51, Ethernet0
```

# NSSAs

The OSPF NSSA feature is described by RFC 1587 and was introduced in Cisco IOS software Release 11.2. It is a nonproprietary extension of the existing stub area feature that allows the injection of external routes in a limited fashion into the stub area.

Redistribution into an NSSA area creates a special type of LSA known as type 7 (see Figure 5-22), which can exist only in an NSSA area. An NSSA ASBR generates this LSA, and an NSSA ABR translates it into a type 5 LSA, which gets propagated into the OSPF domain.

**Figure 5-22**  *NSSA*

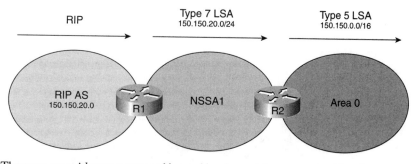

The **area** *area-id* **nssa** command is used in place of the **area** *area-id* **stub** command. Remember that all routers in the NSSA must have this command configured. Routers do not form an adjacency unless both are configured as NSSA.

In Figure 5-23 and Example 5-11, R1 is the ASBR that redistributes RIP routes into area 1, the NSSA. R2 is the NSSA ABR. This router converts LSA type 7 into type 5 for advertisement into backbone area 0. R2 is also configured to summarize the type 5 LSAs that originate from the RIP network. The 150.150.0.0 subnets are summarized to 150.150.0.0/16 and are advertised into area 0. To cause R2 (the NSSA ABR) to generate an O*N2 default route (O*N2 0.0.0.0/0) into the NSSA area, use the **default-information-originate** option with the **area** *area-id* **nssa** command at R2.

**Figure 5-23**  *NSSA*

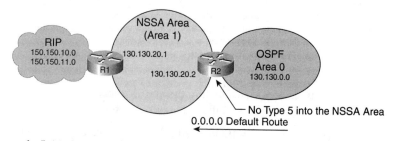

Example 5-11 shows an OSPF NSSA configuration.

**Example 5-11**  *OSPF NSSA Configuration*

```
R1(config)#router ospf 10
R1(config-router)#redistribute rip subnets
R1(config-router)#default metric 150
R1(config-router)#network 130.130.0.0 0.0.255.255 area 1
R1(config-router)#area 1 nssa

R2(config)#router ospf 10
R2(config-router)#summary-address 150.150.0.0 255.255.0.0
R2(config-router)#network 130.130.20.0 0.0.0.255 area 1
R2(config-router)#network 130.130.0.0 0.0.255.255 area 0
R2(config-router)#area 1 nssa default-information-originate
```

Notice in Figure 5-24 that the ABR is using the **area 1 nssa no-summary** command. This command works exactly the same as the totally stubby technique. A single default route replaces both inbound-external (type 5) LSAs and summary (type 3 and 4) LSAs into the area. The NSSA ABR, which is R2, automatically generates the O*N2 default route into the NSSA area with the **no-summary** option configured at the ABR, as shown in Example 5-12.

**Figure 5-24** *NSSA Totally Stubby*

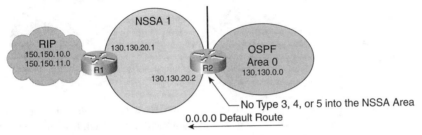

Example 5-12 shows a totally stubby configuration.

**Example 5-12** *NSSA Totally Stubby Configuration*

```
R1(config)#router ospf 10
R1(config-router)#redistribute rip subnets
R1(config-router)#default metric 150
R1(config-router)#network 130.130.0.0 0.0.255.255 area 1
R1(config-router)#area 1 nssa

R2(config)#router ospf 10
R2(config-router)#summary-address 150.150.0.0 255.255.0.0
R2(config-router)#network 130.130.20.0 0.0.0.255 area 1
R2(config-router)#network 130.130.0.0 0.0.255.255 area 0
R2(config-router)#area 1 nssa no-summary
```

All other routers in the NSSA area require the **area 1 nssa** command only. The NSSA totally stubby configuration is a Cisco-specific feature like the totally stubby area feature.

The **show** commands in Table 5-10 are used to display which area type has been configured. NSSA is different from the other area types because the router LSDB includes type 7 LSAs. The type 7 LSA is described in the routing table as an O N2 or O N1 (N stands for NSSA). N1 means that the metric is calculated like E1; N2 means that the metric is calculated like E2. The default is O N2.

**Table 5-10** **show** *Commands for the Stub and NSSA in OSPF*

| Command | Description |
|---|---|
| **show ip ospf** | Displays which areas are normal, stubby, or NSSA. |
| **show ip ospf database** | Displays LSA type 7 updates. |
| **show ip ospf database nssa-external** | Displays specific details of each LSA type 7 update in the database. |
| **show ip route** | Displays NSSA routes with code O N2 or O N1. |

# OSPF Virtual Links

OSPF's two-tiered area hierarchy requires that all areas be directly connected to the backbone area, area 0. In Figure 5-25, area 4 is incorrectly connected to area 1. This incorrect connection leads to LSDB inconsistencies and reachability issues between area 4 networks and area 0.

**Figure 5-25**  *Illegal Area Connections*

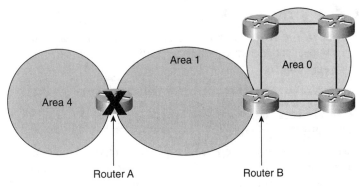

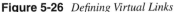
Router A                              Router B

The following are two major reasons for using virtual links:

- **Backup**—Area 4 is normally directly attached to area 0; however, the physical link between area 4 and area 0 is broken. Configure a backup link using area 1 as a transit area to reconnect area 4 temporarily to area 0. The transit area cannot be a stub area. Backup might also be required when area 0 separates into disconnected pieces because of a failed link.

- **Temporary connection**—Because of moves, additions, or changes, area 4 might be a new company acquisition that requires temporary connectivity. A virtual link can be used temporarily until a more correct configuration, connecting area 4 directly to area 0, can be implemented.

Virtual links are part of the OSPF open standard and have been a part of Cisco IOS software since Release 10.0. In Figure 5-26, a logical link (virtual link) is built between the two ABRs, Routers A and B. This virtual link is similar to a standard OSPF adjacency; however, in a virtual link, the routers do not have to be directly attached to neighboring routers.

**Figure 5-26**  *Defining Virtual Links*

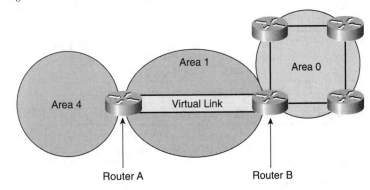

Router A                              Router B

The Hello protocol works over virtual and standard links in the same way: in 10-second intervals. The LSA updates work uniquely on virtual links. An LSA usually refreshes every 30 minutes; however, LSAs learned through the virtual link have the DoNotAge (DNA) option set. If the DNA option is set in the LSA, the LSA does not age out. The DNA technique is required to prevent excessive flooding over the virtual link.

## Configuring OSPF Virtual Links

Use the **area** *area-id* **virtual-link** *router-id* router configuration command, along with any necessary optional parameters, to define an OSPF virtual link. To remove a virtual link, use the **no** form of this command.

```
area area-id virtual-link router-id [authentication [message-digest | null]]
   [hello-interval seconds] [retransmit-interval seconds]
   [transmit-delay seconds] [dead-interval seconds]
   [[authentication-key key] | [message-digest-key key-id md5 key]]
```

The **area** *area-id* **virtual-link** command requires a configured router ID from the far-end router. To find the router ID in the far-end router, use the **show ip ospf** command. Another alternative is to use the **show ip protocol** command. Both these commands display the router ID.

Table 5-11 describes the options available with the **area** *area-id* **virtual-link** command. Make sure you understand the effect of these options before changing them. For instance, the smaller the hello interval, the faster the detection of topological changes; however, more routing traffic ensues. You should be conservative with the setting of the retransmit interval, or the result is needless retransmissions. The value is larger for serial lines and virtual links. The transmit delay value should take into account the interface's transmission and propagation delays. The Cisco IOS software uses the specified authentication key only when authentication is enabled with the **area** *area-id* **authentication** router configuration command. The two authentication schemes (simple text and Message Digest 5 [MD5] authentication) are mutually exclusive.

**Table 5-11**    **area** *area-id* **virtual-link** *Command Parameters*

| Parameter | Description |
|---|---|
| *area-id* | Assigns an area ID to the transit area for the virtual link. This ID can be either a decimal value or in dotted-decimal format, like a valid IP address. There is no default. |
| | The transit area cannot be a stub area. |
| *router-id* | Associates a router ID with the virtual link neighbor. The router ID appears in the **show ip ospf** display. Enter this value in the format of an IP address. There is no default. |
| **authentication** | (Optional) Specifies an authentication type. |
| **message-digest** | (Optional) Specifies the use of message digest authentication. |
| **null** | (Optional) Overrides password or message digest authentication if configured for the area. No use of authentication. |

**Table 5-11**     **area** *area-id* **virtual-link** *Command Parameters (Continued)*

| Parameter | Description |
|---|---|
| **hello-interval** *seconds* | (Optional) Specifies the time (in seconds) between the hello packets that the Cisco IOS software sends on an interface. An unsigned integer value is advertised in the hello packets. The value must be the same for all attached routers and access servers to a common network. The default is 10 seconds. |
| **retransmit-interval** *seconds* | (Optional) Specifies the time (in seconds) between LSA retransmissions for adjacencies belonging to the interface. Expect round-trip delay between any two routers on the attached network. The value must be greater than the expected round-trip delay. The default is 5 seconds. |
| **transmit-delay** *seconds* | (Optional) Specifies the estimated time (in seconds) to send an LSU packet on the interface. The integer value must be greater than 0. LSAs in the update packet have their age incremented by this amount before transmission. The default value is 1 second. |
| **dead-interval** *seconds* | (Optional) Specifies the time (in seconds) that hello packets are not seen before a neighboring router declares the router down. There is an unsigned integer value. The default is four times the default hello interval, or 40 seconds. As with the hello interval, this value must be the same for all routers and access servers attached to a common network. |
| **authentication-key** *key* | (Optional) Specifies the password used by neighboring routers. It is any continuous string of characters up to 8 bytes long that you can enter from the keyboard. This string acts as a key allowing the authentication procedure to generate or verify the authentication field in the OSPF header. Insert this key directly into the OSPF header when originating routing protocol packets. Assign a separate password to each network on a per-interface basis. All neighboring routers on the same network must have the same password to route OSPF traffic. Encrypt the password in the configuration file if the **service password-encryption** command is enabled. There is no default value. |
| **message-digest-key** *key-id* **md5** *key* | (Optional) Identifies the key and password used by neighboring routers and the router for MD5 authentication. The *key-id* argument is a number in the range 1 to 255. The *key* is an alphanumeric string of up to 16 characters. All neighboring routers on the same network must have the same key identifier and key to route OSPF traffic. There is no default value. |

The **area** *area-id* **virtual-link** command for each router must include the transit area ID and the corresponding virtual link neighbor router ID for you to properly configure a virtual link. You should always use the **show ip ospf** command on the far-end router to ensure the correct router ID configuration.

In Figure 5-27, Router 2 builds a virtual link to far-end Router 1. Each router points to the other router ID. Remember that the router ID might not be the nearest interface. Area 1 is configured as the transit area.

| NOTE | Router 2 does not require a network statement that includes area 0. Router 1 does not include area 3. |
|------|------|

**Figure 5-27** *OSPF Virtual Link Configuration: Transit Area*

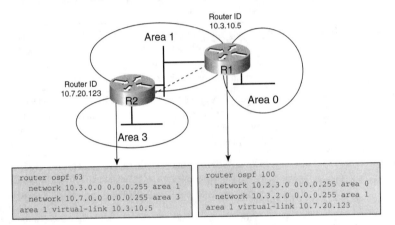

```
router ospf 63
   network 10.3.0.0 0.0.0.255 area 1
   network 10.7.0.0 0.0.0.255 area 3
area 1 virtual-link 10.3.10.5
```

```
router ospf 100
   network 10.2.3.0 0.0.0.255 area 0
   network 10.3.2.0 0.0.0.255 area 1
area 1 virtual-link 10.7.20.123
```

In Figure 5-28, area 0 splits into two pieces because of network failure. A virtual link is used as a backup strategy to temporarily reconnect area 0. Area 1 is used as the transit area.

**Figure 5-28** *OSPF Virtual Link Configuration: Split Area 0*

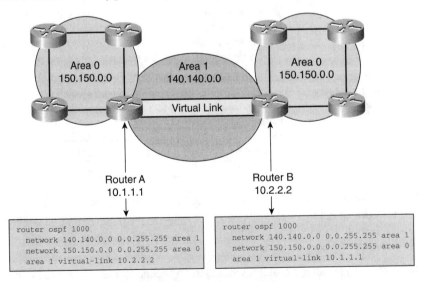

```
router ospf 1000
   network 140.140.0.0 0.0.255.255 area 1
   network 150.150.0.0 0.0.255.255 area 0
area 1 virtual-link 10.2.2.2
```

```
router ospf 1000
   network 140.140.0.0 0.0.255.255 area 1
   network 150.150.0.0 0.0.255.255 area 0
area 1 virtual-link 10.1.1.1
```

Example 5-13 shows the output of the **show ip ospf virtual-links** command.

**Example 5-13** show ip ospf virtual-links *Command Output*

```
Router#show ip ospf virtual-links
Virtual Link to router 192.168.101.2 is up
Transit area 0.0.0.1, via interface Ethernet0, Cost of using 10
Transmit Delay is 1 sec, State POINT_TO_POINT
Timer intervals configured, Hello 10, Dead 40, Wait 40, Retransmit 5
Hello due in 0:00:08
Adjacency State FULL
```

You should use the **show ip ospf virtual-links** command to ensure that the configured virtual link works properly. Table 5-12 describes its fields in detail.

**Table 5-12** show ip ospf *Fields*

| Field | Description |
|---|---|
| Virtual Link to router 10.2.2.2 is up | Specifies the OSPF neighbor and whether the link to that neighbor is up or down. |
| Transit area 0.0.0.1 | Specifies the transit area through which the virtual link is formed. |
| Via interface Ethernet0 | Specifies the interface through which the virtual link is formed. |
| Cost of using 10 | Specifies the cost of reaching the OSPF neighbor through the virtual link. |
| Transmit Delay is 1 second | Specifies the transmit delay on the virtual link. |
| State POINT_TO_POINT | Specifies the state of the OSPF neighbor. |
| Timer intervals configured | Specifies the various timer intervals configured for the link. |
| Hello due in 0:00:08 | Specifies when the next hello is expected from the neighbor. |
| Adjacency State FULL | Specifies the adjacency state between the neighbors. |

## Verifying OSPF Virtual Link Operation

The **debug ip ospf adj** and **show ip ospf database** commands are important for understanding the details of a virtual link and for ensuring that it works properly.

The routers become adjacent and exchange LSAs via the virtual link, similar to a physical link. However, the **show ip ospf neighbor** command does not display neighbor adjacencies over virtual links. The only way to see the neighbor adjacencies is by looking at the router LSA or by using the **debug ip ospf adj** command as the adjacency comes up, as shown in Example 5-14.

**Example 5-14** debug ip ospf adj *Command Output*

```
R3#debug ip ospf adj
1w2d: OSPF: Rcv hello from 1.1.1.1 area 0 from OSPF_VL3 5.0.0.1
1w2d: OSPF: 2 Way Communication to 1.1.1.1 on OSPF_VL3, state 2WAY
1w2d: OSPF: Send DBD to 1.1.1.1 on OSPF_VL3 seq 0xD1C opt 0x62 flag 0x7 len 32
1w2d: OSPF: End of hello processing
1w2d: OSPF: Rcv DBD from 1.1.1.1 on OSPF_VL3 seq 0x1617 opt 0x22 flag 0x7 len
    32  mtu 0 state EXSTART
```

*continues*

**Example 5-14  debug ip ospf adj** *Command Output (Continued)*

```
1w2d: OSPF: First DBD and we are not SLAVE
1w2d: OSPF: Rcv DBD from 1.1.1.1 on OSPF_VL3 seq 0xD1C opt 0x22 flag 0x2 len
    172  mtu 0 state EXSTART
1w2d: OSPF: NBR Negotiation Done. We are the MASTER
1w2d: OSPF: Send DBD to 1.1.1.1 on OSPF_VL3 seq 0xD1D opt 0x62 flag 0x3 len 172
1w2d: OSPF: Database request to 1.1.1.1
1w2d: OSPF: sent LS REQ packet to 5.0.0.1, length 36
1w2d: OSPF: Rcv DBD from 1.1.1.1 on OSPF_VL3 seq 0xD1D opt 0x22 flag 0x0 len
    32  mtu 0 state EXCHANGE
1w2d: OSPF: Send DBD to 1.1.1.1 on OSPF_VL3 seq 0xD1E opt 0x62 flag 0x1 len 32
1w2d: OSPF: Rcv DBD from 1.1.1.1 on OSPF_VL3 seq 0xD1E opt 0x22 flag 0x0 len
    32  mtu 0 state EXCHANGE
1w2d: OSPF: Exchange Done with 1.1.1.1 on OSPF_VL3
1w2d: OSPF: Synchronized with 1.1.1.1 on OSPF_VL3, state FULL
1w2d: OSPF: Build router LSA for area 0, router ID 3.3.3.3, seq 0x80000029
1w2d: OSPF: Dead event ignored for 1.1.1.1 on demand circuit OSPF_VL3
R1#show ip ospf database router 3.3.3.3

        OSPF Router with ID (1.1.1.1) (Process ID 2)

                Router Link States (Area 0)


   Routing Bit Set on this LSA
   LS age: 5 (DoNotAge)
   Options: (No TOS-capability, DC)
   LS Type: Router Links
   Link State ID: 3.3.3.3
   Advertising Router: 3.3.3.3
   LS Seq Number: 80000002
   Checksum: 0x3990
   Length: 36
   Area Border Router
    Number of Links: 1

     Link connected to: a Virtual Link
      (Link ID) Neighboring Router ID: 1.1.1.1
      (Link Data) Router Interface address: 6.0.0.3
       Number of TOS metrics: 0
        TOS 0 Metrics: 65
```

# Summary

In this chapter, you learned that 11 different LSA types are defined in OSPF. The first five are the most commonly used. OSPF defines three kinds of routes: intra-area, interarea, and external. External routes are subdivided into E1 and E2.

You read that route summarization improves CPU utilization, reduces LSA flooding, and reduces LSDB and routing table sizes. You also read that default routes can be used in OSPF to prevent the need for a specific route to all destination networks. The benefit is a much smaller routing table and LSDB, with complete reachability.

You learned that several area types are defined in OSPF and that the backbone is the transit area. You know that stub areas reduce flooding into the area by replacing external LSAs with a default route and that totally stubby areas reduce flooding into the area by replacing both external and summary LSAs with a default route. You will remember that NSSAs are a special case. They allow an area that does not meet a stub's requirements to gain the benefits of a stub.

You also learned that a virtual link is a feature used to *temporarily* mend backbone failures.

# References

For additional information, refer to these resources:

- www.cisco.com article: *OSPF Frequently Asked Questions*
- www.cisco.com article: *OSPF Not-So-Stubby Area (NSSA)*
- www.cisco.com article: *What are OSPF Areas and Virtual Links?*

# Configuration Exercise 5-1: Configuring OSPF for Multiple Areas and Frame Relay NBMA

In this exercise, you will configure OSPF for use over simple Frame Relay networks.

---

### Introduction to the Configuration Exercises

This book uses Configuration Exercises to help you practice configuring routers with the commands and topics presented. If you have access to real hardware, you can try these exercises on your routers. See Appendix H, "Configuration Exercise Equipment Requirements and Initial Configurations," for a list of recommended equipment and initial configuration commands for the routers. However, even if you don't have access to any routers, you can go through the exercises, and keep a log of your own running configurations, or just read through the solution. Commands used and solutions to the Configuration Exercises are provided after the exercises.

In the Configuration Exercises, the network is assumed to consist of two pods, each with four routers. The pods are interconnected to a backbone. You configure pod 1. No interaction between the two pods is required, but you might see some routes from the other pod in your routing tables in some exercises if you have it configured. (The Configuration Exercise answers show the routes from the other pod.) In most of the exercises, the backbone has only one router; in some cases, another router is added to the backbone. Each Configuration Exercise assumes that you have completed the previous chapters' Configuration Exercises on your pod.

---

| NOTE | Throughout this exercise, the pod number is referred to as *x*, and the router number is referred to as *y*. Substitute the appropriate numbers as needed. |
|------|---|

## Objectives

After completing this exercise, you will be able to

- Configure OSPF in a nonbroadcast multiaccess (NBMA) network
- Configure OSPF in a multiarea environment

## Visual Objective

Figure 5-29 illustrates the topology used in this exercise.

**Figure 5-29**  *Configuring OSPF for Multiple Areas and Frame Relay NBMA*

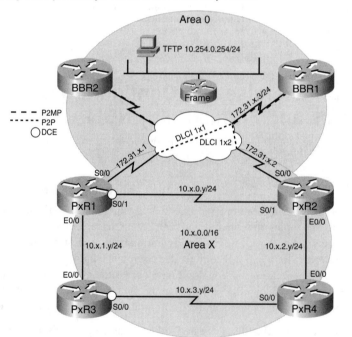

## Command List

In this exercise, you will use the commands in Table 5-13, listed in logical order. Refer to this list if you need configuration command assistance during the exercise.

---

**CAUTION**    Although the command syntax is shown in this table, the addresses shown are typically for the P*x*R1 and P*x*R3 routers. Be careful when addressing your routers! Refer to the exercise instructions and the appropriate visual objective diagram for addressing details.

---

**Table 5-13**    *Configuration Exercise 5-1 Commands*

| Command | Description |
|---|---|
| (config-if)#**ip ospf priority 0** | Sets a port's OSPF priority to 0 to prevent it from participating in DR/BDR election. |
| (config-router)#**network 172.31.*x*.0 0.0.0.255 area 0** | Places a set of interfaces in an OSPF area. |

## Task: Using the Nonbroadcast Network Type Over Frame Relay

In this task, you will configure ABRs, allowing OSPF to pass routes between areas. Follow these steps:

**Step 1**    Configure the edge routers (P*x*R1 and P*x*R2) as ABRs. You do this by placing the Frame Relay connection (the S0 interface on the edge routers) into OSPF area 0. Remember that the default OSPF network type for a Frame Relay interface is NBMA (nonbroadcast).

**Step 2**    It is important that the core (BBR1) is the DR, because this is a hub-and-spoke network, and only the core (BBR1) has full connectivity to the spoke routers. Set the OSPF priority to 0 on the edge router's S0 interface to ensure this.

---

**NOTE**    In an NBMA network, neighbor statements are required only on the DR and BDR. In this hub-and-spoke topology, neighbor statements must be configured on the hub (which must become the DR) and are not mandatory on the spoke routers. However, in a full-mesh topology, you might need neighbor statements on all routers if you have not specified the DR and BDR with the **priority** command.

---

**Step 3**    Enable serial 0/0 interfaces on edge routers with the **no shut** command (they are still down from the previous exercise).

**Step 4**    View the routing table on the internal routers to ensure that all appropriate OSPF routes are present, and ping the TFTP server from the internal router to verify network connectivity. What is the difference between the O, O IA, and O E2 OSPF routes?

---

**NOTE**    During the testing of this exercise with 25*xx* routers, it took approximately 2 minutes for this DR/BDR election to complete.

---

**Step 5** At the edge routers, verify OSPF neighborship with the command **show ip ospf neighbor**. Is BBR1 the DR for the 172.31.x.0/24 hub-and-spoke network?

**Step 6** BBR1 has been configured with neighbor statements for each of the edge routers. Telnet to BBR1, and view the running configuration to verify the **neighbor** commands for your pod's edge routers, P*x*R1 and P*x*R2. (The enable password on BBR1 is **cat5**.) Close the Telnet connection.

**Step 7** On the pod edge routers, P*x*R1 and P*x*R2, verify the OSPF network type on the Frame Relay interface. What is it? On the HDLC serial interface between P*x*R1 and P*x*R2? On the Ethernet interface?

## Exercise Verification

You have completed this exercise when you achieve these results:

- You have enabled OSPF to the core.
- You have a full set of OSPF routes in your routing tables.
- You can ping the core TFTP server.

# Configuration Exercise 5-2: Configuring OSPF for Multiple Areas and Frame Relay Point-to-Multipoint and Point-to-Point

In this exercise, you will configure OSPF for use over complex Frame Relay networks.

**NOTE** Throughout this exercise, the pod number is referred to as *x*, and the router number is referred to as *y*. Substitute the appropriate numbers as needed.

## Objectives

After completing this exercise, you will be able to

- Configure OSPF over Frame Relay using the point-to-multipoint OSPF network type
- Configure OSPF over Frame Relay using the point-to-point OSPF network type
- Connect to other devices in the core

## Visual Objective

Figure 5-30 illustrates the topology used in this exercise.

**Figure 5-30**  *Configuring OSPF for Multiple Areas and Frame Relay Point-to-Multipoint and Point-to-Point*

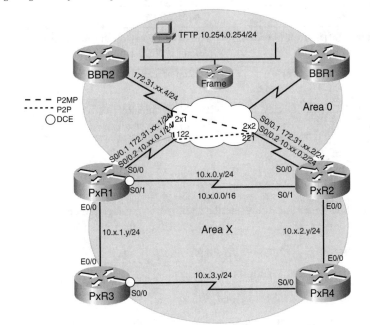

## Command List

In this exercise, you will use the commands in Table 5-14, listed in logical order. Refer to this list if you need configuration command assistance during the exercise.

---

**CAUTION**    Although the command syntax is shown in this table, the addresses shown are typically for the PxR1 and PxR3 routers. Be careful when addressing your routers! Refer to the exercise instructions and the appropriate visual objective diagram for addressing details.

---

**Table 5-14**    *Configuration Exercise 5-2 Commands*

| Command | Description |
|---|---|
| (config)#**default interface S0** | Erases the configuration on an interface. |
| (config-subif)#**frame-relay interface-dlci 122** | Specifies the data-link connection identifier (DLCI) associated with this point-to-point link. |
| (config)#**interface s0.1 multipoint | point-to-point** | Creates a subinterface (either multipoint or point-to-point). |

*continues*

**Table 5-14** *Configuration Exercise 5-2 Commands (Continued)*

| Command | Description |
|---|---|
| (config-subif)#**ip ospf network point-to-multipoint** | Forces OSPF to treat this interface as point-to-multipoint; the default is NBMA. |
| (config-router)#**network 172.31.***xx***.0 0.0.0.255 area 0** | Sets interfaces that match this pattern to be in this OSPF area. |
| (config-if)#**no frame-relay inverse-arp** | Disables Frame Relay inverse Address Resolution Protocol (ARP) on the interface. |

# Task 1: Cleaning Up

Follow these steps:

**Step 1**   Shut the Frame Relay interface, serial 0, on the edge routers. To prepare the interface for use in this exercise, make the following interface configuration changes:

**Step 2**   Remove all Frame Relay map statements.

**Step 3**   Remove the IP address.

**Step 4**   Remove the OSPF **priority** statement.

**Step 5**   View the running configuration to verify that the edge routers' S0/0 interface is configured to use Frame Relay encapsulation and that **frame-relay inverse-arp** is disabled.

**Step 6**   Alternatively, you might remove all the configuration from the interface by issuing the command **default interface s0**.

If you have used the **default interface s0** command, enable Frame Relay encapsulation on the serial 0 interface. Turn off **frame-relay inverse-arp** on that interface.

# Task 2: Configuring OSPF for Multiple Areas and Frame Relay Point-to-Multipoint and Point-to-Point

**NOTE**   For this exercise, you will connect the edge routers to the BBR2 router over the 172.31.*xx*.0/24 network. The connection from the edge routers to the BBR1 router over the 172.31.*x*.0/24 network is not used.

Follow these steps:

**Step 1**   At the edge routers, create a multipoint subinterface numbered s0.1. You will use this interface to explore Frame Relay hub-and-spoke behavior using the OSPF point-to-multipoint network type.

**Step 2**   Change the s0.1 OSPF network type to point-to-multipoint. (The default OSPF network type for a Frame Relay multipoint subinterface is nonbroadcast.)

**Step 3**   Assign the IP address 172.31.*xx.y*/24 to S0.1, where *x* is the pod number and *y* is the router number. For example, for P2R2, the IP address is 172.31.22.2/24.

**Step 4**   Because you are not using **frame relay inverse arp**, you need to manually map the remote IP address to the local DLCI. Create a new Frame Relay **map** statement from each edge router to the BBR2 IP address of 172.31.*xx*.4 using a DLCI number of 2*xy,* where *x* is the pod number and *y* is the router number. Do not forget the **broadcast** option.

For example, for P1R2, the Frame Relay **map** statement is

```
frame-relay map ip 172.31.11.4 212 broadcast
```

For P1R1, the Frame Relay **map** statement is

```
frame-relay map ip 172.31.11.4 211 broadcast
```

**Step 5**   Do not shut the serial 0/0 interface on the edge routers.

**Step 6**   At the edge routers, add a new network statement to OSPF for the 172.31.*xx*.0 network that has been created on s0.1, placing it in area 0.

**Step 7**   On the edge routers, use the proper **show** command to display the OSPF neighbor status. Is there a DR/BDR using the point-to-multipoint OSPF network type?

**Step 8**   View the routing table on the edge routers P*x*R1 and P*x*R2 to verify that they are receiving OSPF routes from the core.

Ping BBR2's Ethernet interface (10.254.0.2) from the edge routers to verify connectivity with the core.

**Step 9**   Create a new point-to-point subinterface to connect the two edge routers. Give the new subinterface the number S0.2. Address it as 10.*xx*.0.*y*/24, where *x* is the pod number and *y* is the router number. Define the DLCI for the subinterface: the DLCI from P*x*R1 to P*x*R2 is 122, and the DLCI from P*x*R2 to P*x*R1 is 221, in every pod.

**Step 10**   At each edge router, ping the s0.2 subinterface of the other edge router to verify connectivity.

**Step 11**   At the edge routers, add the 10.*xx*.0.0 network to OSPF in area *x*.

**Step 12**   At the edge routers, verify the OSPF network type of the two subinterfaces. What is the default OSPF network type on the point-to-point subinterface?

**Step 13**   At the edge routers, use the proper **show** command to verify the OSPF neighbor status. Is there a DR/BDR on s0/0.2 using the point-to-point OSPF network type?

**Step 14** At the edge routers, verify the OSPF routes in the IP routing table. You might not see routes from every pod, depending on the number of pods in use.

**Step 15** At the internal routers, verify the OSPF routes in the IP routing table.

**Step 16** Use the **show ip protocols** command to verify the OSPF routing process at the edge and internal routers. How many areas does the edge router belong to? How many areas does the internal router belong to?

## Exercise Verification

You have successfully completed this exercise when you achieve these results:

- You have configured OSPF over a point-to-multipoint and point-to-point Frame Relay connection.

- You can ping the BBR2 router from your pod.

# Configuration Exercise 5-3: Understanding the OSPF Database and Tuning OSPF

In this exercise, you will use **show** commands to view the LSDB structure. You will also investigate the use of OSPF stub areas.

NOTE    Throughout this exercise, the pod number is referred to as *x*, and the router number is referred to as *y*. Substitute the appropriate numbers as needed.

## Objectives

After completing this exercise, you will be able to

- Understand the OSPF LSDB structure
- Understand the available tools necessary to investigate the LSDB
- Limit routing table size and update traffic using OSPF area route summarization
- Limit routing table size and update traffic using the OSPF stub area

## Visual Objective

Figure 5-31 illustrates the topology used in this exercise.

## Command List

In this exercise, you will use the commands in Table 5-15, listed in logical order. Refer to this list if you need configuration command assistance during the exercise.

**Figure 5-31**  *Examining the OSPF Database*

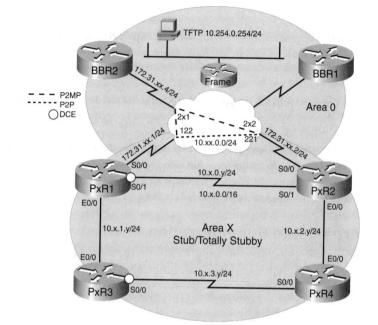

**CAUTION**    Although the command syntax is shown in this table, the addresses shown are typically for the P*x*R1 and P*x*R3 routers. Be careful when addressing your routers! Refer to the exercise instructions and the appropriate visual objective diagram for addressing details.

**Table 5-15**    *Configuration Exercise 5-3 Commands*

| Command | Description |
|---|---|
| (config-router)#**area** *x* **stub** | Configures the area to be stub. Blocks type 5 LSAs (external routes) from reaching this area and substitutes a default route to the ABR. |
| (config-router)#**area** *x* **stub no-summary** | Configures the area to be totally stubby. Blocks type 3, 4, and 5 LSAs (interarea and external routes) from reaching this area and substitutes a default route to the ABR. |
| #**show ip ospf database** | Shows the LSDB. |
| #**show ip ospf database external** | Shows exterior (type 5) LSAs. |
| (config-router)#**area** *x* **range 10.***x***.0.0 255.255.0.0** | Identifies the area subject to route summarization. |

## Task 1: Examining the OSPF Database

Follow these steps:

**Step 1**  On all your pod routers, use the **show ip ospf database** command to display the OSPF database. This database shows all LSAs stored in the router.

Do you see LSA types 1, 2, 3, 4, and 5 in the OSPF database?

On the edge routers, do you see LSA information about area 0 and area *x*?

On the internal routers, do you see LSA information about area *x* only?

**Step 2**  Use the **show ip ospf database external** command on your edge routers to display all the type 5 LSAs in the OSPF database. The core router, BBR2, is redistributing the 10.254.0.0/24 network into OSPF. Determine if there is a type 5 LSA about the 10.254.0.0 network.

## Task 2: OSPF Area Route Summarization

In this task, you will identify how to bring the benefits of summarization to OSPF. Summarization reduces the size of routing tables, reduces routing update traffic, and minimizes the impact of flapping lines. In addition, it minimizes processing and memory requirements for all routers.

Follow these steps:

**Step 1**  At the edge routers, summarize the pod networks to 10.*x*.0.0/16 from area *x* using the **area** *x* **range** command under the OSPF routing process.

**Step 2**  From the edge router, Telnet to the BBR2 router (172.31.*xx*.4), and examine the routing table on BBR2.

Notice that BBR2 recognizes two paths to the pod 10.*x*.0.0/16 network. It no longer recognizes each of the pod /24 links (10.*x*.0.0/24, 10.*x*.1.0/24, 10.*x*.2.0/24, and 10.*x*.3.0/24).

BBR2 still recognizes the 10.*xx*.0.0/24 link, because it is not part of the summarized range.

**Step 3**  Determine the changes summarization made to the routing table on the edge routers. Is the routing table reduced on the edge routers? Explain why there is a route to Null0.

**Step 4**  Configure the pod OSPF area as a stub area (remember to configure both the edge and internal routers, because the **stub** flag is included in hellos). Notice the error messages and that no adjacency is established until both routers agree that they are stubs. What changes do you expect to occur with the implementation of a stub?

**Step 5**  Examine the edge (P*x*R1 or P*x*R2) and internal (P*x*R3 or P*x*R4) routing tables. Determine if any interarea OSPF routes are in the internal routers and the reason for their presence.

Notice that the internal routers do not have any external routes. The ABR (edge router) generates a default route to the internal routers for reaching external networks.

**Step 6**  Configure the OSPF area of the pod as totally stubby. Remember that only the ABR requires the command to configure the area as totally stubby.

**Step 7**  Ping the TFTP server from the internal routers to verify connectivity.

**Step 8**  Examine the edge (P*x*R1 or P*x*R2) and internal (P*x*R3 or P*x*R4) routing tables.

Determine if any interarea OSPF routes are in the internal routers and the reason for their presence.

## Exercise Verification

You have successfully completed this exercise when you achieve these results:

- You have examined the OSPF database, and you understand the tools necessary to investigate the LSDB.

- You have configured your pod router area as an OSPF stub area and as a totally stubby area.

- You have minimized routing table size by using route summarization without affecting reachability. You should still be able to ping all devices in your pod and in the core.

# Configuration Exercise 5-4: Configuring the OSPF Virtual Link

In this exercise, you will investigate OSPF virtual links.

| NOTE | Throughout this exercise, the pod number is referred to as *x*, and the router number is referred to as *y*. Substitute the appropriate numbers as needed. |
| --- | --- |

## Objectives

After completing this exercise, you will be able to use virtual links to connect an area to area 0.

## Visual Objective

Figure 5-32 illustrates the topology used in this exercise.

**Figure 5-32** *Configuring the OSPF Virtual Link*

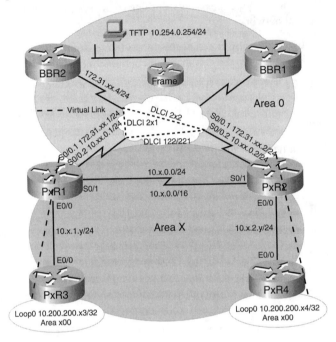

## Command List

In this exercise, you will use the commands in Table 5-16, listed in logical order. Refer to this list if you need configuration command assistance during the exercise.

---

**CAUTION** Although the command syntax is shown in this table, the addresses shown are typically for the PxR1 and PxR3 routers. Be careful when addressing your routers! Refer to the exercise instructions and the appropriate visual objective diagram for addressing details.

---

**Table 5-16** *Configuration Exercise 5-4 Commands*

| Command | Description |
|---------|-------------|
| (config-router)#**area** *x* **virtual-link** | Creates a virtual link. The area number is the transit area. The IP address is the Router ID (RID) of the far end. |
| #**show ip ospf** | Shows information about the OSPF process on the router, including all areas connected to the router. |
| #**show ip ospf neighbor** | Shows a list of OSPF neighbors and their RIDs. |

**Table 5-16**    *Configuration Exercise 5-4 Commands (Continued)*

| Command | Description |
|---------|-------------|
| #show ip ospf virtual-links | Shows the status of virtual links. |
| #show ip route | Shows the router's forwarding table. |

# Task: Configuring the OSPF Virtual Link

OSPF requires that all areas have a connection to area 0, the backbone. In this exercise, you will create a discontiguous area and examine the resulting routing tables. You will then configure a virtual link that connects the new area to area 0.

Follow these steps:

**Step 1**    Remove the OSPF stub configuration from all the pod routers.

**Step 2**    On the internal routers, P*x*R3 and P*x*R4, shut down the serial 0 interface, disconnecting the link between them.

**Step 3**    Place the loopback interface on each internal router into a new OSPF area, using area number *x*00, where *x* is your pod number. This requires an additional network statement under the OSPF router configuration.

**Step 4**    Examine the routing table on the edge routers, P*x*R1 and P*x*R2. Is the network for the internal router's loopback interface (10.200.200.*xy*) present in the routing table?

**Step 5**    Because OSPF assumes that all areas have at least one interface in area 0, the internal routers do not advertise the loopback interface to the edge routers. However, area *x*00 does not border area 0. You remedy this by configuring a virtual link from area *x*00 to area 0. As the first step in configuring the virtual link, discover each router's RID.

**Step 6**    Configure an OSPF virtual link from the internal router to the edge router through area *x*, where *x* is your pod number.

**Step 7**    Verify that the virtual link is functioning.

**Step 8**    Verify that the network for the internal router's loopback interface now appears in the edge router's routing table.

**Step 9**    On the internal router, issue the **show ip ospf** command. Which OSPF areas are active on this router?

# Exercise Verification

You have successfully completed this exercise when you achieve these results:

- You have used virtual links to heal a discontiguous area.
- You have used virtual links to create an arbitrary topology of areas.

# Solution to Configuration Exercise 5-1: Configuring OSPF for Multiple Areas and Frame Relay NBMA

This section provides the answers to the questions in the Configuration Exercise.

---

**NOTE**  Some answers provided cover multiple steps; the answers are given after the last step to which that answer applies.

---

## Solution to Task: Using the Nonbroadcast Network Type Over Frame Relay

In this task, you configure ABRs, allowing OSPF to pass routes between areas.

**Step 1**  Configure the edge routers (P$x$R1 and P$x$R2) as ABRs. You do this by placing the Frame Relay connection (the S0 interface on the edge routers) into OSPF area 0. Remember that the default OSPF network type for a Frame Relay interface is NBMA (nonbroadcast).

**Solution:**

```
P1R1(config)#router ospf 1
P1R1(config-router)#network 172.31.1.0 0.0.0.255 area 0
```

**Step 2**  It is important that the core (BBR1) is the DR, because this is a hub-and-spoke network, and only the core (BBR1) has full connectivity to the spoke routers. Set the OSPF priority to 0 on the edge router's S0 interface to ensure this.

**Solution:**

```
P1R1(config)#interface erial 0
P1R1(config-if)#ip ospf priority 0
```

---

**NOTE**  In an NBMA network, neighbor statements are required only on the DR and BDR. In this hub-and-spoke topology, neighbor statements must be configured on the hub (which must become the DR) and are not mandatory on the spoke routers. However, in a full-mesh topology, you might need neighbor statements on all routers if you have not specified the DR and BDR with the **priority** command.

---

**Step 3**  Enable serial 0/0 interfaces on edge routers with the **no shutdown** command (they are still down from the previous exercise).

**Solution:**

```
P1R1(config)#interface serial 0
P1R1(config-if)#no shutdown
```

**Step 4**  View the routing table on the internal routers to ensure that all appropriate OSPF routes are present, and ping the TFTP server from the internal router to verify network connectivity. What is the difference between the O, O IA, and O E2 OSPF routes?

---

**NOTE**  During the testing of this exercise with 25*xx* routers, it took approximately 2 minutes for this DR/BDR election to complete.

---

**Solution:**

```
P1R1#
P1R1#show ip route
<output omitted>
Gateway of last resort is not set

     172.31.0.0/24 is subnetted, 2 subnets
O       172.31.2.0 [110/3124] via 172.31.1.3, 00:02:10, Serial0
C       172.31.1.0 is directly connected, Serial0
     10.0.0.0/24 is subnetted, 9 subnets
O IA    10.2.0.0 [110/4686] via 172.31.1.3, 00:02:10, Serial0
O       10.1.3.0 [110/1572] via 10.1.1.3, 00:03:41, Ethernet0
O IA    10.2.1.0 [110/3134] via 172.31.1.3, 00:02:10, Serial0
O       10.1.2.0 [110/1572] via 10.1.0.2, 00:03:41, Serial1
O IA    10.2.2.0 [110/3134] via 172.31.1.3, 00:02:10, Serial0
C       10.1.1.0 is directly connected, Ethernet0
O IA    10.2.3.0 [110/4696] via 172.31.1.3, 00:02:12, Serial0
C       10.1.0.0 is directly connected, Serial1
O E2    10.254.0.0 [110/50] via 172.31.1.3, 00:02:12, Serial0
P1R1#
```

O is internal OSPF, O E2 is external from the AS, and O IA is interarea routes—in this case, from area 2.

**Step 5**  At the edge routers, verify OSPF neighborship with the command **show ip ospf neighbor**. Is BBR1 the DR for the 172.31.*x*.0/24 hub-and-spoke network?

**Solution:**

```
P1R1#show ip ospf neighbor
Neighbor ID      Pri   State          Dead Time   Address       Interface
10.200.200.13    0     FULL/DROTHER   00:00:33    10.1.1.3      Ethernet0
100.100.100.100  1     FULL/DR        00:01:50    172.31.1.3    Serial0
10.0.0.12        1     FULL/ -        00:00:37    10.1.0.2      Serial1
P1R1#
```

Yes, BBR1 is the DR (it has a RID of 100.100.100.100).

**Step 6** BBR1 has been configured with neighbor statements for each of the edge routers. Telnet to BBR1, and view the running configuration to verify the **neighbor** commands for your pod's edge routers, P*x*R1 and P*x*R2. (The enable password on BBR1 is **cat5**.) Close the Telnet connection.

**Solution:**

```
!on BBR1:
router ospf 1
 router-id 100.100.100.100
 log-adjacency-changes
 redistribute connected metric 50 subnets
 network 172.31.0.0 0.0.255.255 area 0
 neighbor 172.31.2.2
 neighbor 172.31.2.1
 neighbor 172.31.1.2
 neighbor 172.31.1.1
!
```

**Step 7** On the pod edge routers, P*x*R1 and P*x*R2, verify the OSPF network type on the Frame Relay interface. What is it? On the HDLC serial interface between P*x*R1 and P*x*R2? On the Ethernet interface?

**Solution:**

```
P1R1#show ip ospf interface
Ethernet0 is up, line protocol is up
  Internet Address 10.1.1.1/24, Area 1
  Process ID 1, Router ID 10.0.0.11, Network Type BROADCAST, Cost: 10
  Transmit Delay is 1 sec, State DR, Priority 1
  Designated Router (ID) 10.0.0.11, Interface address 10.1.1.1
  No backup designated router on this network
  Timer intervals configured, Hello 10, Dead 40, Wait 40, Retransmit 5
    Hello due in 00:00:06
  Index 1/1, flood queue length 0
  Next 0x0(0)/0x0(0)
  Last flood scan length is 2, maximum is 4
  Last flood scan time is 0 msec, maximum is 0 msec
  Neighbor Count is 1, Adjacent neighbor count is 1
    Adjacent with neighbor 10.200.200.13
  Suppress hello for 0 neighbor(s)
Serial0 is up, line protocol is up
  Internet Address 172.31.1.1/24, Area 0
  Process ID 1, Router ID 10.0.0.11, Network Type NON_BROADCAST, Cost: 1562
  Transmit Delay is 1 sec, State DROTHER, Priority 0
  Designated Router (ID) 100.100.100.100, Interface address 172.31.1.3
  No backup designated router on this network
  Timer intervals configured, Hello 30, Dead 120, Wait 120, Retransmit 5
    Hello due in 00:00:04
  Index 1/3, flood queue length 0
  Next 0x0(0)/0x0(0)
  Last flood scan length is 1, maximum is 1
```

```
     Last flood scan time is 0 msec, maximum is 0 msec
    Neighbor Count is 1, Adjacent neighbor count is 1
      Adjacent with neighbor 100.100.100.100  (Designated Router)
    Suppress hello for 0 neighbor(s)
  Serial1 is up, line protocol is up
    Internet Address 10.1.0.1/24, Area 1
    Process ID 1, Router ID 10.0.0.11, Network Type POINT_TO_POINT, Cost: 1562
    Transmit Delay is 1 sec, State POINT_TO_POINT,
    Timer intervals configured, Hello 10, Dead 40, Wait 40, Retransmit 5
      Hello due in 00:00:01
    Index 2/2, flood queue length 0
    Next 0x0(0)/0x0(0)
    Last flood scan length is 2, maximum is 4
    Last flood scan time is 0 msec, maximum is 4 msec
    Neighbor Count is 1, Adjacent neighbor count is 1
      Adjacent with neighbor 10.0.0.12
    Suppress hello for 0 neighbor(s)
  P1R1#
```

## Exercise Verification

You have completed this exercise when you achieve these results:

- You have enabled OSPF to the core.
- You have a full set of OSPF routes in your routing tables.
- You can ping the core TFTP server.

# Solution to Configuration Exercise 5-2: Configuring OSPF for Multiple Areas and Frame Relay Point-to-Multipoint and Point-to-Point

This section provides the answers to the questions in the Configuration Exercise.

| NOTE | Some answers provided cover multiple steps; the answers are given after the last step to which that answer applies. |
| --- | --- |

## Solution to Task 1: Cleaning Up

**Step 1**  Shut the Frame Relay interface, serial 0, on the edge routers. To prepare the interface for use in this exercise, make the following interface configuration changes:

**Step 2**  Remove all Frame Relay map statements.

**Step 3**  Remove the IP address.

Step 4    Remove the OSPF priority statement.

Step 5    View the running configuration to verify that the edge routers' S0/0 interface is configured to use Frame Relay encapsulation and that **frame-relay inverse-arp** is disabled.

Step 6    Alternatively, you might remove all the configuration from the interface by issuing the command **default interface s0**.

If you have used the **default interface s0** command, enable Frame Relay encapsulation on the serial 0 interface. Turn off **frame-relay inverse-arp** on that interface.

**Solution:**

```
P1R1(config)#interface serial 0
P1R1(config-if)#shutdown
P1R1(config-if)#default interface s0
Building configuration...

Interface Serial0 set to default configuration
Mar  1 16:10:44 EST: %LINK-3-UPDOWN: Interface Serial0, changed state to up
Mar  1 16:10:45 EST: %LINEPROTO-5-UPDOWN: Line protocol on Interface Serial0,
  changed state to up
Mar  1 16:11:06 EST: %LINEPROTO-5-UPDOWN: Line protocol on Interface Serial0,
  changed state to down
P1R1(config)#interface s0
P1R1(config-if)#encapsulation frame-relay
Mar  1 16:11:17 EST: %LINEPROTO-5-UPDOWN: Line protocol on Interface Serial0,
  changed state to up
P1R1(config-if)#no frame-relay inverse-arp
P1R1(config-if)#
```

# Solution to Task 2: Configuring OSPF for Multiple Areas and Frame Relay Point-to-Multipoint and Point-to-Point

NOTE    For this exercise, you connect the edge routers to the BBR2 router over the 172.31.xx.0/24 network. The connection from the edge routers to the BBR1 router over the 172.31.x.0/24 network is not used.

Step 1    At the edge routers, create a multipoint subinterface numbered s0.1. You will use this interface to explore Frame Relay hub-and-spoke behavior using the OSPF point-to-multipoint network type.

**Step 2**   Change the s0.1 OSPF network type to point-to-multipoint. (The default OSPF network type for a Frame Relay multipoint subinterface is nonbroadcast.)

**Step 3**   Assign the IP address 172.31.*xx.y*/24 to s0.1, where *x* is the pod number and *y* is the router number. For example, for P2R2, the IP address is 172.31.22.2/24.

**Step 4**   Because you are not using **frame relay inverse arp**, you need to manually map the remote IP address to the local DLCI. Create a new Frame Relay map statement from each edge router to the BBR2 IP address of 172.31.*xx*.4 using a DLCI number of 2*xy*, where *x* is the pod number and *y* is the router number. Do not forget the **broadcast** option.

For example, for P1R2, the Frame Relay map statement is

```
frame-relay map ip 172.31.11.4 212 broadcast
```

For P1R1, the Frame Relay map statement is

```
frame-relay map ip 172.31.11.4 211 broadcast
```

**Solution:**

```
P1R1(config)#interface s0.1 multipoint
P1R1(config-subif)#ip ospf network point-to-multipoint
P1R1(config-subif)#ip address 172.31.11.1 255.255.255.0
P1R1(config-subif)#frame-relay map ip 172.31.11.4 211 broadcast
P1R1(config-subif)#exit

P1R2(config)#interface s0.1 multipoint
P1R2(config-subif)#ip ospf network point-to-multipoint
P1R2(config-subif)#ip address 172.31.11.2 255.255.255.0
P1R2(config-subif)#frame-relay map ip 172.31.11.4 212 broadcast
P1R2(config-subif)#exit
```

**Step 5**   Do not shut the serial 0/0 interface on the edge routers.

**Solution:**

```
P1R1(config)#interface serial 0
P1R1(config-if)#no shutdown

P1R2(config)#interface serial 0
P1R2(config-if)#no shutdown
```

**Step 6**   At the edge routers, add a new network statement to OSPF for the 172.31.*xx*.0 network that has been created on s0.1, placing it in area 0.

**Solution:**

```
P1R1(config)#router ospf 1
P1R1(config-router)#network 172.31.11.0 0.0.0.255 area 0

P1R2(config)#router ospf 1
P1R2(config-router)#network 172.31.11.0 0.0.0.255 area 0
```

**Step 7** On the edge routers, use the proper **show** command to display the OSPF neighbor status. Is there a DR/BDR using the point-to-multipoint OSPF network type?

**Solution:**

```
P1R1#show ip ospf neighbor

Neighbor ID       Pri   State           Dead Time   Address       Interface
10.200.200.13      0    FULL/DROTHER    00:00:37    10.1.1.3      Ethernet0
200.200.200.200    1    FULL/  -        00:01:42    172.31.11.4   Serial0.1
10.0.0.12          1    FULL/  -        00:00:33    10.1.0.2      Serial1
P1R1#
```

No, there is no DR/BDR on the point-to-multipoint interface.

**Step 8** View the routing table on the edge routers P*x*R1 and P*x*R2 to verify that they are receiving OSPF routes from the core.

**Solution:**

```
P1R1#show ip route
<output omitted>
Gateway of last resort is not set

     172.31.0.0/16 is variably subnetted, 6 subnets, 2 masks
O       172.31.22.4/32 [110/64] via 172.31.11.4, 00:00:51, Serial0.1
O       172.31.22.1/32 [110/1626] via 172.31.11.4, 00:00:51, Serial0.1
O       172.31.22.2/32 [110/1626] via 172.31.11.4, 00:00:51, Serial0.1
C       172.31.11.0/24 is directly connected, Serial0.1
O       172.31.11.2/32 [110/1626] via 172.31.11.4, 00:00:51, Serial0.1
O       172.31.11.4/32 [110/64] via 172.31.11.4, 00:00:51, Serial0.1
     10.0.0.0/24 is subnetted, 9 subnets
O IA    10.2.0.0 [110/3188] via 172.31.11.4, 00:00:53, Serial0.1
O       10.1.3.0 [110/1572] via 10.1.1.3, 00:01:32, Ethernet0
O IA    10.2.1.0 [110/1636] via 172.31.11.4, 00:00:53, Serial0.1
O       10.1.2.0 [110/1572] via 10.1.0.2, 00:01:32, Serial1
O IA    10.2.2.0 [110/1636] via 172.31.11.4, 00:00:53, Serial0.1
C       10.1.1.0 is directly connected, Ethernet0
O IA    10.2.3.0 [110/3198] via 172.31.11.4, 00:00:54, Serial0.1
C       10.1.0.0 is directly connected, Serial1
O E2    10.254.0.0 [110/50] via 172.31.11.4, 00:00:44, Serial0.1
P1R1#
```

Ping BBR2's Ethernet interface (10.254.0.2) from the edge routers to verify connectivity with the core.

**Solution:**

```
P1R1#ping 10.254.0.2

Type escape sequence to abort.
Sending 5, 100-byte ICMP Echos to 10.254.0.2, timeout is 2 seconds:
!!!!!
Success rate is 100 percent (5/5), round-trip min/avg/max = 32/53/128 ms
```

**Step 9**    Create a new point-to-point subinterface to connect the two edge routers. Give the new subinterface the number S0.2. Address it as 10.xx.0.y/24, where x is the pod number and y is the router number. Define the DLCI for the subinterface: the DLCI from PxR1 to PxR2 is 122, and the DLCI from PxR2 to PxR1 is 221, in every pod.

**Solution:**

```
P1R1(config)#interface serial 0.2 point-to-point
P1R1(config-subif)#ip address 10.11.0.1 255.255.255.0
P1R1(config-subif)#frame-relay interface-dlci 122

P1R2(config)#interface serial 0.2 point-to-point
P1R2(config-subif)#ip address 10.11.0.2 255.255.255.0
P1R2(config-subif)#frame-relay interface-dlci 221
```

**Step 10**    At each edge router, ping the s0.2 subinterface of the other edge router to verify connectivity.

**Solution:**

```
P1R1#ping 10.11.0.2

Type escape sequence to abort.
Sending 5, 100-byte ICMP Echos to 10.11.0.2, timeout is 2 seconds:
!!!!!
Success rate is 100 percent (5/5), round-trip min/avg/max = 36/36/36 ms
P1R1#
P1R2#ping 10.11.0.1

Type escape sequence to abort.
Sending 5, 100-byte ICMP Echos to 10.11.0.1, timeout is 2 seconds:
!!!!!
Success rate is 100 percent (5/5), round-trip min/avg/max = 32/32/32 ms
P1R2#
```

**Step 11**    At the edge routers, add the 10.xx.0.0 network to OSPF in area x.

**Solution:**

```
P1R2(config)#router ospf 1
P1R2(config-router)#network 10.11.0.0 0.0.0.255 area 1

P1R1(config)#router ospf 1
P1R1(config-router)#network 10.11.0.0 0.0.0.255 area 1
```

**Step 12**    At the edge routers, verify the OSPF network type of the two subinterfaces. What is the default OSPF network type on the point-to-point subinterface?

**Solution:**

```
P1R1#show ip ospf interface
Ethernet0 is up, line protocol is up
  Internet Address 10.1.1.1/24, Area 1
  Process ID 1, Router ID 10.0.0.11, Network Type BROADCAST, Cost: 10
```

*continues*

```
    Transmit Delay is 1 sec, State DR, Priority 1
    Designated Router (ID) 10.0.0.11, Interface address 10.1.1.1
    No backup designated router on this network
    Timer intervals configured, Hello 10, Dead 40, Wait 40, Retransmit 5
      Hello due in 00:00:04
    Index 1/1, flood queue length 0
    Next 0x0(0)/0x0(0)
    Last flood scan length is 1, maximum is 10
    Last flood scan time is 0 msec, maximum is 4 msec
    Neighbor Count is 1, Adjacent neighbor count is 1
      Adjacent with neighbor 10.200.200.13
    Suppress hello for 0 neighbor(s)
  Serial0.1 is up, line protocol is up
    Internet Address 172.31.11.1/24, Area 0
    Process ID 1, Router ID 10.0.0.11, Network Type POINT_TO_MULTIPOINT, Cost: 64
    Transmit Delay is 1 sec, State POINT_TO_MULTIPOINT,
    Timer intervals configured, Hello 30, Dead 120, Wait 120, Retransmit 5
      Hello due in 00:00:06
    Index 1/3, flood queue length 0
    Next 0x0(0)/0x0(0)
    Last flood scan length is 1, maximum is 1
    Last flood scan time is 0 msec, maximum is 0 msec
    Neighbor Count is 1, Adjacent neighbor count is 1
      Adjacent with neighbor 200.200.200.200
    Suppress hello for 0 neighbor(s)
  Serial0.2 is up, line protocol is up
    Internet Address 10.11.0.1/24, Area 1
    Process ID 1, Router ID 10.0.0.11, Network Type POINT_TO_POINT, Cost: 64
    Transmit Delay is 1 sec, State POINT_TO_POINT,
    Timer intervals configured, Hello 10, Dead 40, Wait 40, Retransmit 5
      Hello due in 00:00:06
    Index 3/4, flood queue length 0
    Next 0x0(0)/0x0(0)
    Last flood scan length is 1, maximum is 1
    Last flood scan time is 0 msec, maximum is 0 msec
    Neighbor Count is 1, Adjacent neighbor count is 1
      Adjacent with neighbor 10.0.0.12
    Suppress hello for 0 neighbor(s)
  Serial1 is up, line protocol is up
    Internet Address 10.1.0.1/24, Area 1
    Process ID 1, Router ID 10.0.0.11, Network Type POINT_TO_POINT, Cost: 1562
    Transmit Delay is 1 sec, State POINT_TO_POINT,
    Timer intervals configured, Hello 10, Dead 40, Wait 40, Retransmit 5
      Hello due in 00:00:01
    Index 2/2, flood queue length 0
    Next 0x0(0)/0x0(0)
    Last flood scan length is 1, maximum is 9
    Last flood scan time is 0 msec, maximum is 4 msec
    Neighbor Count is 1, Adjacent neighbor count is 1
      Adjacent with neighbor 10.0.0.12
    Suppress hello for 0 neighbor(s)
  P1R1#
```

**Step 13**  At the edge routers, use the proper **show** command to verify the OSPF neighbor status. Is there a DR/BDR on s0/0.2 using the point-to-point OSPF network type?

**Solution:**

```
P1R1#show ip ospf neighbor

Neighbor ID      Pri   State           Dead Time   Address       Interface
10.200.200.13     0    FULL/DROTHER    00:00:34    10.1.1.3      Ethernet0
200.200.200.200   1    FULL/  -        00:01:30    172.31.11.4   Serial0.1
10.0.0.12         1    FULL/  -        00:00:37    10.11.0.2     Serial0.2
10.0.0.12         1    FULL/  -        00:00:30    10.1.0.2      Serial1
P1R1#
```

No, there is no DR/BDR on the S0.2 subinterface.

**Step 14**  At the edge routers, verify the OSPF routes in the IP routing table. You might not see routes from every pod, depending on the number of pods in use.

**Solution:**

```
P1R1#show ip route
<output omitted>
Gateway of last resort is not set

     172.31.0.0/16 is variably subnetted, 6 subnets, 2 masks
O       172.31.22.4/32 [110/64] via 172.31.11.4, 00:04:26, Serial0.1
O       172.31.22.1/32 [110/1626] via 172.31.11.4, 00:04:26, Serial0.1
O       172.31.22.2/32 [110/1626] via 172.31.11.4, 00:04:26, Serial0.1
C       172.31.11.0/24 is directly connected, Serial0.1
O       172.31.11.2/32 [110/1626] via 172.31.11.4, 00:04:26, Serial0.1
O       172.31.11.4/32 [110/64] via 172.31.11.4, 00:04:26, Serial0.1
     10.0.0.0/24 is subnetted, 11 subnets
C       10.11.0.0 is directly connected, Serial0.2
O IA    10.2.0.0 [110/3188] via 172.31.11.4, 00:04:17, Serial0.1
O       10.1.3.0 [110/1572] via 10.1.1.3, 00:04:17, Ethernet0
O IA    10.2.1.0 [110/1636] via 172.31.11.4, 00:04:17, Serial0.1
O       10.1.2.0 [110/74] via 10.11.0.2, 00:04:17, Serial0.2
O IA    10.2.2.0 [110/1636] via 172.31.11.4, 00:04:18, Serial0.1
C       10.1.1.0 is directly connected, Ethernet0
O IA    10.2.3.0 [110/3198] via 172.31.11.4, 00:04:18, Serial0.1
C       10.1.0.0 is directly connected, Serial1
O IA    10.22.0.0 [110/1690] via 172.31.11.4, 00:04:18, Serial0.1
O E2    10.254.0.0 [110/50] via 172.31.11.4, 00:04:18, Serial0.1
P1R1#
```

**Step 15**  At the internal routers, verify the OSPF routes in the IP routing table.

**Solution:**

```
P1R3#show ip route
<output omitted>
Gateway of last resort is not set

     172.31.0.0/32 is subnetted, 6 subnets
```

*continues*

```
O IA    172.31.22.4 [110/74] via 10.1.1.1, 00:05:41, Ethernet0
O IA    172.31.22.1 [110/1636] via 10.1.1.1, 00:05:41, Ethernet0
O IA    172.31.22.2 [110/1636] via 10.1.1.1, 00:05:41, Ethernet0
O IA    172.31.11.1 [110/10] via 10.1.1.1, 00:05:41, Ethernet0
O IA    172.31.11.2 [110/74] via 10.1.1.1, 00:05:41, Ethernet0
O IA    172.31.11.4 [110/74] via 10.1.1.1, 00:05:41, Ethernet0
        10.0.0.0/8 is variably subnetted, 12 subnets, 2 masks
O       10.11.0.0/24 [110/74] via 10.1.1.1, 00:05:42, Ethernet0
C       10.200.200.13/32 is directly connected, Loopback0
O IA    10.2.0.0/24 [110/3198] via 10.1.1.1, 00:05:42, Ethernet0
C       10.1.3.0/24 is directly connected, Serial0
O IA    10.2.1.0/24 [110/1646] via 10.1.1.1, 00:05:42, Ethernet0
O       10.1.2.0/24 [110/84] via 10.1.1.1, 00:05:43, Ethernet0
O IA    10.2.2.0/24 [110/1646] via 10.1.1.1, 00:05:43, Ethernet0
C       10.1.1.0/24 is directly connected, Ethernet0
O IA    10.2.3.0/24 [110/3208] via 10.1.1.1, 00:05:43, Ethernet0
O       10.1.0.0/24 [110/1572] via 10.1.1.1, 00:05:43, Ethernet0
O IA    10.22.0.0/24 [110/1700] via 10.1.1.1, 00:05:43, Ethernet0
O E2    10.254.0.0/24 [110/50] via 10.1.1.1, 00:05:43, Ethernet0
P1R3#
```

**Step 16** Use the **show ip protocols** command to verify the OSPF routing process at the edge and internal routers. How many areas does the edge router belong to? How many areas does the internal router belong to?

**Solution:**

```
P1R1#show ip protocols
Routing Protocol is "ospf 1"
  Outgoing update filter list for all interfaces is not set
  Incoming update filter list for all interfaces is not set
  Router ID 10.0.0.11
  It is an area border router
  Number of areas in this router is 2. 2 normal 0 stub 0 nssa
  Maximum path: 4
  Routing for Networks:
    10.1.0.0 0.0.255.255 area 1
    10.11.0.0 0.0.0.255 area 1
    172.31.1.0 0.0.0.255 area 0
    172.31.11.0 0.0.0.255 area 0
  Routing Information Sources:
    Gateway         Distance      Last Update
    200.200.200.200     110       00:09:24
    100.100.100.100     110       00:45:37
    10.0.0.11           110       00:09:24
    10.200.200.14       110       01:06:52
    10.0.0.12           110       00:09:24
    10.200.200.13       110       00:09:24
    10.1.2.2            110       01:32:16
    10.1.3.3            110       01:40:32
    10.1.1.1            110       01:36:50
    Gateway         Distance      Last Update
    10.1.3.4            110       01:50:15
    10.0.0.22           110       00:09:26
```

```
     10.0.0.21          110      00:09:26
     172.31.1.2         110      01:50:25
     172.31.1.1         110      01:50:25
   Distance: (default is 110)

P1R1#
P1R3#show ip protocols
Routing Protocol is "ospf 1"
  Outgoing update filter list for all interfaces is not set
  Incoming update filter list for all interfaces is not set
  Router ID 10.200.200.13
  Number of areas in this router is 1. 1 normal 0 stub 0 nssa
  Maximum path: 4
  Routing for Networks:
    10.1.0.0 0.0.255.255 area 1
  Routing Information Sources:
    Gateway          Distance      Last Update
    200.200.200.200     110        00:09:31
    100.100.100.100     110        00:45:45
    10.0.0.11           110        00:09:31
    10.200.200.14       110        01:07:00
    10.0.0.12           110        00:09:31
    10.200.200.13       110        00:09:32
    10.1.2.2            110        01:32:24
    10.1.1.1            110        01:37:07
  Distance: (default is 110)

P1R3#
```

The edge router belongs to two areas; the internal router belongs to one area.

## Exercise Verification

You have successfully completed this exercise when you achieve these results:

- You have configured OSPF over a point-to-multipoint and point-to-point Frame Relay connection.

- You can ping the BBR2 router from your pod.

# Solution to Configuration Exercise 5-3: Understanding the OSPF Database and Tuning OSPF

This section provides the answers to the questions in the Configuration Exercise.

---

**NOTE**   Some answers provided cover multiple steps; the answers are given after the last step to which that answer applies.

---

# Solution to Task 1: Examining the OSPF Database

**Step 1** On all of your pod routers, use the **show ip ospf database** command to display the OSPF database. This database shows all LSAs stored in the router.

**Solution:**

```
P1R1#show ip ospf database
        OSPF Router with ID (10.0.0.11) (Process ID 1)
                Router Link States (Area 0)

Link ID             ADV Router          Age     Seq#        Checksum Link count
10.0.0.11           10.0.0.11           1474    0x80000006 0x9051   2
10.0.0.12           10.0.0.12           1415    0x80000006 0xA439   2
10.0.0.21           10.0.0.21           1606    0x80000006 0x6750   2
10.0.0.22           10.0.0.22           1606    0x80000006 0x7B38   2
100.100.100.100 100.100.100.100 2865            0x80000047 0x13F7   2
200.200.200.200 200.200.200.200 1415            0x80000046 0x66C9   6


                Net Link States (Area 0)

Link ID             ADV Router          Age     Seq#        Checksum
172.31.1.3          100.100.100.100 2790        0x80000002 0xE24D
172.31.2.3          100.100.100.100 3745        0x80000001 0x8082


                Summary Net Link States (Area 0)

Link ID             ADV Router          Age     Seq#        Checksum
10.1.0.0            10.0.0.11           1486    0x80000001 0x9963
10.1.0.0            10.0.0.12           1453    0x80000001 0x9368
10.1.1.0            10.0.0.11           1494    0x80000001 0xB75A
10.1.1.0            10.0.0.12           699     0x80000002 0x329D
10.1.2.0            10.0.0.11           697     0x80000002 0x2DA2
10.1.2.0            10.0.0.12           1453    0x80000001 0xA669
10.1.3.0            10.0.0.11           1494    0x80000001 0xDC13
10.1.3.0            10.0.0.12           1453    0x80000001 0xD618
10.2.0.0            10.0.0.21           1640    0x80000001 0x51A0
10.2.0.0            10.0.0.22           1622    0x80000001 0x4BA5
10.2.1.0            10.0.0.21           1640    0x80000001 0x6F97
10.2.1.0            10.0.0.22           1261    0x80000002 0xE9DA
10.2.2.0            10.0.0.21           1262    0x80000002 0xE4DF
10.2.2.0            10.0.0.22           1622    0x80000001 0x5EA6
10.2.3.0            10.0.0.21           1640    0x80000001 0x9450
10.2.3.0            10.0.0.22           1622    0x80000001 0x8E55
10.11.0.0           10.0.0.11           709     0x80000002 0x666B
10.11.0.0           10.0.0.12           732     0x80000001 0x626F
10.22.0.0           10.0.0.21           1273    0x80000001 0xA716
10.22.0.0           10.0.0.22           1262    0x80000002 0x9F1C


                Router Link States (Area 1)

Link ID             ADV Router          Age     Seq#        Checksum Link count
10.0.0.11           10.0.0.11           704     0x8000000C 0x630B   5
10.0.0.12           10.0.0.12           706     0x8000000C 0x4A1E   5
```

```
10.200.200.13    10.200.200.13    212      0x8000000A 0x7418   3
10.200.200.14    10.200.200.14    437      0x80000009 0xF88E   3

                 Net Link States (Area 1)

Link ID          ADV Router       Age      Seq#       Checksum
10.1.1.1         10.0.0.11        501      0x80000003 0xD087
10.1.2.2         10.0.0.12        256      0x80000003 0xCD85

                 Summary Net Link States (Area 1)

Link ID          ADV Router       Age      Seq#       Checksum
10.2.0.0         10.0.0.11        1476     0x80000001 0x4B50
10.2.0.0         10.0.0.12        1410     0x80000001 0x4555
10.2.1.0         10.0.0.11        1476     0x80000001 0x6947
10.2.1.0         10.0.0.12        1410     0x80000001 0x634C
10.2.2.0         10.0.0.11        1476     0x80000001 0x5E51
10.2.2.0         10.0.0.12        1411     0x80000001 0x5856
10.2.3.0         10.0.0.11        1477     0x80000001 0x8EFF
10.2.3.0         10.0.0.12        1411     0x80000001 0x8805
10.22.0.0        10.0.0.11        1273     0x80000001 0xA1C5
10.22.0.0        10.0.0.12        1274     0x80000001 0x9BCA
172.31.11.1      10.0.0.11        1488     0x80000001 0x2F21
172.31.11.1      10.0.0.12        1412     0x80000001 0xE608
172.31.11.2      10.0.0.11        1411     0x80000001 0xE20C
172.31.11.2      10.0.0.12        1447     0x80000001 0x1F2F
172.31.11.4      10.0.0.11        1478     0x80000001 0x9379
172.31.11.4      10.0.0.12        1412     0x80000001 0x8D7E
172.31.22.1      10.0.0.11        1478     0x80000001 0x7371
172.31.22.1      10.0.0.12        1412     0x80000001 0x6D76
172.31.22.2      10.0.0.11        1478     0x80000001 0x697A
172.31.22.2      10.0.0.12        1412     0x80000001 0x637F
172.31.22.4      10.0.0.11        1478     0x80000001 0x1AE7
172.31.22.4      10.0.0.12        1412     0x80000001 0x14EC

                 Summary ASB Link States (Area 1)

Link ID          ADV Router       Age      Seq#       Checksum
200.200.200.200 10.0.0.11        1478     0x80000001 0x4D76
200.200.200.200 10.0.0.12        1413     0x80000001 0x477B

                 Type-5 AS External Link States

Link ID          ADV Router       Age      Seq#       Checksum Tag
10.254.0.0       100.100.100.100 3431     0x80000026 0x9032    0
10.254.0.0       200.200.200.200 1339     0x80000024 0xD062    0
P1R1#

P1R3#show ip ospf database

        OSPF Router with ID (10.200.200.13) (Process ID 1)
```

*continues*

```
                        Router Link States (Area 1)

Link ID             ADV Router          Age          Seq#         Checksum Link count
10.0.0.11           10.0.0.11           883          0x8000000C 0x630B    5
10.0.0.12           10.0.0.12           884          0x8000000C 0x4A1E    5
10.200.200.13       10.200.200.13       388          0x8000000A 0x7418    3
10.200.200.14       10.200.200.14       613          0x80000009 0xF88E    3

                        Net Link States (Area 1)

Link ID             ADV Router          Age          Seq#         Checksum
10.1.1.1            10.0.0.11           678          0x80000003 0xD087
10.1.2.2            10.0.0.12           434          0x80000003 0xCD85

                        Summary Net Link States (Area 1)

Link ID             ADV Router          Age          Seq#         Checksum
10.2.0.0            10.0.0.11           1654         0x80000001 0x4B50
10.2.0.0            10.0.0.12           1588         0x80000001 0x4555
10.2.1.0            10.0.0.11           1654         0x80000001 0x6947
10.2.1.0            10.0.0.12           1589         0x80000001 0x634C
10.2.2.0            10.0.0.11           1655         0x80000001 0x5E51
10.2.2.0            10.0.0.12           1589         0x80000001 0x5856
10.2.3.0            10.0.0.11           1655         0x80000001 0x8EFF
10.2.3.0            10.0.0.12           1589         0x80000001 0x8805
10.22.0.0           10.0.0.11           1451         0x80000001 0xA1C5
10.22.0.0           10.0.0.12           1452         0x80000001 0x9BCA
172.31.11.1         10.0.0.11           1665         0x80000001 0x2F21
172.31.11.1         10.0.0.12           1589         0x80000001 0xE608
172.31.11.2         10.0.0.11           1588         0x80000001 0xE20C
172.31.11.2         10.0.0.12           1625         0x80000001 0x1F2F
172.31.11.4         10.0.0.11           1655         0x80000001 0x9379
172.31.11.4         10.0.0.12           1589         0x80000001 0x8D7E
172.31.22.1         10.0.0.11           1655         0x80000001 0x7371
172.31.22.1         10.0.0.12           1589         0x80000001 0x6D76
172.31.22.2         10.0.0.11           1656         0x80000001 0x697A
172.31.22.2         10.0.0.12           1590         0x80000001 0x637F
172.31.22.4         10.0.0.11           1656         0x80000001 0x1AE7
172.31.22.4         10.0.0.12           1590         0x80000001 0x14EC

                        Summary ASB Link States (Area 1)

Link ID             ADV Router          Age          Seq#         Checksum
200.200.200.200 10.0.0.11              1656         0x80000001 0x4D76
200.200.200.200 10.0.0.12              1591         0x80000001 0x477B

                        Type-5 AS External Link States

Link ID             ADV Router          Age          Seq#         Checksum Tag
10.254.0.0          100.100.100.100 3609            0x80000026 0x9032    0
10.254.0.0          200.200.200.200 1517            0x80000024 0xD062    0
P1R3#
```

Table 5-17 explains some of the displayed fields.

**Table 5-17**    *Displayed Fields*

| Field | Description |
|-------|-------------|
| ADV Router | The advertising router's RID. |
| Age | The LSA's age. |
| Checksum | The checksum of the LSA's contents. |
| Link Count | The number of interfaces on the router. Each serial interface counts as two links, and each Ethernet interface counts as one link. |
| Link ID | A value that uniquely identifies a specific LSA. |
| Seq# | The sequence number, used to detect older or duplicate LSAs. |
| Tag | Administratively used to recognize routes introduced through a specific redistribution process. |

Do you see LSA types 1, 2, 3, 4, and 5 in the OSPF database?

You see types 1, 2, 3, and 5.

On the edge routers, do you see LSA information about area 0 and area *x*?

Yes. For example, P1R1 sees information about area 0 and area 1.

On the internal routers, do you see LSA information about area *x* only?

Yes.

**Step 2**    Use the **show ip ospf database external** command on your edge routers to display all of the type 5 LSAs in the OSPF database. The core router, BBR2, is redistributing the 10.254.0.0/24 network into OSPF. Determine if there is a type 5 LSA about the 10.254.0.0 network.

**Solution:**

```
P1R1#show ip ospf database external

        OSPF Router with ID (10.0.0.11) (Process ID 1)


                Type-5 AS External Link States

  Routing Bit Set on this LSA
  LS age: 1599
  Options: (No TOS-capability, DC)
  LS Type: AS External Link
  Link State ID: 10.254.0.0 (External Network Number )
  Advertising Router: 200.200.200.200
  LS Seq Number: 80000024
  Checksum: 0xD062
  Length: 36
```

```
Network Mask: /24
      Metric Type: 2 (Larger than any link state path)
      TOS: 0
      Metric: 50
      Forward Address: 0.0.0.0
      External Route Tag: 0

P1R1#
```

# Solution to Task 2: OSPF Area Route Summarization

In this task, you identify how to bring the benefits of summarization to OSPF. Summarization reduces the size of routing tables, reduces routing update traffic, and minimizes the impact of flapping lines. In addition, it minimizes processing and memory requirements for all routers.

**Step 1**    At the edge routers, summarize the pod networks to $10.x.0.0/16$ from area $x$ using the **area $x$ range** command under the OSPF routing process.

**Solution:**

```
P1R1(config)#router ospf 1
P1R1(config-router)#area 1 range 10.1.0.0 255.255.0.0

P1R2(config)#router ospf 1
P1R2(config-router)#area 1 range 10.1.0.0 255.255.0.0
```

**Step 2**    From the edge router, Telnet to the BBR2 router ($172.31.xx.4$), and examine the routing table on BBR2.

**Solution:**

```
BBR2>show ip route
<output omitted>
Gateway of last resort is not set

     172.31.0.0/16 is variably subnetted, 9 subnets, 3 masks
O       172.31.22.1/32 [110/1562] via 172.31.22.1, 00:35:02, Serial0.2
C       172.31.22.0/24 is directly connected, Serial0.2
O       172.31.22.2/32 [110/1562] via 172.31.22.2, 00:35:02, Serial0.2
B       172.31.2.0/24 [20/0] via 10.254.0.1, 00:59:05
B       172.31.1.0/24 [20/0] via 10.254.0.1, 01:16:34
R       172.31.0.0/16 [120/1] via 10.254.0.1, 00:00:03, Ethernet0
C       172.31.11.0/24 is directly connected, Serial0.1
O       172.31.11.1/32 [110/1562] via 172.31.11.1, 00:35:02, Serial0.1
O       172.31.11.2/32 [110/1562] via 172.31.11.2, 00:35:02, Serial0.1
     10.0.0.0/8 is variably subnetted, 7 subnets, 2 masks
O IA    10.11.0.0/24 [110/1626] via 172.31.11.2, 00:23:22, Serial0.1
                     [110/1626] via 172.31.11.1, 00:23:22, Serial0.1
O IA    10.2.0.0/24 [110/3124] via 172.31.22.2, 00:00:03, Serial0.2
O IA    10.2.0.0/16 [110/1572] via 172.31.22.1, 00:00:03, Serial0.2
                    [110/1572] via 172.31.22.2, 00:00:03, Serial0.2
B       10.97.97.0/24 [20/0] via 10.254.0.3, 20:10:02
O IA    10.1.0.0/16 [110/1572] via 172.31.11.1, 00:01:14, Serial0.1
                    [110/1572] via 172.31.11.2, 00:01:14, Serial0.1
```

```
O IA    10.22.0.0/24 [110/1626] via 172.31.22.1, 00:32:36, Serial0.2
                     [110/1626] via 172.31.22.2, 00:32:36, Serial0.2
C       10.254.0.0/24 is directly connected, Ethernet0
BBR2>
```

Notice that BBR2 recognizes two paths to the pod 10.x.0.0/16 network. It no longer recognizes each of the pod /24 links (10.x.0.0/24, 10.x.1.0/24, 10.x.2.0/24, and 10.x.3.0/24).

BBR2 still recognizes the 10.xx.0.0/24 link, because it is not part of the summarized range.

**Step 3**  Determine the changes summarization made to the routing table on the edge routers. Is the routing table reduced on the edge routers? Explain why there is a route to Null0.

**Solution**:

The routing table is smaller following summarization. P1R1 knows how to get to the 10.1.x.0 subnets—it uses a mask of 24 bits for those routes. P1R1 routes to interface Null0 (in other words, it discards) packets that belong to network 10.1.x.0 for which it doesn't have a more precise match of 24 bits. This Null0 route is the result of having "told the world" that you know how to get to any subnetworks 10.1.x.0 when you summarized earlier.

```
P1R1#show ip route
<output omitted>
Gateway of last resort is not set

     172.31.0.0/16 is variably subnetted, 6 subnets, 2 masks
O        172.31.22.4/32 [110/64] via 172.31.11.4, 00:04:03, Serial0.1
O        172.31.22.1/32 [110/1626] via 172.31.11.4, 00:04:03, Serial0.1
O        172.31.22.2/32 [110/1626] via 172.31.11.4, 00:04:03, Serial0.1
C        172.31.11.0/24 is directly connected, Serial0.1
O        172.31.11.2/32 [110/1626] via 172.31.11.4, 00:04:03, Serial0.1
O        172.31.11.4/32 [110/64] via 172.31.11.4, 00:04:03, Serial0.1
     10.0.0.0/8 is variably subnetted, 9 subnets, 2 masks
C        10.11.0.0/24 is directly connected, Serial0.2
O IA     10.2.0.0/16 [110/1636] via 172.31.11.4, 00:02:25, Serial0.1
O        10.1.3.0/24 [110/1572] via 10.1.1.3, 00:04:04, Ethernet0
O        10.1.2.0/24 [110/74] via 10.11.0.2, 00:04:04, Serial0.2
C        10.1.1.0/24 is directly connected, Ethernet0
O        10.1.0.0/16 is a summary, 00:04:05, Null0
C        10.1.0.0/24 is directly connected, Serial1
O IA     10.22.0.0/24 [110/1690] via 172.31.11.4, 00:04:05, Serial0.1
O E2     10.254.0.0/24 [110/50] via 172.31.11.4, 00:04:05, Serial0.1
```

**Step 4**  Configure the pod OSPF area as a stub area (remember to configure both the edge and internal routers, because the **stub** flag is included in hellos). Notice the error messages and that no adjacency is established until both routers agree that they are stubs. What changes do you expect to occur with the implementation of a stub?

**Solution:**

```
P1R1(config)#router ospf 1
P1R1(config-router)#area 1 stub

P1R2(config)#router ospf 1
P1R2(config-router)#area 1 stub
P1R2(config-router)#
Mar  1 17:08:42 EST: %OSPF-5-ADJCHG: Process 1, Nbr 10.0.0.11 on Serial0.2 from
    FULL to DOWN, Neighbor Down: Adjacency forced to reset
Mar  1 17:08:42 EST: %OSPF-5-ADJCHG: Process 1, Nbr 10.0.0.11 on Serial1 from
    FULL to DOWN, Neighbor Down: Adjacency forced to reset
Mar  1 17:08:42 EST: %OSPF-5-ADJCHG: Process 1, Nbr 10.200.200.14 on
    Ethernet0 from FULL to DOWN, Neighbor Down: Adjacency forced to reset
Mar  1 17:08:49 EST: %OSPF-5-ADJCHG: Process 1, Nbr 10.0.0.11 on Serial1 from
    LOADING to FULL, Loading Done
P1R2(config-router)#

P1R3(config)#router ospf 1
P1R3(config-router)#area 1 stub

P1R4(config)#router ospf 1
P1R4(config-router)#area 1 stub
P1R4(config-router)#
Mar  1 17:09:19 EST: %OSPF-5-ADJCHG: Process 1, Nbr 10.200.200.13 on
    Serial0 from FULL to DOWN, Neighbor Down: Adjacency forced to reset
Mar  1 17:09:26 EST: %OSPF-5-ADJCHG: Process 1, Nbr 10.0.0.12 on Ethernet0 from
    LOADING to FULL, Loading Done
Mar  1 17:09:28 EST: %OSPF-5-ADJCHG: Process 1, Nbr 10.200.200.13 on
    Serial0 from LOADING to FULL, Loading Done
P1R4#
```

With the implementation of the stub network, you expect the routing tables of all routers in the pod to be smaller.

**Step 5**   Examine the edge (P*x*R1 or P*x*R2) and internal (P*x*R3 or P*x*R4) routing tables. Determine if any interarea OSPF routes are in the internal routers and the reason for their presence.

Notice that the internal routers do not have any external routes. The ABR (edge router) generates a default route to the internal routers for reaching external networks.

**Solution:**

```
P1R1#show ip route
<output omitted>
Gateway of last resort is not set

     172.31.0.0/16 is variably subnetted, 6 subnets, 2 masks
O       172.31.22.4/32 [110/64] via 172.31.11.4, 00:06:43, Serial0.1
O       172.31.22.1/32 [110/1626] via 172.31.11.4, 00:06:43, Serial0.1
O       172.31.22.2/32 [110/1626] via 172.31.11.4, 00:06:43, Serial0.1
```

```
C       172.31.11.0/24 is directly connected, Serial0.1
O       172.31.11.2/32 [110/1626] via 172.31.11.4, 00:06:43, Serial0.1
O       172.31.11.4/32 [110/64] via 172.31.11.4, 00:06:43, Serial0.1
        10.0.0.0/8 is variably subnetted, 9 subnets, 2 masks
C       10.11.0.0/24 is directly connected, Serial0.2
O       10.1.3.0/24 [110/1572] via 10.1.1.3, 00:05:34, Ethernet0
O IA    10.2.0.0/16 [110/1636] via 172.31.11.4, 00:00:04, Serial0.1
O       10.1.2.0/24 [110/74] via 10.11.0.2, 00:05:34, Serial0.2
C       10.1.1.0/24 is directly connected, Ethernet0
O       10.1.0.0/16 is a summary, 00:05:35, Null0
C       10.1.0.0/24 is directly connected, Serial1
O IA    10.22.0.0/24 [110/1690] via 172.31.11.4, 00:05:35, Serial0.1
O E2    10.254.0.0/24 [110/50] via 172.31.11.4, 00:05:35, Serial0.1
P1R1#


P1R3#show ip route
<output omitted>
Gateway of last resort is 10.1.1.1 to network 0.0.0.0

        172.31.0.0/32 is subnetted, 6 subnets
O IA    172.31.22.4 [110/74] via 10.1.1.1, 00:05:45, Ethernet0
O IA    172.31.22.1 [110/1636] via 10.1.1.1, 00:05:45, Ethernet0
O IA    172.31.22.2 [110/1636] via 10.1.1.1, 00:05:45, Ethernet0
O IA    172.31.11.1 [110/10] via 10.1.1.1, 00:05:45, Ethernet0
O IA    172.31.11.2 [110/74] via 10.1.1.1, 00:05:45, Ethernet0
O IA    172.31.11.4 [110/74] via 10.1.1.1, 00:05:45, Ethernet0
        10.0.0.0/8 is variably subnetted, 8 subnets, 3 masks
O       10.11.0.0/24 [110/74] via 10.1.1.1, 00:05:46, Ethernet0
C       10.200.200.13/32 is directly connected, Loopback0
O IA    10.2.0.0/16 [110/1646] via 10.1.1.1, 00:05:46, Ethernet0
C       10.1.3.0/24 is directly connected, Serial0
O       10.1.2.0/24 [110/84] via 10.1.1.1, 00:05:46, Ethernet0
C       10.1.1.0/24 is directly connected, Ethernet0
O       10.1.0.0/24 [110/1572] via 10.1.1.1, 00:05:47, Ethernet0
O IA    10.22.0.0/24 [110/1700] via 10.1.1.1, 00:05:47, Ethernet0
O*IA 0.0.0.0/0 [110/11] via 10.1.1.1, 00:05:47, Ethernet0
P1R3#
```

There are IA routes on the internal router, showing routes in the other pod and the backbone.

The internal routers do not have any external (E2) routes, only a default (0.0.0.0) IA route.

**Step 6**    Configure the OSPF area of the pod as totally stubby. Remember that only the ABR requires the command to configure the area as totally stubby.

**Solution:**

```
P1R1(config)#router ospf 1
P1R1(config-router)#area 1 stub no-summary
Mar  1 17:19:32 EST: %OSPF-5-ADJCHG: Process 1, Nbr 10.0.0.12 on Serial0.2 from
    FULL to DOWN, Neighbor Down: Adjacency forced to reset
Mar  1 17:19:32 EST: %OSPF-5-ADJCHG: Process 1, Nbr 10.0.0.12 on Serial1 from
    FULL to DOWN, Neighbor Down: Adjacency forced to reset
```

*continues*

```
Mar  1 17:19:32 EST: %OSPF-5-ADJCHG: Process 1, Nbr 10.200.200.13 on
    Ethernet0 from FULL to DOWN, Neighbor Down: Adjacency forced to reset

P1R2(config)#router ospf 1
Mar  1 17:19:35 EST: %OSPF-5-ADJCHG: Process 1, Nbr 10.0.0.11 on Serial1 from
    LOADING to FULL, Loading Done
Mar  1 17:19:40 EST: %OSPF-5-ADJCHG: Process 1, Nbr 10.0.0.11 on Serial0.2 from
    LOADING to FULL, Loading Done
P1R2(config-router)#area 1 stub no-summary
Mar  1 17:19:49 EST: %OSPF-5-ADJCHG: Process 1, Nbr 10.0.0.11 on Serial0.2 from
    FULL to DOWN, Neighbor Down: Adjacency forced to reset
Mar  1 17:19:49 EST: %OSPF-5-ADJCHG: Process 1, Nbr 10.0.0.11 on Serial1 from
    FULL to DOWN, Neighbor Down: Adjacency forced to reset
Mar  1 17:19:49 EST: %OSPF-5-ADJCHG: Process 1, Nbr 10.200.200.14 on
    Ethernet0 from FULL to DOWN, Neighbor Down: Adjacency forced to reset
Mar  1 17:19:52 EST: %OSPF-5-ADJCHG: Process 1, Nbr 10.0.0.11 on Serial0.2 from
    LOADING to FULL, Loading Done
```

**Step 7**  Ping the TFTP server from the internal routers to verify connectivity.

**Solution:**

```
P1R1#ping 10.254.0.254

Type escape sequence to abort.
Sending 5, 100-byte ICMP Echos to 10.254.0.254, timeout is 2 seconds:
!!!!!
Success rate is 100 percent (5/5), round-trip min/avg/max = 32/76/240 ms
P1R1#
BBR2>exit

[Connection to bbr2 closed by foreign host]
P1R2#ping 10.254.0.254

Type escape sequence to abort.
Sending 5, 100-byte ICMP Echos to 10.254.0.254, timeout is 2 seconds:
!!!!!
Success rate is 100 percent (5/5), round-trip min/avg/max = 32/32/36 ms
P1R2#
P1R3#ping 10.254.0.254

Type escape sequence to abort.
Sending 5, 100-byte ICMP Echos to 10.254.0.254, timeout is 2 seconds:
!!!!!
Success rate is 100 percent (5/5), round-trip min/avg/max = 48/50/56 ms
P1R3#
P1R4>ping 10.254.0.254

Type escape sequence to abort.
Sending 5, 100-byte ICMP Echos to 10.254.0.254, timeout is 2 seconds:
!!!!!
Success rate is 100 percent (5/5), round-trip min/avg/max = 48/91/256 ms
P1R4>
```

**Step 8**   Examine the edge (P*x*R1 or P*x*R2) and internal (P*x*R3 or P*x*R4) routing
tables.

Determine if any interarea OSPF routes are in the internal routers and the
reason for their presence.

**Solution:**

The internal routers have, as an interarea route, a default route pointing to their ABR.

```
P1R1#show ip route
<output omitted>
Gateway of last resort is not set

     172.31.0.0/16 is variably subnetted, 6 subnets, 2 masks
O       172.31.22.4/32 [110/64] via 172.31.11.4, 00:03:56, Serial0.1
O       172.31.22.1/32 [110/1626] via 172.31.11.4, 00:03:56, Serial0.1
O       172.31.22.2/32 [110/1626] via 172.31.11.4, 00:03:56, Serial0.1
C       172.31.11.0/24 is directly connected, Serial0.1
O       172.31.11.2/32 [110/1626] via 172.31.11.4, 00:03:56, Serial0.1
O       172.31.11.4/32 [110/64] via 172.31.11.4, 00:03:56, Serial0.1
     10.0.0.0/8 is variably subnetted, 9 subnets, 2 masks
C       10.11.0.0/24 is directly connected, Serial0.2
O IA    10.2.0.0/16 [110/1636] via 172.31.11.4, 00:03:57, Serial0.1
O       10.1.3.0/24 [110/1572] via 10.1.1.3, 00:03:58, Ethernet0
O       10.1.2.0/24 [110/74] via 10.11.0.2, 00:03:58, Serial0.2
C       10.1.1.0/24 is directly connected, Ethernet0
O       10.1.0.0/16 is a summary, 00:03:58, Null0
C       10.1.0.0/24 is directly connected, Serial1
O IA    10.22.0.0/24 [110/1690] via 172.31.11.4, 00:03:58, Serial0.1
O E2    10.254.0.0/24 [110/50] via 172.31.11.4, 00:03:58, Serial0.1
P1R1#

P1R2#show ip route
<output omitted>
Gateway of last resort is not set

     172.31.0.0/16 is variably subnetted, 6 subnets, 2 masks
O       172.31.22.4/32 [110/64] via 172.31.11.4, 00:04:06, Serial0.1
O       172.31.22.1/32 [110/1626] via 172.31.11.4, 00:04:06, Serial0.1
O       172.31.22.2/32 [110/1626] via 172.31.11.4, 00:04:06, Serial0.1
C       172.31.11.0/24 is directly connected, Serial0.1
O       172.31.11.1/32 [110/1626] via 172.31.11.4, 00:04:06, Serial0.1
O       172.31.11.4/32 [110/64] via 172.31.11.4, 00:04:06, Serial0.1
     10.0.0.0/8 is variably subnetted, 9 subnets, 2 masks
C       10.11.0.0/24 is directly connected, Serial0.2
O IA    10.2.0.0/16 [110/1636] via 172.31.11.4, 00:04:07, Serial0.1
O       10.1.3.0/24 [110/1572] via 10.1.2.4, 00:04:07, Ethernet0
C       10.1.2.0/24 is directly connected, Ethernet0
O       10.1.1.0/24 [110/74] via 10.11.0.1, 00:04:07, Serial0.2
O       10.1.0.0/16 is a summary, 00:04:08, Null0
C       10.1.0.0/24 is directly connected, Serial1
O IA    10.22.0.0/24 [110/1690] via 172.31.11.4, 00:04:09, Serial0.1
```

*continues*

```
O E2    10.254.0.0/24 [110/50] via 172.31.11.4, 00:04:09, Serial0.1
P1R2#
P1R3#show ip route
<output omitted>
Gateway of last resort is 10.1.1.1 to network 0.0.0.0

     10.0.0.0/8 is variably subnetted, 6 subnets, 2 masks
O       10.11.0.0/24 [110/74] via 10.1.1.1, 00:04:10, Ethernet0
C       10.200.200.13/32 is directly connected, Loopback0
C       10.1.3.0/24 is directly connected, Serial0
O       10.1.2.0/24 [110/84] via 10.1.1.1, 00:04:10, Ethernet0
C       10.1.1.0/24 is directly connected, Ethernet0
O       10.1.0.0/24 [110/1572] via 10.1.1.1, 00:04:11, Ethernet0
O*IA 0.0.0.0/0 [110/11] via 10.1.1.1, 00:04:11, Ethernet0
P1R3#
P1R4>show ip route
<output omitted>
Gateway of last resort is 10.1.2.2 to network 0.0.0.0

     10.0.0.0/8 is variably subnetted, 6 subnets, 2 masks
O       10.11.0.0/24 [110/74] via 10.1.2.2, 00:04:16, Ethernet0
C       10.200.200.14/32 is directly connected, Loopback0
C       10.1.3.0/24 is directly connected, Serial0
C       10.1.2.0/24 is directly connected, Ethernet0
O       10.1.1.0/24 [110/84] via 10.1.2.2, 00:04:16, Ethernet0
O       10.1.0.0/24 [110/1572] via 10.1.2.2, 00:04:16, Ethernet0
O*IA 0.0.0.0/0 [110/11] via 10.1.2.2, 00:04:16, Ethernet0
P1R4>
P1R1#bbr2
Translating "bbr2"
Trying bbr2 (172.31.11.4)... Open


User Access Verification


Password:
BBR2>show ip route
<output omitted>
Gateway of last resort is not set

     172.31.0.0/16 is variably subnetted, 9 subnets, 3 masks
O       172.31.22.1/32 [110/1562] via 172.31.22.1, 00:04:37, Serial0.2
C       172.31.22.0/24 is directly connected, Serial0.2
O       172.31.22.2/32 [110/1562] via 172.31.22.2, 00:04:37, Serial0.2
B       172.31.2.0/24 [20/0] via 10.254.0.1, 00:06:49
B       172.31.1.0/24 [20/0] via 10.254.0.1, 00:06:49
R       172.31.0.0/16 [120/1] via 10.254.0.1, 00:00:10, Ethernet0
C       172.31.11.0/24 is directly connected, Serial0.1
O       172.31.11.1/32 [110/1562] via 172.31.11.1, 00:04:37, Serial0.1
O       172.31.11.2/32 [110/1562] via 172.31.11.2, 00:04:37, Serial0.1
     10.0.0.0/8 is variably subnetted, 6 subnets, 2 masks
O IA    10.11.0.0/24 [110/1626] via 172.31.11.1, 00:04:37, Serial0.1
                     [110/1626] via 172.31.11.2, 00:04:37, Serial0.1
```

```
O IA    10.2.0.0/16 [110/1572] via 172.31.22.1, 00:04:39, Serial0.2
                    [110/1572] via 172.31.22.2, 00:04:39, Serial0.2
B       10.97.97.0/24 [20/0] via 10.254.0.3, 00:06:51
O IA    10.1.0.0/16 [110/1572] via 172.31.11.1, 00:04:39, Serial0.1
                    [110/1572] via 172.31.11.2, 00:04:39, Serial0.1
O IA    10.22.0.0/24 [110/1626] via 172.31.22.1, 00:04:39, Serial0.2
                    [110/1626] via 172.31.22.2, 00:04:39, Serial0.2
C       10.254.0.0/24 is directly connected, Ethernet0
BBR2>
```

## Exercise Verification

You have successfully completed this exercise when you achieve these results:

- You have examined the OSPF database, and you understand the tools necessary to investigate the LSDB.

- You have configured your pod router area as an OSPF stub area and as a totally stub area.

- You have minimized routing table size by using route summarization without affecting reachability. You should still be able to ping all devices in your pod and in the core.

# Solution to Configuration Exercise 5-4: Configuring the OSPF Virtual Link

This section provides the answers to the questions in the Configuration Exercise.

---

**NOTE**    Some answers provided cover multiple steps; the answers are given after the last step to which that answer applies.

---

## Solution to Task: Configuring the OSPF Virtual Link

OSPF requires that all areas have a connection to area 0, the backbone. In this exercise, you create a discontiguous area and examine the resulting routing tables. You then configure a virtual link that connects the new area to area 0.

**Step 1**    Remove the OSPF stub configuration from all of the pod routers.

**Solution:**

```
P1R1(config)#router ospf 1
P1R1(config-router)#no area 1 stub no-summary
P1R1(config-router)#no area 1 stub
P1R2(config)#router ospf 1
P1R2(config-router)#no area 1 stub no-summary
```

*continues*

```
P1R2(config-router)#no area 1 stub
P1R3(config)#router ospf 1
P1R3(config-router)#no area 1 stub
P1R3(config-router)#
P1R4(config)#router ospf 1
P1R4(config-router)#no area 1 stub
```

**Step 2**  On the internal routers, P*x*R3 and P*x*R4, shut down the serial 0 interface, disconnecting the link between them.

**Solution:**

```
P1R3(config)#interface serial 0
P1R3(config-if)#shutdown
P1R4(config)#interface serial 0
P1R4(config-if)#shutdown
```

**Step 3**  Place the loopback interface on each internal router into a new OSPF area, using area number *x*00, where *x* is your pod number. This requires an additional network statement under the OSPF router configuration.

**Solution:**

```
P1R3(config)#router ospf 1
P1R3(config-router)#network 10.200.200.13 0.0.0.0 area 100
P1R3(config-router)#
P1R4#conf t
Enter configuration commands, one per line.  End with CNTL/Z.
P1R4(config)#router ospf 1
P1R4(config-router)#network 10.200.200.14 0.0.0.0 area 100
P1R4(config-router)#
```

**Step 4**  Examine the routing table on the edge routers, P*x*R1 and P*x*R2. Is the network for the internal router's loopback interface (10.200.200.*xy*) present in the routing table?

**Solution:**

```
P1R1#show ip route
<output omitted>
Gateway of last resort is not set

     172.31.0.0/16 is variably subnetted, 6 subnets, 2 masks
O       172.31.22.4/32 [110/64] via 172.31.11.4, 00:12:36, Serial0.1
O       172.31.22.1/32 [110/1626] via 172.31.11.4, 00:12:36, Serial0.1
O       172.31.22.2/32 [110/1626] via 172.31.11.4, 00:12:36, Serial0.1
C       172.31.11.0/24 is directly connected, Serial0.1
O       172.31.11.2/32 [110/1626] via 172.31.11.4, 00:12:36, Serial0.1
O       172.31.11.4/32 [110/64] via 172.31.11.4, 00:12:36, Serial0.1
     10.0.0.0/8 is variably subnetted, 8 subnets, 2 masks
C       10.11.0.0/24 is directly connected, Serial0.2
O IA    10.2.0.0/16 [110/1636] via 172.31.11.4, 00:10:13, Serial0.1
```

```
O       10.1.2.0/24 [110/74] via 10.11.0.2, 00:10:13, Serial0.2
C       10.1.1.0/24 is directly connected, Ethernet0
O       10.1.0.0/16 is a summary, 00:10:13, Null0
C       10.1.0.0/24 is directly connected, Serial1
O IA    10.22.0.0/24 [110/1690] via 172.31.11.4, 00:10:15, Serial0.1
O E2    10.254.0.0/24 [110/50] via 172.31.11.4, 00:10:15, Serial0.1
P1R1#

P1R3#show ip route
<output omitted>
Gateway of last resort is not set

     172.31.0.0/32 is subnetted, 6 subnets
O IA    172.31.22.4 [110/74] via 10.1.1.1, 00:07:09, Ethernet0
O IA    172.31.22.1 [110/1636] via 10.1.1.1, 00:07:09, Ethernet0
O IA    172.31.22.2 [110/1636] via 10.1.1.1, 00:07:09, Ethernet0
O IA    172.31.11.1 [110/10] via 10.1.1.1, 00:07:09, Ethernet0
O IA    172.31.11.2 [110/74] via 10.1.1.1, 00:07:09, Ethernet0
O IA    172.31.11.4 [110/74] via 10.1.1.1, 00:07:09, Ethernet0
     10.0.0.0/8 is variably subnetted, 8 subnets, 3 masks
O       10.11.0.0/24 [110/74] via 10.1.1.1, 00:10:22, Ethernet0
C       10.200.200.13/32 is directly connected, Loopback0
O IA    10.2.0.0/16 [110/1646] via 10.1.1.1, 00:07:10, Ethernet0
O       10.1.2.0/24 [110/84] via 10.1.1.1, 00:10:22, Ethernet0
C       10.1.1.0/24 is directly connected, Ethernet0
O       10.1.0.0/24 [110/1572] via 10.1.1.1, 00:10:23, Ethernet0
O IA    10.22.0.0/24 [110/1700] via 10.1.1.1, 00:07:10, Ethernet0
O E2    10.254.0.0/24 [110/50] via 10.1.1.1, 00:07:10, Ethernet0
P1R3#
```

No, there is not a route for the loopback interface of the internal routers on the edge routers.

**Step 5**   Because OSPF assumes that all areas have at least one interface in area 0, the internal routers do not advertise the loopback interface to the edge routers. However, area *x*00 does not border area 0. You remedy this by configuring a virtual link from area *x*00 to area 0. As the first step in configuring the virtual link, discover each router's RID.

**Solution:**

```
P1R1#show ip ospf neighbors

Neighbor ID      Pri   State          Dead Time   Address       Interface
10.200.200.13     0    FULL/DROTHER   00:00:39    10.1.1.3      Ethernet0
200.200.200.200   1    FULL/  -       00:01:51    172.31.11.4   Serial0.1
10.0.0.12         1    FULL/  -       00:00:31    10.11.0.2     Serial0.2
10.0.0.12         1    FULL/  -       00:00:31    10.1.0.2      Serial1
P1R1#
P1R2#show ip ospf neighbors

Neighbor ID      Pri   State          Dead Time   Address       Interface
10.200.200.14     0    FULL/DROTHER   00:00:38    10.1.2.4      Ethernet0
```

*continues*

```
200.200.200.200    1   FULL/  -      00:01:52   172.31.11.4   Serial0.1
10.0.0.11          1   FULL/  -      00:00:32   10.11.0.1     Serial0.2
10.0.0.11          1   FULL/  -      00:00:32   10.1.0.1      Serial1
P1R2#
P1R3#show ip ospf neighbors

Neighbor ID     Pri  State        Dead Time   Address      Interface
10.0.0.11         1  FULL/DR      00:00:37    10.1.1.1     Ethernet0
P1R3#
P1R4#show ip ospf neighbors

Neighbor ID     Pri  State        Dead Time   Address      Interface
10.0.0.12         1  FULL/DR      00:00:31    10.1.2.2     Ethernet0
P1R1#show ip ospf
 Routing Process "ospf 1" with ID 10.0.0.11 and Domain ID 0.0.0.1
 Supports only single TOS(TOS0) routes
[output deleted]
P1R2#show ip ospf
 Routing Process "ospf 1" with ID 10.0.0.12 and Domain ID 0.0.0.1
[output deleted]
P1R3#show ip ospf
 Routing Process "ospf 1" with ID 10.200.200.13 and Domain ID 0.0.0.1
[output deleted]
P1R4#show ip ospf
 Routing Process "ospf 1" with ID 10.200.200.14 and Domain ID 0.0.0.1
```

**Step 6**  Configure an OSPF virtual link from the internal router to the edge router through area *x*, where *x* is your pod number.

**Solution:**

```
P1R1(config)#router ospf 1
P1R1(config-router)#area 1 virtual-link 10.200.200.13

P1R3(config)#router ospf 1
P1R3(config-router)#area 1 virtual-link 10.0.0.11

P1R2(config)#router ospf 1
P1R2(config-router)#area 1 virtual-link 10.200.200.14

P1R4(config)#router ospf 1
P1R4(config-router)#area 1 virtual-link 10.0.0.12
```

**Step 7**  Verify that the virtual link is functioning.

**Solution:**

```
P1R3#show ip ospf virtual-link
Virtual Link OSPF_VL0 to router 10.0.0.11 is up
  Run as demand circuit
  DoNotAge LSA allowed.
  Transit area 1, via interface Ethernet0, Cost of using 10
  Transmit Delay is 1 sec, State POINT_TO_POINT,
```

```
Timer intervals configured, Hello 10, Dead 40, Wait 40, Retransmit 5
  Hello due in 00:00:04
  Adjacency State FULL (Hello suppressed)
  Index 1/2, retransmission queue length 0, number of retransmission 0
  First 0x0(0)/0x0(0) Next 0x0(0)/0x0(0)
  Last retransmission scan length is 0, maximum is 0
  Last retransmission scan time is 0 msec, maximum is 0 msec
```

**Step 8**  Verify that the network for the internal router's loopback interface now appears in the edge router's routing table.

**Solution:**

```
P1R1#show ip route
<output omitted>
Gateway of last resort is not set

     172.31.0.0/16 is variably subnetted, 6 subnets, 2 masks
O       172.31.22.4/32 [110/64] via 172.31.11.4, 00:00:11, Serial0.1
O       172.31.22.1/32 [110/1626] via 172.31.11.4, 00:00:11, Serial0.1
O       172.31.22.2/32 [110/1626] via 172.31.11.4, 00:00:11, Serial0.1
C       172.31.11.0/24 is directly connected, Serial0.1
O       172.31.11.2/32 [110/1626] via 172.31.11.4, 00:00:11, Serial0.1
O       172.31.11.4/32 [110/64] via 172.31.11.4, 00:00:11, Serial0.1
     10.0.0.0/8 is variably subnetted, 15 subnets, 3 masks
C       10.11.0.0/24 is directly connected, Serial0.2
O IA    10.200.200.14/32 [110/1637] via 172.31.11.4, 00:00:12, Serial0.1
O IA    10.200.200.13/32 [110/11] via 10.1.1.3, 00:00:12, Ethernet0
O IA    10.2.0.0/24 [110/3208] via 172.31.11.4, 00:00:12, Serial0.1
O IA    10.2.0.0/16 [110/1636] via 172.31.11.4, 00:00:12, Serial0.1
O IA    10.2.1.0/24 [110/1646] via 172.31.11.4, 00:00:13, Serial0.1
O       10.1.2.0/24 [110/74] via 10.11.0.2, 00:11:07, Serial0.2
O IA    10.2.2.0/24 [110/1646] via 172.31.11.4, 00:00:13, Serial0.1
C       10.1.1.0/24 is directly connected, Ethernet0
O       10.1.0.0/16 is a summary, 00:11:07, Null0
C       10.1.0.0/24 is directly connected, Serial1
O IA    10.200.200.24/32 [110/1637] via 172.31.11.4, 00:00:13, Serial0.1
O IA    10.22.0.0/24 [110/1690] via 172.31.11.4, 00:00:13, Serial0.1
O IA    10.200.200.23/32 [110/1637] via 172.31.11.4, 00:00:13, Serial0.1
O E2    10.254.0.0/24 [110/50] via 172.31.11.4, 00:00:13, Serial0.1
P1R1#
```

**Step 9**  On the internal router, issue the **show ip ospf** command. Which OSPF areas are active on this router?

**Solution:**

```
P1R3#show ip ospf
 Routing Process "ospf 1" with ID 10.200.200.13 and Domain ID 0.0.0.1
 Supports only single TOS(TOS0) routes
 Supports opaque LSA
 It is an area border router
```

*continues*

```
    SPF schedule delay 5 secs, Hold time between two SPFs 10 secs
    Minimum LSA interval 5 secs. Minimum LSA arrival 1 secs
    Number of external LSA 1. Checksum Sum 0xC468
    Number of opaque AS LSA 0. Checksum Sum 0x0
    Number of DCbitless external and opaque AS LSA 0
    Number of DoNotAge external and opaque AS LSA 0
    Number of areas in this router is 3. 3 normal 0 stub 0 nssa
    External flood list length 0
        Area BACKBONE(0)
            Number of interfaces in this area is 1
            Area has no authentication
            SPF algorithm executed 8 times
            Area ranges are
            Number of LSA 37. Checksum Sum 0x145E33
            Number of opaque link LSA 0. Checksum Sum 0x0
            Number of DCbitless LSA 0
            Number of indication LSA 0
            Number of DoNotAge LSA 31
            Flood list length 0
        Area 1
            Number of interfaces in this area is 2
            Area has no authentication
            SPF algorithm executed 59 times
            Area ranges are
            Number of LSA 72. Checksum Sum 0x200AEA
            Number of opaque link LSA 0. Checksum Sum 0x0
            Number of DCbitless LSA 0
            Number of indication LSA 0
            Number of DoNotAge LSA 0
            Flood list length 0
        Area 100
            Number of interfaces in this area is 1
            Area has no authentication
            SPF algorithm executed 3 times
            Area ranges are
            Number of LSA 21. Checksum Sum 0xA6235
            Number of opaque link LSA 0. Checksum Sum 0x0
            Number of DCbitless LSA 0
            Number of indication LSA 0
            Number of DoNotAge LSA 0
            Flood list length 0

P1R3#
```

OSPF treats the virtual link as if it was an interface belonging to area 0. Thus, you will see three areas active on the router—area $x$, area $x00$, and area 0.

# Exercise Verification

You have successfully completed this exercise when you achieve these results:

- You have used virtual links to heal a discontiguous area.

- You have used virtual links to create an arbitrary topology of areas.

# Review Questions

Answer the following questions, and then refer to Appendix G, "Answers to Review Questions," for the answers.

1 True or false: OSPF performs route summarization by default.

2 True or false: In a large network where topological changes are frequent, routers spend many CPU cycles recalculating the SPF algorithm and updating the routing table.

3 Match the type of router with its description:

| Type of Router | Description |
| --- | --- |
| 1—Internal router | A—A router that sits in the perimeter of the backbone area and that has at least one interface connected to area 0. It maintains OSPF routing information using the same procedures and algorithms as an internal router. |
| 2—Backbone router | B—A router that has interfaces attached to multiple areas, maintains separate LSDBs for each area to which it connects, and routes traffic destined for or arriving from other areas. This router is an exit point for the area, which means that routing information destined for another area can get there only via the local area's router. This kind of router can be configured to summarize the routing information from the LSDBs of its attached areas. This router distributes the routing information into the backbone. The backbone routers then forward the information to the other ABRs. An area can have one or more ABRs. |
| 3—ABR | C—A router that has all its interfaces in the same area with identical LSDBs. |
| 4—ASBR | D—A router that has at least one interface attached to an external internetwork (another AS), such as a non-OSPF network. This router can import non-OSPF network information to the OSPF network and vice versa; this process is called route redistribution. |

4 How many different types of LSAs are there?

    a. 5

    b. 9

    c. 10

    d. 11

5 What kind of router generates LSA type 5?

    a. DR

    b. ABR

    c. ASBR

    d. ADR

**6** True or false: By default, OSPF does not automatically summarize groups of contiguous subnets.

**7** A router advertises a type 1 LSA that floods to what?

    a. Immediate peers

    b. All other routers in the area where it originated

    c. Routers located in other areas

    d. All areas

**8** How does a routing table reflect the link-state information of an intra-area route?

    a. The route is marked with O.

    b. The route is marked with I.

    c. The route is marked with IO.

    d. The route is marked with EA.

**9** Which type of external route is the default?

    a. E1

    b. E2

    c. E5

    d. There is no default external route. OSPF adapts and chooses the most accurate one.

**10** E1 external routes calculate the cost by adding what?

    a. The internal cost of each link the packet crosses

    b. The external cost to the internal cost of each link the packet crosses

    c. The external cost only

    d. All area costs, even those that aren't used

**11** With OSPF, how is the OSPF metric calculated by default?

    a. OSPF calculates the OSPF metric for a router according to the bandwidth of all its interfaces.

    b. OSPF calculates the OSPF metric by referencing the DR.

    c. OSPF calculates the OSPF metric for an interface according to the interface's inverse bandwidth.

    d. OSPF calculates the OSPF metric by using the lowest bandwidth value among all of its interfaces.

**12** Why is configuring a stub area advantageous?

    a. It reduces the size of the LSDB inside an area.

    b. It increases the memory requirements for routers in that area.

    c. It further segments the hierarchy.

    d. It starts to behave like a distance vector routing protocol, thus speeding up convergence.

**13** A stub area is typically created using what kind of topology?

    a. Point-to-point

    b. Broadcast

    c. Hub-and-spoke

    d. Full-mesh

**14** True or false: By default, in normal areas, routers generate default routes.

**15** What command makes an OSPF router generate a default route?

    a. **ospf default-initiate**

    b. **default-information originate**

    c. **default information-initiate**

    d. **ospf information-originate**

**16** If your router has an interface faster than 100 Mbps that is used with OSPF, consider using the _____ command under the _____ process.

    a. **auto-cost reference-bandwidth**, OSPF

    b. **auto-cost reference-bandwidth**, interface

    c. **autocost reference-speed**, OSPF

    d. **autocost reference-speed**, interface

**17** True or false: OSPF design requires that all areas be directly connect to the backbone.

**18** True or false: Virtual links are very useful, and you should include them in your network architecture when designing a completely new OSPF network.

This chapter covers the following topics:

- Overview of IS-IS Routing and CLNS
- Understanding CLNS Addressing
- Basic Operations of IS-IS in a CLNS Environment
- Basic Operations of Integrated IS-IS in an IP and CLNS Environment
- Configuring Basic Integrated IS-IS

CHAPTER **6**

# Configuring the Intermediate System-to-Intermediate System Protocol

This chapter provides an overview of Intermediate System-to-Intermediate System (IS-IS) technology structures and protocols, as well as basic configuration examples. IS-IS is a part of the Open System Interconnection (OSI) suite of protocols. The OSI suite uses Connectionless Network Service (CLNS) to provide connectionless delivery of data, and the actual Layer 3 protocol is Connectionless Network Protocol (CLNP). CLNP is the solution for unreliable delivery of data, similar to IP. IS-IS uses CLNS addresses to identify the routers and build the link-state database. An understanding of CLNS address portions is required to configure and troubleshoot IS-IS.

### What's the Difference Between ISO and OSI?

The International Organization for Standardization (ISO) has been constituted to develop standards for data networking.

OSI protocols represent an international standardization program that facilitates multivendor equipment interoperability.

IS-IS operates in strictly CLNS terms; however, Integrated IS-IS supports IP routing as well as CLNS. IS-IS conforms itself to different data-link environments, such as Ethernet and Frame Relay.

Integrated IS-IS is also an IP routing protocol and requires knowledge of the configuration information for integrated IS-IS in a LAN environment and in a nonbroadcast multiaccess (NBMA) environment.

IS-IS contains the most important characteristics of Open Shortest Path First (OSPF) and Enhanced Interior Gateway Routing Protocol (EIGRP), because it supports variable-length subnet masking (VLSM) and converges quickly. Each protocol has advantages and disadvantages, but this commonality makes any of the three scalable and appropriate for supporting today's large-scale networks.

## Overview of IS-IS Routing and CLNS

IS-IS is a proven and extensible IP routing protocol that converges quickly and supports VLSM. IS-IS is a public standard, originally published as ISO 9542 and republished as RFC 995, *End System to Intermediate System Routing Exchange Protocol*. IS-IS offers support for IP and OSI protocols, called Integrated IS-IS or Dual IS-IS. Although not as common, IS-IS is comparable and in some cases preferred to OSPF. The following addresses some of the concepts necessary to develop an understanding of Integrated IS-IS.

# IS-IS Routing

IS-IS is the most popular and stable IP routing protocol in the Internet service provider (ISP) industry. The simplicity and stability of IS-IS make it robust in large internetworks. IS-IS is found in large ISPs and in some networks that support OSI protocols.

IS-IS development began before OSPF. Large ISPs chose IS-IS because of their unique requirement for scalability, convergence, and stability. The U.S. government also required support for OSI protocols in the early Internet. Later, businesses typically chose OSPF because it was a more widely supported native IP protocol. Today it is hard to find information and expertise on IS-IS. Some of the largest networks in the world still persist with IS-IS, which is a tribute to its capabilities.

IS-IS has its own packets; IS-IS information is not carried within another routed protocol. Because IS-IS is protocol-independent, it can support IP version 4 (IPv4), IP version 6 (IPv6), and the OSI CLNS protocol.

ISO specifications call routers "intermediate systems." Thus, IS-IS is a protocol that allows routers to communicate with routers. IS-IS serves as an Interior Gateway Protocol (IGP) for the CLNS, which is part of the OSI family of protocols.

IS-IS was adapted for use with IP; this version is called Integrated IS-IS (RFC 1195 and ISO 10589). Integrated IS-IS uses its own protocol data units (PDUs) to transport information between routers, including IP reachability information.

IS-IS routers use IS-IS Hellos (IIHs) to establish and maintain neighbor relationships between routers. As soon as the neighbor adjacency is established, IS-IS routers exchange link-state information using link-state packets (LSPs).

IS-IS functions similarly to OSPF when using totally stubby areas. There is a minimal amount of communication of information between areas, which reduces the burden on routers supporting the protocol.

IS-IS is the dynamic link-state routing protocol for the OSI protocol stack. As such, it distributes routing information for routing CLNP data for the ISO CLNS environment.

Integrated IS-IS is an implementation of the IS-IS protocol for routing multiple network protocols. Integrated IS-IS tags CLNP routes with information about IP networks and subnets. Integrated IS-IS provides IP with an alternative to OSPF and combines ISO CLNS and IP routing into one protocol. Integrated IS-IS can be used for IP routing, CLNS routing, or a combination of the two.

Both IS-IS and OSPF obtain adjacency information using a Hello protocol and distribute a list of neighboring routers for each intermediate system (IS) throughout the area as an LSP. Each router then runs the Dijkstra algorithm against its link-state database (LSDB) to pick the best paths.

OSI routing takes place at two levels. Level 1 (L1) routing within an IS-IS area is responsible for routing to end systems (ESs) inside an area. This is similar to OSPF internal nonbackbone routers in a totally stubby area. All devices in an L1 routing area have the same area address. Looking at the locally significant address portion (system IDs within the area) and choosing the lowest-cost path accomplishes routing. The routing to a destination with a different area address is done by a Level 1/Level 2 router, which is the equivalent of an Area Border Router (ABR) in OSPF. L1/L2 routers are discussed later.

L2 routers learn the locations of L1 neighbors and build an interarea routing table. All ISs in an L2 relationship use the destination area address to route traffic using the lowest-cost path.

---

**Key Point: IS-IS Features**

IS-IS supports two routing levels:

- Level 1 builds a common topology of system IDs in the local area. It routes traffic to other areas through the nearest border router.

- Level 2 exchanges prefix information between areas. It routes traffic to an area using the lowest-cost path.

---

IS-IS is a link-state protocol that lets you partition a routing domain into areas. As shown in Figure 6-1, there are three types of routers:

- Level 1 (L1) routers learn about paths within the areas they connect to (intraarea).

- Level 2 (L2) routers learn about paths among areas (interarea).

- Level 1/Level 2 (L1/L2) routers learn about paths both within and between areas. L1/L2 is equivalent to an ABR in OSPF.

**Figure 6-1**  *IS-IS Link-State Operation*

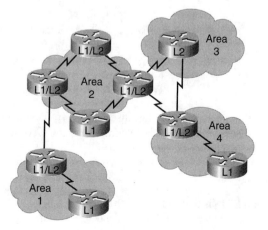

The path of connected L2 and L1/L2 routers is called the backbone. All L1/L2 and L2 routers must be contiguous.

## Integrated IS-IS Design Principles

Effective networks are well-planned. The first and most important step in building a scalable network is developing a good addressing plan. Scalability occurs when you use route summarization, and route summarization occurs when you use a hierarchical addressing structure.

Effective address planning presents opportunities to group devices into areas. Using areas confines the scope of LSP propagation and saves bandwidth. L1/L2 routers, which border an L1 area and the L2 backbone, are logical places to implement route summarization, as shown in Figure 6-2.

**Figure 6-2**   *Integrated IS-IS Design Principles*

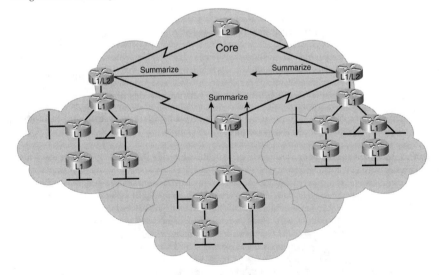

Route summarization saves memory because each IS (router) is no longer responsible for the LSPs of the entire routing domain. Route summarization also saves CPU usage, because a smaller routing table is easier to maintain.

## Issues with Integrated IS-IS

The first issue with IS-IS is that older implementations (those using narrow metrics) are limited to a maximum interface metric of 63 (6 bits) and a maximum total path metric of 1023 (10 bits).

There is little room to distinguish between paths. Cisco IOS software, beginning in Release 12.0, supports wide metrics, which allow a 24-bit interface and 32-bit path metrics. The default, however, is still narrow metrics.

---

**NOTE**    Complications can occur when you use this new capability if you are working with older routers or in a multivendor environment.

---

IS-IS, as implemented on Cisco routers, does not automatically scale the interface metric. Instead, all IS-IS interfaces have a default metric of 10, as shown in Figure 6-3. You can change this manually. If the default metric is not adjusted on each interface, the IS-IS metric becomes similar to the hop count used by Routing Information Protocol (RIP) as the metric.

**Figure 6-3**    *Path Metric Calculation*

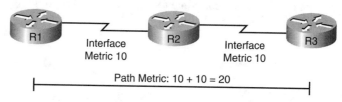

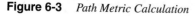

## ES-IS Discovery Protocol Operations

Hosts in OSI terminology are called end systems (ESs). End System-to-Intermediate System (ES-IS) handles topology information discovery and exchange between ISO end systems (hosts) and intermediate systems (routers).

ESs send End System Hellos (ESHs) to well-known addresses that announce their presence to routers (ISs), as shown in Figure 6-4. Routers listen to ESHs to find the ESs on a segment. Routers include information on ESs in LSPs.

**Figure 6-4**    *End System-to-Intermediate System*

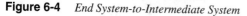

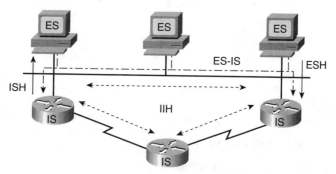

Routers transmit Intermediate System Hellos (ISHs) to well-known addresses, announcing their presence to other ESs. ESs listen for these ISHs and randomly pick an IS to which they forward all their packets. When an ES needs to send a packet to another ES, it sends the packet to one of the (router) ISs on its directly attached network.

Routers also use IIHs to establish adjacency between ISs.

IP end host systems do not use ES-IS. IP has its own processes and applications to handle the same functions as ES-IS, such as Internet Control Message Protocol (ICMP), Address Resolution Protocol (ARP), and Dynamic Host Configuration Protocol (DHCP).

Although Integrated IS-IS can support IP exclusively, IS-IS still uses CLNS to transmit reachability information and still forms adjacencies using ES-IS.

## OSI Routing Levels

The OSI specifications discuss four unique types of routing operations, numbered 0 to 3, as shown in Figure 6-5. IS-IS is responsible for L1 and L2 OSI routing.

**Figure 6-5**    *OSI Routing*

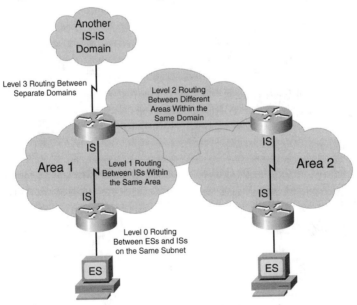

### IS-IS Level 0 Routing

OSI routing begins when the ESs discover the nearest IS by listening to ISH packets.

ES-IS performs the following tasks:

- It identifies the area prefix to ESs.

- It creates adjacencies between ESs and ISs.
- It creates data link-to-network address mappings.

When an ES needs to send a packet to another ES, it sends the packet to an IS on an attached network. This process is called Level 0 (L0) routing.

## IS-IS L1 Routing

Each ES and IS resides in a particular area. To pass traffic, the router looks up the destination address and forwards the packet along the best route. If the destination is on the same subnetwork, the IS knows the location (from listening to the ESH) and forwards the packet appropriately. The IS can also provide a redirect message back to the source that tells it that a more direct route is available. If the destination is on a different subnetwork but within the same area, the router identifies the best path using the system ID and forwards the traffic appropriately.

| NOTE | L1 routing is also called intra-area routing. |
|------|------------------------------------------------|

## IS-IS L2 Routing

If a destination address is in another area, the L1 IS sends the packet to the nearest L1/L2 IS (L2 routing). Packet forwarding continues through L2 ISs until the packet reaches an L1/L2 IS in the destination area. Within the destination area, ISs forward the packet along the best path, based on system ID, until the packet reaches the destination.

| NOTE | L2 routing is also called interarea routing. |
|------|-----------------------------------------------|

## IS-IS L3 Routing

Routing between separate domains is called L3 routing. L3 routing is comparable to Border Gateway Protocol (BGP) interdomain routing in IP. Level 3 routing passes traffic between different autonomous systems. These areas might have different routing logic, so metrics cannot be directly compared. L3 OSI routing is not implemented on Cisco routers but is specified as being accomplished through the Interdomain Routing Protocol (IDRP).

---

**Key Point: Routing Levels**

Level 0 routing is conducted by ES-IS.

L1 and L2 routing is a function of IS-IS.

IDRP conducts L3 routing. IDRP is similar in purpose to BGP. Cisco routers do not support IDRP.

---

## Comparing IS-IS and OSPF

OSPF and IS-IS protocols are link-state IGPs using Dijkstra's algorithm. Most of the development of these two protocols was done concurrently. The cooperation and competition between the development groups produced two protocols that are very similar, and each is better because of the other. The practical differences between the two protocols deal with perceived issues of resource usage and customization.

IS-IS and OSPF share the following critical traits:

- They are open-standard link-state routing protocols.
- They support VLSMs.
- They converge quickly.

Most debates of the merits of these protocols are colored by their mutual history; different groups with different cultures developed them.

Digital Equipment Corporation (DEC) originally developed IS-IS for DECnet Phase V. In 1987, the American National Standards Institute (ANSI) chose it to be the OSI IGP. At that time it could route CLNP only.

---

**A Condensed History of IS-IS**

IS-IS was ad hoc in its evolution, whereas OSPF was more formal.

1985: Originally called DECnet Phase V Routing

1988: Adopted by ISO and renamed IS-IS

1990: Publication of RFC 1142, *OSI IS-IS Intradomain Routing Protocol*

1990: Publication of RFC 1195, *Use of OSI IS-IS for Routing in TCP/IP and Dual Environments*

1991: Cisco IOS software starts supporting IS-IS

1995: ISPs start adopting IS-IS

2000: Publication of IETF draft "IS-IS Extensions for Traffic Engineering"

2001: Publication of IETF draft "IS-IS Extensions in Support of Generalized MPLS"

---

The ISO process is an international standards development process. According to an account given by Christian Huitema in his book *Routing in the Internet*, groups within ISO and outside the U.S. did not approve of TCP/IP because of its origin (it was also called the U.S. Department of Defense [DoD] protocol). From the perspective of ISO, IP development was chaotic and imprecise, based on the famous maxim of "loose consensus and running code." From the perspective of the early Internet engineers, the ISO process was slow, irritating, and disenfranchising.

In 1988, the National Science Foundation Network (NSFNET) was created. The IGP used was based on an early draft of IS-IS. The extensions to IS-IS for handling IP were developed in 1988. OSPF development began during this time; it was loosely based on IS-IS.

In 1989, OSPF version 1 (OSPF v1) was published, and much conflict ensued between the proponents of IS-IS and OSPF. The Internet Engineering Task Force (IETF) eventually supported both, although it continued to favor OSPF. With the unofficial endorsement of the IETF, OSPF eventually became more popular.

By the mid-'90s, large ISPs in need of an IGP selected IS-IS for two reasons. IS-IS supported IP as well as CLNS, and OSPF was seen as immature at the time.

## Similarities Between IS-IS and OSPF

IS-IS and OSPF are more similar than dissimilar. Both routing protocols have the following characteristics:

- They are link-state routing protocols.
- They use similar mechanisms (link-state advertisements [LSAs], link-state timers, and database synchronization) to maintain the LSDB's health.
- They are successful in the largest and most demanding deployments (ISP networks).
- They converge quickly after network changes.

## Differences Between Integrated IS-IS and OSPF

Integrated IS-IS and OSPF are both link-state protocols with similarities and also differences, as explained in the following sections.

### Area Design

Certain design constraints exist because OSPF's configuration is based on a central backbone, area 0, with all other areas being physically attached to area 0, as shown in Figure 6-6. When you use this type of hierarchical model, you need a consistent IP addressing structure to summarize addresses into the backbone. This type of hierarchical model also reduces the amount of information carried in the backbone and advertised across the network.

**Figure 6-6**  *OSPF Design*

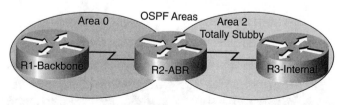

In comparison, IS-IS has a hierarchy with L1, L2/L1, and L2 routers, and the area borders lie on links, as shown in Figure 6-7. However, significantly fewer LSPs are used; therefore, more routers, at least 1000, can reside in a single area. This capability makes IS-IS more scalable than OSPF. IS-IS permits a more flexible approach to extending the backbone. The backbone can be extended by simply adding more L2/L1 or L2 routers, a less-complex process than with OSPF.

**Figure 6-7** *Integrated IS-IS Design*

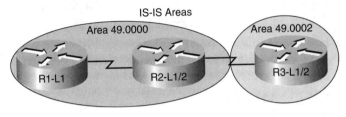

## Advantages of IS-IS

The differences between OSPF and IS-IS are small, but they do exist. OSPF produces many small LSAs. The router groups IS-IS updates and sends them as one LSP. Thus, as network complexity increases, update packet size is not an issue. Each packet must be routed, though, and routing takes network resources, so more packets represent a larger impact on the network. OSPF runs on top of IP, whereas IS-IS runs through CLNS.

IS-IS is also more efficient than OSPF in the use of CPU resources and in how it processes routing updates, as shown in Figure 6-8. For one thing, there fewer LSPs to process (LSAs in OSPF terminology). Also, the mechanism by which IS-IS installs and withdraws prefixes is less intensive, because it revolves around network entity title (NET) addresses, which are already heavily summarized.

**Figure 6-8** *Comparing IS-IS and OSPF Routing Updates*

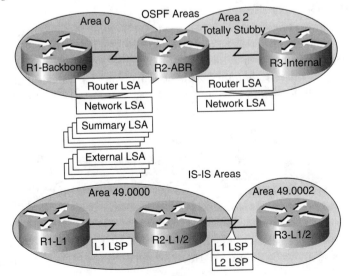

Both OSPF and IS-IS are link-state protocols and thus provide fast convergence. The convergence time depends on a number of factors, such as timers, number of nodes, and type of router. Based on the default timers, IS-IS detects a failure faster than OSPF; therefore, convergence occurs more rapidly. If there are many neighboring routers and adjacencies, the convergence time also might depend on the router's processing power. IS-IS is less CPU-intensive than OSPF.

The IS-IS default timers permit more fine-tuning than OSPF. There are more timers to adjust, so you can achieve finer granularity. By fine-tuning the timers, you can decrease convergence time significantly. It is important to note that stability can be affected by this speed.

New ideas are not easily expressed in OSPF packets; they require the creation of a new LSA. The OSPF description schema is difficult to extend, because of compatibility issues, and because it was developed exclusively for IPv4. IS-IS is easy to extend through the Type, Length, and Value (TLV) mechanism. TLV strings, called tuples, encode all IS-IS updates. IS-IS can easily grow to cover IPv6 or any other protocol, because extending IS-IS consists of simply creating new type codes.

### Advantages of OSPF

An organization might choose OSPF over IS-IS because OSPF is more optimized and is designed exclusively as an IP routing protocol.

Networking equipment must support OSPF, and network engineers must be familiar with OSPF theory and operation. It is relatively easy to find equipment and personnel to support an OSPF infrastructure. Furthermore, OSPF documentation is much more available than IS-IS.

# Understanding CLNS Addressing

Unlike IP addresses, CLNS addresses apply to entire nodes and not to interfaces. Because IS-IS was originally designed for CLNS, it requires CLNS node addresses to function properly.

CLNS addresses used by routers are called network service access points (NSAPs). One part of an NSAP address is the NSAP selector (NSEL) byte. When an NSAP is specified with an NSEL of 0, the NSAP is called the network entity title (NET). An NSEL of 0 identifies network services.

# NSAP Addresses

NSAP addresses have a maximum size of 20 bytes. Various uses require definition of different address structures; the high-order bits describe interarea structure, and the low-order bits identify unique systems within an area.

LSAs (also called LSPs in IS-IS), hello PDUs, and other routing PDUs are OSI-format PDUs; therefore, every IS-IS router requires an OSI address. These IS-IS PDUs are encapsulated directly into an OSI data-link frame. There is no CLNP header and no IP header. IS-IS uses the OSI address in the LSPs to identify the router and build the topology table and the underlying IS-IS routing tree.

OSI addresses are NSAPs. They contain the following:

- The device's OSI address
- A link to the higher-layer process

The NSAP address is equivalent to the combination of the IP address and upper-layer protocol in an IP header.

## IS-IS NSAP Address Structure

The Cisco implementation of Integrated IS-IS divides the NSAP address into three fields: the area address, the system ID, and the NSEL, as shown in Figure 6-9.

**Figure 6-9**   *IS-IS NSAP Address Structure*

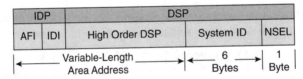

However, Cisco routers routing CLNS data use addressing that conforms to the ISO 10589 standard. ISO NSAP addresses consist of the following:

- The initial domain identifier (IDI) identifies the domain of the NSAP address. The authority and format identifier (AFI) and IDI make up the initial domain part (IDP) of the NSAP address. The IDP corresponds roughly to an IP classful major network.
- The AFI byte specifies the format of the address and the authority that assigned that address. Some valid values are shown in Table 6-1.

**Table 6-1**   *Examples of AFI Values*

| AFI | Address Domain |
| --- | --- |
| 39 | ISO Data Country Code (DCC) |
| 45 | E.164 |
| 47 | ISO 6523 International Code Designation (ICD) |
| 49 | Locally administered (private) |

The IDI identifies a subdomain under the AFI. For instance, 47.0005 is assigned to civilian departments of the U.S. Government and 47.0006 to the U.S. Department of Defense.

The domain-specific part (DSP) contributes to routing within an IS-IS routing domain. The high-order domain-specific part (HODSP), system ID, and NSEL make up the DSP of the NSAP address.

The HODSP subdivides the domain into areas. The HODSP is more or less the OSI equivalent of a subnet in IP.

The system ID identifies an individual OSI device. In OSI, a device has an address, just as it does in DECnet, whereas in IP, each interface has an address.

The NSEL identifies a process on the device. It corresponds roughly to a port or socket in IP. The NSEL is not used in routing decisions.

The simplest NSAP format, when using IS-IS as an IGP, is as follows:

- AFI set to 49, which signifies that the AFI is locally administered and individual addresses can be assigned.
- The area ID, which must be at least 1 byte.
- System ID. Cisco routers compliant with the U.S. Government OSI Profile (GOSIP) version 2.0 standard require a 6-byte system ID.
- NSEL, which must always be set to 0 for a router.

For example, you might assign 49.0001.0000.0c12.3456.00, which represents the following:

- AFI of 49.
- Area ID of 0001.
- System ID of 0000.0c12.3456, Media Access Control (MAC) address of a LAN interface.
- NSEL of 0. The NSAP is called the NET when it has an NSEL of 0. Routers use the NET to identify themselves in the IS-IS PDUs.

## Identifying Systems in IS-IS

The first part of a NET is the area ID. The area ID is associated with the IS-IS routing process. Unlike OSPF, an IS-IS router can be a member of only one area, as shown in Figure 6-10. Other address restrictions are as follows:

- All routers in an area must use the same area address, which actually defines the area.
- ESs recognize only ISs and other ESs on the same subnetwork that share the same area address.
- L1 intra-area routing is based on system IDs. Therefore, each ES and IS must have a unique system ID within the area.
- All L2 ISs eventually recognize all other L2 or L1/L2 ISs in the L2 backbone. Therefore, they must also have unique system IDs.

**Figure 6-10** *IS-IS Routers Are Members of Only One Area*

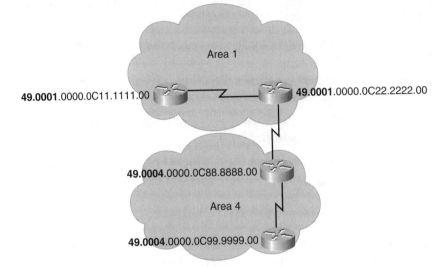

The low-order 6 bytes of an NSAP are the system ID. The system ID must be unique within an area. It is customary to use a MAC address from the router, as shown in Figure 6-11, or, for Integrated IS-IS, to code an IP address into the system ID.

**Figure 6-11** *System IDs Are Often the System MAC Address*

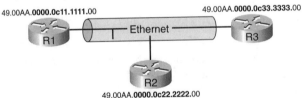

System IDs should remain unique across the domain. If the system IDs remain unique, there can never be a conflict at L1 or L2 if, for example, a device moves into a different area.

All the system IDs in a domain must be of equal length. Cisco enforces this OSI directive by fixing the length of the system ID at 6 bytes in all cases.

## NET Addresses

NET addresses are NSAP addresses with an NSEL value of 0. A NET address is used to uniquely identify an OSI host within an IS-IS routing domain. Because IS-IS originates from the OSI world, NET addresses are required even if the only routed protocol is IP.

If the upper-layer process ID (NSEL) is 00, as shown in Figure 6-12, the NSAP refers to the device itself; that is, it is the equivalent of that device's Layer 3 OSI address. The Layer 3 OSI address is called the NET.

**Figure 6-12**  *Subnetwork Point of Attachment and Local Circuit ID*

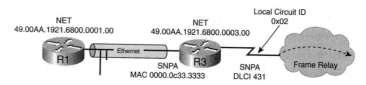

Routers use the NET to identify themselves in the LSPs and, therefore, form the basis for the OSI routing calculation.

Addresses starting with the AFI value of 49 are private addresses, analogous to RFC 1918 for IP addresses. IS-IS routes these addresses. However, this group of addresses should not be advertised to other CLNS networks because they are ad hoc addresses. Other companies that use 49 might have created different numbering schemes that, when used together, could create confusion.

Addresses starting with AFI values 39 and 47 represent the ISO DCC and ISO ICD, respectively.

Additional IS-IS terms introduced in Figure 6-12 include the following:

- The subnetwork point of attachment (SNPA) is the point that provides subnetwork services. SNPA is the equivalent of the Layer 2 address corresponding to the Layer 3, NET, or NSAP address. It is usually a MAC address on a LAN or a virtual circuit ID in X.25, Frame Relay, or ATM.

- A circuit is the IS-IS term for an interface. NSAP and NET refer to the entire device, so a circuit ID is used to distinguish a particular interface.

A link is the path between two neighbor ISs and is defined as being up when communication is possible between the two neighbor SNPAs.

SNPA is taken from

- The MAC address on a LAN interface.

- The virtual circuit ID from X.25 or ATM and the data-link connection identifier (DLCI) from Frame Relay.

- For High-Level Data Link Control (HDLC) interfaces, the SNPA is simply HDLC.

A circuit ID allows interfaces and networks to be distinguished by the router. The router assigns a circuit ID (one octet) to each interface on the router as follows:

In the case of point-to-point interfaces, the SNPA is the circuit's sole identifier; for example, on HDLC point-to-point links, the circuit ID is 0x00.

In the case of LAN interfaces, the circuit ID is appended to the end of the system ID of the designated IS to form a 7-byte LAN ID, such as 1921.6800.0001.01. Designated IS (DIS) is covered in more detail later in this chapter. On Cisco routers, the router host name is used instead of the system ID; therefore, the circuit ID of a LAN interface might look like P6R4.01.

# Basic Operations of IS-IS in a CLNS Environment

This section introduces the concepts used by IS-IS in a CLNS environment, the first step to understanding Integrated IS-IS.

IS-IS runs directly on the data link layer and does not use IP or CLNS as a network protocol. IS-IS is similar to OSPF in the following ways:

- It supports different media in different ways.
- It recognizes neighbors and advertises links to build a link-state table.

This section describes how CLNS addressing affects IS-IS operation. In addition, it describes how the IS-IS protocol learns topology, makes routing decisions, and handles different data links.

## Intra-Area and Interarea Addressing and Routing

IS-IS routing is effortlessly achieved from the OSI address plan. Areas are identified, and unique system IDs are given to each device.

An OSI NSAP address can be up to 20 octets long. The final byte is the selector byte, the preceding 6 bytes are the system ID, and the leading bytes are the area ID. The system ID can be set to any arbitrary value. However, it must be unique within the routing area, and it is recommended that every system ID be globally unique.

The area ID can range from 1 to 13 bytes in length, as specified by the ISO standard. Therefore, an NSAP for an IS-IS network can be as little as 8 bytes in length. However, the NSAP is usually longer to permit some granularity in the allocation of areas. The Area ID prefix is common to all devices in an area and is unique from all other areas. Sets of ISs and ESs are in the same area if they share the same area ID.

Routing within an area involves collecting system IDs and adjacencies for all ISs and ESs in an area and using Dijkstra's algorithm to compute best paths between devices. L1 routers are only aware of the local area topology. They pass the traffic bound outside the area to the closest L1/L2 ABR.

Routing between areas is based on area ID. L2 routers in different areas exchange area ID information and use Dijkstra's algorithm to compute best paths between areas. They pass traffic between areas to the closest L1/L2 router.

---

**Key Point: Addressing and Routing**

Communication is only between an ES and IS in the same area.

The area portion is used to route between areas. System ID is not considered.

System ID is used to route within an area. Area ID is not considered.

---

When an ES is required to send a packet to another ES, the packet goes to one of the ISs on a network directly attached to the ES. The router then searches for the destination address and forwards the packet along the best route. If the destination ES is in the same area, the local IS recognizes the location by listening to ESH packets and forwards the packet appropriately. If the destination address is an ES in another area, the L1 IS sends the packet to the nearest L1/L2 IS.

Forwarding through L2 ISs continues until the packet reaches an L2 IS in the destination area. Within the destination area, ISs forward the packet along the best path until the destination ES is reached.

Because each router makes its own best-path decisions at every hop along the way, there is a significant chance that paths will not be reciprocal, meaning that return traffic will not necessarily take the exact same path as the originating traffic. That is, return traffic can take a different path than the outgoing traffic. For this reason, it is important to know the traffic patterns within your network and tune IS-IS for optimal path selection if necessary.

Using Figure 6-13, the following list analyzes traffic from Router 7 (R7) to Router 9 (R9):

   **1**  R7 recognizes that R9's prefix (49.00AA) is not the same as R7's prefix (49.00BB). R7 therefore passes the traffic to the closest L1/L2 ABR, Router 5 (R5). R7 uses its L1 topology database to find the best path to R5.

   **2**  R5 uses its L2 topology database to pick the best next hop to reach the prefix 49.00CC: R3. R5 does not use the destination system ID in this decision.

   **3**  R3 uses its L2 topology database to pick the best next hop to reach the prefix 49.00CC: R1. R3 does not use the destination system ID in this decision.

   **4**  R1 uses its L2 topology database to pick the best next hop to reach the prefix 49.00CC: R8. R1 does not use the destination system ID in this decision.

   **5**  R8 recognizes that R9's prefix (49.00AA) is the same as R8's prefix (49.00CC). R8 therefore passes the traffic to R9 using its L1 topology database to find the best path.

**Figure 6-13**  *Identifying Systems: OSI Addressing in Networks*

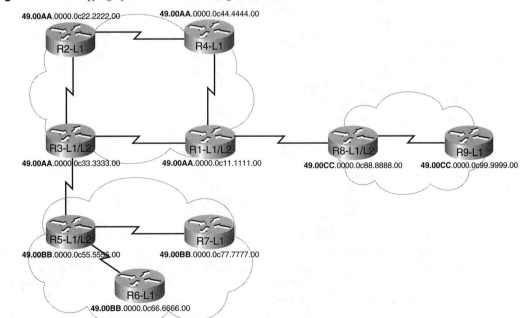

## IS-IS Routing Levels

IS-IS is a link-state protocol that permits partitioning of a routing domain into areas. Routers (ISs) are of two types: L1 and L2. L1 routers, explained earlier in this chapter, recognize paths within the areas to which they are connected (intra-area). L2 routers learn about paths among areas (interarea). A router can be L1 or L2, or L1/L2.

---

**NOTE**    Area boundaries fall on the links. Neighboring routers recognize whether they are in the same or different areas and negotiate appropriate adjacencies (L1, L2, or both).

---

In Figure 6-14, area 1 contains the following two routers:

- One router borders area 2 and is an L1/L2 IS.

- The other router is contained within the area and is an L1 only.

**Figure 6-14** *OSI Area Routing*

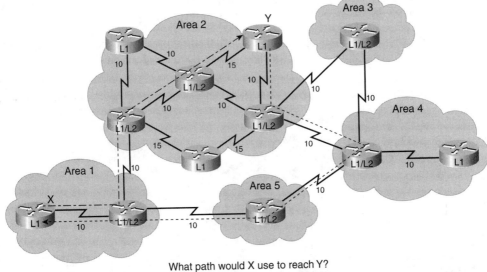

What path would X use to reach Y?
What path would Y use to reach X?

Area 2 has many routers:

- A selection of routers is specified as L1. The routers route either internally to that area or to the exit points (the L1/L2 IS).

- L1/L2 routers form a chain across the area linking to the neighbor areas. Although the middle router of the three L1/L2 routers does not link directly to another area, the middle router must support L2 routing to ensure that the backbone is contiguous. If the middle router fails, the other L1-only routers cannot perform the L2 function (despite providing a physical path across the area), and the backbone is broken.

Area 3 contains one router that borders areas 2 and 4, yet it has no intra-area neighbors and is currently performing L2 functions only. If you add another router to area 3, the border router reverts to L1/L2 functions.

As shown in Figure 6-14, the border between the areas in an IS-IS network is the link between L2 routers. (Figure 6-14 is in contrast to OSPF, where the border exists inside the ABR itself.)

In Figure 6-14, symmetric routing cannot occur, because L2 details are hidden from L1 routers, which only recognize a default route to the nearest L1/L2 router.

Traffic from Router X to Router Y flows from Router X to its closest L1/L2 router. The L1/L2 router then forwards the traffic along the shortest path to the destination area (area 2). After the traffic flows into area 2, it is routed along the shortest intra-area path to Router Y.

Router Y routes return packets to Router X to its nearest L1/L2 router. The L1/L2 router recognizes the best route to area 1 via area 4 based on the lowest-cost L2 path.

Because L1 and L2 computations are separate, the path taken from Router Y back to Router X is not necessarily the least cost from Router X to Router Y.

Asymmetric routing (packets taking different paths in different directions) is not detrimental to the network. However, troubleshooting can be difficult, and this type of routing is sometimes a symptom of bad design. Like EIGRP and OSPF, a good IS-IS design is generally hierarchical and symmetrical.

A feature available since Cisco IOS Release 12.0 allows L2 routes to leak in a controlled manner to L1 routers, which helps avoid asymmetric routing.

# IS-IS PDUs

IS-IS PDUs are encapsulated directly into an OSI data-link frame. There is no CLNP and IP header.

IS-IS has the following four types of PDUs:

- **Hello PDU (ESH, ISH, IIH)**—Used to establish and maintain adjacencies.
- **Link-state PDU (LSP)**—Used to distribute link-state information.
- **Partial sequence number PDU (PSNP)**—Used to acknowledge and request missing pieces of link-state information.
- **Complete sequence number PDU (CSNP)**—Used to describe the complete list of LSPs in a router's LSDB.

The OSI stack defines a unit of data as a PDU. OSI recognizes a frame as a data-link PDU and a packet (or datagram, in the IP environment) as a network PDU.

Figure 6-15 shows three types of PDUs (802.2 Logical Link Control [LLC] encapsulation). IS-IS and ES-IS PDUs are encapsulated directly in a data-link PDU. True CLNP (data) packets contain a full CLNP header between the data-link header and any higher-layer CLNS information.

**Figure 6-15** *OSI IS-IS PDUs*

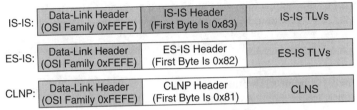

The IS-IS and ES-IS PDUs contain variable-length fields, depending on the PDU's function. Each field contains a type code, a length, and the appropriate values (TLV).

---

### Key Point: IS-IS PDU Types

PDU between peers:

- A network PDU is also called a datagram or packet.
- A data-link PDU is also called a frame.

---

## Link-State Packets

In IS-IS, router characteristics are defined by an LSP. The router's LSP contains an LSP header and TLV fields, as shown in Figure 6-16.

**Figure 6-16** *Link-State Packets Representing Routers*

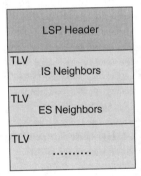

An LSP header describes the following:

- The PDU type and length
- The LSP ID and sequence number used to identify duplicate LSPs and to ensure that the latest LSP information is stored in the topology table
- The LSP's remaining lifetime, which is used to age out LSPs

TLV variable-length fields contain the following:

- The router's neighbor ISs, which are used to build the map of the network
- The router's neighbor ESs

- Authentication information that is used to secure routing updates
- Attached IP subnets (optional for Integrated IS-IS)

LSPs are given sequence numbers that allow receiving routers to do the following:

- Ensure that they use the latest LSPs in their route calculations
- Avoid the entering of duplicate LSPs in the topology tables

When a router reloads, the sequence number is set to 1. The router then gets its previous LSPs back from its neighbors. These LSPs have the last valid sequence number before the router reloaded. The router records this number and reissues its own LSPs with the next-highest sequence number.

Each LSP has a remaining lifetime that is used by the LSP aging process to ensure the removal of outdated and invalid LSPs from the topology table after a suitable time period. This process is known as the count-to-zero operation; 1200 seconds is the default start value.

Each LSP includes specific information about networks and stations attached to a router. This information is found in multiple TLV fields that follow the LSP's common header. TLV is sometimes also called Code, Length, Value (CLV). The TLV structure is a flexible way to add data to the LSP and an easy way to add new data fields that might be required in the future. Table 6-2 shows examples of TLVs.

**Table 6-2**    *Routing Protocol Route Summarization Support*

| TLV | Type Code | Length Field | Value Variable Length |
|-----|-----------|--------------|-----------------------|
| Area address | 1 | Area ID length + 1 | Areas |
| Intermediate system neighbors | 2 | Neighbor count + 1 | List of IS neighbors |

You can find documentation on important TLVs in ISO 10589 and RFC 1195.

Network topologies can be divided into two general types:

- **Point-to-point networks**—Point-to-point links that are either permanently established (leased line, permanent virtual circuit [PVC]) or dynamically established (ISDN, switched virtual circuit [SVC])
- **Broadcast networks**—Multipoint WAN links or LAN links, such as Ethernet, Token Ring, or Fiber Distributed Data Interface (FDDI)

IS-IS supports the following two media representations for its link states:

- Broadcast for LANs and multipoint WAN links
- Point-to-point for all other media

**NOTE**    IS-IS has no concept of an NBMA network. It is recommended that you use point-to-point links such as point-to-point subinterfaces, over NBMA networks, such as ATM, Frame Relay, or X.25.

# Topologies

Cisco IOS software automatically uses broadcast mode for LAN links and multipoint WAN links. It uses point-to-point topology for point-to-point links, such as point-to-point subinterfaces and dialer interfaces.

IS-IS has no specific support for NBMA networks. When implemented in broadcast mode, Cisco IOS software assumes that the NBMA environment features a full mesh of PVCs. You should use the **broadcast** keyword when creating the static maps, because broadcast mode uses multicast updates. You use the **broadcast** keyword when mapping the remote IP address to the local DLCI on a Frame Relay interface.

When you use multipoint WAN links such as multipoint Frame Relay interfaces, you must also create static CLNS maps (in addition to the IP maps), such as by using the command **frame-relay map clns** *dlci-number* **broadcast**.

It is highly recommended that you implement NBMA environments, such as Frame Relay, as point-to-point links instead of multipoint links.

## Broadcast Networks

Broadcast networks are LAN interfaces or multipoint WAN interfaces.

---

**CAUTION**   Broadcast mode is recommended for use only on LAN interfaces.

---

You establish separate adjacencies for L1 and L2. If two neighboring routers in the same area run both L1 and L2, they establish two adjacencies, one for each level. The router stores the L1 and L2 adjacencies in separate L1 and L2 adjacency tables.

On LANs, routers establish the two adjacencies with specific Layer 1 and Layer 2 IIH PDUs. Routers on a LAN establish adjacencies with all other routers on the LAN (unlike OSPF, where routers establish full adjacencies only with the designated router [DR] and backup designated router [BDR]).

IIH PDUs announce the area ID. Separate IIH packets announce the L1 and L2 neighbors. Adjacencies form based on the area address communicated in the incoming IIH and the type of router (L1 or L2). Here's an example:

- L1 routers accept L1 IIH PDUs from their own area and establish adjacencies with other routers in their own area.

- L2 routers (or the L2 process within any L1/L2 router) accept only L2 IIH PDUs and establish only Level 2 adjacencies.

Dijkstra's algorithm requires a virtual router (pseudonode) called the DIS to build a directed graph for broadcast media. Criteria for DIS selection are first, highest priority (the priority value can be configured) and second, highest MAC address. The elected DIS then generates an LSP representing a virtual router connecting all attached routers to a star-shaped topology.

During the DIS election, a set of adjacent routers compare interface priority values. The router with the highest interface priority is the preferred selection. The SNPA address or MAC address breaks any ties. Cisco router interfaces have a default L1 and L2 priority of 64. You can configure the priority from 0 to 127 using the **isis priority** command. The L1 DIS and L2 DIS on a LAN might or might not be the same router, because an interface can have different L1 and L2 priorities.

A selected router is not guaranteed to remain the DIS. Any adjacent IS with a higher priority automatically takes over the DIS role. This behavior is called preemptive. Because the IS-IS LSDB is synchronized frequently on a LAN, giving priority to another IS over the DIS is not a significant issue. Unlike OSPF, IS-IS does not use a backup DIS, and routers on a LAN establish adjacencies with all other routers and with the DIS.

Rather than having each router connected to the LAN advertise an adjacency with every other router on the LAN, the entire network is considered a router, called the pseudonode. Each router just advertises a single adjacency to the pseudonode. Otherwise, each IS on a broadcast subnetwork with $n$-connected ISs requires $(n)(n - 1)/2$ adjacency advertisements. Generating LSPs for each adjacency creates considerable overhead in terms of LSDB synchronization.

When you use a pseudonode, each IS is required to advertise only a single adjacency to the pseudonode. The pseudonode is represented by a DIS, as shown in Figure 6-17, which generates the pseudonode LSPs. A pseudonode LSP details only the adjacent ISs (for example, the ISs connected to that LAN). The pseudonode LSP is used to build the map of the network and to calculate the shortest path first (SPF) tree. The pseudonode LSP is the equivalent of a network LSA in OSPF.

**Figure 6-17**  *LSP Representing Routers: LAN Representation*

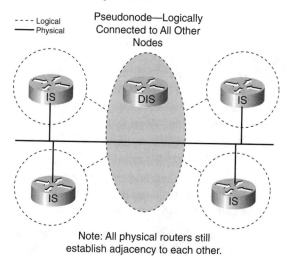

In IS-IS, all routers on the LAN establish adjacencies with all other routers and with the DIS. Therefore, if the DIS fails, another router takes over immediately with little or no impact on the network's topology. There is no backup DIS.

In OSPF, as soon as the DR and BDR are selected, the other routers on the LAN establish full adjacencies with the DR and BDR. In case of DR failure, the BDR is promoted to DR, and a new BDR is elected.

## Point-to-Point Networks

When a network consists of only two routers connected over broadcast media that route using integrated IS-IS, it is more efficient to treat the connection as a point-to-point link instead of as a broadcast link. The following section explains IS-IS point-to-point adjacencies.

### L1 and L2 LSP

IS-IS uses a two-level area hierarchy. The link-state information for these two levels is distributed separately, which results in L1 LSPs and L2 LSPs. Each IS originates its own LSPs (one for L1 and one for L2).

On a LAN, one router (the DIS) sends out LSP information on behalf of the LAN. The DIS creates a pseudonode, which is the representation of the LAN. The DIS sends out the separate L1 and L2 LSPs for the pseudonode. The L1 DIS and the L2 DIS on a LAN might or might not be the same router, because an interface can have different L1 and L2 priorities.

LSPs on broadcast media (LANs) are sent as multicast, and LSPs on point-to-point links are sent as unicast.

### L1 and L2 IIHs

IIHs are used to establish and maintain neighbor adjacency between ISs.

On a LAN, separate L1 and L2 IIHs are sent periodically as multicasts. The default hello interval is every 10 seconds; however, the hello interval timer is adjustable. On a LAN, the hello packets are multicast to a multicast MAC address. L1 announcements are sent to the AllL1IS multicast MAC address 0180.C200.0014, and L2 announcements are sent to the AllL2IS multicast MAC address 0180.C200.0015. The default hello interval for the DIS is 3 times faster than the interval for the other routers so that DIS failures can be detected quickly. Unlike DR/BDR in OSPF, there is no backup DIS in IS-IS.

A neighbor is declared dead if two hellos are not received within the hold time. Hold time is calculated as the product of the hello multiplier and hello time. The default hello time is 10 seconds, and the default multiplier is 3. Therefore, the default hold time is 30 seconds.

Unlike LAN interfaces with separate L1 and L2 IIHs, point-to-point links have a common point-to-point IIH format that specifies whether the hello relates to L1 or L2 or both. Point-to-point hellos are sent to the unicast address of the connected router.

# Link-State Database Synchronization and Adjacency

Table 6-3 summarizes the differences between broadcast and point-to-point links.

**Table 6-3**   *Comparing Broadcast and Point-to-Point Topologies*

|  | **Broadcast** | **Point-to-Point** |
|---|---|---|
| **Usage** | LAN, full-mesh WAN | PPP, HDLC, partial-mesh WAN |
| **Hello timer** | 3.3 seconds for DIS<br>Else 10 seconds | 10 seconds |
| **Adjacencies** | $n(n-1)/2$ | $n-1$ |
| **Uses DIS?** | Yes | No |
| **IIH type** | Level 1 IIH<br>Level 2 IIH | Point-to-point IIH |

## Flooding Subprotocol

An IS-IS update process is responsible for flooding the LSPs throughout the IS-IS domain. An LSP is typically flooded to all adjacent neighbors except the neighbor from which it was received. L1 LSPs are flooded within their local areas. L2 LSPs are flooded throughout the backbone.

Each IS originates its own LSP (one for L1 and one for L2). These LSPs are identified by the originator's system ID and an LSP number starting at 0. If an LSP exceeds the maximum transmission unit (MTU), it is fragmented into several LSPs, numbered 1, 2, 3, and so on.

IS-IS maintains the L1 and L2 LSPs in separate LSDBs.

When an IS receives an LSP, it examines the checksum and discards any invalid LSPs, flooding them with an expired lifetime age. If the LSP is valid and newer than what is currently in the LSDB, it is retained, acknowledged, and given a lifetime of 1200 seconds. The age is decremented every second until it reaches 0, at which point the LSP is considered expired. As soon as the LSP expires, it is kept for an additional 60 seconds before it is flooded as an expired LSP.

## LSDB Synchronization

Sequence number PDUs (SNPs) are used to acknowledge the receipt of LSPs and to maintain LSDB synchronization. There are two types of SNPs: complete SNP (CSNP) and partial SNP (PSNP). The use of SNPs differs between point-to-point and broadcast media.

CSNPs and PSNPs share the same format; that is, each carries summarized LSP information. The main difference is that CSNPs contain summaries of all LSPs in the LSDB, whereas PSNPs contain only a subset of LSP entries.

Separate CSNPs and PSNPs are used for L1 and L2 adjacencies.

Adjacent IS-IS routers exchange CSNPs to compare their LSDB. In broadcast subnetworks, only the DIS transmits CSNPs. All adjacent neighbors compare the LSP summaries received in the CSNP with the contents of their local link-state databases to determine if their LSDBs are synchronized or have the same copies of LSPs as other routers for the appropriate levels and area of routing. CSNPs are periodically multicast (every 10 seconds) by the DIS on a LAN to ensure LSDB accuracy.

If there are too many LSPs to include in one CSNP, they are sent in ranges. The CSNP header indicates the starting and ending LSP ID in the range. If all LSPs fit the CSNP, the range is set to default values.

Adjacent IS-IS routers use PSNPs to acknowledge the receipt of LSPs and to request transmission of missing or newer LSPs.

### LSDB Synchronization: LAN

The DIS periodically (every 10 seconds) sends CSNPs that list the LSPs it holds in its LSDB. This update is a broadcast to all IS-IS routers on the LAN.

As shown in Figure 6-18, the bottom-left router (R1) compares this list of LSPs with its topology table and realizes it is missing one LSP. Therefore, it sends a PSNP to the DIS (R2) to request the missing LSP.

**Figure 6-18**  *LSDB Synchronization: LAN*

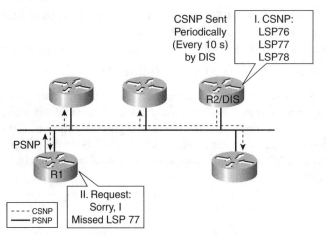

The DIS reissues only that missing LSP (LSP 77), and R1 acknowledges it with a PSNP (not shown).

### LSDB Synchronization: Point-to-Point

Unlike broadcast links, such as LAN links, CSNPs are not periodically sent on point-to-point links. A CSNP is sent only once, when the point-to-point link first comes up. After that, LSPs are sent to describe topology changes, and they are acknowledged with a PSNP.

Figure 6-19 shows what happens on a point-to-point link when a link failure is detected.

**Figure 6-19**  *LSDB Synchronization: Point-to-Point*

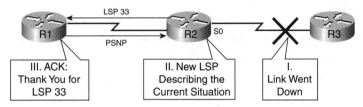

The steps are as follows:

1   A link fails.

2   The middle router (R2) notices this failure and issues a new LSP noting the change.

3   The left router (R1) receives the LSP, stores it in its topology table, and sends a PSNP back
    to R2 to acknowledge receipt of the LSP.

## LAN Adjacency

IIH PDUs announce the area ID. On LANs, separate IIH packets announce the L1 and L2
neighbors.

For example, when a LAN has routers from two areas attached, as shown in Figure 6-20, the
following process takes place:

* The routers from one area accept L1 IIH PDUs only from their own area and therefore
  establish adjacencies only with their own area routers.

* The routers from a second area similarly accept L1 IIH PDUs only from their own area.

**Figure 6-20**  *L1 and L2 Adjacencies on a LAN*

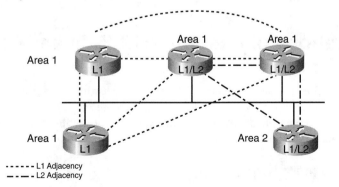

The L2 routers (or the L2 process within any L1/L2 router) accept only L2 IIH PDUs and
establish only L2 adjacencies.

## WAN Adjacency

On point-to-point links (that is, on a point-to-point WAN link), the IIH PDUs are common to both levels but announce the level type and the area ID in the hellos.

L1 routers in the same area (which includes links between L1 and L1/L2 routers) exchange IIH PDUs that specify L1 and establish an L1 adjacency.

L2 routers (in the same area or between areas, and including links between L2 only and L1/L2 routers) exchange IIH PDUs that specify L2 and establish an L2 adjacency.

Two L1/L2 routers in the same area establish both L1 and L2 adjacencies and maintain these with a common IIH PDU that specifies the L1 and L2 information.

Two L1 routers that are physically connected but are not in the same area can exchange IIHs, but they do not establish an adjacency, because the area IDs do not match.

Figure 6-21 shows the different permutations for WAN adjacencies.

**Figure 6-21** *WAN Adjacencies*

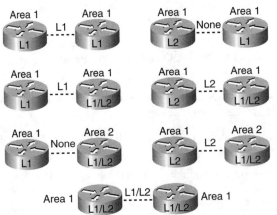

# Basic Operations of Integrated IS-IS in an IP and CLNS Environment

When IS-IS is installed to support IP exclusively, network devices must also be configured to use the OSI CLNS protocol. Each IS-IS router requires a NET, and IS-IS packets are directly encapsulated onto the data link layer instead of traveling inside IP packets. You should understand OSI CLNS characteristics before you configure Integrated IS-IS.

## Integrated IS-IS NET Addressing

A NET address identifies a device (an IS or ES), not an interface. In this way, a NET address is critically different from an IP address. Although we are discussing supporting IS-IS for IP routing, each router still requires a NET.

Cisco routers can use IS-IS for the following two purposes:

- CLNS support
- IP support (Integrated IS-IS) in addition to CLNS or for IP only

Even if you use IP routing only over Integrated IS-IS, each IS-IS router must have a NET address configured, because Integrated IS-IS depends on the support of CLNS routing.

OSI protocols (hello PDUs) are used to form the neighbor relationship between routers.

SPF calculations rely on a configured NET address to identify the routers.

When you are implementing IP addressing, you should do so at the interface, and each interface must belong to a different subnet. A NET address applies to the entire IS-IS router. Each router has a unique NET address that identifies the entire router, not a particular interface. Recall that the NET contains both the area address and the unique device address. These two portions of the address form the basis of IS-IS routing. A device identifies other devices within its own area based on matching area addresses in their NET. It then knows that it can communicate with these other devices without using a default route. A default route is injected into the area by the L1/L2 router. If the area addresses do not match, the device knows that it must forward that traffic to its nearest L1/L2 router.

When you are using IS-IS to route IP traffic, IP subnets are treated as leaf objects associated with IS-IS areas. When you use IP to transmit, the router looks up the destination network in its routing table. If the network belongs to a different area, that traffic must also be forwarded to the nearest L1/L2 router. Scalability is achieved by minimizing the size of the LSDB and routing tables, the amount of processing, and the amount of network updates—in other words, using route summarization wherever possible. Route summarization can be accomplished only where the address planning permits grouping addresses by a common prefix. This condition is true for OSI and IP. Therefore, it is very important to carefully plan the IS-IS areas, NET addresses, and IP addresses.

## Criteria and Path Selection for IS-IS Area Routing

IS-IS adjacencies and path selection processes center on the OSI-based understanding of network topology.

IS-IS uses an OSI forwarding database (routing table) to select the best path to a destination. To build the OSI forwarding database, which is the CLNS routing table, routers use the following process:

1 Use the LSDB to calculate the SPF tree to OSI destinations (NETs). The total of the link metrics along each path determines the shortest path to any given destination.

2 Understand that L1 and L2 routes have separate LSDBs; therefore, routers run SPF twice, once for each level, and create separate SPF trees for each level.

3 Calculate ES reachability with a partial route calculation (PRC) based on the L1 and L2 SPF trees. There are no OSI ESs in a pure IP Integrated IS-IS environment.

4 Insert the best paths in the CLNS routing table (OSI forwarding database).

## Building an IP Forwarding Database

Integrated IS-IS includes IP prefix reachability information in the LSPs, treating it as if it were ES information. For IS-IS, IP is information regarding the leaf connections to the SPF tree. Therefore, updating IP reachability requires only a PRC, similar to ES reachability.

The PRC generates best-path choices for IP routes and offers the routes to the routing table, where they are accepted based on normal IP routing table rules. For example, if more than one routing protocol is running, the router compares administrative distance. When the IP IS-IS routes are entered into the routing table, they are shown as via L1 or L2, as appropriate.

The separation of IP reachability from the core IS-IS network architecture offers Integrated IS-IS better scalability than, for example, OSPF, as follows:

- OSPF sends LSAs for individual IP subnets. If an IP subnet fails, the LSA floods through the network. In all circumstances, all routers must run a full SPF calculation, which is extremely CPU-intensive.

- Integrated IS-IS builds the SPF tree from CLNS information. If an IP subnet fails in an Integrated IS-IS, the LSP floods through the network, which is the same for OSPF. If this is a leaf (stub) IP subnet (that is, the loss of the subnet does not affect the underlying CLNS architecture), the SPF tree is unaffected; therefore, only a PRC occurs.

---

**Key Point: Building an IP Forwarding Table**

PRC is also run to calculate IP reachability.

Because the IP prefix and ES are represented as leaf objects, they do not participate in SPF.

Best paths are placed in the IP forwarding table following IP preferential rules.

They appear as i L1 or i L2 IP routes in the IP routing table.

---

In Figure 6-22, the **show ip route** command has been given to display the IP IS-IS routes in the IP routing table. The table in Example 6-1 shows routes to loopback interfaces on each router. The i indicates that the route sources are from IS-IS. The L1 and L2 show whether the IS-IS path to these destination IP networks is via IS-IS L1 or L2 routing. The next-hop IP addresses are matched from the corresponding next-hop IS-IS neighbor routers.

**Figure 6-22** *Building an IP Forwarding Table*

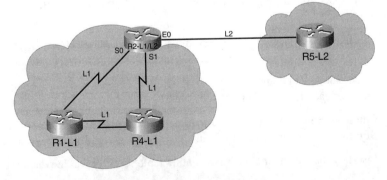

Example 6-1 shows the routing table of R2 associated with Figure 6-22. The IP addresses on loopbacks of routers are 1.0.0.1/8 for R1, 2.0.0.1/8 for R2, 4.0.0.1/8 for R4, and 5.0.0.1/8 for R5.

**Example 6-1**  *Building an IP Forwarding Table*

```
R2#show ip route
i L1 1.0.0.0/8 [115/10] via 10.12.0.1, Serial0-(R1)
i L1 4.0.0.0/8 [115/10] via 10.24.0.4, Serial1-(R4)
i L2 5.0.0.0/8 [115/10] via 11.0.0.10, Ethernet0-(R5)
```

For example, network 1.0.0.0 (the loopback interface on R1) is considered a leaf node attached to R1. For R2 to reach network 1.0.0.0, R2 computes the shortest path to reach the system ID of R1 based on the IS-IS LSDB. Because R1 and R2 are in the same area, routing between R1 and R2 is based on system ID. In this case, the best path for R2 to reach R1's system ID is via the serial 0 interface that directly connects to R1.

# Using show Commands

Many **show** commands are helpful when troubleshooting CLNS and Integrated IS-IS. These specific commands are covered in this section.

## Troubleshooting Commands: CLNS

You can use the following **show clns** commands to verify the router configuration and to troubleshoot the CLNS configuration:

- **show clns**—This command displays general information about the CLNS network.

- **show clns protocol**—This command displays information for the specific IS-IS processes in the router.

- **show clns interface**—This command displays information about the interfaces that currently run IS-IS.

- **show clns neighbors**—This command displays IS and ES neighbors, if there are any. The neighbors are the routers with which this router has IS-IS adjacencies. The optional keyword **detail** displays comprehensive information about the neighbors. If **detail** is not specified, the neighbors are listed without any details. You can reduce the list of those neighbors across a particular interface if you specify the interface in the command.

## Troubleshooting Commands: CLNS and IS-IS

You can use the following **show** commands to verify the router configuration and to troubleshoot the Integrated IS-IS network:

- **show isis route**—This command displays the IS-IS L1 routing table, which includes all other system IDs in the area. This command is available only if CLNS routing is enabled both globally and at the interface level.

- **show clns route**—This command displays the IS-IS L2 routing table.

- **show isis database**—This command displays the contents of the IS-IS LSDB. To force IS-IS to refresh its LSDB and recalculate all routes, issue the **clear isis** command, specifying the IS-IS process tag or using an asterisk (*) to clear all IS-IS processes.

- **show isis topology**—This command displays the L1 and L2 topology tables, which show the least-cost IS-IS paths to the ISs.

## OSI Intra-Area and Interarea Routing Example

Figure 6-23 shows four routers in two areas. Routers R1, R2, and R4 belong to area 49.0001. Router R5 belongs to area 49.0002. Routers R1 and R4 are L1 routers doing only L1 routing. R2 is an L1/L2 router doing both L1 and L2 routing. R5 is an L2 router doing only L2 routing.

**Figure 6-23** *Routing in a Two-Level Area Structure*

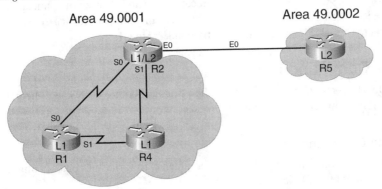

Figure 6-23 forms the basis of the following **show** examples.

## Level 1 and Level 2 Topology Table

The **show isis topology** command, as shown in Example 6-2, displays the topology databases with the least-cost paths to destination ISs.

**Example 6-2** **show isis topology** *Command*

```
R1#show isis topology
IS-IS paths to level-1 routers
System Id        Metric  Next-Hop    Interface   SNPA
R1                --
R2                10      R2          Se0         *HDLC*
R4                10      R4          Se1         *HDLC*


R2#show isis topology
IS-IS paths to level-1 routers
System Id        Metric  Next-Hop    Interface   SNPA
R1                10      R1          Se0         *HDLC*
R2                --
R4                10      R4          Se1         *HDLC*
IS-IS paths to level-2 routers
System Id        Metric  Next-Hop    Interface   SNPA
R2                --
R5                10      R5          Et0         0010.7bb5.9e20
```

Notice in Example 6-2 that the output for Router R1 (an L1 router) shows the topology database for L1 only and the output for Router R2 (an L1/L2 router) shows that separate topology databases exist for L1 and L2.

The fields in the topology database are common for both levels of routing. They are as follows:

- The System ID column shows the NET of the destination IS. Cisco IOS software uses dynamic host name mapping (RFC 2763) to map the system ID to a host name that is available to the router.

- The Metric column displays the sum of the metrics on the least-cost path to the destination.

- The Next-Hop column displays the next IS along the path to a destination.

- The Interface column shows the output interface that leads to the system listed in Next-Hop.

- The SNPA column contains the OSI Layer 2 address of the next hop. HDLC is shown as the SNPA across an HDLC serial interface. The SNPA across an Ethernet interface will be the system ID (MAC address). The SNPA can also be the DLCI if it is across a Frame Relay interface.

The topology database on R1 (an L1 router) in Example 6-2 shows only routers within the local area. R1 is doing only L1 routing, so it does not know of any routers outside its area. Traffic bound for other areas is forwarded to the nearest router doing L2 routing—in this case, R2.

R2 is doing both levels of routing. It thus maintains two topology databases. The L1 database looks very much like the R1 database; only routers within the local area are listed. The L2 database is where the external area router, R5, finally shows up.

### Intra-Area Routing on R1

In Example 6-3, the **show clns route** command on R1 displays the CLNS destinations to which this router routes packets. R1 displays only its local NET entry because it is an L1-only router; therefore, R1 has no L2 area routes to display.

**Example 6-3**  **show clns route** *and* **show isis route** *Commands on R1*

```
R1#show clns route
CLNS Prefix Routing Table
49.0001.0000.0000.0001.00, Local NET Entry

R1#show isis route
IS-IS Level-1 Routing Table - version 312
System Id Next-Hop  Interface   SNPA   Metric State
R2        R2        Se0        *HDLC*  10     Up    L2-IS
R4        R4        Se1        *HDLC*  10     Up
R1         --
Default route out of area - (via 1 L2-attached IS)
System Id Next-Hop  Interface   SNPA   Metric State
          R2        Se0        *HDLC*  10     Up
```

The **show isis route** command on R1 in Example 6-3 shows the L1 routes to IS-IS neighbors. R1 is aware of the other L1 routers in its area.

The L1/L2 routers (R2) appear in the L1 routing table by virtue of their L1 connection, with a note at the end of their entry to show that they also act as L2 routers. The closest L1/L2 router also appears as the default route out of the area.

The next-hop IS, the interface over which the next hop is reached, the SNPA, and the summed metric to that destination for all IS routes are shown. The neighbors show that their state is up to indicate that the hello process has successfully established an adjacency.

The same **show clns route** and **show isis route** commands executed on R2 and shown in Example 6-4 (the L1/L2 router) present these results:

- **show clns route**—This command displays the CLNS prefix routing table and the local NET entry. It displays the L2 routes to its own and neighbor areas. The [110/10] number next to the area ID represents the administrative distance of IS-IS for CLNS—that is, 110 and the IS-IS metric.

---

**NOTE**      The administrative distance of IS-IS for IP is 115.

---

- **show isis route**—This command displays the Level 1 IS-IS routing table. Notice that no default route is listed.

---

**NOTE**      From the **show clns route** output, you can see that R2 regards the route to its own area (49.0001) as being through itself, further emphasizing that the L1 and L2 processes operate separately.

---

**Example 6-4**   **show clns route** *and* **show isis route** *Commands on R2*

```
R2#show clns route
CLNS Prefix Routing Table
49.0001.0000.0000.0002.00, Local NET Entry
49.0002 [110/10]
  via R5, IS-IS, Up, Ethernet0
49.0001 [110/0]
  via R2, IS-IS, Up

R2#show isis route
IS-IS Level-1 Routing Table - version 47
System Id    Next-Hop    Interface    SNPA     Metric   State
R4           R4          Se1          *HDLC*   10       Up
R1           R1          Se0          *HDLC*   10       Up
```

Comparing the R1 and R2 outputs, notice that R2, as a Level 2 IS, has a prefix table that contains routes outside the local area and that R1 (an L1 router) has a default route. You also notice that each router, acting as an L1 IS, has all area neighbors in its IS-IS route table.

In Example 6-5, the output from the **show clns protocol** command shows the following:

- The integrated IS-IS process, its tag, if present, and the level types on the router
- The system ID and area ID for this router
- The interfaces using Integrated IS-IS for routing, including whether they are routing for IP, CLNS, or both
- Any redistribution of other route sources
- The information regarding the distances for L2 CLNS routes and the acceptance and generation of metrics

**Example 6-5**  **show clns protocol** *Command as a Troubleshooting Tool*

```
R2#show clns protocol

IS-IS Router: <Null Tag>
  System Id: 1921.6800.1006.00  IS-Type: level-1-2
  Manual area address(es):
        49.0001
  Routing for area address(es):
        49.0001
  Interfaces supported by IS-IS:
        Serial0 - IP
    Ethernet0 - IP
  Redistribute:
   static (on by default)
  Distance for L2 CLNS routes: 110
  RRR level: level-1
  Generate narrow metrics: level-1-2
  Accept narrow metrics:   level-1-2
  Generate wide metrics:   none
  Accept wide metrics:     none
```

In the output of Example 6-6, the **show clns neighbors** command shows the following:

- The IS-IS neighbors
- The SNPAs and state
- The holdtime, which is the timeout for receipt of no hellos, after which the neighbor is declared down
- The neighbor level and type

Also in Example 6-6, the output from the **show clns interface** command shows the following:

- The interface runs IS-IS and attempts to establish L1 adjacencies.
- The interface numbers and circuit ID for IS-IS purposes.
- The metric(s) for the interface.
- The priority for DIS negotiation. Priority is irrelevant in this case because it is a serial HDLC interface.
- Information about hello timers and the number of established adjacencies.

**Example 6-6** show clns neighbors *Command to Verify Adjacencies*

```
R2#show clns neighbors
System Id     Interface SNPA              State Holdtime  Type  Protocol
R1            Se0       *HDLC*             Up    28        L1    IS-IS
R5            Et0       0000.0c92.de4c     Up    20        L2    IS-IS

R2#show clns interface serial 0
Serial0 is up, line protocol is up
  Checksums enabled, MTU 1500, Encapsulation HDLC
  ERPDUs enabled, min. interval 10 msec.
  RDPDUs enabled, min. interval 100 msec., Addr Mask enabled
  Congestion Experienced bit set at 4 packets
  CLNS fast switching disabled
  CLNS SSE switching disabled
  DEC compatibility mode OFF for this interface
  Next ESH/ISH in 12 seconds
  Routing Protocol: IS-IS
    Circuit Type: level-1
    Interface number 0x1, local circuit ID 0x101
    Level-1 Metric: 10, Priority: 64, Circuit ID: R2.00
    Number of active level-1 adjacencies: 1
    Next IS-IS Hello in 5 seconds
```

# Configuring Basic Integrated IS-IS

This section outlines specific commands necessary to implement IS-IS on a Cisco router. The commands for IS-IS are a bit different from those of the other IP routing protocols you have read about so far, so it is important to understand how to enable IS-IS processes. Additionally, the default settings for IS-IS can result in the inefficient use of router and network resources, and suboptimal routing. Therefore, a network administrator also needs to know how to effectively tune IS-IS for optimum performance.

## Integrated IS-IS Configuration Steps

Four steps are required for the basic setup of Integrated IS-IS. Additional commands are available for fine-tuning the configuration.

Step 1   Define areas, prepare the addressing plan (NETs) for routers, and determine which interfaces to enable Integrated IS-IS on.

Step 2   Enable IS-IS on the router.

Step 3   Configure the router's NET.

Step 4   Enable Integrated IS-IS on the proper interfaces. Do not forget interfaces to stub IP networks, such as loopbacks (although there are no CLNS neighbors).

Before you configure Integrated IS-IS, you must map out the areas and plan the addressing. After that is done, you need three commands (see Table 6-4) to enable Integrated IS-IS on a router for IP routing. You can then use additional commands to fine-tune the IS-IS processes.

**Table 6-4**    *Commands Necessary to Configure Integrated IS-IS*

| Command | Description |
| --- | --- |
| **router isis** | Enables IS-IS as an IP routing protocol and assigns a tag to the process (optional). Given in global configuration mode. |
| **net** [*number*] | Identifies the router for IS-IS by assigning a NET to the router. Given in router configuration mode. |
| **ip router isis** | Enables IS-IS on the interfaces that run IS-IS. (This approach is slightly different from most other IP routing protocols, where the interfaces are defined by network statements; no network statement exists under the IS-IS process.) Given in interface configuration mode. |

## Step 1: Define the Area and Addressing

Recall that all inter-area traffic in IS-IS must traverse the L2 backbone area. Thus, CLNS addresses must be planned to execute a two-level hierarchy. You must decide which routers will be backbone (L2) routers, which routers will be L1/L2 ABRs, and which will be internal area (L1) routers. If some routers must do both L1 and L2 routing, the specific interfaces that will participate in each type of routing should be identified.

Remember that a router's CLNS address is called the NET, and it consists of three main parts:

- The prefix, which identifies the area that the router is a part of
- The system ID, which uniquely identifies each device
- The NSEL, which must be 0

It is not enough to plan the IS-IS area addressing. You must also plan IP addressing to have a scalable network. The IP addresses must be planned to allow for summarization of addresses. Route summarization is the key idea that enables all the benefits of the hierarchical addressing design. Route summarization minimizes routing update traffic and resource utilization.

Be particularly careful when you configure the IP addressing on the router, because it is more difficult to troubleshoot IP address misconfigurations with IS-IS. The IS-IS neighbor relationships are established over OSI CLNS, not over IP. Because of this approach, two ends of a CLNS adjacency can have IP addresses on different subnets, with no impact on the operation of IS-IS.

## Step 2: Enable IS-IS on the Router

The **router isis** global configuration command enables Integrated IS-IS on the router. Optionally, you can apply a tag to identify multiple IS-IS processes.

```
Router(config)#router isis area-tag
```

Just as multiple OSPF processes can be present on the same router, multiple IS-IS processes are possible. The process name is significant only to the local router. If it is omitted, the Cisco IOS software assumes a null tag. If more than one IS-IS process is used, the network plan should indicate which interfaces will participate in which IS-IS process.

CLNS routing is disabled by default but is automatically enabled when the **router isis** command is given. To enable CLNS routing in addition to IP routing, use the **clns routing** global configuration command. Additionally, you must enable the IS-IS routing process on an interface to support CLNS routing.

---

**NOTE**    By default, the Cisco IOS software makes the router an L1/L2 router.

---

## Step 3: Configure the NET

After the IS-IS process is enabled, you must identify the router for IS-IS by assigning a NET to the router with the **net** command given in router configuration mode:

```
Router(config-router)#net network-entity-title
```

Even when you use IS-IS for IP routing only (and not for the purpose of CLNS addressing), you must still configure a NET. The NET is a combination of area number and a unique system identification number for each particular router, plus an NSEL of 00 at the end. The area number must be between 1 and 13 bytes in length. The system ID has a fixed length of 6 bytes in Cisco routers. The system ID must be unique throughout each area (L1) and throughout the backbone (L2).

## Step 4: Enable Integrated IS-IS

The final step is to select which interfaces participate in IS-IS routing. Interfaces that use IS-IS to distribute their IP information (and thus that can also be used to establish IS-IS adjacencies) must be configured using the **ip router isis** interface command:

```
Router(config-if)#ip router isis area-tag
Router(config-if)#clns router isis area-tag tag
```

If there is more than one IS-IS process, interfaces must state the IS-IS process to which they belong by specifying the appropriate process name in the optional *tag* field. If no tag is listed, the Cisco IOS software assumes a tag value of 0. If only one IS-IS process is active on the router, no *tag* value is needed.

Use the **clns router isis** interface command to enable the IS-IS routing process on an interface to support CLNS routing.

Example 6-7 shows a simple Integrated IS-IS configuration for IP routing only; CLNS routing is not enabled. It specifies only one IS-IS process, so the optional tag is not used. The NET configures the router to be in area 49.0001 and assigns a system ID of 0000.0000.0002. IS-IS is enabled on the Ethernet 0 and serial 0 interfaces. Because no level is configured under the IS-IS routing process, this router acts as an L1/L2 router by default.

**Example 6-7**  *IS-IS Configuration Steps: Simple Integrated IS-IS Example*

```
router isis
 net 49.0001.0000.0000.0002.00
 !
interface ethernet 0
 ip address 10.1.1.1 255.255.255.0
 ip router isis
 !
interface serial 0
 ip address 10.1.2.1 255.255.255.0
 ip router isis
```

# Optimizing IS-IS

Optimizing IS-IS facilitates its proper functioning and maximizes its efficiency. Three commands that help optimize IS-IS operation are discussed next.

## Changing the IS-IS Router Level

Remember that the default configuration of IS-IS leaves the router with an IS type of L1/L2. Although this configuration has the advantage of allowing all routers to learn of each other and pass routes without too much administrative oversight, it is not the most efficient way to build an IS-IS network. Routers with the default configuration send out both L1 and L2 hellos and maintain both L1 and L2 LSDBs. Each router should be configured to support the minimum level of routing required, which does the following:

- **Saves memory**—If a router does not need the LSDB for one of the levels, it does not maintain one.

- **Saves bandwidth**—Hellos and LSPs are sent only for the necessary level.

If a router is to operate only as an internal-area router or a backbone router, specify this configuration by entering the **is-type** router configuration command. To specify that the router act only as an internal area (L1) router, use **is-type level-1**. To specify that the router act only as a backbone (L2) router, use **is-type level-2-only**. If the level type has been changed from the default, and the router needs to return to acting as an L1/L2 router, use **is-type level-1-2**:

```
Router(config-router)#is-type {level-1 | level-1-2 | level-2-only}
```

## Changing the IS-IS Interface Level

Although the router can be an L1/L2 router, it might not be required to establish both types of adjacencies over all interfaces. If an L1 router is connected out a particular interface, there is no need for your router to send L2 hellos out that interface. Similarly, if only an L2 router is connected to an interface, there is no need to send L1 hellos out that interface. It wastes bandwidth and router resources to try to establish adjacencies that do not exist. To make IS-IS more efficient in these types of situations, configure the interface to send only the needed type of hellos. This configuration is done with the interface command **isis circuit-type**, and then you specify either **level-1** or **level-2-only**. If the circuit type is not configured by default, the Cisco IOS software attempts to establish both types of adjacencies over the interface (**level-1-2**).

```
Router(config-if)#isis circuit-type {level-1 | level-1-2 | level-2-only}
```

## Changing the IS-IS Metric

Unlike most other IP protocols, IS-IS takes no account of line speed or bandwidth when it sets its link metrics. All interfaces are assigned a metric value of 10. In a network with links of varying types and speeds, this assignment can result in suboptimal routing. To change the metric value, use the **isis metric** *metric* {**level-1** I **level-2**} interface command. The metric can have different values for L1 and L2 over the same interface. The *metric* value is from 1 to 63.

## Tuning IS-IS Example

Figure 6-24 shows two different areas, with their respective configuration in Example 6-8. Area 49.0002 contains only one router (R5) and needs to do only L2 routing. It is appropriate to change Router R5's IS type to L2-only.

**Figure 6-24** *Tuning IS-IS*

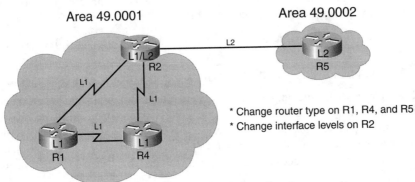

**Example 6-8** *Tuning IS-IS Configuration*

```
R1(config)#router isis
R1(config-router)#net 49.0001.0000.0000.0001.00
R1(config-router)#is-type level-1
R1(config)#interface serial 0
R1(config-if)#ip router isis
R1(config-if)#isis metric 35 level-1
R1(config)#interface serial 1
R1(config-if)#ip router isis
R1(config-if)#isis metric 35 level-1
```

**Example 6-8**  *Tuning IS-IS Configuration (Continued)*

```
R2(config)#router isis
R2(config-router)#net 49.0001.0000.0000.0002.00
R2 (config)#interface Ethernet 0
R2 (config-if)#ip router isis
R2 (config-if)#isis circuit-type level-2-only
R2 (config)#interface serial 0
R2 (config-if)#ip router isis
R2 (config-if)#isis circuit-type level-1
R2 (config-if)#isis metric 35 level-1
R2 (config)#interface serial 1
R2 (config-if)#ip router isis
R2 (config-if)#isis circuit-type level-1
R2 (config-if)#isis metric 35 level-1
```

Area 49.0001 has three routers. R1 and R4 are strictly internal area routers; they do not connect to routers in any other area. It is appropriate to configure the routers as IS type L1. R2 connects to the internal area routers and also to R5, in a different area. R2 must do both L1 and L2 routing, so it is left at the default setting. However, there is no need for R2 to send L2 hellos out the interfaces connected to R1 and R4. It is appropriate to set the IS-IS circuit type of R2's serial 0 and serial 1 interfaces to L1. Similarly, because R2's Ethernet 0 interface connects only to an L2 router, you should set the IS-IS circuit type to L2-only.

Remember that the IS-IS metric for all interfaces is 10. In the topology shown, the serial links are slower than the Ethernet link. Additionally, it is possible that the serial links themselves all have different bandwidths. Using the default metric does not give the routers a true picture of the value of each link, so the routers cannot make truly informed routing decisions. As shown in the sample configuration, you should change the IS-IS metric at each interface to reflect your preference for a link.

# Scalable IS-IS in Large Networks and IP Summarization

Routing protocol scalability is a function of the appropriate use of route summarization.

An intermediate system, IS-IS router, can be configured to aggregate a range of IP addresses into a summary address. The router summarizes IP routes into L1, L2, or both. The default is **level-2**.

```
Router(config-router)#summary-address prefix mask [level-1 | level-2 |
   level-1-2]
```

The benefits of summarization include the following:

- Reduced routing table size
- Reduced LSP traffic and protection from flapping routes
- Reduced memory requirements
- Reduced CPU usage

The following is an example of the command summarizing 10.3.2.0/23 into Level 2:

```
P3R1(config-router)#summary-address 10.3.2.0 255.255.254.0 level-2
```

Route summarization is removed with the **no** form of the command.

# Verifying IS-IS Configuration and Troubleshooting IS-IS Operations

To verify the IS-IS configuration and IP functionality of the Integrated IS-IS network, use the following commands. They can also be useful for troubleshooting problems with the IS-IS network.

- **show ip protocols**—Displays the active IP routing protocols, the interfaces on which they are active, and the networks for which they are routing.

- **show ip route**—Displays the IP routing table. You can specify the details for a particular route or a list of all routes in the routing table from a particular process.

Example 6-9 is sample output from the **show ip protocols** command that shows information about IP routing being done over Integrated IS-IS. IS-IS is running, it is not redistributing any other protocols, and address summarization has not been configured. Example 6-9 also shows that interfaces Serial 0 and Ethernet 0 are taking part in Integrated IS-IS, that there are three sources of routing information (the neighbor routers), and that the administrative distance of Integrated IS-IS is 115.

**Example 6-9**   **show ip protocols** *Command to Examine IS-IS*

```
R2#show ip protocols

Routing Protocol is "isis"
  Sending updates every 0 seconds
  Invalid after 0 seconds, hold down 0, flushed after 0
  Outgoing update filter list for all interfaces is
  Incoming update filter list for all interfaces is
  Redistributing: isis
  Address Summarization:
    None
  Routing for Networks:
    Serial0
    Ethernet0
Routing Information Sources:
    Gateway         Distance      Last Update
    11.0.0.1              115      00:11:44
    13.0.0.1              115      00:11:44
    14.0.0.1              115      00:11:44
Distance: (default is 115)
```

In Example 6-10, the sample output from the **show ip route isis** command shows only the IS-IS routes. These routes are all from L1, as indicated by the **i L1** tag.

**Example 6-10 show ip route isis** *Command*

```
R2#show ip route isis
i L1 11.0.0.0/8 [115/10] via 192.168.20.1, Serial0
i L1 13.0.0.0/8 [115/10] via 192.168.220.3, Ethernet0
i L1 14.0.0.0/8 [115/20] via 192.168.220.3, Ethernet0
```

Integrated IS-IS uses, by default, an administrative distance of 115. The metric shown for each route is taken from the IS-IS cost to the destination.

In Example 6-10, for the value of [115/20], 115 is the Integrated IS-IS administrative distance, and 20 is the IS-IS metric.

# Summary

In this chapter, you learned that IS-IS is the most popular and stable IP routing protocol in the ISP industry. It allows routers to communicate with routers, and it serves as an IGP for the CLNS. You also read that IS-IS and OSPF are both open standards and that they support VLSM and converge quickly. You now know how to select and implement the most effective method of IP routing for your network's topology and its requirements. You read about the various uses of NSAP addresses. You learned that adjacency forms based on the area address announced in the incoming IIH and the type of router. You know that the update process floods LSPs throughout the domain, that NET addresses identify a device, and that IP addresses identify an interface. You learned the four steps for basic IS-IS setup and the additional commands for fine-tuning the IS-IS processes.

# References

For additional information, refer to these resources:

*Dictionary of Internetworking Terms and Acronyms*, Cisco Press, ISBN: 1587200457

Cisco Systems IS-IS Tech notes:

www.cisco.com/en/US/tech/tk365/tk381/tech_tech_notes_list.html

# Configuration Exercise: Configuring Integrated IS-IS in Multiple Areas

In this exercise, you will configure routers for IS-IS routing.

---

### Introduction to the Configuration Exercises

This book uses Configuration Exercises to help you practice configuring routers with the commands and topics presented. If you have access to real hardware, you can try these exercises on your routers. See Appendix H, "Configuration Exercise Equipment Requirements and Initial Configurations," for a list of recommended equipment and initial configuration commands for the routers. However, even if you don't have access to any routers, you can go through the exercises and keep a log of your own running configurations or just read through the solution. Commands used and solutions to the Configuration Exercises are provided after the exercises.

In the Configuration Exercises, the network is assumed to consist of two pods, each with four routers. The pods are interconnected to a backbone. You configure pod 1. No interaction between the two pods is required, but you might see some routes from the other pod in your routing tables in some exercises if you have it configured (the Configuration Exercise answers show the routes from the other pod). In most of the exercises, the backbone has only one router; in some cases, another router is added to the backbone. Each Configuration Exercise assumes that you have completed the previous chapters' Configuration Exercises on your pod.

**NOTE**
Throughout this exercise, the pod number is referred to as *x*, and the router number is referred to as *y*. Substitute the appropriate numbers as needed.

## Objectives

After completing this exercise, you will be able to connect to other devices using IS-IS routes.

## Visual Objective

Figure 6-25 illustrates the topology used in this exercise.

**Figure 6-25** *Configuration Exercise Topology*

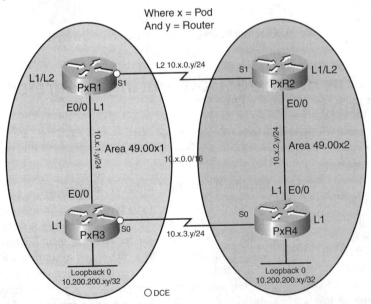

## Command List

In this exercise, you will use the commands in Table 6-4, listed in logical order. Refer to this list if you need configuration command assistance during the exercise.

---

**CAUTION**    Although the command syntax is shown in Table 6-5, the addresses shown are typically for the P*x*R1 and P*x*R3 routers. Be careful when addressing your routers! Refer to the exercise instructions and the appropriate visual objective diagram for addressing details.

---

**Table 6-5**    *Configuration Exercise Commands*

| Command | Description |
|---|---|
| (config)#**router isis** | Turns on IS-IS. |
| (config-router)#**net 49.0031.3333.3333.3333.00** | Identifies the NET to be used for this device. CLNS addresses identify a device, not an interface. |
| (config-if)#**ip router isis** | Enables IS-IS routing on an interface. |
| (config-router)#**is-type level-1** | Sets this router to participate in only Level 1 routing (on internal routers only). |
| (config-if)#**isis circuit level-2-only** | Sets this interface to participate in only Level 2 routing. |
| (config-router)#**summary-address 10.3.2.0 255.255.254.0 level-2** | Creates a summary route into L2. |

## Task 1: Cleaning Up and Preparing

**Step 1**    Remove all OSPF configuration from the edge routers. Remember to remove the **ip ospf network point-to-multipoint** command on the S0.1 subinterface.

**Step 2**    Shut down the serial 0 interface on the edge routers (P*x*R1 and P*x*R2) to isolate your pod from the core for this lab. Enable the serial S1 interface between these two routers.

**Step 3**    Remove all OSPF configurations from the internal routers (P*x*R3 and P*x*R4). Verify that interface S0 is enabled on these routers. If the interface is shut, enable it.

## Task 2: Configuring Integrated IS-IS in Multiple Areas

**Step 1**    Configure IS-IS on the pod routers. Then assign a NET address to each router, as shown in Table 6-6. P*x*R1 and P*x*R3 should be in area 49.00*x*1. P*x*R2 and P*x*R4 should be in area 49.00*x*2.

**Table 6-6**   *Assigning NET Addresses*

| Router | NET | Example (Pod 2) |
|--------|-----|-----------------|
| P*x*R1 | 49.00*x*1.*yyyy.yyyy.yyyy*.00 | 49.0021.1111.1111.1111.00 |
| P*x*R2 | 49.00*x*2.*yyyy.yyyy.yyyy*.00 | 49.0022.2222.2222.2222.00 |
| P*x*R3 | 49.00*x*1.*yyyy.yyyy.yyyy*.00 | 49.0021.3333.3333.3333.00 |
| P*x*R4 | 49.00*x*2.*yyyy.yyyy.yyyy*.00 | 49.0022.4444.4444.4444.00 |

**Step 2**   Leave the edge routers as the default IS type of L1/L2; however, set up internal routers to participate only in L1 using the proper IS-IS router configuration command. When the setup is complete, all communication between the areas will go through the edge routers.

**Step 3**   All routers are L1/L2 by default. L1 communication takes place only if the areas match, however. Therefore, P*x*R3 and P*x*R4 do not form an L1 adjacency with each other, because they are in different areas. They form an adjacency only with their directly connected edge router. P*x*R1 and P*x*R2 form an L2 communication.

Look at the IS-IS topology for an internal router. Note that it should have an L1 adjacency with the edge router. Trace the path from one internal router to the loopback address of the opposite internal router. The trace should show that the path to reach the opposite internal router loopback goes through the edge router.

**Step 4**   Look at the routing table on the internal routers. Notice that IS-IS L1 routing tables resemble OSPF totally stubby areas. For instance, where is the route to the loopback address you just pinged?

**Step 5**   Look at the IS-IS topology table on the edge routers. Although these routers participate in L1 and L2 routing, they use only L1 on the Ethernet interface and only L2 on the serial interface.

**Step 6**   Use the proper IS-IS interface configuration command to remove the redundant and unused hellos by forcing P*x*R1 and P*x*R2 to participate in a single routing level on each interface (Ethernet = L1 only and serial = L2 only). Redundancy wastes bandwidth and router resources to form both L1 and L2 adjacencies.

**Step 7**   On P*x*R1, summarize the 10.*x*.0.0 and 10.*x*.1.0 networks to 10.*x*.0.0/23. On P*x*R2, summarize the 10.*x*.2.0/24 and 10.*x*.3.0/24 networks to 10.*x*.2.0/23. Examine the routing tables on P*x*R1 and P*x*R2 to verify that the summary route appears.

## Exercise Verification

You have successfully completed this exercise when you achieve these results:

- IS-IS is configured properly and exchanging routes.
- IS-IS has been optimized to use only one type of hello over each link.
- IS-IS has been optimized to pass a summary route.

# Solution to Configuration Exercise: Configuring Integrated IS-IS in Multiple Areas

This section provides the answers to the questions in the Configuration Exercise.

**NOTE**   Some answers provided cover multiple steps; the answers are given after the last step to which that answer applies.

## Solution to Task 1: Cleaning Up and Preparing

**Step 1**   Remove all OSPF configuration from the edge routers. Remember to remove the **ip ospf network point-to-multipoint** command on the S0.1 subinterface.

**Step 2**   Shut down the serial 0 interface on the edge routers (P*x*R1 and P*x*R2) to isolate your pod from the core for this lab. Enable the serial S1 interface between these two routers.

**Solution:**

```
P1R1(config)#no router ospf 1
P1R1(config)#interface serial 0.1
P1R1(config-subif)#no ip ospf network point-to-multipoint
P1R1(config-subif)#exit
P1R1(config)#interface serial 0
P1R1(config-if)#shutdown
P1R1(config-if)#exit
P1R1(config)#interface serial 1
P1R1(config-if)#no shutdowm
```

**Step 3**   Remove all OSPF configurations from the internal routers (P*x*R3 and P*x*R4). Verify that interface S0 is enabled on these routers. If the interface is shut, enable it.

**Solution:**

```
P1R3(config)#no router ospf 1
P1R3(config)#interface serial 0
P1R3(config-if)#no shutdown
```

## Solution to Task 2: Configuring Integrated IS-IS in Multiple Areas

**Step 1**   Configure IS-IS on the pod routers. Then assign a NET address to each router, as shown in Table 6-6. P*x*R1 and P*x*R3 should be in area 49.00*x*1. P*x*R2 and P*x*R4 should be in area 49.00*x*2.

**Table 6-6**    *Assigning NET Addresses*

| Router | NET | Example (Pod 2) |
|--------|-----|-----------------|
| P*x*R1 | 49.00*x*1.*yyyy.yyyy.yyyy*.00 | 49.0021.1111.1111.1111.00 |
| P*x*R2 | 49.00*x*2.*yyyy.yyyy.yyyy*.00 | 49.0022.2222.2222.2222.00 |
| P*x*R3 | 49.00*x*1.*yyyy.yyyy.yyyy*.00 | 49.0021.3333.3333.3333.00 |
| P*x*R4 | 49.00*x*2.*yyyy.yyyy.yyyy*.00 | 49.0022.4444.4444.4444.00 |

**Solution**:

For Router P1R1:

```
P1R1(config)#router isis
P1R1(config-router)#net 49.0011.1111.1111.1111.00
```

For Router P1R2:

```
P1R2(config)#router isis
P1R2(config-router)#net 49.0012.2222.2222.2222.00
```

For Router P1R3:

```
P1R3(config)#router isis
P1R3(config-router)#net 49.0011.3333.3333.3333.00
```

For Router P1R4:

```
P1R4(config)#router isis
P1R4(config-router)#net 49.0012.4444.4444.4444.00
```

Enable IS-IS on the active serial, loopback, and Ethernet interfaces of all the routers in your pod using the **ip router isis** command.

For Router P1R1:

```
P1R1(config)#interface ethernet 0
P1R1(config-if)#ip router isis
P1R1(config-if)#exit
P1R1(config)#interface serial 1
P1R1(config-if)#ip router isis
```

For Router P1R2:

```
P1R2(config)#interface e0
P1R2(config-if)#ip router isis
P1R2(config-if)#exit
P1R2(config)#interface serial 1
P1R2(config-if)#ip router isis
```

For Router P1R3:

```
P1R3(config)#interface e0
P1R3(config-if)#ip router isis
P1R3(config-if)#exit
P1R3(config)#interface serial 0
P1R3(config-if)#ip router isis
P1R3(config-if)#exit
P1R3(config)#interface loopback 0
P1R3(config-if)#ip router isis
```

For Router P1R4:

```
P1R4(config)#interface ethernet 0
P1R4(config-if)#ip router isis
P1R4(config-if)#exit
P1R4(config)#interface s0
P1R4(config-if)#ip router isis
P1R4(config-if)#exit
P1R4(config)#interface loopback 0
P1R4(config-if)#ip router isis
```

**Step 2**    Leave the edge routers as the default IS type of L1/L2; however, set up internal routers to participate only in L1 using the proper IS-IS router configuration command. When the setup is complete, all communication between the areas will go through the edge routers.

**Solution:**

For Router P1R3:

```
P1R3(config)#router isis
P1R3(config-router)#is-type level-1
```

For Router P1R4:

```
P1R4(config)#router isis
P1R4(config-router)#is-type level-1
```

**Step 3**    All routers are L1/L2 by default. L1 communication takes place only if the areas match, however. Therefore, P*x*R3 and P*x*R4 do not form an L1 adjacency with each other, because they are in different areas. They form an adjacency only with their directly connected edge router. P*x*R1 and P*x*R2 form an L2 communication.

Look at the IS-IS topology for an internal router. Note that it should have an L1 adjacency with the edge router. Trace the path from one internal router to the loopback address of the opposite internal router. The trace should show that the path to reach the opposite internal router loopback goes through the edge router.

**Solution:**

```
P1R3#show isis topology
IS-IS paths to level-1 routers
System Id            Metric  Next-Hop          Interface   SNPA
P1R1                 10      P1R1              Et0         0060.4740.e8de
P1R3                 --
P1R3#

P1R3#trace 10.200.200.14

Type escape sequence to abort.
Tracing the route to P1R4 (10.200.200.14)

  1 P1R1 (10.1.1.1) 4 msec 4 msec 4 msec
  2 P1R2 (10.1.0.2) 24 msec 16 msec 20 msec
  3 P1R4 (10.1.2.4) 24 msec *  16 msec
P1R3#
```

**Step 4**  Look at the routing table on the internal routers. Notice that IS-IS L1 routing tables resemble OSPF totally stubby areas. For instance, where is the route to the loopback address you just pinged?

**Solution:**

```
P1R3#show ip route
Codes: C - connected, S - static, I - IGRP, R - RIP, M - mobile, B - BGP
       D - EIGRP, EX - EIGRP external, O - OSPF, IA - OSPF inter area
       N1 - OSPF NSSA external type 1, N2 - OSPF NSSA external type 2
       E1 - OSPF external type 1, E2 - OSPF external type 2, E - EGP
       i - IS-IS, L1 - IS-IS level-1, L2 - IS-IS level-2, ia - IS-IS inter area
       * - candidate default, U - per-user static route, o - ODR
       P - periodic downloaded static route

Gateway of last resort is 10.1.1.1 to network 0.0.0.0

     10.0.0.0/8 is variably subnetted, 4 subnets, 2 masks
C       10.200.200.13/32 is directly connected, Loopback0
C       10.1.3.0/24 is directly connected, Serial0
C       10.1.1.0/24 is directly connected, Ethernet0
i L1    10.1.0.0/24 [115/20] via 10.1.1.1, Ethernet0
i*L1 0.0.0.0/0 [115/10] via 10.1.1.1, Ethernet0
P1R3#
```

**Step 5**  Look at the IS-IS topology table on the edge routers. Although these routers participate in L1 and L2 routing, they use only L1 on the Ethernet interface and only L2 on the serial interface.

**Solution:**

```
P1R1#show isis topology

IS-IS paths to level-1 routers
System Id            Metric  Next-Hop          Interface   SNPA
P1R1                 --
P1R3                 10      P1R3              Et0         0060.4740.efb6
```

```
IS-IS paths to level-2 routers
System Id          Metric  Next-Hop        Interface   SNPA
P1R1                 --
P1R2                 10     P1R2            Se1         *HDLC*
P1R3                 **
P1R4                 **
P1R1#
```

**Step 6**    Use the proper IS-IS interface configuration command to remove the redundant
and unused hellos by forcing PxR1 and PxR2 to participate in a single routing
level on each interface (Ethernet = L1 only and serial = L2 only). Redundancy
wastes bandwidth and router resources to form both L1 and L2 adjacencies.

**Solution:**

For Router P1R1:

```
P1R1(config)#interface serial 1
P1R1(config-if)#isis circuit ?
  level-1       Level-1 only adjacencies are formed
  level-1-2     Level-1-2 adjacencies are formed
  level-2-only  Level-2 only adjacencies are formed
  <cr>

P1R1(config-if)#isis circuit level-2-only
P1R1(config-if)#exit
P1R1(config)#interface ethernet 0
P1R1(config-if)#isis circuit level-1
```

For Router P1R2:

```
P1R2(config)#interface serial 1
P1R2(config-if)#isis circuit level-2-only
P1R2(config-if)#exit
P1R2(config)#interface ethernet 0
P1R2(config-if)#isis circuit level-1
```

**Step 7**    On PxR1, summarize the 10.x.0.0 and 10.x.1.0 networks to 10.x.0.0/23. On
PxR2, summarize the 10.x.2.0/24 and 10.x.3.0/24 networks to 10.x.2.0/23.
Examine the routing tables on PxR1 and PxR2 to verify that the summary
route appears.

**Solution:**

For Router P1R1:

```
P1R1(config)#router isis
P1R1(config-router)#summary-address 10.1.0.0 255.255.254.0
```

For Router P1R2:

```
P1R2(config)#router isis
P1R2(config-router)#summary-address 10.1.2.0 255.255.254.0
```

For Router P1R1:

```
P1R1#show ip route
Codes: C - connected, S - static, I - IGRP, R - RIP, M - mobile, B - BGP
       D - EIGRP, EX - EIGRP external, O - OSPF, IA - OSPF inter area
       N1 - OSPF NSSA external type 1, N2 - OSPF NSSA external type 2
       E1 - OSPF external type 1, E2 - OSPF external type 2, E - EGP
       i - IS-IS, L1 - IS-IS level-1, L2 - IS-IS level-2, ia - IS-IS inter area
       * - candidate default, U - per-user static route, o - ODR
       P - periodic downloaded static route

Gateway of last resort is not set

     10.0.0.0/8 is variably subnetted, 7 subnets, 3 masks
i L2    10.200.200.14/32 [115/30] via 10.1.0.2, Serial1
i L1    10.200.200.13/32 [115/20] via 10.1.1.3, Ethernet0
i L1    10.1.3.0/24 [115/20] via 10.1.1.3, Ethernet0
i L2    10.1.2.0/23 [115/20] via 10.1.0.2, Serial1
C       10.1.1.0/24 is directly connected, Ethernet0
i su    10.1.0.0/23 [115/10] via 0.0.0.0, Null0
C       10.1.0.0/24 is directly connected, Serial1
P1R1#
```

For Router P1R2:

```
P1R2#show ip route
Codes: C - connected, S - static, I - IGRP, R - RIP, M - mobile, B - BGP
       D - EIGRP, EX - EIGRP external, O - OSPF, IA - OSPF inter area
       N1 - OSPF NSSA external type 1, N2 - OSPF NSSA external type 2
       E1 - OSPF external type 1, E2 - OSPF external type 2, E - EGP
       i - IS-IS, L1 - IS-IS level-1, L2 - IS-IS level-2, ia - IS-IS inter area
       * - candidate default, U - per-user static route, o - ODR
       P - periodic downloaded static route

Gateway of last resort is not set

     10.0.0.0/8 is variably subnetted, 7 subnets, 3 masks
i L1    10.200.200.14/32 [115/20] via 10.1.2.4, Ethernet0
i L2    10.200.200.13/32 [115/30] via 10.1.0.1, Serial1
i L1    10.1.3.0/24 [115/20] via 10.1.2.4, Ethernet0
i su    10.1.2.0/23 [115/10] via 0.0.0.0, Null0
C       10.1.2.0/24 is directly connected, Ethernet0
i L2    10.1.0.0/23 [115/20] via 10.1.0.1, Serial1
C       10.1.0.0/24 is directly connected, Serial1
P1R2#
```

# Exercise Verification

You have successfully completed this exercise when you achieve these results:

- IS-IS is configured properly and exchanging routes.
- IS-IS has been optimized to use only one type of hello over each link.
- IS-IS has been optimized to pass a summary route.

# Review Questions

Answer the following questions, and then refer to Appendix G, "Answers to Review Questions," for the answers.

**1** What does Integrated IS-IS support?

a. BGP

b. IP

c. OSPF

d. IPX

**2** IS-IS is the most popular routing protocol for which of the following?

a. Small businesses

b. Government organizations

c. ISPs

d. Military establishments

**3** Because IS-IS is protocol-independent, it can support which of the following?

a. IPv4

b. IPv6

c. OSI CLNS

d. All of the above

**4** IS-IS routers use what to establish and maintain neighbor relationships?

a. OSHs

b. IIHs

c. ISKs

d. CLHs

**5** As soon as neighbor adjacency is established, IS-IS routers exchange link-state information using what?

a. Link-state packets

b. Logical state packets

c. Adjacency state packets

d. Reachability state packets

**6** Why can IS-IS be considered superior to OSPF? (Select the two best answers.)

a. More commands need to be configured.

b. More timers can be fine-tuned.

c. Faster router CPUs are required.

d. It aggregates router updates.

**7**  What are CLNS addresses used by routers called?

    a.  DSAPs

    b.  ESAPs

    c.  MSAPs

    d.  NSAPs

**8**  What are NSAP addresses equivalent to?

    a.  A combination of the IP address and upper-layer protocol in an IP header

    b.  Layer 2 addresses

    c.  A combination of the transport layer address and data link address

    d.  Layer 4 addresses

**9**  The Cisco implementation of Integrated IS-IS divides the NSAP address into what three fields?

    a.  The data-link address, the logical address, and the upper-layer address

    b.  The PDU address, the NSAP selector, and the cluster ID

    c.  The area address, the system ID, and the NSAP selector

    d.  The transport layer address, the CPU ID, and the NSAP selector

**10**  True or false: Cisco routers routing CLNS data do not use addressing that conforms to the ISO 10589 standard.

**11**  What is the first part of a NET?

    a.  Zone ID

    b.  Area ID

    c.  Cluster ID

    d.  ISO ID

**12**  What kind of address is used to uniquely identify an OSI host within an IS-IS routing domain?

    a.  NET

    b.  CLSN

    c.  Area

    d.  IP

**13**  What kind of router is aware of only the local area topology?

    a.  External

    b.  Level 2

    c.  Internal

    d.  Level 1

**14**  Routing between areas is based on what?

    a.  Area ID

    b.  IP address

    c.  Level 2

    d.  Level 1/Level 2

**15**  True or false: In IS-IS, area boundaries fall on the links.

**16**  True or false: Symmetrical routing is a feature of IS-IS.

**17**  In IS-IS, PDUs are encapsulated directly into an OSI data-link frame, so there is no what?

    a.  ISO or area ID header

    b.  CLNP or IP header

    c.  ES or IP header

    d.  CLNS or area ID header

**18**  Cisco IOS software automatically uses broadcast mode for which two of the following?

    a.  Dialer interfaces

    b.  LAN interfaces

    c.  Multipoint WAN interfaces

    d.  Point-to-point subinterfaces

**19**  True or false: IS-IS offers support specifically for NBMA networks.

**20**  In IS-IS, rather than having each router connected to the LAN advertise an adjacency with every other router on the LAN, the entire network is considered a router. This is called what?

    a.  Area

    b.  Cluster

    c.  LSDB

    d.  Pseudonode

**21**  True or false: IS-IS maintains the L1 and L2 LSPs in different LSDBs.

**22**  True or false: CSNPs are periodically sent on point-to-point links.

This chapter discusses different means of controlling routing update information. It covers the following topics:

- Migrating to Multiple IP Routing Protocols
- Controlling Routing Update Traffic
- Using Administrative Distance to Influence the Route-Selection Process
- Policy-Based Routing

# CHAPTER 7

# Manipulating Routing Updates

This chapter discusses different means of controlling routing update information and route redistribution between different routing protocols. Methods of controlling the routing information sent between these routing protocols include using distribute lists, using route maps, and changing the administrative distance. This chapter discusses route redistribution and each of these methods and also explains the configuration of policy-based routing using route maps.

After completing this chapter, you will be able to describe how to migrate to using multiple IP routing protocols, describe how route selection is done when multiple routing protocols are running, and configure route redistribution between those routing protocols. You will also be able to configure passive interfaces and distribute lists for dynamic routing protocols. You will be able to use route maps to control and filter routing updates and redistribution and change the default administrative distance of certain routes to control which updates are selected. You will also be able to configure policy-based routing using route maps.

**NOTE**   This chapter on manipulating routing updates is placed before the chapters on Border Gateway Protocol (BGP) because knowledge of route redistribution is required for the BGP discussion.

## Migrating to Multiple IP Routing Protocols

Simple routing protocols work well for simple networks, but as networks grow and become more complex, it might be necessary to change routing protocols. Often the transition between routing protocols takes place gradually, so multiple routing protocols might run in the network for variable lengths of time. This section examines several reasons for using more than one routing protocol. The goal is for you to understand how routing information is exchanged between them and how Cisco routers operate in a multiple routing protocol environment.

# Considerations When Migrating to Another Routing Protocol

There are many reasons why a change in routing protocols might be required. For example, as a network grows and becomes more complex, the original routing protocol might not be the best choice anymore. For example, Routing Information Protocol (RIP) and Interior Gateway Routing Protocol (IGRP) periodically send their entire routing tables in their updates; as the network grows larger, the traffic from those updates can slow the network down, indicating that a change to a more scalable routing protocol might be necessary. The network might be using Cisco's IGRP or Enhanced IGRP (EIGRP) and now a protocol that supports multiple vendors might be required, or a new policy that specifies a particular routing protocol might be introduced.

Whatever the reason for the change, network administrators must manage the migration from one routing protocol to another carefully and thoughtfully. An accurate topology map of the network and an inventory of all network devices are also critical for success. The new routing protocol will most likely have different requirements and capabilities from the old one; it is important for network administrators to understand what must be changed and create a detailed plan before making any changes. For example, link-state routing protocols, such as Open Shortest Path First (OSPF) and Intermediate System-to-Intermediate System (IS-IS), require a hierarchical network structure. Network administrators need to decide which routers will reside in the backbone area and how to divide the other routers into areas. Although EIGRP does not require a hierarchical structure, it operates much more effectively within one.

During the transition, there will likely be a time when both routing protocols are running in the network; it might be necessary to redistribute routing information between the two protocols. If so, the redistribution strategy must be carefully planned to avoid disrupting network traffic or causing suboptimal routing. The timing of the migration must also be determined. For example, will the entire network change all at once, or will it be done in stages? Where will the migration start? An administrator must understand the network to make these decisions.

Note that networks may run multiple routing protocols as part of their design, not only as part of a migration. Thus, redistribution of routing information might be required in other cases as well. The "Redistribution Overview" section discusses the need for redistribution.

Figure 7-1 shows a sample network migration. This network initially used RIP version 1 (RIPv1) and is migrating to OSPF, necessitating the following changes:

- Conversion of the old fixed-length subnet mask (FLSM) addressing scheme to a variable-length subnet mask (VLSM) configuration

- Use of a hierarchical addressing scheme to facilitate route summarization and make the network more scalable

- Division of the network from one large area into a transit backbone area and two other areas

**Figure 7-1**    *Network Migration Might Require Readdressing and Other Changes*

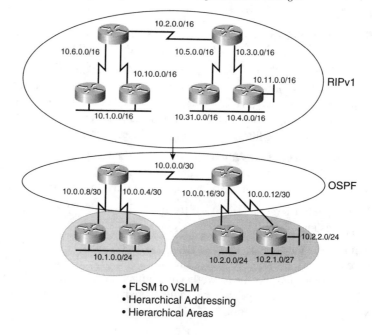

- FLSM to VSLM
- Herarchical Addressing
- Hierarchical Areas

# Planning for a New IP Address Allocation

If the migration to a new routing protocol requires the IP address scheme to be changed, this must also be carefully planned. One of the first steps when migrating to a new address space is to determine the timeframe for the changeover: Will it be a gradual change, with migration of different remote sites each weekend? Or will the new addressing be put in all at once? Resources and schedules must be considered when migrating multiple remote sites to a new address space.

The address plan created for the migration needs to be well-documented and accessible for review and reference by all internetworking personnel. If there are any questions or conflicts, this document helps settle the differences. The plan should include the new addresses for the entire network and should be reviewed by all internetworking personnel so that they can add comments or identify conflicts with existing addressing. For example, the new address space might have portions already in use, unbeknownst to the designer. Having remote personnel review and agree to the address assignments for the entire network helps prevent problems in the implementation stage.

After the IP addressing scheme has been determined, you must plan its implementation. In most situations, the network must stay operational during the transition from one protocol to another and from one IP addressing plan to another. For successful implementation, carefully consider the following:

- **Host addressing**—If host IP addresses are statically assigned, this is an excellent time to migrate to using Dynamic Host Configuration Protocol (DHCP). If DHCP is already in use, changes in IP addressing are transparent to most end users.

- **Access lists and other filters**—Firewalls and other types of traffic filters will have been configured using the old IP addresses. It is important to have complete documentation of all the traffic filters within the network so that they can be updated to use the new IP addresses. Any route filtering based on the old addresses also needs to be updated.

- **Network Address Translation (NAT)**—If you're using NAT, it needs to be configured to recognize and use the new IP addresses. The new addresses also might need to be translated to different outside addresses, depending on the network configuration.

- **Domain Name System (DNS)**—If the network contains DNS servers, decide which mappings must be redone to reflect the new addresses.

- **Timing**—In a large network, changes are typically done in stages. You might start at the core and work outward or start at the edges and work inward; base the decision on a thorough knowledge of the network. Other important decisions are the time of day and day of the week when changes will be implemented; be sure to allow enough time to test and verify the new configuration.

---

**NOTE**  In this section, *core* and *edge* are generic terms used to simplify the discussion of redistribution.

---

- **Transition strategy**—Decide whether you will change sections of the network to use only the new routing protocol and IP addressing or whether you will run the new routing protocol and IP addresses in tandem with the old ones during the transition. If both old and new IP addresses will be used for a time, you might need to configure secondary addresses on the router's interfaces.

---

**NOTE**  This list includes some of the items your transition plan needs to address. Depending on your network, there might be others.

---

For example, suppose that the migration shown in Figure 7-1 is being done because there are frequent changes in the network. These frequent changes cause frequent RIP updates to be sent, which uses up bandwidth. Network convergence is also slow with RIP. If OSPF were implemented in this network without changing the addressing so that route summarization could be implemented, triggered updates would still be sent frequently whenever any part of the network topology changed. The changes would cause the shortest path first (SPF) algorithm to be recomputed frequently, which in turn would disrupt routing. In this case, OSPF would probably be a worse choice than RIP. However, if a proper addressing plan were implemented, this same network could run very efficiently. With route summarization in the right places, changes in the network topology would be hidden from most of the other routers, and the SPF algorithm would not need to run for every topology change.

## Migrating to a New IP Address Space

As soon as the plans for transitioning to a new IP addressing scheme are complete and approved, they can be implemented. Transitioning an IP address space can involve the following steps:

**Step 1**   Select the router and subnet to be transitioned.

**Step 2**   Assign secondary IP addresses to the router's interfaces.

**Step 3**   Configure new **network** commands under the routing process.

**Step 4**   Update DNS for the new addresses.

**Step 5**   Implement DHCP if it isn't already being used.

**Step 6**   Configure the DHCP server to assign new addresses, masks, and default gateways.

**Step 7**   Allow enough time for the transition.

**Step 8**   After the transition has occurred, change the secondary IP addresses to be primary addresses.

**Step 9**   Remove the old **network** commands from the routing process.

**Step 10**  Remove old DNS entries.

**Step 11**  Begin migrating to the new routing protocol on part of the network. Use route redistribution to pass routing information between the old and new routing protocol.

Here are some of the tasks involved in implementing new IP addressing:

- **Host addressing**—Configure the DHCP server to start assigning the new IP addresses to individual hosts. Configure new static IP addresses on devices such as servers. Remember to also change the assigned default gateways on devices.

- **Access lists and other filters**—It is important to keep complete and detailed documentation of all access lists, firewall configurations, routing updates, and other filters in the network. You must update all these elements to use the new IP address ranges. If you are keeping the old and new address ranges active during the transition, the access lists and filters need modification to add the new addresses. After the transition is complete, you must remove the old addresses.

- **NAT**—It is also important to have complete documentation of all devices performing NAT within the network. Servers, routers, and firewall devices can all perform translation, and they might need to have their configurations changed. If you are using both old and new address ranges during the transition, just add the new addresses. Again, if you use this approach, after the transition is complete, you must remove the old addresses.

- **DNS**—Any DNS used for internal addresses needs mappings for the new IP addresses. Be sure to include the changes for any static hosts, such as web or application servers.

- **Timing and transition strategy**—If some portions of the network will be using both the old and new IP addresses for any length of time during the transition, configure the affected routers to recognize and use both address ranges. Secondary addresses may be used on the router interfaces.

## Configuring a Secondary IP Address

If secondary addresses are required in the transition, they must be configured before any of the host addressing, NAT, or access lists can be changed. The old routing protocol also might need updating to include the new networks in its **network** commands if you want it to route for these networks.

Use the **ip address** *address mask* **secondary** interface configuration command to assign a secondary IP address to an interface.

Example 7-1 shows a sample configuration on a router. The **ip address 172.17.1.3 255.255.255.240 secondary** command is applied to interface Ethernet 0 on this router; the resulting configuration is shown in Example 7-2.

**Example 7-1** *Configuration Before the Secondary Address Is Applied*

```
Router#show run

<output omitted>
interface Ethernet0
 ip address 10.1.2.3 255.255.255.0
```

**Example 7-2** *Configuration with a Secondary Address Applied*

```
Router#show run

<output omitted>
interface Ethernet0
 ip address 172.17.1.3 255.255.255.240 secondary
 ip address 10.1.2.3 255.255.255.0
```

Some routing protocols have issues with secondary addresses.

---

### Key Point: EIGRP and OSPF Use Primary Interface Addresses

EIGRP and OSPF use an interface's primary IP address as the source of their updates. They expect the routers on both sides of a link to belong to the same subnet.

---

EIGRP and OSPF do not accept an update from, or form a neighbor relationship with, a router on the wrong subnet; EIGRP generates error messages constantly in this situation. Therefore, you must use the same subnet for the primary addresses on neighbor routers; do not use the same subnet for the secondary address on one router and the primary address on its neighbor.

---

### Key Point: Make New Addresses Primary Addresses

As soon as all the routers in a portion of the network are using the new routing protocol and the new IP address ranges, the routers can be reconfigured to use the new IP addresses as primary. One way to introduce more fault tolerance into this process, and to make the final transition easier, is to configure the original addresses as secondary addresses and the new addresses as the primary addresses until the entire network has transitioned, everything has been tested, and the network is stable. The original IP addresses, now the secondary addresses, should be removed when they are no longer needed.

---

## Migrating to a New Routing Protocol

After planning and implementing the new IP addressing scheme, planning for the migration to the new routing protocol can begin.

Before making any changes to the network, plan an escape route: Make sure you have backup copies of all device configurations. Network documentation should include information on packet-flow paths so that you can be sure that the changes will not create suboptimal paths or routing loops. Documentation should also include baseline statistics for data flows.

When planning the migration, consider the following steps:

**Step 1**    To avoid delays, you need a clear and comprehensive timeline for all steps in the migration, including for implementing and testing the new router configurations. Consider the impact of the changes on user traffic, and make changes when traffic is least likely to be affected (for example, during off-peak hours).

Be sure to allow time for testing and verifying changes as well as configuration. The migration to a new routing protocol typically is gradual—one section of the network is changed at a time. When the network's IP addressing was planned, the network was probably divided into either logical or physical hierarchical areas; plan when each of these areas will be migrated to the new routing protocol.

**Step 2**    Determine which routing protocol is the core and which is the edge. Usually, a choice must be made between starting the migration at the core of the network and working out to the edges, or starting at an edge router and working in toward the network core. Each approach has its pros and cons. For example, if you start at an edge, you can install and test the protocol without disrupting the main network traffic, and you can work out problems that might not have shown up in a testing lab in a more realistic, smaller-scale environment before progressing with the migration.

Migrations to protocols that require a backbone area (such as OSPF) should begin at the core of the network. Because all interarea traffic goes through the backbone, the backbone must be in place before the areas can communicate. Other reasons to begin with the network core include the fact that there are typically fewer devices at the core, and that redundancy is usually built into the core design, which helps minimize the effects of any problems. The most experienced network staff is also usually at the same location as the core network devices.

**Step 3**   Identify the boundary routers where the multiple routing protocols will run. Part of migrating to a new routing protocol includes redistribution between the old and new routing protocol. As part of the timeline, you must determine how many routers will be converted to the new routing protocol at one time. The routers that are the gateways between the old and the new routing protocols are the ones that may perform redistribution.

**Step 4**   Determine how you want to redistribute information between the core and edge routing protocols. Redistribution is covered in detail in the following sections.

**Step 5**   Verify that all devices support the new routing protocol. If not, you need to download, install, and test any required Cisco IOS software upgrades before beginning the migration.

**Step 6**   Implement and test the routing solution in a lab environment. The migration strategy should be tested in as realistic an environment as possible to identify and correct any bugs ahead of time.

Each step of the migration must be documented, tested, and verified.

## Redistribution Overview

The following are possible reasons why you might need multiple routing protocols:

- You are migrating from an older Interior Gateway Protocol (IGP) to a new IGP. Multiple redistribution boundaries may exist until the new protocol has displaced the old protocol completely. Running multiple routing protocols during a migration is effectively the same as a network that has multiple routing protocols running as part of its design.

- You want to use another protocol but need to keep the old routing protocol because of the host system's needs. For example, UNIX host-based routers might run only RIP.

- Different departments might not want to upgrade their routers to support a new routing protocol, or they might not implement a sufficiently strict filtering policy. In these cases, you can protect yourself by terminating the other routing protocol on one of your routers.

- If you have a mixed-router vendor environment, you can use a Cisco-specific routing protocol, such as EIGRP, in the Cisco portion of the network and then use a common standards-based routing protocol, such as OSPF, to communicate with non-Cisco devices.

When multiple routing protocols are running in different parts of the network, hosts in one part of the network might need to reach hosts in the other part. One way to accomplish this is to advertise a default route into each routing protocol. Default routes might not always be the best policy. For example, the network design might not allow default routes, and if there is more than one way to get to a destination network, routers might need information about routes in the other parts of the network to determine the best path to that destination. Additionally, if multiple paths exist, a router must have sufficient information to determine a loop-free path to the remote networks.

When any of these situations arise, Cisco routers allow internetworks using different routing protocols (referred to as routing domains or autonomous systems) to exchange routing information through a feature called route redistribution.

---

**Key Point: Redistribution**

Redistribution is defined as the capability of boundary routers connecting different routing domains to exchange and advertise routing information between autonomous systems.

---

**NOTE**     The term autonomous system (AS) as used here denotes internetworks using different routing protocols. These routing protocols may be IGPs or Exterior Gateway Protocols (EGPs). This use of the term *autonomous system* is different than when discussing BGP.

In some cases the same protocol may be used in multiple different domains or autonomous systems within a network. The multiple instances of the protocol are treated no differently than if they were distinct protocols; redistribution is required to exchange routes between them.

---

Within each AS, the internal routers have complete knowledge of their network. The router that interconnects the autonomous systems is called a *boundary router*. The boundary router must be running all the routing protocols that will exchange routes. In most cases, route redistribution must be configured to redistribute routes from one routing protocol to another. The only time redistribution is automatic in IP routing protocols is between IGRP and EIGRP processes running on the same router and using the same AS number.

When a router redistributes routes, it allows a routing protocol to advertise routes that were not learned through that routing protocol. These redistributed routes could have been learned via a different routing protocol, such as when redistributing between EIGRP and OSPF, or they could have been learned from static routes or by a direct connection to a network. Routers can redistribute static and connected routes as well as routes from other routing protocols.

Redistribution is always performed *outbound*. The router doing redistribution does not change its routing table. For example, when redistribution between OSPF and EIGRP is configured, the OSPF process on the boundary router takes the EIGRP routes in the routing table and advertises them as OSPF routes to its OSPF neighbors. Likewise, the EIGRP process on the boundary router takes the OSPF routes in the routing table and advertises them as EIGRP routes to its EIGRP neighbors. Both autonomous systems know about the routes of the other, and each AS can then make informed routing decisions for these networks. The boundary router's neighbors see the redistributed routes as external routes.

In this example, if a packet destined for one of the networks in the OSPF domain arrives from the EIGRP AS, the boundary router must have the OSPF routes for the networks in the OSPF domain in its routing table to be able to forward the traffic.

---

### Key Point: Redistributed Routes

Routes must be in the routing table for them to be redistributed.

---

This requirement might seem self-evident, but it can be a source of confusion. For instance, if a router learns about a network via EIGRP and OSPF, only the EIGRP route is put in the routing table because it has a lower administrative distance. Suppose RIP is also running on this router, and you want to redistribute OSPF routes into RIP. That network is not redistributed into RIP, because it is placed in the routing table as an EIGRP route, not as an OSPF route.

Figure 7-2 illustrates an AS running OSPF that is connected to an AS running EIGRP. The internal routers within each AS have complete knowledge of their networks, but without redistribution, they do not know about the routes present in the other AS. Router A is the boundary router, and it has active OSPF and EIGRP processes.

**Figure 7-2**  *Redistribution Between OSPF and EIGRP*

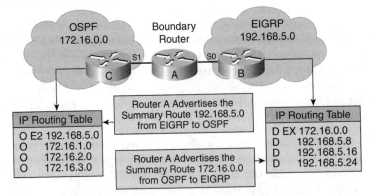

Without redistribution, Router A performs ships-in-the-night (SIN) routing: Router A passes OSPF route updates to its OSPF neighbors on the interfaces participating in OSPF, and it passes EIGRP route updates to its EIGRP neighbors on the interfaces participating in EIGRP. Router A does not exchange information between EIGRP and OSPF. If routers in the OSPF routing domain need to learn about the routes in the EIGRP domain, or vice versa, Router A must redistribute routes between EIGRP and OSPF.

Router A learns about network 192.168.5.0 from Router B via the EIGRP routing protocol running on its S0 interface. After redistribution is configured, Router A redistributes that information to Router C via OSPF on its S1 interface. Routing information is also passed in the other direction, from OSPF to EIGRP.

The routing table in Router B shows that it has learned about network 172.16.0.0 via EIGRP (as indicated by the D in the routing table) and that the route is external to this AS (as indicated by the EX in the routing table). The routing table in Router C shows that it has learned about network 192.168.5.0 via OSPF (as indicated by the O in the routing table) and that the route is external (type 2) to this AS (as indicated by the E2 in the routing table).

Note that in this example, Router A is redistributing routes that are summarized on the network class boundary. (Recall that EIGRP automatically summarizes on the class boundary, whereas OSPF must be configured to summarize.) This approach helps improve routing table stability and decreases the routing tables' size.

# Redistribution Implementation Considerations

Redistribution of routing information, although powerful, adds to a network's complexity and increases the potential for routing confusion, so it should be used only when necessary. The key issues that arise when using redistribution are as follows:

- **Routing feedback (loops)**—Depending on how you employ redistribution—for example, if more than one boundary router is performing route redistribution—routers can send routing information received from one AS back into that same AS. The feedback is similar to the routing loop problem that occurs in distance vector topologies.

- **Incompatible routing information**—Because each routing protocol uses different metrics to determine the best path and because the metric information about a route cannot be translated exactly into a different protocol, path selection using the redistributed route information might not be optimal. To prevent suboptimal routing, as a rule, redistributed routes should be assigned a seed metric that is higher than the metric for any routes in the receiving AS. For example, if RIP routes are being redistributed into OSPF, and the highest OSPF metric in the AS is 50, the redistributed RIP routes should be assigned an OSPF metric higher than 50.

- **Inconsistent convergence times**—Different routing protocols converge at different rates. For example, RIP converges more slowly than EIGRP, so if a link goes down, the EIGRP network learns about it before the RIP network.

| NOTE | Good planning ensures that these issues do not cause problems in your network. |

To understand why some of these problems might occur, you must first understand how Cisco routers select the best path when more than one routing protocol is running and how they convert the metrics used when importing routes from one autonomous system into another. These topics are discussed in the following sections.

## Selecting the Best Route

Most routing protocols have metric structures and algorithms that are incompatible with other protocols. In a network in which multiple routing protocols are present, the exchange of route information and the capability to select the best path across the multiple protocols is critical. For routers to select the best path when they learn two or more routes to the same destination from different routing protocols, Cisco uses the following two parameters:

- **Administrative distance**—As discussed in Chapter 2, "Routing Principles," administrative distance is used to rate a routing protocol's believability. Each routing protocol is prioritized in order from most to least believable (or reliable or trustworthy) using a value called the administrative distance. This criterion is the first thing a router uses to determine which routing protocol to believe if more than one protocol provides route information for the same destination.

- **Routing metric**—This is a value representing the path between the local router and the destination network. The metric is usually a hop or cost value, depending on the protocol being used.

## Administrative Distance

Table 7-1 lists the default believability (administrative distance) of protocols supported by Cisco.

**Table 7-1**   *Default Administrative Distances of Routing Protocols*

| Routing Protocol | Default Administrative Distance Value |
|---|---|
| Connected interface | 0 |
| Static route out an interface | 0 |
| Static route to a next-hop address | 1 |
| EIGRP summary route | 5 |
| External BGP | 20 |
| Internal EIGRP | 90 |
| IGRP | 100 |
| OSPF | 110 |
| IS-IS | 115 |
| RIP version 1 and RIP version 2 | 120 |

**Table 7-1**    *Default Administrative Distances of Routing Protocols (Continued)*

| Routing Protocol | Default Administrative Distance Value |
|---|---|
| EGP | 140 |
| On-Demand Routing (ODR) | 160 |
| External EIGRP | 170 |
| Internal BGP | 200 |
| Unknown | 255 |

---

**Key Point: Administrative Distance**

Lower administrative distances are considered more believable (better).

---

**NOTE**    Static routes are configured with the **ip route** *prefix mask* {*address* | *interface*} [*distance*] [**permanent**] [**tag** *tag*] global configuration command, described in the "Static and Default Routes" section later in this chapter. If the *address* parameter is used in this command, it specifies the address of the next-hop router to use to get to the destination network, and the default administrative distance is 1. If the *interface* parameter is used instead, specifying the local router outbound interface to use to reach the destination network, the router considers this a directly connected route, and the default administrative distance is 0.

For example, if a router receives a route to network 10.0.0.0 from IGRP (administrative distance 100) and then receives a route to the same network from OSPF (administrative distance 110), the router uses the administrative distance to determine that IGRP is more believable and adds the IGRP version of the route to the routing table.

When using route redistribution, you might occasionally need to modify a protocol's administrative distance so that it is preferred. For example, if you want the router to select RIP-learned routes rather than IGRP-learned routes to the same destination, you must increase the administrative distance for IGRP or decrease the administrative distance for RIP. Modifying the administrative distance is discussed in the later section "Using Administrative Distance to Influence the Route-Selection Process."

## Seed Metrics

When a router is redistributing, it must assign a metric to the redistributed routes.

---

**Key Point: Seed Metric for Directly Connected Networks**

When a router advertises a link that is directly connected to one of its interfaces, the initial, or seed, metric that is used is derived from the characteristics of that interface, and the metric increments as the routing information is passed to other routers.

---

For OSPF, the seed metric is based on the interface's bandwidth. For IS-IS, each interface has a default IS-IS metric of 10. For EIGRP and IGRP, the seed metric is based on the interface bandwidth and delay. For RIP, the seed metric starts with a hop count of 0 and increases in increments from router to router.

Redistributed routes are not physically connected to a router; rather, they are learned from other routing protocols. If a boundary router is to redistribute information between routing protocols, it must be capable of translating the metric of the received route from the source routing protocol into the other routing protocol. For example, if a boundary router receives a RIP route, the route has hop count as a metric. To redistribute the route into OSPF, the router must translate the hop count into a cost metric that the other OSPF routers will understand.

This metric, referred to as the seed or default metric, is defined during redistribution configuration. After the seed metric for a redistributed route is established, the metric increments normally within the AS. (The exception to this rule is OSPF E2 routes, which hold their initial metric regardless of how far they are propagated across an AS.)

The **default-metric** router configuration command establishes the seed metric for all redistributed routes. Cisco routers also allow the seed metric to be specified as part of the **redistribution** command, either with the *metric* option or by using a route map. These commands are discussed in detail in the section "Configuring Redistribution."

---

### Key Point: The Seed Metric Should Be Larger Than the Largest Native Metric

When redistributing routing information, set the seed metric to a value larger than the largest metric within the receiving AS to help prevent suboptimal routing and routing loops.

---

### Default Seed Metrics

Table 7-2 illustrates the default seed metric value for routes that are redistributed into each IP routing protocol. RIP, IGRP, and EIGRP interpret the seed metric of 0 as infinity by default. A metric of infinity tells the router that the route is unreachable and, therefore, should not be advertised. Therefore, when redistributing routes into RIP, IGRP, and EIGRP, you must specify a seed metric, or the redistributed routes will not be advertised.

**Table 7-2** *Default Seed Metrics*

| Protocol That Route Is Redistributed Into | Default Seed Metric |
|---|---|
| RIP | Infinity |
| IGRP/EIGRP | Infinity |
| OSPF | 20 for all except BGP, which is 1 |
| IS-IS | 0 |
| BGP | BGP metric is set to IGP metric value |

For OSPF, the redistributed routes have a default type 2 (E2) metric of 20, except for redistributed BGP routes, which have a default type 2 metric of 1.

For IS-IS, the redistributed routes have a default metric of 0. But unlike RIP, IGRP, or EIGRP, a seed metric of 0 is not treated as unreachable by IS-IS.

For BGP, the redistributed routes maintain the IGP routing metrics.

## Redistribution Techniques

The following two methods of redistribution are available:

* **Two-way redistribution**—Redistributes all routes between the two routing processes.
* **One-way redistribution**—Passes a default route into one routing protocol and redistributes only the networks learned from that routing protocol into the other routing protocol.

---

### Key Point: One-Way Redistribution Is Safest

The safest way to perform redistribution is to redistribute routes in only one direction, on only one boundary router within the network. (Note, however, that this results in a single point of failure in the network.)

---

To redistribute, you must first determine which routing protocol is the core routing protocol and which ones are edge routing protocols. The core routing protocol is the main routing protocol running in the network. During a transition between routing protocols, the core is the new routing protocol, and the edge is the old routing protocol; in networks that run multiple routing protocols all the time, the core is usually the more advanced routing protocol.

If redistribution must be done in both directions, or on multiple boundary routers, the redistribution should be tuned to avoid problems such as suboptimal routing and routing loops.

Depending on your network design, you may use any of the following redistribution techniques, as illustrated in Figure 7-3:

* Redistribute a default route from the core AS into the edge AS, and redistribute routes from the edge routing protocols into the core routing protocol. This technique helps prevent route feedback, suboptimal routing, and routing loops.
* Redistribute multiple static routes about the core AS networks into the edge AS, and redistribute routes from the edge routing protocols into the core routing protocol. This method works if there is only one redistribution point; multiple redistribution points might cause route feedback.
* Redistribute routes from the core AS into the edge AS with filtering to block out inappropriate routes. For example, when there are multiple boundary routers, routes redistributed from the edge AS at one boundary router should not be redistributed back into the edge AS from the core at another redistribution point.
* Redistribute all routes from the core AS into the edge AS, and from the edge AS into the core AS, and then modify the administrative distance associated with redistributed routes so that they are not the selected routes when multiple routes exist for the same destination. For example, the administrative distance might need to be modified if the route learned by the native routing protocol is faster but has a higher (less believable) administrative

distance. Recall that if two routing protocols advertise routes to the same destination, information from the routing protocol with the lowest administrative distance is placed in the routing table. A route redistributed into a routing protocol inherits that protocol's default administrative distance by default. (Note, however, that some routing protocols assign a different default administrative distance for external routes learned.)

**Figure 7-3**  *Redistribution Techniques*

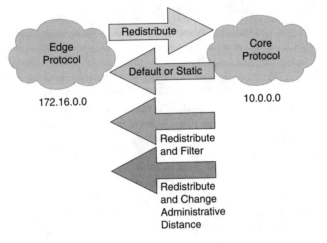

## Configuring Redistribution

As shown in Example 7-3, redistribution supports all routing protocols. Static and connected routes can also be redistributed to allow the routing protocol to advertise these routes.

**Example 7-3**  *Redistribution Supports All Protocols*

```
RtrA(config-router)#redistribute ?
bgp         Border Gateway Protocol (BGP)
connected   Connected
egp         Exterior Gateway Protocol (EGP)
eigrp       Enhanced Interior Gateway Routing Protocol (EIGRP)
igrp        Interior Gateway Routing Protocol (IGRP)
isis        ISO IS-IS
iso-igrp    IGRP for OSI networks
mobile      Mobile routes
odr         On Demand stub Routes
ospf        Open Shortest Path First (OSPF)
rip         Routing Information Protocol (RIP)
static      Static routes
```

---

### Key Point: Routes Are Redistributed into a Protocol

Routes are redistributed *into* a routing protocol, so the **redistribute** command is configured under the routing process that is to *receive* the redistributed routes.

---

Before implementing redistribution, consider the following points:

- You can only redistribute protocols that support the same protocol stack. For example, you can redistribute between IP RIP and OSPF because they both support the TCP/IP stack. You cannot redistribute between Internetwork Packet Exchange (IPX) RIP and OSPF because IPX RIP supports the IPX/Sequenced Packet Exchange (SPX) stack and OSPF does not. Although there are different protocol-dependent modules of EIGRP for IP, IPX, and AppleTalk, routes cannot be redistributed between them, because each protocol-dependent module supports a different protocol stack.

- The method you use to configure redistribution varies among combinations of routing protocols. For example, redistribution occurs automatically between IGRP and EIGRP when they have the same AS number, but redistribution must be configured between all other routing protocols. Some routing protocols require a metric to be configured during redistribution, but others do not.

The following steps for configuring redistribution are generic enough to apply to all routing protocol combinations. However, the commands used to implement the steps might vary. It is highly recommended that you review the Cisco IOS documentation for the configuration commands that apply to the specific routing protocols you want to redistribute.

---

**NOTE**    In this section, the terms *core* and *edge* are generic terms used to simplify the discussion of redistribution.

---

**Step 1**    Locate the boundary router(s) on which redistribution needs to be configured. Selecting a single boundary router for redistribution minimizes the likelihood of routing loops caused by feedback.

**Step 2**    Determine which routing protocol is the core or backbone protocol. Typically, this protocol is OSPF, IS-IS, or EIGRP.

**Step 3**    Determine which routing protocol is the edge or short-term (if you are migrating) protocol. Determine if all routes from the edge protocol need to be propagated into the core. Consider methods that reduce the number of routes.

**Step 4**    Access the core routing protocol, and select a method for injecting the required edge protocol routes into the core. Simple redistribution using summarized routes at network boundaries minimizes the number of new entries in the routing table of the core routers.

**Step 5**    After you have planned the edge-to-core redistribution, consider how to inject the core routing information into the edge protocol. Your choice depends on your network.

The following sections examine the specific commands for redistributing routes into the various IP routing protocols.

## The **redistribute** Command for RIP

Use the **redistribute** *protocol* [*process-id*] [**match** *route-type*] [**metric** *metric-value*] [**route-map** *map-tag*] router configuration command to redistribute routes into RIP. This command is explained in Table 7-3.

**Table 7-3**    **redistribute** *Command for RIP*

| Parameter | Description |
|---|---|
| *protocol* | The source protocol from which routes are redistributed. It can be one of the following keywords: **bgp**, **connected**, **egp**, **eigrp**, **igrp**, **isis**, **iso-igrp**, **mobile**, **odr**, **ospf**, **rip**, or **static**. |
| *process-id* | For BGP, EGP, EIGRP, or IGRP, this value is an AS number. For OSPF, this value is an OSPF process ID. This parameter is not required for IS-IS. |
| *route-type* | An optional parameter used when redistributing OSPF routes into another routing protocol. It is the criterion by which OSPF routes are redistributed into other routing domains. It can be any of the following: <br><br> **internal**—Redistributes routes that are internal to a specific AS. <br><br> **external 1**—Redistributes routes that are external to the AS but are imported into OSPF as a type 1 external route. <br><br> **external 2**—Redistributes routes that are external to the AS but are imported into OSPF as a type 2 external route. |
| *metric-value* | An optional parameter used to specify the RIP seed metric for the redistributed route. When redistributing into protocols other than OSPF (including RIP), if this value is not specified and no value is specified using the **default-metric** router configuration command, the default metric is 0. For protocols other than IS-IS (including RIP), the default metric of 0 is interpreted as infinity, and routes are not redistributed. The metric for RIP is hop count. |
| *map-tag* | An optional identifier of a configured route map to be interrogated to filter the importation of routes from this source routing protocol to the current routing protocol. |

Example 7-4 shows how to configure redistribution from OSPF process 1 into RIP. This example uses the **router rip** command to access the routing process *into* which routes need to be redistributed—the RIP routing process.

**Example 7-4**    *Configuring Redistribution into RIP*

```
RtrA(config)#router rip
RtrA(config-router)#redistribute ospf ?

  <1-65535>  Process ID
RtrA(config-router)#redistribute ospf 1 ?
  match      Redistribution of OSPF routes
  metric     Metric for redistributed routes
  route-map  Route map reference
...
  <cr>
```

The **redistribute** command is then used to specify the routing protocol to be redistributed into RIP. In this case, it is OSPF routing process number 1.

| NOTE | When redistributing into RIP, the default metric is infinity except when redistributing a static (including a default static route defined using the **ip route 0.0.0.0 0.0.0.0** command) or connected route. In that case, the default metric is 1. |
|---|---|

Figure 7-4 provides an example of redistributing routes into RIP. On Router A, routes from OSPF process 1 are redistributed into RIP and are given a seed metric of 3. Because no route type is specified, both internal and external OSPF routes are redistributed into RIP. Notice that Router B learns about the 172.16.1.0 network from Router A via RIP; Router B's routing table has 172.16.1.0 installed as a RIP route.

**Figure 7-4**  *Routes Redistributed into RIP*

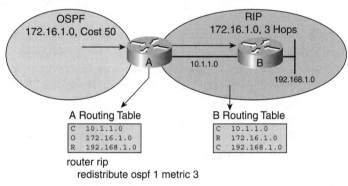

## The **redistribute** Command for OSPF

Use the **redistribute** *protocol* [*process-id*] [**metric** *metric-value*] [**metric-type** *type-value*] [**route-map** *map-tag*] [**subnets**] [**tag** *tag-value*] router configuration command to redistribute routes into OSPF. This command is explained in Table 7-4.

**Table 7-4**  **redistribute** *Command for OSPF*

| Parameter | Description |
|---|---|
| *protocol* | The source protocol from which routes are redistributed. It can be one of the following keywords: **bgp**, **connected**, **egp**, **eigrp**, **igrp**, **isis**, **iso-igrp**, **mobile**, **odr**, **ospf**, **rip**, or **static**. |
| *process-id* | For BGP, EGP, EIGRP, or IGRP, this value is an AS number. For OSPF, this value is an OSPF process ID. This parameter is not required for RIP or IS-IS. |
| *metric-value* | An optional parameter that specifies the OSPF seed metric used for the redistributed route. When redistributing into OSPF, the default metric is 20 (except for BGP, which is 1). Use a value consistent with the destination protocol—in this case, the OSPF cost. |

*continues*

**Table 7-4**     redistribute *Command for OSPF (Continued)*

| Parameter | Description |
|---|---|
| *type-value* | An optional OSPF parameter that specifies the external link type associated with the external route advertised into the OSPF routing domain. This value can be **1** for type 1 external routes or **2** for type 2 external routes. The default is 2. |
| *map-tag* | An optional identifier of a configured route map to be interrogated to filter the importation of routes from this source routing protocol to the current routing protocol. |
| **subnets** | An optional OSPF parameter that specifies that subnetted routes should also be redistributed. Only routes that are not subnetted are redistributed if the **subnets** keyword is not specified. |
| *tag-value* | An optional 32-bit decimal value attached to each external route. The OSPF protocol itself does not use this parameter. It may be used to communicate information between AS boundary routers (ASBRs). |

Example 7-5 shows how to configure redistribution from EIGRP AS 100 into OSPF. This example uses the **router ospf 1** command to access the OSPF routing process 1 into which routes need to be redistributed. The **redistribute** command is then used to specify the routing protocol to be redistributed into OSPF—in this case, the EIGRP routing process for AS 100.

**Example 7-5** *Configuring Redistribution into OSPF*

```
RtrA(config)#router ospf 1
RtrA(config-router)#redistribute eigrp ?

  <1-65535>  Autonomous system number
RtrA(config-router)#redistribute eigrp 100 ?

  metric        Metric for redistributed routes
  metric-type   OSPF/IS-IS exterior metric type for redistributed routes
  route-map     Route map reference
  subnets       Consider subnets for redistribution into OSPF
  tag           Set tag for routes redistributed into OSPF
  ...
  <cr>
```

**NOTE**     When redistributing into OSPF, the default metric is 20, the default metric type is 2, and subnets are not redistributed by default.

Figure 7-5 illustrates an example of redistributing EIGRP routes into OSPF. In this example, the default metric of 20 for OSPF is being used. The metric type is set to 1 (type 1 external [E1] routes), meaning that the metric increments whenever updates are passed through the network. The command contains the **subnets** option, so subnets are redistributed.

**Figure 7-5**   *Routes Redistributed into OSPF*

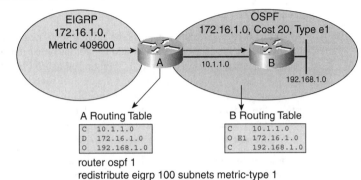

router ospf 1
redistribute eigrp 100 subnets metric-type 1

---

**Key Point: Redistributing Subnets into OSPF**

In Figure 7-5, the **subnets** keyword is used. If this keyword were omitted, *no* subnets would be redistributed into the OSPF domain (including the 172.16.1.0 subnet). Omitting this keyword is a common configuration error.

---

## The **redistribute** Command for EIGRP

Use the **redistribute** *protocol* [*process-id*] [**match** *route-type*] [**metric** *metric-value*] [**route-map** *map-tag*] router configuration command to redistribute routes into EIGRP. This command is explained in Table 7-5.

**Table 7-5**   **redistribute** *Command for EIGRP*

| Parameter | Description |
|-----------|-------------|
| *protocol* | The source protocol from which routes are redistributed. It can be one of the following keywords: **bgp**, **connected**, **egp**, **eigrp**, **igrp**, **isis**, **iso-igrp**, **mobile**, **odr**, **ospf**, **rip**, or **static**. |
| *process-id* | For BGP, EGP, EIGRP, or IGRP, this value is an AS number. For OSPF, this value is an OSPF process ID. This parameter is not required for RIP or IS-IS. |
| *route-type* | An optional parameter used when redistributing OSPF routes into another routing protocol. It is the criterion by which OSPF routes are redistributed into other routing domains. It can be one of the following: <br><br> **internal**—Redistributes routes that are internal to a specific AS. <br><br> **external 1**—Redistributes routes that are external to the AS but are imported into OSPF as a type 1 external route. <br><br> **external 2**—Redistributes routes that are external to the AS but are imported into OSPF as a type 2 external route. |

*continues*

**Table 7-5** **redistribute** *Command for EIGRP (Continued)*

| Parameter | Description |
|-----------|-------------|
| *metric-value* | An optional parameter that specifies the EIGRP seed metric, in the order of bandwidth, delay, reliability, load, and MTU, for the redistributed route. When redistributing into protocols other than OSPF (including EIGRP), if this value is not specified and no value is specified using the **default-metric** router configuration command, the default metric is 0. For protocols other than IS-IS (including EIGRP), the default metric of 0 is interpreted as infinity, and routes are not redistributed. Use a value consistent with the destination protocol. The metric for EIGRP is calculated based only on bandwidth and delay by default. |
| *map-tag* | Optional identifier of a configured route map that is interrogated to filter the importation of routes from this source routing protocol to the current routing protocol. |

Example 7-6 shows how to configure redistribution from OSPF into EIGRP AS 100. This example uses the **router eigrp 100** command to access the routing process into which routes need to be redistributed—in this case, the EIGRP routing process for AS100. The **redistribute** command is then used to specify the routing protocol to be redistributed into EIGRP AS 100— in this case, OSPF routing process 1.

**Example 7-6** *Configuring Redistribution into EIGRP*

```
RtrA(config)#router eigrp 100
RtrA(config-router)#redistribute ospf ?

  <1-65535>  Process ID
RtrA(config-router)#redistribute ospf 1 ?

  match       Redistribution of OSPF routes
  metric      Metric for redistributed routes
  route-map   Route map reference
...
<cr>
```

**NOTE**  When redistributing routes from another routing protocol into EIGRP, the default metric is infinity. When redistributing a static or connected route into EIGRP, the default metric is equal to the metric of the associated static or connected interface.

Table 7-6 shows the five parameters that comprise *metric-value* when redistributing into EIGRP (or IGRP).

**Table 7-6** *metric-value Parameters for EIGRP (and IGRP)*

| *metric-value* Parameter | Description |
|--------------------------|-------------|
| *bandwidth* | The route's minimum bandwidth in kilobits per second (kbps). |
| *delay* | Route delay in tens of microseconds. |

**Table 7-6**    *metric-value Parameters for EIGRP (and IGRP) (Continued)*

| metric-value Parameter | Description |
|---|---|
| *reliability* | The likelihood of successful packet transmission, expressed as a number from 0 to 255, where 255 means that the route is 100 percent reliable. |
| *loading* | The route's effective loading, expressed as a number from 1 to 255, where 255 means that the route is 100 percent loaded. |
| *mtu* | Maximum transmission unit. The maximum packet size in bytes along the route; an integer greater than or equal to 1. |

Figure 7-6 illustrates an example of redistributing OSPF routes into EIGRP AS 100. In this case, a metric is specified to ensure that routes are redistributed. The redistributed routes appear in Router B's table as external EIGRP (D EX) routes. External EIGRP routes have a higher administrative distance than internal EIGRP (D) routes, so internal EIGRP routes are preferred over external EIGRP routes.

**Figure 7-6**    *Routes Redistributed into EIGRP*

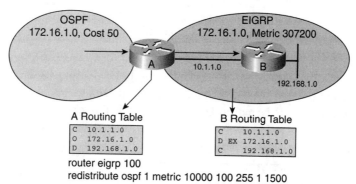

The metric used in this example is interpreted as follows:

- Bandwidth in kbps = 10,000
- Delay in tens of microseconds = 100
- Reliability = 255 (maximum)
- Load = 1 (minimum)
- MTU = 1500 bytes

## The **redistribute** Command for IS-IS

Use the **redistribute** *protocol* [*process-id*] [**level** *level-value*] [**metric** *metric-value*] [**metric-type** *type-value*] [**route-map** *map-tag*] router configuration command to redistribute routes into IS-IS. This command is explained in Table 7-7.

**Table 7-7** **redistribute** *Command for IS-IS*

| Parameter | Description |
|---|---|
| *protocol* | The source protocol from which routes are redistributed. It can be one of the following keywords: **bgp**, **connected**, **egp**, **eigrp**, **igrp**, **isis**, **iso-igrp**, **mobile**, **odr**, **ospf**, **rip**, or **static**. |
| *process-id* | For BGP, EGP, EIGRP, or IGRP, this value is an AS number. For OSPF, this value is an OSPF process ID. This parameter is not required for RIP. |
| *level-value* | An optional parameter that specifies how external routes are redistributed. They can be level 1 (**level-1**), level 1 and level 2 (**level-1-2**), or level 2 (**level-2**) routes. The default is **level-2**. |
| *metric-value* | An optional parameter that specifies the IS-IS seed metric used for the redistributed route. IS-IS uses a default metric of 0. Unlike RIP, IGRP, and EIGRP, a default metric of 0 is not treated as unreachable and is redistributed. The metric is incremented as the route is propagated into the IS-IS domain. Use a value consistent with the destination protocol—in this case, the IS-IS cost. |
| *type-value* | An optional parameter that specifies the IS-IS metric type as **external** or **internal**. The default is **internal**. |
| *map-tag* | An optional identifier of a configured route map to be interrogated to filter the importation of routes from this source routing protocol to the current routing protocol. |

Example 7-7 shows how to configure redistribution from EIGRP AS 100 into IS-IS. This example uses the **router isis** command to access the routing process into which routes need to be redistributed—the IS-IS routing process. The **redistribute** command is then used to specify the routing protocol to be redistributed into IS-IS—in this case, the EIGRP routing process for AS 100.

**Example 7-7** *Configuring Redistribution into IS-IS*

```
RtrA(config)#router isis
RtrA(config-router)#redistribute eigrp 100 ?

  level-1      IS-IS level-1 routes only
  level-1-2    IS-IS level-1 and level-2 routes
  level-2      IS-IS level-2 routes only
  metric       Metric for redistributed routes
  metric-type  OSPF/IS-IS exterior metric type for redistributed routes
  route-map    Route map reference
  ...
  <cr>
```

By default, routes are introduced into IS-IS as level 2, with a metric of 0.

**NOTE**   When redistributing IS-IS routes into other routing protocols, you have the option to include level 1, level 2, or both level 1 and level 2 routes. Example 7-8 shows the commands for choosing these routes. If no level is specified, all routes are redistributed.

**Example 7-8**    *Choosing the Level of Routes to Redistribute into IS-IS*

```
Router(config)#router ospf 1
Router(config-router)#redistribute isis ?

  level-1             IS-IS level-1 routes only
  level-1-2           IS-IS level-1 and level-2 routes
  level-2             IS-IS level-2 routes only
```

Figure 7-7 illustrates an example of redistributing from EIGRP AS 100 into IS-IS, on Router A. No metric is configured, so these routes have a seed metric of 0. No level type is given, so the routes are redistributed as level 2 routes (as shown by the L2 in the Router B routing table).

**Figure 7-7**    *Routes Redistributed into IS-IS*

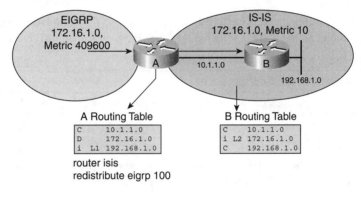

## The **default-metric** Command

---

### Key Point: Changing Default Metrics

You can affect how routes are redistributed by changing the default metric associated with a protocol. You either specify the default metric with the **default-metric** command or use the *metric-value* parameters in the **redistribute** command.

---

If you use the **default-metric** command, the default metric you specify applies to all protocols being redistributed into this protocol.

If you use the **metric** parameter in the **redistribute** command, you can set a different default metric for each protocol being redistributed. A metric configured in a **redistribute** command overrides the value in the **default-metric** command for that one protocol.

When redistributing *into* IGRP or EIGRP, use the **default-metric** *bandwidth delay reliability loading mtu* router configuration command, explained in Table 7-8, to set the seed metric for all protocols.

**Table 7-8** **default-metric** *Command for IGRP and EIGRP*

| Parameter | Description |
|---|---|
| *bandwidth* | The route's minimum bandwidth in kbps. |
| *delay* | The route delay in tens of microseconds. |
| *reliability* | The likelihood of successful packet transmission, expressed as a number from 0 to 255, where 255 means that the route is 100 percent reliable. |
| *loading* | The route's effective loading, expressed as a number from 1 to 255, where 255 means that the route is 100 percent loaded. |
| *mtu* | The maximum transmission unit. The maximum packet size along the route in bytes; an integer greater than or equal to 1. |

When redistributing into OSPF, RIP, EGP, and BGP, use the **default-metric** *number* router configuration command for setting the seed metric, as explained in Table 7-9.

**Table 7-9** **default-metric** *Command for OSPF, RIP, EGP, and BGP*

| Parameter | Description |
|---|---|
| *number* | The value of the metric, such as the number of hops for RIP. |

## The **passive-interface** Command

There are times when you must include an interface in a **network** command, although you do not want that interface to participate in the routing protocol.

---

**Key Point: passive-interface Command**

The **passive-interface** command prevents routing updates for a routing protocol from being sent through a router interface. The **passive-interface** command can set either a particular interface or all router interfaces to passive; use the **default** option to set all router interfaces.

---

When you use the **passive-interface** command with RIP and IGRP, routing updates are not sent out of the specified interface. However, the router still receives routing updates on that interface.

When you use the **passive-interface** command with EIGRP, hello messages are not sent to the specified interface. Neighboring router relationships do not form with other routers that can be reached through that interface (because the hello protocol is used to verify bidirectional communication between routers). Because no neighbors are found on an interface, no other EIGRP traffic is sent.

Using the **passive-interface** command on a router running a link-state routing protocol also prevents the router from establishing neighboring router adjacencies with other routers connected to the interface specified in the command.

| | |
|---|---|
| **NOTE** | During testing with **debug** commands, it was found that in some IOS versions OSPF sends Hello and DBD packets on passive interfaces but does not send link state updates (LSUs). EIGRP does not send anything on passive interfaces. |

To configure a passive interface, regardless of the routing protocol, use the following procedure:

**Step 1**  Select the router and routing protocol that require the passive interface.

**Step 2**  Determine which interfaces you do not want routing update traffic to be sent through.

**Step 3**  Configure the router using the **passive-interface** *type number* [**default**] router configuration command, as shown in Table 7-10.

**Table 7-10**    **passive-interface** *Command*

| Parameter | Description |
|---|---|
| *type number* | The type of interface and interface number that do not send routing updates (or establish neighbor relationships for link-state routing protocols and EIGRP). |
| **default** | An optional parameter that sets all interfaces on the router as passive by default. |

In Internet service providers (ISPs) and large enterprise networks, many distribution routers have more than 200 interfaces. Before the introduction of the passive interface default feature in Cisco IOS Release 12.0, network administrators would configure the routing protocol on all interfaces and then manually set the **passive-interface** command on the interfaces where they did not require adjacency. However, this solution meant entering many **passive-interface** commands. A single **passive-interface default** command can now be used to set all interfaces to passive by default. You then enable routing on individual interfaces where you require adjacencies using the **no passive-interface** command.

For example, in Figure 7-8, Routers A and B run RIP and have a **network** command that encompasses all their interfaces. However, you want to run RIP only on the link between Router A and Router B. Router A has several interfaces, so the **passive-interface default** command is configured, and then the **no passive-interface** command is used for the one interface from where RIP updates are advertised. Router B has only two interfaces, so the **passive-interface** command is used for the one interface that does not participate in RIP routing.

It is important to understand how this configuration affects the information exchanged between Routers A, B, and C. Unless you configure another routing protocol and redistribute between it and RIP, Router A does not tell Router C about the networks it learned from Router B via RIP. Likewise, Router B does not tell Router C that it has a way to reach the networks advertised by Router A via RIP. Redundancy is built into this network; however, the three routers might not be able to use redundancy effectively if they aren't configured properly. For example, if the link between Routers C and A fails, Router C does not know that it has an alternative route through Router B to reach Router A.

**Figure 7-8** *passive-interface Command Restricts Routing Traffic on an Interface*

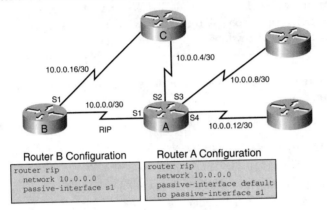

Router B Configuration
```
router rip
  network 10.0.0.0
  passive-interface s1
```

Router A Configuration
```
router rip
  network 10.0.0.0
  passive-interface default
  no passive-interface s1
```

## Route Redistribution Example

This section shows an example of route redistribution in a network using multiple routing protocols.

Figure 7-9 shows the network of a hypothetical company. The network begins with two routing domains (or autonomous systems)—one using OSPF and one using RIPv2. Router B is the boundary router; it connects directly to one router within each routing domain and runs both protocols. Router A is in the RIPv2 domain and advertises subnets 10.1.0.0, 10.2.0.0, and 10.3.0.0 to Router B. Router C is in the OSPF domain and advertises subnets 10.8.0.0, 10.9.0.0, 10.10.0.0, and 10.11.0.0 to Router B.

**Figure 7-9** *Sample Network Before Redistribution*

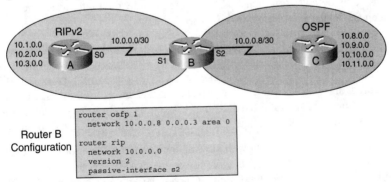

Router B Configuration
```
router osfp 1
  network 10.0.0.8 0.0.0.3 area 0

router rip
  network 10.0.0.0
  version 2
  passive-interface s2
```

Figure 7-9 also shows the configuration of Router B. RIP is required to run on the serial 1 interface only, so the **passive-interface** command is configured for interface serial 2 to prevent RIP from sending route advertisements out that interface. OSPF is configured on interface serial 2.

Figure 7-10 shows the routing tables for Routers A, B, and C. Each routing domain is separate, and routers within them only recognize routes communicated from their own routing protocols. The only router with information on all the routes is Router B, the boundary router that runs both routing protocols and connects to both routing domains.

**Figure 7-10** *Routing Tables Before Redistribution*

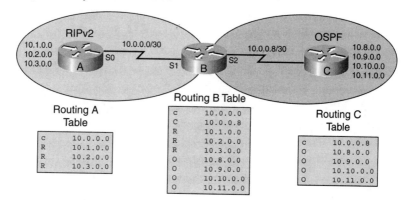

The goal of redistribution in this network is for all routers to recognize all routes within the company. To accomplish this goal, RIP routes are redistributed into OSPF, and OSPF routes are redistributed into RIP. Router B is the boundary router, so the redistribution is configured on it, as shown in Figure 7-11.

**Figure 7-11** *Redistribution Configured on Router B*

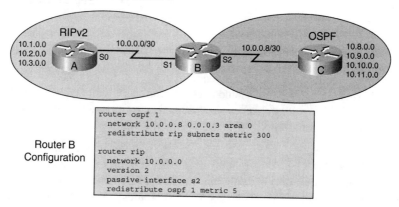

RIP is redistributed into the OSPF process, and the metric is set using the **redistribute** command. A metric value of 300 is selected because it is a worse metric than any belonging to a native OSPF route.

Routes from OSPF process 1 are redistributed into the RIP process with a metric of 5. A value of 5 is chosen because it is higher than any metric in the RIP network.

Figure 7-12 shows the routing tables of all three routers after redistribution is complete; Routers A and C now have routes to all the subnets that Router B learned from the other routing protocol. However, Routers A and C now have many more routes to keep track of than before. They also will be affected by any topology changes in the other routing domain.

**Figure 7-12** *Routing Tables After Redistribution*

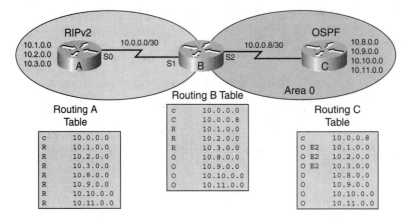

**NOTE**

Notice in Figure 7-12 that Router A does not see the 10.0.0.8/30 subnet, and Router C does not see the 10.0.0.0/30 subnet; these subnets are directly connected to Router B and therefore are not redistributed by the **redistribute rip** or **redistribute ospf** commands. You would need to add a **redistribute connected** command to Router B to redistribute these subnets.

Depending on the network requirements, you can increase efficiency by summarizing the routes before redistributing them. Remember that route summarization hides information, so if routers in the other autonomous systems are required to track topology changes within the entire network, route summarization should not be performed. A more typical case is that the routers need to recognize topology changes only within their own routing domains, so performing route summarization is appropriate.

If routes are summarized before redistribution, the routing tables of each router are significantly smaller. Figure 7-13 shows the routing tables after summarization has been configured. Router B benefits the most; it now has only four routes to keep track of instead of nine. Router A has five routes instead of eight, and Router C has six routes to keep track of instead of eight. The configurations on Routers A and C are also shown in Figure 7-13.

For RIPv2 on Router A, the summarization command is configured on the interface connecting Router B with Router A, interface S0. Interface S0 advertises the summary address instead of the individual subnets. (Note that when RIPv2 is configured, the subnet mask of the summary address must be greater than or equal to the default mask for the major classful network.) 10.0.0.0 255.252.0.0 summarizes the four subnets on Router A.

**Figure 7-13** *Routing Tables After Summarization*

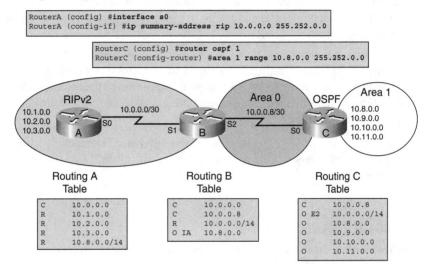

For OSPF on Router C, summarization must be configured on an area border router (ABR) or an ASBR. Therefore, OSPF Area 1 is created to include the four subnets to be summarized. Router C becomes an ABR, and the summarization command is configured under the OSPF process on Router C. 10.8.0.0 255.252.0.0 summarizes the four subnets on Router C.

# Controlling Routing Update Traffic

Routing updates compete with user data for bandwidth and router resources, yet routing updates are critical because they carry the information that routers need to make sound routing decisions. To ensure that the network operates efficiently, you must control and tune routing updates. Information about networks must be sent where it is needed and filtered from where it is not needed. No one type of route filter is appropriate for every situation; therefore, the more techniques you have at your disposal, the better your chance of having a smooth, well-run network.

This section discusses controlling the updates sent and received by dynamic routing protocols and controlling the routes redistributed into routing protocols. The following are some ways to control or prevent dynamic routing updates from being generated:

- **Passive interface**—A passive interface prevents routing updates for the specified protocol from being sent through an interface.

- **Default routes**—A default route instructs the router that if it does not have a route for a given destination, it should send the packet to the default route. Therefore, no dynamic routing updates about the remote destinations are necessary.

- **Static routes**—A static route allows routes to remote destinations to be manually configured in the router. Therefore, no dynamic routing updates about the remote destinations are necessary.

In many cases, you do not want to prevent all routing information from being advertised; you might want to block the advertisement of only certain routes. For example, you could use such a solution to prevent routing loops when implementing two-way route redistribution with dual redistribution points. Other ways to control routing updates include creating and applying distribute lists or route maps.

Passive interfaces were discussed in "The **passive-interface** Command" section. Static and default routes are discussed in the next section, which is followed by a discussion of distribute lists and route maps.

## Static and Default Routes

Static routes are routes that you manually configure on a router. Static routes are used most often to do the following:

- Define specific routes to use when two autonomous systems must exchange routing information, rather than having entire routing tables exchanged.

- Define routes to destinations over a WAN link to eliminate the need for a dynamic routing protocol—that is, when you do not want routing updates to enable or cross the link.

To configure a static route for IP, use the **ip route** *prefix mask {address | interface} [distance]* **[permanent] [tag** *tag*] global configuration command, as explained in Table 7-11.

**Table 7-11**   **ip route** *Command to Configure Static Routes*

| Parameter | Description |
| --- | --- |
| *prefix* | The route prefix for the destination network to be entered into the IP routing table. |
| *mask* | The prefix mask for the destination network to be entered into the IP routing table. |
| *address* | The IP address of the next-hop router that can be used to reach the destination network. |
| *interface* | The local router outbound interface that can be used to reach the destination network. |
| *distance* | The optional administrative distance to assign to this route. (Recall that administrative distance refers to how believable the routing protocol is.) |

**Table 7-11**    **ip route** *Command to Configure Static Routes (Continued)*

| Parameter | Description |
|---|---|
| *tag* | An optional value that can be used as a match value in route maps. |
| **permanent** | Optional. Specifies that the route will not be removed from the routing table even if the interface associated with the route goes down. |

**NOTE**    Static routes pointing to an interface should be used only on point-to-point interfaces, because on other interfaces the router will not know the specific address to which to send the information. On point-to-point interfaces, the information is sent to the only other device on the network.

When configuring static routes, keep in mind the following considerations:

- When using static routes instead of dynamic routing updates, all participating routers must have static routes defined so that they can advertise their remote networks. Static route entries must be defined for all routes for which a router is responsible. To reduce the number of static route entries, you can define a default static route—for example, **ip route 0.0.0.0 0.0.0.0 s1**.

- If you want a router to advertise a static route in a routing protocol, you might need to redistribute it.

Cisco lets you configure default routes for protocols. For example, when you create a default route on a router running RIP, the router advertises an address of 0.0.0.0. When a router receives this default route, it forwards any packets destined for a destination that does not appear in its routing table to the default route you configured.

You can also configure a default route by using the **ip default-network** *network-number* global configuration command. Figure 7-14 and Examples 7-9 and 7-10 demonstrate the use of this command on a router running RIP. With the **ip default-network** command, you designate an actual network currently available in the routing table as the default path to use.

**Figure 7-14**    *Using the* **ip default-network** *Command*

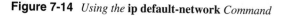
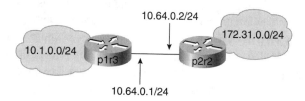

In Examples 7-9 and 7-10, the P2R2 router has a directly connected interface onto the network specified in the **ip default-network** *network-number* command. RIP generates (sources) a default route, which appears as a 0.0.0.0 0.0.0.0 route to its RIP neighbor routers.

**Example 7-9** *Configuration on Router P2R2 in Figure 7-14*

```
router rip
 network 10.0.0.0
 network 172.31.0.0
!
ip classless
ip default-network 10.0.0.0
```

**Example 7-10** *Routing Table on P1R3 in Figure 7-14*

```
<Output Omitted>
Gateway of last resort is 10.64.0.2 to network 0.0.0.0
       10.0.0.0/8 is variably subnetted, 7 subnets, 2 masks
<Output Omitted>
R        10.2.3.0/24 [120/1] via 10.64.0.2, 00:00:05, Ethernet0
C        10.64.0.0/24 is directly connected, Ethernet0
R      172.31.0.0/16 [120/1] via 10.64.0.2, 00:00:16, Ethernet0
R*     0.0.0.0/0 [120/1] via 10.64.0.2, 00:00:05, Ethernet0
```

**NOTE**  The **ip default-network** command is used to distribute default route information to *other* routers. This command provides no functionality for the router on which it is configured.

Other protocols behave differently than RIP with the **ip route 0.0.0.0 0.0.0.0** and **ip default-network** commands. For example, EIGRP does not redistribute the 0.0.0.0 0.0.0.0 default route by default. However, if the **network 0.0.0.0** command is added to the EIGRP configuration, it redistributes a default route as a result of the **ip route 0.0.0.0 0.0.0.0** *interface* command (but not as a result of the **ip route 0.0.0.0 0.0.0.0** *address* or **ip default-network** commands). Refer to the Cisco IOS documentation for further information.

## ip default-network and Other Commands

The **ip default-network** command is used when routers do not know how to get to the outside world. This command is configured at the router that connects to the outside world. This router goes through a different major network to reach the outside world. If your environment is all one major network address, you probably would not want to use the **ip default-network** command, but rather a static route to 0.0.0.0 via a border router.

The **ip route 0.0.0.0 0.0.0.0** command is used on routers with IP routing enabled that point to the outside world for Internet connectivity. This route is advertised as the "gateway of last resort" if running RIP. The router that is directly connected to the border of the outside world is the preferred router, with the static route pointing to 0.0.0.0.

The **ip default-gateway** command is used on routers or communication servers that have IP routing turned off. The router or communication server acts just like a host on the network.

# Using Distribute Lists to Control Routing Updates

One way to control routing updates is to use a distribute list.

---

**Key Point: Distribute List**

A distribute list allows the application of an access list to routing updates.

---

Access lists are usually associated with interfaces and are usually used to control user traffic. However, routers can have many interfaces, and route information can also be obtained through route redistribution, which does not involve a specific interface. Additionally, access lists do not affect traffic originated by the router, so applying one on an interface has no effect on outgoing routing advertisements. However, when you configure an access list for a distribute list, routing updates can be controlled, no matter what their source is.

Access lists are configured in global configuration mode; the associated distribute list is configured under the routing protocol process. The access list should permit the networks that will be advertised or redistributed and deny the networks that will remain hidden. The router then applies the access list to routing updates for that protocol. Options in the **distribute-list** command allow updates to be filtered based on the following three factors:

- Incoming interface
- Outgoing interface
- Redistribution from another routing protocol

Using a distribute list gives the administrator great flexibility in determining just which routes will be permitted and which will be denied.

## Distribute List Processing

Figure 7-15 shows the general process that a router uses when filtering routing updates using a distribute list that is based on the incoming or outgoing interface. The process includes the following steps:

**Step 1**   The router receives a routing update or prepares to send an update about one or more networks.

**Step 2**   The router looks at the interface involved with the action: the interface on which an incoming update has arrived, or, for an update that must be advertised, the interface out of which it should be advertised.

**Step 3**   The router determines if a filter (distribute list) is associated with the interface.

**Step 4**   If a filter (distribute list) is not associated with the interface, the packet is processed normally.

**Step 5**   If a filter (distribute list) is associated with the interface, the router scans the access list referenced by the distribute list for a match for the given routing update.

**Step 6**   If there is a match in the access list, the route entry is processed as configured; it is either permitted or denied by the matching access list statement.

**Step 7**   If no match is found in the access list, the implicit deny any at the end of the access list causes the route entry to be dropped.

**Figure 7-15**   *Route Filters Using a Distribute List*

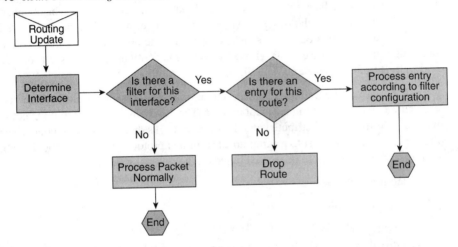

## Configuring Distribute Lists

You can filter routing update traffic for any protocol by defining an access list and applying it to a specific routing protocol using the **distribute-list** command. A distribute list enables the filtering of routing updates coming into or out of a specific interface from neighboring routers using the same routing protocol. A distribute list also allows the filtering of routes redistributed from other routing protocols or sources. To configure a distribute list, follow this procedure:

**Step 1**   Identify the network addresses you want to filter, and create an access list.

**Step 2**   Determine whether you want to filter traffic on an incoming interface, traffic on an outgoing interface, or routes being redistributed from another routing source.

**Step 3**   Use the **distribute-list** {*access-list-number* | *name*} **out** [*interface-name* | *routing-process* | *autonomous-system-number*] router configuration command to assign the access list to filter outgoing routing updates. Table 7-12 explains this command. The **distribute-list out** command cannot be used with link-state routing protocols to block outbound link state advertisements (LSAs) on an interface.

**Step 4**  Use the **distribute-list** {*access-list-number* | *name*} **in** [*type number*] router configuration command to assign the access list to filter routing updates coming in through an interface. Table 7-13 explains this command. This command prevents most routing protocols from placing the filtered routes in their database. When this command is used with OSPF, the routes are placed in the database, but not the routing table.

**Table 7-12**    **distribute-list out** *Command*

| Parameter | Description |
| --- | --- |
| *access-list-number* | *name* | The standard access list number or name. |
| **out** | Applies the access list to outgoing routing updates. |
| *interface-name* | The optional name of the interface out of which updates are filtered. |
| *routing-process* | The optional name of the routing process, or the keyword **static** or **connected**, that is being redistributed and from which updates are filtered. |
| *autonomous-system-number* | The optional AS number of the routing process. |

**NOTE**    OSPF outgoing updates cannot be filtered out of an interface.

**Table 7-13**    **distribute-list in** *Command*

| Parameter | Description |
| --- | --- |
| *access-list-number* | *name* | The standard access list number or name. |
| **in** | Applies the access list to incoming routing updates. |
| *type number* | (Optional) The interface type and number from which updates are filtered. |

### Key Point: Distribute List in Versus Out

The **distribute-list out** command filters updates going out of the interface or routing protocol specified in the command, into the routing process under which it is configured.

The **distribute-list in** command filters updates going into the interface specified in the command, into the routing process under which it is configured.

## IP Route Filtering Configuration Example

Figure 7-16 shows the topology of a WAN in which network 10.0.0.0 must be hidden from the devices in network 192.168.5.0.

**Figure 7-16** *Network 10.0.0.0 Needs to Be Hidden from Network 192.168.5.0*

Example 7-11 is the configuration of Router B in Figure 7-16. In this example, the **distribute-list out** command applies access list 7 to packets going out interface S0. The access list allows only routing information about network 172.16.0.0 to be distributed out Router B's S0 interface. As a result, network 10.0.0.0 is hidden.

**Example 7-11** *Filtering Out Network 10.0.0.0 on Router B in Figure 7-16*

```
router eigrp 1
  network 172.16.0.0
  network 192.168.5.0
  distribute-list 7 out s0
!
access-list 7 permit 172.16.0.0  0.0.255.255
```

**NOTE**   Another way to achieve the filtering of network 10.0.0.0 would be to deny network 10.0.0.0 and permit any other networks. This method would be particularly efficient if the routing information contained multiple networks but only network 10.0.0.0 needed filtering.

Table 7-14 describes some of the commands shown in Example 7-11.

**Table 7-14**   *Redistribution Commands*

| Command | Description |
|---|---|
| **distribute-list 7 out s0** | Applies access list 7 as a route redistribution filter on EIGRP routing updates sent out on interface serial 0. |

**Table 7-14** *Redistribution Commands (Continued)*

| Command | Description |
|---|---|
| **access-list 7 permit 172.16.0.0 0.0.255.255** | |
| **access list 7** | Specifies the access list number. |
| **permit** | Enables routes matching the parameters to be forwarded. |
| **172.16.0.0 0.0.255.255** | Specifies the network number and wildcard mask used to match routes. The first two address octets must match, and the rest are masked. |

## Controlling Redistribution with Distribute Lists

Using a distribute list with redistribution helps prevent route feedback and routing loops. Route feedback occurs when routes originally learned from one routing protocol get redistributed back into that protocol. Figure 7-17 illustrates an example in which two-way redistribution is configured both ways between RIPv2 and OSPF. The configuration on Router B is shown in Example 7-12.

**Figure 7-17** *Router B Controls Redistribution*

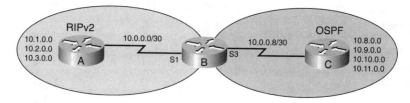

**Example 7-12** *Configuration of Router B in Figure 7-17*

```
router ospf 1
  network 10.0.0.8 0.0.0.3 area 0
  redistribute rip subnets
  distribute-list 2 out rip

router rip
  network 10.0.0.0
  version 2
  passive-interface s3
  redistribute ospf 1 metric 5
  distribute-list 3 out ospf 1

access-list 2 deny 10.8.0.0 0.3.255.255
access-list 2 permit any

access-list 3 permit 10.9.0.0
```

Networks 10.1.0.0 to 10.3.0.0 are redistributed from RIPv2 into OSPF. Route feedback could occur if another redistribution point were configured in the future and OSPF then redistributed those same networks back into RIP.

Although there is currently a single redistribution point, the configuration in Example 7-12 shows a distribute list configuration that prevents route feedback. Access list 2 denies the original OSPF routes and permits all others; the distribute list configured under OSPF refers to this access list. The result is that networks 10.8.0.0 to 10.11.0.0, originated by OSPF, are not redistributed back into OSPF from RIPv2. All other routes are redistributed into OSPF. Redistribution from OSPF into RIPv2 is filtered with access list 3; note that this is a more restrictive filter that permits only one route, 10.9.0.0, to be redistributed into RIPv2.

A distribute list hides network information, which could be considered a drawback in some circumstances. For example, in a network with redundant paths, a distribute list might permit routing updates for only specific paths to avoid routing loops. In this case, other routers in the network might not know about the other ways to reach the filtered networks, so if the primary path goes down, the backup paths are not used because the rest of the network does not know they exist. When redundant paths exist, you should use other techniques, such as manipulating the administrative distance or metric, instead of distribute lists, to enable the use of an alternative path (with a worse administrative distance or metric) when the primary path goes down.

# Using Route Maps to Control Routing Updates

Using route maps to manipulate and control routing protocol updates is the technique preferred by Cisco Systems. It is important that network operators understand the use of route maps when redistributing routes between routing protocols.

Route maps are used for a variety of purposes. This section explores the use of route maps as a tool to filter and manipulate routing updates. All the IP routing protocols can use route maps for redistribution filtering.

## Route Map Operation

---

**Key Point: Route Map Operation**

Route maps were introduced in Chapter 1, "Advanced IP Addressing," in the "Understanding Route Maps" section. If necessary, review that section before continuing with this section on using route maps to control updates.

---

The following is a brief review of general route map features:

- Route maps are complex access lists that allow some conditions to be tested against the packet or route in question using **match** commands. If the conditions match, some actions can be taken to modify attributes of the packet or route; these actions are specified by **set** commands.

- A collection of route map statements that have the same route map name are considered one route map. Within a route map, each route map statement is numbered and therefore can be edited individually.

- The statements in a route map correspond to the lines of an access list. One big difference between route maps and access lists is that route maps can modify the route by using **set** commands.

- A route map may be made up of multiple route map statements. The statements are processed top-down, similar to an access list. The sequence number specifies the order in which conditions are checked. The first match found for a route is applied. The sequence number is used to insert or delete specific route map statements in a specific place in the route map.

- A single match statement may contain multiple conditions. At least one condition in the match statement must be true for that match statement to be considered a match.

- A route map statement may contain multiple match statements. All match statements in the route map statement must be considered true for the route map statement to be considered a match.

- Like an access list, there is an implicit deny any at the end of a route map. The consequences of this deny depend on how the route map is being used.

## Route Map Applications

Network administrators use route maps for a variety of purposes. Several of the more common applications for route maps are as follows:

- **Route filtering during redistribution**—Redistribution nearly always requires some amount of route filtering. Whereas distribute lists can be used for this purpose, route maps offer the added benefit of manipulating routing metrics through the use of **set** commands.

- **Policy-based routing (PBR)**—Route maps can be used to match source and destination addresses, protocol types, and end-user applications. When a match occurs, a **set** command can be used to define the interface or next-hop address to which the packet should be sent. PBR allows the operator to define routing policy other than basic destination-based routing using the routing table. PBR is discussed in the "Policy-Based Routing" section later in this chapter.

- **NAT**—Route maps can better control which private addresses are translated to public addresses. Using a route map with NAT also provides more detailed **show** commands that describe the address-translation process. NAT is discussed in Chapter 1.

- **BGP**—Route maps are the primary tools for implementing BGP policy. Network administrators assign route maps to specific BGP sessions (neighbors) to control which routes are allowed to flow in and out of the BGP process. In addition to filtering, route maps provide sophisticated manipulation of BGP path attributes. Route maps for BGP are discussed in Chapter 9, "Advanced Border Gateway Protocol Configuration."

## Configuring Route Maps

The **redistribute** commands discussed in the "Configuring Redistribution" section all have a **route-map** option with a *map-tag* parameter. This parameter refers to a route map configured with the **route-map** *map-tag* [**permit** I **deny**] [*sequence-number*] global configuration command. Table 7-15 describes the parameters of the **route-map** command.

**Table 7-15**     **route-map** *Command*

| Parameter | Description |
|-----------|-------------|
| *map-tag* | The name of the route map. |
| **permit** I **deny** | An optional parameter that specifies the action to be taken if the **route-map** match conditions are met:<br><br>**permit**—Permits the matched route to be redistributed.<br><br>**deny**—Keeps the matched route from being redistributed. |
| *sequence-number* | An optional sequence number that indicates the position that a new route map statement will have in the list of route map statements already configured with the same route map name. |

The default for the **route-map** command is **permit**, with a sequence number of 10.

---

### Route Map Sequence Numbering

If you leave out the sequence number when configuring all statements for the same route map name, the router assumes that you are editing and adding to the first statement, sequence number 10. Route map sequence numbers do not automatically increment!

---

The **match** {*conditions*} route map configuration commands are used to define the conditions to be checked. Table 7-16 lists a variety of match criteria that can be defined; some of these commands are used for BGP policy, some for PBR, and some for redistribution filtering.

**Table 7-16**     **match** *Commands*

| match Command | Description |
|---------------|-------------|
| **match ip address** *ip-access-list* | Distributes any routes that have a destination network number address that is permitted by a standard or extended access list. |
| **match length** *min max* | Bases policy routing on a packet's Layer 3 length. |
| **match interface** *type number* | Distributes any routes that have the next hop out of one of the interfaces specified. |
| **match ip next-hop** *ip-address-list* | Redistributes any routes that have a next-hop router address passed by one of the access lists specified. |
| **match ip** *route-source* *ip-access-list* | Redistributes routes that have been advertised by routers and access servers that have an address specified by the access list. |
| **match metric** *metric-value* | Redistributes routes that have the metric specified. |

**Table 7-16**    **match** *Commands (Continued)*

| match Command | Description |
|---|---|
| **match route-type [external \| internal \| level-1 \| level-2 \| local]** | Redistributes routes of the specified type. |
| **match community** *list-number \| list-name* | Matches a BGP community. |

The **set** {*condition*} route map configuration commands change or add characteristics, such as metrics, to any routes that have met a match criterion and the action to be taken is permit. (The consequences of a deny action depend on how the route map is being used.) Table 7-17 lists the variety of **set** commands that are available. Not all the **set** commands listed here are used for redistribution purposes; the table includes commands for BGP and PBR.

**Table 7-17**    **set** *Commands*

| set Command | Description |
|---|---|
| **set metric** *metric-value* | Sets the metric value for a routing protocol. |
| **set metric-type [type-1 \| type-2 \| internal \| external]** | Sets the metric type for the destination routing protocol. |
| **set default interface** *type number* | Indicates where to send output packets that pass a match clause of a route map for policy routing and for which the Cisco IOS software has no explicit route to the destination. |
| **set interface** *type number* | Indicates where to send output packets that pass a match clause of a route map for policy routing. |
| **set ip default next-hop** *ip-address* | Indicates where to send output packets that pass a match clause of a route map for policy routing and for which the Cisco IOS software has no explicit route to the destination. |
| **set ip next-hop** *next-hop-address* | Indicates where to send output packets that pass a match clause of a route map for policy routing. |
| **set level [level-1 \| level-2 \| stub-area \| backbone]** | Indicates at what level or type of area to import routes into (for IS-IS and OSPF routes). |
| **set as-path {tag \| prepend** *as-path-string*} | Modifies an AS path for BGP routes. |
| **set automatic-tag** | Automatically computes the BGP tag value. |
| **set community {***community-number* **[additive]** [*well-known-community*] \| **none**} | Sets the BGP communities attribute. |
| **set local-preference** *bgp-path-attributes* | Specifies a local preference value for the BGP AS path. |
| **set weight** *bgp-weight* | Specifies the BGP weight for the routing table. |
| **set origin** *bgp-origin-code* | Specifies the BGP origin code. |

## Using Route Maps with Redistribution

Example 7-13 illustrates configuring a route map used to redistribute RIPv1 into OSPF 10. The route map, called redis-rip, is used in the **redistribute rip route-map redis-rip subnets** command under the OSPF process.

**Example 7-13** *Route Map Used to Redistribute RIPv1 into OSPF*

```
route-map redis-rip permit 10
  match ip address 23  29
  set metric 500
  set metric-type type-1

route-map redis-rip deny 20
  match ip address 37

route-map redis-rip permit 30
  set metric 5000
  set metric-type type-2

access-list 23 permit 10.1.0.0 0.0.255.255
access-list 29 permit 172.16.1.0 0.0.0.255
access-list 37 permit 10.0.0.0 0.255.255.255
```

Sequence number 10 of the route map is looking for an IP address match in access list 23 or access list 29. Routes 10.1.0.0/16 and 172.16.1.0/24 match these lists. If a match is found, the router redistributes the route into OSPF with a cost metric of 500 and sets the new OSPF route to external type 1.

If there is no match to sequence number 10, sequence number 20 is checked. If there is a match in access list 37 (10.0.0.0/8), that route is not redistributed into OSPF, because sequence number 20 specifies **deny**.

If there is no match to sequence number 20, sequence number 30 is checked. Because sequence number 30 is a **permit** and there is no match criterion, all remaining routes are redistributed into OSPF with a cost metric of 5000 and an external metric of type 2.

## Route Maps to Avoid Route Feedback

There is a possibility that routing feedback might cause suboptimal routing or a routing loop when routes are redistributed at more than one router. Figure 7-18 illustrates a network in which mutual redistribution (redistribution in both directions) is configured on Routers A and B. To prevent redistribution feedback loops, route maps are configured on both routers.

The potential for routing feedback becomes apparent if you follow the advertisements for a specific network before route maps are configured. For example, RIPv2 on Router C advertises network 192.168.1.0. Routers A and B redistribute the network into OSPF. OSPF then advertises the route to its neighbor OSPF routers as an OSPF external route. The route passes through the OSPF AS and eventually makes its way back to the other edge router. Router B (or A) then redistributes 192.168.1.0 from OSPF back into the original RIPv2 network; this is a routing feedback loop.

**Figure 7-18** *Route Maps Can Help Avoid Route Feedback Loops*

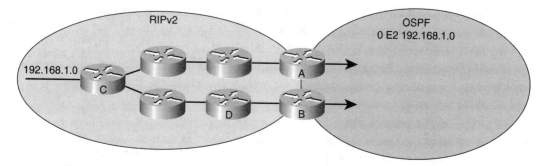

To prevent the routing feedback loop, a route map has been applied to Routers A and B, as shown in Example 7-14. The **route-map** statement with sequence number 10 refers to access list 1, which matches the original RIPv2 network. This statement is a **deny**, so the 192.168.1.0 route is denied from being redistributed back into RIPv2. If the route does not match sequence number 10, the router then checks sequence number 20, which is an empty **permit** statement. This statement matches all routes, so all other routes are redistributed into RIP.

**Example 7-14** *Partial Configuration on Routers A and B in Figure 7-18*

```
access-list 1 permit 192.168.1.0 0.0.0.255

route-map pacific deny 10
  match ip address 1

route-map pacific permit 20

router rip
  redistribute ospf 10 route-map pacific

router ospf 10
  redistribute rip subnets
```

# Using Administrative Distance to Influence the Route-Selection Process

Route selection is sometimes confusing because of redistribution. The redistribution point is a demarcation between two different methods of resolving the best path. As a result, important information is lost during redistribution—namely, the relative metrics of routes. One approach for correcting wayward choices is by controlling the administrative distance so that route selection is unambiguous. This approach does not always guarantee the best route selection, only a consistent choice for route selection.

Controlling administrative distance is an important way to indicate route selection preference. You should change the default administrative distance carefully and by considering the network's specific requirements.

## Administrative Distance Review

Multiple sources of routing information may be active at the same time, including static routes and routing protocols that use various methods of operation and metrics. Routers must identify which routing information source is trustworthy and reliable, given several sources of information that supply ambiguous next-hop information for a particular network.

Recall that administrative distance is a way of ranking the trustworthiness of the sources of routing information. Administrative distance is expressed as an integer from 0 to 255; lower values indicate greater believability.

For example, in Figure 7-19, R1 chooses different paths to get to the 10.0.0.0/8 network on R6, depending on the routing protocol configured. If RIP, IS-IS, OSPF, and EIGRP are all configured on all routers in this network, the protocols make the following path decisions:

- RIP, with an administrative distance of 120, chooses the R1 to R4 to R6 path based on hop count (two hops versus four hops the other way).

- IS-IS, with an administrative distance of 115 and using the default metric of 10 for each interface, also chooses the R1 to R4 to R6 path based on a metric of 20 versus 40 the other way. You can modify the IS-IS metrics to portray a more accurate view of the network. IS-IS is more trustworthy than RIP because it is a link-state routing protocol with fast convergence, so its routing information is more complete and up to date.

- OSPF, with an administrative distance of 110, typically calculates the default metric as 100 Mbps divided by the interface bandwidth, where the interface bandwidth is the speed of each link in Mbps. The path R1 to R4 to R6 default metric is (100 Mbps / 64 kbps) + (100 Mbps / 1.544 Mbps) = (100 Mbps / .064 Mbps) + (100 Mbps / 1.544 Mbps) = (1562 + 64) = 1626. The R1 to R2 to R3 to R5 to R6 path default metric is 64 + 64 + 64 + 64 = 256. Therefore, OSPF chooses the R1 to R2 to R3 to R5 to R6 path. Although OSPF and IS-IS are both link-state routing protocols that converge quickly, OSPF is more trustworthy than IS-IS because OSPF bases its default metric on bandwidth and therefore is more likely to pick a faster path.

---

**NOTE**   In general, the Cisco routers calculate the OSPF cost using the formula 100 Mbps / bandwidth. However, this formula is based on a maximum bandwidth of 100 Mbps, resulting in a cost of 1. If you have faster interfaces, you might want to recalibrate the cost of 1 to a higher bandwidth. Chapter 5, "Interconnecting Multiple Open Shortest Path First Areas," provides details about OSPF cost calculations.

---

- EIGRP, with an administrative distance of 90, calculates the default metric as BW + delay, where BW is ($10^7$ / least bandwidth in the path in kbps) * 256, and delay is cumulative across the path, in tens of microseconds. Assuming a uniform link delay of 100 tens of microseconds, the R1 to R4 to R6 path default metric is (($10^7$ / 64) * 256) + 200 = 40,000,200. The R1 to R2 to R3 to R5 to R6 path default metric is (($10^7$ / 1544) * 256) + 400 = 4,706,282.

Therefore, EIGRP chooses the R1 to R2 to R3 to R5 to R6 path. Although EIGRP and OSPF routing protocols both converge quickly and consider bandwidth, EIGRP is more trustworthy than OSPF because EIGRP takes more information into account in its calculation.

**Figure 7-19** *Path Selected Through a Network Depends on the Routing Protocols Configured*

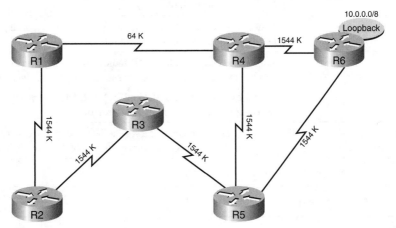

Because EIGRP has the lowest administrative distance of the four protocols, only the EIGRP path to 10.0.0.0/8 is put into the routing table.

---

**NOTE**    The administrative distance affects only the choice of path for identical IP routes—in other words, for routes with the same prefix and mask. For example, because OSPF does not summarize by default, and all the other protocols do, the protocols might potentially provide different routing information. In this example, if OSPF advertised a route to 10.1.0.0/16 that was not advertised by any of the other protocols (because they automatically summarized to 10.0.0.0/8), the 10.1.0.0/16 route would be in the routing tables from OSPF, and the 10.0.0.0/8 route would be in the routing tables from EIGRP. Typically multiple routing protocols are run only on the boundary routers in a network, not on *all* routers, so this situation should not be common.

---

# Modifying Administrative Distance

In some cases, you will find that a router selects a suboptimal path because it believes a routing protocol that actually has a poorer route, because it has a better administrative distance. One way to make sure that routes from the desired routing protocol are selected is to give the undesired route(s) from a routing protocol a larger administrative distance.

For all protocols except EIGRP and BGP, use the **distance** *weight* [*address mask* [*ip-standard-list*] [*ip-extended-list*]] router configuration command, as explained in Table 7-18, to change the default administrative distances.

**Table 7-18**    distance *Command (Except for EIGRP and BGP)*

| Parameter | Description |
|---|---|
| *weight* | The administrative distance as an integer from 10 to 255. (The values 0 to 9 are reserved for internal use and should not be used, even though values from 1 to 9 can be configured.) Routes with a distance of 255 are not installed in the routing table. |
| *address* | The optional IP address. Allows filtering of networks according to the IP address of the router supplying the routing information. |
| *mask* | An optional wildcard mask for the IP address. A bit set to 1 in the *mask* argument instructs the software to ignore the corresponding bit in the *address* value. Use an address/mask of 0.0.0.0 255.255.255.255 to match any IP address (any source router supplying the routing information). |
| *ip-standard-list* *ip-extended-list* | The optional number or name of a standard or extended access list to be applied to the incoming routing updates. Allows filtering of the networks being advertised. |

**NOTE**    The *ip-extended-list* parameter was added in Cisco IOS Release 12.0.

For EIGRP, use the **distance eigrp** *internal-distance external-distance* router configuration command, as explained in Table 7-19. By default, natively learned routes have an administrative distance of 90, but external routes have an administrative distance of 170.

**Table 7-19**    distance eigrp *Command*

| Parameter | Description |
|---|---|
| *internal-distance* | The administrative distance for EIGRP internal routes. Internal routes are those that are learned from another entity within the same autonomous system. The distance can be a value from 1 to 255; the default is 90. |
| *external-distance* | The administrative distance for EIGRP external routes. External routes are those for which the best path is learned from a neighbor external to the autonomous system. The distance can be a value from 1 to 255; the default is 170. |

For BGP, use the **distance bgp** *external-distance internal-distance local-distance* router configuration command to change the administrative distances, as explained in Table 7-20.

**Table 7-20**    distance bgp *Command*

| Parameter | Description |
|---|---|
| *external-distance* | The administrative distance for BGP external routes. External routes are routes for which the best path is learned from a neighbor external to the autonomous system. Acceptable values are from 1 to 255. The default is 20. Routes with a distance of 255 are not installed in the routing table. |

**Table 7-20**　distance bgp *Command (Continued)*

| Parameter | Description |
|---|---|
| *internal-distance* | The administrative distance for BGP internal routes. Internal routes are learned from another BGP entity within the same autonomous system. Acceptable values are from 1 to 255. The default is 200. Routes with a distance of 255 are not installed in the routing table. |
| *local-distance* | The administrative distance for BGP local routes. Local routes are networks that are listed with a **network** router configuration command, often as back doors, for that router or for networks that are redistributed from another process. Acceptable values are from 1 to 255. The default is 200. Routes with a distance of 255 are not installed in the routing table. |

For OSPF, you can also use the **distance ospf** {[**intra-area** *dist1*] [**inter-area** *dist2*] [**external** *dist3*]} router configuration command to define the OSPF administrative distances based on route type, as explained in Table 7-21.

**Table 7-21**　distance ospf *Command*

| Parameter | Description |
|---|---|
| *dist1* | (Optional) The administrative distance for all OSPF routes within an area. Acceptable values are from 1 to 255. The default is 110. |
| *dist2* | (Optional) The administrative distance for all OSPF routes from one area to another area. Acceptable values are from 1 to 255. The default is 110. |
| *dist3* | (Optional) The administrative distance for all routes from other routing domains, learned by redistribution. Acceptable values are from 1 to 255. The default is 110. |

# An Example of Redistribution Using Administrative Distance

Figure 7-20 illustrates a network using multiple routing protocols, RIPv2 and OSPF. There are a number of ways to correct path-selection problems in a redistribution environment. The purpose of this example is to show how a problem can occur, where it appears, and one possible way to resolve it.

Recall that OSPF is more believable than RIPv2 because it has an administrative distance of 110 and RIPv2 has an administrative distance of 120. For example, if the boundary router (P3R1 or P3R2) learns about network 10.3.3.0 via RIPv2 and also via OSPF, the OSPF route is inserted into the routing table. This route is used because OSPF has a lower administrative distance than RIPv2, even though the path via OSPF might be the longer (worse) path.

Examples 7-15 and 7-16 illustrate the configurations for the P3R1 and P3R2 routers. These configurations redistribute RIP into OSPF and OSPF into RIP on both routers.

**Figure 7-20** *Sample Redistribution Network Topology*

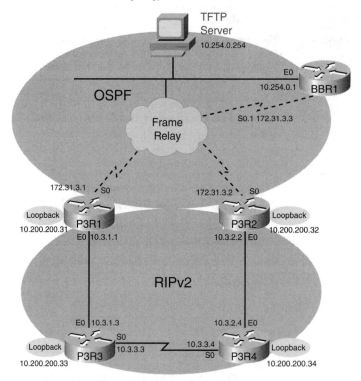

**Example 7-15** *Configuration of Redistribution on Router P3R1 in Figure 7-20*

```
router ospf 1
 redistribute rip metric 10000 metric-type 1 subnets
 network 172.31.0.0 0.0.255.255 area 0
!
router rip
 version 2
 redistribute ospf 1 metric 5
 network 10.0.0.0
 no auto-summary
```

**Example 7-16** *Configuration of Redistribution on Router P3R2 in Figure 7-20*

```
router ospf 1
 redistribute rip metric 10000 metric-type 1 subnets
 network 172.31.0.0 0.0.255.255 area 0
!
router rip
 version 2
 redistribute ospf 1 metric 5
 network 10.0.0.0
 no auto-summary
```

The RIPv2 routes redistributed into OSPF have a default OSPF metric of 10,000 to make these routes less preferred than native OSPF routes and to protect against route feedback. The **redistribute** command also sets the metric type to 1 (external type 1) so that the route metrics continue to accrue. The router also redistributes subnet information.

The OSPF routes redistributed into RIPv2 have a default RIP metric of five hops to also protect against route feedback.

Example 7-17 displays the routing table on the P3R2 router after redistribution has occurred. Even though the P3R2 router learns RIPv2 and OSPF routes, it lists only OSPF routes in the routing table, because they have a lower administrative distance.

**Example 7-17** *Routing Table on Router P3R2 in Figure 7-20 with Redistribution Configured*

```
P3R2#sh ip route
<output omitted>
Gateway of last resort is not set

     172.31.0.0/24 is subnetted, 1 subnet
C        172.31.3.0/24 is directly connected, Serial0
     10.0.0.0/8 is variably subnetted, 8 subnets, 2 masks
O E1    10.3.1.0/24 [110/10781] via 172.31.3.1, 00:09:47, Serial0
O E1    10.3.3.0/24 [110/10781] via 172.31.3.1, 00:04:51, Serial0
C       10.3.2.0/24 is directly connected, Ethernet0
O E1    10.200.200.31/32 [110/10781] via 172.31.3.1, 00:09:48, Serial0
O E1    10.200.200.34/32 [110/10781] via 172.31.3.1, 00:04:52, Serial0
C       10.200.200.32/32 is directly connected, Loopback0
O E1    10.200.200.33/32 [110/10781] via 172.31.3.1, 00:04:52, Serial0
O E2    10.254.0.0/24 [110/50] via 172.31.3.3, 00:09:48, Serial0
P1R2#
```

First, OSPF is configured on the P3R1 router. Then P3R2 receives information about the internal (native RIPv2) routes from both OSPF and RIPv2. P3R2 prefers the OSPF routes because OSPF has a lower administrative distance; therefore, none of the RIPv2 routes appears in the P3R2 routing table. The P3R1 routing table contains both OSPF and RIPv2 routes, as you would expect.

Refer back to Figure 7-20 to trace some of the routes. The redistribution has resulted in suboptimal paths to many of the networks. For instance, 10.200.200.34 is a loopback interface on router P3R4. P3R4 is directly attached to P3R2; however, from P3R2 the OSPF path to that loopback interface goes through P3R1, and then P3R3, and then P3R4 before it reaches its destination. The OSPF path taken is actually a longer (worse) path than the more direct RIP path.

You can change the administrative distance of the redistributed RIPv2 routes to ensure that the boundary routers select the native RIPv2 routes. Examples 7-18 and 7-19 show the configurations on the P3R1 and P3R2 routers. The **distance** command changes the administrative distance of the OSPF routes to the networks that match access list 64 to 125 (from 110). Table 7-22 describes some of the command parameters used in the examples.

**Example 7-18** *Configuration to Change the Administrative Distance on Router P3R1 in Figure 7-20*

```
hostname P3R1
!
router ospf 1
 redistribute rip metric 10000 metric-type 1 subnets
 network 172.31.0.0 0.0.255.255 area 0
 distance 125 0.0.0.0 255.255.255.255 64
!
router rip
 version 2
 redistribute ospf 1 metric 5
 network 10.0.0.0
 no auto-summary
!
access-list 64 permit 10.3.1.0
access-list 64 permit 10.3.3.0
access-list 64 permit 10.3.2.0
access-list 64 permit 10.200.200.31
access-list 64 permit 10.200.200.34
access-list 64 permit 10.200.200.32
access-list 64 permit 10.200.200.33
```

**Example 7-19** *Configuration to Change the Administrative Distance on Router P3R2 in Figure 7-20*

```
hostname P3R2
!
router ospf 1
 redistribute rip metric 10000 metric-type 1 subnets
 network 172.31.0.0 0.0.255.255 area 0
 distance 125 0.0.0.0 255.255.255.255 64
!
router rip
 version 2
 redistribute ospf 1 metric 5
 network 10.0.0.0
 no auto-summary
!
access-list 64 permit 10.3.1.0
access-list 64 permit 10.3.3.0
access-list 64 permit 10.3.2.0
access-list 64 permit 10.200.200.31
access-list 64 permit 10.200.200.34
access-list 64 permit 10.200.200.32
access-list 64 permit 10.200.200.33
```

**Table 7-22** **distance** *Command Parameters Used in Examples 7-18 and 7-19*

| Parameter | Description |
|---|---|
| 125 | Defines the administrative distance that specified routes are assigned. |
| 0.0.0.0 255.255.255.255 | Defines the source address of the router supplying the routing information—in this case, any router. |
| 64 | Defines the access list to be used to filter incoming routing updates to determine which will have their administrative distance changed. |

Access list 64 is used to match all the native RIPv2 routes. The **access-list 64 permit 10.3.1.0** command configures a standard access list to permit the 10.3.1.0 network; similar access list statements permit the other internal native RIPv2 networks. Table 7-23 describes some of the command parameters used in the examples.

**Table 7-23**    **access-list** *Command Parameters Used in Examples 7-18 and 7-19*

| Parameter | Description |
|-----------|-------------|
| 64 | The access list number. |
| permit | Allows all networks that match the address to be permitted—in this case, to have their administrative distance changed. |
| 10.3.1.0 | A network to be permitted—in this case, to have its administrative distance changed. |

Both P3R1 and P3R2 are configured to assign an administrative distance of 125 to routes listed in access list 64, which it learns from OSPF. Access list 64 has permit statements for the internal native RIPv2 networks 10.3.1.0, 10.3.2.0, and 10.3.3.0 and the loopback networks 10.200.200.31, 10.200.200.32, 10.200.200.33, and 10.200.200.34. Therefore, when either of these routers learns about these networks from both RIPv2 and OSPF, it selects the routes learned from RIPv2—with a lower administrative distance of 120—over the same routes learned from OSPF (via redistribution from the other boundary router)—with an administrative distance of 125—and puts only the RIPv2 routes in the routing table.

---

**Key Point: The distance Command**

Notice in this example that the **distance** command is part of the OSPF routing process configuration because the administrative distance should be changed for these routes when they are learned by OSPF, not by RIPv2.

---

You need to configure the **distance** on both redistributing routers because either one can have suboptimal routes, depending on which redistributing router sends the OSPF updates about the RIPv2 networks to the other redistributing router first.

Example 7-20 shows that Router P3R2 now retains the more direct paths to the internal networks by learning them from RIPv2.

**Example 7-20** *Routing Table on Router P3R2 in Figure 7-20 with the Administrative Distance Changed*

```
P3R2#sh ip route
<output omitted>
Gateway of last resort is not set

     172.31.0.0/24 is subnetted, 1 subnet
C       172.31.3.0/24 is directly connected, Serial0
     10.0.0.0/8 is variably subnetted, 8 subnets, 2 masks
R       10.3.1.0/24 [120/2] via 10.3.2.4, 00:00:03, Ethernet0
R       10.3.3.0/24 [120/1] via 10.3.2.4, 00:00:03, Ethernet0
```

*continues*

**Example 7-20** *Routing Table on Router P3R2 in Figure 7-20 with the Administrative Distance Changed (Continued)*

```
C      10.3.2.0/24 is directly connected, Ethernet0
R      10.200.200.31/32 [120/3] via 10.3.2.4, 00:00:04, Ethernet0
R      10.200.200.34/32 [120/1] via 10.3.2.4, 00:00:04, Ethernet0
C      10.200.200.32/32 is directly connected, Loopback0
R      10.200.200.33/32 [120/2] via 10.3.2.4, 00:00:04, Ethernet0
O E2   10.254.0.0/24 [110/50] via 172.31.3.3, 00:00:04, Serial0
P1R2#
```

However, some routing information is lost with this configuration. For example, depending on the actual bandwidths, the OSPF path might have been better for the 10.3.1.0 network. It might have made sense not to include 10.3.1.0 in the access list for P3R2.

This example illustrates the importance of knowing your network before implementing redistribution and closely examining which routes the routers select after redistribution is enabled. You should pay particular attention to routers that can select from a number of possible redundant paths to a network, because they are more likely to select suboptimal paths.

---

**Key Point: No Path Information Is Lost When You Modify the Administrative Distance**

The most important feature of using administrative distance to control route preference is that no path information is lost; in this example, the OSPF information is still in the OSPF database. If the primary path (via the RIPv2 routes) is lost, the OSPF path reasserts itself, and the router maintains connectivity with those networks.

---

# Verifying Redistribution Operation

The best way to verify redistribution operation is as follows:

- Know your network topology, particularly where redundant routes exist.

- Study the routing tables on a variety of routers in the internetwork using the **show ip route** [*ip-address*] EXEC command. For example, check the routing table on the boundary router as well as on some of the internal routers in each autonomous system.

- Perform a trace using the **traceroute** [*ip-address*] EXEC command on some of the routes that go across the autonomous systems to verify that the shortest path is being used for routing. Be sure to run traces to networks for which redundant routes exist.

---

**NOTE**     The **traceroute** command appears in the Cisco IOS documentation as **trace**; on the routers, however, **traceroute** is the full command.

---

- If you encounter routing problems, use the **traceroute** and **debug** commands to observe the routing update traffic on the boundary routers and on the internal routers.

---

**NOTE**     Running **debug** requires extra processing by the router, so if the router is already overloaded, initiating **debug** is not recommended.

---

# Policy-Based Routing

In today's high-performance internetworks, organizations need the freedom to implement packet forwarding and routing according to their own defined policies in a way that goes beyond traditional routing protocol concerns. By using policy-based routing, introduced in Cisco IOS Release 11.0, you can implement policies that selectively cause packets to take different paths based on source address, protocol types, or application types.

PBR also provides a mechanism to mark packets with different types of service (ToS). This feature can be used in conjunction with Cisco IOS queuing techniques so that certain kinds of traffic can receive preferential service.

PBR provides an extremely powerful, simple, and flexible tool to implement solutions in cases where legal, contractual, or political constraints dictate that traffic be routed through specific paths. Here are some of the benefits you can achieve by implementing PBR in networks:

- **Source-based transit provider selection**—ISPs and other organizations can use PBR to route traffic originating from different sets of users through different Internet connections across policy routers.

- **Quality of service (QoS)**—Organizations can provide QoS to differentiated traffic by setting the precedence or ToS values in the IP packet headers in routers at the periphery of the network and then leveraging queuing mechanisms to prioritize traffic in the network's core or backbone. This setup improves network performance by eliminating the need to classify the traffic explicitly at each WAN interface in the network's core or backbone.

- **Cost savings**—An organization can direct the bulk traffic associated with a specific activity to use a higher-bandwidth, high-cost link for a short time and to continue basic connectivity over a lower-bandwidth, low-cost link for interactive traffic. For example, a dial-on-demand ISDN line could be brought up in response to traffic destined for a finance server; PBR would select this link.

- **Load sharing**—In addition to the dynamic load-sharing capabilities offered by destination-based routing that the Cisco IOS software has always supported, network managers can implement policies to distribute traffic among multiple paths based on the traffic characteristics.

---

**Key Point: PBR Is Applied to Incoming Packets**

PBR is applied to *incoming* packets. Enabling PBR causes the router to evaluate all packets incoming on the interface using a route map configured for that purpose.

---

Based on the criteria defined in the route map, packets are forwarded to the appropriate next hop. Therefore, PBR overrides the router's normal routing procedures.

Routers normally forward packets to the destination addresses based on information in their routing tables. Instead of routing by the destination address, PBR allows network administrators to determine and implement routing policies based on the following criteria:

- A source system's identity
- The application being run
- The protocol in use
- The size of packets

# Configuring Policy-Based Routing

Configuring PBR involves configuring a route map with **match** and **set** commands and then applying the route map to the interface.

---

### Key Point: PBR Permit and Deny Statements

The route map statements used for PBR can be configured as **permit** or **deny**.

If the statement is marked as **deny**, a packet meeting the match criteria is sent through the normal forwarding channels (in other words, destination-based routing is performed).

Only if the statement is marked as **permit** and the packet meets all the match criteria are the **set** commands applied.

If no match is found in the route map, the packet is not dropped; it is forwarded through the normal routing channel, which means that destination-based routing is performed.

If you do not want to revert to normal forwarding but instead want to drop a packet that does not match the specified criteria, configure a **set** statement to route the packets to interface null 0 as the last entry in the route map.

---

## Policy-Based Routing **match** Commands

IP standard or extended access lists can be used to establish PBR match criteria using the **match ip address** {*access-list-number* | *name*} [*...access-list-number* | *name*] route map configuration command, as explained in Table 7-24. A standard IP access list can be used to specify match criteria for a packet's source address; extended access lists can be used to specify match criteria based on source and destination addresses, application, protocol type, ToS, and precedence.

**Table 7-24**     **match ip address** *Command*

| Parameter | Description |
| --- | --- |
| *access-list-number* | *name* | The number or name of a standard or extended access list to be used to test incoming packets. If multiple access lists are specified, matching any one results in a match. |

The **match length** *min max* route map configuration command, explained in Table 7-25, can be used to establish criteria based on the packet length between specified minimum and maximum values. For example, a network administrator could use the match length as the criterion that distinguishes between interactive and file transfer traffic, because file transfer traffic usually has larger packet sizes.

**Table 7-25**    **match length** *Command*

| Parameter | Description |
|-----------|-------------|
| *min* | The packet's minimum Layer 3 length, inclusive, allowed for a match. |
| *max* | The packet's maximum Layer 3 length, inclusive, allowed for a match. |

## Policy-Based Routing **set** Commands

If the match statements are satisfied, one or more of the following set statements can be used to specify the criteria for forwarding packets through the router.

---

**Key Point: Using the set Commands for PBR**

The router evaluates the first four **set** commands for PBR shown here in the order they are presented. As soon as a destination address or interface has been chosen, other **set** commands for changing the destination address or interface are ignored. Note, however, that some of these commands affect only packets for which there is an explicit route in the routing table, and others affect only packets for which there is *no* explicit route in the routing table.

A packet that is not affected by any of the **set** commands in a route map statement it has matched is not policy routed and is forwarded normally (in other words, destination-based routing is performed).

---

The **set ip next-hop** *ip-address* [*...ip-address*] route map configuration command provides a list of IP addresses used to specify the adjacent next-hop router in the path toward the destination to which the packets should be forwarded. If more than one IP address is specified, the first IP address associated with a currently up connected interface is used to route the packets. The **set ip next-hop** command is explained in Table 7-26.

---

**NOTE**    With the **set ip next-hop** command, the routing table is checked only to determine if the next hop can be reached. It is not checked to determine if there is an explicit route for the packet's destination address.

The **set ip next-hop** command affects all packet types and is always used if configured.

---

**Table 7-26**      **set ip next-hop** *Command*

| Parameter | Description |
|-----------|-------------|
| *ip-address* | The IP address of the next hop to which packets are output. It must be the address of an adjacent router. |

The **set interface** *type number* [*...type number*] route map configuration command provides a list of interfaces through which the packets can be routed. If more than one interface is specified, the first interface that is found to be up is used to forward the packets. This command is explained in Table 7-27.

---

**NOTE**      If there is *no* explicit route for the destination address of the packet in the routing table (for example, if the packet is a broadcast or is destined for an unknown address), the **set interface** command has no effect and is ignored.

A default route in the routing table is not considered an explicit route for an unknown destination address.

---

**Table 7-27**      **set interface** *Command*

| Parameter | Description |
|-----------|-------------|
| *type number* | The interface type and number to which packets are output. |

The **set ip default next-hop** *ip-address* [*...ip-address*] route map configuration command provides a list of default next-hop IP addresses. If more than one IP address is specified, the first next hop specified that appears to be adjacent to the router is used. The optional specified IP addresses are tried in turn. Table 7-28 explains this command.

---

**NOTE**      A packet is routed to the next hop specified by the **set ip default next-hop** command only if there is *no* explicit route for the packet's destination address in the routing table.

A default route in the routing table is not considered an explicit route for an unknown destination address.

---

**Table 7-28**      **set ip default next-hop** *Command*

| Parameter | Description |
|-----------|-------------|
| *ip-address* | The IP address of the next hop to which packets are output. It must be the address of an adjacent router. |

The **set default interface** *type number* [...*type number*] route map configuration command provides a list of default interfaces. If no explicit route is available to the destination address of the packet being considered for policy routing, it is routed to the first up interface in the list of specified default interfaces. Table 7-29 provides information about this command.

**NOTE**    A packet is routed to the next hop specified by the **set default interface** command only if there is *no* explicit route for the packet's destination address in the routing table.

A default route in the routing table is not considered an explicit route for an unknown destination address.

**Table 7-29**    **set default interface** *Command*

| Parameter | Description |
|---|---|
| *type number* | The interface type and number to which packets are output. |

PBR also provides a mechanism to mark packets using the **set ip tos** and **set ip precedence** commands.

The **set ip tos** [*number* | *name*] route map configuration command is used to set the IP ToS value in the IP packets. The ToS field is 8 bits long in the IP header, with 5 bits for setting the Class of Service (CoS) and 3 bits for the IP precedence. The CoS bits are used to set the delay, throughput, reliability, and cost. The **set ip tos** command is used to set the 5 CoS bits; values 0 through 15 are used (one of the bits is reserved). Table 7-30 provides the names and numbers of the defined ToS values used in this command.

**Table 7-30**    **set ip tos** *Command*

| Parameter *number* | *name* | Description |
|---|---|
| **0 | normal** | Sets the normal ToS. |
| **1 | min-monetary-cost** | Sets the min-monetary-cost ToS. |
| **2 | max-reliability** | Sets the max reliable ToS. |
| **4 | max-throughput** | Sets the max throughput ToS. |
| **8 | min-delay** | Sets the min delay ToS. |

The **set ip precedence** [*number* | *name*] route map configuration command is used to set the IP precedence bits in the IP packets. With 3 bits, there are eight possible values for the IP precedence; values 0 through 7 are defined. This command is used when implementing QoS and can be used by other QoS services, such as weighted fair queuing (WFQ) and weighted random early detection (WRED). Table 7-31 provides the names and numbers of the defined IP precedence values used in this command.

**Table 7-31**    set ip precedence *Command*

| Parameter *number | name* | Description |
|---|---|
| 0 | routine | Sets the routine precedence. |
| 1 | priority | Sets the priority precedence. |
| 2 | immediate | Sets the immediate precedence. |
| 3 | flash | Sets the Flash precedence. |
| 4 | flash-override | Sets the Flash override precedence. |
| 5 | critical | Sets the critical precedence. |
| 6 | internet | Sets the internetwork control precedence. |
| 7 | network | Sets the network control precedence. |

The **set** commands can be used in conjunction with each other.

## Configuring Policy-Based Routing on an Interface

To identify a route map to use for policy routing on an interface, use the **ip policy route-map** *map-tag* interface configuration command, explained in Table 7-32.

**Table 7-32**    ip policy route-map *Command*

| Parameter | Description |
|---|---|
| *map-tag* | The name of the route map to use for policy routing. It must match a map tag specified by the **route-map** command. |

---

### Key Point: PBR Is Configured on the Receiving Interface

Policy-based routing is configured on the interface that *receives* the packets, not on the interface from which the packets are sent.

---

Since Cisco IOS Release 12.0, IP PBR can now be fast-switched. Before this feature, policy routing could only be process-switched, which meant that on most platforms, the switching rate was approximately 1000 to 10,000 packets per second. This was not fast enough for many applications. Users who need policy routing to occur at faster speeds can now implement policy routing without slowing down the router.

PBR must be configured before you configure fast-switched policy routing. Fast switching of policy routing is disabled by default. To have policy routing be fast-switched, use the **ip route-cache policy** interface configuration command.

Fast-switched PBR supports all the **match** commands and most of the **set** commands, except for the following restrictions:

- The **set ip default next-hop** command is not supported.

- The **set interface** command is supported only over point-to-point links unless a route-cache entry exists using the same interface specified in the **set interface** command in the route map. Also, when process switching, the routing table is checked to determine whether the interface is on a reasonable path to the destination. The software does not make this check during fast switching. Instead, if the packet matches, the software blindly forwards the packet to the specified interface.

## Verifying Policy-Based Routing

To display the route maps used for policy routing on the router's interfaces, use the **show ip policy** EXEC command.

To display configured route maps, use the **show route-map** [*map-name*] EXEC command. *map-name* is an optional name of a specific route map.

Use the **debug ip policy** EXEC command to display IP policy routing packet activity. This command shows in detail what policy routing is doing. It displays information about whether a packet matches the criteria and, if so, the resulting routing information for the packet.

| NOTE | Because the **debug ip policy** command generates a significant amount of output, use it only when traffic on the IP network is low so that other activity on the system is not adversely affected. |
| --- | --- |

To discover the routes that the packets follow when traveling to their destination from the router, use the **traceroute** privileged EXEC command. To change the default parameters and invoke an extended **traceroute**, enter the command without a destination argument. You will be stepped through a dialog to select the desired parameters.

To check host reachability and network connectivity, use the **ping** privileged EXEC command. You can use the **ping** command's extended command mode to specify the supported header options by entering the command without any arguments.

## Policy-Based Routing Examples

This section provides two examples of PBR.

### Using Policy-Based Routing When Connecting Two ISPs

In Figure 7-21, Router A provides Internet access for a private enterprise. Router A is connected to two different ISPs. This router is advertising a 0.0.0.0 default route into the enterprise network to avoid a large Internet routing table. The problem is that when traffic from the enterprise networks 10.1.0.0 and 10.2.0.0 reaches Router A, the traffic can go to ISP A or ISP B.

**Figure 7-21** *Router A Is Connected to Two ISPs*

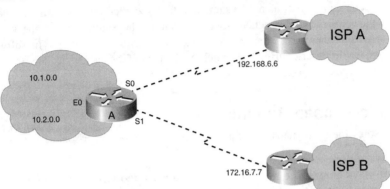

The company prefers to have ISP A and ISP B receive approximately equal amounts of traffic. PBR is implemented on Router A to shape, or load-balance, traffic from Router A to each of the ISPs. All traffic sourced from the 10.1.0.0 subnet is forwarded to ISP A if there is no specific route to the destination in the routing table (the default route is not used). All traffic sourced from the 10.2.0.0 subnet is forwarded to ISP B if there is no specific route to the destination in the routing table.

---

**CAUTION**    Remember, this policy provides for an outbound traffic policy from the enterprise to its ISPs only. It does not determine the inbound traffic policy for Router A. It is possible that traffic from 10.1.0.0 going out to ISP A will receive responses through ISP B.

---

The configuration for Router A is shown in Example 7-21. Route map **equal-access** is configured.

**Example 7-21** *Configuration of Router A in Figure 7-21*

```
RouterA(config)#access-list 1 permit ip 10.1.0.0 0.0.255.255
RouterA(config)#access-list 2 permit ip 10.2.0.0 0.0.255.255

RouterA(config)#route-map equal-access permit 10
RouterA(config-route-map)#match ip address 1
RouterA(config-route-map)#set ip default next-hop 192.168.6.6

RouterA(config-route-map)#route-map equal-access permit 20
RouterA(config-route-map)#match ip address 2
RouterA(config-route-map)#set ip default next-hop 172.16.7.7

RouterA(config-route-map)#route-map equal-access permit 30
RouterA(config-route-map)#set default interface null0

RouterA(config)#interface ethernet 0
RouterA(config-if)#ip address 10.1.1.1 255.255.255.0
RouterA(config-if)#ip policy route-map equal-access

RouterA(config)#interface serial 0
RouterA(config-if)#ip address 192.168.6.5 255.255.255.0
```

**Example 7-21** *Configuration of Router A in Figure 7-21 (Continued)*

```
RouterA(config)#interface serial 1
RouterA(config-if)#ip address 172.16.7.6 255.255.255.0
```

The **ip policy route-map equal-access** command is applied to the Ethernet 0 interface, the *incoming* interface receiving the packets to be policy-routed.

Sequence number 10 in route map **equal-access** is used to match all packets sourced from any host in subnet 10.1.0.0. If there is a match, and if the router has no explicit route for the packet's destination, it is sent to next-hop address 192.168.6.6 (ISP A's router).

Sequence number 20 in route map **equal-access** is used to match all packets sourced from any host in subnet 10.2.0.0. If there is a match, and if the router has no explicit route for the packet's destination, it is sent to next-hop address 172.16.7.7 (ISP B's router).

Sequence number 30 in route map **equal-access** is used to drop all traffic not sourced from subnet 10.1.0.0 or 10.2.0.0. The null0 interface is a route to nowhere (dropped).

The outputs shown in Examples 7-22, 7-23, and 7-24 are from Router A in Figure 7-21.

Example 7-22 provides an example of **show ip policy** command output, indicating that the route map called **equal-access** is used for PBR on the router's Ethernet 0 interface.

**Example 7-22** **show ip policy** *on Router A in Figure 7-21*

```
RouterA#show ip policy

Interface        Route map
Ethernet0        equal-access
```

Example 7-23 provides an example of **show route-map** command output, indicating that three packets have matched sequence 10 of the **equal-access** route map.

**Example 7-23** **show route-map** *on Router A in Figure 7-21*

```
RouterA#show route-map
route-map equal-access, permit, sequence 10
  Match clauses:
    ip address (access-lists): 1
  Set clauses:
    ip default next-hop 192.168.6.6
Policy routing matches: 3 packets, 168 bytes
route-map equal-access, permit, sequence 20
  Match clauses:
    ip address (access-lists): 2
  Set clauses:
    ip default next-hop 172.16.7.7
route-map equal-access, permit, sequence 30
Set clauses:
    default interface null0
```

Example 7-24 provides an example of the **debug ip policy** command. The output indicates that a packet from 10.1.1.1 destined for 172.19.1.1 has been received on interface Ethernet 0 and that it is policy-routed on serial 0 to next hop 192.168.6.6. The source address of 10.1.1.1 matches line 10 of route map **equal-access**.

**Example 7-24** **debug ip policy** *on Router A in Figure 7-21*

```
RouterA#debug ip policy
Policy routing debugging is on

11:51:25: IP: s=10.1.1.1 (Ethernet0), d=172.19.1.1, len 100, policy match
11:51:25: IP: route map equal-access, item 10, permit
11:51:25: IP: s=10.1.1.1 (Ethernet0), d=172.19.1.1 (Serial0), len 100, policy routed
11:51:25: IP: Ethernet0 to Serial0 192.168.6.6
```

**NOTE**  The **show logging** command shows the logging buffer, including the output of the **debug** command.

## Using Policy-Based Routing Based on Source Address

In Figure 7-22, Router A has a policy that packets from 192.168.2.1 should go out to Router C's interface serial 1. All other packets should be routed according to their destination address. The relevant part of the configuration for Router A is shown in Example 7-25.

**Figure 7-22**  *Router A Has a Policy That Packets from 192.168.2.1 Go to Router C's Interface S1*

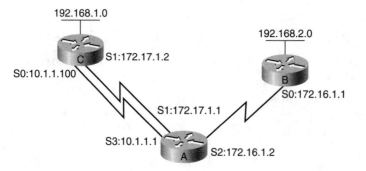

**Example 7-25**  *Configuration of Router A in Figure 7-22*

```
RouterA(config)#interface Serial2
RouterA(config-if)#ip address 172.16.1.2 255.255.255.0
RouterA(config-if)#ip policy route-map test
RouterA(config)#route-map test permit 10
RouterA(config-route-map)#match ip address 1
RouterA(config-route-map)#set ip next-hop 172.17.1.2
RouterA(config-route-map)#exit
RouterA(config)#access-list 1 permit 192.168.2.1 0.0.0.0
```

Router A's serial 2 interface, where packets from 192.168.2.1 go into Router A, is configured to do policy routing with the **ip policy route-map** command. The route map **test** is used for this policy routing. It tests the IP addresses in packets against access list 1 to determine which packets will be policy-routed.

Access list 1 specifies that packets with a source address of 192.168.2.1 are policy-routed. Packets that match access list 1 are sent to the next-hop address 172.17.1.2, which is Router C's serial 1 interface. All other packets are forwarded normally, according to their destination address. (Recall that access lists have an implicit deny any at the end, so no other packets are permitted by access list 1.)

The outputs shown in Examples 7-26, 7-27, and 7-28 are from Router A in Figure 7-22.

Example 7-26 provides an example of the **show ip policy** command. It indicates that the route map called test is used for policy routing on the router's interface serial 2.

**Example 7-26** **show ip policy** *Output on Router A in Figure 7-22*

```
RouterA#show ip policy
Interface       Route map
Serial2         test
```

The **show route-map** command, shown in Example 7-27, indicates that three packets have matched sequence 10 of the test route map.

**Example 7-27** **show route-map** *Output on Router A in Figure 7-22*

```
RouterA#show route-map
route-map test, permit, sequence 10
  Match clauses:
    ip address (access-lists): 1
  Set clauses:
    ip next-hop 172.17.1.2
  Policy routing matches: 3 packets, 168 bytes
```

Example 7-28 provides an example of the output of the **debug ip policy** command. The output indicates that a packet from 172.16.1.1 destined for 192.168.1.1 was received on interface serial 2 and that it was rejected by the policy on that interface. The packet is routed normally (by destination). Another packet, from 192.168.2.1 destined for 192.168.1.1, was later received on the same interface, serial 2. This packet matched the policy on that interface and therefore was policy-routed and sent out interface serial 1 to 172.17.1.2.

**Example 7-28** *Example of* **debug ip policy** *on Router A in Figure 7-22*

```
RouterA#debug ip policy
Policy routing debugging is on

...
11:50:51: IP: s=172.16.1.1 (Serial2), d=192.168.1.1 (Serial3), len 100, policy
  rejected -- normal forwarding
...
11:51:25: IP: s=192.168.2.1 (Serial2), d=192.168.1.1, len 100, policy match
11:51:25: IP: route map test, item 10, permit
11:51:25: IP: s=192.168.2.1 (Serial2), d=192.168.1.1 (Serial1), len 100, policy
  routed
11:51:25: IP: Serial2 to Serial1 172.17.1.2
```

# Summary

In this chapter, you learned about why multiple routing protocols may run in a network and how to control routing update information between them.

Migration from one protocol to another requires a detailed plan, an accurate topology map of the network, and an inventory of all network devices. Redistribution of routing information between the protocols might be required, and this must also be carefully planned.

Migration to a new routing protocol might also require the IP addressing scheme to be modified. Some considerations when changing the IP addresses in a network include host addressing, access lists, the effect on NAT and DNS, and the timing and strategy for the transition. Secondary addresses may be used if both the old and new addresses are required during the transition period.

Migration to a new routing protocol is typically gradual—one section of the network at a time. It is very important that you have backup copies of all device configurations before starting the migration in case you need to revert to the original network.

You might need multiple routing protocols in your network for a number of reasons, including the following:

- You are migrating from an older IGP to a new IGP.

- You want to use another protocol but you need to keep the old routing protocol because of the host system's needs.

- Different departments might not want to upgrade their routers to support a new routing protocol, or they might not implement a sufficiently strict filtering policy.

- If you have a mixed-router vendor environment, you can use a Cisco-specific routing protocol, such as EIGRP, in the Cisco portion of the network and then use a common standards-based routing protocol, such as OSPF, to communicate with non-Cisco devices.

Redistribution is defined as the capability for boundary routers connecting different routing domains to exchange and advertise routing information between autonomous systems. Redistribution allows a routing protocol to advertise routes that were not learned through that protocol.

Redistribution of routing information adds to a network's complexity and increases the potential for routing confusion. Routing feedback, incompatible routing information, and inconsistent convergence times are the key issues that arise with redistribution.

Cisco routers use the administrative distance and routing metric to select the best path when they learn two or more routes to the same destination from different routing protocols.

When a router advertises a link directly connected to one of its interfaces, the initial, or seed, metric used is derived from the characteristics of that interface, and the metric increments as the routing information is passed to other routers.

When redistributing routing information, set the seed metric to a value larger than the largest metric within the receiving AS to help prevent suboptimal routing and routing loops.

The safest way to perform redistribution is to redistribute routes in only one direction on only one boundary router within the network.

Redistribution supports all protocols and allows the routing protocols to advertise the routes without using a **network** command for them. Routes are redistributed *into* a routing protocol, so the **redistribute** command is configured under the routing process that is to *receive* the redistributed routes.

You can affect how routes are redistributed by changing the default metric associated with a protocol by either specifying the default metric with the **default-metric** command or using the *metric-value* parameters in the **redistribute** command.

Some ways to control or prevent dynamic routing updates from being generated are as follows:

- Passive interface
- Default routes
- Static routes
- Distribute lists
- Route maps

The **passive-interface** command prevents routing updates for a routing protocol from being sent through a router interface. The **passive-interface** command can set either a particular interface or all router interfaces to passive; use the **default** option to set all router interfaces.

A distribute list allows the application of an access list to routing updates. The **distribute-list out** command filters updates going out of the interface or routing protocol specified in the command into the routing process under which it is configured. The **distribute-list in** command filters updates going into the interface specified in the command into the routing process under which it is configured.

Route maps are used for a variety of purposes; several of the more common applications for route maps are as follows:

- Route filtering during redistribution
- Policy-based routing
- NAT
- BGP

Route maps work similarly to access lists but offer better editing features and complex **match** and **set** commands for route manipulation.

When used for redistribution, route maps match routes. These routes are either permitted or denied to be redistributed. If permitted, the metric value can be specified as the route is redistributed into the new protocol.

Administrative distance is a way of ranking the trustworthiness of the sources of routing information; lower values indicate greater believability. Administrative distance can be changed for certain routes by using the **distance** command.

Policy-based routing offers significant benefits in terms of implementing user-defined policies to control traffic in the internetwork, including source-based transit provider selection, QoS, cost savings, and load sharing.

PBR is applied to *incoming* packets. PBR uses route maps to implement routing policy. The **match ip address** and **match length** commands determine which packets will be policy-routed. Various **set** commands are used to specify the criteria for forwarding packets through the router.

# Reference

For additional information, refer to Cisco's command reference and configuration guides, available at www.cisco.com/univercd/home/home.htm.

# Configuration Exercise 7-1: Configuring Basic Redistribution

In this Configuration Exercise, you will configure your routers to redistribute routes from RIPv2 into OSPF and to supply a default route to the RIPv2 routing domain. You will also configure a distribute list to filter routes into the core.

---

**Introduction to the Configuration Exercises**

This book uses Configuration Exercises to help you practice configuring routers with the commands and topics presented. If you have access to real hardware, you can try these exercises on your routers; see Appendix H, "Configuration Exercise Equipment Requirements and Initial Configurations," for a list of recommended equipment and initial configuration commands for the routers. However, even if you don't have access to any routers, you can go through the exercises and keep a log of your own running configurations or just read through the solution. Commands used and solutions to the Configuration Exercises are provided after the exercises.

In the Configuration Exercises, the network is assumed to consist of two pods, each with four routers. The pods are interconnected to a backbone. You configure pod 1. No interaction between the two pods is required, but you might see some routes from the other pod in your routing tables in some exercises if you have it configured (the Configuration Exercise answers show the routes from the other pod). In most of the exercises, the backbone has only one router; in some cases, another router is added to the backbone. Each Configuration Exercise assumes that you have completed the previous chapters' Configuration Exercises on your pod.

---

**NOTE**    Throughout this exercise, the pod number is referred to as *x,* and the router number is referred to as *y.* Substitute the appropriate numbers as needed.

---

## Objectives

Your task in this Configuration Exercise is to redistribute routes from RIPv2 into OSPF and to supply a default route to the RIPv2 routing domain.

## Visual Objective

Figure 7-23 illustrates the topology used in this exercise.

**Figure 7-23**   *Basic Redistribution Configuration Exercise Topology*

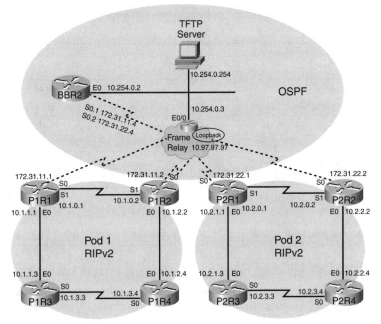

On All Pod Routers Loopback 0: 10.200.200.xy/32

## Command List

In this exercise, you will use the commands in Table 7-33, listed in logical order. Refer to this list if you need configuration command assistance during the exercise.

---

**CAUTION**    Although the command syntax is shown in this table, the addresses shown are typically for the P*x*R1 and P*x*R3 routers. Be careful when addressing your routers! Refer to the exercise instructions and the appropriate visual objective diagram for addressing details.

---

**Table 7-33**    *Basic Redistribution Configuration Exercise Commands*

| Command | Description |
|---|---|
| (config-router)#**network 172.31.***xx***.0 0.0.0.255 area 0** | Configures OSPF to run for interfaces 172.31.*xx*.0/24 in Area 0. |
| (config-router)#**version 2** | Configures RIPv2. |
| (config-router)#**network 10.0.0.0** | Configures RIP to run on interfaces that belong to network 10.0.0.0. |

*continues*

**Table 7-33**   *Basic Redistribution Configuration Exercise Commands (Continued)*

| Command | Description |
|---|---|
| (config-router)#**no auto-summary** | Turns off automatic summarization of routes at classful boundaries. |
| (config-if)#**ip ospf network point-to-multipoint** | Configures the point-to-multipoint network type for OSPF. |
| (config)#**ip route 0.0.0.0 0.0.0.0 172.31.xx.4** | Creates a static default route. |
| (config-router)#**default-information originate** | Advertises the default route through RIP. |
| (config-router)#**redistribute rip subnets** | Redistributes RIP routes into OSPF. The **subnets** keyword enables the passing of subnetted routes into OSPF. |
| (config)#**access-list 1 deny 10.200.200.0 0.0.0.255** | Configures access list 1 to deny any IP address that matches the first 24 bits of 10.200.200.0. |
| (config-router)#**distribute-list 1 out rip** | Configures a distribute list to use access list 1 to determine which routes will be distributed from RIP (into OSPF). |
| **show ip ospf database** | Displays the OSPF database. |

# Task 1: Cleaning Up

In this task, you will remove IS-IS and configure the appropriate addresses before configuring redistribution. Follow these steps:

**Step 1**   Remove the IS-IS configuration from all the pod routers using the **no router isis** global configuration command.

**Step 2**   Check the configuration of S0 on the edge routers. It should include an IP address, Frame Relay encapsulation, and a Frame Relay static map, and it should have Frame Relay Inverse Address Resolution Protocol (ARP) turned off. The IP address should be 172.31.xx.y /24, and the data-link connection identifier (DLCI) should be 2xy, where x is the pod number and y is the router number. One way to do this is to remove all configuration commands on the S0 interfaces by using the **default interface s0** global configuration command, and then put the required configuration on those interfaces.

**Step 3**   Create a loopback interface on your edge routers with the IP address of 10.200.200.xy /32, where x is the pod number and y is the router number. (Your internal routers already have similar loopback addresses.)

# Task 2: Setting Up the Routing Protocols

In this task, you will configure OSPF and RIPv2 on your pod routers. Follow these steps:

**Step 1**   BBR2 is in OSPF area 0. Each pod's edge routers will run both OSPF and RIPv2.

On the edge routers, put the S0 interface in OSPF Area 0. Because BBR2 is configured with a point-to-multipoint interface, configure the edge router's S0 interface with the OSPF point-to-multipoint network type.

Configure the edge routers to also run RIPv2 internally to the pod. Turn off autosummarization for RIPv2.

Configure the internal routers to run only RIPv2.

**Step 2**  Show the IP routing table on both edge routers. Verify that both edge routers are learning both OSPF and RIPv2 routes. What is the highest hop count on the RIPv2 routes to the networks within your pod?

## Task 3: Configuring Basic Redistribution

In this task, you will configure basic redistribution between OSPF and RIPv2. Follow these steps:

**Step 1**  Configure both edge routers to pass a default route into RIPv2. RIPv2 needs a static default route configured to advertise it to other RIPv2 routers.

Examine the routing table on the internal routers. Is the default route present? What are its path and metric?

**Step 2**  Configure both edge routers to redistribute RIPv2 routes into OSPF without specifying a metric value. What default metric will OSPF use when the RIPv2 routes are redistributed? (Remember to include the **subnets** keyword in the **redistribute** command.)

**Step 3**  Telnet to the core router, BBR2 (the password is **cisco**), and examine the OSPF database. What type of routes do the networks from your pod appear as?

**Step 4**  Examine the IP routing table on both internal routers.

**Step 5**  Verify that the internal routers can ping the TFTP server.

## Task 4: Filtering Routing Updates

In this task, you will configure your edge routers to filter information about the loopback addresses to the core. Because the core is exchanging OSPF routes with your pod, you will use a distribute list to block these routes from being redistributed into OSPF. Follow these steps:

**Step 1**  Examine the routing table on the BBR2 router for comparison after the filters are put into place.

**Step 2**  Create an access list that matches the four loopback addresses in your pod.

**Step 3** Use a distribute list to block the RIPv2 routes in this access list from being redistributed into OSPF.

**Step 4** Examine the routing table on the BBR2 router again. Verify that the loopback addresses are not listed.

**Step 5** Can the BBR2 router ping your loopback addresses?

## Exercise Verification

You have successfully completed this exercise when you achieve the following results:

- You can establish OSPF adjacencies between the edge routers and the core BBR2 router and exchange the routing updates.

- You can establish that the RIPv2 updates are exchanged between the internal routers and edge routers.

- You can establish that redistribution is configured from RIPv2 to OSPF.

- You can demonstrate that a default route has been injected into the RIPv2 routing domain.

# Configuration Exercise 7-2: Tuning Basic Redistribution

In this exercise, you will configure a route map to change the metric of redistributed routes.

---

**NOTE** Throughout this exercise, the pod number is referred to as *x*, and the router number is referred to as *y*. Substitute the appropriate numbers as needed.

---

## Objectives

Your task in this Configuration Exercise is to configure a route map to control redistribution.

## Visual Objective

Figure 7-24 illustrates the topology used in this exercise.

---

**NOTE** In this Configuration Exercise, the serial connection between P*x*R1 and P*x*R2 will be shut down.

---

**Figure 7-24**  *Basic Redistribution Configuration Exercise Topology*

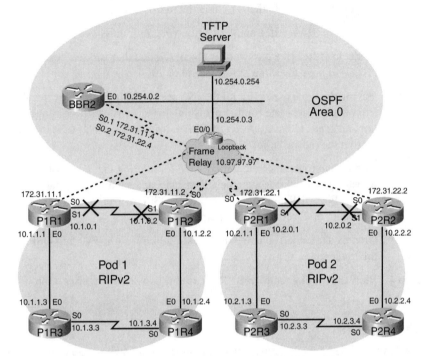

On All Pod Routers Loopback 0: 10.200.200.xy/32

## Command List

In this exercise, you will use the commands in Table 7-34, listed in logical order. Refer to this list if you need configuration command assistance during the exercise.

**CAUTION**    Although the command syntax is shown in this table, the addresses shown are typically for the P*x*R1 and P*x*R3 routers. Be careful when addressing your routers! Refer to the exercise instructions and the appropriate visual objective diagram for addressing details.

**Table 7-34**    *Tuning Basic Redistribution Exercise Commands*

| Command | Description |
|---|---|
| (config)#**route-map CONVERT permit 10** | Creates a route map statement. |
| (config-route-map)#**match metric 1** | Matches the source protocol metric. |
| (config-route-map)#**set metric 1000** | Sets the destination protocol metric. |
| (config-router)#**redistribute rip subnets route-map CONVERT** | Redistributes RIP routes using the route map. |

## Task: Tuning Basic Redistribution with Route Maps

In this task, you will use route maps to tune the redistribution. Follow these steps:

**Step 1**   Shut down S1 on PxR1 and PxR2 (to avoid a routing loop in this task).

**Step 2**   Telnet to BBR2 (the password is **cisco**). Notice that all your pod routes (10.x.0.0) have the same OSPF metric of 20.

**Step 3**   Having the same metric for all the redistributed RIP routes prevents the core from making accurate routing decisions for those routes. The central OSPF domain needs to have different OSPF metrics based on how far the network is from the redistribution point.

At the edge routers, create a route map for altering the metric of the redistributed routes. Match the RIP metric, and set an appropriate OSPF metric: For a RIP hop count of 1, set the OSPF metric to 1000, and for a RIP hop count of 2, set the OSPF metric to 2000.

On the edge routers, change the redistribution from RIPv2 into OSPF to use this route map.

**Step 4**   View the routing table on BBR2. Did this convert the metrics appropriately?

## Exercise Verification

You have completed this exercise when you understand how to use a route map to control redistribution.

# Configuration Exercise 7-3: Configuring Policy-Based Routing

In this exercise, you will use policy-based routing to force traffic from the loopback interfaces to take a certain path through the network.

---

**NOTE**   Throughout this exercise, the pod number is referred to as $x$, and the router number is referred to as $y$. Substitute the appropriate numbers as needed.

---

## Objectives

Your task in this Configuration Exercise is to use policy-based routing to exert the maximum administrative control over how traffic is handled.

## Visual Objective

Figure 7-25 illustrates the topology used in this exercise.

**Figure 7-25**  *Policy-Based Routing Configuration Exercise Topology*

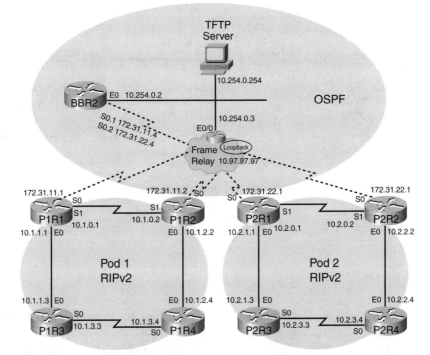

On All Pod Routers Loopback 0: 10.200.200.xy/32

## Command List

In this exercise, you will use the commands in Table 7-35, listed in logical order. Refer to this list if you need configuration command assistance during the exercise.

---

**CAUTION**   Although the command syntax is shown in this table, the addresses shown are typically for the P*x*R1 and P*x*R3 routers. Be careful when addressing your routers! Refer to the exercise instructions and the appropriate visual objective diagram for addressing details.

---

**Table 7-35**   *Policy-Based Routing Configuration Exercise Commands*

| Command | Description |
|---|---|
| (config)#**access-list 2 permit 10.200.200.0 0.0.0.255** | Creates an access list to match any IP address that matches the first 24 bits of 10.200.200.0 to use for policy routing. |
| (config)#**route-map PBR permit 10** | Creates a route map for use with policy routing. |

*continues*

**Table 7-35**    *Policy-Based Routing Configuration Exercise Commands (Continued)*

| Command | Description |
|---|---|
| (config-route-map)#**match ip address 2** | Links access list 2 to the route map to identify traffic to be policy-routed. |
| (config-route-map)#**set interface s1** | Policy-routes traffic matching access list 2 out interface s1. |
| (config-if)#**ip policy route-map PBR** | Uses the PBR route map on this interface for policy-based routing. |
| (config-route-map)#**set ip next-hop 10.x.0.2** | Uses the listed IP address as the next hop for traffic matching access list 2. |
| **show ip policy** | Displays the route maps used for policy routing on the router's interfaces. |
| **show route-map** | Displays configured route maps. |
| **debug ip policy** | Starts the display of IP policy routing packet activity. |

# Task: Configuring PBR

The goal of this exercise is to show that PBR can be used to set an arbitrary path rather than relying on the router's normal path-selection procedure. For the purposes of this exercise, suppose you want to control the path taken by traffic sourced from the internal router's loopback interface (P*x*R3 or P*x*R4). Normally, traffic from the loopback interface of P*x*R3, bound out of the pod, would go to P*x*R1 and then to the backbone router. Similarly, traffic from the loopback of P*x*R4, bound out of the pod, would go to P*x*R2 and then to the backbone.

In this exercise, you will force traffic from the loopback interface of P*x*R3 to go through P*x*R1, and then to P*x*R2, and then to the backbone router. Traffic sourced from the loopback interface of P*x*R4 will be forced to go through P*x*R2, and then to P*x*R1, and then to the backbone router.

Follow these steps:

**Step 1**    Reenable the S1 interfaces on the P*x*R1 and P*x*R2 routers.

**Step 2**    Remove the distribute list from the OSPF router configuration so that BBR2 will have a route to your loopback interfaces.

**Step 3**    On both the edge routers, create an access list 2 to match the loopback address on the directly connected internal router.

**Step 4**    On the edge routers, create a route map. Match the source address of loopback0 of the internal router by referencing the access list created in the preceding step. Set the outbound interface so that this traffic is sent out interface serial 1 to the other edge router. Thus, traffic sourced from the loopback interface of the internal router is forced to go to the other edge router before going out to the core router.

What happens to traffic sourced from IP addresses not listed in the access list?

**Step 5**  Recall that policies are applied on the interface where that traffic enters the router. What is the incoming interface for traffic from the internal router? Apply the policy to that interface.

**Step 6**  Verify that the policy is in place and applied to the correct interface with the **show ip policy** command.

**Step 7**  Go to the internal routers and use **traceroute** to test the policy. First, trace from the internal router to BBR2 (172.31.*xx*.4).

**Step 8**  Use extended traceroute, sourced from loopback0, from the internal router to BBR2 (172.31.*xx*.4). How are the results different from the preceding step?

**Step 9**  View the configured route map to see what traffic has been policy-routed.

**Step 10**  On the edge router, turn on debugging of the policy routing. Then go to the internal router and repeat the traceroutes from the internal router to BBR2. You should see the edge router choosing to policy-route or not.

## Exercise Verification

You have successfully completed this exercise when you control traffic sourced from the loopback interfaces of the internal router through PBR while maintaining reachability to the core router.

# Solution to Configuration Exercise 7-1: Configuring Basic Redistribution

This section provides the answers to the questions in the Configuration Exercise.

---

**NOTE**  Some answers provided cover multiple steps; the answers are given after the last step to which that answer applies.

---

## Solution to Task 1: Cleaning Up

**Step 1**  Remove the IS-IS configuration from all the pod routers using the **no router isis** global configuration command.

**Step 2**  Check the configuration of S0 on the edge routers. It should include an IP address, Frame Relay encapsulation, and a Frame Relay static map, and it should have Frame Relay Inverse Address Resolution Protocol (ARP) turned off. The IP address should be 172.31.*xx*.*y* /24, and the data-link connection identifier (DLCI) should be 2*xy*, where *x* is the pod number and *y* is the router number. One way to do this is to remove all configuration commands on the S0 interfaces by using the **default interface s0** global configuration command, and then put the required configuration on those interfaces.

> **Step 3**    Create a loopback interface on your edge routers with the IP address of
> 10.200.200.*xy* /32, where *x* is the pod number and *y* is the router number.
> (Your internal routers already have similar loopback addresses.)

**Solution:**

The following shows the required configuration on the pod 1 routers:

```
P1R1(config)#no router isis
P1R1(config)#default int s0
Building configuration...

Interface Serial0 set to default configuration
P1R1(config)#int s0
P1R1(config-if)#ip address 172.31.11.1 255.255.255.0
P1R1(config-if)#encapsulation frame-relay
P1R1(config-if)#frame-relay map ip 172.31.11.4 211 broadcast
P1R1(config-if)#no frame-relay inverse-arp
P1R1(config)#int loop 0
P1R1(config-if)#ip address 10.200.200.11 255.255.255.255

P1R2(config)#no router isis
P1R2(config)#default interface s0
Building configuration...

Interface Serial0 set to default configuration
P1R2(config)#int s0
P1R2(config-if)#ip address 172.31.11.2 255.255.255.0
P1R2(config-if)#encapsulation frame-relay
P1R2(config-if)#frame-relay map ip 172.31.11.4 212 broadcast
P1R2(config-if)#no frame-relay inverse-arp
P1R2(config-if)#exit
P1R2(config)#int loop 0
P1R2(config-if)#ip address 10.200.200.12 255.255.255.255
P1R2(config-if)#

P1R3(config)#no router isis

P1R4(config)#no router isis
```

# Solution to Task 2: Setting Up the Routing Protocols

> **Step 1**    BBR2 is in OSPF area 0. Each pod's edge routers will run both OSPF and
> RIPv2.
>
> On the edge routers, put the S0 interface in OSPF area 0. Because BBR2 is
> configured with a point-to-multipoint interface, configure the edge router's
> S0 interface with the OSPF point-to-multipoint network type.
>
> Configure the edge routers to also run RIPv2 internally to the pod. Turn off
> autosummarization for RIPv2.
>
> Configure the internal routers to run only RIPv2.

**Solution:**

The following examples show the configuration for the pod 1 routers:

```
P1R1(config)#router ospf 1
P1R1(config-router)#network 172.31.11.0 0.0.0.255 area 0
P1R1(config-router)#exit
P1R1(config)#router rip
P1R1(config-router)#version 2
P1R1(config-router)#network 10.0.0.0
P1R1(config-router)#no auto-summary
P1R1(config-router)#exit
P1R1(config)#int s0
P1R1(config-if)#ip ospf network point-to-multipoint

P1R2(config)#router ospf 1
P1R2(config-router)#network 172.31.11.0 0.0.0.255 area 0
P1R2(config-router)#exit
P1R2(config)#router rip
P1R2(config-router)#version 2
P1R2(config-router)#network 10.0.0.0
P1R2(config-router)#no auto-summary
P1R2(config-router)#exit
P1R2(config)#int s0
P1R2(config-if)#ip ospf network point-to-multipoint

P1R3(config)#router rip
P1R3(config-router)#version 2
P1R3(config-router)#network 10.0.0.0

P1R4(config)#router rip
P1R4(config-router)#version 2
P1R4(config-router)#network 10.0.0.0
```

**Step 2**    Show the IP routing table on both edge routers. Verify that both edge routers
are learning both OSPF and RIPv2 routes. What is the highest hop count on
the RIPv2 routes to the networks within your pod?

**Solution:**

The following sample output is from the P1R1 and P1R2 routers:

```
P1R1#show ip route
<output omitted>
Gateway of last resort is not set

     172.31.0.0/16 is variably subnetted, 6 subnets, 2 masks
O       172.31.22.4/32 [110/64] via 172.31.11.4, 00:00:13, Serial0
O       172.31.22.1/32 [110/1626] via 172.31.11.4, 00:00:13, Serial0
O       172.31.22.2/32 [110/1626] via 172.31.11.4, 00:00:13, Serial0
C       172.31.11.0/24 is directly connected, Serial0
O       172.31.11.2/32 [110/1626] via 172.31.11.4, 00:00:13, Serial0
O       172.31.11.4/32 [110/64] via 172.31.11.4, 00:00:13, Serial0
     10.0.0.0/8 is variably subnetted, 9 subnets, 2 masks
```

*continues*

```
C        10.200.200.11/32 is directly connected, Loopback0
R        10.200.200.14/32 [120/2] via 10.1.0.2, 00:00:12, Serial1
                          [120/2] via 10.1.1.3, 00:00:02, Ethernet0
R        10.200.200.12/32 [120/1] via 10.1.0.2, 00:00:12, Serial1
R        10.200.200.13/32 [120/1] via 10.1.1.3, 00:00:02, Ethernet0
R        10.1.3.0/24 [120/1] via 10.1.1.3, 00:00:02, Ethernet0
R        10.1.2.0/24 [120/1] via 10.1.0.2, 00:00:12, Serial1
C        10.1.1.0/24 is directly connected, Ethernet0
C        10.1.0.0/24 is directly connected, Serial1
O E2     10.254.0.0/24 [110/50] via 172.31.11.4, 00:00:15, Serial0
P1R1#

P1R2#show ip route
<output omitted>
Gateway of last resort is not set

     172.31.0.0/16 is variably subnetted, 6 subnets, 2 masks
O        172.31.22.4/32 [110/64] via 172.31.11.4, 00:01:34, Serial0
O        172.31.22.1/32 [110/1626] via 172.31.11.4, 00:01:34, Serial0
O        172.31.22.2/32 [110/1626] via 172.31.11.4, 00:01:34, Serial0
C        172.31.11.0/24 is directly connected, Serial0
O        172.31.11.1/32 [110/1626] via 172.31.11.4, 00:01:34, Serial0
O        172.31.11.4/32 [110/64] via 172.31.11.4, 00:01:34, Serial0
     10.0.0.0/8 is variably subnetted, 9 subnets, 2 masks
R        10.200.200.11/32 [120/1] via 10.1.0.1, 00:00:05, Serial1
R        10.200.200.14/32 [120/1] via 10.1.2.4, 00:00:09, Ethernet0
C        10.200.200.12/32 is directly connected, Loopback0
R        10.200.200.13/32 [120/2] via 10.1.0.1, 00:00:05, Serial1
                          [120/2] via 10.1.2.4, 00:00:09, Ethernet0
R        10.1.3.0/24 [120/1] via 10.1.2.4, 00:00:10, Ethernet0
C        10.1.2.0/24 is directly connected, Ethernet0
R        10.1.1.0/24 [120/1] via 10.1.0.1, 00:00:06, Serial1
C        10.1.0.0/24 is directly connected, Serial1
O E2     10.254.0.0/24 [110/50] via 172.31.11.4, 00:01:36, Serial0
P1R2#
```

Both edge routers are learning OSPF and RIPv2 routes.

The highest RIP hop count is two hops.

## Solution to Task 3: Configuring Basic Redistribution

**Step 1**   Configure both edge routers to pass a default route into RIPv2. RIPv2 needs a static default route configured to advertise it to other RIPv2 routers.

Examine the routing table on the internal routers. Is the default route present? What are its path and metric?

**Solution:**

The following sample configuration is on the P1R1 and P1R2 routers:

```
P1R1(config)#ip route 0.0.0.0 0.0.0.0 172.31.11.4
P1R1(config)#router rip
P1R1(config-router)#default-information originate
```

```
P1R2(config)#ip route 0.0.0.0 0.0.0.0 172.31.11.4
P1R2(config)#router rip
P1R2(config-router)#default-information originate
```

The following output shows the routing tables on the P1R3 and P1R4 routers. The default route is present on the internal routers with a metric of 120/1.

```
P1R3#show ip route
<output omitted>
Gateway of last resort is 10.1.1.1 to network 0.0.0.0

     10.0.0.0/8 is variably subnetted, 8 subnets, 2 masks
R       10.200.200.11/32 [120/1] via 10.1.1.1, 00:00:06, Ethernet0
R       10.200.200.14/32 [120/1] via 10.1.3.4, 00:00:21, Serial0
R       10.200.200.12/32 [120/2] via 10.1.3.4, 00:00:21, Serial0
C       10.200.200.13/32 is directly connected, Loopback0
C       10.1.3.0/24 is directly connected, Serial0
R       10.1.2.0/24 [120/1] via 10.1.3.4, 00:00:21, Serial0
C       10.1.1.0/24 is directly connected, Ethernet0
R       10.1.0.0/24 [120/1] via 10.1.1.1, 00:00:07, Ethernet0
R*   0.0.0.0/0 [120/1] via 10.1.1.1, 00:00:07, Ethernet0
P1R3#
P1R4#show ip route
<output omitted>
Gateway of last resort is 10.1.2.2 to network 0.0.0.0

     10.0.0.0/8 is variably subnetted, 8 subnets, 2 masks
R       10.200.200.11/32 [120/2] via 10.1.3.3, 00:00:18, Serial0
C       10.200.200.14/32 is directly connected, Loopback0
R       10.200.200.12/32 [120/1] via 10.1.2.2, 00:00:07, Ethernet0
R       10.200.200.13/32 [120/1] via 10.1.3.3, 00:00:18, Serial0
C       10.1.3.0/24 is directly connected, Serial0
C       10.1.2.0/24 is directly connected, Ethernet0
R       10.1.1.0/24 [120/1] via 10.1.3.3, 00:00:18, Serial0
R       10.1.0.0/24 [120/1] via 10.1.2.2, 00:00:08, Ethernet0
R*   0.0.0.0/0 [120/1] via 10.1.2.2, 00:00:08, Ethernet0
P1R4#
```

**Step 2**    Configure both edge routers to redistribute RIPv2 routes into OSPF without specifying a metric value. What default metric will OSPF use when the RIPv2 routes are redistributed? (Remember to include the **subnets** keyword in the **redistribute** command.)

**Solution:**

The following sample configuration is on the P1R1 and P1R2 routers:

```
P1R1(config)#router ospf 1
P1R1(config-router)#redistribute rip subnets

P1R2(config)#router ospf 1
P1R2(config-router)#redistribute rip subnets
```

The default metric used by OSPF is 20.

**Step 3** Telnet to the core router, BBR2 (the password is **cisco**), and examine the OSPF
database. What type of routes do the networks from your pod appear as?

**Solution:**

The following output is from the BBR2 router. The pod 1 routes appear as type 5 LSAs.

```
BBR2>show ip ospf database

        OSPF Router with ID (200.200.200.200) (Process ID 1)


                Router Link States (Area 0)

Link ID          ADV Router       Age       Seq#       Checksum Link count
10.200.200.11    10.200.200.11    1141      0x80000004 0xC9F5   2
10.200.200.12    10.200.200.12    1119      0x80000004 0xDDDD   2
10.200.200.21    10.200.200.21    1347      0x80000003 0xA2F3   2
10.200.200.22    10.200.200.22    1388      0x80000004 0xB4DC   2
200.200.200.200  200.200.200.200  1576      0x80000062 0x1AB3   6

                Type-5 AS External Link States

Link ID          ADV Router       Age       Seq#       Checksum Tag
10.1.0.0         10.200.200.11    1140      0x80000001 0xF8F5   0
10.1.0.0         10.200.200.12    1119      0x80000001 0xF2FA   0
10.1.1.0         10.200.200.11    1140      0x80000001 0xEDFF   0
10.1.2.0         10.200.200.12    1119      0x80000001 0xDC0F   0
10.1.3.0         10.200.200.11    1140      0x80000001 0xD714   0
10.2.0.0         10.200.200.21    1346      0x80000001 0xB033   0
10.2.0.0         10.200.200.22    1387      0x80000001 0xAA38   0
10.2.1.0         10.200.200.21    1346      0x80000001 0xA53D   0
10.2.2.0         10.200.200.22    1388      0x80000001 0x944C   0
10.2.3.0         10.200.200.21    629       0x80000001 0x8F51   0
10.200.200.11    10.200.200.11    1141      0x80000001 0x8CC6   0
10.200.200.12    10.200.200.12    1120      0x80000001 0x7CD4   0
10.200.200.13    10.200.200.11    1141      0x80000001 0x78D8   0
10.200.200.14    10.200.200.11    1141      0x80000001 0x6EE1   0
10.200.200.21    10.200.200.21    1347      0x80000001 0xEB53   0
10.200.200.22    10.200.200.22    1388      0x80000001 0xDB61   0
10.200.200.23    10.200.200.21    1307      0x80000001 0xD765   0
10.200.200.24    10.200.200.22    1388      0x80000001 0xC773   0
10.254.0.0       200.200.200.200  628       0x8000002D 0xBE6B   0
BBR2>
```

**Step 4** Examine the IP routing table on both internal routers.

**Solution:**

The following output shows the routing tables on the P1R3 and P1R4 routers. These routers are
receiving default routes from the edge routers.

```
P1R3#show ip route
<output omitted>
Gateway of last resort is 10.1.1.1 to network 0.0.0.0
```

```
        10.0.0.0/8 is variably subnetted, 8 subnets, 2 masks
R       10.200.200.11/32 [120/1] via 10.1.1.1, 00:00:06, Ethernet0
R       10.200.200.14/32 [120/1] via 10.1.3.4, 00:00:21, Serial0
R       10.200.200.12/32 [120/2] via 10.1.3.4, 00:00:21, Serial0
C       10.200.200.13/32 is directly connected, Loopback0
C       10.1.3.0/24 is directly connected, Serial0
R       10.1.2.0/24 [120/1] via 10.1.3.4, 00:00:21, Serial0
C       10.1.1.0/24 is directly connected, Ethernet0
R       10.1.0.0/24 [120/1] via 10.1.1.1, 00:00:07, Ethernet0
R*   0.0.0.0/0 [120/1] via 10.1.1.1, 00:00:07, Ethernet0
P1R3#
P1R4#show ip route
<output omitted>
Gateway of last resort is 10.1.2.2 to network 0.0.0.0

        10.0.0.0/8 is variably subnetted, 8 subnets, 2 masks
R       10.200.200.11/32 [120/2] via 10.1.3.3, 00:00:18, Serial0
C       10.200.200.14/32 is directly connected, Loopback0
R       10.200.200.12/32 [120/1] via 10.1.2.2, 00:00:07, Ethernet0
R       10.200.200.13/32 [120/1] via 10.1.3.3, 00:00:18, Serial0
C       10.1.3.0/24 is directly connected, Serial0
C       10.1.2.0/24 is directly connected, Ethernet0
R       10.1.1.0/24 [120/1] via 10.1.3.3, 00:00:18, Serial0
R       10.1.0.0/24 [120/1] via 10.1.2.2, 00:00:08, Ethernet0
R*   0.0.0.0/0 [120/1] via 10.1.2.2, 00:00:08, Ethernet0
P1R4#
```

**Step 5**   Verify that the internal routers can ping the TFTP server.

**Solution:**

The following pings were performed on the P1R3 and P1R4 routers. Both can successfully ping
the TFTP server.

```
P1R3#ping 10.254.0.254

Type escape sequence to abort.
Sending 5, 100-byte ICMP Echos to 10.254.0.254, timeout is 2 seconds:
!!!!!
Success rate is 100 percent (5/5), round-trip min/avg/max = 32/125/328 ms

P1R4#ping 10.254.0.254

Type escape sequence to abort.
Sending 5, 100-byte ICMP Echos to 10.254.0.254, timeout is 2 seconds:
!!!!!
Success rate is 100 percent (5/5), round-trip min/avg/max = 32/48/68 ms
```

# Solution to Task 4: Filtering Routing Updates

**Step 1**   Examine the routing table on the BBR2 router for comparison after the filters
are put into place.

**Solution:**

The following output shows the routing table on the BBR2 router. The loopback routes are highlighted.

```
BBR2>show ip route
<output omitted>
Gateway of last resort is not set

     172.31.0.0/16 is variably subnetted, 9 subnets, 3 masks
O       172.31.22.1/32 [110/1562] via 172.31.22.1, 00:19:22, Serial0.2
C       172.31.22.0/24 is directly connected, Serial0.2
O       172.31.22.2/32 [110/1562] via 172.31.22.2, 00:19:22, Serial0.2
B       172.31.2.0/24 [20/0] via 10.254.0.1, 00:47:03
B       172.31.1.0/24 [20/0] via 10.254.0.1, 00:51:11
R       172.31.0.0/16 [120/1] via 10.254.0.1, 00:00:06, Ethernet0
C       172.31.11.0/24 is directly connected, Serial0.1
O       172.31.11.1/32 [110/1562] via 172.31.11.1, 00:19:23, Serial0.1
O       172.31.11.2/32 [110/1562] via 172.31.11.2, 00:19:23, Serial0.1
     10.0.0.0/8 is variably subnetted, 18 subnets, 2 masks
O E2    10.200.200.11/32 [110/20] via 172.31.11.1, 00:19:23, Serial0.1
O E2    10.200.200.14/32 [110/20] via 172.31.11.1, 00:19:23, Serial0.1
O E2    10.200.200.12/32 [110/20] via 172.31.11.2, 00:19:24, Serial0.1
O E2    10.200.200.13/32 [110/20] via 172.31.11.1, 00:19:24, Serial0.1
O E2    10.1.3.0/24 [110/20] via 172.31.11.1, 00:19:24, Serial0.1
O E2    10.2.0.0/24 [110/20] via 172.31.22.2, 00:19:24, Serial0.2
                    [110/20] via 172.31.22.1, 00:19:24, Serial0.2
O E2    10.1.2.0/24 [110/20] via 172.31.11.2, 00:19:24, Serial0.1
O E2    10.2.1.0/24 [110/20] via 172.31.22.1, 00:19:25, Serial0.2
O E2    10.1.1.0/24 [110/20] via 172.31.11.1, 00:19:25, Serial0.1
O E2    10.2.2.0/24 [110/20] via 172.31.22.2, 00:19:25, Serial0.2
B       10.97.97.0/24 [20/0] via 10.254.0.3, 02:29:17
O E2    10.2.3.0/24 [110/20] via 172.31.22.1, 00:11:19, Serial0.2
O E2    10.1.0.0/24 [110/20] via 172.31.11.1, 00:19:25, Serial0.1
                    [110/20] via 172.31.11.2, 00:19:25, Serial0.1
O E2    10.200.200.24/32 [110/20] via 172.31.22.2, 00:19:25, Serial0.2
O E2    10.200.200.22/32 [110/20] via 172.31.22.2, 00:19:25, Serial0.2
O E2    10.200.200.23/32 [110/20] via 172.31.22.1, 00:19:25, Serial0.2
O E2    10.200.200.21/32 [110/20] via 172.31.22.1, 00:19:25, Serial0.2
C       10.254.0.0/24 is directly connected, Ethernet0
BBR2>
```

**Step 2**  Create an access list that matches the four loopback addresses in your pod.

**Solution:**

The following example shows the required configuration on the P1R1 and P1R2 routers:

```
P1R1(config)#access-list 1 deny 10.200.200.0 0.0.0.255
P1R1(config)#access-list 1 permit any

P1R2(config)#access-list 1 deny 10.200.200.0 0.0.0.255
P1R2(config)#access-list 1 permit any
```

**Step 3**    Use a distribute list to block the RIPv2 routes in this access list from being redistributed into OSPF.

**Solution:**

The following example shows the required configuration on the P1R1 and P1R2 routers:

```
P1R1(config)#router ospf 1
P1R1(config-router)#distribute-list 1 out rip

P1R2(config)#router ospf 1
P1R2(config-router)#distribute-list 1 out rip
```

**Step 4**    Examine the routing table on the BBR2 router again. Verify that the loopback addresses are not listed.

**Solution:**

The following output shows the routing table on the BBR2 router. The loopback routes are not listed. (Note that the pod 2 routers are configured similar to the pod 1 routers.)

```
BBR2>show ip route
<output omitted>
Gateway of last resort is not set

     172.31.0.0/16 is variably subnetted, 9 subnets, 3 masks
O       172.31.22.1/32 [110/1562] via 172.31.22.1, 00:27:58, Serial0.2
C       172.31.22.0/24 is directly connected, Serial0.2
O       172.31.22.2/32 [110/1562] via 172.31.22.2, 00:27:58, Serial0.2
B       172.31.2.0/24 [20/0] via 10.254.0.1, 00:55:38
B       172.31.1.0/24 [20/0] via 10.254.0.1, 00:59:47
R       172.31.0.0/16 [120/1] via 10.254.0.1, 00:00:23, Ethernet0
C       172.31.11.0/24 is directly connected, Serial0.1
O       172.31.11.1/32 [110/1562] via 172.31.11.1, 00:27:58, Serial0.1
O       172.31.11.2/32 [110/1562] via 172.31.11.2, 00:27:58, Serial0.1
     10.0.0.0/24 is subnetted, 10 subnets
O E2    10.1.3.0 [110/20] via 172.31.11.1, 00:27:58, Serial0.1
O E2    10.2.0.0 [110/20] via 172.31.22.2, 00:27:58, Serial0.2
                 [110/20] via 172.31.22.1, 00:27:58, Serial0.2
O E2    10.1.2.0 [110/20] via 172.31.11.2, 00:28:00, Serial0.1
O E2    10.2.1.0 [110/20] via 172.31.22.1, 00:28:00, Serial0.2
O E2    10.1.1.0 [110/20] via 172.31.11.1, 00:28:00, Serial0.1
O E2    10.2.2.0 [110/20] via 172.31.22.2, 00:28:00, Serial0.2
B       10.97.97.0 [20/0] via 10.254.0.3, 02:37:53
O E2    10.2.3.0 [110/20] via 172.31.22.1, 00:19:54, Serial0.2
O E2    10.1.0.0 [110/20] via 172.31.11.1, 00:28:00, Serial0.1
                 [110/20] via 172.31.11.2, 00:28:00, Serial0.1
C       10.254.0.0 is directly connected, Ethernet0
```

**Step 5**    Can the BBR2 router ping your loopback addresses?

**Solution:**

The following output is from the BBR2 router. Because the core cannot see the loopback addresses, the pings do not work.

```
BBR2>ping 10.200.200.13
Type escape sequence to abort.
Sending 5, 100-byte ICMP Echos to 10.200.200.13, timeout is 2 seconds:
.....
Success rate is 0 percent (0/5)

BBR2>ping 10.200.200.22
Type escape sequence to abort.
Sending 5, 100-byte ICMP Echos to 10.200.200.22, timeout is 2 seconds:
.....
Success rate is 0 percent (0/5)
```

## Exercise Verification

You have successfully completed this exercise when you achieve the following results:

- You can establish OSPF adjacencies between the edge routers and the core BBR2 router and exchange the routing updates.

- You can establish that the RIPv2 updates are exchanged between the internal routers and edge routers.

- You can establish that redistribution is configured from RIPv2 to OSPF.

- You can demonstrate that a default route has been injected into the RIPv2 routing domain.

# Solution to Configuration Exercise 7-2: Tuning Basic Redistribution

This section provides the answers to the questions in the Configuration Exercise.

**NOTE**  Some answers provided cover multiple steps; the answers are given after the last step to which that answer applies.

## Solution to Task: Tuning Basic Redistribution with Route Maps

**Step 1**  Shut down S1 on P*x*R1 and P*x*R2 (to avoid a routing loop in this task).

**Solution:**

The following sample configuration is on the P1R1 and P1R2 routers:

```
P1R1(config)#int s1
P1R1(config-if)#shut
P1R2(config)#int s1
P1R2(config-if)#shut
```

**Step 2**    Telnet to BBR2 (the password is **cisco**). Notice that all your pod routes
(10.x.0.0) have the same OSPF metric of 20.

**Solution:**

The following output is from the BBR2 router. All the pod 1 routes have an OSPF metric of 20.

```
BBR2>show ip route
<output omitted>
Gateway of last resort is not set

     172.31.0.0/16 is variably subnetted, 9 subnets, 3 masks
O       172.31.22.1/32 [110/1562] via 172.31.22.1, 00:02:16, Serial0.2
C       172.31.22.0/24 is directly connected, Serial0.2
O       172.31.22.2/32 [110/1562] via 172.31.22.2, 00:02:16, Serial0.2
B       172.31.2.0/24 [20/0] via 10.254.0.1, 00:02:16
B       172.31.1.0/24 [20/0] via 10.254.0.1, 00:02:16
R       172.31.0.0/16 [120/1] via 10.254.0.1, 00:00:01, Ethernet0
C       172.31.11.0/24 is directly connected, Serial0.1
O       172.31.11.1/32 [110/1562] via 172.31.11.1, 00:02:16, Serial0.1
O       172.31.11.2/32 [110/1562] via 172.31.11.2, 00:02:16, Serial0.1
     10.0.0.0/24 is subnetted, 8 subnets
O E2    10.1.3.0 [110/20] via 172.31.11.2, 00:00:36, Serial0.1
O E2    10.1.2.0 [110/20] via 172.31.11.2, 00:00:36, Serial0.1
O E2    10.2.1.0 [110/20] via 172.31.22.1, 00:00:49, Serial0.2
O E2    10.1.1.0 [110/20] via 172.31.11.1, 00:00:24, Serial0.1
O E2    10.2.2.0 [110/20] via 172.31.22.2, 00:00:30, Serial0.2
B       10.97.97.0 [20/0] via 10.254.0.3, 00:02:18
O E2    10.2.3.0 [110/20] via 172.31.22.1, 00:00:49, Serial0.2
C       10.254.0.0 is directly connected, Ethernet0
BBR2>
```

**Step 3**    Having the same metric for all the redistributed RIPv2 routes prevents the
core from making accurate routing decisions for those routes. The central
OSPF domain needs to have different OSPF metrics based on how far the
network is from the redistribution point.

At the edge routers, create a route map for altering the metric of the
redistributed routes. Match the RIPv2 metric and set an appropriate OSPF
metric: For a RIPv2 hop count of 1, set the OSPF metric to 1000, and for a
RIPv2 hop count of 2, set the OSPF metric to 2000.

On the edge routers, change the redistribution from RIPv2 into OSPF to use
this route map.

**Solution:**

The following sample configuration is on the P1R1 and P1R2 routers:

```
P1R1(config)#route-map CONVERT permit 10
P1R1(config-route-map)#match metric 1
P1R1(config-route-map)#set metric 1000
P1R1(config-route-map)#exit
```

*continues*

```
P1R1(config)#route-map CONVERT permit 20
P1R1(config-route-map)#match metric 2
P1R1(config-route-map)#set metric 2000
P1R1(config-route-map)#exit
P1R1(config)#router ospf 1
P1R1(config-router)#redistributes rip subnets route-map CONVERT

P1R2(config)#route-map CONVERT permit 10
P1R2(config-route-map)#match metric 1
P1R2(config-route-map)#set metric 1000
P1R2(config-route-map)#exit
P1R2(config)#route-map CONVERT permit 20
P1R2(config-route-map)#match metric 2
P1R2(config-route-map)#set metric 2000
P1R2(config-route-map)#exit
P1R2(config)#router ospf 1
P1R2(config-router)#redistribute rip subnets route-map CONVERT
```

**Step 4**   View the routing table on BBR2. Did this convert the metrics appropriately?

**Solution:**

The following output is from the BBR2 router. The metrics have been changed appropriately.
(Note that a similar configuration has been put on the pod 2 routers.)

```
BBR2>show ip route
<output omitted>
Gateway of last resort is not set

     172.31.0.0/16 is variably subnetted, 9 subnets, 3 masks
O       172.31.22.1/32 [110/1562] via 172.31.22.1, 00:09:31, Serial0.2
C       172.31.22.0/24 is directly connected, Serial0.2
O       172.31.22.2/32 [110/1562] via 172.31.22.2, 00:09:31, Serial0.2
B       172.31.2.0/24 [20/0] via 10.254.0.1, 00:09:31
B       172.31.1.0/24 [20/0] via 10.254.0.1, 00:09:31
R       172.31.0.0/16 [120/1] via 10.254.0.1, 00:00:24, Ethernet0
C       172.31.11.0/24 is directly connected, Serial0.1
O       172.31.11.1/32 [110/1562] via 172.31.11.1, 00:09:31, Serial0.1
O       172.31.11.2/32 [110/1562] via 172.31.11.2, 00:09:31, Serial0.1
     10.0.0.0/24 is subnetted, 8 subnets
O E2    10.1.3.0 [110/1000] via 172.31.11.1, 00:09:31, Serial0.1
O E2    10.1.2.0 [110/2000] via 172.31.11.1, 00:01:05, Serial0.1
O E2    10.2.1.0 [110/2000] via 172.31.22.2, 00:02:38, Serial0.2
O E2    10.1.1.0 [110/2000] via 172.31.11.2, 00:00:53, Serial0.1
O E2    10.2.2.0 [110/2000] via 172.31.22.1, 00:02:18, Serial0.2
B       10.97.97.0 [20/0] via 10.254.0.3, 00:09:39
O E2    10.2.3.0 [110/1000] via 172.31.22.1, 00:09:39, Serial0.2
C       10.254.0.0 is directly connected, Ethernet0
BBR2>
```

# Exercise Verification

You have completed this exercise when you understand how to use a route map to control
redistribution.

# Solution to Configuration Exercise 7-3: Configuring Policy-Based Routing

This section provides the answers to the questions in the Configuration Exercise.

**NOTE**    Some answers provided cover multiple steps; the answers are given after the last step to which that answer applies.

## Solution to Task: Configuring PBR

**Step 1**    Reenable the S1 interfaces on the P*x*R1 and P*x*R2 routers.

**Solution:**

The following example shows the required configuration on the P1R1 and P1R2 routers:

```
P1R1(config)#int s1
P1R1(config-if)#no shut
P1R2(config)#int s1
P1R2(config-if)#no shut
```

**Step 2**    Remove the distribute list from the OSPF router configuration so that BBR2 will have a route to your loopback interfaces.

**Solution:**

The following example shows the required configuration on the P1R1 and P1R2 routers:

```
P1R1(config)#router ospf 1
P1R1(config-router)#no distribute-list 1 out rip

P1R2(config)#router ospf 1
P1R2(config-router)#no distribute-list 1 out rip
```

**Step 3**    On both the edge routers, create an access list 2 to match the loopback address on the directly connected internal router.

**Solution:**

The following example shows the required configuration on the P1R1 and P1R2 routers:

```
P1R1(config)#access-list 2 permit 10.200.200.0 0.0.0.255

P1R2(config)#access-list 2 permit 10.200.200.0 0.0.0.255
```

**Step 4**    On the edge routers, create a route map. Match the source address of loopback0 of the internal router by referencing the access list created in the preceding step. Set the outbound interface so that this traffic is sent out interface serial 1 to the other edge router. Thus, traffic sourced from the loopback interface of the internal router is forced to go to the other edge router before going out to the core router.

What happens to traffic sourced from IP addresses not listed in the access list?

**Solution:**

The following example shows the required configuration on the P1R1 and P1R2 routers:

```
P1R1(config)#route-map PBR permit 10
P1R1(config-route-map)#match ip address 2
P1R1(config-route-map)#set interface s1

P1R2(config)#route-map PBR permit 10
P1R2(config-route-map)#match ip address 2
P1R2(config-route-map)#set interface s1
```

Traffic sourced from other addresses is routed normally.

**Step 5**   Recall that policies are applied on the interface where that traffic enters the router. What is the incoming interface for traffic from the internal router? Apply the policy to that interface.

**Solution:**

The following example shows the required configuration on the P1R1 and P1R2 routers. The policy is applied to the Ethernet 0 interface.

```
P1R1(config)#int e0
P1R1(config-if)#ip policy route-map PBR

P1R2(config)#int e0
P1R2(config-if)#ip policy route-map PBR
```

**Step 6**   Verify that the policy is in place and applied to the correct interface with the **show ip policy** command.

**Solution:**

The following sample outputs are from the P1R1 and P1R2 routers. The appropriate policies are in place.

```
P1R1#show ip policy
Interface       Route map
Ethernet0       PBR
P1R1#

P1R2#show ip policy
Interface       Route map
Ethernet0       PBR
P1R2#
```

**Step 7**   Go to the internal routers and use **traceroute** to test the policy. First, trace from the internal router to BBR2 (172.31.xx.4).

**Solution:**

The following output is from the P1R3 router. The trace packet is sourced from the e0 interface of the internal router by default, so it is routed normally to the BBR2 router.

```
P1R3>traceroute 172.31.11.4

Type escape sequence to abort.
Tracing the route to bbr2 (172.31.11.4)

  1 P1R1 (10.1.1.1) 4 msec 4 msec 4 msec
  2 bbr2 (172.31.11.4) 128 msec *  28 msec
P1R3>
```

**Step 8**    Use extended traceroute, sourced from loopback0, from the internal router to BBR2 (172.31.xx.4). How are the results different from the preceding step?

**Solution:**

The following output is from the P1R3 router. Because the trace packet is sourced from the internal router's loopback interface, it is policy-routed via the other edge router to the BBR2 router.

```
P1R3#trace
Protocol [ip]:
Target IP address: 172.31.11.4
Source address: 10.200.200.13
Numeric display [n]:
Timeout in seconds [3]:
Probe count [3]:
Minimum Time to Live [1]:
Maximum Time to Live [30]:
Port Number [33434]:
Loose, Strict, Record, Timestamp, Verbose[none]:
Type escape sequence to abort.
Tracing the route to bbr2 (172.31.11.4)

  1 P1R1 (10.1.1.1) 4 msec 4 msec 4 msec
  2 P1R2 (10.1.0.2) 88 msec 32 msec 32 msec
  3 bbr2 (172.31.11.4) 28 msec *  24 msec
P1R3#
```

**Step 9**    View the configured route map to see what traffic has been policy-routed.

**Solution:**

The following output is from the P1R1 router. Some packets have been policy-routed.

```
P1R1#show route-map
route-map PBR, permit, sequence 10
  Match clauses:
    ip address (access-lists): 2
  Set clauses:
    interface Serial1
  Policy routing matches: 6 packets, 360 bytes
route-map CONVERT, permit, sequence 10
```

*continues*

```
 Match clauses:
   metric 1
 Set clauses:
   metric 1000
 Policy routing matches: 0 packets, 0 bytes
route-map CONVERT, permit, sequence 20
 Match clauses:
   metric 2
 Set clauses:
   metric 2000
 Policy routing matches: 0 packets, 0 bytes
```

**Step 10** On the edge router, turn on debugging of the policy routing. Then go to the internal router and repeat the traceroutes from the internal router to BBR2. You should see the edge router choosing to policy route or not.

**Solution:**

The following output is from the P1R1 router. The first section shows the results of the extended trace, with some traffic being policy-routed.

```
P1R1#debug ip policy
Policy routing debugging is on
P1R1#
Mar  1 22:40:58 EST: IP: s=10.200.200.13 (Ethernet0), d=172.31.11.4, len 28,
  policy match
Mar  1 22:40:58 EST: IP: route map PBR, item 10, permit
Mar  1 22:40:58 EST: IP: s=10.200.200.13 (Ethernet0), d=172.31.11.4 (Serial1),
  len 28, policy routed
Mar  1 22:40:58 EST: IP: Ethernet0 to Serial1 172.31.11.4
Mar  1 22:40:58 EST: IP: s=10.200.200.13 (Ethernet0), d=172.31.11.4, len 28,
  policy match
Mar  1 22:40:58 EST: IP: route map PBR, item 10, permit
Mar  1 22:40:58 EST: IP: s=10.200.200.13 (Ethernet0), d=172.31.11.4 (Serial1),
  len 28, policy routed
Mar  1 22:40:59 EST: IP: Ethernet0 to Serial1 172.31.11.4

! The second section shows the result of the normal trace, with no policy routing.
P1R1#
Mar  1 22:41:44 EST: IP: s=10.1.1.3 (Ethernet0), d=172.31.11.4 (Serial0), len 28,
  policy rejected -- normal forwarding
Mar  1 22:41:44 EST: IP: s=10.1.1.3 (Ethernet0), d=172.31.11.4 (Serial0), len 28,
  policy rejected -- normal forwarding
Mar  1 22:41:47 EST: IP: s=10.1.1.3 (Ethernet0), d=172.31.11.4 (Serial0), len 28,
  policy rejected -- normal forwarding
P1R1#
```

# Exercise Verification

You have successfully completed this exercise when you control traffic sourced from the loopback interfaces of the internal router through PBR while maintaining reachability to the core router.

# Review Questions

Answer the following questions, and then refer to Appendix G, "Answers to Review Questions," for the answers.

**1**   What are some of the things you need to consider when migrating to another routing protocol?

**2**   List some considerations when transitioning to a new IP addressing plan.

**3**   A router is configured with a primary and secondary address on its Ethernet 0 interface. It is also configured to run EIGRP on this interface. How will the secondary address interact with EIGRP?

**4**   What are the steps when migrating to a new routing protocol?

**5**   List some reasons why you might use multiple routing protocols in a network.

**6**   What is redistribution?

**7**   Does redistributing between two routing protocols change the routing table on the router that is doing the redistribution?

**8**   What are some issues that arise with redistribution?

**9**   How can a routing loop result in a network that has redundant paths between two routing processes?

**10**   What two parameters do routers use to select the best path when they learn two or more routes to the same destination from different routing protocols?

**11**   Fill in the default administrative distances for the following routing protocols:

| Routing Protocol | Default Administrative Distance Value |
|---|---|
| Connected interface | |
| Static route out an interface | |
| Static route to a next-hop address | |
| EIGRP summary route | |
| External BGP | |
| Internal EIGRP | |
| IGRP | |
| OSPF | |
| IS-IS | |
| RIP version 1 and RIP version 2 | |
| EGP | |
| On-Demand Routing (ODR) | |

*continues*

| Routing Protocol | Default Administrative Distance Value |
|---|---|
| External EIGRP | |
| Internal BGP | |
| Unknown | |

**12** When configuring a default metric for redistributed routes, should the metric be set to a value *larger* or *smaller* than the largest metric within the receiving AS?

**13** Fill in the default seed metrics for the following protocols:

| Protocol That the Route Is Redistributed Into | Default Seed Metric |
|---|---|
| RIP | |
| IGRP/EIGRP | |
| OSPF | |
| IS-IS | |
| BGP | |

**14** What is the safest way to perform redistribution between two routing protocols?

**15** Can redistribution be configured between IPX RIP and IP RIP? Between IPX EIGRP and IP EIGRP? Between IGRP and OSPF?

**16** When configuring redistribution into RIP, what is the *metric-value* parameter?

**17** Router A is running RIP and OSPF. In the RIP domain, it learns about the 10.1.0.0/16 and 10.3.0.0/16 routes. In the OSPF domain, it learns about the 10.5.0.0/16 and 172.16.1.0/24 routes. What is the result of the following configuration on Router A?

```
router ospf 1
  redistribute rip metric 20
```

**18** What are the five components of the EIGRP routing metric?

**19** When redistributing routes into IS-IS, what is the default *level-value* parameter?

**20** What happens if you use the **metric** parameter in the **redistribute** command and you use the **default-metric** command?

**21** What does the **passive-interface default** command do?

**22** Suppose you have a dialup WAN connection between site A and site B. What can you do to prevent excess routing update traffic from crossing the link but still have the boundary routers know the networks that are at the remote sites?

**23** What command causes RIP to source a default route?

24  A distribute list allows routing updates to be filtered based on what?

25  What is the difference between the **distribute-list out** and **distribute-list in** commands?

26  What command is used to configure filtering of the routing update traffic from an interface? At what prompt is this command entered?

27  True or false: In a route map statement with multiple **match** commands, all match statements in the route map statement must be considered true for the route map statement to be considered matched.

28  True or false: In a match statement with multiple conditions, all conditions in the match statement must be true for that match statement to be considered a match.

29  What are some applications of route maps?

30  What is the *map-tag* parameter in a **route-map** command?

31  What commands would be used to configure the use of a route map called TESTING when redistributing OSPF 10 traffic into RIP?

32  What does the following command do?

```
distance 150 0.0.0.0 255.255.255.255 3
```

33  What command can be used to discover the path that a packet takes through a network?

34  What are some benefits of PBR?

35  Which parameters can PBR use to determine how a packet is routed?

36  An interface configured for PBR includes a **deny** statement in the route map. What happens to a packet that matches the criteria in this statement?

37  In which order are the following **set** commands evaluated for PBR?

   — **set ip default next-hop**

   — **set default interface**

   — **set interface**

   — **set ip next-hop**

38  When is a packet routed to the next hop specified by the **set ip default next-hop** command?

39  What command is used for policy-based routing to establish criteria based on the packet length?

40  Policy-based routing is applied to which packets on an interface?

41  What command is used to display the route maps used for policy routing?

This chapter introduces Border Gateway Protocol (BGP), including the fundamentals of BGP operation. This chapter covers the following topics:

- BGP Overview
- BGP Terminology and Concepts
- BGP Operation
- Configuring BGP
- Verifying and Troubleshooting BGP

# CHAPTER 8

# Configuring Basic Border Gateway Protocol

The Internet is becoming a vital resource in many organizations, resulting in redundant connections to multiple Internet service providers (ISPs). With multiple connections, Border Gateway Protocol (BGP) is an alternative to using default routes to control path selections.

Configuring and troubleshooting BGP can be complex. A BGP administrator must understand the various options involved in properly configuring BGP for scalable internetworking. This chapter introduces BGP terminology and concepts, as well as basic BGP configuration and troubleshooting.

When you finish this chapter, you will be able to define BGP characteristics, describe BGP concepts and terminology, configure BGP operations for scalable internetworks, and explain the BGP path-selection process and the role of BGP attributes.

## BGP Overview

This section provides an overview of BGP. Understanding BGP first requires an understanding of autonomous systems.

## Autonomous Systems

One way to categorize routing protocols is by whether they are interior or exterior:

- **Interior Gateway Protocol (IGP)**—This routing protocol is used to exchange routing information *within* an autonomous system (AS). Routing Information Protocol (RIP), Interior Gateway Routing Protocol (IGRP), Open Shortest Path First (OSPF), Intermediate System-to-Intermediate System (IS-IS), and Enhanced Interior Gateway Routing Protocol (EIGRP) are examples of IGPs for IP.

- **Exterior Gateway Protocol (EGP)**—This routing protocol is used to connect *between* autonomous systems. BGP is an example of an EGP.

This concept is illustrated in Figure 8-1.

**Figure 8-1** *IGPs Operate Within an Autonomous System, and EGPs Operate Between Autonomous Systems*

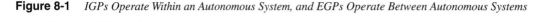

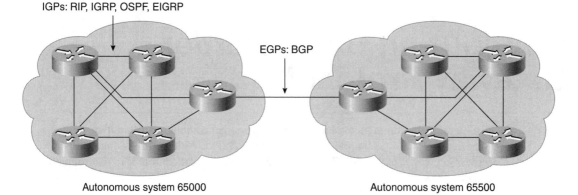

BGP is an Interdomain Routing Protocol (IDRP), which is also known as an EGP. All of the routing protocols you have seen so far in this book are interior routing protocols, also known as IGPs.

---

**NOTE**     The term IDRP as used in this sense is a generic term, not the IDRP defined in ISO/IEC International Standard 10747, *Protocol for the Exchange of Inter-Domain Routing Information Among Intermediate Systems to Support Forwarding of ISO 8473 PDUs*.

---

BGP version 4 (BGP-4) is the latest version of BGP. It is defined in RFC 1771, *A Border Gateway Protocol (BGP-4)*. As noted in this RFC, the classic definition of an AS is "a set of routers under a single technical administration, using an Interior Gateway Protocol and common metrics to route packets within the AS, and using an Exterior Gateway Protocol to route packets to other [autonomous systems]."

---

**NOTE**     Recently, extensions to BGP-4, known as BGP4+, have been defined to support multiple protocols, including IP version 6 (IPv6). These multiprotocol extensions to BGP are defined in RFC 2858, *Multiprotocol Extensions for BGP-4*, available at www.cis.ohio-state.edu/cgi-bin /rfc/rfc2858.html.

---

Today, autonomous systems might use more than one IGP, with potentially several sets of metrics. The important characteristic of an AS from the BGP point of view is that the AS appears to other autonomous systems to have a single coherent interior routing plan, and it presents a consistent picture of which destinations can be reached through it. All parts of the AS must be connected to each other.

The Internet Assigned Numbers Authority (IANA) is the umbrella organization responsible for allocating AS numbers. Specifically, the American Registry for Internet Numbers (ARIN) has jurisdiction over assigning numbers for the Americas, the Caribbean, and Africa. Reseaux IP Europeennes-Network Information Center (RIPE-NIC) administers the numbers for Europe, and the Asia Pacific-NIC (AP-NIC) administers the autonomous system numbers for the Asia-Pacific region.

This AS designator is a 16-bit number, with a range of 1 to 65535. RFC 1930, *Guidelines for Creation, Selection, and Registration of an Autonomous System (AS)*, provides guidelines for the use of AS numbers. A range of AS numbers, 64512 to 65535, is reserved for private use, much like the private IP addresses. All of the examples and exercises in this book use private AS numbers.

You need to use the IANA-assigned AS number, rather than some other number, only if your organization plans to use an EGP, such as BGP to connect to the Internet.

## BGP Use Between Autonomous Systems

BGP is used between autonomous systems, as illustrated in Figure 8-2.

---

### Key Point: BGP Provides Interdomain Routing

The main goal of BGP is to provide an interdomain routing system that guarantees the loop-free exchange of routing information between autonomous systems. BGP routers exchange information about paths to destination networks.

---

**Figure 8-2**    *BGP-4 Is Used Between Autonomous Systems on the Internet*

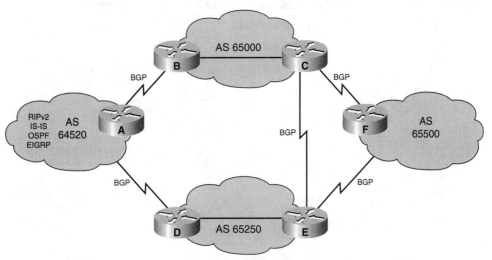

BGP is a successor to Exterior Gateway Protocol (EGP). (Note the dual use of the EGP acronym). The EGP protocol was developed to isolate networks from each other at the early stages of the Internet.

The use of the term *autonomous system* in connection with BGP stresses that the administration of an autonomous system appears to other autonomous systems to have a single, coherent, interior routing plan, and it presents a consistent picture of the networks that can be reached through it. There is also a distinction between an ordinary autonomous system and one that has been configured with BGP to implement a transit policy. The latter is called an ISP or a service provider.

Many RFCs relate to BGP-4, including those listed in Table 8-1.

**Table 8-1**    *RFCs Relating to BGP-4*

| RFC Number | RFC Title |
|---|---|
| RFC 1771 | *A Border Gateway Protocol 4 (BGP-4)* |
| RFC 1772 | *An Application of BGP on the Internet* |
| RFC 1773 | *Experience with the BGP-4 Protocol* |
| RFC 1774 | *BGP-4 Protocol Analysis* |
| RFC 1863 | *A BGP/IDRP Route Server Alternative to a Full-Mesh Routing* |
| RFC 1930 | *Guidelines for Creation, Selection, and Registration of an Autonomous System (AS)* |
| RFC 1965 | *AS Confederations for BGP* (made obsolete by RFC 3065) |
| RFC 1966 | *BGP Route Reflection—An Alternative to Full-Mesh IBGP* (updated by RFC 2796) |
| RFC 1997 | *BGP Communities Attribute* |
| RFC 1998 | *Application of the BGP Community Attribute in Multihome Routing* |
| RFC 2042 | *Registering New BGP Attribute Types* |
| RFC 2283 | *Multiprotocol Extensions for BGP-4* (made obsolete by RFC 2858) |
| RFC 2385 | *Protection of BGP Sessions via TCP MD5 Signature Option* |
| RFC 2439 | *BGP Route Flap Damping* |
| RFC 2545 | *Use of BGP-4 Multiprotocol Extensions for IPv6 Inter domain Routing* |
| RFC 2547 | *BGP/MPLS VPNs* |
| RFC 2796 | *BGP Route Reflection—An Alternative to Full-Mesh IBGP* (updates RFC 1966) |
| RFC 2842 | *Capabilities Advertisement with BGP-4* |
| RFC 2858 | *Multiprotocol Extensions for BGP-4* (makes RFC 2283 obsolete) |
| RFC 2918 | *Route Refresh Capability for BGP-4* |
| RFC 3065 | *Autonomous System Confederations for BGP* (makes RFC 1965 obsolete) |
| RFC 3107 | *Carrying Label Information in BGP-4* |

**NOTE**    For BGP technical support, see the following URL on Cisco's website: www.cisco.com/cgi-bin /Support/browse/psp_view.pl?p=Internetworking:BGP. (You must have an account on Cisco's web site to access this information.)

BGP-4 has many enhancements over earlier protocols. It is used extensively on the Internet today to connect ISPs and to interconnect enterprises to ISPs.

BGP-4 and its extensions are the only acceptable version of BGP available for use on the public-based Internet. BGP-4 carries a network mask for each advertised network and supports both variable-length subnet mask (VLSM) and classless interdomain routing (CIDR). BGP-4 predecessors did not support these capabilities, which are currently mandatory on the Internet. When using CIDR on a core router for a major ISP, the IP routing table, which is composed mostly of BGP routes, has more than 120,000 CIDR blocks; not using CIDR at the Internet level will cause the IP routing table to have more than 2,000,000 entries. Using CIDR, and, therefore, BGP-4, prevents the Internet routing table from becoming too large for interconnecting millions of users.

**NOTE**    The routing tables on the BGP routers on the Internet use more than 32 MB and include knowledge of more than 15,000 AS numbers. These numbers represent a snapshot of the Internet's size. Because the Internet is constantly growing, these numbers are constantly changing (increasing).

# Comparison with Other Scalable Routing Protocols

Table 8-2 compares some of BGP's key characteristics to the other scalable routing protocols discussed in this book.

**Table 8-2**    *Comparison of Scalable Routing Protocols*

| Protocol | Interior or Exterior | Type | Hierarchy Required? | Metric |
|----------|---------------------|------|---------------------|--------|
| OSPF | Interior | Link-state | Yes | Cost |
| IS-IS | Interior | Link-state | Yes | Metric |
| EIGRP | Interior | Advanced distance-vector | No | Composite |
| BGP | Exterior | Path-vector | No | Path-vectors (attributes) |

As shown in Table 8-2, OSPF, IS-IS, and EIGRP are interior protocols, whereas BGP is an exterior protocol.

Chapter 2, "Routing Principles," discusses the characteristics of distance vector and link-state routing protocols. OSPF and IS-IS are link-state protocols, whereas EIGRP is an advanced distance-vector protocol. BGP is also a distance-vector protocol, with many enhancements. It is also called a path-vector protocol.

Most link-state routing protocols, including OSPF and IS-IS, require a hierarchical design, especially to support proper address summarization. OSPF and IS-IS let you separate a large internetwork into smaller internetworks called areas. EIGRP and BGP do not require a hierarchical topology.

OSPF uses cost, which on Cisco routers is based on bandwidth, as its metric. The IS-IS metric is typically based on bandwidth (but it defaults to 10 on all interfaces). EIGRP uses a composite metric, similar to the IGRP metric, with bandwidth and accumulated delay considered by default. In contrast, BGP is a policy-based routing protocol that allows an AS to control traffic flow using multiple BGP attributes. Routers running BGP exchange network reachability information, called path vectors or attributes, including a list of the full path (of BGP AS numbers) that a route should take to reach a destination network. BGP allows a provider to fully use its bandwidth.

## Policy-Based Routing

BGP allows policy decisions at the AS level to be enforced. This setting of policies or rules for routing is known as *policy-based routing*. These policies can be implemented for all networks owned by an AS, for a certain CIDR block of network numbers (prefixes), or for individual networks or subnetworks.

BGP allows policies to be defined to determine how data will flow through the AS. These policies are based on the attributes carried in the routing information and configured on the routers.

---

### Key Point: BGP Can Advertise Only the Routes It Uses

BGP specifies that a BGP router can advertise to its peers in neighboring autonomous systems only those routes that it uses. This rule reflects the hop-by-hop routing paradigm generally used throughout the current Internet.

---

Some policies cannot be supported by the hop-by-hop routing paradigm and, thus, require techniques such as source routing to enforce. For example, BGP does not allow one AS to send traffic to a neighboring AS, intending that the traffic take a different route from that taken by traffic originating in that neighboring AS. However, BGP can support any policy conforming to the hop-by-hop routing paradigm. In other words, you cannot influence how the neighbor AS will route your traffic, but you can influence how your traffic gets to a neighbor AS.

Because the current Internet uses only the hop-by-hop routing paradigm, and because BGP can support any policy that conforms to that paradigm, BGP is highly applicable as an inter-AS routing protocol for the current Internet.

For example, in Figure 8-3, the following paths are possible for AS 64512 to reach networks in AS 64700, through AS 64520:

- 64520 64600 64700
- 64520 64600 64540 64550 64700

- 64520 64540 64600 64700

- 64520 64540 64550 64700

**Figure 8-3**  *BGP Supports Policy-Based Routing*

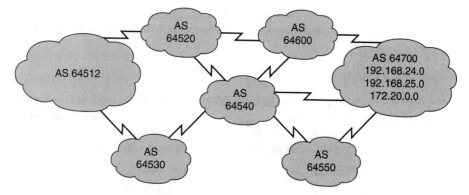

AS 64512 does not see all these possibilities. AS 64520 advertises to AS 64512 only its best path, 64520 64600 64700, the same way that IGPs announce only their best least-cost routes. This path is the only path through AS 64520 that AS 64512 sees. All packets that are destined for 64700 to 64520 take this path, because it is the AS-by-AS (hop-by-hop) path that AS 64520 uses to reach the networks in AS 64700. AS 64520 does not announce the other paths, such as 64520 64540 64600 64700, because it does not choose any of those paths as the best path, based on the BGP routing policy in AS 64520.

AS 64512 does not learn of the second-best path, or any other paths from 64520, unless the best path through AS 64520 becomes unavailable.

Even if AS 64512 were aware of another path through AS 64520 and wanted to use it, AS 64520 would not route packets along that other path, because AS 64520 selected 64520 64600 64700 as its best path, and all AS 64520 routers will use that path as a matter of BGP policy. BGP does not let one AS send traffic to a neighboring AS, intending that the traffic take a different route from that taken by traffic originating in the neighboring AS.

AS 64512 learns of another path to AS 64700, through AS 64530. AS 64512 selects the best path to take based on its own BGP routing policies.

# When to Use BGP

BGP use in an AS is most appropriate when the effects of BGP are well understood and at least one of the following conditions exists:

- The AS allows packets to transit through it to reach other autonomous systems (for example, it is a service provider).

- The AS has multiple connections to other autonomous systems.

- The flow of traffic entering and leaving the AS must be manipulated.

If an enterprise has a policy that requires it to differentiate between traffic from an AS and traffic from its ISP, the AS must connect to its ISP using BGP. If, instead, an AS is connected to its ISP with a static route, traffic from that AS is indistinguishable from traffic from the ISP for policy decision-making purposes.

BGP was designed to allow ISPs to communicate and exchange packets. These ISPs have multiple connections to one another and have agreements to exchange updates. BGP is the protocol that is used to implement these agreements between two or more autonomous systems.

If BGP is not properly controlled and filtered, it has the potential to allow an outside AS to affect the traffic flow to your AS. For example, if you are a customer connected to ISP-A and ISP-B (for redundancy), you want to implement a routing policy to ensure that ISP-A does not send traffic to ISP-B via your AS. You want to be able to receive traffic destined for your AS through each ISP, but you do not want to waste valuable resources and bandwidth within your AS to route traffic for your ISPs. This chapter and the next focus on how BGP operates and how to configure it properly so that you can prevent this from happening.

# When Not to Use BGP

BGP is not always the appropriate solution to interconnect autonomous systems. For example, if there is only one exit path from the AS, a default or static route is appropriate; using BGP will not accomplish anything except to use router CPU resources and memory. If the routing policy that will be implemented in an AS is consistent with the policy implemented in the ISP AS, it is not necessary or even desirable to configure BGP in that AS. The only time BGP will be required is when the local policy differs from the ISP policy.

Do not use BGP if one or more of the following conditions exist:

- A single connection to the Internet or another AS
- Lack of memory or processor power on routers to handle constant BGP updates
- You have a limited understanding of route filtering and the BGP path-selection process
- Low bandwidth between autonomous systems

In these cases, use static or default routes instead, as discussed in the following section.

## Static Routes

Use the **ip route** *prefix mask* {*address* | *interface*} [*distance*] [**permanent**] [**tag** *tag*] global configuration command to define a static route entry in the IP routing table, as described in Table 8-3.

**Table 8-3**  **ip route** *Command Description*

| Parameter | Description |
|---|---|
| *prefix* | The route prefix for the destination network to be entered into the IP routing table. |
| *mask* | The prefix mask for the destination network to be entered into the IP routing table. |

**Table 8-3**    **ip route** *Command Description (Continued)*

| Parameter | Description |
|-----------|-------------|
| *address* | The IP address of the next-hop router to be used to reach the destination network. |
| *interface* | The local router outbound interface that can be used to reach the destination network. |
| *distance* | The optional administrative distance to assign to this route. (Recall that administrative distance refers to how believable the routing protocol is.) |
| *tag* | The optional value that can be used as a match value in route maps. |
| **permanent** | (Optional) Specifies that the route will not be removed from the routing table even if the interface associated with the route goes down. |

As discussed in Chapter 2, if there is more than one route to a destination from different sources (from different routing protocols, or because it is defined as a static route), the administrative distance determines which one is put in the routing table, with the lower administrative distance preferred. By default, the administrative distance of a static route specified with the next-hop *address* parameter is set to 1. The default administrative distance of a static route specified with the *interface* parameter is set to 0.

You can establish a *floating static route* by using an administrative distance that is larger than the default administrative distance of the dynamic routing protocol in use in your network. A floating static route is a statically configured route that can be overridden by dynamically learned routing information. Thus, a floating static route can be used to create a *path of last resort* that is used only when no dynamic information is available.

### ip route Command Parameters

The **ip route** command has two configuration options for configuring a static route: specifying the destination by adjacent-router IP address, and specifying the destination by the local-router interface name. There are a few differences in these two methods. As mentioned, in the case of the IP address parameter, the default administrative distance is 1; in the case of the interface format, the default administrative distance is 0. The distinction is that using the next-hop *address* parameter makes the route look like a standard statically defined route, but under certain conditions, using the *interface* parameter treats the link as if it is locally attached to the router.

You must use the next-hop *address* in the **ip route** command if you're using multiaccess media (for example, on LANs, Frame Relay, X.25, ISDN, and so on) so that the router knows exactly where to go to reach the destination, not just which interface to go out. (An exception is when you're using a dial-on-demand interface, such as ISDN, and you're using a **dialer string** command on the interface, so that the interface knows how to get to only one place.) You can use the *interface* syntax if the adjacent router interface is part of a serial unnumbered link and, therefore, has no IP address. The *interface* syntax is also a very quick way to establish connectivity when you're trying to recover from routing problems in a network, because you do not have to know the IP addresses on the link you want to traverse.

## Static Route Examples

Figure 8-4 shows a network running RIP and using a default static route. The configuration for Router A in Figure 8-4 is provided in Example 8-1.

**Figure 8-4**  *Example of Using RIP and a Default Static Route*

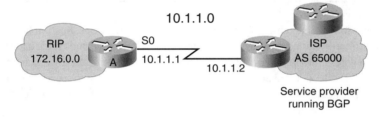

**Example 8-1**  *Configuration of Router A in Figure 8-4*

```
ip route 0.0.0.0 0.0.0.0 S0
!
router rip
  network 172.16.0.0
```

The route 0.0.0.0 is a default route that is included in Router A's IP routing table. If there is no matching route for the destination IP address in the routing table, 0.0.0.0 matches the address and causes the packet to be routed out interface serial 0. The default route is automatically propagated into the RIP domain.

---

**A Caution About Default Routes**

The default route 0.0.0.0 matches only networks that the router knows *nothing* about. When using classful routing protocols such as RIP or IGRP, use the **ip classless** command if you want it to also match unknown subnets of known networks. Note that **ip classless** is on by default in Cisco IOS Release 12.0 and later (it is off by default in earlier releases).

---

Figure 8-5 illustrates a network running OSPF and using a default static route. The configuration for Router A in Figure 8-5 is provided in Example 8-2.

**Figure 8-5** *Example of Using OSPF and a Default Static Route*

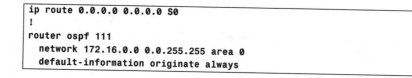

**Example 8-2** *Configuration of Router A in Figure 8-5*

```
ip route 0.0.0.0 0.0.0.0 S0
!
router ospf 111
  network 172.16.0.0 0.0.255.255 area 0
  default-information originate always
```

The **default-information originate always** command in OSPF propagates a default route into the OSPF routing domain. The configuration in this example has an effect similar to the RIP example. The **always** keyword causes the default route to always be advertised, whether or not the router has a default route. This ensures that the default route gets advertised into OSPF, even if the path to the default route (in this case, interface serial 0) goes down.

# BGP Terminology and Concepts

BGP has many concepts that become clearer if you understand the terminology. This section discusses BGP characteristics, neighbors, tables, message types, and attributes.

## BGP Characteristics

What type of protocol is BGP? Chapter 2 covers the characteristics of distance-vector and link-state routing protocols. BGP is sometimes categorized as an advanced distance-vector protocol, but it is actually a path-vector protocol. BGP has many differences from standard distance-vector protocols, such as RIP.

BGP uses TCP as its transport protocol, which provides connection-oriented reliable delivery. In this way, BGP assumes that its communication is reliable and, therefore, doesn't have to implement any retransmission or error-recovery mechanisms, like EIGRP. BGP information is carried inside TCP segments using protocol 179; these segments are carried inside IP packets. Figure 8-6 illustrates this concept.

**Figure 8-6** *BGP Is Carried Inside TCP Segments, Which Are Inside IP Packets*

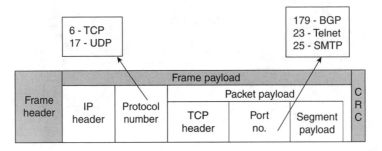

| NOTE | BGP is the only IP routing protocol to use TCP as its transport layer. OSPF, IGRP, and EIGRP reside directly above the IP layer. IS-IS is at the network layer. RIP uses UDP for its transport layer. |
| --- | --- |

### Key Point: BGP Uses TCP to Communicate Between Neighbors

Two routers speaking BGP establish a TCP connection with one another and exchange messages to open and confirm the connection parameters. These two routers are called BGP peer routers or BGP neighbors.

After the TCP connection is made, full BGP routing tables (described in the "BGP Tables" section) are exchanged. However, because the connection is reliable, BGP routers need to send only changes (incremental updates) after that. Periodic routing updates are also not required on a reliable link, so triggered updates are used. BGP sends keepalive messages, similar to the hello messages sent by OSPF, IS-IS, and EIGRP.

OSPF and EIGRP have their own internal function to ensure that update packets are explicitly acknowledged. These protocols use a one-for-one window so that if either OSPF or EIGRP has multiple packets to send, the next packet cannot be sent until an acknowledgment from the first update packet is received. This process can be very inefficient and cause latency issues if thousands of update packets must be exchanged over relatively slow serial links; however, OSPF and EIGRP rarely have thousands of update packets to send. EIGRP can hold more than 100 networks in one EIGRP update packet, so 100 EIGRP update packets can hold up to 10,000 networks. Most organizations do not have 10,000 subnets.

BGP, on the other hand, has more than 120,000 networks on the Internet to advertise, and it uses TCP to handle the acknowledgment function. TCP uses a dynamic window, which allows for 65,576 bytes to be outstanding before it stops and waits for an acknowledgment. For example, if 1000-byte packets are being sent, 65 packets will need to have not been acknowledged for BGP to have to stop and wait for an acknowledgment when using the maximum window size.

TCP is designed to use a sliding window, where the receiver acknowledges at the halfway point of the sending window. This method allows any TCP application, such as BGP, to continue streaming packets without having to stop and wait, as OSPF or EIGRP would require. TCP was selected as the transport layer for BGP because TCP can move a large volume of data reliably. With the full Internet routing table exceeding 32 MB in size and exceeding 1000 bytes of BGP changes per minute, using TCP for windowing and reliability, as opposed to developing a BGP one-for-one windowing capability like OSPF or EIGRP, is the best solution.

## BGP Path Vector

Internal routing protocols announce a list of networks and the metrics to get to each network. BGP routers exchange network reachability information, called path vectors, made up of path attributes, as illustrated in Figure 8-7. The path-vector information includes a list of the full path (of BGP AS numbers) necessary to reach a destination network. Other attributes include the IP address to get to the next AS (the *next-hop* attribute) and how the networks at the end of the path were introduced into BGP (the *origin code* attribute).

**Figure 8-7**    *BGP Uses Path-Vector Routing*

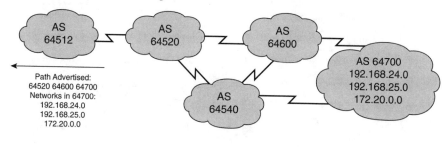

---

### Key Point: The BGP AS Path Is Guaranteed to Be Loop-Free

The BGP AS path is guaranteed to always be loop-free. A router running BGP does not accept a routing update that already includes its AS number in the path list, because the update has already passed through its AS, and accepting it again will result in a routing loop.

---

Routing policies can also be applied to the path of BGP AS numbers to enforce some restrictions on routing behavior.

BGP is designed to scale to huge internetworks, such as the Internet.

## BGP Neighbor Relationships

More than 20,000 routers run BGP and are connected to the Internet, representing more than 15,000 autonomous systems. No one router can handle communications with all the routers that run BGP; a BGP router forms a direct neighbor relationship with a limited number of other BGP routers. Through these BGP neighbors, a BGP router learns of the paths through the Internet to reach any advertised network.

Any router that runs BGP is called a BGP speaker.

---

### Key Point: BGP Peer = BGP Neighbor

A BGP peer, also known as a BGP neighbor, is a BGP speaker that is configured to form a neighbor relationship with another BGP speaker for the purpose of directly exchanging BGP routing information with one another.

---

A BGP speaker has a limited number of BGP neighbors with which it peers and forms a TCP-based relationship, as illustrated in Figure 8-8. BGP peers can be either internal or external to the AS.

**Figure 8-8**    *Routers That Have Formed a BGP Connection Are BGP Neighbors or Peers*

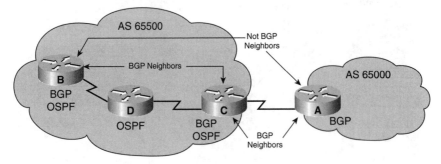

**NOTE**    A BGP peer must be configured under the BGP process with a **neighbor** command. This command instructs the BGP process to establish a relationship with the address listed in the command and to exchange BGP routing updates with that neighbor.

BGP configuration is described later, in the "Configuring BGP" section.

### External BGP Neighbors

When BGP is running between routers in different autonomous systems, it is called External BGP (EBGP). Routers running EBGP are usually directly connected to each other, as shown in Figure 8-9.

**Figure 8-9**  *EBGP Neighbors Belong to Different Autonomous Systems*

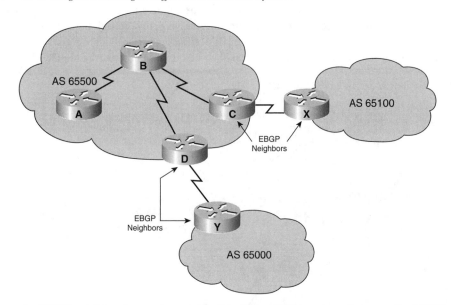

An EBGP neighbor is a router outside this AS; an IGP is not run between the EBGP neighbors. For two routers to exchange BGP routing updates, the TCP reliable-transport layer on each side must successfully pass the TCP three-way handshake before the BGP session can be established. Therefore, the IP address used in the **neighbor** command must be reachable without using an IGP. This can be accomplished by pointing at an address that can be reached through a directly connected network or by using static routes to that IP address. Generally, the neighbor address used is the address of the directly connected network.

## Internal BGP Neighbors

When BGP is running between routers within the same AS, it is called Internal BGP (IBGP). IBGP is run within an AS to exchange BGP information so that all internal BGP speakers have the same BGP routing information about outside autonomous systems and so this information can be passed to other autonomous systems.

Routers running IBGP do not have to be directly connected to each other, as long as they can reach each other so that TCP handshaking can be performed to set up the BGP neighbor relationships. The IBGP neighbor can be reached by a directly connected network, static routes, or an internal routing protocol. Because multiple paths generally exist within an AS to reach other routers, a loopback address is usually used in the BGP **neighbor** command to establish the IBGP sessions.

For example, in Figure 8-10, Routers A, D, and C learn the paths to the external autonomous systems from their respective EBGP neighbors (Routers Z, Y, and X). If the link between Routers D and Y goes down, Router D must learn new routes to the external autonomous systems. Other BGP routers within AS 65500 that were using Router D to get to external networks must also be informed that the path through Router D is unavailable. Those BGP routers within AS 65500 need to have the alternative paths through Routers A and C in their BGP topology database. You must set up IBGP sessions between all routers in AS 65500 so that each router within the AS learns about paths to the external networks via IBGP.

**Figure 8-10** *IBGP Neighbors Are in the Same AS*

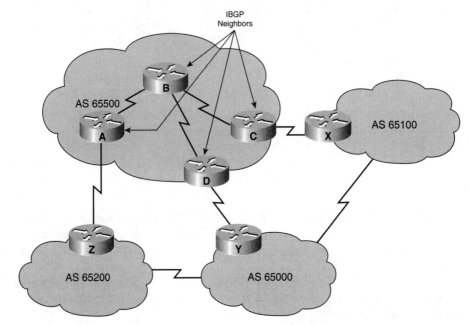

## BGP Tables

As shown in Figure 8-11, a router running BGP keeps its own table for storing BGP information received from and sent to other routers.

**Figure 8-11** *Router Running BGP Keeps a BGP Table, Separate from the IP Routing Table*

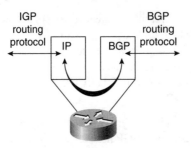

---

**Key Point: BGP Table**

This table of BGP information is known by many names in various documents, including

— BGP table

— BGP topology table

— BGP topology database

— BGP routing table

— BGP forwarding database

This table is separate from the IP routing table in the router.

---

The router can be configured to share information between the BGP table and the IP routing table. BGP also keeps a neighbor table containing a list of neighbors that it has a BGP connection with. For BGP to establish an adjacency, you must configure it explicitly for each neighbor. BGP forms a TCP relationship with each of the configured neighbors and keeps track of the state of these relationships by periodically sending a BGP/TCP keepalive message.

After establishing an adjacency, the neighbors exchange their BGP routes. Each router collects these routes from each neighbor that successfully established an adjacency and places them in its BGP topology database. All routes learned from each neighbor are placed in the BGP topology database. The best routes for each network are selected from the BGP topology database using the BGP route selection process (discussed in the later section "The Route Selection Decision Process") and then are offered to the IP routing table.

Each router compares the offered BGP routes to any other possible paths to those networks in its IP routing table, and the best route, based on administrative distance, is installed in the IP routing table. EBGP routes (BGP routes learned from an external AS) have an administrative distance of 20. IBGP routes (BGP routes learned from within the AS) have an administrative distance of 200.

# BGP Message Types

BGP defines the following message types:

- Open
- Keepalive
- Update
- Notification

After a TCP connection is established, the first message sent by each side is an open message. If the open message is acceptable, a keepalive message confirming the open is sent back.

When the open is confirmed, the BGP connection is established, and update, keepalive, and notification messages might be exchanged.

BGP peers initially exchange their full BGP routing tables. From then on, incremental updates are sent as the routing table changes. Keepalive packets are sent to ensure that the connection is alive between the BGP peers, and notification packets are sent in response to errors or special conditions.

An open message includes the following information:

- **Version**—This 8-bit field indicates the message's BGP version number. The highest common version that both routers support is used. Most BGP implementations today use the current version, BGP-4.

- **My autonomous system**—This 16-bit field indicates the sender's AS number. The peer router verifies this information; if it is not the AS number expected, the BGP session is torn down.

- **Hold time**—This 16-bit field indicates the maximum number of seconds that might elapse between the receipt of successive keepalive or update messages by the sender. Upon receipt of an open message, the router calculates the value of the hold timer to use by using the smaller of its configured hold time and the hold time received in the open message.

- **BGP router identifier (router ID)**—This 32-bit field indicates the sender's BGP identifier. The BGP identifier is an IP address assigned to that router and is determined at startup. The BGP router ID is chosen the same way the OSPF router ID is chosen. It is the highest active IP address on the router, unless a loopback interface with an IP address exists, in which case it is the highest such loopback IP address. Alternatively, the router ID can be statically configured, overriding the automatic selection.

- **Optional parameters**—A length field indicates the total length of the optional parameters field in octets. The optional parameters field might contain a list of optional parameters (currently, only authentication is defined).

BGP does not use any transport protocol-based keepalive mechanism to determine whether peers can be reached. Instead, keepalive messages are exchanged between peers often enough to keep the hold timer from expiring. If the negotiated hold time interval is 0, periodic keepalive messages are not sent.

An update message has information on one path only; multiple paths require multiple messages. All the attributes in the message refer to that path, and the networks are those that can be reached through it. An update message might include the following fields:

- **Withdrawn routes**—A list of IP address prefixes for routes that are being withdrawn from service, if any.

- **Path attributes**—The AS-path, origin, local preference, and the like, as discussed in the next section. Each path attribute includes the attribute type, attribute length, and attribute value. The attribute type consists of the attribute flags, followed by the attribute-type code.

- **Network layer reachability information**—This field contains a list of IP address prefixes that can be reached by this path.

A notification message is sent when an error condition is detected. The BGP connection is closed immediately after this is sent. Notification messages include an error code, an error subcode, and data related to the error.

---

### BGP Neighbor States

BGP is a state machine that takes a router through the following states with its neighbors:

- Idle
- Connect
- Active
- Open sent
- Open confirm
- Established

Only when the connection is in the established state are update, keepalive, and notification messages exchanged.

(Neighbor states are discussed in more detail in the "Understanding and Troubleshooting BGP Neighbor States" section later in this chapter.)

---

**NOTE**     Keepalive messages consist of only a message header and have a length of 19 bytes; they are sent every 60 seconds by default. Other messages might be between 19 and 4096 bytes long. The default hold time is 180 seconds.

---

## BGP Attributes

Routers send BGP update messages about destination networks. These update messages include information about BGP metrics, which are called path attributes. The following are some terms defining how these attributes are implemented:

- An attribute is either well-known or optional, mandatory or discretionary, and transitive or nontransitive. An attribute might also be partial.

- Not all combinations of these characteristics are valid; path attributes fall into four separate categories:

  — Well-known mandatory

> — Well-known discretionary
>
> — Optional transitive
>
> — Optional nontransitive

- Only optional transitive attributes might be marked as partial.

These characteristics are described in the following sections.

---

### BGP Update Message Contents

A BGP update message includes a variable-length sequence of path attributes describing the route. A path attribute is of variable length and consists of three fields:

> — Attribute type, which consists of a 1-byte attribute flags field and a 1-byte attribute-type code field
>
> — Attribute length
>
> — Attribute value

The first bit of the attribute flags field indicates whether the attribute is optional or well-known. The second bit indicates whether an optional attribute is transitive or nontransitive. The third bit indicates whether a transitive attribute is partial or complete. The fourth bit indicates whether the attribute length field is 1 or 2 bytes. The rest of the flag bits are unused and are set to 0.

---

## Well-Known Attributes

A well-known attribute is one that all BGP implementations must recognize. These attributes are propagated to BGP neighbors.

A well-known mandatory attribute *must* appear in a route's description. A well-known discretionary attribute does not need to appear in a route description.

## Optional Attributes

Attributes that are not well-known are called optional. Optional attributes are either transitive or nontransitive.

An optional attribute need not be supported by all BGP implementations; it could be a private attribute. If it is supported, it might be propagated to BGP neighbors based on its meaning.

An optional transitive attribute that is not implemented in a router should be passed to other BGP routers untouched. In this case, the attribute is marked as partial.

An optional nontransitive attribute must be deleted by a router that has not implemented the attribute. The attribute is not passed to other BGP routers.

## Defined BGP Attributes

The attributes defined by BGP include the following:

- Well-known mandatory attributes:
    - AS-path
    - Next-hop
    - Origin
- Well-known discretionary attributes:
    - Local preference
    - Atomic aggregate
- Optional transitive attributes:
    - Aggregator
    - Community
- Optional nontransitive attribute:
    - Multiexit-discriminator (MED)

In addition, Cisco has defined a weight attribute for BGP.

The AS-path, next-hop, origin, local preference, community, MED, and weight attributes are expanded upon in the following sections. The atomic aggregate and aggregator attributes are discussed in Chapter 9, "Advanced Border Gateway Protocol Configuration."

---

### BGP Attribute Type Codes

Cisco uses the following attribute type codes:

- Origin—type code 1
- AS-path—type code 2
- Next-hop—type code 3
- MED—type code 4
- Local-preference—type code 5
- Atomic-aggregate—type code 6
- Aggregator—type code 7
- Community—type code 8 (Cisco-defined)
- Originator-ID—type code 9 (Cisco-defined)
- Cluster list—type code 10 (Cisco-defined)

---

## The AS-Path Attribute

The AS-path attribute is a well-known mandatory attribute. Whenever a route update passes through an AS, the AS number is *prepended* to that update (in other words, it is put at the beginning of the list).

---

### Key Point: AS-Path Attribute

The AS-path attribute is the list of AS numbers that a route has traversed to reach a destination, with the number of the AS that originated the route at the end of the list.

---

In Figure 8-12, Router A advertises network 192.168.1.0 in AS 64520. When that route traverses AS 65500, Router C prepends its own AS number to it. When the route to 192.168.1.0 reaches Router B, it has two AS numbers attached to it. From Router B's perspective, the path to reach 192.168.1.0 is (65500, 64520).

**Figure 8-12**  *Router C Prepends Its Own AS Number as It Passes Routes from Router A to Router B*

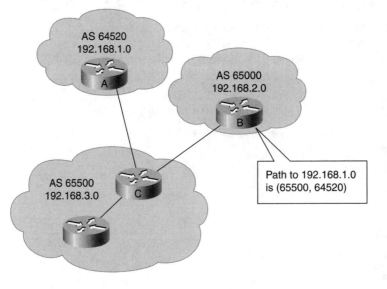

The same applies for 192.168.2.0 and 192.168.3.0. Router A's path to 192.168.2.0 is (65500 65000)—it traverses AS 65500 and then AS 65000. Router C has to traverse path (65000) to reach 192.168.2.0 and path (64520) to reach 192.168.1.0.

BGP routers use the AS-path attribute to ensure a loop-free environment. If a BGP router receives a route in which its own AS is part of the AS-path attribute, it does not accept the route.

AS numbers are prepended only by routers advertising routes to EBGP neighbors. Routers advertising routes to IBGP neighbors do not change the AS-path attribute.

## The Next-Hop Attribute

The BGP next-hop attribute is a well-known mandatory attribute that indicates the next-hop IP address that is to be used to reach a destination. BGP, like IGPs, is a hop-by-hop routing protocol. However, unlike IGPs, BGP routes AS-by-AS, not router-by-router, and the default next hop is the next AS. The next-hop address for a network from another AS is an IP address of the entry point of the next AS along the path to that destination network.

---

**Key Point: EBGP Next Hop**

For EBGP, the next hop is the IP address of the neighbor that sent the update.

---

In Figure 8-13, Router A advertises 172.16.0.0 to Router B, with a next hop of 10.10.10.3, and Router B advertises 172.20.0.0 to Router A, with a next hop of 10.10.10.1. Therefore, Router A uses 10.10.10.1 as the next-hop attribute to get to 172.20.0.0, and Router B uses 10.10.10.3 as the next-hop attribute to get to 172.16.0.0.

**Figure 8-13** *BGP Next-Hop Attribute*

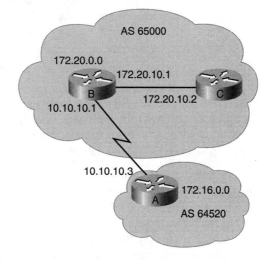

---

**Key Point: IBGP Next Hop**

For IBGP, the protocol states that *the next hop advertised by EBGP should be carried into IBGP.*

---

Because of this IBGP next-hop rule, Router B in Figure 8-13 advertises 172.16.0.0 to its IBGP peer Router C, with a next hop of 10.10.10.3 (Router A's address). Therefore, Router C knows that the next hop to reach 172.16.0.0 is 10.10.10.3, not 172.20.10.1, as you might expect.

It is very important, therefore, that Router C knows how to reach the 10.10.10.0 subnet, either via an IGP or a static route; otherwise, it will drop packets destined for 172.16.0.0, because it will not be able to get to the next-hop address for that network.

The IBGP neighboring router performs a recursive lookup to find out how to reach that BGP next-hop address by using its IGP entries in the routing table. For example, Router C in Figure 8-13 learns in a BGP update about network 172.16.0.0/16 from the route source 172.20.10.1, Router B, with a next hop of 10.10.10.3, Router A. Router C installs the route to 172.16.0.0/16 in the routing table with a next hop of 10.10.10.3. Assuming that Router B announces network 10.10.10.0/24 using its IGP to Router C, Router C installs that route in its routing table with a next hop of 172.20.10.1. An IGP uses the source IP address of a routing update (route source) as the next-hop address, and BGP uses a separate field for each network to record the next-hop address. If Router C has a packet to send to 172.16.100.1, it looks up the network in the routing table and finds a BGP route with a next hop of 10.10.10.3. Because it is a BGP entry, Router C completes a recursive lookup in the routing table for a path to network 10.10.10.3; there is an IGP route to network 10.10.10.0 in the routing table with a next hop of 172.20.10.1. Router C then forwards the packet destined for 172.16.100.1 to 172.20.10.1.

When running BGP over a multiaccess network such as Ethernet, a BGP router uses the appropriate address as the next-hop address (by changing the next-hop attribute) to avoid inserting additional hops into the network. This feature is sometimes called a *third-party next hop*.

For example, in Figure 8-14, assume that Routers B and C in AS 65000 are running an IGP. Router B can reach network 172.30.0.0 via 10.10.10.2. Router B is also running EBGP with Router A. When Router B sends a BGP update to Router A about 172.30.0.0, it uses 10.10.10.2 as the next hop, not its own IP address (10.10.10.1). This is because the network among the three routers is a multiaccess network, and it makes more sense for Router A to use Router C as a next hop to reach 172.30.0.0, rather than making an extra hop via Router B.

The third-party next-hop address issue also makes sense when you review it from an ISP perspective. A large ISP at a public peering point has multiple routers peering with different neighboring routers; it is not possible for one router to peer with every neighboring router at the major public peering points. For example, in Figure 8-14, Router B might peer with AS 64520, and Router C might peer with AS 64600; however, each router must inform the other IBGP neighbor of reachable networks from other autonomous systems. From the perspective of Router A, it must transit AS 65000 to get to networks in and behind AS 64600. Router A has a neighbor relationship with only Router B in AS 65000; however, Router B does not handle

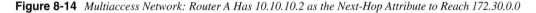

traffic going to AS 64600. Router B gets to AS 64600 through Router C, 10.10.10.2, and Router B must advertise the networks for AS 64600 to Router A, 10.10.10.3. Router B notices that Routers A and C are on the same subnet, so Router B tells Router A to install the AS 64600 networks with a next hop of 10.10.10.2, not 10.10.10.1.

**Figure 8-14**   *Multiaccess Network: Router A Has 10.10.10.2 as the Next-Hop Attribute to Reach 172.30.0.0*

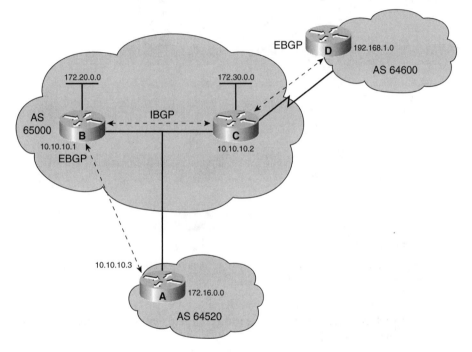

However, if the common medium between routers is a nonbroadcast multiaccess (NBMA) medium, complications might occur.

For example, in Figure 8-15, Routers A, B, and C are connected by Frame Relay. Router B can reach network 172.30.0.0 via 10.10.10.2. When Router B sends a BGP update to Router A about 172.30.0.0, it uses 10.10.10.2 as the next hop, not its own IP address (10.10.10.1). A problem arises if Routers A and C do not know how to communicate directly—in other words, if Routers A and C do not have a Frame Relay map entry to reach each other. Router A does not know how to reach the next-hop address on Router C.

This behavior can be overridden in Router B by configuring it to advertise itself as the next-hop address for routes sent to Router A; this configuration is described in the later section "Changing the Next-Hop Attribute."

**Figure 8-15** *NBMA Medium: Router A Has 10.10.10.2 as the Next-Hop Attribute to Reach 172.30.0.0, But It Might Be Unreachable*

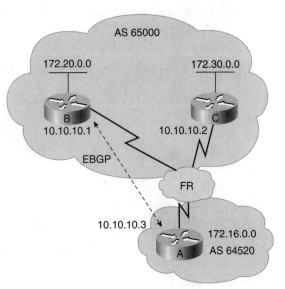

## The Origin Attribute

The origin is a well-known mandatory attribute that defines the origin of the path information. The origin attribute can be one of three values:

- **IGP**—The route is interior to the originating AS. This normally happens when the **network** command is used to advertise the route via BGP. An origin of IGP is indicated with an i in the BGP table.

- **EGP**—The route is learned via EGP. This is indicated with an e in the BGP table. (EGP is considered a historic routing protocol and is not supported on the Internet because it performs only classful routing and does not support CIDR.)

- **Incomplete**—The route's origin is unknown or is learned via some other means. This usually occurs when a route is redistributed into BGP. (Redistribution is discussed in Chapter 7, "Manipulating Routing Updates," and Chapter 9.) An incomplete origin is indicated with a ? in the BGP table.

## The Local Preference Attribute

Local preference is a well-known discretionary attribute that indicates to routers in the AS which path is preferred to exit the AS.

---

### Key Point: Higher Local Preference Is Preferred

A path with a *higher* local preference is preferred.

---

Local preference is an attribute that is configured on a router and exchanged only among routers within the same AS. The default value for local preference on a Cisco router is 100.

---

**Key Point: Local Preference Is Only for Internal Neighbors**

The term *local* refers to *inside the AS*. The local preference attribute is sent only to internal BGP neighbors; it is not passed to EBGP peers.

---

For example, in Figure 8-16, AS 64520 receives updates about network 172.16.0.0 from two directions. Router A and Router B are IBGP neighbors. Assume that the local preference on Router A for network 172.16.0.0 is set to 200 and that the local preference on Router B for network 172.16.0.0 is set to 150. Because the local preference information is exchanged within AS 64520, all traffic in AS 64520 addressed to network 172.16.0.0 is sent to Router A as an exit point from AS 64520.

**Figure 8-16**  *Local Preference Attribute: Router A Is the Preferred Router to Get to 172.16.0.0*

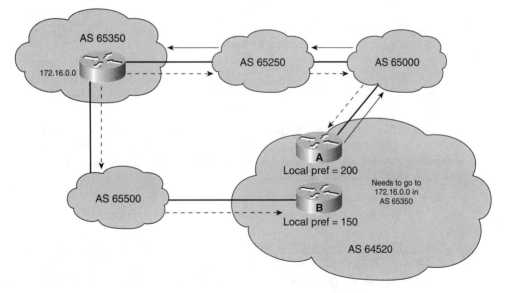

## The Community Attribute

BGP communities are one way to filter incoming or outgoing routes. BGP communities allow routers to *tag* routes with an indicator (the *community*) and allow other routers to make decisions based on that tag. Any BGP router can tag routes in incoming and outgoing routing updates, or when doing redistribution. Any BGP router can filter routes in incoming or outgoing updates or can select preferred routes based on communities (the tag).

BGP communities are used for destinations (routes) that share some common properties and, therefore, share common policies; thus, routers act on the community rather than on individual routes. Communities are not restricted to one network or one AS, and they have no physical boundaries.

Communities are optional transitive attributes. If a router does not understand the concept of communities, it defers to the next router. However, if the router does understand the concept, it must be configured to propagate the community; otherwise, communities are dropped by default.

---

**NOTE**    BGP community configuration is detailed in Appendix A, "Job Aids and Supplements."

---

### The MED Attribute

The MED attribute, also called the *metric*, is an optional nontransitive attribute. The MED was known as the inter-AS attribute in BGP-3.

---

**NOTE**    The MED attribute is called the *metric* in the Cisco IOS.

---

**Key Point: MED**

The MED indicates to *external* neighbors the preferred path into an AS. This is a dynamic way for an AS to try to influence another AS as to which way it should choose to reach a certain route if there are multiple entry points into an AS. Within BGP, the MED is the only attribute that can try to affect how data is sent *into* an AS.

A *lower* metric value is preferred.

---

Unlike local preference, the MED is exchanged between autonomous systems. The MED is carried into an AS and is used there but is not passed on to the next AS. When the same update is passed on to another AS, the metric is removed from the update. MED influences inbound traffic to an AS, and local preference influences outbound traffic from an AS.

By default, a router compares the MED attribute only for paths from neighbors in the same AS.

For example, in Figure 8-17, Router B has set the MED attribute to 150, and Router C has set the MED attribute to 200. When Router A receives updates from Routers B and C, it picks Router B as the best next hop to get to AS 65500, because 150 is less than 200.

**Figure 8-17**  *MED Attribute: Router B Is the Best Next Hop to Get to AS 65500*

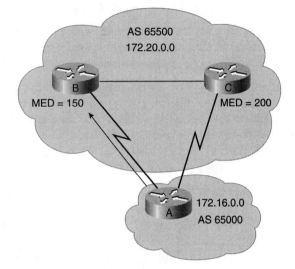

By default, the MED comparison is done only if the neighboring autonomous system is the same for all routes considered. For the router to compare metrics from neighbors coming from different autonomous systems, the **bgp always-compare-med** command must be configured on the router.

Configuring the MED is described in Chapter 9.

## The Weight Attribute (Cisco Only)

The weight attribute is a Cisco-defined attribute used for the path-selection process. The weight is configured locally to a router on a per-neighbor basis.

### Key Point: Weight Attribute

The weight attribute provides local routing policy only and is *not* propagated to *any* BGP neighbors.

Routes with a *higher* weight are preferred when multiple routes to the same destination exist.

The weight can have a value from 0 to 65535. Paths that the router originates have a weight of 32768 by default, and other paths have a weight of 0 by default.

The weight attribute applies when using one router with multiple exit points out an AS, as compared to the local preference attribute, which is used when two or more routers provide multiple exit points.

In Figure 8-18, Routers B and C learn about network 172.20.0.0 from AS 65250 and propagate the update to Router A. Router A has two ways to reach 172.20.0.0 and must decide which way to go. In the example, Router A sets the weight of updates coming from Router B to 200 and the weight of those coming from Router C to 150. Because the weight for Router B is higher than the weight for Router C, Router A is forced to use Router B as a next hop to reach 172.20.0.0.

**Figure 8-18**   *Weight Attribute: Router A Uses Router B as the Next Hop to Reach 172.20.0.0*

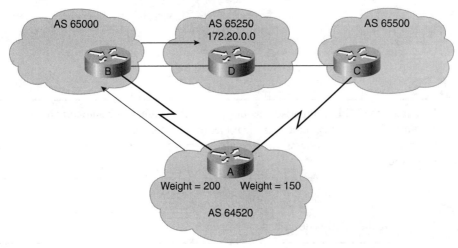

# BGP Operation

This section describes BGP's operation. The following topics are covered:

- Split horizon and full mesh of IBGP neighbors
- Synchronization
- The route selection decision process

## BGP Split Horizon and Full Mesh of IBGP Neighbors

BGP was originally intended to run along the borders of an AS, with the routers in the middle of the AS ignorant of the details of BGP—hence the name "*Border Gateway* Protocol." A transit AS is an AS that routes traffic from one external AS to another external AS. Typically, transit autonomous systems are ISPs. All routers in a transit AS must have complete knowledge of external routes. One way to achieve this goal is to redistribute BGP routes into an IGP at the edge routers; however, this approach has problems.

In 1994 the size of the Internet routing table was only about 4 to 8 MB, so BGP could be redistributed into the local IGP, such as OSPF or EIGRP. The edge routers running BGP would hold the full Internet routing table, and the routers in the middle, running only the IGP, would not incur the overhead of running BGP but would still know about all the routes.

Because the current Internet routing table is very large, redistributing all the BGP routes into an IGP is not a scalable way for the interior routers within an AS to learn about the external networks. Running full-mesh IBGP within the AS is a viable alternative.

## BGP Split Horizon

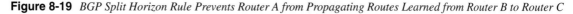

### Key Point: BGP Split Horizon Rule

The BGP split horizon rule governs IBGP behavior. This BGP rule specifies that routes learned via IBGP are never propagated to other IBGP peers.

---

The BGP split horizon is illustrated in Figure 8-19. In this figure, Router A learns routes from Router B via IBGP but does not propagate these routes to Router C.

**Figure 8-19**  *BGP Split Horizon Rule Prevents Router A from Propagating Routes Learned from Router B to Router C*

Similar to the distance-vector routing protocol split-horizon rule, BGP split horizon is necessary to ensure that routing loops are not started within the AS. The result is that a full mesh of IBGP peers is required within an AS for all the routers within the AS to learn about the BGP routes.

## IGP Adjacencies

Interior routing protocols such as RIP and OSPF form adjacency relationships with directly connected neighbors. With RIP, a router sends an update to all directly connected neighbors, which in turn advertise these routes to their directly attached neighbors. OSPF has a formal adjacency relationship; when a change occurs on an OSPF router, that router sends the update to all directly connected routers with which it has a full adjacency. Those routers then flood the change to all their adjacent neighbors.

RIP, OSPF, and EIGRP use broadcast or multicast to propagate changes across an AS; all routers along the path need to use the same protocol to be able to handle the routing updates. All routers running an IGP need the same information. For example, in an OSPF area, if one OSPF router has a 32-MB routing table, all OSPF routers in that area need the same 32-MB routing table.

## IBGP Full Mesh

BGP does not work in the same manner as IGPs. Because the designers of BGP could not guarantee that an AS would run BGP on all routers, a method had to be developed to ensure that IBGP speakers could pass updates to one another. By fully meshing all IBGP neighbors, when a change is received from an external AS, the BGP router for this AS is responsible for informing all of its IBGP neighbors of the change. IBGP neighbors that receive this update do not send it to any other IBGP neighbor, because they assume the sending IBGP neighbor is fully meshed with all other IBGP speakers and has sent each IBGP neighbor the update.

The main reason that an AS needs to fully mesh its IBGP neighbors is because of the BGP split-horizon rule, to prevent routing loops or routing black holes.

---

**NOTE**    TCP sessions cannot be multicast or broadcast because TCP has to ensure the delivery of packets to each recipient. Because TCP cannot use broadcasting, BGP cannot use it either, so BGP has to use fully meshed TCP sessions.

---

If the sending IBGP neighbor is not fully meshed with each IBGP router, the routers that are not peering with this router have different IP routing tables than the routers that are peering with the router that received the original BGP update. The inconsistent routing tables can cause routing loops or routing black holes, because the default assumption by all routers running BGP within an AS is that each BGP router exchanges IBGP information directly with all other BGP routers in the AS.

## BGP Partial-Mesh and Full-Mesh Examples

The top network in Figure 8-20 shows IBGP update behavior in a partially meshed neighbor environment. Router B receives a BGP update from Router A. Router B has two IBGP neighbors, Routers C and D, but does not have an IBGP neighbor relationship with Router E. Routers C and D learn about any networks that were added or withdrawn behind Router B. Even if Routers C and D have IBGP neighbor sessions with Router E, they assume that the AS is fully meshed for IBGP and do not replicate the update and send it to Router E because of the BGP split-horizon rule. Sending an IBGP update to Router E is Router B's responsibility, because it is the router with firsthand knowledge of the networks in and beyond AS 65101. Router E does not learn of any networks through Router B and does not use Router B to reach any networks in AS 65101 or other autonomous systems behind AS 65101.

**Figure 8-20**  *Partial-Mesh Versus Full-Mesh IBGP*

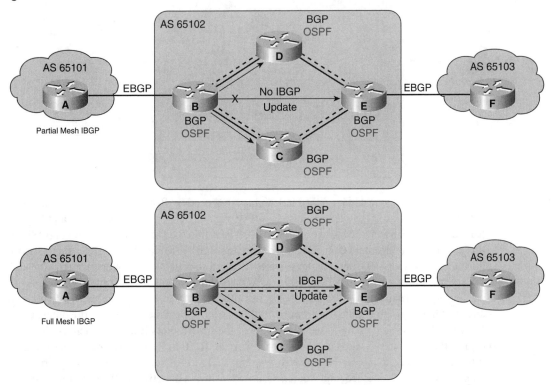

In the lower network in Figure 8-20, IBGP is fully meshed, so when an IBGP neighbor learns of a change from an EBGP neighbor, that router sends the update to all of the other IBGP speakers in the AS. The update is sent once to each neighbor and is not duplicated by any other IBGP neighbor, reducing unnecessary traffic.

Each IBGP neighbor needs to know all of the other IBGP neighbors in the same AS so that it can have a complete picture of how to exit the AS. Because all routers running BGP in an AS are fully meshed and have the same database because of a consistent routing policy, they can apply the same path-selection formula, and the path-selection results will be uniform across the AS. This means no routing loops and a consistent policy for exiting and entering this AS.

In Figure 8-21, Routers A, B, E, and F are the only ones running BGP. Router B has an EBGP **neighbor** statement for Router A and an IBGP **neighbor** statement for Router E. Router E has an EBGP **neighbor** statement for Router F and an IBGP **neighbor** statement for Router B. Routers C and D are not running BGP. Routers B, C, D and E are also running OSPF as their IGP.

**Figure 8-21**  *Without Full-Mesh IBGP, Routing Might Not Work*

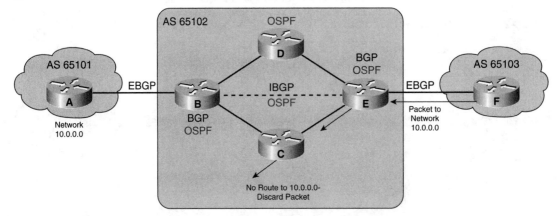

Network 10.0.0.0 is owned by AS 65101 and is advertised by Router A to Router B via an EBGP session. Router B advertises it to Router E via an IBGP session. Routers C and D never learn about this network because it is not redistributed into the local routing protocol (OSPF in this example), and Routers C and D are not running BGP. If Router E advertises this network to Router F in AS 65103, and Router F starts forwarding packets to network 10.0.0.0 through AS 65102, where will Router E send the packets to reach Router B? If Router E forwards packets with a destination address of 10.1.1.1 to either Routers C or D, those routers do not have an entry in their routing table for network 10.0.0.0, so they discard the packet. If Routers C and D have a default route going to the exit points of the AS (Routers B and E), there is a good chance that if Router E sends a packet for network 10.0.0.0 to Routers C or D, those routers might send it back to Router E, which forwards it again to Routers C or D, causing a routing loop. If BGP is fully meshed, and Routers C and D are aware of network 10.0.0.0 from Router B, this problem does not occur.

In Figure 8-21, AS 65102 is responsible for moving packets between AS 65101 and AS 65103, much as an ISP would. AS 65102 (and any ISP network) is a transit AS, responsible for passing packets from one AS to another. Many autonomous systems have multiple connections to the Internet but do not use their bandwidth to transport packets of other autonomous systems; these autonomous systems are called stub autonomous systems, not transit autonomous systems. Most enterprise autonomous systems connected to the Internet are stub autonomous systems: You can enter the enterprise AS to purchase services or products from their web pages, but they do not allow transit to other autonomous systems. In other words, the enterprise does not act as an ISP.

For example, large e-commerce companies can have connections to ten or more ISPs; however, they are in business to sell a product, not to provide transport between autonomous systems. An ISP's function is to provide this transport. You must configure an ISP as a transit AS by running BGP on all of its routers and fully meshing the IBGP sessions so that packets transiting the AS can reach networks and other autonomous systems on the other side of the transit AS.

# BGP Synchronization

---

### Key Point: BGP Synchronization Rule

The BGP synchronization rule states that a BGP router should not use or advertise to an external neighbor a route learned by IBGP, unless that route is local or is learned from the IGP.

---

If your AS is passing traffic from one AS to another, BGP should not advertise a route before all routers in your AS have learned about the route via IGP.

A router learning a route via IBGP waits until the IGP has propagated the route within the AS and then advertises it to external peers. This is done so that all routers in the AS are synchronized and can route traffic that the AS advertises to other autonomous systems it can route. The BGP synchronization rule also ensures consistency of information throughout the AS and avoids *black holes* (for example, advertising a destination to an external neighbor when not all of the routers within the AS can reach the destination) within the AS.

BGP synchronization is on by default in current IOS releases.

---

### Key Point: Turning Off Synchronization

It is safe to turn off synchronization only if all routers in the transit path in the AS (in other words, in the path between the BGP border routers) are running BGP.

---

(Indications are that in future IOS releases, BGP synchronization will be off by default, because most ISPs run BGP on all routers.)

In Figure 8-22, Routers A, B, C, and D are all running BGP with each other (full-mesh IBGP). There are no matching IGP routes for the BGP routes (Routers A and B are not redistributing the BGP routes into the IGP). Routers A, B, C, and D have IGP routes to the internal networks of AS 65500 but do not have routes to external networks, such as 172.16.0.0.

**Figure 8-22** *BGP Synchronization Example*

All routers in AS 65500 are running BGP; there are no matching IGP routes

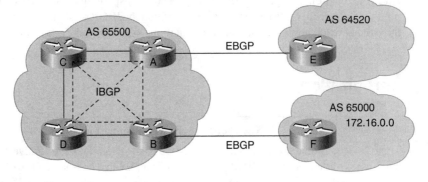

If synchronization is on (the default) in AS 65500 in Figure 8-22, the following happens:

- Router B advertises the route to 172.16.0.0 to the other routers in AS 65500 using IBGP.

- Router B uses the route to 172.16.0.0 and installs it in its routing table.

- Routers A, C, and D do not use or advertise the route to 172.16.0.0 until they receive the matching route via an IGP. Because Router B does not redistribute the BGP routes into the IGP, these routers never use or advertise the route.

- Router E does not hear about 172.16.0.0. If Router E receives traffic destined for network 172.16.0.0, it does not have a route for that network and cannot forward the traffic.

If synchronization is turned off in AS 65500 in Figure 8-22, the following happens:

- Router B advertises the route to 172.16.0.0 to the other routers in AS 65500 using IBGP.

- Routers A, C, and D use and advertise the route to 172.16.0.0 that they receive via IBGP and install it in their routing tables (assuming, of course, that Routers A, C, and D can reach the next-hop address for 172.16.0.0).

- Router E hears about 172.16.0.0 from Router A. Router E has a route to 172.16.0.0 and can send traffic destined for that network.

- If Router E sends traffic for 172.16.0.0, Routers A, C, and D route the packets correctly to Router B. Router E sends the packets to Router A, and Router A forwards them to Router C. Router C has learned a route to 172.16.0.0 via IBGP and, therefore, forwards the packets to Router D. Router D forwards the packets to Router B. Router B forwards the packets to Router F, which routes them to network 172.16.0.0.

In modern autonomous systems, because the size of the Internet routing table is large, redistributing from BGP into an IGP is not scalable; therefore, most modern transit autonomous systems run full-mesh IBGP and disable synchronization. Some advanced BGP configuration methods, such as route reflectors and confederations, reduce the IBGP full-mesh requirements (route reflectors are discussed in Appendix A).

# The Route Selection Decision Process

After BGP receives updates about different destinations from different autonomous systems, it decides which path to choose to reach a specific destination. Multiple paths might exist to reach a given network; these are kept in the BGP table. As paths for the network are evaluated and determined not to be the best path, they are eliminated from the selection criteria but kept in the BGP table in case the best path becomes inaccessible.

---

**Key Point: BGP Chooses Only a Single Best Path**

BGP chooses only a single best path to reach a specific destination.

---

BGP is not designed to perform load balancing; paths are chosen because of policy, not based on bandwidth. The BGP selection process eliminates any multiple paths until a single best path is left.

The best path is submitted to the routing table manager process and is evaluated against any other routing protocols that can also reach that network. The route from the routing protocol with the lowest administrative distance is installed in the routing table.

The decision process is based on the attributes discussed earlier in the "BGP Attributes" section. When faced with multiple routes to the same destination, BGP chooses the best route for routing traffic toward the destination. A path is not considered if it is internal, synchronization is on, and the route is not synchronized (in other words, the route is not in the IGP routing table), or if the path's next-hop address can't be reached. To choose the best route, BGP considers only synchronized routes with no AS loops and a valid next-hop address. The following process summarizes how BGP chooses the best route on a Cisco router:

**Step 1**  Prefer the route with the highest weight. (Recall that the weight is Cisco-proprietary and is local to the router only.)

**Step 2**  If multiple routes have the same weight, prefer the route with the highest local preference. (Recall that the local preference is used within an AS.)

**Step 3**  If multiple routes have the same local preference, prefer the route that was originated by the local router. (A locally originated route has a next hop of 0.0.0.0 in the BGP table.)

**Step 4**  If none of the routes were originated by the local router, prefer the route with the shortest AS-path.

**Step 5**  If the AS-path length is the same, prefer the lowest-origin code (IGP < EGP < incomplete).

**Step 6**  If all origin codes are the same, prefer the path with the lowest MED. (Recall that the MED is sent from other autonomous systems.)

The MED comparison is done only if the neighboring AS is the same for all routes considered, unless the **bgp always-compare-med** command is enabled.

---

**NOTE**  The most recent Internet Engineering Task Force (IETF) decision about BGP MED assigns a value of infinity to a missing MED, making a route lacking the MED variable the least preferred. The default behavior of BGP routers running Cisco IOS software is to treat routes without the MED attribute as having a MED of 0, making a route lacking the MED variable the most preferred. To configure the router to conform to the IETF standard, use the **bgp bestpath med missing-as-worst** router configuration command. In this case, routes without the MED attribute are treated as having a MED of $2^{32} - 2 = 4,294,967,294$.

---

**Step 7**  If the routes have the same MED, prefer external paths (EBGP) over internal paths (IBGP).

**Step 8**  If synchronization is disabled and only internal paths remain, prefer the path through the closest IGP neighbor. This means that the router prefers the shortest internal path within the AS to reach the destination (the shortest path to the BGP next hop).

**Step 9**  For EBGP paths, select the oldest route to minimize the effect of routes going up and down (flapping).

**Step 10**  Prefer the route with the lowest neighbor BGP router-ID value.

**Step 11**  If the BGP router IDs are the same, prefer the route with the lowest neighbor IP address.

Only the best path is put in the routing table and is propagated to the router's BGP neighbors.

---

**NOTE**  The route selection decision process summarized here does not cover all cases, but it is sufficient for a basic understanding of how BGP selects routes.

Further information on the BGP path-selection process can be found in *BGP Best Path Selection Algorithm*, available at www.cisco.com/en/US/tech/tk365/tk80 /technologies_tech_note09186a0080094431.shtml.

---

For example, suppose that there are seven paths to reach network 10.0.0.0. All paths have no AS loops and valid next-hop addresses, so all seven paths proceed to Step 1, which examines the weight of the paths. All seven paths have a weight of 0, so they all proceed to Step 2, which examines the paths' local preference. Four of the paths have a local preference of 200, and the other three have a local preference of 100, 100, and 150. The four with a local preference of 200 continue the evaluation process to the next step. The other three are still in the BGP forwarding table but are currently disqualified as the best path.

BGP continues the evaluation process until only a single best path remains. The single best path that remains is offered to the IP routing table as the best BGP path.

### Multiple Path Selection

BGP chooses only a single best path for each destination.

The **maximum-paths** *paths* router configuration command for BGP works if your router has multiple parallel paths to different routers in the same remote AS. For example, consider three routers: P1R1 is in AS 65201, and both P1R2 and P1R3 are in AS 65301. P1R1 is running EBGP to P1R2 and P1R3. P1R2 and P1R3 are advertising network 10.0.0.0. Without the **maximum-paths** command under the **router bgp 65201** command on P1R1, there is only one path to 10.0.0.0 in P1R1's routing table. After the **maximum-paths 2** command is added to the P1R1 BGP configuration, both paths appear in the IP routing table, as shown in Example 8-3. However, as also shown in Example 8-3, only one path is still selected as the best in the BGP table (as indicated by the > symbol); this is the path the router advertises to its BGP neighbors.

**Example 8-3**  *Output from Testing of the* **maximum-paths** *Command for BGP*

```
p1r1#show ip route bgp
B    10.0.0.0/8 [20/0] via 192.168.1.18, 00:00:41
               [20/0] via 192.168.1.50, 00:00:41

p1r1#show ip bgp
BGP table version is 3, local router ID is 192.168.1.49
Status codes: s suppressed, d damped, h history, * valid, > best, i ->internal
Origin codes: i - IGP, e - EGP, ? - incomplete

   Network          Next Hop          Metric LocPrf Weight Path
*> 10.0.0.0         192.168.1.18           0             0 65301 i
*                   192.168.1.50           0             0 65301 i
```

# Configuring BGP

This section covers the commands used to configure some of the BGP features discussed in this chapter. The concept of peer groups is described first, because peer groups appear in many of the configuration commands.

---

| NOTE | The syntax of some BGP configuration commands is similar to the syntax of commands used to configure internal routing protocols. However, there are significant differences in how an external protocol functions. |
|------|---|

---

# Peer Groups

In BGP, many neighbors are often configured with the same update policies (for example, they have the same filtering applied). On a Cisco router, neighbors with the same update policies can be grouped into peer groups to simplify configuration and, more importantly, to make updating more efficient. When you have many peers, this approach is highly recommended.

---

**Key Point: BGP Peer Group**

A BGP peer group is a group of BGP neighbors of the router being configured that all have the same update policies.

---

Instead of separately defining the same policies for each neighbor, a peer group can be defined with these policies assigned to the peer group. Individual neighbors are then made members of the peer group. The policies of the peer group are similar to a template; the template is then applied to the individual members of the peer group.

Members of the peer group inherit all of the peer group's configuration options. The router can also be configured to override these options for some members of the peer group if these options do not affect outbound updates. In other words, only options that affect the inbound updates can be overridden.

---

| NOTE | Some earlier IOS releases had a restriction that all EBGP neighbors in a peer group had to be reachable over the same interface. This is because the next-hop attribute would be different for EBGP neighbors accessible on different interfaces. You can get around this restriction by configuring a loopback source address for EBGP peers. This restriction was removed starting in IOS Releases 11.1(18)CC, 11.3(4), and 12.0. |
|------|---|

---

Peer groups are useful when many neighbors have the same policy, because they simplify the configuration, and make it easier to read. They are also more efficient because updates are generated only once per peer group, rather than once for each neighbor.

The peer group name is local only to the router it is configured on; it is not passed to any other router.

The **neighbor** *peer-group-name* **peer-group** router configuration command is used to create a BGP peer group. The *peer-group-name* is the name of the BGP peer group to be created.

Another syntax of the **neighbor peer-group** command, the **neighbor** *ip-address* **peer-group** *peer-group-name* router configuration command, is used to assign neighbors as part of the group after the group has been created. The details of this command are shown in Table 8-4.

**Table 8-4**    **neighbor peer-group** *Command Description*

| Parameter | Description |
|---|---|
| *ip-address* | The IP address of the neighbor that is to be assigned as a member of the peer group. |
| *peer-group-name* | The name of the BGP peer group. |

A neighboring router can be part of only one peer group.

The **clear ip bgp peer-group** *peer-group-name* EXEC command is used to clear the BGP connections for all members of a BGP peer group. *peer-group-name* is the name of the BGP peer group for which connections are to be cleared.

**NOTE**    The Cisco documentation says that the **clear ip bgp peer-group** command is used to *remove* all of the members of a BGP peer group; however, it actually clears the connections.

## Entering BGP Configuration Mode

Use the **router bgp** *autonomous-system* global configuration command to enter BGP configuration mode, and identify the local AS. In the command, *autonomous-system* identifies the local AS. The BGP process needs to be informed of its AS so that when BGP neighbors are configured it can determine if they are IBGP or EBGP neighbors.

The **router bgp** command alone cannot activate BGP on a router. You must enter at least one subcommand under the **router bgp** command to activate the BGP process on the router.

Only one instance of BGP can be configured on a router at a time. For example, if you configure your router in AS 65000 and then try to configure the **router bgp 65100** command, the router informs you that you are currently configured for AS 65000.

## Defining BGP Neighbors

Use the **neighbor** {*ip-address* | *peer-group-name*} **remote-as** *autonomous-system* router configuration command to identify a peer router with which the local router will establish a session, as described in Table 8-5.

**Table 8-5** **neighbor remote-as** *Command Description*

| Parameter | Description |
|---|---|
| *ip-address* | Identifies the peer router. |
| *peer-group-name* | Identifies the name of a BGP peer group. |
| *autonomous-system* | Identifies the peer router's AS. |

The value placed in the *autonomous-system* field of the **neighbor remote-as** command determines whether the communication with the neighbor is an EBGP or IBGP session. If the *autonomous-system* field configured in the **router bgp** command is identical to the field in the **neighbor remote-as** command, BGP initiates an internal session. If the field values are different, BGP initiates an external session.

You use the **neighbor remote-as** command to activate a BGP session for external and internal neighboring routers. The IP address used in this command is the destination address for all BGP packets going to this neighboring router. For a BGP relationship to be established, this address must be reachable, because BGP attempts to establish a TCP session and exchange BGP updates with the device at this IP address.

The network shown in Figure 8-23 uses the BGP **neighbor** commands; the configurations of Routers A, B, and C are shown in Examples 8-4, 8-5, and 8-6. Router A in AS 65101 has two **neighbor** statements. In the first statement, neighbor 10.2.2.2 (Router B) is in the same AS as Router A (65101); this **neighbor** statement defines Router B as an IBGP neighbor. AS 65101 runs EIGRP between all internal routers. Router A has an EIGRP path to reach IP address 10.2.2.2; as an IBGP neighbor, Router B can be multiple routers away from Router A.

**Figure 8-23** *BGP Network with IBGP and EBGP Neighbor Relationships*

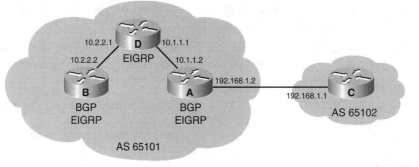

**Example 8-4** *Configuration of Router A in Figure 8-23*

```
router bgp 65101
  neighbor 10.2.2.2 remote-as 65101
  neighbor 192.168.1.1 remote-as 65102
```

**Example 8-5**  *Configuration of Router B in Figure 8-23*

```
router bgp 65101
  neighbor 10.1.1.2 remote-as 65101
```

**Example 8-6**  *Configuration of Router C in Figure 8-23*

```
router bgp 65102
  neighbor 192.168.1.2 remote-as 65101
```

Router A in Figure 8-23 knows that Router C is an external neighbor because the **neighbor** statement for Router C uses AS 65102, which is different from the AS number of Router A, AS 65101. Router A can reach AS 65102 via 192.168.1.1, which is directly connected to Router A.

To disable (administratively shut down) an existing BGP neighbor or peer group, use the **neighbor** {*ip-address* | *peer-group-name*} **shutdown** router configuration command. To enable a previously existing neighbor or peer group that had been disabled using the **neighbor shutdown** command, use the **no neighbor** {*ip-address* | *peer-group-name*} **shutdown** router configuration command. If you implement major policy changes to a neighboring router, and you change multiple parameters, you must administratively shut down the neighboring router, implement the changes, and then bring the neighboring router back up.

## Defining the Source IP Address

The BGP **neighbor** statement tells the BGP process the destination IP address of each update packet. The router must decide which IP address to use as the source IP address in the BGP routing update.

When a router creates a packet, whether it is a routing update, a ping, or any other type of IP packet, the router does a lookup in the routing table for the destination address; the routing table lists the appropriate interface to get to the destination address. The address of this outbound interface is used as that packet's source address by default.

For BGP packets, this source IP address must match the address in the corresponding **neighbor** statement on the other router. (In other words, the router must have a BGP relationship with the packet's source IP address.) Otherwise, the routers will not be able to establish the BGP session, and the packet will be ignored. BGP does not accept unsolicited updates; it must be aware of every neighboring router and have a neighbor statement for it.

For example, in Figure 8-24, assume that Router D uses the **neighbor 10.3.3.1 remote-as 65102** command to establish a relationship with Router A. If Router A is sending the BGP packets to Router D via Router B, the source IP address is 10.1.1.1. When Router D receives this BGP packet via Router B, it does not recognize this BGP packet, because 10.1.1.1 is not configured as a neighbor of Router D. Therefore, the IBGP session between Router A and Router D cannot be established.

A solution to this problem is to establish the IBGP session using a loopback interface when there are multiple paths between the IBGP neighbors.

If the IP address of a loopback interface is used in the **neighbor** command, some extra configuration must be done on the neighbor router. The neighbor router needs to tell BGP that it is using a loopback interface rather than a physical interface to initiate the BGP neighbor TCP connection. Use the **neighbor** {*ip-address* | *peer-group-name*} **update-source loopback** *interface-number* command to cause the router to use its loopback interface as the source for BGP connections to its neighbors.

**Figure 8-24** *BGP Source Address Must Match the Address in the* **neighbor** *Command*

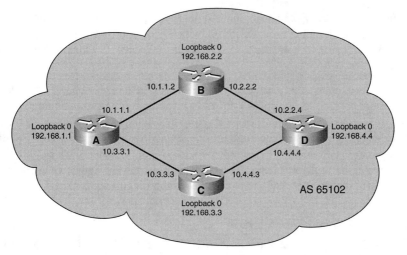

The **update-source** option in the **neighbor** command overrides the default-source IP address for BGP packets. This peering arrangement also adds resiliency to the IBGP sessions, because the routers are not tied into a physical interface, which might go down for any number of reasons. For example, if a BGP router is using a neighbor address that is assigned to a specific physical interface on another router, and that interface goes down, the router pointing at that address loses its BGP session with that other BGP neighbor. If, instead, the router peers with the loopback interface of the other router, the BGP session is not lost, because the loopback interface is always available as long as the router itself does not fail.

To peer with the loopback interface of an IBGP neighbor, configure each router with a **neighbor** command using the loopback address of the other neighbor. Both routers must have a route to the loopback address of the other neighbor in their routing table; check to ensure that both routers are announcing their loopback addresses into their local routing protocol. The **neighbor update-source** command is necessary for both routers.

For example, in Figure 8-25, Router B has Router A as an EBGP neighbor and Router C as an IBGP neighbor. The configurations for Routers B and C are shown in Examples 8-7 and 8-8. The only reachable address that Router B can use to establish a BGP neighbor relationship with Router A is the directly connected address 172.16.1.1. However, Router B has multiple paths to reach Router C, an IBGP neighbor. All networks, including the IP network for Router C's loopback interface, can be reached from Router B because these two routers exchange EIGRP updates. (Router B and Router A do not exchange EIGRP updates.) The neighbor relationship between Routers B and C is not tied to a physical interface, because each router peers with the loopback interface on the other router and uses its loopback address as the BGP source IP address. If Router B instead peered with 10.1.1.2 on Router C and that interface went down, the BGP neighbor relationship would be lost.

**Figure 8-25**  *BGP Sample Network Using Loopback Addresses*

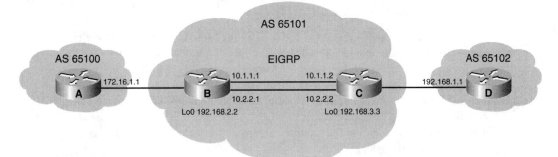

**Example 8-7**  *Configuration of Router B in Figure 8-25*

```
router bgp 65101
  neighbor 172.16.1.1 remote-as 65100
  neighbor 192.168.3.3 remote-as 65101
  neighbor 192.168.3.3 update-source loopback0
!
router eigrp 1
  network 10.0.0.0
  network 192.168.2.0
```

**Example 8-8**  *Configuration of Router C in Figure 8-25*

```
router bgp 65101
  neighbor 192.168.1.1 remote-as 65102
  neighbor 192.168.2.2 remote-as 65101
  neighbor 192.168.2.2 update-source loopback0
!
router eigrp 1
  network 10.0.0.0
  network 192.168.3.0
```

If Router B points at loopback address 192.168.3.3 on Router C and Router C points at loopback address 192.168.2.2 on Router B, but neither uses the **neighbor update-source** command, a BGP session is not established between these routers. Without this command, Router B will send a BGP open packet to Router C with a source IP address of either 10.1.1.1 or 10.2.2.1. Router C will examine the source IP address and attempt to match it against its list of known neighbors; because Router C will not find a match, it will not respond to the open message from Router B.

# EBGP Multihop

When peering with an external neighbor, the only address that an EBGP router can reach without further configuration is the interface that is directly connected to that external BGP router. Because IGP routing information is not exchanged with external peers, the router must point to a directly connected address for external neighbors. The loopback is never directly connected. Therefore, if you want to use a loopback interface instead, you have to add a static route pointing to the physical address of the directly connected network (the next-hop address). You must also enable multihop EBGP.

EBGP assumes a Time To Live (TTL) of 1. The **neighbor** {*ip-address* | *peer-group-name*} **ebgp-multihop** [*ttl*] command must be used for EBGP neighbors that are not directly connected. Whenever the EBGP neighbors are more than one hop away (which includes connections to loopback interfaces), the **neighbor ebgp-multihop** command by default sets the TTL to 255. This allows BGP to create an inter-AS connection. Note that IBGP already assumes a TTL of 255. If you have multiple physical connections between EBGP neighbors, using a loopback interface and static routes to the loopback interface allows you to load-balance the traffic between the multiple connections.

For example, in Figure 8-26, Router A in AS 65102 has two paths to Router B in AS 65101. If Router A uses a single **neighbor** statement that points to 192.168.1.18 on Router B and that link goes down, the BGP session between these autonomous systems is lost, and no packets pass from one AS to the next, even though another link exists. This problem can be solved if Router A uses two **neighbor** statements pointing to 192.168.1.18 and 192.168.1.34 on Router B. However, every BGP update that Router A receives will be sent to Router B twice because of the two **neighbor** statements.

**Figure 8-26** *EBGP Multihop Is Required if Loopback Is Used Between External Neighbors*

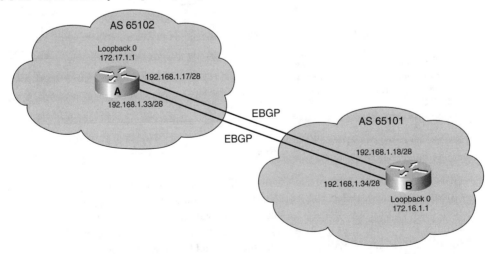

The configurations of Routers A and B are shown in Examples 8-9 and 8-10. As these configurations show, each router instead points to the loopback address of the other router and uses its loopback address as the source IP address for its BGP updates. Because an IGP is not used between autonomous systems, neither router can reach the loopback of the other router without assistance. Each router needs to use two static routes to define the paths available to reach the loopback address of the other router. The **neighbor ebgp-multihop** command must also be configured to change the default setting of BGP and inform the BGP process that this neighbor IP address is more than one hop away. In this example, the command used on Router A informs BGP that the neighbor address of 172.16.1.1 is two hops away.

**Example 8-9**  *Configuration of Router A in Figure 8-26*

```
router bgp 65102
  neighbor 172.16.1.1 remote-as 65101
  neighbor 172.16.1.1 update-source loopback0
  neighbor 172.16.1.1 ebgp-multihop 2
ip route 172.16.1.1 255.255.255.255 192.168.1.18
ip route 172.16.1.1 255.255.255.255 192.168.1.34
```

**Example 8-10**  *Configuration of Router B in Figure 8-26*

```
router bgp 65101
  neighbor 172.17.1.1 remote-as 65102
  neighbor 172.17.1.1 update-source loopback0
  neighbor 172.17.1.1 ebgp-multihop 2
ip route 172.17.1.1 255.255.255.255 192.168.1.17
ip route 172.17.1.1 255.255.255.255 192.168.1.33
```

## Changing the Next-Hop Attribute

As discussed in the section "The Next-Hop Attribute" earlier in this chapter, it is sometimes necessary (for example, in an NBMA environment) to override a router's default behavior and force it to advertise itself as the next-hop address for routes sent to a neighbor.

An internal protocol, such as RIP, EIGRP, or OSPF, always uses the source IP address of a routing update as the next-hop address for each network from that update that is placed in the routing table. The **neighbor** {*ip-address* | *peer-group-name*} **next-hop-self** router configuration command is used to force BGP to use its own IP address as the next hop for each network it advertises to the neighbor, rather than letting the protocol choose the next-hop address to use. This command is described in Table 8-6.

**Table 8-6**    **neighbor next-hop-self** *Command Description*

| Parameter | Description |
|---|---|
| *ip-address* | Identifies the peer router to which advertisements will be sent, with this router identified as the next hop. |
| *peer-group-name* | Gives the name of a BGP peer group to which advertisements will be sent, with this router identified as the next hop. |

For example, in Figure 8-27, Router B views all routes learned from AS 65100 as having a next hop of 172.16.1.1, which is the entrance to AS 65100 for Router B. When Router B announces those networks to its IBGP neighbors in AS 65101, the BGP default setting is to announce that the next hop to reach each of those networks is the entrance to AS 65100 (172.16.1.1), because BGP is an AS-by-AS routing protocol. With the default settings, a BGP router needs to reach the 172.16.1.1 next hop to reach networks in or behind AS 65100. Therefore, the network that represents 172.16.1.1 will have to be advertised in the internal routing protocol.

**Figure 8-27**    **next-hop-self** *Command Allows Router B to Advertise Itself as the Next Hop*

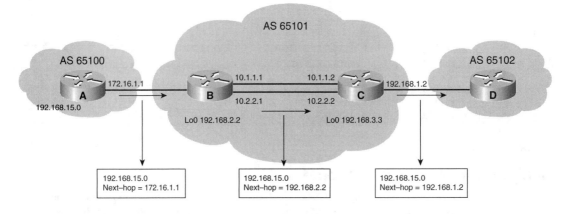

In this example, however, the configuration for Router B is as shown in Example 8-11. Router B uses the **neighbor next-hop-self** command to change the default BGP next-hop settings. After this command is given, Router B advertises a next hop of 192.168.2.2 (the IP address of its loopback interface) to its IBGP neighbor, because that is the source IP address of the routing update to its IBGP neighbor (set with the **neighbor update-source** command).

**Example 8-11** *Configuration of Router B in Figure 8-27*

```
router bgp 65101
  neighbor 172.16.1.1 remote-as 65100
  neighbor 192.168.3.3 remote-as 65101
```

**Example 8-11** *Configuration of Router B in Figure 8-27 (Continued)*

```
   neighbor 192.168.3.3 update-source loopback0
   neighbor 192.168.3.3 next-hop-self
 !
router eigrp 1
  network 10.0.0.0
  network 192.168.2.0
```

When Router C announces networks that are in or behind AS 65101 to its EBGP neighbors, such as Router D in AS 65102, Router C, by default, uses its outbound interface address 192.168.1.2 as the next-hop address. This address is the default next-hop address for Router D to use to reach any networks in or behind AS 65101.

# Defining the Networks That BGP Advertises

Use the **network** *network-number* [**mask** *network-mask*] router configuration command to permit BGP to advertise a network if it is present in the IP routing table, as described in Table 8-7.

**Table 8-7**     **network** *Command Description*

| Parameter | Description |
|---|---|
| *network-number* | Identifies an IP network to be advertised by BGP. |
| *network-mask* | (Optional) Identifies the subnet mask to be advertised by BGP. If the network mask is not specified, the default mask is the classful mask. |

---

### Key Point: The BGP network Command

The BGP **network** command determines in which networks this router originates. This is a different concept from what you are used to when configuring IGPs. The **network** command does not start up BGP on certain interfaces; rather, it indicates to BGP which networks it should originate from this router. The **mask** parameter is used because BGP-4 can handle subnetting and supernetting. The list of **network** commands must include all networks in your AS that you want to advertise, not just those locally connected to your router.

---

The **network** command allows classless prefixes; the router can advertise individual subnets, networks, or supernets. Note that the prefix must exactly match (address and mask) an entry in the IP routing table. A static route to null 0 might be used to create a supernet entry in the IP routing table.

Before Cisco IOS Release 12.0, there was a limit of 200 **network** commands per BGP router; this limit has now been removed. The router's resources, such as the configured NVRAM or RAM, determine the maximum number of **network** commands that you can now use.

---

**Key Point: The network Command Versus the neighbor Command**

The **neighbor** command tells BGP *where* to advertise. The **network** command tells BGP *what* to advertise.

---

The sole purpose of the **network** command is to notify BGP which networks to advertise. If the mask is not specified, this command announces only the classful network number; at least one subnet of the specified major network must be present in the IP routing table to allow BGP to start announcing the classful network as a BGP route. However, if you specify the *network-mask*, an exact match to the network (both address and mask) must exist in the routing table for the network to be advertised. Before BGP announces a route, it checks to see if it can reach it.

For example, if you configure **network 198.1.1.1 mask 255.255.255.0** by mistake, BGP looks for 198.1.1.1/24 in the routing table. It might find 198.1.1.0/24 or 198.1.1.1/32, but it will never find 198.1.1.1/24. Because the routing table does not contain a specific match to the network, BGP does not announce the 198.1.1.1/24 network to any neighbors.

In another example, if you configure **network 198.1.0.0 mask 255.255.0.0** to advertise a CIDR block, BGP looks for 198.1.0.0/16 in the routing table. It might find 198.1.1.0/24 or 198.1.1.1/32; however, if it never finds 198.1.0.0/16, BGP does not announce the 198.1.0.0/16 network to any neighbors. In this case, you can configure the static route **ip route 198.1.0.0 255.255.0.0 null0** toward the null interface so that BGP can find an exact match in the routing table. After finding an exact match in the routing table, BGP announces the 198.1.0.0/16 network to any neighbors.

# Disabling BGP Synchronization

Before a BGP process can place networks it learned through an IBGP neighbor in the IP routing table, the route must be in the local routing table. The BGP and the IGP must be synchronized before the networks learned from an IBGP neighbor can be used. If you disable synchronization, BGP can use networks learned from an IBGP neighbor that are not present in the local routing table.

In some cases, you do not need BGP synchronization. If you will not be passing traffic from a different AS through your AS (in other words, if your AS is not a transit AS), or if all routers in the BGP transit path in your AS will be running BGP, you can disable synchronization.

Disabling this feature can allow you to carry fewer routes in your IGP and allow BGP to converge more quickly. Use synchronization if some routers in the BGP transit path in the AS are not running BGP (and, therefore, do not have a full-mesh IBGP).

Synchronization is on by default; use the **no synchronization** router configuration command to disable it. This command allows a router to use and advertise to an external BGP neighbor routes learned by IBGP before learning them in an IGP.

## Resetting BGP Sessions

BGP can potentially handle huge volumes of routing information. When a BGP policy configuration change occurs (such as when access lists, timers, or attributes are changed), the router cannot go through the huge table of BGP information and recalculate which entry is no longer valid in the local table. Nor can the router determine which route or routes, already advertised, should be withdrawn from a neighbor. There is an obvious risk that the first configuration change will immediately be followed by a second, which would cause the whole process to start all over again. To avoid such a problem, the Cisco IOS software applies changes on only those updates received or transmitted after the BGP policy configuration change has been performed. The new policy, enforced by the new filters, is applied only on routes received or sent after the change.

If the network administrator wants the policy change to be applied on all routes, he or she must force the router to let all routes pass through the new filter. If the filter is applied to outgoing information, the router has to resend the BGP table through the new filter. If the filter is applied to incoming information, the router wants its neighbor to resend its BGP table so that it passes through the new filter. Resetting the affected BGP sessions after a BGP policy configuration change has been completed does this. As soon as the BGP sessions reset, all information received on those sessions is invalidated and removed from the BGP table. The remote neighbor detects a BGP session down state and, likewise, invalidates the received routes. After a period of 30 to 60 seconds, the BGP sessions are reestablished automatically, and the BGP table is exchanged again, but through the new filters. However, resetting the BGP session disrupts packet forwarding.

Use the **clear ip bgp** {* | *address*} [**soft** [**in** | **out**]] privileged EXEC command to remove entries from the BGP table and reset BGP sessions, as described in Table 8-8. Use this command after every BGP configuration change to ensure that the change is activated and that peer routers are informed.

**Table 8-8**    **clear ip bgp** *Command Description*

| Parameter | Description |
|---|---|
| * | Resets all current BGP sessions. |
| *address* | Identifies the address of a specific neighbor for which the BGP sessions will be reset. |

*continues*

**Table 8-8**    **clear ip bgp** *Command Description (Continued)*

| Parameter | Description |
|-----------|-------------|
| **soft** | (Optional) Does a soft reconfiguration, as explained later in this section. |
| **in | out** | (Optional) Triggers inbound or outbound soft reconfiguration. If the **in** or **out** option is not specified, both inbound and outbound soft reconfigurations are triggered. |

**WARNING**    Clearing the BGP table and resetting BGP sessions will disrupt routing, so do not use this command unless you have to.

**NOTE**    The Cisco IOS documentation says that the **clear ip bgp** command can have {* | *address* | *peer-group-name*} parameters. However, the command for peer groups is actually **clear ip bgp peer-group** *peer-group-name*.

The Cisco IOS documentation does not list any other options for this command; however, some IOS versions have more. For example, Example 8-12 shows the options available on a router running Release 12.2(15)T5.

**Example 8-12** **clear ip bgp** *Command Options*

```
clear ip bgp ?
  *                Clear all peers
  <1-65535>        Clear peers with the AS number
  A.B.C.D          BGP neighbor address to clear
  dampening        Clear route flap dampening information
  external         Clear all external peers
  flap-statistics  Clear route flap statistics
  ipmcast          Address family
  ipv4             Address family
  ipv6             Address family
  nsap             Address family
  peer-group       Clear all members of peer-group
  vpnv4            Address family
```

Resetting a session is a method of informing the neighbor or neighbors of a policy change. Without the **soft** keyword, the **clear ip bgp** command causes a hard reset of the BGP neighbors involved. A hard reset means that the router issuing this command closes the appropriate TCP connections, reestablishes those TCP sessions as appropriate, and resends all information to each of the neighbors affected by the particular command used.

If you use **clear ip bgp *****, the BGP forwarding table on the router that issued this command is completely deleted, and all networks must be relearned from every neighbor. If a router has multiple neighbors, this action is a very dramatic event. This command forces all neighbors to resend their entire tables simultaneously.

For example, assume that Router A has eight neighbors and that each neighbor sends Router A the full Internet table that is about 32 MB in size. If Router A issues the **clear ip bgp \*** command, all eight routers resend their 32-MB table at the same time. To hold all of these updates, Router A will need 256 MB of RAM. Router A will also need to be able to process all of this information. Processing 256 MB of updates will take a considerable number of CPU cycles for Router A, further delaying the routing of user data.

If, instead, the **clear ip bgp** *address* command is used, one neighbor is reset at a time. The impact is less severe on the router issuing this command; however, it takes longer to change policy to all the neighbors, because each must be done individually rather than all at once using the **clear ip bgp \*** command. The **clear ip bgp** *address* command still performs a hard reset and must reestablish the TCP session with the specified address used in the command, but this command affects only a single neighbor at a time, not all neighbors at once.

The **soft out** option on the **clear ip bgp** command allows BGP to do a soft reset for outbound updates. The router issuing the **soft out** command does not reset the BGP session; instead, the router creates a new update and sends the whole table to the specified neighbors. This update includes withdrawal commands for networks that the other neighbor will not see anymore based on the new outbound policy. Outbound BGP soft configuration does not have any memory overhead. To make the new inbound policy take effect, you can trigger an outbound reconfiguration on the other side of the BGP session.

The **soft in** option generates new inbound updates without resetting the BGP session, but it can be memory-intensive. BGP does not allow a router to force another BGP speaker to resend its entire table. If you will be changing the inbound BGP policy, and you do not want to complete a hard reset, configure the router so that it can perform a soft reconfiguration.

There are two ways to perform an inbound soft reconfiguration: using stored routing update information and dynamically.

The **neighbor** [*ip-address*] **soft-reconfiguration inbound** router configuration command tells the BGP process to save all updates learned from the neighbor specified in case the inbound policy is changed. The BGP router retains an unfiltered table of what that neighbor has sent. This unfiltered table is used when an inbound policy is changed; the new results are placed in the BGP topology database. Thus, if you make changes, you do not have to force the other side to resend everything. (After configuring the **neighbor soft-reconfiguration** command for the first time, clear all current BGP sessions so that all updates will be resent by all neighbors and can then be stored in the local router.)

Cisco IOS software Releases 12.0 and later contain a BGP soft reset enhancement feature (route-refresh) that provides automatic support for dynamic soft reset of inbound BGP routing table updates that is not dependent on stored routing table update information. This new method requires no preconfiguration (using the **neighbor soft-reconfiguration** command) and requires significantly less memory than the previous soft reset method for inbound routing table updates. The **clear ip bgp soft in** command is the only command required for this dynamic soft reconfiguration. You can find more information on this feature at www.cisco.com/en/US /products/sw/iosswrel/ps1830/products_feature_guide09186a0080087b3a.html#wp19507.

# BGP Configuration Examples

This section provides some configuration examples using the commands discussed.

## Basic BGP Example

Figure 8-28 shows a sample BGP network. Example 8-13 provides the configuration of Router A in Figure 8-28, and Example 8-14 provides the configuration of Router B.

**Figure 8-28** *Sample BGP Network*

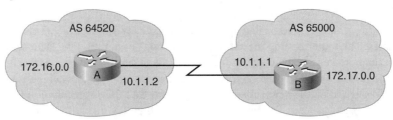

**Example 8-13** *Configuration of Router A in Figure 8-28*

```
router bgp 64520
  neighbor 10.1.1.1 remote-as 65000
  network 172.16.0.0
```

**Example 8-14** *Configuration of Router B in Figure 8-28*

```
router bgp 65000
  neighbor 10.1.1.2 remote-as 64520
  network 172.17.0.0
```

In this example, Routers A and B define each other as BGP neighbors, and start an EBGP session. Router A advertises the network 172.16.0.0/16, and Router B advertises the network 172.17.0.0/16.

## Peer Group Example

In Figure 8-29, AS 65100 has four routers running IBGP. All of these IBGP neighbors are peering with each others' loopback 0 interface (shown in the figure) and are using the IP address of their loopback 0 interface as the source IP address for all BGP packets. Each router is using one of its own IP addresses as the next-hop address for each network advertised through BGP. These are outbound policies.

**Figure 8-29**  *Peer Groups Simplify Configuration*

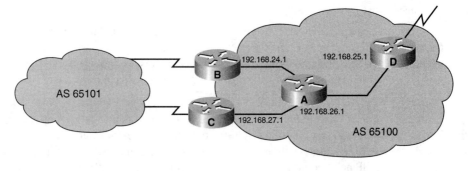

Example 8-15 shows the configuration of Router C when it is not using a peer group.

**Example 8-15**  *Configuration of Router C in Figure 8-29 Without Using a Peer Group*

```
router bgp 65100
  neighbor 192.168.24.1 remote-as 65100
  neighbor 192.168.24.1 update-source loopback 0
  neighbor 192.168.24.1 next-hop-self
  neighbor 198.168.24.1 distribute-list 20 out
  neighbor 192.168.25.1 remote-as 65100
  neighbor 192.168.25.1 update-source loopback 0
  neighbor 192.168.25.1 next-hop-self
  neighbor 198.168.25.1 distribute-list 20 out
  neighbor 192.168.26.1 remote-as 65100
  neighbor 192.168.26.1 update-source loopback 0
  neighbor 192.168.26.1 next-hop-self
  neighbor 198.168.26.1 distribute-list 20 out
```

Router C has an outbound distribution list associated with each IBGP neighbor. This outbound filter performs the same function as the **distribute-list** command you use for internal routing protocols; however, when used for BGP, it is linked to a specific neighbor. For example, the ISP behind Router C might be announcing private address space to Router C, and Router C does not want to pass these networks to other routers running BGP in AS 65100.

---

**NOTE**    Refer to Appendix A, "Job Aids and Supplements," for a discussion of the BGP **neighbor distribute-list** command.

---

To accomplish this, **access-list 20** might look like the following:

- **access-list 20 deny 10.0.0.0 0.255.255.255**
- **access-list 20 deny 172.16.0.0 0.31.255.255**

- **access-list 20 deny 192.168.0.0 0.0.255.255**

- **access-list 20 permit any**

As shown in Example 8-15, all IBGP neighbors have the outbound distribution list linked to them individually. If Router C receives a change from AS 65101, it must generate an individual update for each IBGP neighbor and run each update against distribute-list 20. If Router C has a large number of IBGP neighbors, the processing power needed to inform the IBGP neighbors of the changes in AS 65101 could be extensive.

Example 8-16 shows the configuration of Router C when it is using a peer group called *internal*. The **neighbor remote-as**, **neighbor update-source**, **neighbor next-hop-self**, and **neighbor distribute-list 20 out** commands are all linked to peer group internal, which in turn is linked to each of the IBGP neighbors. If Router C receives a change from AS 65101, it creates a single update and processes it through distribute-list 20 once. The update is replicated for each neighbor that is part of the internal peer group. This action saves processing time in generating the updates for all IBGP neighbors. Thus, the use of peer groups can improve efficiency when processing updates for BGP neighbors that have a common outbound BGP policy.

**Example 8-16** *Configuration of Router C in Figure 8-29 Using a Peer Group*

```
router bgp 65100
  neighbor internal peer-group
  neighbor internal remote-as 65100
  neighbor internal update-source loopback 0
  neighbor internal next-hop-self
  neighbor internal distribute-list 20 out
  neighbor 192.168.24.1 peer-group internal
  neighbor 192.168.25.1 peer-group internal
  neighbor 192.168.26.1 peer-group internal
```

Adding a new neighbor with the same policies as the other IBGP neighbors to Router C when it is using a peer group requires adding only a single **neighbor** statement to link the new neighbor to the peer group. Adding that same neighbor to Router C if it does not use a peer group requires four **neighbor** statements.

Using a peer group also makes the configuration easier to read and change. If you need to add a new policy, such as a route map, to all IBGP neighbors on Router C, and you are using a peer group, you need only to link the route map to the peer group. If Router C does not use a peer group, you need to add the new policy to each neighbor.

## No Synchronization Example

Figure 8-30 shows another BGP example.

Example 8-17 shows the configuration for Router B in Figure 8-30. The first two commands under the **router bgp 65000** command establish that Router B has the following two BGP neighbors:

- Router A in AS 64520

- Router C in AS 65000

**Figure 8-30**  *BGP Example Using No Synchronization*

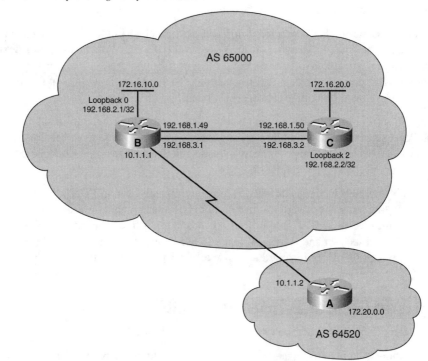

**Example 8-17**  *Configuration of Router B in Figure 8-30*

```
1.    router bgp 65000
2.    neighbor 10.1.1.2 remote-as 64520
3.    neighbor 192.168.2.2 remote-as 65000
4.    neighbor 192.168.2.2 update-source loopback 0
5.    neighbor 192.168.2.2 next-hop-self
6.    network 172.16.10.0 mask 255.255.255.0
7.    network 192.168.1.0
8.    network 192.168.3.0
9.    no synchronization
```

From the perspective of Router B, Router A is an EBGP neighbor, and Router C is an IBGP neighbor.

The **neighbor** statement on Router B for Router A is pointing to the directly connected IP address to reach Router A. However, the **neighbor** statement on Router B for Router C points to Router C's loopback interface. Router B has multiple paths to reach Router C. If Router B pointed to the 192.168.3.2 IP address of Router C and that interface went down, Router B would be unable to reestablish the BGP session until the link came back up. By pointing to the loopback interface of Router C, the link stays established as long as any path to Router C is available. (Router C should also point to Router B's loopback address in its configuration.)

Line 4 in the configuration forces Router B to use its loopback 0 address, 192.168.2.1, as the source IP address when sending an update to Router C, 192.168.2.2.

In line 5, Router B changes the next-hop address for networks that can be reached through it. The default next hop for networks from AS 64520 is 10.1.1.2. With the **neighbor next-hop-self** command, Router B advertises to Router C a next-hop address of Router B's loopback 0 address. This command sets the next-hop address to the source IP address of the routing update, as set by the **neighbor update-source** command.

Lines 6, 7, and 8 tell BGP which networks to advertise. Line 6 contains a subnet of a Class B address using the **mask** option. Lines 7 and 8 contain two **network** statements for the two Class C networks that connect Routers B and C. The default mask for these networks is 255.255.255.0, so it is not needed in the command.

In line 9, synchronization is turned off. If Router A is advertising 172.20.0.0 in BGP, Router B receives that route and advertises it to Router C. Router C cannot use this route unless it has synchronization turned off. Router C also needs to turn off synchronization if it has EBGP neighbors of its own and Router B wants to use Router C as the path to those networks. Synchronization can be disabled, because all the routers within the AS are running IBGP.

# Verifying and Troubleshooting BGP

You can verify BGP operation using the following **show** EXEC commands:

- **show ip bgp**—Displays entries in the BGP topology database (BGP table). Specify a network number to get more specific information about a particular network.
- **show ip bgp neighbors**—Displays detailed information about the TCP and BGP connections to neighbors.
- **show ip bgp summary**—Displays the status on all BGP connections.

Other BGP **show** commands can be found in the BGP documentation on Cisco's website (www.cisco.com). Use the **show ip bgp ?** command on a router to see other BGP **show** commands.

**debug** commands display events as they happen on the router. For BGP, the **debug ip bgp** privileged EXEC command includes the following options:

- **dampening**—BGP dampening
- **events**—BGP events
- **keepalives**—BGP keepalives
- **updates**—BGP updates

## show ip bgp Command Output Example

Use the **show ip bgp** command to display the BGP topology database (the BGP table).

Example 8-18 is a sample output for the **show ip bgp** command. The status codes are shown at the beginning of each line of output, and the origin codes are shown at the end of each line. In this output, the first column has an asterisk (*). This means that the next-hop address (in the fifth column) is valid. The next-hop address is not always the router that is directly connected to this router. Other options for the first column are as follows:

- An s indicates that route summarization has been done and that the specified routes are suppressed.

- A d, for dampening, indicates that the route is being dampened (penalized) for going up and down too often. Although the route might be up right now, it is not advertised until the penalty has expired.

- An h, for history, indicates that the route is unavailable and is probably down; historic information about the route exists, but a best route does not exist.

**Example 8-18** show ip bgp *Command Output*

```
RouterA#show ip bgp
BGP table version is 23, local router ID is 192.168.1.49
Status codes: s suppressed, d damped, h history, * valid, > best, i - internal
Origin codes: i - IGP, e - EGP, ? - incomplete

   Network          Next Hop         Metric LocPrf Weight Path
*> 10.0.0.0         10.1.1.100            0             0 65200 i
*> 172.16.10.0/24   10.1.1.100            0             0 65200 i
*> 172.16.11.0/24   10.1.1.100            0             0 65200 i
*>i172.26.1.16/28   192.168.1.50         0    100      0 i
*>i172.26.1.32/28   192.168.1.50         0    100      0 i
*>i172.26.1.48/28   192.168.1.50         0    100      0 i
*> 192.168.1.0      0.0.0.0              0         32768 i
*> 192.168.2.0      10.1.1.100                         0 65200 65102 i
*> 192.168.2.64/28  10.1.1.100                         0 65200 65102 i
*  i192.168.101.0   192.168.1.34         0    100      0 i
*>i                 192.168.1.18         0    100      0 i
```

A greater-than sign (>) in the second column indicates the best path for a route selected by BGP; this route is offered to the IP routing table.

The third column is either blank or has an i in it. If it is blank, BGP learned that route from an external peer. If it has an i, an IBGP neighbor advertised this route to this router.

The fourth column lists the networks that the router learned.

The fifth column lists all the next-hop addresses for each route. The next-hop address column might contain 0.0.0.0, which signifies that this router originated the route.

The next three columns list three BGP path attributes associated with the path: metric (MED), local preference, and weight.

The next column contains the AS path information. The first AS listed is the adjacent AS that this network was learned from. The last number (the rightmost AS number) is this network's originating AS. The AS numbers between these two represent the exact path that a packet takes back to the originating AS. If the path column is blank, the route is from the current AS.

The last column signifies how this route was entered into BGP on the original router. If the last column has an i in it, the original router probably used a **network** command to introduce this network into BGP. The character e signifies that the original router learned this network from EGP, which is the historic predecessor to BGP. A question mark (?) signifies that the original BGP process cannot absolutely verify this network's availability, because it is redistributed from an IGP into the BGP process.

Example 8-19 shows the additional information displayed when a network is specified in the **show ip bgp** command. (Note that this example is from a different network than the command output shown in Example 8-18.)

**Example 8-19** show ip bgp *Command Output*

```
p1r1#show ip bgp 172.31.20.0/24
BGP routing table entry for 172.31.20.0/24, version 211
Paths: (1 available, best #1)
  Advertised to non peer-group peers:
    192.168.1.18 192.168.1.34 192.168.1.50
  65200 65106 65201
    10.1.1.100 from 10.1.1.100 (172.16.11.100)
      Origin IGP, localpref 100, valid, external, best, ref 2
p1r1#exit
```

# show ip bgp neighbors Command Output Example

Use the **show ip bgp neighbors** command to display information about the BGP connections to neighbors. Example 8-20 provides sample output of the **show ip bgp neighbors** command. In the output, the BGP state is Established, which means that the neighbors have established a TCP connection and that the two peers have agreed to speak BGP with each other.

**Example 8-20** show ip bgp neighbors *Command Output*

```
RouterA#show ip bgp neighbors
BGP neighbor is 10.1.1.1,  remote AS 65000, external link
 Index 1, Offset 0, Mask 0x2
  BGP version 4, remote router ID 172.16.10.1
  BGP state = Established, table version = 5, up for 00:10:47
  Last read 00:00:48, hold time is 180, keepalive interval is 60 seconds
  Minimum time between advertisement runs is 30 seconds
  Received 16 messages, 0 notifications, 0 in queue
  Sent 15 messages, 1 notifications, 0 in queue
  Prefix advertised 1, suppressed 0, withdrawn 0
  Connections established 1; dropped 0
  Last reset 00:16:35, due to Peer closed the session
  2 accepted prefixes consume 64 bytes
  0 history paths consume 0 bytes
 --More--
```

**NOTE**    Refer to the Command Reference documentation in the technical documents section on Cisco's website (www.cisco.com) for a complete description of the fields in the output of this command.

# show ip bgp summary Command Output Example

The **show ip bgp summary** command is one way to verify the neighbor relationship. Example 8-21 presents a sample capture of the output from this command. Here are some of the highlights:

- **BGP table version**—Increments when the BGP table changes.
- **Neighbor**—The IP address used in the **neighbor** statement with which this router is setting up a relationship.
- **Version (V)**—The version of BGP this router is running with the listed neighbor.
- **AS**—The neighbor's AS number.
- **Messages received (MsgRcvd)**—The number of BGP messages received from this neighbor.
- **Messages sent (MsgSent)**—The number of BGP messages sent to this neighbor.
- **TblVer**—The last version of the BGP table that was sent to that neighbor.
- **In queue (InQ)**—The number of messages from this neighbor that are waiting to be processed.
- **Out queue (OutQ)**—The number of messages queued up and waiting to be sent to this neighbor. TCP flow control prevents this router from overwhelming a neighbor with a large update.
- **Up/Down**—The length of time this neighbor has been in the current BGP state (established, active, or idle).
- **State**—The current state of the BGP session—active, idle, open sent, open confirm, or idle (admin). The admin state is new to Cisco IOS software Release 12.0; it indicates that the neighbor is administratively shut down. This state is created by using the **neighbor** *ip-address* **shutdown** router configuration command. Note that if the session is in the established state, a state is not displayed; instead, a number representing the PfxRcd is displayed, as described next.

    **NOTE**    If the state field of the **show ip bgp summary** command indicates Active, the router is attempting to create a TCP connection to that neighbor.

- **Prefix received (PfxRcd)**—When the session is in the established state, this number represents how many BGP network entries have been received from this neighbor.

**Example 8-21** show ip bgp summary *Command Output*

```
RouterA#show ip bgp summary
BGP table version is 23, main routing table version 23
10 network entries and 11 paths using 1242 bytes of memory
4 BGP path attribute entries using 380 bytes of memory
BGP activity 23/13 prefixes, 38/27 paths
0 prefixes revised.

Neighbor        V    AS MsgRcvd MsgSent   TblVer  InQ OutQ Up/Down  State/PfxRcd
10.1.1.100      4 65200     211     211       13    0    0 00:01:53            5
192.168.1.18    4 65101     214     226       23    0    0 00:00:13            1
192.168.1.34    4 65101     214     226       23    0    0 00:00:09            1
192.168.1.50    4 65101     214     225       23    0    0 00:00:06            3
```

# debug ip bgp updates Command Output Example

Example 8-22 shows update messages being received from and sent to neighbor 10.1.1.1. The **clear ip bgp** * command is used to force Router A to reset all of its BGP connections. (Line numbers have been added to the output to simplify the discussion.)

**Example 8-22** debug ip bgp updates *Command Output*

```
RouterA#debug ip bgp updates

BGP updates debugging is on
RouterA#clear ip bgp *

1. 3w5d: BGP: 10.1.1.1 computing updates, neighbor version 0, table version 1,
   starting at 0.0.0.0
2. 3w5d: BGP: 10.1.1.1 update run completed, ran for 0ms, neighbor version 0,
   start version 1, throttled to 1, check point net 0.0.0.0
3. 3w5d: BGP: 10.1.1.1 rcv UPDATE w/ attr: nexthop 10.1.1.1, origin i,
   aggregated by 65000 172.16.10.1, path 65000
4. 3w5d: BGP: 10.1.1.1 rcv UPDATE about 172.16.0.0/16
5. 3w5d: BGP: nettable_walker 172.16.0.0/16 calling revise_route
6. 3w5d: BGP: revise route installing 172.16.0.0/16 -> 10.1.1.1
7. 3w5d: BGP: 10.1.1.1 rcv UPDATE w/ attr: nexthop 10.1.1.1, origin i,
   metric 0, path 65000
8. 3w5d: BGP: 10.1.1.1 rcv UPDATE about 192.168.1.0/24
9. 3w5d: BGP: nettable_walker 192.168.1.0/24 calling revise_route
10. 3w5d: BGP: revise route installing 192.168.1.0/24 -> 10.1.1.1
```

In line 1, Router A reacts to the **clear ip bgp** * command by recomputing and generating a new BGP routing update for neighbor 10.1.1.1. Router A recomputes starting with the lowest network number of 0.0.0.0 and continues until all networks have been examined.

In line 2, Router A finishes computing the routing update. This takes less than 0 milliseconds.

In line 3, Router A receives an update from 10.1.1.1 with the next-hop, origin, and AS-path attributes set for AS 65000, which is summarized by Router ID 172.16.10.1 in AS 65000.

In line 4, you see that one of the networks in the update from 10.1.1.1 is 172.16.0.0 with a prefix mask of /16.

To install this network in the routing table for Router A, the next-hop address must be reachable. To reach network 172.16.0.0/16, line 5 shows that Router A examines the routing table to ensure that a valid path exists to the next-hop address.

A valid path exists to the next-hop address of 10.1.1.1, so the route to 172.16.0.0/16 is installed in the routing table, as shown in line 6.

**NOTE**    Debugging uses up router resources and should be turned on only when necessary.

# Understanding and Troubleshooting BGP Neighbor States

After the TCP handshake is complete, the BGP application tries to set up a session with the neighbor. BGP is a state machine that takes a router through the following states with its neighbors:

- Idle
- Connect
- Active
- Open sent
- Open confirm
- Established

After you enter the **neighbor** command, BGP starts in the idle state, and the BGP process checks that it has a route to the IP address listed. BGP should be in the idle state for only a few seconds. If BGP does not find a route to the neighboring IP address, it stays in the idle state. If it finds a route, it goes to the connect state when the TCP handshaking synchronize acknowledge (SYN ACK) packet returns (when the TCP three-way handshake is complete).

After the TCP connection has finished, the BGP process creates a BGP open message and sends it to the neighbor. After BGP dispatches this open message, the BGP peering session changes to the open sent state. If there is no response for 5 seconds, the state changes to the active state. If a response does come back in a timely manner, BGP goes to the open confirm state and starts scanning (evaluating) the routing table for the paths to send to the neighbor. BGP then goes to the established state and begins routing between the neighbors.

The BGP state is shown in the last column of the **show ip bgp summary** command output.

## Debugging Session Establishment

Use the **debug ip bgp events** command to view BGP handshaking for neighbor establishment. Example 8-23 shows a sample debug session. In this example, notice that BGP does not go into the active state, because it receives the open confirm from its neighbor in a timely manner.

**Example 8-23 debug ip bgp events** *Command Output*

```
RouterA#debug ip bgp events
BGP events debugging is on
BGP :  172.16.1.2 passive open
BGP :  172.16.1.2 went from idle to connect
BGP :  172.16.1.2 open rcvd, version 4
BGP :  172.16.1.2 went from connect to open sent
BGP :  172.16.1.2 sending open, version 4
BGP :  172.16.1.2 went from open sent to open confirm
BGP :  Scanning routing tables
BGP :  172.16.1.2 went from open confirm to established
```

In this example, BGP is trying to set up the session with a neighbor at address 172.16.1.2. The 172.16.1.2 address is the address in the **neighbor** statement under the BGP process for this router.

In the first line of the output, BGP is passive open, which means that it is looking for that address (172.16.1.2) in the routing table. The BGP state at this point is idle.

The second line indicates that the BGP process has found a route to 172.16.1.2 in the routing table and is now performing the TCP handshake with that neighbor. This line also shows the BGP state changing from idle to connect.

The third line signifies that this router has received an open message from 172.16.1.2.

The fourth line shows this router creating its open message to 172.16.1.2 and changing its BGP state to open sent.

The fifth line shows this router sending its open message to 172.16.1.2.

The sixth line shows this router receiving an acknowledgment for the open message that was sent to 172.16.1.2 and going to the open confirm state.

The seventh line indicates that the router is scanning (evaluating) the routing table for the paths to send to the neighbor.

The last line shows that this router has agreed to form a BGP session with 172.16.1.2 and is going to the established state.

## Idle State Troubleshooting

The idle state indicates that the router does not know how to reach the IP address listed in the **neighbor** statement. The router is idle for one of the following reasons:

- It is waiting for a static route to that IP address or network to be configured.
- It is waiting for the local routing protocol (IGP) to learn about this network through an advertisement from another router.

The most common reason for the idle state is that the neighbor is not announcing the IP address or network that the **neighbor** statement of the router is pointing to. Check the following two conditions to troubleshoot this problem:

* Ensure that the neighbor announces the route in its local routing protocol (IGP).

* Verify that you have not entered an incorrect IP address in the **neighbor** statement.

## Active State Troubleshooting

If the router is in the active state, this means that it has found the IP address in the **neighbor** statement and has created and sent out a BGP open packet but has not received a response (open confirm packet) back from the neighbor.

One common cause of this is when the neighbor does not have a return route to the source IP address. Ensure that the source IP address or network of the packets is advertised into the local routing protocol (IGP) on the neighboring router.

Another common problem associated with the active state is when a BGP router attempts to peer with another BGP router that does not have a **neighbor** statement peering back at the first router, or the other router is peering with the wrong IP address on the first router. Check to ensure that the other router has a **neighbor** statement peering at the correct address of the router that is in the active state.

If the state toggles between idle and active, the AS numbers might be misconfigured. You see the following console message at the router with the wrong remote AS number configured in the **neighbor** statement:

```
6w0d: %BGP-3-NOTIFICATION: sent to neighbor 172.31.6.3 2/2
    (peer in wrong AS) 2 bytes FDE6
```

At the remote router, you see the following message:

```
6w0d: %BGP-3-NOTIFICATION: received from neighbor 172.31.6.1 2/2
    (peer in wrong AS) 2 bytes FDE6
```

## Established State

The established state is the state in which you want the neighbor relationship. This state means that both routers agree to exchange BGP updates with one another and routing has begun. If the state column in the **show ip bgp summary** command output is blank or has a number in it, BGP is in the established state. The number shown is the number of routes that have been learned from this neighbor.

# Summary

In this chapter, you learned the basics of BGP.

BGP is an exterior routing protocol used to route between autonomous systems. BGP-4 is the latest version of BGP and is used throughout the Internet. The main goal of BGP is to provide an interdomain routing system that guarantees the loop-free exchange of routing information between autonomous systems. BGP routers exchange information about paths to destination networks.

BGP is an advanced distance-vector protocol and is also called a path-vector protocol. BGP uses TCP as its transport protocol; port 179 is used for BGP. The BGP metrics are path attributes that indicate a variety of information about a route.

BGP specifies that a BGP router can advertise to its peers in neighboring autonomous systems only those routes that it uses.

Two routers speaking BGP establish a TCP connection with one another and exchange messages to open and confirm the connection parameters. These two routers are called BGP peer routers or BGP neighbors.

The BGP AS path is guaranteed to always be loop-free. A router running BGP does not accept a routing update that already includes its AS number in the path list, because the update has already passed through its AS, and accepting it again will result in a routing loop.

When BGP is running between routers in different autonomous systems, it is called EBGP. Routers running EBGP are usually directly connected to each other. When BGP is running between routers within the same AS, it is called IBGP. Routers running IBGP do not have to be directly connected to each other, as long as they can reach each other so that TCP handshaking can be performed to set up the BGP neighbor relationships.

BGP defines the following message types:

- Open
- Keepalive
- Update
- Notification

BGP is a state machine that takes a router through the following states with its neighbors:

- Idle
- Connect
- Active
- Open sent
- Open confirm
- Established

Only when the connection is in the established state are update, keepalive, and notification messages exchanged.

The attributes defined by BGP include the following:

- Well-known mandatory attributes:
    - AS-path
    - Next-hop
    - Origin
- Well-known discretionary attributes:
    - Local preference
    - Atomic aggregate
- Optional transitive attributes:
    - Aggregator
    - Community
- Optional nontransitive attribute:
    - MED

In addition, Cisco has defined a weight attribute for BGP.

BGP split horizon specifies that routes learned via IBGP are never propagated to other IBGP peers.

The BGP synchronization rule states that a BGP router should not use or advertise to an external neighbor a route learned by IBGP, unless that route is local or is learned from the IGP.

BGP chooses only a single best path to reach a specific destination. Multiple paths might exist to reach a given network; these are kept in the BGP table. As paths for the network are evaluated and determined not to be the best path, they are eliminated from the selection criteria but are kept in the BGP table in case the best path becomes inaccessible. To choose the best route, BGP considers only synchronized routes with no AS loops and a valid next hop and then prefers the following characteristics in the following order:

- Highest weight (local to router)
- Highest local preference (global within AS)
- Route originated by the local router
- Shortest AS path
- Lowest origin code (IGP < EGP < incomplete)
- Lowest MED (from the other AS)
- EBGP path over IBGP path
- Path through the closest IGP neighbor
- Oldest route for EBGP paths
- Path with the lowest neighbor BGP router ID
- Path with lowest neighbor IP address

# References

For additional information, refer to these resources:

- Cisco's command reference and configuration guides:
  www.cisco.com/univercd/home/home.htm

- BGP Technical Documentation:
  www.cisco.com/en/US/tech/tk365/tk80/tech_tech_notes_list.html

# Configuration Exercise 8-1: Configuring EBGP and IBGP for Two Neighbors

In this Configuration Exercise, you will configure IBGP between your P*x*R1 and P*x*R2 routers, and configure EBGP between these routers and the two backbone routers, BBR1 and BBR2.

---

### Introduction to the Configuration Exercises

This book uses Configuration Exercises to help you practice configuring routers with the commands and topics presented. If you have access to real hardware, you can try these exercises on your routers. See Appendix H, "Configuration Exercise Equipment Requirements and Initial Configurations," for a list of recommended equipment and initial configuration commands for the routers. However, even if you don't have access to any routers, you can go through the exercises, and keep a log of your own running configurations, or just read through the solution. Commands used and solutions to the Configuration Exercises are provided after the exercises.

In the Configuration Exercises, the network is assumed to consist of two pods, each with four routers. The pods are interconnected to a backbone. You configure pod 1. No interaction between the two pods is required, but you might see some routes from the other pod in your routing tables in some exercises if you have it configured (the Configuration Exercise answers show the routes from the other pod). In most of the exercises, the backbone has only one router; in some cases, another router is added to the backbone. Each Configuration Exercise assumes that you have completed the previous chapters' Configuration Exercises on your pod.

---

**NOTE**    Throughout this exercise, the pod number is referred to as *x*, and the router number is referred to as *y*. Substitute the appropriate numbers as needed.

---

## Objectives

Your task in this Configuration Exercise is to configure a simple IBGP and EBGP network.

## Visual Objective

Figure 8-31 illustrates the topology used in this exercise. You will configure only the P*x*R1 and P*x*R2 routers in this exercise.

**Figure 8-31**  *EBGP and IBGP Configuration Exercise Topology*

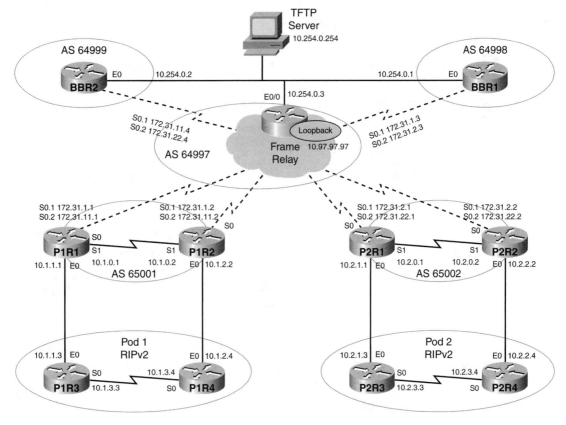

On all pod routers loopback 0:  10.200.200.xy/32

---

**NOTE**    The Frame Relay router is in AS 64997. However, it is provided only for communication with the backbone routers; it is not used in this exercise.

---

## Command List

In this exercise, you will use the commands in Table 8-9, listed in logical order. Refer to this list if you need configuration command assistance during the exercise.

---

**CAUTION**   Although the command syntax is shown in this table, the addresses shown are typically for the P*x*R1 and P*x*R3 routers. Be careful when addressing your routers! Refer to the exercise instructions and the appropriate visual objective diagram for addressing details.

---

**Table 8-9**   *EBGP and IBGP Configuration Exercise Commands*

| Command | Description |
|---|---|
| (config)#**router bgp 65001** | Enters BGP router configuration mode. This router is in AS 65001. |
| (config-router)#**neighbor 10.*x*.0.2 remote-as 65001** | Identifies a BGP neighbor. |
| (config-router)#**network 10.*x*.1.0 mask 255.255.255.0** | Advertises a network in BGP. |
| #**show ip bgp summary** | Shows a summary of BGP neighbor status and activities. |
| #**show ip bgp** | Shows the BGP table. |
| #**show ip route** | Shows the IP routing table. |
| (config-router)#**passive-interface s1** | Configures a routing protocol not to send updates or hellos out the specified interface. |
| #**show ip protocols** | Shows a summary of the IP routing protocols running on the router. |

---

**NOTE**   The commands used in Task 1: Cleaning Up are not shown in Table 8-9.

---

# Task 1: Cleaning Up

In this task, you will use a terminal utility to establish a console connection to the equipment. You will remove some of the configuration from the previous exercises, and create two multipoint subinterfaces on your edge routers in preparation for configuring BGP in the next task. Follow these steps:

**Step 1**   Connect to each of your pod edge routers (P*x*R1 and P*x*R2). Remove all OSPF configurations from these edge routers, but leave RIPv2 enabled on them.

**Step 2**   Disable IP policy-based routing on the e0 interfaces of the edge routers. Remove any route maps and access lists that were configured on these routers in the previous exercises.

**Step 3**  On the edge routers, shut down interface S0 and remove all configuration commands on that interface by using the **default interface s0** global configuration command.

**Step 4**  On the edge routers' S0 interface, enable Frame Relay encapsulation, and then disable Frame Relay Inverse Address Resolution Protocol (ARP).

**Step 5**  Create two multipoint subinterfaces on each edge router's serial 0 interface. (These will be used to connect to both core routers [BBR1 and BBR2] in this exercise.)

**Step 6**  Configure subinterface S0.1 with an IP address of 172.31.$x.y$/24 and a Frame Relay map statement pointing to the BBR1 address of 172.31.$x$.3.

**Step 7**  Configure the second subinterface, S0.2, with an IP address of 172.31.$xx.y$/24 and a Frame Relay map statement pointing to the BBR2 address of 172.31.$xx$.4.

**Step 8**  Test each subinterface by pinging the BBR1 and BBR2 routers from both edge routers.

---

**NOTE**    Using the **default interface s0** command does not remove the subinterface configuration from the router's memory. Therefore, when you try to create a subinterface S0.2 with the multipoint type (in a previous exercise it was point-to-point), you get an error message. The only way to do this is to save your configuration after using the **default interface s0** command, reload your router, and then reconfigure the interface. (Alternatively, you can use a different subinterface number.)

---

## Task 2: Configuring BGP

In this task, you will configure basic BGP on the edge routers. Follow these steps:

**Step 1**  Configure BGP on the edge routers in the pod (P$x$R1 and P$x$R2) using AS 6500$x$, where $x$ is the pod number.

---

**NOTE**    Only the edge routers run BGP in this exercise. The internal routers continue to use RIPv2.

---

**Step 2**  Configure P$x$R1 and P$x$R2 with two external BGP neighbors, BBR1 (AS 64998) and BBR2 (AS 64999), and as internal BGP neighbors to each other. BBR1 has IP address 172.31.$x$.3, and BBR2 has IP address 172.31.$xx$.4. Use the 10.$x$.0.y addresses (the addresses of the S1 interfaces) to establish the IBGP session between the two edge routers.

**Step 3**    Configure the edge routers to advertise your pod networks 10.x.0.0/24, 10.x.1.0/24, 10.x.2.0/24, and 10.x.3.0/24 to the core routers. There are two points to remember:

- The 10.0.0.0 network is subnetted, so you need to use the **mask** option of the **network** command to announce the subnets.

- The networks listed in the **network** command must match the networks in the routing table exactly.

**Step 4**    At the edge routers, verify that all three BGP neighbor relationships are established using the **show ip bgp summary** command.

**Step 5**    Do you see one IBGP neighbor and two EBGP neighbors on each edge router?

**Step 6**    How many prefixes have been learned from each BGP neighbor?

**Step 7**    At the edge routers, display the BGP routing information base using the **show ip bgp** command. Verify that you have received routes from the core and from the other edge router. Look at the IP routing table on the edge routers. Are the BGP routes present?

**Step 8**    Telnet to the core routers, BBR1 (172.31.x.3) and BBR2 (172.31.xx.4); the password is **cisco**. Look at the IP routing table. Are the BGP routes present for your pod? Exit the Telnet session.

**Step 9**    RIPv2 is running between PxR1 and PxR2, because the network statement for RIPv2 includes the entire 10.0.0.0 network. For this exercise, you only want to run IBGP between PxR1 and PxR2. Configure interface serial 1 as a passive interface for RIPv2 on both edge routers.

**Step 10**    At the edge routers, use the **show ip protocols** command to verify the RIPv2 passive interface and the BGP configuration.

**Step 11**    You are not redistributing BGP into RIPv2, so the internal routers PxR3 and PxR4 do not know any routes outside your pod. In a previous exercise, you configured RIPv2 to pass a default route to the internal pod routers using the **default-information originate** command under the RIP router configuration. Verify that this command is still present.

**Step 12**    Verify connectivity by pinging the TFTP server (10.254.0.254) from the edge routers. If this works, ping the TFTP server from internal routers.

## Exercise Verification

You have successfully completed this exercise when you achieve the following results:

- You have successfully configured IBGP on PxR1 and PxR2 and EBGP between PxR1, PxR2, BBR1, and BBR2.

- You can ping the TFTP server from all pod routers.

# Configuration Exercise 8-2: Configuring Full-Mesh IBGP

In this exercise, you will configure and verify full-mesh IBGP in your pod.

**NOTE**    Throughout this exercise, the pod number is referred to as *x*, and the router number is referred to as *y*. Substitute the appropriate numbers as needed.

## Objectives

Your task in this Configuration Exercise is to configure a full-mesh IBGP network.

## Visual Objective

Figure 8-32 illustrates the topology used in this exercise.

**Figure 8-32**   *Full-Mesh IBGP Configuration Exercise Topology*

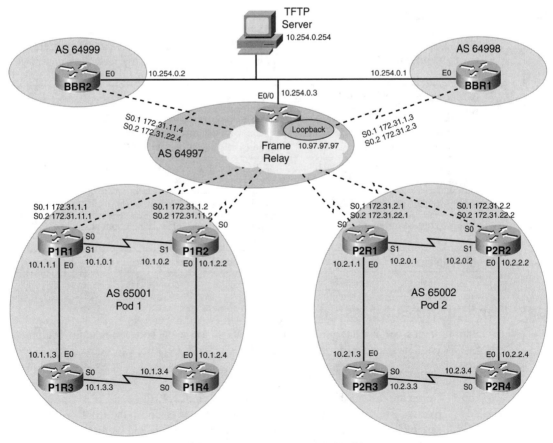

On all pod routers loopback 0: 10.200.200.xy/32

| NOTE | The Frame Relay router is in AS 64997. However, it is provided only for communication with the backbone routers; it is not used in this exercise. |

## Command List

In this exercise, you will use the commands in Table 8-10, listed in logical order. Refer to this list if you need configuration command assistance during the exercise.

| CAUTION | Although the command syntax is shown in this table, the addresses shown are typically for the P*x*R1 and P*x*R3 routers. Be careful when addressing your routers! Refer to the exercise instructions and the appropriate visual objective diagram for addressing details. |

**Table 8-10**    *Full-Mesh IBGP Configuration Exercise Commands*

| Command | Description |
|---|---|
| (config)#**router bgp 65001** | Enters BGP router configuration mode. This router is in AS 65001. |
| (config-router)#**neighbor 10.200.200.***xy* **remote-as 65001** | Identifies a BGP neighbor. |
| (config-router)#**neighbor 10.200.200.***xy* **update-source loopback0** | Peers with a neighbor using a loopback interface address as the source address. |
| (config-router)#**neighbor 10.200.200.***xy* **next-hop-self** | Advertises yourself as the next hop to this neighbor. |
| (config-router)#**no synchronization** | Turns off the synchronization rule. |
| #**show ip bgp summary** | Shows a summary of BGP neighbor status and activities. |
| #**show ip bgp** | Shows the BGP routing table. |

## Task: Configuring Full-Mesh IBGP

In this task, you will use a terminal utility to establish a console connection to the equipment. You will configure and verify full-mesh IBGP in your pod. Follow these steps:

**Step 1**   Remove the RIPv2 default route on the edge routers.

**Step 2**   Configure full-mesh IBGP between the P*x*R1, P*x*R2, P*x*R3, and P*x*R4 routers. Use the loopback address 10.200.200.*xy* to establish the IBGP session between the edge routers and the internal routers and the IBGP session between the internal routers. Recall that RIPv2 is advertising this network, so the routers can use their loopback IP address to establish the IBGP sessions.

For example, Figure 8-33 illustrates the BGP peering sessions for pod 1. The dotted lines indicate EBGP peers, and the solid lines indicate IBGP peers. There are six IBGP sessions; the one between the two edge routers was configured in the preceding exercise, along with the EBGP sessions.

**Figure 8-33**  *BGP Peering Sessions for Pod 1*

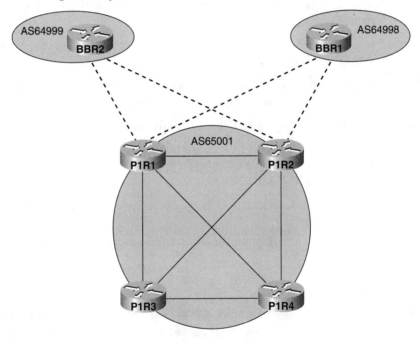

**Step 3**   Configure each internal router to send its BGP updates from its loopback interface (10.200.200.*xy*/32).

**Step 4**   Verify that the appropriate BGP neighbor relationships have been established. Each edge router should see two EBGP neighbors and three IBGP neighbors. Each internal router should see three IBGP neighbors.

**Step 5**   Use the **show ip bgp** command on the internal routers to determine the next hop for the route to the 10.254.0.0/24 network in the core.

**Step 6**   Which path on the internal routers is selected as the best path to the 10.254.0.0/24 network?

**Step 7**   Display the IP routing table of the edge routers. Is there a route to the 10.254.0.0/24 network?

**Step 8** Display the IP routing table of the internal routers. Is there a route to the 10.254.0.0/24 network? Why or why not?

**Step 9** The internal routers do not know how to reach the next-hop address. To correct this problem, you can either advertise the next-hop network via an IBGP or configure the edge routers to advertise themselves as the next hop. Choose the second alternative. Use the **neighbor next-hop self** command to change the next hop advertised into the pod on the edge routers.

**Step 10** On the internal routers, use the **show ip bgp** command once more to see the BGP route to 10.254.0.0/24. What are the next-hop IP addresses for the routes to the 10.254.0.0/24 network now?

**Step 11** Have the internal routers installed these BGP routes in their routing table? Why or why not?

**Step 12** The BGP synchronization rule is stopping BGP from installing the routes in the routing table. What is the BGP synchronization rule?

**Step 13** Because the AS is running full-mesh IBGP, BGP synchronization can safely be turned off in all of the pod routers. Turn off synchronization.

**Step 14** Look again at the routing tables on the internal routers. You should see the BGP route to 10.254.0.0/24.

**Step 15** From the internal routers, ping the TFTP server (10.254.0.254) to test connectivity.

**Step 16** What is the path each internal router is using to reach the TFTP server?

## Exercise Verification

You have successfully completed this exercise if you have configured full-mesh IBGP within your pod and your routing tables contain BGP routes to the networks advertised by the core.

# Solution to Configuration Exercise 8-1: Configuring EBGP and IBGP for Two Neighbors

This section provides the answers to the questions in the Configuration Exercise.

---

**NOTE** Some answers provided cover multiple steps; the answers are given after the last step to which that answer applies.

---

## Solution to Task 1: Cleaning Up

**Step 1**    Connect to each of your pod edge routers (P*x*R1 and P*x*R2). Remove all OSPF configurations from these edge routers, but leave RIPv2 enabled on them.

**Step 2**    Disable IP policy-based routing on the e0 interfaces of the edge routers. Remove any route maps and access lists that were configured on these routers in the previous exercises.

**Step 3**    On the edge routers, shut down interface s0 and remove all configuration commands on that interface by using the **default interface s0** global configuration command.

**Step 4**    On the edge routers' S0 interface, enable Frame Relay encapsulation, and then disable Frame Relay Inverse Address Resolution Protocol (ARP).

**Step 5**    Create two multipoint subinterfaces on each edge router's serial 0 interface. (These will be used to connect to both core routers [BBR1 and BBR2] in this exercise.)

**Step 6**    Configure subinterface S0.1 with an IP address of 172.31.*x*.y/24 and a Frame Relay map statement pointing to the BBR1 address of 172.31.*x*.3.

**Step 7**    Configure the second subinterface, S0.2, with an IP address of 172.31.*xx*.y/24 and a Frame Relay map statement pointing to the BBR2 address of 172.31.*xx*.4.

**Step 8**    Test each subinterface by pinging the BBR1 and BBR2 routers from both edge routers.

---

**NOTE**    Using the **default interface s0** command does not remove the subinterface configuration from the router's memory. Therefore, when you try to create a subinterface S0.2 with the multipoint type (in a previous exercise it was point-to-point), you get an error message. The only way to do this is to save your configuration after using the **default interface s0** command, reload your router, and then reconfigure the interface. (Alternatively, you can use a different subinterface number.)

---

**Solution:**

The following shows how to perform the required steps on the P1R1 router:

```
P1R1(config)#no router ospf 1
P1R1(config)#int e0
P1R1(config-if)#no ip policy route-map PBR
P1R1(config-if)#no access-list 1
P1R1(config)#no access-list 2
```

*continues*

```
P1R1(config)#no route-map PBR
P1R1(config)#no route-map CONVERT
P1R1(config)#int s0
P1R1(config-if)#shutdown
P1R1(config-if)#default interface s0
P1R1(config)#int s0
P1R1(config-if)#encapsulation frame-relay
P1R1(config-if)#no frame-relay inverse-arp
P1R1(config)#int s0.1 multipoint
P1R1(config-subif)#ip address 172.31.1.1 255.255.255.0
P1R1(config-subif)#frame-relay map ip 172.31.1.3 111 broadcast
P1R1(config-subif)#int s0.2 multipoint
P1R1(config-subif)#ip address 172.31.11.1 255.255.255.0
P1R1(config-subif)#frame-relay map ip 172.31.11.4 211 broadcast

P1R2(config)#no router ospf 1
P1R2(config)#int e0
P1R2(config-if)#no ip policy route-map PBR
P1R2(config-if)#no access-list 1
P1R2(config)#no access-list 2
P1R2(config)#no route-map PBR
P1R2(config)#no route-map CONVERT
P1R2(config)#int s0
P1R2(config-if)#shutdown
P1R2(config-if)#default interface s0
P1R2(config)#int s0
P1R2(config-if)#encapsulation frame-relay
P1R2(config-if)#no frame-relay inverse-arp
P1R2(config-if)#int s0.1 multipoint
P1R2(config-subif)#ip address 172.31.1.2 255.255.255.0
P1R2(config-subif)#frame-relay map ip 172.31.1.3 112 broadcast
P1R2(config-subif)#int s0.2 multipoint
P1R2(config-subif)#ip address 172.31.11.2 255.255.255.0
P1R2(config-subif)#frame-relay map ip 172.31.11.4 212 broadcast
```

## Solution to Task 2: Configuring BGP

**Step 1**  Configure BGP on the edge routers in the pod (P$x$R1 and P$x$R2) using
AS 6500$x$, where $x$ is the pod number.

---

**NOTE**  Only the edge routers run BGP in this exercise. The internal
routers continue to use RIPv2.

---

**Step 2**  Configure P$x$R1 and P$x$R2 with two external BGP neighbors, BBR1
(AS 64998) and BBR2 (AS 64999), and as internal BGP neighbors to each
other. BBR1 has IP address 172.31.$x$.3, and BBR2 has IP address 172.31.$xx$.4.
Use the 10.$x$.0.$y$ addresses (the addresses of the S1 interfaces) to establish the
IBGP session between the two edge routers.

**Solution:**

The following shows how to perform the required steps on the P1R1 and P1R2 routers:

```
P1R1(config)#router bgp 65001
P1R1(config-router)#neighbor 172.31.1.3 remote-as 64998
P1R1(config-router)#neighbor 172.31.11.4 remote-as 64999
P1R1(config-router)#neighbor 10.1.0.2 remote-as 65001

P1R2(config)#router bgp 65001
P1R2(config-router)#neighbor 172.31.1.3 remote-as 64998
P1R2(config-router)#neighbor 172.31.11.4 remote-as 64999
P1R2(config-router)#neighbor 10.1.0.1 remote-as 65001
```

**Step 3**   Configure the edge routers to advertise your pod networks 10.x.0.0/24, 10.x.1.0/24, 10.x.2.0/24, and 10.x.3.0/24 to the core routers. There are two points to remember:

- The 10.0.0.0 network is subnetted, so you need to use the **mask** option of the **network** command to announce the subnets.

- The networks listed in the **network** command must match the networks in the routing table exactly.

**Solution:**

The following shows how to perform the required steps on the P1R1 and P1R2 routers:

```
P1R1(config)#router bgp 65001
P1R1(config-router)#network 10.1.0.0 mask 255.255.255.0
P1R1(config-router)#network 10.1.1.0 mask 255.255.255.0
P1R1(config-router)#network 10.1.2.0 mask 255.255.255.0
P1R1(config-router)#network 10.1.3.0 mask 255.255.255.0
P1R2(config)#router bgp 65001
P1R2(config-router)#network 10.1.0.0 mask 255.255.255.0
P1R2(config-router)#network 10.1.1.0 mask 255.255.255.0
P1R2(config-router)#network 10.1.2.0 mask 255.255.255.0
P1R2(config-router)#network 10.1.3.0 mask 255.255.255.0
```

**Step 4**   At the edge routers, verify that all three BGP neighbor relationships are established using the **show ip bgp summary** command.

**Solution:**

The following output is from the P1R1 and P1R2 routers. The number in the State/PfxRcd column indicates the number of prefixes received from the neighbor. A number in that column means that the BGP session with that neighbor is in the established state.

```
P1R1#show ip bgp summary
BGP router identifier 10.200.200.11, local AS number 65001
BGP table version is 20, main routing table version 20
14 network entries and 34 paths using 2582 bytes of memory
```

*continues*

```
15 BGP path attribute entries using 900 bytes of memory
8 BGP AS-PATH entries using 192 bytes of memory
0 BGP route-map cache entries using 0 bytes of memory
0 BGP filter-list cache entries using 0 bytes of memory
BGP activity 14/0 prefixes, 35/1 paths, scan interval 15 secs

Neighbor        V     AS MsgRcvd MsgSent   TblVer  InQ OutQ Up/Down  State/PfxRcd
10.1.0.2        4 65001      16      22       20     0    0 00:05:06        10
172.31.1.3      4 64998      22      20       20     0    0 00:07:30        10
172.31.11.4     4 64999      16      19       20     0    0 00:04:25        10

P1R2#show ip bgp summary
BGP router identifier 10.200.200.12, local AS number 65001
BGP table version is 23, main routing table version 23
14 network entries and 38 paths using 2726 bytes of memory
17 BGP path attribute entries using 1020 bytes of memory
8 BGP AS-PATH entries using 192 bytes of memory
0 BGP route-map cache entries using 0 bytes of memory
0 BGP filter-list cache entries using 0 bytes of memory
BGP activity 15/1 prefixes, 40/2 paths, scan interval 15 secs

Neighbor        V     AS MsgRcvd MsgSent   TblVer  InQ OutQ Up/Down  State/PfxRcd
10.1.0.1        4 65001      22      19       23     0    0 00:05:37        14
172.31.1.3      4 64998      23      21       23     0    0 00:06:04        10
172.31.11.4     4 64999      23      22       23     0    0 00:05:37        10
P1R2#
```

**Step 5**   Do you see one IBGP neighbor and two EBGP neighbors on each edge router?

**Solution:**

Yes, each edge router sees two EBGP neighbors and one IBGP neighbor.

**Step 6**   How many prefixes have been learned from each BGP neighbor?

**Solution:**

The number of prefixes is shown in the State/PfxRcd column. The routers have each received ten prefixes from each of the EBGP neighbors (BBR1 and BBR2). P1R1 has received ten prefixes from P1R2; P1R2 has received 14 prefixes from P1R1.

**Step 7**   At the edge routers, display the BGP routing information base using the **show ip bgp** command. Verify that you have received routes from the core and from the other edge router. Look at the IP routing table on the edge routers. Are the BGP routes present?

**Solution:**

The following output is from the P1R1 router:

```
P1R1#show ip bgp
BGP table version is 20, local router ID is 10.200.200.11
Status codes: s suppressed, d damped, h history, * valid, > best, i - internal
```

```
Origin codes: i - IGP, e - EGP, ? - incomplete

   Network          Next Hop          Metric LocPrf Weight Path
 * i10.1.0.0/24     10.1.0.2               0    100      0 i
 *>                 0.0.0.0                0          32768 i
 * i10.1.1.0/24     10.1.0.2               1    100      0 i
 *>                 0.0.0.0                0          32768 i
 * i10.1.2.0/24     10.1.0.2               0    100      0 i
 *>                 0.0.0.0                1          32768 i
 * i10.1.3.0/24     10.1.2.4               1    100      0 i
 *>                 0.0.0.0                1          32768 i
 *   10.2.0.0/24    172.31.11.4                        0 64999 65002 i
 * i                172.31.1.3                  100    0 64998 65002 i
 *>                 172.31.1.3                         0 64998 65002 i
 *   10.2.1.0/24    172.31.11.4                        0 64999 65002 i
 * i                172.31.1.3                  100    0 64998 65002 i
 *>                 172.31.1.3                         0 64998 65002 i
 *   10.2.2.0/24    172.31.1.3                         0 64998 65002 i
 *>                 172.31.11.4                        0 64999 65002 i
 * i                172.31.11.4                 100    0 64999 65002 i
 * i10.2.3.0/24     172.31.11.4                 100    0 64999 65002 i
 *                  172.31.1.3                         0 64998 65002 i
   Network          Next Hop          Metric LocPrf Weight Path
 *>                 172.31.11.4                        0 64999 65002 i
 *   10.97.97.0/24  172.31.11.4                        0 64999 64997 i
 * i                172.31.1.3                  100    0 64998 64997 i
 *>                 172.31.1.3                         0 64998 64997 i
 *   10.254.0.0/24  172.31.11.4                        0 64999 64998 i
 * i                172.31.1.3             0    100    0 64998 i
 *>                 172.31.1.3             0           0 64998 i
 *   172.31.1.0/24  172.31.11.4                        0 64999 64998 i
 * i                172.31.1.3             0    100    0 64998 i
 *>                 172.31.1.3             0           0 64998 i
 *   172.31.2.0/24  172.31.11.4                        0 64999 64998 i
 * i                172.31.1.3             0    100    0 64998 i
 *>                 172.31.1.3             0           0 64998 i
 *> 172.31.11.0/24  172.31.11.4            0           0 64999 i
 * i                172.31.11.4            0    100    0 64999 i
 *                  172.31.1.3                         0 64998 64999 i
 *> 172.31.22.0/24  172.31.11.4            0           0 64999 i
 * i                172.31.11.4            0    100    0 64999 i
 *                  172.31.1.3                         0 64998 64999 i

P1R1#show ip route
<output omitted>
Gateway of last resort is 172.31.11.4 to network 0.0.0.0

     172.31.0.0/24 is subnetted, 4 subnets
B        172.31.22.0 [20/0] via 172.31.11.4, 00:06:23
B        172.31.2.0 [20/0] via 172.31.1.3, 00:09:27
C        172.31.1.0 is directly connected, Serial0.1
C        172.31.11.0 is directly connected, Serial0.2
     10.0.0.0/8 is variably subnetted, 14 subnets, 2 masks
```

*continues*

```
C       10.200.200.11/32 is directly connected, Loopback0
R       10.200.200.14/32 [120/2] via 10.1.1.3, 00:00:01, Ethernet0
                         [120/2] via 10.1.0.2, 00:00:16, Serial1
R       10.200.200.12/32 [120/1] via 10.1.0.2, 00:00:17, Serial1
R       10.200.200.13/32 [120/1] via 10.1.1.3, 00:00:02, Ethernet0
B       10.2.0.0/24 [20/0] via 172.31.1.3, 00:06:41
R       10.1.3.0/24 [120/1] via 10.1.1.3, 00:00:02, Ethernet0
B       10.2.1.0/24 [20/0] via 172.31.1.3, 00:06:42
R       10.1.2.0/24 [120/1] via 10.1.0.2, 00:00:18, Serial1
B       10.2.2.0/24 [20/0] via 172.31.11.4, 00:06:25
B       10.97.97.0/24 [20/0] via 172.31.1.3, 00:09:29
C       10.1.1.0/24 is directly connected, Ethernet0
B       10.2.3.0/24 [20/0] via 172.31.11.4, 00:05:42
C       10.1.0.0/24 is directly connected, Serial1
B       10.254.0.0/24 [20/0] via 172.31.1.3, 00:09:29
S*   0.0.0.0/0 [1/0] via 172.31.11.4
P1R1#
```

The BGP table for P1R1 indicates that routes have been received from BBR1, BBR2, and P1R2, because the next-hop addresses in the BGP table include the addresses of these neighbors.

The IP routing table on P1R1 shows some BGP routes, as indicated by the B in the first column.

**Step 8**   Telnet to the core routers, BBR1 (172.31.*x*.3) and BBR2 (172.31.*xx*.4); the password is **cisco**. Look at the IP routing table. Are the BGP routes present for your pod? Exit the Telnet session.

**Solution:**

The following output shows the IP routing table on the BBR1 and BBR2 routers. The routes from pod 1 are highlighted. (Note that pod 2 is also configured and that the routes for that pod are also in the BBR1 and BBR2 routing tables.)

```
BBR1>show ip route
<output omitted>
Gateway of last resort is not set

     172.31.0.0/24 is subnetted, 4 subnets
B       172.31.22.0 [20/0] via 10.254.0.2, 00:16:30
C       172.31.2.0 is directly connected, Serial0.2
C       172.31.1.0 is directly connected, Serial0.1
B       172.31.11.0 [20/0] via 10.254.0.2, 00:16:30
S    192.168.11.0/24 [1/0] via 172.31.1.2
     10.0.0.0/24 is subnetted, 10 subnets
B       10.1.3.0 [20/0] via 172.31.1.2, 00:03:03
B       10.2.0.0 [20/0] via 172.31.2.1, 00:07:09
B       10.1.2.0 [20/0] via 172.31.1.2, 00:02:35
B       10.2.1.0 [20/0] via 172.31.2.1, 00:07:09
B       10.1.1.0 [20/0] via 172.31.1.1, 00:03:03
B       10.2.2.0 [20/0] via 172.31.2.2, 00:04:23
```

```
B        10.97.97.0 [20/0] via 10.254.0.3, 05:38:52
B        10.1.0.0 [20/0] via 172.31.1.1, 00:03:05
B        10.2.3.0 [20/1] via 172.31.2.1, 00:06:11
C        10.254.0.0 is directly connected, Ethernet0
S     192.168.22.0/24 [1/0] via 172.31.2.2
S     192.168.1.0/24 [1/0] via 172.31.1.1
S     192.168.2.0/24 [1/0] via 172.31.2.1
BBR1>

BBR2>show ip route
<output omitted>
Gateway of last resort is not set

     172.31.0.0/16 is variably subnetted, 5 subnets, 2 masks
C        172.31.22.0/24 is directly connected, Serial0.2
B        172.31.2.0/24 [20/0] via 10.254.0.1, 00:17:05
B        172.31.1.0/24 [20/0] via 10.254.0.1, 00:17:05
R        172.31.0.0/16 [120/1] via 10.254.0.1, 00:00:01, Ethernet0
C        172.31.11.0/24 is directly connected, Serial0.1
     10.0.0.0/24 is subnetted, 10 subnets
B        10.1.3.0 [20/0] via 172.31.11.2, 00:03:31
B        10.2.0.0 [20/0] via 172.31.22.1, 00:07:37
B        10.1.2.0 [20/0] via 172.31.11.2, 00:03:02
B        10.2.1.0 [20/0] via 172.31.22.1, 00:07:37
B        10.1.1.0 [20/0] via 172.31.11.1, 00:03:31
B        10.2.2.0 [20/0] via 172.31.22.2, 00:04:33
B        10.97.97.0 [20/0] via 10.254.0.3, 00:58:56
B        10.1.0.0 [20/0] via 172.31.11.1, 00:03:33
B        10.2.3.0 [20/1] via 172.31.22.1, 00:06:39
C        10.254.0.0 is directly connected, Ethernet0
BBR2>
```

**Step 9**   RIPv2 is running between PxR1 and PxR2, because the network statement for RIPv2 includes the entire 10.0.0.0 network. For this exercise, you only want to run IBGP between PxR1 and PxR2. Configure interface serial 1 as a passive interface for RIPv2 on both edge routers.

**Solution:**

The following shows the configuration for the P1R1 and P1R2 routers:

```
P1R1(config)#router rip
P1R1(config-router)#passive-interface s1

P1R2(config)#router rip
P1R2(config-router)#passive-interface s1
```

**Step 10**   At the edge routers, use the **show ip protocols** command to verify the RIPv2 passive interface and the BGP configuration.

**Solution:**

The following shows the output on the P1R1 router. The passive interface for RIPv2 is indicated, as is BGP.

```
P1R1#sh ip protocols
Routing Protocol is "rip"
  Sending updates every 30 seconds, next due in 1 seconds
  Invalid after 180 seconds, hold down 180, flushed after 240
  Outgoing update filter list for all interfaces is not set
  Incoming update filter list for all interfaces is not set
  Redistributing: rip
  Default version control: send version 2, receive version 2
    Interface              Send  Recv  Triggered RIP  Key-chain
    Ethernet0              2     2
    Loopback0             2     2
  Automatic network summarization is not in effect
  Maximum path: 4
  Routing for Networks:
    10.0.0.0
  Passive Interface(s):
    Serial1
  Routing Information Sources:
    Gateway         Distance      Last Update
    10.1.0.2          120         00:01:20
    10.1.1.3          120         00:00:06
  Distance: (default is 120)

Routing Protocol is "bgp 65001"
  Outgoing update filter list for all interfaces is not set
  Incoming update filter list for all interfaces is not set
  IGP synchronization is enabled
  Automatic route summarization is enabled
  Neighbor(s):
    Address         FiltIn FiltOut DistIn DistOut Weight RouteMap
    10.1.0.2
    172.31.1.3
    172.31.11.4
  Maximum path: 1
  Routing for Networks:
  Routing Information Sources:
    Gateway         Distance      Last Update
    10.1.0.2            200       00:10:03
    172.31.1.3          20        00:09:45
    172.31.11.4         20        00:08:45
  Distance: external 20 internal 200 local 200
```

**Step 11**   You are not redistributing BGP into RIPv2, so the internal routers P*x*R3 and P*x*R4 do not know any routes outside your pod. In a previous exercise, you configured RIPv2 to pass a default route to the internal pod routers using the **default-information originate** command under the RIP router configuration. Verify that this command is still present.

**Step 12** Verify connectivity by pinging the TFTP server (10.254.0.254) from the edge
routers. If this works, ping the TFTP server from internal routers.

**Solution:**

The following output indicates that the TFTP server can be reached from all four routers
in pod 1:

```
P1R1#ping 10.254.0.254
Type escape sequence to abort.
Sending 5, 100-byte ICMP Echos to 10.254.0.254, timeout is 2 seconds:
!!!!!
Success rate is 100 percent (5/5), round-trip min/avg/max = 32/50/120 ms
P1R1#

P1R2#ping 10.254.0.254
Type escape sequence to abort.
Sending 5, 100-byte ICMP Echos to 10.254.0.254, timeout is 2 seconds:
!!!!!
Success rate is 100 percent (5/5), round-trip min/avg/max = 32/33/40 ms
P1R2#

P1R3>ping 10.254.0.254
Type escape sequence to abort.
Sending 5, 100-byte ICMP Echos to 10.254.0.254, timeout is 2 seconds:
.!!!!
Success rate is 80 percent (4/5), round-trip min/avg/max = 32/143/304 ms
P1R3>

P1R4>ping 10.254.0.254
Type escape sequence to abort.
Sending 5, 100-byte ICMP Echos to 10.254.0.254, timeout is 2 seconds:
!!!!!
Success rate is 100 percent (5/5), round-trip min/avg/max = 32/36/44 ms
P1R4>
```

## Exercise Verification

You have successfully completed this exercise when you achieve the following results:

- You have successfully configured IBGP on P*x*R1 and P*x*R2 and EBGP between P*x*R1,
  P*x*R2, BBR1, and BBR2.

- You can ping the TFTP server from all pod routers.

# Solution to Configuration Exercise 8-2: Configuring Full-Mesh IBGP

This section provides the answers to the questions in the Configuration Exercise.

**NOTE**    Some answers provided cover multiple steps; the answers are given after the last step to which that answer applies.

# Solution to Task: Configuring Full-Mesh IBGP

**Step 1**    Remove the RIPv2 default route on the edge routers.

**Solution:**

The following shows the required steps on P1R1 and P1R2:

```
P1R1(config)#no ip route 0.0.0.0 0.0.0.0 172.31.11.4
P1R1(config)#router rip
P1R1(config-router)#no default-info orig
P1R2(config)#no ip route 0.0.0.0 0.0.0.0 172.31.11.4
P1R2(config)#router rip
P1R2(config-router)#no default-info orig
```

**Step 2**    Configure full-mesh IBGP between the P*x*R1, P*x*R2, P*x*R3, and P*x*R4 routers. Use the loopback address 10.200.200.*xy* to establish the IBGP session between the edge routers and the internal routers and the IBGP session between the internal routers. Recall that RIPv2 is advertising this network, so the routers can use their loopback IP address to establish the IBGP sessions.

**Solution:**

The following shows the required configuration on the pod 1 routers:

```
P1R1(config)#router bgp 65001
P1R1(config-router)#neighbor 10.200.200.13 remote-as 65001
P1R1(config-router)#neighbor 10.200.200.14 remote-as 65001

P1R2(config)#router bgp 65001
P1R2(config-router)#neighbor 10.200.200.13 remote-as 65001
P1R2(config-router)#neighbor 10.200.200.14 remote-as 65001

P1R3(config)#router bgp 65001
P1R3(config-router)#neighbor 10.200.200.11 remote-as 65001
P1R3(config-router)#neighbor 10.200.200.12 remote-as 65001
P1R3(config-router)#neighbor 10.200.200.14 remote-as 65001

P1R4(config)#router bgp 65001
P1R4(config-router)#neighbor 10.200.200.11 remote-as 65001
P1R4(config-router)#neighbor 10.200.200.12 remote-as 65001
P1R4(config-router)#neighbor 10.200.200.13 remote-as 65001
```

**Step 3**    Configure each internal router to send its BGP updates from its loopback interface (10.200.200.*xy*/32).

**Solution:**

The following shows the required configuration on the P1R3 and P1R4 routers:

```
P1R3(config)#router bgp 65001
P1R3(config-router)#neighbor 10.200.200.11 update-source loopback0
P1R3(config-router)#neighbor 10.200.200.12 update-source loopback0
P1R3(config-router)#neighbor 10.200.200.14 update-source loopback0

P1R4(config)#router bgp 65001
P1R4(config-router)#neighbor 10.200.200.11 update-source loopback0
P1R4(config-router)#neighbor 10.200.200.12 update-source loopback0
P1R4(config-router)#neighbor 10.200.200.13 update-source loopback0
```

**Step 4**    Verify that the appropriate BGP neighbor relationships have been
established. Each edge router should see two EBGP neighbors and three
IBGP neighbors. Each internal router should see three IBGP neighbors.

**Solution:**

The following output is from the P1R1 router (an edge router) and the P1R3 router (an internal
router). P1R1 sees two EBGP neighbors and three IBGP neighbors; P1R3 sees three IBGP
neighbors.

```
P1R1#show ip bgp summary
BGP router identifier 10.200.200.11, local AS number 65001
BGP table version is 23, main routing table version 23
14 network entries and 38 paths using 2726 bytes of memory
19 BGP path attribute entries using 1140 bytes of memory
8 BGP AS-PATH entries using 192 bytes of memory
0 BGP route-map cache entries using 0 bytes of memory
0 BGP filter-list cache entries using 0 bytes of memory
BGP activity 14/28 prefixes, 41/3 paths, scan interval 15 secs

Neighbor        V    AS MsgRcvd MsgSent  TblVer  InQ OutQ Up/Down  State/PfxRcd
10.1.0.2        4 65001      43      46      23    0    0 00:27:44        14
10.200.200.13   4 65001       4      12      23    0    0 00:00:44         0
10.200.200.14   4 65001       4      12      23    0    0 00:00:26         0
172.31.1.3      4 64998      45      46      23    0    0 00:30:08        10
172.31.11.4     4 64999      41      45      23    0    0 00:27:04        10
P1R1#

P1R3#show ip bgp summary
BGP router identifier 10.200.200.13, local AS number 65001
BGP table version is 5, main routing table version 5
14 network entries and 26 paths using 2294 bytes of memory
8 BGP path attribute entries using 480 bytes of memory
5 BGP AS-PATH entries using 120 bytes of memory
0 BGP route-map cache entries using 0 bytes of memory
0 BGP filter-list cache entries using 0 bytes of memory
BGP activity 14/0 prefixes, 26/0 paths, scan interval 15 secs
```

*continues*

```
Neighbor          V    AS MsgRcvd MsgSent   TblVer  InQ OutQ Up/Down  State/PfxRcd
10.200.200.11     4 65001     13       5        5    0    0 00:01:43          12
10.200.200.12     4 65001     13       5        5    0    0 00:01:41          14
10.200.200.14     4 65001      6       6        5    0    0 00:02:24           0
P1R3#
```

**Step 5**  Use the **show ip bgp** command on the internal routers to determine the next
hop for the route to the 10.254.0.0/24 network in the core.

**Solution:**

The following output is from the P1R3 router. It shows that the next-hop route to the 10.254.0.0/24
network is 172.31.1.3, the BBR1 router.

```
P1R3#show ip bgp
BGP table version is 7, local router ID is 10.200.200.13
Status codes: s suppressed, d damped, h history, * valid, > best, i - internal
Origin codes: i - IGP, e - EGP, ? - incomplete

   Network          Next Hop          Metric LocPrf Weight Path
* i10.1.0.0/24      10.200.200.12          0    100      0 i
*>i                 10.200.200.11          0    100      0 i
* i10.1.1.0/24      10.1.2.4               2    100      0 i
*>i                 10.200.200.11          0    100      0 i
*>i10.1.2.0/24      10.200.200.12          0    100      0 i
*>i10.1.3.0/24      10.1.2.4               1    100      0 i
* i10.2.0.0/24      172.31.1.3                  100      0 64998 65002 i
* i                 172.31.1.3                  100      0 64998 65002 i
* i10.2.1.0/24      172.31.1.3                  100      0 64998 65002 i
* i                 172.31.1.3                  100      0 64998 65002 i
* i10.2.2.0/24      172.31.11.4                 100      0 64999 65002 i
* i                 172.31.11.4                 100      0 64999 65002 i
* i10.2.3.0/24      172.31.11.4                 100      0 64999 65002 i
* i                 172.31.11.4                 100      0 64999 65002 i
* i10.97.97.0/24    172.31.1.3                  100      0 64998 64997 i
* i                 172.31.1.3                  100      0 64998 64997 i
* i10.254.0.0/24    172.31.1.3             0    100      0 64998 i
* i                 172.31.1.3             0    100      0 64998 i
* i172.31.1.0/24    172.31.1.3             0    100      0 64998 i
* i                 172.31.1.3             0    100      0 64998 i
* i172.31.2.0/24    172.31.1.3             0    100      0 64998 i
* i                 172.31.1.3             0    100      0 64998 i
* i172.31.11.0/24   172.31.11.4            0    100      0 64999 i
* i                 172.31.11.4            0    100      0 64999 i
* i172.31.22.0/24   172.31.11.4            0    100      0 64999 i
* i                 172.31.11.4            0    100      0 64999 i
P1R3#
```

**Step 6**  Which path on the internal routers is selected as the best path to the
10.254.0.0/24 network?

**Solution:**

There is no > beside either of the routes to the 10.254.0.0/24 network, so no path is selected as the best path to this network.

**Step 7**   Display the IP routing table of the edge routers. Is there a route to the 10.254.0.0/24 network?

**Solution:**

The following output is from the P1R1 router. There is a route to the 10.254.0.0/24 network.

```
P1R1#show ip route
<output omitted>
Gateway of last resort is not set

     172.31.0.0/24 is subnetted, 4 subnets
B       172.31.22.0 [20/0] via 172.31.11.4, 00:06:05
B       172.31.2.0 [20/0] via 172.31.1.3, 00:06:05
C       172.31.1.0 is directly connected, Serial0.1
C       172.31.11.0 is directly connected, Serial0.2
     10.0.0.0/8 is variably subnetted, 14 subnets, 2 masks
C       10.200.200.11/32 is directly connected, Loopback0
R       10.200.200.14/32 [120/2] via 10.1.1.3, 00:00:12, Ethernet0
R       10.200.200.12/32 [120/3] via 10.1.1.3, 00:00:12, Ethernet0
R       10.200.200.13/32 [120/1] via 10.1.1.3, 00:00:13, Ethernet0
R       10.1.3.0/24 [120/1] via 10.1.1.3, 00:00:13, Ethernet0
B       10.2.0.0/24 [20/0] via 172.31.1.3, 00:06:06
R       10.1.2.0/24 [120/2] via 10.1.1.3, 00:00:13, Ethernet0
B       10.2.1.0/24 [20/0] via 172.31.1.3, 00:06:07
B       10.97.97.0/24 [20/0] via 172.31.1.3, 00:06:07
B       10.2.2.0/24 [20/0] via 172.31.11.4, 00:06:07
C       10.1.1.0/24 is directly connected, Ethernet0
B       10.2.3.0/24 [20/0] via 172.31.11.4, 00:06:07
C       10.1.0.0/24 is directly connected, Serial1
B       10.254.0.0/24 [20/0] via 172.31.1.3, 00:06:07
P1R1#
```

**Step 8**   Display the IP routing table of the internal routers. Is there a route to the 10.254.0.0/24 network? Why or why not?

**Solution:**

The following output is from the P1R3 router. There is no route to the 10.254.0.0/24 network. The internal routers do not know how to reach the next-hop address for the 10.254.0.0/24 network. The routers do not install the route in their routing tables if the next hop cannot be reached.

```
P1R3#show ip route
<output omitted>
Gateway of last resort is not set

     10.0.0.0/8 is variably subnetted, 8 subnets, 2 masks
R       10.200.200.11/32 [120/1] via 10.1.1.1, 00:00:13, Ethernet0
```

*continues*

```
R        10.200.200.14/32 [120/1] via 10.1.3.4, 00:00:21, Serial0
R        10.200.200.12/32 [120/2] via 10.1.3.4, 00:00:21, Serial0
C        10.200.200.13/32 is directly connected, Loopback0
C        10.1.3.0/24 is directly connected, Serial0
R        10.1.2.0/24 [120/1] via 10.1.3.4, 00:00:21, Serial0
C        10.1.1.0/24 is directly connected, Ethernet0
R        10.1.0.0/24 [120/1] via 10.1.1.1, 00:00:14, Ethernet0
```

**Step 9**    The internal routers do not know how to reach the next-hop address. To correct this problem, you can either advertise the next-hop network via an IBGP or configure the edge routers to advertise themselves as the next hop. Choose the second alternative. Use the **neighbor next-hop self** command to change the next hop advertised into the pod on the edge routers.

**Solution:**

The following shows the required configuration on the P1R1 and P1R2 routers:

```
P1R1(config)#router bgp 65001
P1R1(config-router)#neighbor 10.200.200.13 next-hop-self
P1R1(config-router)#neighbor 10.200.200.14 next-hop-self

P1R2(config)#router bgp 65001
P1R2(config-router)#neighbor 10.200.200.13 next-hop-self
P1R2(config-router)#neighbor 10.200.200.14 next-hop-self
```

**Step 10**   On the internal routers, use the **show ip bgp** command once more to see the BGP route to 10.254.0.0/24. What are the next-hop IP addresses for the routes to the 10.254.0.0/24 network now?

**Solution:**

The following output is from the P1R3 router. The next-hop addresses for the routes to the 10.254.0.0/24 network are 10.200.200.12 and 10.200.200.11.

```
P1R3#show ip bgp
BGP table version is 8, local router ID is 10.200.200.13
Status codes: s suppressed, d damped, h history, * valid, > best, i - internal
Origin codes: i - IGP, e - EGP, ? - incomplete

   Network          Next Hop            Metric LocPrf Weight Path
* i10.1.0.0/24      10.200.200.12            0    100      0 i
*>i                 10.200.200.11            0    100      0 i
* i10.1.1.0/24      10.200.200.12            2    100      0 i
*>i                 10.200.200.11            0    100      0 i
* i10.1.2.0/24      10.200.200.11            2    100      0 i
*>i                 10.200.200.12            0    100      0 i
*>i10.1.3.0/24      10.200.200.11            1    100      0 i
* i                 10.200.200.12            1    100      0 i
* i10.2.0.0/24      10.200.200.12                 100      0 64998 65002 i
```

```
* i                   10.200.200.11              100      0 64998 65002 i
* i10.2.1.0/24        10.200.200.12              100      0 64998 65002 i
* i                   10.200.200.11              100      0 64998 65002 i
* i10.2.2.0/24        10.200.200.12              100      0 64999 65002 i
* i                   10.200.200.11              100      0 64999 65002 i
* i10.2.3.0/24        10.200.200.12              100      0 64999 65002 i
* i                   10.200.200.11              100      0 64999 65002 i
* i10.97.97.0/24      10.200.200.12              100      0 64998 64997 i
* i                   10.200.200.11              100      0 64998 64997 i
* i10.254.0.0/24      10.200.200.12          0   100      0 64998 i
* i                   10.200.200.11          0   100      0 64998 i
* i172.31.1.0/24      10.200.200.12          0   100      0 64998 i
* i                   10.200.200.11          0   100      0 64998 i
* i172.31.2.0/24      10.200.200.12          0   100      0 64998 i
* i                   10.200.200.11          0   100      0 64998 i
* i172.31.11.0/24     10.200.200.12          0   100      0 64999 i
* i                   10.200.200.11          0   100      0 64999 i
* i172.31.22.0/24     10.200.200.12          0   100      0 64999 i
* i                   10.200.200.11          0   100      0 64999 i
P1R3#
```

**Step 11**  Have the internal routers installed these BGP routes in their routing table?
Why or why not?

**Solution:**

The following output shows the IP routing table on the P1R3 router. The route to 10.254.0.0/24
is still not in the routing table, because synchronization is on, but the routes are not synchronized.

```
P1R3#show ip route
<output omitted>
Gateway of last resort is not set

     10.0.0.0/8 is variably subnetted, 8 subnets, 2 masks
R       10.200.200.11/32 [120/1] via 10.1.1.1, 00:00:13, Ethernet0
R       10.200.200.14/32 [120/1] via 10.1.3.4, 00:00:10, Serial0
R       10.200.200.12/32 [120/2] via 10.1.3.4, 00:00:10, Serial0
C       10.200.200.13/32 is directly connected, Loopback0
C       10.1.3.0/24 is directly connected, Serial0
R       10.1.2.0/24 [120/1] via 10.1.3.4, 00:00:10, Serial0
C       10.1.1.0/24 is directly connected, Ethernet0
R       10.1.0.0/24 [120/1] via 10.1.1.1, 00:00:14, Ethernet0
P1R3#
```

**Step 12**  The BGP synchronization rule is stopping BGP from installing the routes in
the routing table. What is the BGP synchronization rule?

**Solution:**

The BGP synchronization rule states that a BGP router should not use or advertise to an external
neighbor a route learned by IBGP, unless that route is local or is learned from the IGP.

**Step 13** Because the AS is running full-mesh IBGP, BGP synchronization can safely be turned off in all of the pod routers. Turn off synchronization.

**Solution:**

The following shows the required configuration on all of the pod 1 routers:

```
P1R1(config)#router bgp 65001
P1R1(config-router)#no synchronization
P1R2(config)#router bgp 65001
P1R2(config-router)#no synchronization
P1R3(config)#router bgp 65001
P1R3(config-router)#no synchronization
P1R4(config)#router bgp 65001
P1R4(config-router)#no synchronization
```

**Step 14** Look again at the routing tables on the internal routers. You should see the BGP route to 10.254.0.0/24.

**Solution:**

The following output is from the P1R3 router. The route to 10.254.0.0/24 is in the routing table with a next-hop address of 10.200.200.11.

```
P1R3#show ip route
<output omitted>
Gateway of last resort is not set

     172.31.0.0/24 is subnetted, 4 subnets
B       172.31.22.0 [200/0] via 10.200.200.11, 00:00:46
B       172.31.2.0 [200/0] via 10.200.200.11, 00:00:46
B       172.31.1.0 [200/0] via 10.200.200.11, 00:00:46
B       172.31.11.0 [200/0] via 10.200.200.11, 00:00:46
     10.0.0.0/8 is variably subnetted, 14 subnets, 2 masks
R       10.200.200.11/32 [120/1] via 10.1.1.1, 00:00:24, Ethernet0
R       10.200.200.14/32 [120/1] via 10.1.3.4, 00:00:16, Serial0
R       10.200.200.12/32 [120/2] via 10.1.3.4, 00:00:17, Serial0
C       10.200.200.13/32 is directly connected, Loopback0
B       10.2.0.0/24 [200/0] via 10.200.200.11, 00:00:47
C       10.1.3.0/24 is directly connected, Serial0
B       10.2.1.0/24 [200/0] via 10.200.200.11, 00:00:48
R       10.1.2.0/24 [120/1] via 10.1.3.4, 00:00:18, Serial0
B       10.97.97.0/24 [200/0] via 10.200.200.11, 00:00:48
B       10.2.2.0/24 [200/0] via 10.200.200.11, 00:00:48
C       10.1.1.0/24 is directly connected, Ethernet0
B       10.2.3.0/24 [200/0] via 10.200.200.11, 00:00:48
R       10.1.0.0/24 [120/1] via 10.1.1.1, 00:00:26, Ethernet0
B       10.254.0.0/24 [200/0] via 10.200.200.11, 00:00:48
P1R3#
```

**Step 15** From the internal routers, ping the TFTP server (10.254.0.254) to test connectivity.

**Solution:**

The following output from P1R3 and P1R4 shows that the routers can reach the TFTP server:

```
P1R3#ping 10.254.0.254
Type escape sequence to abort.
Sending 5, 100-byte ICMP Echos to 10.254.0.254, timeout is 2 seconds:
!!!!!
Success rate is 100 percent (5/5), round-trip min/avg/max = 32/35/44 ms
P1R3#

P1R4#ping 10.254.0.254
Type escape sequence to abort.
Sending 5, 100-byte ICMP Echos to 10.254.0.254, timeout is 2 seconds:
!!!!!
Success rate is 100 percent (5/5), round-trip min/avg/max = 32/47/96 ms
P1R4#
```

**Step 16** What is the path each internal router is using to reach the TFTP server?

**Solution:**

The following output from the pod 1 internal routers shows that P1R3 is using the path through 10.200.200.11 (P1R1) and that P1R4 is using the path through 10.200.200.12 (P1R2):

```
P1R3#show ip bgp
BGP table version is 18, local router ID is 10.200.200.13
Status codes: s suppressed, d damped, h history, * valid, > best, i - internal
Origin codes: i - IGP, e - EGP, ? - incomplete

   Network          Next Hop          Metric LocPrf Weight Path
* i10.1.0.0/24      10.200.200.12          0    100      0 i
*>i                 10.200.200.11          0    100      0 i
* i10.1.1.0/24      10.200.200.12          2    100      0 i
*>i                 10.200.200.11          0    100      0 i
* i10.1.2.0/24      10.200.200.11          2    100      0 i
*>i                 10.200.200.12          0    100      0 i
*>i10.1.3.0/24      10.200.200.11          1    100      0 i
* i                 10.200.200.12          1    100      0 i
* i10.2.0.0/24      10.200.200.12             100      0 64998 65002 i
*>i                 10.200.200.11             100      0 64998 65002 i
* i10.2.1.0/24      10.200.200.12             100      0 64998 65002 i
*>i                 10.200.200.11             100      0 64998 65002 i
* i10.2.2.0/24      10.200.200.12             100      0 64999 65002 i
*>i                 10.200.200.11             100      0 64999 65002 i
* i10.2.3.0/24      10.200.200.12             100      0 64999 65002 i
*>i                 10.200.200.11             100      0 64999 65002 i
* i10.97.97.0/24    10.200.200.12             100      0 64998 64997 i
*>i                 10.200.200.11             100      0 64998 64997 i
```

*continues*

```
* i10.254.0.0/24      10.200.200.12           0    100      0 64998 i
*>i                   10.200.200.11           0    100      0 64998 i
* i172.31.1.0/24      10.200.200.12           0    100      0 64998 i
*>i                   10.200.200.11           0    100      0 64998 i
* i172.31.2.0/24      10.200.200.12           0    100      0 64998 i
*>i                   10.200.200.11           0    100      0 64998 i
* i172.31.11.0/24     10.200.200.12           0    100      0 64999 i
*>i                   10.200.200.11           0    100      0 64999 i
* i172.31.22.0/24     10.200.200.12           0    100      0 64999 i
*>i                   10.200.200.11           0    100      0 64999 i
P1R3#
P1R4#show ip bgp
BGP table version is 19, local router ID is 10.200.200.14
Status codes: s suppressed, d damped, h history, * valid, > best, i - internal
Origin codes: i - IGP, e - EGP, ? - incomplete

   Network           Next Hop          Metric LocPrf Weight Path
*>i10.1.0.0/24       10.200.200.12          0    100      0 i
* i                  10.200.200.11          0    100      0 i
* i10.1.1.0/24       10.200.200.12          2    100      0 i
*>i                  10.200.200.11          0    100      0 i
*>i10.1.2.0/24       10.200.200.12          0    100      0 i
* i                  10.200.200.11          2    100      0 i
*>i10.1.3.0/24       10.200.200.12          1    100      0 i
* i                  10.200.200.11          1    100      0 i
*>i10.2.0.0/24       10.200.200.12               100      0 64998 65002 i
* i                  10.200.200.11               100      0 64998 65002 i
*>i10.2.1.0/24       10.200.200.12               100      0 64998 65002 i
* i                  10.200.200.11               100      0 64998 65002 i
*>i10.2.2.0/24       10.200.200.12               100      0 64999 65002 i
* i                  10.200.200.11               100      0 64999 65002 i
*>i10.2.3.0/24       10.200.200.12               100      0 64999 65002 i
* i                  10.200.200.11               100      0 64999 65002 i
*>i10.97.97.0/24     10.200.200.12               100      0 64998 64997 i
* i                  10.200.200.11               100      0 64998 64997 i
*>i10.254.0.0/24     10.200.200.12          0    100      0 64998 i
* i                  10.200.200.11          0    100      0 64998 i
*>i172.31.1.0/24     10.200.200.12          0    100      0 64998 i
* i                  10.200.200.11          0    100      0 64998 i
*>i172.31.2.0/24     10.200.200.12          0    100      0 64998 i
* i                  10.200.200.11          0    100      0 64998 i
*>i172.31.11.0/24    10.200.200.12          0    100      0 64999 i
* i                  10.200.200.11          0    100      0 64999 i
*>i172.31.22.0/24    10.200.200.12          0    100      0 64999 i
* i                  10.200.200.11          0    100      0 64999 i
P1R4#
```

# Exercise Verification

You have successfully completed this exercise if you have configured full-mesh IBGP within your pod, and your routing tables contain BGP routes to the networks advertised by the core.

# Review Questions

Answer the following questions, and then refer to Appendix G, "Answers to Review Questions," for the answers.

**1**  What is the difference between an IGP and an EGP?

**2**  What type of routing protocol is BGP?

**3**  A BGP router knows of three paths to a network and has chosen the best path. Can this BGP router advertise to its peer routers a route to that network other than the best path?

**4**  When is it appropriate to use BGP to connect to other autonomous systems?

**5**  When is it appropriate to use static routes rather than BGP to interconnect autonomous systems?

**6**  What protocol does BGP use as its transport protocol? What port number does BGP use?

**7**  How does BGP guarantee a loop-free AS path?

**8**  Any two routers that have formed a BGP connection can be referred to by what two terms?

**9**  Write a brief definition for each of the following:

— IBGP

— EBGP

— Well-known attribute

— Transitive attribute

— BGP synchronization

**10**  What tables are used by BGP?

**11**  What are the four BGP message types?

**12**  How is the BGP router ID selected?

**13**  What are the BGP states a router can be in with its neighbors?

**14**  What type of BGP attributes are the following?

— AS-path

— Next-hop

— Origin

— Local preference

— Atomic aggregate

— Aggregator

— Community

— Multiexit-discriminator

**15** When IBGP advertises an external update, where does the value for the next-hop attribute of an update come from?

**16** Describe the complication that an NBMA network can cause for an update's next-hop attribute.

**17** Complete the following table to answer these questions about three BGP attributes:

— In which order are the attributes preferred (1, 2, or 3)?

— For the attribute, is the highest or lowest value preferred?

— Which other routers, if any, is the attribute sent to?

| Attribute | Order Preferred In | Highest or Lowest Value Preferred? | Sent to Which Other Routers? |
|---|---|---|---|
| Local preference | | | |
| MED | | | |
| Weight | | | |

**18** What is the BGP split-horizon rule?

**19** When is it safe to turn off BGP synchronization?

**20** What does the **neighbor 10.1.1.1 ebgp-multihop** command do?

**21** Which commands are used to configure Routers A and B if Router A is to run BGP in AS 65000 and establish a neighbor relationship with Router B in AS 65001? The two routers should use their loopback 0 addresses to establish the BGP connection; Router A has loopback 0 address 10.1.1.1/24, and Router B has loopback 0 address 10.2.2.2/24.

**22** What command disables BGP synchronization?

**23** Which command would Router A in AS 65000 use to activate an IBGP session with Router B, 10.1.1.1, also in AS 65000?

**24** What is the difference between the BGP **neighbor** command and the BGP **network** command?

**25** What does the BGP command **network 198.1.1.1 mask 255.255.255.0** do?

**26** What does the **clear ip bgp 10.1.1.1 soft out** command do?

This chapter discusses some advanced features of Border Gateway Protocol (BGP). It covers the following topics:

- BGP Route Summarization
- Basic BGP Path Manipulation Using Route Maps
- Multihoming Design Options
- Redistribution with IGPs

# CHAPTER 9

# Advanced Border Gateway Protocol Configuration

After reading this chapter, you will be able to configure Border Gateway Protocol (BGP) route summarization and set the BGP local preference and multiexit-discriminator (MED) attributes. You will also be able to select the best implementation when using BGP to multihome to other autonomous systems.

## BGP Route Summarization

This section reviews classless interdomain routing (CIDR) and describes how BGP supports CIDR and summarization of addresses. Both the **network** and **aggregate-address** commands are described.

### CIDR and Aggregate Addresses

As discussed in Chapter 1, "Advanced IP Addressing," CIDR is a mechanism developed to help alleviate the problem of exhaustion of IP addresses and the growth of routing tables. The idea behind CIDR is that blocks of multiple addresses (for example, blocks of Class C address) can be combined, or aggregated, to create a larger classless set of IP addresses. These multiple addresses can then be summarized in routing tables, resulting in fewer route advertisements.

Earlier versions of BGP did not support CIDR; BGP-4 does. BGP-4 support includes the following:

- The BGP update message includes both the prefix and the prefix length. Previous versions included only the prefix; the length was assumed from the address class.

- Addresses can be aggregated when advertised by a BGP router.

- The autonomous system (AS)-path attribute can include a combined unordered list of all autonomous systems that all the aggregated routes have passed through. This combined list should be considered to ensure that the route is loop-free.

For example, in Figure 9-1, Router C is advertising network 192.168.2.0/24, and Router D is advertising network 192.168.1.0/24. Router A could pass those advertisements to Router B; however, Router A could reduce the size of the routing tables by aggregating the two routes into one—for example, 192.168.0.0/16.

**Figure 9-1** *Using CIDR with BGP*

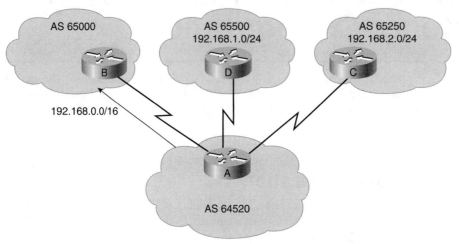

---

**NOTE**    In Figure 9-1, the aggregate route that Router A is sending covers more than the two routes from Routers C and D. The example assumes that Router A also has jurisdiction over all the other routes covered by this aggregate route.

---

Two BGP attributes are related to aggregate addressing:

- **Atomic aggregate**—A well-known discretionary attribute that informs the neighbor AS that the originating router has aggregated the routes.

- **Aggregator**—An optional transitive attribute that specifies the BGP router ID and AS number of the router that performed the route aggregation.

---

**Key Point: Aggregate Routes**

By default, the aggregate route is advertised as coming from the AS that did the aggregation and has the atomic aggregate attribute set to show that information might be missing. The AS numbers from the nonaggregated routes are not listed.

---

The router can be configured to include the unordered list of all autonomous systems contained in all paths that are being summarized.

In Figure 9-1, by default the aggregated route 192.168.0.0/16 has an AS path attribute of (64520). If Router A were configured to include the combined unordered list, it would include the set {65250 65500} as well as (64520) in the AS path attribute.

# Network Boundary Summarization

BGP was originally not intended to be used to advertise subnets. Its intended purpose was to advertise classful, or better, networks. Better in this case means that BGP can summarize blocks of individual classful networks into a few large blocks that represent the same amount of address space as the individual network blocks—in other words, CIDR blocks. For example, 32 contiguous Class C networks can be advertised individually as 32 separate entries, with each having a network mask of /24. Or it might be possible to announce these same networks as a single entry with a /19 mask.

The Routing Information Protocol version 1 (RIPv1), Routing Information Protocol version 2 (RIPv2), Interior Gateway Routing Protocol (IGRP), and Enhanced IGRP (EIGRP) protocols all summarize routes on the classful network boundary by default. In contrast, Open Shortest Path First (OSPF) and Intermediate System-to-Intermediate System (IS-IS) do not summarize by default, but summarization can be configured manually.

Autosummarization can be turned off for RIPv2 and EIGRP. For example, if you are assigned a portion of a Class A, B, or C address, summarization needs to be turned off, or you risk claiming ownership of the whole Class A, B, or C address.

BGP works differently than the other protocols. As discussed in Chapter 8, "Configuring Basic Border Gateway Protocol," the **network** *network-number* [**mask** *network-mask*] router configuration command for BGP permits BGP to advertise a network if it is present in the IP routing table. This command allows classless prefixes; the router can advertise individual subnets, networks, or supernets. The default mask is the classful mask and results in only the classful network number being announced. Note that at least one subnet of the specified major network must be present in the IP routing table for BGP to start announcing the classful network. However, if you specify the *network-mask*, an exact match to the network (both address and mask) must exist in the routing table for the network to be advertised.

The BGP **auto-summary** command determines how BGP handles redistributed routes. The **no auto-summary** router configuration command turns off BGP autosummarization. When it is enabled (with **auto-summary**), all redistributed subnets are summarized to their classful boundaries in the BGP table. When it is disabled (with **no auto-summary**), all redistributed subnets are present in their original form in the BGP table. For example, if an ISP assigns a network of 64.100.50.0/24 to an AS, and that AS then uses the **redistribute connected** command to introduce this network into BGP, BGP announces that the AS owns 64.0.0.0/8 if the **auto-summary** command is on. To the Internet, this AS owns all the Class A network 64.0.0.0/8, which is not true. Other organizations that own a portion of the 64.0.0.0 /8 address space might have connectivity problems because of this AS claiming ownership for the whole block of addresses. This outcome is undesirable if the AS does not own the entire address space. Using the **network 64.100.50.0 mask 255.255.255.0** command instead of the **redistributed connected** command ensures that this assigned network is announced correctly.

---

**CAUTION**　　In Cisco IOS Release 12.2(8)T, the default behavior of the **auto-summary** command was changed to disabled. In other words:

- Before 12.2(8)T, the default is **auto-summary**.

- Starting in 12.2(8)T, the default is **no auto-summary**.

---

# BGP Route Summarization Using the network Command

The **network** command with the **mask** option installs a prefix into the BGP table when a matching Interior Gateway Protocol (IGP) prefix exists in the IP routing table. If the IGP prefix flaps (the route is removed from routing table), the BGP prefix also flaps.

To advertise a simple classful network number, use the **network** *network-number* command without the **mask** option. To advertise an aggregate of prefixes that originate in this AS, use the **network** *network-number* [**mask** *network-mask*] router configuration command (but remember that the prefix must exactly match [both address and mask] an entry in the IP routing table for the network to be advertised).

When BGP has a **network** command for a classful address and it has at least one subnet of that classful address space in its routing table, it announces the classful network and not the subnet. For example, if a BGP router has network 172.16.22.0/24 in the routing table as a directly connected network, and a BGP **network 172.16.0.0** command, BGP announces the 172.16.0.0/16 network to all neighbors. If 172.16.22.0 is the only subnet for this network in the routing table and it becomes unavailable, BGP will withdraw 172.16.0.0/16 from all neighbors. If instead the command **network 172.16.22.0 mask 255.255.255.0** is used, BGP will announce 172.16.22.0/24 and not 172.16.0.0/16.

---

### Key Point: The network Command

The **network** command requires that there be an exact match in the routing table for the prefix or mask that is specified. This exact match can be accomplished by using a static route with a null0 interface, or it might already exist in the routing table, such as because of the IGP performing the summarization.

---

## Cautions When Using the **network** Command for Summarization

The **network** command tells BGP what to advertise but not how to advertise it. When using the BGP **network** command, the network number specified must also be in the IP routing table before BGP can announce it.

For example, consider Router C in Figure 9-2; it has the group of addresses 192.168.24.0/24, 192.168.25.0/24, 192.168.26.0/24, and 192.168.27.0/24 already in its routing table. The configuration in Example 9-1 is put on Router C.

**Figure 9-2**    *BGP Network for Summarization Examples*

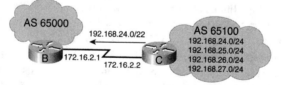

**Example 9-1**    *Sample BGP Configuration for Router C in Figure 9-2*

```
router bgp 65100
  network 192.168.24.0
  network 192.168.25.0
  network 192.168.26.0
  network 192.168.27.0
  neighbor 172.16.2.1 remote-as 65000
```

Each of the four Class C networks is announced because they already exist in the routing table. These networks can be summarized with the following command: **network 192.168.24.0 mask 255.255.252.0**.

However, the 192.168.24.0/22 route is not announced because that route is not in the routing table. If the local routing protocol supports summarization (such as EIGRP or OSPF), and summarization is performed using the local interior routing protocol command, BGP announces that route. If route summarization is not performed with the local interior routing protocol, and BGP is required to announce this route, a static route should be created that allows this network to be installed in the routing table. The static route should point to the null 0 interface (using the command **ip route 192.168.24.0 255.255.252.0 null0**). Remember that 192.168.24.0/24, 192.168.25.0/24, 192.168.26.0/24, and 192.168.27.0/24 addresses are already in the routing table. This command creates an additional entry of 192.168.24.0/22 as a static route to null 0.

If a network, such as 192.168.25.0/24, is unreachable, and packets arrive for 192.168.25.1, the destination address is compared to the current entries in the routing table using the longest-match criteria. Because 192.168.25.0/24 no longer exists in the routing table, the best match is 192.168.24.0/22, which points to the null 0 interface. The packet is sent to the null 0 interface, and an Internet Control Message Protocol (ICMP) unreachable message is generated and sent to the packet's originator. Dropping these packets prevents traffic from using up bandwidth following a default route that is either deeper into your AS or (in a worst-case scenario) back out to the ISP (when the ISP would route it back to the AS because of the summarized route advertised to the ISP, causing a routing loop).

In this example, five networks are announced using **network** commands: the four Class C plus the summary route. The purpose of summarization is to reduce the advertisement's size, as well as the size of the Internet routing table. Announcing these more specific networks along with the summarized route actually increases the table's size.

Example 9-2 shows a more efficient configuration. A single entry represents all four networks, and a static route to null0 installs the summarized route in the IP routing table so that BGP can find a match. The AS 65100 router advertises a summarized route for the four Class C addresses (192.168.24.0/24, 192.168.25.0/24, 192.168.26.0/24, and 192.168.27.0/24) assigned to the AS with the **network** command. For this new **network** command (192.168.24.0/22) to be advertised, it must first appear in the local routing table. Because only the more specific networks exist in the IP routing table, a static route pointing to null 0 has been created to allow BGP to announce this network (192.168.24.0/22) to AS 65000.

**Example 9-2**   *More Efficient BGP Configuration for Router C in Figure 9-2*

```
router bgp 65100
  network 192.168.24.0 mask 255.255.252.0
  neighbor 172.16.2.1 remote-as 65000
ip route 192.168.24.0 255.255.252.0 null 0
```

The **network** command was not designed to perform summarization by itself; the **aggregate-address** command, described in the next section, was designed for summarization.

## Creating a Summary Address in the BGP Table Using the aggregate-address Command

The **aggregate-address** *ip-address mask* [**summary-only**] [**as-set**] router configuration command is used to create an aggregate, or summary, entry in the BGP table, as described in Table 9-1.

**Table 9-1**    **aggregate-address** *Command Description*

| Parameter | Description |
|---|---|
| *ip-address* | Identifies the aggregate address to be created. |
| *mask* | Identifies the mask of the aggregate address to be created. |
| **summary-only** | (Optional) Causes the router to advertise only the aggregated route. The default is to advertise both the aggregate and the more specific routes. |
| **as-set** | (Optional) Generates AS path information with the aggregate route to include all the AS numbers listed in all the paths of the more specific routes. The default for the aggregate route is to list only the AS number of the router that generated the aggregate route. |

---

### Key Point: aggregate-address Versus network Commands

The **aggregate-address** command aggregates only networks that are already in the *BGP table*. This is different from the requirement for advertising summaries with the BGP **network** command, in which case the network must exist in the *IP routing table*.

---

When you use this command without the **as-set** keyword, the aggregate route is advertised as coming from your autonomous system, and the atomic aggregate attribute is set to show that information might be missing. The atomic aggregate attribute is set unless you specify the **as-set** keyword.

Without the **summary-only** keyword, the router still advertises the individual networks. This can be useful for redundant ISP links. For example, if one ISP is advertising only summaries, and the other is advertising a summary plus the more specific routes, the more specific routes are followed. However, if the ISP advertising the more specific routes becomes inaccessible, the other ISP advertising only the summary is followed.

When the **aggregate-address** command is used, a BGP route to null0 is automatically installed in the IP routing table for the summarized route.

If any route already in the BGP table is within the range indicated by the **aggregate-address**, the summary route is inserted into the BGP table and is advertised to other routers. This process creates more information in the BGP table. To get any benefits from the aggregation, the more specific routes covered by the route summary should be suppressed using the **summary-only** option. When the more specific routes are suppressed, they are still present in the BGP table of the router doing the aggregation. However, because the routes are marked as suppressed, they are never advertised to any other router.

For BGP to announce a summary route using the **aggregate-address** command, at least one of the more specific routes must be in the BGP table; this is usually a result of having **network** commands for those routes.

If you use only the **summary-only** keyword on the **aggregate-address** command, the summary route is advertised, and the path indicates only the AS that is summarized (all other path information is missing). If you use only the **as-set** keyword on the **aggregate-address** command, the set of AS numbers is included in the path information (and the command with the **summary-only** keyword is deleted if it existed). However, you may use *both* keywords on one command; this causes only the summary address to be sent and all the autonomous systems to be listed in the path information.

Figure 9-3 illustrates a sample network (it is the same network as in Figure 9-2, repeated here for your convenience). It shows the configuration of Router C using the **aggregate-address** command.

**Figure 9-3** *BGP Network for Summarization Examples*

**Example 9-3** *Configuration for Router C in Figure 9-3 Using the **aggregate-address** Command*

```
router bgp 65100
  network 192.168.24.0
  network 192.168.25.0
  network 192.168.26.0
  network 192.168.27.0
  neighbor 172.16.2.1 remote-as 65000
  aggregate-address 192.168.24.0 255.255.252.0 summary-only
```

This configuration on Router C shows the following:

- **router bgp 65100**—Configures a BGP process for AS 65100.

- **network** commands—Configure BGP to advertise the four Class C networks in AS 65100.

- **neighbor 172.16.2.1 remote-as 65000**—Specifies the router at this address (Router B) as a neighbor in AS 65000. This part of the configuration describes *where* to send the advertisements.

- **aggregate-address 192.168.24.0 255.255.252.0 summary-only**—Specifies the aggregate route to be created but suppresses advertisements of more specific routes to all neighbors. This part of the configuration describes *how* to advertise. Without the **summary-only** option, the new summarized route would be advertised along with the more specific routes. In this example, though, Router B receives only one route (192.168.24.0/22) from Router C. The **aggregate-address** command tells the BGP process to perform route summarization and automatically installs the null route representing the new summarized route.

---

### Key Point: BGP Commands

The following summarizes the differences between the main BGP commands:

— The **network** command tells BGP *what* to advertise.

— The **neighbor** command tells BGP *where* to advertise.

— The **aggregate-address** command tells BGP *how* to advertise the networks.

---

The **aggregate-address** command does not replace the **network** command; at least one of the more specific routes to be summarized must be in the BGP table. In some situations, the more specific routes are injected into the BGP table by other routers, and the aggregation is done in another router or even in another AS. This approach is called *proxy aggregation*. In this case, the aggregation router needs only the proper **aggregate-address** command, not the **network** commands, to advertise the more specific routes.

The **show ip bgp** command provides information about route summarization and displays the local router ID, the networks recognized by the BGP process, the accessibility to remote networks, and AS path information. In Example 9-4, notice the s in the first column for the lower four networks. These networks are being suppressed. They were learned from a **network** command on this router; the next-hop address is 0.0.0.0, which indicates that this router created these entries in BGP. Notice that this router also created the summarized route 192.168.24.0/22 in BGP (this route also has a next hop of 0.0.0.0, indicating that the router created it). The more specific routes are suppressed, and only the summarized route is announced.

**Example 9-4**    **show ip bgp** *Command Output with Routes Suppressed*

```
RouterC#show ip bgp
BGP table version is 28, local router ID is 172.16.2.1
Status codes: s = suppressed, * = valid, > = best, and i = internal
Origin codes : i = IGP, e = EGP, and ? = incomplete
Network             Next Hop         Metric   LocPrf     Weight     Path
*>192.168.24.0/22   0.0.0.0          0                   32768      i
s>192.168.24.0      0.0.0.0          0                   32768      i
s>192.168.25.0      0.0.0.0          0                   32768      i
s>192.168.26.0      0.0.0.0          0                   32768      i
s>192.168.27.0      0.0.0.0          0                   32768      i
```

# Basic BGP Path Manipulation Using Route Maps

Manipulating path selection criteria can affect the inbound and outbound traffic policies of an AS. This section discusses path manipulation and how to configure an AS using route maps to manipulate the BGP local preference and MED attributes.

## BGP Path Manipulation

Unlike local routing protocols, BGP was never designed to choose the quickest path. It was designed to manipulate traffic flow to maximize or minimize bandwidth use. Figure 9-4 demonstrates a common situation that can result when using BGP without any policy manipulation.

**Figure 9-4**  *BGP Network Without Policy Manipulation*

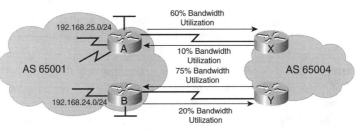

Using default settings for path selection in BGP might cause uneven use of bandwidth. In Figure 9-4, Router A in AS 65001 is using 60 percent of its outbound bandwidth to Router X in 65004, but Router B is using only 20 percent of its outbound bandwidth. If this utilization is acceptable to the administrator, no manipulation is needed. But if the load averages 60 percent and has temporary bursts above 100 percent of the bandwidth, this situation will cause lost packets, higher latency, and higher CPU usage because of the number of packets being routed. When another link to the same locations exists and is not heavily used, it makes sense to divert some of the traffic to the other path. To change outbound path selection from AS 65001, the local preference attribute must be manipulated. Recall from Chapter 8 that a higher local preference is preferred.

To determine which path to manipulate, the administrator performs a traffic analysis on Internet-bound traffic by examining the most heavily visited addresses, web pages, or domain names. This information can usually be found by examining network management records or firewall accounting information.

Assume that in Figure 9-4, 35 percent of all traffic from AS 65001 has been heading to www.cisco.com. The administrator can obtain Cisco's address or AS number by performing a reverse Domain Name System (DNS) lookup or by going to www.arin.net (the American Registry for Internet Numbers [ARIN]) and looking up the AS number of Cisco Systems or the address space assigned to the company. After this information has been determined, the administrator can use route maps to change the local preference to manipulate path selection for the Cisco network. Using a route map, Router B can announce, to all routers within AS 65001, all networks associated with the Cisco Systems AS that have a higher local preference than Router A announces for those networks. Other routers in AS 65001 running BGP prefer the routes with the highest local preference, so all traffic destined for the Cisco Systems AS exits AS 65001 via Router B. The outbound load for Router B increases from its previous load of 20 percent to 35 percent to account for the extra traffic destined for Cisco-owned networks. The outbound load for Router A, which was originally 60 percent, should decrease. This change will make the outbound load on both links more balanced.

Just as there was a loading issue outbound from AS 65001, there can be a similar problem inbound. For example, if the inbound load to Router B has a much higher utilization than the inbound load to Router A, the BGP MED attribute can be used to manipulate how traffic enters AS 65001. Router A in AS 65001 can announce a lower MED for network 192.168.25.0/24 to AS 65004 than Router B announces. This MED recommends to the next AS how to enter AS 65001. However, MED is not considered until later in the BGP path-selection process than local preference. Therefore, if AS 65004 prefers to leave its AS via Router Y (to Router B in AS 65001), Router Y should be configured to announce a higher local preference to the BGP routers in AS 65004 for network 192.168.25.0/24 than Router X announces. The local preference that Routers X and Y advertise to other BGP routers in AS 65004 is evaluated before the MED coming from Routers A and B. MED is considered a *recommendation*, because the receiving AS can override it by manipulating another variable that is considered before the MED is evaluated.

As another example using Figure 9-4, assume that 55 percent of all traffic is going to the 192.168.25.0/24 subnet (on Router A). The inbound utilization to Router A is averaging only 10 percent, but the inbound utilization to Router B is averaging 75 percent. The problem is that if the inbound load for Router B spikes to more than 100 percent and causes the link to flap, all the sessions crossing that link could be lost. For example, if these sessions were purchases being made on AS 65001 web servers, revenue would be lost, which is something administrators want to avoid. If AS 65001 were set to prefer to have all traffic that is going to 192.168.25.0/24 enter through Router A, the load inbound on Router A should increase, and the load inbound on Router B should decrease.

If load averages less than 50 percent for an outbound or inbound case, path manipulation might not be needed. However, as soon as a link starts to spike up to its capacity for an extended period of time, either more bandwidth is needed or path manipulation should be considered.

## The Route Selection Decision Process

An AS rarely implements BGP with only one External Border Gateway Protocol (EBGP) connection, so generally multiple paths exist for each network in the BGP forwarding database.

**NOTE**   If you are running BGP in a network with only one EBGP connection, it is loop-free. If it is synchronized with the IGP for Internal Border Gateway Protocol (IBGP) connections, and the next hop can be reached, the path is submitted to the IP routing table. Because there is only path, there is no benefit to manipulating its attributes.

Recall from the "The Route Selection Decision Process" section in Chapter 8 that, when faced with multiple routes to the same destination, BGP chooses the best route for routing traffic toward the destination. A path is not considered if it is internal, synchronization is on, and the route is not synchronized (in other words, the route is not in the IGP routing table), or if the path's next-hop address cannot be reached. To choose the best route, BGP on a Cisco router considers only synchronized routes with no AS loops and a valid next-hop address and then uses the following process:

**Step 1** Prefer the route with the highest weight. (Recall that the weight is Cisco-proprietary and is local to the router only.)

**Step 2** If multiple routes have the same weight, prefer the route with the highest local preference. (Recall that the local preference is used within an AS.)

**Step 3** If multiple routes have the same local preference, prefer the route that was originated by the local router. (A locally originated route has a next hop of 0.0.0.0 in the BGP table.)

**Step 4** If none of the routes were originated by the local router, prefer the route with the shortest AS path.

**Step 5** If the AS path length is the same, prefer the lowest origin code (IGP < EGP < incomplete).

**Step 6** If all origin codes are the same, prefer the path with the lowest MED. (Recall that the MED is sent from other autonomous systems.)

The MED comparison is done only if the neighboring autonomous system is the same for all routes considered, unless the **bgp always-comparemed** command is enabled.

**Step 7** If the routes have the same MED, prefer external paths (EBGP) over internal paths (IBGP).

**Step 8** If synchronization is disabled and only internal paths remain, prefer the path through the closest IGP neighbor. This means that the router prefers the shortest internal path within the AS to reach the destination (the shortest path to the BGP next hop).

**Step 9** For EBGP paths, select the oldest route to minimize the effect of routes going up and down (flapping).

**Step 10** Prefer the route with the lowest neighbor BGP router ID value.

**Step 11** If the BGP router IDs are the same, prefer the route with the lowest neighbor IP address.

Only the best path is put in the routing table and is propagated to the router's BGP neighbors.

| NOTE | The route selection decision process summarized here does not cover all cases, but it is sufficient for a basic understanding of how BGP selects routes. |
| --- | --- |
| | Further information on the BGP path-selection process can be found in *BGP Best Path Selection Algorithm,* available at www.cisco.com/en/US/tech/tk365/tk80/technologies_tech_note09186a0080094431.shtml. |

Without route manipulation, the most common reason for path selection is Step 4, prefer the shortest AS path.

Step 1 looks at weight, which by default is set to 0 for routes that were not originated by this router.

Step 2 compares local preference, which by default is set to 100 for all networks. Both these steps have an effect only if the network administrator configures the weight or local preference to a nondefault value.

Step 3 looks at networks that are owned by this AS. If one of the routes is injected into the BGP table by the local router, the local router prefers it to any routes received from other BGP routers.

Step 4 selects the path that has the fewest autonomous systems to cross. This is the most common reason a path is selected in BGP. If a network administrator does not like the path with the fewest autonomous systems, he or she needs to manipulate weight or local preference to change which outbound path BGP chooses.

Step 5 looks at how a network was introduced into BGP. This introduction is usually either with network statements (i for an origin code) or through redistribution (? for an origin code).

Step 6 looks at MED to judge where the neighbor AS wants this AS to send packets for a given network. Cisco sets the MED to 0 by default on any route advertised to an external neighbor; therefore, MED does not participate in path selection unless the network administrator of the neighbor AS manipulates the paths using MED.

If multiple paths have the same number of autonomous systems to traverse, the second most common decision point is Step 7, which states that an externally learned path from an EBGP neighbor is preferred over a path learned from an IBGP neighbor. A router in an AS prefers to use the ISP's bandwidth to reach a network rather than using internal bandwidth to reach an IBGP neighbor on the other side of its own AS.

If the AS path is equal and the router in an AS has no EBGP neighbors for that network (only IBGP neighbors), it makes sense to take the quickest path to the nearest exit point. Step 8 looks for the closest IBGP neighbor; the IGP metric determines what closest means (for example, RIP uses hop count, and OSPF uses the least cost based on bandwidth).

If the AS path is equal and the costs via all IBGP neighbors are equal, or if all neighbors for this network are EBGP, the oldest path is the next common reason for selecting one path over another. EBGP neighbors rarely establish sessions at the exact same time. One session is likely older than another, so the paths through that older neighbor are considered more stable, because they have been up longer.

If all these criteria are equal, the next most common decision is to take the neighbor with the lowest BGP router ID, which is Step 10.

If the BGP router IDs are the same (for example, if the paths are to the same BGP router), Step 11 states that the route with the lowest neighbor IP address is used.

# Setting Local Preference

Local preference is used only within an AS between IBGP speakers to determine the best path to leave the AS to reach an outside network. The local preference is set to 100 by default; higher values are preferred. (If for some reason an EBGP neighbor did receive a local preference value [such as because of faulty software], the EBGP neighbor ignores it.)

## Changing Local Preference for All Routes

The **bgp default local-preference** *value* router configuration command changes the default local preference to the value specified for all external BGP routes received by this router; this local preference value is advertised to the IBGP neighbors with the routes. The value can be set to a number between 0 and 4294967295.

Manipulating the default local preference can have an immediate and dramatic effect on traffic flow leaving an AS. Before making any changes to manipulate paths, the network administrator should perform a thorough traffic analysis to understand the effects of the change. For example, the configurations for Routers A and B in Figure 9-5 are shown in Examples 9-5 and 9-6, respectively. In this network, the administrator changed the default local preference for all routes on Router B to 500 and on Router A to 200. All BGP routers in AS 65001 send all traffic destined for the Internet to Router B, causing its outbound utilization to be much higher and the utilization out Router A to be reduced to a minimal amount. This change is probably not what the network administrator intended. Instead, the network administrator should use route maps to set only certain networks to have a higher local preference through Router B to decrease some of the original outbound load that was being sent out Router A.

**Figure 9-5** *Setting a Default Local Preference for All Routes*

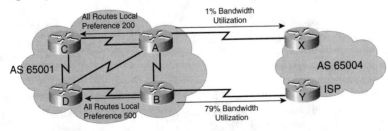

**Example 9-5**  *Configuration for Router A in Figure 9-5*

```
router bgp 65001
  bgp default local-preference 200
```

**Example 9-6**  *Configuration for Router B in Figure 9-5*

```
router bgp 65001
  bgp default local-preference 500
```

## Local Preference Example

Figure 9-6 illustrates a sample network running BGP. This network initially has no commands configured to change the local preference. Neither Router A or B in this example uses the **neighbor next-hop-self** command.

**Figure 9-6**  *Network for Local Preference Examples*

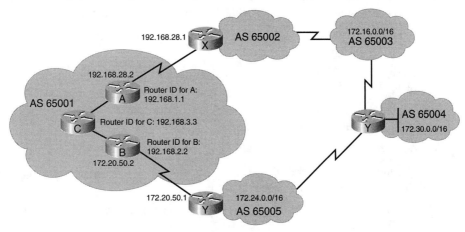

Example 9-7 illustrates the BGP forwarding table on Router C in Figure 9-6, showing only the networks of interest to this example:

- 172.16.0.0 in AS 65003

- 172.24.0.0 in AS 65005

- 172.30.0.0 in AS 65004

**Example 9-7**  *BGP Table for Router C in Figure 9-6 Without Path Manipulation*

```
RouterC#show ip bgp
BGP table version is 7, local router ID is 192.168.3.3
Status codes: s suppressed, d damped, h history, * valid, > best, i - internal
Origin codes: i - IGP, e - EGP, ? - incomplete
```

*continues*

**Example 9-7** *BGP Table for Router C in Figure 9-6 Without Path Manipulation (Continued)*

```
    Network          Next Hop      Metric LocPrf Weight Path
 * i172.16.0.0       172.20.50.1          100       0 65005 65004 65003 i
 *>i                 192.168.28.1         100       0 65002 65003 i
 *>i172.24.0.0       172.20.50.1          100       0 65005 i
 * i                 192.168.28.1         100       0 65002 65003 65004 65005 i
 *>i172.30.0.0       172.20.50.1          100       0 65005 65004 i
 * i                 192.168.28.1         100       0 65002 65003 65004i
```

The best path is indicated with a > in the second column of the output.

Each network has two paths that are loop-free and synchronization-disabled and that have a valid next-hop address (that can be reached from Router C). All routes have a weight of 0 and a default local preference of 100, so Steps 1 and 2 in the BGP path-selection process do not select the best route.

This router does not originate any of the routes (Step 3), so the process moves to Step 4, and BGP uses the shortest AS path to select the best routes as follows:

- For network 172.16.0.0, the shortest AS path of two autonomous systems (65002 65003) is through the next hop of 192.168.28.1.

- For network 172.24.0.0, the shortest AS path of one AS (65005) is through the next hop of 172.20.50.1.

- For network 172.30.0.0, the shortest AS path of two autonomous systems (65005 65004) is through the next hop of 172.20.50.1.

A traffic analysis reveals the following:

- The link going through Router B to 172.20.50.1 is heavily used, and the link through Router A to 192.168.28.1 is hardly used at all.

- The three largest volume destination networks on the Internet from AS 65001 are 172.30.0.0, 172.24.0.0, and 172.16.0.0.

- 30 percent of all Internet traffic is going to network 172.24.0.0 (via Router B), 20 percent is going to network 172.30.0.0 (via Router B), and 10 percent is going to network 172.16.0.0 (via Router A). Therefore, only 10 percent of all traffic is using the link out Router A to 192.168.28.1, and 50 percent of all traffic is using the link out Router B to 172.20.50.1.

The network administrator has decided to divert traffic to network 172.30.0.0 and send it out Router A to the next hop of 192.168.28.1 so that the loading between Routers A and B is more balanced.

## Changing Local Preference Using Route Maps

A route map is added to Router A in Figure 9-6, as shown in the BGP configuration in Example 9-8. The route map alters the network 172.30.0.0 BGP update from Router X (192.168.28.1) to have a high local preference value of 400 so that it will be more preferred.

**Example 9-8** *BGP Configuration for Router A in Figure 9-6 with a Route Map*

```
router bgp 65001
  neighbor 192.168.2.2 remote-as 65001
  neighbor 192.168.3.3 remote-as 65001
  neighbor 192.168.2.2 remote-as 65001 update-source loopback0
  neighbor 192.168.3.3 remote-as 65001 update-source loopback0
  neighbor 192.168.28.1 remote-as 65002
  neighbor 192.168.28.1 route-map local_pref in
!
route-map local_pref permit 10
  match ip address 65
  set local-preference 400
!
route-map local_pref permit 20
!
access-list 65 permit 172.30.0.0 0.0.255.255
```

The first line of the route map is a **permit** statement with a sequence number of 10 for a route map called local_pref; this defines the first **route-map** statement. The match condition for this statement checks all networks that are permitted by access list 65. Access list 65 permits all networks that start with the first two octets of 172.30.0.0; the route map sets these networks to a local preference of 400.

The second statement in the route map is a **permit** statement with a sequence number of 20 for the route map called local_pref, but it does not have any **match** or **set** statements. This statement is similar to a **permit any** statement in an access list. Because there are no match conditions for the remaining networks, they are all permitted with their current settings. In this case, the local preference for networks 172.16.0.0 and 172.24.0.0 stays set at the default of 100. The sequence number 20 (rather than 11) is chosen for the second statement in case other policies have to be implemented later before this **permit any** statement.

This route map is linked to neighbor 192.168.28.1 as an inbound route map. Therefore, as Router A receives updates from 192.168.28.1, it processes them through the local_pref route map and sets the local preference accordingly as the networks are placed in Router A's BGP forwarding table.

Example 9-9 illustrates the BGP table on Router C in Figure 9-6, after the route map has been applied on Router A and the BGP sessions have been reset. Router C learns about the new local preference value (400) coming from Router A for network 172.30.0.0. The only difference in this table compared to the original in Example 9-7 is that the best route to network 172.30.0.0 is now through 192.168.28.1 because its local preference of 400 is higher than the local preference of 100 for the next hop of 172.20.50.1. The AS path through 172.20.50.1 is still shorter than the path through 192.168.28.1, but AS path length is not evaluated until Step 4, whereas local preference was examined in Step 2. Therefore, the higher local preference path was chosen as the best path.

**Example 9-9** *BGP Table for Router C in Figure 9-6 with a Route Map for Local Preference*

```
RouterC#show ip bgp
BGP table version is 7, local router ID is 192.168.3.3
Status codes: s suppressed, d damped, h history, * valid, > best, i - internal
```

*continues*

**Example 9-9** *BGP Table for Router C in Figure 9-6 with a Route Map for Local Preference (Continued)*

```
Origin codes: i - IGP, e - EGP, ? - incomplete
   Network          Next Hop        Metric LocPrf Weight Path
* i172.16.0.0       172.20.50.1        100       0 65005 65004 65003 i
*>i                 192.168.28.1       100       0 65002 65003 i
*>i172.24.0.0       172.20.50.1        100       0 65005 i
* i                 192.168.28.1       100       0 65002 65003 65004 65005 i
* i172.30.0.0       172.20.50.1        100       0 65005 65004 i
*>i                 192.168.28.1       400       0 65002 65003 65004i
```

# Setting the MED with Route Maps

MED is used to decide how to enter an AS when multiple paths exist between two autonomous systems and one AS is trying to influence the incoming path from the other AS. Because MED is evaluated late in the BGP path-selection process (Step 6), it usually has no influence on the process. For example, an AS receiving a MED for a route can change its local preference on how to leave the AS to override what the other AS is advertising with its MED value.

When comparing MED values for the same destination network in the BGP path-selection process, the lowest MED value is preferred.

The MED is exchanged between autonomous systems. The MED is carried into an AS and is used there but is not passed on to the next AS. When the same update is passed on to another AS, the MED is removed from the update.

---

**NOTE**    When an EBGP router receives an update without a MED, it must interpret what that means. BGP routers running Cisco IOS software treat a route without the MED attribute as having a MED of 0, making it the most preferred. The IETF says a missing MED should be treated as an infinite value, making a route lacking the MED variable the least preferred. Use the **bgp bestpath med missing-as-worst** router configuration command to configure a Cisco IOS router to conform to the IETF standard. With this command, routes without the MED attribute are treated as having a MED of $2^{32} - 2 = 4,294,967,294$.

---

## Changing the MED for All Routes

The default MED value for each network an AS owns and advertises to an EBGP neighbor is set to 0. To change this value, use the **default-metric** *number* router configuration command. The *number* parameter is the MED value.

Manipulating the default MED value can have an immediate and dramatic effect on traffic flow entering your AS. Before making any changes to manipulate the path, you should perform a thorough traffic analysis to ensure that you understand the effects of the change.

For example, the configurations of Routers A and B in Figure 9-7 are shown in Examples 9-10 and 9-11, respectively. The network administrator in AS 65001 tries to manipulate how

AS 65004 chooses its path to reach routes in AS 65001. By changing the default metric under the BGP process on Router A to 1001, Router A advertises a MED of 1001 for all routes to Router X. Router X then informs all the other routers in AS 65004 of the MED through Router X to reach networks originating in AS 65001. A similar event happens on Router B, but Router B advertises a MED of 99 for all routes to Router Y. All routers in AS 65004 see a MED of 1001 through the next hop of Router A and a MED of 99 through the next hop of Router B to reach networks in AS 65001. (The **next-hop self** command is not used on Routers X and Y.) If AS 65004 has no overriding policy, all routers in AS 65004 choose to exit their AS through Router Y to reach the networks in AS 65001; this traffic goes through Router B. This selection causes Router A's inbound bandwidth utilization to decrease to almost nothing except for BGP routing updates, and it causes the inbound utilization on Router B to increase and account for all returning packets from AS 65004 to AS 65001.

**Figure 9-7**    *Changing the Default MED for All Routes*

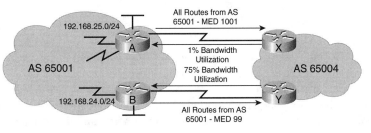

**Example 9-10** *BGP Configuration for Router A in Figure 9-7*

```
router bgp 65001
  default-metric 1001
```

**Example 9-11** *BGP Configuration for Router B in Figure 9-7*

```
router bgp 65001
  default-metric 99
```

This situation is probably not what the network administrator intended. Instead, to load-share the inbound traffic to AS 65001, the AS 65001 network administrator should configure some networks to have a lower MED through Router B and other networks to have a lower MED through Router A. Route maps should be used to set the appropriate MED values for various networks.

## Changing the MED Using Route Maps

The network shown in Figure 9-8 is used as an example to demonstrate how to manipulate inbound traffic using route maps to change the BGP MED attribute. The intention of these route maps is to designate Router A as the preferred entry point to reach networks 192.168.25.0/24 and 192.168.26.0/24 and Router B as the preferred entry point to reach network 192.168.24.0/24. The other networks should still be reachable through each router in case of a link or router failure.

**Figure 9-8**   *Network for MED Examples*

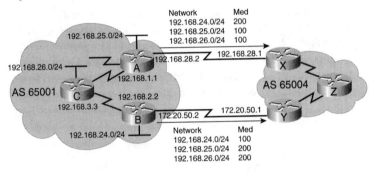

MED is set outbound when advertising to an EBGP neighbor. In the configuration for Router A shown in Example 9-12, a route map named med_65004 is linked to neighbor 192.168.28.1 (Router X) as an outbound route map. When Router A sends an update to neighbor 192.168.28.1, it processes the outbound update through route map med_65004 and changes any values specified in a **set** command as long as the corresponding **match** command conditions are met.

**Example 9-12** *BGP Configuration for Router A in Figure 9-8 with a Route Map*

```
router bgp 65001
  neighbor 192.168.2.2 remote-as 65001
  neighbor 192.168.3.3 remote-as 65001
  neighbor 192.168.2.2 update-source loopback0
  neighbor 192.168.3.3 update-source loopback0
  neighbor 192.168.28.1 remote-as 65004
  neighbor 192.168.28.1 route-map med_65004 out
!
route-map med_65004 permit 10
  match ip address 66
  set metric 100
route-map med_65004 permit 100
  set metric 200
!
access-list 66 permit 192.168.25.0.0 0.0.0.255
access-list 66 permit 192.168.26.0.0 0.0.0.255
```

The first line of the route map is a **permit** statement with a sequence number of 10 for a route map called med_65004; this defines the first **route-map** statement. The **match** condition for this statement checks all networks that are permitted by access list 66. The first line of access list 66 permits any networks that start with the first three octets of 192.168.25.0, and the second line of access list 66 permits networks that start with the first three octets of 192.168.26.0.

Any networks that are permitted by either of these lines will have the MED set to 100 by the route map. No other networks are permitted by this access list (there is an implicit deny all at the end of all access lists), so their MED is not changed. These other networks must proceed to the next **route-map** statement in the med_65004 route map.

The route map's second statement is a **permit** statement with a sequence number of 100 for the route map called med_65004. The route map does not have any **match** statements, just a **set metric 200** statement. This statement is a **permit any** statement for route maps. Because the network administrator does not specify a **match** condition for this portion of the route map, all networks being processed through this section of the route map (sequence number 100) are permitted, and they are set to a MED of 200. If the network administrator did not set the MED to 200, by default it would have been set to a MED of 0. Because 0 is less than 100, the routes with a MED of 0 would have been the preferred paths to the networks in AS 65001.

Similarly, the configuration for Router B is shown in Example 9-13. A route map named med_65004 is linked to neighbor 172.20.50.1 as an outbound route map. Before Router B sends an update to neighbor 172.20.50.1, it processes the outbound update through route map med_65004 and changes any values specified in a **set** command as long as the preceding **match** command conditions are met.

**Example 9-13** *BGP Configuration for Router B in Figure 9-8 with a Route Map*

```
router bgp 65001
  neighbor 192.168.1.1 remote-as 65001
  neighbor 192.168.3.3 remote-as 65001
  neighbor 192.168.1.1 update-source loopback0
  neighbor 192.168.3.3 update-source loopback0
  neighbor 172.20.50.1 remote-as 65004
  neighbor 172.20.50.1 route-map med_65004 out
!
route-map med_65004 permit 10
  match ip address 66
  set metric 100
route-map med_65004 permit 100
  set metric 200
!
access-list 66 permit 192.168.24.0.0 0.0.0.255
```

The first line of the route map is a **permit** statement with a sequence number of 10 for a route map called med_65004; this defines the first **route-map** statement. The **match** condition for this statement checks all networks that are permitted by access list 66. Access list 66 on Router B permits any networks that start with the first three octets of 192.168.24.0. Any networks that are permitted by this line have the MED set to 100 by the route map. No other networks are permitted by this access list, so their MED is unchanged. These other networks must proceed to the next **route-map** statement in the med_65004 route map.

The second statement of the route map is a **permit** statement with a sequence number of 100 for the route map called med_65004, but it does not have any **match** statements, just a **set**

**metric 200** statement. This statement is a **permit any** statement for route maps. Because the network administrator does not specify a **match** condition for this portion of the route map, all networks being processed through this section of the route map are permitted, but they are set to a MED of 200. If the network administrator did not set the MED to 200, by default it would have been set to a MED of 0. Because 0 is less than 100, the routes with a MED of 0 would have been the preferred paths to the networks in AS 65001.

Example 9-14 shows the BGP forwarding table on Router Z in AS 65004 indicating the networks learned from AS 65001. (Other networks that do not affect this example have been omitted.) Note that in this command output, the MED is shown in the column labeled Metric.

**Example 9-14** *BGP Table for Router Z in Figure 9-8 with a Route Map*

```
RouterZ#show ip bgp
BGP table version is 7, local router ID is 192.168.1.1
Status codes: s suppressed, d damped, h history, * valid, > best, i - internal
Origin codes: i - IGP, e - EGP, ? - incomplete
   Network          Next Hop        Metric LocPrf Weight Path
*>i192.168.24.0     172.20.50.2       100    100      0 65001 i
*  i                192.168.28.2      200    100      0 65001 i
*  i192.168.25.0    172.20.50.2       200    100      0 65001 i
*>i                 192.168.28.2      100    100      0 65001 i
*  i192.168.26.0    172.20.50.2       200    100      0 65001 i
*>i                 192.168.28.2      100    100      0 65001 i
```

Router Z has multiple paths to reach each network. These paths all have valid next-hop addresses and synchronization disabled and are loop-free. All networks have a weight of 0 and a local preference of 100, so Steps 1 and 2 in the route-selection decision process do not determine the best path. None of the routes were originated by this router or any router in AS 65004; all networks came from AS 65001, so Step 3 does not apply. All networks have an AS path of one AS (65001) and were introduced into BGP with **network** statements (i is the origin code), so Steps 4 and 5 are equal. The route selection decision process therefore gets to Step 6, which states that BGP chooses the lowest MED if all preceding steps are equal or do not apply.

For network 192.168.24.0, the next hop of 172.20.50.2 has a lower MED than the next hop of 192.168.28.2. Therefore, for network 192.168.24.0, the path through 172.20.50.2 is the preferred path. For networks 192.168.25.0 and 192.168.26.0, the next hop of 192.168.28.2 has a lower MED (100) than the next hop of 172.20.50.2 (with a MED of 200). Therefore, 192.168.28.2 is the preferred path for those two networks.

## Configuring Weight

Recall that the weight attribute influences only the local router. Routes with a higher weight are preferred.

The **neighbor** {*ip-address* | *peer-group-name*} **weight** *weight* router configuration command is used to assign a weight to a neighbor connection, as described in Table 9-2.

**Table 9-2**    **neighbor weight** *Command Description*

| Parameter | Description |
|-----------|-------------|
| *ip-address* | The BGP neighbor's IP address. |
| *peer-group-name* | The name of a BGP peer group. |
| *weight* | The weight to assign. Acceptable values are 0 to 65535. The default is 32768 for local routes (routes that the router originates). Other routes have a weight of 0 by default. |

# Multihoming Design Options

*Multihoming* is the term used to describe when an AS is connected to more than one ISP. This is usually done for one of the following reasons:

- To increase the reliability of the connection to the Internet so that if one connection fails, another will still be available

- To increase the performance so that better paths to certain destinations can be used

If a company has only a single link to the Internet, BGP is inappropriate, and a default route is the recommended design. When all packets go out the same interface to the ISP, BGP's overhead does not provide enough benefits for most single-link implementations.

BGP's benefits are apparent when an AS has multiple EBGP connections to either a single AS or multiple autonomous systems. Having multiple connections allows an organization to have redundant connections to the Internet so that connectivity can still be maintained if a single path becomes unavailable.

A drawback of having all EBGP connections to a single ISP is that connectivity issues in that single ISP could cause your AS to lose connectivity to the Internet.

By having connections to multiple ISPs, an AS has the following characteristics:

- It has redundancy with the multiple connections.

- It is not tied to the routing policy of a single ISP.

- It has more paths to the same networks, allowing better policy manipulation.

The following sections discuss multihoming options.

## Types of Multihoming

You have three design options for implementing BGP multihoming. The configuration of the multiple connections to the ISPs can be classified according to the routes that are provided to the AS from the ISPs. Three common ways of configuring the connections are as follows:

- All ISPs pass only default routes to the AS.

- All ISPs pass default routes and selected specific routes to the AS.
- All ISPs pass all routes to the AS.

Each of these scenarios is examined in the following sections.

---

**NOTE**    When multihoming, the ISPs you connect to should announce your prefixes to the Internet. For example, if the prefixes assigned to you are part of only one of the ISP address ranges, the other ISPs (which do not own your prefixes) should also advertise your specific prefixes to the Internet.

---

## Default Routes from All Providers

The first design option is when all ISPs pass only default routes to the AS. This requires the fewest resources (memory and CPU usage) within the routers in the AS because only default routes have to be processed. The AS sends all its routes to the ISPs, which process them and pass them on to other autonomous systems as appropriate.

The ISP that a specific router within the AS uses to reach the Internet is decided by the IGP metric used to reach the default route within the AS. The default route with the least-cost IGP metric is used. This IGP default route routes packets destined for the external networks to an edge router of this AS, which is running EBGP with the ISPs. The edge router uses the BGP default route to reach all external networks.

The route that inbound packets take to get to the AS is decided outside the AS (within the ISPs and other autonomous systems).

Regional ISPs that have multiple connections to national or international ISPs commonly implement this option. The regional ISPs do not use BGP for path manipulation; however, they need to be able to add new customers and the networks of their customers. By running EBGP with the national or international ISPs, the regional ISP simply adds its customers' new networks to its BGP process; these new networks automatically propagate across the Internet with minimal delay. If the regional ISP does not use BGP, each time it needs to add a new set of networks, it must wait until the national ISPs add these networks to their BGP process and configure static routes pointing to the regional ISP.

When choosing to receive default routes from all providers, you must understand the following limitations of this option:

- Path manipulation cannot be performed, because only a single route is received from each ISP.
- Bandwidth manipulation is extremely difficult and can be accomplished only by manipulating the default route's IGP metric.
- Diverting some of the traffic from one exit point to another is challenging, because all destinations use the same default route for path selection.

In Figure 9-9, AS 65000 and AS 65250 send default routes into AS 65500.

**Figure 9-9**    *AS 65500 Receives Default Routes from All Providers*

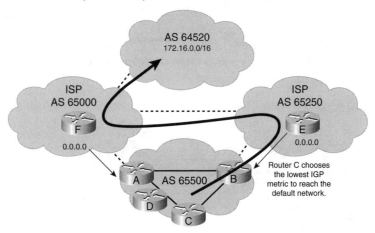

The ISP that a specific router within AS 65500 uses to reach any external address is decided by the IGP metric used to reach the default route within the AS. For example, if RIP is used within AS 65500, Router C selects the route with the lowest hop count to the default route, through Router B, when it wants to send packets to network 172.16.0.0. Packets travel to 172.16.0.0, as indicated by the arrow in Figure 9-9.

# A Partial Routing Table from Each Provider

The second design option is when all ISPs pass default routes and selected specific routes (for example, from customers with whom the AS exchanges a lot of traffic) to the AS.

A customer running EBGP with an ISP that wants a partial routing table generally receives the networks that the ISP and its other customers own. The customer can also receive the routes from any other AS the customer wants; these are known as customer-specified routes and networks.

Major ISPs are assigned between 2000 and 10,000 CIDR blocks of IP addresses from the IANA. An ISP reassigns this address space to its customers. If the ISP passes this information to one of its customers (that wants only a partial BGP routing table), the customer can redistribute these routes into its IGP. Then the customer's internal routers (the routers that are not running BGP) can receive these routes via redistribution. They then can take the nearest exit point based on the best metric of specific networks instead of taking the nearest exit point based on the default route.

Acquiring a partial BGP table from each provider is beneficial because path selection for outbound and inbound traffic is more predictable than using a default route. For example, in the network shown in Figure 9-10, first assume that AS64515 receives only a default route from ISPs A and B. The internal routers in AS 64515 that are closer to ISP A than ISP B send all packets with a destination address outside this AS to ISP A. ISP A forwards the packets to the rest of the Internet, including the networks owned by ISP B. Taking the path through ISP A to reach the AS of ISP B is a longer AS path than going directly to ISP B. (Note that ISP B must also send reply packets to the originating AS. ISP B has a direct connection to that AS and likely will use it. Therefore, the reply packet enters the AS at a different point than the original packet exited.)

**Figure 9-10** *AS 64515 Is Receiving Default Routes and Partial Tables from All Providers*

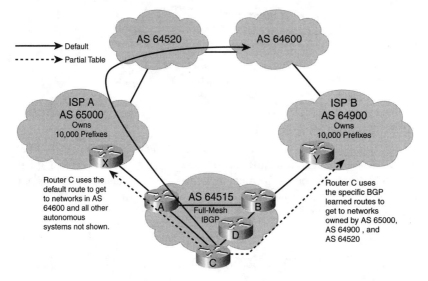

In Figure 9-10, now assume that ISPs A and B send default routes and the routes that each ISP owns to AS 64515. The customer (AS 64515) also has asked both providers to pass networks from AS 64520 (customer-specified networks) because of the amount of traffic between AS 64520 and AS 64515.

By running IBGP between the internal routers within AS 64515, the ISP that a specific router within AS 64515 uses to reach the AS 64520 networks is usually the shortest AS path. The shortest AS path to AS 64520 is via AS 65000 through Router A.

The routes to AS 64600 and to other autonomous systems (not shown in the figure) that are not specifically advertised to AS 64515 by ISP A and ISP B are decided by the IGP metric used to reach the default route within AS 64515.

This design option requires more resources within the AS than just passing the default route to the AS, because the default and all external routes provided must be processed. The AS sends all its routes to the ISPs, which process and pass them to other autonomous systems as appropriate. By limiting the size of the BGP update received from each ISP, this option is less CPU- and bandwidth-intensive than receiving the full BGP table.

An AS that is receiving a partial Internet routing table has two choices for the internal routers: Redistribute BGP into the internal routing protocol, or run BGP on at least the core routers, if not all routers, in the AS.

With the first choice, the internal routers use the IGP metric of the redistributed routes to decide the best way to exit the AS. The paths to all other external destinations that are not explicitly known through redistribution are decided by the IGP metric used to reach the default route within the AS.

Running BGP on routers in the AS allows the network administrator to more easily manipulate the path-selection process than when using just the IGP routing metric. For example, local preference can be used on a per-network basis rather than manipulating the bandwidth statement or interface cost for OSPF or EIGRP. In IGPs such as OSPF, manipulating individual routes can be difficult, because best paths are chosen based on the least-cost bandwidth for an interface that applies to all networks using that path. Changing the bandwidth or interface cost to affect how another router chooses the best path for a specific network will probably change how the IGP on the other router selects the best path for multiple networks. If BGP is running, it is easier to manipulate individual networks for path selection; however, all router administrators need enough knowledge about BGP and its path-selection process to troubleshoot any routing problems across the AS.

In either case, the route that the inbound packets take to reach the AS is decided outside the AS (within the ISPs and other autonomous systems).

# A Full Routing Table from Each Provider

In the third multihoming design option, all ISPs pass all routes to the AS, and IBGP is run on at least the core routers in this AS. (The core routers are the equivalent of area 0 routers in an OSPF network or the backbone of a large internetwork.) Handling the full BGP routing table requires a high-end processor and at least 256 MB of RAM; these are usually found on Cisco 7200 or larger routers. The routers found at the distribution layer and access layer do not need to process BGP's constant updates or handle the full Internet routing table; usually, these routers are in an OSPF stub or totally stubby area and have a default route for all externally learned networks.

This configuration requires a lot of resources within the AS because it must process all the external routes. The AS sends all its routes to the ISPs, which process the routes and pass them to other autonomous systems as appropriate.

The ISP that a specific router within the AS uses to reach the external networks is usually the shortest AS path; however, this can be overridden.

The route that inbound packets take to reach the AS is decided outside the AS (within the ISPs and other autonomous systems); it can be influenced by using the MED.

## Example of Full Routes from All Providers

In Figure 9-11, ISPs A and B send all routes into AS 64515. The ISP that a specific router within AS 64515 uses to reach the external networks is usually the shortest AS path. However, you can configure the routers in AS 64515 to influence the path to certain networks. For example, Routers A and B can use a route map to set the local preference of certain routes to influence the outbound traffic from AS 64515.

**Figure 9-11** *AS 64515 Receives Full Routes from All Providers*

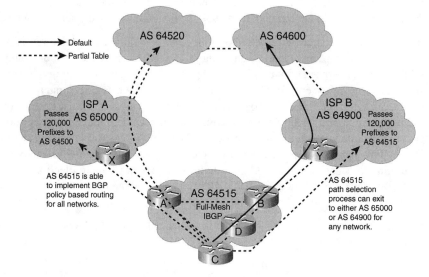

Redistribution is not performed between BGP and the IGP in AS 64515. Therefore, synchronization between the IGP and BGP needs to be turned off, because the IGP will never have the BGP routes introduced into it. Because AS 64515 is running a full mesh of IBGP, synchronization can be turned off.

## OSPF and BGP Example

In Figure 9-12, all routers in AS 65001 run both OSPF and BGP. BGP processes the routing between local clients and the Internet and handles how traffic enters and leaves AS 65001. OSPF handles how traffic is routed between local clients and servers in AS 65001.

Problems on the Internet do not affect employees in AS 65001 accessing corporate resources, because OSPF and BGP are not communicating with each other. This approach is known as *ships in the night* (SIN) routing because OSPF and BGP updates share the same bandwidth and routers, but each is performing a different and unrelated function. OSPF handles traffic local to the AS, and BGP handles traffic between this AS and other autonomous systems. BGP, with its TCP flow control, is designed to process the constant changes that occur on the Internet.

BGP synchronization is turned off in all routers because full-mesh IBGP is being run, and routes are not redistributed from BGP into IGP.

**Figure 9-12**  *AS 65001 Runs OSPF and BGP*

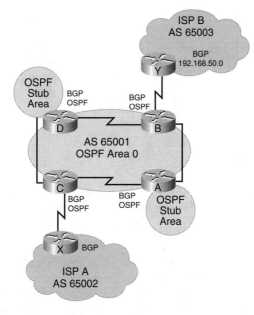

ISPs usually run BGP on every router. For a non-ISP AS, BGP is configured on the core routers, or the Area 0 routers if the network is running OSPF. In this case, OSPF should be configured on all routers, and default routes should be sent into the other OSPF areas, which should be configured as OSPF stub or totally stubby areas (or not-so-stubby areas [NSSAs] if necessary—NSSAs are described in Appendix A, "Job Aids and Supplements").

## Filtering BGP Advertisements to ISPs

In Figure 9-13, BGP is running on all routers in AS 64515 to allow the routers in AS 64515 to manipulate the flow of traffic to and from AS 64515. A dual-homed customer, such as AS 64515 in Figure 9-13, should not pass the BGP routes learned from one ISP to the other. If it does, the customer AS becomes a transit AS, and the two ISPs may pass traffic through the customer AS. This situation is very undesirable for the dual-homed customer. The dual-homed customer only wants to have a redundant Internet connection; it does not want to act as a transit AS between the two ISPs.

In Figure 9-13, Router B learns about network 172.16.0.0/16 from Router Y in AS 64900 (ISP B). Router B passes the 172.16.0.0/16 network advertisement through IBGP to Router A. Assume that Router A then passes the 172.16.0.0/16 network advertisement through EBGP to Router X in AS 65000 (ISP A). The routers in AS 65000 now have two paths to reach AS 64900—one path through ISP C (AS 64520) and the other through AS 64515, the dual-homed customer that is not an ISP.

**Figure 9-13** *BGP Advertisements Can Be Filtered*

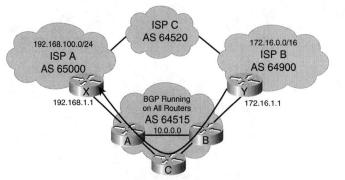

To avoid using the bandwidth of AS 64515 as a path between the ISPs, the routers in AS 64515 should allow only the networks that they own to be advertised to their ISPs.

Example 9-15 is the configuration put on Router A, and Example 9-16 is the configuration put on Router B. These configurations use a **distribute-list** linked to a specific BGP neighbor to determine which networks are announced to that neighbor. (This outbound filter performs the same function as the **distribute-list** command you use for internal routing protocols; however, when used for BGP, it is linked to a specific neighbor.) AS 64515 owns network 10.0.0.0/8. It announces only this network to both EBGP neighbors and denies all other networks. The distribution list filter is applied to only the EBGP neighbors, so the information learned from the other autonomous systems still propagates to other BGP routers in AS 64515. The edge routers do not forward any networks external to AS 64515 to other autonomous systems.

**NOTE**     Refer to Appendix A for a discussion of the BGP **neighbor distribute-list** command.

**Example 9-15** *BGP Configuration for Router A in Figure 9-13*

```
router bgp 64515
  network 10.0.0.0
  neighbor 192.168.1.1 remote-as 65000
  neighbor 192.168.1.1 distribute-list 7 out
 (text omitted)
access-list 7 permit 10.0.0.0 0.255.255.255
```

**Example 9-16** *BGP Configuration for Router B in Figure 9-13*

```
router bgp 64515
  network 10.0.0.0
  neighbor 172.16.1.1 remote-as 64900
  neighbor 172.16.1.1 distribute-list 7 out
(text omitted)
access-list 7 permit 10.0.0.0 0.255.255.255
```

With these configurations applied, other autonomous systems do not learn about networks and autonomous systems behind AS 64515, so those autonomous systems cannot use AS 64515 as a transit AS to reach other networks.

# More Multihoming Examples

In Figure 9-14, AS 64520 is connected to two ISPs: AS 65000 and AS 65250. Both ISPs are sending full routes to AS 64520.

**Figure 9-14**  *AS 64520 Is Multihomed*

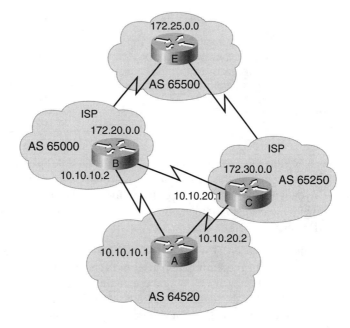

## Multihoming Example with No Special Tuning

In the first sample configuration shown in Example 9-17, Router A is configured with two EBGP neighbors: Router B (10.10.10.2) and Router C (10.10.20.1). No special tuning is done to influence how AS 64520 gets to the other autonomous systems.

**Example 9-17**  *Configuration for Router A in Figure 9-14 with No Special Tuning*

```
RtrA(config)#router bgp 64520
RtrA(config-router)#network 10.10.10.0 mask 255.255.255.0
RtrA(config-router)#network 10.10.20.0 mask 255.255.255.0
RtrA(config-router)#neighbor 10.10.10.2 remote-as 65000
RtrA(config-router)#neighbor 10.10.20.1 remote-as 65250
```

Example 9-18 provides the **show ip bgp** command output on Router A in the network shown in Figure 9-14. In this example, Router A selects the route via 10.10.10.2 (Router B) to get to 172.20.0.0 and the route via 10.10.20.1 (Router C) to get to 172.30.0.0 because these paths have the shortest AS path length (of one AS). (Recall that the selected route is indicated with the > symbol on the left of the **show ip bgp** output.)

**Example 9-18 show** *Output from Router A in Figure 9-14 with No Special Tuning*

```
RtrA#show ip bgp
BGP table version is 7, local router ID is 172.16.10.1
Status codes: s suppressed, d damped, h history, * valid, > best, i - internal
Origin codes: i - IGP, e - EGP, ? - incomplete

   Network          Next Hop          Metric LocPrf Weight Path
*> 10.10.10.0/24    0.0.0.0                0        32768 i
*> 10.10.20.0/24    0.0.0.0                0        32768 i
*  172.20.0.0       10.10.20.1                         0 65250 65000 i
*>                  10.10.10.2             0           0 65000 i
*> 172.25.0.0       10.10.10.2                         0 65000 65500 i
*                   10.10.20.1                         0 65250 65500 i
*  172.30.0.0       10.10.10.2                         0 65000 65250 i
*>                  10.10.20.1             0           0 65250 i
```

Router A has two paths to 172.25.0.0, and both have the same AS path length (each path has two autonomous systems). In this case, if all other attributes are equal, Router A selects the oldest path. If you ignore this oldest-path criterion for now (because you cannot determine which router will send the path to Router A first), Router A selects the path that has the lowest BGP router ID value.

Unfortunately, the BGP router ID values of Routers B and C are not displayed in the output of the **show ip bgp** command. The **show ip bgp neighbors** command or the **show ip bgp 172.25.0.0** command can provide these values. Using these commands, the router ID for Router B is found to be 172.20.0.1, and the router ID for Router C is found to be 172.30.0.1. Router A selects the lower of these router IDs, so it chooses the path through Router B (172.20.0.1) to get to 172.25.0.0.

## Multihoming Example with Weight Attributes Changed

In the sample configuration for Router A in Figure 9-14 shown in Example 9-19, Router A is configured with two EBGP neighbors: Router B (10.10.10.2) and Router C (10.10.20.1). The weights used for routes from each neighbor have been changed from their default of 0. Routes received from 10.10.10.2 (Router B) have a weight of 100, and routes received from 10.10.20.1 (Router C) have a weight of 150.

**Example 9-19** *Configuration for Router A in Figure 9-14 with Weights Changed*

```
RtrA(config)#router bgp 64520
RtrA(config-router)#network 10.10.10.0 mask 255.255.255.0
RtrA(config-router)#network 10.10.20.0 mask 255.255.255.0
```

**Example 9-19** *Configuration for Router A in Figure 9-14 with Weights Changed (Continued)*

```
RtrA(config-router)#neighbor 10.10.10.2 remote-as 65000
RtrA(config-router)#neighbor 10.10.10.2 weight 100
RtrA(config-router)#neighbor 10.10.20.1 remote-as 65250
RtrA(config-router)#neighbor 10.10.20.1 weight 150
```

Example 9-20 provides the **show ip bgp** command output on Router A in the network shown in Figure 9-14, with the weights changed. In this example, because the weight for Router C is higher than the weight for Router B, Router A is forced to use Router C as a next hop to reach all external routes. Recall that the **weight** attribute is looked at before the AS path length, so the AS path length is ignored in this case.

**Example 9-20 show** *Output from Router A in Figure 9-14 with Weights Changed*

```
RtrA#show ip bgp
BGP table version is 9, local router ID is 172.16.10.1
Status codes: s suppressed, d damped, h history, * valid, > best, i - internal
Origin codes: i - IGP, e - EGP, ? - incomplete

   Network          Next Hop         Metric LocPrf Weight Path
*> 10.10.10.0/24    0.0.0.0               0         32768 i
*> 10.10.20.0/24    0.0.0.0               0         32768 i
*> 172.20.0.0       10.10.20.1                        150 65250 65000 i
*                   10.10.10.2            0           100 65000 i
*> 172.25.0.0       10.10.20.1                        150 65250 65500 i
*                   10.10.10.2                        100 65000 65500 i
*> 172.30.0.0       10.10.20.1            0           150 65250 i
*                   10.10.10.2                        100 65000 65250 i
```

# Redistribution with IGPs

Chapter 7, "Manipulating Routing Updates," discusses route redistribution and how it is configured. This section examines the specifics of when redistribution between BGP and IGPs is appropriate.

As noted in Chapter 8, and as shown in Figure 9-15, a router running BGP keeps a table of BGP information, separate from the IP routing table. The router can be configured to share information between the BGP table and the IP routing table.

**Figure 9-15** *A Router Running BGP Keeps Its Own Table, Separate from the IP Routing Table*

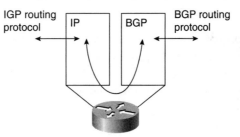

IGP routing protocol — IP — BGP — BGP routing protocol

## Advertising Networks into BGP

Route information is sent from an autonomous system into BGP in one of the following ways:

- **Using the network command**—As discussed, the **network** command allows BGP to advertise a network that is already in the IP table. The list of **network** commands must include all the networks in the AS you want to advertise.

- **By redistributing static routes to interface null 0 into BGP**—Redistribution occurs when a router running different protocols advertises routing information received between the protocols. Static routes in this case are considered a protocol, and static information is advertised to BGP. (The use of the null 0 interface is discussed in the earlier section "Cautions When Using the **network** Command for Summarization.")

- **By redistributing dynamic IGP routes into BGP**—This solution is not recommended because it might cause instability.

Redistributing from an IGP into BGP is not recommended because any change in the IGP routes—for example, if a link goes down—might cause a BGP update. This method could result in unstable BGP tables.

If redistribution is used, care must be taken that only local routes are redistributed. For example, routes learned from other autonomous systems (that were learned by redistributing BGP into the IGP) must not be sent out again from the IGP, or routing loops could result. Configuring this filtering can be complex.

Using a **redistribute** command into BGP results in an incomplete origin attribute for the route, as indicated by the **?** in the **show ip bgp** command output.

## Advertising from BGP into an IGP

Route information may be sent from BGP into an autonomous system by redistributing the BGP routes into the IGP.

Because BGP is an external routing protocol, care must be taken when exchanging information with internal protocols because of the amount of information in BGP tables.

For ISP autonomous systems, redistributing from BGP normally isn't required. Other autonomous systems may use redistribution, but the number of routes means that filtering normally is required.

Each of these situations is examined in the following sections.

### ISP: No Redistribution from BGP into IGP Is Required

An ISP typically has all routers in the AS (or at least all routers in the transit path within the AS) running BGP. Of course, this would be a full-mesh IBGP environment, and IBGP would be used to carry the EBGP routes across the AS. All the BGP routers in the AS would be configured with the **no synchronization** command, because synchronization between IGP and

BGP is not required. The BGP information then would not need to be redistributed into the IGP. The IGP would need to route only information local to the AS and routes to the next-hop addresses of the BGP routes.

One advantage of this approach is that the IGP protocol does not have to be concerned with all the BGP routes; BGP takes care of them. BGP also converges faster in this environment because it does not have to wait for the IGP to advertise the routes.

### Non-ISP: Redistribution from BGP into IGP Might Be Required

A non-ISP AS typically does not have all routers in the AS running BGP, and it might not have a full-mesh IBGP environment. If this is the case, and if knowledge of external routes is required inside the AS, redistributing BGP into the IGP is necessary. However, because of the number of routes that would be in the BGP tables, filtering normally is required.

As discussed in the section "Multihoming Design Options," an alternative to receiving full routes from BGP is that the ISP could send only default routes, or default routes and some external routes, to the AS.

---

**NOTE**    An example of when redistributing into an IGP might be necessary is in an AS that is running BGP only on its border routers and that has other routers in the AS that do not run BGP but that require knowledge of external routes.

Redistribution between routing protocols is discussed in detail in Chapter 7.

---

# Summary

In this chapter, you learned about some advanced BGP features.

CIDR is a mechanism developed to help alleviate the problem of IP address exhaustion and the growth of routing tables. The idea behind CIDR is that blocks of multiple addresses (such as blocks of Class C addresses) can be combined, or aggregated, to create a larger classless set of IP addresses. These multiple addresses can then be summarized in routing tables, resulting in fewer route advertisements. BGP-4 supports CIDR.

By default, BGP aggregate routes are advertised as coming from the autonomous system that did the aggregation. Their atomic aggregate attribute is set to show that information might be missing. The AS numbers from the nonaggregated routes are not listed.

BGP's **network** command permits BGP to advertise a network if it is present in the IP routing table. This command allows classless prefixes; the router can advertise individual subnets, networks, or supernets. The default mask is the classful mask, and it causes only the classful network number to be announced. Note that at least one subnet of the specified major network must be present in the IP routing table for BGP to start announcing the classful network. However, if you specify the *network-mask*, an exact match to the network (both address and mask) must exist in the routing table for the network to be advertised.

The BGP **auto-summary** command determines how BGP handles redistributed routes. The **no auto-summary** router configuration command turns off BGP autosummarization. When it is enabled (with **auto-summary**), all redistributed subnets are summarized to their classful boundaries in the BGP table. When it is disabled (with **no auto-summary**), all redistributed subnets are present in their original form in the BGP table.

The **network** command tells BGP *what* to advertise. The **neighbor** command tells BGP *where* to advertise. The **aggregate-address** command tells BGP *how* to advertise the networks.

BGP attributes can be manipulated using commands that change them for all routes or using route maps to change them for specific routes.

Local preference is used only within an AS between IBGP speakers to determine the best path to leave the AS to reach an outside network. Local preference is set to 100 by default; higher values are preferred.

MED is used to decide how to enter an AS when multiple paths exist between two autonomous systems and one AS is trying to influence the incoming path from the other AS. The lowest MED value is preferred.

The weight attribute influences only the local router. Routes with a higher weight are preferred.

Multihoming is the term used to describe when an AS is connected to more than one ISP. Three common ways of configuring the connections are as follows:

- All ISPs pass only default routes to the AS. This requires the least resources (memory and CPU usage) within the routers in the AS because only default routes have to be processed. The AS sends all its routes to the ISPs, which process them and pass them on to other autonomous systems as appropriate. The ISP that a specific router within the AS uses to reach the Internet is decided by the IGP metric used to reach the default route within the AS.

- All ISPs pass default routes and selected specific routes to the AS. A customer generally receives the networks that the ISP and its other customers own. It also might receive the routes from any other AS the customer wants. This design option requires more resources within the AS than just passing the default route to the AS, because the default and all external routes provided must be processed. There are two choices for the internal routers in the AS: redistribute BGP into the internal routing protocol, or run BGP on at least the core routers, if not all routers, in the AS.

- All ISPs pass all routes to the AS, and IBGP is run on at least the core routers in this AS. Handling the full BGP routing table requires a high-end processor. The ISP that a specific router within the AS uses to reach the external networks is usually the shortest AS path; however, this can be overridden.

# References

For additional information, refer to these resources:

- Cisco's command reference and configuration guides:
  www.cisco.com/univercd/home/home.htm

- BGP Technical Documentation:
  www.cisco.com/en/US/tech/tk365/tk80/tech_tech_notes_list.html

# Configuration Exercise 9-1: Configuring BGP Route Summarization and Examining the BGP Path-Selection Process

In this exercise, you will configure route aggregation on your edge routers and investigate the BGP path-selection process.

---

### Introduction to the Configuration Exercises

This book uses Configuration Exercises to help you practice configuring routers with the commands and topics presented. If you have access to real hardware, you can try these exercises on your routers. See Appendix H, "Configuration Exercise Equipment Requirements and Initial Configurations," for a list of recommended equipment and initial configuration commands for the routers. However, even if you don't have access to any routers, you can go through the exercises and keep a log of your own running configurations or just read through the solution. Commands used and solutions to the Configuration Exercises are provided after the exercises.

In the Configuration Exercises, the network is assumed to consist of two pods, each with four routers. The pods are interconnected to a backbone. You configure pod 1. No interaction between the two pods is required, but you might see some routes from the other pod in your routing tables in some exercises if you have it configured (the Configuration Exercise answers show the routes from the other pod). In most of the exercises, the backbone has only one router; in some cases, another router is added to the backbone. Each Configuration Exercise assumes that you have completed the previous chapters' Configuration Exercises on your pod.

---

**NOTE**     Throughout this exercise, the pod number is referred to as *x*, and the router number is referred to as *y*. Substitute the appropriate numbers as needed.

## Objectives

Your task in this Configuration Exercise is to optimize BGP using route aggregation and to investigate the BGP path-selection process.

## Visual Objective

Figure 9-16 illustrates the topology used in this exercise.

**Figure 9-16** *BGP Route Summarization Configuration Exercise Topology*

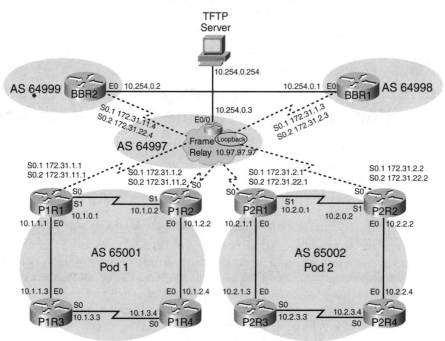

On All Pod Routers Loopback 0: 10.200.200.xy/32

## Command List

In this exercise, you will use the commands in Table 9-3, listed in logical order. Refer to this list if you need configuration command assistance during the exercise.

**CAUTION** Although the command syntax is shown in this table, the addresses shown are typically for the P*x*R1 and P*x*R3 routers. Be careful when addressing your routers! Refer to the exercise instructions and the appropriate visual objective diagram for addressing details.

**Table 9-3** *BGP Route Summarization Configuration Exercise Commands*

| Command | Description |
|---|---|
| (config-router)#**aggregate-address 10.*x*.0.0 255.255.0.0 summary-only** | Advertises a summary route and suppresses all the more specific routes. |
| #**show ip bgp** | Shows the BGP table. |

## Task: Configuring BGP Summarization and Investigating the Path-Selection Process

In this task, you will use a terminal utility to establish a console connection to the equipment. You will configure BGP summarization and see the results of the BGP path-selection process. Follow these steps:

**Step 1**   On edge routers P*x*R1 and P*x*R2, summarize your pod network to 10.*x*.0.0/16 to the core autonomous systems using the **aggregate-address** command with the **summary-only** option. You do not need to include the loopback interfaces on P*x*R3 and P*x*R4 in the summary.

**Step 2**   Telnet to either BBR1 or BBR2, and view the routing table. Is the aggregate address for your pod present?

---

**NOTE**   It might take a while to see the aggregate routes in the backbone routers.

---

**Step 3**   From the BBR1 or BBR2 router, ping 10.*x*.3.3 and 10.*x*.3.4 to test connectivity.

**Step 4**   On the edge routers, display the BGP table with the **show ip bgp** command. Do you see your pod subnets being suppressed because of the **summary-only** option used with the **aggregate-address** command?

**Step 5**   Examine the best path selected for network 10.97.97.0 in AS 64997. (The 10.97.97.0 subnet in AS 64997 is a loopback address, configured on the Frame Relay switch router.) What is the next hop for this network?

**Step 6**   Based on the BGP path-selection process, why was that path chosen?

## Exercise Verification

You have successfully completed this exercise when you achieve the following results:

* You have summarized the pod network in BGP advertisements.
* You have determined the BGP path-selection process used by your BGP routers.

# Configuration Exercise 9-2: BGP Path Manipulation Using MED and Local Preference with Route Maps

In this exercise, you will use route maps to change BGP MED and local preference values and verify how this changes the path selection.

| NOTE | Throughout this exercise, the pod number is referred to as $x$, and the router number is referred to as $y$. Substitute the appropriate numbers as needed. |
|------|------|

## Objectives

Your task in this Configuration Exercise is to use route maps to change BGP MED and local preference values, affecting path selection.

## Visual Objective

Figure 9-17 illustrates the topology used in this exercise.

**Figure 9-17** *BGP Path Manipulation Configuration Exercise Topology*

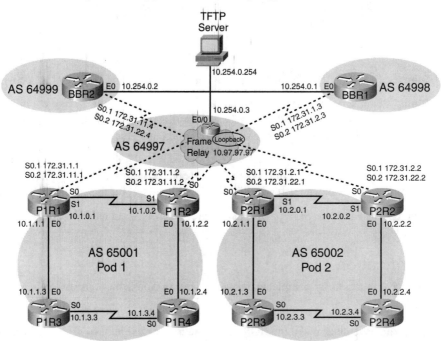

On All Pod Routers Loopback 0: 10.200.200.xy/32

## Command List

In this exercise, you will use the commands in Table 9-4, listed in logical order. Refer to this list if you need configuration command assistance during the exercise.

CAUTION    Although the command syntax is shown in this table, the addresses shown are typically for the P*x*R1 and P*x*R3 routers. Be careful when addressing your routers! Refer to the exercise instructions and the appropriate visual objective diagram for addressing details.

**Table 9-4**    *BGP Path Selection Configuration Exercise Commands*

| Command | Description |
|---|---|
| (config)#**route-map SET_PREF permit 10** | Creates a route map named SET_PREF. |
| (config-route-map)#**match ip address 3** | Used in a route map to match an IP address to routes that are permitted by access list 3. |
| (config-route-map)#**set local-preference 300** | Used in a route map to set the BGP local preference. |
| (config)#**access-list 3 permit 172.31.0.0 0.0.255.255** | Creates access list 3. |
| (config-router)#**neighbor 172.31.***xx***.4 route-map SET_PREF in** | Applies the route map to the incoming updates from a BGP neighbor. |
| (config-route-map)#**set metric 200** | Used in a route map to set the BGP MED. |
| #**clear ip bgp 172.31.***xx***.4 soft in** | Performs a BGP soft in reconfiguration. Applies a policy change to existing routes without resetting the BGP sessions. |
| #**clear ip bgp 172.31.11.4 soft out** | Performs a BGP soft out reconfiguration. The router creates a new update and sends the whole table to the specified neighbors. |
| #**show ip bgp** | Shows the BGP table. |

# Task: Using MED and Local Preference with Route Maps for BGP Path Manipulation

In this task, you will use a terminal utility to establish a console connection to the equipment. You will change the MED and local preference to manipulate the BGP path-selection process.

Step 1    On the edge routers, look at the BGP table, and notice the next hop for routes to the 172.31.*x*.0 and 172.31.*xx*.0 networks in the *other* pod (in other words, the networks that connect the BBR1 and BBR2 routers to the other pod).

Step 2    Which path does the edge router use to reach the remote 172.31.*x*.0 networks? Why does BGP choose that path? Which path does the edge router use to reach the remote 172.31.*xx*.0 networks? Why does BGP choose that path?

**Step 3**  This company has established a policy that all traffic exiting the AS bound for any of the remote 172.31.x.0 and 172.31.xx.0 networks should take the path through BBR2.

To comply with this policy, configure the edge routers, P$x$R1 and P$x$R2, with a route map setting local preference to 300 for any routes to the remote 172.31.x.0 and 172.31.xx.0 networks that are advertised by BBR2.

**Step 4**  Look at the BGP table on the edge routers. Has the local preference for the routes learned from BBR2 changed?

**Step 5**  When you configure a policy, it is not automatically applied to routes already in the BGP table. You can either reset the BGP relationship with BBR2 or configure the router to apply the policy to existing routes without resetting the relationship; the latter solution is called a *soft* reconfiguration. Use a soft reconfiguration to apply the policy to the routes that come in from BBR2 using the command **clear ip bgp 172.31.xx.4 soft in**.

**Step 6**  Look at the BGP table again. Have the local preference values changed?

**Step 7**  Which path does the edge router use to reach the remote 172.31.x.0 networks now? Why does BGP choose that path even though the AS path is longer? Which path does the edge router use to reach the remote 172.31.xx.0 networks now? Why does BGP choose that path?

**Step 8**  Both of the core routers (BBR1 and BBR2) have multiple ways into each pod. For example, BBR1 could take the direct path through your pod's P$x$R1 or P$x$R2 router, or it could take a path through BBR2 and then to one of the pod's edge routers.

**Step 9**  Telnet to BBR1 (the password is **cisco**), and examine the BGP table. Which path does the BBR1 router use to reach your pod's 10.x.0.0 network? Why does BGP choose that path?

**Step 10**  Telnet to BBR2 (the password is **cisco**), and examine the BGP table. Which path does the BBR2 router use to reach your pod's 10.x.0.0 network? Why does BGP choose that path?

**Step 11**  Suppose this company has also established a policy for traffic inbound from the core. This policy states the following:

- Traffic from BBR1 to your pod 10.x.0.0 network should enter your pod through P$x$R1.

- Traffic from BBR2 to your pod 10.x.0.0 network should enter your pod through P$x$R2.

To accomplish this policy, you will do the following:

- Make the paths through P*x*R1 look unattractive to BBR2.

- Make the paths through P*x*R2 look unattractive to BBR1.

Currently, the MED for both paths is 0 in the BGP table of both BBR1 and BBR2, so BBR1 and BBR2 pick the oldest EBGP path.

On P*x*R1, configure a route map that sets the MED to 200 for routes to your pod's internal network (10.*x*.0.0); apply the route map to updates sent to BBR2. (Remember that a lower MED is more attractive to BGP.)

On P*x*R2, configure a route map that sets the MED to 200 for routes to your pod's internal network (10.*x*.0.0); apply the route map to updates sent to BBR1.

**Step 12**   Perform a soft reconfiguration after you apply the policy to the BGP neighbor (BBR1 or BBR2) by using the **clear ip bgp** *ip-address* **soft out** command.

**Step 13**   Telnet to the core routers, and examine the BGP table. Verify that the MED changes have taken effect.

**Step 14**   Notice that the path with a MED of 200 is not chosen as the best path. What is the best path from BBR1 to your pod 10.*x*.0.0 network now? What is the best path from BBR2 to your pod 10.*x*.0.0 network now?

## Exercise Verification

You have successfully completed this exercise when you achieve the following results:

- You have changed the local preference of the specified routes.

- You have changed the MED of the specified routes.

# Solution to Configuration Exercise 9-1: Configuring BGP Route Summarization and Examining the BGP Path-Selection Process

This section provides the answers to the questions in the Configuration Exercise.

| NOTE | Some answers provided cover multiple steps; the answers are given after the last step to which that answer applies. |
|------|--------------------------------------------------------------------------------------------------------------------|

## Solution to Task: Configuring BGP Summarization and Investigating the Path-Selection Process

**Step 1**　On edge routers P*x*R1 and P*x*R2, summarize your pod network to 10.*x*.0.0/16 to the core autonomous systems using the **aggregate-address** command with the **summary-only** option. You do not need to include the loopback interfaces on P*x*R3 and P*x*R4 in the summary.

**Solution:**

The following shows the configuration on the P1R1 and P1R2 routers:

```
P1R1(config)#router bgp 65001
P1R1(config-router)#aggregate-address 10.1.0.0 255.255.0.0 summary-only

P1R2(config)#router bgp 65001
P1R2(config-router)#aggregate-address 10.1.0.0 255.255.0.0 summary-only
```

**Step 2**　Telnet to either BBR1 or BBR2, and view the routing table. Is the aggregate address for your pod present?

---

**Note**　It might take a while to see the aggregate routes in the backbone routers.

---

**Solution:**

The following output is from the BBR1 router. The pod 1 summary route is in the BBR1 routing table:

```
BBR1>show ip route
<output omitted>
Gateway of last resort is not set

     172.31.0.0/24 is subnetted, 4 subnets
B       172.31.22.0 [20/0] via 10.254.0.2, 01:25:57
C       172.31.2.0 is directly connected, Serial0.2
C       172.31.1.0 is directly connected, Serial0.1
B       172.31.11.0 [20/0] via 10.254.0.2, 01:25:57
S    192.168.11.0/24 [1/0] via 172.31.1.2
     10.0.0.0/8 is variably subnetted, 4 subnets, 2 masks
B       10.2.0.0/16 [20/0] via 172.31.2.1, 00:02:11
B       10.97.97.0/24 [20/0] via 10.254.0.3, 06:48:18
B       10.1.0.0/16 [20/0] via 172.31.1.1, 00:01:56
C       10.254.0.0/24 is directly connected, Ethernet0
S    192.168.22.0/24 [1/0] via 172.31.2.2
S    192.168.1.0/24 [1/0] via 172.31.1.1
S    192.168.2.0/24 [1/0] via 172.31.2.1
BBR1>
```

**Step 3**　From the BBR1 or BBR2 router, ping 10.*x*.3.3 and 10.*x*.3.4 to test connectivity.

**Solution:**

The following output is from the BBR1 router, pinging to the pod 1 addresses. All the pings work.

```
BBR1>ping 10.1.3.3
Type escape sequence to abort.
Sending 5, 100-byte ICMP Echos to 10.1.3.3, timeout is 2 seconds:
!!!!!
Success rate is 100 percent (5/5), round-trip min/avg/max = 36/75/132 ms

BBR1>ping 10.1.3.4
Type escape sequence to abort.
Sending 5, 100-byte ICMP Echos to 10.1.3.4, timeout is 2 seconds:
!!!!!
Success rate is 100 percent (5/5), round-trip min/avg/max = 52/103/240 ms
BBR1>
```

**Step 4**   On the edge routers, display the BGP table with the **show ip bgp** command. Do you see your pod subnets being suppressed because of the **summary-only** option used with the **aggregate-address** command?

**Solution:**

The following output is from the P1R1 router. The pod subnets have an s in the first column, indicating that they are being suppressed. Note that the aggregate address, 10.1.0.0/16, does not have an s in the first column.

```
P1R1#show ip bgp
BGP table version is 49, local router ID is 10.200.200.11
Status codes: s suppressed, d damped, h history, * valid, > best, i - internal
Origin codes: i - IGP, e - EGP, ? - incomplete

     Network          Next Hop         Metric LocPrf Weight Path
 s> 10.1.0.0/24       0.0.0.0               0         32768 i
 *  i10.1.0.0/16      10.1.0.2                    100     0 i
 *>                   0.0.0.0                         32768 i
 s> 10.1.1.0/24       0.0.0.0               0         32768 i
 s> 10.1.2.0/24       0.0.0.0               2         32768 i
 s> 10.1.3.0/24       0.0.0.0               1         32768 i
 *  i10.2.0.0/16      172.31.11.4                 100     0 64999 65002 i
 *                    172.31.1.3                          0 64998 65002 i
 *>                   172.31.11.4                         0 64999 65002 i
 *   10.97.97.0/24    172.31.11.4                         0 64999 64997 i
 *  i                 172.31.1.3                  100     0 64998 64997 i
 *>                   172.31.1.3                          0 64998 64997 i
 *   10.254.0.0/24    172.31.11.4                         0 64999 64998 i
 *  i                 172.31.1.3            0      100     0 64998 i
 *>                   172.31.1.3            0              0 64998 i
 *   172.31.1.0/24    172.31.11.4                         0 64999 64998 i
 *  i                 172.31.1.3            0      100     0 64998 i
 *>                   172.31.1.3            0              0 64998 i
 *   172.31.2.0/24    172.31.11.4                         0 64999 64998 i
```

*continues*

```
* i                    172.31.1.3          0    100     0 64998 i
*>                     172.31.1.3          0            0 64998 i
*> 172.31.11.0/24      172.31.11.4         0            0 64999 i
* i                    172.31.11.4         0    100     0 64999 i
*                      172.31.1.3                       0 64998 64999 i
*> 172.31.22.0/24      172.31.11.4         0            0 64999 i
* i                    172.31.11.4         0    100     0 64999 i
*                      172.31.1.3                       0 64998 64999 i
P1R1#
```

**Step 5**  Examine the best path selected for network 10.97.97.0 in AS 64997. (The 10.97.97.0 subnet in AS 64997 is a loopback address, configured on the Frame Relay switch router.) What is the next hop for this network?

**Solution:**

As shown in the P1R1 BGP table, the best path selected for the 10.97.97.0 network is the third path, through 172.31.1.3.

**Step 6**  Based on the BGP path-selection process, why was that path chosen?

**Solution:**

The three routes to 10.97.97.0 are shown in the **show ip bgp** output. The weight and local preference are the same for all routes and therefore do not determine the best route. None of the routes is originated by the local router. The AS paths are all the same length, and the origin codes are all i. The MEDs are all the same. Therefore, the path-selection process looks at EBGP versus IBGP routes, and EBGP routes are preferred. Two EBGP routes exist. Therefore, the route with the lower neighbor BGP router ID is preferred. The route through 172.31.1.3 is preferred over the route through 172.31.11.4.

## Exercise Verification

You have successfully completed this exercise when you achieve the following results:

- You have summarized the pod network in BGP advertisements.
- You have determined the BGP path-selection process used by your BGP routers.

# Solution to Configuration Exercise 9-2: BGP Path Manipulation Using MED and Local Preference with Route Maps

This section provides the answers to the questions in the Configuration Exercise.

---

**NOTE**  Some answers provided cover multiple steps; the answers are given after the last step to which that answer applies.

---

## Solution to Task: Using MED and Local Preference with Route Maps for BGP Path Manipulation

**Step 1**    On the edge routers, look at the BGP table, and notice the next hop for routes to the 172.31.*x*.0 and 172.31.*xx*.0 networks in the *other* pod (in other words, the networks that connect the BBR1 and BBR2 routers to the other pod).

**Solution:**

The following output is from the P1R1 and P1R2 routers. The highlighted lines show the networks 172.31.2.0 and 172.31.22.0, which are the networks that connect pod 2 to the BBR1 and BBR2 routers.

```
P1R1#show ip bgp
BGP table version is 49, local router ID is 10.200.200.11
Status codes: s suppressed, d damped, h history, * valid, > best, i - internal
Origin codes: i - IGP, e - EGP, ? - incomplete

   Network          Next Hop          Metric LocPrf Weight Path
s> 10.1.0.0/24      0.0.0.0               0          32768 i
* i10.1.0.0/16      10.1.0.2                    100      0 i
*>                  0.0.0.0                          32768 i
s> 10.1.1.0/24      0.0.0.0               0          32768 i
s> 10.1.2.0/24      0.0.0.0               2          32768 i
s> 10.1.3.0/24      0.0.0.0               1          32768 i
* i10.2.0.0/16      172.31.11.4                 100      0 64999 65002 i
*                   172.31.1.3                           0 64998 65002 i
*>                  172.31.11.4                          0 64999 65002 i
*   10.97.97.0/24   172.31.11.4                          0 64999 64997 i
* i                 172.31.1.3                  100      0 64998 64997 i
*>                  172.31.1.3                            0 64998 64997 i
*   10.254.0.0/24   172.31.11.4                          0 64999 64998 i
* i                 172.31.1.3            0      100      0 64998 i
*>                  172.31.1.3            0               0 64998 i
*   172.31.1.0/24   172.31.11.4                          0 64999 64998 i
* i                 172.31.1.3            0      100      0 64998 i
*>                  172.31.1.3            0               0 64998 i
*   172.31.2.0/24   172.31.11.4                          0 64999 64998 i
* i                 172.31.1.3            0      100      0 64998 i
*>                  172.31.1.3            0               0 64998 i
*> 172.31.11.0/24   172.31.11.4          0               0 64999 i
* i                 172.31.11.4          0      100      0 64999 i
*                   172.31.1.3                           0 64998 64999 i
*> 172.31.22.0/24   172.31.11.4          0               0 64999 i
* i                 172.31.11.4          0      100      0 64999 i
*                   172.31.1.3                           0 64998 64999 i
P1R1#
P1R2#show ip bgp
BGP table version is 46, local router ID is 10.200.200.12
Status codes: s suppressed, d damped, h history, * valid, > best, i - internal
Origin codes: i - IGP, e - EGP, ? - incomplete
```

*continues*

```
        Network          Next Hop          Metric LocPrf Weight Path
 s> 10.1.0.0/24          0.0.0.0                0           32768 i
 *> 10.1.0.0/16          0.0.0.0                            32768 i
 * i                     10.1.0.1                      100      0 i
 s> 10.1.1.0/24          0.0.0.0                2           32768 i
 s> 10.1.2.0/24          0.0.0.0                0           32768 i
 s> 10.1.3.0/24          0.0.0.0                1           32768 i
 *    10.2.0.0/16        172.31.1.3                             0 64998 65002 i
 *>                      172.31.11.4                            0 64999 65002 i
 * i                     172.31.11.4                   100      0 64999 65002 i
 *    10.97.97.0/24      172.31.11.4                            0 64999 64997 i
 * i                     172.31.1.3                    100      0 64998 64997 i
 *>                      172.31.1.3                             0 64998 64997 i
 *    10.254.0.0/24      172.31.11.4                            0 64999 64998 i
 * i                     172.31.1.3             0      100      0 64998 i
 *>                      172.31.1.3             0                0 64998 i
 *    172.31.1.0/24      172.31.11.4                            0 64999 64998 i
 * i                     172.31.1.3             0      100      0 64998 i
 *>                      172.31.1.3             0                0 64998 i
 *    172.31.2.0/24      172.31.11.4                            0 64999 64998 i
 * i                     172.31.1.3             0      100      0 64998 i
 *>                      172.31.1.3             0                0 64998 i
 * i172.31.11.0/24       172.31.11.4            0      100      0 64999 i
 *>                      172.31.11.4            0                0 64999 i
 *                       172.31.1.3                             0 64998 64999 i
 *> 172.31.22.0/24       172.31.11.4            0                0 64999 i
 * i                     172.31.11.4            0      100      0 64999 i
 *                       172.31.1.3                             0 64998 64999 i
P1R2#
```

**Step 2**   Which path does the edge router use to reach the remote 172.31.x.0 networks? Why does BGP choose that path? Which path does the edge router use to reach the remote 172.31.xx.0 networks? Why does BGP choose that path?

**Solution:**

P1R1 and P1R2 use 172.31.1.3 (BBR1) to reach 172.31.2.0/24 and use 172.31.11.4 (BBR2) to reach 172.31.22.0/24. These are the shortest AS path external routes to these networks; there is one AS in the selected path.

**Step 3**   This company has established a policy that all traffic exiting the AS bound for any of the remote 172.31.x.0 and 172.31.xx.0 networks should take the path through BBR2.

To comply with this policy, configure the edge routers, PxR1 and PxR2, with a route map setting local preference to 300 for any routes to the remote 172.31.x.0 and 172.31.xx.0 networks that are advertised by BBR2.

**Solution:**

The following shows the required configuration on the P1R1 and P1R2 routers:

```
P1R1(config)#route-map SET_PREF permit 10
P1R1(config-route-map)#match ip address 3
```

```
P1R1(config-route-map)#set local-preference 300
P1R1(config-route-map)#route-map SET_PREF permit 20
P1R1(config-route-map)#exit
P1R1(config)#access-list 3 permit 172.31.0.0 0.0.255.255
P1R1(config)#router bgp 65001
P1R1(config-router)#neighbor 172.31.11.4 route-map SET_PREF in

P1R2(config)#route-map SET_PREF permit 10
P1R2(config-route-map)#match ip address 3
P1R2(config-route-map)#set local-preference 300
P1R2(config-route-map)#route-map SET_PREF permit 20
P1R2(config-route-map)#exit
P1R2(config)#access-list 3 permit 172.31.0.0 0.0.255.255
P1R2(config)#router bgp 65001
P1R2(config-router)#neighbor 172.31.11.4 route-map SET_PREF in
```

**Step 4**  Look at the BGP table on the edge routers. Has the local preference for the routes learned from BBR2 changed?

**Solution:**

The following shows the BGP table on the P1R1 router. The local preference has not changed.

```
P1R1#show ip bgp
BGP table version is 49, local router ID is 10.200.200.11
Status codes: s suppressed, d damped, h history, * valid, > best, i - internal
Origin codes: i - IGP, e - EGP, ? - incomplete

   Network          Next Hop         Metric LocPrf Weight Path
s> 10.1.0.0/24      0.0.0.0              0           32768 i
*  i10.1.0.0/16     10.1.0.2                    100      0 i
*>                  0.0.0.0                          32768 i
s> 10.1.1.0/24      0.0.0.0              0           32768 i
s> 10.1.2.0/24      0.0.0.0              2           32768 i
s> 10.1.3.0/24      0.0.0.0              1           32768 i
*  i10.2.0.0/16     172.31.11.4                100      0 64999 65002 i
*                   172.31.1.3                           0 64998 65002 i
*>                  172.31.11.4                          0 64999 65002 i
*  10.97.97.0/24    172.31.11.4                          0 64999 64997 i
*  i                172.31.1.3                 100      0 64998 64997 i
*>                  172.31.1.3                           0 64998 64997 i
*  10.254.0.0/24    172.31.11.4                          0 64999 64998 i
*  i                172.31.1.3           0     100      0 64998 i
*>                  172.31.1.3           0              0 64998 i
*  172.31.1.0/24    172.31.11.4                          0 64999 64998 i
*  i                172.31.1.3           0     100      0 64998 i
*>                  172.31.1.3           0              0 64998 i
   Network          Next Hop         Metric LocPrf Weight Path
*  172.31.2.0/24    172.31.11.4                          0 64999 64998 i
*  i                172.31.1.3           0     100      0 64998 i
*>                  172.31.1.3           0              0 64998 i
*> 172.31.11.0/24   172.31.11.4          0              0 64999 i
*  i                172.31.11.4          0     100      0 64999 i
```

*continues*

```
*                        172.31.1.3                             0 64998 64999 i
*> 172.31.22.0/24        172.31.11.4            0               0 64999 i
* i                      172.31.11.4            0      100       0 64999 i
*                        172.31.1.3                             0 64998 64999 i
P1R1#
```

**Step 5**   When you configure a policy, it is not automatically applied to routes already in the BGP table. You can either reset the BGP relationship with BBR2 or configure the router to apply the policy to existing routes without resetting the relationship; the latter solution is called a *soft* reconfiguration. Use a soft reconfiguration to apply the policy to the routes that come in from BBR2 using the command **clear ip bgp 172.31.*xx*.4 soft in**.

**Solution:**

The following shows the required command on the P1R1 and P1R2 routers:

```
P1R1#clear ip bgp 172.31.11.4 soft in
P1R2#clear ip bgp 172.31.11.4 soft in
```

**Step 6**   Look at the BGP table again. Have the local preference values changed?

**Solution:**

The following output is from the P1R1 router. The local preference value for the routes learned from BBR2 is now 300.

```
P1R1#show ip bgp
BGP table version is 58, local router ID is 10.200.200.11
Status codes: s suppressed, d damped, h history, * valid, > best, i - internal
Origin codes: i - IGP, e - EGP, ? - incomplete

   Network           Next Hop            Metric LocPrf Weight Path
s> 10.1.0.0/24       0.0.0.0                  0         32768 i
* i10.1.0.0/16       10.1.0.2                    100       0 i
*>                   0.0.0.0                           32768 i
s> 10.1.1.0/24       0.0.0.0                  0         32768 i
s> 10.1.2.0/24       0.0.0.0                  2         32768 i
s> 10.1.3.0/24       0.0.0.0                  1         32768 i
* i10.2.0.0/16       172.31.1.3                  100       0 64998 65002 i
*                    172.31.1.3                           0 64998 65002 i
*>                   172.31.11.4                          0 64999 65002 i
* i10.97.97.0/24     172.31.1.3                  100       0 64998 64997 i
*                    172.31.11.4                          0 64999 64997 i
*>                   172.31.1.3                           0 64998 64997 i
* i10.254.0.0/24     172.31.1.3               0  100       0 64998 i
*                    172.31.11.4                          0 64999 64998 i
*>                   172.31.1.3               0             0 64998 i
* i172.31.1.0/24     172.31.11.4                 300       0 64999 64998 i
*>                   172.31.11.4                 300       0 64999 64998 i
*                    172.31.1.3               0             0 64998 i
* i172.31.2.0/24     172.31.11.4                 300       0 64999 64998 i
*>                   172.31.11.4                 300       0 64999 64998 i
```

```
*                      172.31.1.3        0              0 64998 i
* i172.31.11.0/24      172.31.11.4       0    300       0 64999 i
*>                     172.31.11.4       0    300       0 64999 i
*                      172.31.1.3                        0 64998 64999 i
* i172.31.22.0/24      172.31.11.4       0    300       0 64999 i
*>                     172.31.11.4       0    300       0 64999 i
*                      172.31.1.3                        0 64998 64999 i
P1R1#
```

**Step 7**   Which path does the edge router use to reach the remote 172.31.*x*.0 networks now? Why does BGP choose that path even though the AS path is longer? Which path does the edge router use to reach the remote 172.31.*xx*.0 networks now? Why does BGP choose that path?

**Solution:**

P1R1 is using 172.31.11.4 (BBR2) to reach the 172.31.2.0 and 172.31.22.0 networks. The path to 172.31.2.0 through BBR2 was chosen because the local preference is higher; local preference is looked at before AS path length. Of the two routes with the same local preference, the EBGP route is chosen, because EBGP routes are preferred over IBGP routes.

**Step 8**   Both of the core routers (BBR1 and BBR2) have multiple ways into each pod. For example, BBR1 could take the direct path through your pod's P*x*R1 or P*x*R2 router, or it could take a path through BBR2 and then to one of the pod's edge routers.

**Step 9**   Telnet to BBR1 (the password is **cisco**), and examine the BGP table. Which path does the BBR1 router use to reach your pod's 10.*x*.0.0 network? Why does BGP choose that path?

**Solution:**

The following output is from the BBR1 router. BBR1 uses the 172.31.1.1 path (through P1R1) to get to 10.1.0.0/16. This path is chosen because all the other parameters are equal, so the AS path is considered. Of the two routes with an AS path length of 1, either this route is older, or, if they are the same age, the lower neighbor router ID is considered. The BGP router IDs are the routers' loopback addresses: P1R1 has a router ID of 10.200.200.11, and P1R2 (172.31.1.2) has a router ID of 10.200.200.12.

```
BBR1>show ip bgp
BGP table version is 138, local router ID is 172.31.2.3
Status codes: s suppressed, d damped, h history, * valid, > best, i - internal
Origin codes: i - IGP, e - EGP, ? - incomplete

   Network          Next Hop          Metric LocPrf Weight Path
*  10.1.0.0/16      172.31.1.2                        0 65001 i
*                   172.31.2.1                        0 65002 64999 65001 i
*                   10.254.0.2                        0 64999 65001 i
*>                  172.31.1.1                        0 65001 i
*  10.2.0.0/16      172.31.2.2                        0 65002 i
*                   10.254.0.2                        0 64997 64999 65002 i
```

*continues*

```
*                        10.254.0.2                          0 64999 65002 i
*                        172.31.1.1                          0 65001 64999 65002 i
*>                       172.31.2.1                          0 65002 i
*   10.97.97.0/24        172.31.2.1                          0 65002 64999 64997 i
*>                       10.254.0.3           0              0 64997 i
*                        10.254.0.3                          0 64999 64997 i
*>  10.254.0.0/24        0.0.0.0              0          32768 i
*>  172.31.1.0/24        0.0.0.0              0          32768 i
*>  172.31.2.0/24        0.0.0.0              0          32768 i
*   172.31.11.0/24       172.31.1.2                          0 65001 64999 i
*                        172.31.2.2                          0 65002 64999 i
*                        172.31.2.1                          0 65002 64999 i
*                        172.31.1.1                          0 65001 64999 i
*>                       10.254.0.2           0              0 64999 i
*                        10.254.0.2                          0 64997 64999 i
*   172.31.22.0/24       172.31.1.2                          0 65001 64999 i
*                        172.31.2.2                          0 65002 64999 i
*                        172.31.2.1                          0 65002 64999 i
*                        172.31.1.1                          0 65001 64999 i
*>                       10.254.0.2           0              0 64999 i
*                        10.254.0.2                          0 64997 64999 i
BBR1>
```

**Step 10** Telnet to BBR2 (the password is **cisco**), and examine the BGP table. Which path does the BBR2 router use to reach your pod's 10.x.0.0 network? Why does BGP choose that path?

**Solution:**

The following output is from the BBR2 router. BBR2 uses the 172.31.11.1 path (through P1R1) to get to 10.1.0.0/16. This path is chosen because all the other parameters are equal, so the AS path is considered. Of the two routes with an AS path length of 1, either this route is older, or, if they are the same age, the lower neighbor router ID is considered. The BGP router IDs are the routers' loopback addresses: P1R1 has a router ID of 10.200.200.11, and P1R2 (172.31.11.2) has a router ID of 10.200.200.12.

```
BBR2>show ip bgp
BGP table version is 199, local router ID is 172.31.22.4
Status codes: s suppressed, d damped, h history, * valid, > best, i - internal
Origin codes: i - IGP, e - EGP, ? - incomplete

    Network          Next Hop            Metric LocPrf Weight Path
*   10.1.0.0/16      172.31.11.2                          0 65001 i
*                    172.31.22.2                          0 65002 64998 65001 i
*                    10.254.0.1                           0 64998 65001 i
*                    10.254.0.1                           0 64997 64998 65001 i
*>                   172.31.11.1                          0 65001 i
*   10.2.0.0/16      172.31.11.2                          0 65001 64998 65002 i
*                    172.31.22.2                          0 65002 i
*                    10.254.0.1                           0 64998 65002 i
*>                   172.31.22.1                          0 65002 i
```

```
*   10.97.97.0/24   172.31.11.2                      0 65001 64998 64997 i
*                   172.31.22.2                      0 65002 64998 64997 i
*                   172.31.11.1                      0 65001 64998 64997 i
*                   10.254.0.3                       0 64998 64997 i
*>                  10.254.0.3          0            0 64997 i
*   10.254.0.0/24   172.31.11.2                      0 65001 64998 i
*                   172.31.22.2                      0 65002 64998 i
*                   172.31.22.1                      0 65002 64998 i
*                   172.31.11.1                      0 65001 64998 i
*                   10.254.0.1                       0 64997 64998 i
*>                  10.254.0.1          0            0 64998 i
*   172.31.1.0/24   10.254.0.1                       0 64997 64998 i
*>                  10.254.0.1          0            0 64998 i
*   172.31.2.0/24   10.254.0.1                       0 64997 64998 i
*>                  10.254.0.1          0            0 64998 i
*> 172.31.11.0/24   0.0.0.0             0        32768 i
*> 172.31.22.0/24   0.0.0.0             0        32768 i
BBR2>
```

**Step 11** Suppose this company has also established a policy for traffic inbound from the core. This policy states the following:

- Traffic from BBR1 to your pod 10.x.0.0 network should enter your pod through PxR1.

- Traffic from BBR2 to your pod 10.x.0.0 network should enter your pod through PxR2.

To accomplish this policy, you will do the following:

- Make the paths through PxR1 look unattractive to BBR2.

- Make the paths through PxR2 look unattractive to BBR1.

Currently, the MED for both paths is 0 in the BGP table of both BBR1 and BBR2, so BBR1 and BBR2 pick the oldest EBGP path.

On PxR1, configure a route map that sets the MED to 200 for routes to your pod's internal network (10.x.0.0); apply the route map to updates sent to BBR2. (Remember that a lower MED is more attractive to BGP.)

**Solution:**

The following shows the required configuration on P1R1:

```
P1R1(config)#route-map SET_MED_HI permit 10
P1R1(config-route-map)#match ip address 4
P1R1(config-route-map)#set metric 200
P1R1(config-route-map)#route-map SET_MED_HI permit 20
P1R1(config-route-map)#exit
P1R1(config)#access-list 4 permit 10.1.0.0 0.0.255.255
P1R1(config)#router bgp 65001
P1R1(config-router)#neighbor 172.31.11.4 route-map SET_MED_HI out
```

On P*x*R2, configure a route map that sets the MED to 200 for routes to your pod's internal network (10.*x*.0.0); apply the route map to updates sent to BBR1.

**Solution:**

The following shows the required configuration on P1R2:

```
P1R2(config)#route-map SET_MED_HI permit 10
P1R2(config-route-map)#match ip address 4
P1R2(config-route-map)#set metric 200
P1R2(config-route-map)#route-map SET_MED_HI permit 20
P1R2(config-route-map)#exit
P1R2(config)#access-list 4 permit 10.1.0.0 0.0.255.255
P1R2(config)#router bgp 65001
P1R2(config-router)#neighbor 172.31.1.3 route-map SET_MED_HI out
```

**Step 12** Perform a soft reconfiguration after you apply the policy to the BGP neighbor (BBR1 or BBR2) by using the **clear ip bgp** *ip-address* **soft out** command.

**Solution:**

The following shows the required command applied to the P1R1 and P1R2 routers:

```
P1R1#clear ip bgp 172.31.11.4 soft out
P1R2#clear ip bgp 172.31.1.3 soft out
```

**Step 13** Telnet to the core routers, and examine the BGP table. Verify that the MED changes have taken effect.

**Solution:**

The following output from the BBR1 and BBR2 routers shows that the MED changes have taken effect:

```
BBR1>show ip bgp
BGP table version is 141, local router ID is 172.31.2.3
Status codes: s suppressed, d damped, h history, * valid, > best, i - internal
Origin codes: i - IGP, e - EGP, ? - incomplete

   Network          Next Hop         Metric LocPrf Weight Path
*  10.1.0.0/16      172.31.2.2          200            0 65002 64999 65001 i
*                   172.31.2.1                         0 65002 64999 65001 i
*                   172.31.1.2          200            0 65001 i
*                   10.254.0.2                         0 64999 65001 i
*>                  172.31.1.1                         0 65001 i
*  10.2.0.0/16      172.31.2.2          200            0 65002 i
*                   10.254.0.2                         0 64999 65002 i
*>                  172.31.2.1                         0 65002 i
*  10.97.97.0/24    172.31.2.2          200            0 65002 64999 64997 i
*                   172.31.2.1                         0 65002 64999 64997 i
*>                  10.254.0.3            0             0 64997 i
*                   10.254.0.3                         0 64999 64997 i
*> 10.254.0.0/24    0.0.0.0              0         32768 i
```

```
*> 172.31.1.0/24    0.0.0.0              0          32768 i
*> 172.31.2.0/24    0.0.0.0              0          32768 i
*  172.31.11.0/24   172.31.2.2         200            0 65002 64999 i
*                   172.31.2.1                        0 65002 64999 i
*                   172.31.1.2                        0 65001 64999 i
*                   172.31.1.1                        0 65001 64999 i
*>                  10.254.0.2           0            0 64999 i
*                   10.254.0.2                        0 64997 64999 i
*  172.31.22.0/24   172.31.2.2         200            0 65002 64999 i
*                   172.31.2.1                        0 65002 64999 i
*                   172.31.1.2                        0 65001 64999 i
*                   172.31.1.1                        0 65001 64999 i
*>                  10.254.0.2           0            0 64999 i
*                   10.254.0.2                        0 64997 64999 i
BBR1>      exit

BBR2>      show ip bgp
BGP table version is 204, local router ID is 172.31.22.4
Status codes: s suppressed, d damped, h history, * valid, > best, i - internal
Origin codes: i - IGP, e - EGP, ? - incomplete

    Network          Next Hop         Metric LocPrf Weight Path
*> 10.1.0.0/16       172.31.11.2                        0 65001 i
*                    10.254.0.1                         0 64998 65001 i
*                    10.254.0.1                         0 64997 64998 65001 i
*                    172.31.11.1        200             0 65001 i
*> 10.2.0.0/16       172.31.22.2                        0 65002 i
*                    172.31.22.1        200             0 65002 i
*                    10.254.0.1                         0 64997 64998 65002 i
*                    172.31.11.1                        0 65001 64998 65002 i
*                    172.31.11.2                        0 65001 64998 65002 i
*                    10.254.0.1                         0 64998 65002 i
*  10.97.97.0/24     172.31.11.2                        0 65001 64998 64997 i
*                    172.31.11.1                        0 65001 64998 64997 i
*                    10.254.0.3                         0 64998 64997 i
*>                   10.254.0.3           0             0 64997 i
*  10.254.0.0/24     172.31.22.2                        0 65002 64998 i
*                    172.31.22.1                        0 65002 64998 i
*                    172.31.11.2                        0 65001 64998 i
*                    172.31.11.1                        0 65001 64998 i
*                    10.254.0.1                         0 64997 64998 i
*>                   10.254.0.1           0             0 64998 i
*  172.31.1.0/24     10.254.0.1                         0 64997 64998 i
*>                   10.254.0.1           0             0 64998 i
*  172.31.2.0/24     10.254.0.1                         0 64997 64998 i
*>                   10.254.0.1           0             0 64998 i
*> 172.31.11.0/24    0.0.0.0              0          32768 i
*> 172.31.22.0/24    0.0.0.0              0          32768 i
BBR2>
```

**Step 14**   Notice that the path with a MED of 200 is not chosen as the best path. What is the best path from BBR1 to your pod 10.x.0.0 network now? What is the best path from BBR2 to your pod 10.x.0.0 network now?

**Solution:**

The best path from BBR1 to 10.1.0.0 is via 172.31.1.1 (P1R1). This path is chosen because the AS path length is considered before the MED. The two routes with an AS path length of 1 have the same MED, so either this route is older, or, if they are the same age, the lower neighbor router ID is considered. The BGP router IDs are the routers' loopback addresses: P1R1 has a router ID of 10.200.200.11, and P1R2 (172.31.1.2) has a router ID of 10.200.200.12.

The best path from BBR2 to 10.1.0.0 is via 172.31.11.2 (P1R2). The AS path is considered before the MED, so the two routes with an AS path length of 1, through 172.31.11.2 and 172.31.11.1, are considered. The latter has a MED of 200, and the former has a default MED of 0. Because a lower MED is preferred, the route through 172.31.11.2 is selected as the best path.

## Exercise Verification

You have successfully completed this exercise when you achieve the following results:

- You have changed the local preference of the specified routes.
- You have changed the MED of the specified routes.

# Review Questions

Answer the following questions, and then refer to Appendix G, "Answers to Review Questions," for the answers.

1  How does BGP-4 support CIDR?

2  Describe the BGP atomic aggregate and aggregator attributes.

3  What is the default mask on the BGP **network** *network-number* [**mask** *network-mask*] router configuration command?

4  A BGP router has network 172.16.25.0/24 in the routing table as a directly connected network. The BGP command **network 172.16.0.0** is configured on the router. What network does the router announce to its BGP neighbors?

5  What is the preferred method to use to advertise an aggregated route from an AS into BGP?

6  What is the difference between using the **network** command and using the **aggregate-address** command for summarization?

7  Which option of the **aggregate-address** command affects the atomic aggregate attribute?

8  Which option in the **aggregate-address** command affects the number of routes advertised to other routers?

9  Describe the different functions of the BGP **network**, **neighbor**, and **aggregate-address** commands.

10  How can BGP path manipulation affect the relative bandwidth used between two connections to the Internet?

**11** Complete the following table to answer these questions about BGP attributes:

— In which order are the attributes preferred (1, 2, or 3)?

— For the attribute, is the highest or lowest value preferred?

— What is the attribute's default value?

— Which other routers, if any, is the attribute sent to?

| Attribute | Order in Which It Is Preferred | Highest or Lowest Value Preferred? | Default Value | Sent to Which Other Routers? |
|-----------|-------------------------------|-----------------------------------|---------------|------------------------------|
| Local preference | | | | |
| MED | | | | |
| Weight | | | | |

**12** Describe what the following configuration on Router A does:

```
route-map local_pref permit 10
match ip address 65
set local-preference 300
route-map local_pref permit 20
router bgp 65001
neighbor 192.168.5.3 remote-as 65002
neighbor 192.168.5.3 route-map local_pref in
```

**13** Place the BGP route selection criteria in order from the first step to the last step evaluated by placing a number in the blank provided.

_____ Prefer the path with the lowest neighbor BGP router ID.

_____ Prefer the lowest MED.

_____ Prefer the shortest AS path.

_____ Prefer the oldest route for EBGP paths.

_____ Prefer the lowest origin code.

_____ Prefer the highest weight.

_____ Prefer the path through the closest IGP neighbor.

_____ Prefer the highest local preference.

_____ Prefer the route originated by the local router.

_____ Prefer the EBGP path over the IBGP path.

**14** What command is used to assign a weight to a BGP neighbor connection?

**15** What is BGP multihoming?

**16** What are three common design options for BGP multihoming?

**17** What are some advantages of getting default routes and selected specific routes from your ISPs?

**18** What is a disadvantage of having all ISPs pass all BGP routes into your AS?

This appendix contains job aids and supplements for the following topics:

- Supplement 1: IPv4 Addressing
- Supplement 2: EIGRP
- Supplement 3: OSPF
- Supplement 4: IS-IS
- Supplement 5: BGP
- Supplement 6: Route Optimization

# Job Aids and Supplements

The job aids and supplements in this appendix give you some background information on and additional examples of the concepts covered in this book.

The Internet Protocol version 4 (IPv4) addressing supplement includes job aids and supplements that are intended for your use when working with IP addresses. The other supplements contain examples of and additional material on Enhanced Interior Gateway Routing Protocol (EIGRP), Open Shortest Path First (OSPF) protocol, Intermediate System-Intermediate System (IS-IS) protocol, Border Gateway Protocol (BGP), and route optimization.

---

**NOTE**     In this appendix, the term IP refers to IPv4.

---

## Supplement 1: IPv4 Addressing

This section includes an IP addressing and subnetting job aid, as well as a decimal-to-binary conversion chart. The information in the sections "IPv4 Addressing Review" and "IPv4 Access Lists" should serve as a review of the fundamentals of IP addressing and of the concepts and configuration of access lists, respectively. The "IP Features" section includes supplemental information on IP unnumbered serial interfaces, IP helper addresses, and Hot Standby Router Protocol (HSRP).

### IPv4 Addresses and Subnetting Job Aid

Figure A-1 is a job aid to help you with various aspects of IP addressing, including how to distinguish address classes, the number of subnets and hosts available with various subnet masks, and how to interpret IP addresses.

**Figure A-1** *IP Addresses and Subnetting Job Aid*

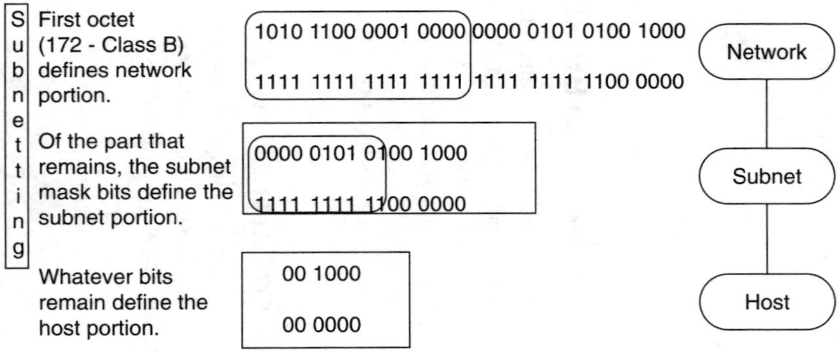

| Subnet Bits | Subnet Mask | Number of Subnets | Number of Hosts |
|---|---|---|---|
| Class B | | | |
| 2 | 255.255.192.0 | 4 | 16382 |
| 3 | 255.255.224.0 | 8 | 8190 |
| 4 | 255.255.240.0 | 16 | 4094 |
| 5 | 255.255.248.0 | 32 | 2046 |
| 6 | 255.255.252.0 | 64 | 1022 |
| 7 | 255.255.254.0 | 128 | 510 |
| 8 | 255.255.255.0 | 256 | 254 |
| 9 | 255.255.255.128 | 512 | 126 |
| 10 | 255.255.255.192 | 1024 | 62 |
| 11 | 255.255.255.224 | 2048 | 30 |
| 12 | 255.255.255.240 | 4096 | 14 |
| 13 | 255.255.255.248 | 8192 | 6 |
| 14 | 255.255.255.252 | 16384 | 2 |
| Class C | | | |
| 2 | 255.255.255.192 | 4 | 62 |
| 3 | 255.255.255.224 | 8 | 30 |
| 4 | 255.255.255.240 | 16 | 14 |
| 5 | 255.255.255.248 | 32 | 6 |
| 6 | 255.255.255.252 | 64 | 2 |

| Class | Net Host | First Octet | Standard Mask Binary |
|---|---|---|---|
| A | N.H.H.H | 1–126 | 1111 1111 0000 0000 0000 0000 0000 0000 |
| B | N.N.H.H | 128–191 | 1111 1111 1111 1111 0000 0000 0000 0000 |
| C | N.N.N.H | 192–223 | 1111 1111 1111 1111 1111 1111 0000 0000 |

Address       172.16.5.72       1010 1100 0001 0000 0000 0101 0100 1000
Subnet mask   255.255.255.192   1111 1111 1111 1111 1111 1111 1100 0000

S   First octet
u   (172 - Class B)
b   defines network
n   portion.
e
t   Of the part that
t   remains, the subnet
i   mask bits define the
n   subnet portion.
g

Network — Subnet — Host

1010 1100 0001 0000 0000 0101 0100 1000
1111 1111 1111 1111 1111 1111 1100 0000

0000 0101 0100 1000
1111 1111 1100 0000

00 1000
00 0000

Whatever bits
remain define the
host portion.

# Decimal-to-Binary Conversion Chart

Table A-1 can be used to convert from decimal to binary and from binary to decimal.

**Table A-1**    *Decimal-to-Binary Conversion Chart*

| Decimal | Binary | Decimal | Binary | Decimal | Binary | Decimal | Binary |
|---------|----------|---------|----------|---------|----------|---------|----------|
| 0 | 00000000 | 28 | 00011100 | 56 | 00111000 | 84 | 01010100 |
| 1 | 00000001 | 29 | 00011101 | 57 | 00111001 | 85 | 01010101 |
| 2 | 00000010 | 30 | 00011110 | 58 | 00111010 | 86 | 01010110 |
| 3 | 00000011 | 31 | 00011111 | 59 | 00111011 | 87 | 01010111 |
| 4 | 00000100 | 32 | 00100000 | 60 | 00111100 | 88 | 01011000 |
| 5 | 00000101 | 33 | 00100001 | 61 | 00111101 | 89 | 01011001 |
| 6 | 00000110 | 34 | 00100010 | 62 | 00111110 | 90 | 01011010 |
| 7 | 00000111 | 35 | 00100011 | 63 | 00111111 | 91 | 01011011 |
| 8 | 00001000 | 36 | 00100100 | 64 | 01000000 | 92 | 01011100 |
| 9 | 00001001 | 37 | 00100101 | 65 | 01000001 | 93 | 01011101 |
| 10 | 00001010 | 38 | 00100110 | 66 | 01000010 | 94 | 01011110 |
| 11 | 00001011 | 39 | 00100111 | 67 | 01000011 | 95 | 01011111 |
| 12 | 00001100 | 40 | 00101000 | 68 | 01000100 | 96 | 01100000 |
| 13 | 00001101 | 41 | 00101001 | 69 | 01000101 | 97 | 01100001 |
| 14 | 00001110 | 42 | 00101010 | 70 | 01000110 | 98 | 01100010 |
| 15 | 00001111 | 43 | 00101011 | 71 | 01000111 | 99 | 01100011 |
| 16 | 00010000 | 44 | 00101100 | 72 | 01001000 | 100 | 01100100 |
| 17 | 00010001 | 45 | 00101101 | 73 | 01001001 | 101 | 01100101 |
| 18 | 00010010 | 46 | 00101110 | 74 | 01001010 | 102 | 01100110 |
| 19 | 00010011 | 47 | 00101111 | 75 | 01001011 | 103 | 01100111 |
| 20 | 00010100 | 48 | 00110000 | 76 | 01001100 | 104 | 01101000 |
| 21 | 00010101 | 49 | 00110001 | 77 | 01001101 | 105 | 01101001 |
| 22 | 00010110 | 50 | 00110010 | 78 | 01001110 | 106 | 01101010 |
| 23 | 00010111 | 51 | 00110011 | 79 | 01001111 | 107 | 01101011 |
| 24 | 00011000 | 52 | 00110100 | 80 | 01010000 | 108 | 01101100 |
| 25 | 00011001 | 53 | 00110101 | 81 | 01010001 | 109 | 01101101 |
| 26 | 00011010 | 54 | 00110110 | 82 | 01010010 | 110 | 01101110 |
| 27 | 00011011 | 55 | 00110111 | 83 | 01010011 | 111 | 01101111 |

*continues*

**Table A-1** *Decimal-to-Binary Conversion Chart (Continued)*

| Decimal | Binary | Decimal | Binary | Decimal | Binary | Decimal | Binary |
|---------|----------|---------|----------|---------|----------|---------|----------|
| 112 | 01110000 | 143 | 10001111 | 174 | 10101110 | 205 | 11001101 |
| 113 | 01110001 | 144 | 10010000 | 175 | 10101111 | 206 | 11001110 |
| 114 | 01110010 | 145 | 10010001 | 176 | 10110000 | 207 | 11001111 |
| 115 | 01110011 | 146 | 10010010 | 177 | 10110001 | 208 | 11010000 |
| 116 | 01110100 | 147 | 10010011 | 178 | 10110010 | 209 | 11010001 |
| 117 | 01110101 | 148 | 10010100 | 179 | 10110011 | 210 | 11010010 |
| 118 | 01110110 | 149 | 10010101 | 180 | 10110100 | 211 | 11010011 |
| 119 | 01110111 | 150 | 10010110 | 181 | 10110101 | 212 | 11010100 |
| 120 | 01111000 | 151 | 10010111 | 182 | 10110110 | 213 | 11010101 |
| 121 | 01111001 | 152 | 10011000 | 183 | 10110111 | 214 | 11010110 |
| 122 | 01111010 | 153 | 10011001 | 184 | 10111000 | 215 | 11010111 |
| 123 | 01111011 | 154 | 10011010 | 185 | 10111001 | 216 | 11011000 |
| 124 | 01111100 | 155 | 10011011 | 186 | 10111010 | 217 | 11011001 |
| 125 | 01111101 | 156 | 10011100 | 187 | 10111011 | 218 | 11011010 |
| 126 | 01111110 | 157 | 10011101 | 188 | 10111100 | 219 | 11011011 |
| 127 | 01111111 | 158 | 10011110 | 189 | 10111101 | 220 | 11011100 |
| 128 | 10000000 | 159 | 10011111 | 190 | 10111110 | 221 | 11011101 |
| 129 | 10000001 | 160 | 10100000 | 191 | 10111111 | 222 | 11011110 |
| 130 | 10000010 | 161 | 10100001 | 192 | 11000000 | 223 | 11011111 |
| 131 | 10000011 | 162 | 10100010 | 193 | 11000001 | 224 | 11100000 |
| 132 | 10000100 | 163 | 10100011 | 194 | 11000010 | 225 | 11100001 |
| 133 | 10000101 | 164 | 10100100 | 195 | 11000011 | 226 | 11100010 |
| 134 | 10000110 | 165 | 10100101 | 196 | 11000100 | 227 | 11100011 |
| 135 | 10000111 | 166 | 10100110 | 197 | 11000101 | 228 | 11100100 |
| 136 | 10001000 | 167 | 10100111 | 198 | 11000110 | 229 | 11100101 |
| 137 | 10001001 | 168 | 10101000 | 199 | 11000111 | 230 | 11100110 |
| 138 | 10001010 | 169 | 10101001 | 200 | 11001000 | 231 | 11100111 |
| 139 | 10001011 | 170 | 10101010 | 201 | 11001001 | 232 | 11101000 |
| 140 | 10001100 | 171 | 10101011 | 202 | 11001010 | 233 | 11101001 |
| 141 | 10001101 | 172 | 10101100 | 203 | 11001011 | 234 | 11101010 |
| 142 | 10001110 | 173 | 10101101 | 204 | 11001100 | 235 | 11101011 |

**Table A-1**    *Decimal-to-Binary Conversion Chart (Continued)*

| Decimal | Binary | Decimal | Binary | Decimal | Binary | Decimal | Binary |
|---------|--------|---------|--------|---------|--------|---------|--------|
| 236 | 11101100 | 241 | 11110001 | 246 | 11110110 | 251 | 11111011 |
| 237 | 11101101 | 242 | 11110010 | 247 | 11110111 | 252 | 11111100 |
| 238 | 11101110 | 243 | 11110011 | 248 | 11111000 | 253 | 11111101 |
| 239 | 11101111 | 244 | 11110100 | 249 | 11111001 | 254 | 11111110 |
| 240 | 11110000 | 245 | 11110101 | 250 | 11111010 | 255 | 11111111 |

# IPv4 Addressing Review

This section reviews the basics of IPv4 addresses:

- Converting IP addresses between decimal and binary
- Determining an IP address class
- Extending an IP classful address using subnet masks
- Calculating a subnet mask
- Calculating the networks for a subnet mask
- Using prefixes to represent a subnet mask

## Converting IP Addresses Between Decimal and Binary

An *IP address* is a 32-bit, two-level hierarchical number. It is hierarchical because the first portion of the address represents the network, and the second portion of the address represents the node (or host).

The 32 bits are grouped into four octets, with 8 bits per octet. The value of each octet ranges from 0 to 255 decimal, or 00000000 to 11111111 binary. IP addresses are usually written in dotted-decimal notation. Each octet is written in decimal notation, and dots are placed between the octets. Figure A-2 shows how you convert an octet of an IP address in binary to decimal notation.

**Figure A-2**    *Converting an Octet of an IP Address from Binary to Decimal*

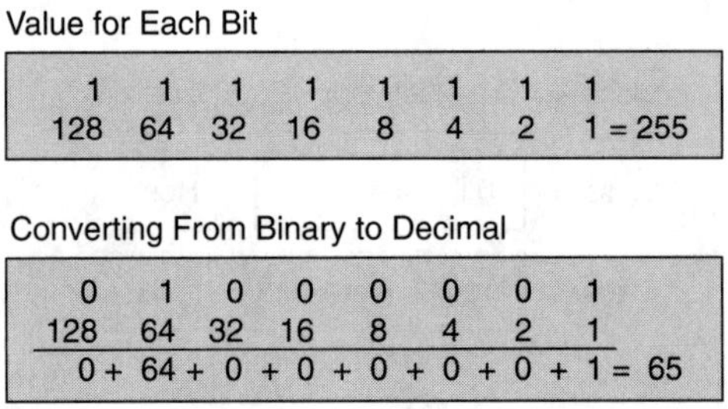

Value for Each Bit

| 1 | 1 | 1 | 1 | 1 | 1 | 1 | 1 |
|---|---|---|---|---|---|---|---|
| 128 | 64 | 32 | 16 | 8 | 4 | 2 | 1 = 255 |

Converting From Binary to Decimal

| 0 | 1 | 0 | 0 | 0 | 0 | 0 | 1 |
|---|---|---|---|---|---|---|---|
| 128 | 64 | 32 | 16 | 8 | 4 | 2 | 1 |

0 + 64 + 0 + 0 + 0 + 0 + 0 + 1 = 65

It is important that you understand how this conversion is done, because it is used when calculating subnet masks, a topic discussed later in this section.

Figure A-3 shows three examples of converting IP addresses between binary and decimal.

**Figure A-3**   *Converting IP Addresses Between Binary and Decimal*

Binary
Address:   00001010.00000001.00010111.00010011

Decimal
Address:   ___10___ . ___1___ . ___23___ . ___19___

Binary
Address:   10101100.00010010.01000001.10101010

Decimal
Address:   172 . 18 . 65 . 170

Binary
Address:   11000000.10101000.00001110.00000110

Decimal
Address:   ___192___ . ___168___ . ___14___ . ___6___

Now that you understand the decimal-to-binary and binary-to-decimal conversion processes, use the following sections to review address classes and the uses of subnet masks.

## Determining an IP Address Class

To accommodate large and small networks, the Network Information Center (NIC) segregated the 32-bit IP address into Classes A through E. The first few bits of the first octet determine the class of an address; this then determines how many network bits and host bits are in the address. Figure A-4 illustrates the bits for Class A, B, and C addresses. Each address class allows for a certain number of network addresses and a certain number of host addresses within a network. Table A-2 shows the address range, the number of networks, and the number of hosts for each of the classes. (Note that Class D and E addresses are used for purposes other than addressing hosts.)

**Figure A-4**   *Determining an IP Address Class from the First Few Bits of an Address*

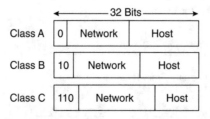

**Table A-2**    *IP Address Classes*

| Class | Address Range | Number of Networks | Number of Hosts |
|---|---|---|---|
| A | 1.0.0.0 to 126.0.0.0 | 128 ($2^7$) | 16,777,214 |
| B | 128.0.0.0 to 191.255.0.0 | 16,386 ($2^{14}$) | 65,532 |
| C | 192.0.0.0 to 223.255.255.0 | Approximately 2 million ($2^{21}$) | 254 |
| D | 224.0.0.0 to 239.255.255.254 | Reserved for multicast addresses | — |
| E | 240.0.0.0 to 254.255.255.255 | Reserved for research | — |

**NOTE**    The network 127.0.0.0 (any address starting with decimal 127) is reserved for loopback.

Using classes to denote which portion of the address represents the network number and which portion represents the node or host address is called *classful addressing*. Several issues must be addressed with classful addressing. First, the number of available Class A, B, and C addresses is finite. Another problem is that not all classes are useful for a midsize organization, as illustrated in Table A-2. As can be expected, the Class B range best accommodates a majority of today's organizational network topologies. Subnet masks were introduced to maximize the use of the IP addresses an organization receives, regardless of the class.

## Extending an IP Classful Address Using Subnet Masks

RFC 950, *Internet Standard Subnetting Procedure* (available at www.cis.ohio-state.edu/cgi-bin /rfc/rfc0950.html), was written to address the IP address shortage. It proposed a procedure, called *subnet masking*, for dividing Class A, B, and C addresses into smaller pieces, thereby increasing the number of possible networks. A subnet mask is a 32-bit value that identifies which address bits represent network bits and which represent host bits. In other words, the router does not determine the network portion of the address by looking at the value of the first octet; rather, it looks at the subnet mask that is associated with the address. In this way, subnet masks let you extend the usage of an IP address. This is one way of making an IP address a three-level hierarchy, as shown in Figure A-5.

**Figure A-5**    *A Subnet Mask Determines How an IP Address Is Interpreted*

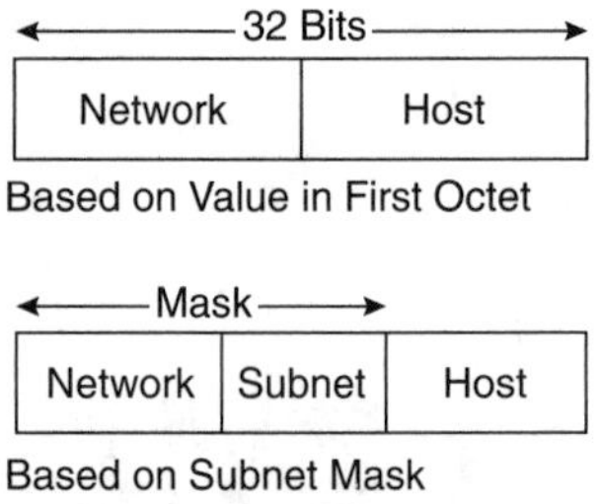

To create a subnet mask for an address, use a 1 for each bit that you want to represent the network or subnet portion of the address, and use a 0 for each bit that you want to represent the node portion of the address. Note that the 1s in the mask are contiguous. The default subnet masks for Class A, B, and C addresses are as shown Table A-3.

**Table A-3**     *IP Address Default Subnet Masks*

| Class | Default Mask in Binary | Default Mask in Decimal |
|-------|------------------------|-------------------------|
| A | 11111111.00000000.00000000.00000000 | 255.0.0.0 |
| B | 11111111.11111111.00000000.00000000 | 255.255.0.0 |
| C | 11111111.11111111.11111111.00000000 | 255.255.255.0 |

## Calculating a Subnet Mask

Because subnet masks extend the number of network addresses you can use by using bits from the host portion, you do not want to randomly decide how many additional bits to use for the network portion. Instead, you want to do some research to determine how many network addresses you need to derive from your given IP address. For example, suppose you have the IP address 172.16.0.0, and you want to configure the network shown in Figure A-6. To establish your subnet mask, do the following:

**Step 1**     Determine the number of networks (subnets) needed. Figure A-6, for example, has five networks.

**Figure A-6**     *Network Used in the Subnet Mask Example*

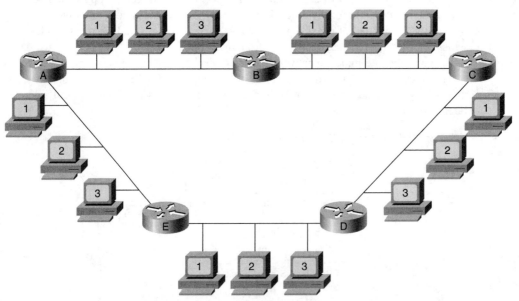

IP Address = 172.16.0.0

**Step 2**   Determine how many nodes per subnet must be defined. This example has five nodes (two routers and three workstations) on each subnet.

**Step 3**   Determine future network and node requirements. For example, assume 100 percent growth.

**Step 4**   Given the information gathered in Steps 1 to 3, determine the total number of subnets required. For this example, ten subnets are required. Refer to the earlier section "IPv4 Addresses and Subnetting Job Aid" to select the appropriate subnet mask value that can accommodate ten networks.

No mask accommodates exactly ten subnets. Depending on your network growth trends, you might select subnet bits, resulting in a subnet mask of 255.255.240.0. The binary representation of this subnet mask is as follows:

   11111111.11111111.11110000.00000000

The number of additional subnets given by $n$ additional bits is $2^n$. For example, the additional 4 subnet bits would give you $2^4 = 16$ subnets.

## Calculating the Networks for a Subnet Mask

Refer to Figure A-6. After you identify your subnet mask, you must calculate the ten subnetted network addresses to use with 172.16.0.0 255.255.240.0. One way to do this is as follows:

**Step 1**   Write the subnetted address in binary format, as shown at the top of Figure A-7. If necessary, use the decimal-to-binary conversion chart provided in Table A-1.

**Figure A-7**   *Calculating the Subnets Shown in Figure A-6*

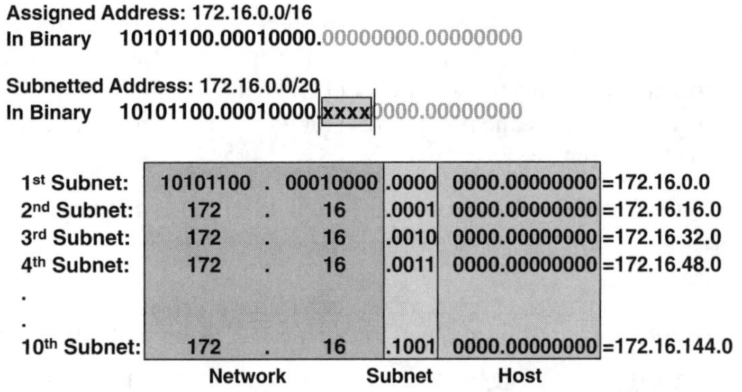

**Step 2**   On the binary address, draw a line between the 16th and 17th bits, as shown in Figure A-7. Then draw a line between the 20th and 21st bits. Now you can focus on the target subnet bits.

**Step 3** Historically, it was recommended that you begin choosing subnets from highest (from the leftmost bit) to lowest, so that you could have available network addresses. However, this strategy does not allow you to adequately summarize subnet addresses, so the present recommendation is to choose subnets from lowest to highest (right to left).

When you calculate the subnet address, all host bits are set to 0. To convert back to decimal, it is important to note that you must always convert an entire octet, 8 bits. For the first subnet, your subnet bits are 0000, and the rest of the octet (all host bits) is 0000.

If necessary, use the decimal-to-binary conversion chart provided in Table A-1, and locate this first subnet number. The first subnet number is 00000000, or decimal 0.

**Step 4** (Optional) List each subnet in binary form to reduce the number of errors. This way, you will not forget where you left off in your subnet address selection.

**Step 5** Locate the second-lowest subnet number. In this case, it is 0001. When combined with the next 4 bits (the host bits) of 0000, this is subnet binary 00010000, or decimal 16.

**Step 6** Continue locating subnet numbers until you have as many as you need—in this case, ten subnets, as shown in Figure A-7.

## Using Prefixes to Represent a Subnet Mask

As discussed, subnet masks identify the number of bits in an address that represent the network, subnet, and host portions of the address. Another way of indicating this information is to use a *prefix*. A prefix is a slash (/) followed by a numeric value that is the number of bits in the network and subnet portion of the address. In other words, it is the number of contiguous 1s in the subnet mask. For example, assume you are using a subnet mask of 255.255.255.0. The binary representation of this mask is 11111111.11111111.11111111.00000000, which is 24 1s followed by eight 0s. Thus, the prefix is /24, for the 24 bits of network and subnet information, the number of 1s in the mask.

Table A-4 shows some examples of the different ways you can represent a prefix and subnet mask.

**Table A-4** *Representing Subnet Masks*

| IP Address/Prefix | Subnet Mask in Decimal | Subnet Mask in Binary |
|---|---|---|
| 192.168.112.0/21 | 255.255.248.0 | 11111111.11111111.11111000.00000000 |
| 172.16.0.0/16 | 255.255.0.0 | 11111111.11111111.00000000.00000000 |
| 10.1.1.0/27 | 255.255.255.224 | 11111111.11111111.11111111.11100000 |

It is important to know how to write subnet masks and prefixes because Cisco routers use both, as shown in Example A-1. You will typically be asked to input a subnet mask when configuring an IP address, but the output generated using **show** commands typically displays an IP address with a prefix.

**Example A-1** *Examples of Subnet Mask and Prefix Use on Cisco Routers*

```
p1r3#show run
<Output Omitted>
interface Ethernet0
 ip address 10.64.4.1 255.255.255.0
!
interface Serial0
 ip address 10.1.3.2 255.255.255.0
<Output Omitted>

P1r3#show interface ethernet0
Ethernet0 is administratively down, line protocol is down
  Hardware is Lance, address is 00e0.b05a.d504 (bia 00e0.b05a.d504)
   Internet address is 10.64.4.1/24
<Output Omitted>

p1r3#show interface serial0
Serial0 is down, line protocol is down
  Hardware is HD64570
   Internet address is 10.1.3.2/24
<Output Omitted>
```

# IPv4 Access Lists

This section reviews IPv4 access lists. It includes the following topics:

- IP access list overview
- IP standard access lists
- IP extended access lists
- Restricting virtual terminal access
- Verifying access list configuration

## IP Access List Overview

Packet filtering helps control packet movement through the network, as shown in Figure A-8. Such control can help limit network traffic and restrict network use by certain users or devices. To permit packets to cross or deny packets from crossing specified router interfaces, Cisco provides access lists. An IP access list is a sequential collection of permit and deny conditions that apply to IP addresses or upper-layer IP protocols.

**Figure A-8** *Access Lists Control Packet Movement Through a Network*

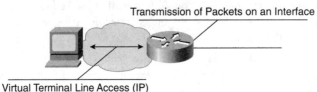

Table A-5 shows some of the available types of access lists on a Cisco router and their access list numbers.

**Table A-5** *Access List Numbers*

| Type of Access List | Range of Access List Numbers |
|---|---|
| IP standard | 1 to 99 |
| IP extended | 100 to 199 |
| Bridge-type code | 200 to 299 |
| IPX standard | 800 to 899 |
| IPX extended | 900 to 999 |
| IPX Service Advertising Protocol (SAP) | 1000 to 1099 |

This section covers IP standard and extended access lists. For information on other types of access lists, refer to the technical documentation on Cisco's website at www.cisco.com.

---

**WARNING** Cisco IOS Release 10.3 introduced substantial additions to IP access lists. These extensions are backward-compatible. Migrating from existing releases to the Cisco IOS Release 10.3 or a later image will convert your access lists automatically. However, previous releases are not upwardly compatible with these changes. Thus, if you save an access list with the Cisco IOS Release 10.3 or a later image and then use older software, the resulting access list will not be interpreted correctly. This incompatibility can cause security problems. Save your old configuration file before booting Cisco IOS Release 10.3 (or later) images in case you need to revert to an earlier version.

---

## IP Standard Access Lists

Standard access lists permit or deny packets based only on the packet's source IP address, as shown in Figure A-9. The access list number range for standard IP access lists is 1 to 99. Standard access lists are easier to configure than their more robust counterparts, extended access lists.

**Figure A-9**  *Standard IP Access Lists Filter Based Only on the Source Address*

A standard access list is a sequential collection of permit and deny conditions that apply to source IP addresses. The router tests addresses against the conditions in an access list one by one. The first match determines whether the router accepts or rejects the packet. Because the router stops testing conditions after the first match, the order of the conditions is critical. If no conditions match, the router rejects the packet.

Figure A-10 shows the processing of inbound standard access lists. After receiving a packet, the router checks the packet's source address against the access list. If the access list permits the address, the router exits the access list and continues to process the packet. If the access list rejects the address, the router discards the packet and returns an Internet Control Message Protocol (ICMP) administratively prohibited message.

**Figure A-10**  *Inbound Standard IP Access List Processing*

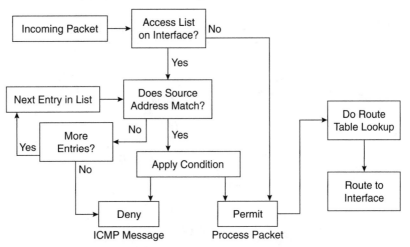

Note that the action taken if no more entries are found in the access list is to deny the packet; this illustrates an important rule to remember when creating access lists. For example, consider what will happen if you create a list that simply denies traffic that you do not want to let into your network, and you configure this on an interface. If you forget about this rule, *all* of your traffic is denied—the traffic explicitly denied by your list, and the rest of the traffic that is implicitly denied because the access list is applied to the interface.

**Key Point: Implicit deny any at the End of the Access List**

The last entry in an access list is known as an *implicit deny any*. All traffic not explicitly permitted is implicitly denied.

**Key Point: Order Is Important When Configuring Access Lists**

When configuring access lists, order is important. Make sure that you list the entries in order from specific to general. For example, if you want to deny a specific host address and permit all other addresses, make sure that your entry about the specific host appears first.

Figure A-11 illustrates the processing of outbound standard IP access lists. After receiving and routing a packet to a controlled interface, the router checks the packet's source address against the access list. If the access list permits the address, the router transmits the packet. If the access list denies the address, the router discards the packet and returns an ICMP administratively prohibited message.

**Figure A-11** *Outbound Standard IP Access List Processing*

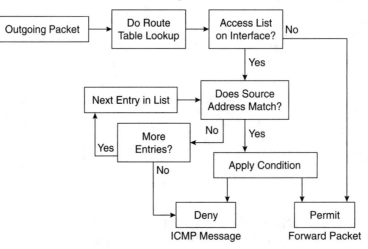

Both standard and extended IP access lists use a wildcard mask. Like an IP address, a *wildcard mask* is a 32-bit quantity written in dotted-decimal format. The wildcard mask tells the router which bits of the address to use in comparisons.

**Key Point: Wildcard Mask Used to Interpret the IP Address**

Address bits corresponding to wildcard mask bits set to 1 are ignored in comparisons; address bits corresponding to wildcard mask bits set to 0 are used in comparisons.

An alternative way to think of the wildcard mask is as follows. If a 0 bit appears in the wildcard mask, the corresponding bit location in the access list address and the same bit location in the packet address must match (both must be 0 or both must be 1). If a 1 bit appears in the wildcard mask, the corresponding bit location in the packet matches (whether it is 0 or 1), and that bit location in the access list address is ignored. For this reason, bits set to 1 in the wildcard mask are sometimes called *don't care bits*.

Remember that the order of the access list statements is important, because the access list is not processed further after a match is found.

---

### Wildcard Masks

The concept of a wildcard mask is similar to the wildcard character used in DOS-based computers. For example, to delete all files on your computer that begin with the letter f, you would enter

**delete f\*.\***

The * character is the wildcard; any files that start with f, followed by any other characters, and then a dot, and then any other characters, are deleted.

Instead of using wildcard characters, routers use wildcard masks to implement this concept.

---

Examples of addresses and wildcard masks, and what they match, are shown in Table A-6.

**Table A-6**    *Access List Wildcard Mask Examples*

| Address | Wildcard Mask | What It Matches |
|---|---|---|
| 0.0.0.0 | 255.255.255.255 | Any address |
| 172.16.0.0/16 | 0.0.255.255 | Any host on network 172.16.0.0 |
| 172.16.7.11/16 | 0.0.0.0 | Host address 172.16.7.11 |
| 255.255.255.255 | 0.0.0.0 | Local broadcast address 255.255.255.255 |
| 172.16.8.0/21 | 0.0.7.255 | Any host on subnet 172.16.8.0/21 |

Whether you are creating a standard or extended access list, you need to complete the following two tasks:

**Step 1**    Create an access list in global configuration mode by specifying an access list number and access conditions.

         Define a standard IP access list using a source address and wildcard, as shown later in this section.

         Define an extended access list using source and destination addresses, as well as optional protocol-type information for finer granularity of control, as discussed in the "IP Extended Access Lists" section later in this supplement.

**Step 2** Apply the access list in interface configuration mode to interfaces or terminal lines.

After creating an access list, you can apply it to one or more interfaces. Access lists can be applied either outbound or inbound on interfaces.

## IP Standard Access List Configuration

Use the **access-list** *access-list-number* {**permit** | **deny**} {*source source-wildcard* | **any**} [**log**] global configuration command to create an entry in a standard traffic filter list, as detailed in Table A-7.

**Table A-7** *Standard IP* **access-list** *Command Description*

| Parameter | Description |
|---|---|
| *access-list-number* | Identifies the list to which the entry belongs. A number from 1 to 99. |
| **permit** | **deny** | Indicates whether this entry allows or blocks traffic from the specified address. |
| *source* | Identifies the source IP address. |
| *source-wildcard* | (Optional) Identifies which bits in the address field must match. A 1 in any bit position indicates don't care bits, and a 0 in any bit position indicates that the bit must strictly match. If this field is omitted, the wildcard mask 0.0.0.0 is assumed. |
| **any** | Use this keyword as an abbreviation for a source and source wildcard of 0.0.0.0 255.255.255.255. |
| **log** | (Optional) Causes an informational logging message about the packet that matches the entry to be sent to the console. Exercise caution when using this keyword, because it consumes CPU cycles. |

When a packet does not match any of the configured lines in an access list, the packet is denied by default, because there is an invisible line at the end of the access list that is equivalent to **deny any**. (**deny any** is the same as denying an address of 0.0.0.0 with a wildcard mask of 255.255.255.255.)

The keyword **host** can also be used in an access list. It causes the address that immediately follows it to be treated as if it were specified with a mask of 0.0.0.0. For example, configuring **host 10.1.1.1** in an access list is equivalent to configuring **10.1.1.1 0.0.0.0**.

Use the **ip access-group** *access-list-number* {**in** | **out**} interface configuration command to link an existing access list to an interface, as shown in Table A-8. Each interface might have both an inbound and an outbound IP access list.

**Table A-8** **ip access-group** *Command Description*

| Parameter | Description |
|---|---|
| *access-list-number* | Indicates the number of the access list to be linked to this interface. |
| **in** | **out** | Processes packets arriving on or leaving from this interface. The default is **out**. |

Eliminate the entire list by entering the **no access-list** *access-list-number* global configuration command. Remove an access list from an interface with the **no ip access-group** *access-list-number* {**in** | **out**} interface configuration command.

## Implicit Wildcard Masks

Implicit, or default, wildcard masks reduce typing and simplify configuration, but you must take care when relying on the default mask.

The access list line shown in Example A-2 is an example of a specific host configuration. For standard access lists, if no wildcard mask is specified, the wildcard mask is assumed to be 0.0.0.0. The implicit mask makes it easier to enter a large number of individual addresses.

**Example A-2** *Standard Access List Using the Default Wildcard Mask*

```
access-list 1 permit 172.16.5.17
```

Example A-3 shows common errors found in access list lines.

**Example A-3** *Common Errors Found in Access Lists*

```
access-list 1 permit 0.0.0.0
access-list 2 permit 172.16.0.0
access-list 3 deny any
access-list 3 deny 0.0.0.0 255.255.255.255
```

The first list in Example A-3—**permit 0.0.0.0**—would exactly match the address 0.0.0.0 and then permit it. In most cases, this address is illegal, so this list would prevent all traffic from getting through (because of the implicit **deny any** at the end of the list).

The second list in Example A-3—**permit 172.16.0.0**—is probably a configuration error. The intention was probably 172.16.0.0 0.0.255.255. The exact address 172.16.0.0 refers to the network and would never be assigned to a host. As a result, nothing would get through with this list, again because of the implicit **deny any** at the end of the list. To filter networks or subnets, use an explicit wildcard mask.

The next two lines in Example A-3—**deny any** and **deny 0.0.0.0 255.255.255.255**—are unnecessary to configure because they duplicate the function of the implicit deny that occurs when a packet fails to match all of the configured lines in an access list. Although they aren't necessary, you might want to add one of these entries for record-keeping purposes.

## Configuration Principles

The following general principles help ensure that the access lists you create have the intended results:

- Top-down processing
  - Organize your access list so that more specific references in a network or subnet appear before more general ones.
  - Place more frequently occurring conditions before less frequent conditions.

- Implicit **deny any**
  - Unless you end your access list with an explicit **permit any**, it denies all traffic that fails to match any of the access list lines by default.
- New lines added to the end
  - Subsequent additions are always added to the end of the access list.
  - You cannot selectively add or remove lines when using numbered access lists, but you can when using IP-named access lists (a feature that is available in Cisco IOS Release 11.2 and later).
- An undefined access list equals **permit any**
  - If you apply an access list with the **ip access-group** command to an interface before any access list lines have been created, the result is **permit any**. The list is live, so if you enter only one line, it goes from a **permit any** to a **deny most** (because of the implicit **deny any**) as soon as you press **Enter**. For this reason, you should create your access list before applying it to an interface.

## Standard Access List Example

Figure A-12 shows a sample network, and Example A-4 shows the configuration on Router X in that figure.

**Figure A-12**  *Network Used for the Standard IP Access List Example*

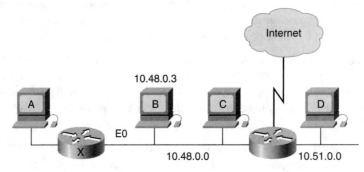

**Example A-4**  *Standard Access List Configuration of Router X in Figure A-12*

```
Router(config)#access-list 2 permit 10.48.0.3
Router(config)#access-list 2 deny 10.48.0.0 0.0.255.255
Router(config)#access-list 2 permit 10.0.0.0 0.255.255.255
Router(config)#!(Note: all other access implicitly denied)
Router(config)#interface ethernet 0
Router(config-if)#ip access-group 2 in
```

Consider which devices can communicate with Host A in this example:

- Host B can communicate with Host A. It is permitted by the first line of the access list, which uses an implicit host mask.

- Host C cannot communicate with Host A. Host C is in the subnet that is denied by the second line in the access list.

- Host D can communicate with Host A. Host D is on a subnet that is explicitly permitted by the third line of the access list.

- Users on the Internet cannot communicate with Host A. Users outside this network are not explicitly permitted, so they are denied by default with the implicit **deny any** at the end of the access list.

## Location of Standard Access Lists

Access list location can be more of an art than a science. Consider the network in Figure A-13 and the access list configuration in Example A-5 to illustrate some general guidelines. If the policy goal is to deny Host Z access to Host V on another network, and not to change any other access policy, determine on which interface of which router this access list should be configured.

**Figure A-13** *Location of the Standard IP Access List Example*

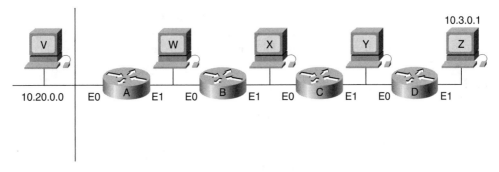

**Example A-5** *Standard Access List to Be Configured on a Router in Figure A-13*

```
access-list 3 deny 10.3.0.1
access-list 3 permit any
```

The access list should be placed on Router A because a standard access list can specify only a source address. No hosts beyond the point in the path where the traffic is denied can connect.

The access list could be configured as an outbound list on E0 of Router A. However, it would most likely be configured as an inbound list on E1 so that packets to be denied would not have to be routed through Router A first.

Consider the effect of placing the access list on other routers:

- **Router B**—Host Z could not connect with Host W (and Host V).

- **Router C**—Host Z could not connect with Hosts W and X (and Host V).

- **Router D**—Host Z could not connect with Hosts W, X, and Y (and Host V).

---

**Key Point: Place Standard Access Lists Close to the Destination**

For standard access lists, the rule is to place them as close to the *destination* router as possible to exercise the most control. Note, however, that this means that traffic is routed through the network, only to be denied close to its destination.

---

## IP Extended Access Lists

Standard access lists offer quick configuration and low overhead in limiting traffic based on source addresses in a network. *Extended access lists* provide a higher degree of control by enabling filtering based on the source and destination addresses, transport layer protocol, and application port number. These features make it possible to limit traffic based on the uses of the network.

### Extended Access List Processing

As shown in Figure A-14, every condition tested in a line of an extended access list must match for the line of the access list to match and for the permit or deny condition to be applied. As soon as one parameter or condition fails, the next line in the access list is compared.

**Figure A-14** *Extended IP Access List Processing Flow*

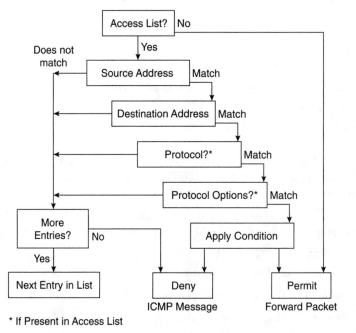

* If Present in Access List

The extended access list checks source address, destination address, and protocol. Depending on the configured protocol, more protocol-dependent options might be tested. For example, a TCP port might be checked, which allows routers to filter at the application layer.

## Extended IP Access List Configuration

Use the **access-list** *access-list-number* {**permit** I **deny**} *protocol* {*source source-wildcard* I **any**} {*destination destination-wildcard* I **any**} [*protocol-specific options*] [**log**] global configuration command to create an entry in an extended-traffic filter list. Table A-9 describes this command.

**Table A-9**    *Extended IP* **access-list** *Command Description*

| Parameter | Description |
|---|---|
| *access-list-number* | Identifies the list to which the entry belongs (a number from 100 to 199). |
| **permit** I **deny** | Indicates whether this entry allows or blocks traffic. |
| *protocol* | **ip**, **tcp**, **udp**, **icmp**, **igmp**, **gre**, **igrp**, **eigrp**, **ospf**, **nos**, or a number from 0 to 255. To match any Internet protocol, use the keyword **ip**. As shown later in this section, some protocols allow more options that are supported by an alternative syntax for this command. |
| *source* and *destination* | Identifies the source and destination IP addresses. |
| *source-wildcard* and *destination-wildcard* | Identifies which bits in the address field must match. A 1 in any bit position indicates don't care bits, and a 0 in any bit position indicates that the bit must strictly match. |
| **any** | Use this keyword as an abbreviation for a source and source wildcard or destination and destination wildcard of 0.0.0.0 255.255.255.255. |
| **log** | (Optional) Causes informational logging messages about a packet that matches the entry to be sent to the console. Exercise caution when using this keyword, because it consumes CPU cycles. |

The wildcard masks in an extended access list operate the same way as they do in standard access lists. The keyword **any** in either the source or the destination position matches any address and is equivalent to configuring an address of 0.0.0.0 with a wildcard mask of 255.255.255.255. An example of an extended access list is shown in Example A-6.

**Example A-6**    *Use of the Keyword* **any**

```
access-list 101 permit ip  0.0.0.0  255.255.255.255  0.0.0.0  255.255.255.255
! (alternative configuration)
access-list 101 permit ip any any
```

The keyword **host** can be used in either the source or the destination position. It causes the address that immediately follows it to be treated as if it were specified with a mask of 0.0.0.0. An example is shown in Example A-7.

**Example A-7** *Use of the Keyword* **host**

```
access-list 101 permit ip  0.0.0.0  255.255.255.255  172.16.5.17  0.0.0.0
! (alternative configuration)
access-list 101 permit ip any host 172.16.5.17
```

Use the **access-list** *access-list-number* {**permit** | **deny**} **icmp** {*source source-wildcard* | **any**} {*destination destination-wildcard* | **any**} [*icmp-type* [*icmp-code*] | *icmp-message*] global configuration command to filter ICMP traffic. The protocol keyword **icmp** indicates that an alternative syntax is being used for this command and that protocol-specific options are available, as described in Table A-10.

**Table A-10**    *Extended IP* **access-list icmp** *Command Description*

| Parameter | Description |
|---|---|
| *access-list-number* | Identifies the list to which the entry belongs (a number from 100 to 199). |
| **permit** | **deny** | Indicates whether this entry allows or blocks traffic. |
| *source* and *destination* | Identifies the source and destination IP addresses. |
| *source-wildcard* and *destination-wildcard* | Identifies which bits in the address field must match. A 1 in any bit position indicates don't care bits, and a 0 in any bit position indicates that the bit must strictly match. |
| **any** | Use this keyword as an abbreviation for a source and source wildcard or destination and destination wildcard of 0.0.0.0 255.255.255.255. |
| *icmp-type* | (Optional) Packets can be filtered by ICMP message type. The type is a number from 0 to 255. |
| *icmp-code* | (Optional) Packets that have been filtered by ICMP message type can also be filtered by ICMP message code. The code is a number from 0 to 255. |
| *icmp-message* | (Optional) Packets can be filtered by a symbolic name representing an ICMP message type or a combination of ICMP message type and ICMP message code. These names are listed in Table A-11. |

Cisco IOS Release 10.3 and later versions provide symbolic names that make configuring and reading complex access lists easier. With symbolic names, it is no longer critical to understand the meaning of the ICMP message type and code (for example, message 8 and message 0 can be used to filter the **ping** command). Instead, the configuration can use symbolic names, as shown in Table A-11. For example, the **echo** and **echo-reply** symbolic names can be used to filter the **ping** command. (You can use the Cisco IOS context-sensitive help feature by entering **?** when entering the **access-list** command to verify the available names and proper command syntax.)

**Table A-11**    *ICMP Message and Type Names*

| Administratively-prohibited | Information-reply | Precedence-unreachable |
|---|---|---|
| Alternate-address | Information-request | Protocol-unreachable |
| Conversion-error | Mask-reply | Reassembly-timeout |

**Table A-11**    *ICMP Message and Type Names (Continued)*

| | | |
|---|---|---|
| Dod-host-prohibited | Mask-request | Redirect |
| Dod-net-prohibited | Mobile-redirect | Router-advertisement |
| Echo | Net-redirect | Router-solicitation |
| Echo-reply | Net-tos-redirect | Source-quench |
| General-parameter-problem | Net-tos-unreachable | Source-route-failed |
| Host-isolated | Net-unreachable | Time-exceeded |
| Host-precedence-unreachable | Network-unknown | Timestamp-reply |
| Host-redirect | No-room-for-option | Timestamp-request |
| Host-tos-redirect | Option-missing | Traceroute |
| Host-tos-unreachable | Packet-too-big | TTL-exceeded |
| Host-unknown | Parameter-problem | Unreachable |
| Host-unreachable | Port-unreachable | |

Use the **access-list** *access-list-number* {**permit** | **deny**} **tcp** {*source source-wildcard* | **any**} [*operator source-port* | *source-port*] {*destination destination-wildcard* | **any**} [*operator destination-port* | *destination-port*] [**established**] global configuration command to filter TCP traffic. The protocol keyword **tcp** indicates that an alternative syntax is being used for this command and that protocol-specific options are available, as described in Table A-12.

**Table A-12**    *Extended IP **access-list tcp** Command Description*

| Parameter | Description |
|---|---|
| *access-list-number* | Identifies the list to which the entry belongs (a number from 100 to 199). |
| **permit** \| **deny** | Indicates whether this entry allows or blocks traffic. |
| *source* and *destination* | Identifies the source and destination IP addresses. |
| *source-wildcard* and *destination-wildcard* | Identifies which bits in the address field must match. A 1 in any bit position indicates don't care bits, and a 0 in any bit position indicates that the bit must strictly match. |
| **any** | Use this keyword as an abbreviation for a source and source wildcard or destination and destination wildcard of 0.0.0.0 255.255.255.255. |
| *operator* | (Optional) A qualifying condition. Can be **lt**, **gt**, **eq**, or **neq**. |
| *source-port* and *destination-port* | (Optional) A decimal number from 0 to 65535 or a name that represents a TCP port number. |
| **established** | (Optional) A match occurs if the TCP segment has the ACK or RST bits set. Use this if you want a Telnet or other activity to be established in one direction only. |

#### established Keyword in Extended Access Lists

When a TCP session is started between two devices, the first segment that is sent has the synchronize (SYN) code bit set but does not have the acknowledge (ACK) code bit set in the segment header, because it is not acknowledging any other segments. All subsequent segments sent do have the ACK code bit set, because they are acknowledging previous segments sent by the other device. This is how a router can distinguish between a segment from a device that is attempting to *start* a TCP session and a segment of an ongoing *established* session. The RST code bit is set when an established session is being terminated.

When you configure the **established** keyword in a TCP extended access list, it indicates that that access list statement should match only TCP segments in which the ACK or RST code bit is set. In other words, only segments that are part of an established session are matched; segments that are attempting to start a session do not match the access list statement.

Table A-13 lists TCP port names that can be used instead of port numbers. You can find the port numbers corresponding to these protocols by entering a **?** in place of a port number or by looking at RFC 1700, *Assigned Numbers* (available at www.cis.ohio-state.edu/cgi-bin/rfc/rfc1700.html).

**NOTE**   RFC 1700 is now outdated, and has been replaced by an online database available at www.iana.org/numbers.html.

**Table A-13**   *TCP Port Names*

| Bgp | Hostname | Syslog |
|---|---|---|
| Chargen | Irc | Tacacs-ds |
| Daytime | Klogin | Talk |
| Discard | Kshell | Telnet |
| Domain | Lpd | Time |
| Echo | Nntp | Uucp |
| Finger | Pop2 | Whois |
| Ftp control | Pop3 | www |
| Ftp-data | Smtp | |
| Gopher | Sunrpc | |

Other port numbers can be found in RFC 1700, *Assigned Numbers*. A partial list of the assigned TCP port numbers is shown in Table A-14.

**Table A-14**    *Some Reserved TCP Port Numbers*

| Port Number (Decimal) | Keyword | Description |
| --- | --- | --- |
| 7 | ECHO | Echo |
| 9 | DISCARD | Discard |
| 13 | DAYTIME | Daytime |
| 19 | CHARGEN | Character generator |
| 20 | FTP-DATA | File Transfer Protocol (data) |
| 21 | FTP-CONTROL | File Transfer Protocol |
| 23 | TELNET | Terminal connection |
| 25 | SMTP | Simple Mail Transfer Protocol |
| 37 | TIME | Time of day |
| 43 | WHOIS | Who is |
| 53 | DOMAIN | Domain name server |
| 79 | FINGER | Finger |
| 80 | WWW | World Wide Web HTTP |
| 101 | HOSTNAME | NIC host name server |

Use the **access-list** *access-list-number* {**permit** I **deny**} **udp** {*source source-wildcard* I **any**} [*operator source-port* I *source-port*] {*destination destination-wildcard* I **any**} [*operator destination-port* I *destination-port*] global configuration command to filter User Datagram Protocol (UDP) traffic. The protocol keyword **udp** indicates that an alternative syntax is being used for this command and that protocol-specific options are available, as described in Table A-15.

**Table A-15**    *Extended IP **access-list udp** Command Description*

| Parameter | Description |
| --- | --- |
| *access-list-number* | Identifies the list to which the entry belongs (a number from 100 to 199). |
| **permit** I **deny** | Indicates whether this entry allows or blocks traffic. |
| *source* and *destination* | Identifies the source and destination IP addresses. |
| *source-wildcard* and *destination-wildcard* | Identifies which bits in the address field must match. A 1 in any bit position indicates don't care bits, and a 0 in any bit position indicates that the bit must strictly match. |
| **any** | Use this keyword as an abbreviation for a source and source wildcard or destination and destination wildcard of 0.0.0.0 255.255.255.255. |

*continues*

**Table A-15**    *Extended IP* **access-list udp** *Command Description (Continued)*

| Parameter | Description |
|---|---|
| *operator* | (Optional) A qualifying condition. Can be **lt**, **gt**, **eq**, or **neq**. |
| *source-port* and *destination-port* | (Optional) A decimal number from 0 to 65535 or a name that represents a UDP port number. |

Table A-16 lists UDP port names that can be used instead of port numbers. You can find port numbers corresponding to these protocols by entering a **?** in place of a port number or by looking at RFC 1700, *Assigned Numbers*.

**Table A-16**    *UDP Port Names*

| | | |
|---|---|---|
| Biff | Nameserver | Syslog |
| Bootpc | NetBios-dgm | Tacacs-ds |
| Bootps | NetBios-ns | Talk |
| Discard | Ntp | Tftp |
| Dns | Rip | Time |
| Dnsix | Snmp | Whois |
| Echo | Snmptrap | Xdmcp |
| Mobile-ip | Sunrpc | |

Other port numbers can be found in RFC 1700, *Assigned Numbers*. A partial list of the assigned UDP port numbers is shown in Table A-17.

**Table A-17**    *Some Reserved UDP Port Numbers*

| Port Number (Decimal) | Keyword | Description |
|---|---|---|
| 7 | ECHO | Echo |
| 9 | DISCARD | Discard |
| 37 | TIME | Time of day |
| 42 | NAMESERVER | Host name server |
| 43 | WHOIS | Who is |
| 53 | DNS | Domain name server |
| 67 | BOOTPS | Bootstrap protocol server |
| 68 | BOOTPC | Bootstrap protocol client |
| 69 | TFTP | Trivial File Transfer Protocol |
| 123 | NTP | Network Time Protocol |

**Table A-17**    *Some Reserved UDP Port Numbers (Continued)*

| Port Number (Decimal) | Keyword | Description |
|---|---|---|
| 137 | NetBios-ns | NetBIOS Name Service |
| 138 | NetBios-dgm | NetBIOS Datagram Service |
| 161 | SNMP | SNMP |
| 162 | SNMPTrap | SNMP Traps |
| 520 | RIP | RIP |

## Extended Access List Examples

In Figure A-15, Router A's interface Ethernet 1 is part of a Class B subnet with the address 172.22.3.0, Router A's interface Serial 0 is connected to the Internet, and the e-mail server's address is 172.22.1.2. The access list configuration applied to Router A is shown in Example A-8.

**Figure A-15** *Network Used for the Extended IP Access List Example*

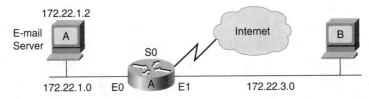

172.22.1.2

E-mail Server    A                                        Internet                        B

S0

172.22.1.0    E0    A    E1        172.22.3.0

**Example A-8**    *Configuration on Router A in Figure A-15*

```
access-list 104 permit tcp any 172.22.0.0 0.0.255.255 established
access-list 104 permit tcp any host 172.22.1.2 eq smtp
access-list 104 permit udp any any eq dns
access-list 104 permit icmp any any echo
access-list 104 permit icmp any any echo-reply
!
interface serial 0
  ip access-group 104 in
```

In Example A-8, access list 104 is applied inbound on Router A's Serial 0 interface. The keyword **established** is used only for the TCP protocol to indicate an established connection. A match occurs if the TCP segment has the ACK or RST bits set, which indicate that the packet belongs to an existing connection. If the session is not already established (the ACK bit is not set and the SYN bit is set), this means that someone on the Internet is attempting to initialize a session, in which case the packet is denied. This configuration also permits SMTP traffic from any address to the e-mail server. UDP domain name server packets and ICMP echo and echo-reply packets are also permitted from any address to any other address.

Another example is shown in Figure A-16. The access list configuration applied to Router A is shown in Example A-9.

**Figure A-16** *Extended IP Access List Example with Many Servers*

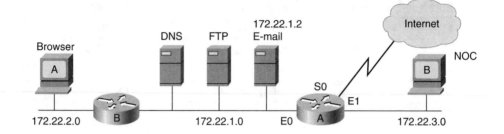

**Example A-9** *Configuration on Router A in Figure A-16*

```
access-list 118 permit tcp any 172.22.0.0  0.0.255.255 eq www established
access-list 118 permit tcp any host 172.22.1.2 eq smtp
access-list 118 permit udp any any eq dns
access-list 118 permit udp 172.22.3.0  0.0.0.255 172.22.1.0 0.0.0.255 eq snmp
access-list 118 deny icmp any 172.22.0.0  0.0.255.255 echo
access-list 118 permit icmp any any echo-reply
!
interface ethernet 0
  ip access-group 118 out
```

In Example A-9, access list 118 is applied outbound on Router A's Ethernet 0 interface. With the configuration shown in Example A-9, *replies* to queries from the Client A browser to the Internet are allowed back into the corporate network (because they are established sessions). Browser queries *from* external sources are not explicitly allowed and are discarded by the implicit **deny any** at the end of the access list.

The access list in Example A-9 also allows e-mail (SMTP) to be delivered exclusively to the mail server. The name server is permitted to resolve DNS requests. The 172.22.1.0 subnet is controlled by the network management group located at the NOC server (Client B), so network-management queries (Simple Network Management Protocol [SNMP]) will be allowed to reach these devices in the server farm. Attempts to ping the corporate network from the outside or from subnet 172.22.3.0 will fail because the access list blocks the echo requests. However, replies to echo requests generated from within the corporate network are allowed to reenter the network.

## Location of Extended Access Lists

Because extended access lists can filter on more than a source address, location is no longer the constraint it was when considering the location of a standard access list. Policy decisions and goals are frequently the driving forces behind extended access list placement.

If your goal is to minimize traffic congestion and maximize performance, you might want to push the access lists close to the source to minimize cross-traffic and administratively prohibited ICMP messages. If your goal is to maintain tight control over access lists as part of your network security strategy, you might want them to be more centrally located. Notice how changing network goals affects access list configuration.

Here are some things to consider when placing extended access lists:

- Minimize distance traveled by traffic that will be denied (and ICMP unreachable messages).
- Keep denied traffic off the backbone.
- Select the router to receive CPU overhead from access lists.
- Consider the number of interfaces affected.
- Consider access list management and security.
- Consider network growth impacts on access list maintenance.

## Restricting Virtual Terminal Access

This section discusses how standard access lists can be used to limit virtual terminal access.

Standard and extended access lists block packets from going *through* the router. They are not designed to block packets that originate within the router. An outbound Telnet extended access list does not prevent router-initiated Telnet sessions by default.

For security purposes, users can be denied virtual terminal (vty) access to the router, or they can be permitted vty access to the router but denied access to destinations from that router. Restricting vty access is less of a traffic-control mechanism than one technique for increasing network security.

Because vty access is accomplished using the Telnet protocol, there is only one type of vty access list.

### How to Control vty Access

Just as a router has physical ports or interfaces such as Ethernet 0 and Ethernet 1, it also has virtual ports. These virtual ports are called virtual terminal lines. By default, there are five such virtual terminal lines, numbered vty 0 to 4, as shown in Figure A-17.

**Figure A-17** *A Router Has Five Virtual Terminal Lines (Virtual Ports) By Default*

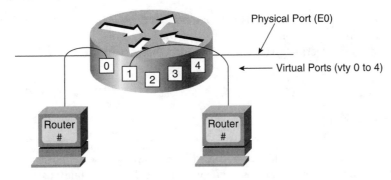

You should set identical restrictions on all virtual terminal lines, because you cannot control on which virtual terminal line a user will connect.

NOTE Some experts recommend that you configure one of the vty terminal lines differently than the others. This gives you a *back door* into the router.

## Virtual Terminal Line Access Configuration

Use the **line vty** {*vty-number* | *vty-range*} global configuration command to place the router in line configuration mode, as described in Table A-18.

**Table A-18**   **line vty** *Command Description*

| Parameter | Description |
|---|---|
| *vty-number* | Indicates the number of the vty line to be configured. |
| *vty-range* | Indicates the range of vty lines to which the configuration applies. |

Use the **access-class** *access-list-number* {**in** | **out**} line configuration command to link an existing access list to a terminal line or range of lines, as described in Table A-19.

**Table A-19**   **access-class** *Command Description*

| Parameter | Description |
|---|---|
| *access-list-number* | Indicates the number of the standard access list to be linked to a terminal line. This is a decimal number from 1 to 99. |
| **in** | Prevents the router from receiving incoming connections *from* the addresses defined in the access list. |
| **out** | Prevents someone from initiating a Telnet *to* the addresses defined in the access list. |

NOTE When you use the **out** keyword in the **access-class** command, the addresses in the specified standard access list are treated as *destination* addresses, rather than as source addresses.

In Example A-10, any device on network 192.168.55.0 is permitted to establish a virtual terminal (Telnet) session with the router. Of course, the user must know the appropriate passwords for entering user mode and privileged mode.

**Example A-10** *Configuration to Restrict Telnet Access to a Router*

```
access-list 12 permit 192.168.55.0 0.0.0.255
!
line vty 0 4
  access-class 12 in
```

Notice that in this example, identical restrictions have been set on all virtual terminal lines (0 to 4), because you cannot control on which virtual terminal line a user will connect. (Note that the implicit **deny any** still applies to this alternative application of access lists.)

## Verifying Access List Configuration

Use the **show access-lists** [*access-list-number* | *name*] privileged EXEC command to display access lists from all protocols, as described in Table A-20. If no parameters are specified, all access lists are displayed.

**Table A-20**    **show access-lists** *Command Description*

| Parameter | Description |
|---|---|
| *access-list-number* | (Optional) Number of the access list to display. |
| *name* | (Optional) Name of the access list to display. |

The system counts how many packets match each line of an extended access list; the counters are displayed by the **show access-lists** command.

Example A-11 illustrates sample output from the **show access-lists** command. In this example, the first line of the access list has been matched three times, and the last line has been matched 629 times. The second line has not been matched.

**Example A-11** *Output of the* **show access-lists** *Command*

```
p1r1#show access-lists
Extended IP access list 100
    deny tcp host 10.1.1.2 host 10.1.1.1 eq telnet (3 matches)
    deny tcp host 10.1.2.2 host 10.1.2.1 eq telnet
    permit ip any any (629 matches)
```

Use the **show ip access-list** [*access-list-number* | *name*] EXEC command to display IP access lists, as described in Table A-21. If no parameters are specified, all IP access lists are displayed.

**Table A-21**    **show ip access-list** *Command Description*

| Parameter | Description |
|---|---|
| *access-list-number* | (Optional) Number of the IP access list to display. |
| *name* | (Optional) Name of the IP access list to display. |

Use the **clear access-list counters** [*access-list-number* | *name*] EXEC command to clear the counters for the number of matches in an extended access list, as described in Table A-22. If no parameters are specified, the counters are cleared for all access lists.

**Table A-22**    **clear access-list counters** *Command Description*

| Parameter | Description |
|---|---|
| *access-list-number* | (Optional) Number of the access list for which to clear the counters. |
| *name* | (Optional) Name of the access list for which to clear the counters. |

Use the **show line** [*line-number*] EXEC command to display information about terminal lines. The *line-number* is optional and indicates the absolute line number of the line for which you want to list parameters. If a line number is not specified, all lines are displayed.

# IP Features

This section includes supplemental information on IP unnumbered serial interfaces, IP helper addresses, and HSRP.

## IP Unnumbered Serial Interfaces

To enable IP processing on a serial interface without assigning an explicit IP address to the interface, use the **ip unnumbered** *type number* interface configuration command. In this command, *type number* indicates the type and number of another interface on which the router has an assigned IP address. It cannot be another unnumbered interface. To disable the IP processing on the interface, use the **no** form of this command.

Whenever the unnumbered interface generates a packet (for example, for a routing update), it uses the address of the specified interface as the source address of the IP packet. The router also uses the address of the specified interface to determine which routing processes are sending updates over the unnumbered interface. (For example, if the **network** command configured for Routing Information Protocol (RIP) indicates that network 10.0.0.0 is running RIP, all interfaces with an address in network 10.0.0.0 will be running RIP, as will all unnumbered interfaces that specify an interface that has an address in network 10.0.0.0.)

Restrictions on unnumbered interfaces include the following:

- Serial interfaces using High-Level Data Link Control (HDLC), PPP, Link Access Procedure, Balanced (LAPB), and Frame Relay encapsulations, as well as Serial Line Internet Protocol (SLIP) and tunnel interfaces, can be unnumbered. You cannot use this interface configuration command with X.25 or Switched Multimegabit Data Service (SMDS) interfaces.

- You cannot use the **ping** EXEC command to determine whether the interface is up, because the interface has no address. SNMP can be used to remotely monitor the interface status.

The interface you specify (by using the *type* and *number* parameters) must be enabled; in other words, it must be listed as up in the **show interfaces** command output.

---

**NOTE**    Using an unnumbered serial line between different major networks requires special care. If at each end of the link different major networks are assigned to the interfaces you specified as unnumbered, any routing protocol running across the serial line must not advertise subnet information.

For example, suppose Router A and Router B are connected via an unnumbered serial line. Router A has all of its interfaces in network 172.16.0.0, so the serial line specifies an interface in network 172.16.0.0. Router B has all of its interfaces in network 172.17.0.0, so the serial line specifies an interface in network 172.17.0.0. If OSPF is configured to run on the unnumbered serial line, it must be configured to summarize the subnet information and not send it across the link.

---

In Figure A-18, interface Serial 0 uses Ethernet 0's address. The configuration for the router in this figure is provided in Example A-12.

**Figure A-18**  **ip unnumbered** *Command*

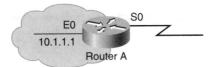

**Example A-12** *Configuration of the Router in Figure A-18*

```
interface Ethernet0
 ip address 10.1.1.1 255.255.255.0
!
interface Serial0
 ip unnumbered Ethernet0
```

A loopback interface is often used as the interface from which unnumbered interfaces get their IP address. Loopback interfaces are virtual interfaces, so after they are defined, they are always active and cannot go down like a real interface.

## IP Helper Addresses

This section covers the use of helper addresses to forward selected broadcasts beyond a router. Routers do not forward broadcasts by default. By doing this, routers prevent broadcast storms—a situation in which a single broadcast triggers an onslaught of other broadcasts, ultimately leading to a disruption in network services. Large, flat networks are notorious for their bouts of broadcast storms.

However, a client might need to reach a server and might not know the server's address. In this situation, the client broadcasts to find the server. If a router is between the client and server, the broadcast does not get through by default. Helper addresses facilitate connectivity by forwarding these broadcasts directly to the target server.

Client hosts interact with a variety of network-support servers such as a Domain Name System (DNS) server, a Bootstrap protocol (BOOTP)/Dynamic Host Configuration Protocol (DHCP) server, or a TFTP server. At startup, the clients often do not know the server's IP address, so they send broadcast packets to find it. Sometimes the clients do not know their own IP address, so they use BOOTP or DHCP to obtain it. If the client and server are on the same network, the server responds to the client's broadcast request. From these replies, the client can glean the server's IP address, and use it in subsequent communication.

However, the server might not be on the same physical medium as the client, as shown in Figure A-19. Remember that a destination IP address of 255.255.255.255 is sent in a link-layer broadcast (FFFFFFFFFFFF). By default, routers never forward such broadcasts, and you would not want them to. A primary reason for implementing routers is to localize broadcast traffic. However, you do want clients to be capable of reaching the appropriate servers. Use helper addresses for this purpose.

**Figure A-19** *Routers Do Not Forward Broadcasts by Default*

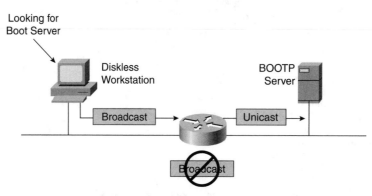

Helper address commands change a destination broadcast address to a unicast address (or a directed broadcast—a local broadcast within a particular subnet) so that the broadcast message can be routed to a specific destination, rather than everywhere. It is important to note that every broadcast (with the default port numbers or with the port numbers you specify) gets sent to all helper addresses, regardless of whether the server can actually help for a certain port.

---

**NOTE**     Helper addresses assist devices in locating necessary services within the network. It is more efficient administratively to allow a client device to broadcast for a service than to hard-code (in the client machines) the IP addresses for devices that might not always be online and available.

---

## Server Location

It is important to consider how you want to get the broadcast, in a controlled way, to the appropriate servers. Such considerations depend on the location of the servers. In practice, server location is implemented in several ways, as shown in Figure A-20:

- **A single server on a single remote medium**—Such a medium might be directly connected to the router that blocks the broadcast, or it might be several routing hops away. In any case, the all-1s broadcast needs to be handled at the first router it encounters and then sent to the server.

- **Multiple servers on a single remote medium, sometimes called a server farm**— Different kinds of servers (for example, DNS and TFTP servers used in the automatic install process [AutoInstall] for Cisco routers) can exist on the same medium. Or perhaps redundant servers of the same type are installed on the same medium. In either case, a directed broadcast can be sent on the server farm subnet so that the multiple devices can see it.

- **Multiple servers on multiple remote media**—In this case, a secondary DNS server could exist on one subnet and the primary DNS server could exist on another subnet, for example. For fault tolerance, client requests need to reach both servers.

**Figure A-20**  *Servers May Be in Many Locations*

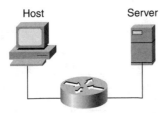

Single Server, Remote Medium

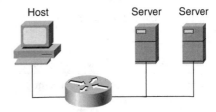

Multiple Servers, Remote Medium

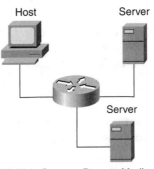

Multiple Servers, Remote Media

| NOTE | In Cisco IOS Release 12.0 and later, the **no ip directed-broadcast** command is on by default, which means that all received IP-directed broadcasts are dropped. To enable the translation of directed broadcasts to physical broadcasts, use the **ip directed broadcast** interface configuration command. |
|------|---|

## IP Helper Address Configuration

Use the **ip helper-address** *address* interface configuration command to configure an interface on which broadcasts are expected or can be received. In this command, *address* indicates the destination address to be used when forwarding UDP broadcasts. The specified address can be the unicast address of a remote server or a directed broadcast address.

If an **ip helper-address** command is defined, forwarding for eight default UDP ports is enabled automatically. The default ports are TFTP (port 69), DNS (port 53), Time (port 37), Network Basic Input/Output System (NetBIOS) name service (port 137), NetBIOS datagram service (port 138), BOOTP server (port 67), BOOTP client (port 68), and TACACS (port 49).

These same eight UDP ports are automatically forwarded if you define an **ip helper-address** and the **ip forward-protocol udp** command with the same ports specified.

Use the **ip forward-protocol** {**udp** [*port*] | **nd** | **sdns**} global configuration command to specify which type of broadcast packets are forwarded, as described in Table A-23.

**Table A-23**   **ip forward-protocol** *Command Description*

| Parameter | Description |
|-----------|-------------|
| **udp** | UDP, the transport-layer protocol. |
| *port* | (Optional) When **udp** is specified, UDP destination port numbers or port names might be specified. |
| **nd** | Network disk, an older protocol used by diskless Sun workstations. |
| **sdns** | Network Security Protocol. |

To forward only one UDP port (whether a default-forwarded port, another UDP port, or a custom port), you must use the **ip forward-protocol udp** *port* command for the ports you want to forward, and then specify **no ip forward-protocol udp** *port* for the default ports you do *not* want forwarded.

---

**NOTE**   There is no easy way to forward all UDP broadcasts. You would need to specify all of the UDP ports in the **ip forward-protocol** command.

DHCP and BOOTP use the same port—port 68—but it is always referred to as the BOOTP port.

---

## IP Helper Address Examples

In Figure A-21, a single server is on a single remote medium. A helper address allows the router to perform the desired function of forwarding a client request to a server. The configuration for the router in this example is shown in Example A-13.

The **ip helper-address** command must be placed on the router interface that receives the original client broadcast. It causes the router to convert the 255.255.255.255 (all-1s) broadcast to a unicast or a directed broadcast. In Example A-13, the **ip helper-address** command placed on interface Ethernet 0 would cause the default eight UDP broadcasts sent by all hosts to be converted into unicasts with a destination address of the boot server, 172.16.2.2. These unicasts would then be forwarded to the boot server.

**Figure A-21** *IP Helper Address with a Single Server on a Remote Medium*

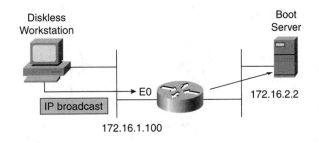

**Example A-13** *Configuration of the Router in Figure A-21*

```
interface ethernet 0
   ip address 172.16.1.100 255.255.255.0
   ip helper-address 172.16.2.2
!
ip forward-protocol udp 3000
no ip forward-protocol udp tftp
```

You might not want to forward all default UDP broadcasts to the server—only those of a protocol type supported on that server. To do this, use the **ip forward-protocol** command followed by the keyword **udp** and a port number or protocol name for UDP broadcasts that are not automatically forwarded. Turn off any automatically forwarded ports with the **no ip forward-protocol udp** *port* or *port name* command. In Example A-13, in addition to the default UDP broadcasts, the configuration has enabled the forwarding of a custom application using UDP port 3000. Because the server does not support TFTP requests, the automatic forwarding of TFTP, port 69, is disabled.

| NOTE | Additional helper addresses are not required on any routers in the middle of a series of routers in the path from the client to the server. This is because the first router has modified the destination address. Modifying the destination address from broadcast to unicast or directed broadcast allows the packet to be routed—over several hops, if necessary—to its final destination. |
|------|---|

To handle forwarding broadcasts to multiple servers on the same remote medium, you can use a directed broadcast into the subnet, instead of using several unicast helper addresses. The most general case is one in which multiple servers are located on different remote media. This case can be handled by a combination of multiple helper statements, some with a unicast and some with a directed-broadcast address. An example of this case is shown in Figure A-22; the configuration for the router in this figure is shown in Example A-14.

**Figure A-22** *IP Helper Address with Multiple Servers on a Remote Medium*

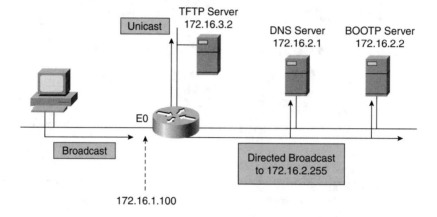

**Example A-14** *Configuration of the Router in Figure A-22*

```
interface ethernet 0
  ip address 172.16.1.100 255.255.255.0
  ip helper-address 172.16.2.255
  ip helper-address 172.16.3.2
```

As shown in Example A-14, a combination of helper addresses can be used on the same interface. Broadcasts arriving on Ethernet 0 are forwarded to all servers on the 172.16.2.0 subnet and to the designated server (172.16.3.2) on the 172.16.3.0 subnet.

---

NOTE   All broadcast traffic for the specified UDP ports (the default ports in Example A-14) is forwarded to both the 172.16.2.0 subnet and the 172.16.3.2 server. This occurs even for traffic that cannot be handled by the servers on that subnet. For example, DNS requests are sent to the 172.16.3.2 TFTP server. Assuming that the DNS service is not enabled on the 172.16.3.2 device, this DNS request is ignored, and an ICMP "port unreachable" message is generated. This sequence consumes bandwidth on the network.

---

## HSRP

Cisco's HSRP provides a way for IP workstations to keep communicating on the internetwork even if their default router becomes unavailable. HSRP works by creating a *phantom router* that has its own IP and MAC addresses. The workstations use this phantom router as their default router.

HSRP routers on a LAN communicate among themselves to designate two routers as *active* and *standby*. The active router sends periodic hello messages. The other HSRP routers listen for hello messages. If the active router fails and the other HSRP routers stop receiving hello messages, the standby router takes over and becomes the active router. Because the new active router assumes both the IP and MAC addresses of the phantom, end nodes see no change at all. They continue to send packets to the phantom router's MAC address, and the new active router delivers those packets.

HSRP also works for proxy Address Resolution Protocol (ARP). When an active HSRP router receives an ARP request for a node that is not on the local LAN, the router replies with the phantom router's MAC address instead of its own. If the router that originally sent the ARP reply later loses its connection, the new active router can still deliver the traffic.

Figure A-23 shows an HSRP implementation.

**Figure A-23** *Example of HSRP: The Phantom Router Represents the Real Routers*

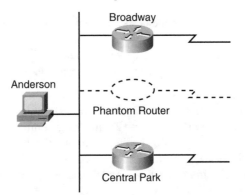

In Figure A-23, the following steps occur:

1  The Anderson workstation is configured to use the Phantom router as its default router.

2  Upon booting, the routers elect Broadway as the HSRP active router. The active router does the work for the HSRP phantom. Central Park is the HSRP standby router.

3  When Anderson sends an ARP frame to find its default router, Broadway responds with the Phantom router's MAC address.

4  If Broadway goes offline, Central Park takes over as the active router, continuing the delivery of Anderson's packets. The change is transparent to Anderson. If there were a third HSRP router on the LAN, that router would begin to act as the new standby router.

HSRP is often used to improve resiliency in networks, but it can result in a decrease in network efficiency. The network shown in Figure A-24 has two paths from the host network to the server network. For redundancy, HSRP runs between R1 and R2, either of which can become the active router. The second router becomes the standby router. It becomes the active router only if the current active router goes down.

**Figure A-24** *Example Using MHSRP So That Both Links Are Used*

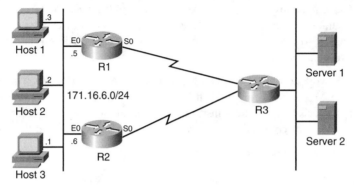

The default gateway address on the hosts has been set to the HSRP virtual IP address. When the hosts need to send packets to the server network, they send them to their default gateway; the packets go to whichever router is active. Because only one router is active, packets from the hosts to the servers traverse only one of the two available paths.

To use *both* paths from the host network to the server network, you can configure Multigroup HSRP (MHSRP) between R1 and R2. With MHSRP, R1 is configured with two HSRP groups (for example, group 1 and group 2), and R2 is configured with the same HSRP groups. For group 1, R1 is the active router, and R2 is the standby router. For group 2, R2 is the active router, and R1 is the standby router. Then you configure half of the hosts' default gateways using HSRP group 1's virtual IP address and the other half of the hosts' default gateways using HSRP group 2's virtual IP address.

## Supplement 1 Review Questions

Answer the following questions, and then refer to Appendix G, "Answers to Review Questions," for the answers.

1 You need to design an IP network for your organization whose IP address is 172.16.0.0. Your assessment indicates that the organization needs at least 130 networks of no more than 100 nodes in each network.

 As a result, you have decided to use a classful subnetting scheme based on the 172.16.0.0/24 scheme. Write down any four IP addresses that are part of the range of subnetwork numbers, and write down the subnet address and subnet mask for these addresses. An example is the address 172.16.1.7/24, which is on subnet 172.16.1.0 255.255.255.0.

2 Your network has the address 172.16.168.0/21. Write eight IP addresses in this network.

3 Write the four IP addresses in the range described by the address 192.168.99.16/30.

**4** Of the four addresses in question 3, which two could you use as host addresses in a point-to-point connection?

**5** Figure A-25 shows the network for this question.

**Figure A-25** *Network for Review Question 5*

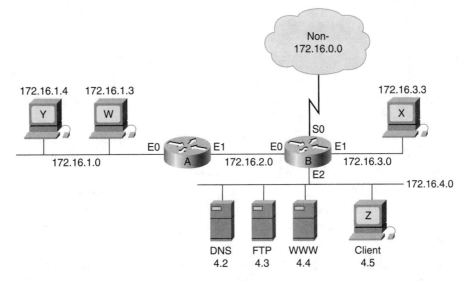

Create an access list and place it in the proper location to satisfy the following requirements:

— Prevent all hosts on subnet 172.16.1.0/24, except host 172.16.1.3, from accessing the web server on subnet 172.16.4.0. Allow all other hosts, including those from the outside world, to access the web server.

— Prevent the outside world from pinging subnet 172.16.4.0.

— Allow all hosts on all subnets of network 172.16.0.0 (using subnet mask 255.255.255.0) to send queries to the DNS server on subnet 172.16.4.0. The outside world is not allowed to access the DNS server.

— Prevent host 172.16.3.3 from accessing subnet 172.16.4.0 for any reason.

— Prevent all other access to the 172.16.4.0 subnet.

In your configuration, be sure to include the router name (A or B), interface name (E0, E1, or E2), and access list direction (in or out).

**6** What do bits set to 1 in a wildcard mask indicate when matching an address?

**7** By default, what happens to all traffic in an access list?

**8** Where should you place an extended access list to save network resources?

**9** Using the keyword **host** in an access list is a substitute for using what value of a wildcard mask?

# Supplement 2: EIGRP

This section covers the following EIGRP-related topics:

- Internetwork Packet Exchange (IPX) and EIGRP
- AppleTalk and EIGRP
- EIGRP configuration examples

## IPX and EIGRP

EIGRP for a Novell IPX network has the same fast routing and partial-update capabilities as EIGRP for IP. In addition, EIGRP has several capabilities that are designed to facilitate the building of large, robust Novell IPX networks.

The first capability is support for incremental SAP updates. Novell IPX RIP routers send out large RIP and SAP updates every 60 seconds. This can consume substantial amounts of bandwidth. EIGRP for IPX sends out SAP updates only when changes occur, and it sends only changed information.

The second capability that EIGRP adds to IPX networks is the capability to build large networks. IPX RIP networks have a diameter limit of 15 hops. EIGRP networks can have a diameter of 224 hops.

The third capability that EIGRP for Novell IPX provides is optimal path selection. The RIP metric for route determination is based on ticks, with hop count used as a tiebreaker. If more than one route has the same value for the tick metric, the route with the least number of hops is preferred. Instead of ticks and hop count, IPX EIGRP uses a combination of delay, bandwidth, reliability, and load.

To add EIGRP to a Novell RIP and SAP network, configure EIGRP on the Cisco router interfaces that connect to other Cisco routers also running EIGRP. Configure RIP and SAP on the interfaces that connect to Novell hosts and/or Novell routers that do not support EIGRP. With EIGRP configured, periodic SAP updates are replaced with EIGRP incremental updates when an EIGRP peer is found. However, note that unless RIP is explicitly disabled for an IPX network number, both RIP and EIGRP are active on the interface associated with that network number.

### Route Selection

IPX EIGRP routes are automatically preferred over RIP routes regardless of metrics, unless a RIP route has a hop count less than the external hop count carried in the EIGRP update—for example, a server advertising its own internal network.

### Redistribution and Metric Handling

Redistribution is automatic between RIP and EIGRP, and vice versa. Automatic redistribution can be turned off using the **no redistribute** command. Redistribution is not automatic between different EIGRP autonomous systems.

## Reducing SAP Traffic

Novell IPX RIP routers send out large RIP and SAP updates every 60 seconds regardless of whether a change has occurred. These updates can consume a substantial amount of bandwidth. You can reduce SAP update traffic by configuring EIGRP to do incremental SAP updates. When EIGRP is configured for incremental SAP updates, the updates consist only of information that has changed, and the updates are sent out only when a change occurs, thus saving bandwidth.

When you configure EIGRP for incremental SAP updates, you can do one of the following:

* Retain RIP, in which case only the reliable transport of EIGRP is used to send incremental SAP updates. (This is the preferred configuration over bandwidth-sensitive connections.)
* Turn off RIP, in which case EIGRP replaces RIP as the routing protocol.

# AppleTalk and EIGRP

Cisco routers support AppleTalk Phase 1 and AppleTalk Phase 2. For AppleTalk Phase 2, Cisco routers support both extended and nonextended networks.

To add EIGRP to an AppleTalk network, configure EIGRP on the Cisco router interfaces that connect to other Cisco routers also running EIGRP. Do not disable Routing Table Maintenance Protocol (RTMP) on the interfaces that connect to AppleTalk hosts or that connect to AppleTalk routers that do not support EIGRP. RTMP is enabled by default when AppleTalk routing is enabled and when an interface is assigned an AppleTalk cable range.

## Route Selection

AppleTalk EIGRP routes are automatically preferred over RTMP routes. Whereas the AppleTalk metric for route determination is based on hop count only, AppleTalk EIGRP uses a combination of the configurable metrics delay, bandwidth, reliability, and load.

## Metric Handling

The formula for converting RTMP metrics to AppleTalk EIGRP metrics is hop count multiplied by 252,524,800. This is a constant based on the bandwidth for a 9.6-kbps serial line and includes an RTMP factor. An RTMP hop distributed into EIGRP appears as a slightly worse path than an EIGRP-native, 9.6-kbps serial link. The formula for converting EIGRP to RTMP is the value of the EIGRP external metric plus 1.

## Redistribution

Redistribution between AppleTalk and EIGRP, and vice versa, is automatic by default. Redistribution involves converting the EIGRP metric back into an RTMP hop count metric. In reality, there is no conversion of an EIGRP composite metric into an RTMP metric. Because a hop count is carried in an EIGRP metric tuple as the EIGRP route spreads through the network, 1 is added to the hop count carried in the EIGRP metric blocks through the network and is put into any RTMP routing tuple generated.

There is no conversion of an EIGRP metric back into an RTMP metric because, in reality, what RTMP uses as a metric (the hop count) is carried along the EIGRP metric all the way through the network. This is true of EIGRP-derived routes and routes propagated through the network that were originally derived from an RTMP route.

# EIGRP Configuration Examples

This section includes configuration and **show** command output examples that result from configuring the network shown in Figure A-26.

**Figure A-26** *Topology for the EIGRP Configuration Examples*

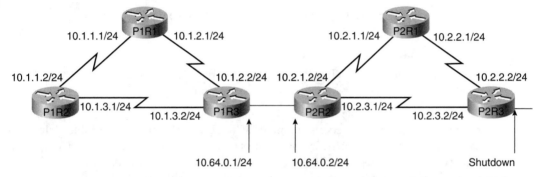

Example A-15 provides the configuration output for Router P1R3 while running EIGRP.

**Example A-15** *P1R3 in Figure A-26 Configured for EIGRP*

```
P1R3#show run
Building configuration...

Current configuration:
!
version 11.2
no service password-encryption
no service udp-small-servers
no service tcp-small-servers
!
hostname P1R3
!
enable password san-fran
!
no ip domain-lookup
ipx routing 0000.0c01.3333
ipx maximum-paths 2
!
interface Loopback0
no ip address
ipx network 1013
!
interface Ethernet0
```

**Example A-15** *P1R3 in Figure A-26 Configured for EIGRP (Continued)*

```
ip address 10.64.0.1 255.255.255.0
!
interface Serial0
 ip address 10.1.3.2 255.255.255.0
 ipx input-sap-filter 1000
 ipx network 1003
!
interface Serial1
 ip address 10.1.2.2 255.255.255.0
 ipx input-sap-filter 1000
 ipx network 1002
 clockrate 56000
!
<Output Omitted>
!
router eigrp 200
 network 10.0.0.0
!
no ip classless
!
!
line con 0
 exec-timeout 0 0
line aux 0
line vty 0 4
 login
!
end
```

Example A-16 shows the topology database of P1R3 running EIGRP before modifying the bandwidth—in other words, all links are equal bandwidth. You can see that in the case of equal-cost paths to the same network (10.1.1.0), both routes appear in the topology table as successors.

**Example A-16** *P1R3 in Figure A-26 EIGRP Topology Database Before the* **bandwidth** *Value Is Changed*

```
P1R3#show ip eigrp topology
IP-EIGRP Topology Table for process 200
Codes: P - Passive, A - Active, U - Update, Q - Query, R - Reply,
       r - Reply status
 P 10.1.3.0/24, 1 successors, FD is 2169856
         via Connected, Serial0
 P 10.1.2.0/24, 1 successors, FD is 2169856
         via Connected, Serial1
 P 10.1.1.0/24, 2 successors, FD is 2681856
         via 10.1.3.1 (2681856/2169856), Serial0
         via 10.1.2.1 (2681856/2169856), Serial1
```

Example A-17 shows the configuration output for P1R3 running EIGRP with **bandwidth** and **ip summary-address** commands configured. The bandwidth on Serial 0 is changed from its default of 1.544 Mbps to 64 kbps.

**Example A-17** *P1R3 in Figure A-26 Configuration for EIGRP with the* **bandwidth** *and* **ip summary-address** *Commands*

```
P1R3#show run
Building configuration...

Current configuration:
!
version 11.2
no service password-encryption
no service udp-small-servers
no service tcp-small-servers
!
hostname P1R3
!
enable password san-fran
!
no ip domain-lookup
ipx routing 0000.0c01.3333
ipx maximum-paths 2
!
interface Loopback0
no ip address
ipx network 1013
!
interface Ethernet0
 ip address 10.64.0.1 255.255.255.0
 ip summary-address eigrp 200 10.1.0.0 255.255.0.0
!
interface Serial0
 ip address 10.1.3.2 255.255.255.0
 ipx input-sap-filter 1000
 ipx network 1003
 bandwidth 64
!
interface Serial1
 ip address 10.1.2.2 255.255.255.0
 ipx input-sap-filter 1000
 ipx network 1002
 clockrate 56000
!
<Output Omitted>
!
router eigrp 200
 network 10.0.0.0
!
no ip classless
!
!
line con 0
 exec-timeout 0 0
line aux 0
line vty 0 4
 login
!
end
```

Example A-18 shows the topology database of P1R3 running EIGRP after modifying the bandwidth on interface Serial 0 and summarizing addresses. You will notice that for network 10.1.1.0, only one route appears as a successor.

**Example A-18** *P1R3 in Figure A-26 EIGRP Topology Database After Applying the* **bandwidth** *and* **ip summary-address** *Commands*

```
P1R3#show ip eigrp topology
IP-EIGRP Topology Table for process 200
Codes: P - Passive, A - Active, U - Update, Q - Query, R - Reply, r - Reply status
  P 10.1.3.0/24, 1 successors, FD is 40512000
          via Connected, Serial0
          via 10.1.2.1 (3193856/2681856), Serial1
  P 10.1.2.0/24, 1 successors, FD is 2169856
          via Connected, Serial1
  P 10.1.1.0/24, 1 successors, FD is 2681856
          via 10.1.2.1 (2681856/2169856), Serial1
```

# Supplement 3: OSPF

This section covers the following OSPF-related topics:

- OSPF not-so-stubby areas
- OSPF single-area configuration example
- OSPF multiarea configuration example

## OSPF Not-So-Stubby Areas

Not-so-stubby areas (NSSAs) were introduced in Cisco IOS Release 11.2. NSSAs are based on RFC 1587, *The OSPF NSSA Option*. NSSAs let you make a hybrid stub area that can accept some autonomous system external routes, called type 7 link-state advertisements (LSAs). Type 7 LSAs may be originated by and advertised throughout an NSSA. Type 7 LSAs are advertised only within a single NSSA; they are not flooded into the backbone area or any other area by Area Border Routers (ABRs), although the information they contain can be propagated into the backbone area by being translated into type 5 LSAs by the ABR. As with stub areas, NSSAs do not receive or originate type 5 LSAs.

Use an NSSA if you are an Internet service provider (ISP) or a network administrator who must connect a central site using OSPF to a remote site using a different protocol, such as RIP or EIGRP, as shown in Figure A-27. You can use an NSSA to simplify the administration of this kind of topology.

Before NSSA, the limitation that a stub area could not import external routes meant that the connection between Router A and Router B in Figure A-27 could not be a stub area. Therefore, if the connection ran OSPF, it would be a standard area and would import the routes learned from RIP or EIGRP as type 5 LSAs. Because it is probably undesirable for the branch office to get all of the type 5 routes from the central site, Router B would be forced to run OSPF and RIP or EIGRP.

**Figure A-27**  *Example of a Topology Where an NSSA Is Used*

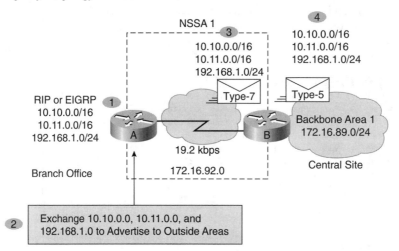

Now, with an NSSA you can extend OSPF to cover the remote connection by defining the area between the corporate router and the remote router as an NSSA, as shown in Figure A-27.

In Figure A-27, Router A is defined as an autonomous system boundary router (ASBR). It is configured to exchange any routes within the RIP/EIGRP domain to the NSSA. The following is what happens when using an NSSA:

1  Router A receives RIP or EIGRP routes for networks 10.10.0.0/16, 10.11.0.0/16, and 192.168.1.0/24.

2  Router A, connected to the NSSA, imports the non-OSPF routes as type 7 LSAs into the NSSA.

3  Router B, an ABR between the NSSA and the backbone area 0, receives the type 7 LSAs.

4  After the SPF calculation on the forwarding database, Router B translates the type 7 LSAs into type 5 LSAs and then floods them throughout backbone area 0.

At this point Router B could have summarized routes 10.10.0.0/16 and 10.11.0.0/16 as 10.0.0.0/8, or it could have filtered one or more of the routes.

## Configuring an NSSA

The steps used to configure the OSPF NSSA are as follows:

**Step 1**    On the ABR connected to the NSSA, configure OSPF, as described in Chapter 4, "Configuring the Open Shortest Path First Protocol in a Single Area," and Chapter 5, "Interconnecting Multiple OSPF Areas."

**Step 2**    Configure an area as an NSSA using the following command, which is explained in Table A-24:

```
router(config-router)#area area-id nssa [no-redistribution]
    [default-information-originate]
```

**Table A-24**    **area nssa** *Command Description*

| Parameter | Description |
|---|---|
| *area-id* | Identifies the area that is to be an NSSA. The identifier can be specified as either a decimal value or an IP address. |
| **no-redistribution** | (Optional) Used when the router is an NSSA ABR and you want the **redistribute** command to import routes only into the normal areas, not into the NSSA area. |
| **default-information-originate** | (Optional) Used to generate a type 7 default into the NSSA area. This argument takes effect only on the NSSA ABR. |

**Step 3**    Every router within the same area must agree that the area is an NSSA; otherwise, the routers will not be able to communicate with each other. Therefore, configure this command on every router in the NSSA area.

**Step 4**    (Optional) Control the summarization or filtering during the translation using the following command, which is explained in Table A-25:

```
router(config-router)#summary-address {{address mask} | {prefix mask}}
    [not-advertise] [tag tag]
```

**Table A-25**    **summary-address** *Command Description*

| Parameter | Description |
|---|---|
| *address* | A summary address designated for a range of addresses. |
| *mask* | An IP subnet mask used for the summary route. |
| *prefix* | An IP route prefix for the destination. |
| *mask* | An IP subnet mask used for the summary route. |
| **not-advertise** | (Optional) Suppresses routes that match the prefix/mask pair. |
| *tag* | (Optional) A tag value that can be used as a match value to control redistribution via route maps. |

Figure A-28 and Example A-19 provide an example of an NSSA configuration.

**Figure A-28**    *Example of an NSSA Topology*

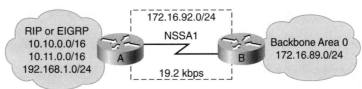

**Example A-19** *Configuring an NSSA on the Routers in Figure A-28*

```
Router A Configuration:
router ospf 1
  redistribute rip subnets
  network 172.16.92.0.0.0.255 area 1
  area 1 nssa

Router B Configuration:
router ospf 1
  summary-address 10.0.0.0.255.0.0.0
  network 172.16.89.0.0.0.255 area 0
  network 172.16.92.0.0.0.255 area 1
  area 1 nssa
```

**NOTE**      The **redistribute** command shown in Example A-19 instructs the router to import RIP packets into the OSPF network. Redistribution is discussed in detail in Chapter 7, "Manipulating Routing Updates."

# OSPF Single-Area Configuration Examples

This section includes configuration and **show** command output examples that result from configuring the network shown in Figure A-29.

**Figure A-29** *OSPF Single-Area Topology*

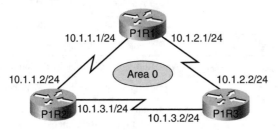

Example A-20 shows a typical configuration for a single-area OSPF for P1R3.

**Example A-20** *Configuration of P1R3 in Figure A-29*

```
P1R3#show run
Building configuration...

Current configuration:
!
version 11.2
no service password-encryption
no service udp-small-servers
no service tcp-small-servers
!
hostname P1R3
!
```

**Example A-20** *Configuration of P1R3 in Figure A-29 (Continued)*

```
interface Ethernet0
 no ip address
 Shutdown
!
interface Ethernet1
 no ip address
 Shutdown
!
interface Serial0
 ip address 10.1.3.2 255.255.255.0
 no fair-queue
 clockrate 64000
!
interface Serial1
 ip address 10.1.2.2 255.255.255.0
!
router ospf 1
 network 10.1.2.0 0.0.0.255 area 0
 network 10.1.3.0 0.0.0.255 area 0
!
no ip classless
!
!
line con 0
 exec-timeout 0 0
line aux 0
line vty 0 4
 login
!
end
```

As shown in Example A-20, OSPF is activated on both Serial 0 and Serial 1 interfaces.

Example A-21 provides output of some **show** commands on P1R3. From the **show ip route** output, you can confirm that OSPF is receiving OSPF routing information. From the **show ip ospf neighbor detail** output, you can confirm that P1R3 has reached the full state with its two neighbors. From the **show ip ospf database** output, you can confirm that P1R3 is receiving only type 1 LSAs—router link state LSAs. No type 2 LSAs are received because all of the connections are point-to-point, so no designated router (DR) was elected.

**Example A-21** *P1R3 in Figure A-29 Output for the* **show ip route**, **show ip ospf neighbor detail**, *and* **show ip ospf database** *Commands*

```
P1R3#show ip route
Codes: C - connected, S - static, I - IGRP, R - RIP, M - mobile, B - BGP
       D - EIGRP, EX - EIGRP external, O - OSPF, IA - OSPF inter area
       N1 - OSPF NSSA external type 1, N2 - OSPF NSSA external type 2
       E1 - OSPF external type 1, E2 - OSPF external type 2, E - EGP
       i - IS-IS, L1 - IS-IS level-1, L2 - IS-IS level-2, * - candidate default
       U - per-user static route, o - ODR
```

*continues*

**Example A-21** *P1R3 in Figure A-29 Output for the* **show ip route***,* **show ip ospf neighbor detail***, and* **show ip ospf database** *Commands (Continued)*

```
Gateway of last resort is not set

     10.0.0.0/24 is subnetted, 3 subnets
C       10.1.3.0 is directly connected, Serial0
C       10.1.2.0 is directly connected, Serial1
O       10.1.1.0 [110/128] via 10.1.3.1, 00:01:56, Serial0
                 [110/128] via 10.1.2.1, 00:01:56, Serial1

P1R3#show ip ospf neighbor detail
 Neighbor 10.1.3.1, interface address 10.1.3.1
    In the area 0 via interface Serial0
    Neighbor priority is 1, State is FULL
    Options 2
    Dead timer due in 00:00:34
 Neighbor 10.1.2.1, interface address 10.1.2.1
    In the area 0 via interface Serial1
    Neighbor priority is 1, State is FULL
    Options 2
    Dead timer due in 00:00:36

P1R3#show ip ospf database
       OSPF Router with ID (10.1.3.2) (Process ID 1)
             Router Link States (Area 0)

Link ID         ADV Router      Age       Seq#        Checksum Link count
10.1.2.1        10.1.2.1        301       0x80000004 0x4A49    4
10.1.3.1        10.1.3.1        292       0x80000004 0x1778    4
10.1.3.2        10.1.3.2        288       0x80000004 0x5D2E    4
P1R3#
```

# OSPF Multiarea Configuration Examples

This section includes configuration and **show** command output examples that result from configuring the network shown in Figure A-30.

**Figure A-30** *OSPF Multiarea Topology*

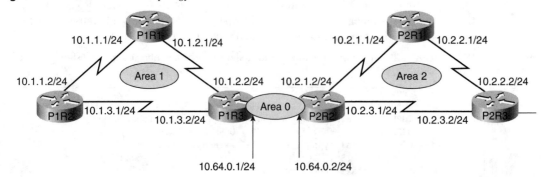

Example A-22 provides output for P1R3 before any areas are configured for stub and route summarization. You can observe that the OSPF database is quite large and has multiple entries from type 1 (Router Link States), type 2 (Net Link States), and type 3 (Summary Net Link States) LSAs.

**Example A-22** *P1R3 in Figure A-30 Output Before Stub and Route Summarization*

```
P1R3#show ip ospf database

        OSPF Router with ID (10.64.0.1) (Process ID 1)

                Router Link States (Area 0)

Link ID         ADV Router      Age       Seq#      Checksum Link count
10.64.0.1       10.64.0.1       84        0x80000009 0x6B87   1
10.64.0.2       10.64.0.2       85        0x8000000C 0x6389   1

                Net Link States (Area 0)

Link ID         ADV Router      Age       Seq#      Checksum
10.64.0.2       10.64.0.2       85        0x80000001 0x7990

                Summary Net Link States (Area 0)

Link ID         ADV Router      Age       Seq#      Checksum
10.1.1.0        10.64.0.1       128       0x80000001 0x92D2
10.1.2.0        10.64.0.1       129       0x80000001 0x59F
10.1.3.0        10.64.0.1       129       0x80000001 0xF9A9
10.2.1.2        10.64.0.2       71        0x80000001 0x716F
10.2.2.1        10.64.0.2       41        0x80000001 0x7070
10.2.3.1        10.64.0.2       51        0x80000001 0x657A

                Router Link States (Area 1)

Link ID         ADV Router      Age       Seq#      Checksum Link count
10.1.2.1        10.1.2.1        859       0x80000004 0xD681   4
10.1.3.1        10.1.3.1        868       0x80000004 0xEB68   4
10.64.0.1       10.64.0.1       133       0x80000007 0xAF61   4

                Summary Net Link States (Area 1)

Link ID         ADV Router      Age       Seq#      Checksum
10.2.1.2        10.64.0.1       74        0x80000001 0xDBFB
10.2.2.1        10.64.0.1       45        0x80000001 0xDAFC
10.2.3.1        10.64.0.1       55        0x80000001 0xCF07
10.64.0.0       10.64.0.1       80        0x80000003 0x299
P1R3#
```

Example A-23 shows the configuration output for P1R3, a router that is an ABR for a stub area and that is doing route summarization.

**Example A-23** *P1R3 in Figure A-30 Configuration*

```
P1R3#show run
Building configuration...

Current configuration:
!
version 11.2
no service password-encryption
no service udp-small-servers
no service tcp-small-servers
!
hostname P1R3
!
interface Ethernet0
 ip address 10.64.0.1 255.255.255.0
!
interface Ethernet1
 no ip address
 shutdown
!
interface Serial0
 ip address 10.1.3.2 255.255.255.0
 no fair-queue
 clockrate 64000
!
interface Serial1
 ip address 10.1.2.2 255.255.255.0
!
router ospf 1
 network 10.64.0.0 0.0.0.255 area 0
 network 10.1.2.0 0.0.0.255 area 1
 network 10.1.3.0 0.0.0.255 area 1
 area 1 stub no-summary
 area 1 range 10.1.0.0 255.255.0.0
!
no ip classless
!
!
line con 0
 exec-timeout 0 0
line aux 0
line vty 0 4
 login
!
end
```

Example A-24 provides output from P1R3 after the network is configured with stub areas and route summarization. The number of entries in the OSPF topology database is reduced.

**Example A-24** *P1R3 in Figure A-30* **show ip ospf database** *Output After Stub and Route Summarization Are Configured*

```
P1R3#show ip ospf database

        OSPF Router with ID (10.64.0.1) (Process ID 1)

                Router Link States (Area 0)

Link ID         ADV Router      Age         Seq#        Checksum Link count
10.64.0.1       10.64.0.1       245         0x80000009 0x6B87    1
10.64.0.2       10.64.0.2       246         0x8000000C 0x6389    1

                Net Link States (Area 0)

Link ID         ADV Router      Age         Seq#        Checksum
10.64.0.2       10.64.0.2       246         0x80000001 0x7990

                Summary Net Link States (Area 0)

Link ID         ADV Router      Age         Seq#        Checksum
10.1.0.0        10.64.0.1       54          0x80000001 0x1B8B
10.2.0.0        10.64.0.2       25          0x80000001 0x9053

                Router Link States (Area 1)

Link ID         ADV Router      Age         Seq#        Checksum Link count
10.1.2.1        10.1.2.1        1016        0x80000004 0xD681    4
10.1.3.1        10.1.3.1        1026        0x80000004 0xEB68    4
10.64.0.1       10.64.0.1       71          0x80000009 0xE9FF    2

                Summary Net Link States (Area 1)

Link ID         ADV Router      Age         Seq#        Checksum
0.0.0.0         10.64.0.1       76          0x80000001 0x4FA3
P1R3#
```

# Supplement 4: IS-IS

This section covers the following IS-IS-related topics:

- IS-IS type, length, and value (TLV)
- Configuring IS-IS authentication
- IS-IS route leaking

## IS-IS TLVs

As explained in Chapter 6, "Configuring the Intermediate System-to-Intermediate System Protocol," IS-IS protocol data units (PDUs) have a fixed and a variable part of the header. The fixed part of the header contains fields that are always present, and the variable part of the header contains the TLV, which permits the flexible encoding of parameters within link state records. These fields are identified by one octet of type T, one octet of length L, and *n* octets of value V. The Type field indicates the type of items in the Value field. The Length field indicates the length of the Value field. The Value field is the data portion of the packet.

Several routing protocols use TLVs to carry a variety of attributes. Cisco Discovery Protocol (CDP), Label Discovery Protocol (LDP), and BGP are examples of protocols that use TLVs. BGP uses TLVs to carry attributes such as Network Layer Reachability Information (NLRI), multiexit-discriminator (MED), and local preference.

## TLV Encoding

Variable-length field encoding is shown in Table A-26.

**Table A-26**    *Variable-Length Field Encoding*

| Field | Number of Octets |
|-------|------------------|
| Type | 1 |
| Length | 1 |
| Value | LENGTH |

## IS-IS PDU and TLV Definitions

ISO 10589 defines IS-IS PDU type codes 1 to 10. RFC 1195 defines type codes 128 to 133.

**NOTE**    TLV code 133 (Authentication Information) is specified in RFC 1195, but Cisco uses ISO code 10 instead. Additionally, TLV code 4 is used for partition repair and is not supported by Cisco.

## TLVs Implemented by Cisco

Cisco implements most TLVs. However, in some cases, draft or low-demand TLVs are not implemented. Table A-27 explains the popular TLVs implemented by Cisco.

**Table A-27**    *Popular TLVs Implemented by Cisco*

| TLV | Name | Description |
|-----|------|-------------|
| 1 | Area Addresses | Includes the area addresses to which the intermediate system is connected. |
| 2 | IIS Neighbors | Includes all of the IS-ISs running interfaces to which the router is connected. |
| 8 | Padding | Primarily used in the IS-IS Hello (IIH) packets to detect maximum transmission unit (MTU) inconsistencies. By default, IIH packets are padded to the interface's fullest MTU. |
| 10 | Authentication | The information that is used to authenticate the PDU. |

**Table A-27**   *Popular TLVs Implemented by Cisco (Continued)*

| TLV | Name | Description |
|---|---|---|
| 22 | TE IIS Neighbors | Increases the maximum metric to 3 bytes (24 bits). Known as the Extended IS Reachability TLV, this TLV addresses a TLV 2 metric limitation. TLV 2 has a maximum metric of 63, but only 6 of 8 bits are used. |
| 128 | IP Int. Reachability | Provides all of the known IP addresses that the given router knows about via one or more internally originated interfaces. This information might appear multiple times. |
| 129 | Protocols Supported | Carries the Network Layer Protocol Identifiers (NLPIDs) for network layer protocols of which the Intermediate System (IS) is capable. It refers to the data protocols that are supported. For example, IPv4 NLPID value 0*x*CC, Connectionless Network Service (CLNS) NLPID value 0*x*81, and/or IPv6 NLPID value 0*x*8E are advertised in this NLPID TLV. |
| 130 | IP Ext. Address | Provides all of the known IP addresses that the given router knows about via one or more externally originated interfaces. This information might appear multiple times. |
| 132 | IP Int. Address | The IP interface address that is used to reach the next-hop address. |
| 134 | TE Router ID | The Multiprotocol Label Switching (MPLS) traffic engineering router ID. |
| 135 | TE IP Reachability | Provides a 32-bit metric and adds a bit for the "up/down" resulting from the route leaking of L2 → L1. Known as the Extended IP Reachability TLV, this TLV addresses the issues with both TLVs 128 and 130. |
| 137 | Dynamic Hostname | Identifies the symbolic name of the router originating the link-state packet (LSP). |
| 10 and 133 | — | TLV 10, not TLV 133, should be used for authentication. If TLV 133 is received, it is ignored on receipt, like any other unknown TLV. TLV 10 should be accepted for authentication only. |

This section was derived from the Cisco website document *Intermediate System-to-Intermediate System (IS-IS) TLVs* (available at www.cisco.com/en/US/tech/tk365/tk381 /technologies_tech_note09186a0080094bbd.shtml).

# Configuring IS-IS Authentication

IS-IS provides for the configuration of a password for a specified link, area, or domain. Routers that want to become neighbors must exchange the same password for their configured level of authentication. A router not in possession of the appropriate password is prohibited from participating in the corresponding function. (In other words, it might not initialize a link, be a member of an area, or be a member of a Level 2 domain.)

Cisco IOS software allows three different types of IS-IS authentication. This section covers only IS-IS clear-text authentication.

- **IS-IS authentication**—For a long time, this was the only way to configure authentication for IS-IS.

- **IS-IS HMAC-MD5 authentication**—This feature adds an HMAC-MD5 digest to each IS-IS PDU. It was introduced in Cisco IOS software version 12.2(13)T and is supported on only a limited number of platforms.

- **Enhanced clear-text authentication**—With this new feature, clear-text authentication can be configured using new commands that allow passwords to be encrypted when the software configuration is displayed. It also makes passwords easier to manage and change.

The IS-IS protocol provides for the authentication of LSPs through the inclusion of authentication information as part of the LSP. This authentication information is encoded as a TLV. The type of the authentication TLV is 10, its length is variable, and its value depends on the authentication type being used. By default, authentication is disabled.

## Interface Authentication

When configuring IS-IS authentication on an interface, you can enable the password for Level 1, Level 2, or Level 1/Level 2 routing. If the level is not specified, the default is Level 1. The level of IS-IS interface authentication should track the type of adjacency on the interface. To find out the type of adjacency, use the **show clns neighbor** command.

Figure A-31 and Example A-25 show interface authentication on Router A, Ethernet 0 and Router B, Ethernet 0. Routers A and B are both configured with **isis password SECr3t** for both Level 1 and Level 2. These passwords are case-sensitive.

**Figure A-31** *Interface Authentication*

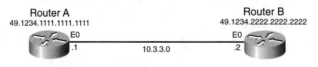

```
        Router A                              Router B
   49.1234.1111.1111.1111                49.1234.2222.2222.2222
              E0                                    E0
              .1          10.3.3.0                  .2
```

**Example A-25** *Interface Authentication Configurations*

```
ROUTER A
interface ethernet 0
ip address 10.3.3.1 255.255.255.0
ip router isis
clns router isis
isis password SECr3t level-1
isis password SECr3t level-2

interface serial0
ip address 10.1.1.1 255.255.255.252
clns router isis
ip router isis
```

**Example A-25** *Interface Authentication Configurations (Continued)*

```
router isis
passive-interface Loopback0
passive-interface Loopback1
net 49.1234.1111.1111.1111.00


ROUTER B
interface ethernet 0
ip address 10.3.3.2 255.255.255.0
ip router isis
clns router isis
isis password SECr3t level-1
isis password SECr3t level-2

interface serial0
ip address 172.16.1.1 255.255.255.252ip router isis
clns router isis

router isis
passive-interface Loopback0
passive-interface Loopback1
net 49.1234.2222.2222.2222.00
```

On Cisco routers configured with CLNS IS-IS, the CLNS adjacency between them is Level 1/
Level 2 by default. So Routers A and B have both types of adjacency, unless configured
specifically for Level 1 or Level 2.

## Area Authentication

Figure A-32 and Example A-26 show area authentication. All of the routers in Figure A-32 are
in the same IS-IS area, 49.1234, and they are all configured with the area password **tiGHter.**

**Figure A-32** *Area Authentication*

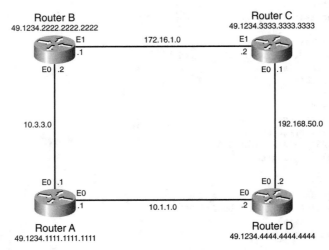

**Example A-26** *Area Authentication Configurations*

```
ROUTER A
interface ethernet 0
ip address 10.3.3.1 255.255.255.0
ip router isis
clns router isis
interface serial0
ip address 10.1.1.1 255.255.255.252
clns router isis
ip router isis

router isis
passive-interface Loopback0
passive-interface Loopback1
net 49.1234.1111.1111.1111.00
area-password tighter

ROUTER B
interface ethernet 0
ip address 10.3.3.2 255.255.255.0
ip router isis
clns router isis

interface serial0
ip address 172.16.1.1 255.255.255.252ip router isis
clns router isis

router isis
passive-interface Loopback0
passive-interface Loopback1
net 49.1234.2222.2222.2222.00
area-password tighter

ROUTER C
interface serial0
ip address 172.16.1.2 255.255.255.252
clns router isis
ip router isis

interface Tokenring0
ip address 192.168.50.1 255.255.255.0
clns router isis
ip router isis

router isis
passive-interface Loopback0
passive-interface Loopback1
net 49.1234.3333.3333.3333.00
area-password tighter

ROUTER D
interface serial0
ip address 10.1.1.2 255.255.255.252
clns router isis
ip router isis
```

**Example A-26** *Area Authentication Configurations (Continued)*

```
interface Tokenring0
ip address 192.168.50.2 255.255.255.0
clns router isis
ip router isis

router isis
passive-interface Loopback0
passive-interface Loopback1
net 49.1234.4444.4444.4444.00
area-password tiGHter
```

## Domain Authentication

Figure A-33 and Example A-27 show domain authentication. Routers A and B are in IS-IS area 49.1234, Router C is in IS-IS area 49.5678, and Router D is in area 49.9999. All of the routers are in the same IS-IS domain (49) and are configured with the domain password **seCurity**.

**Figure A-33** *Domain Authentication*

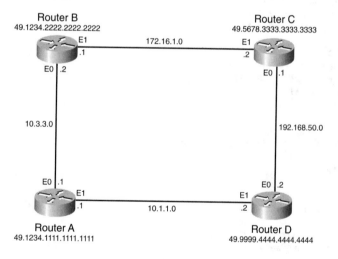

**Example A-27** *Domain Authentication Configurations*

```
ROUTER A
interface ethernet 0
ip address 10.3.3.1 255.255.255.0
ip router isis
clns router isis
interface serial0
ip address 10.1.1.1 255.255.255.252
clns router isis
ip router isis
```

*continues*

**Example A-27** *Domain Authentication Configurations (Continued)*

```
router isis
passive-interface Loopback0
passive-interface Loopback1
net 49.1234.1111.1111.1111.00
domain-password seCurity

ROUTER B
interface ethernet 0
ip address 10.3.3.2 255.255.255.0
ip router isis
clns router isis

interface serial0
ip address 172.16.1.1 255.255.255.252
ip router isis
clns router isis

router isis
passive-interface Loopback0
passive-interface Loopback1
net 49.1234.2222.2222.2222.00
domain-password seCurity

ROUTER C
interface serial0
ip address 172.16.1.2 255.255.255.252
clns router isis
ip router isis

interface Tokenring0
ip address 192.168.50.1 255.255.255.0
clns router isis
ip router isis

router isis
passive-interface Loopback0
passive-interface Loopback1
net 49.5678.3333.3333.3333.00
domain-password seCurity

Router D
interface serial0
ip address 10.1.1.2 255.255.255.252
clns router isis
ip router isis

interface Tokenring0
ip address 192.168.50.2 255.255.255.0
clns router isis
ip router isis
```

**Example A-27** *Domain Authentication Configurations (Continued)*

```
router isis
passive-interface Loopback0
passive-interface Loopback1
net 49.9999.4444.4444.4444.00
domain-password seCurity
```

The preceding information was derived from Cisco website document 13792, *Configuring IS-IS Authentication* (available at www.cisco.com/warp/public/97/isis_authent.html).

## IS-IS Route Leaking

Routing to the closest L1/L2 router can lead to suboptimal routing when the shortest path to the destination is through a different L1/L2 router. Route leaking helps reduce suboptimal routing by providing a mechanism for leaking (redistributing) L2 information into L1 areas. By having more details about interarea routes, an L1 router can make a better choice about which L1/L2 router to forward the packet.

Route leaking is defined in RFC 2966 for use with the narrow metric TLV types 128 and 130, as shown in Figure A-34. *IS-IS Extensions for Traffic Engineering* (available at www.ietf.org /internet-drafts/draft-ietf-isis-traffic-05.txt) defines route leaking for use with the wide metric TLV type 135, shown in Figure A-35. Both drafts define an up/down bit to indicate whether the route defined in the TLV has been leaked. If the up/down bit is set to 0, the route originated within that L1 area. If the up/down bit is set to 1, the route has been redistributed into the area from L2. The up/down bit is used to prevent routing information and forwarding loops. An L1/L2 router does not readvertise into L2 any L1 routes that have the up/down bit set.

**Figure A-34** *TLV Types 128 and 130*

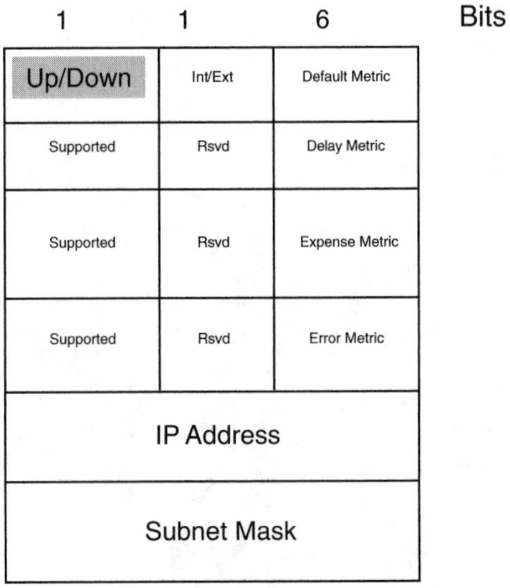

**Figure A-35** *TLV Type 135*

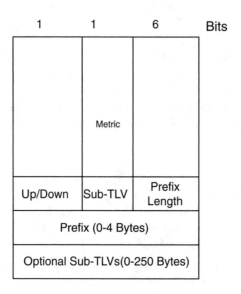

## Using Route Leaking

Typically an L1 router forwards packets destined for an address outside the local area to the closest L1/L2 router, which can lead to suboptimal routing decisions. In Figure A-36, Router C forwards all traffic destined for Routers X and Y to Router A. Assuming an equal cost for all links, this means a cost of 2 to reach Router X and a cost of 4 to reach Router Y. Likewise, Router D routes traffic for Routers X and Y through Router B.

**Figure A-36** *Route Leaking*

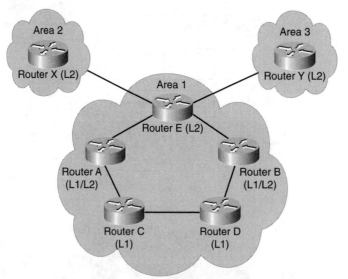

Using route leaking, information about Routers X and Y is redistributed into Area 1 by Routers A and B. With specific information for these routers, Routers C and D can choose optimal paths. Router C now sends traffic to Router Y via Router D, reducing the cost to 3, while still forwarding to Router X through Router A. Likewise, Router D forwards to Router X through Router C while still routing to Router Y via Router B.

By enabling route leaking, Routers C and D can determine the true costs of reaching Routers X and Y and can forward packets accordingly. Two common BGP practices benefit greatly from this ability. One criterion used in the BGP path-selection process is the Interior Gateway Protocol (IGP) cost to the BGP next-hop address. Many ISPs rely on the IGP metric to choose the best path through their autonomous system. This practice is known as *shortest exit routing*. Another common practice is to use the IGP metric for the value of the MED when advertising routes to other autonomous systems. This allows you to request that other autonomous systems use the shortest path through your AS when making routing decisions. Before route leaking, if multiple areas were used within the AS, the IS-IS metric did not represent the true internal cost and did not work well with either of these practices. By leaking routes for each of the BGP next-hop addresses, you can use a multiarea hierarchy while still maintaining accurate end-to-end IGP metrics.

In an MPLS-VPN environment, reachability information is needed for each of the Provider Edge (PE) router's loopback addresses. Leaking routes for the PE loopbacks allows a multiarea hierarchy to be used in this type of implementation.

Route leaking can also be used to implement a crude form of traffic engineering. By leaking routes for individual machines or services from specific L1/L2 routers, you can control the exit point from the L1 area used to reach these addresses.

## Configuring Route Leaking

Route leaking is implemented and supported in Cisco IOS software Releases 12.0S, 12.0T, and 12.1. The 12.0T and 12.1 releases use the same configuration command. The command syntax differs for the 12.0S release, but both commands are entered within the router IS-IS configuration. You must create an IP extended-access list to define which routes will be leaked from Level 2 into Level 1. IOS 12.0S only supports route leaking using type 135 TLVs. If route leaking is configured without configuring wide-style metrics, route leaking does not occur. IOS 12.0T and 12.1 support route leaking using either narrow- or wide-style metrics, but we recommend using wide-style metrics.

The configuration commands for each IOS release are shown in Table A-28.

**Table A-28**    *Route Leaking Commands*

| Release | Command |
|---------|---------|
| 12.0S | **advertise ip l2-into-l1** *100-199*<br>**metric-style wide**<br>The second statement is required. |
| 12.0T and 12.1 | **redistribute isis ip level-2 into level-1 distribute-list** *100-199*<br>**metric-style wide**<br>The second statement is optional but recommended. |

Leaked routes are called *interarea* routes in the routing table and IS-IS database. When you view the routing table, leaked routes are marked with an ia designation, as shown in Example A-28.

**Example A-28** *Leaked Routes Example*

```
RtrB#show ip route
Codes: C - connected, S - static, I - IGRP, R - RIP, M - mobile, B - BGP
       D - EIGRP, EX - EIGRP external, O - OSPF, IA - OSPF inter area
       N1 - OSPF NSSA external type 1, N2 - OSPF NSSA external type 2
       E1 - OSPF external type 1, E2 - OSPF external type 2, E - EGP
       i - IS-IS, L1 - IS-IS level-1, L2 - IS-IS level-2, ia - IS-IS inter area
       * - candidate default, U - per-user static route, o - ODR
       P - periodic downloaded static route

Gateway of last resort is 55.55.55.1 to network 0.0.0.0

i ia 1.0.0.0/8 [115/30] via 55.55.55.1, Serial1/0
i ia 2.0.0.0/8 [115/30] via 55.55.55.1, Serial1/0
i ia 3.0.0.0/8 [115/30] via 55.55.55.1, Serial1/0
i ia 4.0.0.0/8 [115/30] via 55.55.55.1, Serial1/0
     55.0.0.0/24 is subnetted, 1 subnets
C       55.55.55.0 is directly connected, Serial1/0
i ia 5.0.0.0/8 [115/30] via 55.55.55.1, Serial1/0
     7.0.0.0/24 is subnetted, 1 subnets
C       7.7.7.0 is directly connected, FastEthernet0/0
     44.0.0.0/24 is subnetted, 1 subnets
i L1    44.44.44.0 [115/20] via 55.55.55.1, Serial1/0
i*L1 0.0.0.0/0 [115/10] via 55.55.55.1, Serial1/0
In the IS-IS database leaked routes are marked with an IP-Interarea designation.

RtrB#show isis database detail

IS-IS Level-1 Link State Database:
LSPID                   LSP Seq Num  LSP Checksum  LSP Holdtime    ATT/P/OL
rpd-7206g.00-00         0x00000008   0x0855        898             1/0/0
  Area Address: 49.0002
  NLPID:        0xCC
  Hostname: rpd-7206g
  IP Address:   44.44.44.2
  Metric: 10        IP 55.55.55.0/24
  Metric: 10        IP 44.44.44.0/24
  Metric: 10        IS-Extended rpd-7206a.00
  Metric: 20        IP-Interarea 1.0.0.0/8
  Metric: 20        IP-Interarea 2.0.0.0/8
  Metric: 20        IP-Interarea 3.0.0.0/8
  Metric: 20        IP-Interarea 4.0.0.0/8
  Metric: 20        IP-Interarea 5.0.0.0/8
```

Before the introduction of route leaking, the up/down bit for type 128 and 130 TLVs, bit 8 of the default metric, was reserved for the following uses: It should be set to 0 on transmission and ignored upon receipt. Bit 7, the I/E bit, was used to distinguish between internal and external metric types for redistributed routes in TLV 130. The I/E bit set to 0 indicates internal metrics, and the bit set to 1 indicates external metrics. In IOS Release 12.0S and earlier, bit 8 was used as the I/E bit instead of bit 7. This introduces several interoperability discrepancies between the 12.0S and 12.0T/12.1 releases when you use narrow-style metrics.

A router running IOS 12.0T or 12.1 recognizes the up/down bit and treats the route accordingly whether or not route leaking is configured on that router. If an L1 or L1/L2 router not running IOS 12.0T or 12.1 redistributes routes using metric-type external, it sets bit 8 of the default metric to 1. An L1/L2 router running 12.0T or 12.12.1 sees bit 8 (the up/down bit) and interprets it as a route that has been leaked. As a result, the route is not readvertised in that router's L2 LSP. This can cause the undesired effect of routing information not being propagated throughout the network.

Conversely, if a route has been leaked into L1 by a router running IOS 12.0T or 12.1, it sets bit 8 to 1. Routers in the L1 area running IOS Release 12.0S or earlier see that bit 8 is set, and treat the route as having metric-type external. An L1/L2 router running IOS Release 12.0S or earlier readvertises the route in its L2 LSP because it does not recognize bit 8 as the up/down bit. This can lead to the formation of routing loops.

Further details on IS-IS route leaking can be found on Cisco's website. The preceding explanations were derived from Cisco.com document 13796, *IS-IS Route Leaking Overview*.

# Supplement 5: BGP

This section covers the following BGP-related topics:

- BGP configuration output examples
- Distribute lists
- Policy control and prefix lists
- Communities
- Route reflectors

## BGP Configuration Output Examples

This section includes configuration and **show** command output examples that result from configuring the network shown in Figure A-37. RIP is configured as the internal routing protocol within the autonomous systems, and BGP is the external protocol between the autonomous systems. BGP routes are redistributed into RIP.

**Figure A-37** *Sample BGP/RIP Network*

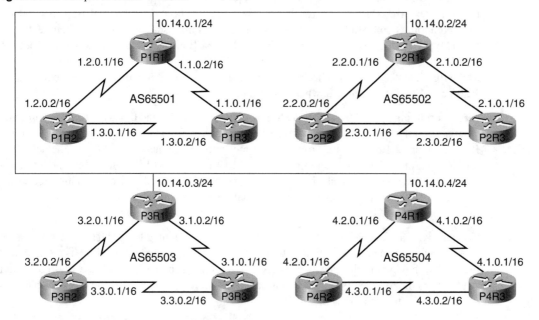

## Example of BGP/RIP Configuration for P1R1

Example A-29 shows part of the configuration for P1R1 in Figure A-37, running both RIP and BGP.

**Example A-29** *Configuration of P1R1 in Figure A-37*

```
P1R1#show run
<output omitted>
!
interface Ethernet0
 ip address 10.14.0.1 255.255.255.0
!
interface Serial0
 ip address 1.1.0.2 255.255.0.0
!

interface Serial1
 ip address 1.2.0.1 255.255.0.0
!
router rip
 network 10.0.0.0
 network 1.0.0.0
 passive-interface e0
 redistribute bgp 65501 metric 3
!
router bgp 65501
 network 1.0.0.0
```

**Example A-29** *Configuration of P1R1 in Figure A-37 (Continued)*

```
 neighbor 10.14.0.2 remote-as 65502
 neighbor 10.14.0.3 remote-as 65503
 neighbor 10.14.0.4 remote-as 65504
!
no ip classless
!
<output omitted>
```

In Example A-29, the **network 10.0.0.0** command advertises network 10.0.0.0 in RIP so that internal routers can see network 10.0.0.0. The **passive-interface e0** command does not allow RIP to advertise any routes on the backbone. The **redistribute bgp 65501 metric 3** command redistributes BGP information into RIP, with a hop count of three. The **network 1.0.0.0** command under the BGP configuration advertises network 1.0.0.0 to each of Router P1R1's three BGP neighbors.

## Sample RIP Configuration for P1R2

Example A-30 shows part of the configuration for P1R2 in Figure A-37, one of the routers running only RIP.

**Example A-30** *Configuration of P1R2 in Figure A-37*

```
P1R2#show run
<output omitted>
!
interface Ethernet0
 Shutdown
!
interface Serial0
 ip address 1.2.0.2 255.255.0.0
!
interface Serial1
 ip address 1.3.0.1 255.255.0.0

!
router rip
 network 1.0.0.0
!
no ip classless
!
<output omitted>
```

In Example A-30, the **network 1.0.0.0** command starts RIP on all interfaces that P1R2 has in network 1.0.0.0 and allows the router to advertise network 1.0.0.0.

## Sample Output of **show ip route** for P1R1

Example A-31 displays the output of the **show ip route** command on P1R1 in Figure A-37.

**Example A-31** show ip route *Command Output on P1R1 in Figure A-37*

```
P1R1#show ip route

<output omitted>

     1.0.0.0/16 is subnetted, 3 subnets
C       1.1.0.0 is directly connected, Serial0
R       1.3.0.0 [120/1] via 1.2.0.2, 00:00:25, Serial1
                [120/1] via 1.1.0.1, 00:00:22, Serial0
C       1.2.0.0 is directly connected, Serial1

B    2.0.0.0/8 [20/0] via 10.14.0.2, 00:03:26
B    3.0.0.0/8 [20/0] via 10.14.0.3, 00:03:26
B    4.0.0.0/8 [20/0] via 10.14.0.4, 00:03:26
     10.0.0.0/24 is subnetted, 1 subnets
C       10.14.0.0 is directly connected, Ethernet0
P1R1#
```

The shaded lines in Example A-31 indicate the routes that P1R1 has learned from its BGP neighbors.

## Sample Output of **show ip route** for P1R2

Example A-32 displays the output of the **show ip route** command on P1R2 in Figure A-37.

**Example A-32** show ip route *Command Output on P1R2 in Figure A-37*

```
P1R2#show ip route
<output omitted>

     1.0.0.0/16 is subnetted, 3 subnets
R       1.1.0.0 [120/1] via 1.2.0.1, 00:00:17, Serial0
                [120/1] via 1.3.0.2, 00:00:26, Serial1
C       1.3.0.0 is directly connected, Serial1

C       1.2.0.0 is directly connected, Serial0
R    2.0.0.0/8 [120/3] via 1.2.0.1, 00:00:17, Serial0
R    3.0.0.0/8 [120/3] via 1.2.0.1, 00:00:17, Serial0
R    4.0.0.0/8 [120/3] via 1.2.0.1, 00:00:17, Serial0
R    10.0.0.0/8 [120/1] via 1.2.0.1, 00:00:17, Serial0
P1R2#
```

The shaded lines in Example A-32 indicate the routes that P1R2 has learned from P1R1 by P1R1's redistributing them from BGP into RIP.

# Distribute Lists

This section details the configuration of distribute lists for filtering BGP information.

The **neighbor distribute-list** {*ip-address* | *peer-group-name*} **distribute-list** *access-list-number* **in** | **out** router configuration command is used to distribute BGP neighbor information as specified in an access list. The parameters for this command are detailed in Table A-29.

**Table A-29**    **neighbor distribute-list** *Command Description*

| Parameter | Description |
|---|---|
| *ip-address* | The IP address of the BGP neighbor for which routes will be filtered. |
| *peer-group-name* | The name of a BGP peer group. |
| *access-list-number* | The number of a standard or extended access list. It can be an integer from 1 to 199. (A named access list can also be referenced.) |
| **in** | Indicates that the access list is applied to incoming advertisements from the neighbor. |
| **out** | Indicates that the access list is applied to outgoing advertisements to the neighbor. |

Example A-33 provides a configuration for Router A in Figure A-38.

**Figure A-38** *Network for the BGP Distribute List Example*

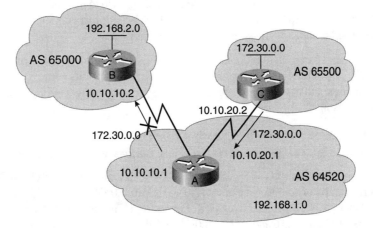

**Example A-33** *Configuration of Router A in Figure A-38*

```
RtrA(config)#router bgp 64520
RtrA(config-router)#network 192.168.1.0
RtrA(config-router)#neighbor 10.10.10.2 remote-as 65000
RtrA(config-router)#neighbor 10.10.20.2 remote-as 65500
RtrA(config-router)#neighbor 10.10.10.2 distribute-list 1 out
RtrA(config-router)#exit
RtrA(config)#access-list 1 deny 172.30.0.0 0.0.255.255
RtrA(config)#access-list 1 permit 0.0.0.0 255.255.255.255
```

In this example, Router A has two neighbors, Router B (10.10.10.2 in AS 65000) and Router C (10.10.20.2 in AS 65500). When Router A sends updates to neighbor Router B, the **neighbor distribute-list** statement specifies that it will use **access-list 1** to determine which updates are to be sent.

Access list 1 specifies that any route starting with 172.30—in this case, the route to 172.30.0.0—should not be sent (it is denied in the access list). All other routes are sent to Router B. (Recall that because access lists have an implicit **deny any** at the end, the **permit** statement is required in the access list for the other routes to be sent.)

As shown in Example A-33, you can use a standard IP access list to control the sending of updates about a specific network number. However, if you need to control updates about subnets and supernets of a network with a distribute list, extended access lists are required.

## Extended Access List Use in a Distribute List

When an IP extended access list is used with a distribute list, the parameters have different meanings than when the extended access list is used in other ways. The syntax of the IP extended access list is the same as usual, with a source address and wildcard, and a destination address and wildcard. However, the meanings of these parameters are different.

The *source* parameters of the extended access list are used to indicate the *address of the network* whose updates are to be permitted or denied. The *destination* parameters of the extended access list are used to indicate the *subnet mask of that network*.

The *wildcard* parameters indicate, for the network and subnet mask, which bits are relevant. Network and subnet mask bits corresponding to wildcard bits set to 1 are ignored during comparisons, and network and subnet mask bits corresponding to wildcard bits set to 0 are used in comparisons.

The following example shows an extended access list:

```
access-list 101 ip permit 172.0.0.0 0.255.255.255 255.0.0.0 0.0.0.0
```

The interpretation of this access list when used with a **neighbor distribute-list** command is to permit only a route to network 172.0.0.0 255.0.0.0. Therefore, this list allows only the supernet 172.0.0.0/8 to be advertised. For example, assume that Router A has routes to networks 172.20.0.0/16 and 172.30.0.0/16 and also has an aggregated route to 172.0.0.0/8. The use of this access list would allow only the supernet 172.0.0.0/8 to be advertised; networks 172.20.0.0/16 and 172.30.0.0/16 would not be advertised.

# Policy Control and Prefix Lists

This section describes how a routing policy is applied to a BGP network using prefix lists.

If you want to restrict the routing information that the Cisco IOS software learns or advertises, you can filter BGP routing updates to and from particular neighbors. To do this, you can define either an access list or a prefix list, and then apply it to the updates.

Distribute lists use access lists to specify what routing information is to be filtered. Distribute lists for BGP have been made obsolete by prefix lists in the Cisco IOS. Prefix lists are available in Cisco IOS Release 12.0 and later.

Figure A-39 shows an example where prefix lists might be used. In this figure, Router C is advertising network 172.30.0.0 to Router A. If you wanted to stop those updates from propagating to AS 65000 (to Router B), you could apply a prefix list on Router A to filter those updates when Router A is talking to Router B.

**Figure A-39**  *Example Where Prefix Lists May Be Used*

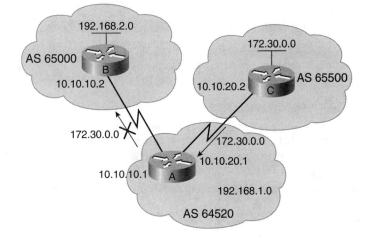

## Prefix List Characteristics

Distribute lists use access lists to do route filtering. However, access lists were originally designed to do packet filtering.

Prefix lists, available in Cisco IOS Release 12.0 and later, can be used as an alternative to access lists in many BGP route filtering commands. The advantages of using prefix lists include the following:

- A significant performance improvement over access lists in loading and route lookup of large lists.

- Support for incremental modifications. Compared to a normal access list in which one **no** command erases the whole access list, prefix list entries can be modified incrementally.

- A more user-friendly command-line interface. The command-line interface for using extended access lists to filter BGP updates is difficult to understand and use.

- Greater flexibility.

## Filtering with Prefix Lists

Filtering by prefix list involves matching the prefixes of routes with those listed in the prefix list, similar to using access lists.

Whether a prefix is permitted or denied is based on the following rules:

- An empty prefix list permits all prefixes.

- If a prefix is permitted, the route is used. If a prefix is denied, the route is not used.

- Prefix lists consist of statements with sequence numbers. The router begins the search for a match at the top of the prefix list, which is the statement with the lowest sequence number.

- When a match occurs, the router does not need to go through the rest of the prefix list. For efficiency, you might want to put the most common matches (permits or denies) near the top of the list by specifying a lower sequence number.

- An implicit deny is assumed if a given prefix does not match any entries in a prefix list.

## Configuring Prefix Lists

**NOTE**    Most of the **prefix-list** commands are *not* documented in the Cisco IOS Command Reference manuals for Release 12.0. The only published documentation is in the *BGP Configuration Guide* for Release 12.0. However, all of the **prefix-list** commands in this book have been tested, and they work on Release 12.0. The commands *are* documented in the Cisco IOS Command Reference manuals for Release 12.1.

The **ip prefix-list** *list-name* [**seq** *seq-value*] {**deny** | **permit**} *network/len* [**ge** *ge-value*] [**le** *le-value*] global configuration command is used to create a prefix list, as described in Table A-30.

**Table A-30**    **ip prefix-list** *Command Description*

| Parameter | Description |
| --- | --- |
| *list-name* | The name of the prefix list that will be created. (It is case-sensitive.) |
| *seq-value* | A 32-bit sequence number of the **prefix-list** statement, used to determine the order in which the statements are processed when filtering. Default sequence numbers are in increments of 5 (5, 10, 15, and so on). |
| **deny** | **permit** | The action taken when a match is found. |
| *network/len* | The prefix to be matched and the length of the prefix. The network is a 32-bit address; the length is a decimal number. |
| *ge-value* | The range of the prefix length to be matched for prefixes that are more specific than *network/len*. The range is assumed to be from *ge-value* to 32 if only the **ge** attribute is specified. |
| *le-value* | The range of the prefix length to be matched for prefixes that are more specific than *network/len*. The range is assumed to be from *len* to *le-value* if only the **le** attribute is specified. |

**ge** and **le** are optional. They can be used to specify the range of the prefix length to be matched for prefixes that are more specific than *network/len*. The value range is

$$len < ge\text{-}value < le\text{-}value < = 32$$

An exact match is assumed when neither **ge** nor **le** is specified.

Prefix list entries can be reconfigured incrementally. In other words, an entry can be deleted or added individually.

The **neighbor** {*ip-address* | *peer-group-name*} **prefix-list** *prefix-listname* {**in** | **out**} router configuration command is used to distribute BGP neighbor information as specified in a prefix list, as described in Table A-31.

**Table A-31**    **neighbor prefix-list** *Command Description*

| Parameter | Description |
|---|---|
| *ip-address* | The IP address of the BGP neighbor for which routes will be filtered. |
| *peer-group-name* | The name of a BGP peer group. |
| *prefix-listname* | The name of the prefix list that will be used to filter the routes. |
| **in** | Indicates that the prefix list is to be applied to incoming advertisements from the neighbor. |
| **out** | Indicates that the prefix list is to be applied to outgoing advertisements to the neighbor. |

**NOTE**    The **neighbor prefix-list** command can be used as an alternative to the **neighbor distribute-list** command, but you cannot use both commands to configure the same BGP peer.

### ip prefix-list Command Options

The use of the **ge** and **le** options in the **ip prefix-list** command can be confusing. The following are results of some testing done to understand these keywords.

Three routers were used in this testing: Router B, Router A, and its neighbor 10.1.1.1, as illustrated in Figure A-40.

Before configuring the prefix list, Router A learns the following routes (from Router B):

```
172.16.0.0 subnetted:
    172.16.10.0/24
    172.16.11.0/24
```

**Figure A-40** *Network Used in Prefix List Option Testing*

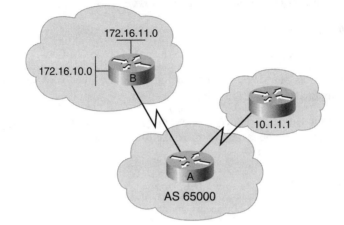

Five scenarios were tested:

**Scenario 1**—In this scenario, the following is configured on Router A:

```
router bgp 65000
    aggregate-address 172.16.0.0 255.255.0.0
    neighbor 10.1.1.1 prefix-list tenonly out
ip prefix-list tenonly permit 172.16.10.0/8 le 24
```

When you view the router's configuration with the **show run** command, you see that the router automatically changes the last line of this configuration to the following:

```
ip prefix-list tenonly permit 172.0.0.0/8 le 24
```

Neighbor 10.1.1.1 learns about 172.16.0.0/16, 172.16.10.0/24, and 172.16.11.0/24.

**Scenario 2**—In this scenario, the following is configured on Router A:

```
router bgp 65000
    aggregate-address 172.16.0.0 255.255.0.0
    neighbor 10.1.1.1 prefix-list tenonly out
ip prefix-list tenonly permit 172.0.0.0/8 le 16
```

Neighbor 10.1.1.1 learns only about 172.16.0.0/16.

**Scenario 3**—In this scenario, the following is configured on Router A:

```
router bgp 65000
    aggregate-address 172.16.0.0 255.255.0.0
    neighbor 10.1.1.1 prefix-list tenonly out
ip prefix-list tenonly permit 172.0.0.0/8 ge 17
```

Neighbor 10.1.1.1 learns only about 172.16.10.0/24 and 172.16.11.0/24. (In other words, it ignores the **/8** parameter and treats the command as if it has the parameters **ge 17 le 32**.)

**Scenario 4**—In this scenario, the following is configured on Router A:

```
router bgp 65000
    aggregate-address 172.16.0.0 255.255.0.0
    neighbor 10.1.1.1 prefix-list tenonly out
ip prefix-list tenonly permit 172.0.0.0/8 ge 16 le 24
```

Neighbor 10.1.1.1 learns about 172.16.0.0/16, 172.16.10.0/24, and 172.16.11.0/24. (In other words, it ignores the **/8** parameter and treats the command as if it has the parameters **ge 16 le 24**.)

**Scenario 5**—In this scenario, the following is configured on Router A:

```
router bgp 65000
    aggregate-address 172.16.0.0 255.255.0.0
    neighbor 10.1.1.1 prefix-list tenonly out
ip prefix-list tenonly permit 172.0.0.0/8 ge 17 le 24
```

Neighbor 10.1.1.1 learns about 172.16.10.0/24 and 172.16.11.0/24. (In other words, it ignores the **/8** parameter and treats the command as if it has the parameters **ge 17 le 24**.)

---

The **no ip prefix-list** *list-name* global configuration command, where *list-name* is the name of a prefix list, is used to delete a prefix list.

The [**no**] **ip prefix-list** *list-name* **description** *text* global configuration command can be used to add or delete a text description for a prefix list.

## Prefix List Sequence Numbers

Prefix list sequence numbers are generated automatically, unless you disable this automatic generation. If you do so, you must specify the sequence number for each entry using the *seq-value* argument of the **ip prefix-list** command.

A prefix list is an ordered list. The sequence number is significant when a given prefix is matched by multiple entries of a prefix list, in which case the one with the smallest sequence number is considered the real match.

Regardless of whether you use the default sequence numbers to configure a prefix list, you don't need to specify a sequence number when removing a configuration entry.

By default, a prefix list's entries have sequence values of 5, 10, 15, and so on. In the absence of a specified sequence value, a new entry is assigned a sequence number equal to the current maximum sequence number plus 5.

Prefix list **show** commands include the sequence numbers in their output.

The **no ip prefix-list sequence-number** global configuration command is used to disable the automatic generation of sequence numbers of prefix list entries. Use the **ip prefix-list sequence-number** global configuration command to reenable the automatic generation of sequence numbers.

## Prefix List Example

The sample network shown in Figure A-41 illustrates the use of a prefix list. In this example, you want Router A to send only the supernet 172.0.0.0/8 to AS 65000; the route to the network 172.30.0.0/16 should not be sent. The configuration for Router A in this figure is provided in Example A-34.

**Figure A-41**  *Prefix List Example*

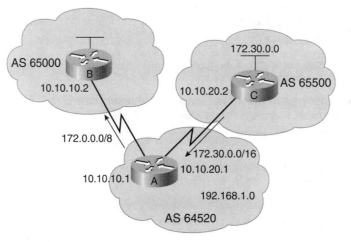

**Example A-34** *Configuration of Router A in Figure A-41*

```
RtrA(config)#ip prefix-list superonly permit 172.0.0.0/8
RtrA(config)#ip prefix-list superonly description only permit supernet
RtrA(config)#router bgp 64520
RtrA(config-router)#network 192.168.1.0
RtrA(config-router)#neighbor 10.10.10.2 remote-as 65000
RtrA(config-router)#neighbor 10.10.20.2 remote-as 65500
RtrA(config-router)#aggregate-address 172.0.0.0 255.0.0.0
RtrA(config-router)#neighbor 10.10.10.2 prefix-list superonly out
RtrA(config-router)#exit
```

In this example, Router A has two neighbors: Router B (10.10.10.2 in AS 65000) and Router C (10.10.20.2 in AS 65500). When Router A sends updates to neighbor Router B, the **neighbor prefix-list** statement specifies that it will use the prefix list called superonly to determine which updates are to be sent.

**ip prefix-list superonly** specifies that only the route 172.0.0.0/8 should be sent (it is permitted in the prefix list). No other routes are sent to Router B, because prefix lists have an implicit deny any at the end.

## Verifying Prefix Lists

The EXEC commands related to prefix lists are described in Table A-32. Use the **show ip prefix-list ?** command to see all of the **show** commands available for prefix lists.

**Table A-32**  *Commands Used to Verify Prefix Lists*

| Command | Description |
|---|---|
| **show ip prefix-list** [**detail** \| **summary**] | Displays information on all prefix lists. Specifying the **detail** keyword includes the description and the hit count (the number of times the entry matches a route) in the display. |
| **show ip prefix-list** [**detail** \| **summary**] *name* | Displays a table showing the entries in a specific prefix list. |
| **show ip prefix-list** *name* [*network/len*] | Displays the policy associated with a specific *prefix/len* in a prefix list. |
| **show ip prefix-list** *name* [**seq** *seq-num*] | Displays the prefix list entry with a given sequence number. |
| **show ip prefix-list** *name* [*network/len*] **longer** | Displays all entries of a prefix list that are more specific than the given network and length. |
| **show ip prefix-list** *name* [*network/len*] **first-match** | Displays the entry of a prefix list that matches the network and length of the given prefix. |
| **clear ip prefix-list** *name* [*network/len*] | Resets the hit count shown on prefix list entries. |

## Verifying Prefix Lists Example

The sample output of the **show ip prefix-list detail** command shown in Example A-35 is from Router A in Figure A-41. Router A has a prefix list called superonly that has only one entry (sequence number 5). The hit count of 0 means that no routes match this entry.

**Example A-35** **show ip prefix-list detail** *Command Output from Router A in Figure A-41*

```
RtrA #show ip prefix-list detail
Prefix-list with the last deletion/insertion: superonly
ip prefix-list superonly:
   Description: only permit supernet
   count: 1, range entries: 0, sequences: 5 - 5, refcount: 1
   seq 5 permit 172.0.0.0/8 (hit count: 0, refcount: 1)
```

# Communities

As discussed in Chapter 8, "Configuring Basic Border Gateway Protocol," BGP communities are another way to filter incoming or outgoing BGP routes. Distribute lists and prefix lists would be cumbersome to configure for a large network with a complex routing policy. For example, individual neighbor statements and access lists or prefix lists would need to be configured for each neighbor on each router involved in the policy.

The BGP communities function allows routers to tag routes with an indicator (the *community*) and allows other routers to make decisions (filter) based on that tag. BGP communities are used for destinations (routes) that share some common properties and that, therefore, share common policies; routers, therefore, act on the community, rather than on individual routes. Communities are not restricted to one network or AS, and they have no physical boundaries.

If a router does not understand the concept of communities, it passes it on to the next router. However, if the router does understand the concept, it must be configured to propagate the community; otherwise, communities are dropped by default.

## Community Attribute

The community attribute is an optional transitive attribute that can have a value in the range 0 to 4,294,967,200. Each network can be a member of more than one community.

The community attribute is a 32-bit number, with the upper 16 bits indicating the AS number of the AS that defined the community. The lower 16 bits are the community number and have local significance. The community value can be entered as one decimal number or in the format *AS:nn,* where *AS* is the AS number and *nn* is the lower 16-bit local number. The community value is displayed as one decimal number by default.

## Setting and Sending the Communities Configuration

Route maps can be used to set the community attributes.

The **set community** {*community-number* [**additive**]} | **none** route map configuration command is used within a route map to set the BGP communities attribute, as described in Table A-33.

**Table A-33**    **set community** *Command Description*

| Parameter | Description |
|---|---|
| *community-number* | The community number. Values are 1 to 4,294,967,200. |
| **additive** | (Optional) Specifies that the community is to be added to the existing communities. |
| **none** | Removes the community attribute from the prefixes that pass the route map. |

The following are predefined, well-known community numbers that can be used in the **set community** command:

- **no-export**—Does not advertise to external BGP (EBGP) peers.
- **no-advertise**—Does not advertise this route to any peer.
- **local-AS**—Does not send outside the local AS.

The **set community** command is used along with the **neighbor route-map** command to apply the route map to updates.

The **neighbor** {*ip-address* | *peer-group-name*} **send-community** router configuration command is used to specify that the BGP communities attribute should be sent to a BGP neighbor. This command is detailed in Table A-34.

**Table A-34**    **neighbor send-community** *Command Description*

| Parameter | Description |
|---|---|
| *ip-address* | The IP address of the BGP neighbor to which the communities attribute is sent. |
| *peer-group-name* | The name of a BGP peer group. |

By default, the communities attribute is not sent to any neighbor (communities are stripped in outgoing BGP updates).

In Figure A-42, Router C is sending BGP updates to Router A, but it does not want Router A to propagate these routes to Router B.

**Figure A-42** *Network for BGP Communities Example*

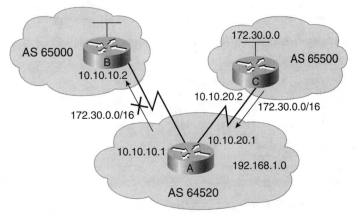

The configuration for Router C, in this example, is provided in Example A-36. Router C sets the community attribute in the BGP routes that it is advertising to Router A. The **no-export** community attribute is used to indicate that Router A should not send the routes to its external BGP peers.

**Example A-36** *Configuration of Router C in Figure A-42*

```
router bgp 65500
  network 172.30.0.0
  neighbor 10.10.20.1 remote-as 64520
  neighbor 10.10.20.1 send-community
  neighbor 10.10.20.1 route-map SETCOMM out
!
route-map SETCOMM permit 10
  match ip address 1
  set community no-export
!
access-list 1 permit 0.0.0.0 255.255.255.255
```

In this example, Router C has one neighbor, 10.10.20.1 (Router A). When communicating with Router A, the community attribute is sent, as specified by the **neighbor send-community** command. The route map SETCOMM is used when sending routes to Router A to set the community attribute. Any route that matches **access-list 1** has the community attribute set to **no-export**. Access list 1 permits any routes; therefore, all routes have the community attribute set to **no-export**.

In this example, Router A receives all of Router C's routes but does not pass them to Router B.

## Using the Communities Configuration

The **ip community-list** *community-list-number* **permit | deny** *community-number* global configuration command is used to create a community list for BGP and to control access to it, as described in Table A-35.

**Table A-35**   **ip community-list** *Command Description*

| Parameter | Description |
|---|---|
| *community-list-number* | The community list number, in the range of 1 to 99. |
| *community-number* | The community number, configured by a **set community** command. |

Here are some predefined well-known community numbers that can be used with the **ip community-list** command:

- **no-export**—Does not advertise to EBGP peers.
- **no-advertise**—Does not advertise this route to any peer.
- **local-AS**—Does not send outside the local AS.
- **internet**—Advertises this route to the Internet community and any router that belongs to it.

The **match community** *community-list-number* [**exact**] route map configuration command is used to match a BGP community attribute to a value in a community list, as described in Table A-36.

**Table A-36**   **match community** *Command Description*

| Parameter | Description |
|---|---|
| *community-list-number* | The community list number, in the range of 1 to 99, that is used to compare the community attribute. |
| **exact** | (Optional) Indicates that an exact match is required. All of the communities and only those communities in the community list must be present in the community attribute. |

**NOTE**   The **match community** command appears in the documentation as the **match community-list** command; however, only **match community** actually works on the routers.

In Figure A-43, Router C is sending BGP updates to Router A. Router A sets the weight of these routes based on the community value set by Router C.

**Figure A-43** *Network for BGP Communities' Example Using Weight*

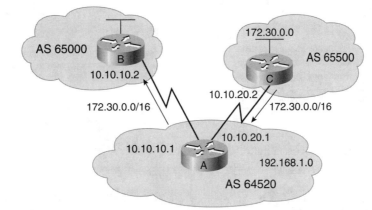

The configuration of Router C in Figure A-43 is shown in Example A-37. Router C has one neighbor, 10.10.20.1 (Router A).

**Example A-37** *Configuration of Router C in Figure A-43*

```
router bgp 65500
  network 172.30.0.0
  neighbor 10.10.20.1 remote-as 64520
  neighbor 10.10.20.1 send-community
  neighbor 10.10.20.1 route-map SETCOMM out
!
route-map SETCOMM permit 10
  match ip address 1
  set community 100 additive
!
access-list 1 permit 0.0.0.0 255.255.255.255
```

In this example, the community attribute is sent to Router A, as specified by the **neighbor send-community** command. The route map SETCOMM is used when sending routes to Router A to set the community attribute. Any route that matches access list 1 has community 100 added to the existing communities in the route's community attribute. In this example, access list 1 permits any routes; therefore, all routes have 100 added to the list of communities. If the **additive** keyword in the **set community** command is not set, 100 replaces any old community that already exits. Because the keyword **additive** is used, the 100 is added to the list of communities that the route is part of.

The configuration of Router A in Figure A-43 is shown in Example A-38.

**Example A-38** *Configuration of Router A in Figure A-43*

```
router bgp 64520
  neighbor 10.10.20.2 remote-as 65500
  neighbor 10.10.20.2 route-map CHKCOMM in
!
```

*continues*

**Example A-38** *Configuration of Router A in Figure A-43 (Continued)*

```
route-map CHKCOMM permit 10
  match community 1
  set weight 20
route-map CHKCOMM permit 20
  match community 2
!
ip community-list 1 permit 100
ip community-list 2 permit internet
```

**NOTE**    Other **router bgp** configuration commands for Router A are not shown in Example A-38.

In this example, Router A has a neighbor, 10.10.20.2 (Router C). The route map CHKCOMM is used when receiving routes from Router C to check the community attribute. Any route whose community attribute matches community list 1 has its weight attribute set to 20. Community list 1 permits routes with a community attribute of 100; therefore, all routes from Router C (which all have 100 in their list of communities) have their weight set to 20.

In this example, any route that does not match community list 1 is checked against community list 2. Any route matching community list 2 is permitted but does not have any of its attributes changed. Community list 2 specifies the **internet** keyword, which means all routes.

The sample output shown in Example A-39 is from Router A in Figure A-43. The output shows the details about the route 172.30.0.0 from Router C, including that its community attribute is 100, and its weight attribute is now 20.

**Example A-39** *Output from Router A in Figure A-43*

```
RtrA #show ip bgp 172.30.0.0/16
BGP routing table entry for 172.30.0.0/16, version 2
Paths: (1 available, best #1)
  Advertised to non peer-group peers:
    10.10.10.2
  65500
    10.10.20.2 from 10.10.20.2 (172.30.0.1)
      Origin IGP, metric 0, localpref 100, weight 20, valid, external, best, ref 2
      Community: 100
```

# Route Reflectors

The BGP split-horizon rule specifies that routes learned via internal BGP (IBGP) are never propagated to other IBGP peers. The result is that a full mesh of IBGP peers is required within an AS. As Figure A-44 illustrates, though, a full mesh of IBGP is not scalable. With only 13 routers, 78 IBGP sessions would need to be maintained. As the number of routers increases, so does the number of sessions required, governed by the following formula, in which *n* is the number of routers:

> # of IGBP sessions = $n(n - 1)/2$

**Figure A-44** *Full-Mesh IBGP Requires Many Sessions and, Therefore, Is Not Scalable*

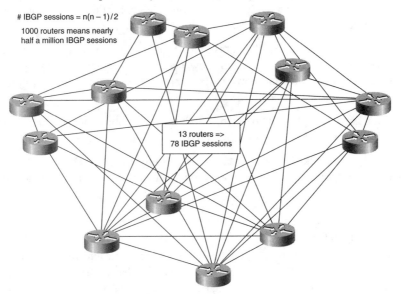

# IBGP sessions = n(n – 1)/2

1000 routers means nearly
half a million IBGP sessions

13 routers =>
78 IBGP sessions

In addition to the number of BGP TCP sessions that must be created and maintained, the
amount of routing traffic also might be a problem. Depending on the AS topology, traffic might
be replicated many times on some links as it travels to each IBGP peer. For example, if the
physical topology of a large AS includes some WAN links, the IBGP sessions running over
those links might consume a significant amount of bandwidth.

A solution to this problem is the use of route reflectors. This section describes what a route
reflector (RR) is, how it works, and how to configure it.

RRs modify the BGP split-horizon rule by allowing the router configured as the RR to propagate
routes learned by IBGP to other IBGP peers, as illustrated in Figure A-45.

**Figure A-45** *When Router A Is a Route Reflector, It Can Propagate Routes Learned From Router B to Router C*

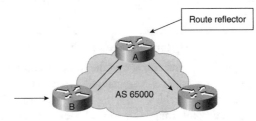

Route reflector

A

AS 65000

B

C

This saves on the number of BGP TCP sessions that must be maintained and also reduces the
BGP routing traffic.

## Route Reflector Benefits

With a BGP RR configured, a full mesh of IBGP peers is no longer required. The RR is allowed
to propagate IBGP routes to other IBGP peers. RRs are used mainly by ISPs when the number

of internal neighbor statements becomes excessive. Route reflectors reduce the number of BGP neighbor relationships in an AS (thus, saving on TCP connections) by having key routers replicate updates to their RR clients.

Route reflectors do not affect the paths that IP packets follow; only the path that routing information is distributed on is affected. However, if route reflectors are configured incorrectly, routing loops might result, as shown in the example later in this appendix in the "Route Reflector Migration Tips" section.

An AS can have multiple route reflectors, both for redundancy and for grouping to further reduce the number of IBGP sessions required.

Migrating to route reflectors involves a minimal configuration and does not have to be done all at once, because routers that are not route reflectors can coexist with route reflectors within an AS.

## Route Reflector Terminology

A *route reflector* is a router that is configured to be the router allowed to advertise (or reflect) routes it learned via IBGP to other IBGP peers. The RR has a partial IBGP peering with other routers, which are called *clients*. Peering between the clients is not needed, because the route reflector passes advertisements between the clients.

The combination of the RR and its clients is called a *cluster*.

Other IBGP peers of the RR that are not clients are called *nonclients*.

The *originator ID* is an optional, nontransitive BGP attribute that is created by the RR. This attribute carries the router ID of the route's originator in the local AS. If the update comes back to the originator because of poor configuration, the originator ignores it.

Usually a cluster has a single RR, in which case the cluster is identified by the RR's router ID. To increase redundancy and avoid single points of failure, a cluster might have more than one RR. When this occurs, all of the RRs in the cluster need to be configured with a *cluster ID*. The cluster ID allows route reflectors to recognize updates from other RRs in the same cluster.

---

### Route Reflector Cluster List

A *cluster list* is a sequence of cluster IDs that the route has passed. When a RR reflects a route from its clients to nonclients outside the cluster, it appends the local cluster ID to the cluster list. If the update has an empty cluster list, the RR creates one. Using this attribute, a RR can tell whether the routing information is looped back to the same cluster because of poor configuration. If the local cluster ID is found in an advertisement's cluster list, the advertisement is ignored.

The originator ID, cluster ID, and cluster list help prevent routing loops in RR configurations.

---

## Route Reflector Design

When using route reflectors in an AS, the AS can be divided into multiple clusters, each having at least one RR and a few clients. Multiple route reflectors can exist in one cluster for redundancy.

The route reflectors must be fully meshed with IBGP to ensure that all routes learned are propagated throughout the AS.

An IGP is still used, just as it was before route reflectors were introduced, to carry local routes and next-hop addresses.

Regular split-horizon rules still apply between a RR and its clients. A RR that receives a route from a client does not advertise that route back to that client.

---

**NOTE**    There is no defined limit to the number of clients a RR might have; it is constrained by the amount of router memory.

---

## Route Reflector Design Example

Figure A-46 provides an example of a BGP RR design.

**Figure A-46**  *Example of a Route Reflector Design*

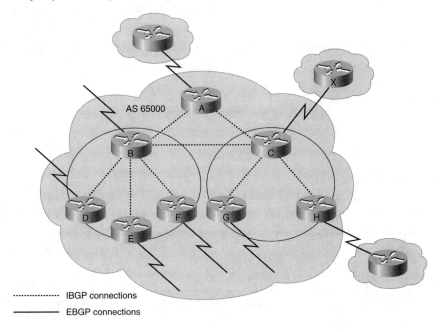

| NOTE | The physical connections within AS 65000 are not shown in Figure A-6. |
| --- | --- |

In Figure A-46, Routers B, D, E, and F form one cluster. Routers C, G, and H form another cluster. Routers B and C are route reflectors. Routers A, B, and C are fully meshed with IBGP. Note that the routers within a cluster are not fully meshed.

## Route Reflector Operation

When a RR receives an update, it takes the following actions, depending on the type of peer that sent the update:

- If the update is from a client peer, it sends the update to all nonclient peers and to all client peers (except the route's originator).
- If the update is from a nonclient peer, it sends the update to all clients in the cluster.
- If the update is from an EBGP peer, it sends the update to all nonclient peers and to all client peers.

For example, in Figure A-46, the following happens:

- If Router C receives an update from Router H (a client), it sends it to Router G, as well as to Routers A and B.
- If Router C receives an update from Router A (a nonclient), it sends it to Routers G and H.
- If Router C receives an update from Router X (via EBGP), it sends it to Routers G and H, as well as to Routers A and B.

| NOTE | Routers also send updates to their EBGP neighbors as appropriate. |
| --- | --- |

## Route Reflector Migration Tips

When migrating to using route reflectors, the first consideration is which routers should be the reflectors and which should be the clients. Following the physical topology in this design decision ensures that the packet-forwarding paths are not affected. Not following the physical topology (for example, configuring RR clients that are not physically connected to the route reflector) might result in routing loops.

Figure A-47 demonstrates what can happen if route reflectors are configured without following the physical topology. In this figure, the bottom router, Router E, is a RR client for both RRs, Routers C and D.

**Figure A-47** *Bad Route Reflector Design*

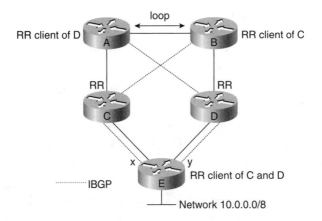

In this *bad design,* which does not follow the physical topology, the following happens:

- Router B knows that the next hop to get to 10.0.0.0 is *x* (because it learns this from its RR, Router C).

- Router A knows that the next hop to get to 10.0.0.0 is *y* (because it learns this from its RR, Router D).

- For Router B to get to *x*, the best route might be through Router A, so Router B sends a packet destined for 10.0.0.0 to Router A.

- For Router A to get to *y*, the best route might be through Router B, so Router A sends a packet destined for 10.0.0.0 to Router B.

- This is a routing loop.

Figure A-48 shows a better design, because it follows the physical topology. Again, in this figure, the bottom router, Router E, is a RR client for both route reflectors.

**Figure A-48** *Good Route Reflector Design*

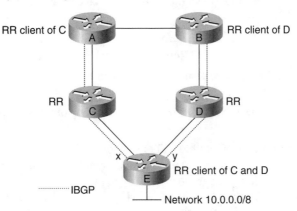

In this *good design,* which follows the physical topology, the following are true:

- Router B knows that the next hop to get to 10.0.0.0 is *y* (because it learns this from its RR, Router D).

- Router A knows that the next hop to get to 10.0.0.0 is *x* (because it learns this from its RR, Router C).

- For Router A to get to *x*, the best route is through Router C, so Router A sends a packet destined for 10.0.0.0 to Router C, and Router C sends it to Router E.

- For Router B to get to *y*, the best route is through Router D, so Router B sends a packet destined for 10.0.0.0 to Router D, and Router D sends it to Router E.

- There is no routing loop.

When migrating to using route reflectors, configure one RR at a time, and then delete the redundant IBGP sessions between the clients. It is recommended that you configure one RR per cluster.

## Route Reflector Configuration

The **neighbor** *ip-address* **route-reflector-client** router configuration command is used to configure the router as a BGP RR and to configure the specified neighbor as its client. This command is described in Table A-37.

**Table A-37**    **neighbor route-reflector-client** *Command Description*

| Parameter | Description |
|---|---|
| *ip-address* | The IP address of the BGP neighbor being identified as a client. |

### Configuring the Cluster ID

To configure the cluster ID if the BGP cluster has more than one RR, use the **bgp cluster-id** *cluster-id* router configuration command on all of the route reflectors in a cluster. You cannot change the cluster ID after the RR clients have been configured.

### Route Reflector Restrictions

Route reflectors cause some restrictions on other commands, including the following:

- When used on route reflectors, the **neighbor next-hop-self** command affects only the next hop of EBGP learned routes, because the next hop of reflected IBGP routes should not be changed.

- RR clients are incompatible with peer groups. This is because a router configured with a peer group must send any update to *all* members of the peer group. If a RR has all of its clients in a peer group and then one of those clients sends an update, the RR is responsible for sharing that update with all *other* clients. The RR must not send the update to the originating client because of the split-horizon rule.

## Route Reflector Example

The network in Figure A-49 illustrates a router configured as a RR in AS 65000. The configuration for Router A in this figure is provided in Example A-40.

**Figure A-49** *Router A Is a Route Reflector*

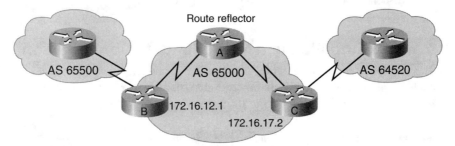

**Example A-40** *Configuration of Router A in Figure A-49*

```
RTRA(config)#router bgp 65000
RTRA(config-router)#neighbor 172.16.12.1 remote-as 65000
RTRA(config-router)#neighbor 172.16.12.1 route-reflector-client
RTRA(config-router)#neighbor 172.16.17.2 remote-as 65000
RTRA(config-router)#neighbor 172.16.17.2 route-reflector-client
```

The **neighbor route-reflector-client** commands are used to configure which neighbors are RR clients. In this example, both Routers B and C are RR clients of Router A, the RR.

## Verifying Route Reflectors

The **show ip bgp neighbors** command indicates that a particular neighbor is a RR client. The sample output for this command, shown in Example A-41, is from Router A in Figure A-49 and shows that 172.16.12.1 (Router B) is a RR client of Router A.

**Example A-41 show ip bgp neighbors** *Output from Router A in Figure A-49*

```
RTRA#show ip bgp neighbors
BGP neighbor is 172.16.12.1,  remote AS 65000, internal link
 Index 1, Offset 0, Mask 0x2
 Route-Reflector Client
 BGP version 4, remote router ID 192.168.101.101
 BGP state = Established, table version = 1, up for 00:05:42
 Last read 00:00:42, hold time is 180, keepalive interval is 60 seconds
 Minimum time between advertisement runs is 5 seconds
 Received 14 messages, 0 notifications, 0 in queue
 Sent 12 messages, 0 notifications, 0 in queue
 Prefix advertised 0, suppressed 0, withdrawn 0
 Connections established 2; dropped 1
 Last reset 00:05:44, due to User reset
 1 accepted prefixes consume 32 bytes
 0 history paths consume 0 bytes
--More--
```

# Supplement 6: Route Optimization

This section reviews the following topics:

- Examples of redistribution in a nonredundant configuration
- Miscellaneous redistribution configuration examples

## Examples of Redistribution in a Nonredundant Configuration

This section includes configuration and **show** command output examples that result from configuring the network shown in Figure A-50. The addresses for this configuration are also shown in Figure A-50; protocols for the example are shown in Figure A-51.

**Figure A-50**  *Addressing for the Redistribution Configuration Example*

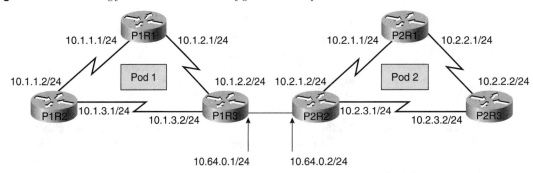

**Figure A-51**  *Nonredundant Redistribution Configuration Example*

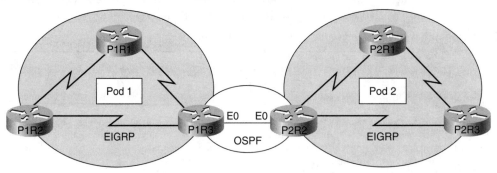

### Example of Redistribution Between EIGRP and OSPF

Example A-42 shows the configuration output for P1R3, an ASBR supporting EIGRP and OSPF.

**Example A-42**  *ASBR in Figures A-50 and A-51, Redistributing Between EIGRP and OSPF*

```
P1R3#show run
Building configuration...
Current configuration:
!
version 11.2
hostname P1R3
!
enable password san-fran
!
no ip domain-lookup
ipx routing 0000.0c01.3333
ipx maximum-paths 2
!
interface Loopback0
 no ip address
 ipx network 1013
!
interface Ethernet0
ip address 10.64.0.1 255.255.255.0
!
interface Serial0
ip address 10.1.3.2 255.255.255.0
bandwidth 64
ipx input-sap-filter 1000
ipx network 1003
!
interface Serial1
ip address 10.1.2.2 255.255.255.0
ipx input-sap-filter 1000
ipx network 1002
clockrate 56000
<Output Omitted>
!

router eigrp 200

redistribute ospf 300 metric 10000 100 255 1 1500
passive-interface Ethernet0
network 10.0.0.0
!
router ospf 300

redistribute eigrp 200 subnets
network 10.64.0.0 0.0.255.255 area 0
!
no ip classless
line con 0
exec-timeout 20 0
password cisco
!
line aux 0
```

*continues*

**Example A-42** *ASBR in Figures A-50 and A-51, Redistributing Between EIGRP and OSPF (Continued)*

```
line vty 0 4
password cisco
!
End
```

In Example A-42, EIGRP in AS 200 is configured for all interfaces in network 10.0.0.0. The
**passive-interface** command is used to disable EIGRP on the Ethernet (because OSPF will
be running there). Routes from OSPF are redistributed into EIGRP with the **redistribute**
command using the defined metrics. OSPF is configured to run on the Ethernet 0 interface in
area 0. Routes from EIGRP are redistributed into EIGRP; the **subnets** keyword is included
so that subnetted routes (in this case, subnets of network 10.0.0.0) are redistributed. If this
keyword were omitted, no routes would be redistributed from OSPF to EIGRP in this example.

Example A-43 shows output verifying that external routes are learned by OSPF and EIGRP,
respectively, on an ASBR.

**Example A-43** *OSPF and EIGRP Topology Databases of P1R3 in Figures A-50 and A-51*

```
P1R3#show ip ospf database

       OSPF Router with ID (10.64.0.1) (Process ID 300)

               Router Link States (Area 0)

Link ID         ADV Router      Age        Seq#       Checksum Link count
10.64.0.1       10.64.0.1       280        0x80000005 0x767F   1
10.64.0.2       10.64.0.2       274        0x80000004 0x767D   1

               Net Link States (Area 0)

Link ID         ADV Router      Age        Seq#       Checksum

10.64.0.2       10.64.0.2       274        0x80000002 0x7791

               Type-5 AS External Link States

Link ID         ADV Router      Age        Seq#       Checksum Tag
10.1.1.0        10.64.0.1       202        0x80000002 0xE95E   0
10.1.2.0        10.64.0.1       202        0x80000002 0xDE68   0
10.1.3.0        10.64.0.1       202        0x80000002 0xD372   0
10.2.1.0        10.64.0.2       1686       0x80000001 0xD96D   0
10.2.2.0        10.64.0.2       1686       0x80000001 0xCE77   0
10.2.3.0        10.64.0.2       1686       0x80000001 0xC381   0
10.64.0.0       10.64.0.1       204        0x80000002 0xFD0C   0
10.64.0.0       10.64.0.2       1688       0x80000001 0xF910   0
P1R3#


P1R3#show ip eigrp topology
IP-EIGRP Topology Table for process 200
```

**Example A-43** *OSPF and EIGRP Topology Databases of P1R3 in Figures A-50 and A-51 (Continued)*

```
Codes: P - Passive, A - Active, U - Update, Q - Query, R - Reply,
       r - Reply status
P 10.1.3.0/24, 1 successors, FD is 40512000
        via Connected, Serial0
        via 10.1.2.1 (3193856/2681856), Serial1
P 10.2.1.0/24, 1 successors, FD is 281600
        via Redistributed (281600/0)
P 10.1.2.0/24, 1 successors, FD is 2169856
        via Connected, Serial
P 10.2.2.0/24, 1 successors, FD is 281600
        via Redistributed (281600/0)
P 10.1.1.0/24, 1 successors, FD is 2681856
        via 10.1.2.1 (2681856/2169856), Serial1
P 10.2.3.0/24, 1 successors, FD is 281600
        via Redistributed (281600/0)
P 10.64.0.0/24, 1 successors, FD is 281600
        via Connected, Ethernet0
```

In Example A-43, you can see from the **show ip ospf database** command output that P1R3
learns external routes (type 5 LSAs) in OSPF. Note that subnetted networks are included.
EIGRP also learns external routes, shown as redistributed routes in the **show ip eigrp topology**
command output.

# Miscellaneous Redistribution Configuration Examples

This section presents examples of one-way redistribution.

## IGRP Redistribution Example

Cisco IOS software supports multiple IGRP autonomous systems. Each autonomous system
maintains its own routing database. You can redistribute routing information among these
routing databases. Table A-38 describes some of the commands shown in Example A-44. Refer
to Figure A-52 for the topology used in Example A-44.

**Figure A-52** *IGRP Redistribution Configuration Example*

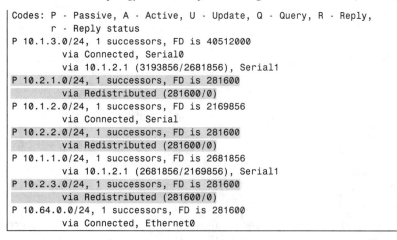

**Example A-44** *Routes Redistributed from AS 109 into AS 71 in Figure A-52*

```
router igrp 71
  redistribute igrp 109
  distribute-list 3 out igrp 109
access-list 3 permit 192.168.7.0 0.0.0.255
```

**Table A-38**    *Redistribution Commands in Example A-44*

| Command | Description |
|---------|-------------|
| **redistribute igrp 109** | Redistributes routes from IGRP 109 into IGRP 71. |
| **distribute-list 3 out igrp 109** | Uses access list 3 to define which routes will be redistributed from IGRP 109 into IGRP 71: <br><br> **3**—Redistributes per access list 3. <br><br> **out**—Applies the access list to outgoing routing updates. <br><br> **igrp 109**—Identifies the IGRP routing process to filter. |
| **access-list 3 permit 192.168.7.0 0.0.0.255** | Permits routes only from network 192.168.7.0. |

In Example A-44, only routing updates from the 192.168.7.0 network are redistributed into autonomous system 71. Updates from other networks are denied.

## RIP/OSPF Redistribution Example

In Example A-45 and Figure A-53, an additional path connects the RIP clouds. These paths, or "back doors," frequently exist, allowing the potential for feedback loops. You can use access lists to determine the routes that are advertised and accepted by each router.

**Figure A-53** *Blocking Paths to Avoid Looping*

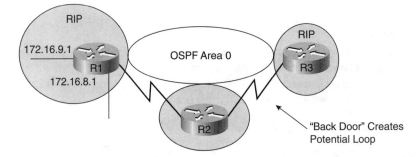

**Example A-45** *Avoiding Loops While Redistributing on Router R1 in Figure A-53*

```
hostname R1
!
router ospf 109
  network 172.16.62.0 0.0.0.255 area 0
  network 172.16.63.0 0.0.0.255 area 0
  redistribute rip subnets metric-type 1 metric 20
  distribute-list 11 out rip

access-list 11 permit 172.16.8.0 0.0.7.255
```

For example, access list 11 in the configuration file for Router R1 allows OSPF to redistribute information learned from RIP only for networks 172.16.8.0 to 172.16.15.0. These commands prevent Router R1 from advertising networks in other RIP domains onto the OSPF backbone, thereby preventing other boundary routers from using false information and forming a loop. You would configure similar access lists on R2 and R3.

## Redistribution Example Using the Default Metric

In Figure A-54 and Example A-46, the router is redistributing IP RIP and EIGRP routes. The 192.168.5.0 network is redistributed to the IP RIP network with a metric of three hops. EIGRP in autonomous system 300 learns routes from IP RIP.

**Figure A-54** *Redistributing RIP and EIGRP*

**Example A-46** *Redistribution Using the Default Metric in Figure A-54*

```
router rip
   network 172.16.0.0
   redistribute eigrp 300
   default-metric 3
router eigrp 300
   network 192.168.5.0
   redistribute rip
   default-metric 56 2000 255 1 1500
```

Table A-39 describes some of the commands shown in Example A-46.

**Table A-39**    *Redistribution Commands in Example A-46*

| Command | Description |
|---|---|
| **redistribute eigrp 300** | Enables redistribution of routes learned from EIGRP autonomous system 300 into the IP RIP network. |
| **default-metric 3** | Specifies that EIGRP-learned routes are three hops away. |
| **redistribute rip** | Enables redistribution of routes learned from the IP RIP network into EIGRP autonomous system 300. |
| **default-metric 56 2000 255 1 1500** | Indicates that the RIP-derived network is being redistributed with the following EIGRP metric values:<br>**56**—Bandwidth is 56 kbps.<br>**2000**—Delay is 2000 tens of microseconds.<br>**255**—Reliability is 100 percent (255 of 255).<br>**1**—Loading is less than 1 percent (1 of 255).<br>**1500**—MTU is 1500 bytes. |

## Redistribution Example Using Filtering

Figure A-55 and Example A-47 provide an example of redistribution filtering.

**Figure A-55** *Redistribution Using Filtering and the Default Metric*

**Example A-47** *R1 in Figure A-53 Hides Network 10.0.0.0 Using Redistribution Filtering*

```
hostname R1
!
router rip
  network 192.168.5.0
  redistribute eigrp 1
  default-metric 3
  distribute-list 7 out eigrp 1
!
router eigrp 1
  network 172.16.0.0
  redistribute rip
  default-metric 56 2000 255 1 1500
!
access-list 7 deny 10.0.0.0 0.255.255.255
access-list 7 permit  0.0.0.0 255.255.255.255
```

Table A-40 describes some of the commands shown in Example A-47.

**Table A-40** *R6 Redistribution Filtering Commands in Example A-47*

| Command | Description |
|---|---|
| **redistribute eigrp 1** | Allows routes learned from EIGRP autonomous system 1 to be redistributed into IP RIP. |
| **default-metric 3** | Specifies that all routes learned from EIGRP will be advertised by RIP as reachable in three hops. |
| **distribute-list 7 out eigrp 1** | Specifies that routes defined by access list 7 leaving the EIGRP process will be filtered before being given to the RIP process. |

## Redistribution Example Using Filtering and the Default Metric

Figure A-56 and Example A-48 provide an example of a redistribution filtering and default metric.

**Figure A-56** *Redistribution Filtering and the Default Metric*

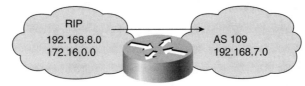

**Example A-48** *Redistributing RIP and IGRP*

```
router rip
  network 192.168.8.0
  network 172.16.0.0
  redistribute igrp 109
  default-metric 4
  distribute-list 11 out igrp 109
!
router igrp 109
  network 192.168.7.0
  redistribute rip
  default-metric 10000 100 255 1 1500
  distribute-list 10 out rip

access-list 10 permit 172.16.0.0 0.0.255.255
access-list 11 permit 192.168.7.0 0.0.0.255
```

Table A-41 describes some of the commands shown in Example A-48.

**Table A-41**    *Redistribution and Route Filtering Commands in Example A-48*

| Command | Description |
|---|---|
| **redistribute igrp 109** | Redistributes IGRP routes into RIP. |
| **default-metric 4** | Sets the metric for IGRP-derived routes to four hops. |
| **redistribute rip** | Redistributes RIP routes into IGRP. |
| **default-metric 10000 100 255 1 1500** | Indicates that the RIP-derived network is being redistributed with the following IGRP metric values: <br><br>**10000**—Bandwidth is 10,000 kbps. <br><br>**100**—Delay is 100 tens of microseconds. <br><br>**255**—Reliability is 100 percent (255 of 255). <br><br>**1**—Loading is less than 1 percent (1 of 255). <br><br>**1500**—MTU is 1500 bytes. |
| **distribute list 10 out rip** | Uses access list 10 to limit updates going out of RIP into IGRP. |

# Router Password Recovery Procedure

This appendix contains the procedure for password recovery on Cisco routers.

**NOTE**  Two different types of commands are used to perform password recovery, depending on the type of router. For example, the 2500 series routers use the more cryptic commands shown in this appendix, while the 1600 series routers use the **confreg** utility. The following lists categorize routers by password recovery. Current listings can be found at www.cisco.com/warp/customer/474/index.shtml.

According to the Cisco documentation (reference: www.cisco.com/warp/customer/474/index.shtml) the following Cisco products use the more cryptic commands:

Cisco 2000
Cisco 2500
Cisco 3000
Cisco 4000
Cisco AccessPro
Cisco 7000 (RP)
Cisco AGS
Cisco IGS
Cisco STS-10x

The following Cisco products use the **confreg** utility:

| | |
|---|---|
| Cisco 1003 | Cisco 7200 |
| Cisco 1004 | Cisco uBR7200 |
| Cisco 1005 | Cisco 7500 |
| Cisco 1600 | Cisco 12000 |
| Cisco 1700 | Cisco LS1010 |
| Cisco 2600 | Catalyst 5500 (RSM) |
| Cisco 3600 | Catalyst 8510-CSR |
| Cisco 4500 | Catalyst 8510-MSR |
| Cisco 4700 | Catalyst 8540-CSR |
| Cisco AS5x00 | Catalyst 8540-MSR |
| Cisco 6x00 | Cisco VG200 Analog Gateway |
| Cisco 7000 (RSP7000) | Cisco MC3810 |
| Cisco 7100 | |

Follow these steps to recover passwords on Cisco routers:

**Step 1**   To enter ROM Monitor mode, power cycle the router; within 60 seconds after the router comes up, press the Break key. (On a PC, the Break key is probably a combination: <Ctrl>+<Break>.)

**Step 2**   Enter the letter **o** or the **e/s 2000002** command to read the original value of the configuration register. (The configuration register default value is 0x2102.) When the configuration register value is displayed, press the Esc key to return to the prompt.

On some routers (see previous listings), you must use the confreg utility to read the configuration register settings. When you use this utility, you won't actually see the value of the configuration register, but you will see what settings are enabled; note what they are.

Set bit 6 in the configuration register (along with the original bit settings) to ignore NVRAM on boot up, using the **o/r** command. (Refer to the "Configuration Register Bits" sidebar later in this appendix for a description of configuration register bits.)

For example, if the original configuration register value was 0x2102, then setting bit 6 means setting a value of 0x2142 for the configuration register. In this example, to set the configuration register, use the following command:

```
>o/r 0x2142
```

On some routers, you must use the confreg utility to set the configuration register. In the utility, enter **y** when asked if you want to enable the system to ignore system configuration information. Keep all other settings the same as you noted in Step 2.

**Step 3**   Initialize and reboot the router, using the **i** command. On some routers, you must use the **boot** command to initialize and reboot the router.

**Step 4**   When the router boots, it will go into setup mode. Answer **no** to all questions.

**Step 5**   When you are back at the Router prompt, enter privileged mode using the following command:

```
Router>enable
```

**Step 6**   Load the configuration that is in NVRAM into active memory using the following command:

```
Router#copy startup-config running-config
```

On releases of the Cisco IOS prior to release 10.3, use the following command:

```
Router#config memory
```

Remember that this operation is a merge, so all interfaces will be shut down at this point because they were shut down when the router loaded without a configuration.

**Step 7** Enable all interfaces that should be enabled using the following commands (where *x/y* represents the appropriate interface name):

```
hostname#config term
hostname(config)#interface x/y
hostname(config-if)#no shutdown
```

For example, to enable the Ethernet 0 interface, use the following commands:

```
hostname#config term
hostname(config)#interface e0
hostname(config-if)#no shutdown
```

**Step 8** Restore the original configuration register value as follows, where *0xvalue* is the original configuration value:

```
hostname#config term
hostname(config)#config-register 0xvalue
```

For example, to restore the configuration value to 0x2102, use the following commands:

```
hostname#config term
hostname(config)#config-register 0x2102
```

**Step 9** To recover or record lost passwords, display the running configuration in RAM using the following command:

```
hostname#show running-config
```

On releases of the Cisco IOS prior to release 10.3, use the following command:

```
hostname#write term
```

To change passwords, use the following commands, inserting the appropriate new passwords (you must use this method if passwords are encrypted):

```
hostname#config term
hostname(config)#enable secret newpassword
```

```
hostname(config)#enable password newpassword
hostname(config)#line con 0
hostname(config-line)#login
hostname(config-line)#password newpassword
```

**Step 10** Save your new configuration into NVRAM using the following command:

```
hostname#copy running-config startup-config
```

On releases of the Cisco IOS prior to release 10.3, use the following command:

```
hostname#write memory
```

## Configuration Register Bits

The configuration register is a 16-bit register. Table B-1 describes the meaning of these bits (source: Cisco Installation and Maintenance of Cisco Routers [IMCR] course student material).

**Table B-1**    *Configuration Register Bit Meanings*

| Bit Number(s) | Hex Value | Meaning |
|---|---|---|
| 0 to 3 | 0x0000 to 0x000f | Boot field |
| 4 | 0x0010 | Fast Boot, 1 = bypass bootstrap image load, boot IOS indicated by boot system |
| 5 | 0x0020 | On 3600, set baud rate up to 115,200 bps |
| 6 | 0x0040 | 1 = ignore startup configuration file |
| 7 | 0x0080 | OEM bit, 1 = disable display of Cisco banner on startup |
| 8 | 0x0100 | 1 = break key disabled after first 60 seconds |
| 9 | 0x0200 | Controls the secondary bootstrap program function used for system debugging |
| 10 | 0x0400 | Netboot broadcast format, 1 = use all 0s broadcast address |
| 11 and 12 | 0x0800 to 0x1000 | Console baud rate, 00 = 9600 bps |

**Table B-1**    *Configuration Register Bit Meanings (Continued)*

| Bit Number(s) | Hex Value | Meaning |
|---|---|---|
| 13 | 0x2000 | Response to netboot failure, 1 = boot from ROM after five failures |
| 14 | 0x4000 | Netboot subnet broadcast, 1 = use subnet broadcast address |
| 15 | 0x8000 | Enable diagnostic messages, 1 = enabled and use test-system configuration |

This appendix is organized into the following sections:

- Summary of ICND Router Commands
- Summary of ICND Switch IOS Commands

# Summary of ICND Router and Switch Commands

This appendix contains a listing of some of the Cisco router IOS, Catalyst 1900, and Catalyst 2950 Switch IOS commands you might find in the Cisco Interconnecting Cisco Network Devices (ICND) course and in Cisco Press's *CCNA Self-Study: Interconnecting Cisco Network Devices* (Steve McQuerry, 2000). The commands are organized into various categories.

---

**NOTE**    Only the commands are listed here; parameters are not included. For details on the parameters and how each command works, please see the *Command Reference Manuals* on the Cisco documentation CD-ROM or on Cisco's website at www.cisco.com.

---

**NOTE**    In the tables in this appendix, words within angled brackets (< >) are single keys that should be pressed, not command words that should be entered. A plus sign (+) between keys indicates that the keys should be pressed simultaneously. For example, **<Ctrl>(+)<a>** indicates that the Ctrl key and the "a" key should be pressed at the same time.

---

## Summary of ICND Router Commands

This section contains a listing of some of the Cisco router IOS commands.

### General Commands

Table C-1 lists general Cisco router EXEC IOS commands.

**Table C-1**    *General Commands*

| Command | Meaning |
|---------|---------|
| ? | Help. |
| <ctrl>+<a> | Moves to the beginning of the command line. |
| <ctrl>+<b> | Moves backward one character. |

*continues*

**Table C-1**    *General Commands (Continued)*

| Command | Meaning |
|---|---|
| **\<ctrl\>+\<c\>** | Aborts from setup mode. |
| **\<ctrl\>+\<e\>** | Moves to the end of the command line. |
| **\<ctrl\>+\<f\>** | Moves forward one character. |
| **\<ctrl\>+\<n\> or \<down arrow\>** | Returns to more recent commands in the history buffer after recalling commands with **\<ctrl\>+\<p\>** or **\<up arrow\>**. Repeat the key sequence to successively recall more recent commands. |
| **\<ctrl\>+\<p\> or \<up arrow\>** | Recalls commands in the history buffer, beginning with the most recent command. Repeat the key sequence to recall successively older commands. |
| **\<ctrl\>+\<Shift\>+\<6\> \<x\>** | The escape sequence, which is used to suspend a Telnet session. |
| **\<ctrl\>+\<r\>** | Redisplays a line. |
| **\<ctrl\>+\<u\>** | Erases a line from the beginning of the line. |
| **\<ctrl\>+\<w\>** | Erases a word. |
| **\<ctrl\>+\<z\>** | Exits from configuration mode back to privileged EXEC mode. |
| **\<esc\>+\<b\>** | Moves to the beginning of the previous word. |
| **\<esc\>+\<f\>** | Moves forward one word. |
| **\<backspace\>** | Removes one character to the left of the cursor. |
| **\<enter\> or \<return\>** | Resumes the last suspended Telnet session. |
| **\<tab\>** | Completes the keyword. |
| **clear counters** | Resets the show interface counters to zero. |
| **clear line** | Disconnects a Telnet session from a foreign host. |
| **clock set** | Sets the router's clock. |
| **configure terminal** | Enters configuration mode. |
| **connect** | Logs on to a host that supports Telnet, rlogin, or Local-Area Transport (LAT). |
| **copy flash tftp** | Copies a file from Flash memory to a Trivial File Transfer Protocol (TFTP) server. |
| **copy running-config startup-config** | Copies configuration from Random Access Memory (RAM) to Nonvolatile RAM (NVRAM) (overwrites). |
| **copy running-config tftp** | Copies configuration from RAM to TFTP server (overwrites). |

**Table C-1**    *General Commands (Continued)*

| Command | Meaning |
| --- | --- |
| **copy startup-config running-config** | Executes configuration from NVRAM into RAM (executes line by line; merges; does not overwrite). |
| **copy startup-config tftp** | Copies configuration from NVRAM to TFTP server (overwrites). |
| **copy tftp flash** | Copies a file from a TFTP server to Flash memory. |
| **copy tftp running-config** | Executes configuration from a TFTP server into RAM (executes line by line; in other words, it merges the commands—it does not overwrite). |
| **copy tftp startup-config** | Copies configuration from a TFTP server to NVRAM (overwrites). |
| **debug** | Starts the console display of the events on the router. |
| **disable** | Exits privileged EXEC mode. |
| **disconnect** | Disconnects a Telnet session. |
| **enable** | Enters privileged mode. |
| **erase startup-config** | Erases the configuration in NVRAM. |
| **exit** | Closes an active terminal session and terminates the EXEC. (Also used to exit any level in configuration mode.) |
| **logout** | Closes an active terminal session and terminates the EXEC. |
| **ping** | Sends an echo and expects an echo reply. The extended **ping** command, accessed by entering **ping** followed by <CR>, also allows ping for protocols other than IP. |
| **reload** | Reloads the operating system. |
| **resume** | Resumes a suspended Telnet session. |
| **setup** | Enters a prompted dialog to establish an initial configuration. |
| **show access-lists** | Displays the contents of all configured access lists. |
| **show cdp entry** | Displays a single cached Cisco Discovery Protocol (CDP) entry; use **show cdp entry \*** to display cached information about all neighbors. |
| **show cdp interface** | Displays values of CDP timers and CDP interface status. |
| **show cdp neighbors** | Displays a summary of CDP information received from neighbors. |
| **show cdp neighbors detail** | Displays detailed CDP information received from neighbors. |

*continues*

**Table C-1** *General Commands (Continued)*

| Command | Meaning |
|---|---|
| **show cdp traffic** | Displays information about interface CDP traffic. |
| **show clock** | Displays the system clock. |
| **show controller** | Displays the Layer 1 information about an interface (including cable type and data circuit-terminating equipment/data terminal equipment [DCE/DTE] status for serial interfaces). |
| **show flash** | Displays information about Flash memory. |
| **show history** | Displays the list of recorded command lines during the current terminal session. |
| **show interfaces** | Displays information about interfaces or an interface, including the state of the interface. |
| **show processes** | Displays the CPU utilization for each process. |
| **show running-config** | Displays the active configuration (in RAM). |
| **show sessions** | Displays a list of hosts to which you have established Telnet connectivity. |
| **show startup-config** | Displays the backup configuration (in NVRAM). |
| **show terminal** | Displays the current terminal settings. |
| **show users** | Displays a list of all active users on the router. |
| **show version** | Displays configuration of system hardware, software version, and configuration register value. |
| **telnet** | Connects to a host. |
| **terminal editing** | Re-enables advanced editing (use **no terminal editing** to disable advanced editing features). Advanced editing is enabled by default. |
| **terminal history size** | Changes the number of command lines the system records during the current terminal session. |
| **terminal monitor** | Forwards debug and error output to your Telnet session (use **terminal no monitor** to turn this off). |
| **traceroute** | Traces the route that packets are taking through the network. (Note that the **traceroute** command appears in the Cisco IOS documentation as **trace**; however, **traceroute** is the full command on the routers.) |
| **undebug** | Turns off debugging (also use **no debug**). |

## Comparison of Configuration File Commands

With Cisco IOS Release 12.0, commands used to copy and transfer configuration and system files have changed to conform to IOS File System (IFS) specifications. The old commands continue to perform their normal functions in the current release, but support for these commands will cease in a future release. Table C-2 contains the old and new commands used for configuration file movement and management.

**Table C-2** *Comparison of Configuration File Commands*

| Old Command | New Command |
|---|---|
| **configure network** (pre-IOS release 10.3)<br>**copy rcp running-config**<br>**copy tftp running-config** | **copy ftp: system:running-config**<br>**copy rcp: system:running-config**<br>**copy tftp: system:running-config** |
| **configure overwrite-network** (pre-IOS release 10.3)<br>**copy rcp startup-config**<br>**copy tftp startup-config** | **copy ftp: nvram:startup-config**<br>**copy rcp: nvram:startup-config**<br>**copy tftp: nvram:startup-config** |
| **show configuration** (pre-IOS release 10.3)<br>**show startup-config** | **more nvram:startup-config** |
| **write erase** (pre-IOS release 10.3)<br>**erase startup-config** | **erase nvram:** |
| **write memory** (pre-IOS release 10.3)<br>**copy running-config startup-config** | **copy system:running-config**<br>**nvram:startup-config** |
| **write network** (pre-IOS release 10.3)<br>**copy running-config rcp**<br>**copy running-config tftp** | **copy system:running-config ftp:**<br>**copy system:running-config rcp:**<br>**copy system:running-config tftp:** |
| **write terminal** (pre-IOS release 10.3)<br>**show running-config** | **more system:running-config** |

## General Configuration Commands

Table C-3 contains some Cisco IOS configuration commands.

**Table C-3** *General Configuration Commands*

| Command | Meaning |
|---|---|
| **<ctrl>+<z>** | Exits from configuration mode back to privileged EXEC mode. |
| **banner** | Specifies a banner for the router (can be a **motd**, **idle**, or **exec** banner). |

*continues*

**Table C-3**    *General Configuration Commands (Continued)*

| Command | Meaning |
| --- | --- |
| **boot system** | Specifies the source of IOS images. |
| **cdp run** | Enables CDP on a router. (CDP is enabled by default; use **no cdp run** to disable it.) |
| **config-register** | Sets the 16-bit configuration register. |
| **enable password** | Specifies the enable password for the router. |
| **enable secret** | Specifies the enable secret password for the router. |
| **end** | Exits from configuration mode. |
| **exec-timeout 0 0** | Sets the timeout for a line EXEC session to zero, preventing the session from timing out and disconnecting. |
| **exit** | Exits any level in configuration mode. |
| **history size** | Specifies the number of command lines the system records on a line. |
| **hostname** | Specifies the router's name. |
| **interface** | Enters interface configuration mode (**ethernet, serial, loopback,** and so on); also used to enter subinterface configuration mode. The first time this command is used for a specific virtual interface (**loopback, tunnel, dialer,** and so on), it creates that virtual interface. |
| **line** | Enters line configuration mode (**console, aux, vty**). |
| **login** | Enables password checking on a line. |
| **logging synchronous** | Used on a line (**console, aux, vty**); causes input to be redisplayed on a single display line at the end of each console message that interrupts the input. |
| **password** | Specifies the password for a line. |
| **service password-encryption** | Specifies that any passwords set subsequent to this command will be encrypted. Use **no service password-encryption** after all such passwords have been set. |
| **service timestamps** | Adds a time stamp to debug or log messages. |

# General Interface Configuration Commands

Table C-4 contains some Cisco IOS interface configuration commands.

**Table C-4**    *General Interface Configuration Commands*

| Command | Meaning |
|---------|---------|
| **bandwidth** | Sets interface bandwidth (used by some routing protocols, including Open Shortest Path First [OSPF], Interior Gateway Routing Protocol [IGRP], and Enhanced IGRP [EIGRP]; also used for load calculations). Note that this command does not change the speed of the interface; it simply changes the number used in calculations. |
| **cdp enable** | Enables CDP on an interface. (CDP is enabled by default; use **no cdp enable** to disable it.) |
| **clock rate** | Sets clock rate in bits per second (used if interface is DCE); note that **clockrate** also works. |
| **description** | Adds a text description to the interface. |
| **encapsulation dot1q** | Defines the data-link encapsulation as 802.1q. |
| **encapsulation isl** | Defines the data-link encapsulation as Inter-switch Link (ISL) and defines a virtual local-area network (VLAN) number for a subinterface. Used for inter-VLAN routing on a Fast Ethernet subinterface. |
| **interface** | Enters interface configuration mode (or subinterface mode, if already in interface mode). |
| **media-type** | Selects the media-type connector for the Ethernet interface (for example, use **10baset** for RJ-45 connectors) on Cisco routers with more than one connector for an Ethernet interface. |
| **shutdown** | Administratively shuts down an interface. (Use **no shutdown** to bring up the interface.) |

# General Internet Protocol (IP) Commands

Table C-5 contains some Cisco IOS EXEC commands that are related to IP.

**Table C-5**    *General IP Commands*

| Command | Meaning |
|---------|---------|
| **clear ip nat translation** | Clears dynamic address translation entries from the Network Address Translation (NAT) table. |
| **debug eigrp neighbors** | Starts the console display of the EIGRP neighbor interaction. |
| **debug ip eigrp** | Starts the console display of the IP EIGRP advertisements and changes to the IP routing table. |

*continues*

**Table C-5** *General IP Commands (Continued)*

| Command | Meaning |
|---|---|
| **debug ip igrp** | Starts the console display of the IP IGRP-related transactions or events on the router. |
| **debug ip ospf events** | Starts the console display of OSPF-related events, such as adjacencies, flooding information, designated router selection, and SPF calculation on the router. |
| **debug ip ospf packet** | Starts the console display about each OSPF packet received. |
| **debug ip rip** | Starts the console display of the IP Routing Information Protocol (RIP)-related events on the router. |
| **debug ip nat** | Starts the console display of NAT translations. |
| **show hosts** | Displays the cached list of host names and addresses (both static and those that are obtained from a DNS server). |
| **show ip access-list** | Displays the IP access lists that are configured. |
| **show ip eigrp neighbors** | Displays the neighbors discovered by IP EIGRP. |
| **show ip eigrp topology** | Displays the IP EIGRP topology table. Use the **all** keyword to display the entire topology table, including those routes that are not feasible successors. |
| **show ip eigrp traffic** | Displays the number of IP EIGRP packets sent and received. |
| **show ip interface** | Displays IP-specific information about an interface, including whether access lists are applied. |
| **show ip ospf interface** | Displays details of the OSPF protocol on the interfaces, including the area, state, timers, neighbors, router ID, and network type. |
| **show ip ospf neighbor** | Displays the list of OSPF neighbors. Use the **detail** keyword to display more details about each neighbor (including priority and state). |
| **show ip protocols** | Displays the IP routing protocols that are running. |
| **show ip route** | Displays the IP routing table. Use other keywords to display specific parts of the routing table. |
| **show ip route eigrp** | Displays the current EIGRP entries in the IP routing table. |
| **show ip nat statistics** | Displays NAT translation statistics. |
| **show ip nat translations** | Displays active NAT translations. |
| **term ip netmask-format** | Specifies the format of how network masks are shown for the current session (bit count, decimal, or hexadecimal). |

# IP Configuration Commands

Table C-6 contains some Cisco IOS configuration commands that are related to IP.

**Table C-6**    *IP Configuration Commands*

| Command | Meaning |
|---|---|
| **access-class** | Activates an access list on a line (**console**, **aux**, **vty**) to restrict incoming and outgoing connections. |
| **access-list** | Defines access lists: IP standard = numbers 1 to 99; IP extended = numbers 100 to 199, or 2000 to 2699. |
| **ip access-group** | Activates an access list on an interface. |
| **ip access-list** | Defines a named access list in Cisco IOS 11.2 or later. |
| **ip address** | Assigns an IP address and subnet mask to an interface. |
| **ip classless** | Specifies that if a packet is received with a destination address within an unknown subnet of a directly attached network, the router matches it to the default route and forwards it to the next hop the default route specifies. |
| **ip domain-lookup** | Turns on name service (DNS) lookups. (Use **no ip domain-lookup** to turn off DNS lookups.) |
| **ip host** | Defines a static host name to IP address mapping. |
| **ip name-server** | Defines one or more (up to six) hosts that supply host name information (DNS). |
| **ip nat** | Defines the NAT parameters (inside and outside addresses, pools of addresses, and access lists). |
| **ip netmask-format** | Specifies how network masks are shown (bit count, decimal, or hexadecimal) for a specific line (**con**, **aux**, **vty**). |
| **ip route** | Defines a static route to an IP destination. |
| **network** | Defines the networks on which the routing protocol runs (for RIP, OSPF, IGRP, and EIGRP). Starts up the routing protocol on all interfaces in that network and allows the router to advertise that network.<br><br>For OSPF, this command also defines the area in which the interface resides. |
| **router eigrp** | Defines EIGRP as an IP routing protocol and enters configuration mode for that protocol. |

*continues*

**Table C-6**    *IP Configuration Commands (Continued)*

| Command | Meaning |
|---------|---------|
| **router igrp** | Defines IGRP as an IP routing protocol and enters configuration mode for that protocol. |
| **router ospf** | Defines OSPF as an IP routing protocol and enters configuration mode for that protocol. |
| **router rip** | Defines RIP as an IP routing protocol and enters configuration mode for that protocol. |
| **traffic-share** | Defines how traffic is distributed among multiple unequal cost routes for the same destination network (for IGRP and EIGRP). |
| **variance** | Defines unequal cost load balancing when using IGRP or EIGRP. |

# General Internetwork Packet Exchange (IPX) Commands

Table C-7 contains some Cisco IOS EXEC commands that are related to IPX.

**Table C-7**    *General IPX Commands*

| Command | Meaning |
|---------|---------|
| **debug ipx routing activity** | Starts the console display of the IPX routing-related events on the router. |
| **debug ipx sap activity** | Starts the console display of the IPX Service Advertisement Protocol (SAP)-related events on the router. |
| **ping ipx** | Sends an echo and expects an echo reply. |
| **show ipx access-list** | Displays the IPX access lists that are configured. |
| **show ipx interface** | Displays IPX-specific information about an interface, including whether access lists are applied. |
| **show ipx route** | Displays the IPX routing table. |
| **show ipx servers** | Displays the IPX server list. |
| **show ipx traffic** | Displays statistics on IPX traffic. |

# IPX Configuration Commands

Table C-8 contains some Cisco IOS configuration commands that are related to IPX.

**Table C-8**    *IPX Configuration Commands*

| Command | Meaning |
|---------|---------|
| **access-list** | Defines access lists: IPX standard = numbers 800 to 899; IPX extended = numbers 900 to 999; IPX SAP = numbers 1000 to 1099. |
| **ipx access-group** | Activates an IPX standard or extended access list on an interface. |

**Table C-8**    *IPX Configuration Commands (Continued)*

| Command | Meaning |
|---------|---------|
| **ipx delay** | Defines the delay tick metric to associate with an interface. |
| **ipx input-sap-filter** | Activates an IPX SAP access list input on an interface. |
| **ipx maximum-paths** | Enables round-robin load sharing over multiple equal metric paths. |
| **ipx network** | Assigns IPX network number and encapsulation type to an interface or subinterface. |
| **ipx output-sap-filter** | Activates an IPX SAP access list output on an interface. |
| **ipx routing** | Enables IPX routing on the router. |

# General AppleTalk Commands

Table C-9 contains some Cisco IOS EXEC commands that are related to AppleTalk.

**Table C-9**    *General AppleTalk Commands*

| Command | Meaning |
|---------|---------|
| **debug appletalk routing** | Starts the console display of the AppleTalk routing-related events on the router. |
| **show appletalk globals** | Displays information and settings regarding the router's global AppleTalk configuration parameters. |
| **show appletalk interface** | Displays AppleTalk-specific information about an interface, including whether access lists are applied. |
| **show appletalk route** | Displays the AppleTalk routing table. |
| **show appletalk zone** | Displays the AppleTalk zone information table. |

# AppleTalk Configuration Commands

Table C-10 contains some Cisco IOS configuration commands that are related to AppleTalk.

**Table C-10**    *AppleTalk Configuration Commands*

| Command | Meaning |
|---------|---------|
| **appletalk cable-range** | Assigns an AppleTalk cable-range to an interface (for phase 2 or extended addressing). |
| **appletalk discovery** | Enables an interface to learn a cable-range and zone name (or use **appletalk cable-range 0-0**). |

*continues*

**Table C-10**    *AppleTalk Configuration Commands (Continued)*

| Command | Meaning |
|---|---|
| **appletalk protocol** | Selects an AppleTalk routing protocol (Routing Table Maintenance Protocol [RTMP], EIGRP, or AppleTalk Update Routing Protocol [AURP]). |
| **appletalk routing** | Enables AppleTalk routing on the router. |
| **appletalk zone** | Assigns an AppleTalk zone name to an interface. |

## General WAN Commands

Table C-11 contains some Cisco IOS EXEC commands that are related to WAN interfaces.

**Table C-11**    *General WAN Commands*

| Command | Meaning |
|---|---|
| **clear frame-relay-inarp** | Clears dynamically created Frame Relay maps, which are created by the use of Inverse Address Resolution Protocol (ARP). |
| **debug dialer** | Starts the console display of dialer events, including the number the interface is dialing. |
| **debug frame-relay lmi** | Starts the console display of Local Management Interface (LMI) packets between the router and the Frame Relay switch. |
| **debug isdn q921** | Starts the console display of data link layer (Layer 2) access procedures that are taking place at the router on the D channel (using the link access procedure for D channel [LAPD]) of its ISDN interface. |
| **debug isdn q931** | Starts the console display of call setup and teardown of ISDN network connections (Layer 3). |
| **debug ppp authentication** | Starts the console display of the Point-to-Point Protocol (PPP) authentication–related events on the router. |
| **debug ppp error** | Starts the console display of errors related to PPP on the router. |
| **debug ppp negotiation** | Starts the console display of the PPP negotiation-related events on the router. |
| **show dialer** | Displays the current status of an interface that is configured for dial-on-demand routing (DDR). |
| **show frame-relay lmi** | Displays the LMI traffic statistics. |
| **show frame-relay map** | Displays the route maps (between network layer addresses and data link connection identifiers [DLCIs]), both static and dynamic. |
| **show frame-relay pvc** | Displays the status of each configured PVC and traffic statistics (including the number of backward explicit congestion notification [BECN] and forward explicit congestion notification [FECN] messages). |

**Table C-11**    *General WAN Commands (Continued)*

| Command | Meaning |
|---------|---------|
| **show frame-relay traffic** | Displays Frame Relay traffic statistics. |
| **show dialer** | Displays the current status of a dialer link, including the amount of time the link has been connected. |
| **show isdn active** | Displays the current call information, including the called number and the time until the call is disconnected. |
| **show isdn status** | Displays the status of an ISDN interface. |

# WAN Configuration Commands

Table C-12 contains some Cisco IOS configuration commands that are related to WAN interfaces.

**Table C-12**    *WAN Configuration Commands*

| Command | Meaning |
|---------|---------|
| **bandwidth** | Defines the bandwidth (in kilobits per second) of the interface (used in routing protocol calculations and load calculations). Note that this command does not change the interface's speed; it simply changes the number used in calculations. |
| **controller** | Enters controller configuration mode. Use when configuring a Primary Rate Interface (PRI). |
| **dialer idle-timeout** | Defines the number of seconds of idle (no interesting data) time before the circuit is disconnected. |
| **dialer load-threshold** | Enables the router to place another call to the same destination (if channels are available), based on the load on the line. |
| **dialer map** | Defines how to reach a destination, maps protocol addresses to the destination's phone number, and defines options, including broadcast, speed, and name of remote device. |
| **dialer pool** | Specifies the pool of physical interfaces that are available for the dialer interface. |
| **dialer pool-member** | Defines the physical interface as a member of a particular dialer pool. |
| **dialer string** | Specifies the destination's phone number on a dialer interface. |
| **dialer-group** | Assigns a dialer list to an interface to determine when to trigger a call. |
| **dialer-list list** | Defines a dialer list to trigger a call based on an access list. (Used only for IP or IPX.) |

*continues*

**Table C-12** *WAN Configuration Commands (Continued)*

| Command | Meaning |
|---|---|
| **dialer-list protocol** | Defines a dialer list to trigger a call based on a protocol type or an access list. |
| **encapsulation** | Defines the data-link encapsulation for an interface (**ppp**, **hldc**, **x25** [**dte** is the default; can use **dce**], **frame-relay**, **smds**, and so on). |
| **frame-relay interface-dlci** | Assigns a DLCI to the subinterface. (Used only on subinterfaces that are defined by the **interface** *type.subinterface number* [**point-to-point** \| **multipoint**] command.) |
| **frame-relay inverse-arp** | Enables Inverse ARP on an interface. (Necessary only if it was disabled at some point; the default is enabled.) |
| **frame-relay lmi-type** | Defines the Local Management Interface (LMI) format (to match the Frame Relay switch). |
| **frame-relay map** | Defines how an interface reaches a destination, maps protocol addresses to the DLCI to the destination, and defines options, including broadcast. |
| **framing** | Defines the framing type on the interface controller; entered in controller configuration mode. |
| **isdn spid1** | Sets a B-channel service profile identifier (SPID) (required by many service providers/ISDN switches). |
| **isdn spid2** | Sets a B-channel SPID for the second B channel (required by many service providers/ISDN switches). |
| **isdn switch-type** | Specifies the ISDN switch to which the router is connected; can be done as a global or interface command from Cisco IOS 11.3 onward. |
| **linecode** | Defines the interface controller's line coding; entered in controller configuration mode. |
| **ppp authentication** | Sets password authentication on an interface (using challenge handshake authentication protocol [CHAP] or password authentication protocol [PAP]). |
| **pri-group** | Defines the interface controller as PRI; entered in controller configuration mode. |
| **username** | Defines a host name and password for verification (used in PAP or CHAP). |

# Summary of ICND Switch IOS Commands

This section contains a listing of some of the Catalyst 1900 and Catalyst 2950 Switch IOS commands.

## General Switch Commands

Table C-13 contains some general Catalyst switch IOS commands.

**Table C-13**    *General Switch Commands*

| Command | Meaning |
|---|---|
| ? | Help. |
| **\<ctrl>+\<a>** | Moves to the beginning of the command line. |
| **\<ctrl>+\<b>** | Moves backward one character. |
| **\<ctrl>+\<e>** | Moves to the end of the command line. |
| **\<ctrl>+\<f>** | Moves forward one character. |
| **\<ctrl>+\<n> or \<down arrow>** | Returns to more recent commands in the history buffer after recalling commands with **\<ctrl>+\<p>** or **\<up arrow>**. Repeat the key sequence to recall successively more recent commands. |
| **\<ctrl>+\<p> or \<up arrow>** | Recalls commands in the history buffer, beginning with the most recent command. Repeat the key sequence to recall successively older commands. |
| **\<ctrl>+\<r>** | Redisplays a line. |
| **\<ctrl>+\<u>** | Erases a line from the beginning of the line. |
| **\<ctrl>+\<w>** | Erases a word. |
| **\<ctrl>+\<z>** | Exits from configuration mode and returns to privileged EXEC mode. |
| **\<esc>+\<b>** | Moves to the beginning of the previous word. |
| **\<esc>+\<f>** | Moves forward one word. |
| **\<backspace>** | Removes one character to the left of the cursor. |
| **\<tab>** | Completes the keyword. |
| **configure terminal** | Enters configuration mode. |
| **copy nvram tftp://{host}/{file}** | Copies switch configuration to a TFTP server (overwrites). (Catalyst 1900) |
| **copy startup-config tftp:// {host}/{file}** | Copies switch configuration to a TFTP server (overwrites). (Catalyst 2950) |
| **copy tftp://{host}/{file} nvram** | Copies switch configuration from a TFTP server (overwrites). (Catalyst 1900) |
| **delete nvram** | Erases the configuration in NVRAM. (Catalyst 1900) |

*continues*

**Table C-13**   *General Switch Commands (Continued)*

| Command | Meaning |
|---|---|
| **delete vtp** | Resets the VTP configuration to factory defaults, including the revision number. Also resets the system, but only VTP configurations are changed. |
| **disable** | Exits privileged EXEC mode. |
| **enable** | Enters privileged mode. |
| **erase startup-config** | Erases the startup configuration in memory. (Catalyst 2950) |
| **ping** | Sends an "echo" and expects an "echo reply." |
| **show CDP interface** | Displays values of CDP timers and CDP interface status. |
| **show CDP neighbors** | Displays a summary of CDP information received from neighbors. |
| **show CDP neighbors detail** | Displays detailed CDP information received from neighbors. |
| **show history** | Displays the list of recorded command lines during the current terminal session. |
| **show ip** | Displays IP information about the switch, including the IP address and subnet mask settings. |
| **show interfaces** | Displays information about interfaces or an interface, including the state of the interface, errors that have occurred, and duplex mode. |
| **show interface vlan 1** | Displays the switch IP address information. (Catalyst 2950) |
| **show interface switchport** | Displays the interface's trunk parameters. (Catalyst 2950) |
| **show mac-address-table** | Displays the MAC address table contents. |
| **show mac-address-table secure** | Displays the port security configuration. (Catalyst 2950) |
| **show mac-address-table security** | Displays the port security configuration. (Catalyst 1900) |
| **show port security** | Displays port security settings. (Catalyst 2950) |
| **show running-config** | Displays the active configuration. |
| **show spanning-tree vlan** | Displays STP configuration status for a particular VLAN. (Catalyst 2950) |
| **show spantree** | Displays the switch's spanning-tree configuration status. (Catalyst 1900) |
| **show trunk** | Displays an interface's trunk configuration. (Catalyst 1900) |
| **show version** | Displays system hardware's software version, uptime, and configuration. |

**Table C-13**    *General Switch Commands (Continued)*

| Command | Meaning |
|---|---|
| **show vlan** | Displays the parameters of a VLAN, including the number, name, and ports. |
| **show vlan brief** | Displays the VLAN assignment and membership type for all switch ports. (Catalyst 2950) |
| **show vlan-membership** | Displays the VLAN assignment and membership type for all switch ports. (Catalyst 1900) |
| **show vtp** | Displays the VTP configuration information. (Catalyst 1900) |
| **show vtp domain** | Displays VTP domain information. |
| **show vtp status** | Displays the VTP configuration information. (Catalyst 2950) |

# General Switch Configuration Commands

Table C-14 contains some general Catalyst switch IOS configuration commands.

**Table C-14**    *General Switch Configuration Commands*

| Command | Meaning |
|---|---|
| **<ctrl>+<z>** | Exits from configuration mode back to privileged EXEC mode. |
| **address-violation** | Specifies the action for a port address violation (suspend, disable, ignore). (Catalyst 1900) |
| **end** | Exits from configuration mode. |
| **hostname** | Specifies the switch's name. |
| **interface** | Enters interface configuration mode. |
| **interface vlan 1** | Enters interface configuration mode for VLAN1 to set the switch management IP address. (Catalyst 2950) |
| **ip address** | Specifies the switch's IP address and subnet mask. |
| **ip default-gateway** | Specifies the default gateway the switch uses to send traffic to a different IP network than that on which its own address resides. |
| **login** | Sets the login identifier on the console or virtual terminal ports. (Catalyst 2950) |
| **mac-address-table permanent** | Specifies a permanent address that is associated with a particular switched port. Permanent addresses do not age out. (Catalyst 1900) |

*continues*

**Table C-14**   *General Switch Configuration Commands (Continued)*

| Command | Meaning |
|---|---|
| **mac-address-table restricted static** | Specifies a restricted static address. The address is associated with a particular switched port, and only devices on specified interfaces can send data to it. Restricted static addresses do not age out. (Catalyst 1900) |
| **mac-address-table secure** | Specifies a secure static address. (Catalyst 2950) |
| **mac-address-table static** | Specifies a static address that is associated with a particular switched port. Permanent addresses do not age out. (Catalyst 2950) |
| **password** | Assigns a password to the console or to virtual terminal ports. (Catalyst 2950) |
| **snmp-server** | Configures the SNMP server in VLAN configuration mode. (Catalyst 2950). |
| **vlan** | Specifies the number and name of a VLAN that is being created or modified. |
| **vlan database** | Enters VLAN configuration mode. (Catalyst 2950) |
| **vtp** | Specifies the VTP operating mode, domain name, password, whether traps are generated, and whether pruning is enabled. (This is done in VLAN configuration mode on Catalyst 2950.) |

# General Switch Interface Configuration Commands

Table C-15 contains some general Catalyst switch IOS interface configuration commands.

**Table C-15**   *General Switch Interface Configuration Commands*

| Command | Meaning |
|---|---|
| **cdp enable** | Enables CDP on an interface (CDP is enabled by default; use **no cdp enable** to disable it). |
| **duplex** | Enables a duplex mode on an interface. |
| **port secure** | Enables addressing security. (Catalyst 1900) |
| **port secure max-mac-count** | Specifies the number of devices on a secured port; the default is 132. (Catalyst 1900) |
| **port security** | Enables addressing security. (Catalyst 2950) |
| **port security action** | Specifies the action to take when an address violation occurs (shutdown, trap). The default is shutdown. (Catalyst 2950) |
| **port security max-mac-count** | Specifies the number of devices on a secured port; the default is 132. (Catalyst 2950) |

**Table C-15**    *General Switch Interface Configuration Commands (Continued)*

| Command | Meaning |
|---|---|
| **shutdown** | Administratively shuts down an interface (use **no shutdown** to bring the interface up). |
| **switchport access** | Specifies the VLAN to which an interface belongs. (Catalyst 2950) |
| **switchport mode** | Specifies the interface's 802.1Q trunk mode. (Catalyst 2950) |
| **trunk** | Specifies the interface's ISL trunk mode (on, off, desirable, auto, or nonegotiate). |
| **vlan-membership** | Specifies the VLAN to which an interface belongs, or specifies dynamic VLAN membership. (Catalyst 1900) |

This appendix is organized in the following sections:

- General Commands
- Comparison of Configuration File Commands
- General Configuration Commands
- General Interface Configuration Commands
- General IP Commands
- IP Configuration Commands
- General WAN Commands
- WAN Configuration Commands
- CLNS Configuration Commands

# Summary of BSCI Router Commands

This appendix contains a listing of some of the Cisco router IOS commands you may find in this book, organized in various categories.

Only the command is listed here; parameters are not included.

For details on the parameters and how the command works, see the *Command Reference Manuals* on the Cisco Documentation CD-ROM or on Cisco's web site at www.cisco.com.

## General Commands

Table D-1 contains some Cisco router EXEC IOS commands.

**Table D-1**  *General Commands*

| Command | Meaning |
| --- | --- |
| clear access-list counters | Clears packet counters in extended access lists. |
| clear logging | Clears the logging buffer. |
| configure terminal | Enters configuration mode. |
| copy running-config startup-config | Copies configuration from random access memory (RAM) to nonvolatile random access memory (NVRAM) (overwrites). |
| debug | Starts the console display of the events on the router. |
| debug eigrp neighbors | Starts the console display of the EIGRP neighbor interaction. |
| debug eigrp packets | Starts the console display of EIGRP packets, both sent and received. |
| erase startup-config | Erases the configuration in NVRAM. |
| ping | Sends an echo and expects an echo reply. Extended **ping** allows specification of the source address and allows **ping** for protocols other than Internet Protocol (IP). |

*continues*

**Table D-1** *General Commands (Continued)*

| Command | Meaning |
|---------|---------|
| **reload** | Reloads the operating system. |
| **setup** | Enters prompted dialog to establish an initial configuration. |
| **show access-lists** | Displays the contents of all access lists configured. |
| **show CDP neighbors** | Displays a summary of Cisco Discovery Protocol (CDP) information received from neighbors. |
| **show CDP neighbors detail** | Displays detailed CDP information received from neighbors. |
| **show controller** | Displays the Layer 1 information about an interface (including cable type and data circuit-terminating equipment/data terminal equipment (DCE/DTE) status for serial interfaces). |
| **show interfaces** | Displays information about interfaces or an interface, including the state of the interface and queuing information. |
| **show line** | Displays information about line (**console**, auxiliary (**aux**), virtual type terminal (**vty**)) configuration. |
| **show logging** | Displays the logging buffer, including logged output of debug commands. |
| **show route-map** | Displays configured route maps; includes number of matches. |
| **show running-config** | Displays the active configuration (in RAM). |
| **show startup-config** | Displays the backup configuration (in NVRAM). |
| **show version** | Displays configuration of system hardware, software version, and configuration register value. |
| **telnet** | Connects to a host. |
| **traceroute** | Traces the route that packets are taking through the network; extended **traceroute** allows specification of the source address. |

# Comparison of Configuration File Commands

With Cisco IOS Release 12.0, commands used to copy and transfer configuration and system files have changed to conform to IOS File System (IFS) specifications. The old commands continue to perform their normal functions in the current release, but support for these commands will cease in a future release. Table D-2 contains the old and new commands used for configuration file movement and management.

**Table D-2**    *Comparison of Configuration File Commands*

| Old Commands | New Commands |
|---|---|
| **configure network** (pre-IOS release 10.3)<br>**copy rcp running-config**<br>**copy tftp running-config** | **copy ftp: system:running-config**<br>**copy rcp: system:running-config**<br>**copy tftp: system:running-config** |
| **configure overwrite-network** (pre-IOS release 10.3)<br>**copy rcp startup-config**<br>**copy tftp startup-config** | **copy ftp: nvram:startup-config**<br>**copy rcp: nvram:startup-config**<br>**copy tftp: nvram:startup-config** |
| **show configuration** (pre-IOS release 10.3)<br>**show startup-config** | **more nvram:startup-config** |
| **write erase** (pre-IOS release 10.3)<br>**erase startup-config** | **erase nvram:** |
| **write memory** (pre-IOS release 10.3)<br>**copy running-config startup-config** | **copy system:running-config nvram:startup-config** |
| **write network** (pre-IOS release 10.3)<br>**copy running-config rcp**<br>**copy running-config tftp** | **copy system:running-config ftp:**<br>**copy system:running-config rcp:**<br>**copy system:running-config tftp:** |
| **write terminal** (pre-IOS release 10.3)<br>**show running-config** | **more system:running-config** |

# General Configuration Commands

Table D-3 contains some Cisco IOS configuration commands.

**Table D-3**    *General Configuration Commands*

| Command | Meaning |
|---|---|
| **config-register** | Changes the value of the configuration register. |
| **enable password** | Specifies the enable password for the router. |
| **enable secret** | Specifies the enable secret password for the router. |
| **exec-timeout 0 0** | Sets the timeout for a line EXEC session to zero, preventing the session from timing out and disconnecting. |
| **hostname** | Specifies the router's name. |

*continues*

**Table D-3**    *General Configuration Commands (Continued)*

| Command | Meaning |
|---------|---------|
| **interface** | Enters interface configuration mode (**ethernet**, **serial**, **loopback**, and so on). Also used to enter subinterface configuration mode. For virtual interfaces (**loopback**, **tunnel**, **dialer**, and so on), the first time that this command is used for a specific virtual interface, it creates that virtual interface. |
| **line** | Enters line configuration mode (**console**, **aux**, **vty**). |
| **logging synchronous** | When used on a line (**console**, **aux**, **vty**), causes input to be redisplayed on a single display line, at the end of each console message that interrupts the input. |
| **login** | Enables password checking on a line. |
| **match** | Defines conditions to be checked within a route map. |
| **password** | Specifies the password for a line. |
| **route-map** | Defines a route map and enters configuration mode for the route map. |
| **set** | Defines actions to be followed if there is a match within a route map. |

# General Interface Configuration Commands

Table D-4 contains some Cisco IOS interface configuration commands.

**Table D-4**    *General Interface Configuration Commands*

| Command | Meaning |
|---------|---------|
| **bandwidth** | Sets bandwidth of interface (used by some routing protocols, including Open Shortest Path First [OSPF], Enhanced Interior Gateway Routing Protocol [EIGRP], Interior Gateway Routing Protocol [IGRP]; also used for load calculations). |
| **clock rate** | Sets clock rate in bits per second (used if interface is DCE). Note that the **clockrate** command also works. |
| **interface** | Enters interface configuration mode (or subinterface mode, if already in interface mode). |
| **interface serial multipoint \| point-to-point** | Enters subinterface configuration mode for a serial interface, and defines whether it is a point-to-multipoint or point-to-point subinterface. |
| **shutdown** | Administratively shuts down an interface (use **no shutdown** to bring up the interface). |

# General IP Commands

Table D-5 contains some Cisco IOS EXEC commands related to IP.

**Table D-5**    *General IP Commands*

| Command | Meaning |
|---|---|
| **clear ip bgp** | Clears entries from the Border Gateway Protocol (BGP) routing table and resets BGP sessions; use the * option to delete all entries. |
| **clear ip bgp peer-group** | Clears the BGP connections for all members of a BGP peer group. |
| **clear ip nat translation** | Removes address translations from the Network Address Translation (NAT) table. |
| **clear ip prefix-list** | Resets the hit count shown on IP prefix list entries. |
| **clear ip route** | Clears the IP routing table; use the * option to delete all routes. |
| **debug eigrp neighbors** | Displays neighbors discovered by EIGRP and the contents of the hello packets. |
| **debug eigrp packets** | Displays the types of EIGRP packets sent and received. A maximum of 11 packet types can be selected for individual or group display. |
| **debug ip bgp** | Starts the console display of BGP-related events on the router, according to the option specified (**dampening**, **events**, **keepalives**, **updates**). |
| **debug ip bgp updates** | Starts the console display of BGP updates. |
| **debug ip eigrp** | Starts the console display of the IP EIGRP advertisements and changes to the IP routing table. |
| **debug ip eigrp summary** | Displays a summarized version of EIGRP activity. It also displays filtering and redistribution numbers, as well as neighbors and distance information. |
| **debug ip icmp** | Starts the console display of Internet Control Message Protocol (ICMP) events. |
| **debug ip igrp** | Starts the console display of the IGRP-related transactions or events on the router. |
| **debug ip nat detailed** | Starts the console display of translation entries being created. |
| **debug ip ospf** | Starts the console display of the OSPF-related events on the router. |
| **debug ip ospf adj** | Starts the console display of OSPF adjacency-related events on the router. |
| **debug ip ospf events** | Starts the console display of OSPF-related events, such as adjacencies, flooding information, designated router selection, and SPF calculation on the router. |
| **debug ip ospf lsa-generation** | Starts the console display of OSFP link-state advertisement (LSA) generation-related events on the router. |
| **debug ip ospf packet** | Starts the console display about each OSPF packet received. |

*continues*

**Table D-5**   *General IP Commands (Continued)*

| Command | Meaning |
|---|---|
| **debug ip ospf spf** | Starts the console display of shortest path first (SPF) calculation-related events on the router. |
| **debug ip packet** | Starts the console display of IP packet events. |
| **debug ip policy** | Starts the console display of IP policy routing events. |
| **debug ip rip** | Starts the console display of IP Routing Information Protocol (RIP)-related events on the router. |
| **debug ip routing** | Starts the console display of IP routing-related events on the router. |
| **debug isis adj-packets** | Displays Intermediate System-to-Intermediate System (IS-IS) adjacency-related packets. |
| **debug isis update-packets** | Displays IS-IS update-related packets. |
| **show eigrp traffic** | Displays the types of EIGRP packets sent and received. This command displays statistics on route compilation. |
| **show ip access-list** | Displays the IP access lists configured. |
| **show ip bgp** | Displays the BGP routing table; specify a network number to get more specific information about a particular network. |
| **show ip bgp neighbors** | Displays information about the Transmission Control Protocol (TCP) and BGP connections to neighbors. |
| **show ip bgp summary** | Displays the status of all BGP connections. |
| **show ip eigrp neighbors** | Displays the neighbors discovered by IP EIGRP. |
| **show ip eigrp topology** | Displays the IP EIGRP topology table; use the **all** keyword to display all of the topology table, including those routes that are not feasible successors. |
| **show ip eigrp traffic** | Displays the number of IP EIGRP packets sent and received. |
| **show ip interface** | Displays IP-specific information about an interface, including whether access lists are applied. |
| **show ip nat translation** | Displays the IP NAT translation table. |
| **show ip ospf** | Displays OSPF-specific parameters on the router, including the router ID, information about each area to which the router is connected, and the number of times the SPF algorithm has been executed. |
| **show ip ospf border-routers** | Displays the internal OSPF routing table entries to area border routers (ABRs) and autonomous system boundary routers (ASBRs). |
| **show ip ospf database** | Displays the contents of the OSPF topological database maintained by the router. This command also shows the router ID and OSPF process ID. Use additional keywords to view detailed information in each part of the database. |

**Table D-5**    *General IP Commands (Continued)*

| Command | Meaning |
|---|---|
| **show ip ospf database nssa-external** | Display specific details of each LSA type 7 update in database. |
| **show ip ospf interface** | Displays details of the OSPF protocol on the interfaces, including the area, state, timers, neighbors, router ID, and network type. |
| **show ip ospf neighbor** | Displays the list of OSPF neighbors; use the **detail** keyword to display more details of each neighbor (including priority and state). |
| **show ip ospf virtual-links** | Displays the OSPF virtual links. |
| **show ip policy** | Displays route maps configured on the routers interfaces for policy routing. |
| **show ip prefix-list** | Displays information on all prefix lists; use the **detail** keyword to include the description and hit count. Other parameters can be used to display other details or specific parts of the prefix lists. |
| **show ip protocols** | Displays the IP routing protocols that are running. |
| **show ip route** | Displays the IP routing table; use other keywords to display specific parts of the routing table. |
| **show ip route eigrp** | Displays the current EIGRP entries in the IP routing table. |
| **show ip route ospf** | Displays the current OSPF entries in the IP routing table. |
| **show clns route** | Displays all the Connectionless Network Service (CLNS) destinations to which this router knows how to route packets. |
| **show isis topology** | Displays a list of the paths to all connected IS-IS routers. |
| **show isis route** | Displays the IS-IS Level 1 forwarding table for IS-IS learned routes. |
| **which-route** | Displays which next-hop IS-IS router will be used to get to a destination. |
| **show clns neighbors** | Displays the neighbor ISs, that is, the routers with which this router has IS-IS adjacencies. End system (ES) neighbors, if there are any, are also displayed. |
| **show clns** | Displays general information about the CLNS network. |
| **show clns protocol** | Displays information for the specific IS-IS processes in the router. |
| **show clns interface** | Displays CLNS-specific information about interfaces running IS-IS. |
| **show clns is-neighbors** | Displays IS-IS related information for IS-IS router adjacencies. |
| **show isis database** | Displays the contents of the IS-IS link-state database. |
| **clear isis** | Forces IS-IS to refresh its link-state database and recalculate all routes. |
| **show isis spf-log** | Displays how often and why the router has run a full SPF calculation. |

# IP Configuration Commands

Table D-6 contains some Cisco IOS configuration commands related to IP.

**Table D-6**   *IP Configuration Commands*

| Command | Meaning |
|---|---|
| **access-class** | Activates an access list on a line (**console**, **aux**, **vty**) to restrict incoming and outgoing connections. |
| **access-list** | Defines access lists: IP standard = numbers 1 to 99; IP extended = numbers 100 to 199. |
| **aggregate-address** | Creates an aggregate, or summary, entry in the BGP table. |
| **area default-cost** | Defines the cost of the default route sent into an OSPF stub area; default is 1. |
| **area nssa** | Defines the OSPF area as a not-so-stubby area (NSSA). |
| **area range** | Defines route summarization of intra-area routes on an OSPF ABR. |
| **area stub** | Defines the OSPF area as a stub area; use the **no-summary** keyword on the ABR to define a totally stubby area. |
| **area virtual-link** | Defines an OSPF virtual link across an area to another OSPF router. |
| **auto-cost reference-bandwidth** | Defines the numerator of the OSPF cost formula (numerator/bandwidth), in megabits per second. The default is 100. |
| **auto-summary** | Enables automatic route summarization for BGP, and determines how redistributed routes are handled by BGP. |
| **bgp always-compare-med** | Forces the comparison of the BGP multi-exit-discriminator (MED) attribute to be done, even if the neighboring autonomous system (AS) is not the same for all the routes considered. |
| **bgp bestpath missing-as-worst** | Forces BGP routes without the MED attribute to have a MED value of infinity, making the route the least preferred. |
| **bgp cluster-id** | Configures the cluster ID; used if a BGP cluster has more than one route reflector. |
| **bgp default local-preference** | Defines the default BGP local-preference attribute value. |
| **default-information originate** | Generates a default external route into an OSPF routing domain. The optional keyword **always** advertises the default route regardless of whether the software has a default route in the routing table. |
| **default-metric** | Defines the seed metric that this routing protocol uses before redistributing a route. |
| **distance** | Defines the administrative distance that will be used for this routing protocol (for all routing protocols except BGP and EIGRP). |
| **distance bgp** | Defines the administrative distance that will be used for BGP. |
| **distance eigrp** | Defines the administrative distance that will be used for EIGRP. |

**Table D-6**    *IP Configuration Commands (Continued)*

| Command | Meaning |
|---|---|
| **distribute-list** | Activates an access list to be used to filter outbound or inbound routing updates for a routing protocol. |
| **eigrp log-neighbor-changes** | Enables the logging of changes in EIGRP neighbor adjacencies. |
| **eigrp stub** | Configures a router as an EIGRP stub. |
| **ip access-group** | Activates an access list on an interface. |
| **ip address** | Assigns an IP address and subnet mask to an interface. Use the **secondary** option to assign a secondary address and mask to the interface. |
| **ip bandwidth-percent eigrp** | Defines the maximum percentage of bandwidth that EIGRP packets will be capable of utilizing on an interface. |
| **ip classless** | Specifies that if a packet is received with a destination address within an unknown subnet of a directly attached network, the router will match it to the default route and forward it to the next hop specified by the default route. |
| **ip community-list** | Creates a community list for BGP and controls access to the list. |
| **ip default-gateway** | Defines a default gateway (router); used on routers or communication servers that have IP routing turned off. The router or communication server acts just like a host on the network. |
| **ip default-network** | Defines a default route. |
| **ip directed-broadcast** | Enables the translation of directed broadcasts to physical broadcasts. In Cisco IOS Release 12.0 and later, the **no ip directed-broadcast** command is on by default. |
| **ip domain-lookup** | Turns on domain name service (DNS) lookups; use **no ip domain-lookup** to turn off DNS lookup. |
| **ip eigrp hello-interval** | Defines the interval at which EIGRP hello packets are sent. |
| **ip eigrp hold-time** | Defines the time that a router will consider an EIGRP neighbor up without receiving a hello (or some other packet). |
| **ip forward-protocol** | Defines the protocols that will be forwarded with the **ip helper-address** command. |
| **ip helper-address** | Defines an address to which the router will forward certain broadcasts (this is usually a server address) that are sent to this interface. |
| **ip host** | Defines a static host name to IP address mapping. |
| **ip nat {inside \| outside}** | Defines the IP networks attached to the interface as either internal or external to the NAT controlled network. Only packets arriving on an interface marked as IP NAT inside or outside are subject to translation. |

*continues*

**Table D-6**  *IP Configuration Commands (Continued)*

| Command | Meaning |
|---|---|
| **ip nat inside source list pool** | Causes the router to compare the source IP address in the packet to the access list referenced in the command to see whether the router should translate that source IP address to the next available address in the pool listed. |
| **ip nat inside source route-map pool** | Causes the router to compare the source IP address in the packet to the route map referenced in the command to see whether the router should translate that source IP address to the next available address in the pool listed. |
| **ip nat pool** | Defines the translation pool used by the other IP NAT commands. |
| **ip ospf cost** | Defines the outgoing OSPF cost of an interface. |
| **ip ospf network** | Defines the OSPF network mode configuration (**non-broadcast**, **point-to-multipoint** [**non-broadcast**], **broadcast**, or **point-to-point**). |
| **ip ospf priority** | Defines the OSPF priority on an interface (the default is 1); used to determine which router will be the designated router (DR) on a multiaccess network. |
| **ip policy route-map** | Defines a route map to use for policy routing on an interface. |
| **ip prefix-list** | Defines a prefix list. |
| **ip prefix-list description** | Defines a description for a prefix list. |
| **ip prefix-list sequence-number** | Re-enables the automatic generation of sequence numbers for a prefix list (automatic generation is the default); use the no form of this command to disable the automatic generation of sequence numbers. |
| **ip route** | Defines a static route to an IP destination. |
| **ip route-cache policy** | Enables fast switching of IP policy routing on an interface. |
| **ip router isis** | Enables interfaces that are to use IS-IS to distribute their IP information. |
| **ip subnet-zero** | Allows use of subnets with all subnet bits equal to zero. |
| **ip summary-address eigrp** | Defines route summarization on an interface for the EIGRP routing protocol. |
| **ip unnumbered** | Enables IP processing on a serial interface without assigning an explicit address to the interface. |
| **ipv6 address** | Assigns an IP version 6 (IPv6) address to an interface and enables IPv6 processing on the interface. |
| **ipv6 unicast-routing** | Enables the forwarding of IPv6 datagrams. |
| **is-type** | Defines which IS-IS level (level-1 | level-1-2 | level-2-only) a router will operate as. |
| **isis priority** | Changes the IS-IS router priority on the interface to influence the DR election. |

**Table D-6**    *IP Configuration Commands (Continued)*

| Command | Meaning |
|---|---|
| **isis circuit-type** | Defines which level of IS-IS adjacency (level-1 I level-1-2 I level-2-only) will be established over an interface. |
| **isis metric** | Defines the IS-IS metric to be used on an interface. The default is 10. |
| **match community** | Matches a BGP community attribute to a value in a community list in a route map. |
| **match interface** | Defines routes to be matched in a route map as those that have a next hop as of one of the interfaces specified. |
| **match ip address** | Defines IP addresses to be matched in a route map, using IP standard or extended access lists. |
| **match ip next-hop** | Defines routes to be matched in a route map as those that have a next-hop router address passed by one of the access lists specified, using IP standard or extended access lists. |
| **match ip route-source** | Defines routes to be matched in a route map as those that have been advertised by routers and access servers at an address passed by one of the access lists specified, using IP standard or extended access lists. |
| **match length** | Defines minimum and maximum packet length values to be matched in a route map. |
| **match metric** | Defines routes to be matched in a route map as those routes that have the metric specified. |
| **match route-type** | Defines routes to be matched in a route map as those of the specified type. |
| **maximum-paths** | Controls the maximum number of parallel routes that an IP routing protocol can support. |
| **metric weights** | Allows tuning of the IGRP or EIGRP metric calculations. |
| **neighbor** (OSPF) | Identifies a peer router with which this OSPF router interconnects over a nonbroadcast network. |
| **neighbor distribute-list** | Distributes BGP neighbor information, as specified in an access list. |
| **neighbor ebgp-multihop** | Allows the router to accept and attempt BGP connections to external peers residing on networks that are not directly connected. |
| **neighbor next-hop-self** | Forces all BGP updates for this neighbor to be advertised with this router as the next-hop address. |
| **neighbor peer-group** | Creates a BGP peer group; assigns neighbors as part of a peer group. |
| **neighbor prefix-list** | Identifies a prefix list to be used to filter BGP routes from or to a peer router. |
| **neighbor remote-as** | Identifies a peer router with which this router will establish a BGP session. |
| **neighbor route-map** | Applies a route map to incoming or outgoing BGP routes. |

*continues*

**Table D-6** *IP Configuration Commands (Continued)*

| Command | Meaning |
|---|---|
| **neighbor route-reflector-client** | Defines the router as a BGP route reflector and identifies the specified neighbor as its route reflector client. |
| **neighbor send-community** | Specifies that the BGP communities attribute should be sent to a BGP neighbor. |
| **neighbor shutdown** | Disables an existing BGP neighbor or neighbor peer group. |
| **neighbor soft-reconfiguration** | Forces the router to store all received BGP updates without modification so that they can be used to do an inbound soft reconfiguration. |
| **neighbor update-source loopback** | Allows internal BGP sessions to use the specified operational loopback interface for TCP connections. |
| **neighbor weight** | Defines the BGP weight attribute to a neighbor connection. |
| **net** | Assigns a Network-entity title (NET) to the router to identify it for IS-IS. |
| **network** | For RIP, IGRP, EIGRP, and OSPF, defines the networks on which the routing protocol will run. Starts up the routing protocol on all interfaces that are in that network and allows the router to advertise that network.<br><br>For OSPF, this command also defines the area that the interface will be in.<br><br>For BGP, this command allows BGP to advertise a route if it is already in the routing table (use the **neighbor** command to start up BGP) and can define the subnet mask of the route. |
| **no auto-summary** | Disables automatic route summarization for the EIGRP, RIP version 2 (RIPv2), and BGP routing protocols. |
| **no ip prefix-list sequence-number** | Disables the automatic generation of sequence numbers for a prefix list. |
| **no synchronization** | Disables BGP synchronization. |
| **passive-interface** | Prevents routing updates from this routing protocol from being generated on an interface. |
| **redistribute** | Defines the protocol that will be redistributed into this routing protocol; the protocol can include static and connected routes. |
| **router bgp** | Defines BGP as an IP routing protocol and enters configuration mode for that protocol. |
| **router eigrp** | Defines EIGRP as an IP routing protocol and enters configuration mode for that protocol. |
| **router igrp** | Defines IGRP as an IP routing protocol and enters configuration mode for that protocol. |
| **router isis** | Defines Integrated IS-IS as an IP routing protocol and enters configuration mode for that protocol. |

**Table D-6**    *IP Configuration Commands (Continued)*

| Command | Meaning |
|---|---|
| **router ospf** | Defines OSPF as an IP routing protocol and enters configuration mode for that protocol. |
| **router rip** | Defines RIP as an IP routing protocol and enters configuration mode for that protocol. |
| **router-id** | To use a fixed OSPF router ID, use the **router-id** command in router configuration mode. |
| **set as-path** | Modifies an AS path for BGP routes. |
| **set automatic-tag** | Automatically computes the BGP tag value. |
| **set community** | Sets the BGP communities attribute within a route map. |
| **set default interface** | Defines the default interface to which packets that have no explicit route to the destination should be forwarded from a route map. |
| **set interface** | Defines the interface to which packets should be forwarded from a route map. |
| **set ip default next-hop** | Defines the default next-hop address to which packets that have no explicit route to the destination should be forwarded from a route map. |
| **set ip next-hop** | Defines the next-hop address to which packets should be forwarded from a route map. |
| **set ip precedence** | Sets the IP precedence in the IP packets from a route map. |
| **set ip tos** | Sets the IP TOS value in the IP packets from a route map. |
| **set level** | Indicates what level or type of area to import routes (for IS-IS and OSPF routes). |
| **set local-preference** | Specifies a BGP local preference value for the autonomous system path from a route map. |
| **set metric** | Sets the BGP metric (MED) value from a route map. |
| **set metric-type** | Sets the metric type for the destination routing protocol. |
| **set origin** | Specifies the BGP origin code. |
| **set weight** | Specifies the BGP weight for the routing table. |
| **summary-address** | Defines route summarization of external routes on an OSPF ASBR. |
| **timers active-time** | Defines the EIGRP active-state time limit (from its default of 3 minutes). |
| **timers spf** | Defines the time that an OSPF router waits before recalculating its routing table and the minimum time between two consecutive SPF calculations. |
| **traffic-share** | Defines how traffic is distributed among multiple unequal cost routes for the same destination network (for IGRP and EIGRP). |
| **variance** | Defines unequal cost load balancing when using IGRP or EIGRP. |

# General WAN Commands

Table D-7 contains a Cisco IOS EXEC command related to WAN interfaces.

**Table D-7**   *General WAN Commands*

| Command | Meaning |
|---------|---------|
| **show frame-relay map** | Displays the mapping between network layer addresses and data-link connection identifiers (DLCIs), both static and dynamic mappings. |

# WAN Configuration Commands

Table D-8 contains some Cisco IOS configuration commands related to WAN interfaces.

**Table D-8**   *WAN Configuration Commands*

| Command | Meaning |
|---------|---------|
| **async default routing** | Enables the router to pass routing updates to other routers over an asynchronous interface. |
| **dialer map** | Configures a serial or Integrated Services Digital Network (ISDN) interface to call one or multiple sites, or to receive calls from multiple sites. |
| **dialer string** | Specifies the destination string (telephone number) to be called for interfaces calling a single site. |
| **encapsulation** | Defines the data-link encapsulation for an interface (**ppp**, **hdlc**, **x25** [**dte** is the default, can use **dce**], **frame-relay**, **smds**, and so on). |
| **frame-relay interface-dlci** | Defines the Frame Relay DLCI number on a subinterface. |
| **frame-relay intf-type dce** | Defines an interface as a Frame Relay DCE device. |
| **frame-relay map** | Maps a next-hop IP address to a permanent virtual circuit (PVC). |
| **frame-relay switching** | Enables Frame Relay switching on the router. |
| **frame-relay route** | Defines a static entry in the Frame Relay switching table. |

# CLNS Configuration Commands

Table D-9 covers CLNS configuration commands.

**Table D-9**    *CLNS Configuration Commands*

| Command | Meaning |
|---|---|
| **clns routing** | Enables routing of CLNS packets. |
| **clns host** | Defines a static host name to CLNS address mapping. |
| **clns router isis** | Configures an IS-IS routing process for International Organization for Standardization (ISO) CLNS on a specified interface and attaches an area designator to the routing process. |

This appendix contains information on the Open System Interconnection (OSI) Reference Model. It includes the following sections:

- Characteristics of the OSI Layers
- Protocols
- OSI Model and Communication Between Systems
- OSI Model's Physical Layer
- OSI Model's Data Link Layer
- OSI Model's Network Layer
- OSI Model's Transport Layer
- OSI Model's Session Layer
- OSI Model's Presentation Layer
- OSI Model's Application Layer
- Information Formats

# Open System Interconnection (OSI) Reference Model

The *Open System Interconnection (OSI)* reference model describes how information from a software application in one computer moves through a network medium to a software application in another computer. The OSI reference model is a conceptual model that is composed of seven layers, each specifying particular network functions. The International Organization for Standardization (ISO) developed the model in 1984. It is now considered the primary architectural model for intercomputer communications. The OSI model divides the tasks involved with moving information between networked computers into seven smaller, more manageable task groups. A task or group of tasks is assigned to each of the seven OSI layers. Each layer is reasonably self-contained so that the tasks assigned to each can be implemented independently. This enables the solutions offered by one layer to be updated without adversely affecting the other layers. The following list details the OSI reference model's seven layers:

- Layer 7 — Application layer
- Layer 6 — Presentation layer
- Layer 5 — Session layer
- Layer 4 — Transport layer
- Layer 3 — Network layer
- Layer 2 — Data link layer
- Layer 1 — Physical layer

Figure E-1 illustrates the seven-layer OSI reference model.

**Figure E-1**  *The OSI Reference Model Contains Seven Independent Layers*

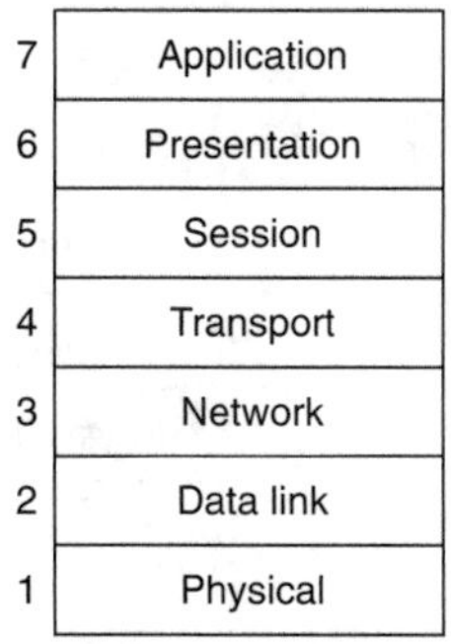

| 7 | Application |
|---|---|
| 6 | Presentation |
| 5 | Session |
| 4 | Transport |
| 3 | Network |
| 2 | Data link |
| 1 | Physical |

# Characteristics of the OSI Layers

The OSI reference model's seven layers can be divided into two categories: upper layers and lower layers.

The upper layers contend with application issues and are generally only implemented in software. The highest layer, the application layer, is closest to the end user. Both users and application layer processes interact with software applications that contain a communications component. The term *upper layer* is sometimes used to refer to any layer above another layer in the OSI model.

---

### Terminology: Upper Layers

Generally speaking, the term *upper layers* is often used to refer to Layers 5, 6, and 7; however, this terminology is relative.

---

The OSI model's *lower layers* handle data transport issues. The physical layer and the data link layer are implemented in hardware and software. The other lower layers are generally only implemented in software. The lowest layer, which is the physical layer, is closest to the physical network medium (for example, the network cabling) and is responsible for actually placing information on the medium.

---

### Terminology: Lower Layers

Generally speaking, the term *lower layers* is often used to refer to Layers 1 through 4; however, this terminology is relative.

---

Figure E-2 illustrates the division between the upper and lower OSI layers.

**Figure E-2**    *Two Sets of Layers Comprise the OSI Layers*

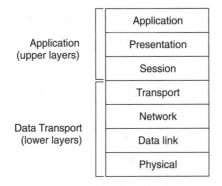

# Protocols

Although the OSI model provides a conceptual framework for communication between computers, the model itself is not a method of communication. Actual communication is made possible through communication protocols. In the context of data networking, a *protocol* is a formal set of rules and conventions that governs how computers exchange information over a network medium. A protocol implements the functions of one or more OSI layers. A wide variety of communication protocols exist, but they all tend to fall into one of the following groups: LAN protocols, WAN protocols, network protocols, or routing protocols. *LAN protocols* operate at the physical and data link layers of the OSI model and define communication over the various LAN media. *WAN protocols* operate at the lowest three layers of the OSI model and define communication over the various wide-area media. *Routing protocols* are network-layer protocols that are responsible for path determination and traffic switching. Finally, *network protocols* are the various upper-layer protocols that exist in a given protocol suite.

# OSI Model and Communication Between Systems

When information is transferred from a software application in one computer system to a software application in another computer system, it must pass through each of the OSI layers. For example, if a software application in System A has information to transmit to a software application in System B, the application program in System A passes its information to System A's application layer (Layer 7). Next, the application layer passes the information to the presentation layer (Layer 6), which relays the data to the session layer (Layer 5), and so on, down to the physical layer (Layer 1). At the physical layer, the information is placed on the physical network medium and sent across the medium to System B. System B's physical layer removes the information from the physical medium. Its physical layer then passes the information up to the data link layer (Layer 2), which passes it to the network layer (Layer 3), and so on, until it reaches System B's application layer (Layer 7). Finally, System B's application layer passes the information to the recipient application program to complete the communication process.

## Interaction Between OSI Model Layers

A given OSI layer generally communicates with three other OSI layers: the layer directly above it, the layer directly below it, and its peer layer in other networked computer systems. For example, System A's data link layer communicates with System A's network layer, System A's physical layer, and System B's data link layer. Figure E-3 illustrates this interaction example.

**Figure E-3** *An OSI Model Layer Communicates with Three Other Layers*

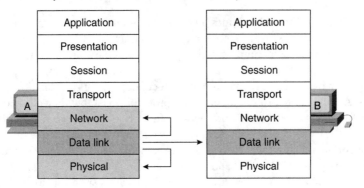

## OSI Layer Services

One OSI layer communicates with another layer to make use of the services provided by the second layer. The services provided by adjacent layers help a given OSI layer communicate with its peer layer in other computer systems. Layer services involves three basic elements: the service user, the service provider, and the service access point (SAP).

In this context, the *service user* is the OSI layer that requests services from an adjacent OSI layer. The *service provider* is the OSI layer that provides services to service users. OSI layers can provide services to multiple service users. The *SAP* is a conceptual location at which one OSI layer can request the services of another OSI layer.

Figure E-4 illustrates how these three elements interact at the network and data link layers.

**Figure E-4** *Service Users, Providers, and SAPs Interact at the Network and Data Link Layers*

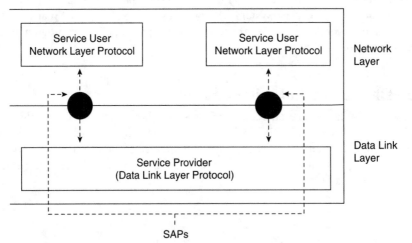

## OSI Model Layers and Information Exchange

The seven OSI layers use various forms of control information to communicate with their peer layers in other computer systems. This control information consists of specific requests and instructions that are exchanged between peer OSI layers.

Control information typically takes one of two forms: headers and trailers. *Headers* are prepended to data that has been passed down from upper layers. *Trailers* are appended to data that has been passed down from upper layers. An OSI layer is not required for attaching a header or trailer to data from upper layers.

Depending on the layer that analyzes the information unit, headers, trailers, and data are relative concepts. An information unit, for example, consists of a Layer 3 header and data at the network layer. At the data link layer, however, all the information passed down by the network layer (the Layer 3 header and the data) is treated as data.

In other words, the data portion of an information unit at a given OSI layer can potentially contain headers, trailers, and data from all the higher layers. This is known as *encapsulation*. Figure E-5 illustrates how the header and data from one layer are encapsulated to become the data of the next lowest layer.

**Figure E-5**  *Headers and Data Are Encapsulated During Information Exchange*

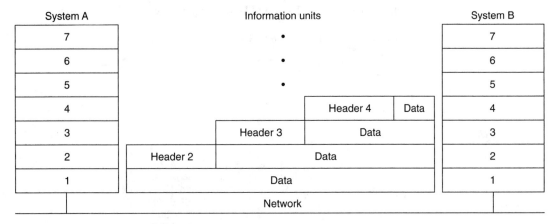

## Information Exchange Process

The information exchange process occurs between peer OSI layers. Each layer in the source system adds control information to data, and each layer in the destination system analyzes and removes the control information from that data.

If System A sends data from a software application to System B, the data is passed to the application layer. System A's application layer then communicates any control information required by System B's application layer by prepending a header to the data. The resulting information unit (a header and the data) is passed to the presentation layer, which prepends its own header that contains control information intended for System B's presentation layer.

The information unit grows in size as each layer prepends its own header (and, in some cases, a trailer), which contains control information to be used by its peer layer in System B. At the physical layer, the entire information unit is placed on the network medium.

System B's physical layer receives the information unit and passes it to the data link layer. Next, System B's data link layer reads the control information contained in the header that was prepended by System A's data link layer. Next, the data link layer removes the header and passes the remainder of the information unit to the network layer. Each layer performs the same actions: the layer reads the header from its peer layer, strips it off, and passes the remaining information unit to the next highest layer. After the application layer performs these actions, the data is passed to System B's recipient software application in exactly the form in which it was transmitted by the application in System A.

# OSI Model's Physical Layer

The *physical layer* defines the electrical, mechanical, procedural, and functional specifications for activating, maintaining, and deactivating the physical link between communicating network systems. Physical layer specifications define characteristics such as voltage levels, timing of voltage changes, physical data rates, maximum transmission distances, and physical connectors. Physical layer implementations can be categorized as either LAN or WAN specifications. Figure E-6 illustrates some common LAN and WAN physical layer implementations.

**Figure E-6**   *Physical Layer Implementations Can Be LAN or WAN Specifications*

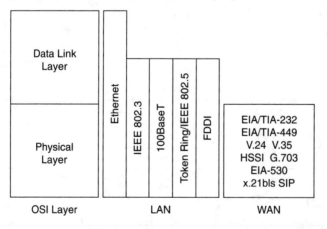

Physical Layer Implementations

# OSI Model's Data Link Layer

The *data link layer* reliably transits data across a physical network link. Different data link layer specifications define different network and protocol characteristics, including physical addressing, network topology, error notification, frame sequencing, and flow control. Physical addressing (as opposed to network addressing) defines how devices are addressed at the data link layer. Network topology consists of the data link layer specifications that often define how devices are to be connected physically, such as in a bus or ring topology. Error notification alerts upper-layer protocols that a transmission error has occurred, and the sequencing of data frames reorders frames that are transmitted out of sequence. Finally, flow control moderates data transmission so that the receiving device is not overwhelmed with more traffic than it can handle at one time.

The Institute of Electrical and Electronics Engineers (IEEE) has subdivided the data link layer into two sublayers: Logical Link Control (LLC) and Media Access Control (MAC). Figure E-7 illustrates the data link layer's IEEE sublayers.

**Figure E-7**  *The Data Link Layer Contains Two Sublayers*

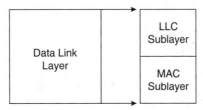

The data link layer's LLC sublayer manages communications between devices over a single network link. LLC, which is defined in the IEEE 802.2 specification, supports both connectionless and connection-oriented services used by higher-layer protocols. IEEE 802.2 defines a number of fields in data link layer frames that enable multiple higher-layer protocols to share a single physical data link. The data link layer's MAC sublayer manages protocol access to the physical network medium. The IEEE MAC specification defines MAC addresses, thereby enabling multiple devices to uniquely identify each other at the data link layer.

# OSI Model's Network Layer

The *network layer* provides routing and related functions that enable multiple data links to be combined into an internetwork. This is accomplished by the logical addressing (as opposed to the physical addressing) of devices. The network layer supports both connection-oriented and connectionless service from higher-layer protocols. Routing protocols, routed protocols, and other types of protocols are implemented at the network layer. Some common routing protocols include *Border Gateway Protocol (BGP)*, which is an Internet interdomain routing protocol; *Open Shortest Path First (OSPF)*, which is a link-state, interior gateway protocol developed for use in Transmission Control Protocol/Internet Protocol (TCP/IP) networks; and *Routing Information Protocol (RIP)*, which is an Internet routing protocol that uses hop count as its metric.

# OSI Model's Transport Layer

The *transport layer* implements optional, reliable internetwork data transport services that are transparent to upper layers. Transport layer functions can include flow control, multiplexing, virtual circuit management, and error checking and recovery.

Flow control manages data transmission between devices so that the transmitting device does not send more data than the receiving device can process. Multiplexing enables the tranmission of data from several applications to a single physical link. The transport layer establishes, maintains, and terminats virtual circuits. Error checking involves creating various mechanisms for detecting transmission errors, while error recovery involves taking an action, such as requesting that data be retransmitted, to resolve any errors.

Some transport layer implementations include *TCP*, which is the protocol in the TCP/IP suite that provides reliable transmission of data; *Name Binding Protocol (NBP)*, the protocol that associates AppleTalk names with addresses; and *OSI transport protocols*, which are a series of transport protocols in the OSI protocol suite.

# OSI Model's Session Layer

The *session layer* establishes, manages, and terminates communication sessions between presentation layer entities. Communication sessions consist of service requests and service responses that occur between applications that are located in different network devices. Protocols that are implemented at the session layer coordinate these requests. Some examples of session layer implementations include *Zone Information Protocol (ZIP)*, which is the AppleTalk protocol that coordinates the name binding process; and *Session Control Protocol (SCP)*, which is the DECnet Phase IV session layer protocol.

# OSI Model's Presentation Layer

The *presentation layer* provides a variety of coding and conversion functions that are applied to application layer data. These functions ensure that information sent from one system's application layer is readable by another system's application layer. Some examples of presentation layer coding and conversion schemes include common data representation formats, conversion of character representation formats, common data compression schemes, and common data encryption schemes.

Common data representation formats, or the use of standard image, sound, and video formats, enable different computer systems to interchange application data. Conversion schemes are used to exchange information with systems by using different text and data representations, such as EBCDIC and ASCII. Standard data compression schemes enable data that is compressed at the source device to be properly decompressed at the destination. Standard data-encryption schemes enable data that is encrypted at the source device to be properly deciphered at the destination.

Presentation layer implementations are not typically associated with a particular protocol stack. Some well-known standards for video include QuickTime and Motion Picture Experts Group (MPEG). *QuickTime* is an Apple Computer specification for video and audio, and *MPEG* is a standard for video compression and coding.

Among the well-known graphic image formats are Graphics Interchange Format (GIF), Joint Photographic Experts Group (JPEG), and Tagged Image File Format (TIFF). *GIF* is a standard for compressing and coding graphic images. *JPEG* is another compression and coding standard for graphic images. Finally, *TIFF* is a standard coding format for graphic images.

# OSI Model's Application Layer

The *application layer* is the OSI layer that is closest to the end user; this means that both the OSI application layer and the user interact directly with the software application.

This layer interacts with software applications that implement a communicating component. Such application programs fall outside the scope of the OSI model. Application layer functions typically include identifying communication partners, determining resource availability, and synchronizing communication.

When identifying communication partners, the application layer determines the identity and availability of communication partners for an application that has data to transmit. When determining resource availability, the application layer must decide whether sufficient network resources for the requested communication exist. In synchronizing communication, all communication between applications requires cooperation that the application layer manages.

TCP/IP applications and OSI applications are two key types of application layer implementations. *TCP/IP applications* are protocols, such as Telnet, File Transfer Protocol (FTP), and Simple Mail Transfer Protocol (SMTP), that exist in the Internet Protocol suite. *OSI applications* are protocols, such as File Transfer, Access, and Management (FTAM), Virtual Terminal Protocol (VTP), and Common Management Information Protocol (CMIP), that exist in the OSI suite.

# Information Formats

The data and control information that is transmitted through internetworks takes various forms. The terms used to refer to these information formats are not used consistently in the internetworking industry, but are sometimes are used interchangeably. Common information formats include the following:

- Frames
- Packets
- Datagrams
- Segments
- Messages
- Cells
- Data units

A *frame* is an information unit whose source and destination are data link layer entities. A frame is composed of the data link layer header (and possibly a trailer) and upper-layer data. The header and trailer contain control information that is intended for the destination system's data link layer entity. The data link layer header and trailer encapsulate data from upper-layer entities. Figure E-8 illustrates the basic components of a data link layer frame.

**Figure E-8**    *Data from Upper-Layer Entities Comprises the Data Link Layer Frame*

Frame

| Data Link Layer Header | Upper Layer Data | Data Link Layer Trailer |
|---|---|---|

A *packet* is an information unit whose source and destination are network layer entities. A packet is composed of the network layer header (and possibly a trailer) and upper-layer data. The header and trailer contain control information that is intended for the destination system's network layer entity. The network layer header and trailer encapsulate data from upper-layer entities. Figure E-9 illustrates the basic components of a network layer packet.

**Figure E-9**    *Three Basic Components Comprise a Network Layer Packet*

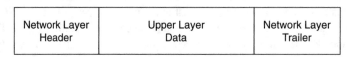

Packet

| Network Layer Header | Upper Layer Data | Network Layer Trailer |
|---|---|---|

The term *datagram* refers to an information unit whose source and destination are network layer entities that use connectionless network service.

The term *segment* refers to an information unit whose source and destination are transport layer entities.

A *message* is an information unit whose source and destination entities exist above the network layer (often in the application layer).

A *cell* is an information unit of a fixed size whose source and destination are data link layer entities. Cells are used in switched environments, such as Asynchronous Transfer Mode (ATM) and Switched Multimegabit Data Service (SMDS) networks. A cell is composed of the header and payload. The header contains control information that is intended for the destination data link layer entity and is typically 5 bytes long. The payload contains upper-layer data that is encapsulated in the cell header and is typically 48 bytes long.

The length of the header and the payload fields are always exactly the same for each cell. Figure E-10 depicts a typical cell's components.

**Figure E-10** *Two Components Comprise a Typical Cell*

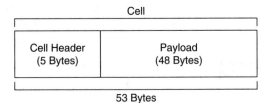

*Data unit* is a generic term that refers to a variety of information units. Some common data units include service data units (SDUs), protocol data units (PDUs), and bridge protocol data units (BPDUs). *SDUs* are information units from upper-layer protocols that define a service request to a lower-layer protocol. *PDU* is OSI terminology for describing the data unit at a given layer; for example, the Layer 3 PDU is also known as a packet, and the Layer 4 PDU is also known as a segment. *BPDUs* are used as hello messages by the spanning-tree algorithm.

# Common Requests for Comments

The Internet Requests For Comments (RFCs) documents are the written definitions of the protocols and policies of the Internet.

## Requests For Comments Information

The following information about RFCs was adapted from RFC 1594, "FYI Q/A—For New Internet Users":

The Internet Architecture Board (IAB) is concerned with technical and policy issues involving the evolution of the Internet architecture.

All decisions of the IAB are made public. The principal vehicle by which IAB decisions are propagated to the parties interested in the Internet and its TCP/IP protocol suite is the Request For Comments (RFC) note series and the Internet Monthly Report.

RFCs are the working notes of the Internet research and development community. A document in this series may be on essentially any topic related to computer communication, and may be anything from a meeting report to the specification of a standard. Submissions for Requests For Comments may be sent to the RFC Editor (RFC-EDITOR@ISI.EDU).

Most RFCs are the descriptions of network protocols or services, often giving detailed procedures and formats for their implementation. Other RFCs report on the results of policy studies or summarize the work of technical committees or workshops. All RFCs are considered public domain unless explicitly marked otherwise.

While RFCs are not refereed publications, they do receive technical review from either the task forces, individual technical experts, or the RFC Editor, as appropriate. Currently, most standards are published as RFCs, but not all RFCs specify standards.

Anyone can submit a document for publication as an RFC. Submissions must be made via electronic mail to the RFC Editor. Please consult RFC 1543, "Instructions to RFC Authors," for further information.

Once a document is assigned an RFC number and published, that RFC is never revised or reissued with the same number. There is never a question of having the most recent version of a particular RFC. However, a protocol (such as File Transfer Protocol [FTP]) may be improved and redocumented many times in several different RFCs. It is important to verify that you have the most recent RFC on a particular protocol. The "Internet Official Protocol Standards" memo is the reference for determining the correct RFC to refer to for the current specification of each protocol.

RFCs are available online at several repositories around the world.

Table F-1 lists some common Requests For Comments (RFCs). A complete list and the documents can be found at www.cis.ohio-state.edu/cs/Services/rfc/index.html.

**Table F-1**    *Common Requests for Comments*

| RFC | Title |
| --- | --- |
| 3107 | Carrying Label Information in BGP-4 |
| 3065 | Autonomous System Confederations for BGP (obsoletes RFC 1965) |
| 2966 | Domain-wide Prefix Distribution with Two-Level IS-IS |
| 2918 | Route Refresh Capability for BGP-4 |
| 2858 | Multiprotocol Extensions for BGP-4 (obsoletes RFC 2283) |
| 2842 | Capabilities Advertisement with BGP-4 |
| 2796 | BGP Route Reflection - An Alternative to Full Mesh IBGP (Updates RFC 1966) |
| 2791 | Scalable Routing Design Principles |
| 2763 | Dynamic Hostname Exchange Mechanism for IS-IS |
| 2740 | OSPF for IPv6 |
| 2547 | BGP/MPLS VPNs |
| 2545 | Use of BGP-4 Multiprotocol Extensions for IPv6 Inter-Domain Routing |
| 2460 | Internet Protocol, Version 6 (IPv6) Specification |
| 2439 | BGP Route Flap Damping |
| 2385 | Protection of BGP Sessions via TCP MD5 Signature Option |
| 2373 | IP Version 6 Addressing Architecture |
| 2370 | The OSPF Opaque LSA Option |
| 2329 | OSPF Standardization Report |
| 2328 | OSPF Version 2 |
| 2283 | Multiprotocol Extensions for BGP-4 (obsoleted by RFC 2858) |
| 2236 | Internet Group Message Protocol (IGMP), Version 2 |
| 2226 | IP Broadcast over ATM Networks |

**Table F-1**    *Common Requests for Comments (Continued)*

| RFC | Title |
| --- | --- |
| 2200 | Internet Official Protocol Standards (obsoletes RFC 2000, RFC 1920, RFC 1880, RFC 1800, RFC 1780, RFC 1720, RFC 1610, RFC 1600, RFC 1540, RFC 1500, RFC 1410, RFC 1360, RFC 1280, RFC 1250, RFC 1200, RFC 1140, RFC 1130, RFC 1100, and RFC 1083) |
| 2185 | Routing Aspects of IPv6 Transition |
| 2178 | OSPF Version 2 (Obsoleted by RFC 2328) |
| 2131 | Dynamic Host Configuration Protocol (DHCP) |
| 2105 | Cisco Systems' Tag Switching Architecture Overview |
| 2080 | RIPng for IPv6 |
| 2050 | Internet Registry IP Allocation Guidelines |
| 2042 | Registering New BGP Attribute Types |
| 1998 | Application of the BGP Community Attribute in Multi-Home Routing |
| 1997 | BGP Communities Attribute |
| 1994 | PPP Challenge Handshake Authentication Protocol (CHAP) |
| 1990 | The PPP Multilink Protocol (MP) |
| 1983 | Internet Users' Glossary |
| 1966 | BGP Route Reflection—An Alternative to Full-Mesh IBGP (updated by RFC 2796) |
| 1965 | AS Confederations for BGP (obsoleted by RFC 3065) |
| 1932 | IP over ATM: A Framework Document |
| 1930 | Guidelines for Creation, Selection, and Registration of an Autonomous System (AS) |
| 1918 | Address Allocation for Private Internets |
| 1863 | A BGP/IDRP Route Server Alternative to a Full-Mesh Routing |
| 1850 | OSPF Version 2 Management Information Base |
| 1817 | CIDR and Classful Routing |
| 1812 | Requirements for IP Version 4 Routers |
| 1793 | Extending OSPF to Support Demand Circuits |
| 1774 | BGP-4 Protocol Analysis |
| 1773 | Experience with the BGP-4 Protocol |
| 1772 | An Application of BGP in the Internet |
| 1771 | A Border Gateway Protocol 4 (BGP-4) |

*continues*

**Table F-1**    *Common Requests for Comments (Continued)*

| RFC | Title |
| --- | --- |
| 1765 | OSPF Database Overflow |
| 1700 | Assigned Numbers (note that this is now obsolete [by RFC 3232], and has been replaced by an online database available at www.iana.org/numbers.html) |
| 1663 | PPP Reliable Transmission |
| 1661 | The Point-to-Point Protocol (PPP) |
| 1631 | The IP Network Address Translator (NAT) |
| 1613 | Cisco Systems X.25 over TCP (XOT) |
| 1587 | OSPF NSSA Option |
| 1586 | Guidelines for Running OSPF over Frame Relay Networks |
| 1583 | OSPF Version 2 (obsoleted by RFC 2178) |
| 1570 | PPP LCP Extensions |
| 1548 | The Point-to-Point Protocol (PPP) |
| 1519 | Classless Interdomain Routing (CIDR): An Address Assignment and Aggregation Strategy |
| 1518 | An Architecture for IP Address Allocation with CIDR |
| 1490 | Multiprotocol Interconnect over Frame Relay |
| 1467 | Status of CIDR Deployment in the Internet |
| 1350 | The TFTP Protocol (Revision 2) |
| 1305 | Network Time Protocol (Version 3) Specification, Implementation |
| 1247 | OSPF Version 2 (obsoleted by RFC 1583) |
| 1246 | Experience with the OSPF Protocol |
| 1245 | OSPF Protocol Analysis |
| 1219 | On the Assignment of Subnet Numbers |
| 1195 | Use of OSI IS-IS for Routing in TCP/IP and Dual Environments |
| 1144 | Compressing TCP/IP Headers for Low-Speed Serial Links |
| 1142 | OSI IS-IS Intra-domain Routing Protocol |
| 1058 | Routing Information Protocol |
| 1042 | Standard for the Transmission of IP Datagrams over IEEE 802 Networks |
| 1020 | Internet Numbers |
| 995 | End System to Intermediate System Routing Exchange Protocol for use in conjunction with ISO 8473 |
| 951 | Bootstrap Protocol |

**Table F-1**    *Common Requests for Comments (Continued)*

| RFC | Title |
|-----|-------|
| 950 | Internet Standard Subnetting Procedure |
| 903 | Reverse Address Resolution Protocol |
| 821 | Simple Mail Transfer Protocol |
| 793 | Transmission Control Protocol |
| 792 | Internet Control Message Protocol |
| 791 | Internet Protocol |

# Answers to Review Questions

## Chapter 1

**1.** When networks are connected based on their location, is this a functional or geographic network design?

**Answer:  This is a geographic network design.**

**2.** Describe the role of each layer in the hierarchical network model.

**Answer:  The access layer provides local and remote workgroup or user access to the network.**

**The distribution layer provides policy-based connectivity.**

**The core (or backbone) layer provides high-speed transport.**

**3.** Name an advantage and a disadvantage of a fully meshed core layer.

**Answer:  In a fully meshed core layer design, each division has redundant routers at the core layer. The core sites are fully meshed, meaning that all routers have direct connections to all other nodes. This connectivity allows the network to react quickly when it must route data flow from a downed link to another path. For a small core with a limited number of divisions, this core layer design provides robust connectivity. However, a fully meshed core layer design is very expensive for a corporation with many divisions because of the number of links required.**

**4.** At what layer are DHCP and DNS servers typically found?

**Answer:  DHCP and DNS servers typically are found at the distribution layer.**

**5.** What are three benefits of a good IP address design?

**Answer:**

**Scalability—A well-designed network allows for large increases in the number of supported sites.**

**Predictability—A well-designed network exhibits predictable behavior and performance.**

**Flexibility—A well-designed network minimizes the impact of additions, changes, or removals within the network.**

**6.** What are private IP addresses, and what are they used for?

**Answer: Private addresses are reserved IPv4 addresses to be used only internally within a company's network. These private addresses are not to be used on the Internet, so they must be mapped to a company's external, registered address when sending anything to a recipient on the Internet. RFC 1918, Address Allocation for Private Internets, has set aside the following IPv4 address space for private use:**

**Class A network—10.0.0.0 to 10.255.255.255**

**Class B network—172.16.0.0 to 172.31.255.255**

**Class C network—192.168.0.0 to 192.168.255.255**

**7.** How does route summarization benefit a network?

**Answer: Route summarization is a way of having a single IP address represent a collection of IP addresses when you employ a hierarchical addressing plan. By summarizing routes, you can keep your routing table entries manageable, which offers the following benefits:**

**More efficient routing**

**Reduced number of CPU cycles when recalculating a routing table or sorting through the routing table entries to find a match**

**Reduced router memory requirements**

**Reduced bandwidth required to send the fewer, smaller routing updates**

**Faster convergence after a change in the network**

**Easier troubleshooting**

**Increased network stability**

**8.** Given a host address 10.1.17.61/28, what is the range of addresses on the subnet that this host is on?

**Answer:**

**The subnet address is 10.1.17.48.**

**The first host address is 10.1.17.49.**

**The last host address is 10.1.17.62.**

**The broadcast address is 10.1.17.63.**

**9.** How does VLSM allow a more efficient use of IP addresses?

**Answer: VLSM allows more than one subnet mask within a major network and enables the subnetting of a previously subnetted network address. Without the use of VLSM, companies are locked into implementing a single subnet mask within an entire Class A, B, or C network number.**

10. What range of addresses is represented by the summary route 172.16.16.0/21?

**Answer:  172.16.16.0 through 172.16.23.255, inclusive.**

11. You are in charge of the network shown in Figure 1-36. It consists of five LANs with 25 users on each LAN and five serial links. You have been assigned the IP address 192.168.49.0/24 to allocate addressing for all links.

**Figure 1-36**  *Network for Address Assignment*

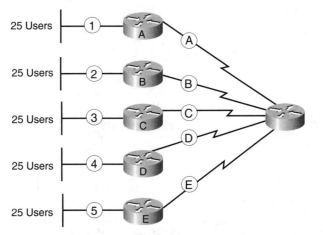

Write down the addresses you would assign to each of the LANs and serial links.

**Answer:  For five LANs with 25 users each, 3 subnet bits and 5 host bits are needed, yielding a maximum of eight subnets with 30 hosts each. Therefore, a prefix of /27 is needed. The following are the available subnets:**

**192.168.49.0/27**

**192.168.49.32/27**

**192.168.49.64/27**

**192.168.49.96/27**

**192.168.49.128/27**

**192.168.49.160/27**

**192.168.49.192/27**

**192.168.49.224/27**

**For the WAN addresses, one of the previous subnets that is not used on the LANs would be further subnetted. A prefix of /30 would be used to allow for two host addresses on each WAN. This would leave 3 bits for additional subnetting, resulting in eight subnets for the WANs. For example, if 192.168.49.160/27 is further subnetted, the following subnets are available for the WANs:**

**192.168.49.160/30**

**192.168.49.164/30**

**192.168.49.168/30**

**192.168.49.172/30**

**192.168.49.176/30**

**192.168.49.180/30**

**192.168.49.184/30**

**192.168.49.188/30**

**One possible allocation of the addresses is as follows:**

| LAN 1 | 192.168.49.0/27 |
|-------|-----------------|
| LAN 2 | 192.168.49.32/27 |
| LAN 3 | 192.168.49.64/27 |
| LAN 4 | 192.168.49.96/27 |
| LAN 5 | 192.168.49.128/27 |
| WAN A | 192.168.49.160/30 |
| WAN B | 192.168.49.164/30 |
| WAN C | 192.168.49.168/30 |
| WAN D | 192.168.49.172/30 |
| WAN E | 192.168.49.176/30 |

**12.** Figure 1-37 shows a network with subnets of the 172.16.0.0 network configured. Indicate in the following table where route summarization can occur in this network and what the summarized addresses would be.

**Figure 1-37** *Network for Route Summarization*

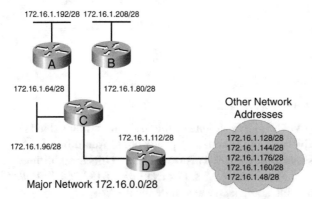

**Answer:**

| Router C Routing Table Entries | Summarized Routes That Can Be Advertised to Router D from Router C |
|---|---|
| **172.16.1.192/28** | **172.16.1.192/27**<br>Summarizes **172.16.1.192/28** and **172.16.1.208/28** |
| **172.16.1.208/28** | — |
| **172.16.1.64/28** | **172.16.1.64/26**<br>Summarizes **172.16.1.64/28, 172.16.1.80/28, 172.16.1.96/28, and 172.16.1.112/28** |
| **172.16.1.80/28** | — |
| **172.16.1.96/28** | — |
| **172.16.1.112/28** | — |

**13.** Figure 1-38 shows a network with subnets of the 172.16.0.0 network configured. Indicate in the following table where route summarization can occur in this network and what the summarized address would be.

**Figure 1-38** *Network for Route Summarization*

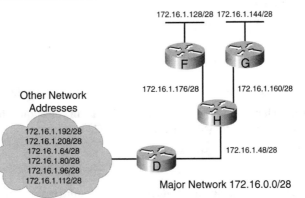

**Answer:**

| Router H Routing Table Entries | Summarized Routes That Can Be Advertised to Router D from Router H |
|---|---|
| **172.16.1.48/28** | **172.16.1.48/28** |
| **172.16.1.128/28** | **172.16.1.128/26**<br>Summarizes **172.16.1.128/28, 172.16.1.144/28, 172.16.1.160/28, and 172.16.1.176/28** |

*continues*

| Router H Routing Table Entries | Summarized Routes That Can Be Advertised to Router D from Router H |
|---|---|
| 172.16.1.144/28 | — |
| 172.16.1.160/28 | — |
| 172.16.1.176/28 | — |

**14.** When selecting a route, which prefix match is used?

**Answer:  The longest prefix match.**

**15.** What is the difference between route summarization and CIDR?

**Answer:  The idea behind CIDR is that blocks of multiple addresses (such as blocks of Class C addresses) can be combined, or aggregated, to create a larger classless set of IP addresses, with more hosts allowed. These multiple Class C addresses can then be summarized in routing tables, resulting in fewer route advertisements. The difference between CIDR and route summarization is that route summarization is generally done within, or up to, a classful boundary, whereas CIDR combines several classful networks.**

**16.** The following networks are in Router A's routing table:

192.168.12.0/24

192.168.13.0/24

192.168.14.0/24

192.168.15.0/24

Using CIDR, what route could Router A advertise to its neighbor?

**Answer:  These routes all have the first 22 bits in common. Therefore, Router A could advertise the summary route 192.168.12.0/22 to its neighbor.**

**17.** What is the difference between a NAT inside local IP address and an inside global IP address?

**Answer:  The inside local IP address is the IP address assigned to a host on the inside network. The inside global IP address is a legitimate IP address (typically assigned by a service provider) that represents one or more inside local IP addresses to the outside world.**

**18.** Which command indicates that NAT translation is to be done for packets arriving on an interface?

**Answer:**

**ip nat {inside | outside}**

**19.** In the following configuration example, what does the first line do? What does the fourth line do?

```
ip nat pool our_pool 192.168.4.1  192.168.4.254 prefix-length 24
ip nat pool their_pool 192.168.5.1 192.168.5.254 prefix-length 24
!
ip nat inside source list 104 pool our_pool
ip nat inside source list 105 pool their_pool
!
interface ethernet 0
 ip address 10.1.1.1 255.255.0.0
 ip nat inside
!
interface serial 0
 ip address 172.16.2.1 255.255.255.0
 ip nat outside
!
access-list 104 permit ip  10.1.1.0 0.0.0.255  172.16.1.0 0.0.0.255
access-list 104 permit ip  10.1.1.0 0.0.0.255  192.168.200.0 0.0.0.255
access-list 105 permit ip  10.1.1.0 0.0.0.255  any
```

**Answer: The first line creates a pool of addresses called our_pool. The addresses in the pool are 192.168.4.1/24 through 192.168.4.254/24. The fourth line specifies that when a packet comes in on an interface marked as IP NAT inside, the source IP address in the packet is compared to access list 104 (defined later in the configuration example). An address that is permitted by access list 104 is translated to the next available address in our_pool.**

**20.** Describe how a route map works.

**Answer:  Route maps are complex access lists that allow some conditions to be tested against the packet or route in question using match commands. If the conditions match, some actions can be taken to modify attributes of the packet or route. These actions are specified by set commands. A collection of route map statements that have the same route map name are considered one route map. Within a route map, each route map statement is numbered and therefore can be edited individually.**

**The statements in a route map correspond to the lines of an access list. Specifying the match conditions in a route map is similar to specifying the source and destination addresses and masks in an access list.**

**One big difference between route maps and access lists is that route maps can modify the route by using set commands.**

**21.** What are some differences between IPv4 and IPv6?

**Answer:**

**IPv6 addresses have 128 bits, compared to the 32 bits in an IPv4 address.**

**IPv6 has a simpler, fixed-size header.**

**In IPv6, mobility is built in, which means that any IPv6 node can use it when necessary. However, mobility is not provided in IPv4; you must add it.**

**IPSec is available for IPv4; IPSec is mandatory in IPv6.**

22. What is the difference between the IPv4 header and the IPv6 header?

    **Answer: The IPv6 header has 40 octets in contrast to the 20 octets in IPv4. IPv6 has a smaller number of fields, and the header is 64-bit aligned to enable fast processing by current processors. The IPv6 address fields are four times larger than in IPv4.**

23. What features does the larger address space of IPv6 provide?

    **Answer: IPv6 addresses have 128 bits, compared to the 32 bits in an IPv4 address, allowing more support for addressing hierarchical levels, a much greater number of addressable nodes, and simpler autoconfiguration of addresses.**

24. Write the shortest legal format for the following IPv6 address:

    2210:0000:0011:ABCD:0000:0000:0000:0101

    **Answer: 2210:0:11:ABCD::101**

25. Write out the following IPv6 address completely:

    2214::15:ABCD

    **Answer: 2214:0000:0000:0000:0000:0000:0015:ABCD**

26. Describe how IPv6 stateless autoconfiguration works.

    **Answer: With stateless autoconfiguration, a router on the local link sends network-type information, such as the prefix of the local link and the default route, to all its nodes. An IPv6-enabled host uses the prefix advertised by the router as the top 64 bits of the address; the remaining 64 bits contain the 48-bit MAC address in the EUI-64 format. This autoconfiguration produces a full 128-bit address that can be used on the local link and that guarantees global uniqueness.**

27. Name two IPv4 packet header fields that are no longer defined in the IPv6 packet header.

    **Answer: The Fragment Offset and Header Checksum fields are not defined in the IPv6 header.**

28. Describe how 6to4 transition works.

    **Answer: The 6to4 tunneling method automatically establishes and enables the connection of IPv6 islands through an IPv4 network. The 6to4 tunnel treats the IPv4 network as a virtual link. Each 6to4 edge router has an IPv6 address with a /48 prefix, which is the concatenation of 2002::/16 and the edge router's IPv4 address (in hexadecimal). 2002::/16 is a specially assigned address range for the purpose of 6to4. The edge routers automatically build the tunnel using the IPv4 addresses imbedded in the IPv6 addresses.**

29. What does dual stack mean?

    **Answer: A dual stack enables both the IPv4 and IPv6 protocols. Cisco IOS software is IPv6-ready; as soon as IPv4 and IPv6 basic configurations are complete on an interface, the interface is dual-stacked, and it forwards IPv4 and IPv6 traffic.**

**30.** What is the difference between an IPv6 anycast address and an IPv6 multicast address?

**Answer:  An IPv6 multicast address is the same as in IPv4 multicast: an address for a set of interfaces (in a given scope) that typically belong to different nodes. A packet sent to a multicast address is delivered to all the interfaces identified by the multicast address. In comparison, the anycast address identifies a list of interfaces that typically belong to different nodes. A packet sent to an anycast address is delivered to the closest interface, as defined by the routing protocols in use, identified by the anycast address.**

**31.** What is the IPv6 broadcast address?

**Answer:  There isn't one. Broadcasts are not supported in IPv6.**

**32.** What does the 2001::/16 summary route mean?

**Answer:  Any IPv6 addresses whose first 16 bits equal 2001 hex match the route.**

**33.** The IPv6 header is aligned on what bit boundary?

**Answer:  The IPv6 header is aligned on a 64-bit boundary.**

# Chapter 2

**1.** Which of the following is not a scenario in which static routes would be used?

   a.  When the administrator needs total control over the routes used by the router

   b.  When a backup to a dynamically recognized route is necessary

   c.  When rapid convergence is needed

   d.  When a route should appear to the router as a directly connected network

**Answer:  c**

**2.** What are two drawbacks of static routes?

   a.  Reconfiguring to reflect topology changes

   b.  Complex metrics

   c.  Involved convergence

   d.  Absence of dynamic route discovery

**Answer:  a, d**

**3.** What is used by traffic for which the destination network is not specifically listed in the routing table?

   a.  Dynamic area

   b.  Default route

   c.  Border getaway

   d.  Black hole

**Answer:  b**

4. The **show ip route** command usually provides information on which of the following two items?

   a. Next hop

   b. Metric

   c. CDP

   d. Host name

   **Answer: a, b**

5. When using dynamic routing protocols, what does the administrator configure the routing protocol on?

   a. Each area

   b. Each intermediate system

   c. Each router

   d. Each gateway of last resort

   **Answer: c**

6. Which of the following is not a dynamic routing protocol?

   a. IS-IS

   b. CDP

   c. EIGRP

   d. BGP

   e. RIPv2

   **Answer: b**

7. What is a metric?

   a. A standard of measurement used by routing algorithms

   b. The set of techniques used to manage network resources

   c. Interdomain routing in TCP/IP networks

   d. Services limit the input or output transmission rate

   **Answer: a**

8. Which two routing protocols use only major classful networks to determine the interfaces participating in the protocol?

   a. RIPv2

   b. EIGRP

   c. RIPv1

d.  IS-IS

e.  BGP

f.  OSPF

g.  IGRP

**Answer: c, g**

9.  ODR uses what to carry network information between spoke (stub) routers and the hub?

a.  Metric

b.  BGP

c.  Convergence

d.  CDP

**Answer: d**

10.  Which of the following is not a classification of routing protocols?

a.  Link-state

b.  Default

c.  Hybrid

d.  Distance-vector

**Answer: b**

11.  What is the default subnet mask of a Class B address?

a.  255.255.255.255

b.  255.255.255.0

c.  255.255.0.0

d.  255.0.0.0

**Answer: c**

12.  What do you call the process when the router, using a classful routing protocol, sends an update about a subnet of a classful network across an interface belonging to a different classful network and assumes that the remote router will use the default subnet mask for that class of IP address?

a.  Autosummarization

b.  Default routing

c.  Classful switching

d.  Tunneling

**Answer: a**

**13.** True or false: Discontiguous subnets are subnets of the same major network that are separated by a different major network.

**Answer: True**

**14.** Classless routing protocols allow _____.

a. QoS

b. VLSM

c. VPN

d. RIP

**Answer: b**

**15.** What is the command to turn off autosummarization?

a. **no auto-summarization**

b. **enable classless**

c. **ip route**

d. **no auto-summary**

**Answer: d**

**16.** What is the OSPF default administrative distance value?

a. 90

b. 100

c. 110

d. 120

**Answer: c**

**17.** When a static route's administrative distance is manually configured to be higher than the default administrative distance of dynamic routing protocols, that static route is called what?

a. Semistatic route

b. Floating static route

c. Semidynamic route

d. Manual route

**Answer: b**

**18.** Which protocols are considered "best-effort"?

a. RIPv1

b. QoS

c.  IS-IS

d.  IGRP

e.  EIGRP

**Answer:  a, d**

19.  Which variables can be used to calculate metrics?

a.  Hops

b.  Convergence time

c.  Administrative distance

d.  Path attributes

e.  Cost

**Answer:  a, d, e**

20.  What is an interval, in seconds, during which routing information about a worse or equivalent metric path is suppressed?

a.  Invalid timer

b.  Holddown timer

c.  Flush timer

d.  Dead-detection timer

**Answer:  b**

# Chapter 3

1.  What are some features of EIGRP?

    **Answer:  Features of EIGRP include rapid convergence, reduced bandwidth usage, multiple network layer support, support for all data-link protocols and topologies, VLSM support, and a guaranteed loop-free topology.**

2.  Is EIGRP operational traffic multicast or broadcast?

    **Answer:  EIGRP operational traffic is multicast (and unicast).**

3.  How do IGRP and EIGRP differ in their metric calculation?

    **Answer:  IGRP and EIGRP use the same algorithm for metric calculation, but EIGRP's metric value is multiplied by 256 to give it more granularity in its decision-making. EIGRP represents its metrics in 32-bit format instead of the 24-bit representation used by IGRP.**

4.  What is in the EIGRP topology table?

    **Answer:  All learned routes to a destination are maintained in the topology table.**

**5.** Describe the five types of EIGRP packets.

**Answer: EIGRP uses the following five types of packets:**

**Hello—Hello packets are used for neighbor discovery. They are sent as multicasts and carry an acknowledgment number of 0.**

**Update—An update is sent to communicate the routes a particular router has used to converge; an update is sent only to affected routers. These updates are sent as multicasts when a new route is discovered and when convergence is completed (when the route becomes passive). To synchronize topology tables, updates are sent as unicasts to neighbors during their EIGRP startup sequence. Updates are sent reliably.**

**Query—When a router is performing route computation and does not find a feasible successor, it sends a query packet to its neighbors, asking if they have a feasible successor to the destination. Queries are always multicast and are sent reliably.**

**Reply—A reply packet is sent in response to a query packet. Replies are unicast to the originator of the query and are sent reliably.**

**Acknowledge (ACK)—The ACK is used to acknowledge updates, queries, and replies. ACKs are hello packets sent as unicasts and contain a nonzero acknowledgment number. (Note that hello and ACK packets do not require acknowledgment.)**

**6.** How often are EIGRP hello packets sent?

**Answer: The time interval of hello packets varies depending on the medium. Hello packets are released every 5 seconds on a LAN link, such as Ethernet, Token Ring, or FDDI. The default interval is also set to 5 seconds for point-to-point links, such as PPP, HDLC, point-to-point Frame Relay, and ATM subinterfaces, and for multipoint circuits with bandwidth greater than T1, including ISDN PRI, SMDS, ATM, and Frame Relay. Hello packets are sent out less frequently on lower-speed links, such as multipoint circuits with a bandwidth less than or equal to T1, including ISDN BRI, Frame Relay, SMDS, ATM, and X.25. Hellos are generated at 60-second intervals on these types of interfaces.**

**7.** What is the difference between the hold time and the hello-time interval?

**Answer:**

**The hello time interval determines how often hello packets are sent. It is 5 or 60 seconds by default, depending on the media type.**

**The hold time is the amount of time a router considers a neighbor up without receiving a hello or some other EIGRP packet from that neighbor. Hello packets report the hold time value. The hold time interval is set by default to 3 times the hello interval.**

**8.** What is the difference between a passive route and an active route? Which is the desired type of route in a stable network?

**Answer:  A route is considered passive when the router is not performing recomputation on that route. A route is active when it is undergoing recomputation (in other words, when it is looking for a new successor). Note that passive is the operational state.**

**9.** Which command is used to see the RTO and hold timers?

**Answer:  The show ip eigrp neighbors command displays this information, along with the rest of the neighbor table.**

**10.** Why are EIGRP routing updates described as reliable?

**Answer:  EIGRP update packets are generated by the Reliable Transport Protocol within EIGRP. Reliable packets have a sequence number assigned to them, and the receiving device must acknowledge them.**

**11.** What units are the bandwidth and delay parameters in the EIGRP metric calculation?

**Answer:**

**The default formula for the EIGRP metric is**

**metric = bandwidth + delay**

**In this formula, the EIGRP delay value is the sum of the delays in the path, in tens of microseconds, multiplied by 256.**

**The bandwidth is calculated using the minimum bandwidth link along the path, represented in kbps. Divide $10^7$ by this value, and then multiply the result by 256.**

**12.** What is the difference between an AD and a FD?

**Answer:**

**The advertised distance is the EIGRP metric for an EIGRP neighbor router to reach a particular network. This is the metric between the next-hop neighbor router and the destination network.**

**The feasible distance is the EIGRP metric for this router to reach a particular network. This is the sum of the advertised distance for the particular network learned from an EIGRP neighbor plus the EIGRP metric to reach that neighbor.**

**13.** What does it mean when a route is marked as an FS?

**Answer:  A route is marked as a feasible successor when the next-hop router's advertised distance is less than the feasible distance of the current successor route for the destination network. A feasible successor route is an alternative or backup route for the successor route in the routing table.**

**14.** In the following table, place the letter of the description next to the term the description describes. The descriptions may be used more than once.

Descriptions:

a. A network protocol that EIGRP supports.

b. A table that contains FS information.

c. The administrative distance determines routing information that is included in this table.

d. A neighbor router that has the best path to a destination.

e. A neighbor router that has the best alternative path to a destination.

f. An algorithm used by EIGRP that ensures fast convergence.

g. A multicast packet used to discover neighbors.

h. A packet sent by EIGRP routers when a new neighbor is discovered and when a change occurs.

**Answer:**

| Term | Description Letter |
|---|---|
| Successor | D |
| Feasible successor | E |
| Hello | G |
| Topology table | B |
| IP | A |
| Update | H |
| AppleTalk | A |
| Routing table | C |
| DUAL | F |
| IPX | A |

**15.** Answer true or false to the following statements.

**Answer:**

**EIGRP performs autosummarization: True**

**EIGRP autosummarization cannot be turned off: False**

**EIGRP supports VLSM: True**

**EIGRP can maintain three independent routing tables: True**

**The EIGRP hello interval is an unchangeable fixed value: False**

16. What is the recommended practice for configuring bandwidth on a Frame Relay point-to-point subinterface?

   **Answer: For Frame Relay point-to-point interfaces and subinterfaces with only one virtual circuit, set the bandwidth to the CIR. For Frame Relay multipoint connections, set the bandwidth to the sum of all CIRs. If the PVCs have different CIRs, set the bandwidth to the lowest CIR multiplied by the number of PVCs for the multipoint connection.**

17. Router A has three interfaces with IP addresses 172.16.1.1/24, 172.16.2.3/24, and 172.16.5.1/24. What commands would be used to configure EIGRP to run in AS 100 on only the interfaces with addresses 172.16.2.3/24 and 172.16.5.1/24?

   **Answer: One EIGRP configuration for Router A is as follows:**

   ```
   RouterA(config)#router eigrp 100
   RouterA(config-router)#network 172.16.2.0 0.0.0.255
   RouterA(config-router)#network 172.16.5.0 0.0.0.255
   ```

18. Router A, connected to Router B, is configured with the **ip default-network 172.17.0.0** command for EIGRP. What does this command do on Router A?

   **Answer: The routing table for Router A does not set the gateway of last resort; the ip default-network command does not benefit Router A directly. Router A needs to have the 172.17.0.0 network listed in a network command under the EIGRP process to pass it to its neighbor, Router B. On Router B, the EIGRP-learned 172.17.0.0 network is flagged as a candidate default network (indicated by * in the routing table). Router B sets the gateway of last resort to Router A's address to reach the default network 172.17.0.0.**

19. Routers A and B are connected and are running EIGRP on all their interfaces. Router A has four interfaces, with IP addresses 172.16.1.1/24, 172.16.2.3/24, 172.16.5.1/24, and 10.1.1.1/24. Router B has two interfaces, with IP addresses 172.16.1.2/24 and 192.168.1.1/24. (Other routers in the network are running EIGRP on each of the interfaces on these two routers.) Which summary routes does Router A generate automatically?

   **Answer: Router A generates two summary routes: 172.16.0.0 and 10.0.0.0. The 10.0.0.0 summary route is sent to the routers connected on the 172.16.0.0 subnets, including Router B (on the 172.16.1.0/24 subnet). The 172.16.0.0 summary route is sent to the router on the 10.1.1.0/24 subnet. Router A does not generate a summary route for 192.168.1.0, because it does not have an interface in that network.**

20. Router A has four EIGRP paths to a destination with the following EIGRP metrics:

   — Path 1: 1100

   — Path 2: 1200

   — Path 3: 2000

   — Path 4: 4000

If the command **variance 3** is configured on Router A, which paths are included for load balancing?

**Answer: Path 1 is chosen as the successor because it is the least-cost path. With the variance 3 command configured, any paths with a metric less than 1100 \* 3 = 3300 are included for load balancing. Therefore, load balancing takes place across Paths 1, 2, and 3.**

21.  Router A has the following configuration:

```
interface s0
  ip bandwidth-percent eigrp 100 40
  bandwidth 256
router eigrp 100
  network 10.0.0.0
```

What is the maximum bandwidth that EIGRP uses on the S0 interface?

**Answer: EIGRP uses 40 percent of the 256-kbps bandwidth configured, so it uses a maximum of 102 kbps.**

22.  What is the default stuck-in-active timer?

**Answer: The default time is 3 minutes. If the router does not receive a reply to all the outstanding queries within this time, the route goes to the stuck-in-active state, and the router then resets the neighbor relationships for the neighbors that failed to reply.**

23.  How can EIGRP queries be limited?

**Answer: Two of the best options are as follows:**

**Configure route summarization using the ip summary-address eigrp command on the outbound interfaces of the appropriate routers.**

**Configure the remote routers as stub EIGRP routers.**

24.  Why does summarization limit the query range?

**Answer: Summarization limits the query range because a remote router extends the query about a network only if it has an exact match in the routing table. Consider a remote router that receives only a summary route, not specific subnet routes. If a subnet route goes down and the router receives a query for the subnet, it immediately replies that the route is unreachable; it does not propagate the query to other routers.**

25.  How does the stub feature limit the query range?

**Answer: Stub routers are not queried. Instead, hub routers connected to the stub router answer the query on behalf of the stub router.**

26.  What does the **eigrp stub receive-only** command do?

**Answer: This command makes the router an EIGRP stub. The receive-only keyword restricts the router from sharing any of its routes with any other router within the EIGRP autonomous system.**

**27.** What command displays EIGRP-learned IP routes?

**Answer: The show ip route eigrp command displays the current EIGRP entries in the IP routing table.**

**28.** The following is part of the output of the **show ip eigrp topology** command:

```
P 10.1.3.0/24, 1 successors, FD is 10514432
         via 10.1.2.2 (10514432/28160), Serial0/0
```

What are the two numbers in parentheses?

**Answer: The first number is the feasible distance for the network, and the second number is the advertised distance from the next-hop router.**

**29.** What command displays the types of EIGRP packets as they are received from EIGRP neighbors?

**Answer: The debug eigrp packets command displays all types of EIGRP packets as they are received and sent to neighbors.**

**30.** What command displays EIGRP packets as they are sent and received?

**Answer: The debug ip eigrp command displays EIGRP packets as they are sent and received.**

# Chapter 4

**1.** Which of the following is not a characteristic of link-state routing protocols?

   a.  They respond quickly to network changes.

   b.  They broadcast every 30 minutes.

   c.  They send triggered updates when a network change occurs.

   d.  They send periodic updates, known as link-state refresh, at long time intervals, such as every 30 minutes.

   **Answer: b**

**2.** For all the routers in the network to make consistent routing decisions, each router must keep a record of all of the following items except which one?

   a.  Its immediate neighbor routers

   b.  All of the other routers in the network, or in its area of the network, and their attached networks

   c.  The best paths to each destination

   d.  The version of the routing protocol used

   **Answer: d**

**3.** Link-state routing protocols use a two-layer area hierarchy composed of which two areas?

   a.  Transit area

   b.  Transmit area

   c.  Regular area

   d.  Linking area

**Answer: a, c**

**4.** Which of the following is not a characteristic of an OSPF area?

   a.  It minimizes routing table entries.

   b.  It requires a flat network design.

   c.  It localizes the impact of a topology change within an area.

   d.  Detailed LSA flooding stops at the area boundary.

**Answer: b**

**5.** True or false: An ABR connects area 0 to the nonbackbone areas.

**Answer: True**

**6.** When each router receives the LSU, it does not do which of the following?

   a.  If the entry does not already exist, the router adds the entry to its LSDB, sends back an LSAck, floods the information to other routers, runs SPF, and updates its routing table.

   b.  If the entry already exists and the received LSU has the same information, the router overwrites the information in the LSDB with the new LSA entry.

   c.  If the entry already exists but the LSU includes newer information, the router adds the entry to its LSDB, sends back an LSAck, floods the information to other routers, runs SPF, and updates its routing table.

   d.  If the entry already exists but the LSU includes older information, it sends an LSU to the sender with its newer information.

**Answer: b**

**7.** What is an OSPF Type 2 packet?

   a.  Database Description (DBD), which checks for database synchronization between routers

   b.  Link-State Request (LSR), which requests specific link-state records from router to router

   c.  Link-State Update (LSU), which sends specifically requested link-state records

   d.  Link-State Acknowledgment (LSAck), which acknowledges the other packet types

**Answer: a**

**8.** Which of the following is true of hellos and dead intervals?

   a. They don't need to be the same on neighboring routers, because the lowest common denominator is adopted

   b. They don't need to be the same on neighboring routers, because the highest common denominator is adopted

   c. They don't need to be the same, because it is a negotiated interval between neighboring routers

   d. They need to be the same

**Answer: d**

**9.** In which state do the DR and BDR establish adjacencies with each router in the network?

   a. Init state

   b. Exstart state

   c. Exchange state

   d. Loading state

   e. Full state

**Answer: a**

**10.** Which IP address is used to send an updated LSA entry to OSPF DRs and BDRs?

   a. **unicast 224.0.0.5**

   b. **unicast 224.0.0.6**

   c. **multicast 224.0.0.5**

   d. **multicast 224.0.0.6**

**Answer: d**

**11.** To ensure an accurate database, how often does OSPF flood (refresh) each LSA record?

   a. Every 60 minutes

   b. Every 30 minutes

   c. Every 60 seconds

   d. Every 30 seconds

   e. Flooding each LSA record would defeat the purpose of a link-state routing protocol, which strives to reduce the amount of routing traffic it generates.

**Answer: b**

**12.** What command is used to display router ID, timers, and statistics?

   a. **show ip ospf**

   b. **show ip ospf neighbors**

   c. **show ip ospf stats**

   d. **show ip ospf neighborship**

   **Answer: a**

**13.** Which of the following is not a way in which the router ID (a unique IP address) can be assigned?

   a. The highest IP address of any physical interface.

   b. The lowest IP address of any physical interface.

   c. A loopback address is always preferred over an interface address, because a loopback address never goes down.

   d. A **router-id** command is the preferred procedure to set the router ID and is always used over the other two procedures.

   **Answer: b**

**14.** True or false: On point-to-point networks, the router dynamically detects its neighboring routers by multicasting its hello packets to all SPF routers using the address 224.0.0.6.

   **Answer: False**

**15.** An adjacency is the relationship that exists where?

   a. Between routers located on the same physical network

   b. Between routers in different OSPF areas

   c. Between a router and its DR and BDR on different networks

   d. Between a backbone DR and a transit BDR

   **Answer: a**

**16.** To elect a DR and BDR, a router does not use which of the following conditions to determine which router to select?

   a. The router with the highest priority value is the DR.

   b. The router with the second-highest priority value is the BDR.

   c. If all routers have the default priority, the router with the lowest router ID becomes the DR.

   d. The router with a priority set to 0 cannot become the DR or BDR.

   **Answer: c**

**17.** Which of the following is not true of point-to-multipoint mode?

    a. It does not require a full-mesh network.

    b. It does not require a static neighbor configuration.

    c. It uses multiple IP subnets.

    d. It duplicates LSA packets.

**Answer: c**

**18.** What is the default OSPF mode on a point-to-point Frame Relay subinterface?

    a. Point-to-point mode

    b. Multipoint mode

    c. Nonbroadcast mode

    d. Broadcast mode

**Answer: a**

**19.** What is the default OSPF mode on a Frame Relay point-to-multipoint subinterface?

    a. Point-to-point mode

    b. Multipoint mode

    c. Nonbroadcast mode

    d. Broadcast mode

**Answer: c**

**20.** What is the default OSPF mode on a main Frame Relay interface?

    a. Point-to-point mode

    b. Multipoint mode

    c. Nonbroadcast mode

    d. Broadcast mode

**Answer: c**

# Chapter 5

**1.** True or false: OSPF performs route summarization by default.

**Answer: False**

**2.** True or false: In a large network where topological changes are frequent, routers spend many CPU cycles recalculating the SPF algorithm and updating the routing table.

**Answer: True**

**3.** Match the type of router with its description:

| Type of Router | Description |
|---|---|
| 1—Internal router | A—A router that sits in the perimeter of the backbone area and that has at least one interface connected to area 0. It maintains OSPF routing information using the same procedures and algorithms as an internal router. |
| 2—Backbone router | B—A router that has interfaces attached to multiple areas, maintains separate LSDBs for each area to which it connects, and routes traffic destined for or arriving from other areas. This router is an exit point for the area, which means that routing information destined for another area can get there only via the local area's router. This kind of router can be configured to summarize the routing information from the LSDBs of its attached areas. This router distributes the routing information into the backbone. The backbone routers then forward the information to the other ABRs. An area can have one or more ABRs. |
| 3—ABR | C—A router that has all its interfaces in the same area with identical LSDBs. |
| 4—ASBR | D—A router that has at least one interface attached to an external internetwork (another AS), such as a non-OSPF network. This router can import non-OSPF network information to the OSPF network and vice versa; this process is called route redistribution. |

**Answer:**

**1—C**

**2—A**

**3—B**

**4—D**

**4.** How many different types of LSAs are there?

a. 5

b. 9

c. 10

d. 11

**Answer: d**

**5.** What kind of router generates LSA type 5?

a. DR

b. ABR

    c.  ASBR

    d.  ADR

    **Answer: c**

**6.** True or false: By default, OSPF does not automatically summarize groups of contiguous subnets.

    **Answer: True**

**7.** A router advertises a type 1 LSA that floods to what?

    a.  Immediate peers

    b.  All other routers in the area where it originated

    c.  Routers located in other areas

    d.  All areas

    **Answer: b**

**8.** How does a routing table reflect the link-state information of an intra-area route?

    a.  The route is marked with O.

    b.  The route is marked with I.

    c.  The route is marked with IO.

    d.  The route is marked with EA.

    **Answer: a**

**9.** Which type of external route is the default?

    a.  E1

    b.  E2

    c.  E5

    d.  There is no default external route. OSPF adapts and chooses the most accurate one.

    **Answer: b**

**10.** E1 external routes calculate the cost by adding what?

    a.  The internal cost of each link the packet crosses

    b.  The external cost to the internal cost of each link the packet crosses

    c.  The external cost only

    d.  All area costs, even those that aren't used

    **Answer: b**

**11.** With OSPF, how is the OSPF metric calculated by default?

    a.  OSPF calculates the OSPF metric for a router according to the bandwidth of all its interfaces.

    b.  OSPF calculates the OSPF metric by referencing the DR.

    c.  OSPF calculates the OSPF metric for an interface according to the interface's inverse bandwidth.

    d.  OSPF calculates the OSPF metric by using the lowest bandwidth value among all of its interfaces.

**Answer: c**

12. Why is configuring a stub area advantageous?

    a.  It reduces the size of the LSDB inside an area.

    b.  It increases the memory requirements for routers in that area.

    c.  It further segments the hierarchy.

    d.  It starts to behave like a distance vector routing protocol, thus speeding up convergence.

**Answer: a**

13. A stub area is typically created using what kind of topology?

    a.  Point-to-point

    b.  Broadcast

    c.  Hub-and-spoke

    d.  Full-mesh

**Answer: c**

14. True or false: By default, in normal areas, routers generate default routes.

**Answer: False**

15. What command makes an OSPF router generate a default route?

    a.  **ospf default-initiate**

    b.  **default-information originate**

    c.  **default information-initiate**

    d.  **ospf information-originate**

**Answer: b**

16. If your router has an interface faster than 100 Mbps that is used with OSPF, consider using the _____ command under the _____ process.

    a.  **auto-cost reference-bandwidth**, OSPF

    b.  **auto-cost reference-bandwidth**, interface

    c. **autocost reference-speed**, OSPF

    d. **autocost reference-speed**, interface

    **Answer: a**

17. True or false: OSPF design requires that all areas be directly connect to the backbone.

    **Answer: True**

18. True or false: Virtual links are very useful, and you should include them in your network architecture when designing a completely new OSPF network.

    **Answer: False**

# Chapter 6

1. What does Integrated IS-IS support?

    a. BGP

    b. IP

    c. OSPF

    d. IPX

    **Answer: b**

2. IS-IS is the most popular routing protocol for which of the following?

    a. Small businesses

    b. Government organizations

    c. ISPs

    d. Military establishments

    **Answer: c**

3. Because IS-IS is protocol-independent, it can support which of the following?

    a. IPv4

    b. IPv6

    c. OSI CLNS

    d. All of the above

    **Answer: d**

4. IS-IS routers use what to establish and maintain neighbor relationships?

    a. OSHs

    b. IIHs

    c. ISKs

    d. CLHs

    **Answer: b**

5. As soon as neighbor adjacency is established, IS-IS routers exchange link-state information using what?

    a. Link-state packets

    b. Logical state packets

    c. Adjacency state packets

    d. Reachability state packets

    **Answer: a**

6. Why can IS-IS be considered superior to OSPF? (Select the two best answers.)

    a. More commands need to be configured.

    b. More timers can be fine-tuned.

    c. Faster router CPUs are required.

    d. It aggregates router updates.

    **Answer: b, d**

7. What are CLNS addresses used by routers called?

    a. DSAPs

    b. ESAPs

    c. MSAPs

    d. NSAPs

    **Answer: d**

8. What are NSAP addresses equivalent to?

    a. A combination of the IP address and upper-layer protocol in an IP header

    b. Layer 2 addresses

    c. A combination of the transport layer address and data link address

    d. Layer 4 addresses

    **Answer: a**

9. The Cisco implementation of Integrated IS-IS divides the NSAP address into what three fields?

    a. The data-link address, the logical address, and the upper-layer address

    b. The PDU address, the NSAP selector, and the cluster ID

c. The area address, the system ID, and the NSAP selector

d. The transport layer address, the CPU ID, and the NSAP selector

**Answer: c**

10. True or false: Cisco routers routing CLNS data do not use addressing that conforms to the ISO 10589 standard.

**Answer: False**

11. What is the first part of a NET?

a. Zone ID

b. Area ID

c. Cluster ID

d. ISO ID

**Answer: b**

12. What kind of address is used to uniquely identify an OSI host within an IS-IS routing domain?

a. NET

b. CLSN

c. Area

d. IP

**Answer: a**

13. What kind of router is aware of only the local area topology?

a. External

b. Level 2

c. Internal

d. Level 1

**Answer: d**

14. Routing between areas is based on what?

a. Area ID

b. IP address

c. Level 2

d. Level 1/Level 2

**Answer: a**

**15.** True or false: In IS-IS, area boundaries fall on the links.

**Answer: True**

**16.** True or false: Symmetrical routing is a feature of IS-IS.

**Answer: False**

**17.** In IS-IS, PDUs are encapsulated directly into an OSI data-link frame, so there is no what?

   a. ISO or area ID header

   b. CLNP or IP header

   c. ES or IP header

   d. CLNS or area ID header

**Answer: b**

**18.** Cisco IOS software automatically uses broadcast mode for which two of the following?

   a. Dialer interfaces

   b. LAN interfaces

   c. Multipoint WAN interfaces

   d. Point-to-point subinterfaces

**Answer: b, c**

**19.** True or false: IS-IS offers support specifically for NBMA networks.

**Answer: False**

**20.** In IS-IS, rather than having each router connected to the LAN advertise an adjacency with every other router on the LAN, the entire network is considered a router. This is called what?

   a. Area

   b. Cluster

   c. LSDB

   d. Pseudonode

**Answer: d**

**21.** True or false: IS-IS maintains the L1 and L2 LSPs in different LSDBs.

**Answer: True**

**22.** True or false: CSNPs are periodically sent on point-to-point links.

**Answer: False**

# Chapter 7

**1.** What are some of the things you need to consider when migrating to another routing protocol?

**Answer:**

**An accurate topology map of the network and an inventory of all network devices**

**A hierarchical network structure**

**A redistribution strategy**

**A new addressing scheme**

**Address summarization**

**2.** List some considerations when transitioning to a new IP addressing plan.

**Answer:**

**Host addressing**

**Access lists**

**NAT**

**DNS**

**Timing of the migration**

**Transition strategy**

**3.** A router is configured with a primary and secondary address on its Ethernet 0 interface. It is also configured to run EIGRP on this interface. How will the secondary address interact with EIGRP?

**Answer:  EIGRP uses an interface's primary IP address as the source of its updates, and it expects the routers on both sides of a link to belong to the same subnet. Therefore, EIGRP will not use the secondary address on the interface.**

**4.** What are the steps when migrating to a new routing protocol?

**Answer:**

**Step 1    To avoid delays, you need a clear and comprehensive timeline for all the steps in the migration, including implementing and testing the new router configurations.**

**Step 2    Determine which routing protocol is the core and which is the edge.**

**Step 3    Identify the boundary routers where the multiple routing protocols will run.**

**Step 4    Determine how you want to redistribute information between the core and edge routing protocols.**

> **Step 5**   Verify that all devices support the new routing protocol.
>
> **Step 6**   Implement and test the routing solution in a lab environment.

5. List some reasons why you might use multiple routing protocols in a network.

   **Answer:**

   **When you are migrating from an older IGP to a new IGP, multiple redistribution boundaries might exist until the new protocol has displaced the old protocol completely.**

   **You want to use another protocol, but you need to keep the old protocol because of the host systems' needs.**

   **Different departments might not want to upgrade their routers, or they might not implement a sufficiently strict filtering policy. In these cases, you can protect yourself by terminating the other routing protocol on one of your routers.**

   **If you have a mixed-router vendor environment, you can use a Cisco-specific protocol in the Cisco portion of the network and use a common protocol to communicate with non-Cisco devices.**

6. What is redistribution?

   **Answer:  Cisco routers allow internetworks using different routing protocols (autonomous systems) to exchange routing information through a feature called route redistribution. Redistribution is defined as the capability of boundary routers connecting different autonomous systems to exchange and advertise routing information between those autonomous systems.**

7. Does redistributing between two routing protocols change the routing table on the router that is doing the redistribution?

   **Answer:  No. Redistribution is always performed outbound. The router doing the redistribution does not change its routing table.**

8. What are some issues that arise with redistribution?

   **Answer:  The key issues that arise with redistribution are routing loops, incompatible routing information, and inconsistent convergence times.**

9. How can a routing loop result in a network that has redundant paths between two routing processes?

   **Answer:  Depending on how you employ redistribution, routers can send routing information received from one autonomous system back into that same autonomous system. The feedback is similar to the routing loop problem that occurs in distance vector protocols.**

10. What two parameters do routers use to select the best path when they learn two or more routes to the same destination from different routing protocols?

Answer:

**Administrative distance is used to rate the believability of a routing protocol. Each routing protocol is prioritized in order from most to least believable (reliable) using a value called administrative distance. This criterion is the first thing a router uses to determine which routing protocol to believe if more than one protocol provides route information for the same destination.**

**The routing metric is a value representing the path between the local router and the destination network. The metric is usually a hop or cost value, depending on the protocol being used.**

**11.** Fill in the default administrative distances for the following routing protocols.

Answer:

| Routing Protocols | Default Administrative Distance Value |
|---|---|
| Connected interface | 0 |
| Static route out an interface | 0 |
| Static route to a next-hop address | 1 |
| EIGRP summary route | 5 |
| External BGP | 20 |
| Internal EIGRP | 90 |
| IGRP | 100 |
| OSPF | 110 |
| IS-IS | 115 |
| RIP version 1 and RIP version 2 | 120 |
| EGP | 140 |
| On-Demand Routing (ODR) | 160 |
| External EIGRP | 170 |
| Internal BGP | 200 |
| Unknown | 255 |

**12.** When configuring a default metric for redistributed routes, should the metric be set to a value *larger* or *smaller* than the largest metric within the receiving AS?

**Answer:  When configuring a default metric for redistributed routes, set the metric to a value larger than the largest metric within the receiving AS.**

**13.** Fill in the default seed metrics for the following protocols.

**Answer:**

| Protocol That the Route Is Redistributed Into | Default Seed Metric |
|---|---|
| RIP | Infinity |
| IGRP/EIGRP | Infinity |
| OSPF | 20 for all except BGP, which is 1 |
| IS-IS | 0 |
| BGP | BGP metric is set to IGP metric value |

14. What is the safest way to perform redistribution between two routing protocols?

    **Answer: The safest way to perform redistribution is to redistribute routes in only one direction on only one boundary router within the network.**

15. Can redistribution be configured between IPX RIP and IP RIP? Between IPX EIGRP and IP EIGRP? Between IGRP and OSPF?

    **Answer: You can redistribute only protocols that support the same protocol stack. Therefore, redistribution cannot be configured between IPX RIP and IP RIP or between IPX EIGRP and IP EIGRP. Redistribution can be configured between IGRP and OSPF.**

16. When configuring redistribution into RIP, what is the *metric-value* parameter?

    **Answer: The *metric-value* parameter in the redistribute command for RIP is an optional parameter used to specify the RIP seed metric for the redistributed route. The default seed metric for RIP is 0, which is interpreted as infinity. The metric for RIP is hop count.**

17. Router A is running RIP and OSPF. In the RIP domain, it learns about the 10.1.0.0/16 and 10.3.0.0/16 routes. In the OSPF domain, it learns about the 10.5.0.0/16 and 172.16.1.0/24 routes. What is the result of the following configuration on Router A?

    ```
    router ospf 1
      redistribute rip metric 20
    ```

    **Answer: The subnets keyword is not configured on this redistribute command. As a result, the 10.1.0.0/16 and 10.3.0.0/16 routes are *not* redistributed into the OSPF domain.**

18. What are the five components of the EIGRP routing metric?

    **Answer:**

    **Bandwidth—The route's minimum bandwidth in kbps.**

    **Delay—Route delay in tens of microseconds.**

**Reliability**—The likelihood of successful packet transmission expressed as a number from 0 to 255, where 255 means that the route is 100 percent reliable.

**Loading**—The route's effective loading, expressed as a number from 1 to 255, where 255 means that the route is 100 percent loaded.

**MTU**—Maximum transmission unit, the maximum packet size along the route in bytes. An integer greater than or equal to 1.

**19.** When redistributing routes into IS-IS, what is the default *level-value* parameter?

**Answer:  The default for *level-value* is level-2.**

**20.** What happens if you use the **metric** parameter in the **redistribute** command and you use the **default-metric** command?

**Answer:  If you use the metric parameter in the redistribute command, you can set a different default metric for each protocol being redistributed. A metric configured in a redistribute command overrides the value in the default-metric command for that one protocol.**

**21.** What does the **passive-interface default** command do?

**Answer:  The passive-interface command prevents routing updates for a routing protocol from being sent through a router interface. The passive-interface default command sets all router interfaces to passive.**

**22.** Suppose you have a dialup WAN connection between site A and site B. What can you do to prevent excess routing update traffic from crossing the link but still have the boundary routers know the networks that are at the remote sites?

**Answer:  Use static routes, possibly in combination with passive interfaces.**

**23.** What command causes RIP to source a default route?

**Answer:  When running RIPv1, you can create the default route by using the ip default-network command. If the router has a directly connected interface onto the network specified in the ip default-network command, RIP generates (sources) a default route to its RIP neighbor routers.**

**24.** A distribute list allows routing updates to be filtered based on what?

**Answer:**

**Incoming interface**

**Outgoing interface**

**Redistribution from another routing protocol**

**25.** What is the difference between the **distribute-list out** and **distribute-list in** commands?

**Answer:**

**The distribute-list out command filters updates going *out of* the interface or routing protocol specified in the command, *into* the routing process under which it is configured.**

**The distribute-list in command filters updates going *into* the interface specified in the command, *into* the routing process under which it is configured.**

26. What command is used to configure filtering of the routing update traffic from an interface? At what prompt is this command entered?

    **Answer:  To assign an access list to filter outgoing routing updates, use the distribute-list {*access-list-number | name*} out *interface-name* command. This command is entered at the Router(config-router)# prompt.**

27. True or false: In a route map statement with multiple **match** commands, all match statements in the route map statement must be considered true for the route map statement to be considered matched.

    **Answer:  True.**

28. True or false: In a match statement with multiple conditions, all conditions in the match statement must be true for that match statement to be considered a match.

    **Answer:  False. In a single match statement that contains multiple conditions, at least one condition in the match statement must be true for that match statement to be considered a match.**

29. What are some applications of route maps?

    **Answer:**

    **Route filtering during redistribution**

    **PBR**

    **NAT**

    **BGP**

30. What is the *map-tag* parameter in a **route-map** command?

    **Answer:  *map-tag* is the name of the route map.**

31. What commands would be used to configure the use of a route map called TESTING when redistributing OSPF 10 traffic into RIP?

    **Answer:**

    ```
    router rip
      redistribute ospf 10 route-map TESTING
    ```

**32.** What does the following command do?

```
distance 150 0.0.0.0 255.255.255.255 3
```

**Answer: The distance command is used to change the default administrative distance of routes from specific source addresses that are permitted by an access list. The parameters in this command are as follows:**

| Parameter | Description |
|---|---|
| 150 | Defines the administrative distance that specified routes are assigned. |
| 0.0.0.0 255.255.255.255 | Defines the source address of the router supplying the routing information—in this case, any router. |
| 3 | Defines the access list to be used to filter incoming routing updates to determine which will have their administrative distance changed. |

**Thus, routes matching access list 3 from any router are assigned an administrative distance of 150.**

**33.** What command can be used to discover the path that a packet takes through a network?

**Answer: The traceroute privileged EXEC command.**

**34.** What are some benefits of PBR?

**Answer:**

**Source-based transit provider selection—ISPs and other organizations can use PBR to route traffic originating from different sets of users through different Internet connections across policy routers.**

**QoS—Organizations can provide QoS to differentiated traffic by setting the precedence or ToS values in the IP packet headers in routers at the network's periphery and then leveraging queuing mechanisms to prioritize traffic in the network's core or backbone.**

**Cost savings—An organization can direct the bulk traffic associated with a specific activity to use a higher-bandwidth, high-cost link for a short time and to continue basic connectivity over a lower-bandwidth, low-cost link for interactive traffic.**

**Load sharing—Network managers can implement policies to distribute traffic among multiple paths based on the traffic characteristics.**

**35.** Which parameters can PBR use to determine how a packet is routed?

**Answer: Instead of routing by the destination address, PBR allows network administrators to determine and implement routing policies based on the following criteria:**

**The identity of a source system**

The application being run

The protocol in use

The size of packets

**36.** An interface configured for PBR includes a **deny** statement in the route map. What happens to a packet that matches the criteria in this statement?

**Answer: When a route map statement is marked as deny, a packet meeting the match criteria is sent through the normal forwarding channels (in other words, destination-based routing is performed).**

**37.** In which order are the following **set** commands evaluated for PBR?

— **set ip default next-hop**

— **set default interface**

— **set interface**

— **set ip next-hop**

**Answer:**

**set ip next-hop**

**set interface**

**set ip default next-hop**

**set default interface**

**38.** When is a packet routed to the next hop specified by the **set ip default next-hop** command?

**Answer: A packet is routed to the next hop specified by the set ip default next-hop command only if there is no explicit route for the packet's destination address in the routing table.**

**39.** What command is used for policy-based routing to establish criteria based on the packet length?

**Answer: The match length *min max* route map configuration command can be used to establish criteria based on the packet length between specified minimum and maximum values.**

**40.** Policy-based routing is applied to which packets on an interface?

**Answer: Policy-based routing is applied to incoming packets on an interface.**

**41.** What command is used to display the route maps used for policy routing?

**Answer: To display the route maps used for policy routing on the router's interfaces, use the show ip policy EXEC command.**

# Chapter 8

1. What is the difference between an IGP and an EGP?

   **Answer:  An IGP is a routing protocol used to exchange routing information within an AS. An EGP is a routing protocol used to connect between autonomous systems.**

2. What type of routing protocol is BGP?

   **Answer:  BGP is an exterior path-vector routing protocol.**

3. A BGP router knows of three paths to a network and has chosen the best path. Can this BGP router advertise to its peer routers a route to that network other than the best path?

   **Answer:  No. BGP specifies that a BGP router can advertise to its peers in neighboring autonomous systems only those routes that it itself uses—in other words, its best path.**

4. When is it appropriate to use BGP to connect to other autonomous systems?

   **Answer:  BGP use in an AS is most appropriate when the effects of BGP are well-understood and at least one of the following conditions exists:**

   **The AS allows packets to transit through it to reach other autonomous systems (for example, it is a service provider).**

   **The AS has multiple connections to other autonomous systems.**

   **The flow of traffic entering and leaving the AS must be manipulated.**

5. When is it appropriate to use static routes rather than BGP to interconnect autonomous systems?

   **Answer:  It is appropriate to use static routes rather than BGP if at least one of the following conditions exists:**

   **A single connection to the Internet or another AS**

   **Lack of memory or processor power on routers to handle constant BGP updates**

   **Limited understanding of route filtering and the BGP path-selection process**

   **Low bandwidth between autonomous systems**

6. What protocol does BGP use as its transport protocol? What port number does BGP use?

   **Answer:  BGP uses TCP as its transport protocol; port 179 has been assigned to BGP.**

7. How does BGP guarantee a loop-free AS path?

   **Answer:  The BGP AS path is guaranteed to always be loop-free, because a router running BGP does not accept a routing update that already includes its AS number in the path list. Because the update has already passed through its AS, accepting it again would result in a routing loop.**

**8.** Any two routers that have formed a BGP connection can be referred to by what two terms?

**Answer: Any two routers that have formed a BGP connection are called BGP peer routers or BGP neighbors.**

**9.** Write a brief definition for each of the following:

— IBGP

— EBGP

— Well-known attribute

— Transitive attribute

— BGP synchronization

**Answer:**

**IBGP—When BGP is running between routers within one AS, it is called IBGP.**

**EBGP—When BGP is running between routers in different autonomous systems, it is called EBGP.**

**Well-known attribute—A well-known attribute is one that all BGP implementations must recognize. Well-known attributes are propagated to BGP neighbors.**

**Transitive attribute—A transitive attribute that is not implemented in a router can be passed to other BGP routers untouched.**

**BGP synchronization—The BGP synchronization rule states that a BGP router should not use or advertise to an external neighbor a route learned by IBGP unless that route is local or is learned from an IGP.**

**10.** What tables are used by BGP?

**Answer: A router running BGP keeps its own table for storing BGP information received from and sent to other routers. This table is separate from the IP routing table in the router. The router can be configured to share information between the BGP table and the IP routing table. BGP also keeps a neighbor table containing a list of neighbors that it has a BGP connection with.**

**11.** What are the four BGP message types?

**Answer: The four BGP message types are open, keepalive, update, and notification.**

**12.** How is the BGP router ID selected?

**Answer: The BGP router ID is an IP address assigned to that router and is determined on startup. The BGP router ID is chosen the same way that the OSPF router ID is chosen—it is the highest active IP address on the router, unless a loopback interface with an IP address exists, in which case it is the highest such loopback IP address. Alternatively, the router ID can be statically configured, overriding the automatic selection.**

**13.** What are the BGP states a router can be in with its neighbors?

**Answer: BGP is a state machine that takes a router through the following states with its neighbors:**

**Idle**

**Connect**

**Active**

**Open sent**

**Open confirm**

**Established**

**Only when the connection is in the established state are update, keepalive, and notification messages exchanged.**

**14.** What type of BGP attributes are the following?

— AS-path

— Next-hop

— Origin

— Local preference

— Atomic aggregate

— Aggregator

— Community

— Multiexit-discriminator

**Answer:**

**The following are well-known mandatory attributes:**

**AS-path**

**Next-hop**

**Origin**

**The following are well-known discretionary attributes:**

**Local preference**

**Atomic aggregate**

**The following are optional transitive attributes:**

**Aggregator**

**Community**

**The multi-exit-discriminator is an optional nontransitive attribute.**

**15.** When IBGP advertises an external update, where does the value for the next-hop attribute of an update come from?

**Answer:  When IBGP advertises an external update, the value of the next-hop attribute is carried from the EBGP update.**

**16.** Describe the complication that an NBMA network can cause for an update's next-hop attribute.

**Answer:  When running BGP over a multiaccess network, a BGP router uses the appropriate address as the next-hop address to avoid inserting additional hops into the network. The address used is of the router on the multiaccess network that advertised the network. On Ethernet networks, that router is accessible to all other routers on the Ethernet. On NBMA media, however, not all routers on the network might be accessible to each other, so the next-hop address used might be unreachable.**

**17.** Complete the following table to answer these questions about three BGP attributes:

— In which order are the attributes preferred (1, 2, or 3)?

— For the attribute, is the highest or lowest value preferred?

— Which other routers, if any, is the attribute sent to?

**Answer:**

| Attribute | Order Preferred In | Highest or Lowest Value Preferred? | Sent to Which Other Routers? |
|---|---|---|---|
| Local preference | 2 | Highest | Internal BGP neighbors only |
| MED | 3 | Lowest | External BGP neighbors only |
| Weight | 1 | Highest | Not sent to any BGP neighbors; local to the router only |

**18.** What is the BGP split-horizon rule?

**Answer:  It specifies that routes learned via IBGP are never propagated to other IBGP peers.**

**19.** When is it safe to turn off BGP synchronization?

**Answer:  It is safe to turn off synchronization only if all routers in the transit path in the AS (in other words, in the path between the BGP border routers) are running BGP.**

**20.** What does the **neighbor 10.1.1.1 ebgp-multihop** command do?

**Answer:  The neighbor 10.1.1.1 ebgp-multihop command sets the time to live for the EBGP connection to 10.1.1.1 to 255 (by default). This command is necessary if the EBGP neighbor address 10.1.1.1 is not directly connected to this router.**

**21.** Which commands are used to configure Routers A and B if Router A is to run BGP in AS 65000 and establish a neighbor relationship with Router B in AS 65001? The two routers should use their loopback 0 addresses to establish the BGP connection; Router A has loopback 0 address 10.1.1.1/24, and Router B has loopback 0 address 10.2.2.2/24.

**Answer: The BGP configuration for Router A is as follows:**

```
RouterA(config)#router bgp 65000
RouterA(config-router)#neighbor 10.2.2.2 remote-as 65001
RouterA(config-router)#neighbor 10.2.2.2 update-source loopback 0
RouterA(config-router)#neighbor 10.2.2.2 ebgp-multihop
```

**The BGP configuration for Router B is as follows:**

```
RouterB(config)#router bgp 65001
RouterB(config-router)#neighbor 10.1.1.1 remote-as 65000
RouterB(config-router)#neighbor 10.1.1.1 update-source loopback 0
RouterB(config-router)#neighbor 10.1.1.1 ebgp-multihop
```

**22.** What command disables BGP synchronization?

**Answer: Use the no synchronization router configuration command to disable BGP synchronization.**

**23.** Which command would Router A in AS 65000 use to activate an IBGP session with Router B, 10.1.1.1, also in AS 65000?

**Answer: The neighbor 10.1.1.1 remote-as 65000 router configuration command would be used.**

**24.** What is the difference between the BGP **neighbor** command and the BGP **network** command?

**Answer: The neighbor command tells BGP *where* to advertise. The network command tells BGP *what* to advertise.**

**25.** What does the BGP command **network 198.1.1.1 mask 255.255.255.0** do?

**Answer: If you configure network 198.1.1.1 mask 255.255.255.0, BGP looks for 198.1.1.1/24 in the routing table. It might find 198.1.1.0/24 or 198.1.1.1/32, but it will never find 198.1.1.1/24. Because the routing table does not contain a specific match to the network, BGP does not announce the 198.1.1.1/24 network to any neighbors.**

**26.** What does the **clear ip bgp 10.1.1.1 soft out** command do?

**Answer: The soft out option of the clear ip bgp command allows BGP to do a soft reset for outbound updates. The router issuing the soft out command does not reset the BGP session; instead, the router creates a new update and sends the whole table to the specified neighbors. This update includes withdrawal commands for networks that the other neighbor will not see anymore based on the new outbound policy. Outbound BGP soft configuration does not have any memory overhead.**

> To make the new inbound policy take effect, you can trigger an outbound reconfiguration on the other side of the BGP session.

27. Which command is used to display detailed information about BGP connections to neighbors?

    **Answer: The show ip bgp neighbors command is used to display detailed information about BGP connections to neighbors.**

28. What does a > in the output of the **show ip bgp** command mean?

    **Answer: The > indicates the best path for a route selected by BGP; this route is offered to the IP routing table.**

29. What column in the **show ip bgp** command output displays the MED?

    **Answer: The metric column displays the MED.**

30. How is the established neighbor state represented in the output of the **show ip bgp summary** command?

    **Answer: If the neighbor state is established, the State/PfxRcd column either is blank or has a number in it. The number represents how many BGP network entries have been received from this neighbor.**

31. What command is used to see a BGP router progress through the various states with its neighbors and see the BGP handshaking?

    **Answer: Use the debug ip bgp events command to view BGP handshaking for neighbor establishment.**

# Chapter 9

1. How does BGP-4 support CIDR?

   **Answer:**

   **BGP-4 support for CIDR includes the following:**

   **The BGP update message includes both the prefix and the prefix length. Previous versions included only the prefix; the length was assumed from the address class.**

   **Addresses can be aggregated when advertised by a BGP router.**

   **The AS path attribute can include a combined unordered list of all autonomous systems that all the aggregated routes have passed through. This combined list should be considered to ensure that the route is loop-free.**

**2.** Describe the BGP atomic aggregate and aggregator attributes.

**Answer:**

**The atomic aggregate is a well-known discretionary attribute that informs the neighbor AS that the originating router has aggregated the routes.**

**The aggregator is an optional transitive attribute that specifies the BGP router ID and AS number of the router that performed the route aggregation.**

**3.** What is the default mask on the BGP **network** *network-number* [**mask** *network-mask*] router configuration command?

**Answer:  The default mask is the classful mask. It causes only the classful network number to be announced. At least one subnet of the specified major network must be present in the IP routing table for BGP to start announcing the classful network.**

**4.** A BGP router has network 172.16.25.0/24 in the routing table as a directly connected network. The BGP command **network 172.16.0.0** is configured on the router. What network does the router announce to its BGP neighbors?

**Answer:  The router announces the 172.16.0.0/16 network to its BGP neighbors.**

**5.** What is the preferred method to use to advertise an aggregated route from an AS into BGP?

**Answer:  The preferred method is to use the aggregate-address command. With this command, as long as a more specific route exists in the BGP table, the aggregate gets sent. If the aggregating router loses all its specific connections to the networks being aggregated, the aggregate route disappears from the BGP table, and the BGP aggregate doesn't get sent.**

**6.** What is the difference between using the **network** command and using the **aggregate-address** command for summarization?

**Answer:  The aggregate-address command aggregates only networks that are already in the BGP table. This is different from the requirement for advertising summaries with the BGP network command, in which case the network must exist in the IP routing table.**

**7.** Which option of the **aggregate-address** command affects the atomic aggregate attribute?

**Answer:  The atomic aggregate attribute is set unless you specify the as-set keyword in the aggregate-address command.**

**8.** Which option in the **aggregate-address** command affects the number of routes advertised to other routers?

**Answer:  The summary-only option of the aggregate-address command suppresses the more specific routes covered by the route summary. When the more specific routes are suppressed, they are still present in the BGP table of the router doing the aggregation.**

**9.** Describe the different functions of the BGP **network**, **neighbor**, and **aggregate-address** commands.

**Answer:  The network command tells BGP *what* to advertise. The neighbor command tells BGP *where* to advertise. The aggregate-address command tells BGP *how* to advertise the networks.**

**10.** How can BGP path manipulation affect the relative bandwidth used between two connections to the Internet?

**Answer:  BGP path manipulation can affect which traffic uses which Internet connection. For example, all traffic going to a particular IP address or AS can be forced to go out one connection to the Internet, and all other traffic can be routed out the other connection. Depending on the volume of Internet traffic, the bandwidth of these connections is affected.**

**11.** Complete the following table to answer these questions about BGP attributes:

— In which order are the attributes preferred (1, 2, or 3)?

— For the attribute, is the highest or lowest value preferred?

— What is the attribute's default value?

— Which other routers, if any, is the attribute sent to?

**Answer:**

| Attribute | Order in Which It Is Preferred | Highest or Lowest Value Preferred? | Default Value | Sent to Which Other Routers? |
|---|---|---|---|---|
| Local preference | 2 | Highest | 100 | Sent to internal BGP neighbors only |
| MED | 3 | Lowest | 0 | Sent to external BGP neighbors only |
| Weight | 1 | Highest | 32768 for local routes (routes that the router originates); other routes have a weight of 0 by default | Not sent to any BGP neighbors; local to the router only |

**12.** Describe what the following configuration on Router A does:

```
route-map local_pref permit 10
match ip address 65
set local-preference 300
route-map local_pref permit 20
router bgp 65001
neighbor 192.168.5.3 remote-as 65002
neighbor 192.168.5.3 route-map local_pref in
```

**Answer:  The first line of the route map is a permit statement with a sequence number of 10 for a route map called local_pref; this defines the first route-map statement. The match condition for this statement checks all networks that are permitted by access list 65. The route map sets these networks to a local preference of 300. The second statement in the route map is a permit statement with a sequence number of 20 for the route map called local_pref, but it does not have any match or set statements. Because there are no match conditions for the remaining networks, they are all permitted with their current settings. In this case, the local preference for the remaining networks stays set at the default of 100. This route map is linked to neighbor 192.168.5.3 as an inbound route map. Therefore, as Router A receives updates from 192.168.5.3, it processes them through the local_pref route map and sets the local preference accordingly as the networks are placed into Router A's BGP forwarding table.**

**13.** Place the BGP route selection criteria in order from the first step to the last step evaluated by placing a number in the blank provided.

**Answer:**

　　**10**　　Prefer the path with the lowest neighbor BGP router ID.

　　**6**　　Prefer the lowest MED.

　　**4**　　Prefer the shortest AS path.

　　**9**　　Prefer the oldest route for EBGP paths.

　　**5**　　Prefer the lowest origin code.

　　**1**　　Prefer the highest weight.

　　**8**　　Prefer the path through the closest IGP neighbor.

　　**2**　　Prefer the highest local preference.

　　**3**　　Prefer the route originated by the local router.

　　**7**　　Prefer the EBGP path over the IBGP path.

**14.** What command is used to assign a weight to a BGP neighbor connection?

**Answer:  The neighbor *ip-address* weight *weight* router configuration command is used to assign a weight to a neighbor connection.**

**15.** What is BGP multihoming?

**Answer:  Multihoming describes when an AS is connected to more than one ISP. This is usually done for one of the following reasons:**

**To increase the reliability of the Internet connection so that if one connection fails, another is still available**

**To increase performance so that better paths to certain destinations can be used**

**16.** What are three common design options for BGP multihoming?

**Answer:**

**All ISPs pass only default routes to the AS.**

**All ISPs pass default routes and selected specific routes to the AS.**

**All ISPs pass all routes to the AS.**

**17.** What are some advantages of getting default routes and selected specific routes from your ISPs?

**Answer:  Acquiring a partial BGP table from each ISP is beneficial because path selection for outbound and inbound traffic is more predictable than using a default route. For example, the ISP that a specific router within the AS uses to reach the networks that are passed into the AS usually is the shortest AS path. If instead only default routes are passed into the AS, the ISP that a specific router within the AS uses to reach any external address is decided by the IGP metric used to reach the default route within the AS.**

**18.** What is a disadvantage of having all ISPs pass all BGP routes into your AS?

**Answer:  This configuration requires a lot of resources within the AS, because it must process all the external routes.**

# Appendix A

**1.** You need to design an IP network for your organization whose IP address is 172.16.0.0. Your assessment indicates that the organization needs at least 130 networks of no more than 100 nodes in each network.

As a result, you have decided to use a classful subnetting scheme based on the 172.16.0.0/24 scheme. Write down any four IP addresses that are part of the range of subnetwork numbers, and write down the subnet address and subnet mask for these addresses. An example is the address 172.16.1.7/24, which is on subnet 172.16.1.0 255.255.255.0.

**Answer:  Four addresses in this subnet are as follows:**

| IP Address | Subnet Address and Mask |
|---|---|
| 172.16.2.9/24 | 172.16.2.0 255.255.255.0 |
| 172.16.3.11/24 | 172.16.3.0 255.255.255.0 |
| 172.16.4.12/24 | 172.16.4.0 255.255.255.0 |
| 172.16.255.2/24 | 172.16.255.0 255.255.255.0 |

2. Your network has the address 172.16.168.0/21. Write eight IP addresses in this network.

   **Answer:**

   **172.16.168.1**

   **172.16.168.255**

   **172.16.169.1**

   **172.16.175.253**

   **172.16.168.2**

   **172.16.169.0**

   **172.16.169.2**

   **172.16.175.254**

3. Write the four IP addresses in the range described by the address 192.168.99.16/30.

   **Answer:**

   **192.168.99.16**

   **192.168.99.17**

   **192.168.99.18**

   **192.168.99.19**

4. Of the four addresses in question 3, which two could you use as host addresses in a point-to-point connection?

   **Answer:  192.168.99.17 and 192.168.99.18.**

5. Figure A-25 shows the network for this question.

**Figure A-25** *Network for Review Question 5*

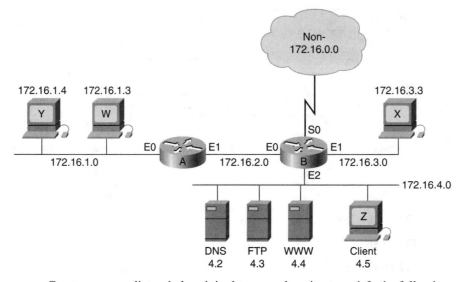

Create an access list and place it in the proper location to satisfy the following requirements:

— Prevent all hosts on subnet 172.16.1.0/24, except host 172.16.1.3, from accessing the web server on subnet 172.16.4.0. Allow all other hosts, including those from the outside world, to access the web server.

— Prevent the outside world from pinging subnet 172.16.4.0.

— Allow all hosts on all subnets of network 172.16.0.0 (using subnet mask 255.255.255.0) to send queries to the DNS server on subnet 172.16.4.0. The outside world is not allowed to access the DNS server.

— Prevent host 172.16.3.3 from accessing subnet 172.16.4.0 for any reason.

— Prevent all other access to the 172.16.4.0 subnet.

In your configuration, be sure to include the router name (A or B), interface name (E0, E1, or E2), and access list direction (in or out).

**Answer:**

**Global commands: Configuration for Router B:**

```
access-list 104 deny ip host 172.16.3.3 172.16.4.0 0.0.0.255
access-list 104 permit tcp host 172.16.1.3 172.16.4.0 0.0.0.255 eq 80
access-list 104 deny tcp 172.16.1.0 0.0.0.255 172.16.4.0 0.0.0.255 eq 80
access-list 104 permit tcp any any eq 80
access-list 104 permit udp 172.16.0.0 0.0.255.255 172.16.4.0 0.0.0.255 eq dns
```

**Interface commands:**

```
interface e2
ip access-group 104 out
```

6. What do bits set to 1 in a wildcard mask indicate when matching an address?

   **Answer:  Bits set to 1 in a wildcard mask indicate that the corresponding bits in the address are ignored when matching an address in a packet to the address in the access list.**

7. By default, what happens to all traffic in an access list?

   **Answer:  By default, all traffic is denied by an access list.**

8. Where should you place an extended access list to save network resources?

   **Answer:  An extended access list should be placed close to the source to save network resources.**

9. Using the keyword **host** in an access list is a substitute for using what value of a wildcard mask?

   **Answer:  The keyword host is a substitute for a wildcard mask of 0.0.0.0.**

This appendix contains information on the equipment requirements for the Configuration Exercises in this book, along with the initial configuration commands for the routers.

This appendix is organized into the following sections:

- Configuration Exercise Equipment Requirements
- Configuration Exercise Setup Diagram
- Configuration Exercise Equipment Wiring
- Backbone Router Configurations
- TFTP Server and Pod Router Configurations

# Configuration Exercise Equipment Requirements and Initial Configurations

This book provides Configuration Exercises to give you practice in configuring routers. If you have access to real hardware, you can try these exercises on your routers; this appendix provides a list of recommended equipment and initial configuration commands for the routers. However, even if you don't have access to any routers, you can go through the exercises and keep a log of your own running configurations. Commands used and solutions to the Configuration Exercises are provided after the exercises in each chapter.

## Configuration Exercise Equipment Requirements

In the Configuration Exercises in this book, the network is assumed to consist of two pods, each with four routers. The pods are interconnected to a backbone. You configure one of the pods, pod 1. No interaction between the two pods is required, although you might see some routes from the other pod in your routing tables in some exercises if you have it configured (the Configuration Exercise answers do show the routes from the other pod). In most of the exercises, the backbone has only one router; in some cases, another router is added to the backbone. Each of the Configuration Exercises in this book assumes that you have completed the previous chapters' Configuration Exercises on your pod.

The equipment listed in Table H-1 is for two pods (each with four routers) and the backbone (with three routers).

The lab diagrams and configurations provided for the 3620 Frame Relay backbone router assume that the serial port network module (NM-8A/S) is installed in slot 1 (on the left).

**Table H-1**    *Configuration Exercise Equipment Requirements for Two Pods and the Backbone*

| Quantity | Required Product Description | Recommended Product Number |
|---|---|---|
| 3 | PC running Windows 95 and Hyperterminal, with one COM port. One per pod and one for the backbone. The backbone PC also functions as the TFTP server and must therefore also have TFTP server software installed. | — |
| 3 | A/B/C/D switch to connect the pod or backbone PC to routers. | — |
| 1 | Hub or switch to interconnect backbone routers. | — |
| 4 | Router with one Ethernet port and one serial port (two per pod). | Cisco 2500 or Cisco 2600 (we used 2514) |
| 4 | Router with two serial ports and one Ethernet port (two per pod). | Cisco 2500 or Cisco 2600 (we used 2514) |
| 2 | Router with one Ethernet port and one serial port (for the backbone). | Cisco 2500 or Cisco 2600 (we used 2520) |
| 1 | Router with one Ethernet port and six serial ports (for the Frame Relay backbone). | Cisco 3620 or 3640 (we used 3620) |
| 10 | Version 12.1(18) or later Cisco IOS Enterprise software for the pod and backbone routers (see the documentation for Flash and RAM memory requirements for your routers). | We used 12.1(19): c2500-js-l.121-9a.bin |
| 1 | Version 12.0(3) or later Cisco IOS Enterprise Plus software for the Frame Relay backbone router (see the documentation for Flash and RAM memory requirements for your router). | We used 12.0(3): c3620-js-mz_120-3c.bin |
| 1 | Eight-port asynchronous/synchronous serial network module (for a Frame Relay backbone router; six serial ports required). | NM-8A/S |
| 11 | Power cord, 110V. | CAB-AC |
| 10 | V.35 cable, DCE, female, 10 feet. | CAB-V35FC |
| 10 | V.35 cable, DTE, male, 10 feet. | CAB-V35MT |
| 4 | Ethernet crossover cable. | — |
| 3 | Ethernet straight-through cable. | — |

# Configuration Exercise Setup Diagram

The network consists of the following:

- Two pods, each with four routers named P$x$R1, P$x$R2, P$x$R3, and P$x$R4, where $x$ = the pod number
- Two backbone routers, named BBR1 and BBR2
- A third backbone router used as a Frame Relay switch, named Frame_Switch

The Configuration Exercise setup diagram is shown in Figure H-1.

**Figure H-1** *Configuration Exercise Setup Diagram*

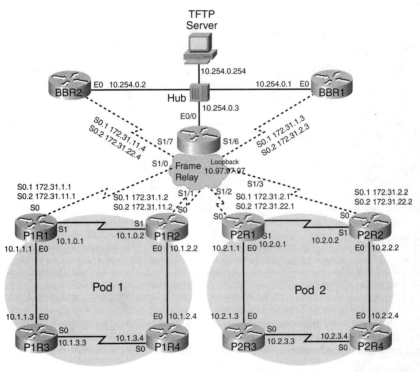

On All Pod Routers Loopback 0: 10.200.200.xy/32

---

**NOTE**  Figure H-1 is also posted on the Cisco Press website, at www.ciscopress.com/158705146X, so that you can print it and copy it when you are doing the Configuration Exercises.

---

The backbone router addresses shown in Figure H-1 are in the configurations provided in the "Backbone Router Configurations" section later in this chapter. The addresses shown for the pod routers will be configured in the Configuration Exercises; part of the pod router configurations will be downloaded from a TFTP server. These TFTP configurations are provided in the "TFTP Server and Pod Router Configurations" section later in this chapter.

---

**NOTE**    The hub shown in Figure H-1 is not shown in subsequent Configuration Exercise network diagrams.

---

# Configuration Exercise Equipment Wiring

The Frame Relay backbone 3620 router requires six serial ports. All interfaces on the 3620 router are DCE. The Serial 1 interfaces on the P*x*R1 routers are DCE. The Serial 0 interfaces on the P*x*R3 routers are DCE. All other serial interfaces are DTE.

The Frame_Switch Frame Relay backbone router interfaces should be cabled as shown in Table H-2. (Note that interfaces S1/4 and S1/5 on Frame_Switch are unused.)

**Table H-2**    *Frame_Switch Cabling*

| Frame_Switch Interface | Pod Router and Interface |
|---|---|
| S1/0 DCE | P1R1 S0 DTE |
| S1/1 DCE | P1R2 S0 DTE |
| S1/2 DCE | P2R1 S0 DTE |
| S1/3 DCE | P2R2 S0 DTE |
| S1/6 DCE | BBR1 S0 DTE |
| S1/7 DCE | BBR2 S0 DTE |
| E0/0 | Hub |

The BBR1 and BBR2 E0 router interfaces should be connected to the hub.

The remaining pod router interfaces should be cabled as shown in Table H-3.

**Table H-3**    *Other Pod Interface Cabling*

| This Interface | Goes to This Interface |
|---|---|
| P*x*R1 S1 (DCE) | P*x*R2 S1 (DTE) |
| P*x*R3 S0 (DCE) | P*x*R4 S0 (DTE) |
| P*x*R1 E0 | P*x*R3 E0 |
| P*x*R2 E0 | P*x*R4 E0 |

# Backbone Router Configurations

The backbone routers need to be configured only once, before the first Configuration Exercise.

The text of the configurations is provided in the following sections. To use the configurations, create text files from the information provided. These configurations are written to be sent using the Transfer, Send Text File menu command in Hyperterminal into the devices' console port. Each configuration assumes that the router has no configuration. In other words, it assumes that the startup configuration has been erased and that the router has been reloaded.

| NOTE | The backbone router configurations are also posted as text files on the Cisco Press website at www.ciscopress.com/158705146X. |
|------|------|

| NOTE | You might need to modify the configurations provided so that they work with the specific routers you are using. For example, if you have routers with modular interfaces where we used routers with fixed interfaces, you have to change how the interfaces are referenced. |
|------|------|

Before sending a configuration file, go into privileged EXEC mode on the router. The configurations have **config t** commands at the beginning, followed by the necessary configuration commands, and then commands to save the configuration into NVRAM.

| NOTE | The last command in each configuration is **copy run start**. If you create your own text files, enter a carriage return after this command and then another carriage return. This ensures that the configuration is saved and that the router returns to the privileged EXEC prompt. |
|------|------|

When testing similar configurations, we ran into a problem on some 3640 routers. Loading the files from Hyperterminal was too fast for the 3640. It would lose some of the commands, and then the rest of the file would get mixed up. To fix this problem in Hyperterminal, do the following:

- Select File, Properties.
- Click the Settings tab.
- Click the ASCII Settings button.
- Set the Line Delay to 200 milliseconds. (You might have to increase the line delay further if you get errors.)

# BBR1 Configuration

Example H-1 provides the text of the configuration file for the BBR1 router.

**Example H-1** *BBR1 Configuration*

```
!
!BBR1 configuration exercise configuration
!
! This file is designed to be copied and pasted into an erased router, at
! the # prompt.
!
! This configuration was tested with the c2500-js-1.121-9a.bin IOS image
!
conf t
service timestamps debug datetime localtime show-timezone
service timestamps log datetime localtime show-timezone
no service password-encryption
!
hostname BBR1
!
enable secret cat5
!
clock timezone EST -5
ip subnet-zero
no ip domain-lookup
ip host bbr1 10.254.0.1 172.31.1.3 172.31.2.3 172.31.3.3 172.31.4.3
ip host bbr2 10.254.0.2 172.31.11.4 172.31.22.4 172.31.33.4 172.31.44.4
ip host Frame_Switch 10.254.0.3
ip host tftp 10.254.0.254
!
!
ip host P2R4 10.2.3.4 10.2.2.4 10.200.200.24
ip host P2R3 10.2.1.3 10.2.3.3 10.200.200.23
ip host P2R2 10.2.2.2 10.2.0.2 10.22.0.2 172.31.2.2 172.31.22.2 10.200.200.22
ip host P2R1 10.2.1.1 10.2.0.1 10.22.0.1 172.31.2.1 172.31.22.1 10.200.200.21
!
ip host P1R4 10.1.3.4 10.1.2.4 10.200.200.14
ip host P1R3 10.1.1.3 10.1.3.3 10.200.200.13
ip host P1R2 10.1.2.2 10.1.0.2 10.11.0.2 172.31.1.2 172.31.11.2 10.200.200.12
ip host P1R1 10.1.1.1 10.1.0.1 10.11.0.1 172.31.1.1 172.31.11.1 10.200.200.11
!
interface Ethernet0
 description - Backbone LAN Connection
 ip address 10.254.0.1 255.255.255.0
 ip router isis
 ip rip send version 2
 ip rip receive version 2
 no shutdown
!
interface Serial0
 description - Interface for Frame Relay Multipoint
 no ip address
 encapsulation frame-relay
 no frame-relay inverse-arp
 no shutdown
```

**Example H-1**  *BBR1 Configuration (Continued)*

```
!
interface Serial0.1 multipoint
 description - Frame Relay DLCI 111 and 112 for Pod 1
 bandwidth 64
 ip address 172.31.1.3 255.255.255.0
 ip rip send version 1 2
 ip rip receive version 1 2
 ip ospf network non-broadcast
 frame-relay map ip 172.31.1.1 111 broadcast
 frame-relay map ip 172.31.1.2 112 broadcast
!
interface Serial0.2 multipoint
 description - Frame Relay DLCI 121 and 122 for Pod 2
 bandwidth 64
 ip address 172.31.2.3 255.255.255.0
 ip rip send version 1 2
 ip rip receive version 1 2
 ip ospf network non-broadcast
 frame-relay map ip 172.31.2.1 121 broadcast
 frame-relay map ip 172.31.2.2 122 broadcast
!
!
router eigrp 1
 network 10.254.0.0 0.0.0.255
 network 172.31.0.0
 distribute-list 1 in
 no auto-summary
 no eigrp log-neighbor-changes
!
router ospf 1
 router-id 100.100.100.100
 log-adjacency-changes
 redistribute connected metric 50 subnets
 network 172.31.0.0 0.0.255.255 area 0
 neighbor 172.31.2.1
 neighbor 172.31.2.2
 neighbor 172.31.1.1
 neighbor 172.31.1.2
!
router isis
 net 49.0999.8888.8888.8888.00
!
router rip
 network 10.0.0.0
 network 172.31.0.0
 distribute-list 1 in
!
router bgp 64998
 bgp log-neighbor-changes
 network 10.254.0.0 mask 255.255.255.0
 network 172.31.1.0 mask 255.255.255.0
 network 172.31.2.0 mask 255.255.255.0
```

*continues*

**Example H-1** *BBR1 Configuration (Continued)*

```
 neighbor 10.254.0.2 remote-as 64999
 neighbor 10.254.0.3 remote-as 64997
 neighbor 172.31.1.1 remote-as 65001
 neighbor 172.31.1.2 remote-as 65001
 neighbor 172.31.2.1 remote-as 65002
 neighbor 172.31.2.2 remote-as 65002
!
ip classless
ip route 192.168.1.0 255.255.255.0 172.31.1.1
ip route 192.168.2.0 255.255.255.0 172.31.2.1
ip route 192.168.11.0 255.255.255.0 172.31.1.2
ip route 192.168.22.0 255.255.255.0 172.31.2.2
no ip http server
!
access-list 1 deny   0.0.0.0
access-list 1 permit any
!
!
line con 0
 exec-timeout 0 0
 privilege level 15
 logging synchronous
line aux 0
line vty 0 4
 exec-timeout 5 0
 password cisco
 logging synchronous
 login
!
ntp server 10.254.0.2
end
copy run start
```

# BBR2 Configuration

Example H-2 provides the text of the configuration file for the BBR2 router.

**Example H-2** *BBR2 Configuration*

```
!
!BBR2 configuration exercise configuration
!
! This file is designed to be copied and pasted into an erased router, at
! the # prompt.
!
! This configuration was tested with the c2500-js-1.121-9a.bin IOS image
!
conf t
service timestamps debug datetime localtime show-timezone
service timestamps log datetime localtime show-timezone
no service password-encryption
!
```

**Example H-2**  *BBR2 Configuration (Continued)*

```
hostname BBR2
!
enable secret cat5
!
!
clock timezone EST -5
ip subnet-zero
no ip domain-lookup
!
ip host bbr1 10.254.0.1 172.31.1.3 172.31.2.3 172.31.3.3 172.31.4.3
ip host bbr2 10.254.0.2 172.31.11.4 172.31.22.4 172.31.33.4 172.31.44.4
ip host Frame_Switch 10.254.0.3
ip host tftp 10.254.0.254
!
!
ip host P2R4 10.2.3.4 10.2.2.4 10.200.200.24
ip host P2R3 10.2.1.3 10.2.3.3 10.200.200.23
ip host P2R2 10.2.2.2 10.2.0.2 10.22.0.2 172.31.2.2 172.31.22.2 10.200.200.22
ip host P2R1 10.2.1.1 10.2.0.1 10.22.0.1 172.31.2.1 172.31.22.1 10.200.200.21
!
ip host P1R4 10.3.3.4 10.1.2.4 10.200.200.14
ip host P1R3 10.1.1.3 10.1.3.3 10.200.200.13
ip host P1R2 10.1.2.2 10.1.0.2 10.11.0.2 172.31.1.2 172.31.11.2 10.200.200.12
ip host P1R1 10.1.1.1 10.1.0.1 10.11.0.1 172.31.1.1 172.31.11.1 10.200.200.11
!
!
!
interface Ethernet0
 description - Backbone LAN Connection
 ip address 10.254.0.2 255.255.255.0
 ip router isis
 no shutdown
!
interface Serial0
 description - Interface for Frame Relay Multipoint for OSPF Lab 4.3
 no ip address
 encapsulation frame-relay
 no frame-relay inverse-arp
 no shutdown
!
interface Serial0.1 multipoint
 description - Frame Relay DLCI 211 and 212 for Pod 1
 bandwidth 64
 ip address 172.31.11.4 255.255.255.0
 ip router isis
 ip ospf network point-to-multipoint
 frame-relay map clns 212 broadcast
 frame-relay map clns 211 broadcast
 frame-relay map ip 172.31.11.1 211 broadcast
 frame-relay map ip 172.31.11.2 212 broadcast
 no frame-relay inverse-arp
!
```

*continues*

**Example H-2** *BBR2 Configuration (Continued)*

```
interface Serial0.2 multipoint
 description - Frame Relay DLCI 221 and 222 for Pod 2
 bandwidth 64
 ip address 172.31.22.4 255.255.255.0
 ip router isis
 ip ospf network point-to-multipoint
 frame-relay map clns 222 broadcast
 frame-relay map clns 221 broadcast
 frame-relay map ip 172.31.22.1 221 broadcast
 frame-relay map ip 172.31.22.2 222 broadcast
!
!
router eigrp 1
 network 10.0.0.0
 no auto-summary
!
router ospf 1
 router-id 200.200.200.200
 log-adjacency-changes
 redistribute connected metric 50 subnets
 network 172.31.0.0 0.0.255.255 area 0
!
router isis
 net 49.0999.9999.9999.9999.00
!
router rip
 version 2
 passive-interface Ethernet0
 passive-interface Serial0.1
 passive-interface Serial0.2
 network 10.0.0.0
!
router bgp 64999
 bgp log-neighbor-changes
 network 172.31.11.0 mask 255.255.255.0
 network 172.31.22.0 mask 255.255.255.0
 neighbor 10.254.0.1 remote-as 64998
 neighbor 10.254.0.3 remote-as 64997
 neighbor 172.31.11.1 remote-as 65001
 neighbor 172.31.11.2 remote-as 65001
 neighbor 172.31.22.1 remote-as 65002
 neighbor 172.31.22.2 remote-as 65002
!
ip classless
no ip http server
!
!
!
line con 0
 exec-timeout 0 0
 privilege level 15
 logging synchronous
           •
```

**Example H-2**  *BBR2 Configuration (Continued)*

```
line aux 0
line vty 0 4
 exec-timeout 5 0
 password cisco
 logging synchronous
 login
!
ntp master 2
!
end
copy run start
```

# Frame_Switch Configuration

Example H-3 provides the text of the configuration file for the Frame_Switch Frame Relay backbone router.

**Example H-3**  *Frame_Switch Configuration*

```
!
!Frame_Switch configuration exercise configuration
!
! This file is designed to be copied and pasted into an erased router, at
! the # prompt. The configuration is based on 3620 Router with Ethernet
! in slot 0 and an 8-port Serial Module in slot 1.
!
! This configuration was tested with the c3620-js-mz_120-3c.bin IOS image
!
conf t
service timestamps debug datetime localtime show-timezone
service timestamps log datetime localtime show-timezone
no service password-encryption
!
hostname Frame_Switch
!
enable secret cat5
!
!
clock timezone EST -5
ip subnet-zero
no ip domain-lookup
ip host bbr1 10.254.0.1
ip host bbr2 10.254.0.2
ip host Frame_Switch 10.254.0.3
ip host tftp 10.254.0.254
!
frame-relay switching
!
!
interface Loopback0
 ip address 10.97.97.97 255.255.255.0
 no ip directed-broadcast
```

*continues*

**Example H-3**   *Frame_Switch Configuration (Continued)*

```
!
interface Ethernet0/0
 description - Backbone LAN Connection
 ip address 10.254.0.3 255.255.255.0
 no shutdown
!
interface Serial1/0
 description - to P1R1 Serial 0
 no ip address
 encapsulation frame-relay
 clockrate 128000
 frame-relay intf-type dce
 frame-relay route 111 interface Serial1/6 111
 frame-relay route 122 interface Serial1/1 221
 frame-relay route 211 interface Serial1/7 211
 no shutdown
!
interface Serial1/1
 description - to P1R2 Serial 0
 no ip address
 encapsulation frame-relay
 clockrate 115200
 frame-relay intf-type dce
 frame-relay route 112 interface Serial1/6 112
 frame-relay route 212 interface Serial1/7 212
 frame-relay route 221 interface Serial1/0 122
 no shutdown
!
interface Serial1/2
 description - to P2R1 Serial 0
 no ip address
 encapsulation frame-relay
 clockrate 115200
 frame-relay intf-type dce
 frame-relay route 121 interface Serial1/6 121
 frame-relay route 122 interface Serial1/3 221
 frame-relay route 221 interface Serial1/7 221
 no shutdown
!
interface Serial1/3
description - to P2R2 Serial 0
 no ip address
 encapsulation frame-relay
 clockrate 115200
 frame-relay intf-type dce
 frame-relay route 122 interface Serial1/6 122
 frame-relay route 221 interface Serial1/2 122
 frame-relay route 222 interface Serial1/7 222
 no shutdown
!
interface Serial 1/6
 description - to BBR1 Serial 0
```

**Example H-3**  *Frame_Switch Configuration (Continued)*

```
 no ip address
 encapsulation frame-relay
 clockrate 115200
 frame-relay intf-type dce
 frame-relay route 111 interface Serial1/0 111
 frame-relay route 112 interface Serial1/1 112
 frame-relay route 121 interface Serial1/2 121
 frame-relay route 122 interface Serial1/3 122
 no shutdown
!
interface Serial 1/7
 description - to BBR2 Serial 0
 no ip address
 encapsulation frame-relay
 clockrate 115200
 frame-relay intf-type dce
 frame-relay route 211 interface Serial1/0 211
 frame-relay route 212 interface Serial1/1 212
 frame-relay route 221 interface Serial1/2 221
 frame-relay route 222 interface Serial1/3 222
 no shutdown
!
interface Serial 1/4
 no ip address
 shutdown
!
interface Serial 1/5
 no ip address
 shutdown
!
router bgp 64997
 bgp log-neighbor-changes
 network 10.97.97.0 mask 255.255.255.0
 neighbor 10.254.0.1 remote-as 64998
 neighbor 10.254.0.2 remote-as 64999
!
ip classless
no ip http server
!
!
!
line con 0
 exec-timeout 0 0
 privilege level 15
 logging synchronous
 transport input none
line aux 0
line vty 0 4
 exec-timeout 5 0
 password cisco
 logging synchronous
 login
```

*continues*

**Example H-3**  *Frame_Switch Configuration (Continued)*

```
!
ntp server 10.254.0.2
!
end
copy run start
```

# TFTP Server and Pod Router Configurations

In the first Configuration Exercise, a minimal configuration will be put on the pod routers so that they can communicate with the TFTP server. Initial configurations will then be downloaded from the TFTP server.

The TFTP server should be configured with the static IP address 10.254.0.254 255.255.255.0. The default gateway on the TFTP server should be set to its own address, 10.254.0.254. (If you set the default gateway to be one of the core routers, you will have to change this setting during the Configuration Exercises, because not all core routers can be reached at all times.)

The configurations in the following sections should be stored on the TFTP server in the appropriate TFTP directory. The filenames should be P*x*R*y*.txt, where *x* is the pod number and *y* is the router number. (For example, the Pod 1 Router 2 file is called P1R2.txt.)

NOTE    The pod router configurations are also posted as text files on the Cisco Press website, at www.ciscopress.com/158705146X.

NOTE    You might need to modify the configurations to work with the specific routers you are using. For example, if you have routers with modular interfaces where we used routers with fixed interfaces, you have to change how the interfaces are referenced.

## P1R1 Configuration

Example H-4 provides the text of the P1R1.txt configuration file.

**Example H-4**  *P1R1.txt Configuration File*

```
hostname P1R1
service timestamps debug datetime localtime show-timezone
service timestamps log datetime localtime show-timezone
no ip domain-lookup
ip host P1R1 10.1.1.1 10.1.0.1 10.11.0.1 172.31.1.1 172.31.11.1 10.200.200.11
```

**Example H-4**  *P1R1.txt Configuration File (Continued)*

```
ip host P1R2 10.1.2.2 10.1.0.2 10.11.0.2 172.31.1.2 172.31.11.2 10.200.200.12
ip host P1R3 10.1.1.3 10.1.3.3 10.200.200.13
ip host P1R4 10.1.3.4 10.1.2.4 10.200.200.14
ip host bbr1 172.31.1.3 172.31.2.3 172.31.3.3 172.31.4.3 10.254.0.1
ip host bbr2 172.31.11.4 172.31.22.4 172.31.33.4 172.31.44.4 10.254.0.2
ip host Frame_Switch 10.254.0.3
ip host tftp 10.254.0.254
clock timezone EST -5
enable password cisco
interface Serial 0
 description - Frame Relay connection to BBR1, DLCI 111
 bandwidth 64
 ip address 172.31.1.1 255.255.255.0
 encapsulation frame-relay
 frame-relay map ip 172.31.1.3 111 broadcast
 no frame-relay inverse-arp
 no shutdown
interface Serial 1
 description - HDLC connection to P1R2
 bandwidth 64
 ip address 10.1.0.1 255.255.255.0
 clock rate 64000
 no shutdown
interface Ethernet 0
 description - LAN connection to P1R3
 ip address 10.1.1.1 255.255.255.0
 no shutdown
no ip classless
no ip http server
line con 0
 logging synchronous
 exec-timeout 20 0
line vty 0 4
 logging synchronous
 no login
 exec-timeout 15 0
ntp server 10.254.0.2
```

## P1R2 Configuration

Example H-5 provides the text of the P1R2.txt configuration file.

**Example H-5**  *P1R2.txt Configuration File*

```
hostname P1R2
service timestamps debug datetime localtime show-timezone
service timestamps log datetime localtime show-timezone
no ip domain-lookup
ip host P1R1 10.1.1.1 10.1.0.1 10.11.0.1 172.31.1.1 172.31.11.1 10.200.200.11
ip host P1R2 10.1.2.2 10.1.0.2 10.11.0.2 172.31.1.2 172.31.11.2 10.200.200.12
ip host P1R3 10.1.1.3 10.1.3.3 10.200.200.13
```

*continues*

**Example H-5** *P1R2.txt Configuration File (Continued)*

```
ip host P1R4 10.1.3.4 10.1.2.4 10.200.200.14
ip host bbr1 172.31.1.3 172.31.2.3 172.31.3.3 172.31.4.3 10.254.0.1
ip host bbr2 172.31.11.4 172.31.22.4 172.31.33.4 172.31.44.4 10.254.0.2
ip host Frame_Switch 10.254.0.3
ip host tftp 10.254.0.254
clock timezone EST -5
enable password cisco
interface Serial 0
 description - Frame Relay connection to BBR1, DLCI 112
 bandwidth 64
 ip address 172.31.1.2 255.255.255.0
 encapsulation frame-relay
 frame-relay map ip 172.31.1.3 112 broadcast
 no frame-relay inverse-arp
 no shutdown
interface Serial 1
 description - HDLC connection to P1R1
 bandwidth 64
 ip address 10.1.0.2 255.255.255.0
 no shutdown
interface Ethernet 0
 description - LAN connection to P1R4
 ip address 10.1.2.2 255.255.255.0
 no shutdown
no ip classless
no ip http server
line con 0
 logging synchronous
 exec-timeout 20 0
line vty 0 4
 logging synchronous
 no login
 exec-timeout 15 0
ntp server 10.254.0.2
```

# P1R3 Configuration

Example H-6 provides the text of the P1R3.txt configuration file.

**Example H-6** *P1R3.txt Configuration File*

```
hostname P1R3
service timestamps debug datetime localtime show-timezone
service timestamps log datetime localtime show-timezone
no ip domain-lookup
ip host P1R1 10.1.1.1 10.1.0.1 10.11.0.1 172.31.1.1 172.31.11.1 10.200.200.11
ip host P1R2 10.1.2.2 10.1.0.2 10.11.0.2 172.31.1.2 172.31.11.2 10.200.200.12
ip host P1R3 10.1.1.3 10.1.3.3 10.200.200.13
ip host P1R4 10.1.3.4 10.1.2.4 10.200.200.14
ip host bbr1 172.31.1.3 172.31.2.3 172.31.3.3 172.31.4.3 10.254.0.1
ip host bbr2 172.31.11.4 172.31.22.4 172.31.33.4 172.31.44.4 10.254.0.2
```

**Example H-6**  *P1R3.txt Configuration File (Continued)*

```
ip host Frame_Switch 10.254.0.3
ip host tftp 10.254.0.254
clock timezone EST -5
enable password cisco
interface Serial 0
 description - HDLC connection to P1R4
 bandwidth 64
 ip address 10.1.3.3 255.255.255.0
 clock rate 64000
 no shutdown
interface Ethernet 0
 description - LAN connection to P1R1
 ip address 10.1.1.3 255.255.255.0
 no shutdown
no ip classless
no ip http server
line con 0
 logging synchronous
 exec-timeout 20 0
line vty 0 4
 logging synchronous
 no login
 exec-timeout 15 0
ntp server 10.254.0.2
```

# P1R4 Configuration

Example H-7 provides the text of the P1R4.txt configuration file.

**Example H-7**  *P1R4.txt Configuration File*

```
hostname P1R4
service timestamps debug datetime localtime show-timezone
service timestamps log datetime localtime show-timezone
no ip domain-lookup
ip host P1R1 10.1.1.1 10.1.0.1 10.11.0.1 172.31.1.1 172.31.11.1 10.200.200.11
ip host P1R2 10.1.2.2 10.1.0.2 10.11.0.2 172.31.1.2 172.31.11.2 10.200.200.12
ip host P1R3 10.1.1.3 10.1.3.3 10.200.200.13
ip host P1R4 10.1.3.4 10.1.2.4 10.200.200.14
ip host bbr1 172.31.1.3 172.31.2.3 172.31.3.3 172.31.4.3 10.254.0.1
ip host bbr2 172.31.11.4 172.31.22.4 172.31.33.4 172.31.44.4 10.254.0.2
ip host Frame_Switch 10.254.0.3
ip host tftp 10.254.0.254
clock timezone EST -5
enable password cisco
interface Serial 0
 description - HDLC connection to P1R3
 bandwidth 64
 ip address 10.1.3.4 255.255.255.0
 no shutdown
```

*continues*

**Example H-7** *P1R4.txt Configuration File (Continued)*

```
interface Ethernet 0
 description - LAN connection to P1R2
 ip address 10.1.2.4 255.255.255.0
 no shutdown
no ip classless
no ip http server
line con 0
 logging synchronous
 exec-timeout 20 0
line vty 0 4
 logging synchronous
 no login
 exec-timeout 15 0
ntp server 10.254.0.2
```

# P2R1 Configuration

Example H-8 provides the text of the P2R1.txt configuration file.

**Example H-8** *P2R1.txt Configuration File*

```
hostname P2R1
service timestamps debug datetime localtime show-timezone
service timestamps log datetime localtime show-timezone
no ip domain-lookup
ip host P2R1 10.2.1.1 10.2.0.1 10.22.0.1 172.31.2.1 172.31.22.1 10.200.200.21
ip host P2R2 10.2.2.2 10.2.0.2 10.22.0.2 172.31.2.2 172.31.22.2 10.200.200.22
ip host P2R3 10.2.1.3 10.2.3.3 10.200.200.23
ip host P2R4 10.2.3.4 10.2.2.4 10.200.200.24
ip host bbr1 172.31.2.3 172.31.1.3 172.31.3.3 172.31.4.3 10.254.0.1
ip host bbr2 172.31.22.4 172.31.11.4 172.31.33.4 172.31.44.4 10.254.0.2
ip host Frame_Switch 10.254.0.3
ip host tftp 10.254.0.254
clock timezone EST -5
enable password cisco
interface Serial 0
 description - Frame Relay connection to BBR1, DLCI 121
 bandwidth 64
 ip address 172.31.2.1 255.255.255.0
 encapsulation frame-relay
 frame-relay map ip 172.31.2.3 121 broadcast
 no frame-relay inverse-arp
 no shutdown
interface Serial 1
 description - HDLC connection to P2R2
 bandwidth 64
 ip address 10.2.0.1 255.255.255.0
 clock rate 64000
 no shutdown
interface Ethernet 0
 description - LAN connection to P2R3
```

**Example H-8**  *P2R1.txt Configuration File (Continued)*

```
 ip address 10.2.1.1 255.255.255.0
 no shutdown
no ip classless
no ip http server
line con 0
 logging synchronous
 exec-timeout 20 0
line vty 0 4
 logging synchronous
 no login
 exec-timeout 15 0
ntp server 10.254.0.2
```

# P2R2 Configuration

Example H-9 provides the text of the P2R2.txt configuration file.

**Example H-9**  *P2R2.txt Configuration File*

```
hostname P2R2
service timestamps debug datetime localtime show-timezone
service timestamps log datetime localtime show-timezone
no ip domain-lookup
ip host P2R1 10.2.1.1 10.2.0.1 10.22.0.1 172.31.2.1 172.31.22.1 10.200.200.21
ip host P2R2 10.2.2.2 10.2.0.2 10.22.0.2 172.31.2.2 172.31.22.2 10.200.200.22
ip host P2R3 10.2.1.3 10.2.3.3 10.200.200.23
ip host P2R4 10.2.3.4 10.2.2.4 10.200.200.24
ip host bbr1 172.31.2.3 172.31.1.3 172.31.3.3 172.31.4.3 10.254.0.1
ip host bbr2 172.31.22.4 172.31.11.4 172.31.33.4 172.31.44.4 10.254.0.2
ip host Frame_Switch 10.254.0.3
ip host tftp 10.254.0.254
clock timezone EST -5
enable password cisco
interface Serial 0
 description - Frame Relay connection to BBR1, DLCI 122
 bandwidth 64
 ip address 172.31.2.2 255.255.255.0
 encapsulation frame-relay
 frame-relay map ip 172.31.2.3 122 broadcast
 no frame-relay inverse-arp
 no shutdown
interface Serial 1
 description - HDLC connection to P2R1
 bandwidth 64
 ip address 10.2.0.2 255.255.255.0
 no shutdown
interface Ethernet 0
 description - LAN connection to P2R4
 ip address 10.2.2.2 255.255.255.0
 no shutdown
```

*continues*

**Example H-9** *P2R2.txt Configuration File (Continued)*

```
no ip classless
no ip http server
line con 0
 logging synchronous
 exec-timeout 20 0
line vty 0 4
 logging synchronous
 no login
 exec-timeout 15 0
ntp server 10.254.0.2
```

## P2R3 Configuration

Example H-10 provides the text of the P2R3.txt configuration file.

**Example H-10** *P2R3.txt Configuration File*

```
hostname P2R3
service timestamps debug datetime localtime show-timezone
service timestamps log datetime localtime show-timezone
no ip domain-lookup
ip host P2R1 10.2.1.1 10.2.0.1 10.22.0.1 172.31.2.1 172.31.22.1 10.200.200.21
ip host P2R2 10.2.2.2 10.2.0.2 10.22.0.2 172.31.2.2 172.31.22.2 10.200.200.22
ip host P2R3 10.2.1.3 10.2.3.3 10.200.200.23
ip host P2R4 10.2.3.4 10.2.2.4 10.200.200.24
ip host bbr1 172.31.2.3 172.31.1.3 172.31.3.3 172.31.4.3 10.254.0.1
ip host bbr2 172.31.22.4 172.31.11.4 172.31.33.4 172.31.44.4 10.254.0.2
ip host Frame_Switch 10.254.0.3
ip host tftp 10.254.0.254
clock timezone EST -5
enable password cisco
interface Serial 0
 description - HDLC connection to P2R4
 bandwidth 64
 ip address 10.2.3.3 255.255.255.0
 clock rate 64000
 no shutdown
interface Ethernet 0
 description - LAN connection to P2R1
 ip address 10.2.1.3 255.255.255.0
 no shutdown
no ip classless
no ip http server
line con 0
 logging synchronous
 exec-timeout 20 0
line vty 0 4
 logging synchronous
 no login
 exec-timeout 15 0
ntp server 10.254.0.2
```

## P2R4 Configuration

Example H-11 provides the text of the P2R4.txt configuration file.

**Example H-11** *P2R4.txt Configuration File*

```
hostname P2R4
service timestamps debug datetime localtime show-timezone
service timestamps log datetime localtime show-timezone
no ip domain-lookup
ip host P2R1 10.2.1.1 10.2.0.1 10.22.0.1 172.31.2.1 172.31.22.1 10.200.200.21
ip host P2R2 10.2.2.2 10.2.0.2 10.22.0.2 172.31.2.2 172.31.22.2 10.200.200.22
ip host P2R3 10.2.1.3 10.2.3.3 10.200.200.23
ip host P2R4 10.2.3.4 10.2.2.4 10.200.200.24
ip host bbr1 172.31.2.3 172.31.1.3 172.31.3.3 172.31.4.3 10.254.0.1
ip host bbr2 172.31.22.4 172.31.11.4 172.31.33.4 172.31.44.4 10.254.0.2
ip host Frame_Switch 10.254.0.3
ip host tftp 10.254.0.254
clock timezone EST -5
enable password cisco
interface Serial 0
 description - HDLC connection to P2R3
 bandwidth 64
 ip address 10.2.3.4 255.255.255.0
 no shutdown
interface Ethernet 0
 description - LAN connection to P2R2
 ip address 10.2.2.4 255.255.255.0
 no shutdown
no ip classless
no ip http server
line con 0
 logging synchronous
 exec-timeout 20 0
line vty 0 4
 logging synchronous
 no login
 exec-timeout 15 0
ntp server 10.254.0.2
```

# GLOSSARY

This glossary assembles and defines terms and acronyms used in this book and in the internetworking industry. Many of the definitions have yet to be standardized, and many terms have several meanings. Multiple definitions and acronym expressions are included where they apply. Many of these definitions can also be found at www.cisco.com by searching "Internetworking Terms and Acronyms."

**10BaseT.** 10-Mbps baseband Ethernet specification using two pairs of twisted-pair cabling (Category 3, 4, or 5): one pair for transmitting data and the other for receiving data. 10BaseT, which is part of the IEEE 802.3 specification, has a distance limit of approximately 328 feet (100 meters) per segment.

**802.x.** Set of IEEE standards for the definition of LAN protocols.

# A

**AAA.** Authentication, authorization, and accounting (pronounced "triple a").

**ABR.** Area Border Router. A router located on the border of one or more OSPF areas that connects those areas to the backbone network. ABRs are considered members of both the OSPF backbone and the attached areas. Therefore, they maintain routing tables describing both the backbone topology and the topology of the other areas.

**access layer.** Layer in a hierarchical network that provides workgroup/user access to the network.

**access list.** List kept by routers to control access to or from the router for a number of services (for example, to prevent packets with a certain IP address from leaving a particular interface on the router).

**access method.** Generally, the way in which network devices access the network medium.

**access server.** Communications processor that connects asynchronous devices to a LAN or WAN through network and terminal emulation software. Performs both synchronous and asynchronous routing of supported protocols. Sometimes called a *network access server (NAS)*.

**accounting management.** One of five categories of network management defined by ISO for management of OSI networks. Accounting management subsystems are responsible for collecting network data relating to resource usage.

**accuracy.** The percentage of useful traffic that is correctly transmitted on the system, relative to total traffic, including transmission errors.

**ACK.** 1. Acknowledgment bit in a TCP segment. 2. See *acknowledgment*.

**Acknowledgment.** Notification sent from one network device to another to acknowledge that some event (for example, receipt of a message) occurred. Sometimes abbreviated *ACK*. Compare with *NAK*.

**ACL.** See access list.

**AD.** 1. Administrative Distance. Rating of the trustworthiness of a routing information source. Administrative distance is often expressed as a numeric value between 0 and 255. The higher the value, the lower the trustworthiness rating. 2. Advertised distance. The cost between the next-hop router and the destination.

**Address.** A data structure or logical convention used to identify a unique entity, such as a particular process or network device.

**address mapping.** A technique that allows different protocols to interoperate by translating addresses from one format to another. For example, when routing IP over X.25, the IP addresses must be mapped to the X.25 addresses so that the IP packets can be transmitted by the X.25 network. See also *address resolution*.

**address resolution.** Generally, a method for resolving differences between computer addressing schemes. Address resolution usually specifies a method for mapping network layer (Layer 3) addresses to data link layer (Layer 2) addresses.

**Adjacency.** A relationship formed between selected neighboring routers and end nodes for the purpose of exchanging routing information. Adjacency is based on the use of a common media segment.

**administrative distance.** A rating of the trustworthiness of a routing information source. The higher the value, the lower the trustworthiness rating.

**Advertised distance.** The cost between the next-hop router and the destination.

**Advertising.** Router process in which routing or service updates are sent so that other routers on the network can maintain lists of usable routes.

**AFI.** Authority and format ID. In OSI NSAP address, specifies the format of the address and the authority that assigned that address. The AFI is 1 byte.

**Agent.** 1. Generally, software that processes queries and returns replies on behalf of an application. 2. In NMSs, a process that resides in all managed devices and reports the values of specified variables to management stations.

**Aggregation.** See *route summarization*.

**Alarm.** A message notifying an operator or administrator of a network problem.

**Algorithm.** Well-defined rule or process for arriving at a solution to a problem. In networking, algorithms are commonly used to determine the best route for traffic from a particular source to a particular destination.

**Analog.** An electrical circuit that is represented by means of continuous, variable physical quantities (such as voltages and frequencies), as opposed to discrete representations (such as the 0/1, off/on representation of digital circuits).

**analog transmission.** Signal transmission over wires or through the air in which information is conveyed through variation of some combination of signal amplitude, frequency, and phase.

**ANSI.** American National Standards Institute. Voluntary organization composed of corporate, government, and other members that coordinates standards-related activities, approves U.S. national standards, and develops positions for the United States in international standards organizations. ANSI helps develop international and U.S. standards relating to, among other things, communications and networking. ANSI is a member of the IEC and the ISO.

**API.** Application programming interface. A specification of function-call conventions that defines an interface to a service.

**APNIC.** Asia Pacific Network Information Center.

**AppleTalk.** A series of communications protocols designed by Apple Computer. Two phases currently exist. Phase 1, the earlier version, supports a single physical network that can have only one network number and be in one zone. Phase 2, the more recent version, supports multiple logical networks on a single physical network and allows networks to be in more than one zone. See also *zone*.

**application layer.** Layer 7 of the OSI reference model. This layer provides services to application processes (such as electronic mail, file transfer, and terminal emulation) that are outside the OSI model. The application layer identifies and establishes the availability of intended communication partners (and the resources required to connect with them), synchronizes cooperating applications, and establishes agreement on procedures for error recovery and control of data integrity. It corresponds roughly with the transaction services layer in the SNA model.

**Area.** A logical set of network segments and their attached devices. Areas are usually connected to other areas via routers, making up a single autonomous system. See also *AS*.

**ARIN.** American Registry for Internet Numbers. Nonprofit organization established for the purpose of administrating and registering IP numbers to the geographical areas currently managed by Network Solutions (InterNIC). Those areas include, but are not limited to, North America, South America, South Africa, and the Caribbean.

**ARP.** Address Resolution Protocol. An Internet protocol used to map an IP address to a MAC address. It is defined in RFC 826.

**ARPA.** Advanced Research Projects Agency. Research and development organization that is part of DoD. ARPA is responsible for numerous technological advances in communications and networking. ARPA evolved into DARPA and then back into ARPA (in 1994).

**ARPANET.** Advanced Research Projects Agency Network. Landmark packet-switching network established in 1969. ARPANET was developed in the 1970s by BBN and was funded by ARPA (and later DARPA). It eventually evolved into the Internet. The term ARPANET was officially retired in 1990.

**AS.** Autonomous system. A collection of networks under a common administration sharing a common routing strategy. Autonomous systems may be subdivided into areas.

**ASBR.** Autonomous System Boundary Router. An ABR located between an OSPF autonomous system and a non-OSPF network. ASBRs run both OSPF and another routing protocol, such as RIP. ASBRs must reside in a non-stub OSPF area.

**ASCII.** American Standard Code for Information Interchange. An 8-bit code for character representation (7 bits plus parity).

**assigned numbers.** The IANA documents the currently assigned values from several series of numbers used in network protocol implementations, at www.iana.org/numbers.html. This site provides a directory of living documents which are updated constantly. If you are developing a protocol or application that will require the use of a link, socket, port, protocol, and so forth, contact the IANA to receive a number assignment.

**asynchronous transmission.** Term describing digital signals that are transmitted without precise clocking. Such signals generally have different frequencies and phase relationships. Asynchronous transmissions usually encapsulate individual characters in control bits (called start and stop bits) that designate the beginning and end of each character.

**ATM.** Asynchronous Transfer Mode. An international standard for cell relay in which multiple service types (such as voice, video, or data) are conveyed in fixed-length (53-byte) cells. Fixed-length cells allow cell processing to occur in hardware, thereby reducing transit delays. ATM is designed to take advantage of high-speed transmission media, such as E3, SONET, and T3.

**AUI.** Attachment unit interface. IEEE 802.3 interface between an MAU and an NIC. The term AUI can also refer to the rear panel port to which an AUI cable might attach.

**Authentication.** In security, the verification of the identity of a person or process.

**AURP.** AppleTalk Update Routing Protocol. A method of encapsulating AppleTalk traffic in the header of a foreign protocol, allowing the connection of two or more discontiguous AppleTalk internetworks through a foreign network (such as TCP/IP) to form an AppleTalk WAN. This connection is called an AURP tunnel. In addition to its encapsulation function, AURP maintains routing tables for the entire AppleTalk WAN by exchanging routing information between exterior routers.

**AUX.** Auxiliary port on Cisco Routers.

**average rate.** Average rate, in kilobits per second (kbps), at which a given virtual circuit will transmit.

# B

**Backbone.** Part of a network that acts as the primary path for traffic that is most often sourced from and destined for other networks.

**backward explicit congestion notification.** See *BECN*.

**Bandwidth.** Difference between the highest and lowest frequencies available for network signals. The term is also used to describe the rated throughput capacity of a given network medium or protocol.

**bandwidth reservation.** Process of assigning bandwidth to users and applications served by a network. It involves assigning priority to different flows of traffic based on how critical and delay-sensitive they are. This makes the best use of available bandwidth; if the network becomes congested, lower-priority traffic can be dropped. This sometimes is called bandwidth allocation.

**Basic Rate Interface.** See *BRI*.

**Baud.** Unit of signaling speed equal to the number of discrete signal elements transmitted per second. Baud is synonymous with bits per second (bps) if each signal element represents exactly 1 bit.

**Bc.** Committed Burst. Negotiated tariff metric in Frame Relay internetworks. The maximum amount of data (in bits) that a Frame Relay internetwork is committed to accept and transmit at the CIR.

**BCRAN.** Building Cisco Remote Access Networks.

**BDR.** Backup Designated Router. The BDR does not perform any DR functions when the DR is operating. Instead, it receives all information, but allows the DR to perform the forwarding and synchronization tasks. The BDR performs DR tasks only if the DR fails.

**Be.** Excess burst. Negotiated tariff metric in Frame Relay internetworks. This is the number of bits that a Frame Relay internetwork will attempt to transmit after Bc is accommodated. Be data is, in general, delivered with a lower probability than Bc data because Be data can be marked as DE by the network. See also *Bc* and *DE*.

**BECN.** Backward explicit congestion notification. A bit set by a Frame Relay network in frames traveling in the opposite direction of frames encountering a congested path. DTE receiving frames with the BECN bit set can request that higher-level protocols take flow control action as appropriate. Compare with *FECN*.

**Bellman-Ford routing algorithm.** See *distance vector routing algorithm*.

**best-effort delivery.** Delivery in a network system that does not use a sophisticated acknowledgment system to guarantee reliable delivery of information.

**BGP.** Border Gateway Protocol. An interdomain routing protocol that replaces EGP. BGP exchanges reachability information with other BGP systems. It is defined in RFC 1163. See also *BGP-4* and *EGP*.

**BGP-4.** BGP version 4. This is version 4 of the predominant interdomain routing protocol used on the Internet. BGP-4 supports CIDR and uses route aggregation mechanisms to reduce the size of routing tables. See also *BGP*.

**BIA.** Burned-in address, another name for a MAC address.

**Binary.** Numbering system characterized by 1s and 0s (1 = on, 0 = off).

**Bit.** Binary digit used in the binary numbering system. This can be 0 or 1.

**BOD.** Bandwidth on demand.

**BOOTP.** Bootstrap Protocol. Protocol used by a network node to determine the IP address of its Ethernet interfaces in order to affect network booting.

**BPDU.** Bridge protocol data unit. A Spanning-Tree Protocol hello packet that is sent out at configurable intervals to exchange information among bridges in the network.

**BRI.** Basic Rate Interface. The most common kind of ISDN interface available in the United States. BRI contains two B channels, each with a capacity of 64 kbps, and a single D channel (with a capacity of 16 kbps) that is used for signaling and call progress messages. Compare with *PRI*.

**Broadcast.** Data packet that will be sent to all nodes on a network. Broadcasts are identified by a broadcast address. Compare with *multicast* and *unicast*.

**BSCN.** Building Scalable Cisco Networks.

**Buffer.** Storage area used for handling data in transit. Buffers are used in internetworking to compensate for differences in processing speed between network devices. Bursts of data can be stored in buffers until they can be handled by slower processing devices. This sometimes is referred to as a packet buffer.

**Byte.** Term used to refer to a series of consecutive binary digits that are operated upon as a unit (for example, an 8-bit byte).

# C

**Cable.** Transmission medium of copper wire or optical fiber wrapped in a protective cover.

**CCITT.** Consultative Committee for International Telegraph and Telephone. International organization responsible for the development of communications standards. It is now called the ITU-T. See *ITU-T*.

**CCDA.** Cisco Certified Design Associate.

**CCDP.** Cisco Certified Design Professional.

**CCNA.** Cisco Certified Network Associate.

**CCNP.** Cisco Certified Network Professional.

**CCO.** Cisco Connection Online. Cisco's web site.

**CDP.** Cisco Discovery Protocol. Media- and protocol-independent device-discovery protocol that runs on all Cisco-manufactured equipment including routers, access servers, bridges, and switches. Using CDP, a device can advertise its existence to other devices and receive information about other devices on the same LAN or on the remote side of a WAN. Runs on all media that supports SNAP including LANs, Frame Relay, and ATM media.

**CHAP.** Challenge Handshake Authentication Protocol. A security feature supported on lines using PPP encapsulation and that prevents unauthorized access. CHAP does not itself prevent unauthorized access; it merely identifies the remote end. The router or access server then determines whether that user is allowed access. Compare with *PAP*.

**Channel.** Communication path. Multiple channels can be multiplexed over a single cable in certain environments.

**Channelized E1.** Access link operating at 2.048 Mbps that is subdivided into 30 B channels and 1 D channel. It supports DDR, Frame Relay, and X.25.

**Channelized T1.** Access link operating at 1.544 Mbps that is subdivided into 24 channels (23 B channels and 1 D channel) of 64 kbps each. The individual channels or groups of channels connect to different destinations. It supports DDR, Frame Relay, and X.25. It is also referred to as fractional T1.

**Checksum.** Method for checking the integrity of transmitted data. A checksum is an integer value computed from a sequence of octets taken through a series of arithmetic operations. The value is recomputed at the receiving end and is compared for verification.

**CIDR.** Classless interdomain routing. Developed for Internet service providers (ISPs). This strategy suggests that the remaining IP addresses be allocated to ISPs in contiguous blocks, using geography as one consideration.

**CIR.** Committed information rate. Rate at which a Frame Relay network agrees to transfer information under normal conditions, averaged over a minimum increment of time. CIR, measured in bits per second, is one of the key negotiated tariff metrics. See also *Bc*.

**Circuit.** Communications path between two or more points.

**CiscoSecure.**  A complete line of access-control software products that complement any dial network solution, enabling the centralization of security policies.

**classful routing protocols.**  Routing protocols that do not transmit any information about the prefix length. Examples are RIPv1 and IGRP.

**classless routing protocols.**  Routing protocols that include the prefix length with routing updates; routers running classless routing protocols do not have to determine the prefix themselves. Classless routing protocols support VLSM.

**CLI.**  Command-line interface. An interface that enables the user to interact with the operating system by entering commands and optional arguments.

**Client.**  A node or software program that requests services from a server. See also *server.*

**client/server computing.**  Computing (processing) network systems in which transaction responsibilities are divided into two parts: client (front end) and server (back end). Both terms (*client* and *server*) can be applied to software programs or actual computing devices. This is also called distributed computing (processing).

**CLNP.**  Connectionless Network Protocol. CLNP is the OSI equivalent of IP.

**CLNS.**  Connectionless Network Service. One of two types of OSI network layer services that are available to the OSI transport layer.

**CMIP.**  Common Management Information Protocol. An OSI protocol suite network management protocol.

**CMNS.**  Connection-Mode Network Service. One of two types of OSI network layer services that are available to the OSI transport layer.

**collapsed backbone.**  A nondistributed backbone in which all network segments are interconnected by way of an internetworking device. A collapsed backbone might be a virtual network segment existing in a device such as a hub, a router, or a switch.

**Collision.**  In Ethernet, the result of two nodes transmitting simultaneously. The frames from each device impact and are damaged when they meet on the physical media.

**Committed burst.**  See *Bc.*

**Committed information rate.**  See *CIR.*

**connectionless.** A transmission without the establishment of an end-to-end connection prior to the exchange of data.

**connection-oriented.** A transmission with the establishment of an end-to-end connection prior to the exchange of data.

**CONP.** Connection-Oriented Network Protocol.

**CoS.** Class of service. 5 bits in the IP header used to set the delay, throughput, reliability, and cost.

**Cost.** An arbitrary value, typically based on hop count, media bandwidth, or other measures, that is assigned by a network administrator and used to compare various paths through an internetwork environment. Cost values are used by routing protocols to determine the most favorable path to a particular destination: The lower the cost, the better the path. In OSPF, this is the value assigned to a link. This metric is based on the speed of the media. It is sometimes called path cost.

**CPE.** Customer premises equipment. Terminating equipment, such as terminals, telephones, and modems, supplied by the telephone company, installed at customer sites, and connected to the telephone company network.

**CPU.** Central Processing Unit. The central processor (chip - brain) of the router, computer, switch, etc.

**CR.** Carriage return.

**CRC.** Cyclic redundancy check. Error-checking technique in which the frame recipient calculates a remainder by dividing frame contents by a prime binary divisor and then compares the calculated remainder to a value stored in the frame by the sending node.

**CSNP.** Complete sequence number PDU. In IS-IS, used to distribute a router's complete link-state database. CSNPs are a list of the LSPs held by a router.

**CSU.** Channel service unit. Digital interface device that connects end-user equipment to the local digital telephone loop. It is often referred to, together with DSU, as CSU/DSU. See also *DSU*.

**customer premises equipment.** See *CPE*.

**cyclic redundancy check.** See *CRC*.

# D

**DARPA.** Defense Advanced Research Projects Agency. U.S. government agency that funded research for and does experimentation with the Internet. It evolved from ARPA and then, in 1994, back to ARPA.

**Data Encryption Standard.** See *DES*.

**Data Network Identification Code.** See *DNIC*.

**data terminal equipment.** See *DTE*.

**Datagram.** Logical grouping of information sent as a network layer unit over a transmission medium without prior establishment of a virtual circuit. IP datagrams are the primary information units in the Internet. The terms *cell*, *frame*, *message*, *packet*, and *segment* are also used to describe logical information groupings at various layers of the OSI reference model and in various technology circles.

**data-link connection identifier.** See *DLCI*.

**DB.** Data bus connector. Type of connector used to connect serial and parallel cables to a data bus. DB connector names are in the format DB-*x*, where *x* represents the number of wires within the connector. Each line is connected to a pin on the connector, but in many cases, not all pins are assigned a function. DB connectors are defined by various EIA/TIA standards.

**DBD.** Database description packets. Describes the contents of the topological database. These messages are exchanged when an adjacency is initialized.

**DCE.** Data circuit-terminating equipment (ITU-T expansion). Devices and connections of a communications network that comprise the network end of the user-to-network interface. The DCE provides a physical connection to the network, forwards traffic, and provides a clocking signal used to synchronize data transmission between DCE and DTE devices. Modems and interface cards are examples of DCE. Compare with *DTE*.

**DDR.** Dial-on-demand routing. Technique whereby a router can automatically initiate and close a circuit-switched session as transmitting stations demand. The router spoofs keepalives so that end stations treat the session as active. DDR permits routing over ISDN or telephone lines using an external ISDN terminal adapter or modem.

**DE.** Discard eligible indicator. When the router detects network congestion, the FR switch will drop packets with the DE bit set first. The DE bit is set on the oversubscribed traffic—that is, the traffic that was received after the CIR was sent.

**Decryption.** Reverse application of an encryption algorithm to encrypted data, thereby restoring that data to its original, unencrypted state. See also *encryption*.

**dedicated line.** Communications line that is indefinitely reserved for transmissions rather than switched as transmission is required. See also *leased line*.

**default route.** A routing table entry that is used to direct frames for which a next hop is not explicitly listed in the routing table.

**default router.** The router to which frames are directed when a next hop is not explicitly listed in the routing table. Also called a default gateway.

**Delay.** Time between the initiation of a transaction by a sender and the first response received by the sender. Also, the time required to move a packet from source to destination over a given path.

**Demarc.** Demarcation point between carrier equipment and CPE.

**DES.** Data Encryption Standard. Standard cryptographic algorithm developed by the U.S. National Bureau of Standards.

**destination address.** Address of a network device that is receiving data. See also *source address*.

**DHCP.** Dynamic Host Configuration Protocol. Provides a mechanism for allocating IP addresses dynamically so that addresses can be reused when hosts no longer need them.

**dial backup.** Feature that provides protection against WAN downtime by allowing the network administrator to configure a backup serial line through a circuit-switched connection.

**dial-on-demand routing.** See *DDR*.

**dialup line.** Communications circuit that is established by a switched-circuit connection using the telephone company network.

**Diffusing Update Algorithm.** DUAL. A convergence algorithm used in EIGRP that provides loop-free operation at every instant throughout a route computation. This allows routers involved in a topology change to synchronize at the same time, while not involving routers that are unaffected by the change.

**Digital.** The use of a binary code to represent information, such as 0/1 or on/off.

**DIS.** Designated intermediate system for IS-IS. The DIS is elected (by configurable priority and then by highest MAC address) to generate an LSP representing a virtual router connecting all attached routers to a star-shape topology.

**distance vector routing algorithm.** A class of routing algorithms that call for each router to send all or some portion of its routing table, but only to its neighbors. This is also called the Bellman-Ford routing algorithm and DBF.

**DLCI.** Data-link connection identifier. Value that specifies a PVC or an SVC in a Frame Relay network. In the basic Frame Relay specification, DLCIs are locally significant (connected devices might use different values to specify the same connection). In the LMI extended specification, DLCIs are globally significant (DLCIs specify individual end devices). See also *LMI*.

**DNIC.** Data Network Identification Code. Part of an X.121 address. DNICs are divided into two parts: the first specifying the country in which the addressed PSN is located, and the second specifying the PSN itself.

**DNS.** Domain Name System. System used in the Internet for translating names of network nodes into addresses.

**DoD.** Department of Defense. U.S. government organization that is responsible for national defense. The DoD has frequently funded communication protocol development.

**Domain.** In the Internet, a portion of the naming hierarchy tree that refers to general groupings of networks based on organization type or geography.

**Domain Name System.** See *DNS*.

**dotted decimal notation.** Syntactic representation for a 32-bit integer that consists of four 8-bit numbers written in base 10 with periods (dots) separating them. It is used to represent IP addresses in the Internet, as in 192.168.67.20. This is also called dotted quad notation.

**DR.** Designated router. OSPF router that generates LSAs for a multiaccess network and has other special responsibilities in running OSPF. Each multiaccess OSPF network that has at least two attached routers has a designated router that is elected by the OSPF Hello protocol. The designated router enables a reduction in the number of adjacencies required on a multiaccess network, which in turn reduces the amount of routing protocol traffic and the size of the topological database.

**DS.** Digital signal.

**DSL.** Digital subscriber line. Public network technology that delivers high bandwidth over conventional copper wiring at limited distances. There are four common types of DSL: Asymmetric Digital Subscriber Line (ADSL), High-data-rate digital subscriber line (HDSL), Single-Line Digital Subscriber Line (SDSL), and Very-high-Data-rate Digital Subscriber Line (VDSL). All are provisioned via modem pairs, with one modem located at a central office and the other at the customer site. Because most DSL technologies do not use the whole bandwidth of the twisted pair, there is room remaining for a voice channel.

**DSP.** Domain-specific part of OSI NSAP address. The HODSP, system ID, and NSEL together make up the DSP of the NSAP address.

**DSU.** Data service unit. Device used in digital transmission that adapts the physical interface on a DTE device to a transmission facility such as T1 or E1. The DSU is also responsible for such functions as signal timing. It is often referred to, together with CSU, as CSU/DSU. See also *CSU*.

**DTE.** Data terminal equipment. Device at the user end of a user-network interface that serves as a data source, a destination, or both. DTE connects to a data network through a DCE device (for example, a modem) and typically uses clocking signals generated by the DCE. DTE includes such devices as computers, protocol translators, and multiplexers. Compare with *DCE*.

**DTR.** Delay, throughput, and reliability bits in the IP ToS field.

**DUAL.** See *Diffusing Update Algorithm*.

**DVMRP.** Distance Vector Multicast Routing Protocol. Internetwork gateway protocol, largely based on RIP, that implements a typical dense mode IP multicast scheme. DVMRP uses IGMP to exchange routing datagrams with its neighbors.

**dynamic address resolution.** Use of an address resolution protocol to determine and store address information on demand.

# E

**E1.** External Type 1. Autonomous system external link entry. Originating from the ASBR, they describe routes to destinations external to the autonomous system. They are flooded throughout an OSPF autonomous system except for stub, totally stubby, and not-so-stubby areas. If a packet is an E1, then the metric is calculated by adding the external cost to the internal cost of each link the packet crosses.

**E2.** External Type 2. Autonomous system external link entry. Originating from the ASBR, they describe routes to destinations external to the autonomous system. They are flooded throughout an OSPF autonomous system except for stub, totally stubby, and not-so-stubby areas. If a packet is an E2, then it will always have only the external cost assigned, no matter where in the area it crosses. Use this packet type if only one router is advertising a route to the autonomous system. Type 2 routes are preferred over type 1 routes unless two same-cost routes exist to the destination.

**EBGP.** External BGP. When BGP is running between routers in different autonomous systems it is called EBGP. Routers running EBGP are usually directly connected to each other.

**EGP.** 1. Exterior Gateway Protocol. An Internet protocol for exchanging routing information between autonomous systems. It is documented in RFC 904. EGP is an obsolete protocol that has been replaced by BGP 2. Exterior gateway protocol. Generic term for a routing protocol used to exchange information between autonomous systems.

**EIA/TIA.** Electronic Industries Association/Telecommunications Industry Association.

**EIGRP.** Enhanced Interior Gateway Routing Protocol. An advanced version of IGRP developed by Cisco. It provides superior convergence properties and operating efficiency, and combines the advantages of link-state protocols with those of distance vector protocols.

**e-mail.** Electronic mail. Widely used network application in which text messages are transmitted electronically between end users over various types of networks using various network protocols.

**Encapsulation.** Wrapping of data in a particular protocol header. For example, Ethernet data is wrapped in a specific Ethernet header before network transit. Also, when bridging dissimilar networks, the entire frame from one network is simply placed in the header used by the data link layer protocol of the other network.

**Encryption.** Application of a specific algorithm to data to alter the appearance of the data, making it incomprehensible to those who are not authorized to see the information. See also *decryption*.

**end system.** In IS-IS, a nonrouting host or node.

**Enhanced IGRP.** See *EIGRP*.

**ES.** End system.

**ES-IS.** End System-to-Intermediate System.

**ESH.**  End system hello. Used in IS-IS. ESs send ESHs.

**EUI-64.**  Extended universal identifier 64-bit. The EUI-64 format interface ID for IPv6 is derived from the 48-bit link-layer MAC address by inserting the hex number FFFE between the upper three bytes and the lower 3 bytes of the link-layer address. To make sure that the chosen address is from a unique MAC address, the $7^{th}$ bit in the high-order byte is set to 1 to indicate the uniqueness of the 48-bit address.

**Excess burst.**  See *Be*.

**Extended Super Frame.**  ESF. Framing type used on T1 circuits that consists of 24 frames of 192 bits each, with the 193rd bit providing timing and other functions. ESF is an enhanced version of SF.

**exterior gateway protocol.**  Any internetwork protocol used to exchange routing information between autonomous systems. This is not to be confused with Exterior Gateway Protocol (EGP), which is a particular instance of an exterior gateway protocol. See also *BGP*.

**exterior routing protocols.**  See *exterior gateway protocol*.

# F

**FCC.**  Federal Communications Commission. U.S. government agency that supervises, licenses, and controls electronic and electromagnetic transmission standards.

**FCS.**  Frame check sequence. Extra characters added to a frame for error control purposes. This is used in HDLC, Frame Relay, and other data link layer protocols.

**FD.**  Feasible Distance. In EIGRP, the FD is the lowest cost route to a destination.

**Feasible Distance.**  See *FD*.

**Feasible Successor.**  See *FS*.

**FECN.**  Forward explicit congestion notification. Bit set by a Frame Relay network to inform the DTE receiving the frame that congestion was experienced in the path from the source to the destination. The DTE receiving frames with the FECN bit set can request that higher-level protocols take flow-control action as appropriate. Compare with *BECN*.

**FIFO.**  First in, first out. With FIFO, transmission occurs in the same order as messages are received.

**Filter.** Generally, a process or device that screens network traffic for certain characteristics, such as source address, destination address, or protocol, and determines whether to forward or discard that traffic based on the established criteria.

**Firewall.** Router or access server, or several routers or access servers, designated as a buffer between any connected public networks and a private network. A firewall router uses access lists and other methods to ensure the security of the private network.

**Flapping.** Intermittent interface failures.

**flash update.** A routing update sent asynchronously in response to a change in the network topology. Compare with *routing update*.

**floating static route.** A static route that has a higher administrative distance than a dynamically learned route so that it can be overridden by dynamically learned routing information.

**Flooding.** A traffic-passing technique used by switches and bridges in which traffic received on an interface is sent out all the interfaces of that device, except the interface on which the information was originally received.

**Flow.** Stream of data traveling between two endpoints across a network (for example, from one LAN station to another). Multiple flows can be transmitted on a single circuit.

**flow control.** Technique for ensuring that a transmitting entity, such as a modem, does not overwhelm a receiving entity with data. When the buffers on the receiving device are full, a message is sent to the sending device to suspend the transmission until the data in the buffers has been processed.

**FLSM.** Fixed Length Subnet Masking. A major network is a class A, B, or C network. FLSM is when all subnet masks in a major network must be the same size.

**FR.** See *Frame Relay*.

**Fragmentation.** Process of breaking a packet into smaller units when transmitting over a network medium that cannot support the original size of the packet.

**Frame.** Logical grouping of information sent as a data link layer unit over a transmission medium. This often refers to the header and trailer, used for synchronization and error control, that surround the user data contained in the unit. The terms *cell*, *datagram*, *message*, *packet*, and *segment* are also used to describe logical information groupings at various layers of the OSI reference model and in various technology circles.

**Frame Relay.** Industry-standard, switched data link layer protocol that handles multiple virtual circuits using HDLC encapsulation between connected devices. Frame Relay is more efficient than X.25, the protocol for which it is generally considered a replacement. See also *X.25.*

**Frequency.** Number of cycles, measured in hertz, of an alternating current signal per unit time.

**FS.** Feasible Successor. EIGRP neighbor that is downstream with respect to the destination, but is not the least cost path and therefore is not used for forwarding data.

**FTAM.** File Transfer, Access, and Management. An OSI protocol suite file transfer application.

**FTP.** File Transfer Protocol. Application protocol, part of the TCP/IP protocol stack, used for transferring files between network nodes. FTP is defined in RFC 959.

**full duplex.** Capability for simultaneous data transmission between a sending station and a receiving station.

**full mesh.** Term describing a network in which devices are organized in a mesh topology, with each network node having either a physical circuit or a virtual circuit connecting it to every other network node. A full mesh provides a great deal of redundancy, but because it can be prohibitively expensive to implement, it is usually reserved for network backbones. See also *mesh* and *partial mesh.*

# G

**Gateway.** In the IP community, an older term referring to a routing device. Today, the term *router* is used to describe nodes that perform this function, and *gateway* refers to a special-purpose device that performs an application layer conversion of information from one protocol stack to another.

**GIF.** Graphics Interchange Format. A common file format for graphic images.

**GRE.** Generic routing encapsulation. Tunneling protocol developed by Cisco that can encapsulate a wide variety of protocol packet types inside IP tunnels, creating a virtual point-to-point link to Cisco routers at remote points over an IP internetwork. By connecting multiprotocol subnetworks in a single-protocol backbone environment, IP tunneling using GRE allows network expansion across a single-protocol backbone environment.

# H

**half duplex.** Capability for data transmission in only one direction at a time between a sending station and a receiving station.

**HDLC.** High-Level Data Link Control. Bit-oriented synchronous data link layer protocol developed by ISO. Derived from SDLC, HDLC specifies a data encapsulation method on synchronous serial links using frame characters and checksums.

**Header.** Control information placed before data when encapsulating that data for network transmission.

**hello packet.** A multicast packet that is used by routers for neighbor discovery and recovery. Hello packets also indicate that a client is still operating and network-ready.

**hello PDU.** In IS-IS, one of ESH, ISH, or IS-IS hello. Used to establish and maintain adjacencies.

**Hello protocol.** A protocol used by OSPF systems for establishing and maintaining neighbor relationships.

**High-Speed Serial Interface.** See *HSSI*.

**HODSP.** High-order domain-specific part of OSI NSAP address. Used for subdividing the domain into areas. This can be considered loosely as the OSI equivalent of a subnet in IP.

**Holddown.** A state into which a route is placed so that routers will neither advertise the route nor accept advertisements about the route for a specific length of time (the holddown period); in this way, the entire network has a chance to learn about the change. Holddown is used to flush bad information about a route from all routers in the network. A route is typically placed in holddown when a link in that route fails.

**Hop.** The passage of a data packet between two network nodes (for example, between two routers). See also *hop count*.

**hop count.** A routing metric used to measure the distance between a source and a destination. IP RIP uses hop count as its sole metric.

**HSRP.** Hot Standby Router Protocol. Provides a way for IP workstations to keep communicating on the internetwork even if their default router becomes unavailable, thereby providing high network availability and transparent network topology changes.

**HSSI.**  High-Speed Serial Interface. Network standard for high-speed (up to 52-Mbps) serial connections over WAN links.

**HTTP.**  Hypertext Transfer Protocol. The TCP/IP protocol used to send hypertext documents.

**Hub.**  Hardware or software device that contains multiple independent but connected modules of network and internetwork equipment. Hubs can be active (when they repeat signals sent through them) or passive (when they do not repeat, but merely split, signals sent through them).

# I

**IANA.**  Internet Assigned Numbers Authority. Organization operated under the auspices of the ISOC as a part of the IAB. IANA delegates authority for IP address-space allocation and domain-name assignment to the InterNIC and other organizations. IANA also maintains a database of assigned protocol identifiers used in the TCP/IP stack, including autonomous system numbers.

**IBGP.**  Internal Border Gateway Protocol. When BGP is running between routers within one AS it is called Internal BGP.

**ICMP.**  Internet Control Message Protocol. Network layer Internet protocol that reports errors and provides other information relevant to IP packet processing. It is documented in RFC 792.

**ICND.**  Interconnection Cisco Network Devices.

**IDI.**  Interdomain identifier. In OSI NSAP address, identifies this domain. The IDI can be up to 10 bytes.

**IDP.**  Interdomain part of OSI NSAP address. The IDP is made up of the AFI and IDI together. This can loosely be equated to an IP classful major network.

**IDRP.**  Interdomain Routing Protocol. A standard OSI routing protocol for pure CLNS environments. IDRP is not supported by the Cisco IOS.

**IEEE.**  Institute of Electrical and Electronic Engineers. Professional organization whose activities include the development of communications and network standards. IEEE LAN standards are the predominant LAN standards today.

**IETF.**  Internet Engineering Task Force. Task force consisting of more than 80 working groups responsible for developing Internet standards. The IETF operates under the auspices of ISOC.

**IGMP.** Internet Group Management Protocol. Used by IP hosts to report their multicast group memberships to an adjacent multicast router.

**IGP.** Interior Gateway Protocol. An Internet protocol used to exchange routing information within an autonomous system. Examples of common Internet IGPs include IGRP, OSPF, and RIP.

**IGRP.** Interior Gateway Routing Protocol. An IGP developed by Cisco to address the problems associated with routing in large, heterogeneous networks. Compare with *EIGRP*.

**IIH.** IS-IS hello. Used between two ISs.

**Integrated IS-IS.** Routing protocol based on the OSI routing protocol IS-IS, but with support for IP and other protocols.

**Integrated Services Digital Network.** See *ISDN*.

**interior routing protocols.** Routing protocols used by routers within the same autonomous system, such as RIP, IGRP, and EIGRP.

**intermediate system.** In IS-IS, a router.

**Internet.** A term that refers to the largest global internetwork, connecting tens of thousands of networks worldwide and having a "culture" that focuses on research and standardization based on real-life use. Many leading-edge network technologies come from the Internet community. The Internet evolved in part from ARPANET. At one time, it was called the DARPA Internet. This is not to be confused with the general term *internet*.

**internet.** Short for internetwork. Not to be confused with the Internet. See also *internetwork*.

**internetwork.** A collection of networks interconnected by routers and other devices that functions (generally) as a single network. It is sometimes called an internet, which is not to be confused with the Internet.

**internetworking.** The industry that has arisen around the problem of connecting networks. The term can refer to products, procedures, and technologies.

**Intranet.** A network, internal to an organization, based on Internet and World Wide Web technology, that delivers immediate, up-to-date information and services to networked employees.

**I/O.** Input/output. Typically used when discussing ports on a device where data comes in or goes out.

**IOS.** Internetwork Operating System. Cisco system software that provides common functionality, scalability, and security for all products under the CiscoFusion architecture. Cisco IOS allows centralized, integrated, and automated installation and management of internetworks, while ensuring support for a wide variety of protocols, media, services, and platforms.

**IP.** Internet Protocol. A network layer protocol in the TCP/IP stack offering a connectionless internetwork service. IP provides features for addressing, type-of-service specification, fragmentation and reassembly, and security. It is documented in RFC 791.

**IP address.** A 32-bit address assigned to hosts using TCP/IP. An IP address belongs to one of five classes (A, B, C, D, or E) and is written as four octets separated with periods (dotted decimal format). Each address consists of a network number, an optional subnetwork number, and a host number. The network and subnetwork numbers together are used for routing, and the host number is used to address an individual host within the network or subnetwork. A subnet mask is used to extract network and subnetwork information from the IP address. It is also called an Internet address.

**IP multicast.** A routing technique that allows IP traffic to be propagated from one source to a number of destinations or from many sources to many destinations. Rather than send one packet to each destination, one packet is sent to a multicast group identified by a single IP destination group address.

**IPSec.** Standards-based method of providing privacy, integrity, and authenticity to information transferred across IP networks. It provides IP network layer encryption.

**IPv4.** IP version 4. The correct name for the current version of IP.

**IPv6.** IP version 6. Replacement for the current version of IP (version 4). IPv6 includes support for flow ID in the packet header, which can be used to identify flows. It formerly was called IPng (IP next generation).

**IPX.** Internetwork Packet Exchange. A NetWare network layer (Layer 3) protocol used for transferring data from servers to workstations.

**IS.** 1. Information systems. A broad term used to describe the use of information technology in organizations. This includes the movement, storage, and use of information. 2. Information services. A broad term used to describe the department in an organization that takes care of information technology. 3. See *intermediate system*.

**IS-IS.** Intermediate System-to-Intermediate System.

**IS-ISv6.** Intermediate System-to-Intermediate System for IP version 6.

**ISH.** Intermediate system hello. Used in IS-IS. ESs discover the nearest IS by listening to ISHs.

**ISL.** Inter-Switch Link. A Cisco-proprietary protocol that maintains VLAN information as traffic flows between switches and routers.

**ISO.** International Organization for Standardization.

**ISO-IGRP.** A Cisco proprietary protocol used in a pure OSI (CLNS) environment.

**ISDN.** Integrated Services Digital Network. Communication protocol offered by telephone companies that permits telephone networks to carry data, voice, and other source traffic.

**IS-IS.** Intermediate System-to-Intermediate System. An OSI link-state hierarchical routing protocol based on DECnet Phase V routing whereby ISs (routers) exchange routing information based on a single metric to determine network topology.

**ISO.** International Organization for Standardization. International organization that is responsible for a wide range of standards, including those relevant to networking. ISO developed the OSI reference model, a popular networking reference model.

**ISOC.** Internet Society. International nonprofit organization, founded in 1992, that coordinates the evolution and use of the Internet. In addition, ISOC delegates authority to other groups related to the Internet, such as the IAB. ISOC is headquartered in Reston, Virginia (United States).

**ISP.** Internet service provider. Company that provides Internet access to other companies and individuals.

**ITU-T.** International Telecommunication Union Telecommunication Standardization Sector. International body that develops worldwide standards for telecommunications technologies. The ITU-T carries out the functions of the former CCITT.

# J

**JPEG.** Joint Photographic Experts Group. Standard for graphic image files.

# K

**Kb.** Kilobit. Approximately 1,000 bits.

**Kbps.** Kilobits per second.

**keepalive message.** A message sent by one network device to inform another network device that the circuit between the two is still active.

**Kerberos.** Developing standard for authenticating network users. Kerberos offers two key benefits: It functions in a multivendor network, and it does not transmit passwords over the network.

# L

**LAN.** Local-area network. High-speed, low-error data network covering a relatively small geographic area (up to a few thousand meters). LANs connect workstations, peripherals, terminals, and other devices in a single building or other geographically limited area. LAN standards specify cabling and signaling at the physical and data link layers of the OSI model. Ethernet, FDDI, and Token Ring are widely used LAN technologies. Also see *MAN* and *WAN*.

**LAPB.** Link Access Procedure, Balanced. Data link layer protocol in the X.25 protocol stack. LAPB is a bit-oriented protocol derived from HDLC.

**LAPD.** Link Access Procedure on the D channel. Used on the ISDN D channel.

**leased line.** Transmission line reserved by a communications carrier for the private use of a customer. A leased line is a type of dedicated line. See also *dedicated line*.

**LED.** Light emitting diode. Semiconductor device that emits light produced by converting electrical energy. Status lights on hardware devices are typically LEDs.

**Level 1 IS.** In IS-IS, the equivalent of an OSPF internal nonbackbone router. These routers are responsible for routing to ESs inside an area.

**Level 1-2 IS.** In IS-IS, the equivalent of an Area Border Routers in OSPF. These routers route between areas and the backbone. They participate in the Level 1 intra-area routing and the Level 2 interarea routing.

**Level 2 IS.** In IS-IS, the equivalent of a backbone router in OSPF. These routers route only between areas.

**Link.** Network communications channel consisting of a circuit or transmission path and all related equipment between a sender and a receiver. It is most often used to refer to a WAN connection and sometimes is referred to as a line or a transmission link.

**link-state routing algorithm.** A routing algorithm in which each router broadcasts or multicasts information regarding the cost of reaching each of its neighbors to all nodes in the internetwork. Compare with *distance vector routing algorithm*.

**LLC.** Logical Link Control. The higher of the two data link layer sublayers defined by the IEEE. The LLC sublayer handles error control, flow control, framing, and MAC-sublayer addressing.

**LMI.** Local Management Interface. Set of enhancements to the basic Frame Relay specification. LMI includes support for a keepalive mechanism, which verifies that data is flowing; a multicast mechanism, which provides the network server with its local DLCI and the multicast DLCI; global addressing, which gives DLCIs global rather than local significance in Frame Relay networks; and a status mechanism, which provides an ongoing status report on the DLCIs known to the switch. It is known as LMT in ANSI terminology.

**load balancing.** In routing, the capability of a router to distribute traffic over all its network ports that are the same distance from the destination address. Good load-balancing algorithms use both line speed and reliability information. Load balancing increases the use of network segments, thus increasing effective network bandwidth.

**local loop.** Also known as "the last mile." Line from the premises of a telephone subscriber to the telephone company CO.

**LSA.** Link-state advertisement. In OSPF, broadcast packet used by link-state protocols that contains information about neighbors and path costs. LSAs are used by the receiving routers to maintain their routing tables.

**LSAck.** Link-state acknowledgment. In OSPF, a packet in which the router acknowledges the receipt of the DBD.

**LSP.** Link-state packet. In OSPF, packet sent to the master router if the DBD has a more up-to-date link-state entry.

**LSU.** Link-state update. In OSPF, the master router responds with the complete information about the requested entry in a LSU packet.

# M

**MAC.** Media Access Control. Lower of the two sublayers of the data link layer defined by the IEEE. The MAC sublayer handles access to shared media, such as whether token passing or contention will be used.

**MAC address.** Standardized data link layer address that is required for every port or device that connects to a LAN. Other devices in the network use these addresses to locate specific ports in the network and to create and update routing tables and data structures. MAC addresses are 6 bytes long and are controlled by the IEEE. Also known as a hardware address, MAC-layer address, and physical address.

**MAN.** Metropolitan-area network. Network that spans a metropolitan area. Generally, a MAN spans a larger geographic area than a LAN, but a smaller geographic area than a WAN. Compare with *LAN* and *WAN*.

**maximum transmission unit.** See *MTU*.

**MD5.** Message digest algorithm 5. Algorithm used for message authentication. MD5 verifies the integrity of the communication, authenticates the origin, and checks for timeliness.

**MED.** Multi-Exit-Discriminator. In BGP, the MED attribute is an optional nontransitive attribute.

**Mesh.** A network topology in which devices are organized in a manageable, segmented manner with many, often redundant, interconnections strategically placed between network nodes. See also *full mesh* and *partial mesh*.

**Message.** An application layer (Layer 7) logical grouping of information, often composed of a number of lower-layer logical groupings such as packets.

**Metric.** A standard of measurement, such as performance, that is used for measuring whether network management goals have been met.

**MHSRP.** Multigroup HSRP. Provides a way to utilize redundant paths while running HSRP.

**Mobile IP.** An IETF standard available for both IPv4 and IPv6 that enables mobile devices to move without breaks in current connections.

**Modem.** Modulator-demodulator. Device that converts digital and analog signals. At the source, a modem converts digital signals to a form suitable for transmission over analog communication facilities. At the destination, the analog signals are returned to their digital form. Modems allow data to be transmitted over voice-grade telephone lines.

**Modulation.** Process by which the characteristics of electrical signals are transformed to represent information. Types of modulation include AM, FM, and PAM.

**MP.** Multilink PPP.

**MPEG.** Motion Picture Experts Group. Standard for compressing video. MPEG1 is a bit stream standard for compressed video and audio optimized to fit into a bandwidth of 1.5 Mbps. MPEG2 is intended for higher quality video-on-demand applications and runs at data rates between 4 and 9 Mbps. MPEG4 is a low-bit-rate compression algorithm intended for 64-kbps connections.

**MTU.** Maximum transmission unit. Maximum packet size, in bytes, that a particular interface can handle.

**multiaccess network.** Network that allows multiple devices to connect and communicate simultaneously.

**Multicast.** Single packets copied by the network and sent to a specific subset of network addresses. These addresses are specified in the Destination Address Field. Compare with *broadcast* and *unicast*.

**Multiplexing.** Scheme that allows multiple logical signals to be transmitted simultaneously across a single physical channel.

# N

**NAK.** negative acknowledgment. Response sent from a receiving device to a sending device indicating that the information received contained errors. Compare to *acknowledgment*.

**NAS.** See *access server*.

**NAT.** Network Address Translation. Mechanism for reducing the need for globally unique IP addresses. NAT allows an organization with addresses that are not globally unique to connect to the Internet by translating those addresses into globally routable address space. Also known as Network Address Translator.

**NBMA.** Nonbroadcast multiaccess. Term describing a multiaccess network that does not support broadcasting (such as X.25) or in which broadcasting is not feasible (for example, an SMDS broadcast group or an extended Ethernet that is too large).

**NBP.** Name Binding Protocol. Appletalk protocol that associates AppleTalk names with addresses.

**neighboring router.** In OSPF, two routers that have interfaces to a common network.

**NET.** Network-entity title.

**NetBEUI.** NetBIOS Extended User Interface. Enhanced version of the NetBIOS protocol used by network operating systems such as LAN Manager, LAN Server, Windows for Workgroups, and Windows NT. NetBEUI formalizes the transport frame and adds additional functions. NetBEUI implements the OSI LLC2 protocol.

**Network.** Collection of computers, printers, routers, switches, and other devices that are capable of communicating with each other over some transmission medium.

**NIC.** 1. Network interface card. A board that provides network communication capabilities to and from a computer system. Also called an adapter. 2. Network Information Center. An organization that serves the Internet community by supplying user assistance, documentation, training, and other services.

**NLSP.** NetWare Link Services Protocol. Link-state routing protocol based on IS-IS.

**NNI.** The standard interface between two Frame Relay switches meeting the same criteria.

**non-stub area.** A resource-intensive OSPF area that carries a default route, static routes, intra-area routes, interarea routes, and external routes. Compare with *stub area*. See also *ASBR*.

**NSAP.** Network service access point.

**NSEL.** NSAP-selector part of OSI NSAP address.

**NSSA.** Not-so-stubby area. In OSPF, a not-so-stubby area imports a limited number of external routes. The number of routes is limited to only those required to provide connectivity between backbone areas.

**NVRAM.** Nonvolatile random access memory.

# O

**OC.** Optical carrier. Series of physical protocols (OC-1, OC-2, OC-3, and so forth) defined for SONET optical signal transmissions. OC signal levels put STS frames onto multimode fiber-optic lines at a variety of speeds. The base rate is 51.84 Mbps (OC-1); each signal level thereafter operates at a speed divisible by that number (thus, OC-3 runs at 155.52 Mbps).

**Octet.** Eight bits. In networking, the term *octet* is often used rather than *byte* because some machine architectures employ bytes that are not 8 bits long.

**ODBC.** Open database connectivity.

**OLE.** Object linking and embedding. Compound document standard developed by Microsoft Corporation. It enables creating objects with one application and then linking or embedding them in a second application. These objects keep their original format and links to the application that created them.

**OSI.** Open System Interconnection. International standardization program created by ISO and ITU-T to develop standards for data networking that facilitate multivendor equipment interoperability.

**OSI reference model.** Open System Interconnection reference model. Network architectural model developed by ISO and ITU-T. The model consists of seven layers, each of which specifies particular network functions such as addressing, flow control, error control, encapsulation, and reliable message transfer. The lowest layer (the physical layer) is closest to the media technology. The lower two layers are implemented in hardware and software, while the upper five layers are implemented only in software. The highest layer (the application layer) is closest to the user. The OSI reference model is used universally as a method for teaching and understanding network functionality.

**OSPF.** Open Shortest Path First. A link-state, hierarchical IGP routing algorithm proposed as a successor to RIP in the Internet community. OSPF features include least-cost routing, multipath routing, and load balancing. OSPF was derived from an early version of the IS-IS protocol. See also *EIGRP*, *IGP*, *IGRP*, *IS-IS*, and *RIP*.

**OSPFv3.** OSPF version 3. A new version of OSPF for IPv6.

**OUI.** Organizationally unique identifier. Three octets assigned by the IEEE, used in the 48-bit MAC addresses.

# P

**Packet.** Logical grouping of information that includes a header containing control information and (usually) user data. Packets are most often used to refer to network layer units of data. The terms *datagram*, *frame*, *message*, and *segment* are also used to describe logical information groupings at various layers of the OSI reference model and in various technology circles. See also *PDU*.

**packet switching.** Networking method in which nodes share bandwidth with each other by sending packets.

**PAP.** Password Authentication Protocol. An authentication protocol that allows PPP peers to authenticate one another. The remote router attempting to connect to the local router is required to send an authentication request. Unlike CHAP, PAP passes the password and host name or username in the clear (unencrypted). PAP does not itself prevent unauthorized access, but merely identifies the remote end. The router or access server then determines whether that user is allowed access. PAP is supported only on PPP lines. Compare with *CHAP*.

**partial mesh.** Network in which devices are organized in a mesh topology, with some network nodes organized in a full mesh, but with others that are connected to only one or two other nodes in the network. A partial mesh does not provide the level of redundancy of a full-mesh topology, but it is less expensive to implement. Partial-mesh topologies are generally used in the peripheral networks that connect to a fully meshed backbone. See also *full mesh* and *mesh*.

**Payload.** Portion of a cell, frame, or packet that contains upper-layer information (data).

**PBR.** Policy-based routing. Using policies to selectively cause packets to take different paths, based on source address, protocol types, or application types.

**PDM.** Protocol-dependent modules. In EIGRP, PDMs are responsible for network layer, protocol-specific requirements for IP, IPX, and AppleTalk.

**PDN.** Public Data Network. Network operated either by a government (as in Europe) or by a private concern to provide computer communications to the public, usually for a fee. PDNs enable small organizations to create a WAN without all the equipment costs of long-distance circuits.

**PDU.** Protocol data unit. An OSI term for packet. A packet of data consisting of control information and user information that is to be exchanged between communicating peers in a network. In general, a PDU is a segment of data generated by a specific layer of a protocol stack, usually containing information from the next higher layer, encapsulated together with header and trailer information generated by the layer in question.

**peak rate.** Maximum rate, in kilobits per second, at which a virtual circuit can transmit.

**permanent virtual circuit.** Virtual circuit that is permanently established. PVCs save bandwidth associated with circuit establishment and teardown in situations in which certain virtual circuits must exist all the time. In ATM terminology, this is called a permanent virtual connection.

**Ping.** Packet internet groper. ICMP echo message and its reply. This is often used in IP networks to test the reachability of a network device.

**PIX.** *Cisco's* Private Internet Exchange firewall. See also *firewall*.

**Playback.** Reuse of a packet captured from a line by a sniffer.

**PLP.** Packet-Layer Protocol. For X.25.

**point of demarcation.** The physical point at which the phone company ends its responsibility with the wiring of the phone line.

**POP.** Point of presence. A long-distance carrier's office in your local community. A POP is the place where your long-distance carrier, or IXC, terminates your long-distance lines just before those lines are connected to your local phone company's lines or to your own direct hookup. Each IXC can have multiple POPs within one LATA. All long-distance phone connections go through the POPs.

**PPP.** Point-to-Point Protocol. Successor to SLIP that provides router-to-router and host-to-network connections over synchronous and asynchronous circuits. Whereas SLIP was designed to work with IP, PPP was designed to work with several network layer protocols, such as IP, IPX, and ARA. PPP also has built-in security mechanisms, such as CHAP and PAP. PPP relies on two protocols: LCP and NCP. See also *CHAP* and *PAP*.

**PRC.** Partial route calculation. Used in IS-IS to calculate ES reachability.

**PRI.** Primary Rate Interface. ISDN interface to primary rate access. Primary rate access consists of a single 64-Kbps D channel plus 23 (T1) or 30 (E1) B channels for voice or data. Compare with *BRI*.

**Pseudonode.** For IS-IS, a virtual router required by Dijkstra's algorithm for broadcast media to build a directed graph.

**PSNP.** Partial sequence number PDU. In IS-IS, used to acknowledge and request link-state information. PSNPs usually contain only one LSP descriptor block.

**PVC.** Permanent virtual circuit. Virtual circuit that is permanently established. PVCs save bandwidth associated with circuit establishment and teardown in situations in which certain virtual circuits must exist all the time. In ATM terminology, this is called a permanent virtual connection. See *SVC*.

# Q

**QoS.**  Quality of service. A measure of performance for a transmission system that reflects its transmission quality and service availability.

**Query.**  Message used to inquire about the value of some variable or set of variables.

**Queue.**  1. Generally, an ordered list of elements waiting to be processed. 2. In routing, a backlog of packets waiting to be forwarded over a router interface.

# R

**RA.**  Router Advertisement. IPv6 routing advertisement.

**RADIUS.**  Database for authenticating modem and ISDN connections and for tracking connection time.

**RAM.**  Random-access memory. Volatile memory that can be read and written by a microprocessor.

**rate enforcement.**  See *traffic policing*.

**Redistribution.**  Allowing routing information discovered through one routing protocol to be distributed in the update messages of another routing protocol. This is sometimes called route redistribution.

**RFC.**  Requests For Comments. Document series used as the primary means for communicating information about the Internet. Some RFCs are designated by the IAB as Internet standards. Most RFCs document protocol specifications such as Telnet and FTP, but some are humorous or historical. RFCs are available online from numerous sources.

**RIP.**  1. Routing Information Protocol. A distance vector IGP, RIP uses hop count as a routing metric. See also *EIGRP*, *hop count*, *IGP*, *IGRP*, and *OSPF*. 2. IPX Routing Information Protocol. A distance vector routing protocol for IPX.

**RIPE-NIC.**  Reseaux IP Europeennes-Network Information Center.

**RIPng.**  Routing Information Protocol next generation. A newer version of RIP for IPv6.

**RIPv1.**  Routing Information Protocol version 1.

**RIPv2.**  Routing Information Protocol Version 2. A newer version of RIP for IP.

**RJ-45.** Registered jack connector. Standard connectors used for 10BaseT and other types of network connections.

**route summarization.** The consolidation of advertised addresses in a routing table. Summarizing routes reduces the number of routes in the routing table, the routing update traffic, and overall router overhead. Also called route aggregation.

**Router.** A network layer device that uses one or more metrics to determine the optimal path along which network traffic should be forwarded. Routers forward packets from one network to another based on network layer information. It is occasionally called a gateway (although this definition of gateway is becoming increasingly outdated).

**Routing.** The process of finding a path to a destination host. Routing is complex in large networks because of the many potential intermediate destinations that a packet might traverse before reaching its destination host. Routing occurs at Layer 3, the network layer.

**routing domain.** A group of end systems and intermediate systems operating under the same set of administrative rules.

**routing metric.** A standard of measurement, such as path length, that is used by routing algorithms to determine the optimal path to a destination. This information is stored in routing tables. Metrics include bandwidth, communication cost, delay, hop count, load, MTU, path cost, and reliability. It is sometimes referred to simply as a metric.

**routing protocol.** A routing protocol supports a routed protocol by providing mechanisms for sharing routing information. Routing protocol messages move between the routers. A routing protocol allows the routers to communicate with other routers to update and maintain routing tables. Routing protocol messages do not carry end-user traffic from network to network. A routing protocol uses the routed protocol to pass information between routers. Examples of routing protocols are IGRP, OSPF, and RIP.

**routing table.** A table stored in a router or some other internetworking device that keeps track of routes to particular network destinations and metrics associated with those routes.

**routing update.** A message sent from a router to indicate network reachability and associated cost information. Routing updates are typically sent at regular intervals and after a change in network topology. Compare with *flash update*.

**RS.** Router Solicitation. An IPv6 packet requesting a router advertisement.

**RTO.** Retransmission timeout. This is the amount of time the EIGRP waits before retransmitting a packet from the retransmission queue to a neighbor.

**RTMP.** Routing Table Maintenance Protocol. AppleTalk routing protocol.

**RTP.** Reliable Transport Protocol. RTP is responsible for guaranteed, ordered delivery of EIGRP packets to all neighbors.

# S

**SA.** Source address.

**SAP.** 1. service access point. A conceptual location at which one OSI layer can request the services of another OSI layer. 2. Service Advertising Protocol. Novell protocol for advertising services available.

**SCP.** Session Control Protocol. The DECnet Phase IV session layer protocol.

**SCTP.** Stream Control Transmission Protocol. IPv6 transport layer protocol for reliable transport services.

**SDLC.** Synchronous Data Link Control. SNA data link layer communications protocol. SDLC is a bit-oriented, full-duplex serial protocol that has spawned numerous similar protocols, including HDLC and LAPB.

**SDU.** Service data unit. SDUs are information units from upper-layer protocols that define a service request to a lower-layer protocol.

**Server.** Node or software program that provides services to clients. See also *client*.

**SIA.** Stuck in active. In some circumstances, it takes a very long time for an EIGRP query to be answered. So long, in fact, that the router that issued the query gives up and clears its connection to the router that isn't answering, effectively restarting the neighbor session. This is known as a SIA route.

**SIN.** Ships-in-the-night. Ships-in-the-night routing advocates the use of a completely separate and distinct routing protocol for each network protocol so that the multiple routing protocols essentially exist independently.

**SMDS.** Switched Multimegabit Data Service. A high-speed, packet-switched, datagram-based WAN networking technology offered by the telephone companies.

**SMTP.** Simple Mail Transfer Protocol. Internet protocol providing e-mail services.

**SNA.** Systems Network Architecture.

**SNAP.** SubNetwork Access Protocol.

**SNMP.** Simple Network Management Protocol.

**SNP.** Sequence number PDUs in IS-IS. SNPs ensure that LSPs are sent reliably. SNPs contain LSP descriptors—not the actual, detailed LSP information, but headers describing the LSPs.

**SNPA.** Subnetwork point of attachment for IS-IS. An SNPA is the point at which subnetwork services are provided. This is the equivalent of the Layer 2 address corresponding to the Layer 3 (NET or NSAP) address.

**SOF.** Start of frame.

**SONET.** Synchronous Optical Network. High-speed (up to 2.5 Gbps) synchronous network specification developed by Bellcore and designed to run on optical fiber. STS-1 is the basic building block of SONET. It was approved as an international standard in 1988.

**source address.** Address of a network device that is sending data. See also *destination address*.

**SPF.** Shortest path first algorithm. Routing algorithm that iterates on length of path to determine a shortest-path spanning tree. Commonly used in link-state routing algorithms. Sometimes called Dijkstra's algorithm. Used in IS-IS and OSPF.

**SPID.** Service profile identifier. A number that some service providers use to define the services to which an ISDN device subscribes. The ISDN device uses the SPID when accessing the switch that initializes the connection to a service provider.

**split-horizon.** Routing technique in which information about routes is prevented from exiting the router interface through which that information was received. Split-horizon updates are useful in preventing routing loops.

**Spoofing.** Scheme used by routers to cause a host to treat an interface as if it were up and supporting a session. The router spoofs replies to keepalive messages from the host to convince that host that the session still exists. Spoofing is useful in routing environments such as DDR, in which a circuit-switched link is taken down when there is no traffic to be sent across it to save toll charges.

**SPX.** Sequenced Packet Exchange. A reliable, connection-oriented protocol that supplements the datagram service provided by the IPX protocol.

**SQL.** Structured Query Language.

**SRAM.** Static RAM.

**SRTT.** Smooth round-trip time. This is the number of milliseconds it takes for an EIGRP packet to be sent to a neighbor and for the local router to receive an acknowledgment of that packet.

**SSAP.** Source service access point (LLC).

**SSE.** Silicon switching engine.

**SSP.** Silicon switch processor.

**static route.** A route that is explicitly configured and entered into the routing table.

**STP.** Shielded twisted-pair; also Spanning-Tree Protocol.

**stub area.** An OSPF area that carries a default route, intra-area routes, and interarea routes, but that does not carry external routes. Compare with *non-stub area*.

**stub network.** Part of an internetwork that can be reached by only one path; a network that has only a single connection to a router.

**Subinterface.** One of a number of virtual interfaces on a single physical interface.

**Subnet.** See *subnetwork*.

**subnet mask.** A 32-bit number that is associated with an IP address; each bit in the subnet mask indicates how to interpret the corresponding bit in the IP address. In binary, a subnet mask bit of 1 indicates that the corresponding bit in the IP address is a network or subnet bit; a subnet mask bit of 0 indicates that the corresponding bit in the IP address is a host bit. The subnet mask then indicates how many bits have been borrowed from the host field for the subnet field. It sometimes is referred to simply as mask.

**Subnetwork.** In IP networks, a network sharing a particular subnet address. Subnetworks are networks arbitrarily segmented by a network administrator to provide a multilevel, hierarchical routing structure while shielding the subnetwork from the addressing complexity of attached networks. It is sometimes called a subnet.

**Successor.** A successor is a neighboring router used for packet forwarding that has a least cost path to a destination that is guaranteed not to be part of a routing loop.

**SVC.** switched virtual circuit. Virtual circuit that is dynamically established on demand and is torn down when transmission is complete. SVCs are used in situations in which data transmission is sporadic. It is called a switched virtual connection in ATM terminology. Compare with *PVC*.

**Switch.** 1. A network device that filters, forwards, and floods frames based on the destination address of each frame. The switch operates at the data link layer of the OSI model. 2. An electronic or mechanical device that allows a connection to be established as necessary and terminated when there is no longer a session to support.

**SYN.** Synchronize (TCP segment).

**Synchronization.** Establishment of common timing between sender and receiver.

# T

**T1.** Digital WAN carrier facility. T1 transmits DS-1-formatted data at 1.544 Mbps through the telephone-switching network using AMI or B8ZS coding.

**TAC.** Technical Assistance Center (Cisco).

**TACACS.** Terminal Access Controller Access Control System.

**TCP.** Transmission Control Protocol. Connection-oriented transport layer protocol that provides reliable full-duplex data transmission. TCP is part of the TCP/IP protocol stack. See also *TCP/IP*.

**TCP/IP.** Transmission Control Protocol/Internet Protocol. Common name for the suite of protocols developed by the U.S. DoD in the 1970s to support the construction of worldwide internetworks. TCP and IP are the two best-known protocols in the suite. See also *IP*, *TCP*, and *UDP*.

**TDM.** Time-division multiplexing.

**Telco.** Telephone company.

**TFTP.** Trivial File Transfer Protocol.

**TIA.** Telecommunications Industry Association.

**TIFF.** Tagged Image File Format. Common format for exchanging graphic images between applications.

**TLV.** Type Length Value. Variable-length field in an IS-IS LSP.

**Topology table.** In EIGRP, the topology table contains all destinations advertised by neighboring routers.

**ToS.** Type of service.

**traffic policing.** Process used to measure the actual traffic flow across a given connection and compare it to the total admissible traffic flow for that connection. Traffic outside of the agreed-upon flow can be tagged (where the CLP bit is set to 1) and can be discarded en route if congestion develops. Traffic policing is used in ATM, Frame Relay, and other types of networks.

**traffic shaping.** The use of queues to limit surges that can congest a network. Data is buffered and then sent into the network in regulated amounts to ensure that the traffic will fit within the promised traffic envelope for the particular connection. Traffic shaping is used in ATM, Frame Relay, and other types of networks. It is also known as metering, shaping, and smoothing.

**Transmission Control Protocol.** See *TCP*.

**TTL.** Time To Live. A field in an IP header that indicates how long a packet is considered valid.

**Tunneling.** An architecture that provides a virtual data link connection between two like networks through a foreign network. The virtual data link is created by encapsulating the network data inside the packets of the foreign network.

**twisted pair.** Two insulated wires, usually copper, twisted together and often bound into a common sheath to form multipair cables. In ISDN, the cables are the basic path between a subscriber's terminal or telephone and the PBX or the central office.

# U

**UDP.** User Datagram Protocol. Connectionless transport layer protocol in the TCP/IP protocol stack. UDP is a simple protocol that exchanges datagrams without acknowledgments or guaranteed delivery, requiring that error processing and retransmission be handled by other protocols.

**UNC.** Universal Naming Convention or Uniform Naming Convention. A PC format for specifying the location of resources on a local-area network (LAN). UNC uses the following format: \\server-name\shared-resource-pathname.

**Unicast.** Message sent to a single network destination. Compare with *broadcast* and *multicast*.

**URL.** Uniform Resource Locator.

**UTC.** Coordinated Universal Time (same as Greenwich Mean Time).

**UTL.** Utilization.

**UTP.** Unshielded twisted-pair wire.

# V

**V.35.** ITU-T standard describing a synchronous, physical layer protocol used for communications between a network access device and a packet network. V.35 is most commonly used in North America and in Europe, and is recommended for speeds up to 48 Kbps.

**VC.** See *virtual circuit*.

**VIP.** Versatile Interface Processor.

**virtual circuit.** Logical circuit created to ensure reliable communication between two network devices. A virtual circuit is defined by a VPI/VCI pair and can be either permanent (PVC) or switched (SVC). Virtual circuits are used in Frame Relay and X.25. In ATM, a virtual circuit is called a virtual channel. It is sometimes abbreviated VC.

**VLAN.** Virtual LAN. A logical, rather than physical, grouping of devices. The devices are grouped using switch management software so that they can communicate as if they were attached to the same wire, when in fact they might be located on a number of different physical LAN segments. Because VLANs are based on logical instead of physical connections, they are extremely flexible.

**VLSM.** Variable-length subnet mask. The capability to specify a different subnet mask for the same network number on different subnets. VLSM can help optimize available address space. Some protocols do not allow the use of VLSM. See also *classless routing protocols*.

**VTP.** VLAN Trunking Protocol. A layer 2 messaging protocol that manages the addition, deletion, and renaming of VLANs.

**Vty.** Virtual terminal.

# W

**WAN.** Wide-area network. Data communications network that serves users across a broad geographic area and often uses transmission devices provided by common carriers. Frame Relay, SMDS, and X.25 are examples of WANs.

**WFQ.** Weighted Fair Queuing. Congestion-management algorithm that identifies conversations (in the form of traffic streams), separates packets that belong to each conversation, and ensures that capacity is shared fairly between these individual conversations. WFQ is an automatic way of stabilizing network behavior during congestion and results in increased performance and reduced retransmission.

**wildcard mask.** A 32-bit quantity used in conjunction with an IP address to determine which bits in an IP address should be ignored when comparing that address with another IP address. A wildcard mask is specified when setting up access lists.

**Window.** The number of data segments that the sender is allowed to have outstanding without yet receiving an acknowledgment.

**Windowing.** A method to control the amount of information transferred end to end, using different window sizes.

**Workgroup.** A collection of workstations and servers on a LAN that are designed to communicate and exchange data with one another.

**World Wide Web.** See *WWW.*

**WRED.** Weighted Random Early Detection. Queuing method that ensures that high-precedence traffic has lower loss rates than other traffic during times of congestion.

**WWW.** World Wide Web. A large network of Internet servers providing hypertext and other services to terminals running client applications such as a WWW browser.

**WWW browser.** A GUI-based hypertext client application, such as Mosaic, used to access hypertext documents and other services located on innumerable remote servers throughout the WWW and Internet. See also *Internet* and *WWW.*

# X

**X.25.** ITU-T standard that defines how connections between DTE and DCE are maintained for remote terminal access and computer communications in PDNs. X.25 specifies LAPB, a data link layer protocol, and PLP, a network layer protocol. To some degree, Frame Relay has superseded X.25.

**XDSL.** Group term used to refer to ADSL, HDSL, SDSL, and VDSL. All are emerging digital technologies using the existing copper infrastructure provided by the telephone companies. xDSL is a high-speed alternative to ISDN.

**XNS.** Xerox Network Systems.

# Z

**ZIP.** Zone Information Protocol. AppleTalk session layer protocol that maps network numbers to zone names. ZIP is used by NBP to determine which networks contain nodes that belong to a zone.

# INDEX

## Symbols

## Numerics

## A

# B

# F

# G

# H

# J – L

# N

# O

# Q – R

# T

# W–Z

CISCO SYSTEMS

**Cisco Press**

# 3 STEPS TO LEARNING

**STEP 1**

**STEP 2**

**STEP 3**

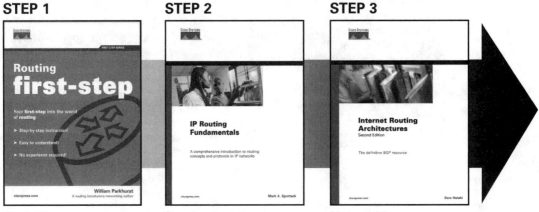

**First-Step**

**Fundamentals**

**Networking Technology Guides**

**STEP 1** **First-Step**—Benefit from easy-to-grasp explanations. No experience required!

**STEP 2** **Fundamentals**—Understand the purpose, application, and management of technology.

**STEP 3** **Networking Technology Guides**—Gain the knowledge to master the challenge of the network.

## NETWORK BUSINESS SERIES

The Network Business series helps professionals tackle the business issues surrounding the network. Whether you are a seasoned IT professional or a business manager with minimal technical expertise, this series will help you understand the business case for technologies.

**Justify Your Network Investment.**

**Look for Cisco Press titles at your favorite bookseller today.**

Visit **www.ciscopress.com/series** for details on each of these book series.

# DISCUSS

## NETWORKING PRODUCTS AND TECHNOLOGIES WITH CISCO EXPERTS AND NETWORKING PROFESSIONALS WORLDWIDE

VISIT NETWORKING PROFESSIONALS
A CISCO ONLINE COMMUNITY
WWW.CISCO.COM/GO/DISCUSS

**CISCO SYSTEMS**

THIS IS THE POWER OF THE NETWORK. now.

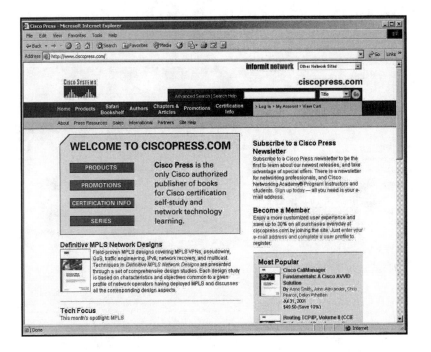

# SEARCH THOUSANDS OF BOOKS FROM LEADING PUBLISHERS

Safari® Bookshelf is a searchable electronic reference library for IT professionals that features thousands of titles from technical publishers, including Cisco Press.

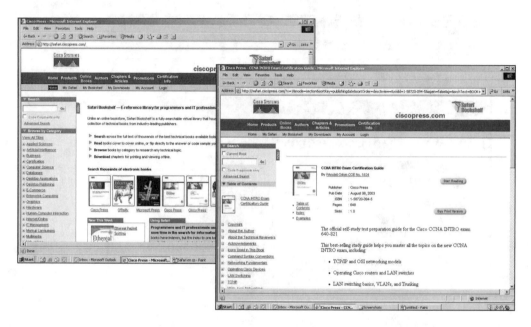

With Safari Bookshelf you can

- **Search** the full text of thousands of technical books, including more than 130 Cisco Press titles from authors such as Wendell Odom, Jeff Doyle, Bill Parkhurst, Sam Halabi, and Dave Hucaby.

- **Read** the books on My Bookshelf from cover to cover, or just flip to the information you need.

- **Browse** books by category to research any technical topic.

- **Download** chapters for printing and viewing offline.

With a customized library, you'll have access to your books when and where you need them—and all you need is a user name and password.